A-Z HAMPSHIRE

CONTENTS

REFERENCE

Motorway	M27
Primary Route	A31
A Road	A335
B Road	B3038
Dual Carriageway	
One-way Street — Traffic flow on A Roads is also indicated by a heavy line on the driver's left.	
Road Under Construction — Opening dates are correct at the time of publication	
Proposed Road	
Restricted Access	
Pedestrianized Road	
Track / Footpath	
Residential Walkway	
Railway	Station / Heritage Sta. / Level Crossing / Tunnel
Built-up Area	ST. IVES / PARK
Local Authority Boundary	
National Park Boundary	
Posttown Boundary	
Postcode Boundary (within Posttowns)	
Map Continuation	16 / Small Scale Mapping 8 / Large Scale Mapping 4
Airport	✈
Berth Number (Southampton Docks)	101

Car Park (selected)	P
Church or Chapel	†
Cycleway (selected)	🚲
Dock Gate Number (Southampton Docks)	8
Fire Station	■
Hospital	H
House Numbers (A & B Roads only)	83 96
Information Centre	i
National Grid Reference	⁴45
Park & Ride	East Winchester (Barfield) P+R
Police Station	▲
Post Office	★
Safety Camera with Speed Limit — Fixed cameras and long term road works cameras. Symbols do not indicate camera direction	30
Toilet: without facilities for the Disabled	▽
with facilities for the Disabled	▽
Disabled use only	▽
Viewpoint	🎍 ☀
Educational Establishment	▢
Hospital or Healthcare Building	▢
Industrial Building	▢
Leisure or Recreational Facility	▢
Place of Interest Building	▢
Public Building	▢
Shopping Centre or Market	▢
Other Selected Buildings	▢

SCALES

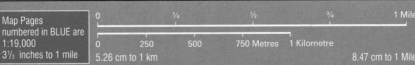

Map Pages numbered in BLUE are 1:19,000 — 3⅓ inches to 1 mile — 5.26 cm to 1 km — 8.47 cm to 1 Mile

Map Pages numbered in RED are 1:9,500 — 6⅔ inches to 1 mile — 10.52 cm to 1 km — 16.94 cm to 1 mile

Map Pages numbered in GREEN are 1:38,000 — 1⅔ inches to 1 mile — 2.63 cm to 1 km — 4.23 cm to 1 mile

Copyright of Geographers' A-Z Map Company Limited

Fairfield Road, Borough Green, Sevenoaks, Kent TN15 8PP
Telephone: 01732 781000 (Enquiries & Trade Sales)
01732 783422 (Retail Sales)
www.az.co.uk
Copyright © Geographers' A-Z Map Co. Ltd.
Edition 3 2012

Ordnance Survey® This product includes mapping data licensed from Ordnance Survey® with the permission of the Controller of Her Majesty's Stationery Office.

© Crown Copyright 2011. All rights reserved. Licence number 100017302

Safety camera information supplied by www.PocketGPSWorld.com
Speed Camera Location Database Copyright 2011 © PocketGPSWorld.com

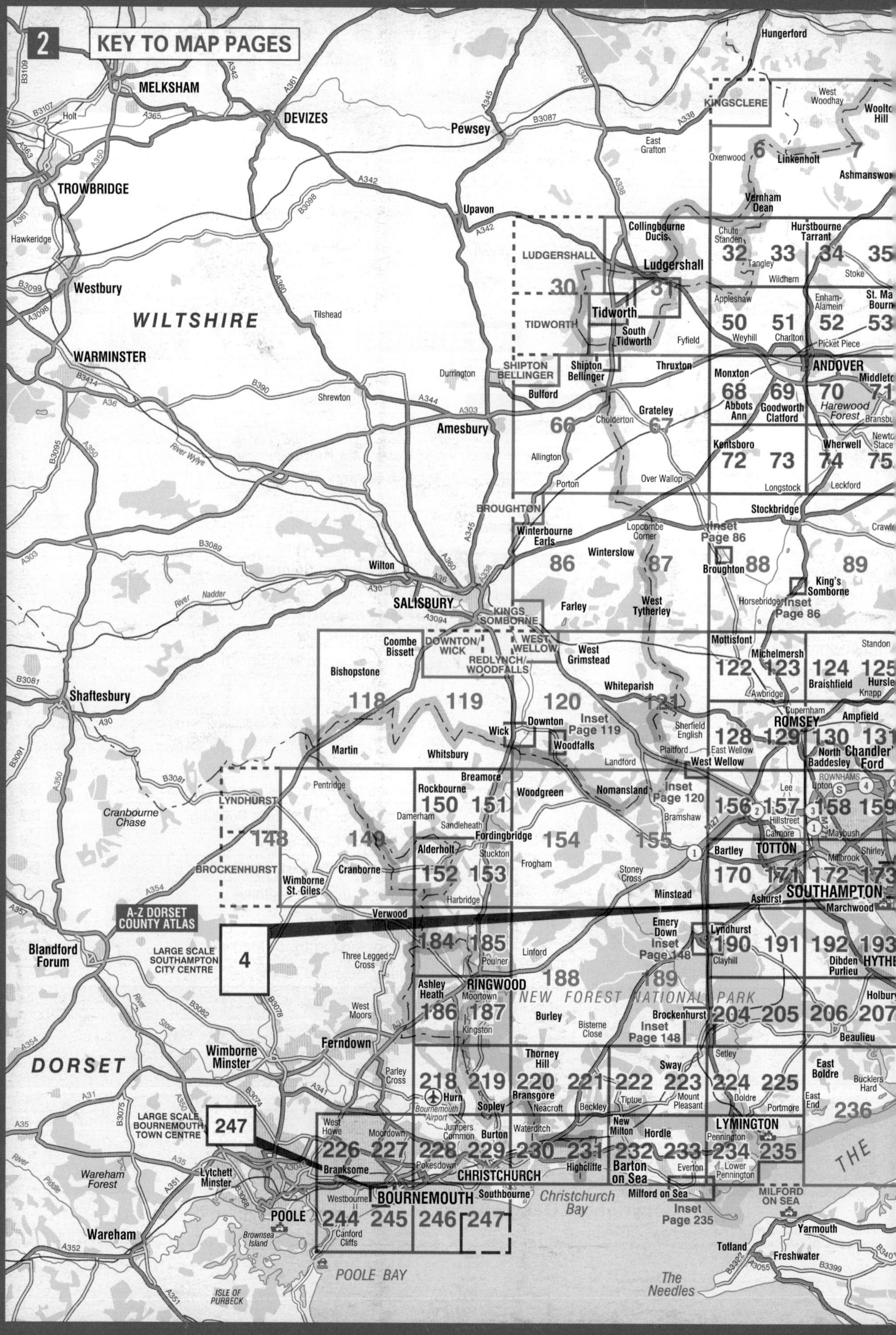

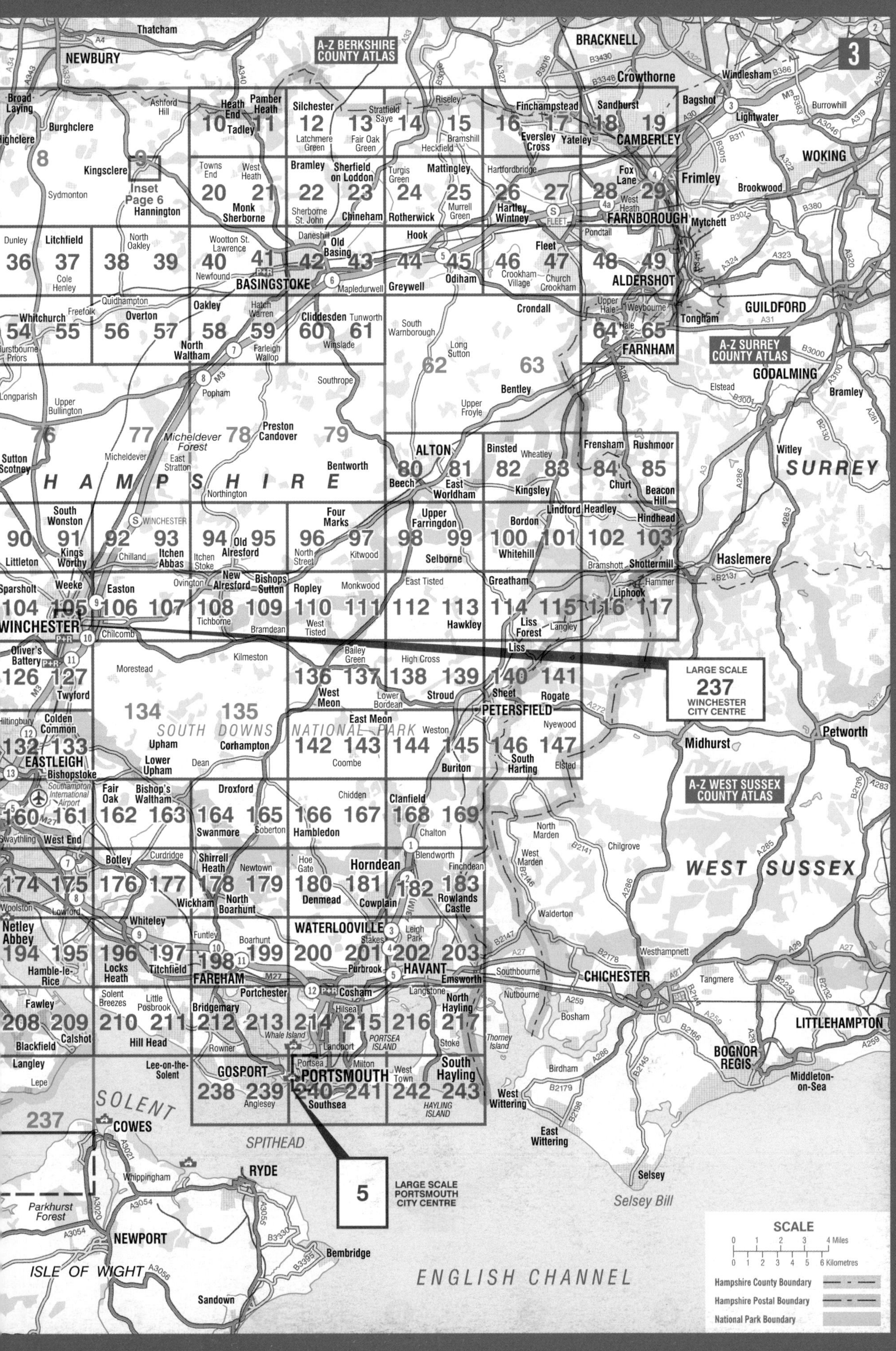
A-Z BERKSHIRE COUNTY ATLAS
A-Z SURREY COUNTY ATLAS
A-Z WEST SUSSEX COUNTY ATLAS
NEWBURY
Thatcham
BRACKNELL
Crowthorne
Windlesham
Bagshot
Lightwater
Burrowhill
WOKING
Sandhurst
CAMBERLEY
Frimley
Brookwood
Mytchett
Fox Lane
West Heath
FARNBOROUGH
Finchampstead
Eversley Cross
Yateley
Hartfordbridge
Hartley Wintney
FLEET
Fleet
Crookham Village
Church Crookham
Pondtail
ALDERSHOT
Upper Hale
Weybourne
Hale
Tongham
GUILDFORD
FARNHAM
GODALMING
Elstead
Bramley
Crondall
Bentley
Upper Froyle
Long Sutton
South Warnborough
Broad Laying
Highclere
Burghclere
Ashford Hill
Kingsclere
Sydmonton
Inset Page 6
Hannington
Heath End
Pamber Heath
Tadley
Silchester
Stratfield Saye
Latchmere Green
Fair Oak Green
Riseley
Heckfield
Bramshill
Towns End
West Heath
Monk Sherborne
Bramley
Sherfield on Loddon
Sherborne St. John
Chineham
Turgis Green
Rotherwick
Mattingley
Murrell Green
Dunley
Litchfield
Cole Henley
North Oakley
Wootton St. Lawrence
Newfound
BASINGSTOKE
Daneshill
Old Basing
Mapledurwell
Hook
Greywell
Odiham
Whitchurch
Freefolk
Quidhampton
Overton
Oakley
Hatch Warren
North Waltham
Farleigh Wallop
Cliddesden
Tunworth
Winslade
Hurstbourne Priors
Longparish
Upper Bullington
Popham
Southrope
Micheldever Forest
Preston Candover
Micheldever
East Stratton
Northington
Sutton Scotney
HAMPSHIRE
Bentworth
ALTON
Beech
East Worldham
Binsted
Wheatley
Kingsley
Frensham
Rushmoor
Churt
Beacon Hill
SURREY
Witley
South Wonston
Kings Worthy
WINCHESTER
Chilland
Itchen Abbas
Itchen Stoke
Old Alresford
Four Marks
Kitwood
North Street
Upper Farringdon
Selborne
Bordon
Whitehill
Lindford
Headley
Hindhead
Bramshott
Shottermill
Haslemere
Littleton
Weeke
Sparsholt
Easton
Ovington
New Alresford
Bishops Sutton
Ropley
Monkwood
East Tisted
Greatham
Liphook
Hammer
Tichborne
Bramdean
West Tisted
Hawkley
Liss Forest
Langley
Liss
Chilcomb
Oliver's Battery
Twyford
Morestead
Kilmeston
Bailey Green
High Cross
West Meon
Lower Bordean
Stroud
Sheet
Rogate
PETERSFIELD
LARGE SCALE 237 WINCHESTER CITY CENTRE
Hiltingbury
Colden Common
EASTLEIGH
Bishopstoke
Upham
Lower Upham
SOUTH DOWNS NATIONAL PARK
Corhampton
Dean
East Meon
Weston
Coombe
Buriton
Nyewood
South Harting
Elsted
Midhurst
Petworth
Southampton International Airport
Fair Oak
Bishop's Waltham
Droxford
Swanmore
Soberton
Chidden
Hambledon
Clanfield
Chalton
North Marden
West Marden
Chilgrove
Swaythling
West End
Botley
Curdridge
Shirrell Heath
Newtown
Hoe Gate
Horndean
Blendworth
Finchdean
Rowlands Castle
Denmead
Cowplain
Wickham
North Boarhunt
WEST SUSSEX
Walderton
Woolston
Lowford
Netley Abbey
Whiteley
Funtley
Boarhunt
WATERLOOVILLE
Leigh Park
Stakes
Purbrook
HAVANT
Emsworth
Southbourne
Westhampnett
CHICHESTER
Tangmere
Hamble-le-Rice
Locks Heath
Titchfield
FAREHAM
Portchester
Cosham
Langstone
North Hayling
Nutbourne
Bosham
Fawley
Solent Breezes
Little Posbrook
Bridgemary
Hilsea
Blackfield
Calshot
Hill Head
Whale Island
Rowner
Landport
PORTSEA ISLAND
Stoke
Thorney Island
LITTLEHAMPTON
Langley
Lee-on-the-Solent
GOSPORT
Portsea
Milton
PORTSMOUTH
West Town
South Hayling
West Wittering
Birdham
BOGNOR REGIS
Middleton-on-Sea
Lepe
Anglesey
Southsea
HAYLING ISLAND
SOLENT
COWES
SPITHEAD
East Wittering
Whippingham
RYDE
LARGE SCALE PORTSMOUTH CITY CENTRE
Selsey
Selsey Bill
Parkhurst Forest
NEWPORT
Bembridge
ISLE OF WIGHT
Sandown
ENGLISH CHANNEL
SCALE
0 1 2 3 4 Miles
0 1 2 3 4 5 6 Kilometres
Hampshire County Boundary
Hampshire Postal Boundary
National Park Boundary

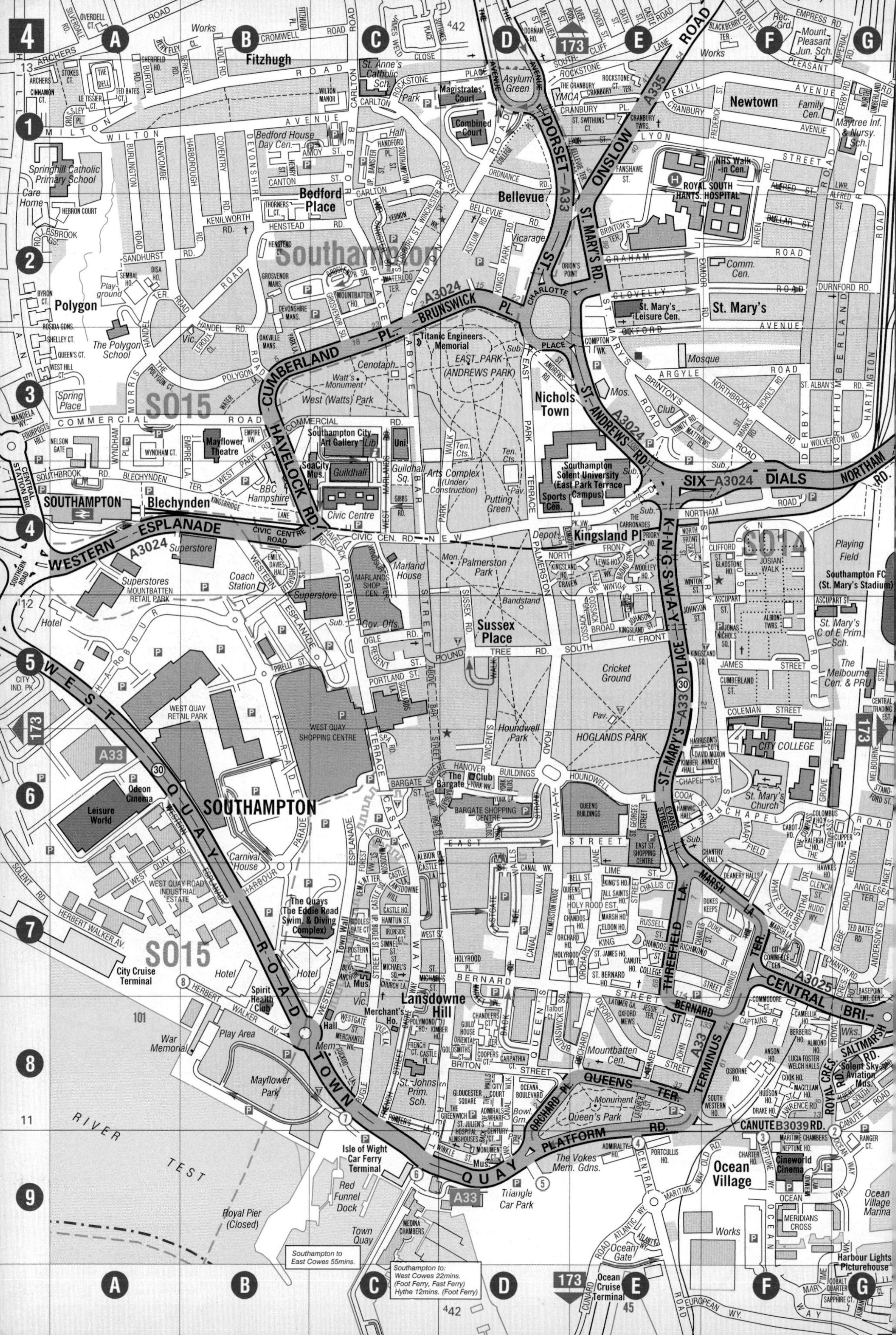

Fitzhugh
Newtown
Bedford Place
Bellevue
Southampton
Polygon
St. Mary's
Nichols Town
SO15
SO14
Blechynden
Kingsland Pl
SOUTHAMPTON
Sussex Place
Lansdowne Hill
Ocean Village
Springhill Catholic Primary School
The Polygon School
Spring Place
Mayflower Theatre
Southampton City Art Gallery
SeaCity Mus.
Guildhall
Civic Centre
Titanic Engineers Memorial
Cenotaph
Watt's Monument
West (Watts) Park
EAST PARK (ANDREWS PARK)
Arts Complex (Under Construction)
Southampton Solent University (East Park Terrace Campus)
Sports Cen.
BBC Hampshire
Superstore
Superstores
MOUNTBATTEN RETAIL PARK
Coach Station
Marland House
MARLANDS SHOP. CEN.
Gov. Offs.
Palmerston Park
Bandstand
Cricket Ground
HOGLANDS PARK
Houndwell Park
WEST QUAY RETAIL PARK
WEST QUAY SHOPPING CENTRE
The Bargate
BARGATE SHOPPING CENTRE
QUEENS BUILDINGS
EAST ST. SHOPPING CENTRE
CITY COLLEGE
St. Mary's Church
Leisure World
Odeon Cinema
Carnival House
WEST QUAY ROAD INDUSTRIAL ESTATE
The Quays (The Eddie Read Swim. & Diving Complex)
City Cruise Terminal
Hotel
Spirit Health Club
Play Area
War Memorial
Mayflower Park
Merchant's Ho.
St. Johns Prim. Sch.
Mountbatten Cen.
Queen's Park
The Vokes Mem. Gdns.
Triangle Car Park
Isle of Wight Car Ferry Terminal
Red Funnel Dock
Royal Pier (Closed)
Town Quay
Ocean Gate
Ocean Cruise Terminal
Cineworld Cinema
MERIDIANS CROSS
Works
Ocean Village Marina
Harbour Lights Picturehouse
Solent Sky Aviation Mus.
Southampton FC (St. Mary's Stadium)
Playing Field
The Melbourne Cen. & PRU
Royal South Hants. Hospital
NHS Walk-in Cen.
Magistrates' Court
Combined Court
Asylum Green
St. Mary's Leisure Cen.
Mosque
RIVER TEST
Southampton to East Cowes 55mins.
Southampton to: West Cowes 22mins. (Foot Ferry, Fast Ferry) Hythe 12mins. (Foot Ferry)
A3024
A33
A335
A3025
B3039
173
WESTERN ESPLANADE
CUMBERLAND PL.
BRUNSWICK PL.
HAVELOCK RD.
COMMERCIAL ROAD
WEST QUAY ROAD
TOWN QUAY
PLATFORM RD.
QUEENS TER.
TERMINUS
ST. MARY'S PLACE
KINGSWAY
SIX DIALS
NORTHAM RD.
ONSLOW ROAD
DORSET ST.
ST. ANDREWS RD.
CENTRAL BRI.
CANUTE RD.
ABOVE BAR STREET
EAST STREET

5
G
H
J
K
L
M
N
214
240
63
464
1
2
3
4
5
6
7
8
9
Basin No. 2
Basin No. 3
Dock No.11
Dock No.8
Dock No.15
Dock No.14
Dock No.12
Dock No.6
Dock No.5
Dock No.4
Basin No. 1
Dock No.1
Middle Slip Jetty
North Railway Jetty
Sheer Jetty
Pitch House Jetty
Kings Stairs Jetty
South Railway Jetty
HM NAVAL BASE
Portsmouth
PO1
Historic Dockyard
Mary Rose Museum
Royal Naval Museum
HMS Victory
Trafalgar Sail
Dockyard Apprentice
Action Stations
Harbour Tours
Visitor Centre
PORTSEA
HMS Warrior 1860
Transport Interchange
Common Hard
Portsea to Gosport 4 mins. (Foot Ferry)
PORTSMOUTH HARBOUR
GUNWHARF QUAYS
Vue Cinema
Bowlplex
The Waterfront
Spinnaker Tower
Gunwharf Marina
Waterbus Terminal
Aspex Art Gall.
Isle of Wight Ferry Terminal (Vehicular)
Outer Camber
Inner Camber
The Point
The Round Tower
Point Battery
OLD PORTSMOUTH
The Square Tower
Victoria Pier
Portsmouth to Fishbourne 40 mins.
Portsmouth to Ryde 22 mins. (Foot Ferry, Fast Ferry)
Portsmouth to Ryde 10 mins. (Foot Ferry, Hovercraft)
SPITHEAD
Cathedral
Governor's Green
Royal Garrison Church
Pembroke Gardens
King's Bastion
Moat
CLARENCE GROUND (Playing Fields)
Clarence Pier Amusement Park
Clarence Pier Pavilion
Hovercraft Terminal
Peel Mon.
SOUTHSEA
SOUTHSEA COMMON
Nelson's Statue
Meteorological Station
St. Jude's C of E Prim. Sch.
Portsmouth Grammar Sch.
City Museum & Art Gallery
University of Portsmouth (Ravelin Pk.)
Frewen Library
Town Mount
Landport Gate
Running Track
Grandstand
HMS Temeraire (Fleet Recreation Ground)
Sports Ground
Portsmouth Indoor Tennis Cen.
Nuffield Sports Centre
Nuffield Centre
King James's Gate
United Services Recreation Ground
Portsmouth Register Off.
Burnaby Terrace
Milldam
St. George's Prim. Sch.
Play Field
Powell Sq.
University of Portsmouth (University Quarter)
Victoria Park
PORTSMOUTH
RC Cathedral
HMS NELSON
Cascades Centre
Superstore
PORTSMOUTH & SOUTHSEA
Guildhall
Civic Offices
Theatre
NHS Walk-in Cen.
Combined Court Centre
Magistrates' Court
University of Portsmouth (Eldon Bldg.)
Southsea
PO5
Portsmouth High Sch. (Senior Sch.)
Portsmouth High Jun. Sch.
MARKETWAY
HOPE STREET
ALFRED RD.
ANGLESEA ROAD
WINSTON CHURCHILL AV.
CAMBRIDGE A3 RD.
HAMPSHIRE T.
LANDPORT TER.
KING'S TER.
KING'S B2154 ROAD
MUSEUM ROAD
HIGH STREET
BROAD STREET
PIER ROAD
SOUTHSEA TER.
WESTERN A288 PDE.
CLARENCE PDE.
ST. GEORGE'S ROAD
THE HARD
B2154
PARK ROAD
QUEEN STREET
CIRCULAR ROAD
A3
A2030
A288

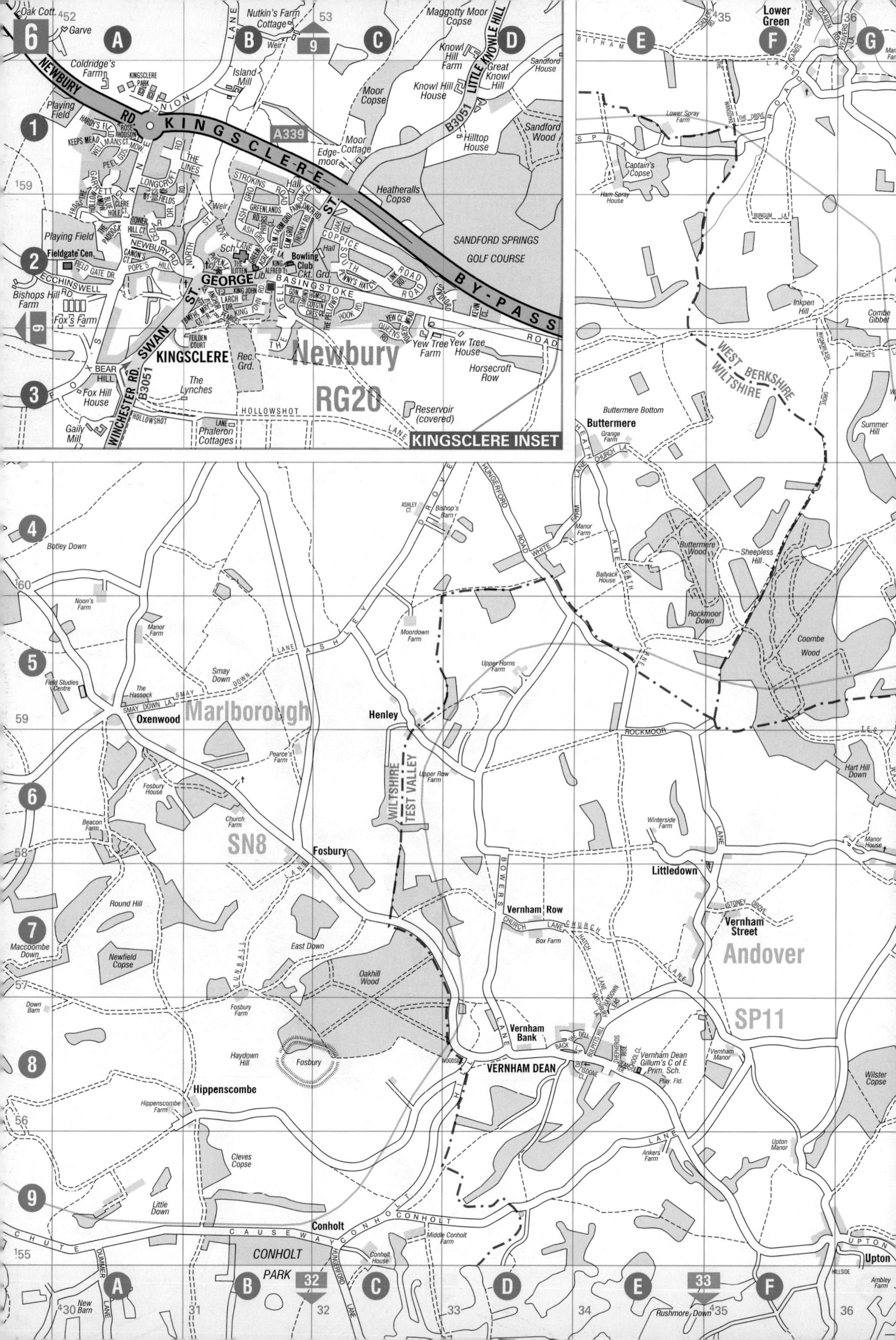

6
KINGSCLERE INSET
Newbury
RG20
KINGSCLERE
Sandford Springs Golf Course
Kingsclere By-Pass
Newbury Rd.
Swan St.
George St.
Basingstoke Road
Winchester Rd.
Hollowshot Lane
A339
B3051
Little Knowle Hill
Nutkin's Farm Cottage
Island Mill
Moor Copse
Moor Cottage
Edgemoor
Heatheralls Copse
Knowl Hill Farm
Knowl Hill House
Great Knowl Hill
Hilltop House
Sandford House
Sandford Wood
Coldridge's Farm
Playing Field
Fieldgate Cen.
Bishops Hill Farm
Fox's Farm
Fox Hill House
Gaily Mill
The Lynches
Rec. Grd.
Phaleron Cottages
Yew Tree Farm
Yew Tree House
Horsecroft Row
Reservoir (covered)
Bowling Club
Ckt. Grd.
Marlborough
SN8
Andover
SP11
West Berkshire
Wiltshire
Test Valley
Lower Green
Lower Spray Farm
Captain's Copse
Ham Spray House
Inkpen Hill
Combe Gibbet
Buttermere Bottom
Buttermere
Grange Farm
Summer Hill
Botley Down
Noon's Farm
Manor Farm
Field Studies Centre
The Hassock
Smay Down
Oxenwood
Pearce's Farm
Ashley Ct.
Bishop's Barn
Moordown Farm
Upper Horns Farm
Henley
Upper Row Farm
Buttermere Wood
Ballyack House
Sheepless Hill
Rockmoor Down
Coombe Wood
Hart Hill Down
Fosbury House
Beacon Farm
Church Farm
Fosbury
Round Hill
Maccoombe Down
Newfield Copse
East Down
Oakhill Wood
Down Barn
Fosbury Farm
Haydown Hill
Hippenscombe
Hippenscombe Farm
Cleves Copse
Little Down
Conholt
Conholt Park
Conholt House
Middle Conholt Farm
New Barn
Vernham Row
Box Farm
Vernham Bank
Vernham Dean
Vernham Dean Gillum's C of E Prim. Sch.
Winterside Farm
Littledown
Vernham Street
Vernham Manor
Manor House
Wilster Copse
Upton Manor
Ankers Farm
Rushmore Down
Upton
Ambley Farm
Causeway
Chute
Hungerford Road
Rockmoor
Bowers
9
32
33

INKPEN
Inkpen Common
Hell Corner
Inkpen Common Nature Reserve
HEAD'S LANE
BURGESS LANE
HOLLY LANE
WATERY LANE
Holtwood
Redhill Wood
Vanner's Farm
VANNERS LA.
Red Hill
Enborne Street Farm
River Enborne
Upper Green
Kirby Farm
Trapshill
Middle Furze Park
Malt House
Hazelby House
HAZELBY COTTS.
Gore End
GORE END VILLAS
Hatt Common
Yew Tree Farm
Ball Hill
Kirby House
WESTFIELDS
West Woodhay House
Fishponds Farm
Smart's Copse
North End
Park House
WEST WOODHAY
Hatch House Farm
BALLHILL COTTS.
Woolton House Stud
Hungerford
Burlyns
Northenby
Woolton House Farm
HOBLEY LANE
WOOLTON HILL
Harwood Lodge
Highwood Farm
Berries Farm
Heath End
Woolton House
WEST BERKSHIRE
BASINGSTOKE and DEANE
West Woodhay Down
Copse Farm
Barn Croft
FULLERS LANE
TRADE STREET
Walbury Hill
RG17
East Woodhay
Church Farm
East End
Primary School
Malverleys
CHURCH ROAD
Combe
Lower Farm
Stargrove
Hollington Herb Garden
Hollington Farm
Manor Farm
CHURCH LA.
Combe Hill
Hollington
Tower House
Hollington Park
Great Copse
Newbury
WAYFARERS WALK
Eastwick
Jones Farm
HOLLINGTON LANE
Hogs Hole
Pilot Hill
RG20
WEST BERKSHIRE
TEST VALLEY
The Oaks
West Down Copse
Kinghams Farm
Pill Hill
Buckhanger Copse
Hollington Cross
Coles Wood
Zell House Farm
Zell House Copse
LINKENHOLT
Manor Farm
ARTHURS LA.
FACCOMBE
Curzon Street Farm
Privet Copse
Netherton
ASHMANSWORTH
Ashmansworth Manor
OX DROVE
CROSS LANE
GREEN LANE
LONDON LANE
HIGHFIELD
Steeles Farm
HIPPLE LANE
NETHERTON ROAD
TEST VALLEY
BASINGSTOKE and DEANE
Church Farm
Alexander Farm
HILL
A343
Crux Easton
Faccombe Wood
Lower Manor Farm
Crux Easton House
Clinchorn Farm
Sidley Wood
Beech Hanger Copse
REDHILL
DOILEY HILL
Doyley Manor
Woodcott
River Swift
G H J K L M N
37 38 39 40 41 42 43
64 63 62 61 60 59 58 57 56 55
1 2 3 4 5 6 7 8 9
8
34
35

Enborne Row
Wash Water
Wash Common
Newtown
Horris Hill
Newtown Common
Burghclere Common
WOOLTON HILL
Broad Layings
Penwood
Tot Hill
Pound Street
Tot Hill Service Area
BURGHCLERE
The Mount
HIGHCLERE
Highclere Street
Hollington Cross
Whitway
Old Burghclere
Sydmonton
Crux Easton
Woodcott
Newbury
Whitchurch
RG14
RG28
A34
A343
A339
B4640
Highclere Castle
Highclere Park
Sidown Hill
Beacon Hill & Nature Reserve
Upper Woodcott Down
Lower Woodcott Down
Great Litchfield Down
Ladle Hill
Earlstone Common
Frith Copse
Great Gasson Copse
Glasshanger Copse
River Enborne
WINCHESTER ROAD
NEWBURY BY-PASS
WAYFARER'S WALK

7
36
37

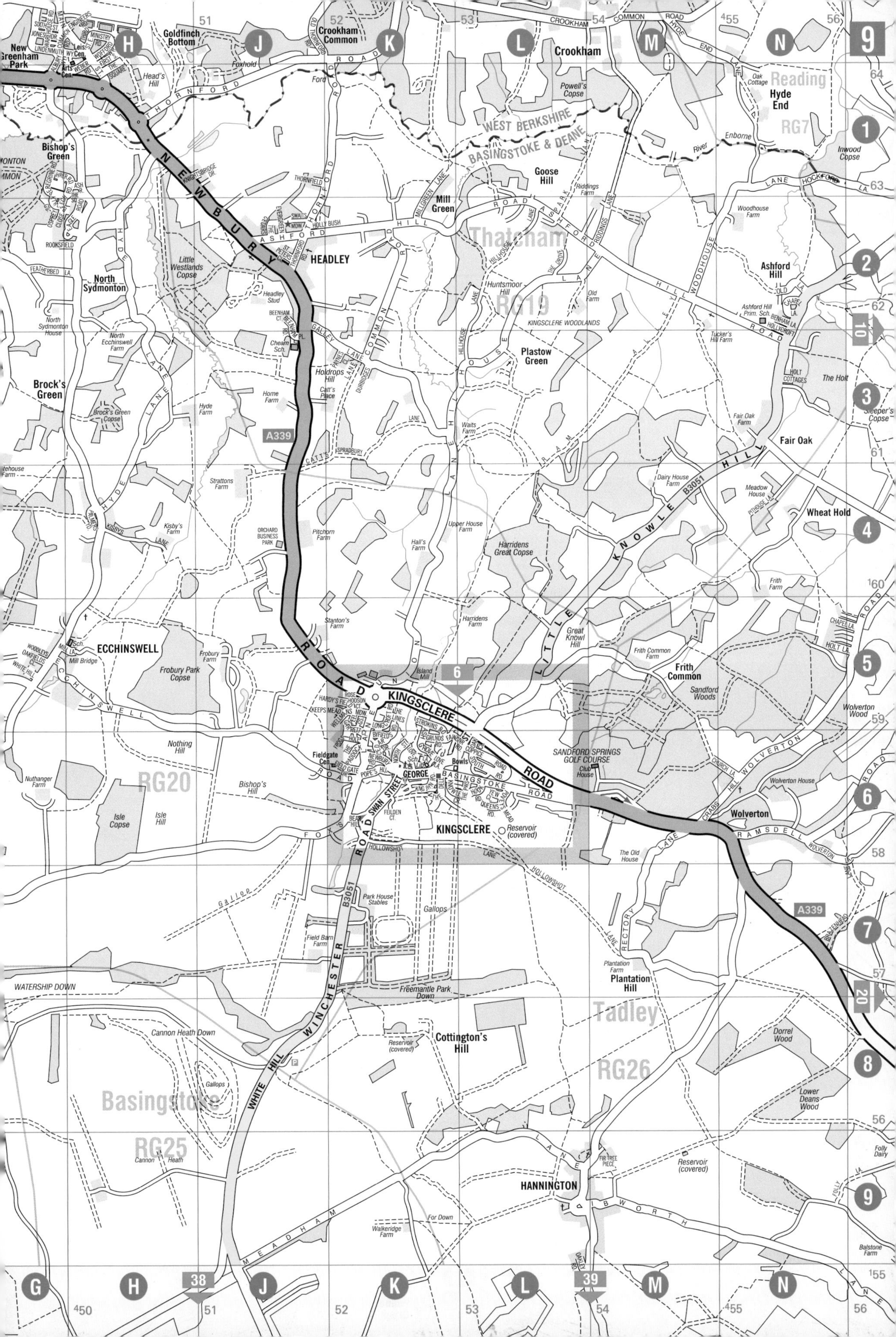
9
New Greenham Park
Goldfinch Bottom
Crookham Common
Crookham
Hyde End
Reading
RG7
WEST BERKSHIRE
BASINGSTOKE & DEANE
Bishop's Green
Goose Hill
Mill Green
Thatcham
HEADLEY
North Sydmonton
RG19
Ashford Hill
Plastow Green
Brock's Green
Holdrops Hill
The Holt
Fair Oak
Wheat Hold
A339
ECCHINSWELL
Frobury Park Copse
Frith Common
Sandford Woods
KINGSCLERE ROAD
SANDFORD SPRINGS GOLF COURSE
RG20
GEORGE
KINGSCLERE
Wolverton
Isle Copse
WATERSHIP DOWN
Freemantle Park Down
Plantation Hill
Tadley
Cottington's Hill
RG26
Basingstoke
RG25
HANNINGTON
WHITE HILL WINCHESTER ROAD
B3051
38
39
10
20

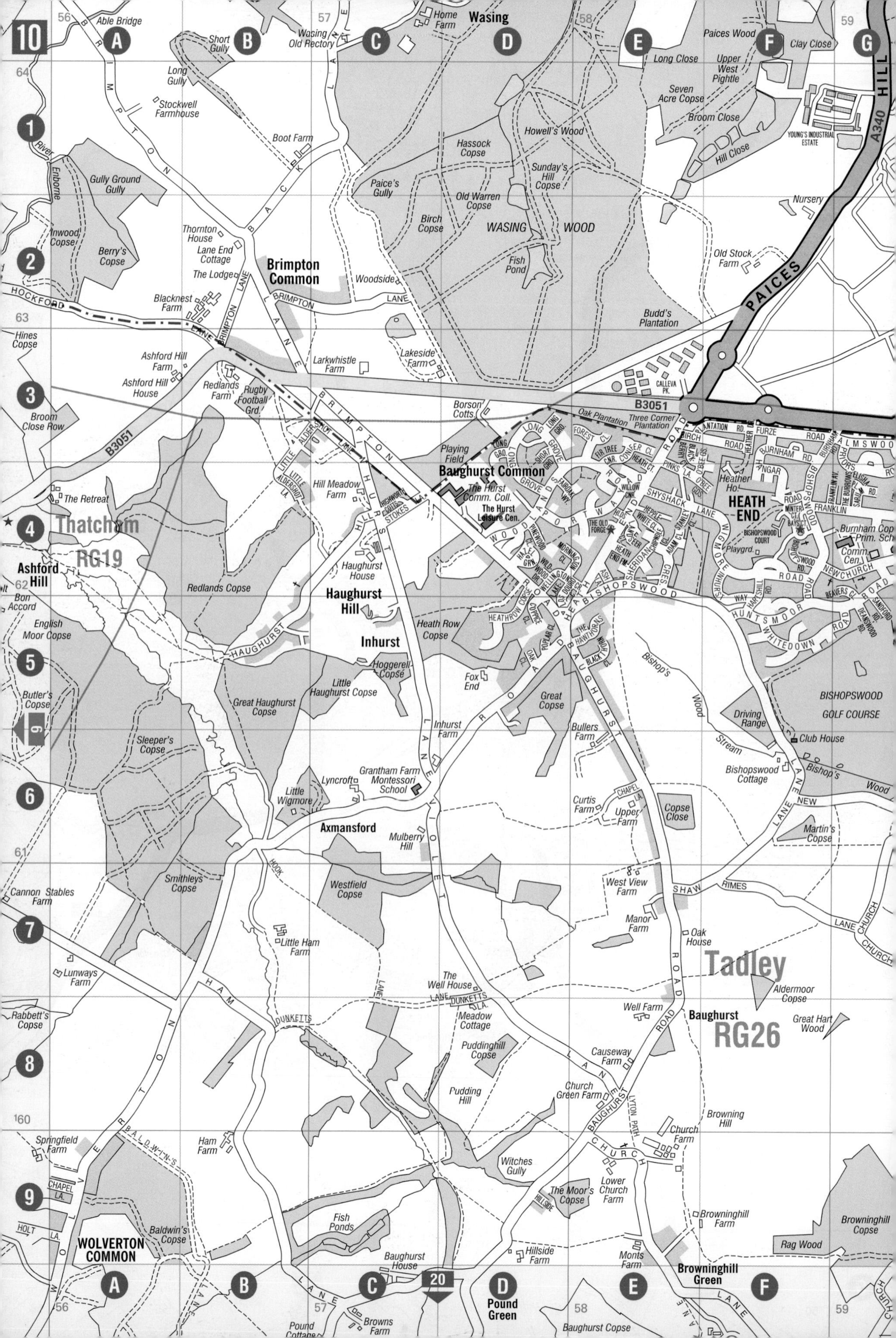

Wasing
Brimpton Common
Baughurst Common
HEATH END
Thatcham
RG19
Ashford Hill
Haughurst Hill
Inhurst
Axmansford
Tadley
RG26
Baughurst
WOLVERTON COMMON
Browninghill Green
Pound Green
WASING WOOD
BISHOPSWOOD GOLF COURSE
A340
B3051
PAICES HILL
The Hurst Comm. Coll.
The Hurst Leisure Cen.
Grantham Farm Montessori School
Great Haughurst Copse
Redlands Copse
Westfield Copse
Baughurst Copse

9
20

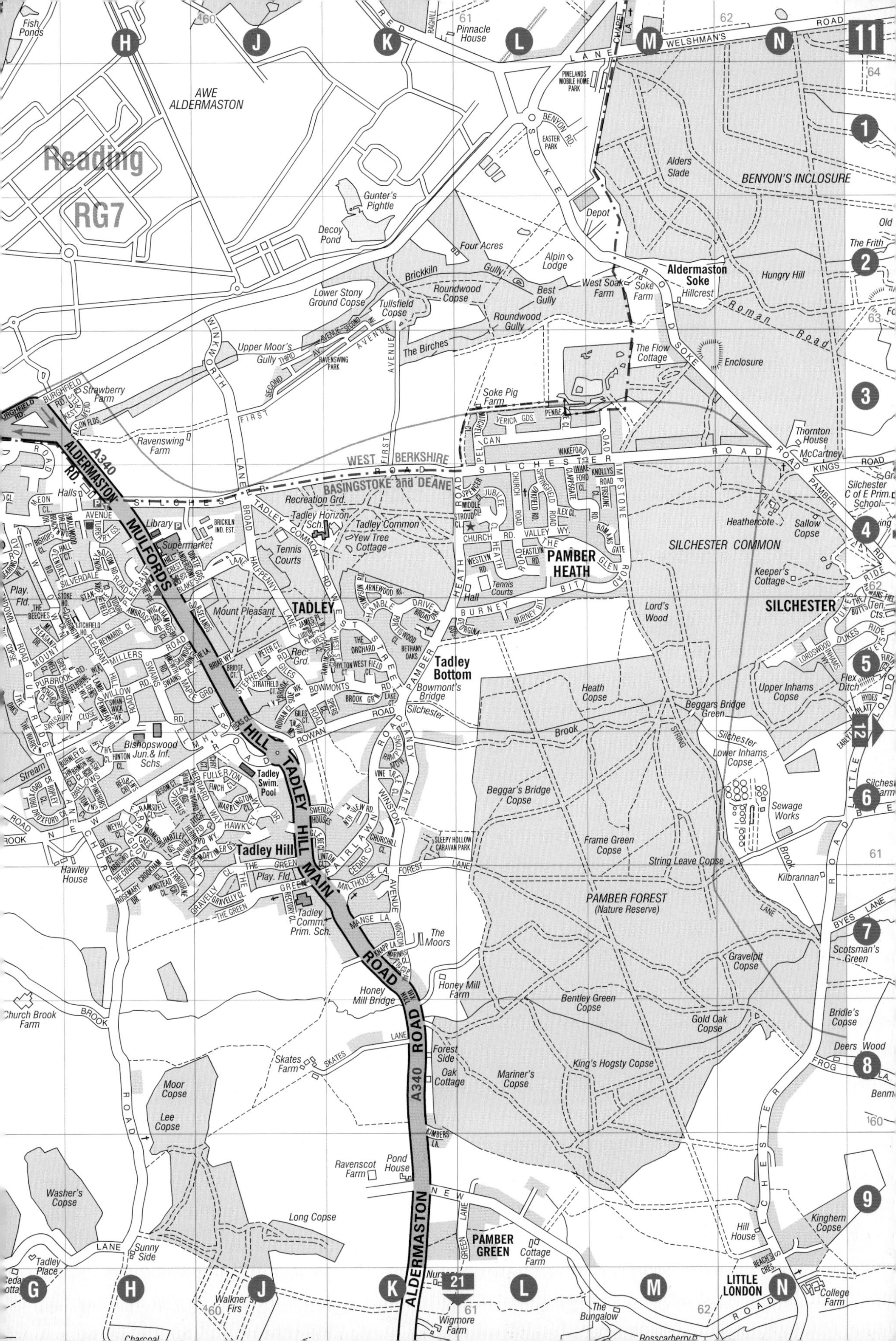
AWE
ALDERMASTON
Reading
RG7
Gunter's Pightle
Decoy Pond
Four Acres
Brickkiln Gully
Roundwood Copse
Best Gully
Roundwood Gully
Lower Stony Ground Copse
Tullsfield Copse
The Birches
Upper Moor's Gully
Alpin Lodge
West Soak Farm
Soke Farm
Aldermaston Soke
Hillcrest
Hungry Hill
Alders Slade
BENYON'S INCLOSURE
The Frith
Depot
Pinnacle House
PINELANDS MOBILE HOME PARK
EASTER PARK
The Flow Cottage
Enclosure
Roman Road
Soke Pig Farm
Strawberry Farm
Ravenswing Farm
WEST BERKSHIRE
BASINGSTOKE and DEANE
Thornton House
McCartney
Silchester C of E Prim. School
Heathercote
Sallow Copse
SILCHESTER COMMON
Keeper's Cottage
SILCHESTER
Lord's Wood
Recreation Grd.
Tadley Horizon Sch.
Tadley Common
Yew Tree Cottage
Tennis Courts
PAMBER HEATH
Library
Supermarket
Mount Pleasant
TADLEY
Tadley Bottom
Bowmont's Bridge
Silchester Brook
Heath Copse
Beggars Bridge Green
Upper Inhams Copse
Flex Ditch
Lower Inhams Copse
Sewage Works
Bishopswood Jun.& Inf. Schs.
Tadley Swim. Pool
Tadley Hill
Play. Fld.
Hawley House
Tadley Comm. Prim. Sch.
The Moors
Beggar's Bridge Copse
Frame Green Copse
String Leave Copse
Kilbrannan
PAMBER FOREST
(Nature Reserve)
SLEEPY HOLLOW CARAVAN PARK
Gravelpit Copse
Scotsman's Green
Honey Mill Bridge
Honey Mill Farm
Bentley Green Copse
Gold Oak Copse
Bridle's Copse
Deers Wood
Church Brook Farm
Skates Farm
Forest Side
Oak Cottage
Mariner's Copse
King's Hogsty Copse
Moor Copse
Lee Copse
Ravenscot Farm
Pond House
Washer's Copse
Long Copse
PAMBER GREEN
Cottage Farm
Hill House
Kinghern Copse
Tadley Place
Sunny Side
LITTLE LONDON
College Farm
Walkner's Firs
Nursery
Wigmore Farm
The Bungalow
A340
ALDERMASTON ROAD
MULFORDS HILL
TADLEY HILL
MAIN ROAD
SILCHESTER ROAD
WELSHMAN'S ROAD
21
12
H
J
K
L
M
N
G
1
2
3
4
5
6
7
8
9
60
61
62
63
64

Mortimer West End
Reading RG7
SILCHESTER
Tadley RG26
BRAMLEY
LITTLE LONDON
Latchmere Green
Three Ashes
Bramley Corner
Silchester Roman City Walls
Calleva Roman Town
Silchester Roman Amphitheatre
The Devil's Highway (Roman Road)
BENYON'S INCLOSURE
Allen's Common
Fox Hill
Great Slade
Old School House
School Piece
Blue Hayes
Cricket Grd.
Pavilion
West End Farm
Lovegrove's Farm
West End Brook
Simms's Copse
Simms Stud Farm
Windabout Copse
Mill Copse
Hilliar's Copse
Long Copse
Nine Acre Copse
Simm's Plantation
Brocas Plantation
Brocas Land Farm
Tanhous Cotts.
Luke's Copse
Stonehill Copse
Stone Hill
Heathland Copse
Coleshill
Kiln Pond
The Frith
Old Kiln Yard
Pond Farm
The Larches
Little Heath
Fort
Catthaw Lands Copse
Catthawlands Farm
Roman Road
Rye House
Tennis Court
North Gate
Roman Burial Ground
Clad Gully
Kiln Yard Copse
Collin's Copse
The Mount
Sheepsgrove Cottages
Sheepgrove Farm
Manor Farm
Old Manor House
The Drove
Sawyers Lands
Edrington Cottages
Edrington
Ten. Ct.
The Rectory
The Grange
Silchester C of E Prim. School
Playing Fields
Thornton House
McCartney
Silchester Hall
Rampier Copse
South Gate
Dicker's Copse
Churchlane Copse
Dicker's Farm
Scrub Copse
The Beeches
Spoil Bank
North Copse
Hasker's Copse
Haskers Farm
Great Scrub Copse
Newersland
Church Lane Farm
Clappers Farm
Ford
Brickledons Farm
Moat
Silchester House
The Cottage
Greenlands Farm
Flex Ditch
Silchester Farm
Byes Farm
Scotsman's Green
Early Bridge Copse
Bridle's Copse
Deers Wood
Holly Bush
Benmore
Froglane Farm
Pound Farm
Brook Farm
Lower Farm Bungalow
Lower Farm
Barnoaks
Park Copse
Park Farm
Old Meadows
The Pound House
Brookside Cottages
Brook
Withy Place
Highfield
Brookbend Kennels
Halls Farm
May Bank
Haines Farm
Latchmere House
Frith View
Latchmere Green Farm
Withy Copse
Little Holdens Copse
Davnage Copse
Electricity Sub Station
Bramley Frith Wood
Minchens
Barefoot's House
Kinghern Copse
Latchmore Farm
College Farm
Recreation Ground
Hall
Bramley Grange
Welshman's Rd.
Ferr Cottage
Bosket
Long View
Windabout
Rose Cottage
Vic.
Back Lane
Farm Lane
Church Road
Wall Lane
Kings Road
Bramley Road
Pamber Road
School La.
Ride Road
Whistlers La.
Holly La.
Dukes Ride
Romans Field
The Butts
Hartleys
Hydes Platt
Lordswood
Firth
Little London Road
Byes Lane
Frog Lane
Silchester Road
Church Lane
Clappers Farm Road
Clappers Road
Park Road
Simms
Turk's Lane
Drury Lane
Minchens Lane
Moat Cl.
Browns Cl.
Bramley La.
Oakmead
Coopers
Street
Pound Cl.
Ringshall Gdns.
Sherfield Road
Longbridge
Bramley
11
22
A B C D E F G
1 2 3 4 5 6 7 8 9
63 64 465
64 63 62 61 160

STRATFIELD MORTIMER
Jun. Sch.
Tun Bri.
Mortimer
STATION ROAD
THE FOREHEAD
Kiln Lane
Pitfield Lane
Foudry Brook
Admiral's Copse
Furze Ground
Ladyfield Copse
New Mow Mead
Perrins Fm.
Smith's Copse
Tanhouse Bridge
Home Wood
Little Park Farm
Ticklecorner Lane
Butlers Lands
Hogs Plat
WEST BERKSHIRE
BASINGSTOKE and DEANE
Park Lane
Wigmore Copse
The Jackdaw
Hilly Meadows
Butler's Lands Copse
Mortimer Lane
Garden Copse
Misselbury Copse
Wigmore Farm
Wigmore Thatch
Foreland's Farm
Hall
Dollery's Copse
Pheasantry Copse
Parson's Farm
Stratfield Saye
New Street
Dollery's Farm
Lavell's Lane
West End Green
The Springs
Green Lane
Lavell's Farm
Herriot's Farm
Lane
14
Broadford Bridge
King's Farm
Goodchilds Hill
Oak Lane
Fairfields
Purdue's Farm
Ives Farm
Purdue Farm Cottage
Fair Oak Green
Fair Oak Lane
Homeleigh
Stratfield Saye Road
Mill Lane
The Well House
New Plantation
Southend Farm
River Loddon
Holly Cross
Holly Cross Farm
Oliver's Lane
Heywood's Farm
Turgis
Ladywell
Hook RG27
Ladyland Copse
Tubbs Copse
Bramley C of E Prim. Sch.
Chute Close
Tottenham Cl.
Strawberry
Osler
Oliver's Farm
Folly Lane
Folly Farm
The Fishery
Potters
23
66
67
68
69
64
63
62
61
60
H J K L M N
G H J K L M N
1 2 3 4 5 6 7 8 9

Beech Hill
Beech Hill Rd.
Park View
Rowe's
Cannon Bridge
Way
West Berkshire
Wokingham
Lane
A33
Spring Lane
Balcombe Cott.
Uplands
Goddard's Farm
Basingstoke
Field Cottage
Elmtree Cottage
Taylor's Lane
Collins Copse
The Lodge
Smithy Cottage
Applegarth
Highgrove Copse
Smith's Copse
Broad Road
Stanford End Farm
Barge
Bull
Collins Copse
River Loddon
B3349
St. Leger's Copse
Russett
Spring
Noah's Ark
Lane
Stanford End
Cosfield
Chapel Lane
Newbarn House
Norton Rd.
Portway
Bull
Sun Lane
Rowe's Lane
Lane
Chequers
Fair Cross
Lodge
Lakepond Copse
Lane
Welsh
Standfordend Bridge
Road
Chequer
The Devil's Highway (Roman Road)
Lake Pond
Coldharbour Wood
B3349
Home Farm
Ten. Ct.
Park Corner
Road
New Inn Copse
Wellington Riding
Stone Bridge
Lower Tumbling Bay
Top Hill Copse
Heckfield Heath
Stratfield Saye Park
A33
Pheasantry Copse
Heck
Basingstoke & Deane
Hart
Stratfield Saye House
London Lodges
Duke of Wellington Commemorative Column
The Plantation
The
Stratfield Saye Park
Pheasantry Lodge
Green La
The Old Rectory
Wellingtonia Cottages
River Loddon
Broadford Bridge
King's Farm
Hall's Copse
The Moor
Sheephouse Copse
Reservoir (covered)
Park Pitham Copse
Highfield Farm
Cattle Copse
Basingstoke
Cottroles
Broadford House
Lower Pitham House
Highfield House
Highfield Park
Lower Pitham Copse
Turgis Court Farm
Lawn Farm
Rose Cottages
Corner Cottage
Stratfield Turgis
Tatlants Copse
A33
Yew Tree Cottage
Thorpe's Copse
Timber Copse
Daneshill School
Home Farm
Browns Farm Cottage
Guyets Copse
24
Cricket Ground
Pav.
Bylands Farmhouse
Wheelers Farm House
Clay's
A B C D E F G
1 2 3 4 5 6 7 8 9
69 470 71 72
64 63 62 61 160

13
24

Reading
RG7
Hook
RG27
RISELEY
HECKFIELD
Bramshill
Hazeley Lea
HAZELEY
Grouse Green
WELLINGTON COUNTRY PARK
BRAMSHILL PLANTATION
GREAT DANMOOR COPSE
Deep Water
Angel Sprints
Springalls Farm
Riseley Farm
Yew Tree Farm
Glasspool Farm
Riseley Gorse Farm
West Graylake
RISELEY BUSINESS PARK
The Marshes
Barossa Fm.
Oak Fruit Farm
Wheelers Fm.
Sandpit Farm
Chill Hill
Dacre Farm
Farley Ct.
Wyvol's Copse
Picket's Copse
Wheeler's Copse
Hill Farm
King's Copse
Jouldings Farm
Bottom Farm House
Well House Farm
Cordery's Farm
Ham's Wood
Vis. Cen.
Birchen Copse
Caravan Park
Riseley Wood
Mill Wood
Pound Copse
Fox Warren
Hall's Farm
Springwater Farm
Reading Lodge
Park Farm
Church Lodge
Heckfield Place Park
Heckfield Place
Wiggins Copse
Heckfield Bridge
BRAMSHILL COUNCIL HOUSES
Holyoak Farm
Alder Wood
Moor Place Farm
Omar Farm
Cemetery
School Farm
Cunningham's Copse
Holdshott House
Holdshott Farm
Vinalls Copse
Netherclifts Copse
Little Danmoor Copse
Bouchiers Copse
Turnpike Cottage
Turnpike Copse
Ivy Cottage
The Bungalow
The Cottage
Coldpiece Farm
Brickkiln Copse
Kiln Farm
Garstones Lodge
Garstones Wood
Moorlane Copse
Alder Moor Farm
Alder Moor
Lea Bridge Pump House
Lea Farm
The Meadows
Stevens Farm
Dell Farm
Peatmoor Copse
Bramshill Park
BRAMSHILL PARK
High Bridge
Rec. Grd.
Hall
Lodge
Ford
The Devil's Highway (Roman Rd.)
THE DEVIL'S HIGHWAY
WOKINGHAM
HART
River Blackwater
River Whitewater
Whitewater River
River Hart
Weir
The Broadwater
TROWES LANE
PART LANE
SCHOOL LANE
SCHOOL ROAD
DEVIL'S MILL LANE
RISELEY ROAD
MILL LANE
ODIHAM ROAD
B3349
B3011
CAUSEWAY
BRAMSHILL
LAUNDRY LANE
CHURCH LANE
CHARTER LAINSMUIR
BENHAM LA.
NUTBEAN LANE
SANDPIT LANE
FORD LANE
WELL HOUSE LANE
JOULDINGS
FORGES
BRAMSHILL ROAD
COPES LANE
HAZELEY LEA
PLOUGH LANE
MANSION DRIVE
LOWER
H J K L M N G
1 2 3 4 5 6 7 8 9
73 74 475
64 63 62 61 60
16
25

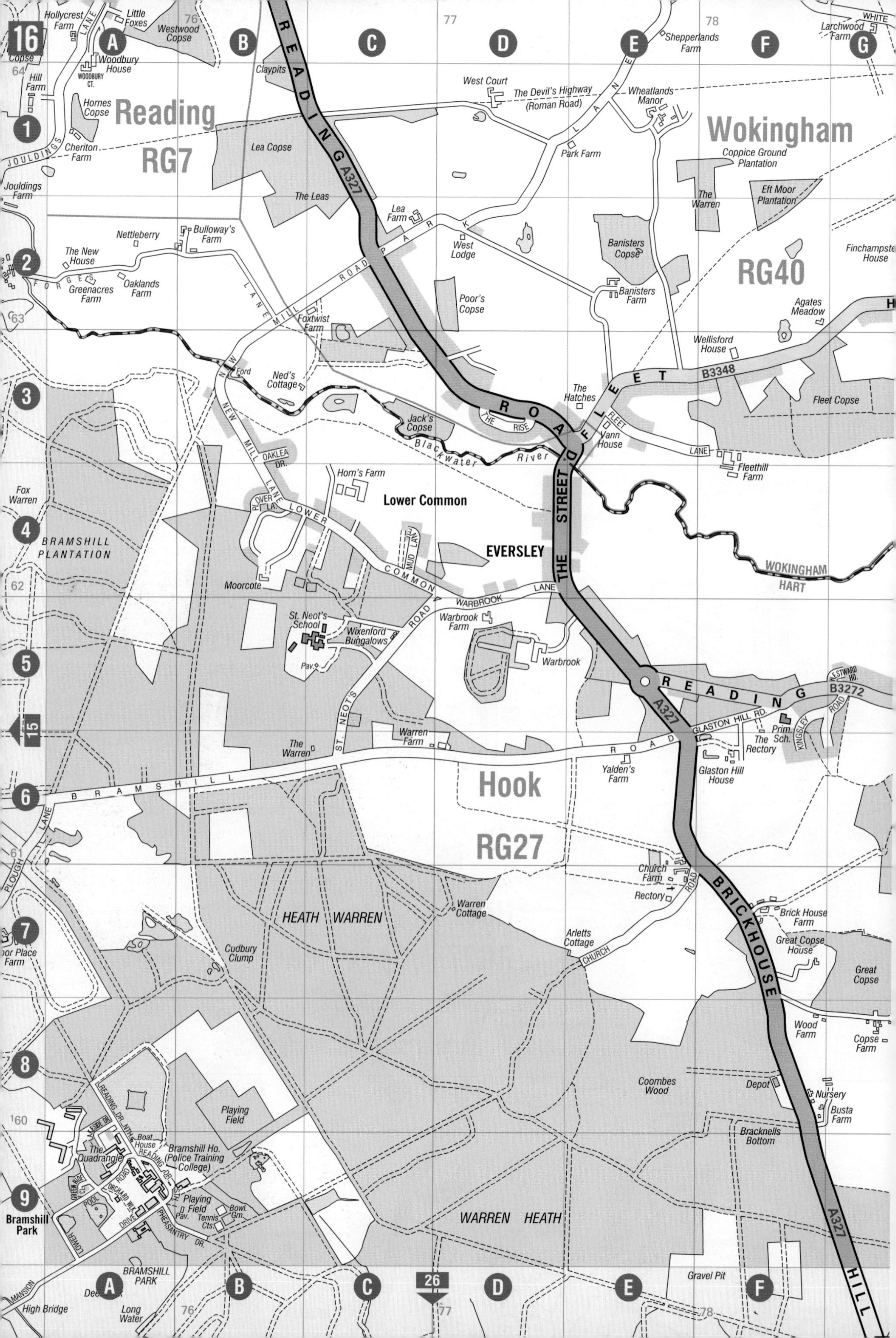

Reading
RG7
Wokingham
RG40
Hook
RG27
EVERSLEY
Lower Common
Hollycrest Farm
Little Foxes
Westwood Copse
Woodbury House
Hill Farm
Hornes Copse
Cheriton Farm
Jouldings Farm
Claypits
Lea Copse
The Leas
West Court
The Devil's Highway (Roman Road)
Shepperlands Farm
Wheatlands Manor
Larchwood Farm
Park Farm
Coppice Ground Plantation
Eft Moor Plantation
The Warren
Banisters Copse
Banisters Farm
Finchampstead House
Agates Meadow
Wellisford House
Lea Farm
West Lodge
Poor's Copse
Nettleberry
Bulloway's Farm
The New House
Greenacres Farm
Oaklands Farm
Foxtwist Farm
Ned's Cottage
Ford
Jack's Copse
Blackwater River
The Hatches
Vann House
Fleet Copse
Fleetfill Farm
Horn's Farm
Fox Warren
BRAMSHILL PLANTATION
Moorcote
St. Neot's School
Wixenford Bungalows
Warbrook Farm
Warbrook
WOKINGHAM
HART
The Warren
Warren Farm
The Rectory
Prim. Sch.
Glaston Hill House
Yalden's Farm
Church Farm
Rectory
Brick House Farm
Great Copse House
Great Copse
Warren Cottage
HEATH WARREN
Arletts Cottage
Cudbury Clump
Moor Place Farm
Wood Farm
Copse Farm
Coombes Wood
Depot
Nursery
Busta Farm
Bracknells Bottom
Playing Field
Boat House
The Quadrangle
Bramshill Ho. (Police Training College)
Playing Field
Pav.
Tennis Cts.
Bowl. Grn.
Bramshill Park
WARREN HEATH
BRAMSHILL PARK
Deer Park
High Bridge
Long Water
Gravel Pit
READING ROAD
A327
THE STREET
FLEET ROAD
B3348
FLEET LANE
READING ROAD
B3272
BRICKHOUSE HILL
BRAMSHILL ROAD
NEW MILL LANE
MILL LANE
PARK ROAD
FORGE LANE
LOWER COMMON ROAD
WARBROOK LANE
ST. NEOT'S ROAD
GLASTON HILL RD.
KINGSLEY ROAD
CHURCH ROAD
PLOUGH LANE
JOULDINGS LANE
MANSION DRIVE
PHEASANTRY DR.

15
26

79
480
81
82
H
J
K
L
M
N
G
1
2
3
4
5
6
7
8
9
Arden House
Ridge Farm
Heath Pond
Simons Wood
HEATH
ROMAN
RIDE
TALISMAN CL.
LWR. WOKINGHAM ROAD
PRIORS WOOD
HORSE
Church Farm
LANE
CHURCH
WICK
HILL
JUBILEE
B3016
Armholes
Rhododendron Corner
THE RIDGES
North Ct. Farm
Manor House
Lower Cottage
High Barn
Pye Hill House
Crowthorne
HOLLYBUSH RIDE
B3348
AVENUE
WELLINGTONIA
RG45
WOKINGHAM
BRACKNELL FOREST
A321
RD. THE
Poor Ridge Cottage
Puckswood House
The Ridges
FINCHAMPSTEAD RIDGES
RIDGES
Rectory Farm
Bowling Green
West View
The Rectory
St. Anthonys Cottage
East Court
Rec. Grd.
Sports Club
Manor Farm
Russets
ROAD
THE
VILLAGE
Prim. Sch.
Breakspear's Farm
LONGWATER LA.
MANOR
BARNS LA.
Spout Pond
Sandhurst
63
Fisher's Copse
CORFIELD CL.
LIDDELL CL.
BURNMOOR
MDW.
WOODMOOR
CRICKET HILL
DELL
BLACKWATER VW.
Beech Hill
LONGWATER
FINCHAMPSTEAD
Sewage Works
LOWER SANDHURST ROAD
LOWER
Hawthorns
Moor Green Farm
Foxglade
Hall Farm
SANDHURST
Hilton Cottage
Grove Farm House
Coalpit Copse
AMBARROW FARM COURTYARD
Ambarrow Farm
Grove Farm
AMBARROW LA.
GU47
LONGWATER
Blackwater River
BRACKNELL FOREST
HART
Horseshoe Lake Watersports Centre
62
BANNISTER GDNS.
LONGWATER LA.
Mill Farm
Mill Bridge
Pavilion
BLACKWATER VALLEY GOLF COURSE
Driving Range
Playing Field
Club House
Club House
Sean Devereaux Park
Pav.
Cross Green
Vann Place Farm
Eversley Centre
PAUL'S FLD.
FOX
COPSE LA.
BLAIRE PARK
MILL BRIDGE RD.
RIVER RD.
COOMBE RD.
MILL LANE
18
Depot
JARVIS CL.
MAYFIELD CT.
HOLLYBUSH
Nurseries
THE FIELDERS
SPARVELLS
CHAPEL MEAD
GRENSELL CL.
SHERLOCK LEA
YEOMANS
EVERSLEY CROSS
MARSH
B3272
Watmore Farm
CANBERRA GDNS.
EXETER
MAYFLOWER
MOULSHAM GREEN
MOULSHAM COPSE LA.
FAREHAM DR.
IVES CLOSE
BROOME CL.
CRONDALL END
CHANDLERS LANE
SHIRES
WEST FRYERNE
LITTLE COPSE
Hollybush Farm
LANE
Nursery
NORTH WICK
NEW RD.
ROAD
EVERSLEY RD.
CROSBY GDNS.
DR.
VICARAGE
Yateley Green
VICARAGE
READING ROAD
Brooklands
CELANDINE CT.
LOWFIELD
WEST GREEN
LANE CT.
CASTOR
Lower Eversley Copse
UP GREEN
B3016
LANE
LOVE
Brookside Farm
FRENSHAM CL.
FIRGROVE
BOWL. Grn.
Tennis Cts.
Pav.
Yateley
Village Hall
B3272
CORONATION RD
Yateley Industries
THE CRESCENT
61
Yateley Manor Sch.
Playing Fields
STILWELL
YATELEY
CHEQUERS
UP GREEN
Up Green Farm
FIRGROVE RD.
FIRGROVE
ROAD
HONEYSUCKLE CL.
CLOVER
BRACKEN
ROBINS GRO.
CRES.
BRAMLING
RIDE
SELWYN
BLAKES RIDE
BROOK COTTS.
SOUTHWARK
OLD SCHOOL CL.
MACRAE RD.
CRANFORD
LAWFORD
ROSARY GDNS.
ST. PETER'S GDNS.
CRESCENT
Alder Copse
HILL
FIRGROVE MANOR
Superstore
TRESHAM
AYLESHAM
PARTRIDGE AV.
SWALLOW
AYLESHAM WAY
CONNAUGHT CL.
Playing Fld.
Yateley School
GU46
Hall
HOME PARK
PARKFIELDS
LANFORD CRES.
Prim. Sch.
HEARMON CL.
ROKES PL.
HOLBECHE CL.
AVENUE
SCHOOL LANE
Lib.
Comm. Centre
YATELEY CENTRE
WISTARIA LA.
WINTON CRES.
Fir Grove Farm
DUNSMORE GDNS.
RYVES AV.
CRESCENT
MORLEY CL.
MONTEAGLE LA.
Westfields Jun. & Inf. Schs.
Yateley Health & Fitness Centre
THE DELL
FARMVIEW
VIEW
CRES.
Kiln Close Copse
HUDDINGTON GLADE
ROAD
THROGMORTON
MORTON RD.
MONTEAGLE
Playing Fields
BYWAYS
HALLTOP
VIEW
HANDFORD
LANE
LUCAS CL.
CHURCHILL
Cricket Hill
Kits Croft
8
GARNET FIELD
CATESBY GDS.
CALLUM
THROGMORTON
BADGERSWORTH
HAWKINS WY.
GREENHAVEN
LIMECROFT
DICKENS WAY
BLACKBUSHE PARK
Newlands Prim. Sch.
MISTLETOE RD.
OAKS CROFT
MAPLE GDNS.
60
Westfield Farm
B3016
THE SETT
BROCK LANDS
STOKES WY.
HARVEST CL.
GIBBS WY.
KEATS WY.
BYRON AVENUE
VIGO LANE
HARDY AVENUE
KIPLING CL.
HERRIOT CT.
CHRISTIE WK.
DUNGELLS
BARTONS DR.
STOCK-BRIDGE WY.
MICHAELMAS CL.
DRIVE
WALNUT CL.
LANE
Darach
The Oaks
Hill House
Castle Bottom National Nature Reserve
GU17
BLACKBUSHE AIRPORT
LITTLE VIGO
GALWAY RD.
ARAGON RD.
GORSELANDS
SAXONY
TUSCANY WAY
BLACKBUSHE BUSINESS PARK
DUNGELLS LANE
FRESHWOOD DR.
SILVER GLADES
BIRCHVIEW CL.
HIGHWOOD CL.
WHITLEY RD.
GLENAYTON
YATELEY COMMON COUNTRY PARK
TUDOR
WOODANDS
HEATHLANDS CT.
Depot
COOPER'S
EVERSLEY COMMON
27
Camberley Karting Club
79
480
81
82

CROWTHORNE
BROADMOOR HOSPITAL
Crowthorne
RG45
WELLINGTON COLLEGE
Wellington Health & Fitness Club
Cricket Ground
Playing Field
Chaucer Woods
Edgbarrow Sch.
Edgbarrow Sports Centre
Pine Hill
Edgbarrow Woods Local Nature Reserve
Edgbarrow Hill
Wildmoor Heath
Smallbrook Bottom
Ambarrow Hill
Ambarrow Wood
Ambarrow Farm
Ambarrow Ct. Local Nature Reserve
Perry Bridge Farm
Horseshoe Lake Watersports Centre
Eagle House School
LITTLE SANDHURST
New Scotland Hill Prim. Sch.
Sandhurst
GU47
Uplands Prim. Sch.
Snaprails Park
Sandhurst Sch. & Open Learning Cen.
Sandhurst Sports Cen.
Community Hall
SANDHURST
Sandhurst Mem. Pk.
Sewage Works
THE YATELEY LAKES
Trilakes Animal Park
Little Angels Playworld
Church Farm
Riverside
Mill Bridge
Yateley Bridge
Blackwater River
DARBY GREEN
Yateley Common
Frogmore Leisure Cen.
Frogmore Community College
Potley Hill Prim. Sch.
Two Oaks Farm
Frogmore Inf. & Jun. Schs.
BLACKWATER
FROGMORE
GU17
YATELEY
Cricket Hill
Yateley
GU46
Heathlands Cemetery
YATELEY COMMON COUNTRY PARK
Wyndham's Pool
Hill Farm
Leafy Oak Farm
Hayward's Cottage
Picnic Area
HAWLEY
Shepherds Meadow
BRACKNELL FOREST
HART
WOKINGHAM ROAD A321
HIGH ROAD
YORKTOWN ROAD
RACKSTRAW ROAD A3095
MARSHALL ROAD
LONDON ROAD A30
READING ROAD
B3272
B3348
DUKE'S RIDE
17
28

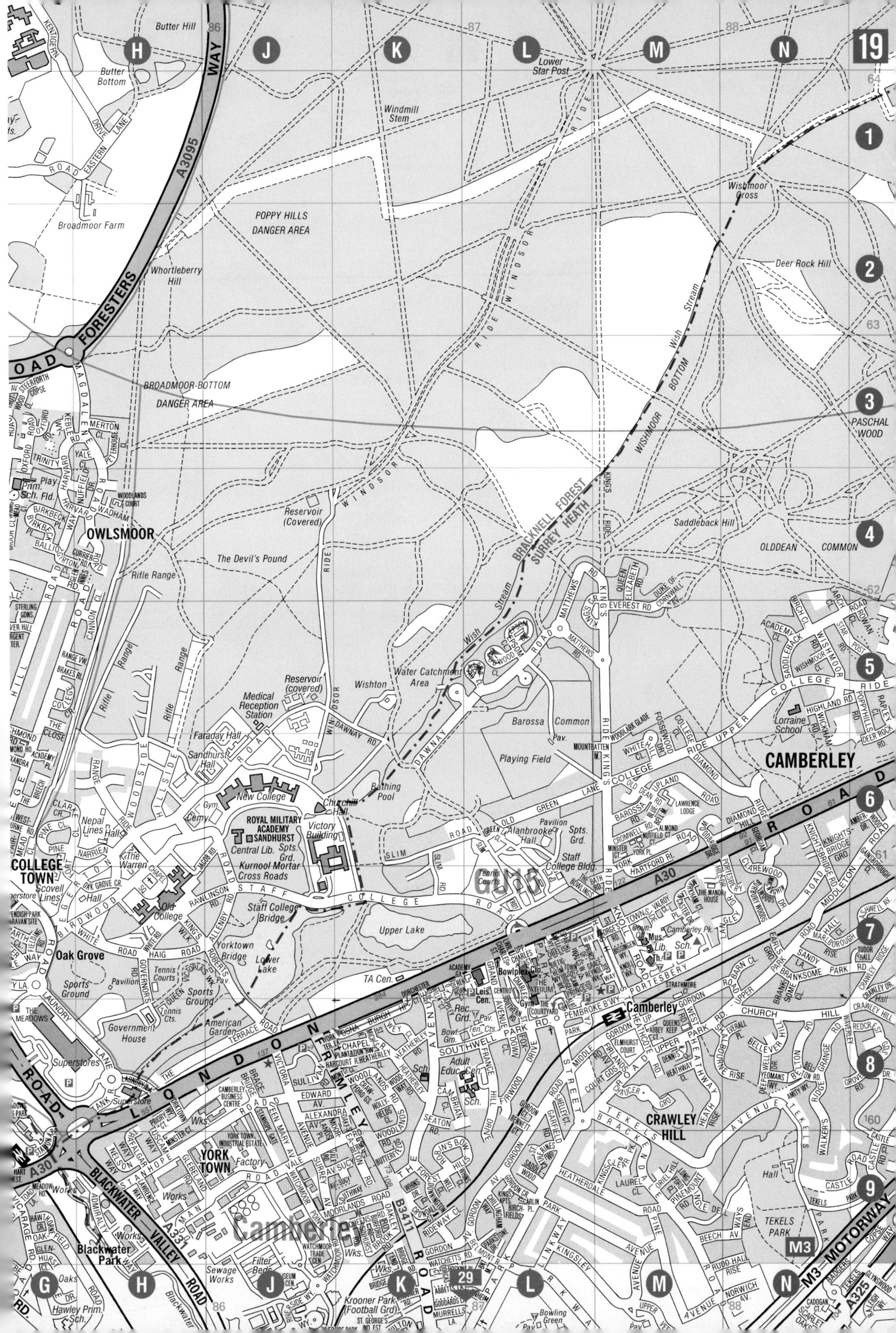

Butter Hill
Butter Bottom
Lower Star Post
Windmill Stem
Broadmoor Farm
POPPY HILLS DANGER AREA
Whortleberry Hill
FORESTERS WAY
A3095
BROADMOOR-BOTTOM DANGER AREA
Wishmoor Cross
Deer Rock Hill
PASCHAL WOOD
WISHMOOR BOTTOM
Wish Stream
BRACKNELL FOREST
SURREY HEATH
Saddleback Hill
OLDDEAN COMMON
OWLSMOOR
Reservoir (Covered)
The Devil's Pound
Rifle Range
Water Catchment Area
Wishton
Medical Reception Station
Faraday Hall
Sandhurst Hall
New College
ROYAL MILITARY ACADEMY SANDHURST
Central Lib.
Kurnool Mortar Cross Roads
Victory Building
Churchill Hall
Bathing Pool
Barossa Common
Playing Field
Alanbrooke Hall
Staff College Bldg.
COLLEGE TOWN
Old College
Staff College Bridge
Upper Lake
Lower Lake
Yorktown Bridge
Oak Grove
Sports Ground
Government House
American Garden
TA Cen.
CAMBERLEY
Lorraine School
Camberley
CRAWLEY HILL
YORK TOWN
Blackwater Park
Sewage Works
Filter Beds
Krooner Park (Football Grd)
TEKELS PARK
M3 MOTORWAY
LONDON ROAD
A30
BLACKWATER VALLEY ROAD
A331
B3411
A325
GU16
29

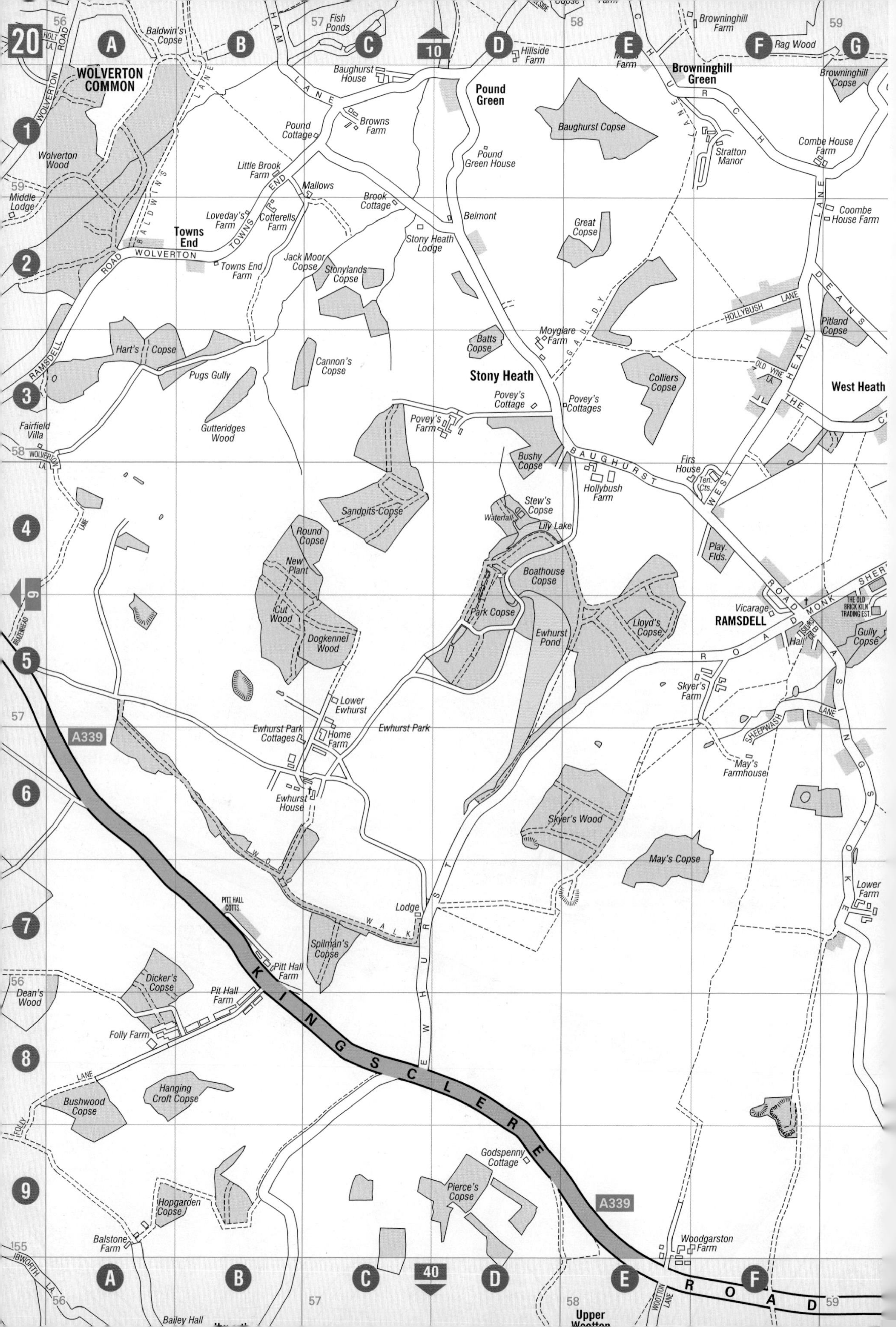
WOLVERTON COMMON
Wolverton Wood
Baldwin's Copse
Fish Ponds
Baughurst House
Browns Farm
Pound Cottage
Little Brook Farm
Mallows
Brook Cottage
Loveday's Farm
Cotterells Farm
Towns End
Towns End Farm
Jack Moor Copse
Stonylands Copse
Stony Heath Lodge
Middle Lodge
Pound Green
Pound Green House
Belmont
Hillside Farm
Browninghill Farm
Rag Wood
Browninghill Green
Browninghill Copse
Baughurst Copse
Stratton Manor
Combe House Farm
Coombe House Farm
Great Copse
HOLLYBUSH LANE
Pitland Copse
West Heath
Moyglare Farm
Batts Copse
Stony Heath
Colliers Copse
Hart's Copse
Pugs Gully
Cannon's Copse
Gutteridges Wood
Povey's Cottage
Povey's Cottages
Povey's Farm
Fairfield Villa
Bushy Copse
Hollybush Farm
Firs House
Ten. Cts.
Sandpits Copse
Stew's Copse
Waterfall
Lily Lake
Round Copse
New Plant
Boathouse Copse
Play. Flds.
Cut Wood
Park Copse
Dogkennel Wood
Ewhurst Pond
Lloyd's Copse
Vicarage
RAMSDELL
THE OLD BRICK KILN TRADING EST.
Gully Copse
Hall
Lower Ewhurst
Skyer's Farm
Ewhurst Park Cottages
Home Farm
Ewhurst Park
A339
May's Farmhouse
Ewhurst House
Skyer's Wood
May's Copse
Lower Farm
PITT HALL COTTS.
Lodge
Spilman's Copse
Pitt Hall Farm
Dicker's Copse
Pit Hall Farm
Dean's Wood
Folly Farm
Hanging Croft Copse
Bushwood Copse
KINGSCLERE ROAD
Godspenny Cottage
Pierce's Copse
Hopgarden Copse
Balstone Farm
Woodgarston Farm
Bailey Hall
Upper Wootton
WOOTTON LANE
IBWORTH LA.
WOLVERTON ROAD
TOWNS END
BALDWINS LANE
RAMSDELL ROAD
WOLVERTON LA.
BAUGHURST ROAD
GAULDY
CHURCH LANE
HEATH LANE
DEANS
WEST HEATH
OLD VYNE LA.
MONK SHERBORNE
SHEEPWASH LANE
KINGS TOKE
EWHURST
WOOD WALK
FOLLY LANE
10
40
9

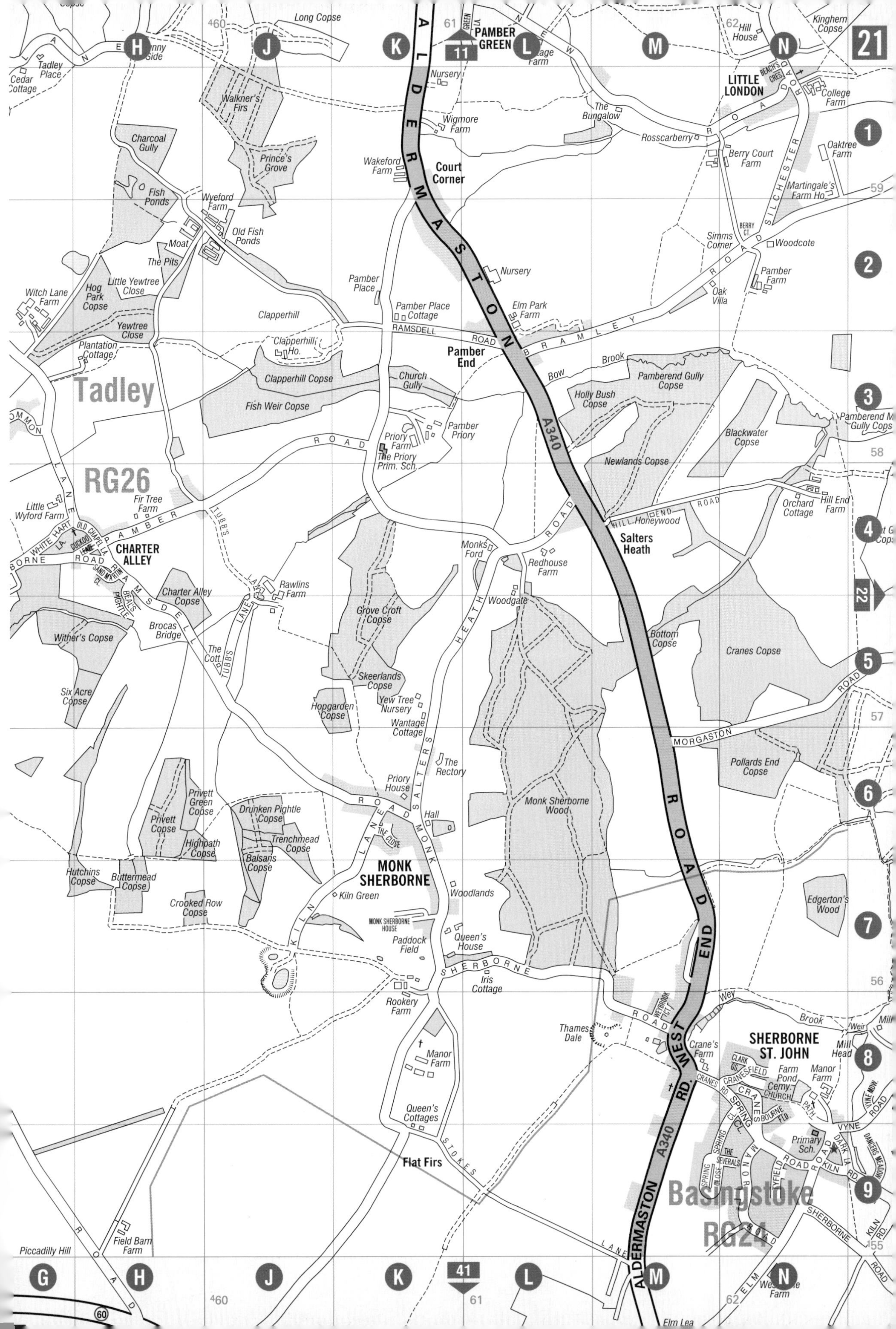
21
Long Copse
Pamber Green
Tadley Place
Cedar Cottage
Walkner's Firs
Nursery
Wigmore Farm
Little London
College Farm
The Bungalow
Rosscarberry
Berry Court Farm
Oaktree Farm
Hill House
Kinghern Copse
Charcoal Gully
Prince's Grove
Wakeford Farm
Court Corner
Fish Ponds
Wyeford Farm
Old Fish Ponds
Moat
The Pits
Martingale's Farm Ho.
Simms Corner
Woodcote
Pamber Farm
Oak Villa
Witch Lane Farm
Hog Park Copse
Little Yewtree Close
Yewtree Close
Plantation Cottage
Clapperhill
Clapperhill Ho.
Pamber Place
Pamber Place Cottage
Elm Park Farm
Nursery
Ramsdell Road
Bramley Road
Pamber End
Aldermaston Road
A340
Tadley
Clapperhill Copse
Church Gully
Fish Weir Copse
Bow Brook
Pamberend Gully Copse
Holly Bush Copse
Blackwater Copse
Pamberend M Gully Cops
Pamber Priory
Priory Farm
The Priory Prim. Sch.
Newlands Copse
RG26
Fir Tree Farm
Little Wyford Farm
Pamber Road
Charter Alley
Hill End Road
Honeywood
Orchard Cottage
Hill End Farm
Salters Heath
Monks Ford
Redhouse Farm
Rawlins Farm
Charter Alley Copse
Brocas Bridge
Wither's Copse
Woodgate
Grove Croft Copse
Bottom Copse
Cranes Copse
The Cott.
Tubb's Lane
Six Acre Copse
Skeerlands Copse
Yew Tree Nursery
Hopgarden Copse
Wantage Cottage
Morgaston Road
Pollards End Copse
The Rectory
Priory House
Salters Heath
Privett Green Copse
Privett Copse
Drunken Pightle Copse
Trenchmead Copse
Highpath Copse
Monk Sherborne Wood
Hall
Balsans Copse
Hutchins Copse
Buttermead Copse
Monk Sherborne
Kiln Green
Woodlands
Edgerton's Wood
Crooked Row Copse
Monk Sherborne House
Paddock Field
Queen's House
Sherborne Road
Iris Cottage
West End Road
Rookery Farm
Thames Dale
Wey
Brook
Crane's Farm
Sherborne St. John
Mill Head
Manor Farm
Farm Pond
Manor Farm
Cemy.
Queen's Cottages
Primary Sch.
Flat Firs
Stokes Lane
Basingstoke
RG24
Field Barn Farm
Piccadilly Hill
Westbrook Farm
Elm Lea
41
22
11
G
H
J
K
L
M
N
1
2
3
4
5
6
7
8
9
460
61
62
59
58
57
56
155
60

Kinghern
Latchmore Farm
12
Little London
College Farm
Bramley Corner
Bramley Grange
Oaktree Farm
Boar's Bridge
Park Gate Farm
Silchester Lodge
Little London Nurseries
Middle Lodge
Bow Brook
Bell's Water Copse
Bowling Alley Copse
Park Copse
Beaurepaire Park
Wiltshire's Gully Copse
Beaurepaire Mill
Beaurepaire Mill Bridge
Pamberend Moor Gully Copse
Beaurepaire House
Tennis Court
Fish Ponds
Hill End Farm
Peat Gully Copse
Beaurepaire Farm
New Road
South Lodge
Pepper Wood
Beech Lodges
Morgaston Road
Beeches
North Lodge
Nursery
Weir
Vine Garden Cottage
The Lake
Morgaston Copse
The Vyne
Vyne Park
Vyne Farm
Vyne Road
Edgerton's Wood
Swingate Hill
Cowdry House
Smiths Green
Sewage Works
Mill House
Kestrel Ct.
Bob's Farm
Chute Rec. Grd.
Tennis Cts.
Pavs.
Vyne Mdw.
Sherborne St. John
Dancers Meadow
Dark La.
Kiln Farm Cottage
Kiln Farm
Vidler's Farm
Sherborne Road
Marnel Lodge (Nursing Home)
Marl's Lane
Spier's Copse
Marl's Copse
Seven Acre Piece
Great Germans Copse
Barn Copse
Basing Forest
Carpenter's Down Wood
Bowling
Comm.
Guernsey Cl.
Barrington Dr.
Tasman
42
Basingstoke
RG24
Collett's Copse
Grub Close Plantation
Martin's Brushes
Russell's Copse
Upper Parrott's Copse
Five Acre Plantation
Five Acre Piece
Four Acre Piece
Inner Maynard's Copse
Maynard's Piece
Parrott's Copse
Upper Plantation
Scours Plantation
Carpenter's Down Piece
Gallary Pightle Copse
Gallaries Copse
Long Swains Row
Razor's Farm
Crockford Lane
Hampshire International Business Park
Lime Tree Way
Petty's Brook
Chineham Business Park
Fitness First
Chineham
Great Binfields Copse
Tadley
RG26
Bramley Road
Locksbridge Road
Cufaude Lane
Vicarage
Grays House
Tudor Farm
Tudor Cl.
Church Farm
Church Lands
Middle Farm
Hall
Football Grd.
Beaurepaire Cl.
Church Farm Cottages
Lantern Courtyard
Ridgewell
King's Copse
Bridge Cottage
Lock's Bridge
Watford Copse
Hunters Moon
Baker's Farm
Works
Bushyplatt Copse
Broad Street
Vyne Lodge Farm
Cufaude Farm
Moat
Cufaude Road
Cufaude
Cufaude Cottage
Sandwick
Upper Cufaude Farm
Recreation Ground
Pav.
Ten. Cts.
Minchens Lane
Sherfield Road
Ringshall Gdns.
Pound Cl.
Oakmead
Coopers
Bramley
BRAMLEY
Yard Copse
The Maltings
Richardson Lane
Moat La.
North Row
Browns Cl.

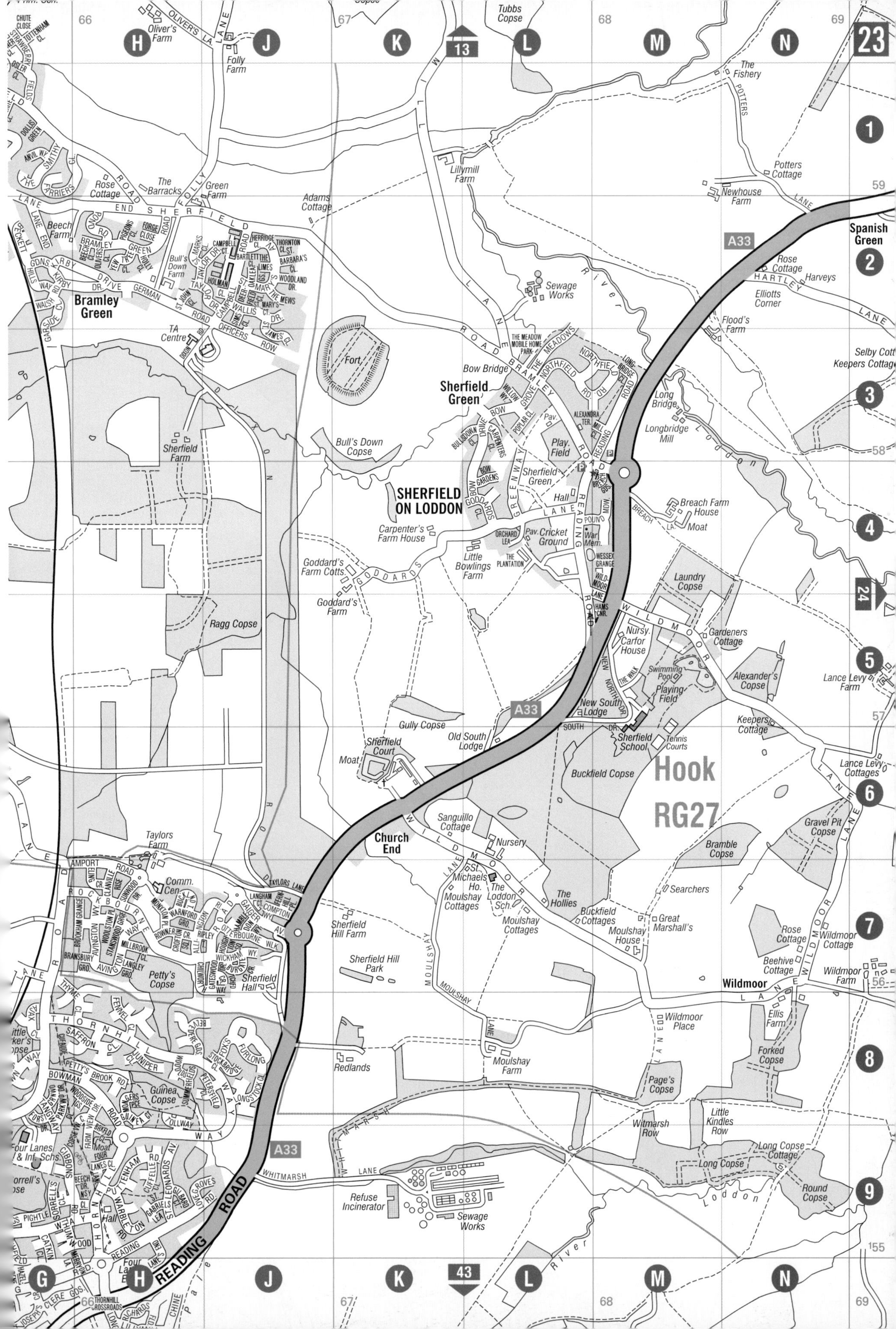
Oliver's Farm
Folly Farm
Tubbs Copse
13
The Fishery
Bramley Green
Rose Cottage
The Barracks
Green Farm
Adams Cottage
Lillymill Farm
Potters Cottage
Newhouse Farm
Spanish Green
A33
Rose Cottage
Harveys
Elliotts Corner
Flood's Farm
Sewage Works
Beech Farm
Bull's Down Farm
TA Centre
Fort
Selby Cott
Keepers Cottage
Bow Bridge
Sherfield Green
Long Bridge
Longbridge Mill
Sherfield Farm
Bull's Down Copse
Sherfield Green
SHERFIELD ON LODDON
Breach Farm House
Moat
Carpenter's Farm House
Cricket Ground
Little Bowlings Farm
Goddard's Farm Cotts.
Goddard's Farm
Ragg Copse
Laundry Copse
24
Nursy.
Carfor House
Gardeners Cottage
Alexander's Copse
Lance Levy Farm
Swimming Pool
Playing Field
New South Lodge
Gully Copse
Sherfield Court
Old South Lodge
Moat
Sherfield School
Tennis Courts
Keepers Cottage
Buckfield Copse
Hook
RG27
Lance Levy Cottages
Sanguillo Cottage
Church End
Nursery
Gravel Pit Copse
Bramble Copse
Taylors Farm
Comm. Cen.
St. Michaels Ho.
The Loddon Sch.
Moulshay Cottages
Searchers
The Hollies
Buckfield Cottages
Great Marshall's
Sherfield Hill Farm
Moulshay Cottages
Moulshay House
Rose Cottage
Wildmoor Cottage
Sherfield Hill Park
Beehive Cottage
Wildmoor
Wildmoor Farm
Petty's Copse
Sherfield Hall
Wildmoor Place
Ellis Farm
Forked Copse
Redlands
Moulshay Farm
Guinea Copse
Page's Copse
Little Kindles Row
Witmarsh Row
Four Lanes Inf. Schs.
Long Copse Cottage
Long Copse
Round Copse
Refuse Incinerator
Sewage Works
Loddon
River
READING ROAD
Hall
Four Lanes
43
66
67
68
69
59
58
57
56
155
H
J
K
L
M
N
G
1
2
3
4
5
6
7
8
9

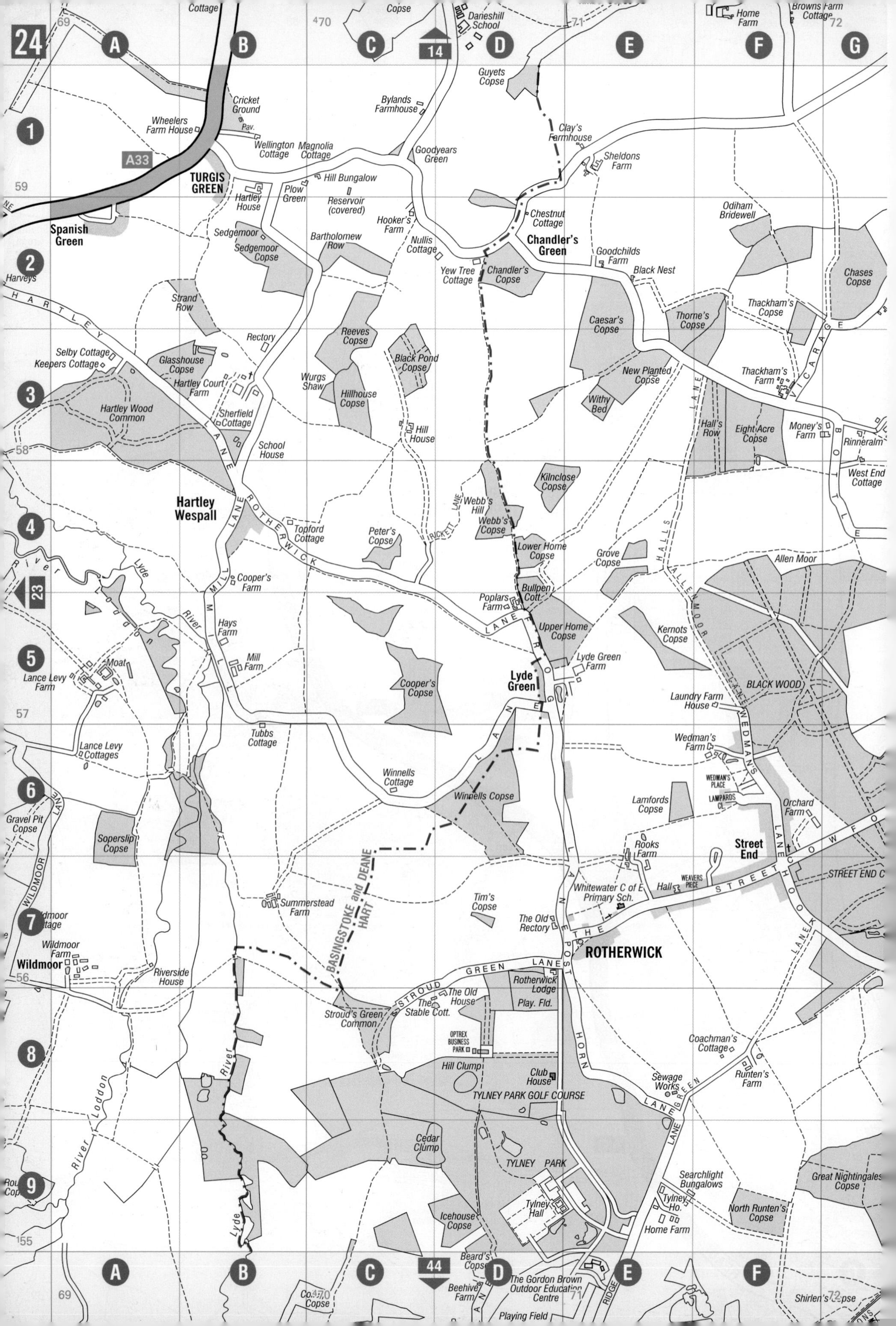

TURGIS GREEN
Spanish Green
Wheelers Farm House
Cricket Ground
Wellington Cottage
Magnolia Cottage
Hill Bungalow
Plow Green
Reservoir (covered)
Hartley House
Daneshill School
Bylands Farmhouse
Goodyears Green
Guyets Copse
Clay's Farmhouse
Sheldons Farm
Chestnut Cottage
Chandler's Green
Hooker's Farm
Nullis Cottage
Yew Tree Cottage
Chandler's Copse
Goodchilds Farm
Black Nest
Odiham Bridewell
Chases Copse
Thackham's Copse
Thorne's Copse
Caesar's Copse
New Planted Copse
Withy Bed
Thackham's Farm
Money's Farm
Rinneralm
West End Cottage
Hall's Row
Eight Acre Copse
Sedgemoor
Sedgemoor Copse
Bartholomew Row
Strand Row
Rectory
Reeves Copse
Black Pond Copse
Selby Cottage
Keepers Cottage
Glasshouse Copse
Hartley Court Farm
Hartley Wood Common
Sherfield Cottage
Wurgs Shaw
Hillhouse Copse
Hill House
School House
Hartley Wespall
Kilnclose Copse
Webb's Hill
Webb's Copse
Topford Cottage
Peter's Copse
Lower Home Copse
Grove Copse
Allen Moor
Cooper's Farm
Poplars Farm
Bullpen Cott.
Upper Home Copse
Kernots Copse
Hays Farm
Mill Farm
Moat
Lance Levy Farm
Lyde Green
Lyde Green Farm
BLACK WOOD
Cooper's Copse
Laundry Farm House
Tubbs Cottage
Lance Levy Cottages
Wedman's Farm
Winnells Cottage
Winnells Copse
Lamfords Copse
Orchard Farm
Gravel Pit Copse
Soperslip Copse
Rooks Farm
Street End
Whitewater C of E Primary Sch.
Hall
STREET END C
Summerstead Farm
Tim's Copse
The Old Rectory
Wildmoor Farm
Wildmoor
Riverside House
ROTHERWICK
Rotherwick Lodge
Play. Fld.
The Old House
The Stable Cott.
Stroud's Green Common
OPTREX BUSINESS PARK
Coachman's Cottage
Hill Clump
Club House
Sewage Works
Runten's Farm
TYLNEY PARK GOLF COURSE
Cedar Clump
TYLNEY PARK
Searchlight Bungalows
Great Nightingales Copse
Tylney Hall
Tylney Ho.
North Runten's Copse
Icehouse Copse
Home Farm
Beard's Copse
The Gordon Brown Outdoor Education Centre
Beehive Farm
Playing Field
Shirlen's Copse
BASINGSTOKE and DEANE
HART
A33
HARTLEY
LANE
ROTHERWICK
MILL LANE
RICKETT LANE
HALLS LANE
ALLEN MOOR LANE
WEDMANS LANE
VICARAGE
BOTTLE LANE
HOOK LANE
THE STREET
STROUD GREEN LANE
HORN LANE
GREEN LANE
WILDMOOR LANE
RIDGE
River Loddon
River Lyde
14
23
44
A B C D E F G
1 2 3 4 5 6 7 8 9
69 470 71 72
59 58 57 56 55

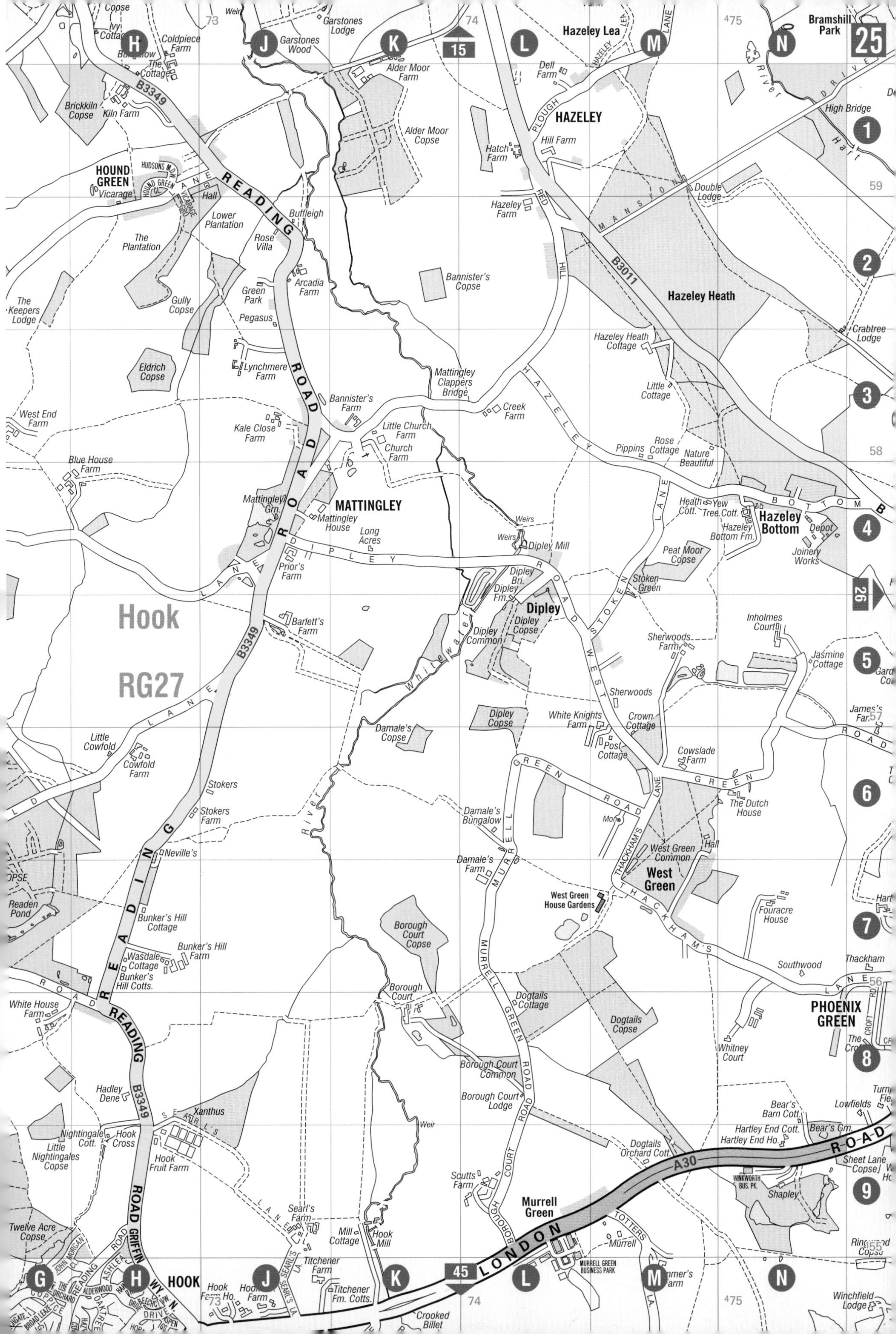
HOUND GREEN
Vicarage
The Plantation
Lower Plantation
Rose Villa
Buffleigh
Arcadia Farm
Green Park
Pegasus
Gully Copse
The Keepers Lodge
Eldrich Copse
Lynchmere Farm
West End Farm
Blue House Farm
Kale Close Farm
Bannister's Farm
Little Church Farm
Church Farm
Mattingley Grn.
MATTINGLEY
Mattingley House
Long Acres
Prior's Farm
Barlett's Farm
Hook
RG27
Little Cowfold
Cowfold Farm
Stokers
Stokers Farm
Neville's
Readen Pond
Bunker's Hill Cottage
Bunker's Hill Farm
Wasdale Cottage
Bunker's Hill Cotts.
White House Farm
Hadley Dene
Xanthus
Nightingale Cott.
Hook Cross
Little Nightingales Copse
Hook Fruit Farm
Twelve Acre Copse
HOOK
Hook Farm Ho.
Searl's Farm
Mill Cottage
Hook Mill
Titchener Farm
Titchener Fm. Cotts.
Crooked Billet
Brickkiln Copse
Kiln Farm
Coldpiece Farm
The Cottage
Garstones Wood
Garstones Lodge
Alder Moor Farm
Alder Moor Copse
Bannister's Copse
Mattingley Clappers Bridge
Creek Farm
Weirs
Dipley Mill
Dipley Bri.
Dipley Fm.
Dipley
Dipley Copse
Dipley Common
Whitewater
Damale's Copse
Dipley Copse
River
Borough Court Copse
Borough Court
Borough Court Common
Borough Court Lodge
Weir
Damale's Bungalow
Damale's Farm
Dogtails Cottage
Dogtails Copse
Dogtails Orchard Cott.
Scutts Farm
Murrell Green
Murrell
MURRELL GREEN BUSINESS PARK
Hazeley Lea
Dell Farm
HAZELEY
Hatch Farm
Hill Farm
Hazeley Farm
Hazeley Heath
Hazeley Heath Cottage
Little Cottage
Double Lodge
Pippins
Rose Cottage
Nature Beautiful
Heath Cott.
Yew Tree Cott.
Hazeley Bottom Fm.
Hazeley Bottom
Depot
Joinery Works
Peat Moor Copse
Stoken Green
Sherwoods Farm
Sherwoods
Crown Cottage
White Knights Farm
Post Cottage
Cowslade Farm
The Dutch House
West Green Common
Hall
West Green
West Green House Gardens
Fouracre House
Southwood
Thackham
PHOENIX GREEN
Whitney Court
Inholmes Court
Jasmine Cottage
Bear's Barn Cott.
Hartley End Cott.
Hartley End Ho.
Bear's Grn.
Lowfields
Sheet Lane Copse
WINKWORTH BUS. PK.
Shapley
Winchfield Lodge
Bramshill Park
High Bridge
Crabtree Lodge
B3349
B3011
A30
READING ROAD
LONDON ROAD
DIPLEY ROAD
HAZELEY
MANSFORD
BOTTOM
PLOUGH LANE
RED HILL
STOKEN LANE
WEST GREEN ROAD
MURRELL GREEN ROAD
BOROUGH COURT ROAD
THACKHAM'S LANE
SEARL'S LANE
TOTTERS LA.
H J K L M N G
1 2 3 4 5 6 7 8 9
73 74 475
59 58 57 56 55
15 26 45

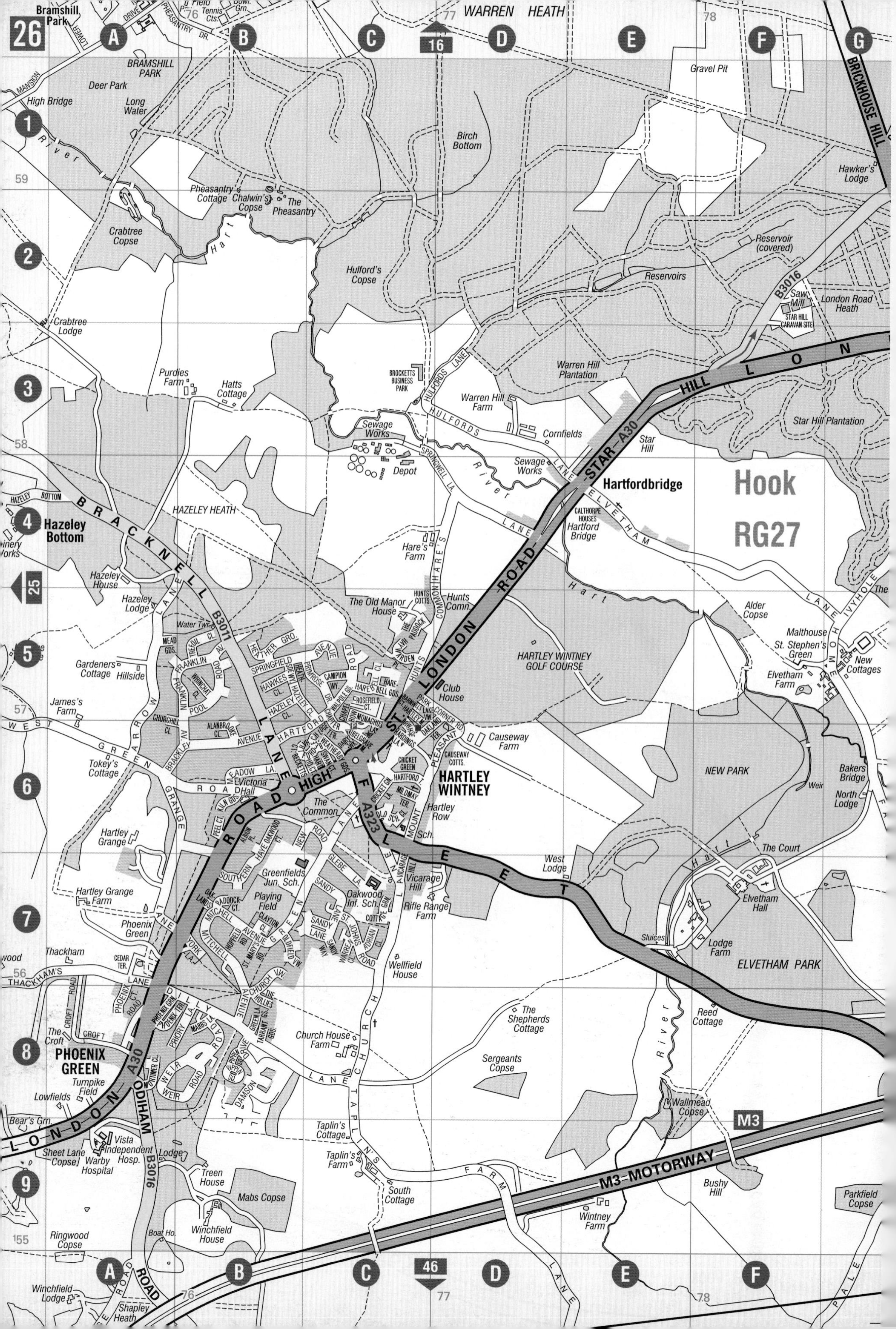
Bramshill Park
WARREN HEATH
16
BRAMSHILL PARK
Deer Park
High Bridge
Long Water
Birch Bottom
Gravel Pit
BRICKHOUSE HILL
Hawker's Lodge
Pheasantry Cottage
Chalwin's Copse
The Pheasantry
Crabtree Copse
Hulford's Copse
Reservoir (covered)
Reservoirs
B3016
Saw Mill
STAR HILL CARAVAN SITE
London Road Heath
Crabtree Lodge
Purdies Farm
Hatts Cottage
BROCKETTS BUSINESS PARK
Warren Hill Plantation
Warren Hill Farm
Star Hill Plantation
Sewage Works
Depot
Cornfields
Star Hill
HULFORDS LANE
SPRINGWELL LA.
STAR HILL
LONDON ROAD
A30
Hartfordbridge
Hook
RG27
HAZELEY HEATH
Hazeley Bottom
BRACKNELL LANE
B3011
CALTHORPE HOUSES
Hartford Bridge
ELVETHAM LANE
Hare's Farm
25
Hazeley House
Hazeley Lodge
The Old Manor House
Hunts Comn.
COMMON HARE'S
Alder Copse
IVYHOLE LANE
Water Twr.
Malthouse
St. Stephen's Green
New Cottages
HARTLEY WINTNEY GOLF COURSE
Gardeners Cottage
Hillside
Club House
Elvetham Farm
James's Farm
WEST GREEN ROAD
HIGH ST.
LONDON ROAD
Causeway Farm
CAUSEWAY COTTS.
Tokey's Cottage
NEW PARK
Bakers Bridge
HARTLEY WINTNEY
Weir
North Lodge
Victoria Hall
The Common
A323
FLEET ROAD
Hartley Row
Hartley Grange
GRANGE
Greenfields Jun. Sch.
Playing Field
Oakwood Inf. Sch.
Vicarage Hill
Rifle Range Farm
West Lodge
The Court
Elvetham Hall
Hartley Grange Farm
Phoenix Green
Sluices
Lodge Farm
ELVETHAM PARK
Thackham
THACKHAM'S LANE
Wellfield House
CHURCH LANE
The Shepherds Cottage
Reed Cottage
River
The Croft
CROFT
PHOENIX GREEN
Church House Farm
Sergeants Copse
Turnpike Field
Lowfields
Bear's Grn.
Wallmead Copse
M3
Taplin's Cottage
Taplin's Farm
TAPLIN'S FARM LANE
M3 MOTORWAY
Bushy Hill
Sheet Lane Copse
Vista Independent Hosp.
Warby Hospital
B3016
ODIHAM ROAD
Lodge
Treen House
Mabs Copse
South Cottage
Wintney Farm
Parkfield Copse
Boat Ho.
Winchfield House
Ringwood Copse
46
Winchfield Lodge
Shapley Heath
PALE LANE

EVERSLEY COMMON
Camberley Karting Club
BLACKBUSHE AIRPORT
Works
Camberley
Auction Market
Camp Plantation
Hartford Bridge Flats
A30 ROAD
GU17
Forest Lodge
PENNY HILL CARAVAN PARK
B3013 ROAD
Yateley
YATELEY COMMON COUNTRY PARK
GU46
Minley
West Minley Farm
Fire Tower
Three Corner Plantation
YATELEY HEATH WOOD
MINLEY WOOD
Minley Farm
Hole Plantation
Ivyhole Hill Wood
Great Butt
The Kennels
Mount Zion Copse
Muddy Grove Hill
Muddy Grove
Adam's Acre
Wright's Copse
Blackbushes Farm
Pont Hill
Ponthill Plantation
Oak Grove
Strip Plantation
Loman's Hill
Lichett Plain
Word Hill Farm
Fleet
Moor Copse
Tobridge Copse
Dogghouse Cottage
Doghouse Bridge
Sewage Works
GU51
Brook House
Elvetham Old Rectory
Turner's Green Farm
Doghouse Copse
Broomhurst Farm
Gilldown Farm
M3 MOTORWAY
Broomhurst Wood
Elvetham
Foresters Cottage
Streetend Copse
School House
Rotten Green
Elvetham Heath Local Nature Reserve
Practice Area
School Plantation
Brickyard Plantation
Fleet Service Area
Club House
Turner's Wood
NORTH HANTS GOLF COURSE
Elvetham Heath
Palelane Farm
A3013
Fleet
FLEET POND (Nature Reserve)
Great Bog Copse
Railroad Copse
FLEET COMM. HOSP.
Landing Stage

28
18
27
48
Junction 4a
LONDON ROAD
A30
MINLEY LANE
MINLEY ROAD
A327
M3 MOTORWAY
M3
A327 MINLEY LINK ROAD
FLEET ROAD
A3013
B3014
A327 IVELY AVENUE
SUMMIT
YATELEY COMMON COUNTRY PARK
GU46
GU17
GU51
BLACKWATER
Minley
Minley Manor
GIBRALTAR BARRACKS
Parade Grd.
HORNLEY COMMON
HAWLEY COMMON
HAWLEY LAKE
Hawley Hard
Hawley Hill
Starve Acre
FOX LANE
COVE
Fleet
SOUTHWOOD
FLEET POND (Nature Reserve)
Ancells Farm Nature Reserve
Ancels Copse
Mallards Copse
Bramshot Copse
Great Bramshot Farm
Little Bramshot Farm
Cove Sch.
Virgin Active
Football Ground
Pinewood Inf. Sch.
Guillemont Jun. Sch.
HART
RUSHMOOR
SOUTHWOOD GOLF COURSE
Peartree Cottages

Blackwater Park
Sewage Works
Filter Beds
Coliseum Bus. Cen.
Watchmoor Trade Cen.
Krooner Park (Football Grd)
St. George's Ind. Est.
Recycling Cen.
Crabtree Park
Camberley Indoor Bowling Club
Skate Park
Superstore
The Oaks
Hawley Prim. Sch.
HAWLEY
HAWLEY PARK
Hawley Park Farm
Camberley
Hawley Bridge
Lodge
All Saints Cottages
GU15
Bowling Green
Tennis Courts
Putting Green
Watchetts Rec. Grd.
Cricket Ground
Watchetts Lakes
The Watchetts Jun. Sch.
Play. Fld.
Kings International College
Tennis Courts
Bristow Inf. Sch.
TEKELS PARK
M3
Warren Wood
FRIMLEY PARK HOSPITAL
Frimley Park
Hall
Sch.
Pav.
Rec. Grd.
Offs.
Prim. Sch.
FRIMLEY
Junc. 4
Warehouse
Hawley Bri.
Fernhill Sch.
Fernhill Prim. Sch.
Rec. Grd.
Test Cen.
Team Sport Karting
A331
Frimley Bus. Pk.
The Quadrangle
Warehouse
Frimley
GU16
Comm. Cen.
Factory
M3 MOTORWAY
Farnborough Gra. Inf. Comm. Sch.
Play. Fld.
Grange Comm. Jun. Sch.
Hawley Lane
Farnborough FC (Rushmoor Stadium)
FRIMLEY GREEN
Frimley C of E School
Blackwater Shopping Pk.
Football Ground
Cemetery
Bowl. Grn.
Playing Field
Sixth Form Coll. Farnborough
Tennis Courts
Manor Inf. & Jun. Schs.
Samuel Cody Sports Coll.
St. Bernadette's Catholic Prim. School
Oak Farm Play. Flds.
Recreation Ground
Cove Jun. Sch.
Farnborough
FARNBOROUGH GREEN
Tennis Courts
Farnborough Hill School
Playing Field
Farnborough North
Cross Farm Inf. Sch.
Cross Fm.
SURREY HEATH
RUSHMOOR
North Farnborough Inf. Sch.
GU14
QUEEN ELIZABETH PARK
WEST HEATH
FARNBOROUGH STREET
Recreation Ground
St. Michael's Abbey
Abbey Ho.
Farnborough Main
Mytchett Rec. Grd.
Skate Park
Leisure Park
Tennis Courts
Cove Green
Cemy.
NORTH FARNBOROUGH
FARNBOROUGH
Superstores
St. Patrick's Cath. Prim. Sch.
C of E Jun. Sch.
Pav.
Playing Fields
RAFBOROUGH
Hotel
Monkey Puzzle Roundabout
Prim. Sch.
Wks.
Works
Farnborough Leisure Cen.
Comm. Cen.
Lib.
Rushmoor BC Offs.
FARNBOROUGH PARK
MYTCHETT
Linsford Business Park
Linsford Farm
Leisure Club
IQ Farnborough
Farnborough Coll. of Technology
Bifrons
Knellwood War Memorial
Club House
BLACKWATER VALLEY ROAD
A331 ROAD
FRIMLEY BY-PASS
PORTSMOUTH ROAD
FARNBOROUGH ROAD
A325
B3411
B3272
B311 RD.
B3014
A327
VICTORIA ROAD
MEUDON AV.
BLACKWATER VALLEY ROUTE
19
49

LUDGERSHALL INSET
TIDWORTH INSET
LUDGERSHALL
Andover
SP11
Faberstown
PERHAM DOWN
Great Shoddesden
Tidworth
SP9
North Tidworth
Tidworth Camp
TIDWORTH
South Tidworth
WILTSHIRE
TEST VALLEY
ANDOVER ROAD
TIDWORTH ROAD
A342
A3026
A338
LUDGERSHALL ROAD
PENNINGS ROAD
PARK ROAD
BULFORD ROAD
COLLINGBOURNE RD.
SALISBURY
The Wellington Academy
Health & Fitness Club
Sports Ground
Depot
Warehouse
Castle Farm
Cemetery
Recreation Ground
Castle Prim. Sch.
Crawlboys Row
Marlins Farm
Poultry Houses
Castledown Business Park
Ludgershall Business Park
Newdrove Plantation
Sewage Works
Willis Wood
South Park
Cachy Barracks
Swinton Barracks
Meadow Copse
Little Perham Copse
Great Perham Copse
Shoddesden Grange
Lamb Down
Hazelberry Plantation
Hougoumont Farm
Barrow Plantation
Sidbury Hill Plantation
Gason Hill
Zouch Prim. Sch.
Half Moon Clump
Chalkpit Hill Plantation
Chalkpit Hill
Chalkpit Wood
Playground
Clarendon Hill Plantation
Clarendon Hill
Reservoir
Miniature Range
Seven Barrows
Football Ground
Mooltan Barracks
Lucknow Barracks
Jellalabad Barracks
Delhi Barracks
Candahar Barracks
Aliwal Barracks
Sports Ground
Clarendon Jun. & Inf. Schools
Training College
Tidworth Leis. Cen.
Superstore
Andover Plantation
Playing Field
Pickpit Hill
Furze Hill
Tidworth Garrison Golf Course
Home Farm
The Cross Belt
Tidworth SP9
Recreation Ground

Collingbourne Kingston
Cow Down
Rag Copse
Limmer Pond
CHUTE CAUSEWAY
Limmer Copse
Mount Cowdown
Herridge Stud Farm
New Barn
Sunton
A338
MARLBOROUGH RD.
HIGH ST.
Lynden Down
Marlborough
Chantry
CHANTRY LANE
CADLEY
Cadley
Dean Farm
Parsonage Farm
UPPER CHUTE
Manor Farm
Sunton Heath
BUTTS HILL
MALTHOUSE LA.
CHICKS
EVERLEIGH
Bauks Hill
Chute Down
FOREST LANE
CHURCH
LUDGERSHALL
Mount Orleans Farm
GRAVELLY ROAD
SN8
COLLINGBOURNE DUCIS
COLLINGBOURNE WOOD
TIDWORTH RD.
Honey Bottom
HATCHETT HILL
Forest House
Wick Down
River Bourne
A346
Coldridge Wood
COLDRIDGE RIDE
WHITEDITCH
Shaw Hill
Stert Copse
BLACKMORE LANE
BOTTOM
Widgerly Down
Coldridge Down
Crawlboys Farm
Sunnyhill Farm
Blackmore Down
CRAWLBOYS ROAD
Longbottom Farm
Ludgershall Castle (remains of)
BULLS DROVE
Castle Farm
A342
LONG
Windmillhill Down
Marlins Farm
Biddesden Farm
Biddesden Ho.
Biddesden
Depot
The Wellington Academy
Fitness Club
Sports Pitch
TIDWORTH ROAD
ANDOVER ROAD
BIDDESDEN LANE
MANKHORN LA.
Faberstown
Lambourne's Hill
CASTLEDOWN BUS. PK.
LUDGERSHALL BUSINESS PARK
LUDGERSHALL
NEWTOWN VILLAS
Pickpit Hill
A3026
REDENHAM DROVE
Sewage Works
SHODDESDEN LANE
LUDGERSHALL ROAD
PERHAM DOWN
South Park
Redenham
Redenham House
COPSE VW.
Sewage Works
Clarendon Jun. & Inf. Schs.
Great Shoddesden
PARK RD.
Little Shoddesden
TIDWORTH
Lamb Down
30
COW
STATION RD.
Andover
Littleton Copse
PLANTATION RD.
FURZE HILL RD.
Newdown Copse
COW LANE
48
50
WARREN HILL
WILTSHIRE TEST VALLEY
Kimpton Down Farm
South Tidworth
PRIVET LANE
SP11
ROAD
DEACON ROAD
A342
ANDOVER ROAD
Ashdown Copse
DOWN DROVE
Kimpton Wood
FYFIELD LA.
Kimpton
THE GREEN
Gallop
FYFIELD ROAD
Pickford Hill
THE RANK
FYFIELD
STANBURY ROAD
Kimpton, Thruxton & Fyfield C of E Prim Sch.
DAUNTSEY LANE
SNODDINGTON ROAD
THRUXTON AIRFIELD RD.
THRUXTON
AMESBURY
COACH ROAD
THRUXTON AERODROME
67
Thruxton Motor Racing
Mullenspond
G H J K L M N
24 ⁴25 26 27 28 29 ⁴30
¹55 54 53 52 51 150 49 48 47 46
1 2 3 4 5 6 7 8 9
32

A
B
C
D
E
F
G
1
2
3
4
5
6
7
8
9
6
31
50
430
31
32
33
55
54
53
52
51
CHUTE CAUSEWAY
DUMMER
Sheephouse Copse
New Barn Cott.
New Barn
Hackney Plantation
Bottomhalves Copse
Mafeking Clump
CONHOLT PARK
Conholt Farm
Conholt House
CHUTE CAUSE-WAY
HUNGERFORD
Hampshire Gate
New Lodge
Old Lodge
Reservoir (covered)
Main Place Row
Standen House
Manor Farm
Chute Standen
BREACH LANE
MALTHOUSE LANE
Round Copse
Fisher's Hanger
Cathanger Wood
Standen Farm
DUMMER LANE
Bottom Copse
Butler's Row
Home Farm
Chute Cadley
NEW BUILDINGS
Collis Farm
HOOKWOOD LANE
Grove Copse
Tolley's Cottages
Croft Hanger
Chessams Copse
Young's Copse
LOWER CHUTE
Holly Cottages
Hookwood Row
HILL
Cadley Lodge
King George's Field
FOREST LANE
Forest Hill Cottage
Forest House
HATCHETT
Jolly's Farm
Tangley Bottom
CLARKE'S LANE
Home Farm Dairy
Scamore
Manor Farm Cottages
HUNGERFORD
Bats Copse
Home Farm
Manor Farm
Tangley House
TANGLEY
Sydney's Copse
Cadley Bottom
Little Pill
Upper Hobbs Row
Great Lodge Copse
Lower Hobbs Row
COLDRIDGE RIDE
Little Lodge Copse
LANE
LIMEKILN ROAD
Highland Copse
WILTSHIRE
TEST VALLEY
BOTTOM
Chalkpit Ride
Brickkiln Ride
Chute Forest
Chute Lodge Farm
Chute Forest Orchard
Sexton's Heath
Big Wood
Chute Lodge
Longbottom Farm
Biddesden Corner Ride
LONG
Cooper's Acre
Cooper's Acre Plantation
Mankhorn Round
Appleshaw Round
Butlersfield Ride
Pollard's Farm
Pollard's Farm Bungalow
ROUNDAWAY LANE
Redhouse Farm
Roundaway Farm
Mankhorn Ride
Mankhorn Cottage
MANKHORN LANE
LODGE
Redhouse Farmhouse
Roundaway Copse
South Lodge
DROVE
Soper's Barn

Lower Conholt Farm

Mascombe Copse

Oakdown Copse

Coholt Down

Rushmore Cottages

Forty Acre Wood

Little Bourne Farm

Rushmore Cottage

Rushmore Farms

Ambley Farm

Upton Common

Hillside

Soper's Farm

Ambley Wood

The B

Rushmore Farm

RUSHMORE DOWN

Bleekfield Firs

Cow Down

Tangley Clumps

Pill Drove Copse

Sheep Down

Lower Down Copse

New Close Wood

54

Dowland's Pit Farm

LANE

Poultry Farm

Whistler's Farm

Poultry Farm

LOCKS

Locke's Barn

DROVE

LOCKS

DROVE

LOCKS DROVE

Windmill Hill Down

Andover

SP11

Eastend Cottages

Eastend Farm

Reservoir (covered)

Pill Heath Farm

53

Greenacres

Holt Copse

Tangley Farm

PILL HEATH

Pill Heath Cottage

5

BLAGDEN COPSE

34

HOLT LANE

Chalkpit Cottages

HUNGERFORD

Stanchels

Pimperne

Blagden Cottage

Blagden Lodge

Blagden House

6

Fox Plantation

52

Dine's Farm

Dine's Cottages

Dine's Copse

Tanglewood

Dilly House

7

White Hill

Middle Acre

Doles Farm

Rag Wood

Ditch

Devil's

8

LANE

WHITE

HILL

51

Sports Ground

THE AVENUE

Peaks Copse

Manor Cottages

Hatherden Manor

Reservoirs (covered)

HUNGERFORD

Wildhern

Little Hatherden

Peaks Cottage

Plough Farm

9

HATCHET

THE CLOSE

LANE

Hatherden House

Old Plough Farm

A343

NEWBURY RD.

GREEN DROVE

Great Stubbage

Upton
Upton Common
Ambley Farm
Ambley Wood
River Swift
Ford
Upton Valley
The Bungalow
York Bungalow
DUNSTAN'S DROVE
Upper Ibthorpe Farm
Ibthorpe
Ibthorpe Manor Farm
HORSESHOE LANE
Yewtree Farm
Stags Cottage
Keepers Cottage
Adams Farm
LOCKS DROVE
HURSTBOURNE TARRANT
DINES CL
DINES MEADOW
KNIGHTS YARD
THE DENE
The Dene
DEAN RISE
THE CRESCENT
THE SQUARE
VICTORIA PLACE
CHURCH ST.
DOLOMANS
Windmills Farm
Windmills
Windmills Lodge
DOCTORS DRO
Hillside
Hurstbourne Hill
Parsonage Farm
Hurstbourne Tarrant C of E Prim. Sch.
Rec. Grd.
Lower Farm
STOKE ROAD
B3048
Herblands
Reservoir
Gossings Cottage
Eden Cottage
Bourne Rivulet
Old Tollgate Bungalow
A343
DOLES WOOD
Wallop Hill Down
Great Wallop Hill Copse
Little Wallop Hill Copse
Reservoir (covered)
TEST VALLEY
BASINGSTOKE and DEANE
Doles Pond
Doles Lodge
Doles Bungalow
Doles House
The Row
BOURNE PARK
Devil's Ditch
Rag Wood
Hay's Copse
Stokehill Farm
The Heath
Frenches Farm
RAG COPSE
Little Leafy Grove
Leafy Grove Copse
Lee's Wood
Frenche's Farm Cottages
Frenche's Lodge
LONG COPSE
Straits Copse
GREEN DROVE
NEWBURY RD.
Great Stubbage
DOIYLEY ROAD
NETHERTON ROAD
Doyley Manor Farm
The Bungalow
The Warren
Fairway
Provost Hill
Prosperous Farm
Spring Row
Windmill Hill Down
7
33
52
37
38
39
55
54
53
52
51
A B C D E F G
1 2 3 4 5 6 7 8 9

Lye Copses
7
Lye Farm
Lye Copses
Easton Park Wood
Essebourne Manor
The Bungalow
Doiley Hill Farm
Doiley Wood
A343
HILL
RED HILL
Splatts Copse
Long Copse
Sladen Green Farm
Sladen Green
White Eastridge Row
Paul's Copse
Lower Doiley Farm
Lower Doiley Cottages
Dairy Cottage
Slade Green Cottage
Highfield House
Eastridge House
Highfield Farm
Mayfield
Binley Farm
SLADEN CORNER
Dene Bungalow
The White House
Mossdall's Copse
Binley Farm
Binley House Farm
Binley House
BINLEY
Binley Cottage
Great Eastwards
Park Copse
Wadwick Ho.
Pit Croft Copse
Hawk Hatch
Wadwick
Andover
SP11
Binley Farm
Old Lawn
Craigdene
New Cottages
Priors Farm
Slade Bottom Farm
The Bungalow
DROVE
Little Downham Copse
Rolf's Copse
36
Reservoir (covered)
Burry Hill Farm
Valley Farm
Elm Farm
Stoke Hollow
Ford
Jasmine Cottage
Summerhayes
Windmill Farm
Jones Farm
Valley Farm
LANE
Manor Farm
Stoke House
STOKE
Garston
Hopgood's Farm
Whitefield Cottage
Quarley Row
April Cott.
Gangbridge House Cottage
Gangbridge House
Beech Tree Bungalow
Hilliers Lodge
Gang Bridge
Little Thatch
Rowe House
Wakes Wood
Wakeswood
Cold Harbour Farm
Ringlands
Stoke Farm
The Green Lodge
Rowe Farm
New Lodge
Garage Bungalow
Willow Tree Farm
Butler's Farm
Cold-Harbour House
Little Hassocks
The Croft
Gaston Wood
Bourne
Rivulet
Bourne Farm
Gaston Wood Farm
Longhouse
B3048
Belle Vue
Breach Farm
Breach Farmhouse
Green Pastures
Breach Farm Bungalow
Gaston Wood
Oak Tree Farm
Hilliers Farm Cottages
St. Mary Bourne Prim. Sch.
Medhurst
Hill House
SWAMPTON
Haven Hill
Oak Tree Farm
Wood Leigh
Birches
Haven Hill Cottages
Little Meadow
War Meml.
Bourne Ho.
Ford
Upper Wyke
53
Coronation Cottages
Upper Wyke Manor
Upper Wyke Cottages
Bowl. Grn.
Rec. Grd.
ST. MARY BOURNE
Portway
WYNDHAM ROAD
EGBURY ROAD
WADWICK
BOTTOM
HEDGE
LONG

Haredown
Upper Woodcott Farm
Res. (cov.)
Reservoir (covered)
Woodcott
Hall Cottage
Hall
Lower Woodcott Farm
Thorndown Copse
WAYFARER'S WALK
Shell's Copse
Danegrove Copse
Woodcott House
Suggeaston Copse
Stubb's Copse
Sowleaze Copse
Buckets Down Farm
Long Copse
Bixley Copse
Old Orchard Copse
High Copse
Dunley
Dunley Manor
The Lodge
Subway
A34
JUBILEE CL.
Sub.
Litchfield Farm
Broadclose Copse
Park Copse
Wadwick Ho.
Wadwick
BOTOM
WADWICK
New Cottages
Hollycroft Copse
Bradley Hill
Werries Copse
Angle Down
Hedgerow Copse
The Hassock
Rolf's Copse
Little Downhams Copse
Reservoir (covered)
Egbury House
Egbury Fm.
New Cottages
Windmill Cottages
EGBURY
Downhams Farm Cottage
Egbury House Cottage
Dunley Park
Bradley Wood Farm
Downhams Farm Cottage
Andover
Downhams Farm
Downhams
SP11
Downhams Copse
Clap Gate Cottage
BRADLEY WOOD
Egbury Castle Farm
Cooper's in the Wood Copse
Bradley Cottage
Cooper's in the Wood Farm
Subway
Cold-Harbour House
ROAD
WYNDHAM
EGBURY RD.
HOGDIGGING COPSE
Jamaica Farm
Newbarn Down Plantation
8
35
54
43
44
445
46
155
54
53
52
51

1

Hare Warren Farm

Hare Warren Cottages

Reservoir (covered)

2

54

Palmer's Bushes

Hare Warren Copse

Little Down

Down Farm

Greenacre Cottages

THE VILLAGE

Old Sewage Works

LITCHFIELD

3

Wormley Copse

Caesar's Belt

The Lodge

Litchfield Down

Whitchurch RG28

4

53

Ridgeway Copse

Keeper's Cottage

Angledown Copse

Ridgeway

Ridgeway Cottages

Ridgeway Farm

Pheasantry

Streetley Copse

Furze Copse

5

Milkhill Wood

Dunn's Wood

38

Bradley Wood

Paul's Wood

6

52

Twinley Manor

7

Reservoir (covered)

Paul's Heath Copse

Little Twinley's Copse

Whitnal Farmhouse

Whitnal

New Barn

Peak House Farm

Cole Henley Manor Farm

8

51

Thatched Cottage

La Bresse

Cole Henley

LARKS

Cole Henley Farm

Square Oaks

Larksborough

9

Down Copse

G H 55 L M N
BARROW HILL
Poultry House
KING'S CLERE RD.
de Hill Copse
48
Oak Cottage
47
Wooldings Farm
49
The Orchards
The Cottage
Harroway Belt

A B C D E F G
1 2 3 4 5 6 7 8 9
450
51
52
155
54
53
52
51
9
37
56
MEADHAM LANE
Polhampton Lodge Plantation
Polhampton Stud Cottages
B3051
Scotland Cottages
Polhampton Lodge Stud
Tidgrove Warren Farm
Robley Belt
Palmer's Bushes
Keepers Cottage
Frost Hill Farm
Frost Hill
Reservoir (covered)
Old Farmhouse
Willesley Warren Farm
New Cottages
RG25
Willesley Warren Cottages
Willesley Warren
Cottages
Whitchurch
RG28
The Peak
HARROW WAY
Basingstoke
KINGSCLERE ROAD
COURT DROVE
New Barn
Overton Mill
Overton
HILLTOP ROAD
STATION ROAD
ELM RD.
COPSE
BEECH CL.
HILL MEADOW
FOXDOWN
Foxdown
NORTH FD.
Kennel Plantation
HILL
Harroway Belt
Quidhampton
Quidhampton Pond
Quidhampton Mill
River Test
Ford

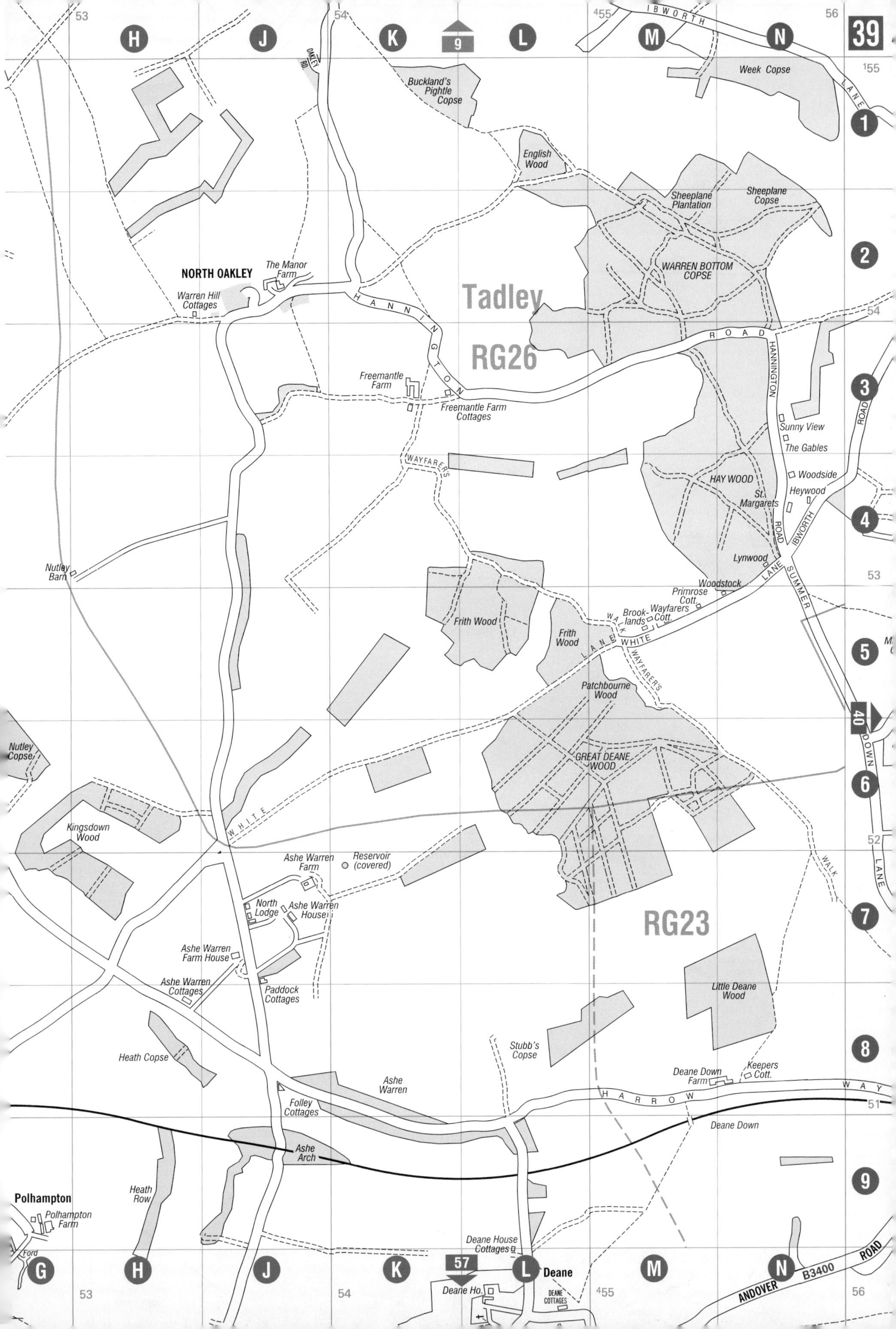

Tadley

RG26

RG23

NORTH OAKLEY

Polhampton

Deane

Week Copse

Buckland's Pightle Copse

English Wood

Sheeplane Plantation

Sheeplane Copse

WARREN BOTTOM COPSE

The Manor Farm

Warren Hill Cottages

Freemantle Farm

Freemantle Farm Cottages

WAYFARERS

Sunny View

The Gables

Woodside

HAY WOOD

Heywood

St. Margarets

Nutley Barn

Lynwood

Woodstock

Primrose Cott.

Brook-lands

Wayfarers Cott.

Frith Wood

Frith Wood

Patchbourne Wood

GREAT DEANE WOOD

Nutley Copse

Kingsdown Wood

Ashe Warren Farm

Reservoir (covered)

North Lodge

Ashe Warren House

Ashe Warren Farm House

Ashe Warren Cottages

Paddock Cottages

Little Deane Wood

Heath Copse

Stubb's Copse

Ashe Warren

Deane Down Farm

Keepers Cott.

Folley Cottages

Ashe Arch

HARROW WAY

Deane Down

Polhampton Farm

Heath Row

Ford

Deane House Cottages

Deane Ho.

DEANE COTTAGES

ANDOVER ROAD B3400

HANNINGTON ROAD

IBWORTH LANE

SUMMER DOWN LANE

WHITE LANE

WAYFARER'S WALK

OMKEY RD.

9

40

57

ROAD

Tadley
RG26
RG23
Ibworth
Upper Wootton
Newfound
Clarken Green
OAKLEY
East Oakley
Balstone Farm
Hopgarden Copse
Bailey Hall Farm
Res.
Manor Farm
Woodgarston Farm
KINGSCLERE
A339
WOOTTON
WOODGARSTON LANE
Field House
Great Yarth
Whitedown Farm
IBWORTH ROAD
LANE
Upper Farm
CORONATION COTTS.
WELL CL.
Hall
Wootton Chase
Wootton House
Tangier House
The Wilderness
Tangier Park
Lodge
Lockley Copse
Sheardown Farm
HOOK
Malshanger Cottages
Bowling Green
Sheardown House
Malshanger House
Wych Hazel Copse
Kirval Lane Row Copse
Firdell Cottages
MANYDOWN PARK
The Firs
Summer Down Copse
MALSHANGER PARK
Little Breach Copse
Manydown Park
Marvel Row Copse
Old Orchard Plantation
New Plantation
Home Farm
Home Farm Cottages
Little Breach Row
Lady Mead Row
The Lodge
Winter Down Coppice
WAYFARERS WALK
Blandy's Farm
Summer Down Farm
MALSHANGER LANE
Winter Down Copse
Sourley Row
Summerdown Cottages
SUMMER DOWN LANE
WORTING ROAD
Playing Fields
Dell Farm
Mother's Copse
Sewage Works
HARROW WAY
B3400
FOXMOOR CL.
HUNTERS CL.
DELLFIELD
TOLLGATE
LONGFIELD
PARK
LIGHTSFIELD
TURNPIKE WY.
BOW WY.
WITHER RI.
SHEPHERDS WLK.
Works
FOX LANE
Cow Down Copse
Ten. Cts.
MALSHANGER ROAD
GLAMIS CL.
HIGHLAND
BRAEMAR
PARK CL.
ARRAN CL.
MULL CL.
LOMOND
OBAN CL.
ASHLEY GDNS.
MEDWAY AV.
THE GREENAWAYS
ST. JOHN'S
St. John's Copse
Battledown Flyover Bri.
Worting Junction
CADNAM
TANNERS WAY
AVON
DEVER WY.
TAMAR DR.
ITCHEN CL.
SPRINGFIELD
ROAD
FROME
OAKLEY
KENNET
MARLBORO GS.
DR. CROFT
The Spinney
RECTORY
ANDOVER
Oakley Lodge
STATION ROAD
Park Farm
Peter Houseman Rec. Grd.
Oakley Inf. Sch.
Oakley C of E Jun. Sch.
Manor House
LYDE CL.
MEON RD
MEDINA
HOOPER
Well's Copse
Battledown Farm
39
20
58

Field Barn Fm.
Piccadilly Hill
West Lane Farm
Elm Lea
Elm Bottom Cross
RG24
Shothanger Works
A339
WEYBROOK PARK GOLF COURSE
Club House
Greatfield Farm
PARKLANDS HOSPITAL
St. Michael's Hospice
BASINGSTOKE & NTH. HAMPSHIRE HOSPITAL
Cemetery
WOOTTON ST. LAWRENCE
Manor Farm
Depot
Hermes Ho.
RINGWAY NORTH
A340
Houndmills
Fort Hill Community School
Winklebury
Winklebury Jun. & Inf. Schs.
Wortingwood Farm
Worting Wood
Wootton Copse
Basingstoke
Castle Hill Jun. & Inf. Schs.
Football Centre
Winklebury Park
West Ham
Planet Ice
Odeon Cinema
Gala Bingo
The Loddon Vale Indoor Bowling Club
Milestones, Hampshire's Living History Mus.
Aquadrome
Bowlplex
BASINGSTOKE GOLF CENTRE
Driving Range
Worting House
Worting
WORTING PARK
Scrapp's Hill Farm
B3400
CHURCHILL WAY
WORTING ROAD
BASINGSTOKE
RG22
Chiltern Prim. Sch.
Buckskin
Limington House Sch.
Russell Howard Pk.
South Ham
Bishop Challoner Catholic Sec. Sch.
St. Anne's Catholic Prim. Sch.
Aldworth Science College
Park View Jun. & Inf. Schs.
Recreation Ground
Stratton Park
Tennis Courts
Fiveways
Battledown
Down Grange Sports Complex
Grangeside School
Brighton Hill
Basingstoke Town F.C.
BRIGHTON HILL RETAIL PARK
WINCHESTER A30 RD.
RINGWAY WEST

A
B
C
D
E
F
G
22
1
2
3
4
5
6
7
8
9
BASINGSTOKE
RG21
Basingstoke
Popley
Oakridge
South View
Houndmills
Daneshill
Eastrop
Black Dam
King's Furlong
Cranbourne
BASING FOREST
Carpenter's Down Wood
Upper Plantation
Scours Plantation
Down Piece
Marnel Lodge (Nursing Home)
Marnel Dell
Everest Comm. Academy
Popley Ponds Local Nature Reserve
Merton Jun. & Inf. Schs.
Chineham Park
Oakridge Jun. & Inf. Schs.
Maple Ridge Sch.
The Vyne Comm. Sch.
South View Jun. & Inf. Schs.
Dove Ho. Sch.
HAMPSHIRE BMI CLINIC
Town Centre
FESTIVAL PLACE
Costello Technology College
War Memorial Park
Playing Field
Kings Furlong Jun. & Inf. Schs.
Cranbourne Business & Enterprise Coll.
Queen Mary's College
Central Studio (Thtre.)
St. John's C of E Prim. Sch.
Rucstall Prim. Sch.
Common Plantation
Upper Mill Farm
Mill Head
Blackdam Nature Reserve
Lower Fish Pond
Upper Fish Pond
Junction 6
M3
M3 MOTORWAY
Oaken Plantation
A340
A339
A33
A3010
A30
B3046
RINGWAY
ALDERMASTON ROAD
READING ROAD
CHURCHILL WAY
Eastrop Park
River Loddon
41
60
Cricket Ground
The Bothy
Home Farm
Viables Craft Cen.

H
J
K
L
M
N
Refuse Incinerator
Sewage Works
23
Four Lane's End
THORNHILL CROSSROADS
A33
ROAD
GREAT BINFIELDS COPSE
CHINEHAM
Great Binfields Prim. Sch.
Centre Ct. Tennis Cen.
Brick Kiln Cottages
Lodge Farm
River Loddon
Lower River Row
Blackland's Farm
Hale Farm
Upper River Row
Rushes Row
Bottom Row
Basingstoke
Pyott's Hill
Lychpit
BINFIELDS
Lower Mill
Mill Head
Lower Mill Farm
Bain's Wood
Gravelly Bottom Copse
Elliot's Copse
Bell's Copse
Poors Farm
Hayden's Pightle
Gold's Farm
Orchard Cott.
Pot Cott.
Wildwood Farm
Oliver's Battery
Hall
Recreation Ground
Bowling Grn.
Playground
Tennis Cts.
RG24
Round Copse
Hodd's Copse
WATER END LANE
Playing Field
Mill Field Local Nature Reserve
Cemetery
OLD BASING
Basing Ho.
Barton's Mill
Weir
Cowdery's Downs
Bushey Lease Copse
Hodd's Copse
New Plantation
Virnell's Copse
Hodd's Farm
The Bungalow
Hodd's Hill
Brown's Farm
St. Mary's C of E Jun. Sch.
Grange Farm
Graveyard
Old Basing Inf. Sch.
Basing House
Childrens Home
Peat Moor
A30
ROAD
Priory Farm
Andwell
Priory (Rems. of)
East Moor Copse
East Moor
Middle Copse
44
Conkers Nursery
Swanhill Nursery
Southville
M3
BASING PARK
Basingstoke Common
LINDEN AVENUE
PARK AVENUE
Ckt. Grd.
Rec. Grd.
Andwell Moor
Burrough Close
Hatch
M3 MOTORWAY
Crabtree Plantation
Lodge
The Farm
Cob Tree Cottages
Mapledurwell House
Webb's Farm
Huish Farm
Cobblers Dell
Huish House
RG25
NEW PARK
Plantation Lane
MAPLEDURWELL
Moorhams Farm
Moorhams Copse
Nunnery Hill
Manor Farm
Sheetlands Copse
Gray's Farm
St. Mary's Church
Dicken's Lane
TUNWORTH ROAD
1
2
3
4
5
6
7
8
9
G
H
J
K
61
L
M
N
66
67
68
69
Polecat Cotts.
Blackdown Cottage
Blackdown Farm

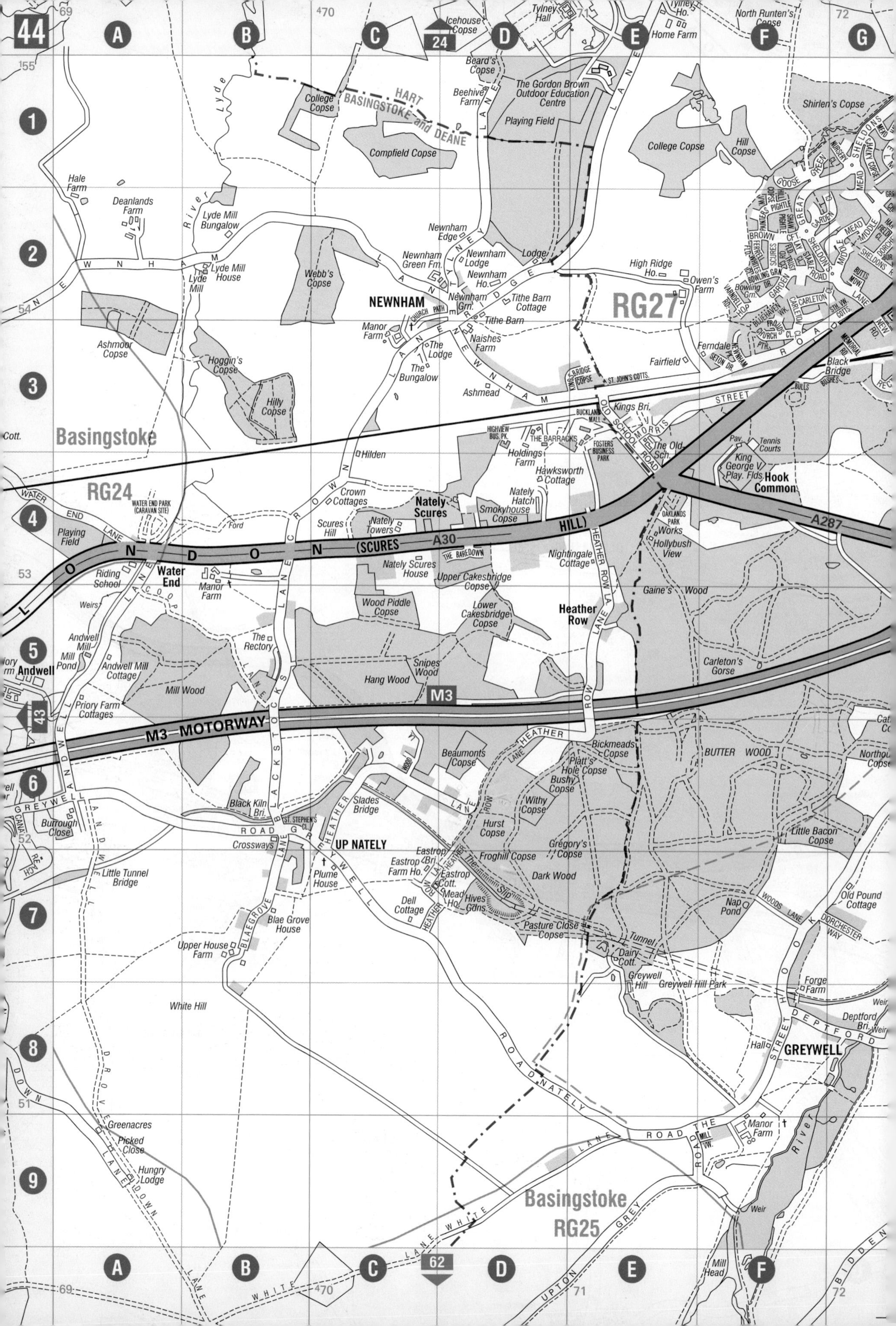

A
B
C
D
E
F
G
470
71
72
69
155
54
53
52
51
24
62
43
Icehouse Copse
Tylney Hall
Tylney Ho.
Home Farm
North Runten's Copse
Beard's Copse
College Copse
HART
BASINGSTOKE and DEANE
Beehive Farm
The Gordon Brown Outdoor Education Centre
Playing Field
Compfield Copse
College Copse
Hill Copse
Shirlen's Copse
Hale Farm
Deanlands Farm
Lyde Mill Bungalow
Newnham Edge
Newnham Green Fm.
Newnham Lodge
Newnham Ho.
Lodge
Lyde Mill House
Lyde Mill
Webb's Copse
NEWNHAM
Newnham Grn.
Tithe Barn Cottage
Tithe Barn
High Ridge Ho.
Owen's Farm
RG27
Manor Farm
The Lodge
The Bungalow
Naishes Farm
Ashmoor Copse
Hoggin's Copse
Hilly Copse
Ashmead
Fairfield
Ferndale
Black Bridge
Basingstoke
RG24
Cott.
Hilden
Kings Bri.
The Old Sch.
Holdings Farm
Hawksworth Cottage
THE BARRACKS
Pav.
Tennis Courts
King George V Play. Flds.
Hook Common
Crown Cottages
Nately Scures
Nately Hatch
Smokyhouse Copse
WATER END PARK (CARAVAN SITE)
Playing Field
Ford
Scures Hill
Nately Towers
A30
A287
Works
Hollybush View
Riding School
Water End
Manor Farm
Nately Scures House
Upper Cakesbridge Copse
Nightingale Cottage
Gaine's Wood
Wood Piddle Copse
Lower Cakesbridge Copse
Heather Row
Weirs
Andwell Mill
Mill Pond
Andwell
The Rectory
Andwell Mill Cottage
Snipes Wood
Carleton's Gorse
Mill Wood
Hang Wood
M3
Priory Farm Cottages
M3 MOTORWAY
Beaumonts Copse
Bickmeads Copse
Platt's Hole Copse
BUTTER WOOD
Bushy Copse
Black Kiln Bri.
Slades Bridge
Withy Copse
Hurst Copse
Burrough Close
Little Bacon Copse
Crossways
UP NATELY
Gregory's Copse
Eastrop Bri.
Eastrop Farm Ho.
Froghill Copse
Plume House
Eastrop Cott.
Dark Wood
Little Tunnel Bridge
Mead Ho.
Hives Gdns.
Dell Cottage
Nap Pond
Old Pound Cottage
Blae Grove House
Pasture Close Copse
Tunnel
Upper House Farm
Dairy Cott.
Greywell Hill
Greywell Hill Park
Forge Farm
White Hill
Deptford Bri.
Hall
GREYWELL
Greenacres
Picked Close
Manor Farm
Hungry Lodge
Basingstoke
RG25
Weir
Mill Head

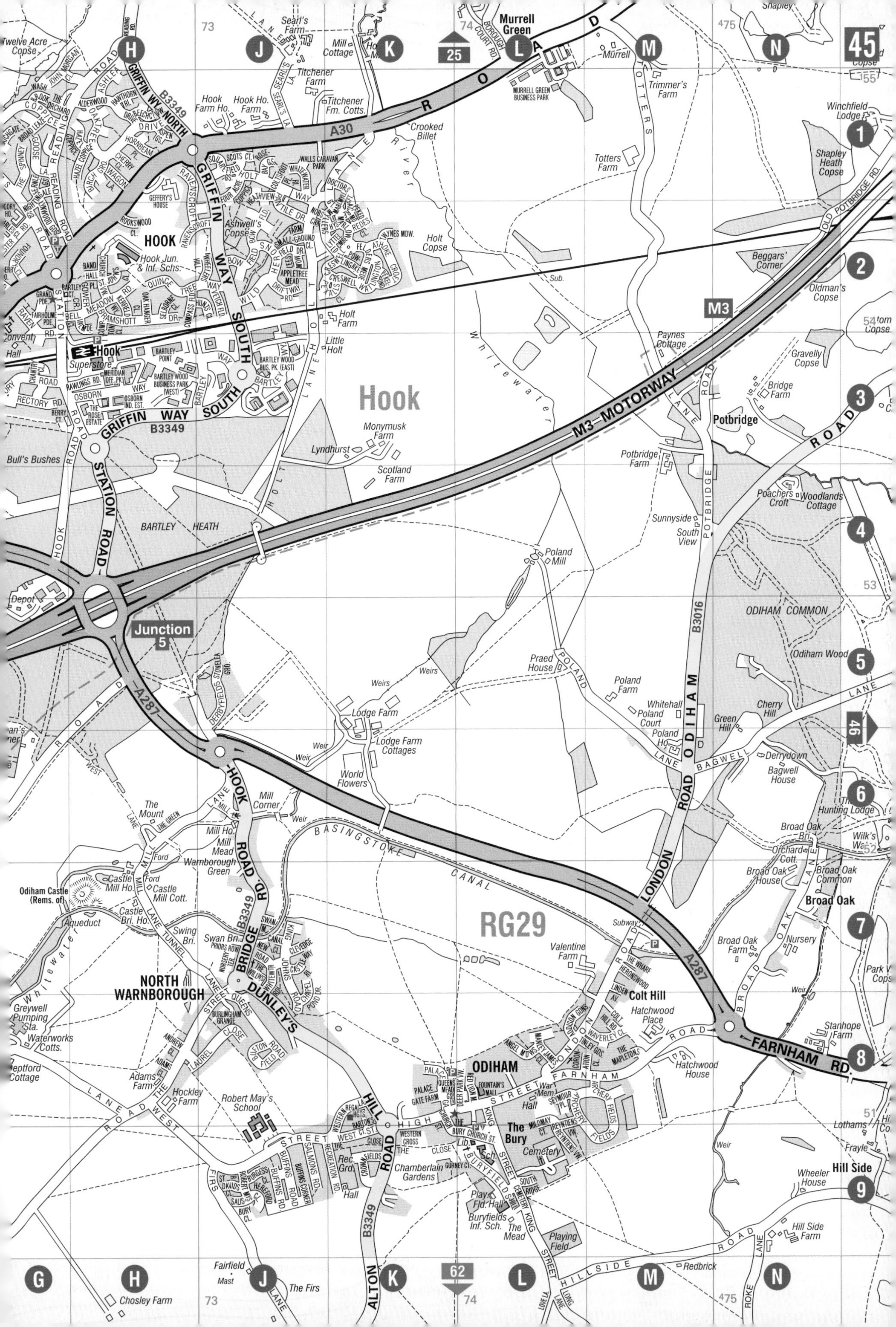
Hook
RG29
HOOK
ODIHAM
NORTH WARNBOROUGH
Murrell Green
Colt Hill
Broad Oak
Potbridge
Hill Side
The Bury
M3 MOTORWAY
Junction 5
A30
A287
B3349
B3016
LONDON ROAD
ODIHAM ROAD
FARNHAM RD.
GRIFFIN WAY NORTH
GRIFFIN WAY SOUTH
STATION ROAD
HOOK ROAD
HIGH STREET
ALTON ROAD
BASINGSTOKE CANAL
BARTLEY HEATH
ODIHAM COMMON
Odiham Wood
Odiham Castle (Rems. of)
Bull's Bushes
Whitewater
Lodge Farm
Poland Mill
Robert May's School
Hook Jun. & Inf. Schs.
Buryfields Inf. Sch.
Chamberlain Gardens
Cemetery
Playing Field
Hockley Farm
Adams Farm
Valentine Farm
Hatchwood House
Shapley Heath Copse
Beggars' Corner
Oldman's Copse
Gravelly Copse
Bridge Farm
Monymusk Farm
Scotland Farm
Lyndhurst
Holt Copse
Holt Farm
Little Holt
Totters Farm
Trimmer's Farm
Crooked Billet
Titchener Farm
Hook Farm Ho.
Searl's Farm
Mill Cottage
Winchfield Lodge
Redbrick
Hill Side Farm
Wheeler House
Chosley Farm
Fairfield
The Firs
25
46
62
73
74
475

M3 MOTORWAY
M3
26
WINCHFIELD
Winchfield
Winchfield Hurst
Hook
RG27
Chatter Alley
DOGMERSFIELD
Pilcot
RG29
GU10
Farnham
Broad Oak
Hill Side
Rye Common
45
63
FARNHAM ROAD
A287
ODIHAM ROAD
B3016
BASINGSTOKE CANAL
GREAT PARK
DOGMERSFIELD PARK
Ringwood Copse
Mabs Copse
Winchfield House
South Cottage
Wintney Farm
Parkfield Copse
Winchfield Lodge
Shapley Heath
Shapley Heath Copse
Shapley Hill
Cranford's Farm
Vale Farm
Furzy Moor
Tossell Wood
Keepers Cottage
Oldman's Copse
Bottom Copse
Brickfield
Tudor Farm
Blacklands Copse
Hurst Farm
Hungerford Farm
Cricket Ground
Gravelly Copse
Withy Bed Copse
Chevertons
The Oast House
Court Ho.
The Cottage
Gunner's Copse
Barley Mow Bridge
Round Copse
Old Barley Mow Farm
Burnbake Copse
The Rectory
Hellet's Copse
Woodlands Cottage
The Old Rectory
Arch Plantation
Chatter Alley Green
Sewage Works
Pilcot Farm
Old Thatch
Oak Hatch
Stacey's Bri.
Greenways Farm
Bagwell Green
Rectory Cottage
Allen's Tree
Baseley's Bri.
Gillet's Copse
Swan's Farm Cottages
Dairy Cottage
Swan's Farm
Cricket Grd.
Dogmersfield C of E Prim. Sch.
Odiham Wood
Bagwell Shaw
Dogmersfield Plat
Yew Tree Copse
The Dower House
Sluice
Sprats Hatch Bri.
Sandy Hill Bri.
Sprats Hatch Farm
Sprats Hatch Cotts.
Tundry Hill
All Saints' Church
Tundry Pond
Lousey Moor
Victory Cottages
Calves Pightle Copse
Peatmoor Copse
Piller's Copse
Parsonage Copse
Blacksmith's Bridge
The Lodge
The Hunting Lodge
Wilk's Water
Old Parsonage
Ormersfield Farm
Lake Head
Double Bridge Farm
Whitlow Alders
Broad Oak Common
Piller's Park
Double Bridge
Ormusfield
Weir
Dogmersfield Lake
Church Lodge
Eastcote House
Hall
Floods Farm
Swing Bridge Copse
Cunningham's Row
Park Wall Copse
Hotel
Reeds Cotts.
Hop Garden Plantation
Stanhope Farm
Forest Park
Fermoy
Coxmoor Bridge
New Bungalow
Harewarren Plantation
Coxmoor Wood
Lothams
Hillside Common
Berry Horn Cottage
Farnham Lodge Plantation
Frayle
Berry Horn House
River's Park
Coxmoor Farm
Electricity Sub Station
Small Acres Farm
Harewarren Farm
Peaked Croft Farm
Wheeler Ho.
Old Green Cottage
Wychwood Carp Farm
Oaks Copse
Peaked Croft Copse
Sewage Works
Hill Side Farm
Bullock's Farm
Varndell's Copse
Varndell House
Rye Common
Nursery
Darwin's Farm
Darwins House
TAPLINS FARM LANE
THE HURST
PALE LANE
CHATTER ALLEY
CHURCH LANE
CHALKY LANE
STATION HILL
STATION ROAD
BEAUCLERK GREEN
BAGWELL LANE
Mousey Row
HATCH LANE
SPRATS HATCH LANE
POTBRIDGE ROAD
SHAPLEY HEATH
RYE COMMON LANE
AQUARIUS CL.
River
55
54
53
52
51
76
77
78
A
B
C
D
E
F
G
1
2
3
4
5
6
7
8
9

FLEET
GU51
GU52
Fleet
CROOKHAM VILLAGE
CHURCH CROOKHAM
Farnham GU10
READING ROAD
A323
NORTH READING ROAD
ALDERSHOT ROAD
FLEET ROAD
A3013
KINGS ROAD
B3010
B3013
SOUTH BEACON HILL ROAD
ELVETHAM ROAD
CRONDALL ROAD
BASINGSTOKE CANAL
FITZROY ROAD
LEAWOOD ROAD
GLEN ROAD
FLEET POND (Nature Reserve)
Landing Stage
Great Bog Copse
Railroad Copse
Culver Copse
FLEET COMMUNITY HOSPITAL
Fitness First
The Harlington Cen.
Oakley Park
Calthorpe Park
Calthorpe Park Sch.
Hart Leisure Cen.
Playing Field
Jack Reid's Copse
Long Copse
All Saints C of E Jun. Sch.
Heatherside Inf. Sch.
Heatherside Junior Sch.
Velmead Jun. Sch.
Fleet Inf. Sch.
Court Moor School
Netherhouse Copse
Pilcot Hill House
Brook Meadow Farm
Brook Hill
Sewage Works
Grove Farm
Basingbourne Park
GRANGE ESTATE (Caravan Site)
Willow Cottage
Riverside Cottage
Peatmoor Copse
Zephon Common
Zebon Copse (Nature Reserve)
Swing-Bridge
Crookham Wharf
Bridge House
Chequers Bridge
Nursery
Poulter's Bridge
Comm. Cen.
The Old Horns
Garden Cen.
Redfields Racing Stables
Dachs Lodge
Blackmore Copse
Wychwood
Redfields Rows
St. Nicholas' School
Redfields Cottage Farm
Tyland
Triggs
Hancock's Farm
Two Ponds
Falker's Copse
Fusney Copse
Leeches Copse
Five Acre Copse
HURST GOLF COURSE
Driving Range
Goose Close
Bowenhurst Copse
Mill Lane
Queen Elizabeth Barracks
Parade Grd.
Crookham Jun. Sch.
Tweseldown Inf. Sch.
Soanes Copse
Wood Copse
Wakefords Copse
Rifle Range
Leipzig Barracks
Stillers Farm
Ridding's Copse
Reservoir (covered)
Beacon Hill Farm
Seymour Farm
Peter Driver Sports Ground
Depot
FLEET BUSINESS PARK
Hart
River Hart
79
80
81
82
55
54
53
52
51
H J K L M N G
1 2 3 4 5 6 7 8 9
27
48
63

FLEET POND
(Nature Reserve)
SOUTHWOOD
SOUTHWOOD GOLF COURSE
Peartree Cottages
Depot
Sewage Works
KENNELS LANE
IVELY ROAD
Pyestock
CODY TECHNOLOGY PARK
Playing Field
Bowling Green
PONDTAIL
GU51
KINGS RD.
ALDERSHOT RD.
NORRIS HILL ROAD
A323
BASINGSTOKE CANAL
Pyestock Hill
Pyestock Wood
Fleet Inf. Sch.
Velmead Jun. Sch.
Norris Hill West
Eelmoor Marsh
WHIRLWIND TRACK
Ball Hill
DSTL Farnborough
Norris Hill East
Gelvert Bottom
Miles Hill
Laffan's Copse
Bridge Hill
Eelmoor Flash
Puckridge Flash
Puckridge Hill
Claycart Flash
Claycart Bridge
Hussar Copses
Norris Hill Copse
Miles Copses
Fleet
Brock's Hill
Aunt's Pool
Eelmoor Hill
Spur Hill
Eelmoor Hill West
Eelmoor Hill East
RUSHMOOR
HART
Ravine Head
Long Hill Copse
Cocked Hat Wood
Aunt's Pool Hill
TWESELDOWN RACE COURSE
Tweseldown Hill
Parade Ring
Grandstand
Peter Driver Sports Ground
Depot
Bickley Oaks
Long Hill
Long Valley
Centre Hill
Bickley Moor
Eelmoor Plain
Claycart Bottom
GU52
Outridden Hill
Chestnut Copse
Jones Acre
Bat's Hogsty (Tumulus)
Wakefords Copse
FLEET BUSINESS PARK
Outridden Copse
Showground
Rushmoor Hill
Greendane Copse
Bickley Copse
Jubilee Plantation
Camping Ground
Six Acre Copse
Bourley Camping Ground
Rifle Range
Sports Ground
Ewshot Camping Grd.
Chandler's Copse
Jubilee Hill
WELLESLEY ROAD
Beacon Hill Cottages
Beacon Hill Copse
Farnham GU10
Parkhurst Hill
Firs Hill
Burn's Hill
Burn's Plain
Pavilion Hill
Royal Pavilion
The Lodge
BOURLEY ROAD
Water Works
Rifle Range
Cheese Hill
Groom's Lodge
Reservoir (covered)
Reservoir
Steep Hill
Steep Bottom
Sunny Hill
BEACON HILL
B3013
Long Gut Copse
TADPOLE LANE
Beacon Hill Farm
Bourley Bottom
Reservoir
Bourley Hill
Rifle Range
Skirmishing Hill
Lookout Post
DANGER AREA
FLEET ROAD
A323
RUSHMOOR ROAD
FARNBOROUGH RD.
ALDERSHOT ROAD
28
47
64
A B C D E F G
1 2 3 4 5 6 7 8 9
82 83 84 485
55 54 53 52 51

49
Farnborough
GU14
FARNBOROUGH AIRPORT
SOUTH FARNBOROUGH
NORTH CAMP
North Camp
Marlborough Park
Ramillies Park
Sewage Works
ARMY GOLF COURSE
WATTS' COMMON
Berkshire Copse
Queen's Parade Recreation Ground
Golf Course
Government House
Blandford House
Rushmore Flash
Aldershot Services Grounds
SOUTH CAMP
Aldershot
GU11
ALDERSHOT
Aldershot Town FC (The EBB Stadium)
Redan Hill
Peaked Hill
Goose Green Park
Military Cemetery
Waterloo Park
Red Hill
Dolly's Hill
NORTH TOWN
GU12
GOLD VALLEY LAKES
Gold Farm
Aldershot Stubs
Gasworks Bri.
Ash Lock
Silvester Bridge
Iron Bridge
Wharf Bridge
BASINGSTOKE CANAL
Blackwater River
BLACKWATER VALLEY ROUTE
A331
A325
FARNBOROUGH ROAD
A327
A3011
LYNCHFORD ROAD
B3403
A323
WELLINGTON AVENUE
HIGH ST.
B3008
VICTORIA ROAD
GROSVENOR RD.
QUEEN'S AVENUE
ALISON'S ROAD
FLEET RD.
CLUBHOUSE RD.
ALEXANDRA ROAD
RUSHMOOR ROAD
GUILDFORD ROAD
NORTH LANE
Farnborough Coll. of Technology
Knellwood War Memorial Old People's Home
Salesian Coll.
The Linden Education Cen.
Military Mus.
Aldershot Military Stadium
Army School of Physical Training
Combat Sports Cen.
Garrison Sports Cen.
Alpine Snowsports Cen.
Aldershot Cen. for Health
Talavera Inf. & Jun. Schs.
St. Omer Barracks
Travers Barracks
Gale Barracks
Buller Barracks
Clayton Barracks
Normandy Barracks
Bruneval Barracks
Arnhem Barracks
Rhine Barracks
McGrigor Barracks
Duchess of Kent Barracks
Malta Barracks
Hammersley Barracks
Browning Barracks
29
65
G H J K L M N
1 2 3 4 5 6 7 8 9
86 87 88

Mankhorn Cottage
MANKHORN LA
LODGE LA
South Lodge
Soper's Bottom
Soper's Barn
Farmhouse
32
Roundaway Copse
DROVE
WILTSHIRE
TEST VALLEY
LANE
HATCHET
Poultry Houses
Bucklands Copse
Woodlands
New Bungalow
Flinty Cottage
FLINT LANE
BOTTOM
ST. MARGARETS
Nutbane Copse
Nutbane
REDENHAM
HOUSE
NEW
The Bungalow
Redenham
Blakes Farm
Tilly Down
Abattoir
Manor Farm
Well Farm
Cooks Farm
COPSE VW.
PRIVET LA
PENTON LANE
Nutbane Farm
NUTBANE LANE
Appleshaw Copse
Manor Farm
Manor House
St. Peter's C of E Primary School
EASTVILLE
SOPER'S
Clanville House
Clanville Farm
Clanville
Rosehill
Reservoir (covered)
BACK
LANE
PENTON
Iron Pear Tree Cottage
APPLESHAW DENE
Ragged Appleshaw
The Old Vicarage
Primrose Hill
Privet Down
Great Copse
APPLESHAW
Harrow Farm
Poplar Farm
Hall
Clanville Lodge Stud Farm
Blissamore Hall
The Orchards
Hall
PIPPIN GRO.
WEST PK.
GREENSEY
Hill House
Vicarage
Pav.
Play. Fld.
Lodge
31
Appleshaw House
SP11
Chalk Croft Farm
RAMRIDGE COPSE
BARNCROFT
Horse Croft Copse
Staddlestones Farm
The Kennels
Springfield
Hazelhurst
Parkside
Staddles Cottag
ANDOVER
Reeds
Ramridge House
Lodges
PENTON MEWSEY
Ashtree Lodge
RAMRIDGE PARK
THE GROVE
TRINITY RI.
Greatfield Lodge
Ramridge Farm
Ramridge Dean
Penton Grafton
GRAFTON PL.
Little Down
Blue Bell Farm
Escote Ho.
SCAMBLERS MEAD
Play. Fld.
Pav.
CHALKCROFT
A342
LANE
DROVE
The White House
Omsk
Weyhill Bottom
Prebbles Lodge
Playing Field
HARROWAY
Whiarsdale
FYFIELD
Poultry Houses
DAUNTSEY
HAYMOUSE LA.
ROAD
FAIRGROUND IND. PK.
FAIRVIEW RD.
CASTERBRIDGE
RECTORY PLACE FLATS
RECTORY PL.
Weyhill Farm
Fairways
FAIRGROUND
BUSS.
MORELA LA.
Craft Cen.
THE RANK
ANCIENT
HARDYFAIR CL.
Braust House
Depot
BUSHES
Greenacre
LANE
ROAD
WEYHILL
MAYFIELD AV. IND. PK.
Works
NEW ABBEY HO.
FAIRWAYS
MONXTON
Weyhill Lodge
LODGE DR.
WEYHILL GDS.
HANGING
Penton Harroway
Aucris House
Depot
ORDNANCE LA.
MACHAEMAS DROVE
War Meml.
SARSON
The Red House
Penton Corner
SHORT LANE
BEECH CL.
MULLENSCOTE PARK HOMES
Mayfield House
DAUNTSEY
A303
Bridge Bungalow
POST
Weyhill Service Area
A303
Nursery
AMESBURY
Weyhill Nurseries & Garden Cen.
46
LANE
MONXTON
68
LANE
Kimber
SARSON LANE
The Limes
430
31
32
33
47
48
49
150

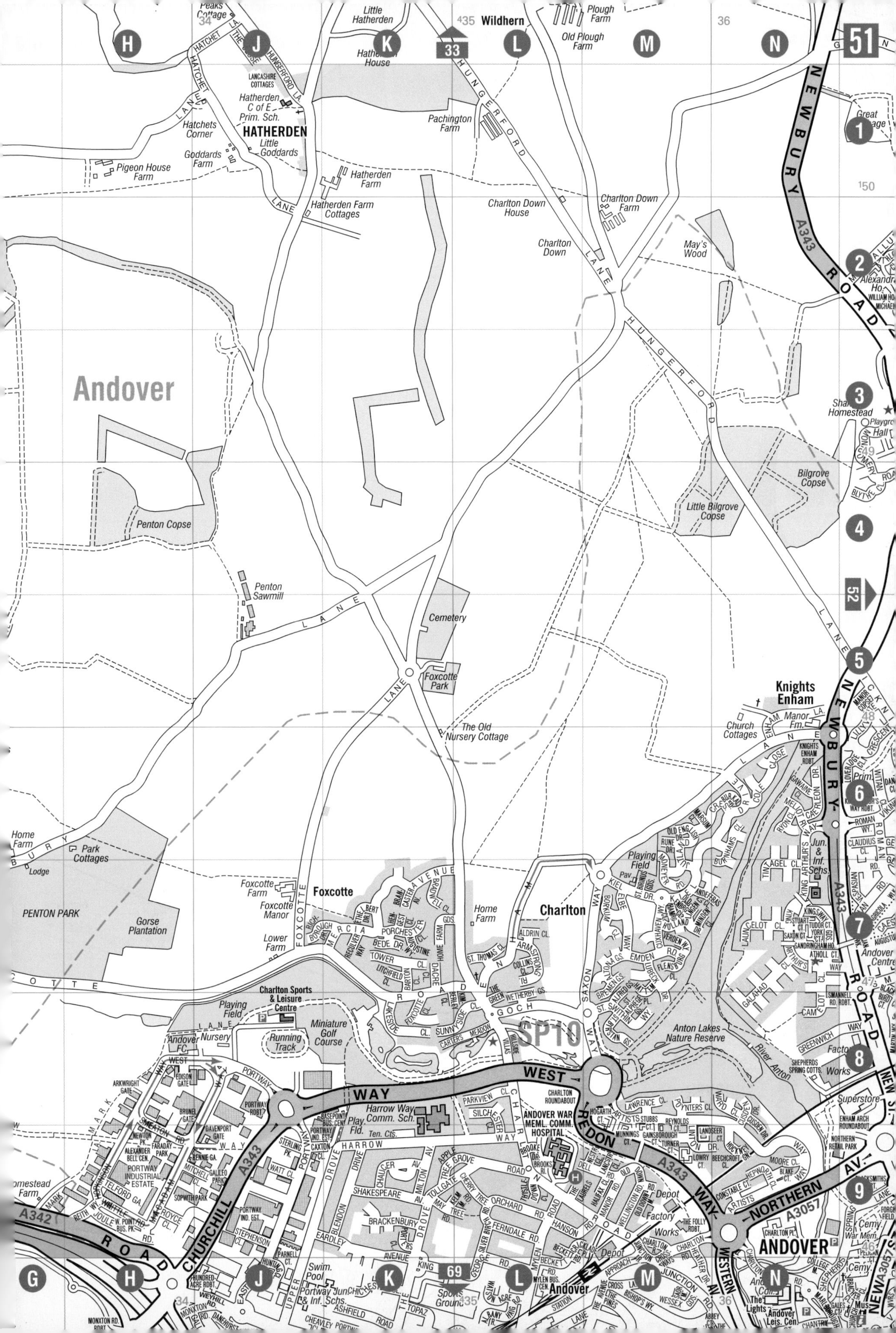
Andover
HATHERDEN
Wildhern
Little Hatherden
Hatherden House
Plough Farm
Old Plough Farm
Hatherden C of E Prim. Sch.
Hatchets Corner
Little Goddards
Goddards Farm
Pigeon House Farm
Hatherden Farm
Hatherden Farm Cottages
Pachington Farm
Charlton Down House
Charlton Down Farm
Charlton Down
May's Wood
Great Cottage
Alexandra Ho.
Penton Copse
Penton Sawmill
Little Bilgrove Copse
Bilgrove Copse
Cemetery
Foxcotte Park
The Old Nursery Cottage
Knights Enham
Church Cottages
Home Farm
Park Cottages
Lodge
PENTON PARK
Gorse Plantation
Foxcotte Farm
Foxcotte Manor
Lower Farm
Foxcotte
Home Farm
Charlton
Playing Field
Charlton Sports & Leisure Centre
Miniature Golf Course
Running Track
Andover FC
Nursery
Anton Lakes Nature Reserve
River Anton
SP10
Harrow Way Comm. Sch.
ANDOVER WAR MEML. COMM. HOSPITAL
CHARLTON ROUNDABOUT
PORTWAY INDUSTRIAL ESTATE
Superstore
ENHAM ARCH ROUNDABOUT
NORTHERN RETAIL PARK
ANDOVER
Andover
Swim. Pool
Portway Jun. & Inf. Schs.
Sports Ground
The Lights
Andover Leis. Cen
NEWBURY ROAD
A343
A342
A3057
WEST WAY
HARROW WAY
CHURCHILL WAY
NORTHERN AV.
WESTERN AV.
HUNGERFORD LANE
FOXCOTTE LANE
33
52
69

Great Stubbage
LONG COPSE
Straits Copse
RIDGES COPSE
Little Camber's Copse
Camber's Copse
Home Farm
Postgrove Farmhouse
Poultry House
Postgrove Copse
Mount Pleasant Farm
Little London
Mongomble Copse
Hackwood Copse
Factory
Resource Cen.
ENHAM ALAMEIN
Poultry Houses
Postgrove House
Shanghai Homestead
Playing Field
Woodhouse Farm
Woodhouse
Smannell & Enham C of E Prim. Sch.
Pound View
Ashley Copse
SMANNELL
Bilgrove Copse
Trinley Buildings
Finkley House
Manor Farm Cotts.
Finkley Manor Farm
Lesleys Cottage
Andover SP11
Eastanton Farm Cottages
Endeavour Primary Sch.
Eastanton Farm
East Anton
Playground
Andover Educ. Centre
Finkley Down Farm Park
Warehouse
Lapstone Farm
Picket Piece
Works
Factory
Depot
Sports Field
Poultry Houses
Melrose Farm
Kennels
Depot
Smallholding
ANDOVER
SP10
Superstore
The Phoenix Cen.
Icknield Sch.
Factories
WALWORTH INDUSTRIAL ESTATE
Recycling Cen.
Harewood Farm
Harewood Mobile Home Park
Vigo Jun. & Inf. Schs.
Norman Gate School
Play. Flds.
The Mark Wy. Sch.
Winton School
Convent Farm
Down Ho.
Down Ho. Farm
Harewood House
NEWBURY ROAD
CHURCHILL WAY
LONDON ROAD
FINKLEY ROAD
SMANNELL ROAD
DROVE LANE
MALTHOUSE LANE
A343
A3057
A3093
B3400
34
51
70

SWAMPTON
ST. MARY BOURNE
Upper Wyke
Derry Down
Oak Tree Farm
Hilliers Farm Cottages
Little Meadow
Coronation Cottages
Upper Wyke Manor
Upper Wyke Cottages
Upper Wyke Farm
Haven Hill
Breach Farm Bungalow
War Meml.
Bourne Ho.
Ford
Bowl. Grn.
Pav.
Rec. Grd.
CHURCH ST.
APPLEGATE
EGBURY ROAD
Portway
FIVE LANES
Bedlam's Copse
Abbatoir
ROAD
Derrydown Copse
Bourne Court
Upper Link
Reservoir (covered)
SOUTH VIEW TERRACE
B3048
Derry Down Cottage
Derrydown Farm
Cress View
Middle Wyke Bungalows
Middle Wyke Farm
Lower Wyke Barn
Moors Wood
Gravel Hill Plantation
Watercress Beds
Lower Link Farm
Keepers Cottage
Middle Wyke Cottages
Lower Wyke Farm
Chapmansford Farm
Lower Wyke Cottages
HARROWAY
ROAD
Apsley Clump
Apsley Farm
The Wooden House
Apsley Cottages
Pickford's Plantation
Pepper Hill Firs
Wyke Down Gold Driving Range
Wyke Down Farm
WYKE DOWN TOURING & CARAVAN PARK
Poultry Houses
WALWORTH
ANDOVER
OX DROVE RI.
Keepers Cottage
Long Plantation
Faulkner's Down Farm
Faulkner's Bushes
BASINGSTOKE and DEANE
TEST VALLEY
Whitchurch
RG28
Tinker's Hill
Harewood Peak House
Harewood Peak
Foxdale House
Fox Cottages
Foxhill Cottages
Andover Down Farm
Saw Mill
B3400
Poultry Houses
Fox Farm
Ridges Plantation
Saw Mill
Bourne Wood
The Ridge
Budgett Farm
ROAD
FOLLY COPSE
Harewood Forest
Andover Down
End Copse
H J K L M N
G H J K L M N
1 2 3 4 5 6 7 8 9
440 41 42 43
150 49 48 47 46
35
54
71

HOGDIGGING COPSE
36
Jamaica Farm
Newbarn Down Plantation
Andover
SP11
Down Farm
Dirty Corner
BLOSWOOD
HARROW WAY
A34
Cress View
New Barn Farm
B3048
Lower Link
Lower Link Farm
Cowdown Lodges
COWDOWN COPSE
Little Cowdown Copse
Inner Tugbury Plantation
The Plantation
Chapmansford Cottage
53
Perry's Croft Row
Tugbury Cottage
The Lawn
Garden Cottages
The Mansion
Spratts Villa
Pickford's Plantation
The Island
Spratt's Down
Subway
Manor Farm
Saw Mill House
Bourne Rivulet
HURSTBOURNE PARK
Cemetery
ANDOVER ROAD
CHURCH ST
Vicarage
Works
Cricket Ground
Park Cottage
The Bungalow
B3400
Long Plantation
THE COMMON
Fulling Mill
Little Bull's
River Test
Tufton
Riverside Cottages
Manor House
The Beeches
Longcroft Moor
Vineyard Plantation
HURSTBOURNE PRIORS
Cricket Grd.
Bourne Wood
The Ridge
Bee House
Manor Farm
LONGPARISH ROAD
Faulkner's Cross
Reservoir (covered)
Testbourne
Testbourne Cottages
Paper Mill Bridge
Paper Mill Farm
76
Three Halves Copse
DRURY CL.
WINCHESTER

Whitchurch
RG28
WHITCHURCH
Bere Hill
Lynch Hill
Freefolk
LAVERSTOKE
LAVERSTOKE PARK
Laverstoke House
Laverstock Mill (Engineering Works)
Mill Pond
Home Farm
Home Plantation
Sports Ground
Gardener's Cottage
Tennis Court
The Warren
Railway Belt
Watt's Plantation
South View Cottages
Tudor Rose Cotts.
Manor Farm
The Rectory
Football Grd.
Bowling Green
Tennis Courts
Cowlease Cottage
Wool Down
Reservoir (covered)
Clapper Copse
Boxams Close
Freefolk House
Freefolk House Lodge
Coombedown Hanger
Spring Pond Farm
Southfield Farm
Knowle Clump
Knowle Hassock
New Barn Cottages
New Barn Farm
Brickkiln Wood
Breach Hassock
Buftons
Sewage Works
Testbourne Community School
Whitchurch C of E Prim. Sch.
Playing Field
Rec. Grd. Hall
Great Town Bridge
Weirs
Weir
River Test
Bere Mill
The Gables
Wells-in-the Field Farm
Winterhill Plantation
Berehill Farm
Sheepcrook Cottages
Poultry House
Oak Cottage
Dairy Unit
Side Hill Copse
Down Copse
Wooldings Farm
Cowlease Copse
Wooldings Cottages
The Orchards
The Cottage
Ash Bed Plantation
Northfield Plantation
Harroway Belt
THE HARROW WAY
LONDON ROAD
LONDON ST.
B3400
ROTTEN HILL
LAVERSTOKE LANE
DEVER ROAD
TWINLEY LANE
WATCH LANE
PRIORY LANE
KINGSCLERE ROAD
LARKS BARROW HILL
NEWBURY STREET
WINCHESTER STREET
BERE HILL
BERE HILL PARK (CARAVAN PK.)
PARK HILL
THE HILLSIDE
FREEFOLK PRIORS
MOUNT PLEASANT
MANOR COTTAGES
MEMORIAL BUNGALOWS
37
76
56
47
48
49
150
46

A
B
C
D
E
F
G
450
51
52
38
77
55
1
2
3
4
5
6
7
8
9
150
49
48
47
46
Harroway Belt
Lordsfield Plantation
Northington Belt
Sewage Works
Lynch
Overton C of E Prim. School
Court Farm
Foxdown
Quidhampton Farm
Kennel Plantation
Quidhampton Mill
Quidhampton Pond
Quidhampton
KINGSCLERE ROAD
B3051
Southington Mill
Glebe House
Spts. Grd.
Sports Ground
Football Ground
Farm Cottages
Northington Farm
Parsonage Farm
Southington
HILL
HIGH STREET
LONDON ROAD
B3400
Home Plantation
River Test
The Lodge
OVERTON
Berrydown Court
Berrydown Farm
South Berrydown
Tennis Court
Icehouse Row
LAVERSTOKE PARK
Mill Pond
ROTTEN
Rotten Hill Copse
Sports Ground
Basingstoke
Jackson's Copse
Sapley Farm House
Woodside
Turrill Hill Farm
Reservoir (covered)
White Hill
Lower Whitehill Cottages
Keepers Cottage
Whitchurch
Pot Bottom Cottage
Southley Farm
RG28
Laverstoke Grange Farm
Quidhampton Southley Copse
Pilgrim's Copse
Copse Farm
Southley Copse
Upper Whitehill Farm
Pilgrim's Farm
LAVERSTOKE WOOD
Breach Hassock
TEST VALLEY GOLF COURSE

Polhampton
Polhampton Farm
Heath Row
39
Deane House Cottages
Deane House
DEANE COTTAGES
DEANE
Manor Farm
DEANE PARK
B3400
ROAD
West Lodge
RG23
Oakley Hall
Home Farm
Lower Ashe Farm
ASHE
Spring (Source of River Test)
Ashe Court
Ashe House
Hyde Hill Plantation
The Ladies' Walk
ANDOVER
Cheesedown Farm
Ash Hill Row
Tidnock Farm
Tidnock House
Ashe Hill
ASHE PARK
Ashe Park Fm.
Ashe Park Cottages
Ashe Park
Burley Lane Farm
Kimber's Copse
Keeper's Cottage
ASHE PARK COPSE
Berrydown Copse
Lampacre Plantation
Burley Wood
Rookery Row
The Arch
Reservoir (covered)
Upper Ashe
Peak Hill House
Steventon Arch
STONEHILLS
Nurshanger Farm
Steventon House
Stoken Farm
Gravelly Bottom Bungalow
Nun's Walk
WHEATLEYS CLOSE
STEVENTON
RG25
BURLEY LANE
Berrydown Copse
Berrydown
Willowdown Farm
OAKLEY RD.
Bramdown Copse
Quintan's Plantation
Stubbs Copse
Basset's Farm
STEVENTON PARK
Oakdown House
Northdown Plantation
WALTHAM LANE
West Wood
Hazeldown Copse
Hatch Gate
Orchard Cottage
Village Farm
West Wood
Sewage Works
Westside Dairy
Shelter Plantation
Crawley Copse
Manor Farm
SEVENTON RD.
CHURCH RD.
ST. MICHAEL'S
Litchfield Tunnel
Litchfield Copse
Folly Farm
Steventon Warren Cott.
Cowage Copse
Ashen Grove Copse
Litchfield Grange
77
G H J K L M N
1 2 3 4 5 6 7 8 9
53 54 455 56
150 49 48 47 46
58

OAKLEY
East Oakley
40
ANDOVER RD.
B3400
The Spinney
RECTORY
Park Farm
Peter Houseman Rec. Grd.
Oakley Inf. Sch.
Oakley C of E Jun. Sch.
Manor House
Oakley Hall
OAKLEY PARK
Spinney Cott.
Ckt. Grd.
St. John's Copse
Well's Copse
Breach Farm
Breach Cottages
Leydown
Jeffery's Copse
Sewage Works
RG23
Pardown
Pardown Copse
Small's Copse
Itchen Row
Bull's Bushes Copse
Bull's Bushes Farm
Basingstoke
57
Round Wood
Little Stubbs Copse
South Wood
Great Stubbs Copse
Berrydown Copse
Dean Heath Copse
Old Cottages
Southwood Farm
Berrydown
Willowdown Farm
New Cottages
Ganderdown Copse
Keepers Cottage
Ganderdown Cottages
Kynance
Oakdown Farm
THE COPSE CARAVAN SITE
Ind. Est.
Junction 7
Subway
Village Farm
Sewage Works
Church Farm
Driving Range
RG25
M3
Club House
Westside Dairy
NORTH WALTHAM
Sports Grd.
Prim. Sch.
Village Farm
MAIDENTHORN LANE
Gaythorne
North Waltham Farm
M3 MOTORWAY
A30
Play. Flds.
The Old Rectory
Paddock Lodge
St. George
DUMMER
Cemy.
The Lodge
Dummer House
Tower Hill
Tower Hill Fm.
Hall
Manor Farm
Claydown
78
NORTH WALTHAM ROAD
PARDOWN
Worting Junction

Battledown Farm
Battledown
BATTLEDOWN COTTAGES
Kempshott
RG22
Down Grange Sports Complex
Playing Fields
Down Grange Farm
Down Grange Track
Beechdown Health and Leisure Club
Grangeside School
Brighton Hill Community College
Powerleague
Superstores
Brighton Hill
Superstore Depot
Manor Field Jun. & Inf. Schs.
Hatch Warren Park
Kempshott Jun. & Inf. Sch.
WINCHESTER ROAD
A30
Hatch Warren Jun. & Inf. Schs.
Hatch Warren
Superstore
St. Mark's C of E Prim. School
Playing Field
Hall
Hatch Warren Fm.
Hatch Hill
Playing Fields
Middle Copse
Reservoirs (covered)
M3
M3 MOTORWAY
New Town Cottage
Kempshott Hill
Club House
Coachroad Belt
Beggarwood
Kempshott Park
BASINGSTOKE GOLF COURSE
Rifle Butts
Farleigh Hill
Northgate
B3046
FARLEIGH ROAD
BROADMERE
Sullenger's Copse
Farleigh Mortimer
Broadmere House
Kennel Farm
Gunavie Cott.
Woodside
The Cedars
Kempshott Copse
Shortwood's Copse
Stable Cotts.
Woodlands
The Old Cott.
Shrub Copse
Fellows House
Farleigh Lodge
FARLEIGH WALLOP
Club Cottages
Home Farm
Playing Field
DUMMER GOLF COURSE
Rowley Copse
Foxhall
Manor Farm
Manor Farm Cottages
Foxhall Cottages
Farleigh Park
Inwood Copse
Dummer Clump
The Clump House
Clump Farm
Reservoir (covered)
Mulberry Cottage
Lowes Wood
GREAT WOOD
41
60
78

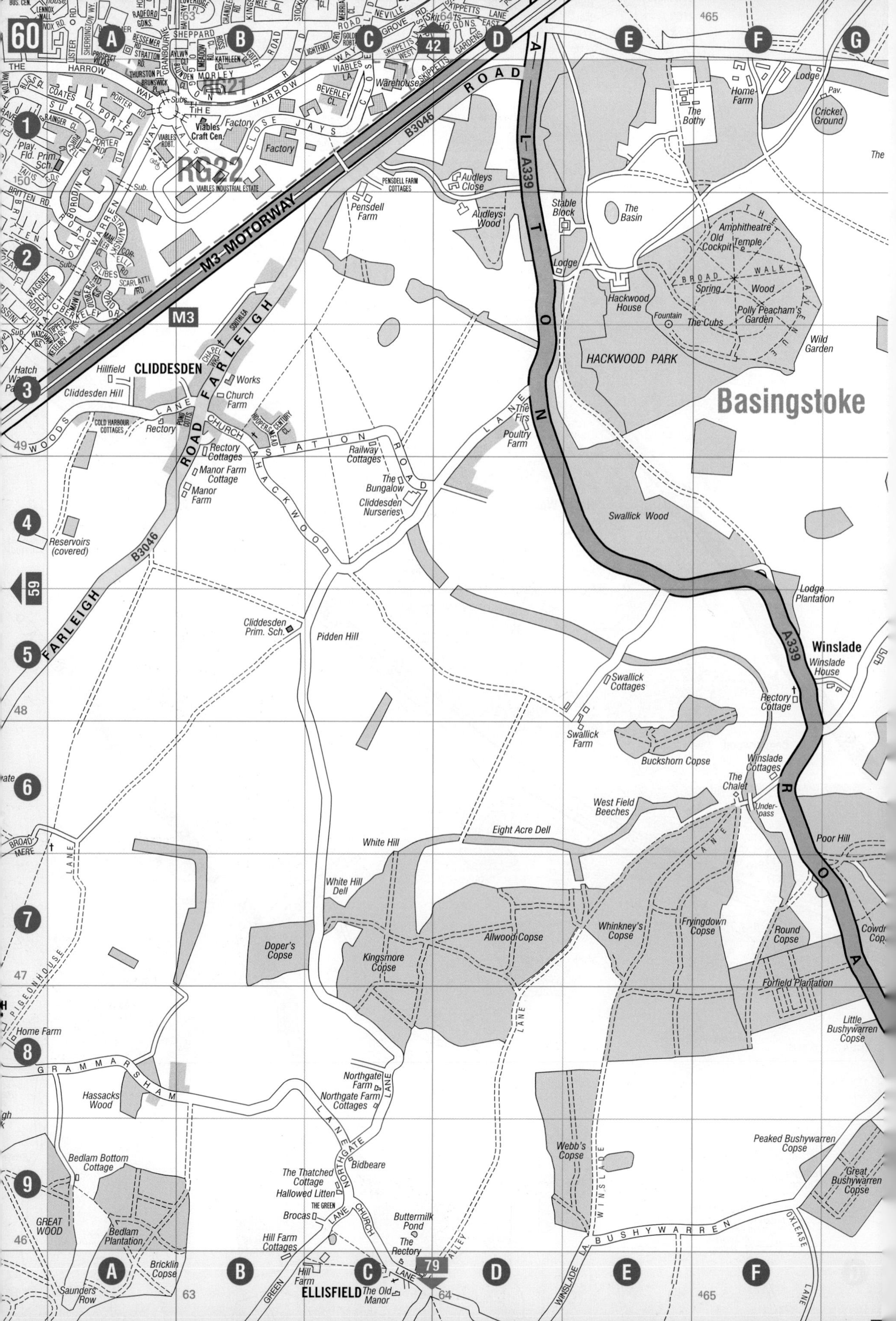

A
B
C
D
E
F
G
1
2
3
4
5
6
7
8
9
63
64
465
150
49
48
47
46
42
59
79
M3
M3–MOTORWAY
A339
B3046
A621
RG22
Basingstoke
CLIDDESDEN
ELLISFIELD
Winslade
HACKWOOD PARK
Hackwood House
The Basin
Stable Block
Lodge
Amphitheatre
Old Cockpit
Temple
BROAD WALK
Spring Wood
Fountain
The Cubs
Polly Peacham's Garden
Wild Garden
Home Farm
The Bothy
Cricket Ground
Pav.
Audleys Close
Audleys Wood
Pensdell Farm
PENSDELL FARM COTTAGES
Viables Craft Cen.
VIABLES INDUSTRIAL ESTATE
VIABLES RDBT.
Factory
Warehouse
THE HARROW WAY
JAYS CLOSE
Hillfield
Works
Church Farm
Cliddesden Hill
COLD HARBOUR COTTAGES
Rectory
Rectory Cottages
Manor Farm Cottage
Manor Farm
CHURCH LANE
STATION ROAD
HACKWOOD LANE
Railway Cottages
The Bungalow
Cliddesden Nurseries
The Firs
Poultry Farm
Swallick Wood
Reservoirs (covered)
FARLEIGH ROAD
Cliddesden Prim. Sch.
Pidden Hill
Lodge Plantation
Winslade House
Rectory Cottage
Swallick Cottages
Swallick Farm
Buckshorn Copse
Winslade Cottages
The Chalet
Under-pass
West Field Beeches
Eight Acre Dell
White Hill
White Hill Dell
Poor Hill
Doper's Copse
Kingsmore Copse
Allwood Copse
Whinkney's Copse
Fryingdown Copse
Round Copse
Forfield Plantation
Little Bushywarren Copse
PIGEONHOUSE LANE
BROAD MERE
Home Farm
GRAMMARSHAM
Hassacks Wood
Northgate Farm
Northgate Farm Cottages
NORTHGATE LANE
Bidbeare
The Thatched Cottage
Hallowed Litten
THE GREEN
Brocas
Buttermilk Pond
The Rectory
Hill Farm Cottages
Hill Farm
The Old Manor
GREEN LANE
ALLEY LANE
Webb's Copse
WINSLADE LANE
BUSHYWARREN LANE
OXLEASE LANE
Peaked Bushywarren Copse
Great Bushywarren Copse
Bedlam Bottom Cottage
GREAT WOOD
Bedlam Plantation
Bricklin Copse
Saunders Row
WOODS LANE
SOUTHLEA
CHAPEL WALK
HOOPERS MEAD
CENTURY CL.
Hatch Warren

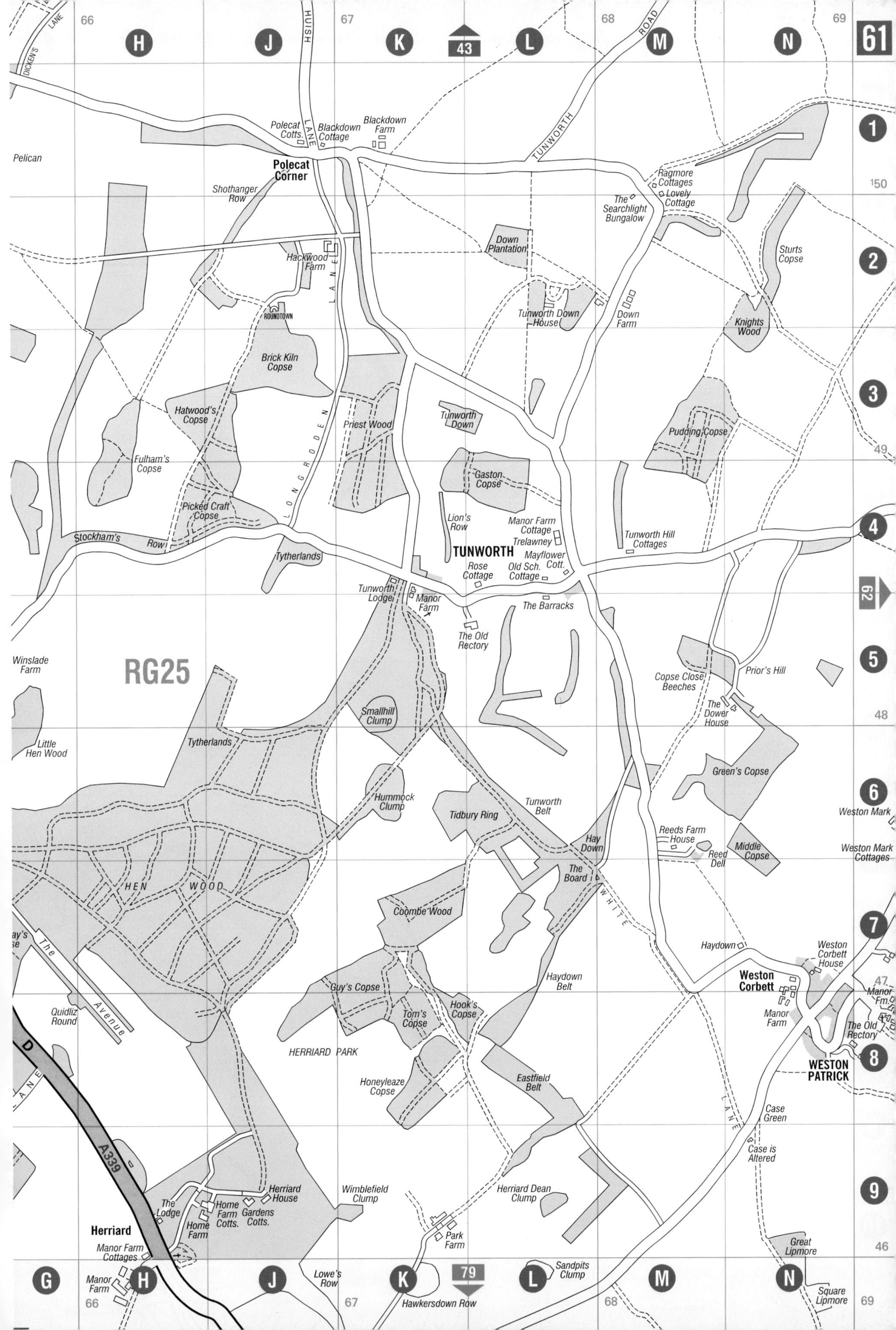

Polecat Corner
Polecat Cotts.
Blackdown Cottage
Blackdown Farm
Pelican
Shothanger Row
Hackwood Farm
Roundtown
Brick Kiln Copse
Hatwood's Copse
Fulham's Copse
Picked Craft Copse
Stockham's Row
Tytherlands
Priest Wood
Longroden Lane
Hush Lane
Tunworth Road
Down Plantation
Tunworth Down House
Down Farm
The Searchlight Bungalow
Ragmore Cottages
Lovely Cottage
Sturts Copse
Knights Wood
Pudding Copse
Tunworth Down
Gaston Copse
Lion's Row
Manor Farm Cottage
Trelawney
Mayflower Cott.
TUNWORTH
Rose Cottage
Old Sch. Cottage
Tunworth Hill Cottages
Tunworth Lodge
Manor Farm
The Barracks
The Old Rectory
Winslade Farm
RG25
Little Hen Wood
Smallhill Clump
Copse Close Beeches
The Dower House
Prior's Hill
Green's Copse
Hummock Clump
Tidbury Ring
Tunworth Belt
Weston Mark
Weston Mark Cottages
Reeds Farm House
Reed Dell
Middle Copse
Hay Down
The Board
HEN WOOD
White Lane
Coombe Wood
Haydown
Weston Corbett House
Weston Corbett
Haydown Belt
Guy's Copse
Tom's Copse
Hook's Copse
Manor Farm
Manor Fm.
The Old Rectory
WESTON PATRICK
The Avenue
Quidliz Round
HERRIARD PARK
Honeyleaze Copse
Eastfield Belt
Case Green
Case is Altered
A339
Herriard House
Wimblefield Clump
Herriard Dean Clump
The Lodge
Home Farm Cotts.
Gardens Cotts.
Home Farm
Herriard
Park Farm
Great Lipmore
Manor Farm Cottages
Manor Farm
Lowe's Row
Sandpits Clump
Hawkersdown Row
Square Lipmore
43
62
79

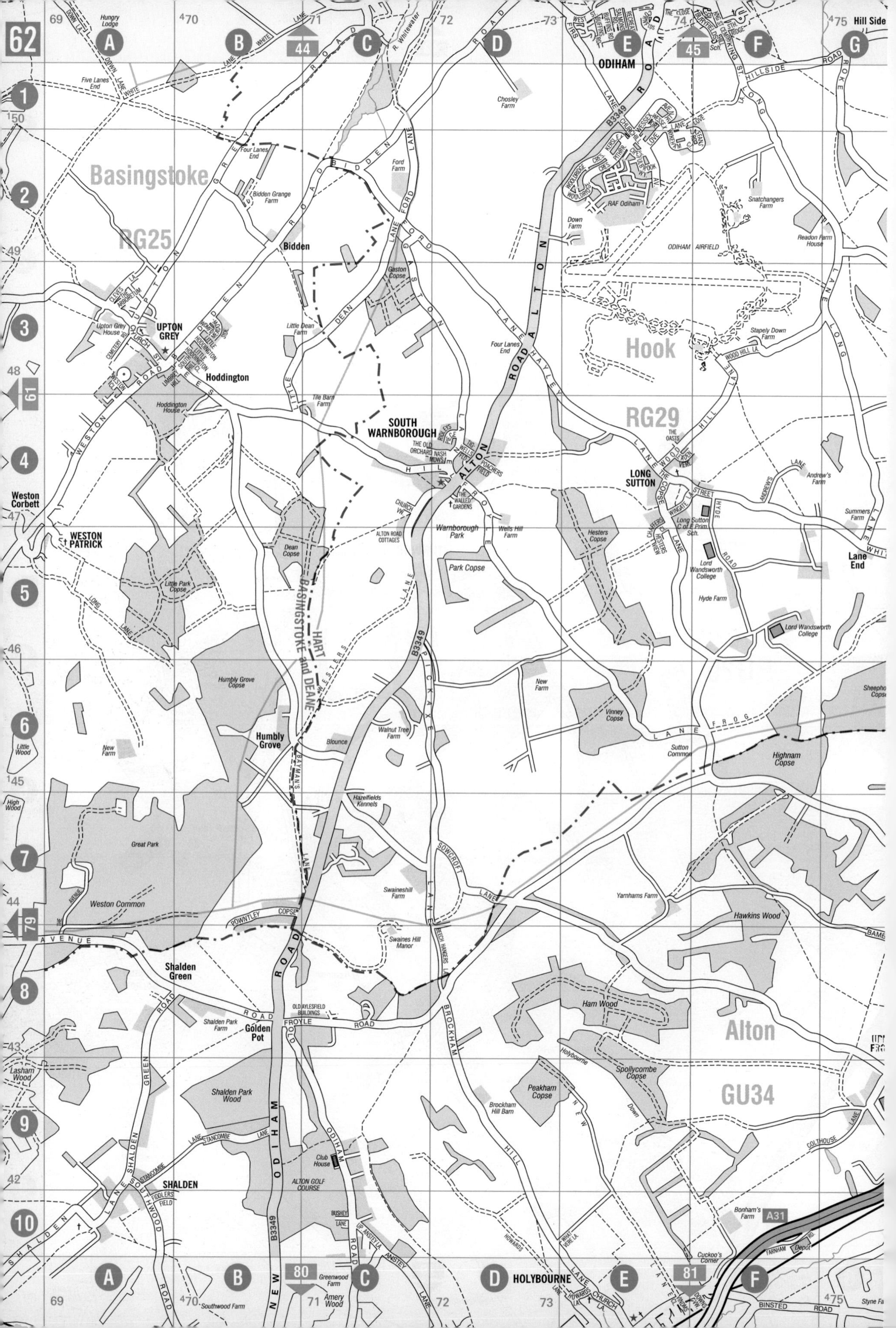
Basingstoke
RG25
UPTON GREY
Hoddington
Bidden
Four Lanes End
Bidden Grange Farm
Ford Farm
Five Lanes End
Hungry Lodge
Chosley Farm
ODIHAM
RAF Odiham
Down Farm
ODIHAM AIRFIELD
Snatchangers Farm
Readon Farm House
Stapely Down Farm
Hook
RG29
LONG SUTTON
Andrew's Farm
Summers Farm
Lane End
Hill Side
Upton Grey House
Hoddington House
Little Dean Farm
Gaston Copse
Four Lanes End
Tile Barn Farm
SOUTH WARNBOROUGH
THE OLD ORCHARD
THE WALLED GARDENS
Warnborough Park
Wells Hill Farm
Park Copse
ALTON ROAD COTTAGES
Hesters Copse
Long Sutton C of E Prim Sch.
Lord Wandsworth College
Hyde Farm
Weston Corbett
WESTON PATRICK
Dean Copse
Little Park Copse
HART
BASINGSTOKE and DEANE
Humbly Grove Copse
Humbly Grove
Walnut Tree Farm
Blounce
New Farm
Vinney Copse
Sutton Common
Highnam Copse
Little Wood
New Farm
High Wood
Great Park
Hazelfields Kennels
Swaineshill Farm
Yarnhams Farm
Hawkins Wood
Weston Common
Swaines Hill Manor
Shalden Green
Ham Wood
Alton
OLD AYLESFIELD BUILDINGS
Shalden Park Farm
Golden Pot
Lasham Wood
Shalden Park Wood
Peakham Copse
Spollycombe Copse
GU34
Brockham Hill Barn
SHALDEN
Club House
ALTON GOLF COURSE
Bonham's Farm
A31
Cuckoo's Corner
Depot
Greenwood Farm
Amery Wood
Southwood Farm
HOLYBOURNE
Styne Farm
B3349
ALTON ROAD
ODIHAM ROAD
NEW ODIHAM ROAD
FROYLE ROAD
BINSTED ROAD
BROCKHAM HILL
FROG LANE
HAYLEY LANE
GASTON LANE
LONG LANE
WOOD HILL LANE
HILLSIDE ROAD
COLTHOUSE LANE
SHALDEN LANE
SOUTHWOOD ROAD
STANCOMBE LANE
GREEN ROAD
PICKAXE LANE
SOWCROFT LANE
WESTON ROAD
THE AVENUE
POWNTLEY COPSE
44
45
61
79
80
81
69
470
71
72
73
74
475
150
49
48
47
46
145
44
43
42

Farnham
GU10
CRONDALL
BENTLEY
EWSHOT
ROWLEDGE
LOWER FROYLE
UPPER FROYLE
BINSTED
Rye Common
Mill Lane
Bowling Alley
Redlands
Warren Corner
Dora's Green
Dippenhall
Wimble Hill
Well
Well Green
Holt Pound
Bucks Horn Oak
Isington
Bentley
Blacknest
East Green
Northbrook
HART
EAST HAMPSHIRE
WAVERLEY
SOUTH DOWNS NATIONAL PARK
ALICE HOLT FOREST
OAK PARK GOLF COURSE
CLARE PARK SPIRE HOSPITAL
BOWENHURST GOLF CENTRE
BLACKNEST GOLF COURSE
BLACKNEST INDUSTRIAL PARK
BENTLEY INDUSTRIAL CENTRE
Birdworld & Underwater World
Alice Holt Forest Centre
Treloar School
Crondall Prim. Sch.
Bentley C of E Prim Sch.
Rowledge C of E Prim. Sch.
FARNHAM ROAD
A287
A31
A325
B3013
ALTON RD.
46
47
64
82
83

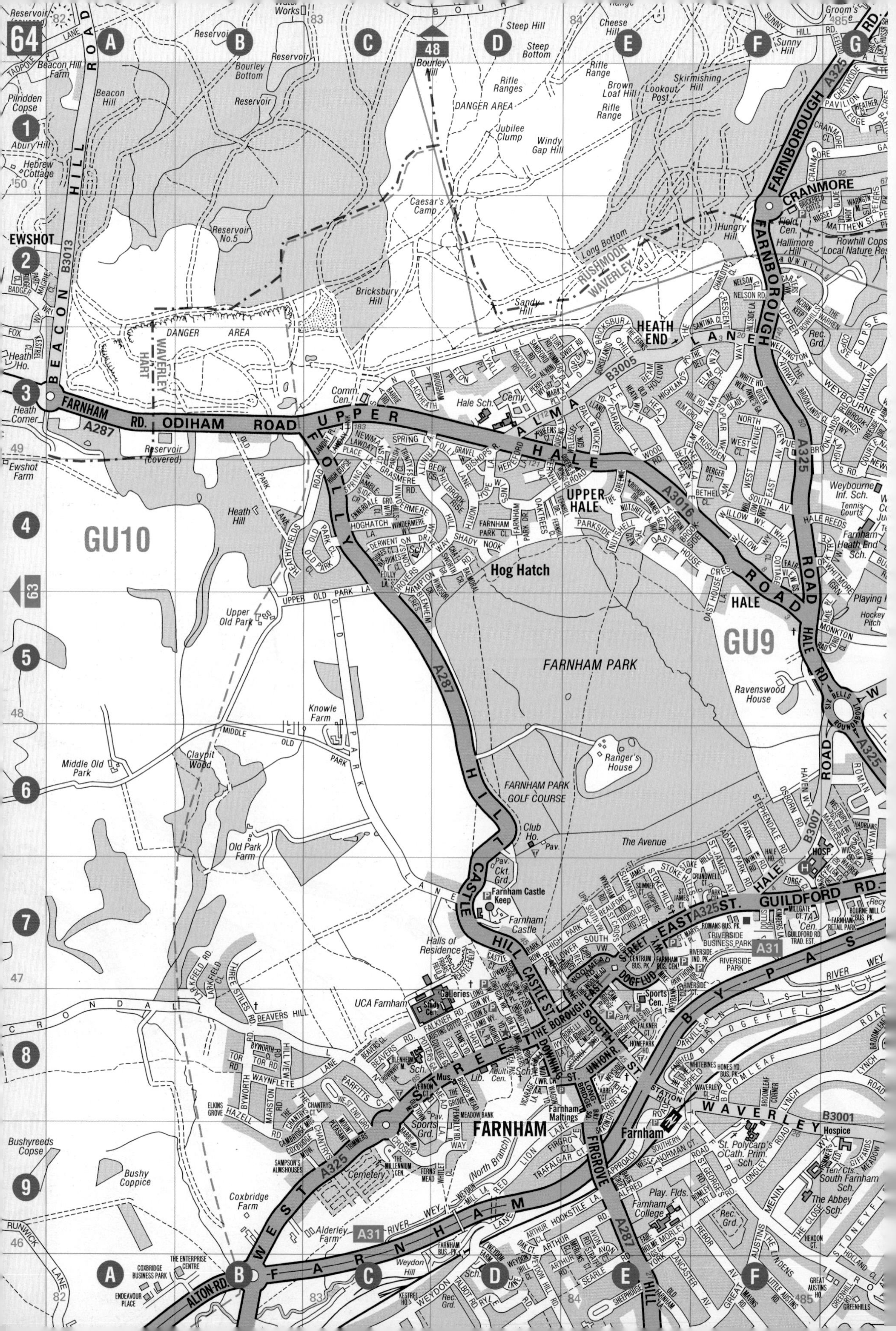
A
B
C
D
E
F
G
1
2
3
4
5
6
7
8
9
48
63
Reservoir
Water Works
Bourley Hill
Bourley Bottom
Beacon Hill Farm
Beacon Hill
Pilridden Copse
Abury Hill
Hebrew Cottage
EWSHOT
Heath Ho.
Heath Corner
Ewshot Farm
BEACON HILL ROAD
B3013
TADPOLE LANE
Steep Hill
Steep Bottom
Cheese Hill
Rifle Range
Rifle Ranges
DANGER AREA
Brown Loaf Hill
Lookout Post
Skirmishing Hill
Sunny Hill
Groom's
SUNNY HILL RD.
Jubilee Clump
Windy Gap Hill
Caesar's Camp
Reservoir No.5
Bricksbury Hill
Long Bottom
Sandy Hill
RUSHMOOR
WAVERLEY
HART
Hungry Hill
CRANMORE
Field Cen.
Hallimore Hill
Rowhill Copse Local Nature Reserve
MATTHEW ST. PETERS
FARNBOROUGH ROAD
A325
HEATH END
LANE
B3005
Comm. Cen.
Hale Sch.
Cemy.
FARNHAM RD.
ODIHAM ROAD
A287
UPPER HALE
ALMA
Reservoir (Covered)
FOLLY HILL
Heath Hill
GU10
UPPER HALE
A3016
Hog Hatch
Sch.
HEATHYFIELDS
OLD PARK LANE
UPPER OLD PARK LA.
Upper Old Park
HALE
GU9
HALE RD.
ROAD
Playing Fld.
Hockey Pitch
Weybourne Inf. Sch.
Farnham Heath End Sch.
Tennis Courts
HALE REEDS
WEYBOURNE
Ravenswood House
SIX BELLS ROUNDABOUT
FARNHAM PARK
Knowle Farm
MIDDLE OLD PARK
Claypit Wood
Middle Old Park
Ranger's House
FARNHAM PARK GOLF COURSE
Club Ho.
Pav.
The Avenue
Old Park Farm
Ckt. Grd.
Farnham Castle Keep
Farnham Castle
CASTLE HILL
B3007
HOSP.
HALE
GUILDFORD RD.
EAST ST.
A325
RIVERSIDE BUSINESS PARK
A31
RIVERSIDE PARK
RIVER WEY
Halls of Residence
UCA Farnham
Galleries
Study Cen.
CRONDALL LANE
BEAVERS HILL
THREE STILES RD.
LARKFIELD RD.
CASTLE ST.
THE BOROUGH
WEST STREET
SOUTH ST.
UNION RD.
DOGFLUD WAY
Sports Cen.
BY PASS
Mus.
Lib.
Adult Cen.
WAYNFLETE LANE
HILL VIEW
TOR RD.
BYWORTH RD.
HAZELL RD.
ELKINS GROVE
Sports Grd.
FARNHAM
Farnham Maltings
FIRGROVE
STATION HILL
Farnham
WAVERLEY
B3001
Hospice
St. Polycarp's Cath. Prim. Sch.
South Farnham Sch.
The Abbey Sch.
Bushyreeds Copse
Bushy Coppice
Coxbridge Farm
SAMPSON'S ALMSHOUSES
Cemetery
(North Branch)
RIVER WEY
FARNHAM
A31
Alderley Farm
Play. Flds.
Farnham College
Rec. Grd.
Weydon Hill
RUNWICK LANE
COXBRIDGE BUSINESS PARK
THE ENTERPRISE CENTRE
ENDEAVOUR PLACE
ALTON RD.
WEYDON
Sch.
Rec. Grd.
HOOKSTILE LA.
ARTHUR
SEARLE
MORLEY
LANCASTER AV.
GREAT AUSTINS
AUSTINS
LITTLE AUSTINS
MENIN
LONGLEY
STONEYFIELDS
82
83
84
485
150
49
48
47
46

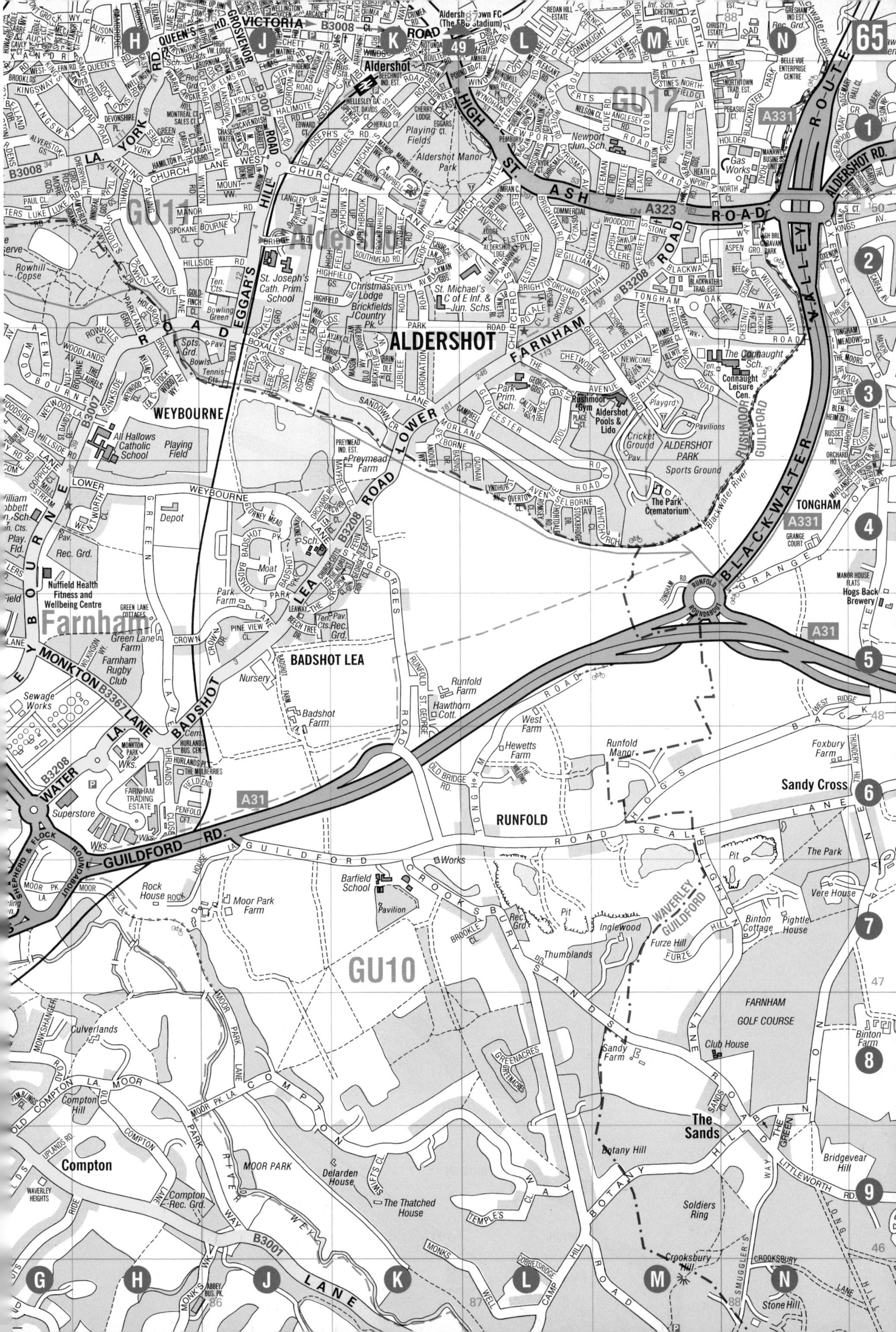
ALDERSHOT
Aldershot
GU11
GU12
GU10
Farnham
WEYBOURNE
BADSHOT LEA
RUNFOLD
TONGHAM
Sandy Cross
The Sands
Compton
MOOR PARK
FARNHAM GOLF COURSE
Crooksbury Hill
Soldiers Ring
Botany Hill
Stone Hill
BLACKWATER VALLEY ROUTE
GUILDFORD RD.
HOGS BACK
SEALE LANE
A31
A331
A323
B3208
B3007
B3008
B3001
B3367
Aldershot Town FC (The EBB Stadium)
Aldershot Manor Park
Aldershot Park
Aldershot Pools & Lido
The Park Crematorium
Runfold Roundabout
Farnham Trading Estate
Nuffield Health Fitness and Wellbeing Centre
Farnham Rugby Club
All Hallows Catholic School
Barfield School
Hogs Back Brewery

SHIPTON BELLINGER INSET
Shipton Bellinger Prim. Sch.
SHIPTON BELLINGER
Tidworth
SP9
Shipton Plantation
Recreation Ground
Parsonage Farm
Manor Fm.
Sewage Works
Factory
Danger Area
Devil's Ditch
Beacon Hill
BULFORD CAMP
BULFORD
AMESBURY
Solstice Park
Earl's Farm Down
Salisbury
Beacon Hill Farm
Reservoir (covered)
Boscombe Down West
Arundel Farm
SP4
MOD Boscombe Down
BOSCOMBE DOWN AIRFIELD
Rare Breeds Farm Park
CHOLDERTON
Cholderton House
Wilbury Park
Three Corner Hat
Cemetery
Newton Tony C of E Primary School
NEWTON TONY
ALLINGTON
Boscombe
Allington Fm.
IDMISTON
PORTON
Birdlymes Farm
Down Barn
Boscombe Down East
Idmiston Down
The Cross Belt
Tower
A303
A338
A3028
SALISBURY ROAD
TIDWORTH ROAD
DOUBLE HEDGES
AMESBURY ROAD
ALLINGTON TRACK
TONEY ROAD
NEWTON TONY

THRUXTON
Kimpton, Thruxton & Fyfield C of E Prim Sch.
THRUXTON AERODROME
Thruxton Motor Racing Circuit
Works
A303
Mullenspond
East Cholderton
ELMSTEAD PARK
London Hill
AMESBURY
AMPORT
Amport House
Bush Farm
Racedown
Snoddington Down Farm
SNODDINGTON LANE
SNODDINGTON ROAD
Snoddington Manor
COACH ROAD
THRUXTON ROAD
AIRFIELD ROAD
Lains Farm
QUARLEY
Thruxton Hill
Middlecot House
Thruxton Farm
B3084
Cholderton Hill
CHOLDERTON ROAD
Amport Wood
FURZEDOWN
Cricket Ground
SKEW ROAD
GRATELEY DROVE
GREEN DROVE
GEORGIA LANE
Sarson Wood
Andover
Fort
Quarley Hill
Quarley Manor Farm
Gunville
Club Ho.
Monxton & Grateley Golf Centre
Gollard Farm
Georgia Farm
Cemetery
GRATELEY
Grateley Prim. Sch.
Grateley Ho. Sch.
Hurst Copse
SP11
CHOLDERTON ROAD
GRATELEY BUSINESS PARK
STATION
Grateley
WALLOP ROAD
OLD
KING LANE
STOCKBRIDGE ROAD
Palestine
STREETWAY
MOUNT HERMON ROAD
PALESTINE ROAD
BOURNEMOUTH RD
CARMEL ROAD
MOUNT ZION
Boar Knoll
DANGER AREA
Hampshire Gap
Red Lodge Farm
Oklahoma Farm
GEORGIA DROVE
Sunnyside Farm
Park Farm
Stockbridge
Castle Farm
SO20
WILTSHIRE
TEST VALLEY
Martin's Clump
DANGER AREA
POTTERY DROVE
Croft Farm
CRAYDOWN LANE
DOWNS RD
PARK
Works
Tunlands Farm
Middle Wallop Airfield
OVER WALLOP
STATION RD.
B3084
Sports Field
SALISBURY LANE
Tower Hill
A343
Middle Wallop
Wallop Prim. Sch.
SCHOOL LANE
KNOCKWOOD LANE
Suddern Hill
Isle of Wight Hill
ROMSEY ROAD B3084
FARLEY STREET
DANGER AREA
Jack's Bush Farm
BENHAM DROVE
Wallop House
24 25 26 27 28 29 30
G H J K L M N
1 2 3 4 5 6 7 8 9
46 45 44 43 42 41 40 39 38 37
31
68
72
87

Weyhill Nurseries Garden Cen.
Bridge Bungalow
House
SARSON LA.
A303
AMESBURY ROAD
Weyhill Service Area
50
ANDOVER AIRFIELD
Melbury
RED POST LANE
MONXTON
Kimber
The Limes
The Hawk Conservancy
Works
Pillhill Brook
Rifle Range
Red Post Bridge
MONXTON ROAD
NEWALL RD.
Manor Farm
East Cholderton
HUNT'S LANE
WIREMEAD
Waterloo Bridge
SARSON LANE
Piper's Hill
SUNNYBANK
Silver Birch Farm
Willow Farm
FARM
Sarson
SARSON CL.
CHAPEL CL.
THE EIGHTS
COB MEWS
MOUNT PLEASANT
Windward
Manor Farm
ANDOVER ROAD
Upper Mill Farm
CATTLE LANE
AMPORT
ABBOTTS LANE
Ford
Weirs
HIGH ST.
CHALKPIT LANE
Sarson Farm
The Green
FURZEDOWN LANE
KEEPERS HILL
Amport C of E Prim. Sch.
AMPORT PK. MEWS
MONXTON
New House
Little
Cricket Grd.
GREEN LANE
The Triangle
ANN ROAD
Keeper's Lodge
DUCK STREET
HILLSIDE
ABBOTTS ANN
SP11
CHURCH LANE
67
Manor Farm
CHURCH CL.
Spts. Grd.
MANOR CL.
CATHERINE'S WLK.
WARREN DR.
BULBERY
TIMOTHY'S FLD.
Sports Ground
OLD COACH ROAD
HOOK LANE
BROAD ROAD
GREAT WOOD
Sarson Wood
The Bungalow
DUNKIRT LANE
WEBBS LANE
CRISWICK CL.
Abbotts Ann C of E Prim. School
Sarson Down
Keeper's Cottage
St. John's Cross
Eastover Farm
Dunkirt Barn
DUNKIRT
Woodlands Prospect Farm
Eastover Farm Cottages
The Groves
The Morrells
Newlands Prospect Farm
Sunnycroft
Eastover Copse
SALISBURY ROAD
A343
Little Prospect
Prospect Farm Cottage
Old Prospect Farm
New Cottage
Cossical Copse
72
Reservoir (covered)
Prospect Farm
Stonehanger Cottages
Stonehanger

ANDOVER
Andover
SP10
UPPER CLATFORD
GOODWORTH CLATFORD
Red Rice
Anna Valley
Barrow Hill
Andover Golf Course
Red Post Junction
Little Park Farm
Little-Ann Bridge Farm
Abbots Law
Little Ann Bridge
Abbottshill Farm
Bury Hill
Fishing Cottage
Norman Court Farm
Clatford Mills House
Clatford Mills
Clatford Mill Farm
Green Meadows
Briar Hill
Orchard Hill Farm
Orchard Hill
The Mile House
Home Farm
Horse Meadow
North Lodge
South Lodge
The Kennels
Farleigh School
Errington House
Home Covert
The Rookery
The White Cottage
Wayside
Red Rice Park
Barrow Hill Barns
Barrow Hill Farm
Reservoir (covered)
Recreation Ground
Clatford C of E Prim. Sch.
Playing Field
Rectory
Rooksbury Mill
Anton Jun. Sch.
Anton Inf. Sch.
Club House
Rookwood School
Beech Hurst Council Offs.
John Hanson Comm. Sch.
Corporation Yard
Gallaghers Copse
Portway Jun. & Inf. Schs.
Sports Ground
Andover Coll.
Guildhall
WEYHILL
A303
A343
A3057
B3402
51
70
73

ANDOVER
SP10
Bere Hill
Cow Down
Andover
HAREWOOD FOREST
A303
A3057
A3093
B3400
B3420
LONDON
WINCHESTER
ROAD
ROMSEY
WINCHESTER RD.
NEW ST.
EAST ST.
EASTERN AV.
MICHELDEVER
LADIES WALK
PICKET TWENTY
FOREST LANE
COWDOWN LANE
NEW BARN LANE
Sports Centre
Norman Gate School
Play. Flds.
The Mark Wy. Sch.
Winton School
Vigo Jun. & Inf. Schs.
Iron Bridge
Reservoirs (covered)
New Grange
The Cottages
Harewood
Poultry Houses
Rent Hay Farm
Convent Farm
Down House
Down Ho. Farm
Playing Field
Depot
Bere Hill Farm
Subway
Club House
ANDOVER GOLF COURSE
The Mile House
Fourways
Old Halls Copse
Round Copse
Pound
Blake's Bushes
Ball's Cottages
Cowdown Farm Cottages
Cowdown Farm Buildings
Wismore Copse
Cowdown Copse
Cowdown Farmhouse
Furzy Croft Copse
Popple Hill Copse
Augers Hill Copse
Hartway Copse
Keeper's Cottage
Park Farm
Park Brow Copse
Upping Copse
Hassock Copse
THE HAMPSHIRE GOLF COURSE
High Cedar
Whitehouse
New Barn
Wilkinson's Bank
Windwhistle Cottage
Sewage Works
Mackrel's Down
The Mount
Playing Field
Wolverdene Special Sch.
Recycling Cen.
Harewood Mobile Home Park
52
69
74

(covered)
Andover Down
FOLLY COPSE
Harewood Forest
53
Whitchurch
RG28
Dane End Copse
Houndshott Copse
Whiteditch Copse
POND COPSE
Tracy's Dell
Wood Walk Plantation
Burnt Copse
Green's Copse
Pheasantry
Deadman's Plack Copse
Deadman's Plack Monument
Ridgeway Copse
Gravelly Bank Copse
Middleton Park Farm
Middleton Green
THE MIDDLE WAY
Cowdown Copse
SP11
A303
ROAD
Middleton Park
Lower Farm
Play. Fld.
GLADSTONE TER.
SUGAR LA.
MIDDLETON
Middleton House
THE WITHIES
River Test
SOUTHSIDE RD.
Longparish C of E Prim. Sch.
Church Farm
The Common
B3048
Burnt Lodge Copse
Gravel Pit
LONGPARISH ROAD
Forton
Forton House
Snows Copse
Forton Farm House
76
Drayton Cottage
MONIER WILLIAMS RD.
AVENUE
Play. Flds.
Parade Ground
Beechen Copse
HAREWOOD FOREST IND. EST.
Longparish Station
Drayton Copse
THUILLER RD.
THE HILL
Drayton Camp
Poultry Houses
Ladies House Copse
Gavelacre Cottage
Adders Corner
Pachington Farm
Rifle Range
Park Clump
Pachington Copse
Gavelacre
Weirs
Woodland Cottage
Winchester
Bransbury Manor Farm
The Keepers Cottage
Stoneyard Copse
Bransbury Manor
Bransbury
Bransbury Mill
Weir
SO21
Church Farm Buildings
Poultry Farm Cottages
River Test
Bransbury Common
River Dever
75
H J K L M N G
1 2 3 4 5 6 7 8 9
440 41 42 43
46 145 44 43 42

A
B
C
D
E
F
G
68
88
67
1
2
3
4
5
6
7
8
9
430
31
32
33
41
140
39
38
37
Little Prospect
Old Prospect Farm
Prospect Farm Cott.
New Cottage
Prospect Farm
Reservoir (covered)
Cossical Copse
SALISBURY ROAD
A343
Stonehanger Cottages
Stonehanger Copse
Chestnut Cottage
Abbotts Ann Down
Down Farm
Down House
Dunkirt House
Monxton Oakcuts
OLD STOCKBRIDGE ROAD
Oakcuts
Larch Gables
Saxley Farm
Kentsboro
Kentsboro Farm
FALAISE ROAD
Playing Field
Upper Oakcuts Copse
Lower Oak Copse
AAC Middle Wallop
Museum of Army Flying
Knock Wood
Down Farm
MIDDLE WALLOP AIRFIELD
Sewage Works
Stockbridge
SO20
Danebury Hill
Danebury Hill Fort (Nature Reserve)
DANEBURY DOWN
The Turret
Blackstake Hill
Dene Farm
Danebury
Gallop

Andover
SP11
Home Covert
Farleigh School
Errington House
Swimming Pool
The White Cottage
Wayside
Red Rice Park
Garden Clump
Silver Clump
Silver Clump Row
New Barn
Flint Farm
Reservoir (covered)
Westover Farm
Pewet Corner
New Plantation
DIPDEN BOTTOM
Rowbury Farm
Clatford Oakcuts
Oakcuts
Rowbury Copse
Nettlebank Copse
Hazel Down
Charity Down Farm
Hazeldown Farm
Garage Cottages
Waters Down Farm
Cleave Hill
New Buildings
Cemetery
War Memorial
Vicarage
Charity Farm House
LONGSTOCK
Church Farm
Aqueduct
FULLERTON
BARROW HILL
LONGSTOCK ROAD
STOCKBRIDGE ROAD
CHURCH ROAD
69
88
74
435
34
36
41
40
39
38
37

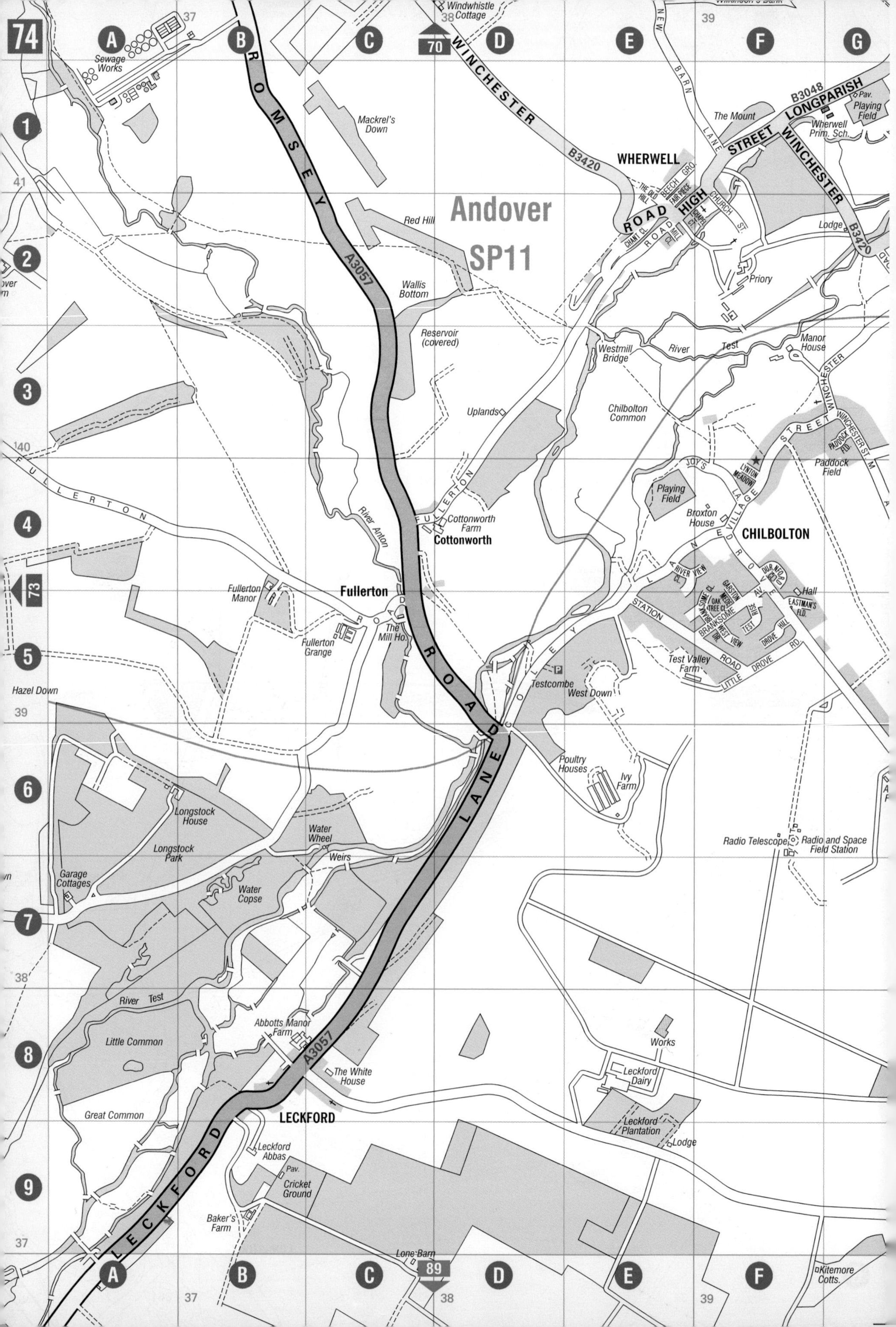
Windwhistle Cottage
70
Sewage Works
ROMSEY ROAD
WINCHESTER
Mackrel's Down
B3420
WHERWELL
The Mount
B3048
LONGPARISH
STREET
Playing Field
Pav.
Wherwell Prim. Sch.
NEW BARN LANE
HIGH ROAD
CHURCH ST.
Lodge
Priory
Andover
SP11
Red Hill
A3057
Wallis Bottom
Reservoir (covered)
Westmill Bridge
River Test
Manor House
Uplands
Chilbolton Common
FULLERTON
Cottonworth Farm
Cottonworth
River Anton
Playing Field
Broxton House
CHILBOLTON
JOY'S LANE
VILLAGE STREET
Paddock Field
Fullerton Manor
Fullerton
Fullerton Grange
The Mill Ho.
STATION ROAD
RIVER VIEW CL.
BRANKSOME AVE.
DROVE HILL
Hall
EASTMAN'S FLD.
Test Valley Farm
LITTLE DROVE RD.
Testcombe
West Down
73
Hazel Down
Poultry Houses
Ivy Farm
LANE
Longstock House
Longstock Park
Water Wheel
Weirs
Radio Telescope
Radio and Space Field Station
Garage Cottages
Water Copse
River Test
Works
Little Common
Abbotts Manor Farm
A3057
The White House
Leckford Dairy
Great Common
LECKFORD
Leckford Plantation
Lodge
Leckford Abbas
LECKFORD
Pav.
Cricket Ground
Baker's Farm
Lone Barn
89
Kitemore Cotts.

ROAD
Dublin Farm
River Dever
Ford
ROAD
Gravel Pit
Rangebourne Cottage
River Cottage
Newton Stacey
Manor House
Hook Cottage
Manor Farm
Windmill Cottage
Gravelhill Cottages
Gravelhill Farm
Gravel Hill
Reservoir (covered)
DANGER AREA
Winchester
SO21
B3420
DANGER AREA
Newton Down Farm
Moody's Down Farm
DRIFT
B3420
BIRCH GROVE
Stockbridge
SO20
Middlebarn Farm
ROAD
STONEFIELD PARK
ROAD
Brockley Cottages
Barton Stacey Belt
A30
LANE
BROCKLEY WARREN
71
76
89
H J K L M N
G H J K L M N
1 2 3 4 5 6 7 8 9
440 41 42 43
41 140 39 38 37

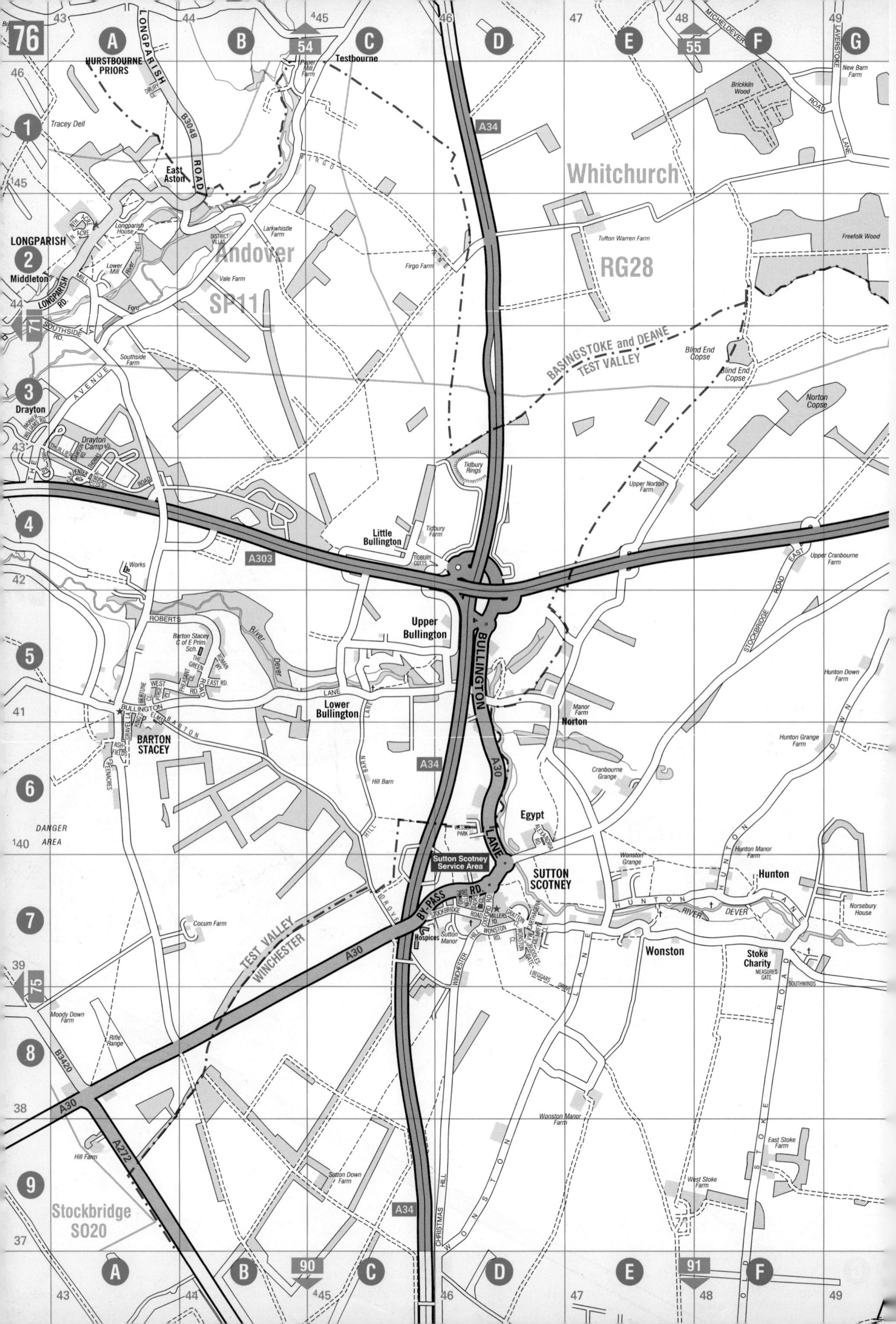

HURSTBOURNE PRIORS
Testbourne
Whitchurch
LONGPARISH
Middleton
East Aston
Andover
SP11
RG28
Drayton
Drayton Camp
Little Bullington
Upper Bullington
Lower Bullington
BARTON STACEY
Norton
Egypt
SUTTON SCOTNEY
Sutton Scotney Service Area
Wonston
Hunton
Stoke Charity
Stockbridge SO20
BASINGSTOKE and DEANE
TEST VALLEY
WINCHESTER
A34
A303
A30
A272
B3048
B3420
Tidbury Rings
Tufton Warren Farm
Freefolk Wood
Norton Copse
Blind End Copse
Upper Norton Farm
Upper Cranbourne Farm
Hunton Down Farm
Hunton Grange Farm
Hunton Manor Farm
Cranbourne Grange
Manor Farm
Wonston Grange
Norsebury House
Wonston Manor Farm
East Stoke Farm
West Stoke Farm
Sutton Down Farm
Hill Farm
Moody Down Farm
Rifle Range
Cocum Farm
Hill Barn
DANGER AREA
Southside Farm
Vale Farm
Firgo Farm
Larkwhistle Farm
Tracey Dell
Longparish House
Lower Mill
Ford
Paper Mill Farm
Brickkiln Wood
New Barn Farm
Tidbury Farm
Works
Hospices
Sutton Manor

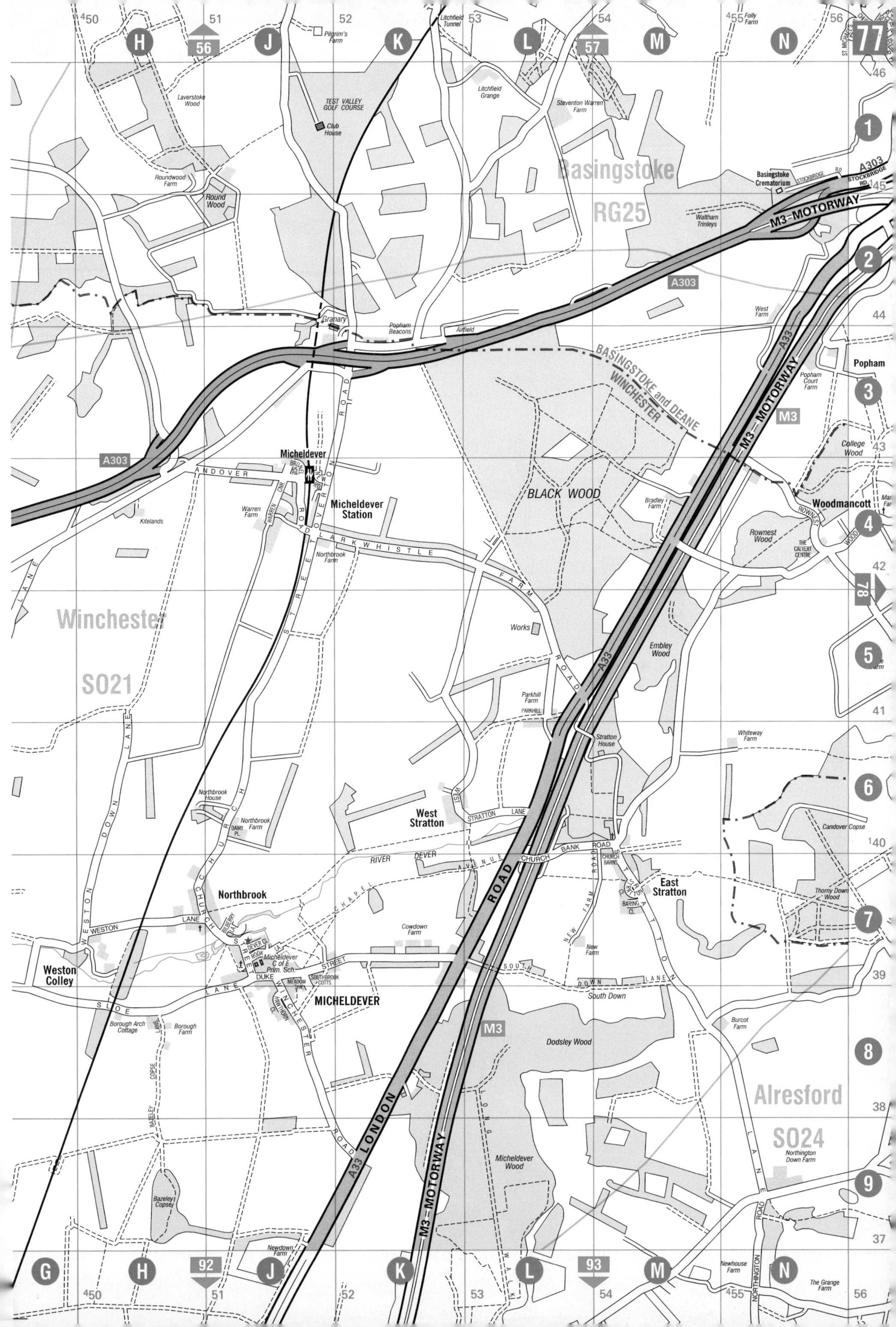
Basingstoke
RG25
Winchester
SO21
Alresford
SO24
M3-MOTORWAY
A303
A33
A33 LONDON ROAD
M3
BASINGSTOKE and DEANE
WINCHESTER
Laverstoke Wood
TEST VALLEY GOLF COURSE
Club House
Pilgrim's Farm
Litchfield Tunnel
Litchfield Grange
Steventon Warren Farm
Folly Farm
Basingstoke Crematorium
STOCKBRIDGE RD.
Waltham Trinleys
Roundwood Farm
Round Wood
Granary
Popham Beacons
Airfield
West Farm
Popham
Popham Court Farm
College Wood
Woodmancott
Rownest Wood
THE CALVERT CENTRE
Micheldever
Micheldever Station
ANDOVER
Warren Farm
Kitelands
LARKWHISTLE FARM ROAD
Northbrook Farm
BLACK WOOD
Bradley Farm
Works
Embley Wood
Parkhill Farm
Stratton House
Whiteway Farm
West Stratton
STRATTON LANE
Candover Copse
RIVER DEVER
CHURCH BANK ROAD
CHURCH BARNS
East Stratton
BARING CL.
Thorny Down Wood
Northbrook House
Northbrook Farm
DAIRY PL.
Northbrook
WESTON DOWN LANE
WESTON LANE
Weston Colley
SLOE LANE
DUKE STREET
Micheldever C of E Prim. Sch.
MEADOW VW.
SOUTHBROOK COTTS.
MICHELDEVER
Cowdown Farm
New Farm
SOUTH DOWN LANE
South Down
Burcot Farm
Borough Arch Cottage
Borough Farm
Dodsley Wood
Micheldever Wood
Northington Down Farm
Bazeley Copse
Newdown Farm
Newhouse Farm
The Grange Farm
NORTHINGTON ROAD
56
57
78
92
93

NORTH WALTHAM
DUMMER
DUMMER GOLF COURSE
M3 MOTORWAY
Junction 8
A303
A33
A30
M3
STOCKBRIDGE ROAD
Popham
College Wood
Manor Farm
Woodmancott
Winchester
SO21
Lone Farm
Candover Copse
Thorny Down Wood
Foxhill
Lone Barn
Church Lane Farm
Alresford
Candover House
Brown Candover
SO24
Totford
Northington
Swarraton
BASINGSTOKE and DEANE
WINCHESTER
Dummer Down Farm
Tidley Hill
Dummer Grange
Dummer Grange Farm
The Holt
Breach Farm
Becket's Down
Chilton Wood
Chilton Manor
Chilton Candover
Flockmoor Cottage
Nutley
Nutley Wood
Gobley Hole
Norton's Wood
Nutley Down
Windmill Hill
Berrydown Farm
Axford
Basingstoke
Fawkners
Preston House
RG25
PRESTON CANDOVER
Preston Candover C of E Prim. Sch.
Preston Grange
Down Farm
Preston Down
B3046
ALRESFORD RD.
Juniper Hill
Wield Wood
Barton Copse
Godsfield Copse
Bugmore Hill
Three Castles Path
Armsworth House
ARMSWORTH PARK
Godsfield
Lower Lanham Copse
Upper Lanham Farm
Hoggs Lodge
Abbotstone Woods
The Grange Farm
Inwood Copse
Clump Farm
Great Wood

60
61
62
80
96
97
H
J
K
L
M
N
G
1
2
3
4
5
6
7
8
9
63
64
65
66
67
68
69
46
45
44
43
42
41
40
39
38
37
ELLISFIELD
Ellisfield Manor
Upper Common
Lower Common
College Farm
High Wood
Merritt's Farm
Herriard Grange
Herriard Park
Herriard House
Herriard
Manor Farm
Park Farm
Nashes Green
Lee Farm
Little Wood
Hurst Farm
Bagmore
Southrope
Hale Farm
High Wood
Great Matt's Copse
Herriard Common
Preston Oak Hills
Moundsmere Manor
Southwood Farm
Bradley Hill
Foster's Copse
Lasham Airfield
Lasham Hill
New Copse
Home Farm
Burkham House
Lasham Wood
Alton
LASHAM
GU34
BRADLEY
EAST HAMPSHIRE
BASINGSTOKE and DEANE
South Lease Copse
Powells Farm
Wadgett's Copse
A339
Summerley
Bentworth Lodge
Binney Copse
Lower Wield
Ashley Farm
BENTWORTH
Primary School
Well Copse
Childer Hill Farm
Thedden Copse
Hall Farm
Heathcroft Farm
WIELD INDUSTRIES
Gaston Wood
Holt End
Gaston Grange
Bentworth Hall
Thedden
Thedden Grange
Upper Wield
Church Farm
Collier's Wood
Wivelrod
BEECH
Medstead Grange
Red Barn Farm
Newmer Farm
Beech Abbey
Bushy Leaze Wood
Old Park Farm
Hattingley
Heath Green
Hattingley Farm
MEDSTEAD
Convent
Grove Wood
Chawton Park Wood
ROAD
LANE
AXFORD LANE
BUSHYWARREN
WINSLADE LANE
CHURCH LANE
RED LA
BAGMORE
SPAIN
BERRYWOOD LANE
RUSHMOOR
ASHLEY ROAD
BULLFIELD LA
DRURY LA
CHURCH ST.
VILLAGE ST.
STATION
MUCKLANDS
JENNIE GREEN LANE
DIRTY LANE
WIELD
HOLT END
HOLT ROAD
TRINITY HILL
NEW COPSE
GREEN
WIVELROD ROAD
KINGS HILL
MEDSTEAD
WELLHOUSE ROAD
SNODE HILL
ABBEY LANE
REDWOOD LA
FERNEY LANE
DROVE WAY
HATTINGLEY
HILL
CASTLE ST.
HIGH ST.
TOWN
HUSSELL
DOWNS RD.
COMMON
CHALKY
WELL
SHALDEN LANE
HALEY LANE
SCRATCHFACE LANE
OXLEASE LANE
LITTLE BAGMORE LA.
BACK LANE
KIT LANE
FURZEN
GREEN LANE
COLLEGE LANE
LIPSCOMBE CLOSE
CAMOYS MEAD
GLEBE FLDS.

80
62
98
79
ALTON
Newtown
Mt. Pleasant
The Butts
CHAWTON
BEECH
Shalden Lane Plantation
Clover Farm
Southwood Parks
Gunner's Plantation
Row Wood
Anstey Copse
Crooksberry Farm
Greenwood Farm
Cadnam Farm
Pancake Copse
Pancake Plantation
Southwood Farm
Amery Wood
Glenville Farm
Highmead Bungalow
Highmead House
Reservoir (covered)
Blanes Farm
Marlfield
Wootey Jun. & Inf. Schs.
Binney Copse
Warren Plantation
Warren Farm
South Wood
Greenmount Farm
North Wood
Applesome Wood
Great Wood
Alton College
Thedden Copse
Cemetery
Anstey Jun. Sch.
Amery Hill School
Alton Inf. Sch.
The Palace Cin.
Tollens
Hungry Copse
Gallery
Mus.
Alton Brewery (Coors Visitor Cen.)
Thedden Park
Keepers Lodge
Wyards Farm
Bowl Grn.
The Public Gds.
Super-store
The Butts Prim. Sch.
Recreation Ground
Dark Wick's Wood
Ackender Wood
ALTON COMMUNITY HOSPITAL
Butts Bridge
Borovere Farm
Alexandra Wood
Chawton Park Indoor Bowls Club
Alton Sports Centre
Mounter's Farm
Stonehill Farm
BUSHY LEAZE WOOD
Lumbry Farm
Jubilee Playing Fields
Pavilion
Little Eastfield Farm
Westbrook Grange
New Cottages
Chalk Dell Cottages
Jane Austen's House Museum
Eastfield Farm
Chawton Park Farm
Pound Farm
Mingledown Plantation
Diamond Jubilee Clump
Eastfield Plantation
Chawton C of E Prim. Sch.
Cricket Grd.
SOUTH DOWNS
NATIONAL PARK
Silver Wedding Clump
Adela Copse
Chawton Glebe
Home Farm
Baigent's Copse
Knickerknocker Copse
Peck Copse
Chawton House Library & Study Centre
Hulvers Row
Reed's Copse
Imbook Copse
Broadlands
A339
A31
A32
B3349
BASINGSTOKE RD.
BASINGSTOKE ROAD
WHITEDOWN LA.
SELBORNE RD.
ODIHAM ROAD
NEW ODIHAM ROAD
WATERCRESS LINE (MID HANTS RAILWAY)
SOUTHWOOD
BRICK KILN LANE
SNODE HILL ROAD
MEDSTEAD
WINCHESTER RD.
GOSPORT
WOLF'S LANE
SELBORNE

Cuckoo's Corner
Holybourne
Neatham
Anstey
Alton
Spitalhatch
Wilsom
GU34
EAST WORLDHAM
West Worldham
SOUTH DOWNS NATIONAL PARK
Manor Farm
Field Cottage
Sports Field
Howards Farm
Playing Fields
Treloar College
Andrews' C of E Prim. Sch.
Eggar's School
Playing Field
Alton Convent School
Anstey Park
Alton Town FC
Tennis Courts
Sports Grd.
Upper Neatham Mill Farm
Neatham Mill Cottage
Baycroft Cottages
Neatham Mill
Neatham Manor
Manor Farm
Haw Bridge
Hawbridge Farm
Hawbridge Cottages
Styne Farm
Malms Farm
Cannon's Copse
Depot
Fulling Mill
Copt Hill
Lynch Hill
Lynch Hill Cottage
Golden Chair Hill
Golden Chair Farm
Stirvill's Copse
Monk Wood
Neatham Down
Sewage Works
Wyck Farm
Clay's Farm
Field House
Redans Copse
Hurdles
Wixes
Club House
WORLDHAM GOLF COURSE
Driving Range
Cox's Copse
Little Caker Bridge
Kiln House
Truncheaunts
Shelley's Barn
Old House Farm
East Worldham House
Park Farm
Smith's Farm
East Worldham Manor
Manor Farm
King John's Hill
Worldham Hanger
Willow Plantation
Hamble Pits Copse
Whitehouse Farm
Wild Duck Copse
Darby's Dell
Copse Close
Manor Farm
Warner's Hanger
Warner's Wood
West Worldham Farm
Paglett's Green Cottages
A31
B3004
B3006
BINSTED ROAD
CAKERS LANE
WORLDHAM HILL
WILSOM ROAD
MILL LANE
CLAY'S LANE
WYCK LANE
WINDMILL HILL
LONDON ROAD
MONTECCHIO WY.
62
99
82

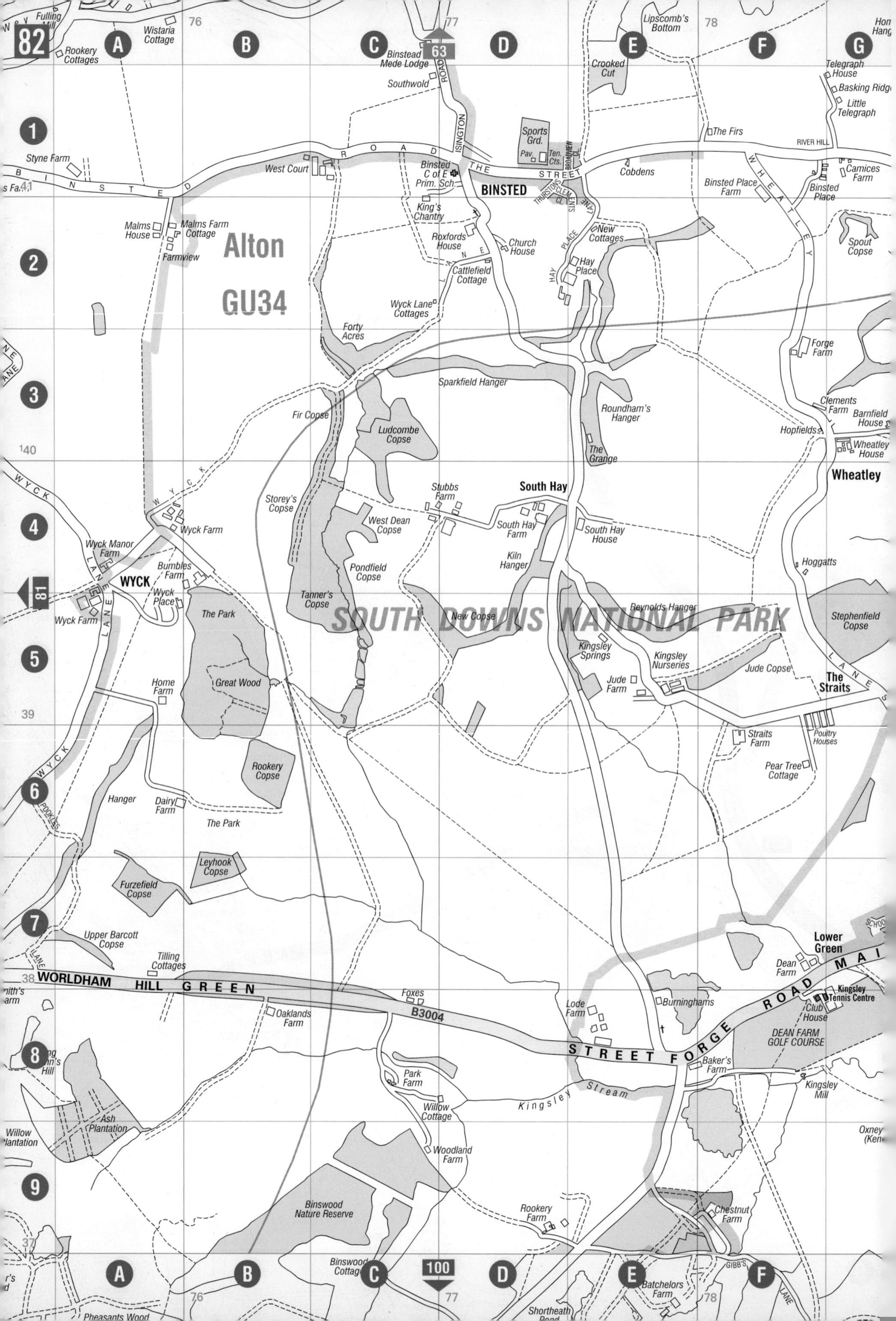
A
B
C
D
E
F
G
76
77
78
63
81
100
140
39
38
37
1
2
3
4
5
6
7
8
9
Fulling Mill
Wistaria Cottage
Rookery Cottages
Binstead Mede Lodge
Southwold
Lipscomb's Bottom
Crooked Cut
Telegraph House
Basking Ridge
Little Telegraph
The Firs
RIVER HILL
Styne Farm
BINSTED ROAD
ISINGTON ROAD
West Court
Binsted C of E Prim. Sch.
THE STREET
BINSTED
Sports Grd.
Pav.
Ten. Cts.
BROADVIEW CL
THURSTONS CL
CLEMENTS
LANE
Cobdens
Binsted Place Farm
WHEATLEY
Camices Farm
Binsted Place
King's Chantry
Malms House
Malms Farm Cottage
Farmview
Alton
GU34
Roxfords House
Church House
HAY PLACE
New Cottages
Spout Copse
Cattlefield Cottage
Hay Place
Wyck Lane Cottages
Forty Acres
Forge Farm
Sparkfield Hanger
Roundham's Hanger
Clements Farm
Barnfield House
Fir Copse
Ludcombe Copse
Hopfields
Wheatley House
The Grange
WYCK
Wheatley
Storey's Copse
Stubbs Farm
South Hay
West Dean Copse
South Hay Farm
South Hay House
Wyck Farm
Wyck Manor Farm
Kiln Hanger
Hoggatts
Bumbles Farm
WYCK
Pondfield Copse
LANE
Wyck Place
Tanner's Copse
SOUTH DOWNS NATIONAL PARK
New Copse
Reynolds Hanger
Stephenfield Copse
Wyck Farm
The Park
Kingsley Springs
Kingsley Nurseries
Jude Copse
Great Wood
Jude Farm
The Straits
Home Farm
Straits Farm
Poultry Houses
Rookery Copse
Pear Tree Cottage
Hanger
Dairy Farm
POOKES
The Park
Leyhook Copse
Furzefield Copse
Upper Barcott Copse
Lower Green
Tilling Cottages
Dean Farm
WORLDHAM HILL GREEN
ROAD
Kingsley Tennis Centre
Foxes
Lode Farm
Burninghams
Club House
Oaklands Farm
B3004
DEAN FARM GOLF COURSE
STREET
FORGE
Baker's Farm
Park Farm
Kingsley Stream
Kingsley Mill
Willow Cottage
Ash Plantation
Willow Plantation
Woodland Farm
Oxney
Binswood Nature Reserve
Rookery Farm
Chestnut Farm
Binswood Cottage
GIBB'S
LANE
Batchelors Farm
Pheasants Wood
Shortheath Pond

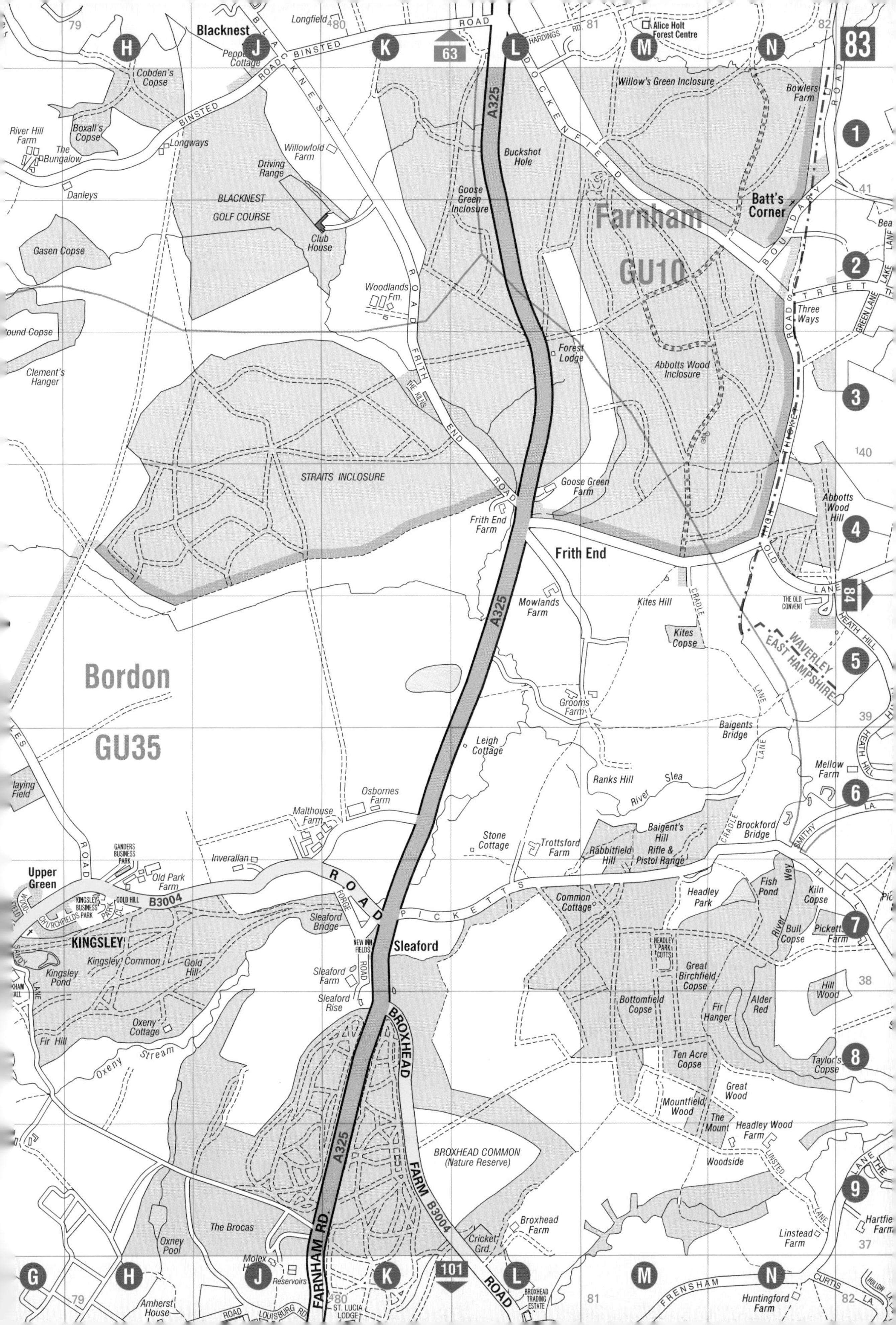
Blacknest
Longfield
Alice Holt Forest Centre
Willow's Green Inclosure
Bowlers Farm
Cobden's Copse
Boxall's Copse
River Hill Farm
The Bungalow
Longways
Danleys
Willowfold Farm
Driving Range
BLACKNEST GOLF COURSE
Club House
Buckshot Hole
Goose Green Inclosure
Farnham
GU10
Batt's Corner
Gasen Copse
Woodlands Fm.
Three Ways
Forest Lodge
Abbotts Wood Inclosure
Clement's Hanger
STRAITS INCLOSURE
Goose Green Farm
Frith End Farm
Frith End
Abbotts Wood Hill
Mowlands Farm
Kites Hill
Kites Copse
THE OLD CONVENT
WAVERLEY
EAST HAMPSHIRE
Bordon
GU35
Grooms Farm
Baigents Bridge
Leigh Cottage
Ranks Hill
River Slea
Mellow Farm
Osbornes Farm
Malthouse Farm
Stone Cottage
Trottsford Farm
Rabbitfield Hill
Baigent's Hill
Rifle & Pistol Range
Brockford Bridge
GANDERS BUSINESS PARK
Inverallan
Upper Green
Old Park Farm
KINGSLEY BUSINESS PARK
B3004
Sleaford Bridge
Common Cottage
Headley Park
Fish Pond
River Wey
Kiln Copse
Bull Copse
Picketts Farm
KINGSLEY
Kingsley Common
Gold Hill
Kingsley Pond
Sleaford
NEW INN FIELDS
Sleaford Farm
Sleaford Rise
HEADLEY PARK COTTS
Great Birchfield Copse
Hill Wood
Bottomfield Copse
Fir Hanger
Alder Red
Oxeny Cottage
Fir Hill
Oxeny Stream
Ten Acre Copse
Taylor's Copse
Great Wood
Mountfield Wood
The Mount
Headley Wood Farm
BROXHEAD COMMON (Nature Reserve)
Woodside
Hartfield Farm
The Brocas
Oxney Pool
Broxhead Farm
Cricket Grd.
Linstead Farm
Molex
Reservoirs
ST. LUCIA LODGE
BROXHEAD TRADING ESTATE
Huntingford Farm
Amherst House
A325
BINSTED ROAD
BLACKNEST ROAD
DOCKENFIELD
HARDINGS RD.
BOUNDARY ROAD
STREET
FRITH END ROAD
THE KILNS
HIGH THICKET ROAD
OLD LANE
HEATH HILL
CRADLE LANE
SMITHY LA.
PICKETTS HILL
FORGE ROAD
BROXHEAD FARM ROAD
FARNHAM RD.
FRENSHAM
CURTIS LA.
LOUISBURG RD
LINSTED LANE
GREEN LANE
63
84
101
H J K L M N G
1 2 3 4 5 6 7 8 9
79 480 81 82
41 140 39 38 37

Ashbeds
Nash's Copse
Grubb's Copse
Falkner's Copse
Swan's Copse
Hallsgrove Copse
The Ham
Rough Copse
Ham Ashbed
Pitt Hanger
Pitthanger
Lane End
St. Mary's C of E Inf. Sch.
FRENSHAM
THE STREET
PEAKFIELD
LOWERS LA.
THE GRANGE
A287
Bowlers Farm
BOUNDARY ROAD
Middle Copse
Jeffrey's Copse
Pitt Farm
MILL LANE
BEALESWOOD
Bealeswood Common
Dockenfield
LAKE LANE
FRENSHAM COMMON
Frensham Manor
DOCKENFIELD ST.
THE STREET
GREEN LANE
Three Ways
ABBOTTS COTTAGES
Westhanger
Flat Copse
Dockenfield Farm
OLD PITT LANE
FRENSHAM COUNTRY
The Hanger
Frensham Great Pond
THICKET ROAD
Abbotts Wood Hill
Dockenfield Manor
MANOR FARM MEWS
Manor Fm.
OLD LANE
River Wey
POND LANE
BACON LANE
Frensham Pond Sailing Club
THE OLD CONVENT
83
HEATH HILL
Rock Barn Cottage
Hales Copse
Furze Hill
Churt House
New Farm
Field House
EAST HAMPSHIRE
WAVERLEY
Kingsmead
Wishanger Common
Dufferin House
The Chase
WAYSIDE COTTAGES
STAR HILL DRIVE
Gum Hill
Wishanger Lodge
FRENSHAM LANE
WISHANGER LANE
Heath Hill
The Oasts
Stream Farm
Wishanger Lake
Wishanger Farm
Symondstone Farm
SIMMONDSTONE LANE
Furze Hills Farm
Mellow Farm
Huntingford Bridge
SMITHY LANE
Stream Copse
Summer House Copse
Caravan Site
Chinton Hanger
LAMPARD LANE
Beech Field Copse
High Field Copse
Fish Pond
Stream Cottage
SMITHFIELD LANE
Firs Close
Hoppery Hill
Hoppery Copse
Ham Copse
Barford Court
Barford Court Farm
Kiln Copse
Pickets Hill House
PICKETTS HILL
Twelve Acre Copse
Dipping Tank Copse
Three Cornered Copse
Stream Forest
Furze Copse
Daniel's Copse
Bull Copse
Picketts Hill Farm
Park Copse
PARK LANE
Ford
Hill Wood
Horseshoe Farm
FRENSHAM LANE
Park View Farm
Hills Copse
Bordon GU35
Saunders Green
High Breck
Opax Farm
SPATS LANE
Elliot's Farm
Plaster Hill Farm
Lower Hearn Cottages
Taylor's Copse
PROSPECT HILL
Prospect Hill Farm
Hearn House Farm
Lower Coombe Farm
Coombe Farm
Hearn Copse
Hearn House
Hungry Coombe
Bayfields Farm
Headley Meadows
Hearn
Dalen Copse
Hartfield House
Brambletye
Chintens Copse
Land of Nod Wood
RED LANE
Little Hearn Copse
HEARN VALE
Cain Farm
Folly Plantation
THE HANGER
Hartfield Farm
Land of Nod
Linstead Farm
LINSTEAD LA.
The Hanger
The Oaks
LANGTON DR.
CHURT ROAD
ARFORD
Curtis Farm
CURTIS LA.
HOLLOW LA.
WHEATSHEAF COURT
BARLEY MOW HILL
COMMON
GLAYSHERS HILL
Community Centre
102

H
J
K
L
M
N
86
87
88
Frensham Little Pond
PRIORY LANE
GRANGE ROAD
Hillside Farm
Greenhills Farm
HANKLEY COMMON
WINCHESTER ROAD
CARLISLE
RUSHMOOR
Melbreck Nursing Home
WELLESLEY ROAD
EGLINTON
LOWICKS RD.
LOWICKS ROAD
Mackenzies
Lowicks
Graywalls
SANDY
Kettlebury Hill
GLEBE LA
Lowicks House
LANE
Gold Hill
Farnham
THE FLASHES (Nature Reserve)
GU10
Crosswater House
Nursery
Crosswater
Millais Gardens
CROSSWATER
Churt Common
The Devil's Jumps
Stony Jump
Stoneyside
Barrow House
Lingwood
THURSLEY ROAD
TILFORD ROAD
Borrowstone
Tylosand
The Sculpture Park
Sundial House
Coombe Ridge
Churt Place Farm
The Cedars
Silverbeck
Silverbeck Farm
OLD KILN LANE
Old Kiln Farm
CRABTREE LANE
Churt Lea
Bookhams
Garden Cottage
Churt Place Nursery
Sunward
Podmore
HOUSE LANE
The Pack House
High Meadow
Hyde Copse
Hyde Farm
OLD BARN LANE
GREEN CROSS LANE
HYDE LANE
Glenhead Farm
CROSSWAYS
Pav.
Rec. Grd.
Hale Ho.
THE MEADOWS
CHURT
Avalon Farm
Green Cross
High Barn
Stock Farm
Marchants Farm
SILVER BIRCH COTTAGES
Fair View Farm
Green Cross Farm
BARFORD LA
St. John's C of E Inf. Sch.
KITTS LANE
EDDYSTONE CT.
PARKHURST FIELDS
GREEN LANE
Willow Farm
Green Farm
Chipstead
GREENHANGER
Barford Farm
Kitts Farm
Barford
Woodbury House
Oak Grove
Hyde Hill
HEATHER COTTAGES
Road Farm
Hill Lodge
Marchants Hill
Gravel Hanger
Hindhead
GU26
Churt Wynde Reservoir (covered)
A287
EIGHT ACRES
HINDHEAD GOLF COURSE
Hatch Hill House
WHITMOOR VALE
HEATH CL.
SANDHEATH RD.
CLOVELLY
Marchant's Hill (Activity Centre)
Hindhead Playing Field
BEACON HILL
Linkside
LINKSIDE NORTH
LINKSIDE WEST
LINKSIDE EAST
LINKSIDE SOUTH
103
The Central Deaconess House
CRICKET CL.
CHURT ROAD
VALE ROAD
Club House
Twizzletwig
Broome Acres
G
1
2
3
4
5
6
7
8
9
41
140
39
38
37

A
B
C
D
E
F
G
1
2
3
4
5
6
7
8
9
88
66
120
BROUGHTON INSET
Broughton Primary School
SCHOOL LANE
NORTH END
HIGH STREET
DIXONS
HINWOOD CL.
PAYNES LANE
CHAPEL LA.
OLD FORGE
RECTORY LANE
Ford
BROUGHTON
Little London
Stockbridge
SO20
Cemetery
Play Fld.
PLOUGH GS.
WHITESHOOT
Greenacre
QUEENWOOD RD.
SALISBURY RD
Cricket Ground
THE POUND
BUCKHOLT ROAD
ROMSEY ROAD
B3084
BEECHCROFT COTTAGES
QUEENW RISE
Weir
Brook
STREET
ROOKERY
HORSEBRIDGE ROAD
LANE
Idmiston
Idmiston C of E Prim. Sch.
PORTON
RECTORY CT.
WINTERSLOW RD.
DANGER AREA
BLACKBARN ROAD
Idmiston Down
Boscombe Down East
SP4
East GOMELDON ROAD
Gomeldon
Broadfield Farm
Porton Down
Winterbourne Dauntsey
Barracks
Winterbourne Gunner
THORNEY BANK
Winterbourne Earls
Winterbourne Earls C of E Prim. Sch.
Hurdcott
SUMMERLUG
A338
MAIN RD
Battery Hill
Thorny Down
Figsbury Ring
LONDON ROAD
A30
Winterbourne Down
Firsdown
MAPLE DR.
JUNIPER RD.
FIRS CL.
FIRS ROAD
GT CROFT
Bracknell Croft
OLD MALTHOUSE LANE
Stock Bottom
Salisbury
New Manor Farm
Dunstable Farm
West Winterslow
THE STREET
Manor Farm
Stanley's New Farm
Cockey Down Nature Reserve
Fussells Lodge Farm
Reservoir (Covered)
QUEEN MANOR ROAD
Queen Manor Farm
Savage's Farm
Clarendon Park
Carverel Copse
PITTON
Pitton C of E Prim. School
Cemy.
WHITE HILL
GREEN
Pitton Lodge
Hound Wood
MANOR
QUEEN
Beechy Dean Copse
PITTON ROAD
CHURCH ROAD
FARLEY
THE STREET
PENNYS LA.
PARSONAGE HILL
LUCEWOOD LANE
GRIMSTEAD
LANE
DROVE
Blackmoor Copse
Nightwood Copse
Clarendon House
CLARENDON
GREEN ROAD
LONG DROVE
East Grimstead
LONG ROAD
BUGMORE LA.
THE CHESTNUTS
LYVERS
KINGS SOMBORNE INSET
Cemetery
Recreation Ground
CONN DROVE HILL
STOCKBRIDGE RD.
Old Fromans Farm
KING'S SOMBORNE
OLD VICARAGE LA.
MUSS LANE
WINCHESTER RD.
FROGHOLE LANE
War Mem.
CHURCH
KINGS ACRE
CAMP FLD.
The Cross
A3057
King's Somborne C of E Prim. Sch.
Hall
Sports Ground
HAYES CL.
PALACE FARM
FURZEDOWN ROAD
Carn Brea
SCOTT CLOSE
ELDON CL.
SOPWITH CL.
Stockbridge
SO20
HUMBERS VW.
HUNTER CL.
ELDON ROAD
ROMSEY
HORSEBRIDGE RD.
431
133
131
436
420
21
22
23
34
33
32

Nether Wallop
Stockbridge
SO20
Lopcombe Corner
East Winterslow
MIDDLE WINTERSLOW
The Common
SP5
WEST TYTHERLEY
The Green
Stony Batter
East Tytherley
Frenchmoor
Easton Down
Roche Court Down
Ashley's Copse
Burretts Grove
Noad's Copse
Hedgemoor Copse
Picked Copse
Norman Ct. Preparatory School
Bentley Wood
Coalpits Copse
Park Copse
Nature Reserve
Barnridge Copse
Howe Copse East
Dean Copse
Tytherley Common
Keepers Cottage
Drove Farm House
Pilgrims Croft
Pug's Hole Farm
Lockerley Hall
Lain Copse
Manor Farm
Stride's Farm
Home Farm
Buckholt Farm
Horseshoe Hill
Whiteshoot Hill
BROUGHTON DOWN
Broughton Down Farm
Warren Farm
Hill Farm
Roche Court
Gutteridge Farm
Woodgate Farmhouse
The Livery
Hollom Down Farm
Jack's Bush Farm
Beech Farm
Wallop House
Berry Court Farm
Church Farm
Queenwood Farm
West Tytherley C of E Primary School
Winterslow C of E Prim. Sch.
DANGER AREA
WILTSHIRE
TEST VALLEY
A343
A30
B3084
STOCKBRIDGE ROAD
SALISBURY ROAD
ROMSEY ROAD
67
88
121

NETHER WALLOP
Danebury
Chattis Hill
Houghton Down
LONGSTOCK
STOCKBRIDGE
Stockbridge SO20
Meon Hill
Houghton Down Farm
Test Valley School
North Houghton
Homestead Farm
Marsh Court
Houghton Lodge & Gardens
Eveley Farm
BROUGHTON
Little London
Manor Farm
Waterloo Farm
Nine Mile Water Farm
Darfield Farm
Berry Court Farm
Garlogs
Church Farm
Broughton Hill
Roakes Farm
HOUGHTON
Houghton Drayton
Bossington
Hoopers Farm
Yew Hill
Works
KING'S SOMBORNE
Horsebridge
Crown Farm
Queenwood Farm
Romsey SO51
Bentley Farms
Pittleworth Farm
Compton
Compton Manor
Humbers Wood
Brook
Lain Copse
Spearywell Wood
Spearywell
Lower Brook
Michelmersh Wood
Lower Eldon Farm
Steepleton House
A30
A3057
B3084
SALISBURY
LECKFORD
ROMSEY
HIGH ST.
WINTON
72
73
87
86
98
122
123

Leckford Abbas
74
75
Club House
LECKFORD GOLF COURSE
New Farm
Brockley Warren
Martins Lane
Chilbolton Down
A30
Fair View Farm
Woolbury
Sandydown Farm
Heath House
Dumper's Oak
Stockbridge Bridge Nature Reserve
Long Copse
Bushy Copse
Crawley Forest
Windmill Hill
CRAWLEY
90
B3049
Somborne Park Road
North Park Farm
Winter Down Copse
North Park Wood
Folly Farm
STOCKBRIDGE ROAD B3049
Kirton Farm
Winchester
SO21
Rookley Farm
Little Somborne House
Whitehall Lane
Little Somborne
WINCHESTER
TEST VALLEY
BALLDOWN CARAVAN & CAMPING PARK
Hatchery
Court La.
Up Somborne
New Lease Farm
Chalk Hill
Vale
Garstons
Track
Sparsholt College
Westley
SPARSHOLT
Chalkvale Farm
Lane Road
Chalk
Ashley
Great Up Somborne Wood
Moor Court Farm
Moor Court Lane
Castle (Remains)
Ashley Wood
Well Copse
104
Forest of Bere Farm
Hoplands
Ashley Down
West Wood
Burrow
Farley Mount Country Park
Beacon Hill
Luke Copse
Farley Mount Road
Parnholt Wood
Mount Down
Romsey
SO51
Farley Down
PITT DOWN
Parnholt La.
Bailey's Down
124
125
Farley Farm
Berrydown Farm
Fishponds Farm
Grovelands Copse
Sparsholt Rd.

76
104
89
Barton Stacey Belt
Barton Ashes
TEST-VALLEY
WINCHESTER
Barton Stacey Belt
OX DROVE
CRAWLEY DOWN
Crawley Clump
A272
A34
CHRISTMAS HILL
WONSTON
Larkwhistle Farm
Reservoir (covered)
STAVEDOWN
MARKSON RD.
ORCHARD CL.
Water Tower
Warren Wood
Warren House
Warren Cottages
NEW BARN LANE
Little Grove
New Barn Cottages
New Barn
Long Barrow
Worthy Grove
Roman Road
WORTHY DOWN
REES RD.
BLACKWELL
WINCHESTER ROAD
CRAWLEY
Whitethorn House
Crawley Pond
SO21
Morns Field Cottages
Morns Field
Gas Valve Compound
Beeches Farm
The Beeches
Littleton House
Lower Farm
Lower Farm Cottages
Lower Farm House
Drovers Way
Earthwork
Long Park
The Paddocks
Long Park Cottage
Long Park Farm
Pumping Station
Littleton Stud
Littleton Stud Cottages
Stud Lodge
STOCKBRIDGE ROAD
B3049
Church Garage
BALLDOWN CARAVAN & CAMPING PARK
Littleton Manor
CHURCH LANE
MAIN RD.
OLD STABLE MEWS
LITTLETON LANE
Cradle Copse
Long Wood
Northwood Cottage
Lyne's Plantation
Winsley Cottage
LITTLETON
NEW RD.
Bowling Green
Tennis Cts.
Playground
Rec. Grd.
FLOWERDOWN MOBILE HOME PARK
Playing Field
PADDOCK VW.
ROZELLE CL.
HOLLANDS CL.
THE HALL WAY
PITTER CL.
Northwood Farm
Chilcott's Plantation
NORTHWOOD PARK
Ball Down Farm
Garston Farm
Garstons Buildings
TRACK
LANE

SOUTH WONSTON
Winchester
Worthy Down
Worthy Down Camp
Springvale
SO23
SO22
KINGS WORTHY
ABBOTS WORTHY
Headbourne Worthy
South Wonston Farm
Windy Nook
Belle Vue
Sanctuary Farm
Ruby Cottage
Greenacres
Bayley's Clump
Wallers Ash
Southridge Copse
ALRESFORD DROVE
OX DROVE
STOKE ROAD
CHARITY
WALLERS ASH TUNNEL
South Wonston Prim. Sch.
Playing Field
Tennis Ct.
Playground
Race Course Cottages
Married Quarters
Gallop
Little Stoke
North Winchester Farm
Kingsway Farm
Depot
Railway Cottages
Southstoke Farm
Down Farm
Sewage Works
Bull Farm
Bank Fm.
Copse Farm
Down Farm
Underpass
Woodhams Farm
A34
WINCHESTER BY PASS
DOWNS FARM
Roman Road
B3420
ANDOVER RD. N.
Sewage Works
Upper Farm
Vokes Cotts.
Watercress Beds
The White Cottage
Kings Worthy Prim.Sch.
Hinton House
Club
Recreation Ground
Playground
Hinton Cott.
Play. Fld.
Nursery
Cornerways
B3047
A33
LONDON RD.
BASINGSTOKE RD.

76
92
105

77
91
106
Bazeley Copse
Harley Hill Cottages
New Down Farm Cottages
Newdown Farm
ALRESFORD DROVE
Reservoir (covered)
WALLERS ASH TUNNEL
ROMAN ROAD
Burnt Wood
M3 MOTORWAY
CHILLANDHAM LANE
Itchen Wood
Winchester Service Area
Shroner Wood
Shroner Wood House
The Beacon
Shroner Hill House
Winchester
SO21
Rutherley Copse
Subway
Chillandham Farm
Southstoke Farm
Yearly Cotts.
Burntwood Cotts.
Burntwood Farm
BRIDGETTS
Pavis Copse
Burntwood Cottages
Bull Farm
Copse Farm
Depot
Meadow Farm
Bridget House
Bridget's Experimental Husbandry Farm
Reservoir (covered)
BASINGSTOKE ROAD
A33
LOVEDON LANE
SHEPHERDS FLD.
Garage Cottages
Chillandham Cottages
Couch Green
Grace's Farm Cottages
Grace's Farm
Freefolk House
Martyr Worthy Place
COUCH GRN.
Rec. Grd.
Sports Grd.
KINGS WORTHY
The New House
Princes Mead Sch.
Homewood
WORTHY PARK
PARK LANE
B3047
Manor House
CHURCH LANE
Hall
MARTYR WORTHY
Cygnet House
Chilland Barn
Upper Chilland House
Chilland
SOUTH DOWNS
Chilland Ho.
Worthy Park Home Farm
The Worthys
Abbotsworthy House
ABBOTS WORTHY
Mill
Ford
New Bridge Cott.
Easton Bridge
EASTON LANE
RIVER ITCHEN
Weir
LONDON RD.
Subway

MICHELDEVER WOOD
Mill Lane Copse
Enclosure
Cross Dyke
Hassock Copse
Hassock Farm
Newhouse
Cricket Ground
Pav.
Newhouse Farm
Northfield Plantation
Northington Lodge
NORTHINGTON ROAD
Reservoir (covered)
Reservoir (covered)
The Grange Farm
THE GRANGE PARK
The Grange (Northington)
Alresford
SO24
ITCHEN WOOD
Courtney's Copse
The Scrubbs
Itchen Stoke Down
Home Covert
Itchen Down House
Itchen Down Farm
NORTHINGTON ROAD
Roman Villa (site of)
Lone Farm
Spreadoak Cottages
Veterinary Centre
RECTORY LANE
Rectory Lane Dairy
New Farm Cottages
Folly Hill Farm
Railway Cottages
Winton Cottages
Abbey House
BARING CL.
The Elms
Hazeldene Gds.
Station Approach
SCHOOL LA.
Little Hayes
LITTLE HAYES LANE
Clock Cottage
ITCHEN ABBAS
STATION RD.
OLD STATION CL.
SHELLEY CL.
NORTHINGTON HILL
The Paddock
Itchen Abbas Prim. Sch.
ABBAS BUS. CEN.
Hall
Itchen Abbas Ho.
Fish Farm
Fish Farm
Park Farm
B3047
AVINGTON LANE
NATIONAL PARK
Waterfall
Chalk Pit
Avington Lodge
AVINGTON PARK GOLF COURSE
Avington House
The Pavilion
The Rectory
Yavington Farm Cottage
ITCHEN STOKE
Longcrate Cottages
Millers Piece
Rectory
ITCHEN VW.
WATER LA.
Itchen House
Cricket Grd.
G H J K L M N
1 2 3 4 5 6 7 8 9
53 54 455 56
37 36 35 34 33
77 94 107

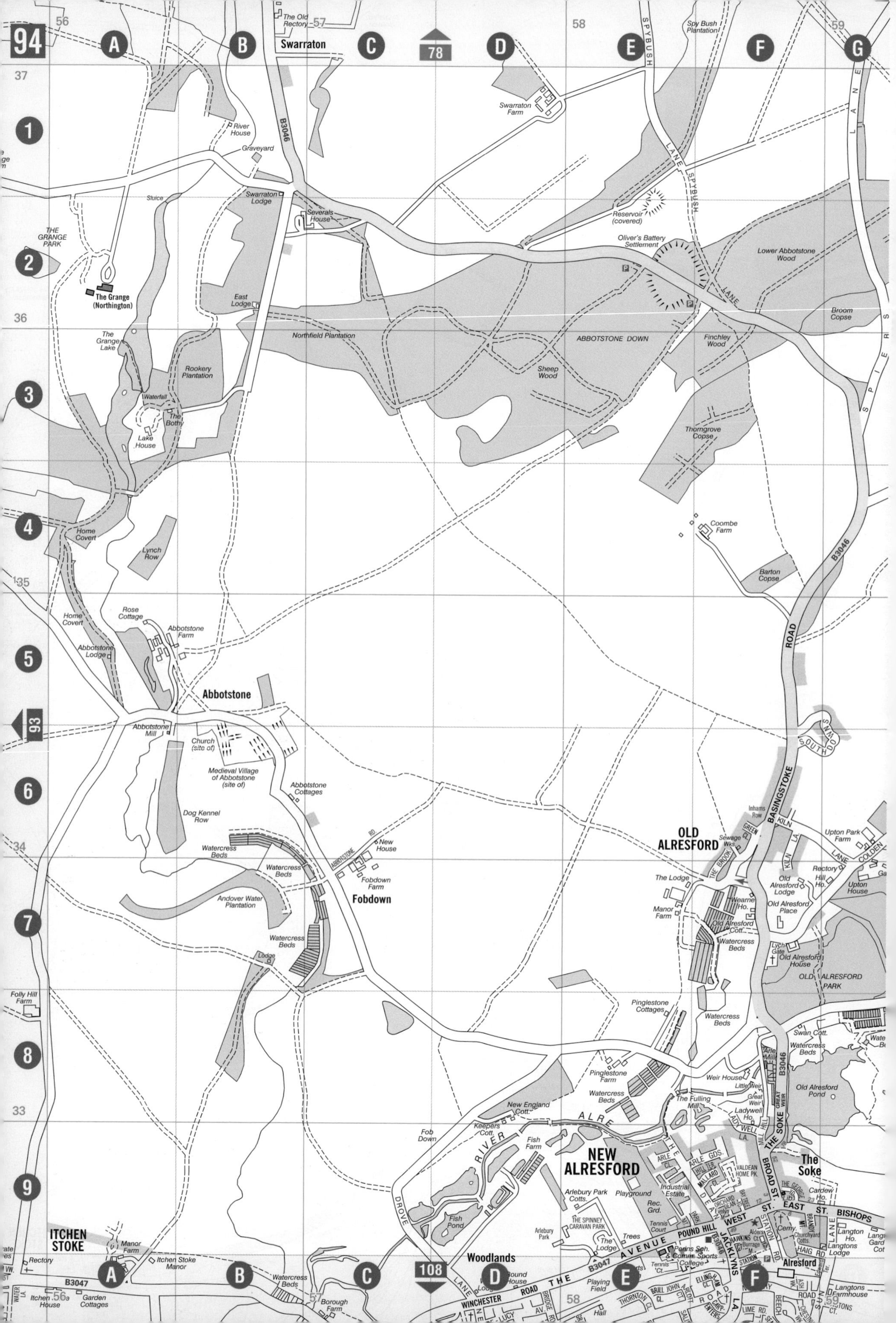

56
57
58
59
A
B
C
D
E
F
G
78
108
93
37
36
35
34
33
1
2
3
4
5
6
7
8
9
The Old Rectory
Swarraton
Spy Bush Plantation
SPYBUSH
Swarraton Farm
River House
Graveyard
B3046
Sluice
Swarraton Lodge
Severals House
THE GRANGE PARK
The Grange (Northington)
Reservoir (covered)
Oliver's Battery Settlement
Lower Abbotstone Wood
East Lodge
Northfield Plantation
ABBOTSTONE DOWN
Finchley Wood
Broom Copse
The Grange Lake
Rookery Plantation
Sheep Wood
Waterfall
The Bothy
Lake House
Thorngrove Copse
Home Covert
Lynch Row
Coombe Farm
Barton Copse
Rose Cottage
Abbotstone Farm
Home Covert
Abbotstone Lodge
ROAD
BASINGSTOKE
Abbotstone
Abbotstone Mill
Church (site of)
Medieval Village of Abbotstone (site of)
SOUTHDOWN
Abbotstone Cottages
Dog Kennel Row
ABBOTSTONE RD
New House
Inhams Row
KILN
Upton Park Farm
COLDEN
OLD ALRESFORD
Sewage Wks.
GREEN
THE BROOK
KILN LA
LANE
Watercress Beds
Fobdown Farm
Fobdown
The Lodge
Rectory Hill Ho.
Upton House
Old Alresford Lodge
Andover Water Plantation
Manor Farm
Wearne Ho.
Old Alresford Place
Old Alresford Cott.
Lych Gate
Old Alresford House
Lodge
OLD ALRESFORD PARK
Folly Hill Farm
Pinglestone Cottages
Swan Cott.
Arle Mill
Pinglestone Farm
Weir House
Little Weir
Great Weir
Ladywell Ho.
Old Alresford Pond
New England Cott.
The Fulling Mill
ALRE
Keepers Cott.
Fob Down
RIVER
Fish Farm
NEW ALRESFORD
ARLE CL.
ARLE GDS.
HILL TER.
MILLARD
VALDEAN HOME PK.
Industrial Estate
GREAT WEIR
MILL HILL
LADYWELL LA.
THE SOKE
The Soke
Cardew Ho.
DROVE
Fish Pond
Arlebury Park Cotts.
Playground
Rec. Grd.
Tennis Court
THE DEAN
PARK
POUND HILL
WEST ST.
BROAD ST.
EAST ST.
BISHOPS
THE SPINNEY CARAVAN PARK
Arlebury Park
The Lodge
Trees
Perins Sch. & Comm. Sports College
JACKLYNS
STATION RD.
HAWKINS CT.
Cemy.
Churchyard Cotts.
Langtons Ho.
Langtons Lodge
ITCHEN STOKE
Manor Farm
Itchen Stoke Manor
Rectory
Woodlands
Round House
AVENUE
THE
B3047
Playing Field
HAIG RD.
Alresford
Langtons Farmhouse
B3047
WATER LA.
Itchen House
Garden Cottages
Watercress Beds
Borough Farm
LANE
WINCHESTER ROAD
THE
BRIDGE RD.
LUCY
THORNTON CL.
BRAIL CL.
JOHN RD.
ELLINGHAM CL.
Hall
LIME RD.
BEECH
SUN LA.

Godsfield Ho.
Godsfield Cott.
Godsfield Farm
78
The Bungalow
Upper Lanham Farm
UPPER LANHAM LANE
The Firs
The Cabin
Upper Abbotstone Wood
Lower Lanham Copse
Seventeen Acres
Upper Lanham Copse
Marks Wood
The Border
Lower Lanham Farm
Lucys Wood
Bighton Wood
Newells Copse
Scrivens Copse
BIGHTON WOOD
The Plantation
Nettlebeds Farm
Nettlebeds Farm Stables
Bighton House
Nettlebeds Cottage
NETTLEBEDS LANE
Gardeners Cottage
Inner Lodge
Alresford
SO24
High Dell Farm
Cricket Ground
Bighton Manor
BIGHTON
Hall
96
Manor Farm
MALTHOUSE LA
BIGHTON DEAN LANE
Cricket Ground
GOLDEN LANE
BIGHTON
FARM LANE
SUTTONWOOD
UPTON HOUSE
Henrys Wood
Goscombs Copse
Upton Lodge
DRAYTON
Drayton Farm
The Nythe House
Watercress Beds
Sutton Wood
Hazel Wood
GOSCOMBE LANE
GUNDLETON
NORTHSIDE LANE
Sutton Beech Wood
Bighton Bottom Farm
Northside Farm
White's Wood
Field Ho.
SUTTON ROAD
B3047
Secundus
WATERCRESS LINE (MID HANTS RAILWAY)
BIGHTON
Watercress Beds
109
Lower Mill Pond Watercress Beds
Upper Mill Pond Watercress Beds
Western Court Farm
G
H
J
K
L
M
N
1
2
3
4
5
6
7
8
9
460
61
62
37
36
35
34
33

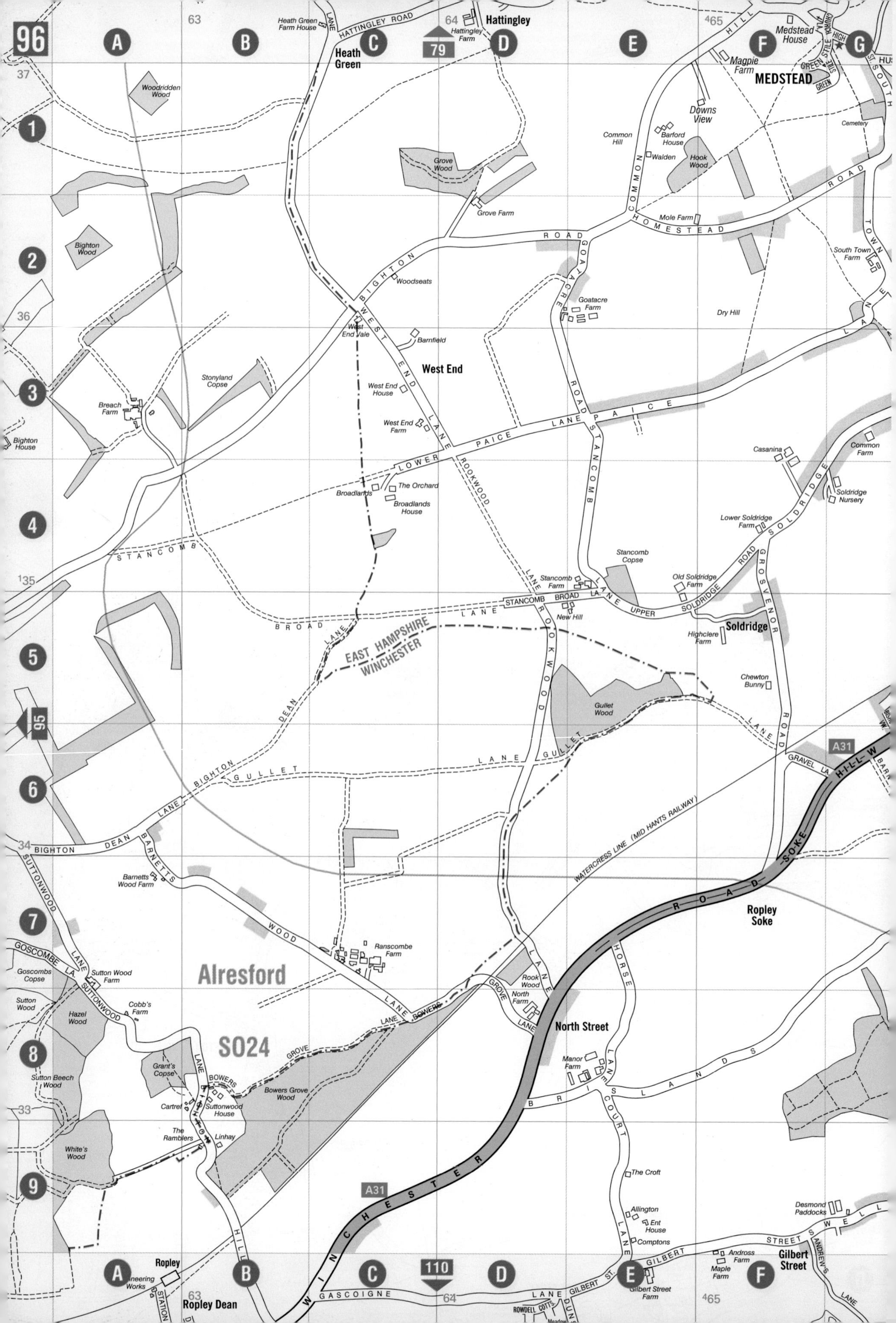
A
B
C
D
E
F
G
1
2
3
4
5
6
7
8
9
63
64
465
37
36
135
34
33
79
95
110
Heath Green Farm House
HATTINGLEY ROAD
LANE
Hattingley
Hattingley Farm
Heath Green
Medstead House
Magpie Farm
MEDSTEAD
CHURCH
HIGH
GREEN STILE
GREEN
HILL
ST.
SOUTH
Woodridden Wood
Downs View
Cemetery
Common Hill
Barford House
Walden
Hook Wood
Grove Wood
Grove Farm
COMMON
HOMESTEAD
ROAD
Mole Farm
Bighton Wood
BIGHTON
Woodseats
GOATACRE
Goatacre Farm
South Town Farm
TOWN
Dry Hill
36
West End Vale
WEST END LANE
Barnfield
West End
Stonyland Copse
Breach Farm
Bighton House
West End House
West End Farm
PAICE LANE
LOWER PAICE
STANCOMB
Casanina
Common Farm
Broadlands
The Orchard
Broadlands House
ROOKWOOD
Soldridge Nursery
Lower Soldridge Farm
SOLDRIDGE ROAD
Stancomb Copse
Stancomb Farm
STANCOMB BROAD LANE
New Hill
Old Soldridge Farm
UPPER SOLDRIDGE
GROSVENOR ROAD
Soldridge
Highclere Farm
BROAD LANE
DEAN
EAST HAMPSHIRE
WINCHESTER
Chewton Bunny
Gullet Wood
GULLET LANE
A31
GRAVEL LA
HILL
BIGHTON DEAN LANE
WATERCRESS LINE (MID HANTS RAILWAY)
ROAD SOKE
BARNETTS
SUTTONWOOD
Barnetts Wood Farm
Ropley Soke
WOOD
Ranscombe Farm
GOSCOMBE LA.
Goscombs Copse
Sutton Wood Farm
Alresford
Rook Wood
GROVE
North Farm
HORSE
Sutton Wood
Hazel Wood
Cobb's Farm
BOWERS LANE
North Street
SO24
Grant's Copse
Manor Farm
BRISLANDS
COURT
Sutton Beech Wood
BOWERS
Bowers Grove Wood
Cartref
Suttonwood House
White's Wood
The Ramblers
Linhay
WINCHESTER
The Croft
A31
Allington
Ent House
Comptons
Desmond Paddocks
WELL
STREET
ST ANDREW'S
GILBERT
Andross Farm
Maple Farm
Gilbert Street
Ropley
Engineering Works
STATION
Ropley Dean
GASCOIGNE LANE
GILBERT ST.
Gilbert Street Farm
ROWDELL COTTS
DUN
LANE

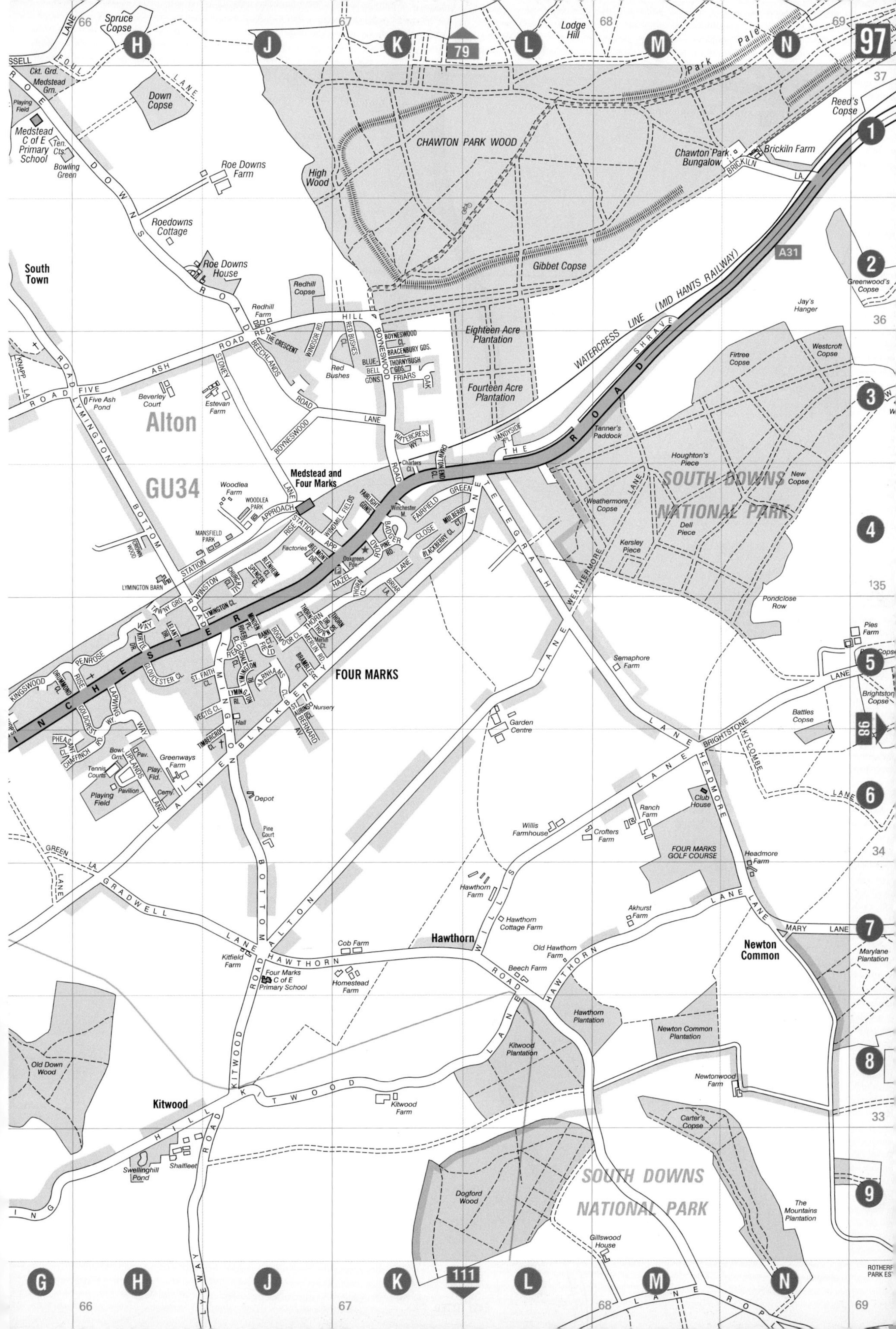

Spruce Copse
Down Copse
Medstead C of E Primary School
Roe Downs Farm
Roedowns Cottage
Roe Downs House
South Town
CHAWTON PARK WOOD
High Wood
Gibbet Copse
Lodge Hill
Chawton Park Bungalow
Brickiln Farm
Reed's Copse
A31
WATERCRESS LINE (MID HANTS RAILWAY)
Redhill Copse
Eighteen Acre Plantation
Fourteen Acre Plantation
Jay's Hanger
Greenwood's Copse
Firtree Copse
Westcroft Copse
Alton
GU34
Medstead and Four Marks
Tanner's Paddock
Houghton's Piece
SOUTH DOWNS NATIONAL PARK
New Copse
Weathermore Copse
Dell Piece
Kersley Piece
Pondclose Row
Pies Farm
FOUR MARKS
Semaphore Farm
Garden Centre
Battles Copse
Brightston Copse
Willis Farmhouse
Crofters Farm
Ranch Farm
Club House
FOUR MARKS GOLF COURSE
Headmore Farm
Hawthorn Farm
Hawthorn Cottage Farm
Hawthorn
Newton Common
Marylane Plantation
Cob Farm
Kitfield Farm
Four Marks C of E Primary School
Homestead Farm
Old Hawthorn Farm
Beech Farm
Hawthorn Plantation
Newton Common Plantation
Old Down Wood
Kitwood Plantation
Newtonwood Farm
Kitwood
Kitwood Farm
Carter's Copse
Swellinghill Pond
Shalfleet
Dogford Wood
SOUTH DOWNS NATIONAL PARK
The Mountains Plantation
Gillswood House

79
98
111

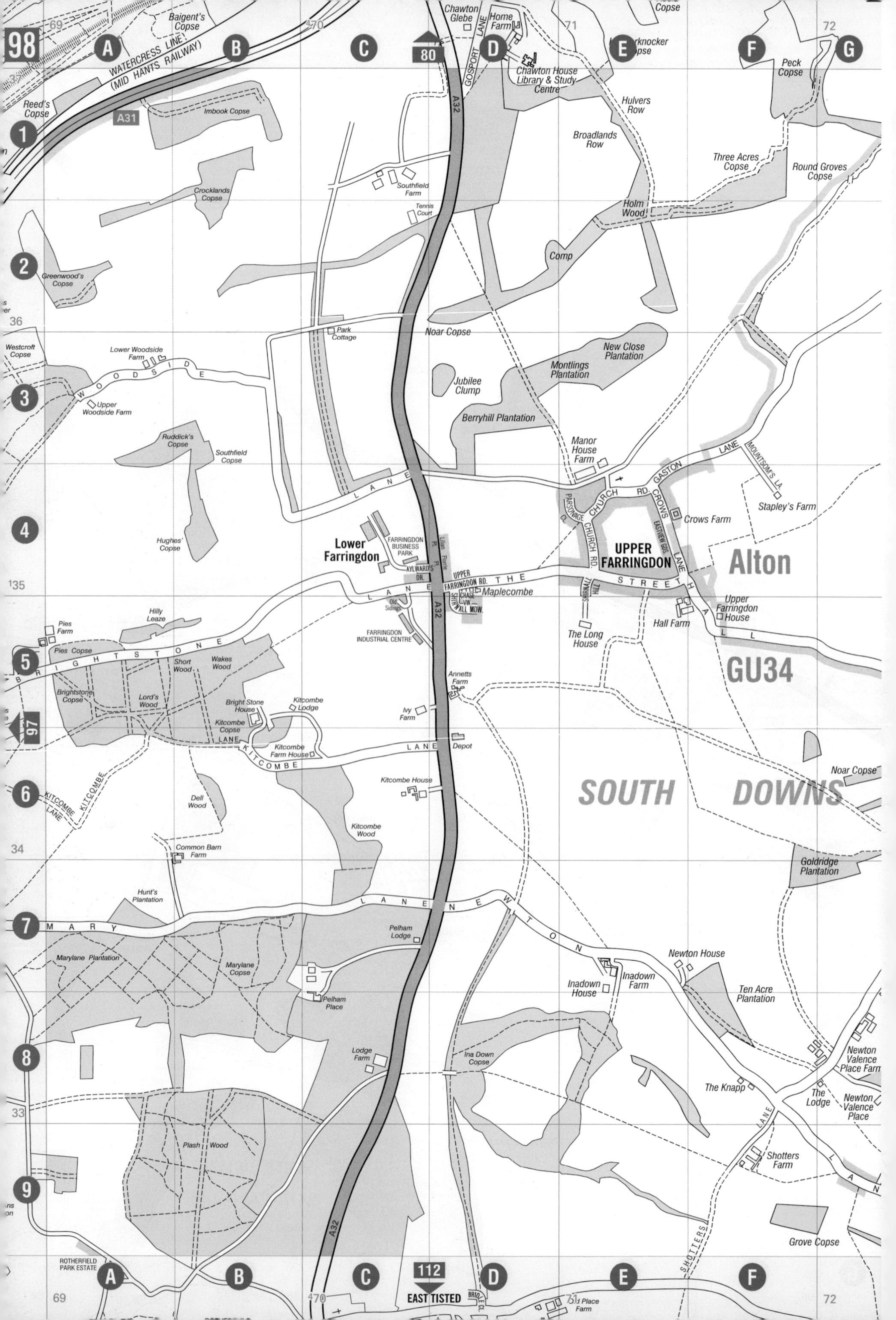
Baigent's Copse
Watercress Line (Mid Hants Railway)
Reed's Copse
A31
Imbook Copse
Chawton Glebe
Home Farm
Gosport Lane
80
Chawton House Library & Study Centre
Hulvers Row
Broadlands Row
Peck Copse
Three Acres Copse
Round Groves Copse
Crocklands Copse
Southfield Farm
Tennis Court
Holm Wood
Comp
Greenwood's Copse
A32
Park Cottage
Noar Copse
New Close Plantation
Westcroft Copse
Lower Woodside Farm
Woodside
Montlings Plantation
Jubilee Clump
Upper Woodside Farm
Berryhill Plantation
Ruddick's Copse
Southfield Copse
Manor House Farm
Gaston Lane
Mountsom's La
Church Rd.
Crows Lane
Parsonage Cl.
Crows Farm
Stapley's Farm
Hughes' Copse
Lower Farringdon
Farringdon Business Park
Aylward's Dr.
Church Rd.
Upper Farringdon
Alton
Upper Farringdon Rd.
The Street
Maplecombe
Old Sidings
Pies Farm
Hilly Leaze
The Long House
Hall Farm
Upper Farringdon House
Farringdon Industrial Centre
Pies Copse
Brightstone
Short Wood
Wakes Wood
GU34
Brightstone Copse
Lord's Wood
Annetts Farm
Bright Stone House
Kitcombe Lodge
Ivy Farm
97
Kitcombe Copse
Kitcombe Farm House
Kitcombe Lane
Depot
Kitcombe House
Noar Copse
Kitcombe Lane
Dell Wood
South Downs
Kitcombe Wood
Common Barn Farm
Goldridge Plantation
Hunt's Plantation
Mary Lane
Newton Lane
Pelham Lodge
Marylane Plantation
Marylane Copse
Newton House
Inadown House
Inadown Farm
Ten Acre Plantation
Pelham Place
Lodge Farm
Ina Down Copse
Newton Valence Place Farm
The Knapp
The Lodge
Newton Valence Place
Plash Wood
Shotters Farm
Shotters Lane
Grove Copse
Rotherfield Park Estate
112
East Tisted

West Worldham
Hartley Mauditt
SELBORNE
Newton Valence
Galley Hill
NATIONAL PARK
SELBORNE ROAD
B3006
HIGH STREET
FOUNTAIN RD.
Darby's Dell
Copse Close
Caker Stream
Round House
Barleywood Farm
Little Wood Copse
West Worldham Farm
Manor Farm
Hartley Mauditt House
Jeffries Cottages
Old Elm
Hartley Pond
Hartley Park
Park Hanger
Warner's Hanger
Warner's Wood
Pagletts Green Cottages
HARTLEY PARK FARM BUSINESS CENTRE
Hartley Park Farm
Windmill Cottages
Wick Hill Cottage
Wick Hill Hanger
Wick Hill Farm
Norton Farm
Frenchmare Copse
LANE
Fielder's Farm
Sunny View
Milking Hanger
Wells Plantation
Wick Wood
Long Copse
Coombe Wood
Priory Fa
PRIORY LA.
Stream
Oakhanger
Bush Down
Long Lythe
Dorton
Nine Acres
Rhodehill Bungalow
Rhode Hill
Northfield Hill
Grange Farm
GOSLINGS CFT.
GANDERS CL.
The Plantation
Short Lythe
GRACIOUS LANE
Coneycroft
Lythe House
WOOD
Selborne C of E Prim. Sch.
THE PLESTOR
Selborne Pottery
HUCKERS LA.
Sparrow's Hanger
Sewage Works
New Barn Farm
The Granary
Coneycroft Hanger
Coneycroft Bottom
STREET
Gilbert White's House & Garden (& the Oates Collection)
HASTARDS LA.
STREAM END DR.
MALTBY'S
Oaktree Farm
Woodside
Pleasure Row Plantation
Coneycroft Hill
Selbourne Hanger
PLUM FELL LANE
Romany Folklore Museum
Under the Hill
HONEY
The Scrubbs
SELBORNE COMMON
Kite Hill
ADAMS LA.
Rec. Grd.
Hopkiln
LANE
Ketcher's Farm
KETCHERS FLD.
Wood Pond
Selborne Hill
Burhunt Cottages
SOTHERINGTON
Manor House
Galley Hill Farm
Burhunt Farm
HULLAM LANE
Longhope
Homestead Farm
GREEN LANE
HILL
NOAR
Burhunt Hanger
Adderh Hang
Outshott Hanger
Charity
81
100
113
H J K L M N G
1 2 3 4 5 6 7 8 9
73 74 475
37 36 35 34 33

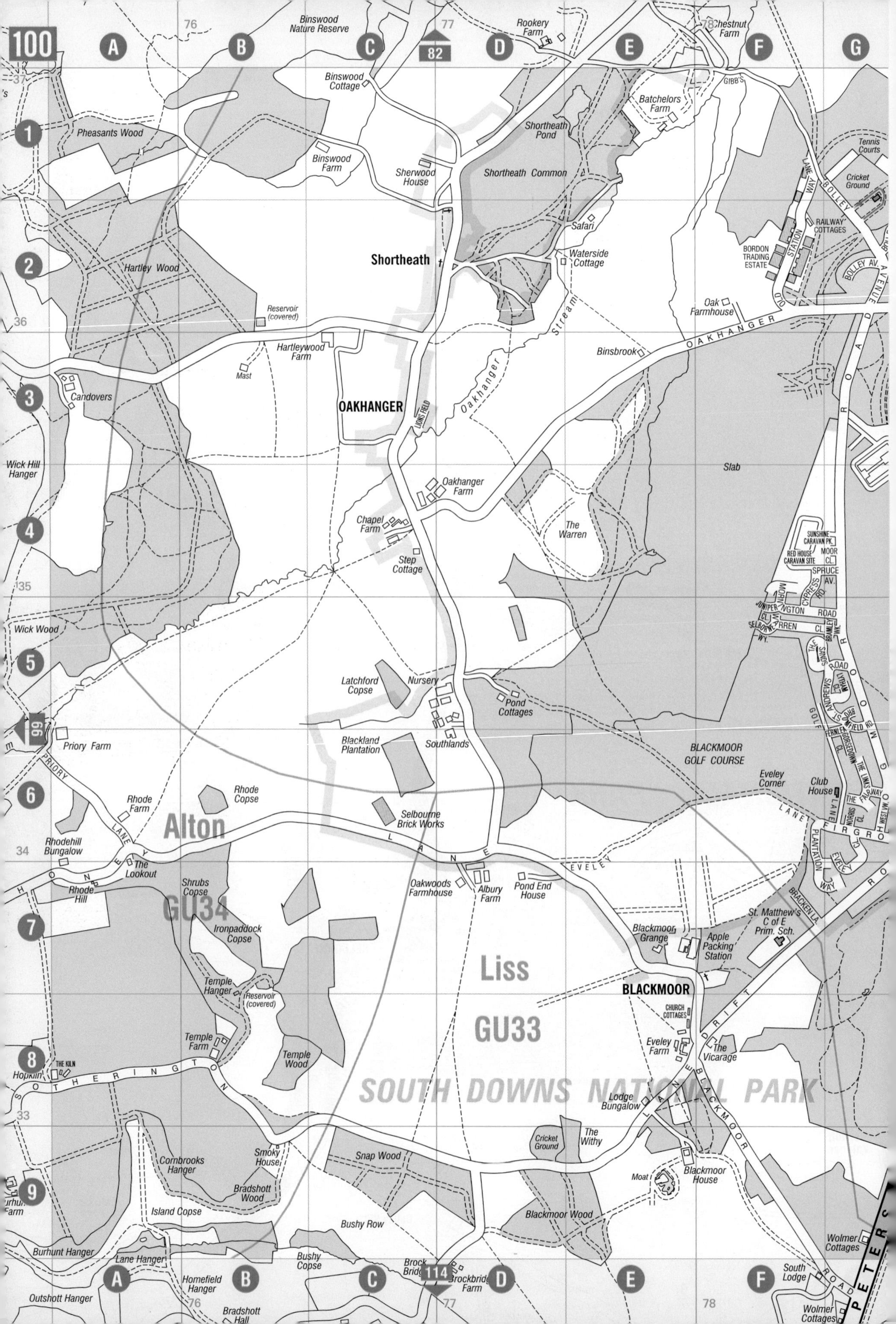
Binswood Nature Reserve
Rookery Farm
Chestnut Farm
82
Binswood Cottage
Batchelors Farm
Pheasants Wood
Shortheath Pond
Binswood Farm
Sherwood House
Shortheath Common
Tennis Courts
Cricket Ground
Safari
RAILWAY COTTAGES
BORDON TRADING ESTATE
Hartley Wood
Shortheath
Waterside Cottage
Reservoir (covered)
Oak Farmhouse
Hartleywood Farm
Binsbrook
OAKHANGER ROAD
Mast
Candovers
OAKHANGER
LIONS FIELD
Oakhanger Stream
Wick Hill Hanger
Slab
Oakhanger Farm
Chapel Farm
The Warren
Step Cottage
SUNSHINE CARAVAN PK.
RED HOUSE CARAVAN SITE
MOOR CL.
SPRUCE AV.
Wick Wood
Latchford Copse
Nursery
Pond Cottages
99
Priory Farm
Blackland Plantation
Southlands
BLACKMOOR GOLF COURSE
Eveley Corner
Club House
Rhode Farm
Rhode Copse
Selbourne Brick Works
Alton
Rhodehill Bungalow
ALTON LANE
EVELEY LANE
The Lookout
Rhode Hill
Shrubs Copse
Oakwoods Farmhouse
Albury Farm
Pond End House
GU34
Ironpaddock Copse
Blackmoor Grange
Apple Packing Station
St. Matthew's C of E Prim. Sch.
Liss
Temple Hanger
Reservoir (covered)
BLACKMOOR
CHURCH COTTAGES
Temple Farm
GU33
Eveley Farm
The Vicarage
THE KILN
Hopkin
Temple Wood
SOTHERINGTON LANE
SOUTH DOWNS NATIONAL PARK
Lodge Bungalow
BLACKMOOR LANE
Cricket Ground
The Withy
Cornbrooks Hanger
Smoky House
Snap Wood
Bradshott Wood
Moat
Blackmoor House
Island Copse
Bushy Row
Blackmoor Wood
Burhunt Hanger
Lane Hanger
Bushy Copse
Brock Bridge
Brockbridge Farm
114
Wolmer Cottages
South Lodge
Homefield Hanger
Outshott Hanger
Bradshott Hall
Wolmer Cottages
76
77
78
36
35
34
33

BORDON
Bordon Camp
Whitehill
Deadwater
LINDFORD
HEADLEY
Standford
Hollywater
Bordon GU35
Liphook GU30
WOOLMER FOREST
HOGMOOR INCLOSURE
PASSFIELD COMMON
BRIMSTONE INCLOSURE
Alexandra Park
Eveley Wood
Deadwater Valley Local Nature Reserve
Hollywater Pond
Lynchborough Wood
Round Hill
Fern Hill
Park Hill
Horsebush Hill
Linchborough Park
Keeper's Hill
Polecat Hill
Thorn Hill
Long Down
Cranmer Pond
Cranmer Bottom
Rifle Range
HIGH STREET CAMP ROAD
FARNHAM ROAD
LINDFORD ROAD
STATION ROAD
BUDDS LANE
LIPHOOK ROAD
HEADLEY ROAD
STANDFORD LANE
HOLLYWATER ROAD
WHITEHILL ROAD
WALLDOWN ROAD
MILL CHASE ROAD
83
102
115

HEADLEY
ARFORD
Beech Hill
GRAYSHOTT
HEADLEY DOWN
Bordon
GU35
Hilland Woods
Headley Grange Farm
Headley Grange
LUDSHOTT COMMON
Gentle's Copse
Dog Kennel Firs
Sheep Grove
The Chestnuts
Passfield
Passfield Common
Liphook
GU30
Long Plantation
The Hanger
Spring Pond Hanger
Conford
BRAMSHOTT
Bramshott Vale
Cold Ash Hill
Hurland Copse
High Hurlands
Coachroad Plantation
Round Clump
The Frith
The Loampits
Woolmead Farm
Woolmer Farm
Garden Clump
Ludshott Manor
Spring Pond Lodge
Spring Pond
Downlands Farm
Downlands House
Downlands Lodge
Glebe House Farm
The Glebe House
Falkners
Playing Field
Bramshott Manor
Nutscale House
Westering
Woodlands
Phoenix House
Penally Farm
Radford Bri.
Conford Park Farm
Conford Park Gate
Griggsgreen Copse
Holm Hills
Conford Moor
Passfield Manor
Waterside Copse
Nursery
Passfield Farm
Passfield House Farm
Garthwaite
Baldpate Cottage
Elm Grove Farm
Cooper's Bridge Farm
Coopers Bri.
Oaklea Farm
The Peppercorn
Quinces
Bramshott Vale Farm
Gunsgreen
Fairlands
North Lodge
Firtree Cottage
Curtis Farm
Curtis's Hill
Hartfield Farm
The Hanger
The Oaks
The Holme C. of E. Prim. Sch.
Hall
Library
Hall
Rec. Grd.
Foxwood Lodge
Benifold
Windridge
Pentlow
Beech Hill Common
Beech Hill Ho.
Community Centre
Cain Farm
Land of Nod
Sewage Works
Playing Field
Tennis Cts.
B3002
B3004
B2171
A3
LIPHOOK BY-PASS
PORTS
LONDON RD.
STANDFORD LANE
HILL HEAD
LANE HILL
HOUSE HILL
TUNBRIDGE LANE
WOOLMER LANE
GENTLES LANE
BRAMSHOTT ROAD
PASSFIELD ROAD
HEADLEY LA.
LIPHOOK ROAD
HURLAND LANE
TULLS LANE
VALE BEECH
POND ROAD
FURZE HILL
FULLERS ROAD
MILL LA.
CRABTREE LA.
LONG CROSS HILL
BARLEY MOW HILL
COMMON HILL
HEADLEY HILL ROAD
BURGH HILL ROAD
CHURCH LANE
RECTORY LANE
CHURCH ROAD
LIMES CL.
HEWSHOTT LA.
102
116
101
84
83
82
84
85
37
36
35
34
33
A B C D E F G
1 2 3 4 5 6 7 8 9

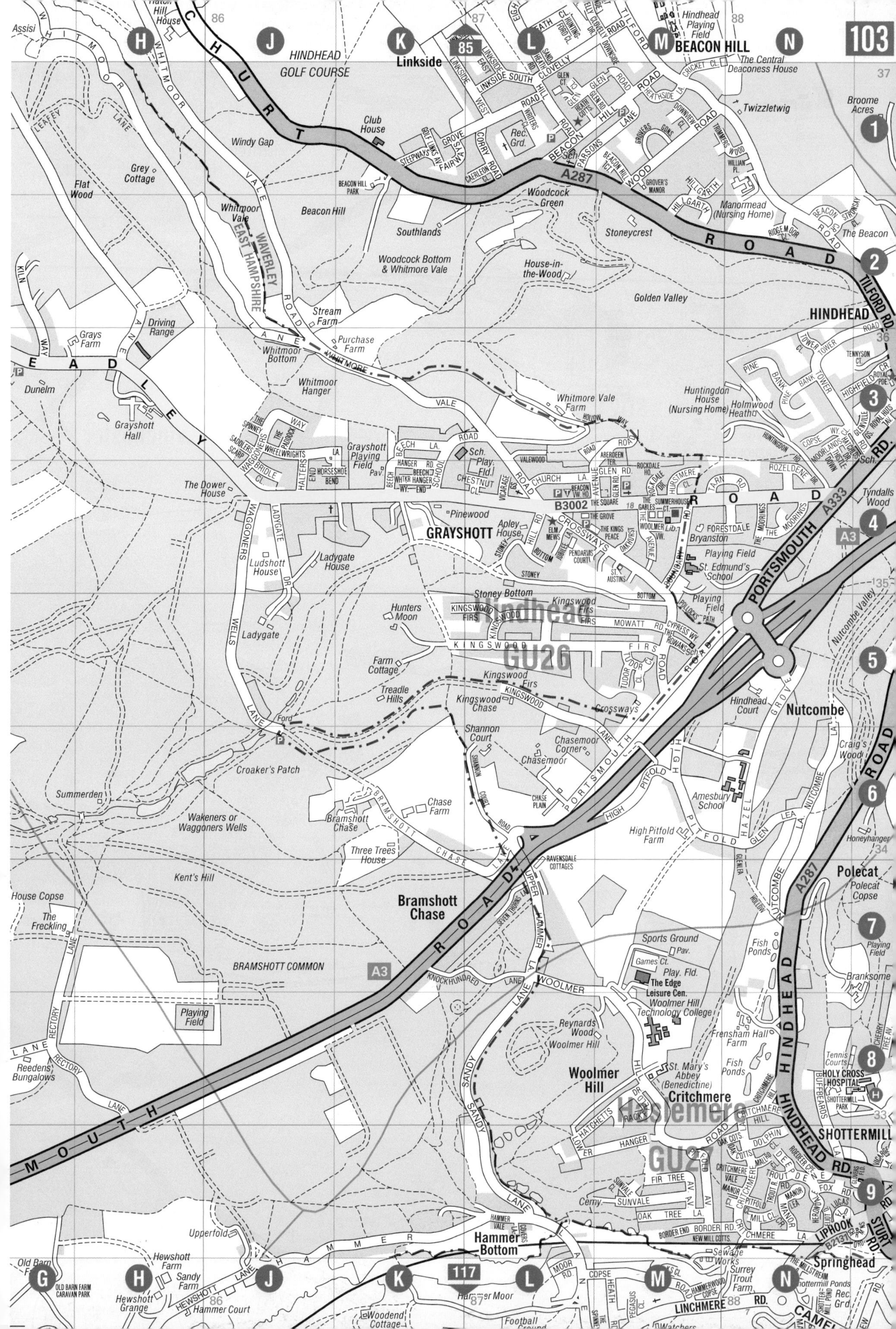
103
85
117
BEACON HILL
Linkside
HINDHEAD GOLF COURSE
Club House
Windy Gap
Grey Cottage
Flat Wood
Whitmoor Vale
Beacon Hill
Southlands
Woodcock Green
Stoneycrest
Manormead (Nursing Home)
The Beacon
The Central Deaconess House
Twizzletwig
Broome Acres
Woodcock Bottom & Whitmore Vale
House-in-the-Wood
Golden Valley
HINDHEAD
Stream Farm
Purchase Farm
Whitmoor Bottom
Driving Range
Grays Farm
Dunelm
Whitmoor Hanger
Grayshott Hall
Whitmore Vale Farm
Huntingdon House (Nursing Home)
Holmwood Heath
Grayshott Playing Field
The Dower House
GRAYSHOTT
Pinewood
Apley House
Bryanston
Playing Field
St. Edmund's School
Tyndalls Wood
Ludshott House
Ladygate House
Ladygate
Hunters Moon
Stoney Bottom
Kingswood Firs
Hindhead GU26
Farm Cottage
Treadle Hills
Kingswood Chase
Crossways
Nutcombe Valley
Hindhead Court
Nutcombe
Craig's Wood
Shannon Court
Chasemoor Corner
Chasemoor
Croaker's Patch
Summerden
Wakeners or Waggoners Wells
Chase Farm
Bramshott Chase
Three Trees House
Amesbury School
High Pitfold Farm
Honeyhanger
Polecat
Polecat Copse
Kent's Hill
House Copse
The Freckling
Bramshott Chase
BRAMSHOTT COMMON
Sports Ground
The Edge Leisure Cen.
Woolmer Hill Technology College
Playing Field
Fish Ponds
Branksome
Reynards Wood
Woolmer Hill
Frensham Hall Farm
Reedens Bungalows
St. Mary's Abbey (Benedictine)
Critchmere
Haslemere GU27
HOLY CROSS HOSPITAL
SHOTTERMILL
Cemy.
Upperfold
Hammer Bottom
Springhead
Hewshott Farm
Sandy Farm
Hewshott Grange
Hammer Court
Old Barn Farm
OLD BARN FARM CARAVAN PARK
Hammer Moor
Sewage Works
Surrey Trout Farm
Woodend Cottage
CHURT ROAD
A287
TILFORD RD.
HEADLEY ROAD
B3002
PORTSMOUTH ROAD
A333
A3
HINDHEAD ROAD
HAMMER LANE
SANDY LANE
LINCHMERE RD.
WAVERLEY LANE
WHITMORE VALE
KINGSWOOD FIRS
BRAMSHOTT CHASE
WOOLMER LANE
HIGH PITFOLD
RECTORY LANE
EAST HAMPSHIRE
H J K L M N G
1 2 3 4 5 6 7 8 9
86 87 88
37 36 35 34 33

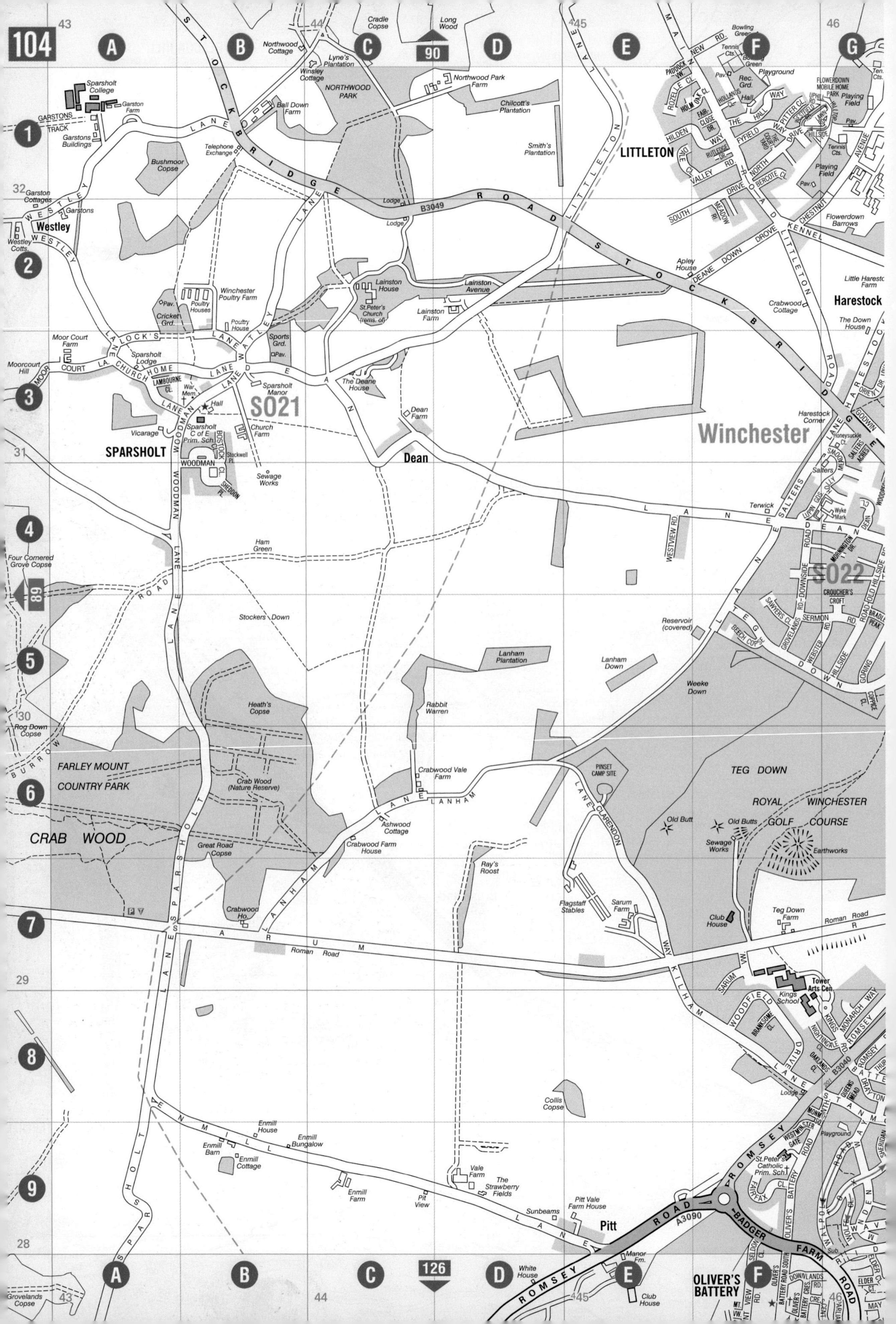

Sparsholt College
Garston Farm
Garstons Track
Garstons Buildings
Westley
Westley Cotts.
Garston Cottages
Bushmoor Copse
Telephone Exchange
Stockbridge Lane
Northwood Cottage
Cradle Copse
Long Wood
Lyne's Plantation
Winsley Cottage
Northwood Park
Ball Down Farm
Northwood Park Farm
Chilcott's Plantation
Smith's Plantation
Littleton
Stockbridge Road
B3049
Lodge
Lainston House
Lainston Avenue
St.Peter's Church (rems. of)
Lainston Farm
Winchester Poultry Farm
Poultry Houses
Poultry House
Cricket Grd.
Sports Grd.
Moor Court Farm
Moorcourt Hill
Sparsholt Lodge
Lambourne Cl.
Lock's Lane
Church Lane
Home Lane
Watley Lane
Deane
Sparsholt Manor
SO21
The Deane House
Dean Farm
Dean
War Mem.
Hall
Sparsholt C of E Prim. Sch.
Vicarage
Church Farm
Sparsholt
Woodman Lane
Bostock Cl.
Stockwell Pl.
Sheddon Pl.
Sewage Works
Apley House
Deane Down Drove
Kennel Lane
Crabwood Cottage
Harestock
Little Harestock Farm
The Down House
Harestock Corner
Winchester
Salters Lane
Terwick
Westview Rd.
Teg Down
SO22
Croucher's Croft
Reservoir (covered)
Beech Copse
Four Cornered Grove Copse
89
Ham Green
Stockers Down
Lanham Plantation
Lanham Down
Weeke Down
Heath's Copse
Rabbit Warren
Rog Down Copse
Burrow
Farley Mount Country Park
Crab Wood (Nature Reserve)
Crab Wood
Crabwood Vale Farm
Lanham Lane
Ashwood Cottage
Crabwood Farm House
Great Road Copse
Pinset Camp Site
Clarendon Lane
Teg Down
Royal Winchester Golf Course
Old Butt
Old Butts
Sewage Works
Earthworks
Ray's Roost
Flagstaff Stables
Sarum Farm
Club House
Teg Down Farm
Roman Road
Crabwood Ho.
Sarum Road
Kilham Lane
Sarum Way
Tower Arts Cen.
Kings School
Woodfield Dr.
Branksome Cl.
Monarch Way
Romsey Road
B3040
Oakland Lane
Lodge
Collis Copse
Enmill Lane
Enmill House
Enmill Bungalow
Enmill Barn
Enmill Cottage
Enmill Farm
Pit View
Vale Farm
The Strawberry Fields
Sunbeams
Pitt Vale Farm House
Pitt
Romsey Road
A3090
Badger Farm Road
St.Peter's Catholic Prim. Sch.
Playground
Fairfax Cl.
Westminster Gate
Manor Fm.
White House
Club House
Oliver's Battery
Grovelands Copse
Sparsholt Lane
Littleton Lane
Main Road
Bowling Green
Tennis Cts.
Rec. Grd.
Playground
Hall
Pav.
The Hall Way
Hilden Way
Valley Rd.
North Drive
Bercote Cl.
South Drive
Meadow Ri.
Pitter Cl.
Flowerdown Mobile Home Park
Playing Field
Tennis Cts.
Flowerdown Barrows
126
90

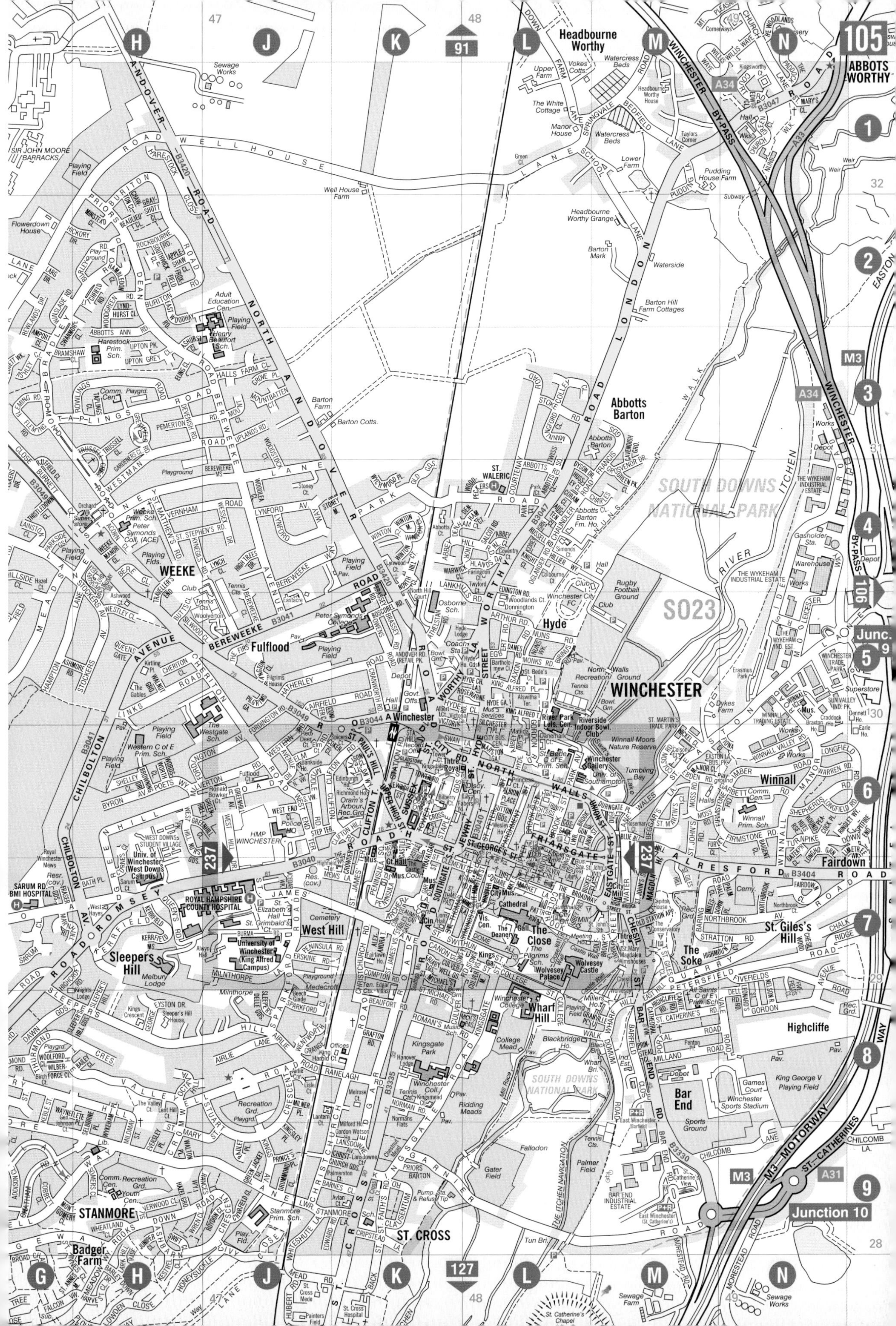

105
91
127
237
106
Headbourne Worthy
ABBOTTS WORTHY
Sewage Works
Well House Farm
WELLHOUSE LANE
SIR JOHN MOORE BARRACKS
Playing Field
Flowerdown House
ANDOVER ROAD
NORTH ANDOVER ROAD
Harestock Prim. Sch.
Adult Education Cen.
Henry Beaufort Sch.
Barton Farm
Barton Cotts.
Upper Farm
Vokes Cotts.
Watercress Beds
The White Cottage
Manor House
Lower Farm
Pudding House Farm
Headbourne Worthy Grange
Barton Mark
Waterside
Barton Hill Farm Cottages
LONDON ROAD
WINCHESTER BY-PASS
Abbotts Barton
SOUTH DOWNS NATIONAL PARK
ST. WALERIC
RIVER ITCHEN
THE WYKEHAM INDUSTRIAL ESTATE
Gasholder Sta.
Warehouse
Depot
Works
WEEKE
Peter Symonds Coll. (ACE)
Fulflood
Peter Symonds College
Osborne Sch.
Hyde
Rugby Football Ground
Winchester City FC
SO23
WINCHESTER
North Walls Recreation Ground
River Park Leis. Cen.
Riverside Indoor Bowl Club
Winnall Moors Nature Reserve
Tumbling Bay
Winchester Gallery
Univ. Southampton
Junc. 9
Winchester Trade Park
Superstore
Sun Valley Ind. Pk.
Dykes Farm
Winnall
Winnall Prim. Sch.
Fairdown
ALRESFORD ROAD
B3404
The Westgate Sch.
Western C of E Prim. Sch.
HMP WINCHESTER
Univ. of Winchester (West Downs Campus)
ROYAL HAMPSHIRE COUNTY HOSPITAL
SARUM RD. BMI HOSPITAL
ROMSEY ROAD
CHILBOLTON AVENUE
Sleepers Hill
Melbury Lodge
University of Winchester (King Alfred Campus)
West Hill
Cemetery
Cathedral
The Close
The Deanery
The Pilgrims Sch.
Wolvesey Castle
Wolvesey Palace
Winchester College
Wharf Hill
College Mead
Kingsgate Park
Winchester Coll.
Ridding Meads
Fallodon
Gater Field
Palmer Field
THE ITCHEN NAVIGATION
St. Giles's Hill
The Soke
Highcliffe
Pav.
King George V Playing Field
Games Court
Winchester Sports Stadium
Bar End
Sports Ground
BAR END INDUSTRIAL ESTATE
East Winchester
M3 MOTORWAY
ST. CATHERINES WAY
A31
M3
A34
Junction 10
CHILCOMB LA.
Recreation Ground
STANMORE
Stanmore Prim. Sch.
Badger Farm
St. Cross
ST. CROSS
Sewage Farm
Sewage Works
St. Catherine's Chapel
St. Cross Hospital
Tun Bri.

ABBOTS WORTHY
Abbotsworthy House
Worthy Park Home Farm
The Worthy
Mill
Ford
Subway
92
Easton Bridge
New Cott.
RIVER ITCHEN
Chilland Ho.
Lower Chilland House
Weir
M3
M3 MOTORWAY
Pumping Station
WATER LA.
The Old Rectory
CHURCH LANE
The Terrace
EASTON
Power House
Easton Lodge
MALTHOUSE
Hall
Sports Grd.
High Down
Chapel Field
Cocket's Mead
Earthwork
Low Grounds
Beech Hill
EASTON DOWN
Dairy Farm
Dairy Cottages
Lone Barn
EASTON LANE
CHAPEL LANE
Easton Manor Farm
DUKES
WINCHESTER BY-PASS
Works
Depot
A33
Winchester
SO21
Winnall Cottage Farm
White Hill Cott.
Shoulder of Mutton Farm
Harfield Farm
Harley Hill
Junction 9
105
Superstore
SUN VALLEY IND. PK.
Dennett Ho.
Earle Ho.
SOUTH DOWNS
Larkwhistle Farm
Pits Copse
Winnall Down Copse
Roseacre
Winnall Down Farm
Pits Farm
Three Acres
A272
SPITFIRE LINK
LONGFIELD RD.
WARREN RD.
St. Swithun's School
No Man's Land
The Holding
MORN HILL CARAVAN SITE
LEIGH HOUSE
Magdalen Hill Farm
Narcunda
Glencross
Green Pastures
Pits Farm House
Tennis Cts.
Fairdown
ALRESFORD ROAD
B3404
Works
Lodge
MAGDALEN HILL DOWN
Magdalen Hill Cemetery
WYKEHAM PARK
The Firs
Satellite Teleport
CHALK RIDGE
PETERSFIELD ROAD
Intech Science Centre & Planetarium
A31
KINGS LANE
The Bungalow
Pav.
Sports Ground
Rec. Grd.
Highcliffe
Chilcomb Down
Works
ST. CATHERINES WAY
CHILCOMB
Range Cott.
The Manor House
Complyns
Chilcomb Manor
St. Kilda's
Hazeldown
Velpins Bank Plantation
Tops and Bottoms Plantation
Telegraph Clump
Telegraph Hill
GYPSY LANE
Hillacre
Chilcomb Ranges
Rookery Cottages
Deacon View
134
Little Golders
450
51
52

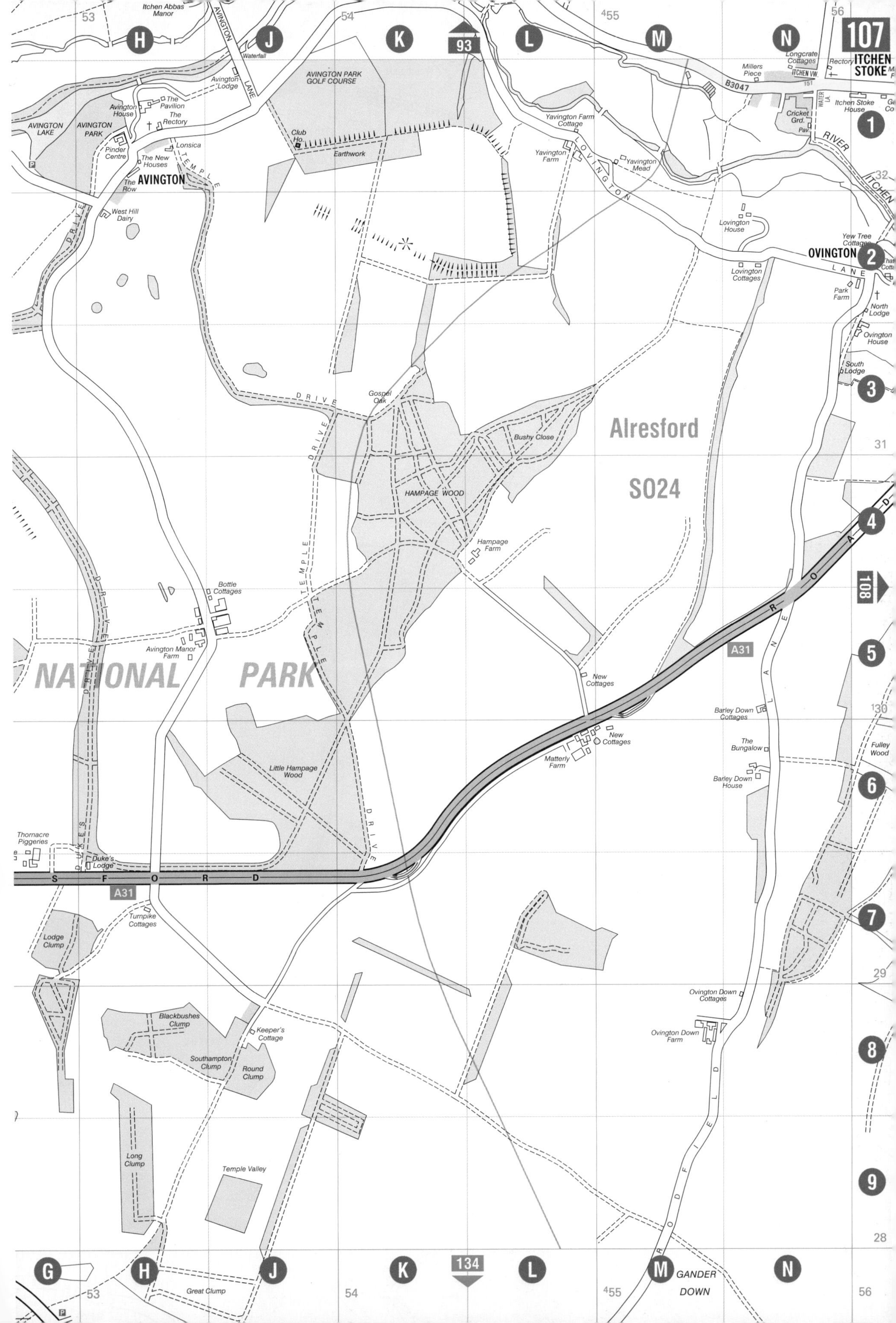

ITCHEN STOKE
Itchen Abbas Manor
Waterfall
Avington Lodge
AVINGTON PARK GOLF COURSE
Club Ho.
Earthwork
AVINGTON LAKE
AVINGTON PARK
Avington House
The Pavilion
The Rectory
Pinder Centre
Lonsica
The New Houses
The Row
AVINGTON
West Hill Dairy
Yavington Farm Cottage
Yavington Farm
Yavington Mead
LOVINGTON
Millers Piece
Longcrate Cottages
ITCHEN VW.
Rectory
B3047
Itchen Stoke House
Cricket Grd.
Pav.
WATER LA.
RIVER ITCHEN
Lovington House
Lovington Cottages
Yew Tree Cottage
OVINGTON
LANE
Park Farm
North Lodge
Ovington House
South Lodge
Gospel Oak
DRIVE
TEMPLE
Bushy Close
HAMPAGE WOOD
Hampage Farm
Alresford
SO24
Bottle Cottages
Avington Manor Farm
NATIONAL PARK
New Cottages
Matterly Farm
A31
ROAD
Barley Down Cottages
The Bungalow
Barley Down House
Fulley Wood
Little Hampage Wood
Thornacre Piggeries
DUKE'S DRIVE
Duke's Lodge
SFORD ROAD
Turnpike Cottages
Lodge Clump
Blackbushes Clump
Keeper's Cottage
Southampton Clump
Round Clump
Ovington Down Cottages
Ovington Down Farm
Long Clump
Temple Valley
ROD FIELD
Great Clump
GANDER DOWN

93
108
134

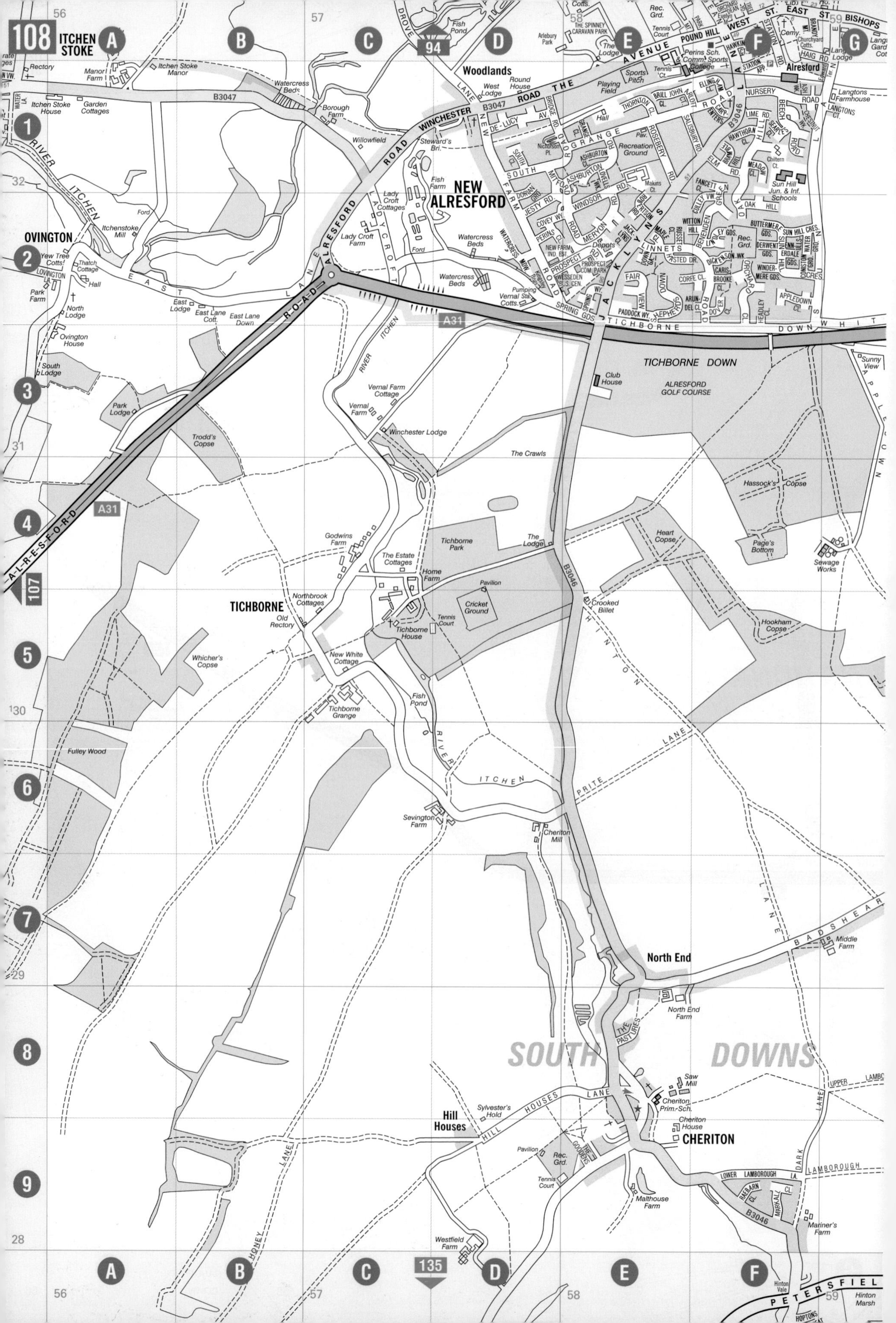
ITCHEN STOKE
OVINGTON
Itchen Stoke House
Garden Cottages
Manor Farm
Itchen Stoke Manor
Rectory
Watercress Beds
Borough Farm
Willowfield
Itchenstoke Mill
Yew Tree Cotts.
Thatch Cottage
Hall
Park Farm
North Lodge
Ovington House
South Lodge
Park Lodge
Trodd's Copse
East Lodge
East Lane Cott.
East Lane Down
Woodlands
West Lodge
Round House
Steward's Bri.
Fish Farm
Lady Croft Cottages
Lady Croft Farm
Ford
Watercress Beds
NEW ALRESFORD
Pumping Vernal Sta. Cotts.
THE SPINNEY CARAVAN PARK
Arlebury Park
The Lodge
Rec. Grd.
Tennis Court
Perins Sch. Comm. Sports College
Tennis Ct.
Sports Pitch
Playing Field
Hall
Pav.
Recreation Ground
Alresford
Cemy.
Churchyard Cotts.
Langtons Farmhouse
Sun Hill Jun. & Inf. Schools
Chiltern Ct.
Rec. Grd.
Depots
NEW FARM IND. EST.
WESSEDEN BUS. CEN.
PROSPECT COM. PARK
TICHBORNE DOWN
Club House
ALRESFORD GOLF COURSE
Sunny View
Vernal Farm Cottage
Vernal Farm
Winchester Lodge
The Crawls
Hassock's Copse
Heart Copse
Page's Bottom
Sewage Works
Tichborne Park
The Lodge
Godwins Farm
The Estate Cottages
Home Farm
Pavilion
Cricket Ground
Crooked Billet
Hookham Copse
TICHBORNE
Northbrook Cottages
Old Rectory
Tichborne House
Tennis Court
Whicher's Copse
New White Cottage
Tichborne Grange
Fish Pond
Fulley Wood
Sevington Farm
Cheriton Mill
North End
Middle Farm
North End Farm
SOUTH DOWNS
Saw Mill
Cheriton Prim. Sch.
Cheriton House
CHERITON
Sylvester's Hold
Hill Houses
Pavilion
Rec. Grd.
Tennis Court
Malthouse Farm
Mariner's Farm
Westfield Farm
Hinton Vale
Hinton Marsh
B3047
B3046
A31
A B C D E F G
56 57 58 59
28 29 30 31 32
1 2 3 4 5 6 7 8 9
94
107
135

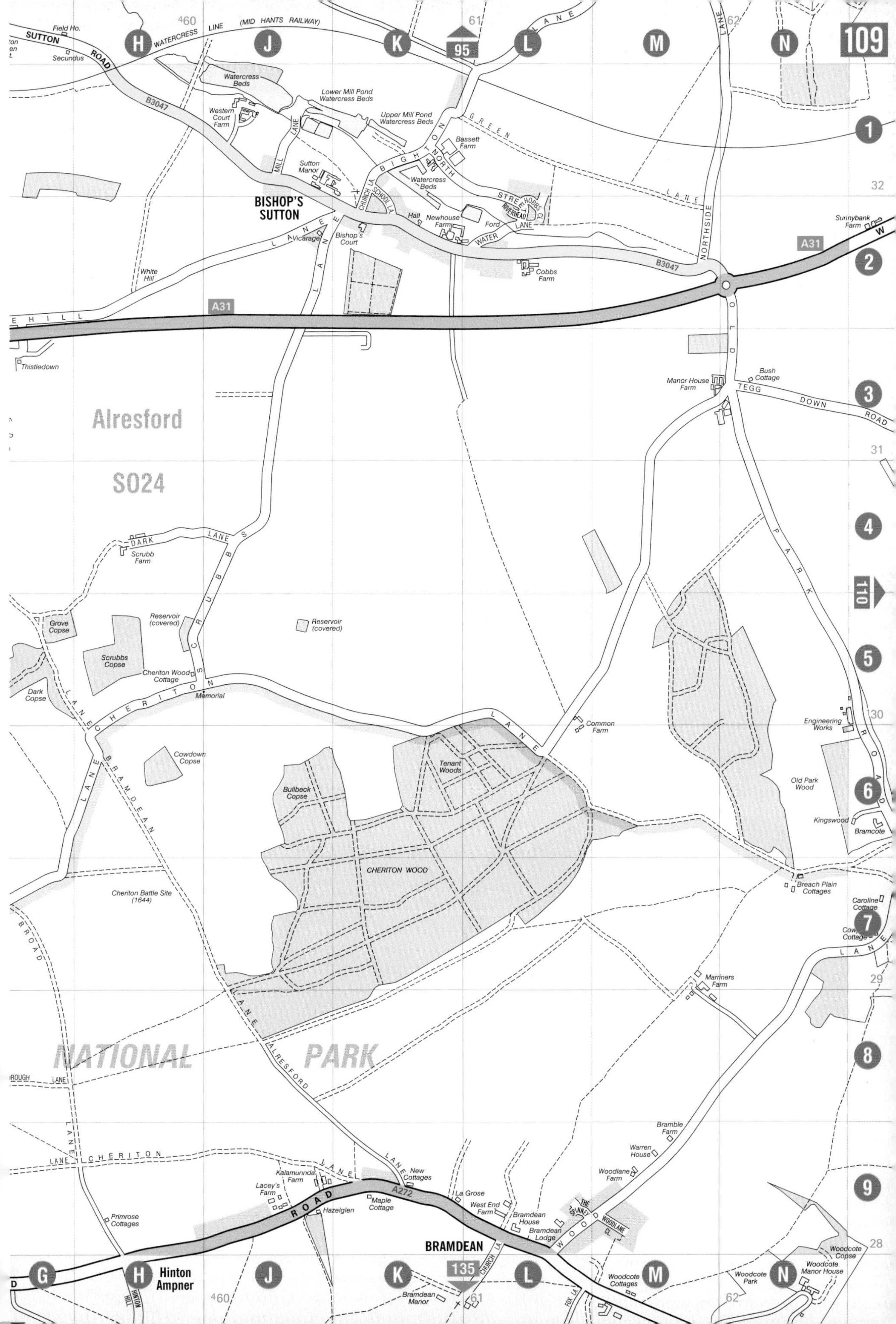
Alresford
SO24
BISHOP'S SUTTON
NATIONAL PARK
BRAMDEAN
Hinton Ampner
CHERITON WOOD
Watercress Beds
Lower Mill Pond Watercress Beds
Upper Mill Pond Watercress Beds
Western Court Farm
Bassett Farm
Sutton Manor
Watercress Beds
Vicarage
Bishop's Court
Hall
Newhouse Farm
Ford
Cobbs Farm
Sunnybank Farm
White Hill
Thistledown
Manor House Farm
Bush Cottage
Field Ho.
Secundus
Scrubb Farm
Reservoir (covered)
Reservoir (covered)
Grove Copse
Scrubbs Copse
Cheriton Wood Cottage
Memorial
Dark Copse
Cowdown Copse
Common Farm
Tenant Woods
Bullbeck Copse
Engineering Works
Old Park Wood
Kingswood
Bramcote
Breach Plain Cottages
Caroline Cottage
Cheriton Battle Site (1644)
Marriners Farm
Bramble Farm
Warren House
Woodlane Farm
Kalamunnda Farm
Lacey's Farm
New Cottages
Maple Cottage
Hazelglen
La Grose
West End Farm
Bramdean House
Bramdean Lodge
Primrose Cottages
Bramdean Manor
Woodcote Cottages
Woodcote Park
Woodcote Copse
Woodcote Manor House
WATERCRESS LINE (MID HANTS RAILWAY)
SUTTON ROAD
B3047
A31
A272
MILL LANE
CHURCH LA.
SCHOOL LA.
BIGHTON LANE
NORTH STREET
GREEN LANE
RIVERHEAD
HOBBS CL.
WATER LANE
NORTHSIDE LANE
OLD PARK ROAD
TEGG DOWN ROAD
DARK LANE
SCRUBBS LANE
CHERITON LANE
BRAMDEAN LANE
ALRESFORD LANE
BROAD ROAD
CHERITON LANE
WOOD LANE
THE SPINNEY
WOODLANE CL.
HINTON HILL
FOX LA.
ROAD
95
110
135
H J K L M N G
1 2 3 4 5 6 7 8 9
460 61 62
32 31 30 29 28

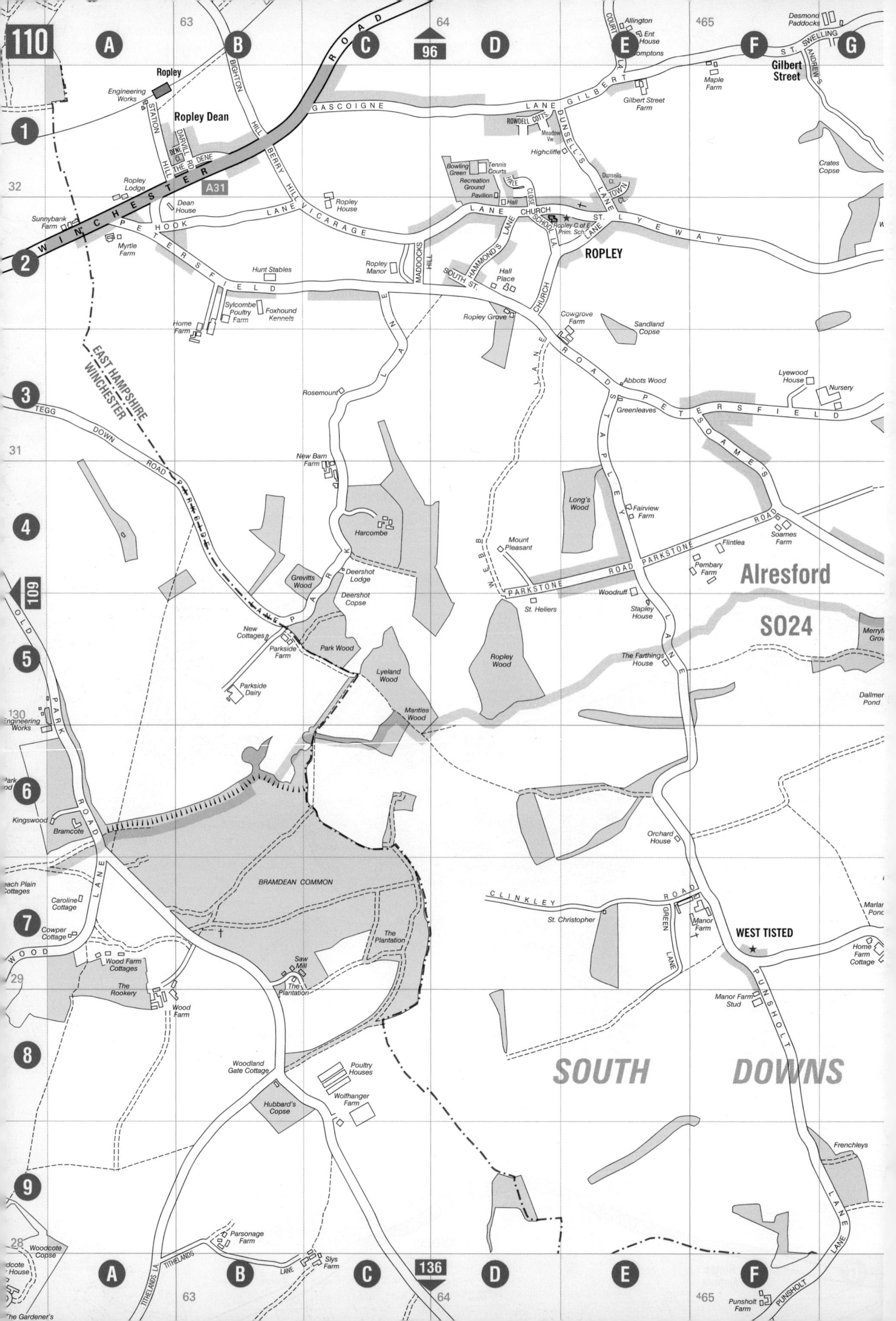

Ropley
Engineering Works
Ropley Dean
Gilbert Street
Allington
Ent House
Comptons
Desmond Paddocks
Maple Farm
Gilbert Street Farm
GASCOIGNE LANE
GILBERT ST.
SWELLING
ST. ANDREW'S
WINCHESTER ROAD
A31
BIGHTON HILL
BERRY HILL
STATION HILL
DARVILL RD
DENE CL.
THE DENE
ROWDELL COTTS.
Meadow Vw.
Highcliffe
DUNSELL'S LANE
Dunsells Ct.
TOWN CL.
Crates Copse
Ropley Lodge
Sunnybank Farm
Dean House
Ropley House
Bowling Green
Tennis Courts
Recreation Ground
Pavilion
Hall
HALE CLOSE
HOOK LANE
VICARAGE LANE
CHURCH ST.
SCHOOL LA.
Ropley C of E Prim. Sch.
LYEWAY
ROPLEY
Myrtle Farm
PETERSFIELD ROAD
Hunt Stables
Ropley Manor
MADDOCKS HILL
SOUTH ST.
HAMMOND'S LANE
Hall Place
CHURCH LANE
Sylcombe Poultry Farm
Foxhound Kennels
Home Farm
Ropley Grove
Cowgrove Farm
Sandland Copse
EAST HAMPSHIRE
WINCHESTER
Abbots Wood
Lyewood House
Nursery
Rosemount
TEGG DOWN ROAD
Greenleaves
PETERSFIELD ROAD
STAPLEY LANE
SOAMES LANE
New Barn Farm
Long's Wood
Fairview Farm
Harcombe
PARK LANE
WEBB LANE
Mount Pleasant
PARKSTONE ROAD
Flintlea
Soames Farm
Pembary Farm
Alresford
SO24
Grevitts Wood
Deershot Lodge
Deershot Copse
St. Heliers
Woodruff
Stapley House
OLD PARK ROAD
New Cottages
Parkside Farm
Park Wood
Ropley Wood
Lyeland Wood
Parkside Dairy
The Farthings House
Mantles Wood
Engineering Works
Dallmer Pond
Kingswood
Bramcote
Orchard House
BRAMDEAN COMMON
Caroline Cottage
Cowper Cottage
CLINKLEY ROAD
St. Christopher
GREEN LANE
Manor Farm
WEST TISTED
The Plantation
Saw Mill
Wood Farm Cottages
The Rookery
Wood Farm
Home Farm Cottage
Manor Farm Stud
PUNSHOLT LANE
WOOD LANE
Woodland Gate Cottage
Poultry Houses
SOUTH DOWNS
Hubbard's Copse
Wolfhanger Farm
Frenchleys
Parsonage Farm
Woodcote Copse
TITHELANDS LA.
TITHELANDS LANE
Slys Farm
Punsholt Farm
The Gardener's

96
109
136

Alton
GU34
Charlwood
MONKWOOD
Lane End
Basing Park
NATIONAL PARK
Winchester Wood
Lyeway Farm
Gillswood House
The Mountains Plantation
Plain Farm
Avenue Bungalow
Pine Cottages
Plaindell
Charlwood Farm
Lawrence House
Little Down
Winton Farm
Monkwood House
Treetops Farm
Dunn's Plantation
Broomfield Plantation
Vale Farm
Maybank Farm
Hill House
Farley Farm
The Priors Way
Stony Brow
Stonybrow Plantation
Stonybrow Wood
Oak Wood
Short Wood
Camouflage Paintball
Hedge Corner Farm
Merryfield Farm
Inham's Wood
Knight's Wood
West Tisted Common
Brewer's Farm
Wyatt's Wood
Woodside Farm
Bottom Farm
Bottom Farm Cottage
Pond Cottage
Long House
Brick Kiln Farm
Bridgefield House
New Copse
Old Lodge
The Grove
Court Farm
Cannon Dell
Railway Cottages
Little Ashen Wood
Ashen Wood House
Oakleigh Farm
Basing Barns
Basing Home Farm
Basing Park
Ashen Wood
The Jumps
Broom Farm
Bagmore Copse
Coles Bungalow
ROTHERFIELD PARK ESTATE
LYEWAY LANE
PETERSFIELD ROAD
FARM ROAD
ROPLEY ROAD
KILN LANE
BREWERS LANE
FAWLEY LANE
BASING DEAN LANE
LANE HILL
SMUGGLER'S LANE
CHARLWOOD LANE
A32
97
112
137

ROTHERFIELD PARK ESTATE
ROTHERFIELD PARK
EAST TISTED
Home Farm
Home Field Cottages
Old Place Farm
SHOTTERS LANE
Grove Copse
Heards Farm
ROPLEY ROAD
Keepers Cottage
Anchor Cottages
A32
Playing Field
Pavilion
SHELL LANE
Monk's Lodge
Goleigh Wood
Alton
GU34
Colemore House
COLEMORE
Manor Farm
Lye Farm
SOUTH DOWNS
Slade Farm
Penny Hill House
Keepers Cottage
Beckstedde Farm House
Beckstedde
Hedge Corner Farm
Common Cottages
COLEMORE
Windmill Farm
COLEMORE LANE
Field Farm Cottage
Lupin Farm
Beech Bungalow
Oaklands Farm
Hermitage House
Hermitage Farm
Hermitage Copse
COLEMORE COMMON
Windmill Copse
Copse Farm
Windmill Farm Cottages
Upper Blackdown Farm
MONKEY LANE
Gunner's Plantation
Hatch Plantation
Little Barnett
Reservoir (covered)
Seven Wells Plantation
CLAYPIT LANE
Barnet Side
Barnet Side Farm
Barnet Side Cottage
Claypit Farm
Severn Wells
Temple Copse
RAGMORE LANE
Hall Place
Alexander's Farm
Ragmore Farm
Chawner's Plantation
Froxfield Drive
KING'S LANE
GREEN LANE
ALEXANDERS LANE
BARNET SIDE LANE
Coles
Coles Bungalow
BASING

98
111
138

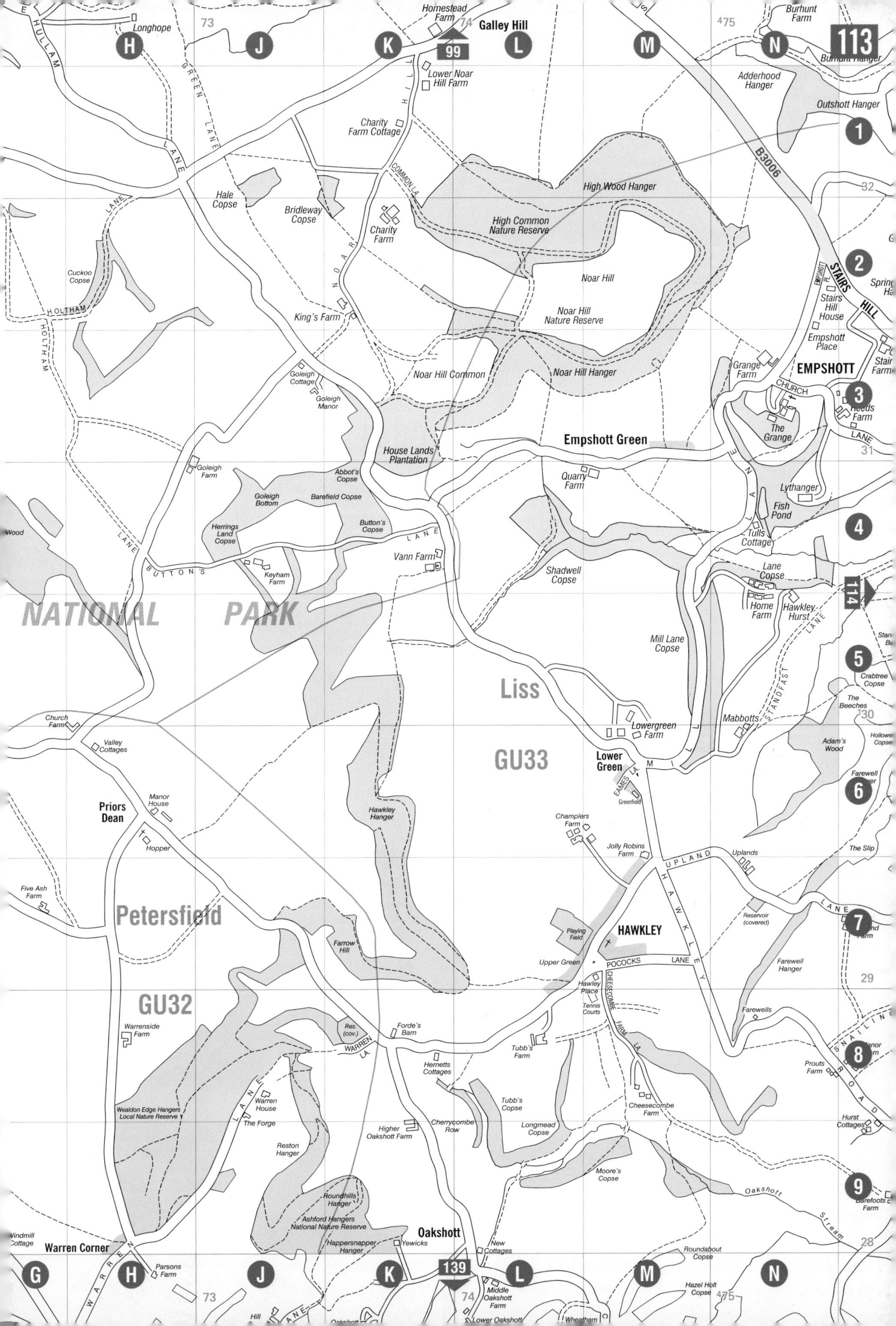
Galley Hill
Homestead Farm
Longhope
Lower Noar Hill Farm
Charity Farm Cottage
Burhunt Farm
Burhunt Hanger
Adderhood Hanger
Outshott Hanger
B3006
High Wood Hanger
High Common Nature Reserve
Hale Copse
Bridleway Copse
Charity Farm
Noar Hill
Noar Hill Nature Reserve
Cuckoo Copse
King's Farm
Stairs Hill House
Empshott Place
EMPSHOTT
Grange Farm
Noar Hill Common
Noar Hill Hanger
Goleigh Cottage
Goleigh Manor
The Grange
Reeds Farm
Empshott Green
House Lands Plantation
Goleigh Farm
Abbot's Copse
Quarry Farm
Lythanger
Goleigh Bottom
Barefield Copse
Fish Pond
Herrings Land Copse
Button's Copse
Tulls Cottage
Vann Farm
Shadwell Copse
Lane Copse
Keyham Farm
Home Farm
Hawkley Hurst
NATIONAL PARK
Mill Lane Copse
Liss
Crabtree Copse
The Beeches
Mabbotts
Church Farm
Valley Cottages
Lowergreen Farm
Adam's Wood
GU33
Lower Green
Farewell
Priors Dean
Manor House
Hawkley Hanger
Greenfield
Champlers Farm
Hopper
Jolly Robins Farm
Uplands
The Slip
Five Ash Farm
Petersfield
Reservoir (covered)
HAWKLEY
Playing Field
Farrow Hill
Upper Green
Hawley Place
Tennis Courts
Farewell Hanger
GU32
Farewells
Warrenside Farm
Res. (cov.)
Forde's Barn
Tubb's Farm
Hernetts Cottages
Prouts Farm
Wealdon Edge Hangers Local Nature Reserve
Warren House
The Forge
Tubb's Copse
Cheesecombe Farm
Cherrycombe Row
Higher Oakshott Farm
Longmead Copse
Hurst Cottages
Reston Hanger
Moore's Copse
Oakshott Stream
Barefoots Farm
Roundhills Hanger
Ashford Hangers National Nature Reserve
Oakshott
Happersnapper Hanger
Yewicks
New Cottages
Windmill Cottage
Warren Corner
Parsons Farm
Roundabout Copse
Hazel Holt Copse
Middle Oakshott Farm
Lower Oakshott
Wheatham
Hill
Oakshott
HULLAM LANE
GREEN LANE
HOLTHAM LANE
HOLTHAM
NOAR HILL
COMMON LA.
STAIRS HILL
EMPSHOTT PL.
CHURCH LANE
BUTTON'S LANE
STANDFAST LANE
MILL LANE
EAMES LA.
UPLAND LANE
HAWKLEY
POCOCKS LANE
CHEESECOMBE FARM LA.
WARREN LA.
WARREN LANE
SNAILING ROAD
99
114
139
73
74
475
32
31
30
29
28
H J K L M N G
1 2 3 4 5 6 7 8 9

Liss
GU33
SOUTH DOWNS
GREATHAM
EMPSHOTT
Burgates
West Liss
Liss Forest
East Liss
Liss
100
113
140
A
B
C
D
E
F
G
1
2
3
4
5
6
7
8
9
76
77
78
32
31
30
29
28
Burhunt Farm
Island Copse
Bushy Row
Blackmoor Wood
Burhunt Hanger
Lane Hanger
Outshott Hanger
Homefield Hanger
Bushy Copse
Brock Bridge
Brockbridge Farm
Bradshott Hall
Bradshott
Lower Hanger
Snap House
Yard Farm
Squiresfield Hanger
North Lodge
Greenwood Farm
Le Court Hanger
Spring Garden Hanger
Laundry Cottage
Lawrence's Copse
LE COURT
Stairs Hill House
Empshott Place
Stairs Hill Farmhouse
STAIRS HILL
B3006
Reeds Farm
Empshott Lodge
CHURCH
Cott's Shaw
South Lodge
Great Wood
Copse House
Little Wood
Cam Green Cottage
Pilgrims Way
CHURCH LANE
River Rother
Mill Farm
Mill Cottage
Greatham Mill Gdn.
SELBORNE RD.
Standfast Barn
Bulls Brook
Kemps Place
Crabtree Copse
The Beeches
Inholms Copse
Adam's Wood
Hollowell Copse
Farewell Hanger
Ford-Arun
Parklands
Hurst Farm
Manor Cottage
Park Lands Farm
Hatchmoor Farm
Ham Barn Farm
Lowerbarn Copse
The Slip
UPLAND LANE
SNAILING LANE
Scotland Farm
Primmers
Warren Pond
Manor Barn
Hurst Common
HAWKLEY ROAD
Hurst Cottages
Brickyard Cottages
Berrygrove Farm
Berrygrove Copse
Park Cottages
Lyss Place Farm
Lyss Place
Barefoots Farm
Stream
WHEATHAM
Hazel Copse
Sheepcrafts Copse
Ridges Cottage
Benhams House
BENHAM'S LANE
Knightsfield Copse
Benhams Farm
Firsplat Copse
Forest Side Farm
Lowergroves Copse
Keepers Cottage
South Lodge
Wolmer Cottages
BLACKMOOR ROAD
PETERSFIELD ROAD
A325
WOOLMER
DIGBY WAY
SILVER BIRCH WAY
Applepie Corner
The Coach House
King's Holt
Play. Fld
LODMOOR
LONGMOOR RD
HOPESWOOD
THE OAKS
WOLFMERE LA.
Moor Cottage
Reservoir
Deal Farm
BAKERS FIELD
Playing Field
Nursery
Rooks Farm
Greatham Prim. Sch.
The Old Rectory
Golds Farm
Manor House
FOREST RD.
Palmer's Ball
Greatham Moor
Goleigh Farm House
Farm Cottage
Weir
Water Works
A3
Moor Park Farm
Bridge Cotts.
ROAD
Greatham Bridge
FOREST CNR.
BRIAR WOOD
BERRYLANDS
WARREN RD
SHERWOOD CL.
NEWFIELD
PINE WALK
BEECHWOOD CT.
TEMPLE RD.
Rec. Ground
ROTHERBANK FM. LA.
FOREST RISE
MINT ROAD
Burgate Cotts.
Berry Grove
CHURCH ST.
Almshouses
FARNHAM ROAD
Playing Field
Pav.
Old Stocks Oak
Kippences
STATION ROAD
KILN FIELD
HAWKS MEAD
BISHEARNE
Rec. Grd.
The Arcade
ST. MARY'S RD
Church Cl.
WESTERN ROAD
Brows Farm
YORKWOOD
MAINLINE BUS. CEN.
SYERS
Chilmark
THE OVAL
ROUNDABOUT
MILL RD
WYLD GREEN LANE
Wyld Green Farm
MILL BROOK
Patrick's Copse
RAKE

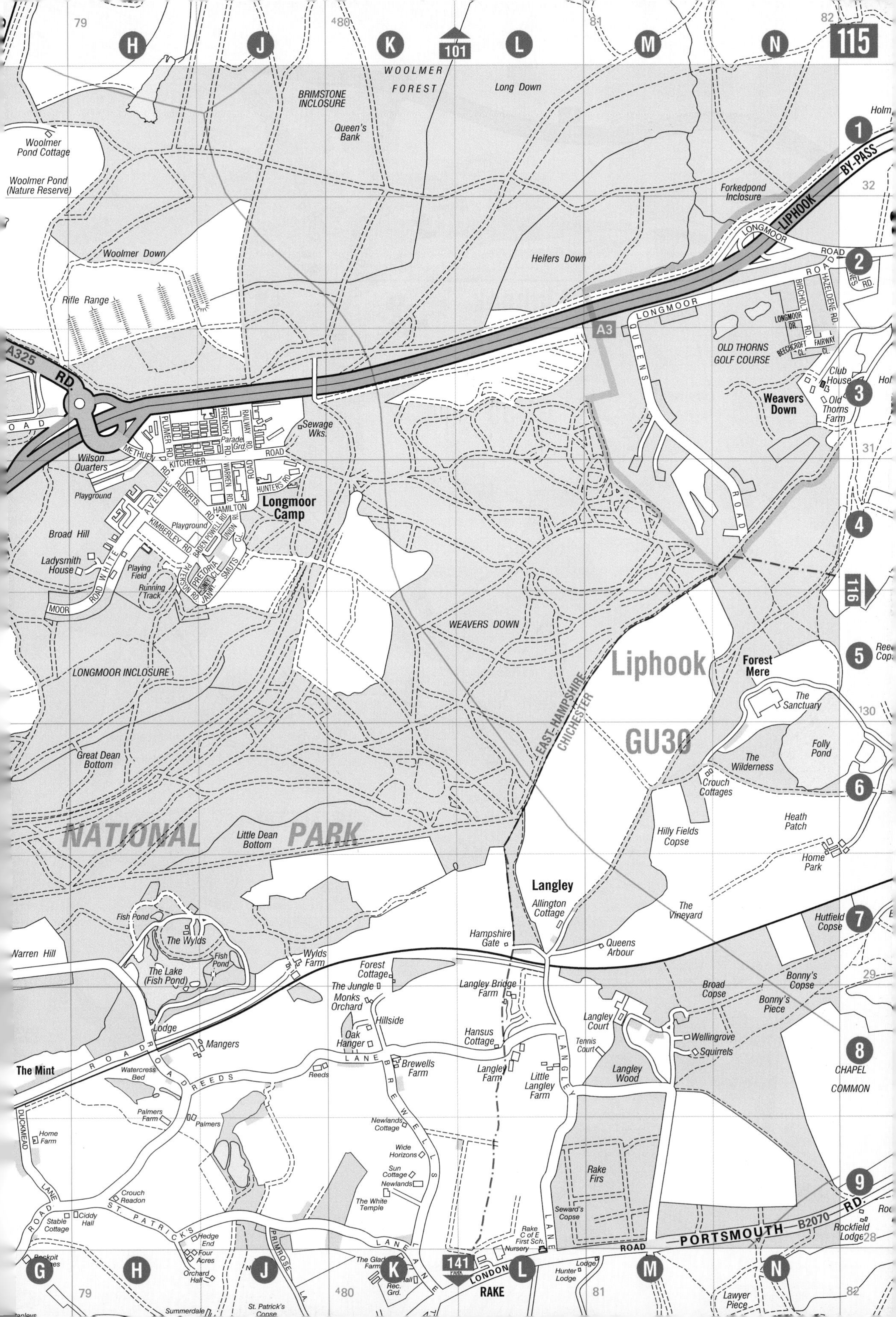
WOOLMER FOREST
BRIMSTONE INCLOSURE
Queen's Bank
Long Down
Woolmer Pond Cottage
Woolmer Pond (Nature Reserve)
Forkedpond Inclosure
LIPHOOK BY-PASS
LONGMOOR ROAD
Woolmer Down
Heifers Down
Rifle Range
A325 RD.
A3
LONGMOOR
QUEENS ROAD
BIRCHOLT RD.
HAZELDENE RD.
LONGMOOR DR.
BEECHCROFT CL.
FAIRWAY CL.
OLD THORNS GOLF COURSE
Club House
Weavers Down
Old Thorns Farm
PLUMER RD.
FRENCH RD.
RAILWAY RD.
Parade Grd.
Sewage Wks.
METHUEN RD.
KITCHENER ROAD
WARREN RD.
HUNTERS RD.
Wilson Quarters
Playground
AVENUE
ROBERTS RD.
HAMILTON
Longmoor Camp
Broad Hill
KIMBERLEY RD.
BADEN POWELL RD.
UNION RD.
PRETORIA RD.
SMUTS CL.
Ladysmith House
WHITE MOOR ROAD
Playing Field
Running Track
PATERSON RD.
WEAVERS DOWN
LONGMOOR INCLOSURE
Liphook
Forest Mere
The Sanctuary
EAST HAMPSHIRE
CHICHESTER
GU30
Great Dean Bottom
The Wilderness
Folly Pond
Crouch Cottages
NATIONAL PARK
Little Dean Bottom
Hilly Fields Copse
Heath Patch
Home Park
Langley
Allington Cottage
The Vineyard
Hutfield Copse
Fish Pond
The Wylds
Hampshire Gate
Queens Arbour
Warren Hill
Fish Pond
Wylds Farm
The Lake (Fish Pond)
Forest Cottage
Langley Bridge Farm
Broad Copse
Bonny's Copse
Bonny's Piece
The Jungle
Monks Orchard
Hillside
Lodge
Oak Hanger
Hansus Cottage
Langley Court
Tennis Court
Wellingrove
Squirrels
CHAPEL COMMON
Mangers
The Mint
ROAD
LANE
Brewells Farm
Langley Farm
Little Langley Farm
Langley Wood
LANGLEY LANE
Watercress Bed
REEDS
Reeds
Palmers Farm
Palmers
DUCKMEAD LANE
Home Farm
Newlands Cottage
Wide Horizons
BREWELLS LANE
Sun Cottage
Newlands
Rake Firs
Crouch Readon
The White Temple
Seward's Copse
ROAD
Stable Cottage
Ciddy Hall
ST. PATRICK'S LANE
Hedge End
Four Acres
PRIMROSE LA
Rake C of E First Sch.
Nursery
PORTSMOUTH RD.
B2070
Rockfield Lodge
Orchard Hall
Lodge
Hunter Lodge
ROAD
LONDON
RAKE
Rec. Grd.
Hall
Lawyer Piece
St. Patrick's Copse
Summerdale
H J K L M N
G H J K L M N
79 480 81 82
1 2 3 4 5 6 7 8 9
32 31 30 29 28
101
116
141

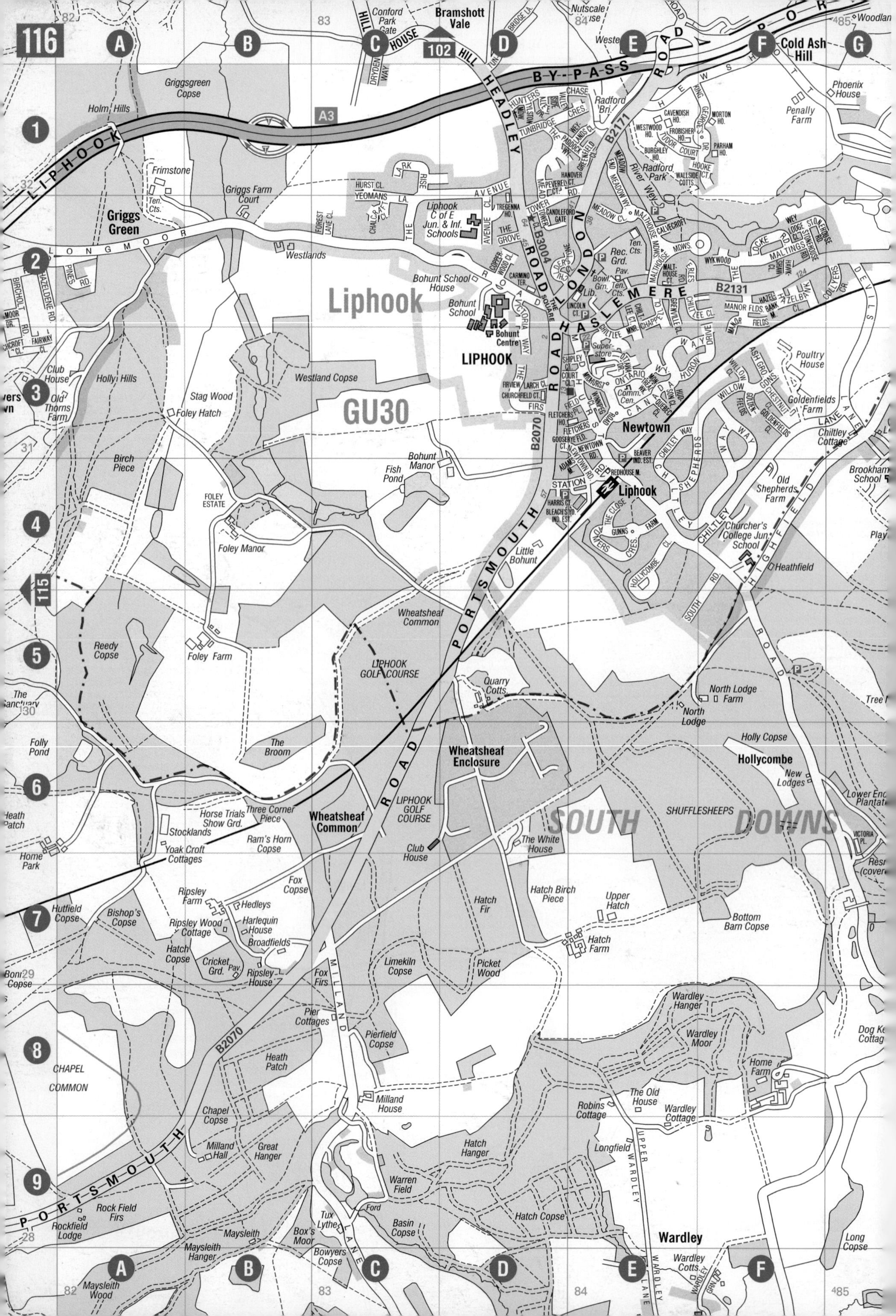

102
115
Bramshott Vale
Conford Park Gate
Cold Ash Hill
Griggsgreen Copse
Holm Hills
Griggs Green
Frimstone
Griggs Farm Court
Westlands
Liphook
GU30
LIPHOOK
Liphook C of E Jun. & Inf. Schools
Bohunt School House
Bohunt School
Bohunt Centre
Westland Copse
Stag Wood
Foley Hatch
Holly Hills
Club House
Old Thorns Farm
Birch Piece
FOLEY ESTATE
Foley Manor
Bohunt Manor
Fish Pond
Little Bohunt
Newtown
Radford Park
Radford Bri.
Phoenix House
Penally Farm
Poultry House
Goldenfields Farm
Chiltley Cottage
Old Shepherds Farm
Churcher's College Jun. School
Heathfield
Brookham School
Reedy Copse
Foley Farm
Wheatsheaf Common
LIPHOOK GOLF COURSE
Quarry Cotts.
North Lodge Farm
North Lodge
Holly Copse
Hollycombe
New Lodges
The Broom
Wheatsheaf Enclosure
SOUTH DOWNS
SHUFFLESHEEPS
The Sanctuary
Folly Pond
Heath Patch
Home Park
Horse Trials Show Grd.
Three Corner Piece
Stocklands
Ram's Horn Copse
Yoak Croft Cottages
Club House
The White House
Hatch Birch Piece
Upper Hatch
Bottom Barn Copse
Lower End Plantation
Hutfield Copse
Bishop's Copse
Ripsley Farm
Hedleys
Harlequin House
Ripsley Wood Cottage
Broadfields
Fox Copse
Hatch Fir
Hatch Farm
Hatch Copse
Cricket Grd.
Ripsley House
Fox Firs
Limekiln Copse
Picket Wood
Wardley Hanger
Wardley Moor
Pier Cottages
Pierfield Copse
CHAPEL COMMON
Heath Patch
Milland House
Chapel Copse
Milland Hall
Great Hanger
Hatch Hanger
Robins Cottage
The Old House
Wardley Cottage
Longfield
Home Farm
Dog Kennel Cottage
Warren Field
Rock Field Firs
Rockfield Lodge
Tux Lythe
Ford
Basin Copse
Maysleith
Maysleith Hanger
Box's Moor
Bowyers Copse
Maysleith Wood
Wardley
Wardley Cotts.
Long Copse
LIPHOOK BY-PASS
A3
LONGMOOR RD.
HEADLEY HILL
LONDON ROAD
HASLEMERE RD.
PORTSMOUTH ROAD
B2070
B3004
B2171
B2131
MILLAND LANE
UPPER WARDLEY LANE
HIGHFIELD LANE
CHILTLEY LANE
DEVILS LANE

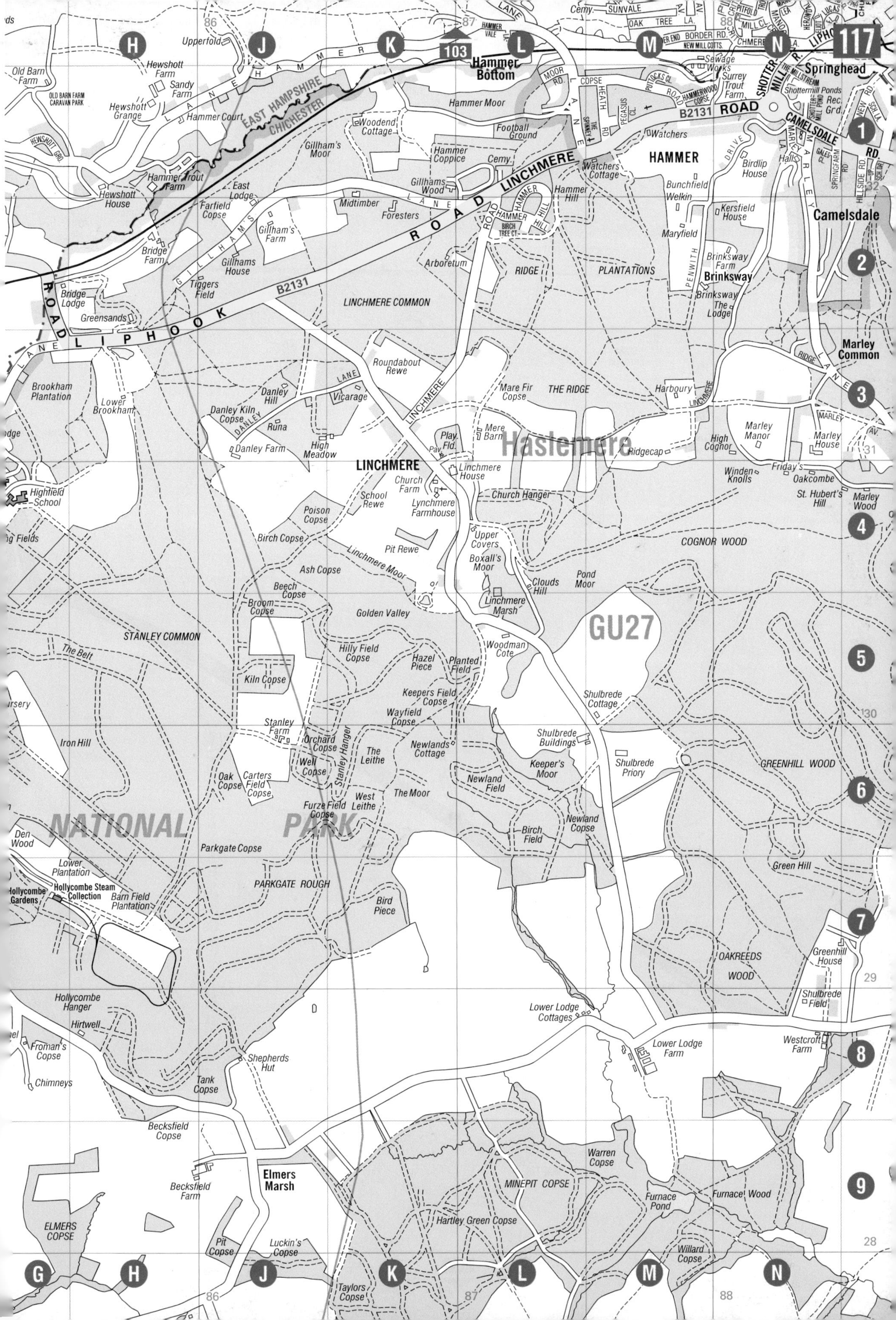
Hammer Bottom
Springhead
Upperfold
Hewshott Farm
Sandy Farm
Old Barn Farm
OLD BARN FARM CARAVAN PARK
Hewshott Grange
Hammer Court
EAST HAMPSHIRE
CHICHESTER
Hammer Moor
Woodend Cottage
Football Ground
Hammer Coppice
Gillham's Moor
Hammer Trout Farm
Hewshott House
East Lodge
Farfield Copse
Gillhams Wood
Cemy.
Midtimber
Foresters
Watchers Cottage
Watchers
HAMMER
Hammer Hill
Bunchfield
Welkin
Birdlip House
Kersfield House
Maryfield
Camelsdale
Gillham's Farm
Bridge Farm
Gillhams House
Tiggers Field
Bridge Lodge
Greensands
Arboretum
RIDGE
PLANTATIONS
Brinksway Farm
Brinksway
Brinksway The Lodge
LINCHMERE COMMON
LIPHOOK ROAD
LINCHMERE ROAD
B2131 ROAD
Marley Common
Roundabout Rewe
Brookham Plantation
Lower Brookham
Danley Hill
Vicarage
Mare Fir Copse
THE RIDGE
Harboury
Danley Kiln Copse
Runa
Mere Barn
Haslemere
Ridgecap
Marley Manor
High Cognor
Marley House
Danley Farm
High Meadow
Play Fld.
LINCHMERE
Linchmere House
Church Farm
Church Hanger
Winden Knolls
Friday's
Oakcombe
St. Hubert's Hill
Marley Wood
Highfield School
School Rewe
Lynchmere Farmhouse
Poison Copse
Birch Copse
Upper Covers
COGNOR WOOD
Pit Rewe
Linchmere Moor
Boxall's Moor
Ash Copse
Clouds Hill
Pond Moor
Beech Copse
Broom Copse
Golden Valley
Linchmere Marsh
GU27
STANLEY COMMON
The Belt
Woodman Cote
Hilly Field Copse
Hazel Piece
Planted Field
Kiln Copse
Keepers Field Copse
Shulbrede Cottage
Wayfield Copse
Stanley Farm
Iron Hill
Orchard Copse
Stanley Hanger
The Leithe
Newlands Cottage
Shulbrede Buildings
Shulbrede Priory
GREENHILL WOOD
Well Copse
Keeper's Moor
Oak Copse
Carters Field Copse
Newland Field
West Leithe
The Moor
Furze Field Copse
NATIONAL PARK
Birch Field
Newland Copse
Den Wood
Parkgate Copse
Green Hill
Lower Plantation
PARKGATE ROUGH
Hollycombe Gardens
Hollycombe Steam Collection
Barn Field Plantation
Bird Piece
OAKREEDS WOOD
Greenhill House
Shulbrede Field
Hollycombe Hanger
Lower Lodge Cottages
Hirtwell
Westcroft Farm
Lower Lodge Farm
Froman's Copse
Shepherds Hut
Chimneys
Tank Copse
Becksfield Copse
Warren Copse
Elmers Marsh
MINEPIT COPSE
Becksfield Farm
Furnace Pond
Furnace Wood
Hartley Green Copse
ELMERS COPSE
Pit Copse
Luckin's Copse
Willard Copse
Taylors Copse
103

Hydon Hill
Hut Bottom
Little Down
Flamstone Farm
NETTON DOWN
Windwhistle
PORTFIELD ROAD
Salisbury Racecourse
COOMBE NURSERIES CARAVAN PARK
RACE PLAIN
Down Barn
Roman Road (course of)
Stoke Down
Stratford Tony
STRATFORD
BROAD CHALKE
BISHOPSTONE
Stoke Farm
Stoke Farthing
The Pitts
MANOR FARM
CHURCH LA.
THREE COLTS LA.
Throope Manor House
BROADCHALKE ROAD
HIGH ROAD
River Ebble
Faulston Ho.
FAULSTON COTTAGES
Faulston
Croucheston
Mill
Broad Chalke C of E Prim. Sch.
THE CHESTNUTS
KNIGHTON ROAD
BULBURY LANE
Chalke Valley Spts. Cen.
Knighton Manor
Salisbury
SP5
Throope Hill
Throope Bottom Cottages
OLD BLANDFORD ROAD
Lower Coombe Farm
Coombe Bissett Down
A354
CROUCHESTON HOLLOW
CROUCHESTON DROVE
FAULSTON DROVE
BISHOPSTONE HOLLOW
Knighton Hill
Church Bottom
HOWGARE ROAD
Stratford Tony Down
Knighton Hill Farm
Faulston Down
Middleton Hill
Faulston Down Farm
OX DROVE
Jervoise Farm
Knowle Hill
Croucheston Down Farm
Grims Lodge Farm
Toyd Clump
Knighton Wood Farm
The Hut
Knighton Wood
BLANDFORD ROAD
Croucheston Down
Lodge Farm
WILTSHIRE
NEW FOREST
Little Toyd Down
ROCKBOURNE ROAD
Rockbourne Down
Fordingbridge
Paradise
Sundown Farm
A354
Martin Drove End
Cranway Farm
Toyd Farm
Haskells Farm
MARTIN DROVE END
SP6
St. Brides Farm
Longbarrow House
MIDDLE LANE
Damer's Farm
TOWNSEND LA.
DOWN VIEW RD.
MARTIN
Talk's Farm
East Martin
Knap Barrow
Toyd Down
Grans Barrow
Down Farm
TOWNSEND LANE
Martin Down
King's Farm
ST. GEORGES COTTAGES
ANGELS LANE
MARTIN DOWN NATIONAL NATURE RESERVE
SILLENS LANE
Knap Barrow Farm
Windmill Hill
Knoll Down
Tidpit
BOKERLEY DITCH
Bokerley Down
Trail

149

119
DOWNTON & WICK INSET
REDLYNCH & WOODFALLS INSET
H
J
K
L
M
N
G
1
2
3
4
5
6
7
8
9
120
119
150
151
A338
B3080
WICK
DOWNTON
Salisbury SP5
Morgan's Vale
REDLYNCH
WOODFALLS
NEW FOREST NATIONAL PARK
Coombe Bissett
New Court Farm
Recreation Ground
Cemetery
Scott's House
Depot
DAVID HART BUSINESS CENTRE
DOWNTON BUSINESS CENTRE
Watermeadows
Weir
Mill Race
Manor House
Parsonage Farm
Vicarage
Horseshoe Cl.
Downton Leis. Cen.
Wick Cottage
Wick House
Sports Ground
Downton C of E Prim. Sch.
The Trafalgar Sch. at Downton
Meadow End Cottage
Barnaby Close
Moot Ho.
Moot Farm
The Moot
Hall
Fish Pond
Boat House
Meadow View
Beech Nut Pit (Disused)
Grove Copse
Park Cotts.
Redlynch House
The Lodge
Morgans Corner
Prim. Sch.
The Barracks
Little Nursery Copse
Lock's Farm
Hart Hill Firs
Street's Copse
Ridge Farm
The Green
Parsonage Barn
Odstock Down
HOMINGTON DOWN
Tottens Down Barn
Southdown Farm
Down Barn
Little Yews
Pennings Farm
COLLEGE FARM CARAVAN SITE
Yews Farm
Clearbury Down
Charlton Manor Farm
Great Yews
Round Clump
Black Hill
New Court Down Barn
New Court Down
Whitsbury Down
Tenantry Farm
Wick Down
Gallows Hill
Botley's Farm
Breamore Down
North Charford Down Farm
Scotland Farm Cottage
Manor Farm
Fort
Manor House
Down Farm
Lower Farm
Breamore Wood
Breamore House
Breamore Park
Countryside Mus.
Glebe Farm
Dunberry Hill
WHITSBURY
Upper Street
North Street
North Charford
South Charford
South Charford Farm
NUNTON DROVE
WICK LANE
NORTH CHARFORD DROVE
SOUTH LANE
BREAMORE ROAD
SALISBURY ROAD
THE HIGHWAY
HIGH ST.
BOROUGH
LODE HILL
BARFORD LANE

WEST WELLOW INSET
WEST WELLOW
Romsey
SO51
NEW FOREST NATIONAL PARK
SALISBURY ROAD
CRAWLEY HILL
East Grimstead
WEST GRIMSTEAD
SOUTHAMPTON ROAD
A36
Salisbury
SP5
Pepperbox Hill
Witherington
Witherington Down
Charlton-All-Saints
SALISBURY HIGHWAY
A338
RIVER AVON
Standlynch Down
BRICKWORTH
A27
DOWNTON
WICK
BRAEMORE RD.
REDLYNCH
Morgan's Vale
WOODFALLS
North Charford
LOVER
Bohemia
WILTSHIRE
NEW FOREST
Hatchet Green
Fordingbridge SP6
HALE
Langley Wood
Shearwood Copse
Loosehanger Copse

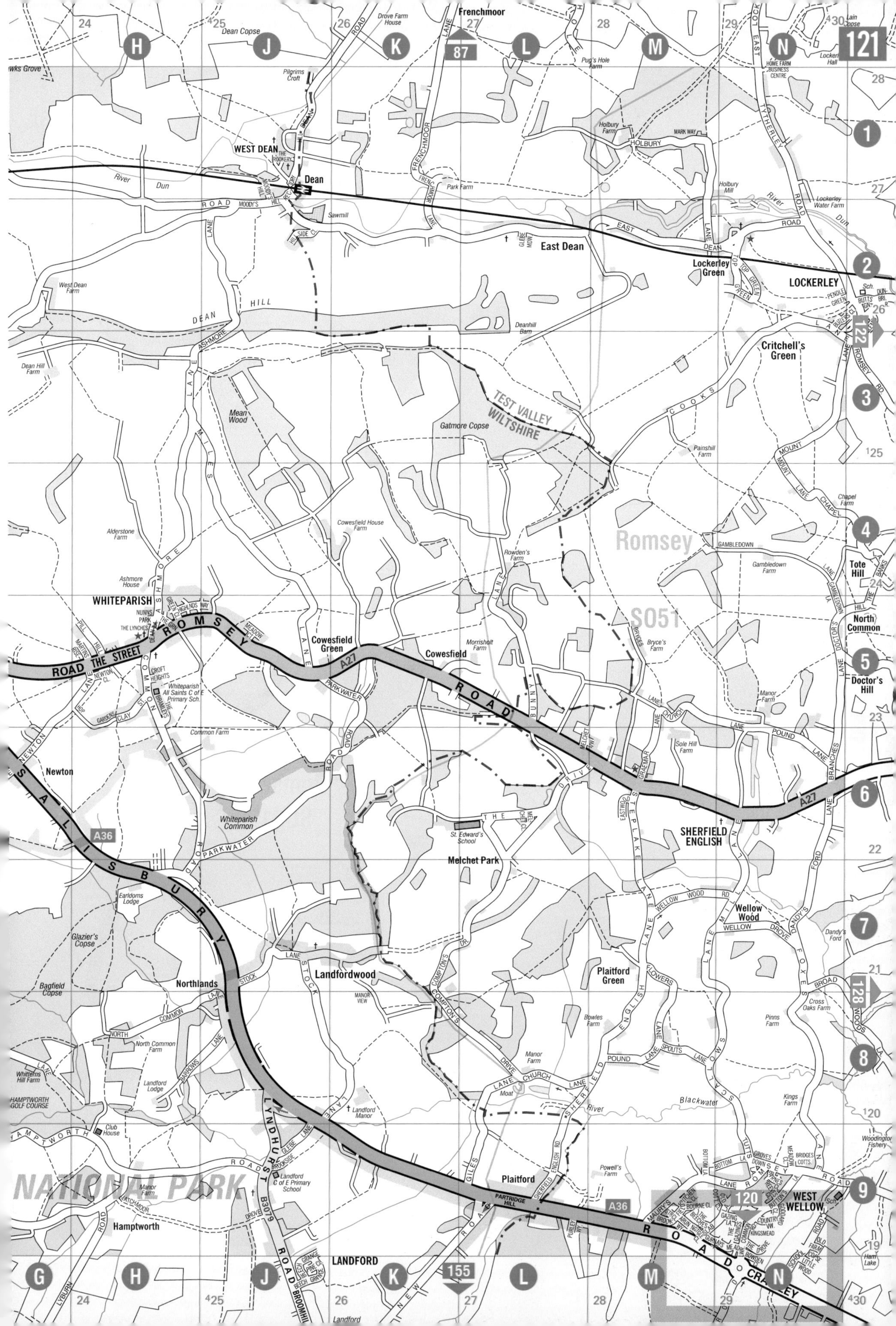
Frenchmoor
87
West Dean
Dean
River Dun
East Dean
Holbury
Holbury Farm
Holbury Mill
Lockerley Green
LOCKERLEY
Lockerley Water Farm
Lockerley Hall
Home Farm Business Centre
Pug's Hole Farm
Park Farm
Sawmill
Pilgrims Croft
Drove Farm House
Dean Copse
West Dean Farm
Dean Hill
Deanhill Barn
Dean Hill Farm
Critchell's Green
Mean Wood
Gatmore Copse
Test Valley
Wiltshire
Painshill Farm
Chapel Farm
Alderstone Farm
Cowesfield House Farm
Rowden's Farm
Romsey
Gambledown Farm
Tote Hill
North Common
Doctor's Hill
Ashmore House
WHITEPARISH
Cowesfield Green
Cowesfield
Morrisholt Farm
Bryce's Farm
S051
Manor Farm
Sole Hill Farm
Whiteparish All Saints C of E Primary Sch.
Common Farm
Newton
Whiteparish Common
St. Edward's School
Melchet Park
SHERFIELD ENGLISH
Wellow Wood
Dandy's Ford
Earldoms Lodge
Glazier's Copse
Bagfield Copse
Northlands
Landfordwood
Plaitford Green
Cross Oaks Farm
Pinns Farm
North Common Farm
Whittens Hill Farm
Hamptworth Golf Course
Landford Lodge
Landford Manor
Bowles Farm
Manor Farm
Moat
River Blackwater
Kings Farm
Woodington Fishery
Club House
Landford C of E Primary School
Powell's Farm
Plaitford
NATIONAL PARK
Manor Farm
Hamptworth
LANDFORD
Partridge Hill
A36
A27
120
WEST WELLOW
Ham Lake
155
Landford
122
128
Salisbury Road
Romsey Road
The Street
Lyndhurst Road
B3079
Cranley Road
H J K L M N G
24 25 26 27 28 29 30
1 2 3 4 5 6 7 8 9
28 27 26 25 24 23 22 21 20 19

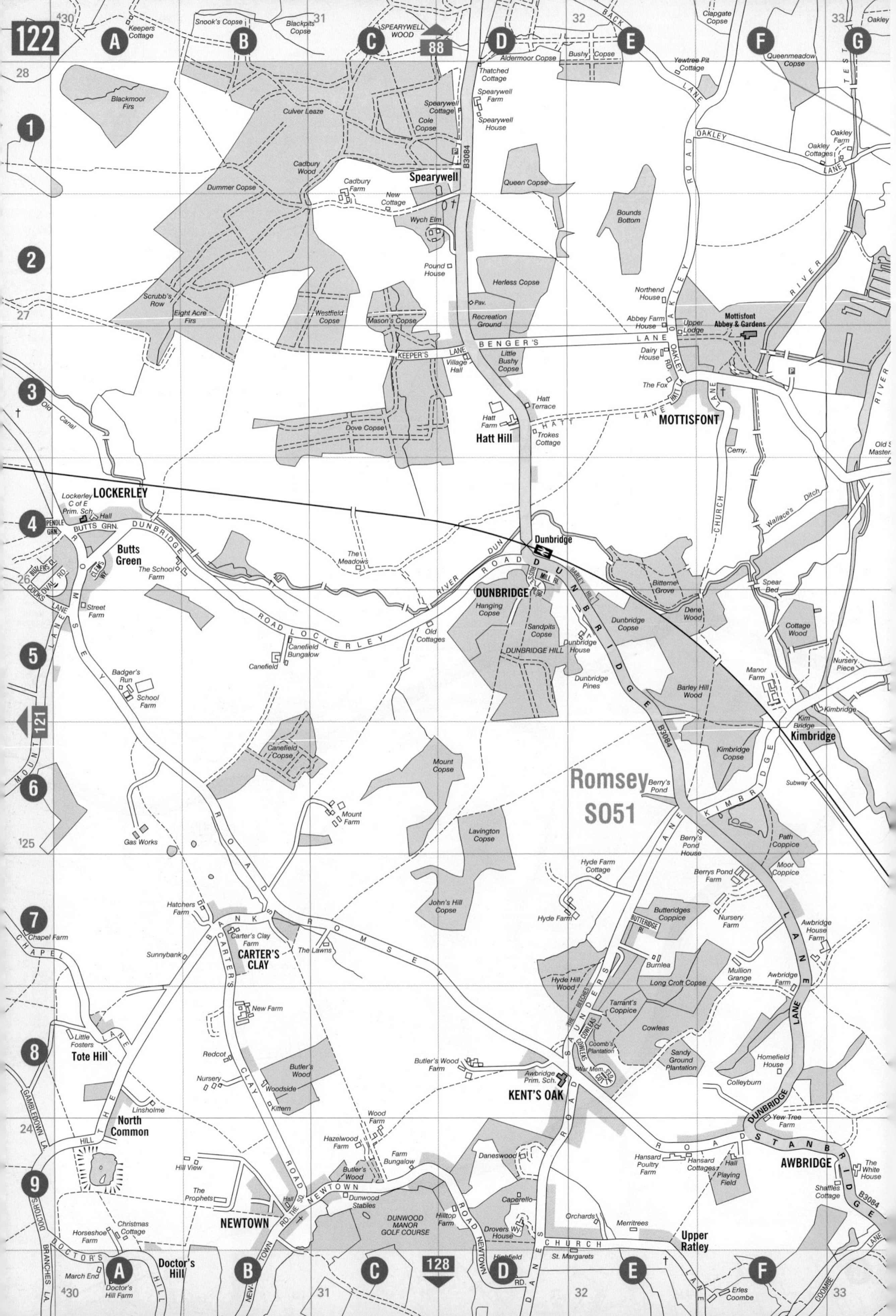

122
88
128
121
Romsey
SO51
Keepers Cottage
Snook's Copse
Blackpits Copse
SPEARYWELL WOOD
Aldermoor Copse
Bushy Copse
BACK LANE
Clapgate Copse
Oakley
Queenmeadow Copse
Yewtree Pit Cottage
Thatched Cottage
Spearywell Farm
Spearywell House
Spearywell Cottage
Cole Copse
Blackmoor Firs
Culver Leaze
Cadbury Wood
Dummer Copse
Spearywell
Cadbury Farm
New Cottage
Wych Elm
Pound House
Queen Copse
Bounds Bottom
OAKLEY LANE
Oakley Farm
Oakley Cottages
OAKLEY ROAD
Herless Copse
Scrubb's Row
Eight Acre Firs
Westfield Copse
Mason's Copse
Pav.
Recreation Ground
Northend House
Abbey Farm House
Upper Lodge
Mottisfont Abbey & Gardens
RIVER TEST
KEEPER'S LANE
BENGER'S LANE
Village Hall
Little Bushy Copse
Dairy House
OAKLEY RD.
The Fox
HATT LA.
Hatt Terrace
Hatt Farm
Hatt Hill
HATT LANE
Trokes Cottage
MOTTISFONT
Cemy.
Dove Copse
Old Canal
Old Salt Master
LOCKERLEY
Lockerley C of E Prim. Sch.
Hall
PENDLE GRN.
BUTTS GRN.
DUNBRIDGE LANE
Butts Green
The School Farm
The Meadows
CHURCH LANE
Wallace's Ditch
Dunbridge
DUN ROAD
RIVER ROAD
DUNBRIDGE
MILL RI.
BARLEY HILL
Bitterne Grove
Spear Bed
Hanging Copse
Sandpits Copse
Dunbridge Copse
Dene Wood
Cottage Wood
Street Farm
COOKS LANE
ROMSEY ROAD
ROAD LOCKERLEY
Canefield Bungalow
Canefield
Old Cottages
DUNBRIDGE HILL
Dunbridge House
Dunbridge Pines
Barley Hill Wood
Manor Farm
Nursery Piece
Badger's Run
School Farm
Kim Bridge
Kimbridge
B3084
Canefield Copse
Mount Copse
Kimbridge Copse
MOUNT LANE
Berry's Pond
Subway
KIMBRIDGE LANE
Mount Farm
Lavington Copse
Gas Works
Berry's Pond House
Path Coppice
Hyde Farm Cottage
Berrys Pond Farm
Moor Coppice
John's Hill Copse
Hatchers Farm
Hyde Farm
Butteridges Coppice
BUTTERIDGE RI.
Nursery Farm
Awbridge House Farm
Chapel Farm
CHAPEL LANE
BANK
Carter's Clay Farm
CARTER'S CLAY
The Lawns
Sunnybank
Burnlea
Mullion Grange
Awbridge Farm
Hyde Hill Wood
Long Croft Copse
SAUNDERS LANE
THE BEECHES
COWLEAS
Tarrant's Coppice
Cowleas
New Farm
Coomb's Plantation
Sandy Ground Plantation
Homefield House
Little Fosters
Tote Hill
Redcot
Butler's Wood
Butler's Wood Farm
War Mem.
Awbridge Prim. Sch.
KENT'S OAK
Colleyburn
Nursery
Woodside
CARTER'S CLAY ROAD
Kittern
GAMBLEDOWN LANE
THE HILL
Linsholme
North Common
Wood Farm
Yew Tree Farm
DUNBRIDGE ROAD
STANBRIDGE LANE
Hazelwood Farm
Farm Bungalow
Daneswood
Hansard Poultry Farm
Hansard Cottages
Hall
Playing Field
AWBRIDGE
The White House
Shaftes Cottage
Hill View
Butler's Wood
NEWTOWN
The Prophets
Hall
Dunwood Stables
DUNWOOD MANOR GOLF COURSE
Hilltop Farm
Caperello
Orchards
Merritrees
Drovers Wy. House
NEWTOWN ROAD
DANES ROAD
CHURCH LANE
Upper Ratley
DOCTOR'S HILL
Horseshoe Farm
Christmas Cottage
Doctor's Hill
NEW TOWN RD.
THE SQ.
Highfield
St. Margarets
March End
Doctor's Hill Farm
BRANCHES LA.
Erles Coombe
COOMBE LANE
A
B
C
D
E
F
G
1
2
3
4
5
6
7
8
9
430
31
32
33
28
27
26
125
24

Stockbridge
SO20
Lower Brook
Brook Down
Eldon Firs
News Wood
The Bungalow
Eldon Ho.
Upper Eldon Farm
Lower Eldon Farm
STROUD'S WOOD
MICHELMERSH WOOD
Park Farm
STUBB'S COPSE
Park Farm Bungalow
Parnell Barn
Orchard Cottage
Michelmersh Court
Barn Cottage
The Forge House
Station House
Stonymarsh Cottage
Corner Barns
Laundry Cott.
Michelmersh House
Manor Farm Cottage
Greenacres
Hall Place Cottage
Stonymarsh
Oak Tree Farm
Four Seasons
Manor Farm
Oak Tree House
Ridgemount
Old School House
Little Hackupps
Woodlands
The Coppice
Mariolaine
Sandy Croft
Hillside
MICHELMERSH
Works
Michelmersh Dairy Farm
Stonymarsh House
Malthouse Farm
Kimbridge Corner
Brick Works
Glenwood Cottages
Glenville
Meadow Cottages
Upper Timsbury
CHAPEL LA
Hunt's Farm
THE MILLBURNS
MANNYNGHAM WAY
Hall
Rec. Grd.
CASBROOK
REDLANDS DR.
LEBOURNE CL.
Springways
Snowdrop Cottage
Stragwyne
Cranford Farm
Wild Acres
Sharpe Farm
Linhay Meads
Sports Grd.
Pav.
Casbrook Common
The Herons
TIMSBURY
Playing Field
Herons Mead
ST ANDREWS CL.
Fairbourne Lake
Round Copse
Fairbourne Cottage
Timsbury Manor
Brook Farm
Timsbury Lake
YOKESFORD HILL ESTATE
WYNFORD INDUSTRIAL PARK
Wynford Farm
Lodge Farm
Eight Acre Copse
Abbotswood Farm
Longacre
The Bog
Los Pinares
Crawland Gate Copse
Parsonage Copse
Common Copse
Parsonage Farm
Awbridge Hill
Stanbridge Earls
Rookwood Copse
Belbin's Copse
Cedar Nursery
Abbotswood
TOLLGATE ESTATES
Hillberry Farm
Tennis Courts
Ashley Meadows
Belbin's House
BELBINS BUSINESS PARK
Timsbury Bridge
A3057
STOCKBRIDGE ROAD
MESH ROAD
CHURCH RD
HACKUPS LANE
STAFF ROAD
HILL VIEW ROAD
MANOR FARM
RUDD LANE
NEW ROAD
PARNELL LANE
ELDON ROAD
LOWER STREET
HERON LANE
MANOR LANE
BUNNY LANE
YOKESFORD HILL
BELBINS
SANDY LANE
CUPERNHAM LA
RIVER TEST
H J K L M N G
1 2 3 4 5 6 7 8 9
34 435 36
28 27 26 25 24
88 124 129

A
B
C
D
E
F
G
37
38
39
89
Parnholt Wood
Tallboys
Bailey's Down
Farley Down
Grass Air Strip
Farley Farm Cottages
Dairy Cottage
Farley Farm
Eldon Ho.
Upper Eldon Farm
Fishponds Farm
Taunton Vale
Hall Copse
Bailey's Down Farm
28
1
2
COPSE
27
Bull Grove Copse
Farley House
The Old School House
Farley Dell
Hall Pond
Oakfield
Glebe Cottage
Blue Haze Farm
Poultry Houses
Church Walk
Parnell Barn
3
Greenacres
Hall Place Cottage
Hall Place
Windmill Cottages
Oaktrees
Pitt Farm
Miller's Copse
Parkfield House
4
Braishfield Manor
Manor Cottage
Braishfield Lodge
Fern Hill
Fernhill Farm
Broom Hill Copse
26
Malthouse Farm
Chalk Pit Cottage
Wyndhams
Necton Cottage
Combe Cottage
5
Braishfield House
Merrie Meade Farm
Fern Hill Copse
WINCHESTER
TEST VALLEY
Lower Slackstead
Laurel Cottage
Paynes Hay Farm
Pond Cottages
BRAISHFIELD
The Close
Meade Hill
Walnut Tree Cottage
The Rectory
Colsons
123
Spinney Corner
Orchard Copse
Slackstead Manor
Berryhill Copse
Romsey
6
Braishvale
War Mem.
Elm Grove Farm
Poultry Houses
Hursley Foxhound Kennels
The Kennels
SO51
Hawkes Farm
Churchers Barn
Woolley Green Farm
Oxlease Copse
125
Cricket Ground
Hall
Rec. Grd.
Braishfield Prim. Sch.
Pucknall Cottage
Pucknall
Pucknall House
Pucknall Farm
CHAPEL CL.
BLACKTHORN CL.
HILL VIEW RD.
7
Round Copse
Red Gate
The Homestead
8
Fairbournes Farm
Crook Hill
MEGANA WAY
24
Crook Bridge
Sir Harold Hillier Gardens & Arboretum
Crookhill Farm
Nursery
Jermyns House
Longacre
The Bog
9
Visitor Centre
Arboretum
Garden Centre
Los Pinares
Sandpits Bungalows
Arboretum
Lodge
Nursery
Plantation Copse
Arboretum
Nursery
Nursery
Outwood Lodge
Ampfield Hill
Tadburn
130
Bracken Wood
Abbotswood
Cemetery
A3090
STRAIGHT MILE
PARNELL LANE
ELDON ROAD
LOWER STREET
FURZEDOWN
PARNHOLT ROAD
SOMBORNE
KING'S
FARLEY LANE
FARLEY ROAD
HAY
PAYNES
FERN HILL LANE
CHURCH LANE
DUMMERS ROAD
DORES LANE
HILL
COMMON
NEWPORT LANE
KILN LANE
RUDD LANE
BRAISHFIELD ROAD
SANDY LANE
JERMYNS LANE

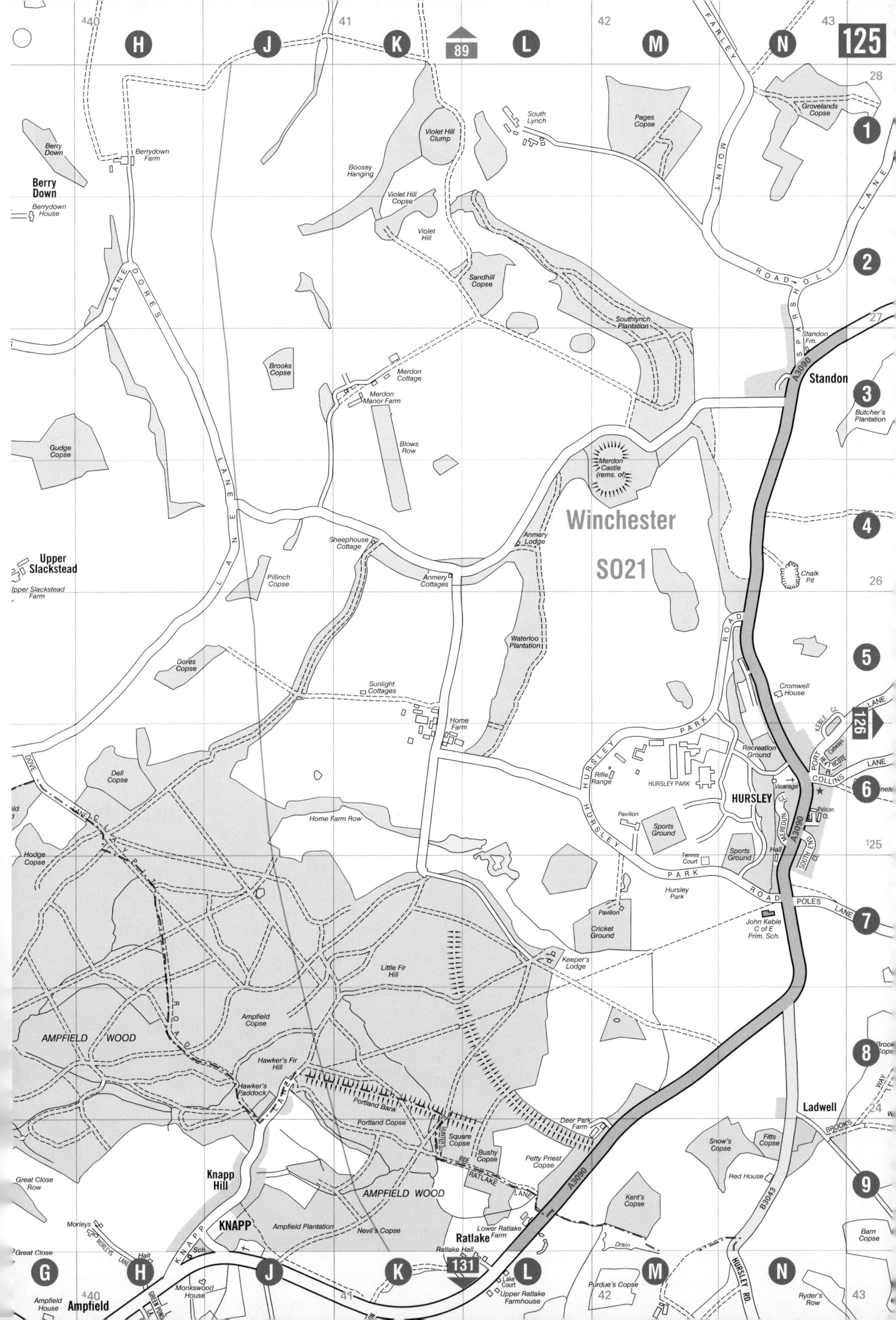
H
J
K
89
L
M
N
Berry Down
Berrydown Farm
Berry Down
Berrydown House
Boosey Hanging
Violet Hill Clump
Violet Hill Copse
Violet Hill
South Lynch
Pages Copse
Grovelands Copse
FARLEY MOUNT ROAD
HOLT LANE
SPARSHOLT ROAD
DORES LANE
Sandhill Copse
Southlynch Plantation
Standon Fm.
Standon
A3090
Butcher's Plantation
Brooks Copse
Merdon Cottage
Merdon Manor Farm
Gudge Copse
Blows Row
Merdon Castle (rems. of)
Winchester
SO21
Sheephouse Cottage
Anmery Lodge
Anmery Cottages
Upper Slackstead
Upper Slackstead Farm
Pillinch Copse
Chalk Pit
Waterloo Plantation
Dores Copse
Sunlight Cottages
Cromwell House
Home Farm
HURSLEY PARK
Rifle Range
Recreation Ground
KEBLE CL.
126
PORT
LANE
COLLINS
Vicarage
HURSLEY
Pelican Cl.
MEREDUN CL.
SOUTH END CL.
DOVE
CLAY PIT ROAD
Dell Copse
Home Farm Row
Pavilion
Sports Ground
Tennis Court
Sports Ground
Hall
Hodge Copse
Hursley Park
POLES LANE
Pavilion
Cricket Ground
John Keble C of E Prim. Sch.
Keeper's Lodge
Little Fir Hill
Ampfield Copse
AMPFIELD WOOD
Hawker's Fir Hill
Hawker's Paddock
Portland Bank
Portland Copse
HUNTERS
Square Copse
Bushy Copse
RIDE
RATLAKE LANE
Deer Park Farm
Petty Priest Copse
Ladwell
BROOKS
WAY
Snow's Copse
Fitts Copse
Red House
Great Close Row
Knapp Hill
AMPFIELD WOOD
Kent's Copse
B3043
Morleys
MORLEYS LANE
KNAPP
KNAPP LANE
Ampfield Plantation
Nevil's Copse
Lower Ratlake Farm
Ratlake
Ratlake Hall
Drain
Barn Copse
Great Close
Hall
Sch.
131
G
H
J
K
L
M
N
Lake Court
Upper Ratlake Farmhouse
Purdue's Copse
HURSLEY RD.
Monkswood House
Ampfield House
Ampfield
GREEN POND
Ryder's Row
440
41
42
43
28
27
26
125
24
1
2
3
4
5
6
7
8
9

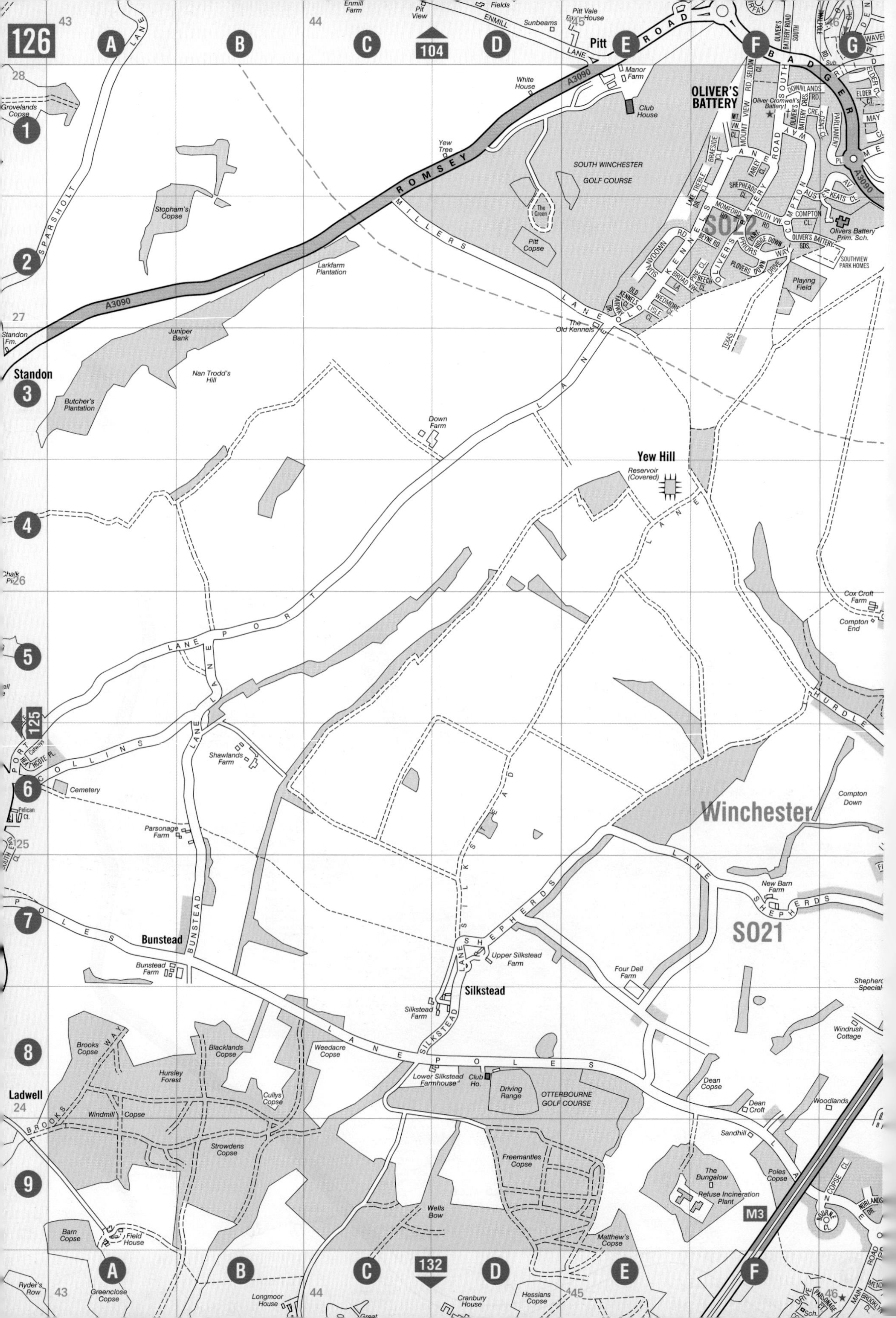

126
A
B
C
D
E
F
G
104
125
132
43
44
45
46
28
27
26
25
24
1
2
3
4
5
6
7
8
9
Grovelands Copse
Enmill Farm
Pit View
Fields
Sunbeams
Pitt Vale House
ENMILL LANE
Pitt
ROMSEY ROAD
A3090
Manor Farm
White House
Club House
OLIVER'S BATTERY
Oliver Cromwell's Battery
BADGER
SPARSHOLT LANE
Stopham's Copse
Yew Tree
SOUTH WINCHESTER GOLF COURSE
The Green
Pitt Copse
MILLERS LANE
Larkfarm Plantation
Olivers Battery Prim. Sch.
SOUTHVIEW PARK HOMES
Playing Field
SO22
The Old Kennels
Standon Fm.
Standon
Juniper Bank
Nan Trodd's Hill
Butcher's Plantation
Down Farm
Yew Hill
Reservoir (Covered)
TEXAS
Chalk Pit
Cox Croft Farm
Compton End
PORT LANE
HURDLE
COLLINS LANE
Shawlands Farm
Cemetery
Pelican Ct.
Parsonage Farm
Winchester
Compton Down
SILKSTEAD LANE
SHEPHERDS LANE
New Barn Farm
SO21
POLES LANE
Bunstead
BUNSTEAD LANE
Bunstead Farm
Upper Silkstead Farm
Four Dell Farm
Shepherds Special
Silkstead
Silkstead Farm
Windrush Cottage
Brooks Copse
Blacklands Copse
Weedacre Copse
Hursley Forest
Lower Silkstead Farmhouse
Club Ho.
Driving Range
OTTERBOURNE GOLF COURSE
Dean Copse
Dean Croft
Woodlands
Ladwell
Windmill Copse
Cullys Copse
BROOKS WAY
Strowdens Copse
Sandhill
Freemantles Copse
The Bungalow
Refuse Incineration Plant
Poles Copse
M3
Wells Bow
Barn Copse
Field House
Matthew's Copse
Ryder's Row
Greenclose Copse
Longmoor House
Cranbury House
Hessians Copse

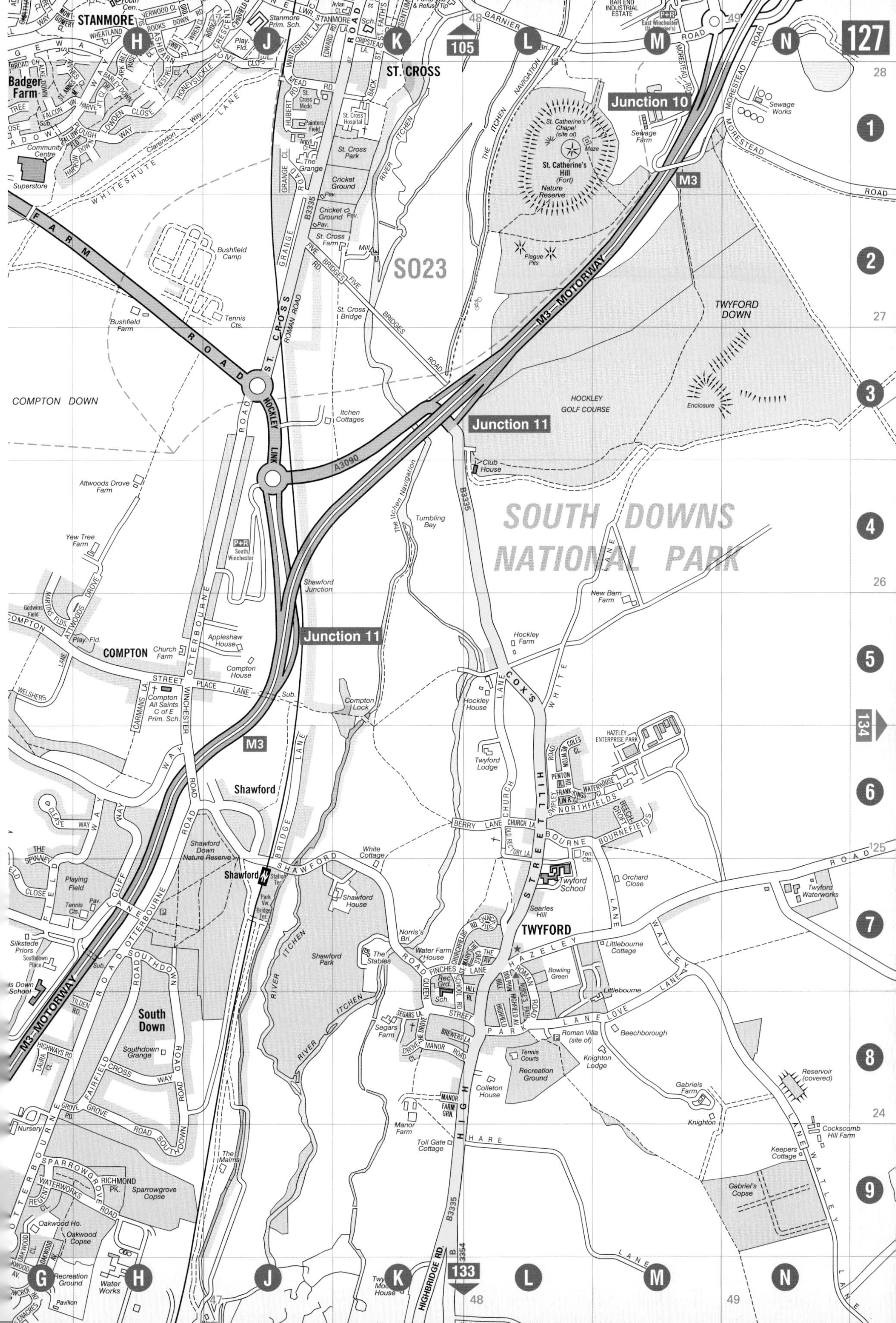
STANMORE
Badger Farm
ST. CROSS
Junction 10
St. Catherine's Hill (Fort)
Nature Reserve
St. Catherine's Chapel (site of)
Maze
Sewage Works
Sewage Farm
M3
MORESTEAD ROAD
BAR END INDUSTRIAL ESTATE
GARNIER ROAD
THE ITCHEN NAVIGATION
RIVER ITCHEN
St. Cross Hospital
St. Cross Park
Cricket Ground
St. Cross Farm
Mill
SO23
Plague Pits
TWYFORD DOWN
Enclosure
HOCKLEY GOLF COURSE
Junction 11
Club House
M3 MOTORWAY
FARM ROAD
Bushfield Camp
Bushfield Farm
Tennis Cts.
COMPTON DOWN
St. Cross Bridge
FIVE BRIDGES ROAD
HOCKLEY LINK
A3090
Itchen Cottages
Attwoods Drove Farm
Yew Tree Farm
South Winchester
Tumbling Bay
SOUTH DOWNS NATIONAL PARK
New Barn Farm
Shawford Junction
Appleshaw House
COMPTON
Church Farm
Compton House
Hockley Farm
COX'S HILL
WHITE LANE
Compton Lock
Hockley House
Compton All Saints C of E Prim. Sch.
HAZELEY ENTERPRISE PARK
Twyford Lodge
Shawford
Shawford Down Nature Reserve
White Cottage
BERRY LANE
CHURCH LANE
NORTHFIELDS
BOURNE
BOURNEFIELDS
Orchard Close
Twyford School
Twyford Waterworks
Shawford House
Shawford Park
Playing Field
Searles Hill
TWYFORD
Littlebourne Cottage
Bowling Green
Littlebourne
Silkstede Priors
Norris's Bri.
Water Farm House
The Stables
South Down
Southdown Grange
Segars Farm
Roman Villa (site of)
Beechborough
Knighton Lodge
Tennis Courts
Recreation Ground
Colleton House
Reservoir (covered)
Gabriels Farm
Knighton
Manor Farm
Toll Gate Cottage
HARE LANE
Cockscomb Hill Farm
Keepers Cottage
Gabriel's Copse
WATLEY LANE
Sparrowgrove Copse
RICHMOND PK.
Oakwood Ho.
Oakwood Copse
The Malms
Recreation Ground
Water Works
Pavilion
HIGHBRIDGE RD.
B3335
B3354
Nursery
OTTERBOURNE ROAD
LOVE LANE
HIGH STREET
Twyford Moors House

105
134
133

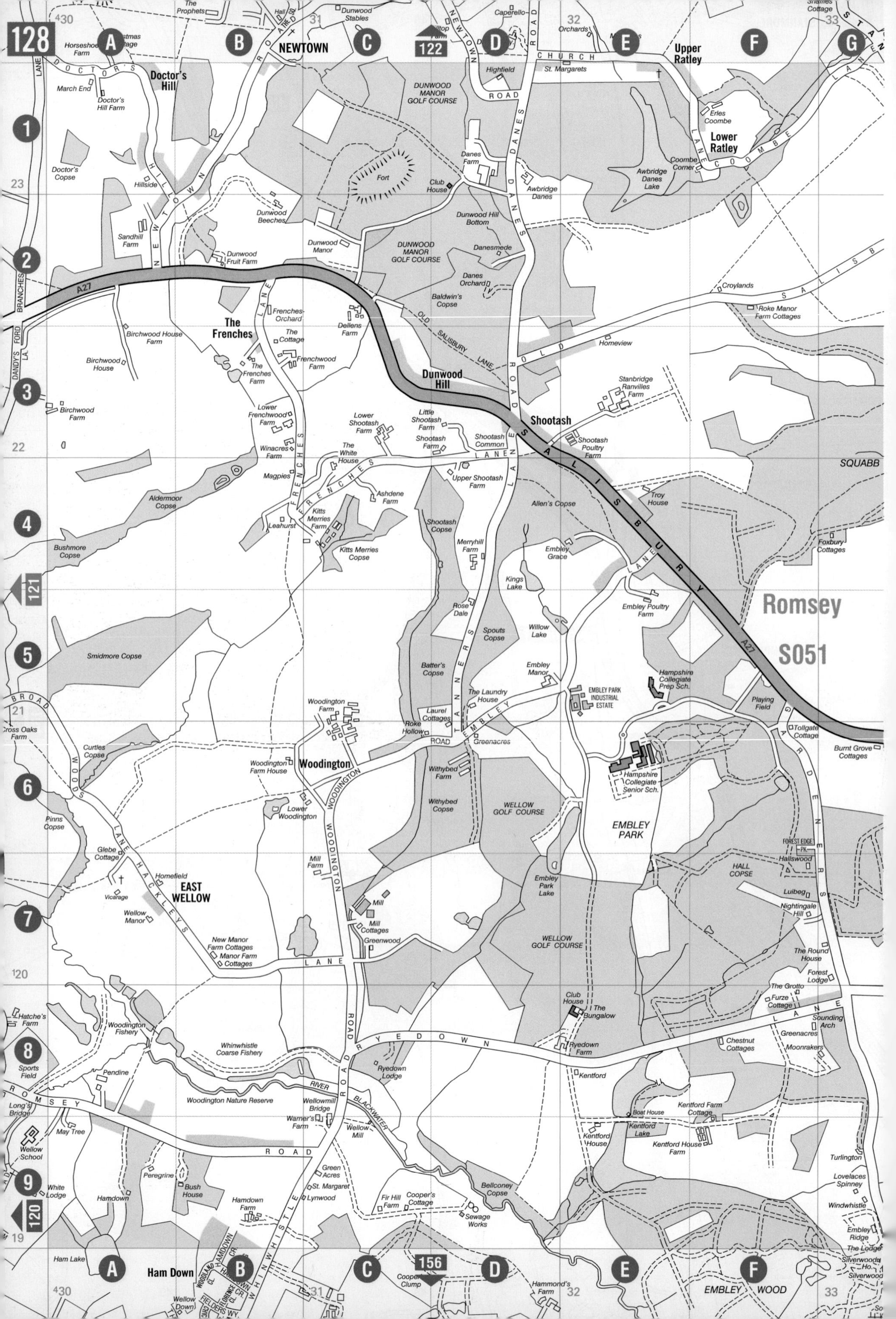

NEWTOWN
Doctor's Hill
Upper Ratley
Lower Ratley
DUNWOOD MANOR GOLF COURSE
The Frenches
Dunwood Hill
Shootash
Romsey
S051
Woodington
EAST WELLOW
WELLOW GOLF COURSE
EMBLEY PARK
Ham Down
EMBLEY WOOD
Smidmore Copse
Aldermoor Copse
Bushmore Copse
Kitts Merries Copse
Shootash Copse
Allen's Copse
Batter's Copse
Withybed Copse
Spouts Copse
HALL COPSE
Bellconey Copse
Woodington Nature Reserve
Whinwhistle Coarse Fishery
Woodington Fishery
RIVER BLACKWATER
Hampshire Collegiate Prep Sch.
Hampshire Collegiate Senior Sch.
EMBLEY PARK INDUSTRIAL ESTATE
Wellow School
Sewage Works
Kings Lake
Willow Lake
Embley Park Lake
Kentford Lake
Ham Lake
Sports Field
Playing Field
FOREST EDGE PK
122
156
121
120

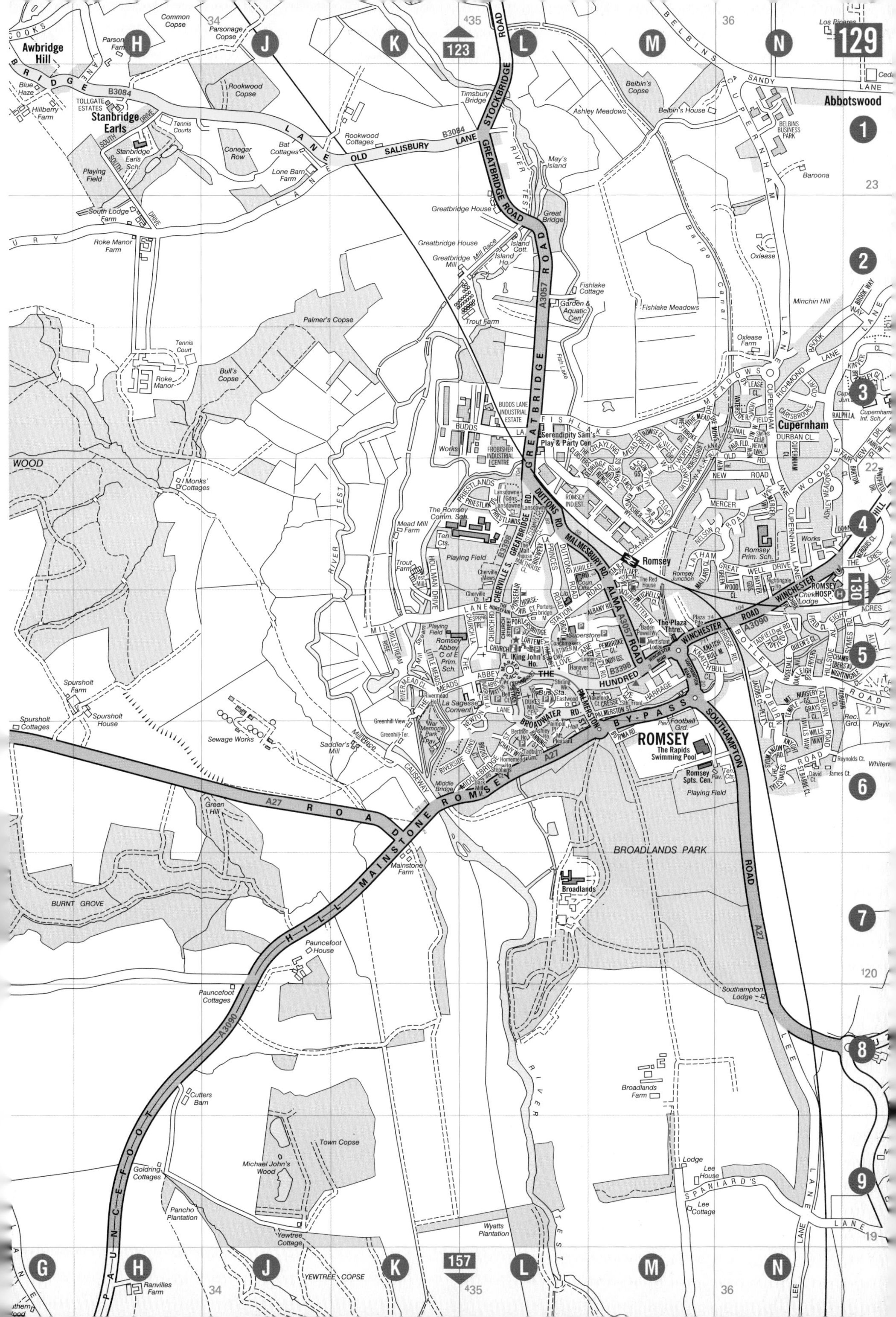

Awbridge Hill
Stanbridge Earls
Abbotswood
Cupernham
ROMSEY
BROADLANDS PARK
Broadlands
Romsey
The Rapids Swimming Pool
Romsey Spts. Cen.
Playing Field
Palmer's Copse
Bull's Copse
Roke Manor
Common Copse
Parsonage Copse
Rookwood Copse
Conegar Row
Belbin's Copse
Ashley Meadows
Fishlake Meadows
Minchin Hill
Oxlease
Oxlease Farm
Mainstone Farm
Pauncefoot House
Pauncefoot Cottages
Cutters Barn
Town Copse
Michael John's Wood
Goldring Cottages
Pancho Plantation
Yewtree Cottage
YEWTREE COPSE
Ranvilles Farm
Wyatts Plantation
Broadlands Farm
Lee House
Lee Cottage
Southampton Lodge
Spursholt Farm
Spursholt House
Spursholt Cottages
Sewage Works
Saddler's Mill
BURNT GROVE
Green Hill
WOOD
Monks' Cottages
Greatbridge House
Greatbridge Mill
Timsbury Bridge
Great Bridge
May's Island
Trout Farm
Mead Mill Farm
The Romsey Comm. Sch.
Romsey Abbey C of E Prim. Sch.
La Sagesse Convent
War Memorial Park
King John's Ho.
The Plaza Thtre.
Romsey Prim. Sch.
ROMSEY HOSP.
BUDDS LANE INDUSTRIAL ESTATE
FROBISHER INDUSTRIAL CENTRE
ROMSEY IND. EST.
Serendipity Sam's Play & Party Cen
BELBINS BUSINESS PARK
A27
A3090
A3057
A3057
B3084
B3398
ROMSEY ROAD
MAINSTONE HILL
PAUNCEFOOT HILL
GREATBRIDGE ROAD
STOCKBRIDGE ROAD
OLD SALISBURY LANE
WINCHESTER ROAD
SOUTHAMPTON ROAD
BY-PASS
MALMESBURY RD.
ALMA ROAD
DUTTONS RD.
FISHLAKE MEADOWS
CUPERNHAM LANE
WOODLEY LANE
SPANIARD'S LANE
LEE LANE
SANDY LANE
BELBINS
123
130
157
34
435
36
23
22
21
120
19
H
J
K
L
M
N
G
1
2
3
4
5
6
7
8
9

Abbotswood
Cupernham
Woodley
Harefield
Halterworth
Whitenap
ROMSEY
Romsey
SO51
Crampmoor
Ampfield Hill
Scrag Hill
NORTH BADDESLEY
Nutburn
Ashfield
BADDESLEY COMMON
LUZBOROUGH PLANTATION
WINCHESTER HILL
STRAIGHT MILE
BOTLEY
CHILWORTH
124
158
129

H
J
K
L
M
N
125
AMPFIELD WOOD
Ampfield Plantation
KNAPP
Morleys
Great Close
Nevil's Copse
Lower Ratlake Farm
Ratlake Hall
Ratlake
Kent's Copse
Drain
Winchester
SO21
Lake Court
Purdue's Copse
Upper Ratlake Farmhouse
White's Copse
Hawstead Farm
Ryder's Row
Ampfield House
Ampfield
Monkswood House
Redburn Farm
Club House
Sports Ground
AMPFIELD GOLF COURSE
A3090
POTTERS HERON LA.
POTTERS HERON CL.
Buddy's Barn
Sandpit Copse
Hook Row
Hocombe Plantation
Hocombe Upper Plantation
HOCOMBE ROAD
Hocombe
Ampfield Common Piece
Broadgate
Nursery
HOOK ROAD
HOOK CRESCENT
HOOKWATER RD
HOCOMBE WOOD
Hocombe Mead Nature Reserve
Purser's Great Copse
Bluebell Copse
Broadgate Clump
WOODLEA WAY
HOOKWOOD LA.
BEECHWOOD CL.
BEECHWOOD CRES
HOCOMBE DR.
Great High Trees
Trodds Copse
HILTINGBURY ROAD
Hiltingbury Playing Fields
B3043
WINCHESTER ROAD
TEST VALLEY
Wheelhouse Pk Caravan Pk
King Edward Park
St James Park
Flexford Nature Reserve
North Hill Copse
Cemetery
BUSHES LANE
Churchers Common Plantation
Broadgate Plantation
Woodend Copse
Monks Brook
Thorn Hill
Flexford
Baddesley Bridge
FURTHER COMMON PLANTATION
Green Acres
Newlands Copse
Flexford House
Apiary
Depot
Ramalley
Ramalley Copse
132
Castle Hill
Clothiers Copse
Keepers Lodge
Bucket Corner
POUND LANE
Elmer Cottage
EASTLEIGH
TEST VALLEY
Ramalley Bri.
Knightwood Prim. Sch.
Ramalley Piece
Knight Wood
CHANDLER'S FORD
Badger's Copse
Sky's Wood
Castlehill Farm
FLEXFORD ROAD
Moss Corner
Knightwood Park
Ryders Farm
Body Farm
Manor Farm
Manor House
Tredgoulds Copse
SHANNON WAY
Eastleigh
SO53
Southampton
SO52
CRUSADERS WAY
Nutburn Cottage
DIRTY DRIVE
Zionshill Copse
Small Profits
ANCHOR BUS.CEN.
MONKS BROOK IND. PARK
Bodysound Fitness Club
BRICKFIELD TRAD. EST.
CHANDLER'S FORD INDUSTRIAL ESTATE
Nutburn Farm
Knightwood Leisure Centre
St. Francis C of E Prim. Sch.
Great Covert
Comm. Cen.
Titlark Copse
Thatched Cottages
Mile Ride
Marlborough Cl.
WARRIOR PK. IND. EST.
CASTLE LANE
Wrens Farm
Littlemead
Zion Hill Cottage
HOGTROUGH WOOD
The Talisman
Wrens Copse
Misslebrooks Copse
TEMPLARS WAY
Castle Lane Farm
MISSELBROOK LANE
Roundabouts
Club Ho.
Range
The Rough
VELMORE RD
GUILDFORD DRIVE
TEMPLARS MEDE
A27
ROAD
GOLF COURSE
Austins Copse
Roman Road (course of)
Velmore Farm
HAMPSHIRE CORPORATE PARK
Hypermarket
BOURNEMOUTH ROAD
G
159
Velmore Farm Cottages
Builders Yard
Rother House
Spring Copse
Marshalls
Offices
440
41
42
43
23
22
21
120
1
2
3
4
5
6
7
8
9

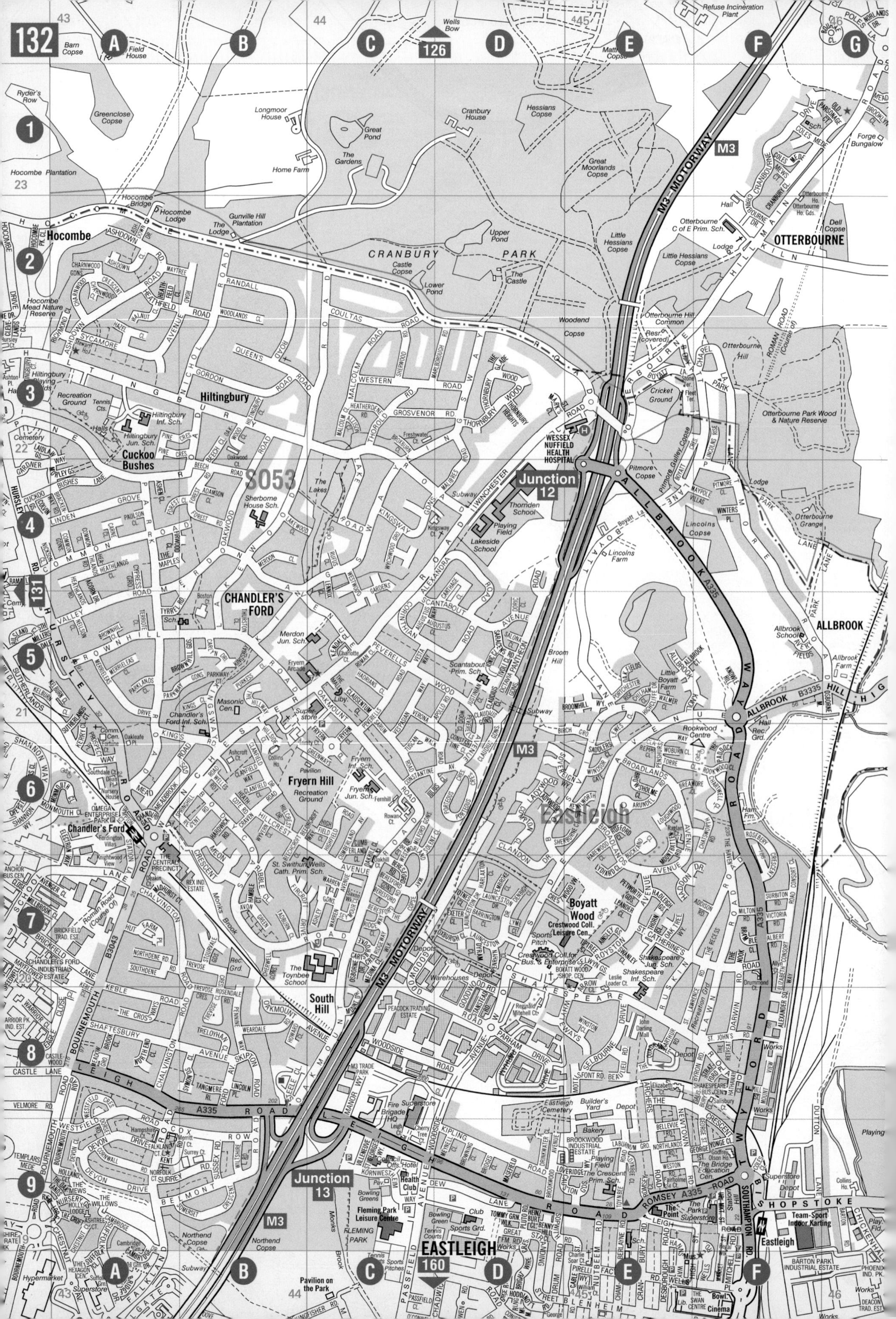

126
131
160
A
B
C
D
E
F
G
1
2
3
4
5
6
7
8
9
Wells Bow
Refuse Incineration Plant
Barn Copse
Field House
Ryder's Row
Greenclose Copse
Hocombe Plantation
Longmoor House
Great Pond
The Gardens
Home Farm
Cranbury House
Hessians Copse
Great Moorlands Copse
M3
M3–MOTORWAY
Forge Bungalow
Hocombe Bridge
Hocombe Lodge
The Lodge
Gunville Hill Plantation
Hocombe
Upper Pond
CRANBURY PARK
Castle Copse
Lower Pond
The Castle
Little Hessians Copse
Little Hessians Copse
Otterbourne C of E Prim. Sch.
OTTERBOURNE
Dell Copse
Hocombe Mead Nature Reserve
Woodend Copse
Otterbourne Hill Common
Otterbourne Hill
Hiltingbury
Recreation Ground
Hiltingbury Inf. Sch.
Hiltingbury Jun. Sch.
Cemetery
Cuckoo Bushes
S053
Sherborne House Sch.
The Lakes
WESSEX NUFFIELD HEALTH HOSPITAL
Junction 12
Thornden School
Playing Field
Lakeside School
Cricket Ground
Otterbourne Park Wood & Nature Reserve
Pitmore Copse
Lincolns Copse
Lincolns Farm
Otterbourne Grange
CHANDLER'S FORD
Merdon Jun. Sch.
Fryern Arcade
Scantabout Prim. Sch.
ALLBROOK
Allbrook School
Allbrook Farm
Broom Hill
Little Boyatt Farm
Masonic Cen.
Chandler's Ford Inf. Sch.
Rookwood Centre
Fryern Hill
Recreation Ground
Fryern Inf. Sch.
Fryern Jun. Sch.
Eastleigh
OMEGA ENTERPRISE PARK
Chandler's Ford
THE CENTRAL PRECINCT
REX IND. ESTATE
St. Swithun Wells Cath. Prim. Sch.
Monks Brook
Boyatt Wood
Crestwood Coll. Leisure Cen.
Crestwood Coll. for Bus. & Enterprise
BOYATT WOOD SHOP. CEN.
Shakespeare Jun. Sch.
Shakespeare Inf. Sch.
BRICKFIELD TRAD. EST.
CHANDLER'S FORD INDUSTRIAL ESTATE
The Toynbee School
South Hill
M3–MOTORWAY
PEACOCK TRADING ESTATE
M3 TRADE PARK
Recreation Ground
Eastleigh Cemetery
Builder's Yard
BROOKWOOD INDUSTRIAL ESTATE
The Crescent Prim. Sch.
The Bridge Education Cen.
Fire Brigade HQ
Superstore
Junction 13
Fleming Park Leisure Centre
FLEMING PARK
Northend Copse
Pavilion on the Park
EASTLEIGH
The Point
Eastleigh
Team-Sport Indoor Karting
BARTON PARK INDUSTRIAL ESTATE
THE SWAN CENTRE
Bowl. Cinema
Hypermarket
Superstore
A335
B3043
B3335
LEIGH ROAD
BOURNEMOUTH ROAD
WINCHESTER ROAD
ALLBROOK WAY
TWYFORD ROAD
SOUTHAMPTON RD.
SHOPSTOKE
43
44
445
46
23
22
21
20
19

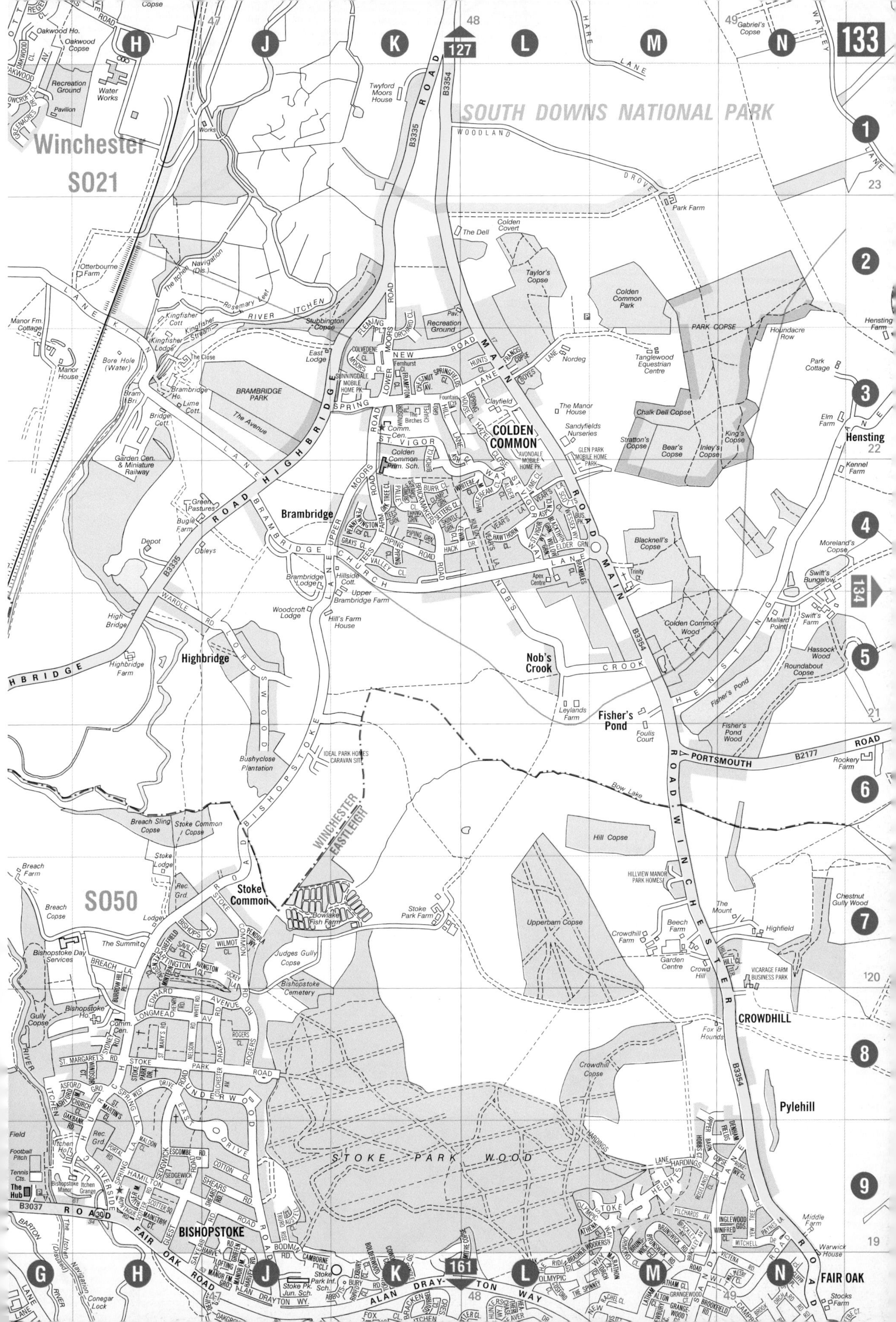
SOUTH DOWNS NATIONAL PARK
Winchester
SO21
SO50
COLDEN COMMON
Brambridge
Highbridge
Nob's Crook
Fisher's Pond
Stoke Common
CROWDHILL
Pylehill
Hensting
BISHOPSTOKE
FAIR OAK
STOKE PARK WOOD
Upperbarn Copse
Hill Copse
Colden Common Park
PARK COPSE
Chalk Dell Copse
Stratton's Copse
Bear's Copse
Inley's Copse
King's Copse
Taylor's Copse
Colden Covert
The Dell
Park Farm
Houndacre Row
Tanglewood Equestrian Centre
Park Cottage
Elm Farm
Kennel Farm
Hensting Farm
Moreland's Copse
Swift's Bungalow
Swift's Farm
Mallard Point
Hassock Wood
Roundabout Copse
Colden Common Wood
Blacknell's Copse
Fisher's Pond Wood
Rookery Farm
Leylands Farm
Foulis Court
Bow Lake
WINCHESTER
EASTLEIGH
Bushyclose Plantation
IDEAL PARK HOMES CARAVAN SITE
Breach Sling Copse
Stoke Common Copse
Stoke Lodge
Breach Farm
Breach Copse
Bishopstoke Day Services
The Summit
Judges Gully Copse
Bishopstoke Cemetery
Bowlake Fish Farm
Stoke Park Farm
HILLVIEW MANOR PARK HOMES
The Mount
Highfield
Chestnut Gully Wood
Beech Farm
Crowdhill Farm
Garden Centre
Crowd Hill
VICARAGE FARM BUSINESS PARK
Fox & Hounds
Crowdhill Copse
Middle Farm
Warwick House
Stocks Farm
Twyford Moors House
Water Works
Recreation Ground
Pavilion
Oakwood Ho.
Oakwood Copse
Otterbourne Farm
Manor Fm. Cottage
Manor House
Bore Hole (Water)
Kingfisher Cott
Kingfisher Lodge
Kingfisher Stream
RIVER ITCHEN
The Itchen Navigation (Dis.)
Rosemary Leet
Stubbington Copse
East Lodge
BRAMBRIDGE PARK
The Avenue
Brambridge Ho.
Lime Cott.
Bridge Cott.
Garden Cen. & Miniature Railway
Green Pastures
Bugle Farm
Depot
Obleys
High Bridge
Highbridge Farm
Brambridge Lodge
Hillside Cott.
Upper Brambridge Farm
Woodcroft Lodge
Hill's Farm House
Comm. Cen.
Colden Common Prim. Sch.
The Birches
The Manor House
Sandyfields Nurseries
GLEN PARK MOBILE HOME PARK
AVONDALE MOBILE HOME PK.
SUNNINGDALE MOBILE HOME PK.
Clayfield
Nordeg
Apex Centre
B3335
B3354
B2177
B3037
HIGHBRIDGE ROAD
MAIN ROAD
PORTSMOUTH ROAD
WINCHESTER ROAD
BISHOPSTOKE ROAD
WOODLAND DROVE
HARE LANE
KILN LANE
CHURCH LANE
SPRING LANE
NEW ROAD
ST. VIGOR WAY
UPPER MOORS ROAD
HENSTING LANE
CROOK
LORDS WOOD
WARDLE RD.
ALAN DRAYTON WAY
FAIR OAK ROAD
RIVERSIDE
STOKE PARK ROAD
UNDERWOOD
EAST DRIVE
Itchen Ho.
Football Pitch
Tennis Cts.
The Hub
Bishopstoke Manor
Itchen Grange
Stoke Pk. Jun. Sch.
Stoke Park Inf. Sch.
Conegar Lock
The Itchen Navigation (Disused)
RIVER ITCHEN
Gully Copse
Bishopstoke Ho.
Comm. Cen.
Rec. Grd.
127
134
161
G
H
J
K
L
M
N
1
2
3
4
5
6
7
8
9
47
48
49
23
22
21
120
19

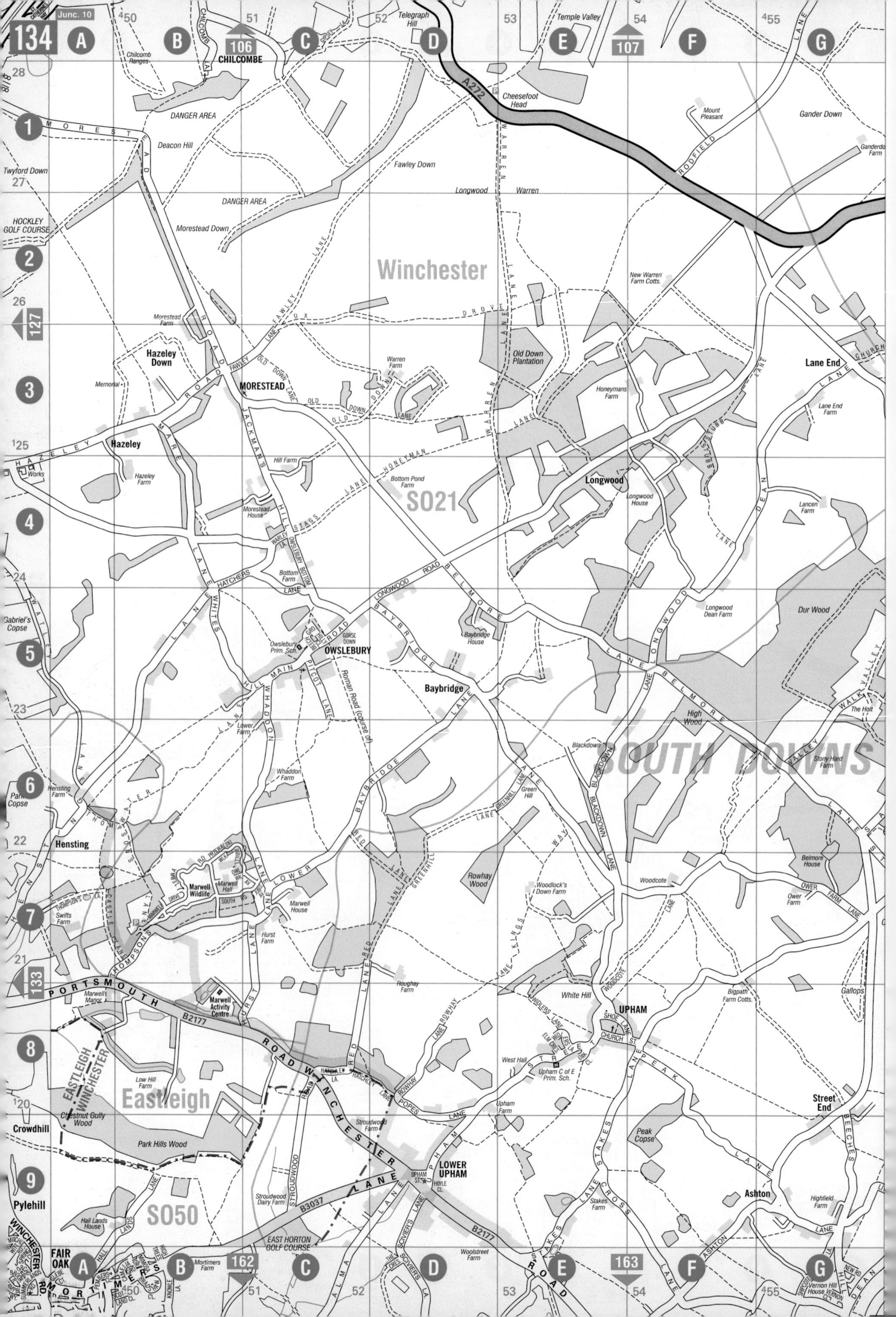
Junc. 10
106
107
127
133
162
163
CHILCOMBE
Chilcomb Ranges
Telegraph Hill
Temple Valley
Cheesefoot Head
A272
DANGER AREA
Deacon Hill
Twyford Down
HOCKLEY GOLF COURSE
Fawley Down
Longwood
Warren
Morestead Down
Mount Pleasant
Gander Down
Winchester
New Warren Farm Cotts.
Morestead Farm
Hazeley Down
Warren Farm
Old Down Plantation
Lane End
MORESTEAD
Honeymans Farm
Lane End Farm
Memorial
Hazeley
Hill Farm
Bottom Pond Farm
Hazeley Farm
SO21
Longwood
Longwood House
Lancen Farm
Morestead House
Bottom Farm
Gabriel's Copse
Longwood Dean Farm
Dur Wood
Owslebury Prim. Sch.
OWSLEBURY
Baybridge House
Baybridge
Roman Road (course of)
Lower Farm
High Wood
The Holt
Blackdown
SOUTH DOWNS
Stony Hard Farm
Whaddon Farm
Hensting Farm
Green Hill
Hensting
Rowhay Wood
Woodlock's Down Farm
Belmore House
Woodcote
Marwell Wildlife
Marwell Hall
Marwell House
Ower Farm
Swifts Farm
Hurst Farm
Roughay Farm
White Hill
UPHAM
Bignath Farm Cotts.
Gallops
Marwell Manor
Marwell Activity Centre
B2177
West Hall
Upham C of E Prim. Sch.
Eastleigh
Winchester
Low Hill Farm
Upham Farm
Street End
Crowdhill
Chestnut Gully Wood
Stroudwood Farm
Peak Copse
Park Hills Wood
LOWER UPHAM
Ashton
Pylehill
Stroudwood Dairy Farm
Stakes Farm
Highfield Farm
Hall Lands House
SO50
B3037
FAIR OAK
EAST HORTON GOLF COURSE
Mortimers Farm
Woolstreet Farm
Vernon Hill House
PORTSMOUTH ROAD
WINCHESTER ROAD
MORESTEAD ROAD
HAZELEY ROAD
JACKMANS HILL
LONGWOOD ROAD
BELMORE LANE
BAYBRIDGE LANE
WARREN LANE
HONEYMAN LANE
OLD DOWN LANE
FAWLEY LANE
STAGS LANE
HATCHERS LANE
WHITES LANE
WHADDON LANE
PITCOT LANE
BLACKDOWN LANE
GREENHILL LANE
RED LANE
HURST LANE
LOWER LANE
THOMPSONS LANE
CASTLE LANE
HENSTING LANE
KINGS LANE
ROWHAY LANE
POPES LANE
STROUDWOOD LANE
LANDS LANE
UPHAM STREET
CHURCH ST
PEAK LANE
STAKES LANE
CROSS LANE
ASHTON LANE
BEECHES LANE
OWER FARM LANE
VALLEY WALK
DEAN LANE
RODFIELD LANE
CHURCH LANE
STUBB LANE
SHOE LANE
ALMA LANE
SCIVIERS LANE
MORTIMERS LANE
WINCHESTER RD
HATCHLEY LA.
HAZELEY
A B C D E F G
1 2 3 4 5 6 7 8 9
450 51 52 53 54 455
28 27 26 125 24 23 22 21 120

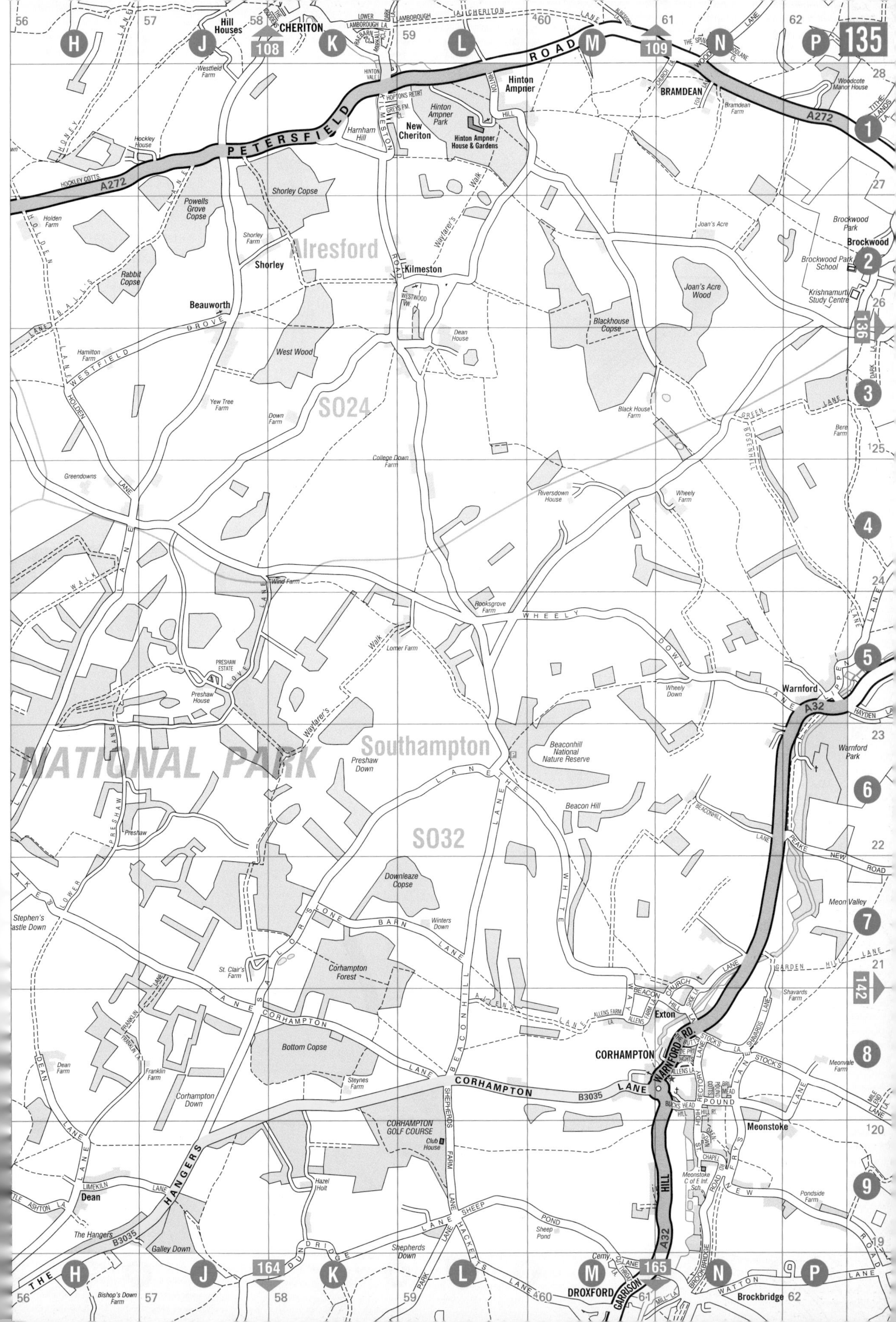
CHERITON
Hill Houses
BRAMDEAN
Hinton Ampner
New Cheriton
Hinton Ampner House & Gardens
PETERSFIELD ROAD
A272
Shorley Copse
Powells Grove Copse
Alresford
Shorley
Beauworth
Kilmeston
Brockwood
Brockwood Park School
Krishnamurti Study Centre
Joan's Acre Wood
Blackhouse Copse
West Wood
SO24
College Down Farm
Riversdown House
Wheely Farm
Rooksgrove Farm
WHEELY DOWN LANE
Warnford
A32
Warnford Park
Preshaw House
NATIONAL PARK
Southampton
Beaconhill National Nature Reserve
Beacon Hill
SO32
Downleaze Copse
Corhampton Forest
Bottom Copse
Exton
CORHAMPTON
CORHAMPTON LANE
B3035
Meonstoke
CORHAMPTON GOLF COURSE
Dean
The Hangers
Galley Down
Shepherds Down
DROXFORD
Brockbridge
Meon Valley
108
109
136
142
164
165

Woodcote Copse
Woodcote Manor House
Slys Farm
TITHELANDS LANE
Hinton Woodlands Cottages
Pursers Lodge
Purser's
Punsholt Farm
Punsholt Cottages
Woodlands Cottages
Hinton Woodlands Farm
Woodlands Farm
Alresford
SO24
A272
Humpty's Down
Three Horse Shoes Farm
PUNSHOLT LANE
PURSER'S LANE
KITT'S LANE
Brockwood Dean
The Grove
Godwin's Copse
Lodge Plantation
The Dean
West Meon Woodlands
Woodlands Cottages
Brockwood Lodge
BROCKWOOD PARK
Brockwood
Upper House Farm
THREE HORSE SHOES LANE
Moon's Spinney
Inwood Copse
Sherwood's Cottage
RIVERDOWN RD.
SOUTH DOWNS
Gardener's Cottage
BrockwoodPark School
Brockwood Park Farm
Sherwood's Grove
Shutt's Copse
Saw House Firs
Moon's Copse
Inwoods
EAST HAMPSHIRE
WINCHESTER
Krishnamurti Study Centre
Dell Cottages
Brockwood Bottom
Rowley Beeches
Brick Kiln Cottage
A32
Brick Kiln Farm
Little Headdon Copse
Stoney Dene
Westwood
Highfield
Headdon Farm
Arnold's Firs
Sutton Park
Brockwood Copse
Marlands Cottage
Marlands
DARK LANE
GREEN LA.
Westwood Cottage
VINNELLS LANE
Little Hayling Wood
Marldell Farm
Hayling Wood
Bere Farm
West Wood
Reservoirs (covered)
Southampton
SO32
Court Farm
Lippen Wood
Lippen Cottages
Garretts Farm
Little Lippen Wood
Little Bottoms Wood
Tennis Courts
Rec. Grd.
Pav.
Hall
LONG PRIORS
KNAPPS HARD
Westbury Cottage
Pav.
Cricket Ground
CHURCH LANE
Floud Cottages
FLOUD LA.
HEADON VW.
Wolverton Gds.
Laurel Dene
WEST MEON
West Meon C of E Prim. Sch.
DOCTORS LA.
East End
MEONWARA CRES.
Westbury Manor Farm Cottages
Westbury Manor Farm
BOSENHILL
HIGH ST.
Home Paddocks
The Court House
West Meon House
St. Nicholas's Chapel (remains of)
Hall Place
Hall Farm
STATION ROAD
LOVE LA.
Westbury House
Chappetts Farm
Chappets Copse
North End Cottages
PEPPER LANE
College Farm
Beaconsfield Farm
LYNCH LANE
OLD WINCHESTER HILL LANE
Brocklands Farm
Sheepbri Copse
Watercress Beds
Bradford's Clump
Gadsfield

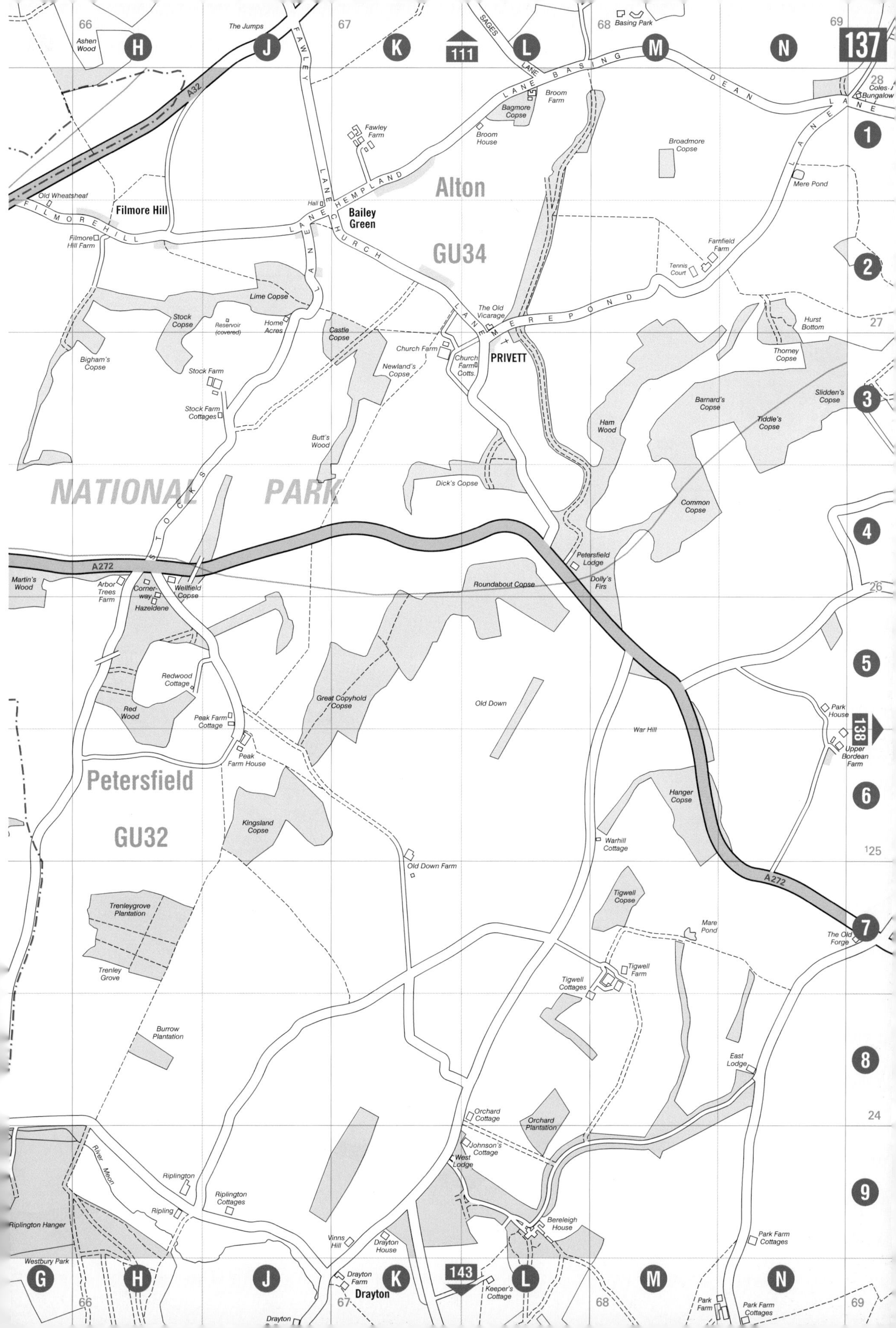

Ashen Wood
The Jumps
A32
Fawley Lane
Sages Lane
Basing Park
Basing Lane
Dean Lane
111
Broom Farm
Bagmore Copse
Coles Bungalow
Fawley Farm
Broom House
Broadmore Copse
Hempland Lane
Alton
Mere Pond
Old Wheatsheaf
Filmore Hill
Hall
Bailey Green
Filmore Hill Farm
Church Lane
GU34
Farnfield Farm
Tennis Court
Lime Copse
The Old Vicarage
Merepond Lane
Hurst Bottom
Stock Copse
Reservoir (covered)
Home Acres
Castle Copse
Church Farm
PRIVETT
Thorney Copse
Bigham's Copse
Church Farm Cotts.
Newland's Copse
Stock Farm
Barnard's Copse
Slidden's Copse
Stock Farm Cottages
Ham Wood
Tiddle's Copse
Butt's Wood
Dick's Copse
NATIONAL PARK
Stocks Lane
Common Copse
A272
Petersfield Lodge
Martin's Wood
Arbor Trees Farm
Corner-way
Wellfield Copse
Hazeldene
Dolly's Firs
Roundabout Copse
Redwood Cottage
Red Wood
Great Copyhold Copse
Old Down
War Hill
Peak Farm Cottage
Park House
Upper Bordean Farm
138
Peak Farm House
Petersfield
Hanger Copse
Kingsland Copse
GU32
Warhill Cottage
Old Down Farm
A272
Tigwell Copse
Trenleygrove Plantation
Mare Pond
The Old Forge
Trenley Grove
Tigwell Farm
Tigwell Cottages
Burrow Plantation
East Lodge
Orchard Cottage
Orchard Plantation
Johnson's Cottage
West Lodge
River Meon
Riplington
Riplington Cottages
Ripling
Riplington Hanger
Bereleigh House
Park Farm Cottages
Vinns Hill
Drayton House
Westbury Park
Drayton Farm
Drayton
143
Keeper's Cottage
Park Farm
Park Farm Cottages
Drayton
66
67
68
69
28
27
26
125
24
G
H
J
K
L
M
N
1
2
3
4
5
6
7
8
9

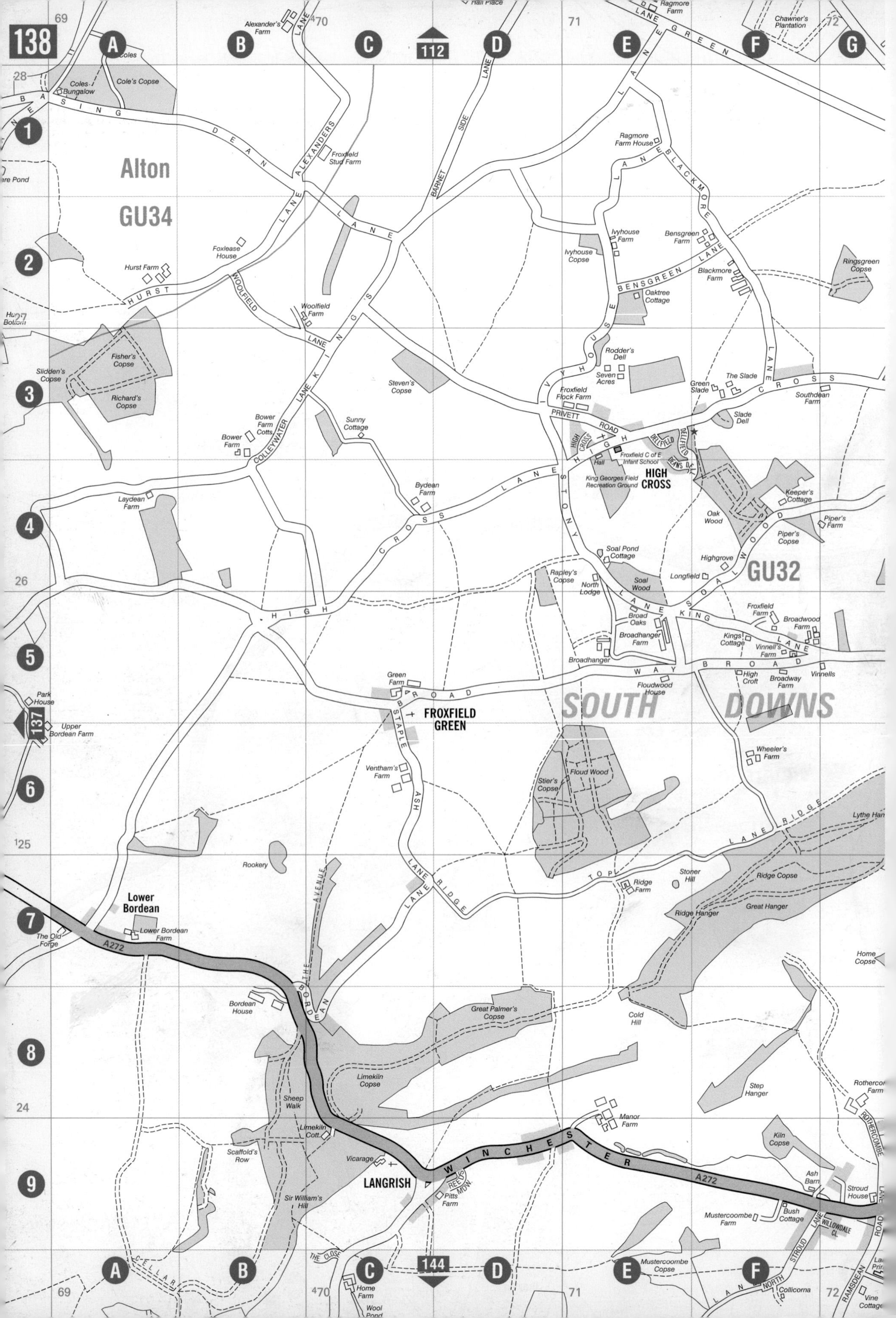
112
144
137
Alton
GU34
GU32
SOUTH DOWNS
HIGH CROSS
FROXFIELD GREEN
Lower Bordean
LANGRISH
Coles
Coles Bungalow
Cole's Copse
Alexander's Farm
Hall Place
Ragmore Farm
Chawner's Plantation
DEAN LANE
ALEXANDERS LANE
Froxfield Stud Farm
BARNET SIDE LANE
Ragmore Farm House
BLACKMORE LANE
GREEN LANE
Foxlease House
Hurst Farm
HURST
WOOLFIELD
Woolfield Farm
Ivyhouse Farm
Ivyhouse Copse
Bensgreen Farm
BENSGREEN LANE
Blackmore Farm
Oaktree Cottage
Ringsgreen Copse
Fisher's Copse
Slidden's Copse
Richard's Copse
Steven's Copse
Rodder's Dell
Seven Acres
Froxfield Flock Farm
The Slade
Green Slade
Southdean Farm
Slade Dell
PRIVETT ROAD
CROSS
KINGS LANE
COLLEYWATER LANE
Bower Farm Cotts
Bower Farm
Sunny Cottage
Froxfield C of E Infant School
Hall
King Georges Field Recreation Ground
DELFIELD
DEANS DELL
Keeper's Cottage
Oak Wood
Piper's Farm
Piper's Copse
Laydean Farm
Bydean Farm
CROSS LANE
STONY LANE
Soal Pond Cottage
Highgrove
Longfield
Rapley's Copse
North Lodge
Soal Wood
SOAL WOOD
HIGH
Froxfield Farm
Broadwood Farm
Broad Oaks
Broadhanger Farm
Kings Cottage
Vinnell's Farm
Broadhanger
BROAD WAY
Vinnells
High Croft
Broadway Farm
Floudwood House
Green Farm
BROAD
Park House
Upper Bordean Farm
STAPLE ASH
Wheeler's Farm
Ventham's Farm
Floud Wood
Stier's Copse
Lythe Han
RIDGE LANE
Rookery
TOP LANE
Ridge Farm
Stoner Hill
Ridge Copse
Great Hanger
Ridge Hanger
THE AVENUE
The Old Forge
Lower Bordean Farm
A272
Home Copse
Bordean House
THE BORDEAN
Great Palmer's Copse
Cold Hill
Limekiln Copse
Step Hanger
Rotherco Farm
Sheep Walk
Manor Farm
ROTHERCOMBE
Limekiln Cott.
Scaffold's Row
Vicarage
WINCHESTER
Kiln Copse
REEDS MDW.
Pitts Farm
Sir William's Hill
Ash Barn
Stroud House
Mustercoombe Farm
Bush Cottage
STROUD LANE
WILLOWDALE CL
CELLAR
THE CLOSE
Mustercoombe Copse
NORTH LANE
Collicorna
Home Farm
Wool Pond
RAMSDEAN
Vine Cottage

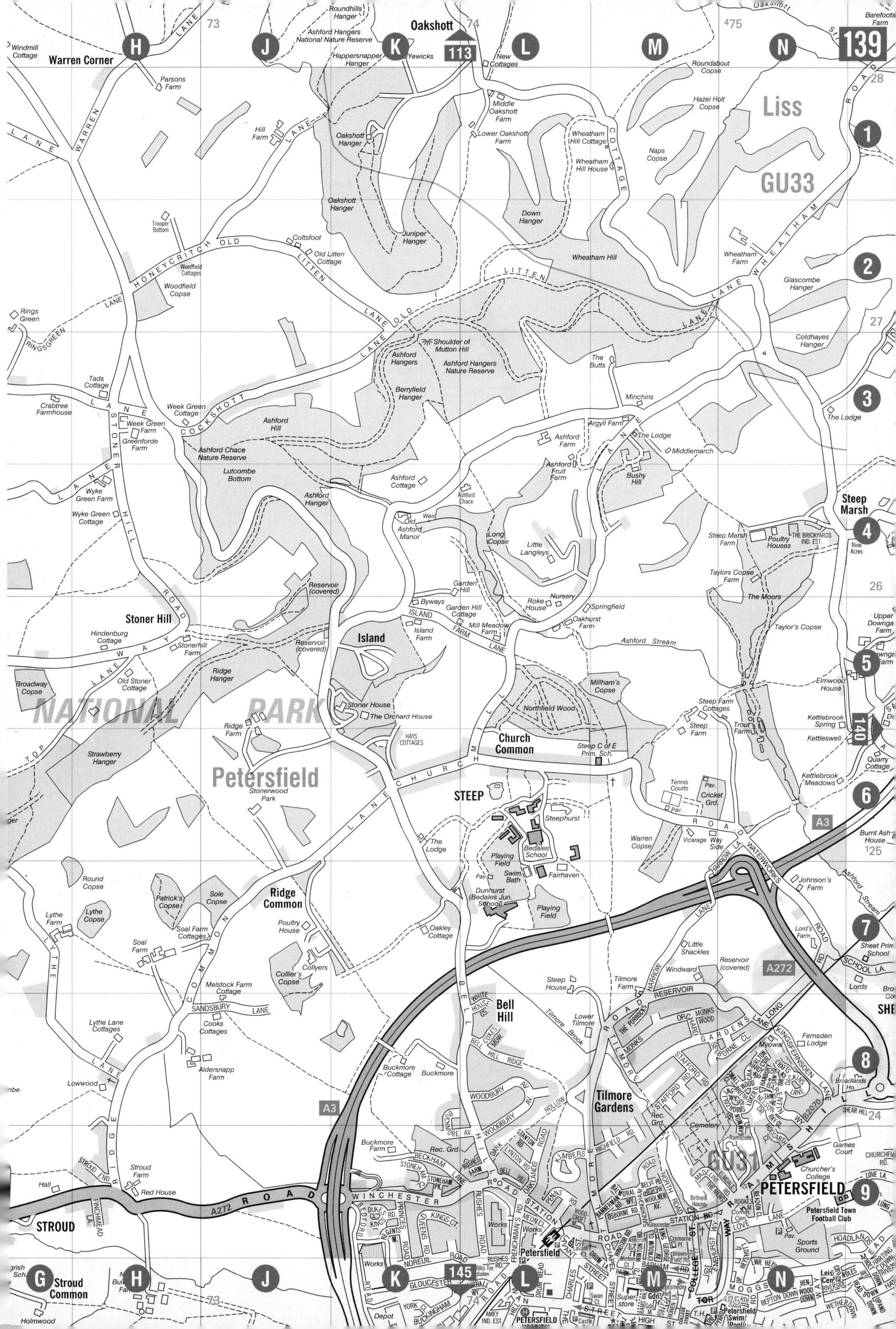

Oakshott
113
Warren Corner
Windmill Cottage
Parsons Farm
Roundhills Hanger
Ashford Hangers National Nature Reserve
Happersnapper Hanger
Yewicks
New Cottages
Roundabout Copse
Barefoots Farm
Liss
GU33
Hazel Holt Copse
Middle Oakshott Farm
Lower Oakshott Farm
Oakshott Hanger
Hill Farm
Wheatham Hill Cottage
Wheatham Hill House
Naps Copse
Down Hanger
Juniper Hanger
Wheatham Hill
Wheatham Farm
Glascombe Hanger
Coldhayes Hanger
Trooper Bottom
Coltsfoot
Old Litten Cottage
Woodfield Cottages
Woodfield Copse
Rings Green
Shoulder of Mutton Hill
Ashford Hangers
Ashford Hangers Nature Reserve
The Butts
Minchins
The Lodge
Tads Cottage
Crabtree Farmhouse
Week Green Cottage
Week Green Farm
Greenforde Farm
Berryfield Hanger
Ashford Hill
Argyll Farm
Ashford Farm
Middlemarch
Ashford Chace Nature Reserve
Lutcombe Bottom
Ashford Fruit Farm
Bushy Hill
Wyke Green Farm
Wyke Green Cottage
Ashford Cottage
Ashford Chace
Ashford Hanger
Steep Marsh
Old Ashford Manor
Weir
Long Copse
Little Langleys
Steep Marsh Farm
Poultry Houses
THE BRICKYARDS IND. EST.
Nine Acres
Taylors Copse Farm
The Moors
Reservoir (covered)
Garden Hill
Byways
Garden Hill Cottage
Roke House
Nursery
Springfield
Stoner Hill
Hindenburg Cottage
Island Farm
Mill Meadow Farm
Oakhurst Farm
Ashford Stream
Taylor's Copse
Upper Downgate Farm
Stonerhill Farm
Island
Reservoir (covered)
Ridge Hanger
Old Stoner Cottage
Broadway Copse
Millham's Copse
Elmwood House
Stoner House
The Orchard House
Northfield Wood
Steep Farm Cottages
Steep Farm
Trout Farm
Kettlebrook Spring
Kettleswell
140
NATIONAL PARK
Ridge Farm
HAYS COTTAGES
Church Common
Steep C of E Prim. Sch.
Quarry Cottage
Strawberry Hanger
Petersfield
Stonerwood Park
STEEP
Tennis Courts
Pav.
Cricket Grd.
Kettlebrook Meadows
Steephurst
A3
The Lodge
Bedales School
Warren Copse
Vicarage
Way Side
Burnt Ash House
Round Copse
Playing Field
Swim. Bath
Fairhaven
Johnson's Farm
Patrick's Copse
Sole Copse
Ridge Common
Dunhurst (Bedales Jun. School)
Playing Field
Lythe Farm
Lythe Copse
Soal Farm Cottages
Poultry House
Oakley Cottage
Lord's Farm
Sheet Primary School
Soal Farm
Collyers
Collier's Copse
Little Shackles
Windward
Reservoir (covered)
A272
Melstock Farm Cottage
Steep House
Tilmore Farm
Lords
Bell Hill
Lower Tilmore
Tilmore Brook
Lythe Lane Cottages
Cooks Cottages
Fernsden Lodge
Myowal
Aldersnapp Farm
Buckmore Cottage
Buckmore
Broadlands Ho.
Lowwood
Tilmore Gardens
Rec. Grd.
Cemetery
Ramscote
Games Court
A3
Buckmore Farm
Rec. Grd.
Stroud Farm
Red House
Churcher's College
PETERSFIELD
Petersfield Town Football Club
Hall
STROUD
Britnell House
Works
Works
Petersfield
Sports Ground
Stroud Common
Holmwood
145
Depot
AMEY IND. EST.
Super store
Swan Cl.
Petersfield Swim. Pool
Leis. Cen.
WARREN
LANE
HONEYCRITCH
OLD
LITTEN
COCKSHOTT
STONER HILL
ROAD
WAY
TOP
RINGSGREEN
COTTAGE
WHEATHAM
ROAD
ISLAND FARM LANE
CHURCH LANE
COMMON
SANDSBURY LANE
LYTHE LANE
RIDGE
STROUD END
FINCHMEAD LA.
A272 ROAD
WINCHESTER
STATION
HARROW LA.
WATERWORKS ROAD
RESERVOIR
HARROW ROAD
TILMORE ROAD
MONKS ORCHARD
MONKS WOOD
GARDENS
SECBORNE CL.
LONG
KINGSFERNSDEN LANE
STAFFORD RD.
BELL HILL RIDGE
WOODBURY AV.
HOLLOW
BUCKMORE AV.
BECKHAM LANE
STONEHAM PK.
RUSHES FARM
BELL HILL
DARK LANE
LYNTON RD.
STANTON ROAD
OAKLANDS
KIMBERS
HIGHFIELD RD.
PENNS RD.
RUSHES ROAD
KINGS CT.
QUEENS RD.
PRINCES ROAD
REGENTS M.
BEDFORD
NOREUIL ROAD
GLOUCESTER
YORK CL.
BUCKINGHAM
FRENCHMAN'S RD.
MEON CL.
DRUM MEAD
CHARLES STREET
CHAPEL STREET
OSBORNE RD.
NORTH ROAD
COLLEGE ST.
RAMSHILL
MOGGS
HIGH
SHEAR HILL
B2070
SCHOOL LA.
CHURCHER'S RD.
LOVE LA.
HOARDLANDS
BEPTON DOWN
WETHERDOWN
GU31
G H J K L M N
1 2 3 4 5 6 7 8 9
73 74 475
28 27 26 125 24

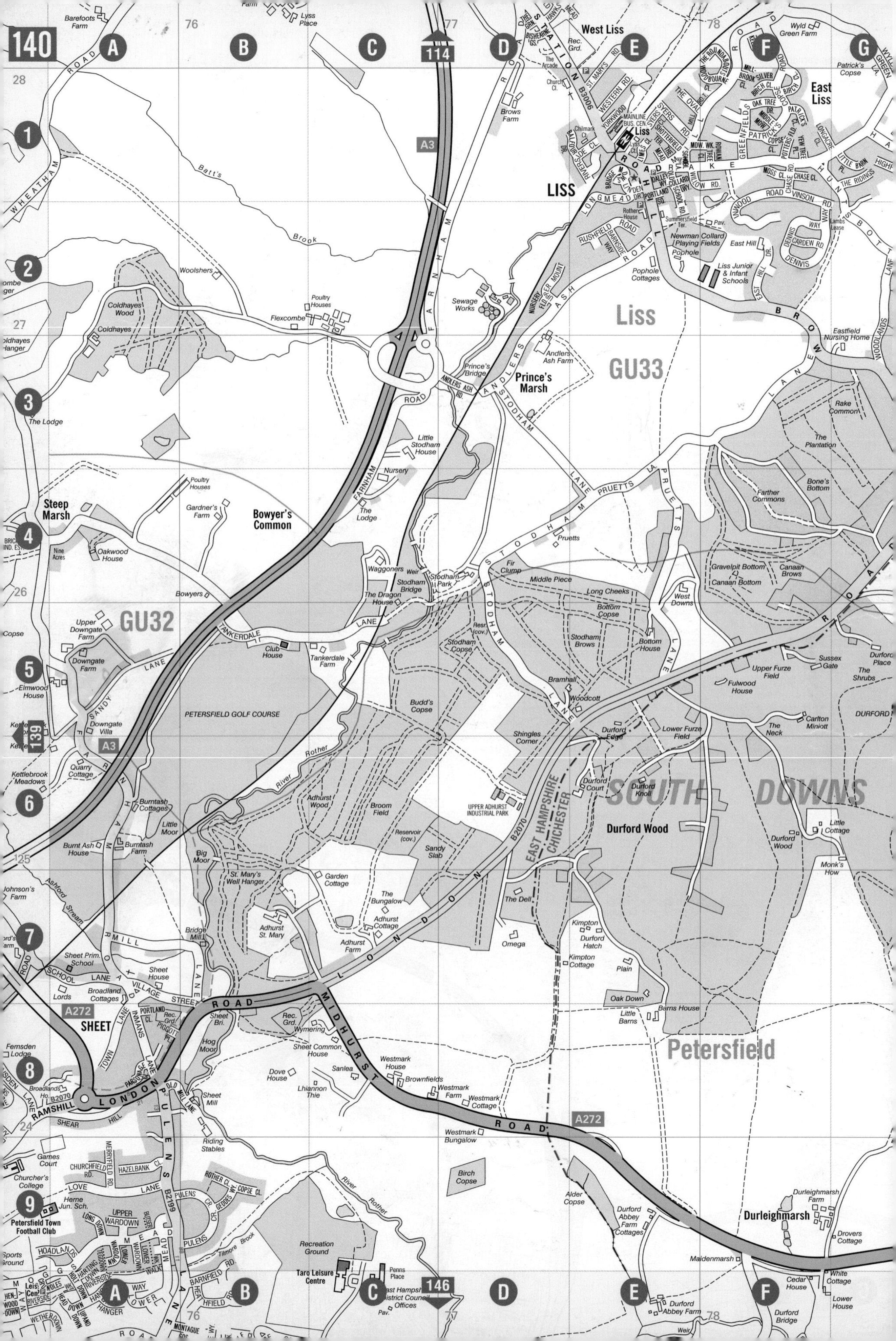

A
B
C
D
E
F
G
114
146
139
West Liss
East Liss
LISS
Liss
GU33
GU32
Prince's Marsh
Bowyer's Common
Steep Marsh
SHEET
SOUTH DOWNS
Durford Wood
Petersfield
Durleighmarsh
PETERSFIELD GOLF COURSE
UPPER ADHURST INDUSTRIAL PARK
EAST HAMPSHIRE
CHICHESTER
A3
A272
B2070
B3006
B2199
LONDON ROAD
MIDHURST ROAD
Liss Junior & Infant Schools
Sheet Prim. School
Taro Leisure Centre
Petersfield Town Football Club
Churcher's College
Recreation Ground
River Rother
Rake Common
The Plantation
Farther Commons
Bone's Bottom
Sewage Works
Little Stodham House
Tankerdale Farm
Adhurst St. Mary
Stodham Park
Westmark Farm
Birch Copse
Durford Abbey Farm

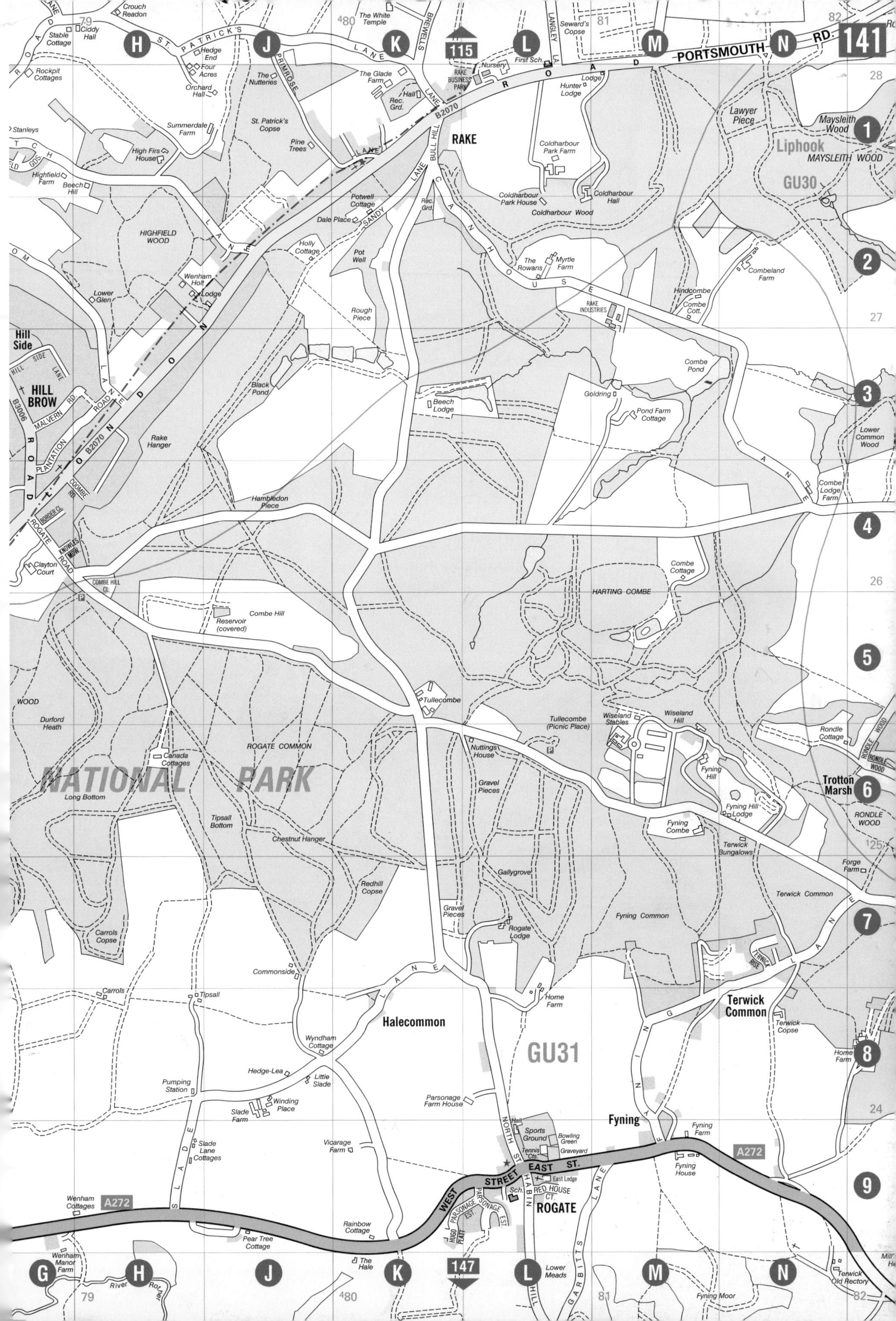
115
147
PORTSMOUTH RD.
B2070
RAKE
Liphook
GU30
MAYSLEITH WOOD
Maysleith Wood
Lawyer Piece
Coldharbour Park Farm
Coldharbour Park House
Coldharbour Hall
Coldharbour Wood
Hunter Lodge
Lodge
Seward's Copse
First Sch.
Nursery
RAKE BUSINESS PARK
Rec. Grd.
The Glade Farm
Hall
The White Temple
BREWELLS
LANGLEY
St. Patrick's Copse
The Nutteries
PRIMROSE
Pine Trees
Crouch Readon
Ciddy Hall
Stable Cottage
Hedge End
Four Acres
Orchard Hall
Rockpit Cottages
Summerdale Farm
High Firs House
Stanleys
Highfield Farm
Beech Hill
HIGHFIELD WOOD
Wenham Holt
Lodge
Lower Glen
Hill Side
HILL BROW
B3006
MALVERN RD
PLANTATION
COOMBE RD
BORDER CL.
ROGATE ROAD
KNOWLES MDW.
Clayton Court
COMBE HILL CL.
Rake Hanger
Potwell Cottage
Dale Place
SANDY LANE
BULL HILL
Holly Cottage
Pot Well
Rough Piece
Black Pond
Hambledon Piece
Reservoir (covered)
Combe Hill
Beech Lodge
The Rowans
Myrtle Farm
RAKE INDUSTRIES
Hindcombe
Combe Cott.
Combeland Farm
Combe Pond
Goldring
Pond Farm Cottage
Lower Common Wood
Combe Lodge Farm
Combe Cottage
HARTING COMBE
Tullecombe
Tullecombe (Picnic Place)
Wiseland Stables
Wiseland Hill
Fyning Hill
Fyning Hill Lodge
Rondle Cottage
RONDLE WOOD
Trotton Marsh
Fyning Combe
Terwick Bungalows
Forge Farm
Terwick Common
WOOD
Durford Heath
NATIONAL PARK
Long Bottom
Canada Cottages
ROGATE COMMON
Nuttings House
Gravel Pieces
Tipsall Bottom
Chestnut Hanger
Gallygrove
Redhill Copse
Carrols Copse
Fyning Common
Gravel Pieces
Rogate Lodge
Commonside
Home Farm
TERWICK RISE
Terwick Common
Terwick Copse
Home Farm
Carrols
Tipsall
Halecommon
Wyndham Cottage
GU31
Hedge-Lea
Little Slade
Pumping Station
Winding Place
Slade Farm
Parsonage Farm House
Fyning
Fyning Farm
Slade Lane Cottages
Vicarage Farm
Hall
Sports Ground
Bowling Green
Tennis Cts.
Graveyard
A272
Fyning House
EAST ST.
WEST STREET
NORTH ST.
East Lodge
Sch.
RED HOUSE CT.
ROGATE
PARSONAGE EST.
HUGO PLATT
HABIN
Wenham Cottages
Pear Tree Cottage
Rainbow Cottage
The Hale
Wenham Manor Farm
River Rother
Lower Meads
GARBITTS LANE
Fyning Moor
Terwick Old Rectory
H J K L M N G
1 2 3 4 5 6 7 8 9
79 480 81 82
28 27 26 25 24

North End Cottages
LIPPEN LANE
River Meon
Brocklands Farm
136
STATION RD
OLD
LYNCH LA
Chappetts Farm
Chappetts Copse
A
B
C
D
E
F
G
63
64
465
Warnford Pond
A32
Sheepbridge Copse
Watercress Beds
Bradford's Clump
Gadsfield
HAYDEN
23
Manor Farm Dairy
Hayden House
Hayden Barn
WARNFORD PARK
ROAD
HAYDEN
WINCHESTER HILL LANE
LANE
1
2
3
4
5
6
7
8
9
22
PEAKE
NEW
ROAD
Lower Peake Cottage
Bullshead Copse
Whitewool Hanger
Henwood Copse
Peake Farm
Peake Wood
Whitewool Pond
Whitewool Lodge
Whitewool Farm
Southampton
135
Roll's Copse
GARDEN HILL LANE
SO32
SOUTH
DOWNS
EAST HAMPSHIRE
WINCHESTER
21
Old Winchester Hill Nature Reserve
Old Winchester Hill
Old Winchester Hill Fort
The Seven Wells
Castle Cottages
Meonvale Farm
END LANE
Harvestgate
MILE
STOCKS
Harvestgate Farm
20
Stocks Cottage
Stocks Farm
LANE
Shogden Wood
Shady Grove
Waterlooville
Teglease Down
Little West End Farm
PO7
Teglease Copse
NEW ROAD
19
166
Westend Down
WATTON LANE
Sheepbarn
Teglease

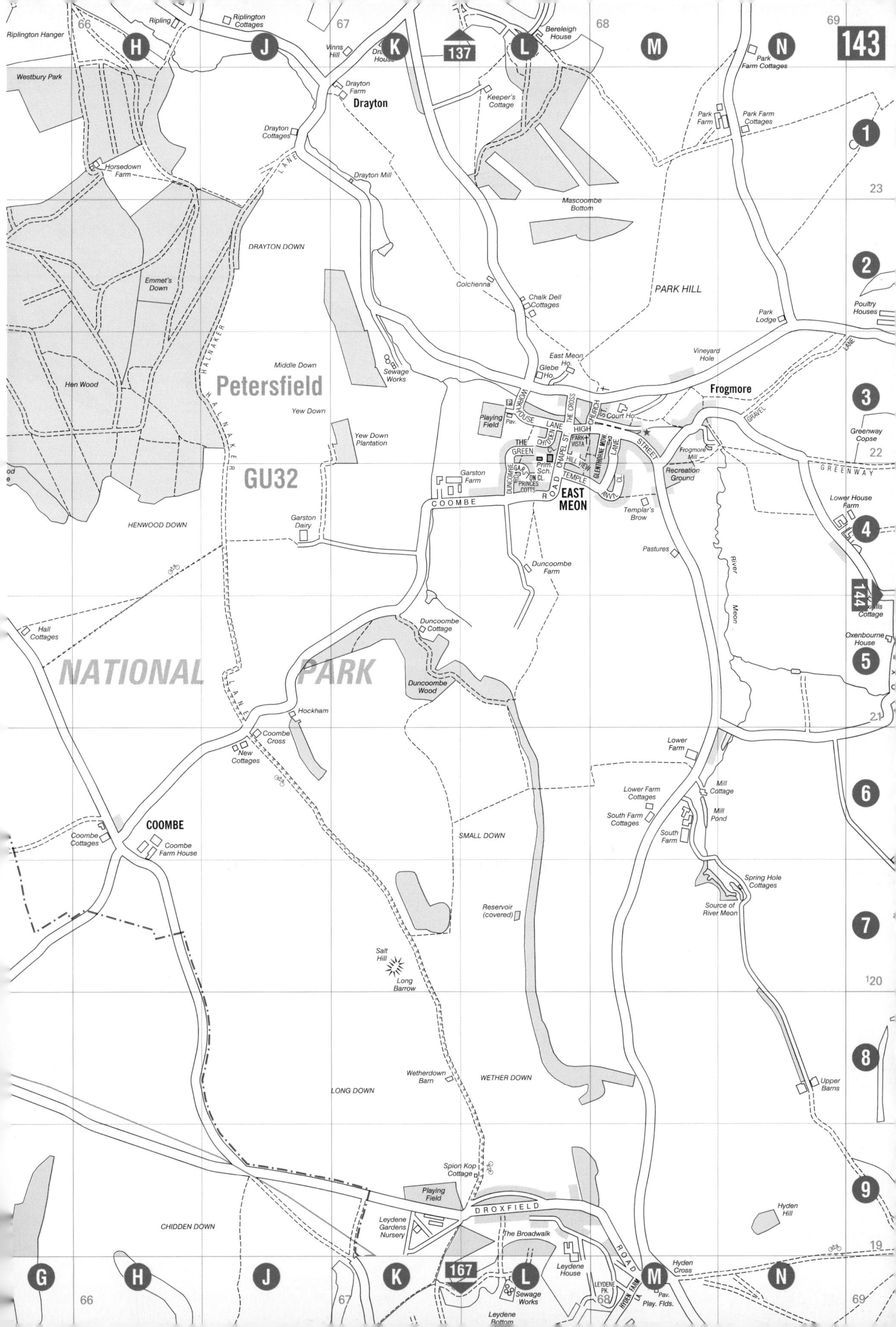

Riplington Hanger
Ripling
Riplington Cottages
Westbury Park
Drayton Farm
Drayton
Keeper's Cottage
Bereleigh House
Park Farm Cottages
Park Farm
Drayton Cottages
Horsedown Farm
Drayton Mill
Mascoombe Bottom
DRAYTON DOWN
Emmet's Down
Colchenna
Chalk Dell Cottages
PARK HILL
Park Lodge
Poultry Houses
Hen Wood
Middle Down
Petersfield
Sewage Works
East Meon Ho.
Glebe Ho.
Vineyard Hole
Frogmore
Yew Down
Yew Down Plantation
Playing Field
Court Ho.
Greenway Copse
GU32
Garston Farm
Frogmore Mill
Recreation Ground
GREENWAY
EAST MEON
Templar's Brow
Lower House Farm
HENWOOD DOWN
Garston Dairy
Pastures
Duncoombe Farm
River Meon
Hall Cottages
Duncoombe Cottage
Oxenbourne House
NATIONAL PARK
Duncoombe Wood
Hockham
Coombe Cross
New Cottages
Lower Farm
Mill Cottage
Lower Farm Cottages
South Farm Cottages
Mill Pond
South Farm
COOMBE
Coombe Cottages
Coombe Farm House
SMALL DOWN
Spring Hole Cottages
Source of River Meon
Reservoir (covered)
Salt Hill
Long Barrow
Wetherdown Barn
WETHER DOWN
LONG DOWN
Upper Barns
Spion Kop Cottage
Playing Field
DROXFIELD
CHIDDEN DOWN
Leydene Gardens Nursery
The Broadwalk
Hyden Hill
Leydene House
Hyden Cross
Sewage Works
Pav. Play. Flds.
Leydene Bottom
137
167
144

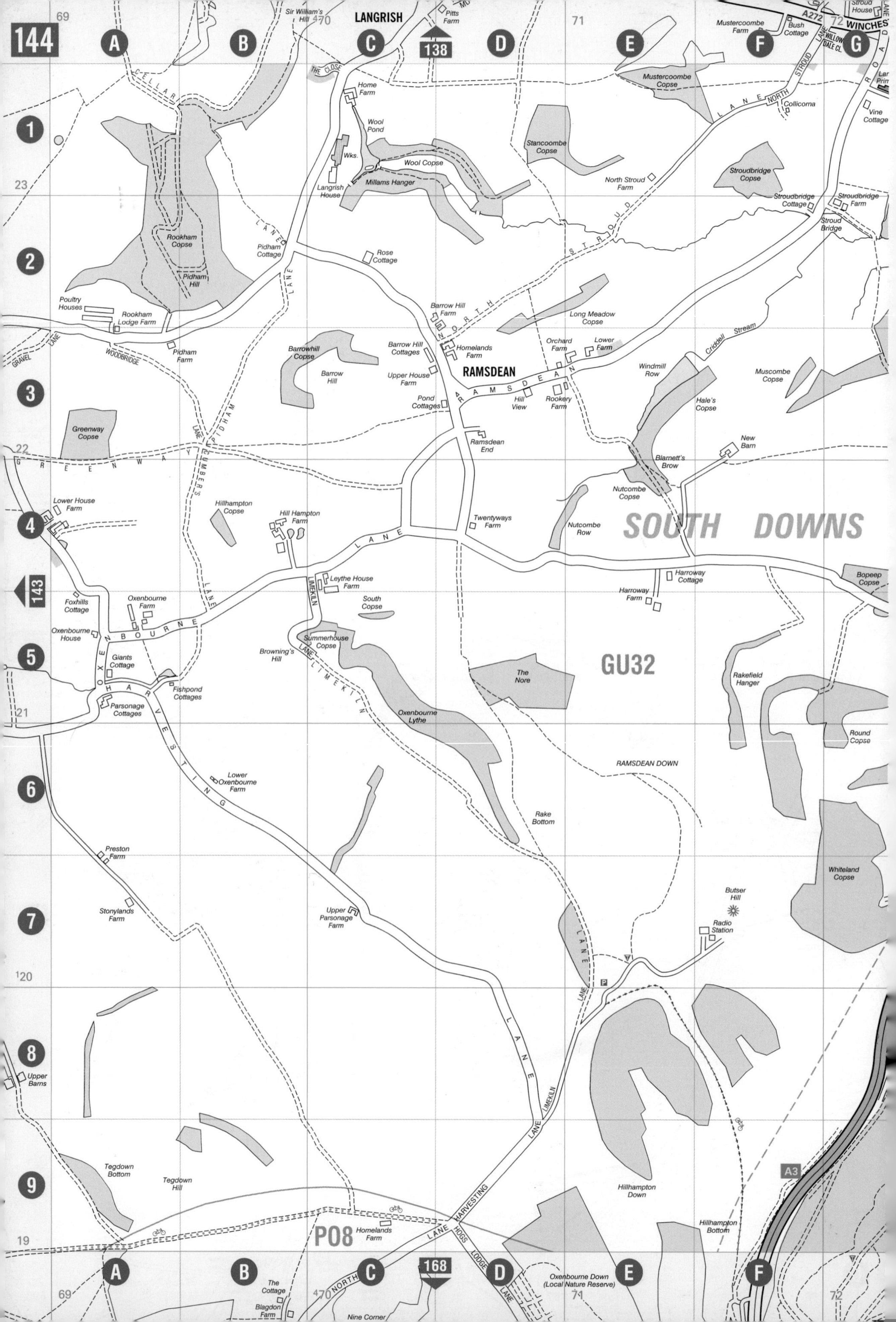
LANGRISH
138
Sir William's Hill
Pitts Farm
Mustercoombe Farm
Bush Cottage
A272
WINCHES
Home Farm
Wool Pond
Wks.
Wool Copse
Millams Hanger
Langrish House
Mustercoombe Copse
Stancoombe Copse
North Stroud Farm
Stroudbridge Copse
Collicorna
Vine Cottage
Stroudbridge Cottage
Stroudbridge Farm
Stroud Bridge
Rookham Copse
Pidham Hill
Pidham Cottage
Rose Cottage
Poultry Houses
Rookham Lodge Farm
Pidham Farm
Barrow Hill Farm
Homelands Farm
Long Meadow Copse
Orchard Farm
Lower Farm
Criddell Stream
Windmill Row
Muscombe Copse
Barrowhill Copse
Barrow Hill
Barrow Hill Cottages
Upper House Farm
Pond Cottages
RAMSDEAN
Hill View
Rookery Farm
Hale's Copse
Ramsdean End
New Barn
Blarnett's Brow
Greenway Copse
GREENWAY
Lower House Farm
Hillhampton Copse
Hill Hampton Farm
Twentyways Farm
Nutcombe Copse
Nutcombe Row
SOUTH DOWNS
Leythe House Farm
Harroway Cottage
Harroway Farm
Bopeep Copse
143
Foxhills Cottage
Oxenbourne Farm
Oxenbourne House
South Copse
Summerhouse Copse
Browning's Hill
GU32
Giants Cottage
Fishpond Cottages
Parsonage Cottages
The Nore
Rakefield Hanger
Oxenbourne Lythe
Round Copse
RAMSDEAN DOWN
Lower Oxenbourne Farm
Rake Bottom
Preston Farm
Whiteland Copse
Butser Hill
Stonylands Farm
Upper Parsonage Farm
Radio Station
Upper Barns
Tegdown Bottom
Tegdown Hill
Hillhampton Down
A3
Homelands Farm
PO8
Hillhampton Bottom
168
The Cottage
Blagdon Farm
Nine Corner
Oxenbourne Down (Local Nature Reserve)
HARVESTING LANE
LIMEKILN LANE
HOGS LODGE LANE
NORTH LANE
STROUD LANE
OXENBOURNE
PIDHAM LANE
CUMBER'S LANE
WOODBRIDGE LANE
GRAVEL LANE
THE CLOSE
CELLAR LANE

STROUD
Stroud Common
New Buildings Farm
Holmwood Cottage
Furzefield Copse
Widow Knight's Copse
Petersfield
Dean's Farm
The Hopkin
Weston Farm
WESTON
Kiln Cottages
Trinity Barns
NATIONAL PARK
Copyhold Barn
New Barn Cottage
Maple Durham
Luxford Cottage
Kiln Cottage
Hundry Copse
Halls Hill
QUEEN ELIZABETH COUNTRY PARK
WAR DOWN
HEAD DOWN PLANTATION
Ludgersham Copse
Gorecombe Hole
Forest Lodge
Fagg's Farm
Appleton's Copse
Dean Barn
Works
Graveyard
Wooliff Pond
Buriton Hanger
Reservoir (covered)
Coulters Dean Farm
Cockshot Wood
The Miscombe
North Lodge
Ditcham Woods
BURITON
Tithe House
Buriton Prim. Sch.
Hall
Rec. Grd.
Tennis Court
Manor House
Pillmead House
Nursery
Lawn Cottage
Buriton House
Jacob's Yard
Cowhouse Farm
Miscombe Manor
Sewage Works
Pillmead Row
Furzefield Copse
Round Copse
Birch Copse
Costerdale Crundle
Black Hill Cottages
Hoadlands Crundle
Binden Cottages
Nursted Cottages
Nursted House
Nursted Farm
Nursted House Lodge
Wood Mead Hanger
Nursted Copse
Hurstle's Copse
GU31
Bolinge Hill Copse
Bolinge Hill Cottages
Bolinge Hill Farm
Bolinge Hill Farm Cottages
Wardown House
Fairview Cotts.
BURITON BUS. PK.
Landpits
Causeway Farm
Causeway
Depository
Fairfield Farm
BROADWAY PARK
PETERSFIELD (OLD) GOLF COURSE
Club House
HEATH COMMON
Heath Pond
Landing Stage
Recreation Ground
PETERSFIELD
Petersfield Swim. Pool
The Petersfield School
Superstore
The Mint
PETERSFIELD HOSPITAL
PETERSFIELD BUSINESS PARK
PARKERS TRADE PARK
RIDGEWAY OFFICE PARK
ROTHERBROOK COURT
AMEY IND. EST.
Depot
Works
Petersfield
Sports Ground
Petersfield Town Football Club
WINCHESTER RD.
RAMSDEAN LA.
WESTON LANE
WYLDS LANE
GREENWAY
BOLINGE HILL
THE CAUSEWAY
B2070
A3
B2146
B2199
SUSSEX RD.
HEATH RD.
HYLTON ROAD
BOROUGH ROAD
HIGH ST.
DRAGON ST.
BEDFORD
GLOUCESTER
BUCKINGHAM
NOREUIL
CRANFORD
GRANGE
PADDOCK WAY
SUMNER RD.
GLEBE ROAD
HEATHERFIELD
BONES LANE
PITCROFT LANE
MILKY WAY
ODWAY LANE
MEAD LANE
KILN LANE
NEW BARN LANE
SOUTH LANE
NORTH LANE
HIGH STREET
PETERSFIELD LANE
MARDEN WAY
RUSSELL WAY
139
146
169

Petersfield
GU31
SOUTH DOWNS
Durleighmarsh
Goose Green
NURSTED
Old Ditcham
Quebec
WEST HARTING
SOUTH HARTING
Taro Leisure Centre
East Hampshire District Council Offices
Recreation Ground
Cricket Ground
HEATH COMMON
WEST HEATH COMMON
EAST HAMPSHIRE
CHICHESTER
River Rother
Sewage Works
The Old House
Durford Abbey Farm
Durford Mill
Holly Cottage
Maidenmarsh
Cedar House
White Cottage
Lower House
Durford Bridge
Drovers Cottage
Oldcroft
Rival Lodge Farm
Rival Lodge
Sand Pit
Down Park Farm Cottages
Down Park Farm House
Killarney Cottage
Brickkiln Copse
Down Park Farm
Park Bridge
Harting Pond
Ryefield
Ryefield Cottages
Goff's Plantation
Heath Farm
Club House
Stanbridge Farm
Nursted House Lodge
Keepers Cottage
Buttermilk Copse
Mill Barn
The Crundle
Nursted Rocks
Nursted Farm
The Plantation
Uphill Cottage
Old House Cottage
Old House Farm
Rock Cottage
Nursted Rock Cottages
Latchett's Copse
Garrett's Copse
Sunnyside
Clappers
Pondtail Plantation
Goosegreen Cottage
Quarry Hill Cottage
Tom Rokes Row
George's Wood
Wheat River Copse
Quebec
Manor Farm
Penpoll
Hill Ash Farm
Old Manor House
Fir Cottage
Dene Cottage
Putmans
Bowers
Oak Cottage
Nutwood Cottage
West Harting Cottage
Weston Farmhouse
Millhanger Copse
Hurst Mill Cottage
Hurst Mill
Hood Cottage
Hurst Cottage
Beech Barn
Mill Dam
The Badgers
Hurst Farm
Hurstle's Copse
Canada Corner
The Old Inn
Poppett
Dell Cottage
Torberry Copse
Torberry Hill
Old Ditcham Farm
Old Ditcham Farm Cottages
Torberry Farm
Torberry Cottages
Little Torberry Hill
Torberryhill Plantation
Coombe Cottage
Noddswood
Pitts Star Brow
Hemner Hill House
Byways
Leith House
The Meads
Playing Fields
Tennis Courts
The Miscombe
Old Ditcham Wood
LEITH COPSE
Hemner Hill
Miscombe Cottages
Church Farm
St. Mary & St. Paul C of E First School
Sunwood Farm
FORTY ACRE LANE
Downlands
Old Copse
South Gardens
Engine Farm
The Bosom
Foxcombe Cottages
PARK ROAD
HEATH ROAD
SUSSEX ROAD
B2146
B2199
A272
EAST PULLENS LANE
DURFORD ROAD
RIVAL MOOR ROAD
COLLINS LANE
PUTMANS LANE
WARRENSIDE
140
145
76
77
78
23
22
21
120
19

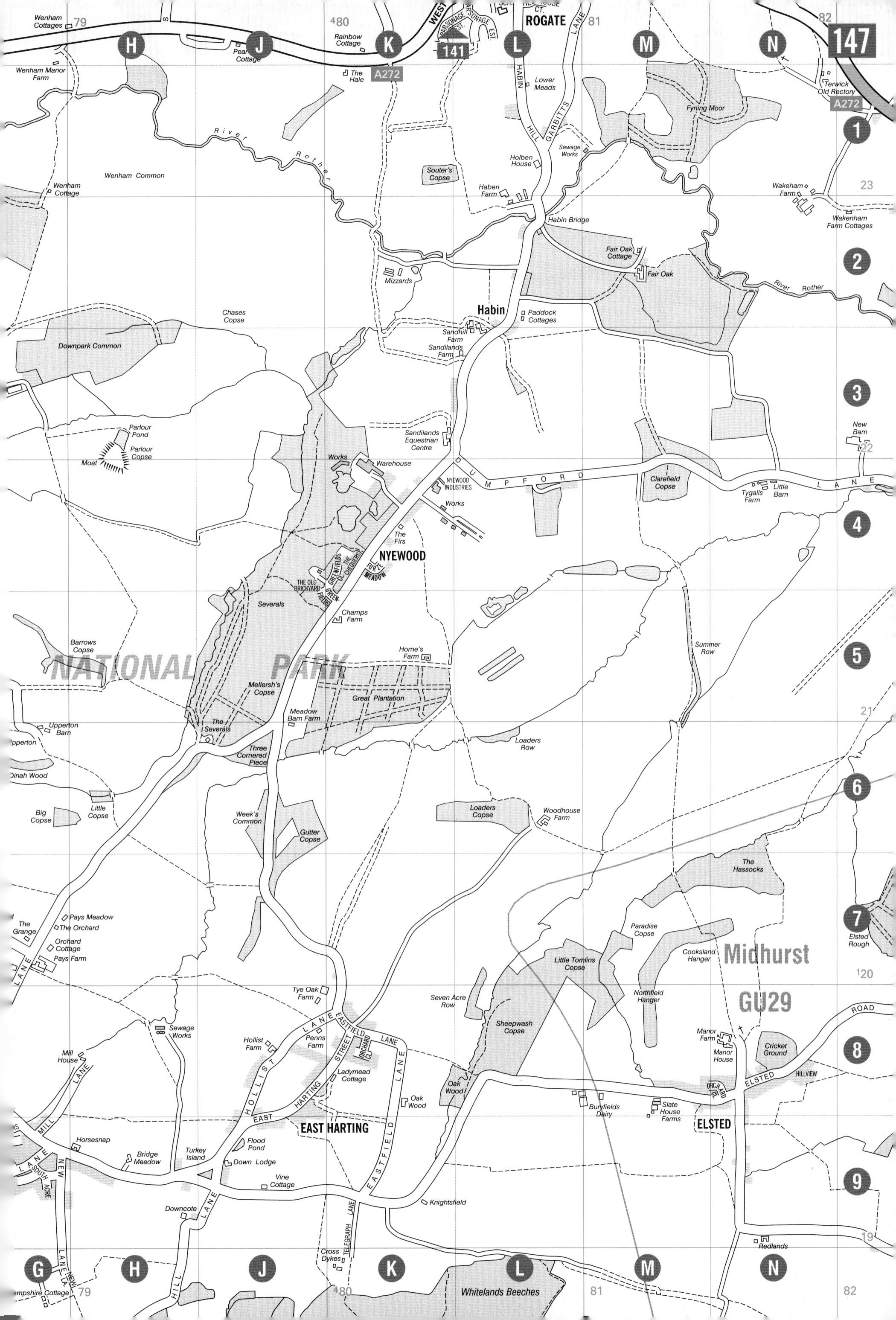
Wenham Cottages
79
480
81
82
ROGATE
H
J
K
L
M
N
141
A272
Pear Cottage
Rainbow Cottage
The Hale
Wenham Manor Farm
PARSONAGE EST.
HABIN HILL
GARBITTS
LANE
Lower Meads
Fyning Moor
Terwick Old Rectory
A272
1
River Rother
Wenham Common
Wenham Cottage
Souter's Copse
Holben House
Sewage Works
Haben Farm
Wakeham Farm
23
Wakenham Farm Cottages
Habin Bridge
Fair Oak Cottage
Fair Oak
2
River Rother
Mizzards
Habin
Paddock Cottages
Chases Copse
Sandhill Farm
Sandilands Farm
Downpark Common
3
New Barn
22
Parlour Pond
Parlour Copse
Moat
Sandilands Equestrian Centre
Works
Warehouse
NYEWOOD INDUSTRIES
Works
DUMPFORD LANE
Clarefield Copse
Tygalls Farm
Little Barn
4
The Firs
NYEWOOD
GREENFIELDS
THE CHEQUERS
FURZE MEADOW
THE OLD BRICKYARD
GREENFIELDS
Severals
Champs Farm
Barrows Copse
Horne's Farm
Summer Row
5
NATIONAL PARK
Mellersh's Copse
Great Plantation
Meadow Barn Farm
21
Upperton Barn
Upperton
The Severals
Three Cornered Piece
Loaders Row
Dinah Wood
6
Big Copse
Little Copse
Week's Common
Loaders Copse
Woodhouse Farm
Gutter Copse
The Hassocks
The Grange
Pays Meadow
The Orchard
Orchard Cottage
Pays Farm
LANE
Paradise Copse
7
Elsted Rough
Cooksland Hanger
Midhurst
Little Tomlins Copse
Northfield Hanger
20
GU29
Tye Oak Farm
Seven Acre Row
ROAD
Sewage Works
Mill House
MILL LANE
Hollist Farm
Penns Farm
EASTFIELD LANE
HOLLIST LANE
STREET
ORCHARD CL.
Sheepwash Copse
Manor Farm
Manor House
Cricket Ground
8
HILLVIEW
ELSTED
ORCHARD
Ladymead Cottage
Oak Wood
Oak Wood
Buryfields Dairy
Slate House Farms
ELSTED
EAST HARTING
EAST HARTING
Horsesnap
Flood Pond
EASTFIELD LANE
Bridge Meadow
Turkey Island
Down Lodge
NEW LANE
SOUTH ACRE
Vine Cottage
9
Downcote
HILL LANE
TELEGRAPH LANE
Knightsfield
19
Redlands
Cross Dykes
G
H
J
K
L
M
N
NEW LA.
Hampshire Cottage
79
480
Whitelands Beeches
81
82

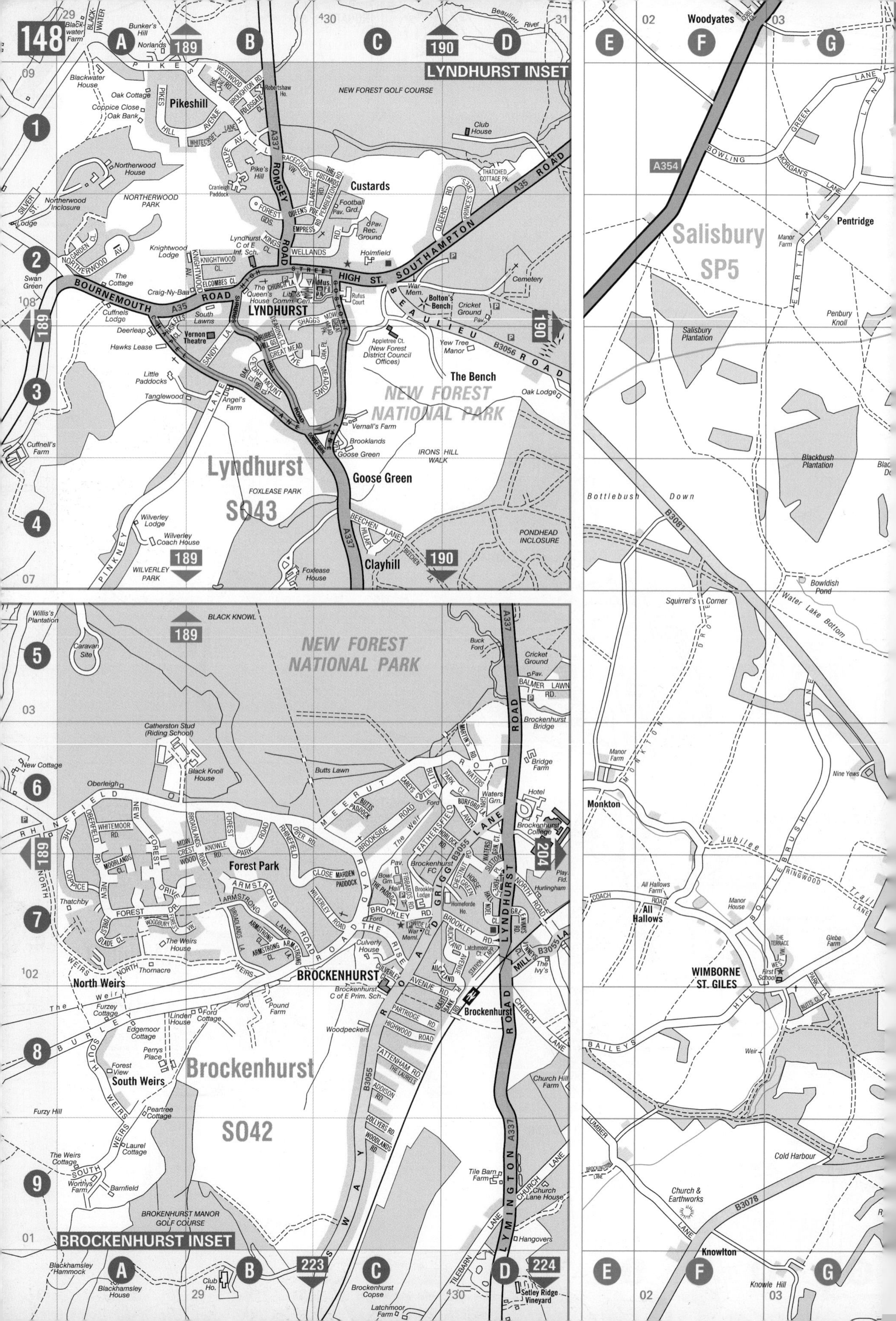
LYNDHURST INSET
Lyndhurst
SO43
Pikeshill
Custards
LYNDHURST
NEW FOREST NATIONAL PARK
Goose Green
Clayhill
The Bench
NEW FOREST GOLF COURSE
BROCKENHURST INSET
Brockenhurst
SO42
BROCKENHURST
Forest Park
North Weirs
South Weirs
NEW FOREST NATIONAL PARK
BROCKENHURST MANOR GOLF COURSE
Salisbury
SP5
Woodyates
Pentridge
Monkton
All Hallows
WIMBORNE ST. GILES
Knowlton
Bottlebush Down
Salisbury Plantation
Blackbush Plantation
Squirrel's Corner
Cold Harbour
A35
A337
A354
B3081
B3078
B3055
B3056
189
190
223
224
204

MARTIN DOWN
NATIONAL NATURE RESERVE
SILLENS LANE
King's Farm
118
Tidpit
Knap Barrow Farm
Windmill Hill
Knoll Down
Bokerley Down
BOKERLEY DITCH
Jubilee Trail
Whitey Top
Blagdon Plantation
Blagdon Hill
Tidpit Common Down
Allen River
North Allenford Farm
Damerham Knoll
Knoll Farm
Knight's Copse
Fordingbridge
Blackheath Down
South Allenford Farm
Blagdon Farm
Kites Nest Farm
Boulsbury Down
SP6
150
Crockerton Hill
West Blagdon
Martin Wood
North End
POUND LANE
HIGH STREET
LITTLEMILL LA.
WEST PARK LA.
ROCKBOURNE LA.
THE TER.
WEST PK. DR.
Wimborne
Boulsbury Farm
Kingland Copse
BROWNS LANE
East End
STONY LANE
DAMERHAM
STEELS LA.
CHURCH LA.
CT. HILL
MILL
Western Downland C of E Prim. Sch.
Toby's Bottom
BH21
Stapleton Farm
Boulsbury Wood
CORNPITS LANE
Ashley Park Farm
South End
THE COMMON
Noddle Hill
Boveridge
Boveridge House
Cranborne Farm
Ashridge Copse
Perry Copse
Biddlesgate Farm
Hyde Farm
Burwood
DROVE
WADLEY'S DROVE
ROAD
Bratch Copse
NEW FOREST
EAST DORSET
Bull Hill Farm
LANE
The Ancient Technology Centre
Cranborne Middle School
Lopshill
CHEATER'S LANE
Manor Farm
Bellows Cross
Ashes Farm
CHURCHILL
DAMERHAM
CRANBORNE
SALISBURY ST.
GRUGS LA.
PENNY'S LA.
THE SQ.
HIGH ST.
WATER ST.
CASTLE ST.
BERKELEY RD.
Lower Daggons
High Wood
Creech Hill House
Manor House
Cranbourne Manor Gardens
Holwell Farm
Holwell
PYE LA.
PYE LANE
Crendell
Hart's Farm
Creech Hill Wood
CASTLE CL.
HILL LANE
MILL
Hither Daggons Wood
Lower Holwell
DROVE
Rushmore Farm
B3078
CASTLE HILL
Motte & Bailey
Cripplestyle
DAGGONS RD.
CRANBORNE RD.
Daggons
HARE LANE
King Barrow
B3081
Castle Hill Wood
Mill Farm
Hare Lane Farm
DROVE
Lower Farm
152
MILL LANE
PURBECK
Vale Acre Farm
Edmondsham House
Edmondsham
ORCHARD CL.
Upper Farm
Cranborne Common (Nature Reserve)
BATTERLEY DROVE
Gotham
Telegraph Plantation
Smallbridge Farm
Maldry Wood
Sandy's Hill
Dorset Heavy Horse Centre
HILLSIDE CAMPING & CARAVAN SITE
Pistle Down
Verwood
BH31
Deer Park Farm
FURZE BRACH LANE
Westworth Farm
Mulberry Lodge
Birches Copse
Burrows Farm
BURROWS LA.
Mount Ararat
Sutton
Six Acre Copse
Park Copse
HORTON ROAD
Sutton Holms
WARWICKS LANE
EDMONDSHAM RD.
Trinity C of E First School
COOPERS LA.
Stephen's Castle
Boveridge Heath
Woodlands Copse
Boys Wood
04 05 06 07 08 09 10
H J K L M N P
19 18 17 16 15 14 13 12 11 10
1 2 3 4 5 6 7 8 9

A B C D E F G
11 12 13
119
Glebe Farm
Provost Farm
DUNBERRY HILL
Round Copse
Major's Farm
WHITSBURY
Lower Farm
Whitsbury Wood
Lime Kiln Farm
Braeside
Sweatfords
Newbourne Farm
Pav.
Sports Ground
The Mushroom Farm
Water
NEW ROAD
Manor Farm
Manor House
Slippery Elm M
Reservoir (covered)
Rectory
ROCKBOURNE
Western Downland C of E Prim. Sch.
Bourne Cottages
Mintys Hill
The Terrace
The Cottage
LOWER GROVE
Hall
ST. LEONARDS VW.
Lower Farm
Nippard's Farm
Long Copse
Three Corner Copse
Whitsbury Firs
Mushroom Farm
Whitsbury Common
Blackmoor Cottage
Drove Barn
Lodge
How Copse
Bare Plots
Whitsbury Cross
Whitsbury House
Fifords Coppice
ROCKSTEAD COPSE
Rockstead Farm
Greenlane Wood
GREEN
Lodges
LANE
ROCKBOURNE
Staddles
Marsh Farm
Lodge
RADNALL WOOD
Whip's Hill Copse
Whipps Hill
CLACK
WEST PARK
Channel Hill
Rockbourne Roman Villa (remains of)
Brookheath
Lodge
Little Wood
Sagles Spring
Seacraft Copse
Water Meadows
LANE
Clack Barn
North End
149
DRIVE
WEST PARK WOOD
Popplepit
Palmers's Copse
Sweatfords
Water
Sir Eyre Coote's Monument
PARK
Mist Farm
DAMERHAM
WEST PARK LANE
Park Villas
The Terrace
WEST
Hall
HIGH ST.
Pav.
Cricket Ground
East End
Court Farm
COURT
Allen's Farm
Court Lodge
Greenbank Farm
GREEN CLOSE
Allen
STEELS LA.
CHURCH LANE
MILL
Sch.
West Park Farm
Brickhill
Vicarage
River
Court Vale
HILL
WILKINS'S COOMB
Hill Farm
END
Lower Breach Copse
South End
CORN PITS LANE
Boardengates Copse
Hurley Farm
Reservoir
MARL LANE
Courtwood Farm
Poultry Farm
Depot
THE COMMON
The Marsh
Lops Copse
TANNERS LA.
Gould's Copse
Lower Court Wood
Sandle Copse
Sandle Home Farm
ROAD
SANDLEHEATH
Fish Farm
Woodlands Lodge
Thorps Farm
Coronation Terrace
ELMS CLOSE
OLD BRICKYARD RD
SANDLEHEATH IND. EST.
Forres Sandle Manor Sch
Ashridge Hill Copse
NEW FOREST
EAST DORSET
Holly Villas
KERRY GDNS.
Sandle Manor Farm
Sandle Lodge
Furze Close Copse
Alder Copse
Ford
ROAD
ALDERHOLT
STATION
SANDLE MNR. DR.
ELMWOOD AV.
SANDLE COPSE
MANOR FARM ROAD
MAYFIELD RD
Hawkhill Mill Farm
Hawkhill Ditch
152
Reeve's Copse
JUBILEE
Alderholt Mill
Alderholt Bridge
Bullhill Copse
Andrew's
Brixey's Copse
Ashford Water
ASHFORD
FORDINGBRIDGE BUS PK.
Dpt.

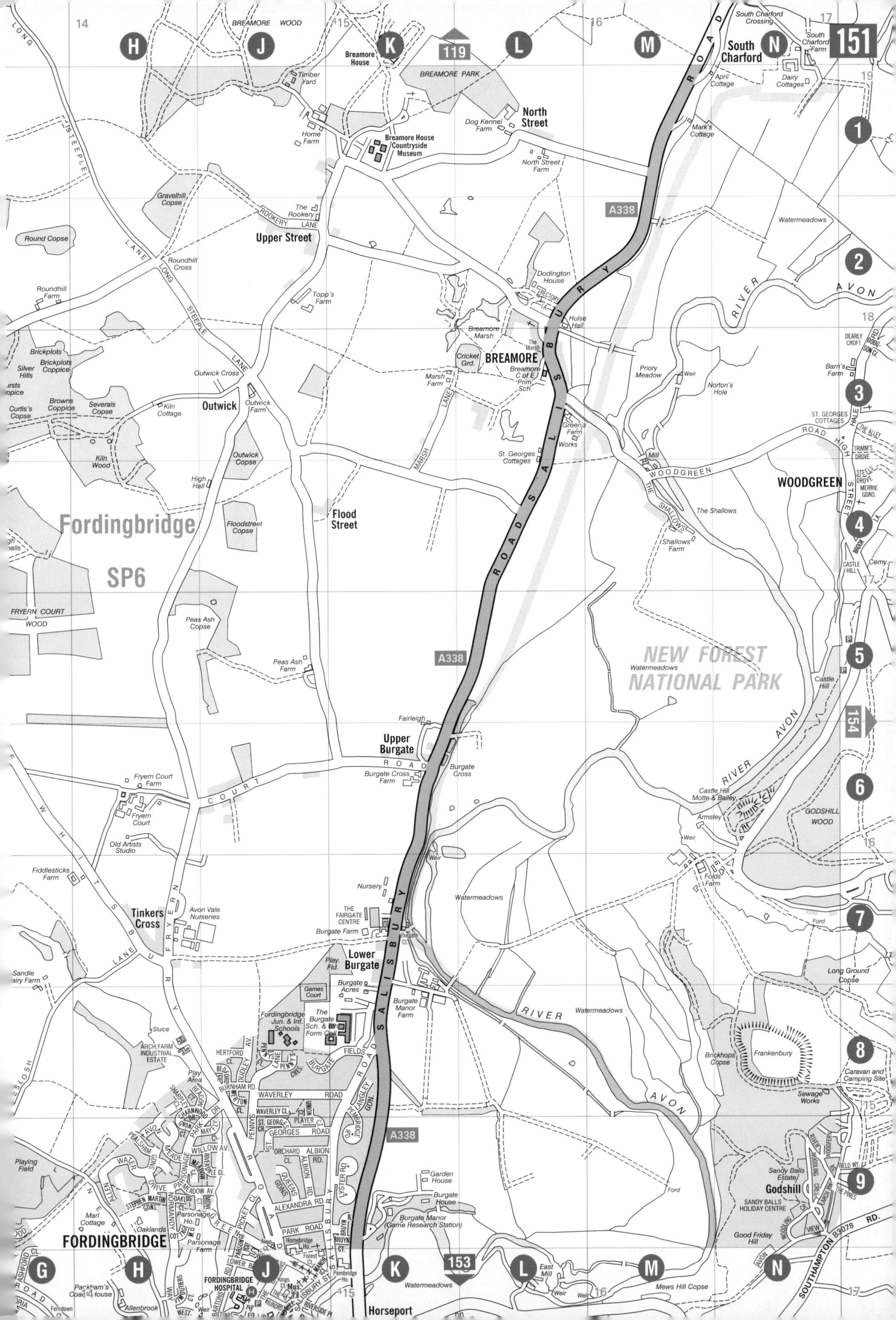
BREAMORE WOOD
Breamore House
119
BREAMORE PARK
South Charford Crossing
South Charford
South Charford Farm
April Cottage
Dairy Cottages
Timber Yard
Home Farm
Breamore House Countryside Museum
North Street
Dog Kennel Farm
North Street Farm
Mark's Cottage
Gravelhill Copse
The Rookery
ROOKERY LANE
Upper Street
Round Copse
Roundhill Cross
Roundhill Farm
LONG STEEPLE LANE
A338
Watermeadows
Dodington House
RECTORY LA.
Hulse Hall
Topp's Farm
RIVER AVON
Breamore Marsh
The Marsh
Cricket Grd.
BREAMORE
Breamore C of E Prim. Sch.
Marsh Farm
MARSH LANE
Priory Meadow
Weir
Norton's Hole
DEARLY CROFT
DOOGSON CL.
Barn's Farm
Brickplots
Brickplots Coppice
Silver Hills
Outwick Cross
Browns Coppice
Severals Copse
Curtis's Copse
Kiln Cottage
Outwick
Outwick Farm
Green's Farm Works
St. Georges Cottages
Mill
WOODGREEN ROAD
ST. GEORGES COTTAGES
HALE
THE ALLEY
TRIMM'S DROVE
STEVELS DROVE
MERRIE GDNS.
HIGH STREET
WOODGREEN
Kiln Wood
Outwick Copse
High Hall
THE SHALLOWS
The Shallows
Shallows Farm
Fordingbridge
Floodstreet Copse
Flood Street
BROOK LA.
CASTLE HILL
Cemy.
SP6
FRYERN COURT WOOD
Peas Ash Copse
NEW FOREST NATIONAL PARK
Watermeadows
Castle Hill
Peas Ash Farm
154
Fairleigh
Upper Burgate
ROAD
Burgate Cross
Burgate Cross Farm
Fryern Court Farm
COURT
Fryern Court
Old Artists Studio
Castle Hill Motte & Bailey
Armsley
GODSHILL WOOD
Weir
Fiddlesticks Farm
Weir
Folds Farm
Nursery
Watermeadows
Tinkers Cross
Avon Vale Nurseries
THE FAIRGATE CENTRE
Burgate Farm
Burgate Ct.
Ford
Lower Burgate
Play. Fld.
Sandle Dairy Farm
WHITSBURY LANE
FRYERN
Long Ground Copse
Games Court
Burgate Acres
Burgate Manor Farm
Watermeadows
Fordingbridge Jun. & Inf. Schools
The Burgate Sch. & 6th Form Coll.
SALISBURY ROAD
Sluice
ARCH FARM INDUSTRIAL ESTATE
Brickhops Copse
Frankenbury
Caravan and Camping Site
Play Area
HERTFORD CL.
DUDLEY AV.
BURGATE FIELDS
BURNHAM RD.
WAVERLEY ROAD
Sewage Works
WAVERLEY CL.
PLAYER CT.
ST. GEORGES ROAD
ORCHARD CL.
ALBION RD.
PEMBRIDGE RD.
AVON
Playing Field
WILLOW AV.
MEADOW AV.
QUEENS GDNS.
LYSTER RD.
Garden House
Sandy Balls Estate
Godshill
SANDY BALLS HOLIDAY CENTRE
FIELD WY.
THE PINES
Ford
ALLEN
STEPHEN MARTIN GDNS.
NORMANDY
Marl Cottage
Oaklands
Parsonage Ho.
ALEXANDRA RD.
Burgate House
Burgate Manor (Game Research Station)
PARK ROAD
FORDINGBRIDGE
Parsonage Farm
Homebridge Ho.
Good Friday Hill
SOUTHAMPTON B3078 RD.
ASHFORD CL.
153
East Mill
Packham's Coach House
FORDINGBRIDGE HOSPITAL
Mus.
Pembridge Ho.
Watermeadows
Weir
Mews Hill Copse
Allenbrook
Horseport
Ferndown
H J K L M N G
1 2 3 4 5 6 7 8 9
14 15 16 17 18 19

150
149
184
A
B
C
D
E
F
G
1
2
3
4
5
6
7
8
9
ALDERHOLT
ASHFORD
Daggons
Camel Green
Charing Cross
Bleak Hill
Verwood
Ringwood
BH31
BH24
ALDERHOLT COMMON
CRANBORNE COMMON
(Nature Reserve)
BOVERIDGE HEATH
NEW FOREST
EAST DORSET
Alderholt Mill
Alderholt Bridge
Alderholt Mill Farm
Hawkhill Mill Farm
Ford
Bullhill Copse
Andrew's Copse
Reeve's Copse
Brixey's Copse
Ashford Water
Perry Copse
Garett's Copse
Lower Bullhill Farm
Higher Bullhill Farm
Avon Farm
North Lodge
Old Manor House
Pond Close
Landlubbers Cottage
Chapel Lodge
Manor Farm Bungalow
Home Farm
East Lodge
Old Vicarage
Manor Farm
Hill Cottage Farm
Hill Cottage
HILL COTTAGE FARM CARAVAN PARK
Alderholt Park
Park Farm
The Rookery
Highwood Cottage
Salisbury Arms Farm
Cross Farm
Presseys Corner
Bonfire Hill
Hill Farm
Hill Copse
Hart's Copse
Wolvercroft Farm
Wolvercrate Copse
Hilbury Wood
Hillbury Farm
Holmwood
Birch Hill
The Piggery
Strouds Firs
St. James C of E First School
Vicarage Farm
Church Cottages
The Grange
Pug's Plantation
Thornes Piece
Maryfield
Nurseries
Recreation Ground
Five Acres
Marsh Lands
St. Annes
Oak Tree Farm
Poultry Houses
Sleepbrook Farm
Drove End Farm
Rifle Range
Ringwood Forest
Cross Roads Plantation
Blackwater
Stanford Point
Warren Park Farm
SLEEP BOTTOM
Sleep Brook
Decoy Pond
Whitefield
Bottom
North Plumley Farmhouse
Plumley
Drove
North
Fire Tower
North Plumley Cottages
PLUMLEY WOOD
Hamer Copse
Hamer
Hamer Brook
Wiggs
Fish Farm
Ashford House
Perry Farm House
Poultry House
Bowerwood Cottages
Pittismoor
The Embers
Edge Hill
Bowerwood House
Pippin Cottage
Highfield Hall
New Farm
Berrylands
Shalotte House
Highfield Farm
Midgham Wood
Saw Mill
Midgham Farm
The Bungalow
Lomer Copse
Bleakhill Farm
Braemoor
The Bungalow
Daffodil Cottage
Christmas Rose Cottage
Primrose Cottage
Hill Crest
Sandp. Cott.
Kent Hill
Cootman's Copse
Kent Hill Plantation
FORDINGBRIDGE BUS. PK.
THE OLD VINERIES
ASHFORD WORKS INDUSTRIAL ESTATE
Sandle Manor Farm
Sandle Lodge
Hawkhill Ditch
Alder Copse
Ashford Water
ALDERHOLT ROAD
SANDLEHEATH ROAD
FORDINGBRIDGE ROAD
B3078
DAGGONS ROAD
STATION ROAD
RINGWOOD ROAD
HILLBURY ROAD
HARBRIDGE DROVE
ROAD
ASHFORD ROAD
BOWERWOOD ROAD
MIDGHAM ROAD
LOMER LANE
NORTH LANE
DROVE
KENT LANE
CHEATER'S LA.
MANOR FARM ROAD
MAYFIELD RD.
SANDLE COPSE
ELMWOOD
JUBILEE
CAMEL
HAYTERS WAY
GREEN
FIR TREE
WINDSOR WAY
DOWN LODGE CL.
COPPERS CL.
SOUTH HILL
ANTELLS WAY
BRAMBLE CL.
ASH CL.
BEECH CL.
TUDOR CL.
SAXON WAY
SILVER
DALE CL.
GREEN DR.
WREN DRIVE
KESTREL
GDS.
HILLBURY PARK (MOBILE HOME PARK)
FERN CL.
HAZEL CL.
BROOMFIELD DRIVE
BIRCHWOOD
EARLSWOOD DRIVE
ALDER DRIVE
APPLE TREE RD.
LIME TREE CL.
PEAR TREE CL.
OAK ROAD
PINE ROAD
ATTWOOD CL.
PARK LANE
STATION YD.
OLD FORGE CL.
JUBILEE CL.
CHURCHILL CL.
GROVE
BLACKWATER
HARTS PL.
HIGHWOOD CL.

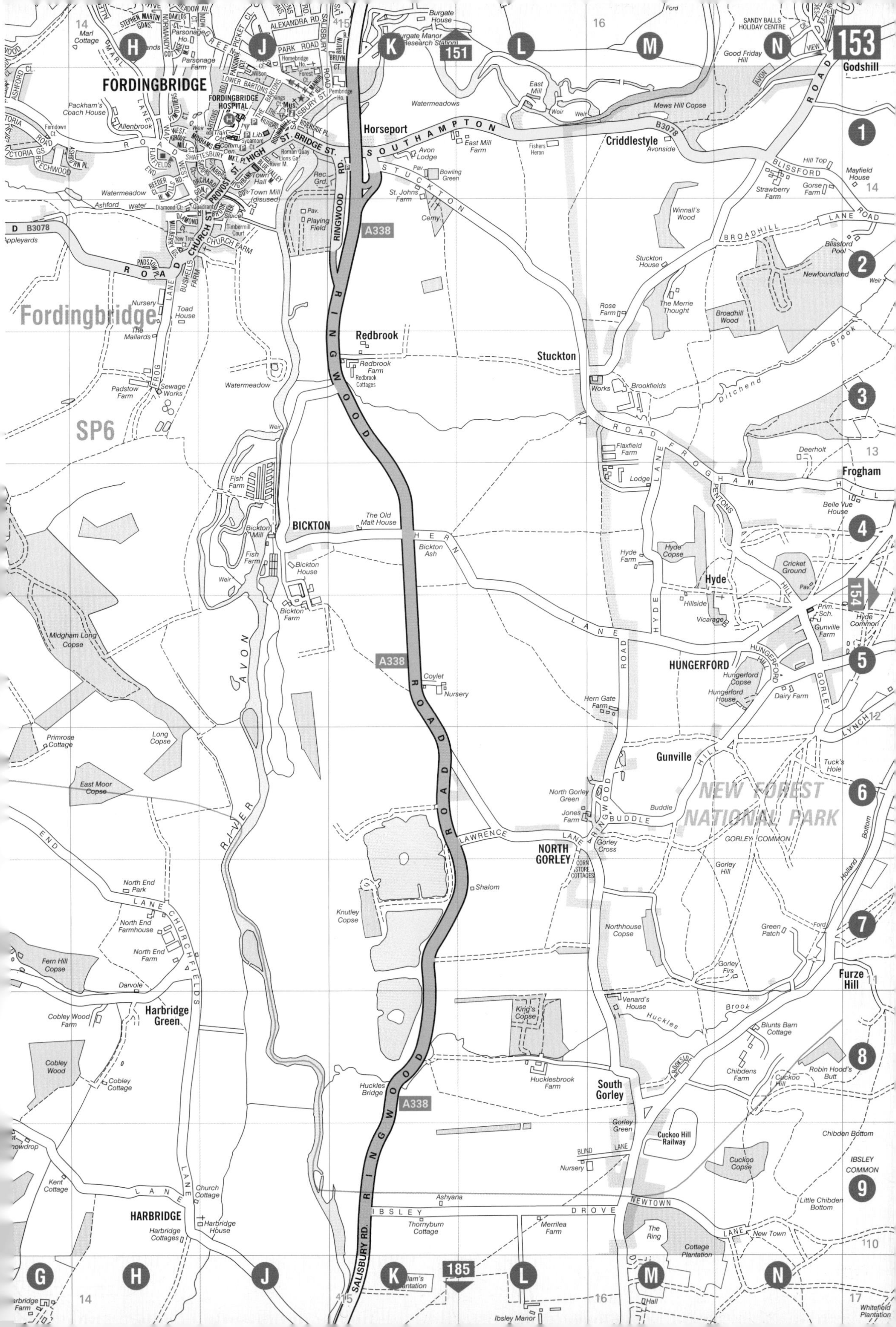

153
FORDINGBRIDGE
Fordingbridge
FORDINGBRIDGE HOSPITAL
SP6
Godshill
Horseport
Criddlestyle
Stuckton
Redbrook
BICKTON
Frogham
Hyde
HUNGERFORD
Gunville
NEW FOREST NATIONAL PARK
GORLEY COMMON
NORTH GORLEY
Furze Hill
South Gorley
Harbridge Green
HARBRIDGE
IBSLEY COMMON
Cuckoo Hill Railway
SANDY BALLS HOLIDAY CENTRE
Good Friday Hill
Burgate House
Burgate Manor Research Station
East Mill
Watermeadows
Mews Hill Copse
East Mill Farm
Fishers Heron
Avonside
Avon Lodge
Bowling Green
St. Johns Farm
Cemy.
Playing Field
Rec. Grd.
Pav.
Hill Top
Mayfield House
Strawberry Farm
Gorse Farm
Winnall's Wood
Blissford Pool
Newfoundland
Stuckton House
The Merrie Thought
Broadhill Wood
Rose Farm
Redbrook Farm
Redbrook Cottages
Works
Brookfields
Ditchend
Brook
Flaxfield Farm
Lodge
Deerholt
Belle Vue House
Cricket Ground
Hyde Copse
Hyde Farm
Hillside
Vicarage
Prim. Sch.
Hyde Common
Gunville Farm
Hungerford Copse
Hungerford House
Dairy Farm
Hern Gate Farm
Tuck's Hole
North Gorley Green
Jones Farm
Buddle
Gorley Cross
CORN STORE COTTAGES
Gorley Hill
Bottom
Holland
Green Patch
Ford
Northhouse Copse
Gorley Firs
Venard's House
Huckles Brook
Blunts Barn Cottage
Chibdens Farm
Robin Hood's Butt
Cuckoo Hill
Chibden Bottom
Cuckoo Copse
Little Chibden Bottom
New Town
NEWTOWN
The Ring
Cottage Plantation
Hall
Whitefield Plantation
Ibsley Manor
Merrilea Farm
Thornyburn Cottage
Ashyana
Nursery
BLIND LANE
Gorley Green
Hucklesbrook Farm
King's Copse
Huckles Bridge
Knutley Copse
Shalom
Coylet
Nursery
Bickton Ash
The Old Malt House
Bickton Mill
Fish Farm
Bickton House
Bickton Farm
Weir
Watermeadow
RIVER AVON
Midgham Long Copse
Primrose Cottage
Long Copse
East Moor Copse
North End Park
North End Farmhouse
North End Farm
Fern Hill Copse
Darvole
Cobley Wood Farm
Cobley Wood
Cobley Cottage
Kent Cottage
Church Cottage
Harbridge House
Harbridge Cottages
Harbridge Farm
Padstow Farm
Sewage Works
Nursery
Toad House
The Mallards
Marl Cottage
Packham's Coach House
Allenbrook
Ashford Water
Watermeadow
Appleyards
Parsonage Farm
Parsonage Ho.
Homebridge Ho.
Forest Ct.
Kings Ct.
Mus.
Pembridge Ho.
Roman Quay
Lions Ga.
River M.
Town Hall
Town Mill (disused)
Sluice
Timbermill Court
Diamond Ct.
Quadrant
Yew Tree Ct.
Lib.
Train. Cen.
Comm. Cen.
Sycamore Ct.
Wilson Ct.
Ferndown Ct.
B3078
A338
RINGWOOD ROAD
SALISBURY RD.
IBSLEY DROVE
SOUTHAMPTON ROAD
STUCKTON ROAD
FROGHAM HILL
BROADHILL LANE
BLISSFORD ROAD
HERN LANE
LAWRENCE LANE
BUDDLE HILL
HYDE LANE
GORLEY ROAD
HUNGERFORD HILL
LYNCH
RINGWOOD ROAD
CHURCHFIELDS
HARBRIDGE LANE
NORTH END LANE
FROG LANE
PADSTOW ROAD
ST. BRIDGE ST.
HIGH ST.
CHURCH ST.
PROVOST ST.
SALISBURY ST.
ALEXANDRA RD.
PARK ROAD
STEPHEN MARTIN GDNS.
FLAXFIELDS
SHAFTESBURY ST.
151
154
185
H J K L M N G
1 2 3 4 5 6 7 8 9
14 15 16 17
10 11 12 13 14

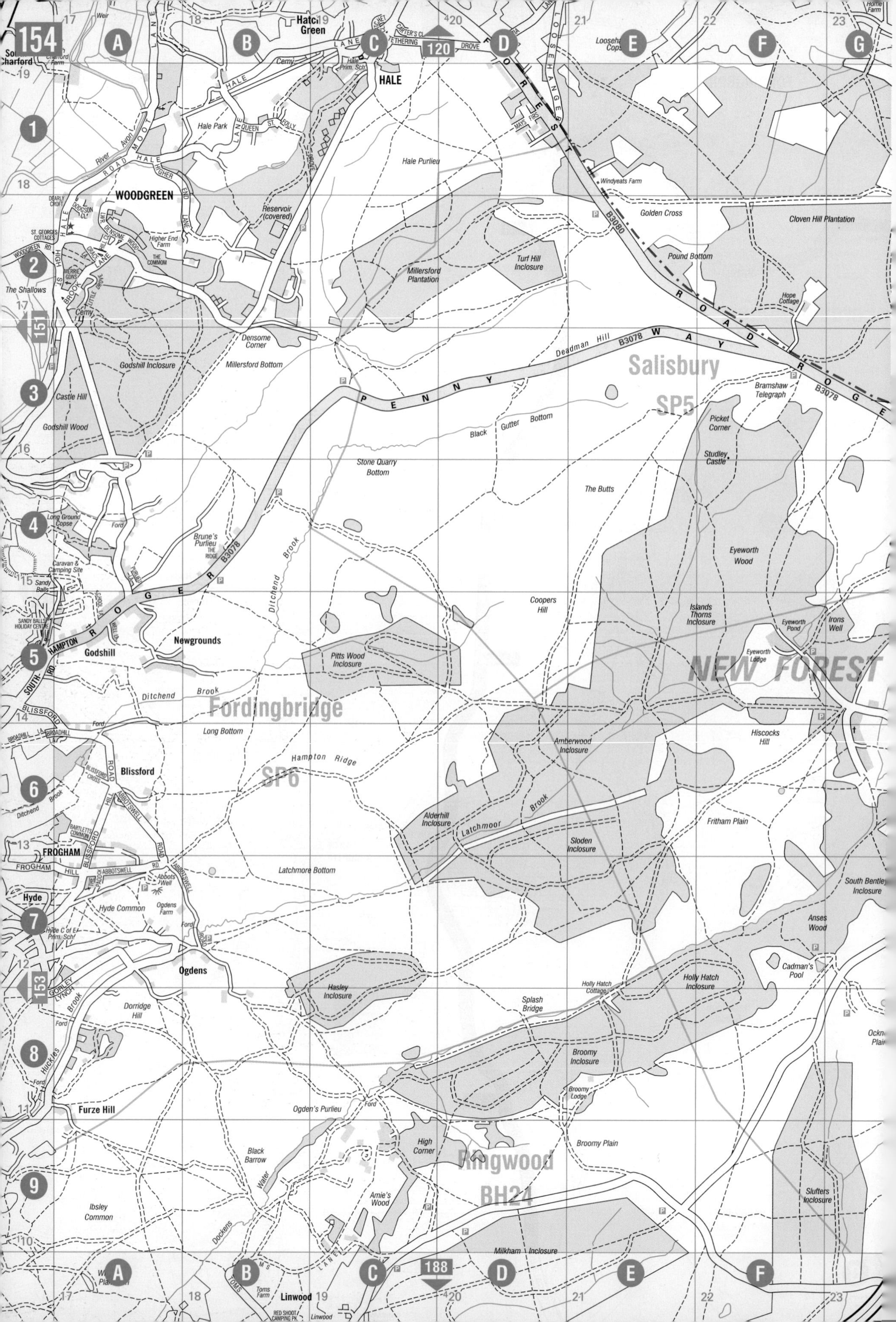
Hatch Green
HALE
WOODGREEN
Hale Park
Hale Purlieu
Reservoir (covered)
Millersford Plantation
Turf Hill Inclosure
Windyeats Farm
Golden Cross
Cloven Hill Plantation
Pound Bottom
Hope Cottage
Densome Corner
Millersford Bottom
Godshill Inclosure
Castle Hill
Godshill Wood
The Shallows
PENNY WAY
ROGER
Deadman Hill
B3078
B3080
Salisbury
SP5
Bramshaw Telegraph
Picket Corner
Studley Castle
Black Gutter Bottom
Stone Quarry Bottom
The Butts
Eyeworth Wood
Long Ground Copse
Caravan & Camping Site
Sandy Balls
Brune's Purlieu
Ditchend Brook
Coopers Hill
Islands Thorns Inclosure
Eyeworth Pond
Irons Well
Eyeworth Lodge
NEW FOREST
Newgrounds
Godshill
Pitts Wood Inclosure
Fordingbridge
Long Bottom
Hampton Ridge
SP6
Amberwood Inclosure
Hiscocks Hill
Blissford
Alderhill Inclosure
Latchmoor Brook
Sloden Inclosure
Fritham Plain
FROGHAM
Latchmore Bottom
South Bentley Inclosure
Hyde
Hyde Common
Ogdens Farm
Anses Wood
Ogdens
Cadman's Pool
Hasley Inclosure
Holly Hatch Cottage
Holly Hatch Inclosure
Splash Bridge
Dorridge Hill
Broomy Inclosure
Broomy Lodge
Furze Hill
Ogden's Purlieu
High Corner
Broomy Plain
Black Barrow
Ringwood
BH24
Ibsley Common
Amie's Wood
Slufters Inclosure
Milkham Inclosure
Linwood
Toms Farm
120
151
153
188

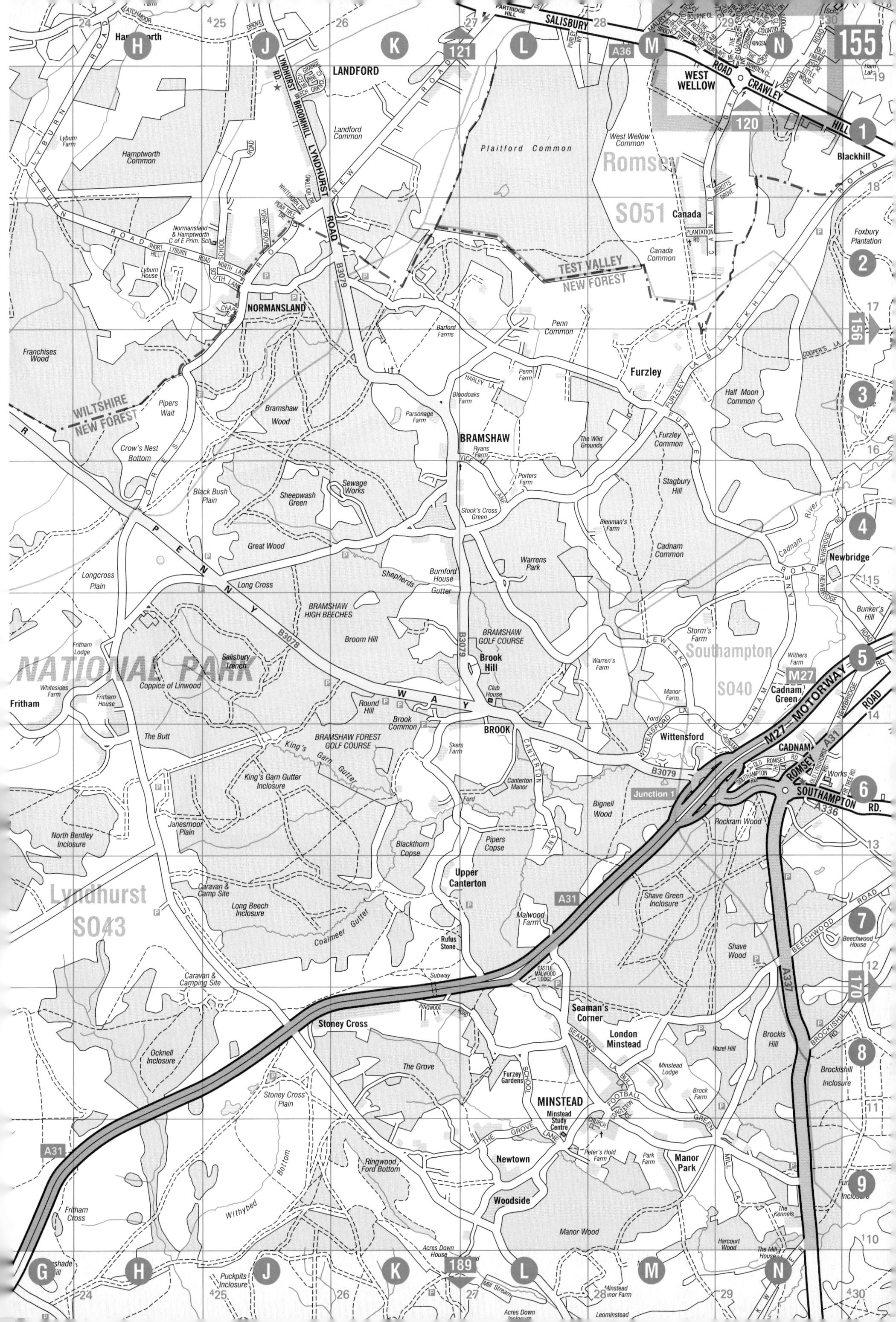
H
J
K
L
M
N
121
120
156
170
189
1
2
3
4
5
6
7
8
9
G
Hamptworth
LANDFORD
SALISBURY
WEST WELLOW
ROAD
CRAWLEY
HILL
A36
Blackhill
Lybum Farm
Hamptworth Common
Landford Common
Plaitford Common
West Wellow Common
Romsey
SO51
Canada
Canada Common
Foxbury Plantation
TEST VALLEY
NEW FOREST
LYNDHURST ROAD
BROOMHILL
LYNDHURST
ROAD
B3079
Normansland & Hamptworth C of E Prim. Sch.
Lyburn House
NORMANSLAND
Franchises Wood
WILTSHIRE
NEW FOREST
Pipers Wait
Crow's Nest Bottom
Bramshaw Wood
Barford Farms
Penn Common
Furzley
Penn Farm
Bloodoaks Farm
Parsonage Farm
BRAMSHAW
Ryans Farm
The Wild Grounds
Furzley Common
Half Moon Common
Black Bush Plain
Sheepwash Green
Sewage Works
Porters Farm
Stagbury Hill
Stock's Cross Green
Blenman's Farm
Cadnam Common
Great Wood
Warrens Park
Newbridge
Longcross Plain
Long Cross
Shepherds Gutter
Burnford House
BRAMSHAW HIGH BEECHES
Broom Hill
BRAMSHAW GOLF COURSE
Brook Hill
Storm's Farm
Southampton
SO40
Bunker's Hill
Withers Farm
Cadnam Green
M27
M27 MOTORWAY
NATIONAL PARK
Fritham Lodge
Salisbury Trench
Coppice of Linwood
Fritham
Whitesides Farm
Fritham House
B3078
PENNY WAY
Round Hill
Brook Common
Club House
BROOK
Warren's Farm
Manor Farm
Wittensford
CADNAM
A31
The Butt
BRAMSHAW FOREST GOLF COURSE
King's Garn Gutter
Skers Farm
King's Garn Gutter Inclosure
Canterton Manor
B3079
Junction 1
SOUTHAMPTON RD.
A336
Rockram Wood
Bignell Wood
North Bentley Inclosure
Janesmoor Plain
Blackthorn Copse
Pipers Copse
Upper Canterton
Lyndhurst
SO43
Caravan & Camp Site
Long Beech Inclosure
Coalmeer Gutter
Shave Green Inclosure
Malwood Farm
Rufus Stone
Shave Wood
Beechwood House
BEECHWOOD
A337
Caravan & Camping Site
Subway
CASTLE MALWOOD LODGE
Seaman's Corner
Stoney Cross
London Minstead
Brockis Hill
Ocknell Inclosure
The Grove
Furzey Gardens
Hazel Hill
Minstead Lodge
Brock Farm
Brockishill Inclosure
Stoney Cross Plain
MINSTEAD
Minstead Study Centre
Newtown
Peter's Hold Farm
Park Farm
Manor Park
Ringwood Ford Bottom
Bottom
Woodside
Withybed
Fritham Cross
Manor Wood
The Kennels
Harcourt Wood
The Mill House
Acres Down House
Puckpits Inclosure
Mill Stream
Minstead Manor Farm
Leominstead
Acres Down Inclosure

Ham Down
Blackhill
Romsey
SO51
Ower Service Area
Wigley
OWER
Junction 2
NEW FOREST NATIONAL PARK
SO43
SO40
Stonyford
Barrow Hill
Newbridge
COPYTHORNE
Pollards Moor
EMBLEY WOOD
SHELLEY COMMON
PAULTONS GOLF CENTRE AND GOLF COURSE
Paultons Park
Paultons Park Watermill
NEWBRIDGE INCLOSURE
COPYTHORNE COMMON
CRAWLEY HILL
SALISBURY ROAD
ROMSEY ROAD
M27 MOTORWAY
A36
A31
A3090
A326
M27
Tilhill
Foxbury Plantation
Fourteen Acre Copse
Pearce's Copse
Allmoor Copse
Middle Copse
High Wood Copse
Larks Lease Copse
Fuzzies Copse
Court Copse
Sandhill Plantation
Cooper's Copse
Robins Copse
Upper Shelley Copse
Lower Shelley Copse
Shorn Hill
Tatchbury Mount Hill Fort
Blackwater Bridge
Ham Lake
Hamdown Farm
Wellow Down
Long Clump
Wyndmoor
Oakdene Farm
Cooper's Clump
Hammond's Farm
Lark Farm
Shelley Lodge
Shelley Farm
Heatherlands
Rough Park
Romsey Lodge
Golden Meadow
Whitemoor Pond
Crowhaven Farm
Moor Farm
Copythorne C of E Infant School
The Hollies
Tatchbury Copse
Tatchbury Manor Farm
James's Farm
Gipsies Fir Plantation
Shornhill Great Fir Plantation
Little Fir Clump
120
155
128
170

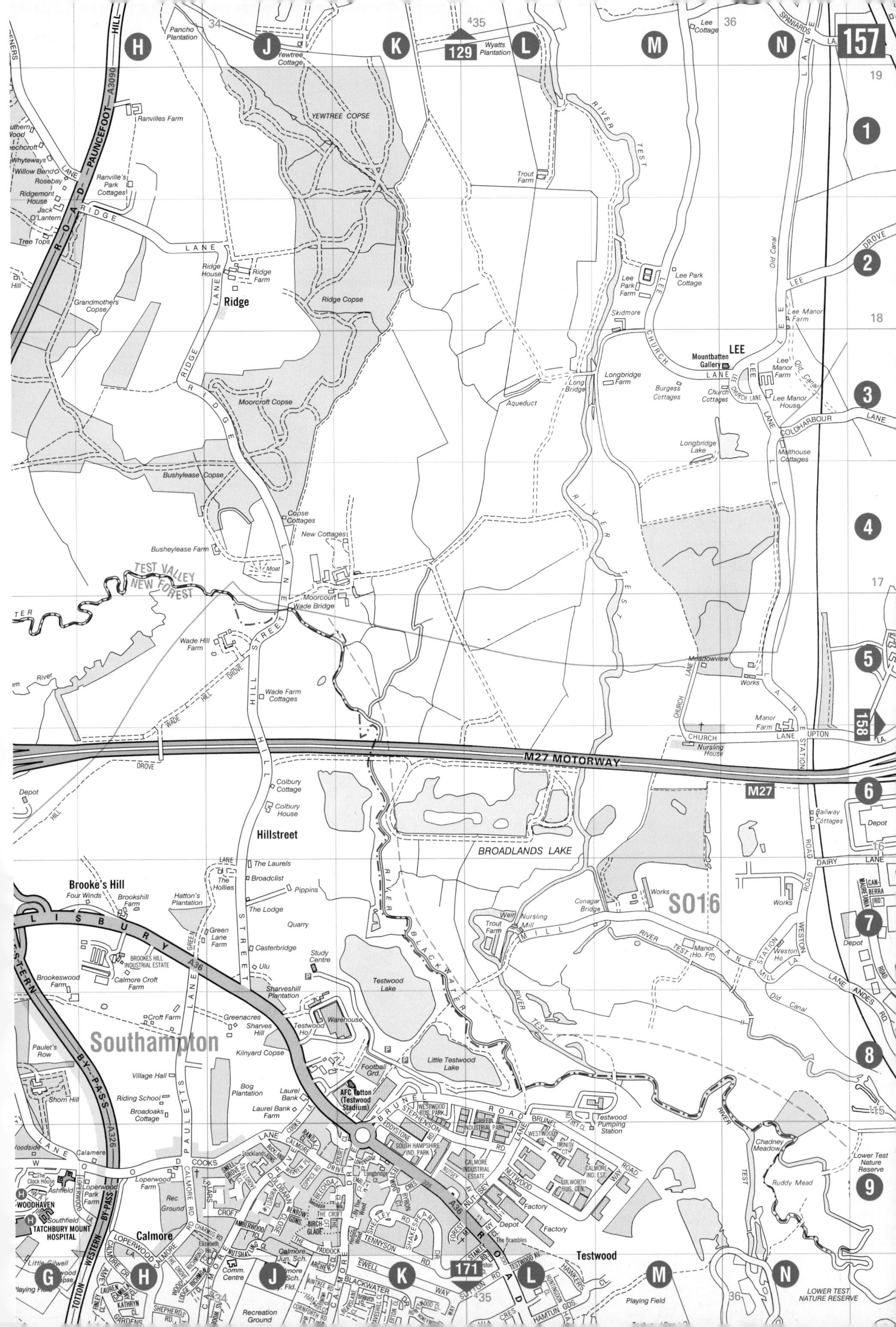
129
Pancho Plantation
Yewtree Cottage
Wyatts Plantation
Lee Cottage
Ranvilles Farm
YEWTREE COPSE
RIVER TEST
PAUNCEFOOT HILL
A3090
Ranville's Park Cottages
Trout Farm
Ridge Lane
Ridge House
Ridge Farm
Ridge
Ridge Copse
Grandmothers Copse
Lee Park Farm
Lee Park Cottage
Old Canal
Lee Drove
Lee Manor Farm
Skidmore
Church Lane
Mountbatten Gallery
LEE
Longbridge Farm
Long Bridge
Aqueduct
Burgess Cottages
Church Cottages
Lee Manor Farm
Lee Manor House
Moorcroft Copse
Coldharbour Lane
Longbridge Lake
Malthouse Cottages
Bushylease Copse
Copse Cottages
New Cottages
Busheylease Farm
Moat
TEST VALLEY
NEW FOREST
Moorcourt
Wade Bridge
Wade Hill Farm
Wade Hill Drove
Hill Street
Wade Farm Cottages
Meadowview
Works
Manor Farm
Church Lane
Upton Lane
Station
Nursling House
158
M27 MOTORWAY
M27
Depot
Colbury Cottage
Colbury House
Railway Cottages
Hillstreet
BROADLANDS LAKE
Dairy Lane
The Laurels
Broadclist
Pippins
The Hollies
Brooke's Hill
Four Winds
Brookshill Farm
Hatton's Plantation
The Lodge
Quarry
Works
Conagar Bridge
SO16
Weir
Nursling Mill
Trout Farm
Mill Lane
River Test
Manor Ho. Fm.
Weston Ho.
Canberra Rd.
Mauretania Rd.
Depot
Weston Lane
Andes Rd
SALISBURY RD
A36
Green Lane
Green Lane Farm
Casterbridge
Study Centre
Ulu
BROOKES HILL INDUSTRIAL ESTATE
Calmore Croft Farm
Brookeswood Farm
Testwood Lake
Sharveshill Plantation
Old Canal
WESTERN BY-PASS
Croft Farm
Greenacres
Sharves Hill
Testwood Ho.
Warehouse
Southampton
Paulet's Row
Kilnyard Copse
Little Testwood Lake
Football Grd.
Village Hall
Shorn Hill
Bog Plantation
AFC Totton (Testwood Stadium)
Laurel Bank
Riding School
Broadoaks Cottage
Laurel Bank Farm
Brunel Road
Westwood Bus. Park
Griffin Industrial Park
Stephenson
Eddystone Rd
South Hampshire Ind. Park
Testwood Pumping Station
Chadney Meadow
Lower Test Nature Reserve
Woodside Lane
Calamere
Cooks Lane
Calmore Industrial Estate
Westwood Ct.
Trinity Ct.
Calmore Ind. Est.
Lulworth Bus. Cen.
Ruddy Mead
Loperwood Farm
Loperwood Park Farm
Ashfield
WOODHAVEN
Southfield
TATCHBURY MOUNT HOSPITAL
Rec. Ground
Calmore Rd
Nutwood Way
Factory
Depot
The Brambles
Testwood
Calmore
Loperwood La.
Little Gilwell
Comm. Centre
Calmore Jun. Sch.
Tennyson Rd
Shakespeare Dr
Ewell Way
Blackwater Dr
171
Totton
Sutton Rd
Hawkers Cl
Playing Field
Recreation Ground
Hamtun Gds
LOWER TEST NATURE RESERVE
Playing Field
Shepherds Rd.
Kathryn Cl.
G H J K L M N
1 2 3 4 5 6 7 8 9
19 18 17 16 15
34 435 36

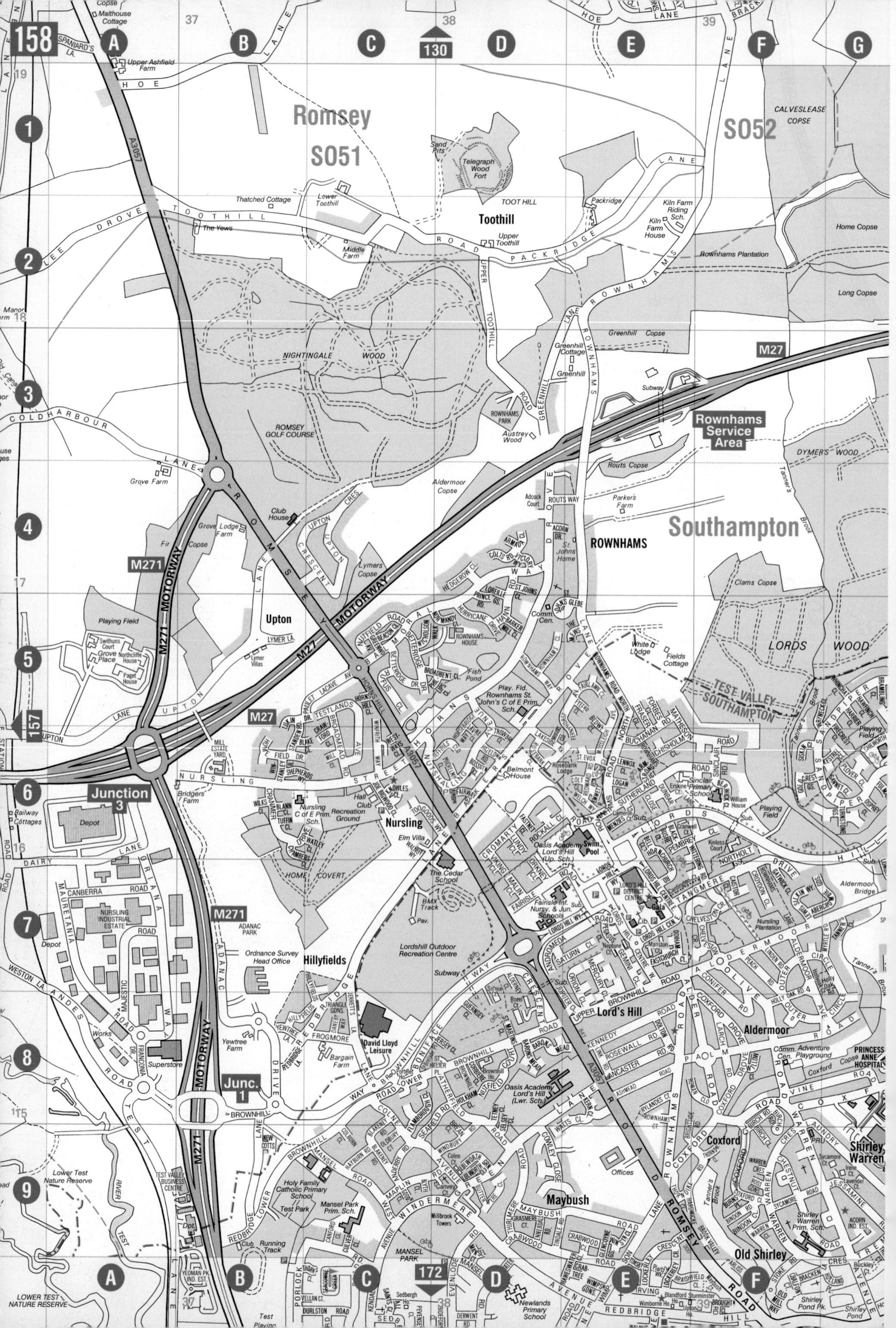

130
172
157
Romsey
SO51
SO52
Southampton
Toothill
TOOT HILL
Telegraph Wood Fort
Sand Pits
Upper Ashfield Farm
Malthouse Cottage
SPANIARD'S LA.
HOE LANE
Thatched Cottage
Lower Toothill
The Yews
Middle Farm
Upper Toothill
TOOTHILL ROAD
PACKRIDGE LANE
Packridge
Kiln Farm Riding Sch.
Kiln Farm House
Rownhams Plantation
CALVESLEASE COPSE
Home Copse
Long Copse
Greenhill Copse
Greenhill Cottage
Greenhill
NIGHTINGALE WOOD
ROMSEY GOLF COURSE
COLDHARBOUR LANE
LEE DROVE
Grove Farm
ROWNHAMS PARK
Austrey Wood
Subway
Rownhams Service Area
Routs Copse
DYMER'S WOOD
Parker's Farm
Aldermoor Copse
Club House
Grove Lodge Farm
Fir Copse
Lymers Copse
Upton
UPTON CRESCENT
LYMER LA
Lymer Villas
M27
M271
M27 MOTORWAY
M271 MOTORWAY
A3057
ROMSEY ROAD
ROWNHAMS
Adcock Court
ROUTS WAY
St. Johns Home
Comm. Cen.
ROWNHAMS HOUSE
Fish Pond
Clams Copse
LORDS WOOD
White Lodge
Fields Cottage
TEST VALLEY
SOUTHAMPTON
Playing Field
Swithuns Court
Grove Place
Northcliffe House
Paget House
Play. Fld. Rownhams St. John's C of E Prim. Sch.
Belmont House
Rosebank Lodge
Sinclair Primary School
William House
NURSLING STREET
Bridgers Farm
MILL ESTATE YARD
Junction 3
Railway Cottages
Depot
DAIRY LANE
CANBERRA ROAD
MAURETANIA ROAD
NURSLING INDUSTRIAL ESTATE
ORIANA WAY
WESTON LA.
ANDES ROAD
MAJESTIC ROAD
FRANCONIA DR.
Works
Superstore
TEST LANE
ADANAC PARK
ADANAC DRIVE
Ordnance Survey Head Office
Nursling C of E Prim. Sch.
Hall
Club
Recreation Ground
Nursling
Elm Villa
HOME COVERT
The Cedar School
BMX Track
Pav.
Lordshill Outdoor Recreation Centre
Hillyfields
Oasis Academy Lord's Hill (Up. Sch.)
Swim Pool
LORD'S HILL DISTRICT CENTRE
Gala
Fairisle Inf. Nursy. & Jun. Schools
Lord's Hill
Aldermoor
Aldermoor Bridge
Nursling Plantation
Comm. Adventure Playground
PRINCESS ANNE HOSPITAL
Coxford
Shirley Warren
Old Shirley
Shirley Warren Prim. Sch.
Junc. 1
BROWNHILL
Yewtree Farm
David Lloyd Leisure
Bargain Farm
FROGMORE
Oasis Academy Lord's Hill (Lwr. Sch.)
Offices
Maybush
Holy Family Catholic Primary School
Mansel Park Prim. Sch.
Test Park
Millbrook Towers
MANSEL PARK
WINDERMERE AVENUE
TEST VALLEY BUSINESS CENTRE
Lower Test Nature Reserve
LOWER TEST NATURE RESERVE
RIVER TEST
YEOMAN PK. IND. EST.
Running Track
REDBRIDGE LANE
REDBRIDGE HILL
Newlands Primary School
ACORN IND. EST.
Shirley Pond Pk.
Shirley Pond

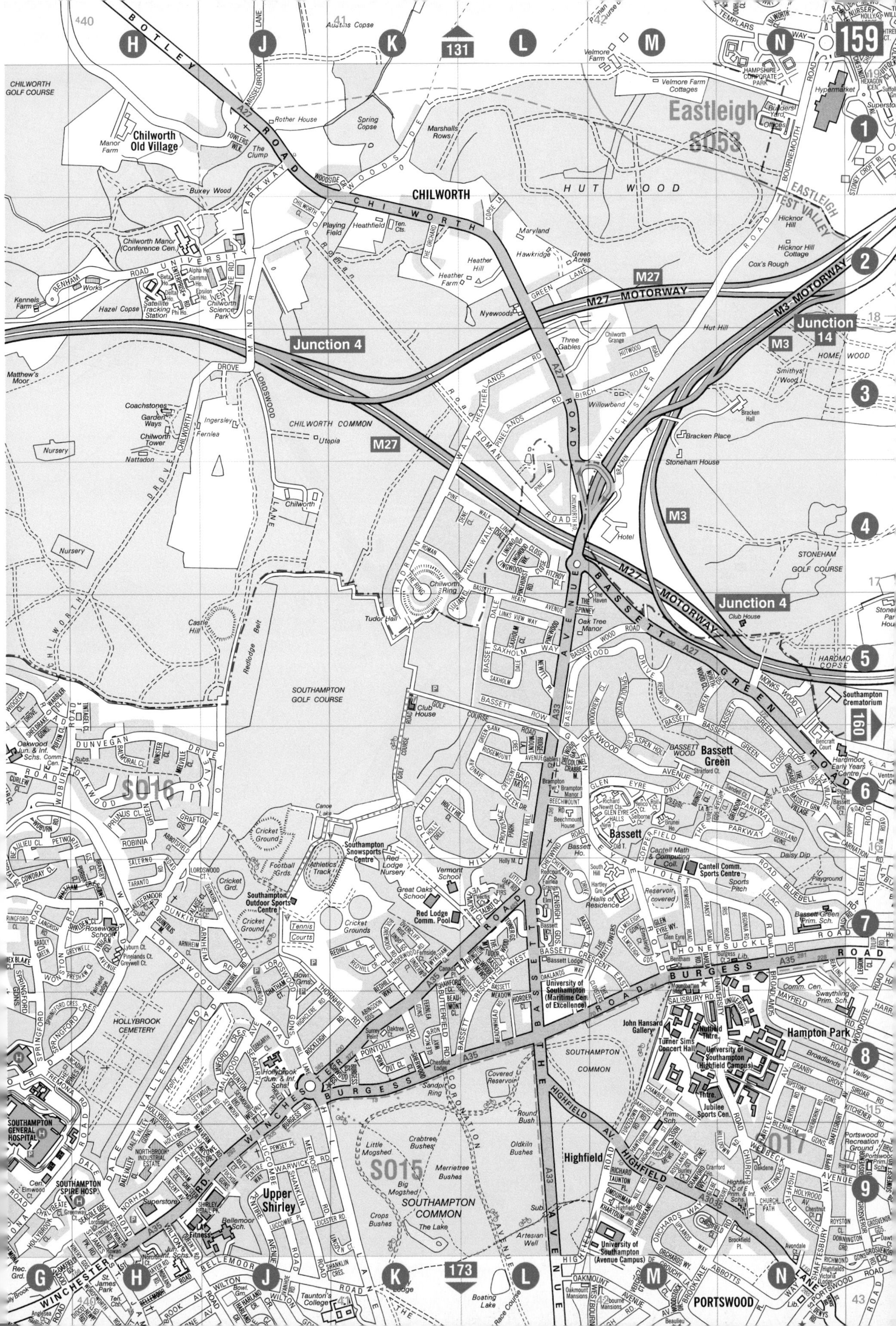
159
131
173
160
H
J
K
L
M
N
G
1
2
3
4
5
6
7
8
9
440
41
42
43
19
18
17
16
115
BOTLEY ROAD
CHILWORTH GOLF COURSE
Chilworth Old Village
Manor Farm
Austins Copse
Rother House
Spring Copse
Velmore Farm
Velmore Farm Cottages
TEMPLARS WAY
HAMPSHIRE CORPORATE PARK
Hypermarket
Eastleigh
SO53
Builders' Yard Offices
BOURNEMOUTH ROAD
Marshalls Rows
The Clump
Buxey Wood
CHILWORTH
HUT WOOD
EASTLEIGH
TEST VALLEY
Hicknor Hill
Hicknor Hill Cottage
Cox's Rough
Playing Field
Heathfield
Ten. Cts.
Maryland
Hawkridge
Green Acres
Heather Hill
Heather Farm
Chilworth Manor (Conference Cen.)
UNIVERSITY ROAD
BENHAM
Works
Kennels Farm
Hazel Copse
Satellite Tracking Station
Chilworth Science Park
M27
M27 MOTORWAY
M3 MOTORWAY
GREEN LANE
Nyewoods
Junction 4
Junction 14
M3
Hut Hill
HOME WOOD
Smithys Wood
Three Gables
Chilworth Grange
HUTWOOD ROAD
BIRCH ROAD
Willowbend
Bracken Hall
Bracken Place
Stoneham House
Matthew's Moor
DROVE
MANOR
LORDSWOOD
Coachstones
Garden Ways
Chilworth Tower
Nattadon
Ingersley
Fernlea
CHILWORTH COMMON
Utopia
Nursery
HEATHERLANDS RD
PINELANDS RD
ROMAN ROAD
WINCHESTER
A27
Hotel
STONEHAM GOLF COURSE
Chilworth
Chilworth Ring
The Ring
Tudor Hall
Castle Hill
Redlodge Belt
BASSETT AVENUE
BASSETT GREEN ROAD
MOTORWAY
Club House
The Haven
The Spinney
Oak Tree Manor
BASSETT WOOD ROAD
SAXHOLM WAY
HARDMOOR COPSE
Southampton Crematorium
SOUTHAMPTON GOLF COURSE
Club House
BASSETT ROW
A33
Bassett Green
BASSETT WOOD
Stratford Ct.
Hardmoor Early Years Centre
DUNVEGAN DRIVE
Oakwood Jun. & Inf. Schs.
WOBURN ROAD
SO16
Canoe Lake
Cricket Ground
Southampton Snowsports Centre
Red Lodge Nursery
Athletics Track
Football Grds.
Vermont School
Great Oaks School
Red Lodge Comm. Pool
Southampton Outdoor Sports Centre
Cricket Grounds
Tennis Courts
Brampton Manor
Beechmount House
GLEN EYRE DRIVE
Bassett
Glen Eyre Halls
Cantell Math & Computing Coll.
Cantell Comm. Sports Centre
Sports Pitch
Halls of Residence
Reservoir (covered)
Daisy Dip
Playground
Basset Green Prim. Sch.
BURGESS ROAD
A35
HONEYSUCKLE ROAD
University of Southampton (Maritime Cen. of Excellence)
John Hansard Gallery
Nuffield Thtre.
Turner Sims Concert Hall
University of Southampton (Highfield Campus)
Thtre.
Jubilee Sports Cen.
Hampton Park
Swaythling Prim. Sch.
Comm. Cen.
HOLLYBROOK CEMETERY
Hollybrook Jun. & Inf. Schs.
SOUTHAMPTON COMMON
Covered Reservoir
Sandpit Ring
Round Bush
Crabtree Bushes
Oldkiln Bushes
Little Mogshed
Big Mogshed
Merrietree Bushes
SO15
Crops Bushes
The Lake
Artesian Well
Highfield
HIGHFIELD AV.
SO17
Portswood Recreation Ground
SOUTHAMPTON GENERAL HOSPITAL
SOUTHAMPTON SPIRE HOSP.
NORTHBROOK INDUSTRIAL ESTATE
Superstore
Shirley Retail Pk.
LA Fitness
Bellemoor Sch.
Upper Shirley
WINCHESTER RD.
WINCHESTER ROAD
BELLEMOOR ROAD
St. James Park
Taunton's College
Boating Lake
Race Course
University of Southampton (Avenue Campus)
PORTSWOOD
Oakmount Mansions
Westbourne Mansions
Lib.

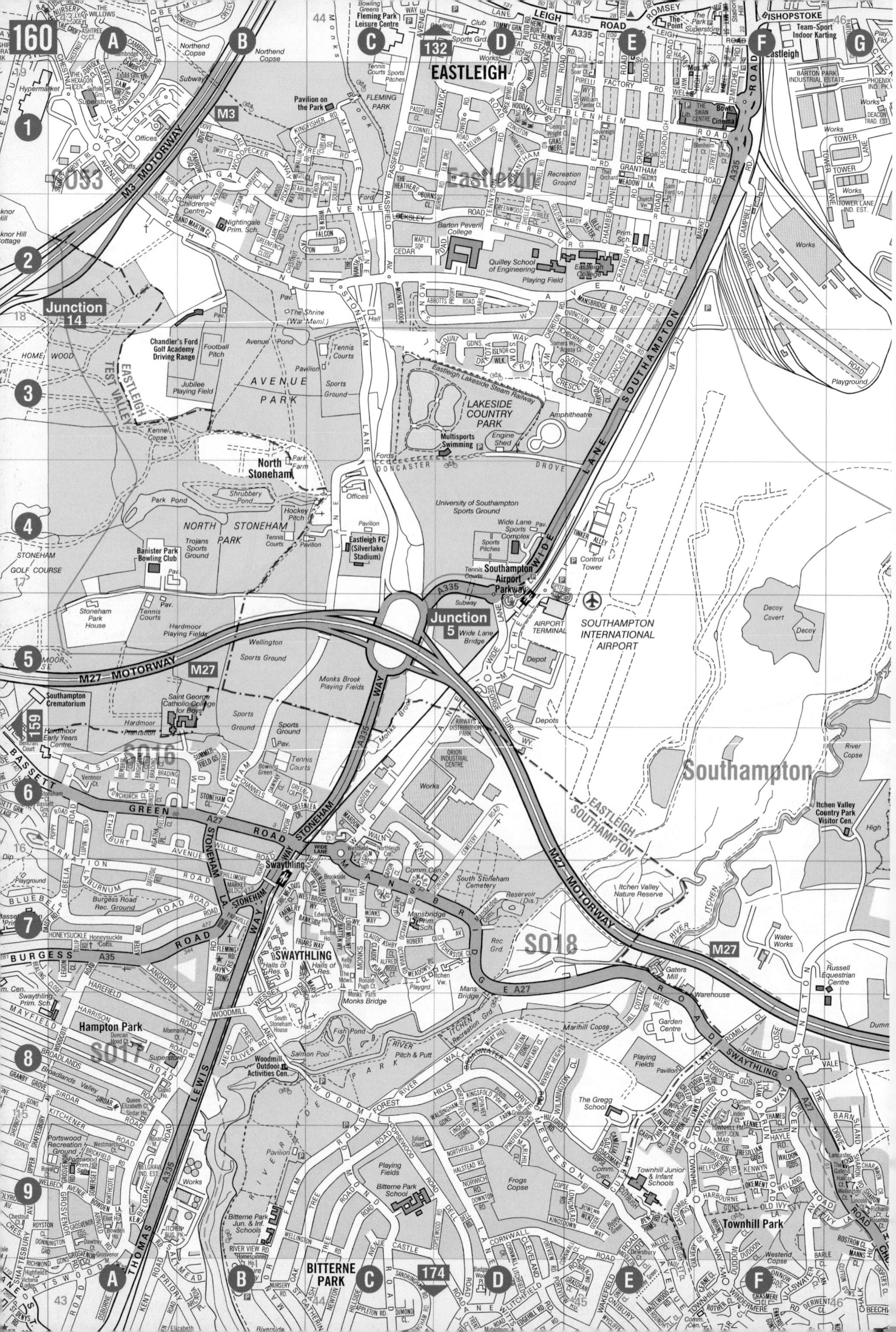

EASTLEIGH
Eastleigh
BISHOPSTOKE
Team-Sport Indoor Karting
LEIGH ROAD
A335
ROMSEY
The Point
The Park Superstore
Fleming Park Leisure Centre
Bowling Greens
Club
Sports Grd.
Works
Northend Copse
Hypermarket
Superstore
Offices
SO53
M3 MOTORWAY
M3
Subway
Pavilion on the Park
FLEMING PARK
Tennis Courts Sports Pitches
Aviary Childrens Centre
Nightingale Prim. Sch.
Barton Peveril College
Quilley School of Engineering
Eastleigh College
Playing Field
Recreation Ground
BARTON PARK INDUSTRIAL ESTATE
TOWER LANE IND. EST.
Works
THE SWAN CENTRE
Bowl
Cinema
Junction 14
Chandler's Ford Golf Academy Driving Range
Football Pitch
Jubilee Playing Field
AVENUE PARK
Tennis Courts
Sports Ground
Pavilion
The Shrine (War Meml.)
EASTLEIGH
TEST VALLEY
Kennel Copse
Eastleigh Lakeside Steam Railway
LAKESIDE COUNTRY PARK
Multisports Swimming
Engine Shed
Amphitheatre
Playground
North Stoneham
Park Farm
Shrubbery Pond
Park Pond
Hockey Pitch
NORTH STONEHAM PARK
Trojans Sports Ground
Tennis Courts
Offices
Pavilion
Eastleigh FC (Silverlake Stadium)
University of Southampton Sports Ground
Wide Lane Sports Complex
Sports Pitches
Southampton Airport Parkway
Control Tower
STONEHAM GOLF COURSE
Banister Park Bowling Club
Stoneham Park House
Tennis Courts
Hardmoor Playing Fields
Junction 5
Wide Lane Bridge
AIRPORT TERMINAL
SOUTHAMPTON INTERNATIONAL AIRPORT
Depot
Depots
Decoy Covert
Decoy
M27 MOTORWAY
M27
Wellington Sports Ground
Monks Brook Playing Fields
Southampton Crematorium
Saint George Catholic College for Boys
Hardmoor Early Years Centre
Sports Ground
Tennis Courts
AIRWAYS DISTRIBUTION PARK
ORION INDUSTRIAL CENTRE
Works
Southampton
River Copse
EASTLEIGH
SOUTHAMPTON
SO16
Itchen Valley Country Park Visitor Cen.
BASSETT GREEN ROAD
A27
Swaythling
South Stoneham Cemetery
Reservoir (Dis.)
Itchen Valley Nature Reserve
Burgess Road Rec. Ground
Mansbridge Prim. Sch.
SO18
Rec. Grd.
Water Works
BURGESS ROAD
A35
SWAYTHLING
Halls of Res.
Gaters Mill
Warehouse
Russell Equestrian Centre
Swaythling Prim. Sch.
Hampton Park
SO17
Superstore
Monks Bridge
Mans Bridge
Itchen Recreation Grd.
Marlhill Copse
Garden Centre
Salmon Pool
Fish Pond
Woodmill Outdoor Activities Cen.
RIVERSIDE PARK
Pitch & Putt
Playing Fields
Pavilion
The Gregg School
Portswood Recreation Ground
SWAYTHLING ROAD
Works
Pavilion
Playing Fields
Bitterne Park School
Frogs Copse
Townhill Junior & Infant Schools
Townhill Park
Bitterne Park Jun. & Inf. Schools
BITTERNE PARK
Westend Copse
LEWIS
THOMAS
A335
132
174
159

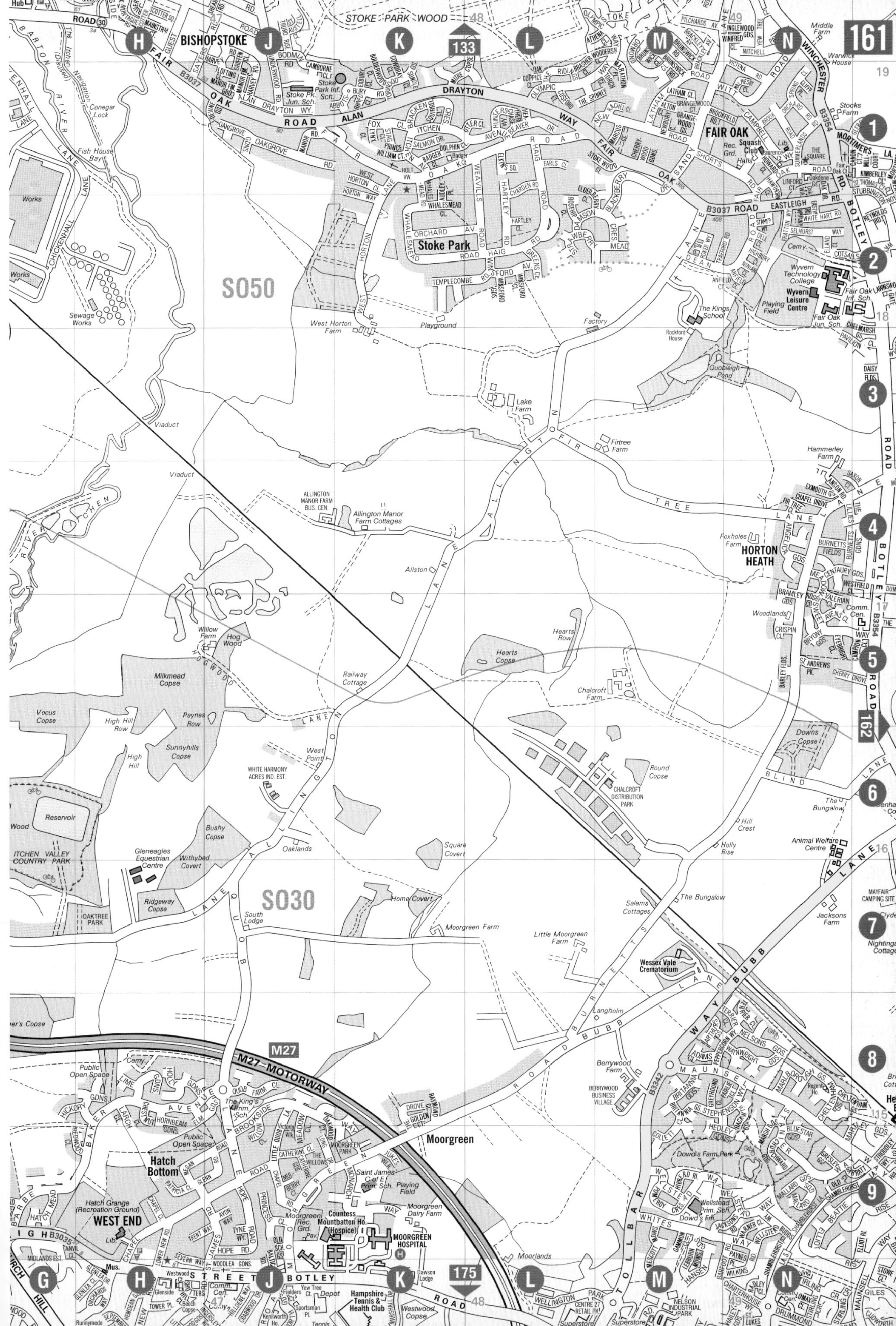
BISHOPSTOKE
FAIR OAK
Stoke Park
SO50
HORTON HEATH
SO30
WEST END
Hatch Bottom
Moorgreen
M27 MOTORWAY
MOORGREEN HOSPITAL
Wessex Vale Crematorium
ITCHEN VALLEY COUNTRY PARK
CHALCROFT DISTRIBUTION PARK
133
162
175

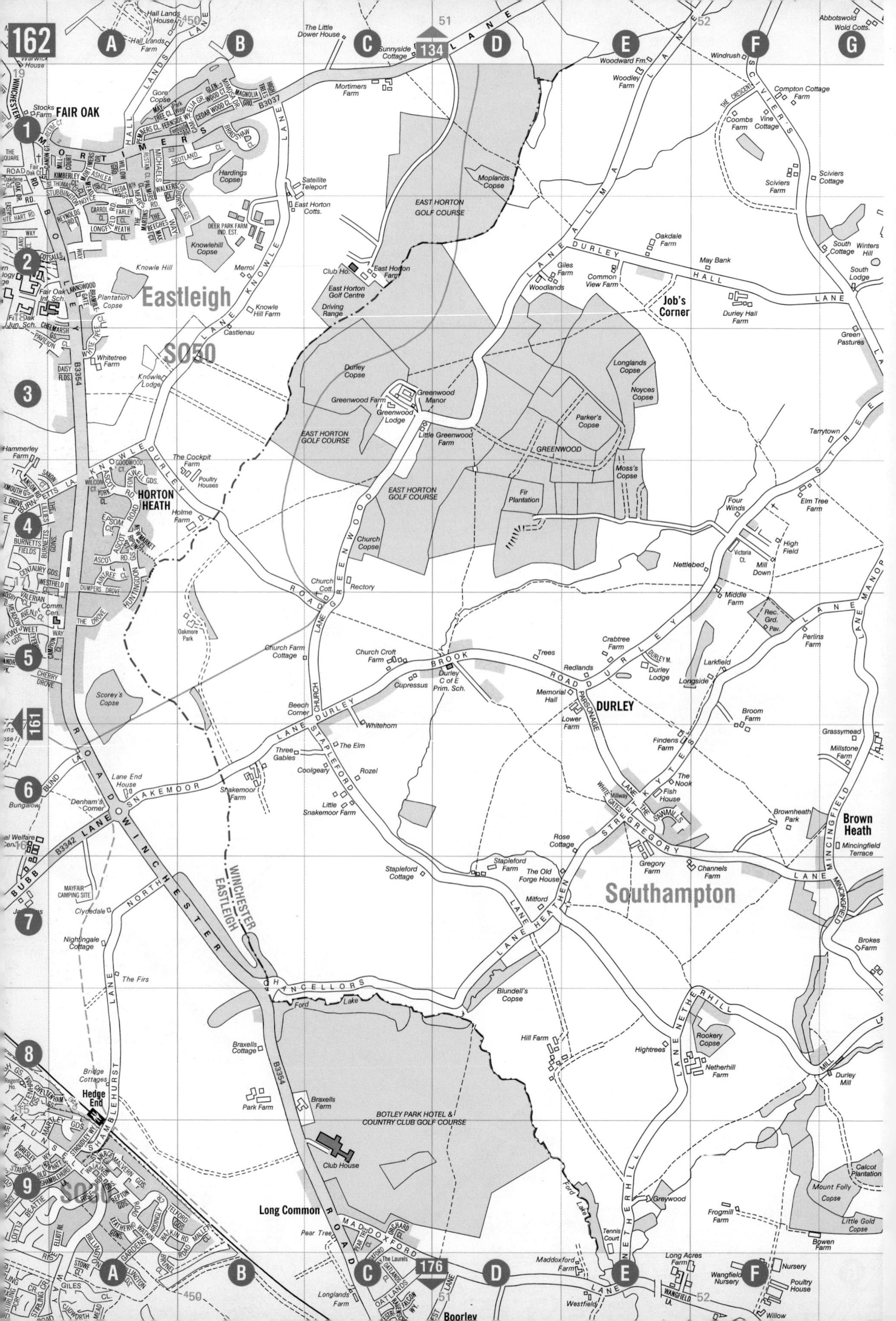

134
176
161
Hall Lands House
Hall Lands Farm
The Little Dower House
Sunnyside Cottage
Mortimers Farm
Woodward Fm.
Woodley Farm
Windrush
Abbotswold
Wold Cotts.
Compton Cottage Farm
Coombs Farm
Vine Cottage
Sciviers Cottage
Sciviers Farm
FAIR OAK
Stocks Farm
Gore Copse
B3037
Hardings Copse
Satellite Teleport
East Horton Cotts.
Moplands Copse
EAST HORTON GOLF COURSE
DEER PARK FARM IND. EST.
Knowlehill Copse
Knowle Hill
Merrol
Club Ho.
East Horton Farm
East Horton Golf Centre
Driving Range
Eastleigh
Knowle Hill Farm
Plantation Copse
Castlenau
SO50
Oakdale Farm
May Bank
Giles Farm
Woodlands
Common View Farm
Job's Corner
Durley Hall Farm
South Cottage
Winters Hill
South Lodge
Green Pastures
DURLEY HALL LANE
Whitetree Farm
Knowle Lodge
Durley Copse
Greenwood Farm
Greenwood Manor
Greenwood Lodge
Little Greenwood Farm
Longlands Copse
Noyces Copse
Parker's Copse
GREENWOOD
Moss's Copse
Tarrytown
Hammerley Farm
The Cockpit Farm
Poultry Houses
HORTON HEATH
Holme Farm
Fir Plantation
Four Winds
Elm Tree Farm
High Field
Victoria Ct.
Mill Down
Nettlebed
Church Copse
Church Cott.
Rectory
Middle Farm
Rec. Grd. Pav.
Perlins Farm
Oakmore Park
Church Farm Cottage
Church Croft Farm
Durley C of E Prim. Sch.
Trees
Crabtree Farm
Redlands
Durley Lodge
Larkfield
Longside
Memorial Hall
DURLEY
Lower Farm
Cupressus
Whitehorn
Beech Corner
Scorey's Copse
Broom Farm
Grassymead
Millstone Farm
Findens Farm
Three Gables
The Elm
Coolgeary
Rozel
Little Snakemoor Farm
Lane End House
Denham's Corner
Bungalow
Shakemoor Farm
The Nook
Fish House
Brownheath Park
Brown Heath
Mincingfield Terrace
Rose Cottage
Stapleford Farm
The Old Forge House
Stapleford Cottage
Gregory Farm
Channels Farm
Southampton
MAYFAIR CAMPING SITE
Clydedale
Nightingale Cottage
Mitford
WINCHESTER
EASTLEIGH
The Firs
Brokes Farm
Ford Lake
Blundell's Copse
Braxells Cottage
Hill Farm
Hightrees
Rookery Copse
Netherhill Farm
Durley Mill
Bridge Cottages
Hedge End
Park Farm
Braxells Farm
BOTLEY PARK HOTEL & COUNTRY CLUB GOLF COURSE
Club House
Calcot Plantation
Mount Folly Copse
Greywood
Frogmill Farm
Little Gold Copse
Bowen Farm
Long Common
Pear Tree
Tennis Court
SO30
Maddoxford Farm
Long Acres Farm
Nursery
Wangfield Nursery
Poultry House
Longlands Farm
Westfield
Willow
Boorley
B3354
B3342
WINCHESTER ROAD
SNAKEMOOR LANE
CHANCELLORS LANE
NETHERHILL LANE
HEATHEN LANE
STAPLEFORD LANE
CHURCH LANE
DURLEY BROOK ROAD
KYTES LANE
GREGORY LANE
MINCINGFIELD LANE
MANOR LANE
NORTH LANE
SHAMBLEHURST LANE
MADDOXFORD LANE
KNOWLE LANE
BUBB LANE
BLIND LANE
DURLEY STREET
SCIVIER'S LANE

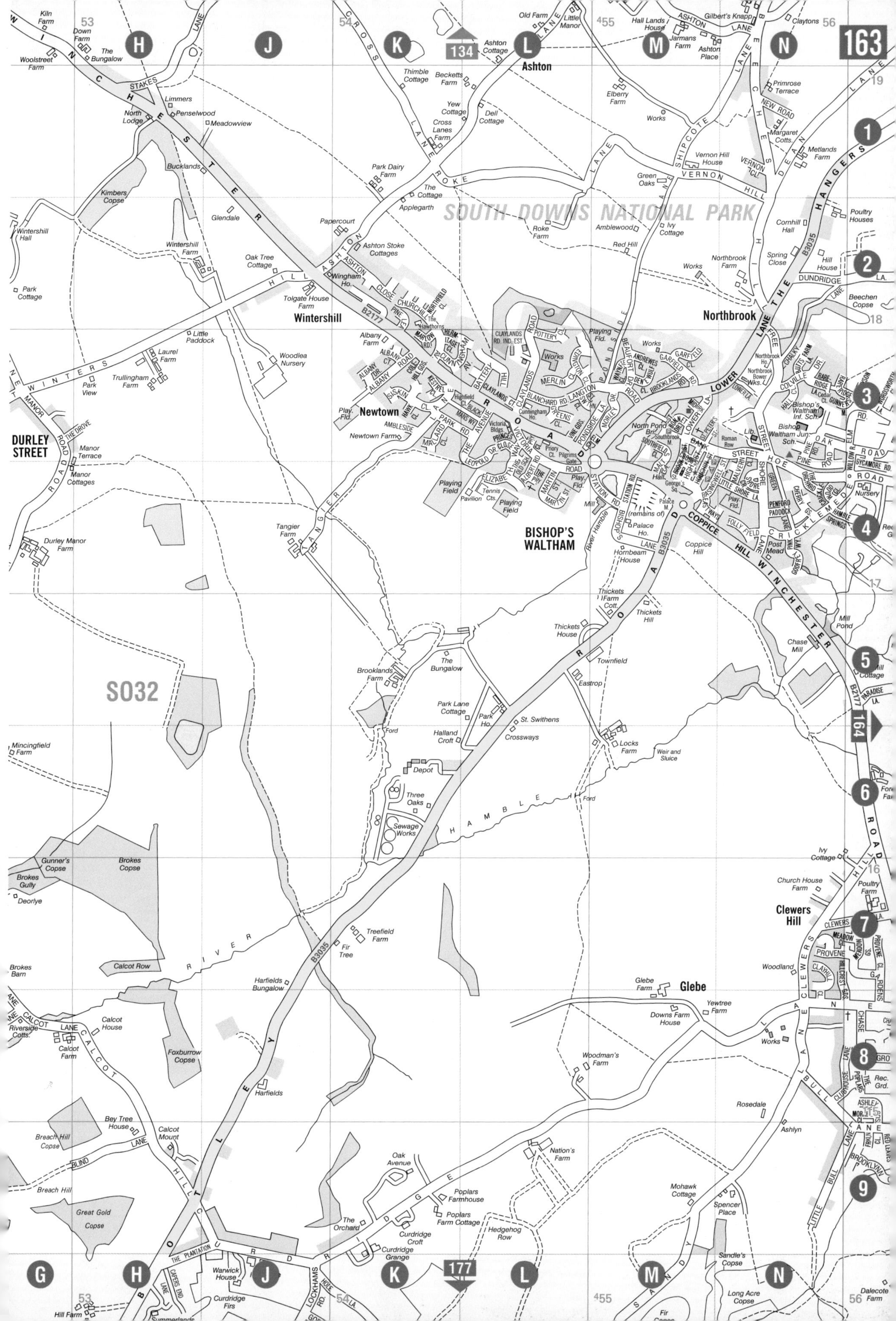
SOUTH DOWNS NATIONAL PARK
Ashton
Wintershill
Newtown
Northbrook
BISHOP'S WALTHAM
DURLEY STREET
Clewers Hill
Glebe
SO32
134
164
177
Kiln Farm
Down Farm
The Bungalow
Woolstreet Farm
Stakes
Limmers
Penselwood
Meadowview
North Lodge
Bucklands
Kimbers Copse
Glendale
Wintershill Hall
Wintershill Farm
Oak Tree Cottage
Park Cottage
Tolgate House Farm
Little Paddock
Laurel Farm
Trullingham Farm
Park View
Woodlea Nursery
Manor Terrace
Manor Cottages
Durley Manor Farm
Old Farm
Little Manor
Ashton Cottage
Hall Lands House
Jarmans Farm
Ashton Place
Gilbert's Knapp
Claytons
Primrose Terrace
New Road
Thimble Cottage
Becketts Farm
Yew Cottage
Cross Lanes Farm
Dell Cottage
Elberry Farm
Works
Margaret Cotts.
Metlands Farm
Vernon Hill House
Green Oaks
Park Dairy Farm
The Cottage
Applegarth
Papercourt
Ashton Stoke Cottages
Roke Farm
Amblewood
Ivy Cottage
Red Hill
Cornhill Hall
Poultry Houses
Spring Close
Hill House
Northbrook Farm
Beechen Copse
Albany Farm
Wingham Ho.
The Hawthorns
Claylands Rd. Ind. Est.
Playing Fld.
Newtown Farm
Victoria Bldgs.
Priory Cl.
Pilgrims Gate
Playing Field
Pavilion
Tennis Cts.
North Pond
Southbrook
Roman Row
Lib.
Bishop's Waltham Inf. Sch.
Bishop's Waltham Jun. Sch.
Nursery
Palace Ho.
Palace (remains of)
George's Sq.
Hornbeam House
Coppice Hill
Post Mead
Tangier Farm
Thickets Farm Cott.
Thickets Hill
Thickets House
Townfield
Eastrop
Mill Pond
Chase Mill
Mill Cottage
Brooklands Farm
The Bungalow
Park Lane Cottage
Park Ho.
Halland Croft
St. Swithens
Crossways
Locks Farm
Weir and Sluice
Ford
Depot
Three Oaks
Sewage Works
Mincingfield Farm
Gunner's Copse
Brokes Copse
Brokes Gully
Deorlye
Ivy Cottage
Church House Farm
Poultry Farm
Treefield Farm
Fir Tree
Calcot Row
Brokes Barn
Harfields Bungalow
Glebe Farm
Yewtree Farm
Downs Farm House
Woodland
Calcot House
Riverside Cotts.
Calcot Farm
Foxburrow Copse
Woodman's Farm
Harfields
Rosedale
Ashlyn
Bey Tree House
Breach Hill Copse
Calcot Mount
Nation's Farm
Oak Avenue
Breach Hill
Great Gold Copse
Mohawk Cottage
Spencer Place
Poplars Farmhouse
Poplars Farm Cottage
Hedgehog Row
The Orchard
Curdridge Croft
Curdridge Grange
Sandle's Copse
Warwick House
Curdridge Firs
Hill Farm
Long Acre Copse
Dalecote Farm
Rec. Grd.

135
163
178
Meadowbank
The Hangers
Hilltop
Galley Down
Shepherds Down
DEAN LANE
HANGERS LANE
B3035
Metlands Farm
Bishop's Down Farm
Poultry Houses
DUNDRIDGE LANE
DUNDRIDGE
Duncombe
The Bungalow
Dundridge Farm
White Cottage
Damson Hill Ho.
Dundridge
Little Phrymph Copse
Beechen Copse
Beechen Copse
Runny Down Copse
Field Farm
The Old Cottage
Sheelds Copse
DAMSON HILL
Damsonhill Cottage
Lycroft
Hillside
Swanmore Barn Farm
Swanmore Park Farm
Little Forest Copse
North Lodge
Dairy Cottage
Poultry Houses
Poultry House
Little Horsecroft Copse
Swanmore Park
The Ranch
Swanmore Park
Hill Top
PARK LANE
Mayhill Copse
South Lodge
Upper Swanmore
GREEN LANE
Cemetery
Upfield
Y Berllan
WEST HOE LANE
JERVIS COURT
Hoe
TENNYSON CL.
WORDSWORTH CL.
BYRON CL.
HAZEL GRO.
RAREBRIDGE
OAK RD.
ELM RD.
PINE RD.
SYCAMORE RD.
WILLOW R.
GUNNERS PK.
THE ORCHARD
CRICKLEMEDE
THE GARDENS
HAMBLE SPRINGS
Nursery
Recreation Ground
Jervis Lodge
Jervis Lodge Cottage
JERVIS COURT LA.
Jervis Court Farm
Swanmore Lodge
Laurel Cottage
Mayhill
Yew Tree Villa
South View
Hoe Farm
Little Hoe Farm
SWANMORE LANE
MOORLANDS RD.
WELL LANE
Well Cott.
Mayhill Barn Farm
Mayhill Farm
Westwo
Hampton Farm
HAMPTON FARM LANE
Hampton Hill
SUETTS
Suetts Farm
Mill Pond
The Moors Nature Reserve
Primrose Hill
Admiral's Copse
MAYHILL LANE
DONIGERS CL.
Donigers
DONIGERS DELL
HAMPTON
CUT THROAT LA.
Tennis Cts.
The Vicarage
Upper Hill Farm
Old Mill Cottage
Works
Alexanders Moors
PARADISE LANE
CHURCH ROAD
MICHAELMAS CL.
VICARAGE LA.
CHURCH LANE
FOXCOMBE CL.
Swanmore C of E Prim. Sch.
STONES CL.
BUCKETTS FARM CL.
Meon Gds.
Hill Place Farm
Hill Place Cottage
Hill Place
Church Cottage
Ivydale
Hill Farm
Forest Farm
SWANMORE BUS. PARK
BROAD
Pav.
Rec. Grd.
LARKSPUR CL.
THE HOLLY
THE DROVE
CORONATION RD.
CHAPEL RD.
DODDS LANE
Ellington
Hill Grove Cottages
Hill Grove
HILL GROVE
Lower Chase Farm
CHASE ROAD
Singleton's Farm
CROFTON WAY
MYERS CL.
GREENWAYS LANE
COBBETT CL.
SWANMORE
COTT
Ivy Cottage
Oaklands Poultry Farm
Swanmore College of Technology
BEVERLEY GS.
ROWAN CL.
Hill Grove Farm
Ludwell's Farm
Swanmore College Sports Complex
Halls
SPRING LANE
VALE
WILLOWS CL.
MEDLICOTT WY.
MARTIN CL.
Poultry Farm
Games Pitch
LOWER CHASE
LUDWELLS LA.
THE LAKES
GLENDALE
Tudor Cottage
CLEWERS LA.
EVELYN
B2177
MEADOW GS.
PROVENE
PROVENE CL.
CLAYHILL
HILLCREST
GARDENS
CURDRIDGE LANE
Hillpound
Hillpound Farm
Kooshkaboot
WALTHAM BUSINESS PARK
Jetty
ORCHARDLEA
NEW BRICKYARD ROAD
FOREST LANE
FOREST GDNS.
CHASE GS.
LINDEN CL.
CLOSE
GROVE
FOREST
WALTHAM CHASE
The Firs
Bekhon Haven
Forest Farm
Heathfield
Woodgreen
Dirty Copse
Filldich Farm
Rec. Grd.
BEAUCROFT RD.
ASHLEY
MORRELL CL.
CHASE FARM CL.
CLUBHOUSE LANE
POPLARS
Wolmer Cottage
Beaulieu
Mellowstones
Longridge Farm
BISHOP'S WOOD ROAD
HILL POUND ROAD
MISLINGFORD ROAD
Forest Lodge
Chasewood
The Bungalow
West Lodge
Coach Road Copse
Hall
BULL LANE
BROOKLYNN CL.
RED LEAVES
Gravelhill Plantation
Gravel Hill
Bishopsmore
SWANMORE GOLF COURSE
Great Lion Copse
WESTFIELD DR.
Res (Cov.)
Hillcot
Beechcroft
Swanmore Golf Cen.
Driving Range
Bishopswood Farm
Fareham
PO17
St. John The Baptist C of E Prim. Sch.
Works
Wassalls Hall Farm
Brookfield Farm
HOLYWELL ROAD
SOLOMONS LANE
Gamblins Farm
Nursery
Depot
Bishop's Inclosure
Bishops Hill House
Hillcrest
Woodview
Hawksnest Farm
Black Horse Farm
Hazelmont Nurseries
Lindfield
HOLYWELL RD.
Dalecote Farm
Stares Farm
GRAVEL HILL
HEARNE GDNS.
BISHOPS LANE
Shirrell Heath Farm
LITTLE BULL LANE
A B C D E F G
1 2 3 4 5 6 7 8 9
56 57 58 59
19 18 17 16 115

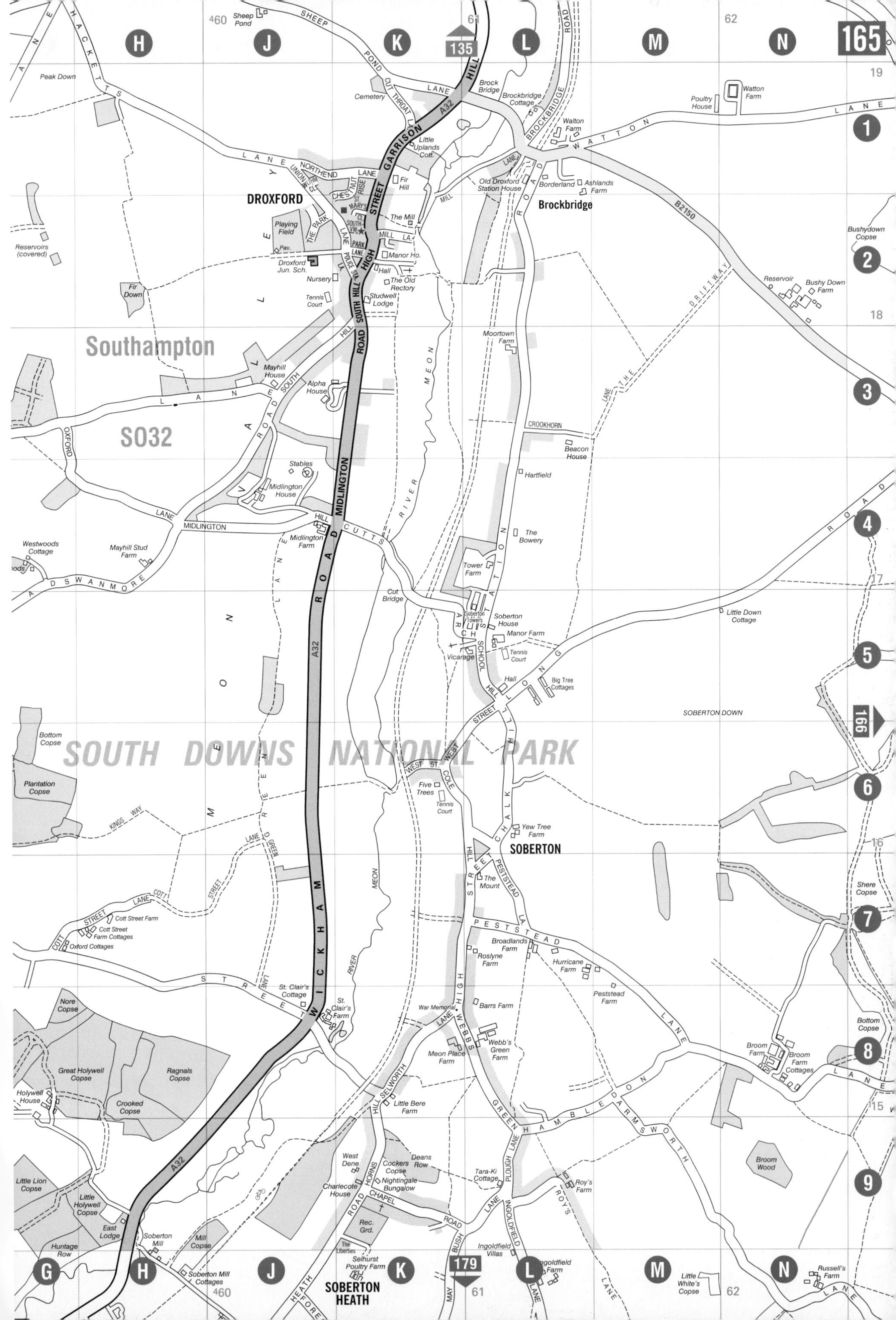

DROXFORD
Brockbridge
Southampton
SO32
SOUTH DOWNS NATIONAL PARK
SOBERTON
SOBERTON HEATH
Peak Down
Sheep Pond
Cemetery
Brock Bridge
Brockbridge Cottage
Watton Farm
Poultry House
Walton Farm
Little Uplands Cott.
Fir Hill
Old Droxford Station House
Borderland
Ashlands Farm
Playing Field
Pav.
Reservoirs (covered)
Droxford Jun. Sch.
Nursery
The Mill
Manor Ho.
Hall
The Old Rectory
Studwell Lodge
Tennis Court
Fir Down
Bushydown Copse
Reservoir
Bushy Down Farm
Moortown Farm
Mayhill House
Alpha House
Beacon House
Hartfield
Stables
Midlington House
Midlington Farm
Westwoods Cottage
Mayhill Stud Farm
The Bowery
Tower Farm
Cut Bridge
Soberton Towers
Soberton House
Manor Farm
Tennis Court
Vicarage
Little Down Cottage
Hall
Big Tree Cottages
SOBERTON DOWN
Bottom Copse
Plantation Copse
Five Trees
Tennis Court
Yew Tree Farm
The Mount
Shere Copse
Cott Street Farm
Cott Street Farm Cottages
Oxford Cottages
Broadlands Farm
Roslyne Farm
Hurricane Farm
Peststead Farm
St. Clair's Cottage
St. Clair's Farm
War Memorial
Barrs Farm
Nore Copse
Webb's Green Farm
Meon Place Farm
Bottom Copse
Broom Farm
Broom Farm Cottages
Great Holywell Copse
Ragnals Copse
Holywell House
Crooked Copse
Little Bere Farm
West Dene
Cockers Copse
Deans Row
Broom Wood
Charlecote House
Nightingale Bungalow
Tara-Ki Cottage
Roy's Farm
Little Lion Copse
Little Holywell Copse
Rec. Grd.
East Lodge
Huntage Row
Soberton Mill
Mill Copse
Soberton Mill Cottages
The Liberties
Selhurst Poultry Farm
Ingoldfield Villas
Ingoldfield Farm
Little White's Copse
Russell's Farm
SHEEP POND LANE
CUT THROAT LANE
GARRISON HILL
A32
WATTON LANE
BROCKBRIDGE ROAD
B2150
NORTHEND LANE
UNION LANE
CHESTNUT RISE
ST. MARY'S CL.
SOUTH VW.
THE PARK
PARK LANE
HIGH STREET
SOUTH HILL
POLICE STA. LA.
MILL LANE
STATION ROAD
MIDLINGTON ROAD
MIDLINGTON HILL
MIDLINGTON LANE
CUTTS ARCH
RIVER MEON
THE DRIFTWAY
LANE
CROOKHORN LANE
OXFORD LANE
SWANMORE ROAD
MEONVALLEY LANE
MEON VALLEY LANE
SCHOOL HILL
LONG ROAD
WEST STREET
WEST ST.
COLE HILL
CHALK HILL
KINGS WAY
GREEN LANE
COTT STREET LANE
STREET HILL
PESTSTEAD LANE
WICKHAM ROAD
HIGH STREET
WEBBS GREEN
HAMBLEDON LANE
SELWORTH LANE
HORNS HILL
HAMBLEDON LANE
DARMSWORTH LANE
ROYS LANE
PLOUGH LANE
INGOLDFIELD LANE
CHAPEL ROAD
BUSH ROAD
MAY LANE
FOREST ROAD
HEATH ROAD
135
179
166
460
61
62
H
J
K
L
M
N
G
1
2
3
4
5
6
7
8
9
15
16
17
18
19

Southampton
SO32
PO7
SOUTH DOWNS
HAMBLEDON
Rushmere
Westend Down
Sheepbarn Copse
Teglease Copse
Teglease Farm
Teglease Cottage
Poultry Houses
Bushydown Copse
Reservoir
Stoke Wood
Little Sheardley Wood
Great Sheardley Wood
Bushy Down Farm
Wallops Wood Farm
Wallops Wood House
Big West End Farm
Westend House
New Cottages
Chidden Farm
Thatch Cottage
Race Course Cottage
Stockram Copse
Wallops Wood Parlour
Dickey Medley's Copse
Grenville Hall
Upper Grenville Copse
Battlegreen Cottages
Hook Cottage
The Nook
Beckless Plantation
Chidden Holt Farm
Lower Grenville Copse
Beckless Farm
Beckless Copse
Brooks Copse
The Holt
Homefield
Brook Cottages
Three Corners
HOME DOWN
Recreation Ground
Pav.
East Hoe House
Windmill Down Farm
WINDMILL DOWN
Park House
Park Farm
Coombe Down
Shere Copse
East Hoe Manor
Tennis Court
Whitedale Farm
Hambledon Vineyard
Whitedale House
Litheys Hanger
Mill Down Cottage
Hambledon Infant Sch.
Bottom Copse
Fairfield House
Vicarage
Folly House
The Old Vicarage
Westfields
Little Symonds
Woodside
Landford Hall
Hambledon House
Manor Farm
Rashmere Gate
Stud Farm
Hoe Cross Farm Cottages
Hoe Cross Farm
Boarhuts Copse
Cams
Hill View
Homelands
Veniss Copse
Rushmere Cottages
Russell's Farm
Hill View Farm
Pilgrims
WATTON LANE
NEW ROAD
B2150
LONG ROAD
SHEARDLEY LANE
WHITELEAF LANE
GREEN LANE
BROOK LANE
HOE ROAD
EAST HOE ROAD
CHURCH LANE
DOGKENNEL LANE
GLIDDEN LANE
HAMBLEDON LANE
EAST STREET
HIGH ST
WEST STREET
SPELTHAM HILL
BACK LANE
CAMS HILL
PITT HILL LANE
LODGE LANE
RUSHMERE LA.
HAMBLEDON ROAD
ARMSWORTH LA.
HOE STREET
LASHLY MDW.
THE GARDENS
VICARAGE LA.
COACHMANS HALT
THE MALTINGS
OLD BARN CRES.
142
165
180
A B C D E F G
1 2 3 4 5 6 7 8 9
63 64 65
15 16 17 18 19

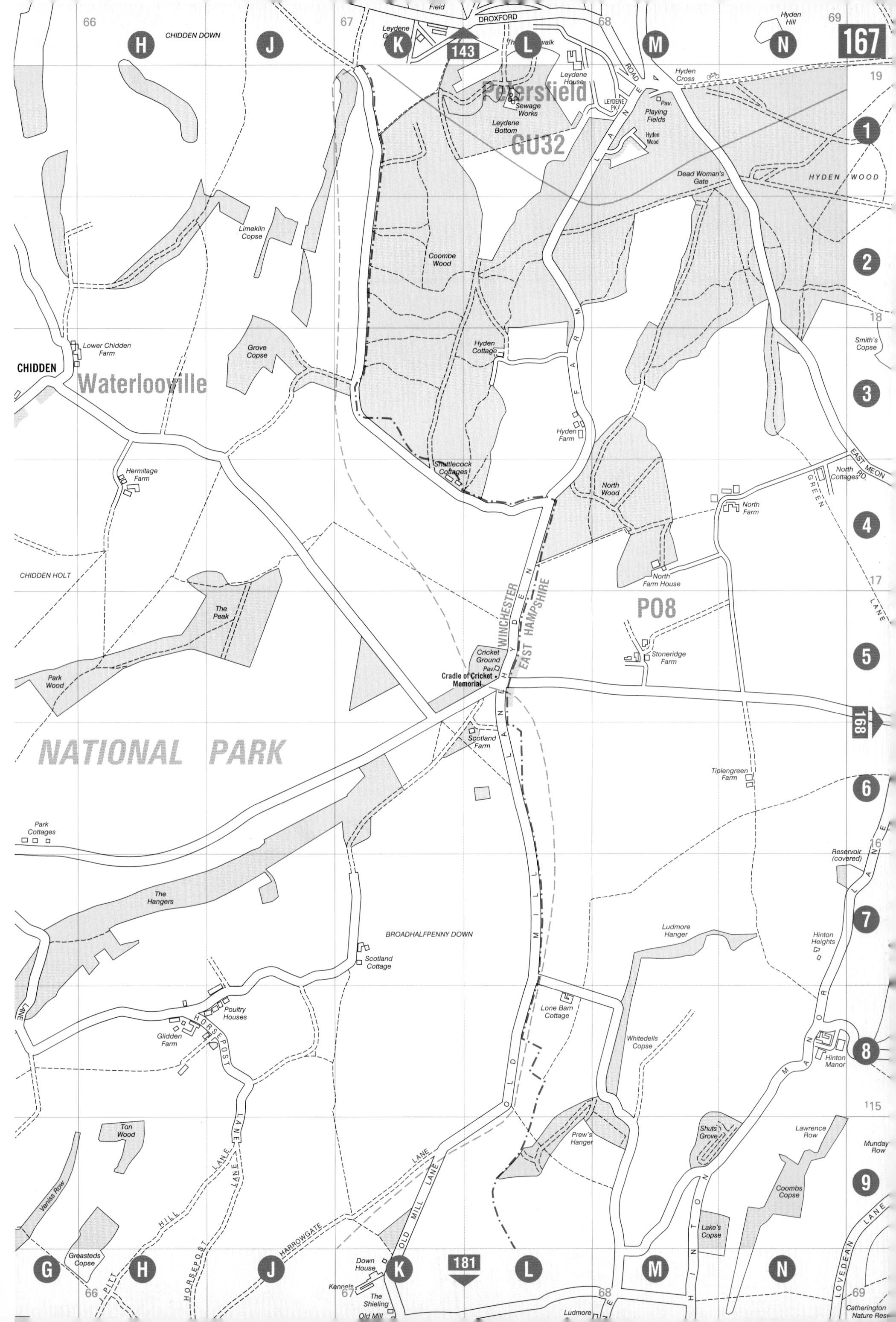

CHIDDEN DOWN
DROXFORD
Leydene House
Petersfield
GU32
Sewage Works
Leydene Bottom
Playing Fields
Hyden Wood
Hyden Cross
Hyden Hill
HYDEN WOOD
Dead Woman's Gate
Limekiln Copse
Coombe Wood
Hyden Cottage
Grove Copse
Lower Chidden Farm
CHIDDEN
Waterlooville
Smith's Copse
Hyden Farm
Shuttlecock Cottages
Hermitage Farm
North Wood
North Farm
North Cottages
EAST MEON RD.
GREEN LANE
CHIDDEN HOLT
North Farm House
The Peak
PO8
WINCHESTER
EAST HAMPSHIRE
HYDEN FARM LANE
Cricket Ground
Pav.
Cradle of Cricket Memorial
Stoneridge Farm
Park Wood
Scotland Farm
NATIONAL PARK
Tiplengreen Farm
Park Cottages
Reservoir (covered)
The Hangers
BROADHALFPENNY DOWN
Ludmore Hanger
Hinton Heights
Scotland Cottage
Poultry Houses
Glidden Farm
HORSEPOST LANE
Lone Barn Cottage
Whitedells Copse
Hinton Manor
MANOR LANE
OLD MILL LANE
Prew's Hanger
Shuts Grove
Lawrence Row
Munday Row
Ton Wood
HILL LANE
HARROWGATE LANE
Coombs Copse
Veniss Row
Lake's Copse
Greasteds Copse
PITT
Down House
Kennels
The Shieling
Old Mill
Ludmore
HINTON
LOVEDEAN LANE
Catherington Nature Res
143
181
168

144
HYDEN WOOD
The Cottage
Blagdon Farm
Nine Corner Hanger
Newmans Farm
Byden Copse
Blagden Copse
Oxenbourne Down (Local Nature Reserve)
Wascoombe Bottom
Hillhampton Bottom
QUEEN ELIZABETH COUNTRY PARK
Queen Elizabeth Country Park Centre
Evadene
Thistledoon
Nexus House
Lambleaze Copse
Ditch Acre Copse
Smith's Copse
Lowton's Copse
Reservoir (covered)
Gravel Hill
Butser House
Bottom Cott.
Highbank
Chapel Farm
North Cottages
Packhurst Farm House
Byden Court
Waterlooville
Sunnyfields
Clanfield Chase
Clanfield Jun. Sch.
Manor Farm
CHALTON
SOUTH
Recreation Ground
PO8
CLANFIELD
Fieldview
Down Farm
Butser Ancient Farm
Barnfield
Meadow Croft Farm
CLANFIELD DOWN
Windmill Hill
Chalton Windmill
Mast
Windmill Hill Farm
Bascomb Copse
Down House
Reservoir (covered)
Nursery
Charity Farm
Petersgate Inf. Sch.
WINDMILL DOWN
Hinton Heights
Greylands Farm and Kennels
Snell's Corner
HORNDEAN DOWN
BLENDWORTH DOWN
Hinton Manor
White Dirt Farm
Kingswood
Lawrence Row
Munday's Row
Hawquins
New Barn Farm
CATHERINGTON
Church House
Reservoir (covered)
Vicarage
Playing Field
Catherington C of E Int. School
St. Catherines
Hall
Catherington Down Nature Reserve
Netherley Down
182
167
A3
HOGS LODGE LANE
EAST MEON ROAD
PETERSFIELD ROAD
CHALTON LANE
HAMBLEDON ROAD
SOUTH LANE
LONDON ROAD
DRIFT ROAD
DOWNHOUSE ROAD
CATHERINGTON LANE
HINTON MANOR LANE
WHITE DIRT LANE
NEW ROAD
BARN FARM LANE
GREEN LANE
THIEVES' LANE
SUNDERTON LANE
NORTH ROAD
SOUTHDOWN ROAD
LOVEDEAN LANE

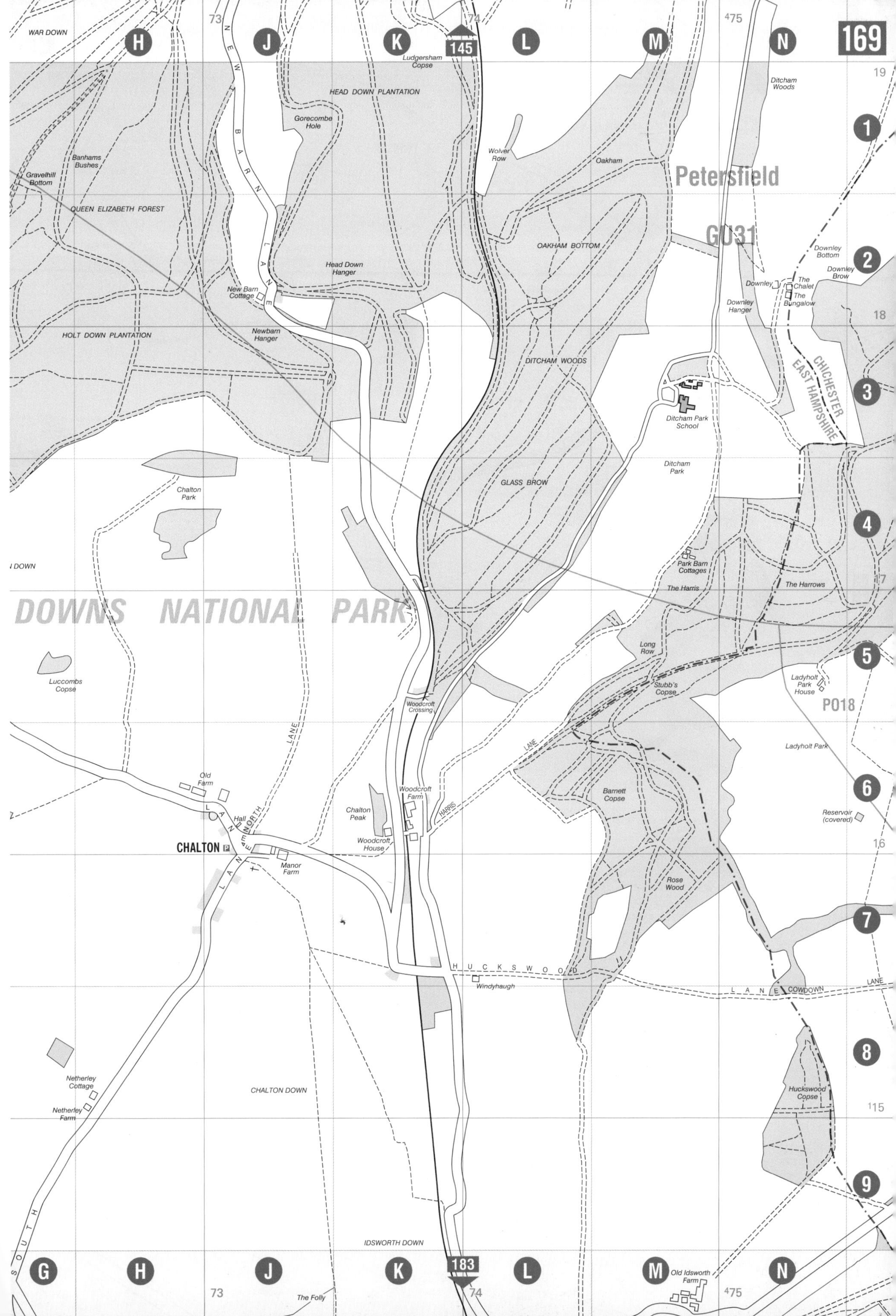
WAR DOWN
145
Ludgersham Copse
HEAD DOWN PLANTATION
Gorecombe Hole
Ditcham Woods
Wolver Row
Oakham
Peterstield
Banhams Bushes
Gravelhill Bottom
QUEEN ELIZABETH FOREST
NEW BARN LANE
OAKHAM BOTTOM
GU31
Downley Bottom
Downley Brow
Head Down Hanger
New Barn Cottage
Downley
The Chalet
The Bungalow
Downley Hanger
HOLT DOWN PLANTATION
Newbarn Hanger
DITCHAM WOODS
CHICHESTER
EAST HAMPSHIRE
Ditcham Park School
Ditcham Park
Chalton Park
GLASS BROW
DOWN
Park Barn Cottages
The Harris
The Harrows
DOWNS NATIONAL PARK
Long Row
Luccombs Copse
Stubb's Copse
Ladyholt Park House
PO18
Woodcroft Crossing
Ladyholt Park
LANE
Old Farm
Woodcroft Farm
Barnett Copse
HARRIS
Chalton Peak
Reservoir (covered)
Hall
NORTH LANE
CHALTON
Woodcroft House
Manor Farm
Rose Wood
HUCKSWOOD
LANE
COWDOWN
LANE
Windyhaugh
Netherley Cottage
Netherley Farm
CHALTON DOWN
Huckswood Copse
IDSWORTH DOWN
SOUTH LANE
183
Old Idsworth Farm
The Folly
H J K L M N
G H J K L M N
1 2 3 4 5 6 7 8 9
73 74 475
19 18 17 16 115

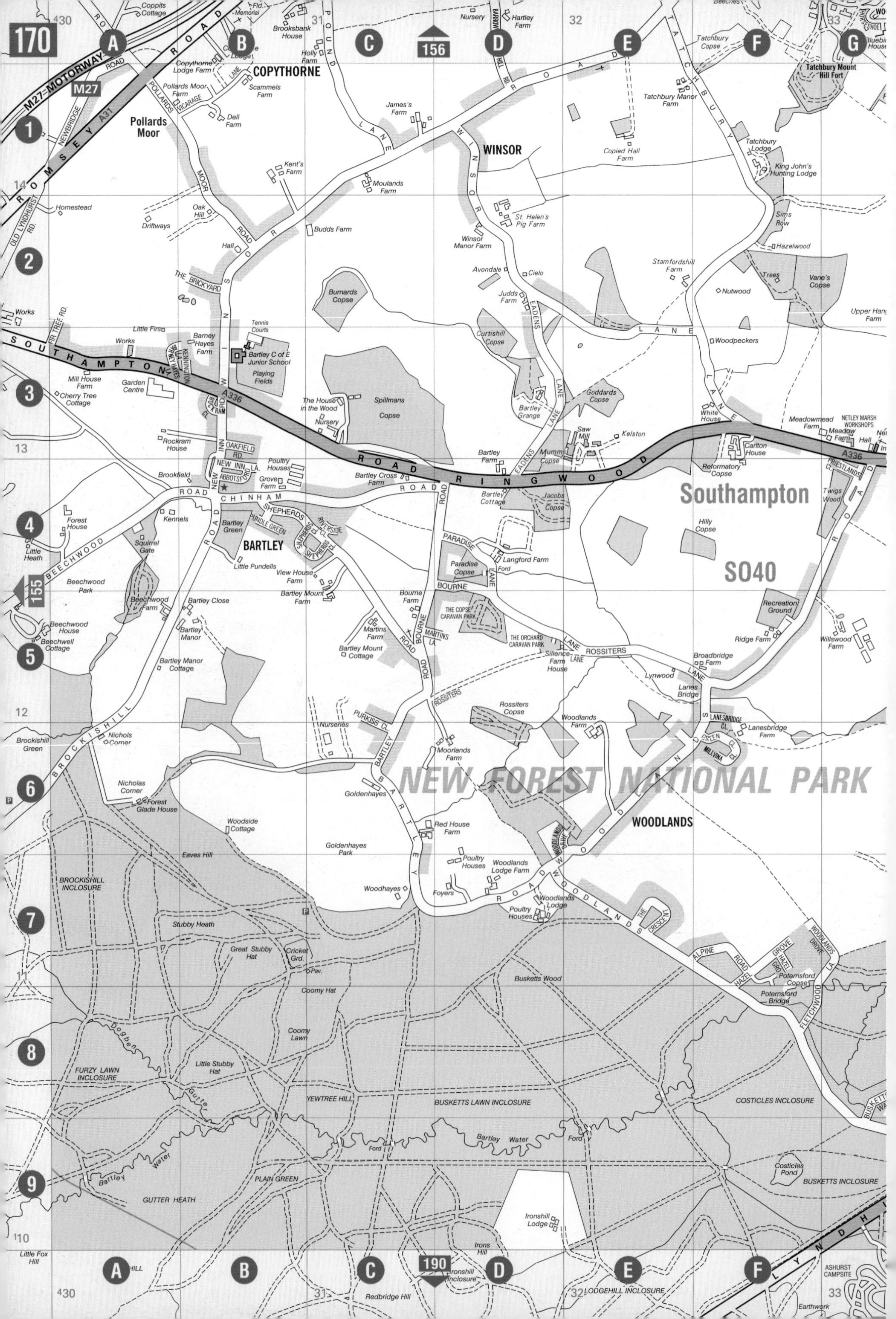
M27 MOTORWAY
M27
ROMSEY ROAD
A31
COPYTHORNE
Pollards Moor
WINSOR
BARTLEY
Southampton
SO40
NEW FOREST NATIONAL PARK
WOODLANDS
SOUTHAMPTON ROAD
A336
RINGWOOD ROAD
CHINHAM ROAD
Copythorne Lodge Farm
Pollards Moor Farm
Scammels Farm
Dell Farm
James's Farm
Kent's Farm
Moulands Farm
Homestead
Oak Hill
Driftways
Budds Farm
Copied Hall Farm
Tatchbury Manor Farm
Tatchbury Copse
Tatchbury Mount Hill Fort
Tatchbury Lodge
King John's Hunting Lodge
St. Helen's Pig Farm
Winsor Manor Farm
Stamfordshill Farm
Hazelwood
Nutwood
Vane's Copse
Upper Hang Farm
Woodpeckers
Burnards Copse
Curtishill Copse
Spillmans Copse
Bartley C of E Junior School
Playing Fields
Tennis Courts
Barney Hayes Farm
Garden Centre
Mill House Farm
Cherry Tree Cottage
Rockram House
Brookfield
Poultry Houses
Grove Farm
Bartley Cross Farm
Bartley Farm
Mumms Copse
Saw Mill
Kelston
Goddards Copse
Bartley Grange
White House
Meadowmead Farm
NETLEY MARSH WORKSHOPS
Carlton House
Reformatory Copse
Twigs Wood
Hilly Copse
Recreation Ground
Ridge Farm
Willswood Farm
Forest House
Little Heath
Kennels
Squirrel Gate
Beechwood Park
Beechwood Farm
Beechwood House
Beechwell Cottage
Bartley Green
Little Pundells
View House Farm
Bartley Mount Farm
Bartley Close
Bartley Manor
Bartley Manor Cottage
Paradise Copse
Langford Farm
Bourne Farm
THE COPSE CARAVAN PARK
THE ORCHARD CARAVAN PARK
Martins Farm
Bartley Mount Cottage
Silence Farm House
Lynwood
Broadbridge Farm
Lanes Bridge
Lanesbridge Farm
Rossiters Copse
Woodlands Farm
Moorlands Farm
Nurseries
Brockishill Green
Nichols Corner
Nicholas Corner
Forest Glade House
Goldenhayes
Goldenhayes Park
Woodside Cottage
Eaves Hill
Red House Farm
Woodlands Lodge Farm
Woodhayes
Foyers
Woodlands Lodge
BROCKISHILL INCLOSURE
Stubby Heath
Great Stubby Hat
Cricket Grd.
Coomy Hat
Coomy Lawn
Busketts Wood
Poternsford Copse
Poternsford Bridge
FURZY LAWN INCLOSURE
Little Stubby Hat
YEWTREE HILL
BUSKETTS LAWN INCLOSURE
COSTICLES INCLOSURE
Bartley Water
Ford
PLAIN GREEN
GUTTER HEATH
Costicles Pond
BUSKETTS INCLOSURE
Ironshill Lodge
Irons Hill
Ironshill Inclosure
LODGEHILL INCLOSURE
Redbridge Hill
Little Fox Hill
ASHURST CAMPSITE
Earthwork
156
155
190

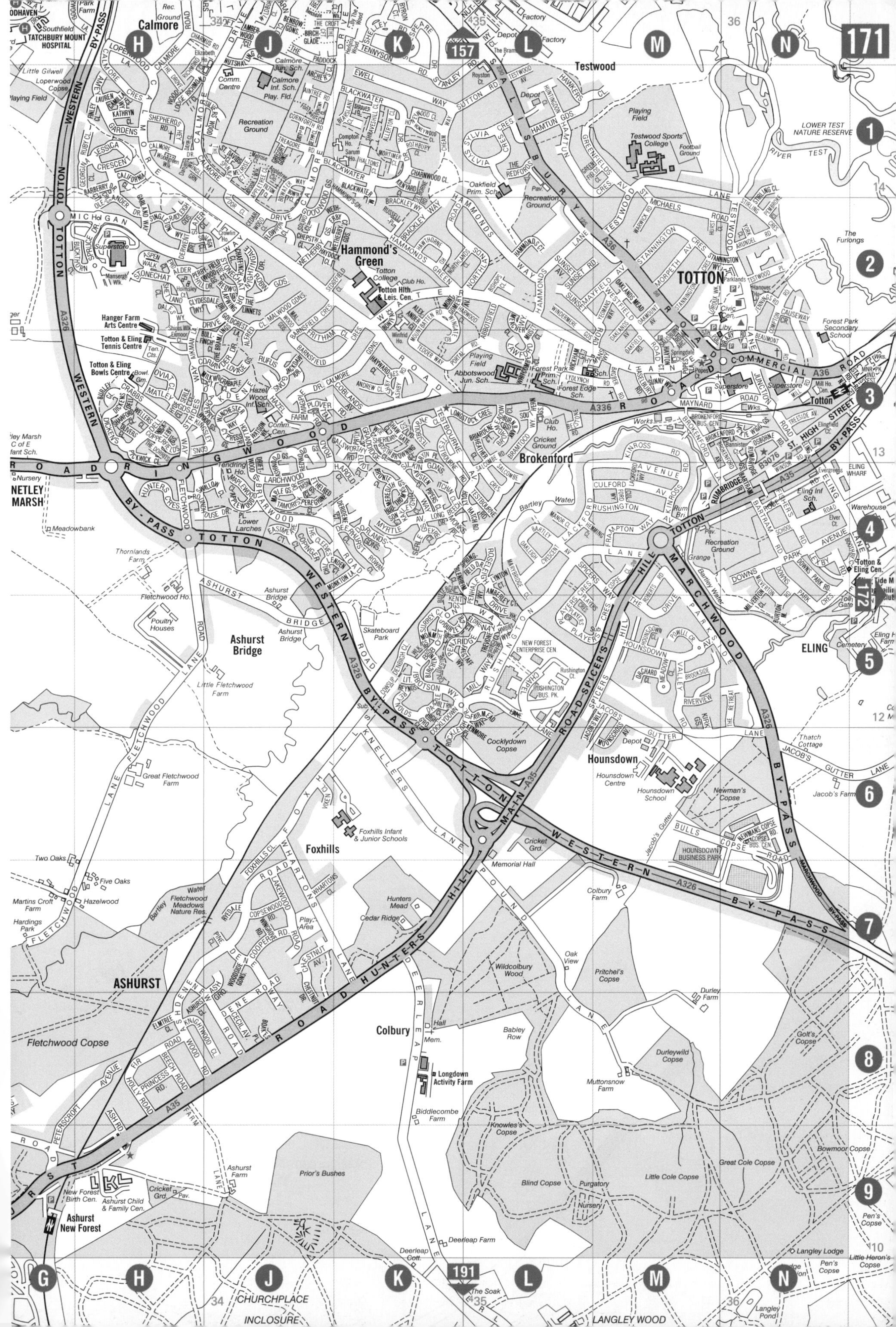
Calmore
TATCHBURY MOUNT HOSPITAL
Testwood
LOWER TEST NATURE RESERVE
RIVER TEST
Testwood Sports College
Playing Field
Football Ground
Oakfield Prim. Sch.
Recreation Ground
Calmore Jun. Sch.
Calmore Inf. Sch.
Comm. Centre
Hammond's Green
Totton College
Totton Hlth. & Leis. Cen.
TOTTON
The Furlongs
Forest Park Secondary School
Hanger Farm Arts Centre
Totton & Eling Tennis Centre
Totton & Eling Bowls Centre
Superstore
Abbotswood Jun. Sch.
Forest Park Prim. Sch.
Forest Edge Sch.
Brokenford
Cricket Ground
NETLEY MARSH
Meadowbank
Thornlands Farm
Fletchwood Ho.
Poultry Houses
Ashurst Bridge
Little Fletchwood Farm
Skateboard Park
NEW FOREST ENTERPRISE CEN.
RUSHINGTON BUS. PK.
Recreation Ground
Eling Inf Sch.
Totton & Eling Cen.
ELING
Cemetery
Cocklydown Copse
Hounsdown
Hounsdown Centre
Hounsdown School
Newman's Copse
HOUNSDOWN BUSINESS PARK
Thatch Cottage
Jacob's Farm
Great Fletchwood Farm
Foxhills Infant & Junior Schools
Foxhills
Cricket Grd.
Memorial Hall
Colbury Farm
Two Oaks
Five Oaks
Martins Croft Farm
Hazelwood
Hardings Park
Fletchwood Meadows Nature Res.
Hunters Mead
Cedar Ridge
Wildcolbury Wood
Oak View
Pritchel's Copse
Durley Farm
ASHURST
Fletchwood Copse
Colbury
Babley Row
Longdown Activity Farm
Durleywild Copse
Muttonsnow Farm
Golt's Copse
Biddlecombe Farm
Knowles's Copse
Prior's Bushes
Ashurst Farm
Blind Copse
Purgatory
Nursery
Little Cole Copse
Great Cole Copse
Bowmoor Copse
New Forest Birth Cen.
Ashurst Child & Family Cen.
Ashurst New Forest
Deerleap Farm
Deerleap Cott.
Langley Lodge
Pen's Copse
Little Heron's Copse
CHURCHPLACE INCLOSURE
The Soak
LANGLEY WOOD
Langley Pond
A326 WESTERN BY-PASS
A35 TOTTON BY-PASS
A336 RINGWOOD ROAD
A36 COMMERCIAL ROAD
A36 SALISBURY ROAD
MARCHWOOD BY-PASS
HUNTERS HILL
157
172
191

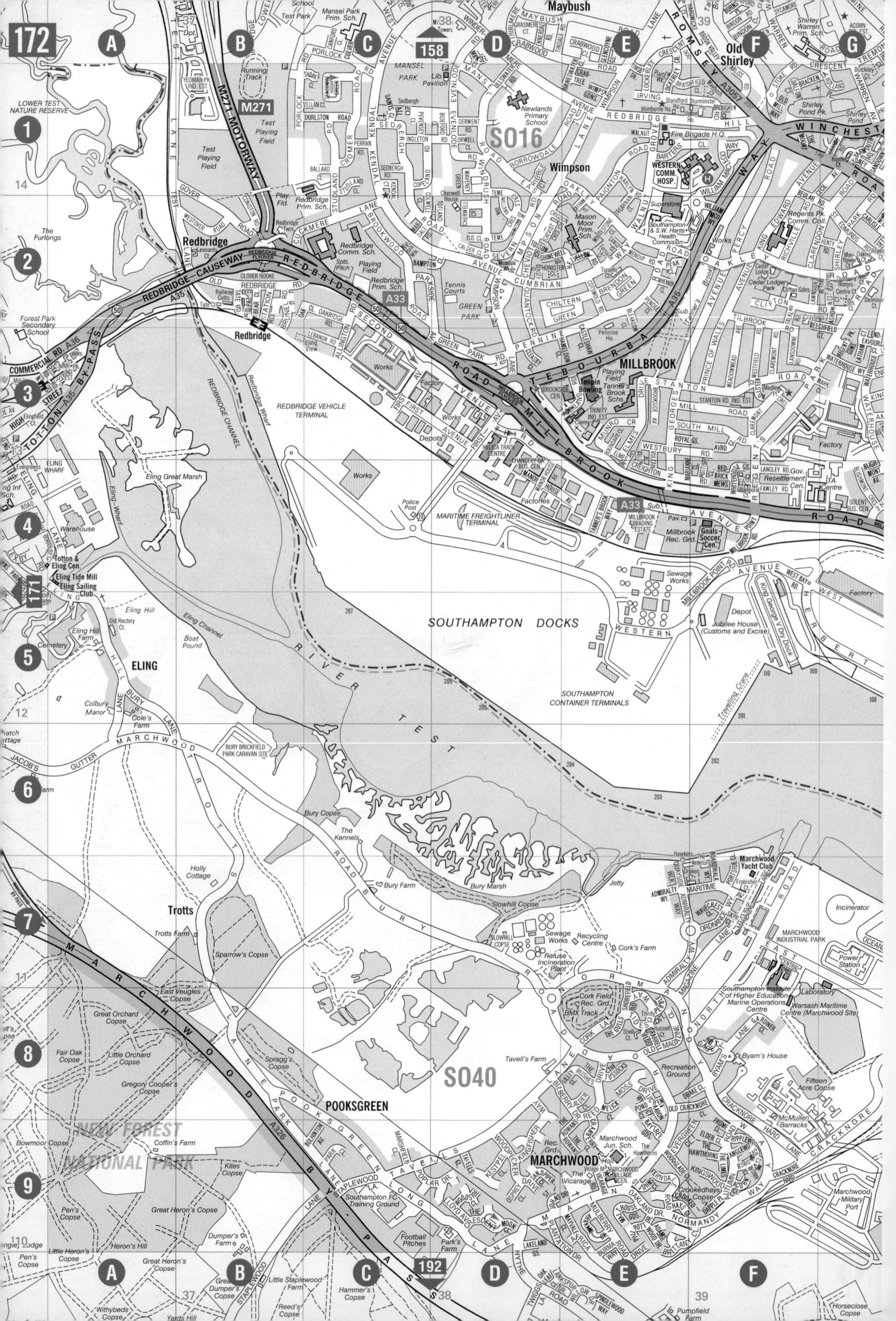

A
B
C
D
E
F
G
1
2
3
4
5
6
7
8
9
158
171
192
Maybush
Old Shirley
Mansel Park Prim. Sch.
MANSEL PARK
Lib. Pavilion
Newlands Primary School
SO16
Wimpson
WESTERN COMM. HOSP.
Fire Brigade H.Q.
Southampton & S.W. Hants Health Commission
Superstore
Mason Moor Prim. Sch.
Regents Pk. Comm. Coll.
Cedar Lodge Park
Shirley Warren Prim. Sch.
Shirley Pond Pk.
LOWER TEST NATURE RESERVE
The Furlongs
Running Track
M271
M271 MOTORWAY
Test Playing Field
Play. Fld.
Redbridge Prim. Sch.
Redbridge
REDBRIDGE CAUSEWAY
REDBRIDGE FLYOVER
REDBRIDGE ROAD
Redbridge Comm. Sch.
Playing Field
Tennis Courts
GREEN PARK
A33
A35
A36
A3057
COMMERCIAL RD.
TOTTON BY-PASS
Forest Park Secondary School
Redbridge
TEBOURBA WAY
MILLBROOK
Tenpin Bowling
Tanner's Brook Schs.
MILLBROOK ROAD
MILLBROOK FLYOVER
Factory
Works
Depots
HELICA TRADE CENTRE
Resettlement Cen.
TA Centre
REDBRIDGE VEHICLE TERMINAL
REDBRIDGE CHANNEL
Redbridge Wharf
Eling Great Marsh
Eling Wharf
ELING WHARF
Warehouse
Totton & Eling Cen.
Eling Tide Mill
Eling Sailing Club
Eling Hill
Old Rectory
Eling Hill Farm
Cemetery
ELING
Eling Channel
Boat Pound
Police Post
MARITIME FREIGHTLINER TERMINAL
MILLBROOK TRADING ESTATE
Millbrook Rec. Grd.
Goals Soccer Cen.
Sewage Works
SOUTHAMPTON DOCKS
Depot
Jubilee House (Customs and Excise)
King George V Dry Dock
SOUTHAMPTON CONTAINER TERMINALS
Travelling Crane
RIVER TEST
Colbury Manor
Cole's Farm
MARCHWOOD ROAD
JACOB'S GUTTER LANE
BURY BRICKFIELD PARK CARAVAN SITE
TROTTS LANE
Bury Copse
The Kennels
BURY ROAD
Bury Farm
Bury Marsh
Holly Cottage
Trotts
Trotts Farm
Sparrow's Copse
Slowhill Copse
Sewage Works
Recycling Centre
Refuse Incineration Plant
Cork's Farm
Jetty
Marchwood Yacht Club
Incinerator
MARCHWOOD INDUSTRIAL PARK
Power Station
Laboratory
Southampton Institute of Higher Education Marine Operations Centre
Warsash Maritime Centre (Marchwood Site)
Cork Field Rec. Grd.
BMX Track
Recreation Ground
Byam's House
Fifteen Acre Copse
McMullen Barracks
MARCHWOOD BY-PASS
A326
East Veugles Copse
Great Orchard Copse
Fair Oak Copse
Little Orchard Copse
Gregory Cooper's Copse
Spragg's Copse
Tavell's Farm
SO40
POOKSGREEN
NEW FOREST NATIONAL PARK
Bowmoor Copse
Coffin's Farm
Kites Copse
Pen's Copse
Great Heron's Copse
Dumper's Farm
Heron's Hill
Little Heron's Copse
Southampton FC Training Ground
Football Pitches
Park's Farm
MARCHWOOD
Marchwood Jun. Sch.
The Hawthorns
Rec. Grd.
The Vicarage
MARCHWOOD VILLAGE CEN.
Crookedhays Copse
Marchwood Military Port
Great Dumper's Copse
Little Staplewood Farm
Hammer's Copse
Reed's Copse
Withybeds Copse
Yards Hill
Pumpfield Farm
Horseclose Copse
37
38
39
14
13
12
11
110

173
159
193
174
H
J
K
L
M
N
G
1
2
3
4
5
6
7
8
9
Upper Shirley
SOUTHAMPTON COMMON
University of Southampton (Avenue Campus)
PORTSWOOD
SO17
Westwood Park
Portswood Park
St. Denys
SHIRLEY
Southampton
The Hawthorns Urban Wildlife Centre
SOUTHAMPTON CEMETERY
King Edward VI School
Bevois Mount
Bevois Town
Bevois Valley
Banister Park
SO15
Fitzhugh
Freemantle
Hill
Polygon
Bedford Place
Bellevue
Newtown
Northam
St. Mary's
ROYAL SOUTH HANTS. HOSP.
Millbrook
MOUNTBATTEN WAY
Nichols Town
Titanic Engineers Meml.
EAST PARK (Andrews Park)
WEST PARK (Watts Park)
Fourposts
SOUTHAMPTON
Blechynden
WESTERN DOCKS
Sussex Place
SO14
Southampton FC (St. Mary's Stadium)
Chapel
Crosshouse
WEST QUAY SHOPPING CENTRE
WEST QUAY RETAIL PARK
Mayflower Cruise Terminal
RIVER TEST
SOUTHAMPTON NEW FOREST
City Cruise Terminal
Lansdowne Hill
Mayflower Park
Isle of Wight Car Ferry Terminal
ROYAL PIER (Closed)
Town Quay
Ocean Village
Harbour Lights Picturehouse
Ocean Cruise Terminal
University of Southampton (National Oceanography Cen.)
Empress Dock
Ocean Dock
EASTERN DOCKS
Marchwood Military Port
Sports Ground
Southampton to East Cowes 55mins.
Southampton to:
West Cowes 22mins.
(Foot Ferry, Fast Ferry)
Hythe 12mins. (Foot Ferry)
A33
A35
A3057
A3024
A335
A3035
40
41
42
43

A
B
C
D
E
F
G
1
2
3
4
5
6
7
8
9
10
160
173
194
43
44
445
46
SO17
SO18
SO14
SO19
Townhill Park
BITTERNE PARK
Miniature Railway
Riverside Park
The Triangle
Cobden Hts.
Midanbury Broadway
Midanbury
Moorlands Prim. Sch.
Westend Copse
ST. DENYS
St. Denys
ST. DENYS ROAD
COBDEN BRIDGE
Priory Hard
Jetties
Itchen Boat Yard
Quay 2000
Bevois Valley
EMPRESS PARK
Clausentum Quay
Bitterne Wharf
Bitterne Manor Ho.
Deep Dene Rec. Grd.
The Deepdene
Dalmally Gs.
St.Mary's College
Playing Field
Beechwood Jun. Sch.
Bitterne
Bitterne Manor Prim. Sch.
Acolade Hlth. & Fitness
CENTURION PARK
Quayside Marina
KEMPS QUAY IND. PK.
Glenfield Inf. Sch.
Hum Hole
BITTERNE
MAYBRAY
BITTERNE ROAD WEST
Bitterne Leis. Cen.
Pure Gym
Sports Ground
Playing Field
Harefield Primary School
Comm. Cen.
NHS
MOUNT PLEASANT INDUSTRIAL ESTATE
ALPHA BUS. PK.
Drivers Wharf
Old Mill Quay
Coalporters Amateur Rowing Club
NORTHAM BUS. CEN.
Northam
Works
BELGRAVE INDUSTRIAL ESTATE
LOWER WILLIAM STREET INDUSTRIAL ESTATE
SHAMROCK QUAY
Millbank
MURIA ESTATE
BAKERS WHARF
MILLBANK WHARF
RIVER ITCHEN
James Wharf
Freemantle Common
Prospect Ho.
Merry Oak
Itchen College Sports Centre
Itchen Sixth Form College
Play. Fld.
Southampton
Sholing Jun. Sch.
Sholing Inf. Sch.
The Sholing Tech. Coll.
Veracity Recreation Ground
Community Centre
Sholing Common
Gas Holders
Belvidere
Belvidere Wharf
Crown Wharf
Southampton F.C. (St. Mary's Stadium)
Leamouth Wharf
BRITANNIA WHARF
Phoenix Wharf
Burnley Wharf
WILLMENT MARINE & BUSINESS PARK
MILL HOUSE BUS. CEN.
SPITFIRE QUAY
THE R.J. MITCHELL CEN.
Peartree Green
Bramdean Mews
Leslie Loader Ho.
Peartree Ho.
Chapel
Victoria Wharf
Sunderland Wharf
Tredegar Wharf
Baltic Wharf
Vancouver Wharf
American Wharf
Chapel Wharf
Corporation Wharf
Crosshouse
MERLIN QUAY
SMITHS QUAY
WILLMENTS IND. EST.
City Coll. (Maritime Tech. Cen.)
ITCHEN
Ludlow Jun. & Inf. Schs.
St. Monica Jun. Sch.
St. Monica Inf. Sch.
Woodland Vale
Sholing
Pleasant View
Cemetery
Botany Bay
Rec. Grd.
Millers Pond Open Space
THE ITCHEN BRIDGE A3025
Woolston
Toll
LONGBRIDGE IND. PARK
Southampton Water Activities Centre
Academy Oasis Mayfield (Up. Sch.)
PORTSMOUTH ROAD
Sholing
Woolston Inf. Sch.
Super-store
Yacht Club
Ocean Village Marina
Ocean Village
Princess Alexandra Dock
Pontoon
Wharf
Lawrence Ct.
Bowl. Grn.
Nursery
MAYFIELD PARK
Fox's Monument
Weston Park Jun. & Inf. Schs.
Chamberlayne Leisure Centre
Newtown
Playing Field
West Wood
Oasis Academy Mayfield (Lower Sch.)
Play. Fld.
WOOLSTON
Works
Jurd's Lake
Jetty
WESTON POINT
Slipway
EASTERN DOCKS
Recreation Ground
Pitch & Putt
Weston
Chamberlayne College for the Arts
Tickleford Gully
Weston Hard
Hampton Towers
Havre Towers
Oslo Towers
Copenhagen Towers

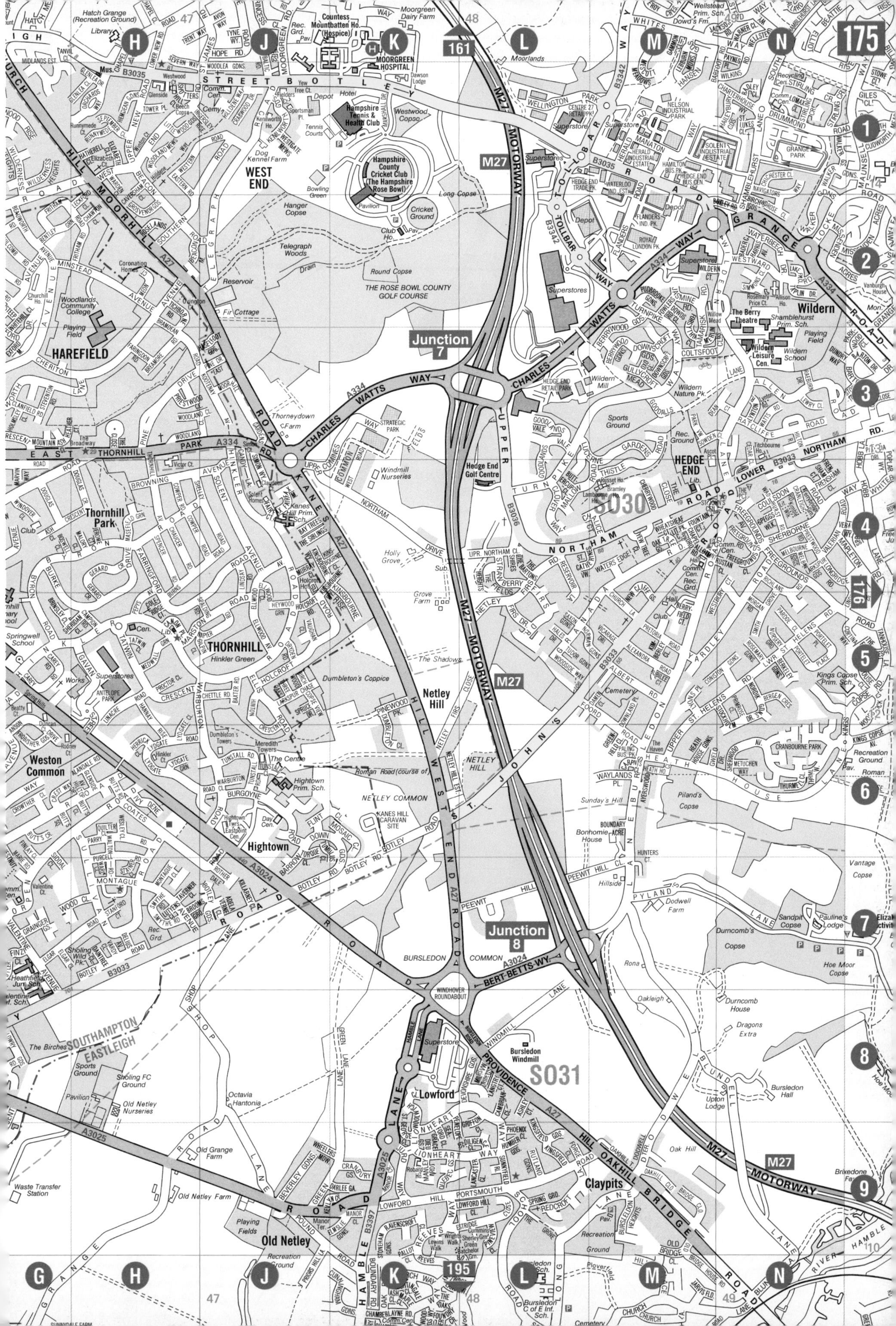

161
176
195
H
J
K
L
M
N
G
1
2
3
4
5
6
7
8
9
47
48
49
Hatch Grange (Recreation Ground)
Library
Countess Mountbatten Ho. (Hospice)
Moorgreen Dairy Farm
MOORGREEN HOSPITAL
Moorlands
STREET
BOTLEY
B3035
Mus.
Hampshire Tennis & Health Club
Westwood Copse
Dawson Lodge
WEST END
Dog Kennel Farm
Hampshire County Cricket Club (The Hampshire Rose Bowl)
Bowling Green
Pavilion
Cricket Ground
Long Copse
Hanger Copse
Telegraph Woods
Round Copse
THE ROSE BOWL COUNTY GOLF COURSE
Reservoir
Fir Cottage
Coronation Homes
Woodlands Community College
Playing Field
HAREFIELD
MOORHILL
A27
M27
MOTORWAY
Junction 7
CHARLES WATTS WAY
A334
STRATEGIC PARK
Thorneydown Farm
Windmill Nurseries
Hedge End Golf Centre
UPPER NORTHAM
B3036
EAST
THORNHILL
PARK
The Broadway
Thornhill Park
THORNHILL
Hinkler Green
KANES
HILL
Kanes Hill Prim. Sch.
Holly Grove
Grove Farm
Dumbleton's Coppice
The Shadows
Netley Hill
NETLEY HILL
NETLEY COMMON
KANES HILL CARAVAN SITE
Roman Road (course of)
Hightown Prim. Sch.
Hightown
Springwell School
Superstores
ANTELOPE PARK
Weston Common
A3024
B3033
Sholing Wild Pk.
Heathfield Jun. Sch.
SOUTHAMPTON
EASTLEIGH
The Birches
Sports Ground
Sholing FC Ground
Pavilion
Old Netley Nurseries
A3025
Octavia Hantonia
Old Grange Farm
Waste Transfer Station
Old Netley Farm
Playing Fields
Old Netley
Recreation Ground
GRANGE
Junction 8
BURSLEDON COMMON
BERT BETTS WY.
WINDHOVER ROUNDABOUT
Superstore
Bursledon Windmill
S031
PROVIDENCE
HILL
Lowford
HAMBLE LANE
B3397
Claypits
OAKHILL
BRIDGE
Recreation Ground
Bursledon C of E Inf. Sch.
Cemetery
HAMBLE RIVER
Brixedone Farm
Bursledon Hall
Upton Lodge
Dragons Extra
Durncomb House
Oakleigh
Rona
Durncomb's Copse
Hoe Moor Copse
Sandpit Copse
Pauline's Lodge
Vantage Copse
Dodwell Farm
PYLAND
PEEWIT HILL
Hillside
Bonhomie House
Sunday's Hill
Piland's Copse
Cemetery
ST. JOHNS
HEATH HOUSE
Recreation Ground
CRANBOURNE PARK
Kings Copse Prim. Sch.
S030
HEDGE END
Lib.
NORTHAM
LOWER NORTHAM RD.
B3033
FREEGROUNDS
Comm. Cen.
Rec. Grd.
Sports Ground
Wildern Nature Pk.
Wildern Mill
HEDGE END RETAIL PARK
Wildern
The Berry Theatre
Shamblehurst Prim. Sch.
Wildern Leisure Cen.
Wildern School
Playing Field
GRANGE ROAD
A334
Superstore
Superstores
Depot
TOLLBAR WAY
B3342
HEDGE END TRADE PK.
WATERLOO IND. EST.
FLANDERS IND. PK.
ROYAL LONDON PK.
HERALD INDUSTRIAL ESTATE
SOLENT INDUSTRIAL ESTATE
NELSON INDUSTRIAL PARK
WELLINGTON PARK
CENTRE 27 RETAIL PK.
HEDGE END BUS. CEN.
HAMILTON BUS. PK.
GRANGE PARK
Recycling Cen.
Wellstead Prim. Sch.
Dowd's Fm.
WHITES WAY

176
A
B
C
D
E
F
G
1
2
3
4
5
6
7
8
9
450
51
52
162
175
196
Long Common
Pear Tree
Greywood
Frogmill Farm
Little Gold Copse
Bowen Farm
Copse
MADDOXFORD
ORCHARD CL.
MADDOXFORD WAY
The Laurels
OATLANDS RD
OATLANDS
FALCON WY.
Maddoxford Farm
Long Acres Farm
Nursery
Wangfield Nursery
Poultry House
WANGFIELD
LANE
Westfield
Lower Wangfield Farm
Willow Farm
Parklands
Longlands Farm
Boorley Green
WEST LANE
Broomley Green Farm
Oak Ridge Farm
CROWS
NETHERHILL LANE
WINCHESTER B3354 ROAD
Berrywood Prim. Sch.
Bushy Copse
BILLINGTON GARDENS
BILLINGTON GDS.
STOWE CL.
GILES CL.
CUDWORTH MEAD
MAUNSELL WAY
ELLIOT RISE
REPTON GDS.
TELFORD GDS.
WATKIN RD
MALLETT CL.
BRUNEL RD
Newhouse Farm
Wangfield Copse
Wangfield Farm
Titlarks Farm
CHURCH LANE
HAMBLE RIVER
MISSENDEN ACRES
FAWN CRES.
STAG DR.
DEER WK.
Sluices
Botleigh Grange Hotel
Burlington Ho.
Vanburgh House
Millbrook Ho.
Poultry Houses
Phoenix Ho.
Jellicoe Ho.
Bottom Copse
The Barn
Grange Nurseries
Uplands Farm
Viaduct
Cold Down Copse
The White House
Coledown Cottage
Coledown House
VICARAGE
BOTLEY HILL
WICKHAM
Wildern
Playing Field
GRANGE ROAD
PAVILION
DRIVE
Mon.
Pav.
Bowling Grn.
Tennis Courts
Depot
Greenlands View
WOODHOUSE LANE
Woodhouse Gully
Holmesland
ROWLEY CT.
LUXTON CL.
AMBERLEY CT.
Sycamore CT.
RECTORY CT.
MAFFEY CT.
GLEBE CT.
APPLETREE CT.
PERN CT.
BOTLEY
B3354
STREET
ALEXANDRA WAY
HOLMESLAND LA.
DOWNLAND CL.
Play. Fld.
Botley C of E Prim. Sch.
MAYFAIR CT.
CYPRESS GDS.
DRIVE
Botley
BOTTINGS INDUSTRIAL ESTATE
HILLSONS ROAD
Blenheim Cottage
Gibbets Corner
A334
ROAD
BROAD
OAK
HIGH
LOWER NORTHERN ROAD
B3033
TRIPPS END CARAVAN SITE
AVENUE
MARVIN WAY
MARLS RD.
ORCHARD CL.
OSTERLEY CL.
BLOSSOM CL.
Broadoak
Comm. Cen.
Hall
Tennis Cts.
Woodhill Schs. Prep. School
Recreation Ground
Pavilion
BOSWELL CL.
MORTIMER
BAILEY CL.
KILFORD CT.
CHEPING GDS.
FOUR ACRES
DONKEY LA.
BOTLEY MILLS CRAFT & BUS. CEN.
Sherecroft Farm
SHERECROFT GDS.
MILL HILL
BOTLEY A334 HILL
STATION
Depot
WOODVIEW PARK CARAVAN PARK
Old Forge
OUTLANDS
BURRIDGE A3051
Botley Hill
Pinkmead Farm
Pudbrook House
Pudbrook Lake
Southbrook Farm
BROOK LANE
West View Nursery
SO30
HAMBLEWOOD CT.
QUAYSIDE
Fir Tree Farm
Wild Grounds
Steeple Court
Club House
FAIRTHORNE MANOR GOLF COURSE
Shawfords Lake
Pinkmead Copse
Trullmill Copse
Fairthorne Manor
(YMCA Training Centre)
Hatts Copse Farm
Gould Copse
Manor Lodge
CHURCH LANE
Boat House
Gully Copse
Curbridge Creek
Manor Farm
Marks Farm
Pinkmead Row
WINCHESTER
EASTLEIGH
Sewage Works
Harmsworth Farm
Curbridge Nature Reserve
HAMBLE RIVER ESTATE
TANHOUSE LANE
Recreation Ground
Roman Road (course of)
Kings Copse
Dockdell Copse
Hill Top
Little Hats Recreation Ground
Kings Copse Prim. Sch.
FREEGROUNDS
Freegrounds Jun. & Inf. Schs.
Laburnum House
HOBB LA.
HAVENDALE
KINGS COPSE AVENUE
SOVEREIGN DR.
MONTROSE CL.
CRANBOURNE PARK
HEATH HOUSE
Vantage Copse
MANOR FARM COUNTRY PARK
Queen Elizabeth II Jubilee Activities Cen.
Bottom Copse
Hoe Moor Copse
Fosters Copse
Dock Copse
HAMBLE
RIVER
EASTLEIGH
FAREHAM
Long Copse
Harmsworth Row
Eversdown Copse
Foxburrow Copse
Suttons Copse
Bury Farm
Bedlams Copse
Hangmans Copse
A3051
BURRIDGE ROAD
Catland Copse
Bloomfield Copse
Hoe Moor Creek
SO31
Burridge Farm
BURRIDGE ROAD
Tennis Courts
Recreation Ground
Club
Works
Eversdown Farm
Poultry Houses
WHITELEY LANE
Beckings Copse
Whiteley Cottages
Brixedone Farm
Oaken Copse
Swanwick Wood
Wellspring Copse
BURRIDGE
GREEN LANE
Nursery
Lynwood
NEW ROAD
EASTLANDS BOATYARD
Works
New Lake
Toms Lake
Swanwick Nature Reserve
Bens Lake
Ladd Little Lake
Centre Lake
Study Cen.
M27 MOTORWAY
M27
Playing Field
Pav.
COAL PARK LANE
Traffic Control Centre
Brick Works
Midfield Nursery
Nursery
SOPWITH
BOTLEY ROAD
Fairlawns
CAIGERS GREEN
KINGSLEY
DICKENS
JEROME
WORDSWORTH
SWEETHILLS
Rec. Grd.
WINCHESTER
FAREHAM
Quaveys Copse
Glassfield Copse
Round Copse
BLUEBELL LANE
RATTIGAN
GARDENS
MARPLE

Great Gold Copse
Curdridge Croft
Curdridge Grange
Warwick House
Furzecote Farm
Curdridge Firs
Hill Farm
Summerlands
Woodpeckers
Woollams
The Lodge
Curdridge House
Curdridge Prim. Sch.
CURDRIDGE
Club
Curdridge Common
Recreation Ground
Lockhams Copse
Tree Cottage
Jasmine Cottage
Scout Training Centre
Woodman's Paddock
Lyons Copse
Decoy Pond
Fir Copse
Long Acre Copse
Sandle's Copse
Spencer Place
Dalecote Farm
MEON VALLEY GOLF COURSE
The Bungalow
Hilly Cantsley
Tennis Courts
Shedfield Grange
Meon Valley Golf and Country Club
SO32
Shedfield House
Park View
SHEDFIELD
Shedfield Lodge
ROAD KITNOCKS
HILL BOTLEY
A334
Kitnocks Lodge
Kitnocks House
Kitnocks
Kitnocks Farm
Southampton
Hedgerows
The Elms
Rowash Cottages
Row Ash House
Row Ash
Wickham Vineyard
Oakes Farm House
Rowash Farm House
Broadcroft
Southside Cottage
Cam Cottage
The Red House
Raglington Farm
Pond
Crooked Row
Biggs Copse
Church Copse
Vicarage
Shirrall House
Little Hall Court
Hall Court
Dunningwell
Hall Court Cottage
Ferny Copse
Upper Dagwells Copse
Nursery
Dagwells Farm
Heathlands Farm
Quagg End
Kitnocks Gully
Shawfords Lake
Triangle Row
SILFORD COPSE
Little Brook Wood
Horse Wood
Hallcourt Wood
Brook Wood
Fairthorne Grange
HOLE COPSE
Gulley Copse
Biddenfield
Biddenfield Cottage
Honeycut Row
Blacklands Copse
Tankerhill Copse
Biddenfield High Wood
St. Swithins
Two Ways
Waller's Close
Mansfield High Wood
Lower Blacklands Copse
Eastcroft Row
Cockshot Row
Bridge Farm
Cur Bridge
Botley Row
Seven Acre Copse
Mansfield Barn
Hangman's Copse
Mountwood House
Cold Harbour Farm
Barn Farm
Meadow Cottage
Alder Gully
Birch Row
Hangman's Row
Nursery
CURBRIDGE
Maids Garden Copse
Round Copse
Jacob's Croft
Treetops Farm
Marvane Cottage Farm
Alder Moor
New Copse
BLACKMOOR COPSE
Coldland Copse
Oakwood
Gravel Pit Copse
Woodlands Farm
Quob Farm
Webb's Land Cottage
Fareham
DIMMOCK'S MOOR
Webb's Land Farm
RIDGE COPSE
Moor Copse
Quob Copse
Bridge Copse
Little Tapnage Farm
Tapnage
Sager's Down
Picked Croft
Greystones Farm
Tapnage
PO17
PO15
Sawpit Copse
Lewd Land
White Cottage Farm
Waterclose Copse
BOTLEY WOOD
Tapnage Wood
WHITELEY FARM ROUNDABOUT
The Lodge
Everett's Coppice
Long Pond
Superstore
WHITELEY VILLAGE SHOPPING CENTRE
Playing Field
Meadowside Leisure Centre
Spring
Lone Cottage
Flagpond Copse
Knowle Hatches Viaduct
Works
Cemy.
TITCHFIELD LANE
BIDDENFIELD LANE
MANSFIELD LANE
SANDY LANE
ST. ANNES LANE
CHURCH RD.
CHAPEL LANE
LOCKHAMS LANE
GORDON ROAD
HOLE LANE
CURDRIDGE LANE
RIDGE LANE
B3035
163
178
197

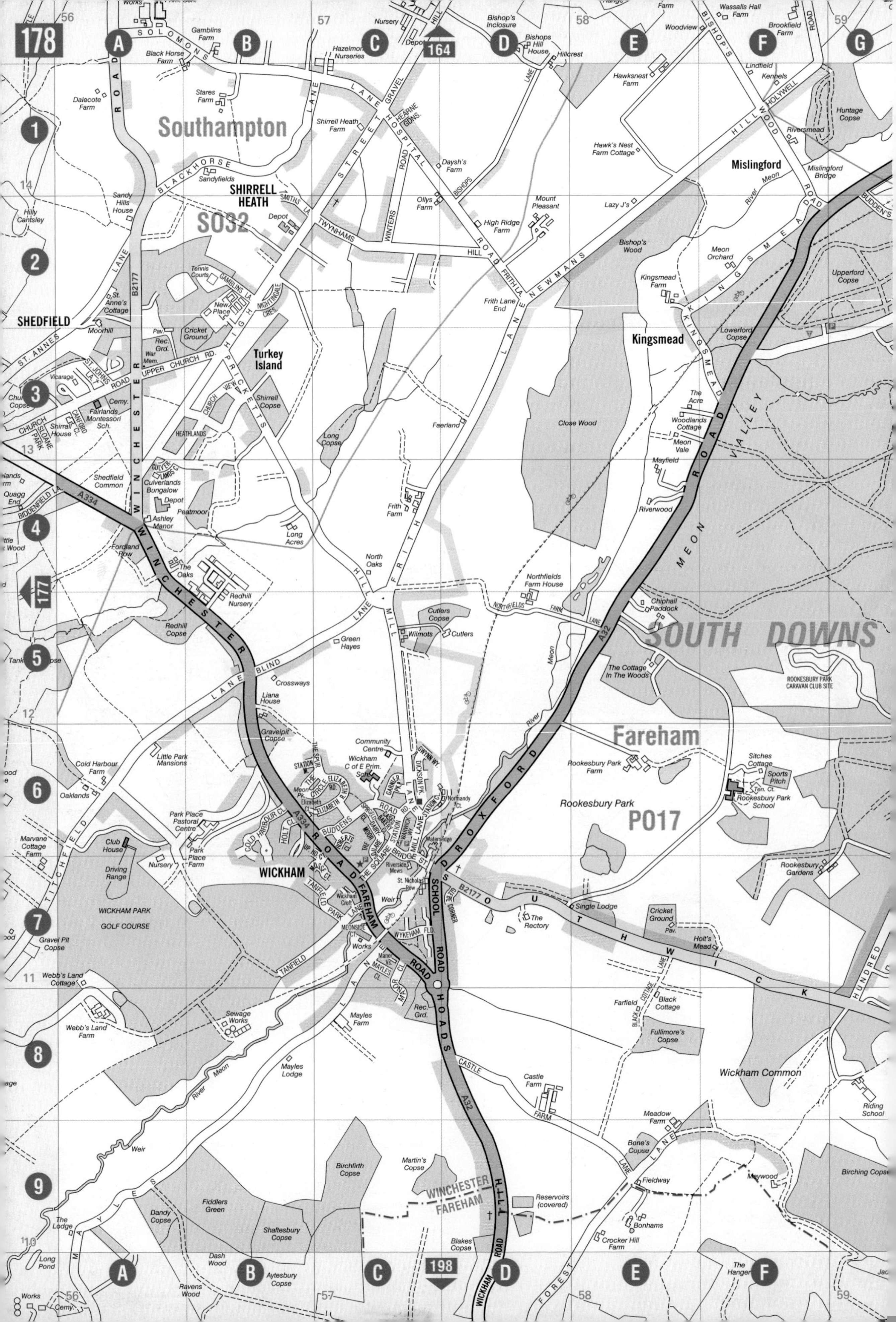
Southampton
SHIRRELL HEATH
SO32
SHEDFIELD
Turkey Island
WICKHAM
Fareham
PO17
SOUTH DOWNS
Mislingford
Kingsmead
Rookesbury Park
Wickham Common
WICKHAM PARK GOLF COURSE
ROOKESBURY PARK CARAVAN CLUB SITE
WINCHESTER ROAD
FAREHAM ROAD
DROXFORD ROAD
MEON VALLEY ROAD
SOUTHWICK
WICKHAM ROAD
HOADS HILL
BLIND LANE
TITCHFIELD LANE
FRITH LANE
NEWMANS LANE
BISHOPS LANE
HOSPITAL ROAD
GRAVEL STREET
SOLOMONS LANE
BLACKHORSE LANE
UPPER CHURCH RD.
CHURCH ROAD
ST. ANNES LA.
MAYLES LANE
FOREST LANE
CASTLE FARM LANE
Close Wood
Bishop's Wood
River Meon
WINCHESTER
FAREHAM
164
177
198

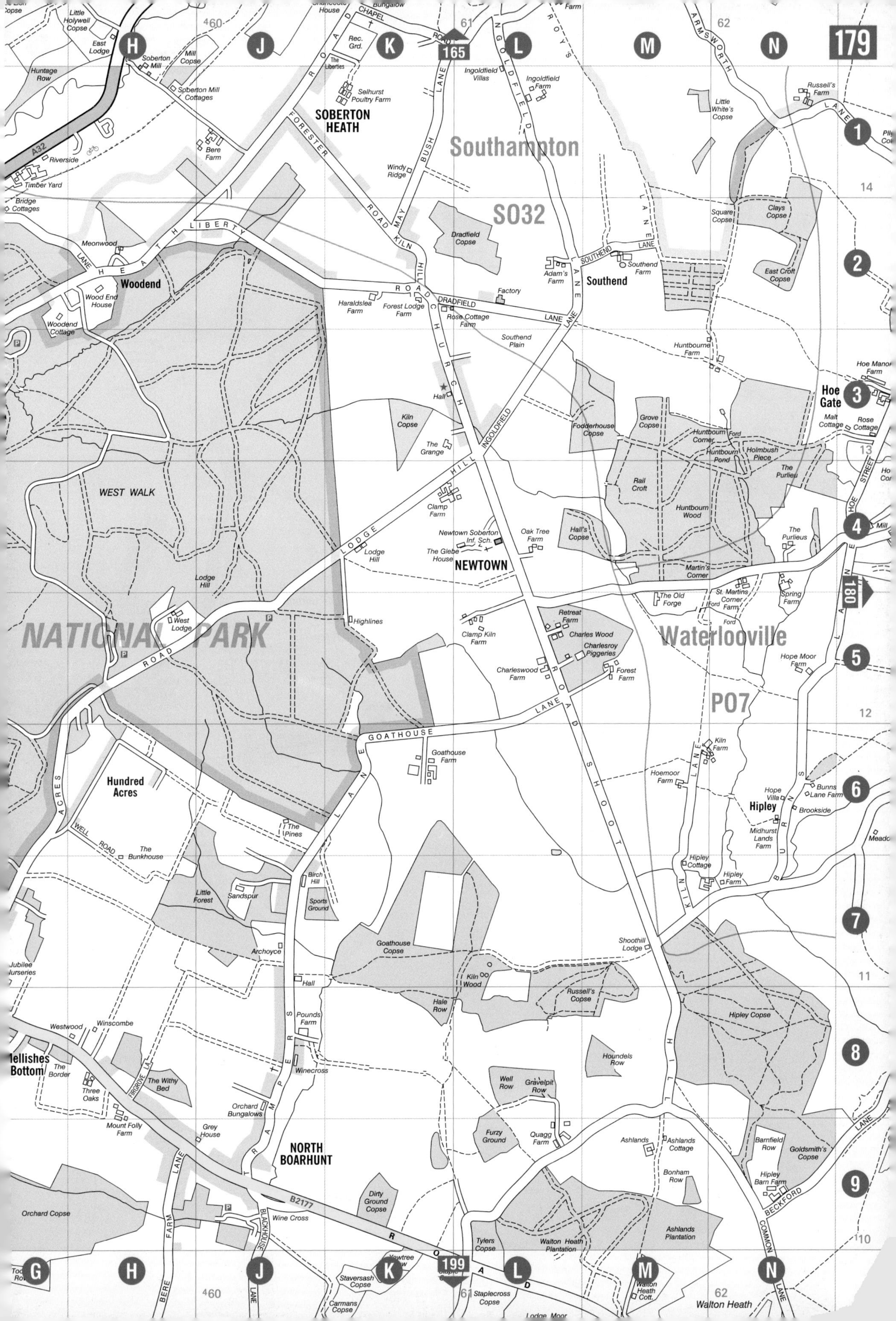
Southampton
SO32
Waterlooville
PO7
NATIONAL PARK
SOBERTON HEATH
Woodend
Southend
NEWTOWN
Hoe Gate
Hipley
NORTH BOARHUNT
Hundred Acres
WEST WALK
165
180
199
Soberton Mill
Mill Copse
Soberton Mill Cottages
East Lodge
Little Holywell Copse
Huntage Row
Riverside
Timber Yard
Bridge Cottages
Bere Farm
Rec. Grd.
The Liberties
Selhurst Poultry Farm
Ingoldfield Villas
Ingoldfield Farm
Little White's Copse
Russell's Farm
Windy Ridge
Dradfield Copse
Clays Copse
Square Copse
East Croft Copse
Southend Farm
Adam's Farm
Factory
Meonwood
Wood End House
Woodend Cottage
Haraldslea Farm
Forest Lodge Farm
Rose Cottage Farm
Southend Plain
Huntbourne Farm
Hoe Manor Farm
Malt Cottage
Rose Cottage
Hall
Kiln Copse
The Grange
Fodderhouse Copse
Grove Copse
Huntbourn Corner
Huntbourn Pond
Holmbush Piece
The Purlieu
Rail Croft
Huntbourn Wood
Clamp Farm
Newtown Soberton Inf. Sch.
The Glebe House
Oak Tree Farm
Hall's Copse
The Purlieus
Mill
Lodge Hill
Martin's Corner
St. Martins Corner Farm
The Old Forge
Spring Farm
Ford
West Lodge
Highlines
Clamp Kiln Farm
Retreat Farm
Charles Wood
Charlesroy Piggeries
Charleswood Farm
Forest Farm
Hope Moor Farm
Goathouse Farm
Kiln Farm
Hoemoor Farm
Hope Villa
Bunns Lane Farm
Brookside
Midhurst Lands Farm
Hipley Cottage
Hipley Farm
The Pines
The Bunkhouse
Birch Hill
Sports Ground
Little Forest
Sandspur
Archoyce
Goathouse Copse
Shoothill Lodge
Jubilee Nurseries
Hall
Kiln Wood
Hale Row
Russell's Copse
Hipley Copse
Westwood
Winscombe
Pounds Farm
Mellishes Bottom
The Border
Three Oaks
The Withy Bed
Winecross
Houndels Row
Well Row
Gravelpit Row
Orchard Bungalows
Mount Folly Farm
Grey House
Furzy Ground
Quagg Farm
Ashlands
Ashlands Cottage
Barnfield Row
Goldsmith's Copse
Bonham Row
Hipley Barn Farm
Orchard Copse
Wine Cross
Dirty Ground Copse
Tylers Copse
Walton Heath Plantation
Ashlands Plantation
Staversash Copse
Staplecross Copse
Carmans Copse
Walton Heath Cott.
Walton Heath
Lodge Moor
A32
B2177
CHAPEL ROAD
MAY BUSH LANE
INGOLDFIELD LANE
ROYS LANE
ARMSWORTH LANE
FORESTER ROAD
KILN ROAD
LIBERTY
HEATH LANE
SOUTHEND LANE
DRADFIELD LANE
CHURCH ROAD
HILL
INGOLDFIELD LANE
LODGE HILL
LODGE ROAD
GOATHOUSE LANE
ROAD SHOOT
ACRES
WELL ROAD
HOE STREET
BUNNS LANE
KILN LANE
FIRGROVE LA
TRAMPERS LANE
FARM LANE
BERE LANE
BLACKHOUSE LANE
ROAD
BECKFORD LANE
COMMON LANE
HILL
H
J
K
L
M
N
G
1
2
3
4
5
6
7
8
9
14
13
12
11
10
460
61
62

180
A
B
C
D
E
F
G
1
2
3
4
5
6
7
8
9
63
64
465
14
13
12
11
110
166
179
200
SOUTH DOWNS
Russell's Farm
ARMSWORTH LANE
Pilgrims Cottages
HOE STREET
Hill View Farm
Hill View
Homelands
CAMS HILL
Cams
WEST ST
OLD BAR CRES.
HAMBLEDON ROAD
B2150
Goldsmith's Plantation
Glebeland Farm
MENSLANDS LANE
Menslands Pond
Shepherds Croft
Madam's Copse
Hole Farm
HOLE LANE
MENSLANDS LANE
Prestfield Stud
HABENS LANE
The Paddocks
Bury Lodge Farm
BURY LODGE LANE
Bury Lodge
Harwood House
PITT HILL LANE
Rushmere Cottages
Rushmere
Rushmere Farm
Veniss Copse
SPELTHAM HILL LANE
Bittles Farm
Vinnell's Wood
Port Copse Plantation
WELL HILL
Rookwood Cottage
Rookwood Farm
RUSHMERE
Forest Gate
The Oaks
Kidburn
FAREHAM ROAD
Hill House
Hoe Manor Farm
Hoe Gate Farm
Hoegate Farm
Hoe Gate
Malt Cottage
Rose Cottage
Halsteads
Bent Farm
BENT LANE
Hoegate Common
Mill
Mill Plain
Mill Copse
The Purlieus
Great Ervills Farm
BROAD LANE
Hambur Lodge
Cherry Copse
The Plantation
Cherryhill Copse
Cherryhill Farm
UPLANDS ROAD
White Lodge
High Wood
Great Ervills Cottage
Drakes Bottom
Lavender Cottage
UPPER CRABBICK LA.
ANTHILL CL.
THOMPSONS LANE
Anthill Common
Anthill Farm
SCHOOL LANE
Comm. Cen.
Harts Copse
B2150
Little Acres
St. Christopher's
CRABBICK LANE
Meadow Farm Cottage
Kimbers
Yew Tree Cottage
Meadows Farm
Worlds End
PO7
Inhams Cottage
Inhams Farm
INHAMS LANE
Crabbick Farm
Woodlake Cottage
Woodlake Farm
Hiltonbury
Lower Crabbick Farm
The Cottage
LOWER
FOREST ROAD
Collyers Farm
Apless View
APLESS LANE
Apless Farm
The Bungalow
Brookside
Meadowsweet
BUNNS LANE
Works
HATCHMORE RD.
HAWTHORN RD.
HARVEST ROAD
GLASSPOOL
MASON'S WK.
GREEN LANE
SOUTHWICK ROAD
King George's Field
Pav.
Ten. Cts.
SOUTHERNHAY
Bowling Green
CLARENDON PARK
ROOKWOOD VW.
Cemy.
Thornbank
Bunkers Hill
Nursery
BUNKERS HILL
ROMAN GN.
FOREST
CREECH VIEW
THE WILLOWS
THE PASTURES
THE LIBERTY
THE TITHE
POND PIECE
HOME
COTTAGE
Mount Edgcumbe Cottage
PARKLANDS BUSINESS PK.
THE SPINNEY
CREECH WOOD
Creech House
Upper Beckford
Drain
Creech Lodge
Fareham
Beckford Green Farmhouse
Wiggs Wood
Beckford Bridge
BECKFORD LANE
Mitchelland Copse
Lovelocks
PO17
Goldsmith's Copse
Furzeley Corner
FURZELEY GOLF COURSE
Furzehill Cottage
Three Oak Farm
Furzehill Farm
SHEEPWASH LANE
Creech Farm
Jays Hummock
Jays Copse
Wynn's Copse
Mitchelland
Jays Copse
Little Belney Copse
Belney Farm
BELNEY
Great Belney

NATIONAL PARK
Waterlooville
LOVEDEAN
PO8
Eastland Gate
Wecock
COWPLAIN
DENMEAD
Anmore
Mead End
Soake
WATERLOOVILLE
WINCHESTER
EAST HAMPSHIRE
HAVANT
Lovedean Electricity Sub Station
FURZELEY GOLF COURSE
THE QUEEN'S INCLOSURE
Borrows Recreation Ground
Waterlooville Leisure Cen.
BRAMBLES ENTERPRISE CENTRE
BRAMBLES FARM INDUSTRIAL ESTATE
PIPERS WOOD INDUSTRIAL PARK
167
182
201

182
168
202
181
Junction 1
Junction 2
CATHERINGTON
HORNDEAN
BLENDWORTH
COWPLAIN
Waterlooville
PO8
PO7
A3(M) MOTORWAY
LONDON ROAD
PORTSMOUTH ROAD
HAVANT ROAD
B2149
DELL PIECE WEST
DELL PIECE EAST
Catherington Down Nature Reserve
Catherington Lith
Blendworth Lith
Horndean Technology College
Recreation Ground
Football Ground Pavilion
Superstore
Hazleton Wood
BLENDWORTH COMMON
WATERLOOVILLE GOLF COURSE
THE QUEEN'S INCLOSURE
BELL'S COPSE
HAVANT THICKET
THE HOLT
STEIN WOOD
Long Wood
Loscott's Plain
Horsefoot Hill
Upper Lake
Furzy Plain
Deadman's Dell
Netherley Down
STAUNTON COUNTRY PARK
EAST HAMPSHIRE
HAVANT
Cowplain Activity Centre
Padnell Jun. Sch.
Padnell Inf. Sch.
Queen's Inclosure Prim. Sch.
Padnell Cuts Wood
Padnell Grange
Club House
Blendworth House
Blendworth Farm
Broxburn House
St. Giles Farm
Nobles Farm
Hook Cottage
Pyle Farm
Soakfield Row
Eastlands
Rushmore Cottages
Redcroft Row
Hazelton Farm
Crookley Park Ho.
The New Blendworth Centre
Cadlington House
The Yews
Blendworth Lodge
Myrtle Farm
Crabden Row
Six Bells Farm
Southview Farm
Hawquins
New Barn Farm
Meadowdown Farm
White Gate Farm
Kinches Farm
Kingscourt School
Randells
Yoells Copse
69
470
71
72

H
J
K
L
M
N
73
74
475
169
IDSWORTH DOWN
Old Idsworth Farm
The Folly
Heberdens
Oxleys Copse
Old Idsworth Garden
Manor Copse
MARKWELLS WOOD
Wick Farm
WICK HANGER
SOUTH DOWNS NATIONAL PARK
Murrants
Murrants Copse
Idsworth House
South Holt Farm
Idsworth Villa
Shortleys Copse
IDSWORTH PARK
ASHCROFT LA
FINCHDEAN
The Old Iron Foundry
Treadwheel Farm
Adam's Copse
Keepers Cottage
Idsworth Lodge
Woodhouse Farm
TREADWHEEL
Finchdean Farm
EAST HAMPSHIRE
CHICHESTER
Bottom Copse
Northwood Farm
Forestside
WOODHOUSE LANE
DEAN
ROAD
MAGPIE ROAD
LANE
Coronation Cottages
Woods Copse
White Hill
Motleys Copse
Ring and Bailey
Deanlane End
Forestside Farm
Holt Pond
Magpie
Magpie Cottages
Diddy Bones Knap
Warren Down
WALK
MAGPIE BROAD
Drews Farm
Cherry Row
WELLSWORTH
WOODHOUSE
Woodhouse Ashes Farm
Great Wellsworth
STANSTED FOREST
Little Woodhouse
BOWES
WELLSWORTH
Little Wellsworth
HOLT GDNS
MEADOWLANDS
UPLANDS ROAD
GREATFIELD WAY
BROADCROFT
FINCHDEAN
ROWLANDS CASTLE GOLF COURSE
ROWLANDS CASTLE
LINKS
THE PEAK
UPLANDS
Rowlands Castle
Old Lodges
Hare Warren
Recreation Ground
FAIRWAY
HILL
Swallow Holes
Tennis Cts.
Pav.
The Sling
Club House
LINKS LANE
THE GREEN
Lodge
Deerleap
WOODBERRY
Beechwood
The Avenue
The Forest
CASTLE ROAD
Motte and Bailey
Works
Rowland's Castle
KINGS CL
ROYAL GS
COLLEGE
GLEN DALE
The Slip
B2149
NIGHTINGALE
KINGFISHER
Red Hill
DUNNOCK CL
Works
Horsepasture Farm
THE DRIFT
LODGE
MALLARD RD
BLACKCAP
Clarke's Dell
Monument
HAZELDEAN DR
HILL BROW
Red Hill Farm
PO9
Nightingale Bottom
Playground
Bettina
HAZELDEAN CT
Lodge
Oaklands House
Lyels Wood
Hall
Mem.
ROAD
REDHILL
Woodberry Cottage
LANE
203
G
H
J
K
L
M
Rowlands Castle St. John's C of E Prim. Sch.
Holme Farm
Animal Home
Gipsies Plain
The
73
74
475
1
2
3
4
5
6
7
8
9
14
13
12
11

BOVERIDGE HEATH
Bailey's Plantation
Fire Tower
PLUMLEY WOOD
Wiggs Copse
Plumley Cottages
Hamer Copse
Hamer
Pond
Hamer Brook
Ford
Kent Hill
Cootman Copse
Kent Hill Plantation
Turmer Hill
Wiggs Cottage
Harefield Lodge
Plumley Farm
Fernbrake Cottage
Lion's Ground
Turmer Cottages
Saw Mill
Turmer House
Lower Turmer
HAREFIELD PLANTATION
Verwood
BH31
Numbers
Nea Cottage
Harbridge Court
Burnt Hill House
SHEPHERDS
Shepherds Cottage
SHEPHERDS LANE
CHESTNUT AVENUE
Home Wood
Nea Lodge
Reservoir Cottage
Whitehoe Belt
Nettle Clump
Dog Kennel
Old Somerley
RINGWOOD FOREST
Whitehoe Cottages
New Barn Cottages
Golf Course
SOMERLEY PARK GOLF COURSE
Club Ho
Nursery Cottages
The Bothy
ELLINGHAM DRIVE
Laundry Cottage
Somerley
Somerley Park
HUNTERS CL
THE CHASE
RINGWOOD
THE FORESTERS
Playing Field
Ebblake
ROSEBERY
VIRGINIA CL
EBBLAKE ENTERPRISE PARK
THE FORELLE CEN.
PARKLANDS CL
B3081
Cemetery
Ebblake Bridge
Chatsworth
Old Laundry Cottage
Park Cottage
ASHLEY DRIVE
BLACKMOOR ROAD
Industrial Estate
EBBLAKE INDUSTRIAL ESTATE
Ebblake Ho.
BESSEMER
Ebblake Stream
Bluehaze
Sand and Gravel Pit
The Belt
Sunderton Wood
Crane Lake
DUNCOMBE
ASHLEY HEATH
Withy Bed
Duncombe Lodge
Ashley Farm
NEW FOREST
EAST DORSET
MOORS VALLEY GOLF COURSE
Kingsmere (Moors Valley Railway)
Club House
Kings Farm
Baker's Hanging
Visitor Cen.
Go Ape
Coach Park
MOORS VALLEY COUNTRY PARK AND FOREST
VERWOOD ROAD
Ashley Lodge
Watchmoor Wood
Style Cottage

152
186

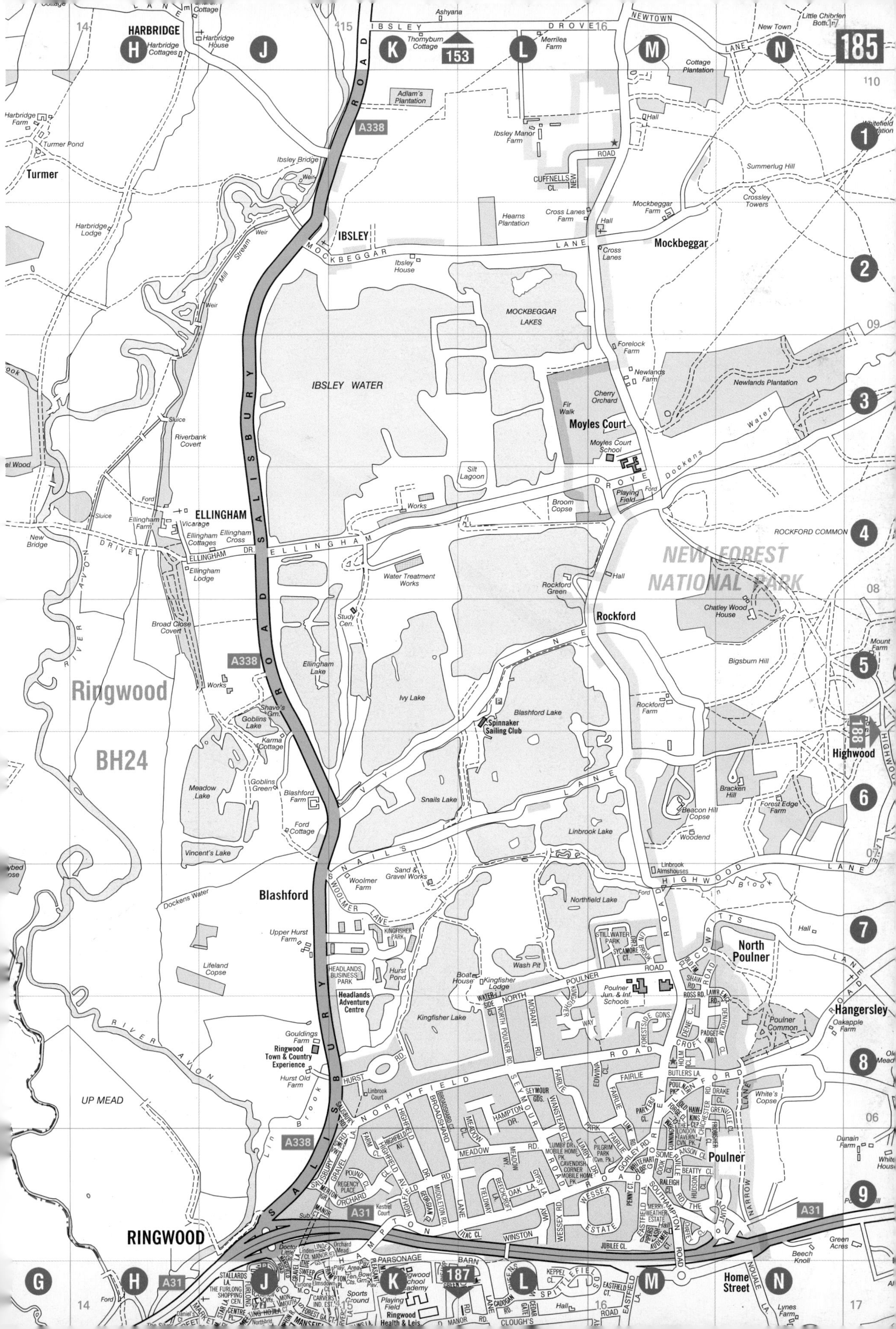

HARBRIDGE
Harbridge House
Harbridge Cottages
Harbridge Farm
Turmer Pond
Turmer
Harbridge Lodge
Ibsley Bridge
Weir
IBSLEY
Mill Stream
Ibsley House
MOCKBEGGAR LANE
Thornyburn Cottage
153
Ashyana
IBSLEY DROVE
Merrilea Farm
NEWTOWN
New Town
Little Chibden Bottom
Cottage Plantation
Adlam's Plantation
A338
Ibsley Manor Farm
CUFFNELLS CL.
NEW ROAD
Hall
Summerlug Hill
Crossley Towers
Mockbeggar Farm
Hearns Plantation
Cross Lanes Farm
Cross Lanes
Mockbeggar
Whitefield Plantation
MOCKBEGGAR LAKES
Forelock Farm
Newlands Farm
Newlands Plantation
IBSLEY WATER
Riverbank Covert
Sluice
Fir Walk
Cherry Orchard
Moyles Court
Moyles Court School
Dockens Water
Silt Lagoon
DROVE
Playing Field
Ford
Works
Broom Copse
ROCKFORD COMMON
Ellingham Farm
Vicarage
ELLINGHAM
Ellingham Cottages
Ellingham Cross
New Bridge
AVON DRIVE
ELLINGHAM DR.
ELLINGHAM
Ellingham Lodge
Water Treatment Works
NEW FOREST NATIONAL PARK
Rockford Green
Hall
Rockford
Chatley Wood House
Broad Close Covert
RIVER AVON
Study Cen.
Ellingham Lake
Ivy Lake
Mount Farm
Bigsburn Hill
Ringwood
Works
Shavo's Grn.
Goblins Lake
Karma Cottage
Blashford Lake
Spinnaker Sailing Club
Rockford Farm
188
Highwood
BH24
Meadow Lake
Goblins Green
Blashford Farm
IVY LANE
Snails Lake
Bracken Hill
Beacon Hill Copse
Forest Edge Farm
Ford Cottage
Linbrook Lake
Woodend
Vincent's Lake
SNAIL'S LANE
Sand & Gravel Works
Woolmer Farm
Linbrook Almshouses
HIGHWOOD LANE
Lin Brook
Blashford
WOOLMER LANE
Northfield Lake
Dockens Water
COWPITTS LANE
Hall
Upper Hurst Farm
KINGFISHER PARK
STILLWATER PARK
SYCAMORE CT.
North Poulner
Lifeland Copse
HEADLANDS BUSINESS PARK
Hurst Pond
Wash Pit
Boat House
Kingfisher Lodge
POULNER ROAD
Poulner Jun. & Inf. Schools
Headlands Adventure Centre
Poulner Common
Hangersley
Oakapple Farm
Kingfisher Lake
NORTH POULNER RD.
MORANT RD.
Gouldings Farm
Ringwood Town & Country Experience
Hurst Old Farm
FORESTSIDE GDNS.
RIVER AVON
HURST RD.
NORTHFIELD
SEYMOUR
FAIRLIE
BUTLERS LA.
White's Copse
UP MEAD
Linbrook Court
BROADSHARD
HAMPTON DR.
WANSTEAD CL.
PARK
FAIRLIE
MEADOW CL.
MEADOW RD.
LUMBY DR. MOBILE HOME PK.
PILGRIM PARK (Cvn. Pk.)
GORLEY RD.
Dunain Farm
White House
A338
SALISBURY RD.
GRAVEL LA.
HIGHFIELD AV.
CAVENDISH CORNER MOBILE HOME PK.
WHITEHART
SOMERVILLE
Poulner
POUND CL.
REGENCY PLACE
ORCHARD
MIDDLETON RD.
FIELDWAY
BEECHCROFT
DAK LA.
GYPSY LA.
WESSEX ESTATE
PENNY CT.
EASTFIELD LA.
SOUTHAMPTON RD.
RALEIGH CL.
HUDSON CL.
THE MOUNT
A31
Kestrel Court
LANE
WINSTON
JUBILEE CL.
NARROW LANE
Green Acres
RINGWOOD
Orchard Mead
HAMPTON
PARSONAGE BARN
Beech Knoll
A31
STALLARDS LA.
THE FURLONG SHOPPING CEN.
Ringwood School Academy
187
KEPPEL CL.
SPITTLEFIELDS
EASTFIELD CT.
Home Street
NOUALE LA.
Sports Ground
Playing Field
Ringwood Health & Leis.
Hall
Lynes Farm
MANOR RD.
CLOUGH'S
Ford

MOORS VALLEY
COUNTRY PARK
AND FOREST
ASHLEY HEATH
ST. IVES
ST. LEONARDS
ASHLEY
AVON HEATH COUNTRY PARK
(NORTH PARK)
AVON HEATH
COUNTRY PARK
(SOUTH PARK)
Grange Estate
Matchams
MATCHAM'S PARK
Leybrook Common
RACECOURSE HEATH
HURN FOREST
RINGWOOD ROAD
HORTON ROAD
BOUNDARY LANE
WAYSIDE ROAD
ST. LEONARD'S COMMUNITY HOSPITAL
Matchams Leisure Park Golf Driving Range
Ringwood Raceway
Ringwood Waldorf School
Holly Grove Farm
Shelling School
SUNNYSIDE PARK (CARAVAN SITE)
A31
A338
B3081

184
218

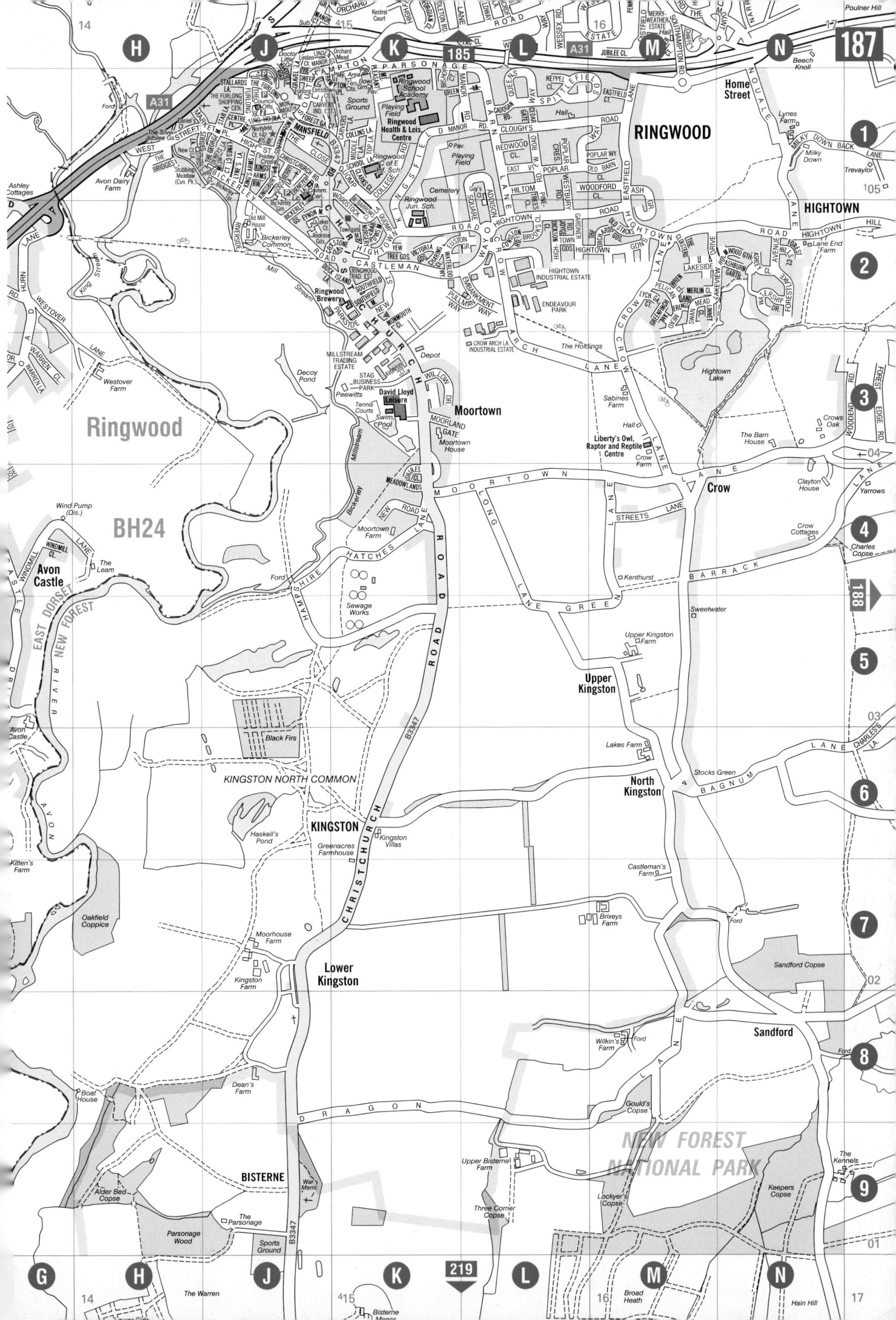

RINGWOOD
Home Street
HIGHTOWN
Poulner Hill
Beech Knoll
Lynes Farm
Milky Down
MILKY DOWN BACK LANE
Trevaylor
HIGHTOWN HILL
Lane End Farm
Ringwood School Academy
Ringwood Health & Lsr. Centre
Sports Ground
Playing Field
MANSFIELD
Ringwood C of E Inf. Sch.
Cemetery
Ringwood Jun. Sch.
Playing Field
THE FURLONG SHOPPING CEN.
The Silver Jubilee Gs.
Avon Dairy Farm
Ashley Cottages
Stubbings Meadow (Cvn. Pk.)
Old Mill House
Bickerley Common
Mill Stream
King Stream
Ringwood Brewery
RINGWOOD TRAD. EST.
HIGHTOWN INDUSTRIAL ESTATE
ENDEAVOUR PARK
CROW ARCH LA. INDUSTRIAL ESTATE
The Holdings
Hightown Lake
MILLSTREAM TRADING ESTATE
STAG BUSINESS PARK
Depot
Decoy Pond
Peewitts
Tennis Courts
David Lloyd Leisure
Swim. Pool
Moortown
Moortown House
Westover Farm
Ringwood
BH24
Wind Pump (Dis.)
Avon Castle
The Leam
EAST DORSET
NEW FOREST
RIVER AVON
Sabines Farm
Hall
Liberty's Owl, Raptor and Reptile Centre
Crow Farm
The Barn House
Crows Oak
Crow
Clayton House
Yarrows
Crow Cottages
Charles Copse
Moortown Farm
Ford
Sewage Works
Kenthurst
Sweetwater
Upper Kingston Farm
Upper Kingston
Lakes Farm
North Kingston
Stocks Green
Black Firs
KINGSTON NORTH COMMON
Haskell's Pond
KINGSTON
Kingston Villas
Greenacres Farmhouse
Castleman's Farm
Brixeys Farm
Kitten's Farm
Oakfield Coppice
Moorhouse Farm
Kingston Farm
Lower Kingston
Sandford Copse
Sandford
Wilkin's Farm
Boat House
Dean's Farm
Gould's Copse
NEW FOREST NATIONAL PARK
Upper Bisterne Farm
BISTERNE
War Meml.
Alder Bed Copse
The Parsonage
Parsonage Wood
Sports Ground
Three Corner Copse
Lockyer's Copse
Keepers Copse
The Kennels
The Warren
Bisterne Manor
Broad Heath
Hain Hill
CHRISTCHURCH ROAD
B3347
MOORTOWN LANE
BARRACK
BAGNUM LANE
DRAGON LANE
HAMPSHIRE HATCHES LANE
GREEN LANE
LONG LANE
STREETS LANE
CROW LANE
CROW ARCH LANE
HIGHTOWN ROAD
A31
185
188
219
H J K L M N G
1 2 3 4 5 6 7 8 9
14 415 16 17
105 04 03 02 01

South Gorley
Ibsley Common
Dockens
Amie's Wood
154
Milkham Inclosure
Slufters Inclosure
Whitefield Plantation
Toms Farm
Linwood
Red Shoot Camping Pk.
Deers Leap Caravan Pk.
Linwood Farm
Digden Bottom
King's Garden
A31
Newlands Plantation
Appleslade Inclosure
Castle Piece
Linford Brook
Bratley Plain
Bratley Inclosure
Pillow Mounds
Roe Inclosure
Rockford Common
Red Shoot Wood
Bratley Wood
Buckherd Bottom
185
Great Linfod Inclosure
Backley Bottom
Mount Farm
Pinnick Wood
Bigsburn Hill
Handy Cross Plain
Handy Cross
Backley Inclosure
Highwood
Little Linford Inclosure
Marrowbones Hill
Linbrook View
North Poulner
Linford
Backley Plain
Ridley Plain
Ringwood
Soarley Beeches
Hangersley
St. Aubyns La.
Hangersley Hill
Burcombe La.
Shobley
Beech Bed Inclosure
Linford Road
Cowpitts Lane
Harvest Slade Bottom
Berry Beeches
Old House
Poulner
Picket Post
Ridley Wood
NEW FOREST
BH24
Picket Plain
Picket Hill
Berry Wood
Milky Down Back Lane
Breach Lane
Sir Dudley's Road
Foulford
Hightown Lower Copse
South Oakley Inclosure
Sunny Down
Verely Hill
Vereley
Turf Croft
Hightown
Forest Lake Av.
Forest Hills
Hightown Forest
Coach Hill
Hurn Farm
Hightown Lake
Woodend Rd.
Forest Edge Rd.
Ravenswood Pk. Caravan Site
Smugglers
Vales Moor
Castle Hill
Ringwood Forest
Chapel Haye
Burley Moor
Lyndhurst Road
Lucy Hill
Forest Farm
Knaves Ash
Randalls La.
Stock's Farm
Burley Street
Clayton House
Crow Hill
Crow Hill Ho.
Crow Hill Fm.
Crow Hill Top
Fort
Castle Hill
Longmead Rd.
Mill Lane
Charles Copse
Barrack Lane
Strodgemoor Bottom
Black Bush
Burley Hill
New Forest Safari
Burley Lawn
BURLEY
Beechwood Lane
Bisterne Close
Cranes Moor
Chapel Lane
Church
Sch.
Club House
Lester Sq.
Bennetts Lane
Southfield
187
Charles
Bagnum
Kingston Great Common
Meadow Cl.
Coppice
New Forest Cider
Shappen Bottom
Cott Lane
Burley Beacon
Burnt Axon
Bagnum Farm
Honey Lane
Pound Lane
Shappen Hill La.
Moorhill
Burley Golf Course
Station Road
Passage
Clay Hill
Sandford Copse
Turf Hill
Slap
Ford
Christchurch
Greenberry Bridge
Goatspen Plain
Clayhill Bottom
Holmsley
Bisterne Common
BH23
Dur Hill Down
Holmsley Ridge
Holmsley Lodge
220
221
A B C D E F G
1 2 3 4 5 6 7 8 9
17 18 19 20 21 22 23
01 02 03 04 05 06 07 08 09 10

Woodside
155
Withybed
Frith Cross
Manor Wood
Inclosure
Mogshade Hill
Puckpits Inclosure
Mill Stream
Minstead Manor Farm
Acres Down Inclosure
Leominstead Lake
Bratley Arch
Wick Wood
Lyndhurst
Pikeshill
NEW FOREST GOLF COURSE
Highland Water Inclosure
Holmhill Inclosure
Pilmore Gate Heath
SO43
Acres Down
Yew Tree Farm
Deer Sanctuary
Forest Walks
Northerwood House
LYNDHURST
Bolderwood Farm
EMERY DOWN
Wood Crates
Highland Water
Bolderwood Cottage
Lyndhurst Hill
BOURNEMOUTH RD.
148
190
Boldrewood
Grounds
White Moor
North Oakley Inclosure
Bolderwood Arboretum
Wooson's Hill
Portuguese Fireplace
Millyford Bridge
Mark Ash Wood
Barrow Moor
Wooson's Hill Inclosure
Holiday's Hill Inclosure
Cuffnell's Farm
Clayhill
Goose Green
New Forest Reptile Centre
Allum Green
Wilverley Coach House
Bratley Water
Bolderwood Arboretum Ornamental Drive
Bank
PINKNEY
Church Moor
Winding Shoot
Knightwood Oak
Warwick Slade
Foxlease
Coxlease Sch.
High Cocklease House
Knightwood Inclosure
Gritnam
Brick Kiln Inclosure
Gritnam Wood
NATIONAL PARK
Anderwood Inclosure
Great Huntley Bank
Eagle Oak
Outer Rails Inclosure
Butts Lawn
Brinken Wood
Hursthill Inclosure
Forest Walks
Whitley Wood
Burley Lodge
Vinney Ridge Inclosure
Dames Slough Inclosure
A35
A337
New Park Plantation
Poundhill Inclosure
Blackwater Bridge
Forest Walks
Burley New Inclosure
Poundhill Heath
New Park Farm
Fletchers Water
Rhinefield Sandy's Inclosure
Fletchers Thorns Inclosure
Bolderford Bridge
Burley Old Inclosure
Kennels
Ober Heath
Lymington River
Red Rise
Caravan & Camping Site
Brockenhurst
Ober Water
Rhinefield House
Aldridgehill Inclosure
148
Black Knowl
Caravan Site
Markway Inclosure
204
Rock Hills
Beachern Wood
Forest Walks
SO42
Markway Hill
Crab Tree Earth
RHINEFIELD ROAD
Forest Park
North Weirs
Duck Hole
Holm Hill
White Moor
Wilverley Post
Naked Man
Hinchesea Moor
Five Thorns Hill
Brockenhurst C of E Prim. School
BROCKENHURST
Brockenhurst
South Weirs
Wilverley Plain
Wilverley Inclosure
BH25
Hincheslea
BURLEY
222
223
Hincheslea Wood
Long Slade Bottom
Club House
BROKENHURST MANOR GOLF COURSE
SWAY ROAD
LYMINGTON ROAD

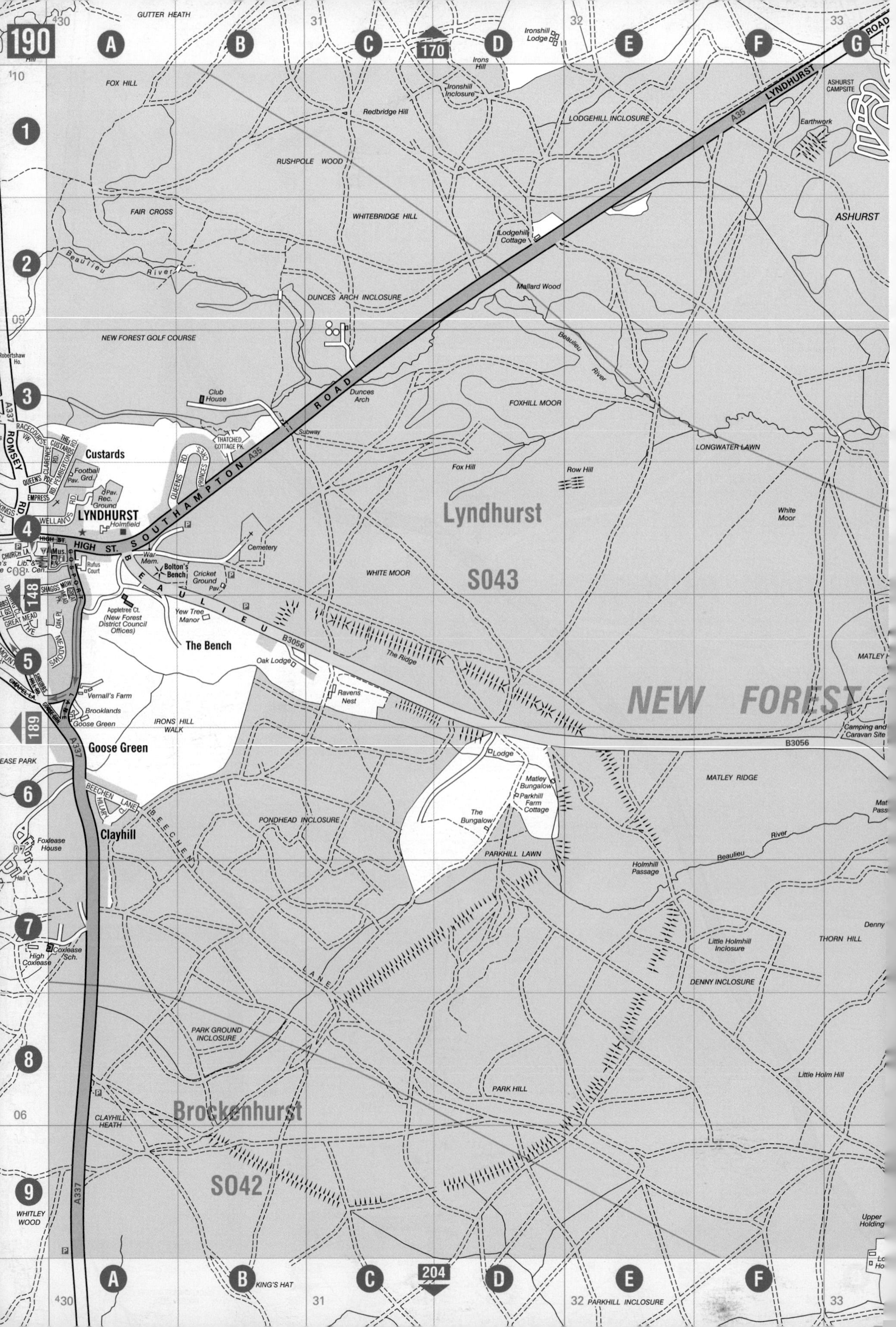

GUTTER HEATH
Ironshill Lodge
170
Irons Hill
Ironshill Inclosure
FOX HILL
Redbridge Hill
LODGEHILL INCLOSURE
LYNDHURST ROAD
A35
ASHURST CAMPSITE
Earthwork
RUSHPOLE WOOD
FAIR CROSS
WHITEBRIDGE HILL
ASHURST
Lodgehill Cottage
Beaulieu River
Mallard Wood
DUNCES ARCH INCLOSURE
NEW FOREST GOLF COURSE
Robertshaw Ho.
SOUTHAMPTON ROAD
Dunces Arch
Club House
FOXHILL MOOR
Subway
THATCHED COTTAGE PK.
LONGWATER LAWN
Custards
ROMSEY RD
Football Grd.
Pav.
Rec. Ground
Fox Hill
Row Hill
LYNDHURST
Holmfield
Lyndhurst
White Moor
HIGH ST.
Cemetery
War Mem.
Bolton's Bench
Cricket Ground
Mus.
Rufus Court
WHITE MOOR
SO43
148
Appletree Ct. (New Forest District Council Offices)
Yew Tree Manor
The Bench
B3056
The Ridge
Oak Lodge
MATLEY
Ravens Nest
NEW FOREST
Vernall's Farm
Brooklands
Goose Green
IRONS HILL WALK
Camping and Caravan Site
189
Goose Green
A337
Lodge
B3056
LEASE PARK
Matley Bungalow
Parkhill Farm Cottage
MATLEY RIDGE
BEECHEN LANE
The Bungalow
PONDHEAD INCLOSURE
Clayhill
Foxlease House
Beaulieu River
Holmhill Passage
PARKHILL LAWN
Coxlease Sch.
High Coxlease
Little Holmhill Inclosure
THORN HILL
Denny
LANE
DENNY INCLOSURE
PARK GROUND INCLOSURE
Little Holm Hill
PARK HILL
Brockenhurst
CLAYHILL HEATH
SO42
WHITLEY WOOD
Upper Holding
KING'S HAT
204
PARKHILL INCLOSURE

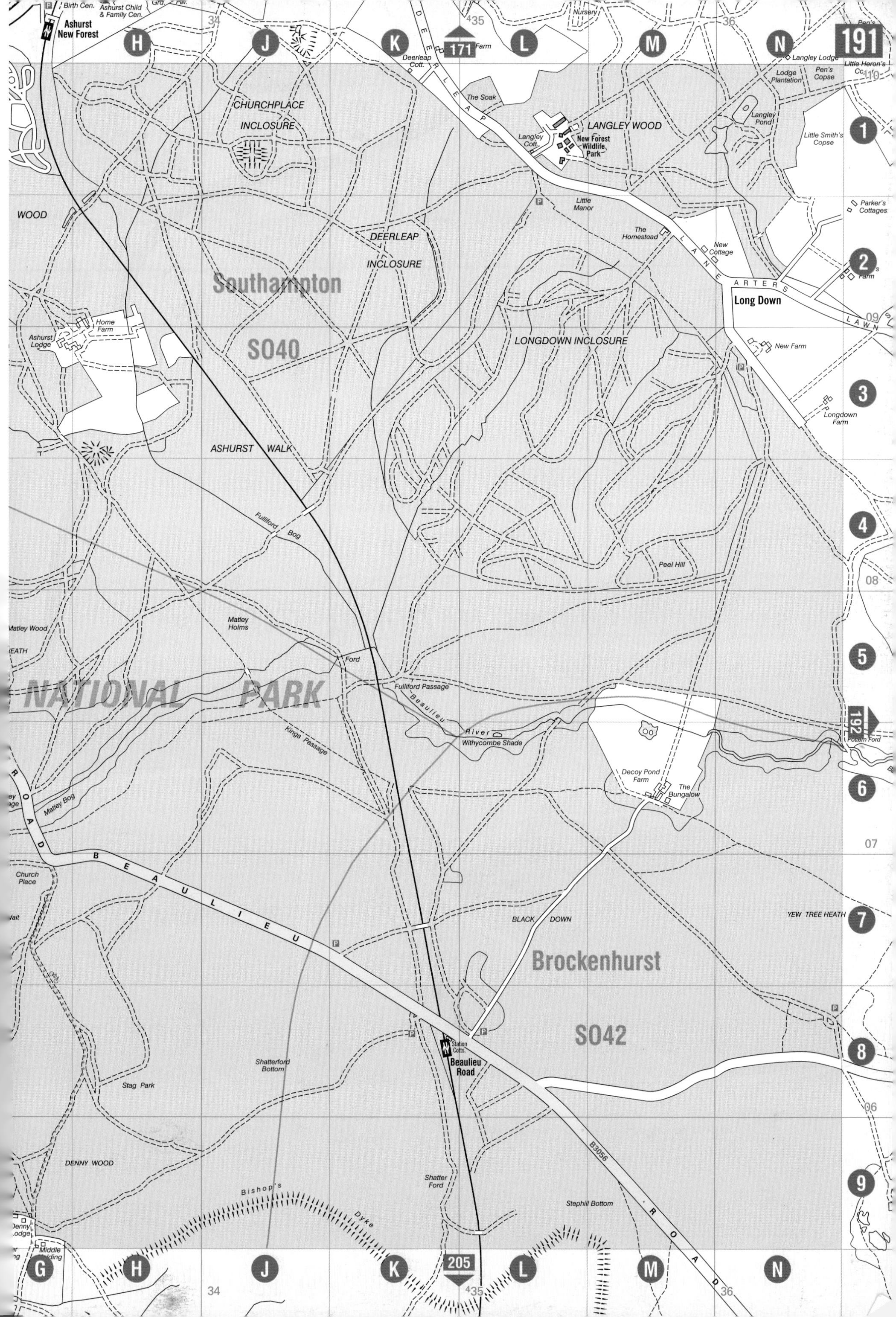

Ashurst New Forest
Birth Cen.
Ashurst Child & Family Cen.
Deerleap Cott.
171
Farm
Nursery
Langley Lodge
Little Heron's Co.
Lodge Plantation
Pen's Copse
CHURCHPLACE INCLOSURE
The Soak
LANGLEY WOOD
Langley Cott.
New Forest Wildlife Park
Langley Pond
Little Smith's Copse
DEERLEAP
WOOD
Little Manor
Parker's Cottages
The Homestead
New Cottage
DEERLEAP INCLOSURE
Southampton
ARTERS LANE
Long Down
LAWN
Home Farm
Ashurst Lodge
SO40
LONGDOWN INCLOSURE
New Farm
Longdown Farm
ASHURST WALK
Fulliford Bog
Peel Hill
Matley Wood
Matley Holms
HEATH
Ford
NATIONAL PARK
Fulliford Passage
Beaulieu River
Withycombe Shade
Kings Passage
192
Pottern Ford
Decoy Pond Farm
The Bungalow
Matley Bog
BEAULIEU ROAD
Church Place
BLACK DOWN
YEW TREE HEATH
Brockenhurst
SO42
Station Cotts.
Beaulieu Road
Shatterford Bottom
Stag Park
B3056
DENNY WOOD
Shatter Ford
Bishop's Dyke
Stephill Bottom
Denny Lodge
Middle
205

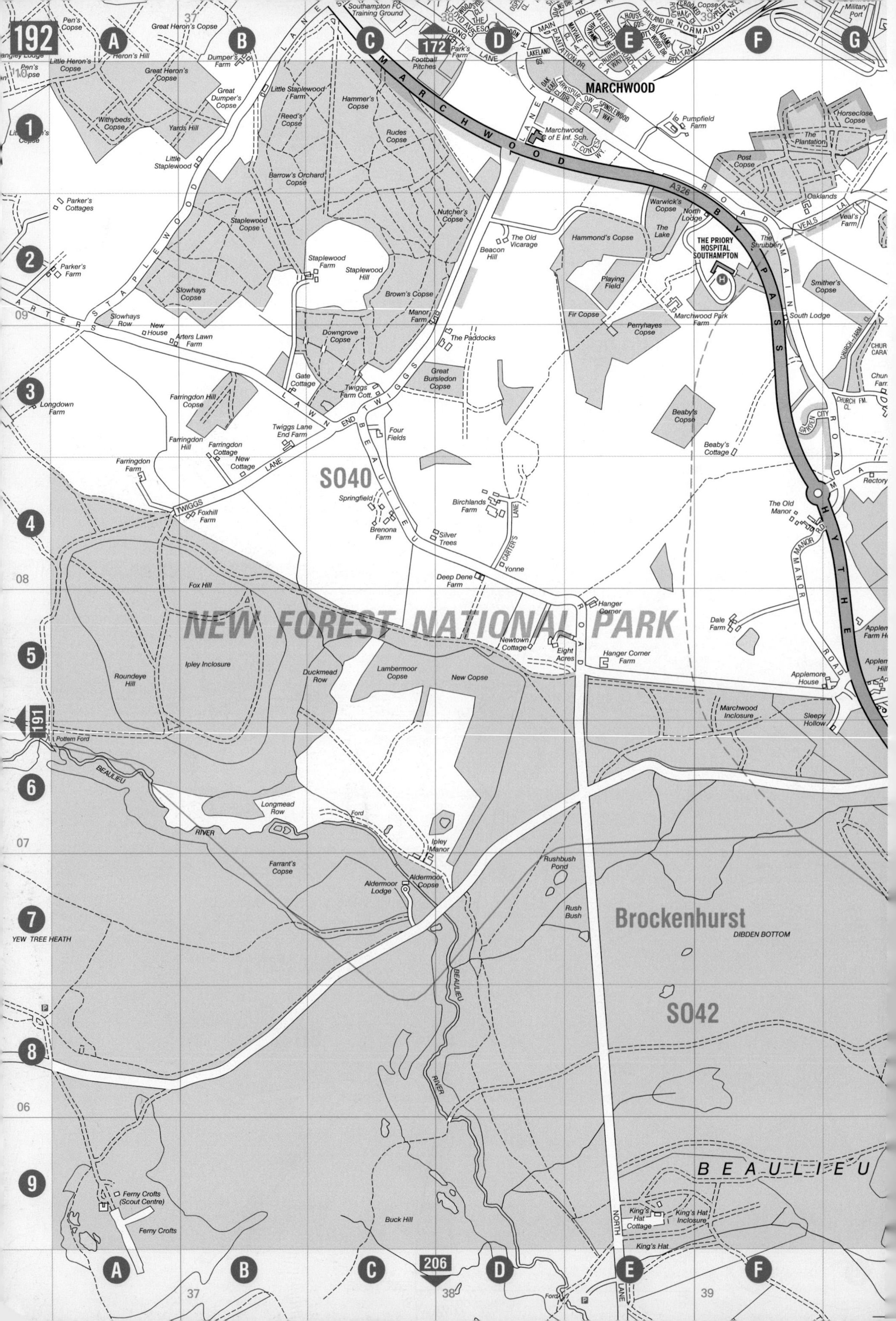

A
B
C
D
E
F
G
1
2
3
4
5
6
7
8
9
37
38
39
10
09
08
07
06
172
191
206
NEW FOREST NATIONAL PARK
MARCHWOOD
SO40
SO42
Brockenhurst
BEAULIEU
DIBDEN BOTTOM
YEW TREE HEATH
Southampton FC Training Ground
Football Pitches
Park's Farm
Military Port
Pen's Copse
Heron's Hill
Great Heron's Copse
Little Heron's Copse
Dumper's Farm
Great Dumper's Copse
Little Staplewood Farm
Hammer's Copse
Reed's Copse
Rudes Copse
Withybeds Copse
Yards Hill
Little Staplewood
Barrow's Orchard Copse
Parker's Cottages
Parker's Farm
Staplewood Copse
Nutcher's Copse
Staplewood Farm
Staplewood Hill
Brown's Copse
Slowhays Copse
Slowhays Row
New House
Arters Lawn Farm
Manor Farm
The Paddocks
Downgrove Copse
Gate Cottage
Twiggs Farm Cott.
Great Bursledon Copse
Longdown Farm
Farringdon Hill Copse
Farringdon Hill
Farringdon Cottage
New Cottage
Twiggs Lane End Farm
Farringdon Farm
Foxhill Farm
Four Fields
Springfield
Brenona Farm
Silver Trees
Birchlands Farm
Yonne
Deep Dene Farm
Hanger Corner
Newtown Cottage
Eight Acres
Hanger Corner Farm
Fox Hill
Roundeye Hill
Ipley Inclosure
Duckmead Row
Lambermoor Copse
New Copse
Pottern Ford
Longmead Row
Ford
Ipley Manor
Farrant's Copse
Aldermoor Lodge
Aldermoor Copse
Rushbush Pond
Rush Bush
Buck Hill
Ferny Crofts (Scout Centre)
Ferny Crofts
King's Hat Cottage
King's Hat Inclosure
King's Hat
Marchwood Inclosure
Sleepy Hollow
Applemore House
Dale Farm
The Old Manor
Rectory
Beaby's Copse
Beaby's Cottage
Marchwood Park Farm
Perryhayes Copse
Fir Copse
Playing Field
Hammond's Copse
The Old Vicarage
Beacon Hill
Warwick's Copse
North Lodge
The Lake
THE PRIORY HOSPITAL SOUTHAMPTON
The Shrubbery
South Lodge
Smither's Copse
Veal's Farm
Oaklands
Post Copse
The Plantation
Horseclose Copse
Pumpfield Farm
Marchwood C of E Inf. Sch.
MARCHWOOD BY PASS
A326
ROAD
MAIN ROAD
HYTHE ROAD
MANOR ROAD
GARDEN CITY
CHURCH FM. CL.
CHURCH FARM CL.
VEALS LA.
STAPLEWOOD LANE
ARTERS LAWN
TWIGGS LANE
TWIGGS END LANE
BEAULIEU ROAD
CARTER'S LANE
NORTH LANE
BEAULIEU RIVER
LONG LANE
LAKELAND GDS.
MAIN RD.
PLANTATION DR.
NORMANDY WY.
OAKLAND DR.
SPINDLEWOOD WAY
ST. CONTES WY.
LARKSPUR DR.
WILLOW DR.
OAK LEA
BURMA WAY
AFRICA DRIVE

Southampton
Dibden
Applemore
HYTHE
S045
S014
RIVER TEST
SOUTHAMPTON
NEW FOREST
DIBDEN PURLIEU
Langdown
Frostlane
Buttsash
DIBDEN GOLF COURSE
DIBDEN INCLOSURE
HEATH
QE II Cruise Terminal
Hythe to Southampton 12 mins (Foot Ferry)
Ferry Landing Stage
Hythe Pier
Hythe Marina
Applemore Health & Leisure Centre
Applemore College
Oak Lodge School
Clayfields Sports Centre
Hythe Hosp.
Veterinary Hospital
Recreation Ground
Football Ground

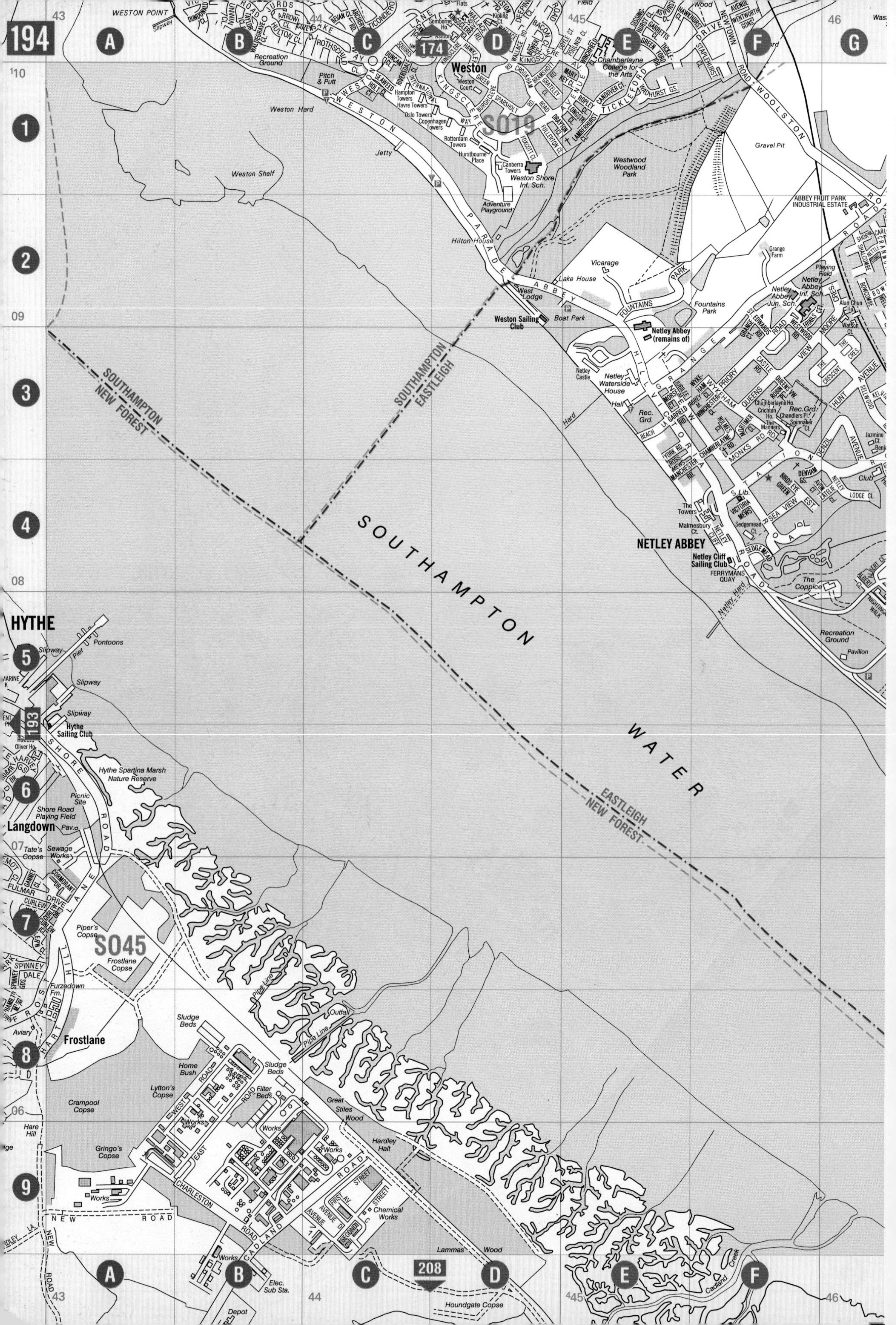
194
174
193
208
Weston
SO19
Weston Point
Weston Hard
Weston Shelf
Weston Shore Inf. Sch.
Recreation Ground
Pitch & Putt
Adventure Playground
Hilton House
Weston Sailing Club
Boat Park
West Lodge
Westwood Woodland Park
Gravel Pit
ABBEY FRUIT PARK INDUSTRIAL ESTATE
Chamberlayne College for the Arts
Vicarage
Lake House
Fountains Park
Netley Abbey (remains of)
Netley Castle
Netley Waterside House
Netley Abbey Inf. Sch.
Netley Abbey Jun. Sch.
Grange Farm
Playing Field
NETLEY ABBEY
Netley Cliff Sailing Club
FERRYMANS QUAY
Netley Hard
The Coppice
Recreation Ground
Pavilion
SOUTHAMPTON WATER
SOUTHAMPTON
NEW FOREST
SOUTHAMPTON
EASTLEIGH
EASTLEIGH
NEW FOREST
HYTHE
Pontoons
Pier
Slipway
Hythe Sailing Club
Hythe Spartina Marsh Nature Reserve
Picnic Site
Shore Road Playing Field
Langdown
Tate's Copse
Sewage Works
Piper's Copse
SO45
Frostlane Copse
Furzedown Fm.
Frostlane
Aviary
Sludge Beds
Home Bush
Lytton's Copse
Crampool Copse
Hare Hill
Gringo's Copse
Filter Beds
Works
Great Stiles Wood
Hardley Halt
Chemical Works
Lammas Wood
Elec. Sub Sta.
Depot
Houndgate Copse
Cadland Creek
Pipe Line
Outfall
SHORE ROAD
HART HILL LANE
NEW ROAD
CHARLESTON ROAD
CADLAND ROAD
WESTON PARADE
ABBEY HILL
WOOLSTON ROAD
VICTORIA ROAD
STATION ROAD
NETLEY ROAD

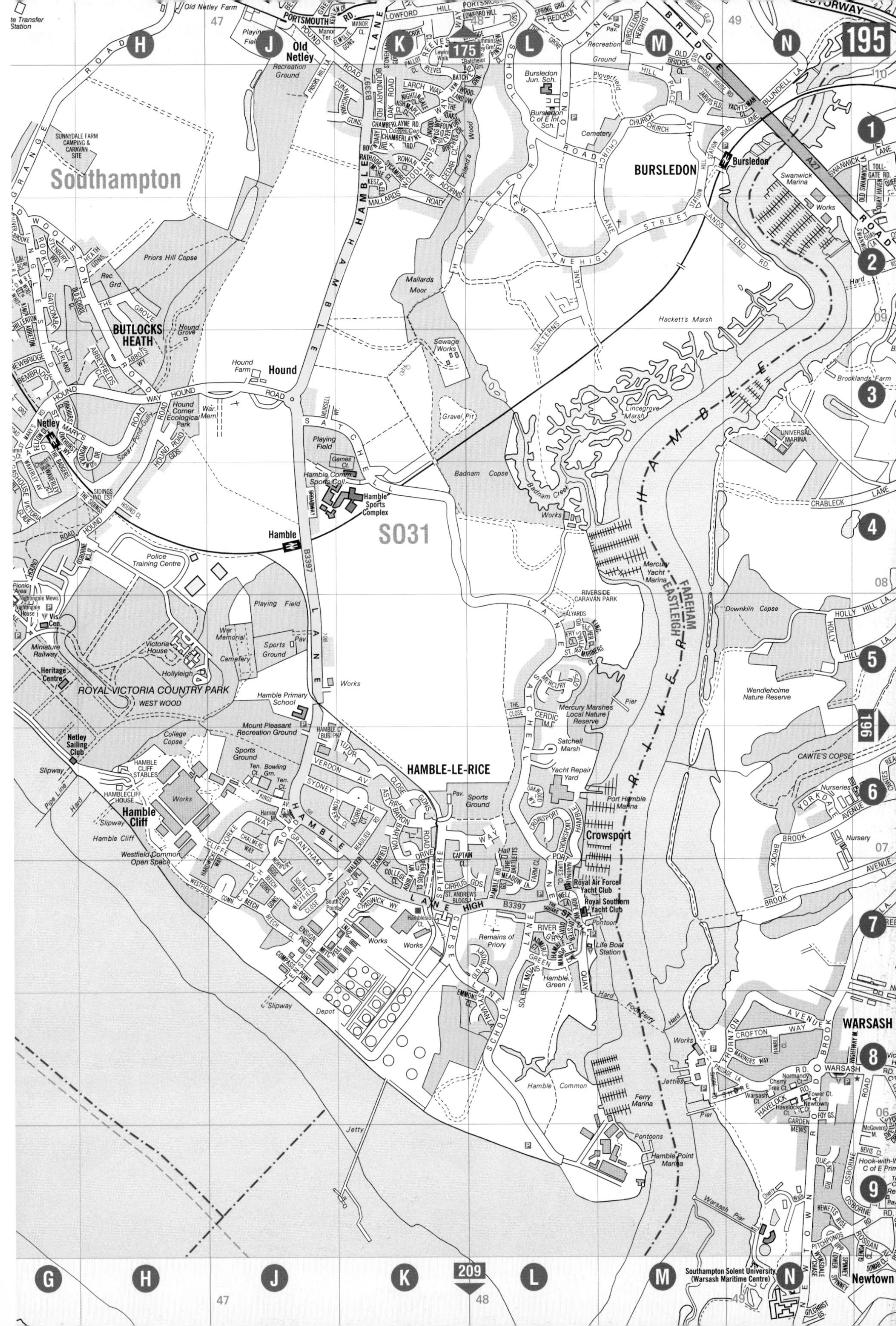
195
175
209
196
Southampton
Old Netley
BUTLOCKS HEATH
Hound
Netley
Hamble
SO31
BURSLEDON
Bursledon
HAMBLE-LE-RICE
Hamble Cliff
Crowsport
WARSASH
Newtown
ROYAL VICTORIA COUNTRY PARK
Old Netley Farm
SUNNYDALE FARM CAMPING & CARAVAN SITE
Priors Hill Copse
Recreation Ground
Bursledon Jun. Sch.
Bursledon C of E Inf. Sch.
Cemetery
Mallards Moor
Sewage Works
Hound Farm
Hound Corner Ecological Park
War. Mem.
Playing Field
Hamble Comm. Sports Coll.
Hamble Sports Complex
Gravel Pit
Badnam Copse
Badnam Creek
Hackett's Marsh
Lincegrove Marsh
Swanwick Marina
UNIVERSAL MARINA
Brooklands Farm
Police Training Centre
Mercury Yacht Marina
RIVERSIDE CARAVAN PARK
Downkiln Copse
Wendleholme Nature Reserve
Victoria House
Hollyleigh
Miniature Railway
Heritage Centre
WEST WOOD
Hamble Primary School
Mount Pleasant Recreation Ground
Mercury Marshes Local Nature Reserve
Satchell Marsh
Yacht Repair Yard
Port Hamble Marina
Netley Sailing Club
College Copse
Sports Ground
HAMBLE CLIFF STABLES
HAMBLECLIFF HOUSE
Works
Westfield Common Open Space
Royal Air Force Yacht Club
Royal Southern Yacht Club
Remains of Priory
Life Boat Station
Hamble Green
Hamble Common
Ferry Marina
Hamble Point Marina
Pontoons
Jetty
Depot
Slipway
Warsash Pier
Southampton Solent University (Warsash Maritime Centre)
CAWTE'S COPSE
Nurseries
Nursery
RIVER HAMBLE
FAREHAM
EASTLEIGH
HAMBLE LANE
SATCHELL LANE
HIGH STREET
B3397
A27
G H J K L M N
1 2 3 4 5 6 7 8 9
47 48 49
06 07 08 09 10

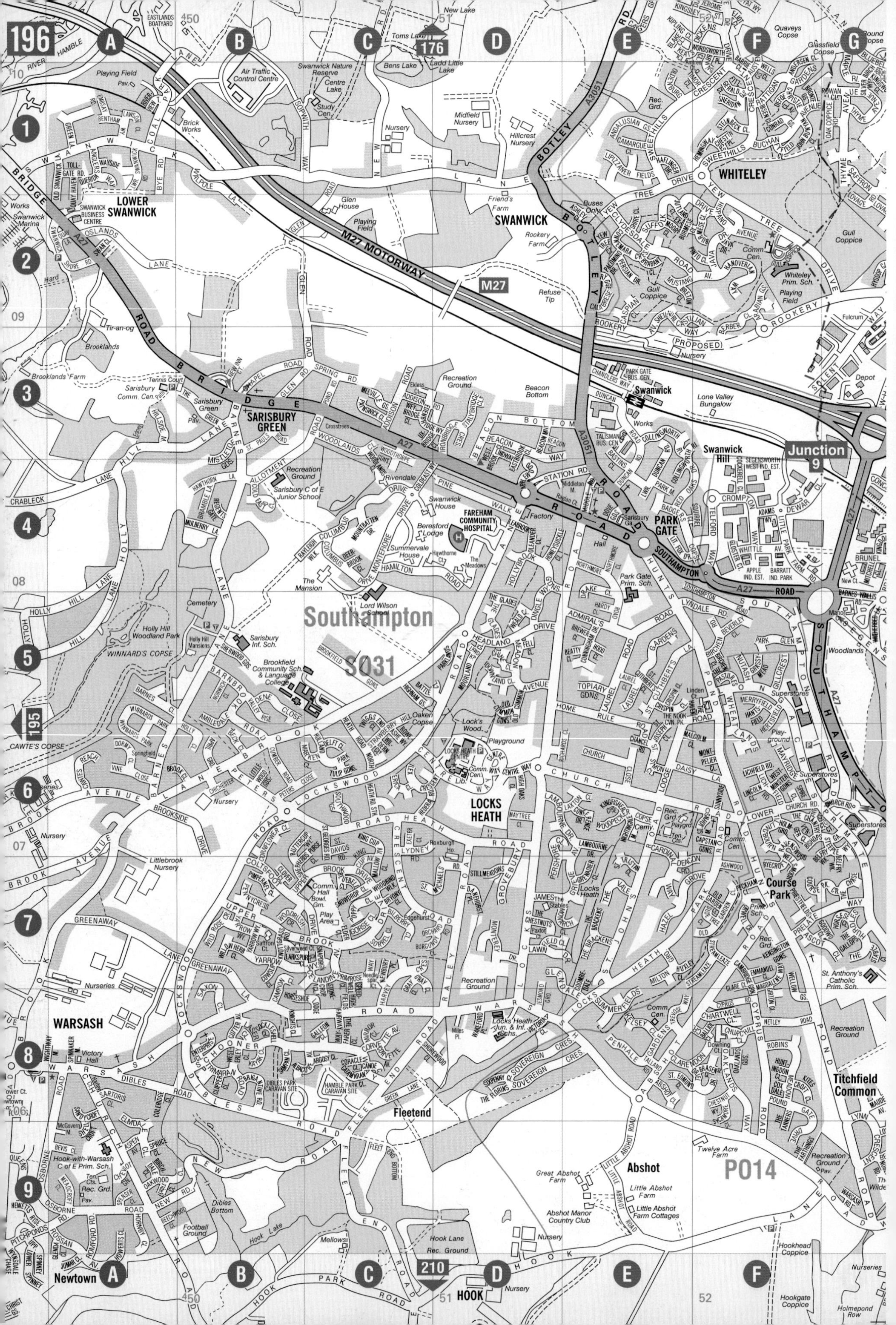

LOWER SWANWICK
SWANWICK
WHITELEY
SARISBURY GREEN
PARK GATE
Swanwick Hill
Junction 9
Southampton
SO31
LOCKS HEATH
Course Park
WARSASH
Fleetend
Abshot
PO14
Titchfield Common
Newtown
HOOK
M27 MOTORWAY
BRIDGE ROAD
FAREHAM COMMUNITY HOSPITAL
Swanwick
176
195
210

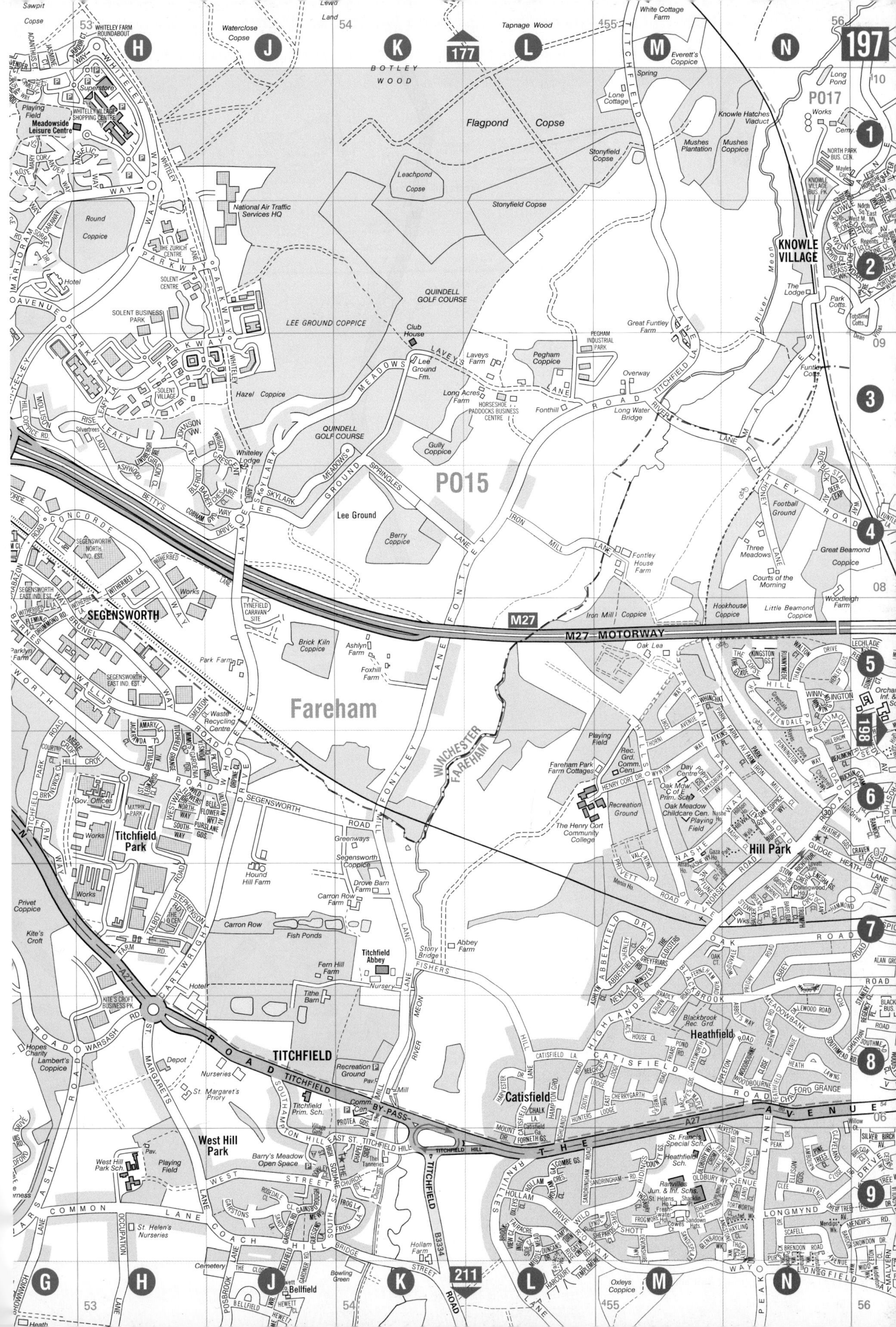

BOTLEY WOOD
Flagpond Copse
Whiteley Village Shopping Centre
Meadowside Leisure Centre
Round Coppice
National Air Traffic Services HQ
Solent Business Park
Quindell Golf Course
Lee Ground Coppice
Hazel Coppice
Knowle Village
P015
P017
Lee Ground
M27 Motorway
Segensworth
Fareham
Titchfield Park
Titchfield Abbey
Titchfield
Hill Park
Heathfield
Catisfield
West Hill Park
Fontley House Farm
Great Beamond Coppice
The Henry Cort Community College
177
211
198

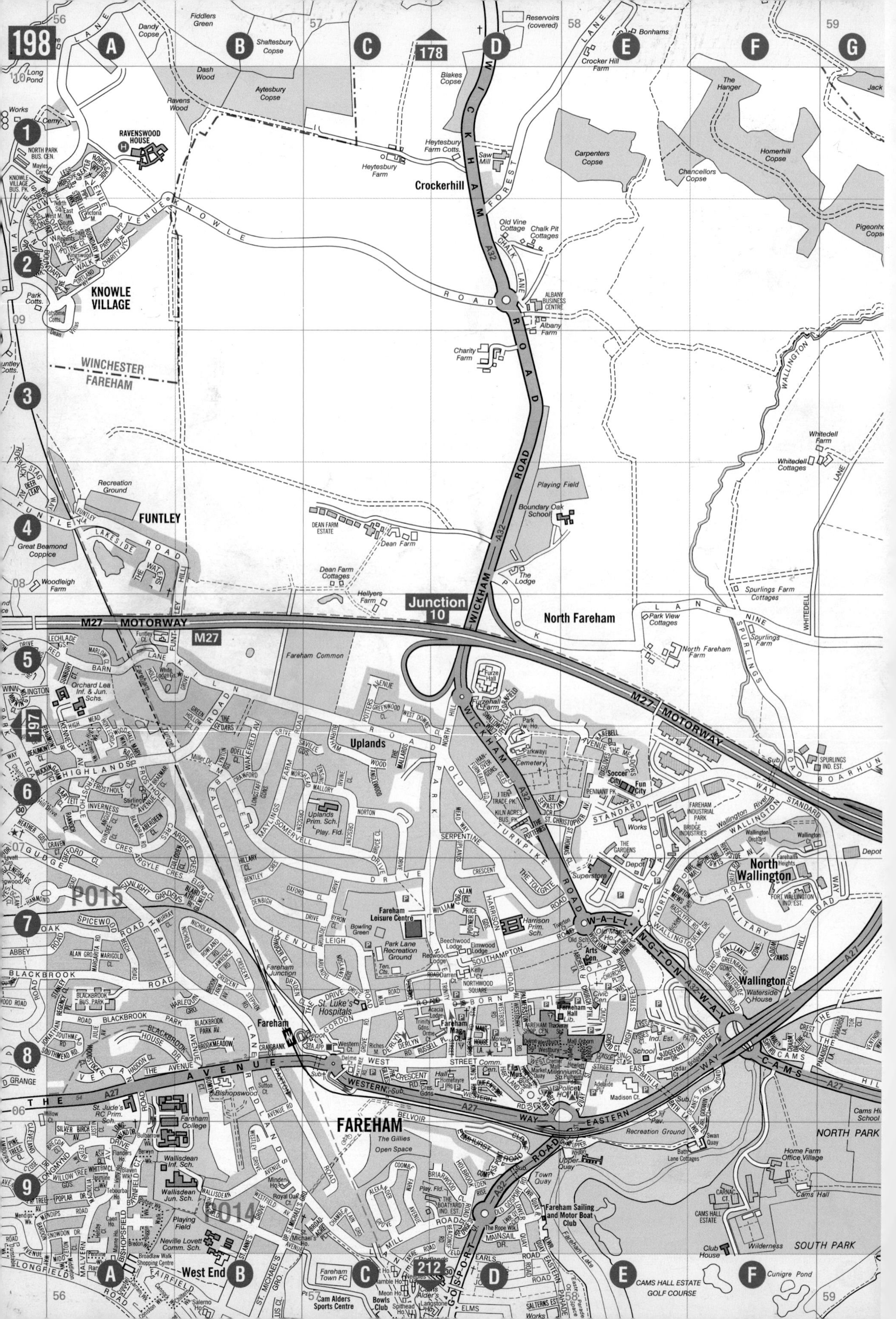
178
Fiddlers Green
Dandy Copse
Shaftesbury Copse
Reservoirs (covered)
Bonhams
Crocker Hill Farm
Dash Wood
Aytesbury Copse
Blakes Copse
The Hanger
Ravens Wood
Long Pond
Works
Cemy.
RAVENSWOOD HOUSE
Heytesbury Farm Cotts.
Heytesbury Farm
Saw Mill
Carpenters Copse
Homerhill Copse
Chancellors Copse
Crockerhill
NORTH PARK BUS. CEN.
KNOWLE VILLAGE BUS. PK.
Old Vine Cottage
Chalk Pit Cottages
KNOWLE VILLAGE
Park Cotts.
ALBANY BUSINESS CENTRE
Albany Farm
Charity Farm
WINCHESTER
FAREHAM
WICKHAM ROAD
A32
KNOWLE ROAD
Whitedell Farm
Whitedell Cottages
Recreation Ground
Playing Field
Boundary Oak School
FUNTLEY
DEAN FARM ESTATE
Dean Farm
Great Beamond Coppice
Dean Farm Cottages
The Lodge
Woodleigh Farm
Hellyers Farm
Junction 10
Spurlings Farm Cottages
North Fareham
M27 MOTORWAY
M27
Park View Cottages
Spurlings Farm
North Fareham Farm
Fareham Common
Furze Hall
Orchard Lea Inf. & Jun. Schs.
197
Uplands
Cemetery
Soccer City
Fun City
SPURLINGS IND. EST.
FAREHAM INDUSTRIAL PARK
BRIDGE INDUSTRIES
Uplands Prim. Sch.
Play. Fld.
North Wallington
FORT WALLINGTON IND. EST.
Superstore
Depot
PO15
Fareham Leisure Centre
Harrison Prim. Sch.
Bowling Green
Park Lane Recreation Ground
Arts Cen.
Wallington
Waterside House
Fareham Junction
St. Luke's Hospitals
Fareham Hall
Lib.
FAREHAM SHOP. CEN.
Civic Cen.
Fareham
BLACKBROOK BUS. PARK
THE AVENUE
A27
Bishopswood
St. Jude's RC Prim. Sch.
Fareham College
Wallisdean Inf. Sch.
Wallisdean Jun. Sch.
FAREHAM
The Gillies Open Space
EASTERN WAY
Recreation Ground
Upper Quay
Town Quay
Swan Quay
Bath Lane Cottages
Cams Hill School
NORTH PARK
Home Farm Office Village
Cams Hall
CAMS HALL ESTATE
PO14
Playing Field
Neville Lovett Comm. Sch.
Broadlaw Walk Shopping Centre
West End
THE BOATYARD IND. EST.
Fareham Sailing and Motor Boat Club
Fareham Lake
Club House
Wilderness
SOUTH PARK
Fareham Town FC
212
Cam Alders Sports Centre
Bowls Club
CAMS HALL ESTATE GOLF COURSE
Cunigre Pond
GOSPORT ROAD
56
57
58
59
09
08
07
06

Orchard Copse
Dirty Ground Copse
Wine Cross
SOUTHWICK
179
Tylers Copse
Walton Heath Plantation
Ashlands Plantation
O' Tooles Row
Yewtree Row
Staple Cross
Staversash Copse
Carmans Copse
Staplecross Copse
Lodge Moor
B2177
Walton Heath Cott.
Walton Heath
Walton Heath Cottages
Vernons Farm
Prior's Hold Farm
Lodge Farm
Bere Farm House
Bere Farm
Bucks Copse
Carmans Farm
Lodge Coppice
Friar's Coppice
Gravelhole Copse
Boarhunt Mill
Grub Coppice
Mill Coppice
RIVER
Moor Coppice
Great Breach Row
Ham Coppice
Snow Hill
BRIDGE
Castle Farm
Bridge House
BERRY-MEADOW COTTS
Newman's Bridge
BACK
The Elms
WEST STREET
Ham Farm
Sewage Works
Old Vicarage
SOUTHWICK
Dirtystile Copse
Fareham
Dell Row
Ashleydown Coppice
Newport Farm
Cheeseman's Bridge
Manor Farm
Collier Row
B2177 BY-PASS
Rook's Bridge
BOARHUNT
Ashley Down Farm
Perrige's Coppice
WINCHESTER
FAREHAM
Ashleydown Cottages
Marl Rows
Stroud Coppice
PO17
Watercress Beds
Offwell Farm
ELMS LANE
Damson Row
BOARHUNT ROAD
SWIVELTON LANE
Monument Farm
200
CROOKED
Gas Valve Compound
Reservoir (covered)
Fort Nelson (Royal Armouries)
Visitors Cen.
Mountemoor's Coppice
Junction 11
Nelson Monument
Research Establishment
PORTSDOWN ROAD
HILL ROAD
JAMES CALLAGHAN DRIVE
Chalk Pit
Solent View
Westmore House
The Mount
Carriden
High Tor
PORTS DOWN
Mount Cottage
FAREHAM
PORTSMOUTH
PO16
M27 MOTORWAY
M27
Ellerslie House
Fitness First
Downend
Red Barn Open Space
Dore Avenue Open Space
Northern Inf. Sch.
Northern Jun. Sch.
Winnhams Farm
Cams Bridge
Portchester Crematorium
Red Barn Prim. Sch.
PO6
Portchester
Play. Grd.
PORTCHESTER ROAD
A27
WEST STREET
PORTCHESTER
EAST STREET
SOUTHAMPTON RD.
Wicor Prim. School
Playing Field
213
Playing Fields
Portchester Comm.
Sports Ground Pavilion
CAMS BAY

Fareham
PO17
SOUTHWICK
PAULSGROVE
WYMERING
Lye Heath
PLACE WOOD
HMS DRYAD
Royal Military Police Museum
Southwick House
SOUTHWICK PARK GOLF COURSE
FORT SOUTHWICK
PORTSDOWN
WINCHESTER
PORTSMOUTH
M27 MOTORWAY
B2177
A27
A3
QUEEN ALEXANDRA HOSP.
King Richard School
Paulsgrove Chalk Pit
DSTL Portsdown West
Sewage Works
Moat & Bailey
Ring Work & Bailey Castle
Pigeon House Farm
Roman Road (Course of)
Mitchelland
Vernons Farm
Assells Coppice
Friar's Coppice
Wynn's Copse
Jays Copse
Jays Hummock
Little Belney Copse
Belney Farm
Great Belney Copse
Sheepwash Farms
Hazelhook Coppice
Graysland Hummock
Shorts Coppice
Ward's Coppice
Lyeheath Farm
Rooks Row
Hobern Coppice
Wanstead Farm
Sheep Park Plantation
Playing Field
Sports Ground
Comphouse Moor Coppice
Comphouse Farm
Sawyer's Wood
Hookheath Farm
Greathunts Coppice
Mallin's Coppice
Littlehunts Coppice
Portland Coppice
Broomfield House
Pitymoor Coppice
Pinsley Coppice
Miller's Coppice
Tree Coppice
Pinsley Plantation
Venables Coppice
Bushy Coppice
Potwell Farm
Potwell House
New Barns Farm
New Barns House
Fort Widley
Equestrian Centre
Ashley Dell

180
199
214

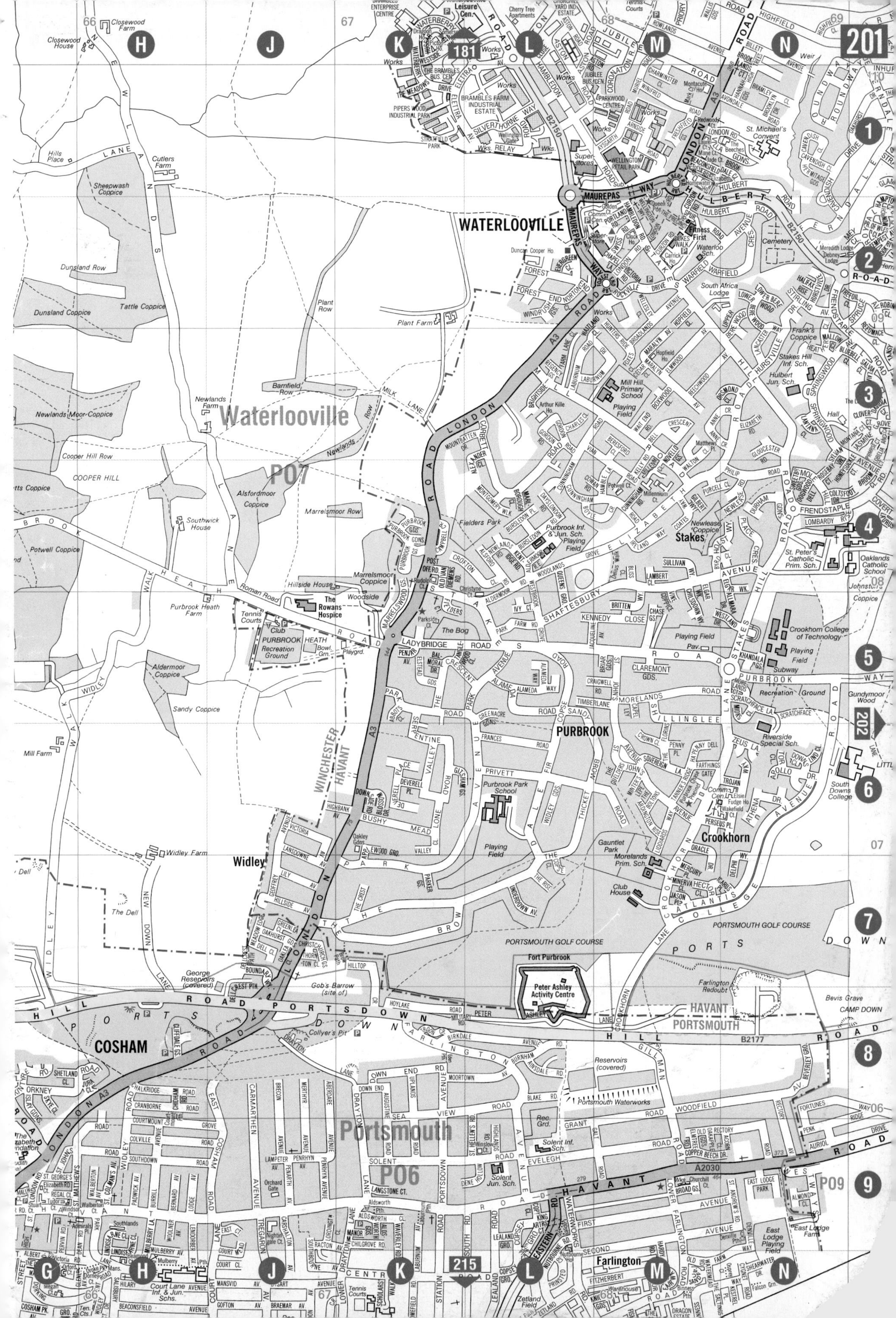
WATERLOOVILLE
Waterlooville
PO7
PURBROOK
Stakes
Crookhorn
Widley
COSHAM
Portsmouth
PO6
PO9
Farlington
PORTSMOUTH GOLF COURSE
Fort Purbrook
Peter Ashley Activity Centre
PORTS DOWN
HAVANT
PORTSMOUTH
WINCHESTER
HAVANT
Newlands Moor Coppice
Cooper Hill Row
COOPER HILL
Dunsland Row
Dunsland Coppice
Tattle Coppice
Sheepwash Coppice
Cutlers Farm
Hills Place
Closewood Farm
Closewood House
Newlands Farm
Alsfordmoor Coppice
Marrelsmoor Row
Southwick House
Potwell Coppice
Purbrook Heath Farm
The Rowans Hospice
Hillside House
Marrelsmoor Coppice
Woodside
PURBROOK HEATH Recreation Ground
Aldermoor Coppice
Sandy Coppice
Mill Farm
Widley Farm
The Dell
Plant Row
Plant Farm
Barnfield Row
Newlands Row
Brambles Farm Industrial Estate
Pipers Wood Industrial Park
Wellington Retail Park
St. Michael's Convent
Cemetery
South Africa Lodge
Frank's Coppice
Stakes Hill Inf. Sch.
Hulbert Jun. Sch.
Mill Hill Primary School
Playing Field
Arthur Kille Ho.
Millennium Ct.
Purbrook Inf. & Jun. Sch.
Fielders Park
Newlease Coppice
St. Peter's Catholic Prim. Sch.
Oaklands Catholic School
Johnston's Coppice
Crookhorn College of Technology
Recreation Ground
Gundymoor Wood
Riverside Special Sch.
South Downs College
Purbrook Park School
Gauntlet Park
Morelands Prim. Sch.
Club House
Gob's Barrow (site of)
George Reservoirs (covered)
Collyer's Pit
Farlington Redoubt
Bevis Grave
CAMP DOWN
Reservoirs (covered)
Portsmouth Waterworks
Rec. Grd.
Solent Inf. Sch.
Solent Jun. Sch.
Court Lane Inf. & Jun. Schs.
East Lodge Farm
East Lodge Playing Field
Zetland Field
LONDON ROAD
A3
B2150
B2177
A2030
PORTSDOWN HILL ROAD
HAVANT ROAD
MAUREPAS WAY
HULBERT ROAD
STAKES ROAD
STAKES HILL ROAD
LADYBRIDGE ROAD
SHAFTESBURY AVENUE
ELIZABETH ROAD
PURBROOK WAY
CROOKHORN LANE
COLLEGE ROAD
SOLENT ROAD
WIDLEY WALK
NEWLANDS LANE
BROOK LANE
HEATH ROAD
MILK LANE
181
202
215
H J K L M N G
1 2 3 4 5 6 7 8 9
66 67 68 69
06 07 08 09
110

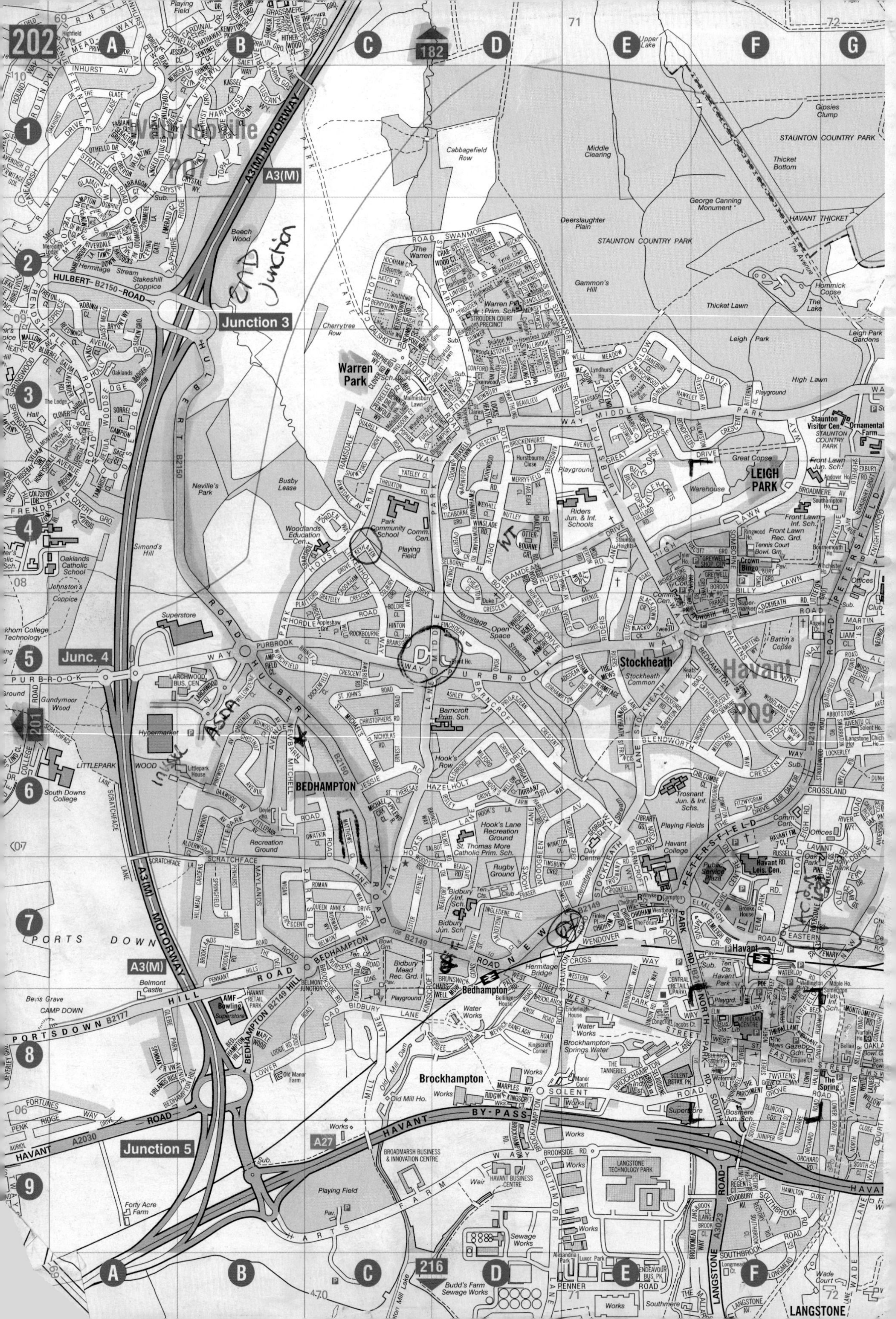
A
B
C
182
D
E
F
G
1
2
3
4
5
6
7
8
9
Waterlooville
PO7
A3(M) MOTORWAY
A3(M)
Junction 3
HULBERT B2150 ROAD
Stakeshill Coppice
Hermitage Stream
Beech Wood
Cherrytree Row
Cabbagefield Row
Middle Clearing
STAUNTON COUNTRY PARK
Gipsies Clump
Thicket Bottom
George Canning Monument
HAVANT THICKET
Deerslaughter Plain
Gammon's Hill
Thicket Lawn
Hammick Copse
The Lake
Leigh Park
Leigh Park Gardens
High Lawn
Staunton Visitor Cen.
Ornamental Farm
Warren Park
Warren Pk. Prim. Sch.
STROUDEN COURT PRECINCT
Great Copse
LEIGH PARK
Warehouse
Front Lawn Jun. Sch.
Front Lawn Inf. Sch.
Front Lawn Rec. Grd.
Tennis Court Bowl. Grn.
Crown Bingo
GREYWELL SHOP. CEN.
Riders Jun. & Inf. Schools
Park Community School
Comm. Cen.
Playing Field
Woodlands Education Cen.
Neville's Park
Busby Lease
Simond's Hill
Oaklands Catholic School
Johnston's Coppice
Superstore
Junc. 4
PURBROOK WAY
Gundymoor Wood
201
LARCHWOOD BUS. CEN.
Hypermarket
LITTLEPARK WOOD
Littlepark House
South Downs College
BEDHAMPTON
Recreation Ground
Hook's Row
Barncroft Prim. Sch.
Stockheath
Stockheath Common
Havant
PO9
Battin's Copse
Trosnant Jun. & Inf. Schs.
Playing Fields
Havant College
Public Service Plaza
Havant Leis. Cen.
Hook's Lane Recreation Ground
St. Thomas More Catholic Prim. Sch.
Rugby Ground
Day Centre
Bidbury Inf. Sch.
Bidbury Jun. Sch.
Bidbury Mead Rec. Grd.
PORTS DOWN
A3(M)
Belmont Castle
Bevis Grave
CAMP DOWN
AMF Bowling
HAVANT RETAIL PARK
BELMONT JUNCTION
Bedhampton
Hermitage Bridge
Water Works
CENTRAL RETAIL PARK
Havant Park
Brockhampton
Brockhampton Springs Water
THE TANNERIES
SOLENT RETAIL PK.
Old Manor Farm
Old Mill Ho.
MARPLES WY.
HAVANT BY-PASS
A27
Junction 5
HAVANT A2030 ROAD
BROADMARSH BUSINESS & INNOVATION CENTRE
HAVANT BUSINESS CENTRE
LANGSTONE TECHNOLOGY PARK
Playing Field
Forty Acre Farm
HARTS FARM WAY
Sewage Works
216
Budd's Farm Sewage Works
ENDEAVOUR BUS. PK.
PENNER ROAD
Bosmere Jun. Sch.
LANGSTONE ROAD A3023
SOUTHBROOK
LANGSTONE
Wade Court
71
72
69
70

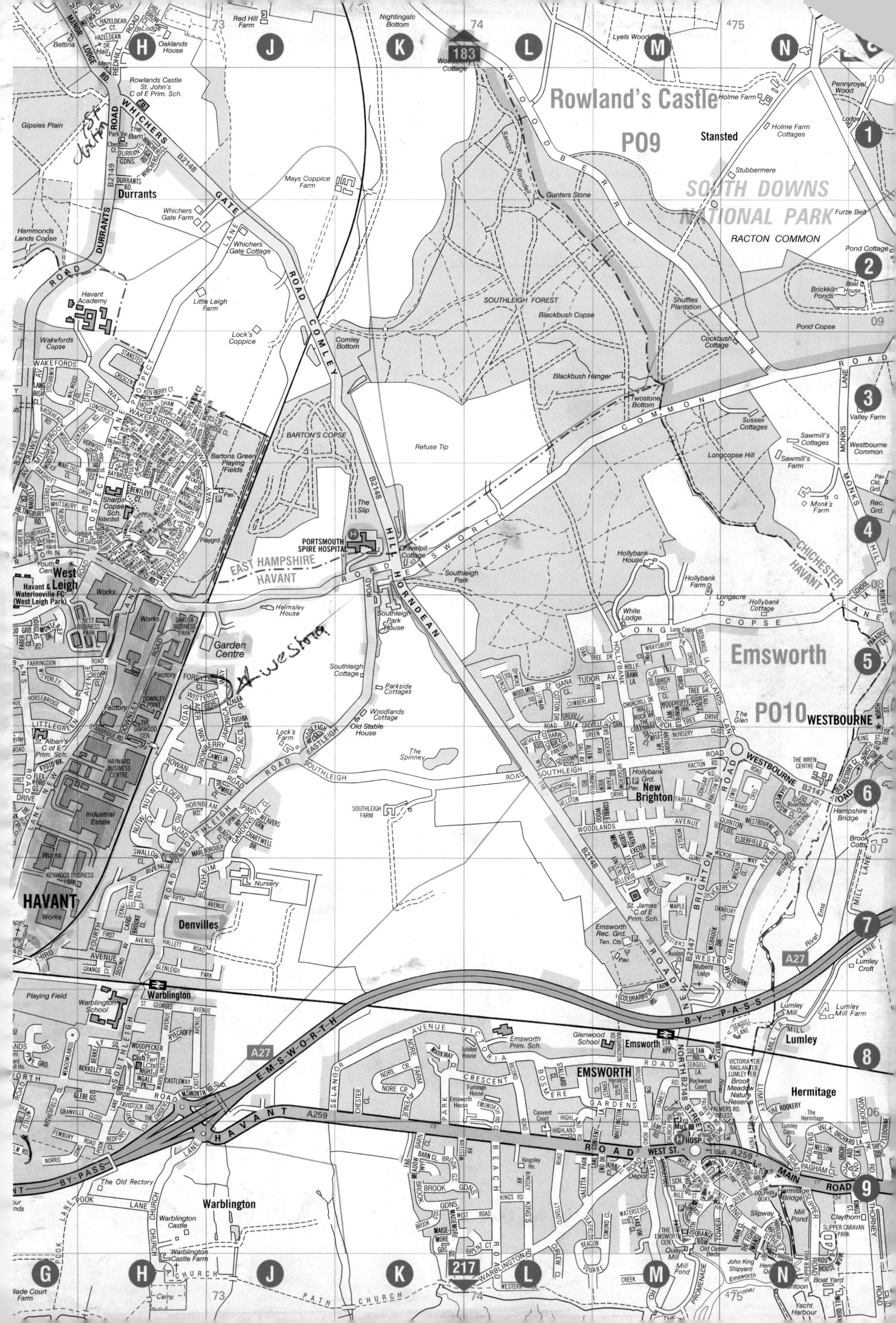

183
217
73
74
475
H
J
K
L
M
N
G
1
2
3
4
5
6
7
8
9
Rowland's Castle
PO9
PO10
Stansted
SOUTH DOWNS NATIONAL PARK
RACTON COMMON
Emsworth
WESTBOURNE
HAVANT
West Leigh
Durrants
Denvilles
New Brighton
Warblington
Lumley
Hermitage
EMSWORTH
Red Hill Farm
Nightingale Bottom
Lyels Wood
Woodberry Cottage
Oaklands House
Rowlands Castle St. John's C of E Prim. Sch.
Gipsies Plain
Mays Coppice Farm
Whichers Gate Farm
Whichers Gate Cottage
Hammonds Lands Copse
Havant Academy
Little Leigh Farm
Lock's Coppice
Wakefords Copse
Comley Bottom
SOUTHLEIGH FOREST
Blackbush Copse
Blackbush Hanger
Gunters Stone
Shuffles Plantation
Cockbush Cottage
Twostone Bottom
Holme Farm
Holme Farm Cottages
Stubbermere
Pennyroyal Wood
Furze Belt
Pond Cottage
Brickkiln Ponds
Boat House
Pond Copse
Valley Farm
Westbourne Common
Sussex Cottages
Sawmill's Cottages
Sawmill's Farm
Longcopse Hill
Monk's Farm
BARTON'S COPSE
Refuse Tip
The Slip
PORTSMOUTH SPIRE HOSPITAL
Gravelpit Cottage
Southleigh Park
Southleigh Park House
Bartons Green Playing Fields
EAST HAMPSHIRE
HAVANT
CHICHESTER
HAVANT
Hollybank House
Hollybank Farm
Longacre
Hollybank Cottage
White Lodge
Helmsley House
Garden Centre
Southleigh Cottage
Parkside Cottages
Woodlands Cottage
Old Stable House
Lock's Farm
The Spinney
SOUTHLEIGH FARM
Nursery
Havant & Waterlooville FC (West Leigh Park)
DAKOTA BUSINESS PARK
NEST BUSINESS PARK
HAYWARD BUSINESS CENTRE
Industrial Estate
KENWOOD BUSINESS PARK
St. Alban's C of E Prim. Sch.
St. James' C of E Prim. Sch.
Emsworth Rec. Grd.
Hampshire Bridge
Brook Cotts
Lumley Croft
Lumley Mill
Lumley Mill Farm
Playing Field
Warblington School
Emsworth Prim. Sch.
Glenwood School
Brook Meadow Nature Reserve
The Old Rectory
Warblington Castle
Warblington Castle Farm
Wade Court Farm
Quay Mill
Mill Pond
John King Shipyard Emsworth
Yacht Harbour
Boat Yard
Slipper Caravan Park
Hermitage Bridge
Mill Pond
A27
A259
B2148
B2149
B2147
WHICHERS GATE ROAD
DURRANTS ROAD
COMLEY HILL
HORNDEAN ROAD
EMSWORTH COMMON ROAD
WOODBERRY LANE
LONG COPSE LANE
SOUTHLEIGH ROAD
WESTBOURNE ROAD
HAVANT ROAD
EMSWORTH BY-PASS
HAVANT BY-PASS
NEW BRIGHTON ROAD
VICTORIA AVENUE
NORTH STREET
WEST ST.
MAIN ROAD
CHURCH PATH

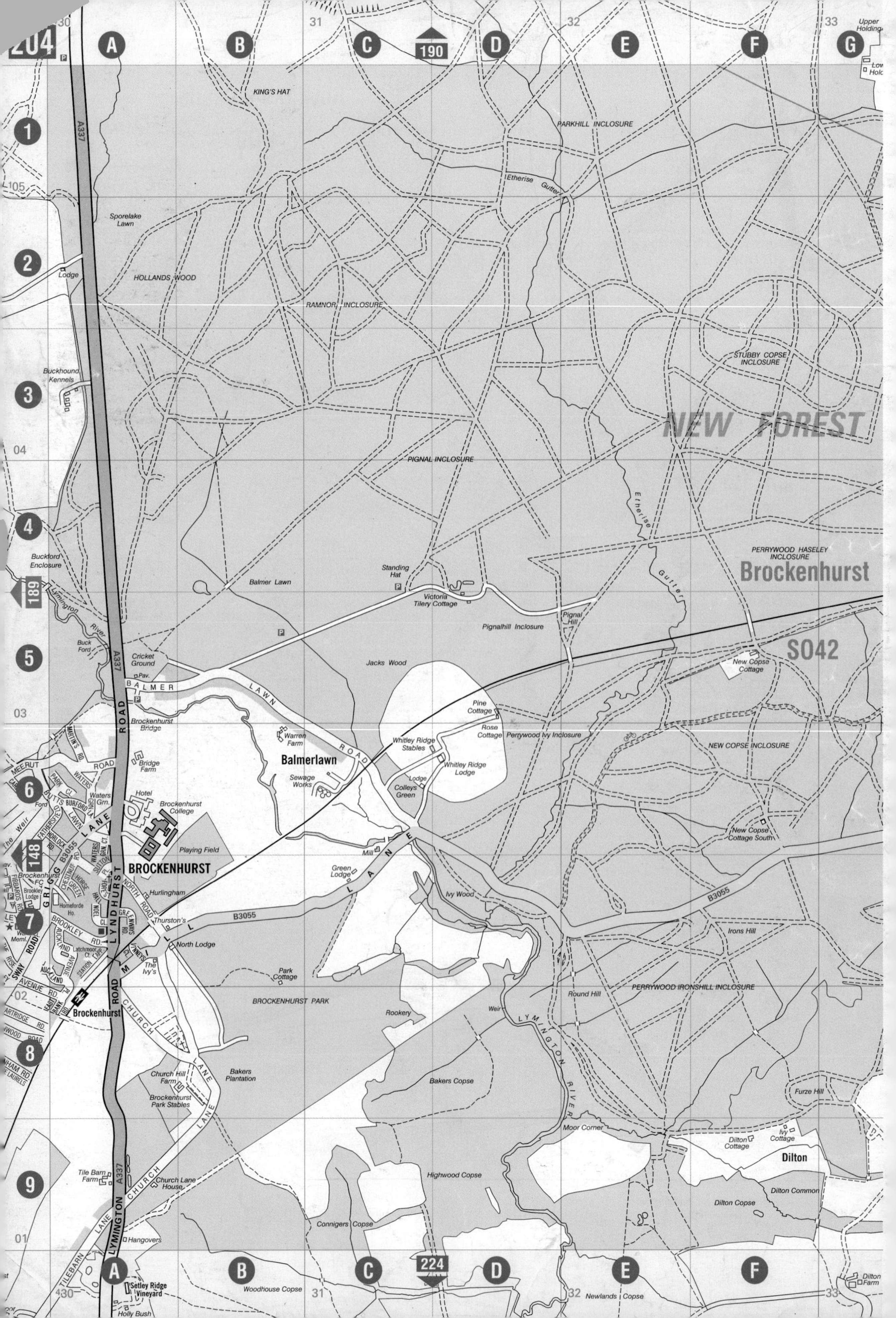
A
B
C
D
E
F
G
190
189
148
224
1
2
3
4
5
6
7
8
9
30
31
32
33
105
04
03
02
01
430
KING'S HAT
PARKHILL INCLOSURE
Etherise Gutter
Sporelake Lawn
HOLLANDS WOOD
RAMNOR INCLOSURE
Lodge
STUBBY COPSE INCLOSURE
Buckhound Kennels
NEW FOREST
PIGNAL INCLOSURE
Etherise Gutter
PERRYWOOD HASELEY INCLOSURE
Brockenhurst
Buckford Enclosure
Standing Hat
Balmer Lawn
Victoria Tilery Cottage
Pignal Hill
Pignalhill Inclosure
Lymington River
Buck Ford
SO42
Cricket Ground
Pav.
Jacks Wood
New Copse Cottage
BALMER LAWN ROAD
A337
Brockenhurst Bridge
Warren Farm
Pine Cottage
Rose Cottage
Perrywood Ivy Inclosure
NEW COPSE INCLOSURE
Whitley Ridge Stables
Whitley Ridge Lodge
Balmerlawn
Sewage Works
Lodge
Colleys Green
Bridge Farm
Hotel
Brockenhurst College
MEERUT ROAD
MARTIN'S RD.
WATERS
PARK CL.
BUTTS
Ford
BURFORD LA.
LAWN
Waters Grn.
The Weir
FATHERSFIELD
HORLOCK RD.
B3055
LANE
Playing Field
BROCKENHURST
New Copse Cottage South
Mill
Green Lodge
MILL LANE
Brockenhurst FC
Brookley Lodge
Homeforde Ho.
GRIGG
Hurlingham
NORTH ROAD
LYNDHURST
Ivy Wood
B3055
Thurston's
B3055
BROOKLEY RD.
Irons Hill
Latchmoor Ct.
North Lodge
SWAY ROAD
AUCKLAND AVENUE
STATION
The Ivy's
Park Cottage
Round Hill
PERRYWOOD IRONSHILL INCLOSURE
AVENUE RD.
Brockenhurst
BROCKENHURST PARK
Weir
ARTRIDGE RD.
ROAD
CHURCH LANE
Rookery
LYMINGTON RIVER
LAURELS
Bakers Plantation
Church Hill Farm
Bakers Copse
Brockenhurst Park Stables
Furze Hill
Moor Corner
Dilton Cottage
Ivy Cottage
Dilton
Tile Barn Farm
Church Lane House
Highwood Copse
Dilton Common
Dilton Copse
LYMINGTON ROAD
A337
TILEBARN LANE
Conniger's Copse
Hangovers
Setley Ridge Vineyard
Woodhouse Copse
Newlands Copse
Dilton Farm
Holly Bush
Upper Holdings
Low Hold

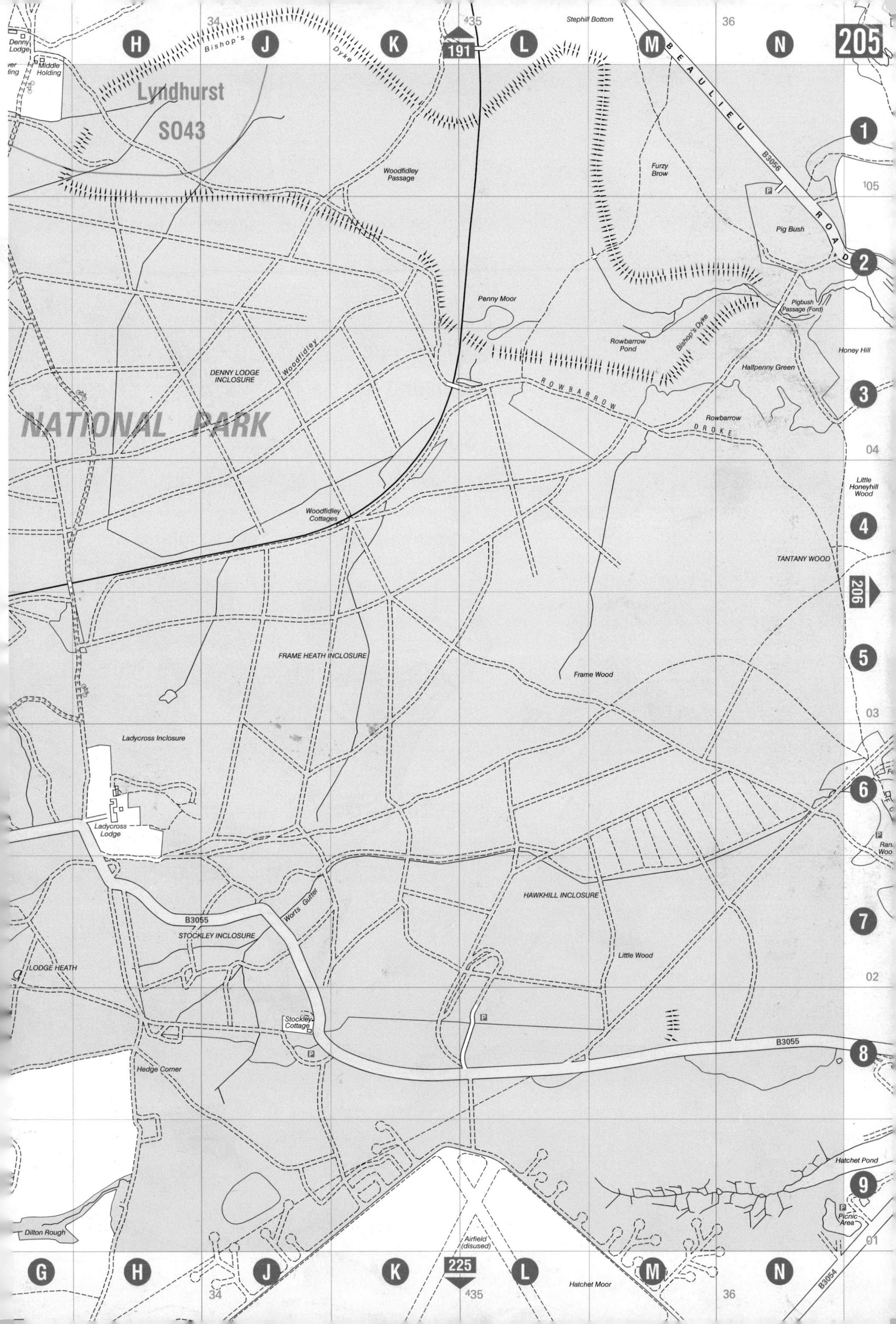
H
J
K
L
M
N
34
435
36
191
Stephill Bottom
Bishop's
Dyke
Denny Lodge
Middle Holding
Lyndhurst
SO43
Woodfidley Passage
BEAULIEU ROAD
B3056
Furzy Brow
105
Pig Bush
Pigbush Passage (Ford)
Penny Moor
Rowbarrow Pond
Bishop's Dyke
Honey Hill
Halfpenny Green
DENNY LODGE INCLOSURE
Woodfidley
ROWBARROW
Rowbarrow
DROKE
NATIONAL PARK
04
Little Honeyhill Wood
Woodfidley Cottages
TANTANY WOOD
206
FRAME HEATH INCLOSURE
Frame Wood
03
Ladycross Inclosure
Ladycross Lodge
HAWKHILL INCLOSURE
B3055
Worts Gutter
STOCKLEY INCLOSURE
LODGE HEATH
Little Wood
02
Stockley Cottage
B3055
Hedge Corner
Hatchet Pond
Picnic Area
Dilton Rough
Airfield (disused)
01
B3054
G
225
Hatchet Moor
1
2
3
4
5
6
7
8
9

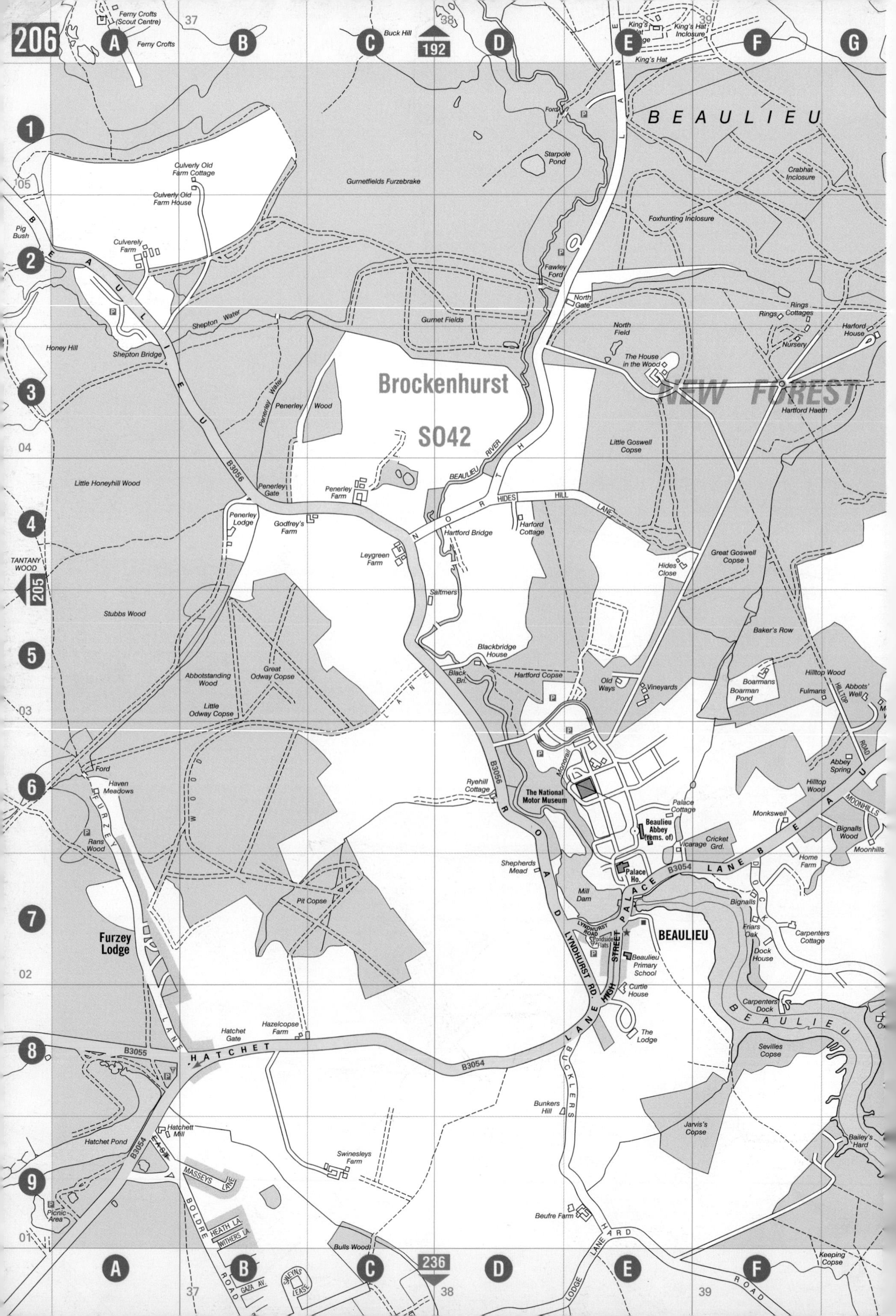

Ferny Crofts (Scout Centre)
Ferny Crofts
Buck Hill
192
King's Hat Inclosure
King's Hat
BEAULIEU
Culverly Old Farm Cottage
Culverly Old Farm House
Gurnetfields Furzebrake
Starpole Pond
Crabhat Inclosure
Foxhunting Inclosure
Pig Bush
Culverely Farm
Fawley Ford
North Gate
Rings Cottages
Rings
Harford House
Nursery
Shepton Water
Gurnet Fields
North Field
The House in the Wood
Honey Hill
Shepton Bridge
Penerley Water
Penerley Wood
Brockenhurst
SO42
NEW FOREST
Hartford Haeth
Little Goswell Copse
Little Honeyhill Wood
B3056
Penerley Gate
Penerley Farm
Beaulieu River
Hides Hill Lane
North
Penerley Lodge
Godfrey's Farm
Hartford Bridge
Harford Cottage
Leygreen Farm
Great Goswell Copse
Hides Close
TANTANY WOOD
205
Saltmers
Stubbs Wood
Baker's Row
Blackbridge House
Abbotstanding Wood
Great Odway Copse
Hartford Copse
Black Br.
Old Ways
Vineyards
Hilltop Wood
Boarmans
Boarman Pond
Fulmans
Abbots' Well
Hilltop Road
Little Odway Copse
Ford
Haven Meadows
Moor Lane
Ryehill Cottage
The National Motor Museum
Monorail
Abbey Spring
Hilltop Wood
Palace Cottage
Monkswell
Moonhills Lane
Furzey Lane
Rans Wood
Beaulieu Abbey (rems. of)
Cricket Grd.
Vicarage
Bignalls Wood
Moonhills
Shepherds Mead
Palace Ho.
B3054
Palace Lane
Beaulieu Lane
Home Farm
Pit Copse
Mill Dam
Bignalls
Dock Lane
Furzey Lodge
Lyndhurst Road
Pondside Flats
High Street
BEAULIEU
Friars Oak
Carpenters Cottage
Beaulieu Primary School
Dock House
Curtle House
Carpenters Dock
Beaulieu
Hatchet Gate
Hazelcopse Farm
The Lodge
Sevilles Copse
B3055
Hatchet
B3054
Hatchet Lane
Bunkers Hill
Bucklers
Hatchett Mill
Hatchet Pond
East
Jarvis's Copse
Swinesleys Farm
Bailey's Hard
Masseys Lane
Picnic Area
Heath La.
Withers La.
Boldre Road
Beufre Farm
Hard Lane
Bulls Wood
Gaza Av.
Sneyns Lease
236
Lodge Lane
Road
Keeping Copse
A
B
C
D
E
F
G
1
2
3
4
5
6
7
8
9
37
38
39
105
04
03
02
01

193
236
208
HEATH
NATIONAL PARK
Buttsash
HARDLEY
Little Holbury
HOLBURY
Hill Top
Otterwood
Southampton
SO45
FAWLEY INCLOSURE
Denny Lodge Walk
Cole's Hole
HYTHE BY-PASS
A326
B3054
Oil Depot
HARDLEY INDUSTRIAL ESTATE
Refuse Tip
CHEVRON BUSINESS PARK
LIME KILN LANE ESTATE
LITTLE HOLBURY PARK HOMES
Reservoir (covered)
Sports Ground
Football Ground
Hardley Bridge (Ford)
Mill Pond
Little Holbury Farmhouse
Stonyford Pond
HOLBURY PURLIEU
Pitts Copse Farm
The Warren
Pitts Copse
Dark Water
Heather Hill
Holbury Manor
Holbury Manor Park
Stonyford Hill Farm
Mount Pleasant Farmhouse
Warren Copse
Ipers Bridge
Ipers Bridge Farm
Rollestone Farm
Rollestone Copse
Green Rollestone Copse
Hilltop Farm
Hilltop Gate
Hilltop House
Moonhills Gate
Moonhills Copse
Cowleys Heath (Nursery)
Otterwood Gate
Otterwood
Otterwood Farm
Cowleys Copse
Stock Water
Stock Copse
KINGS COPSE INCLOSURE
Oxleys Copse
THE HUMMICKS
Stock Bungalow
East Stock Copse
Cuckoo Pens
South Stock Copse
Stock Cottages
Spearbed Copse
Tarks Reach
The Tukal
The River House
Braces Quay
Landing Stage
Landing Stages
Meadow Close Copse
Magazine Fields (Nursery)
Sims Wood
Steerleys Copse
Butney Row
Yard Wood
Miniature Railway
RIVER
The Noads
EXBURY ROAD
SUMMER LANE
COWLEYS LANE
ROLLESTONE RD.
GREEN LANE
PARK LANE
LIME KILN LANE
FAWLEY ROAD
CADLAND RD.
LONG LA.
Playing Field
Manor Inf. Sch.
Depot
Club
Row Down
King's Copse House

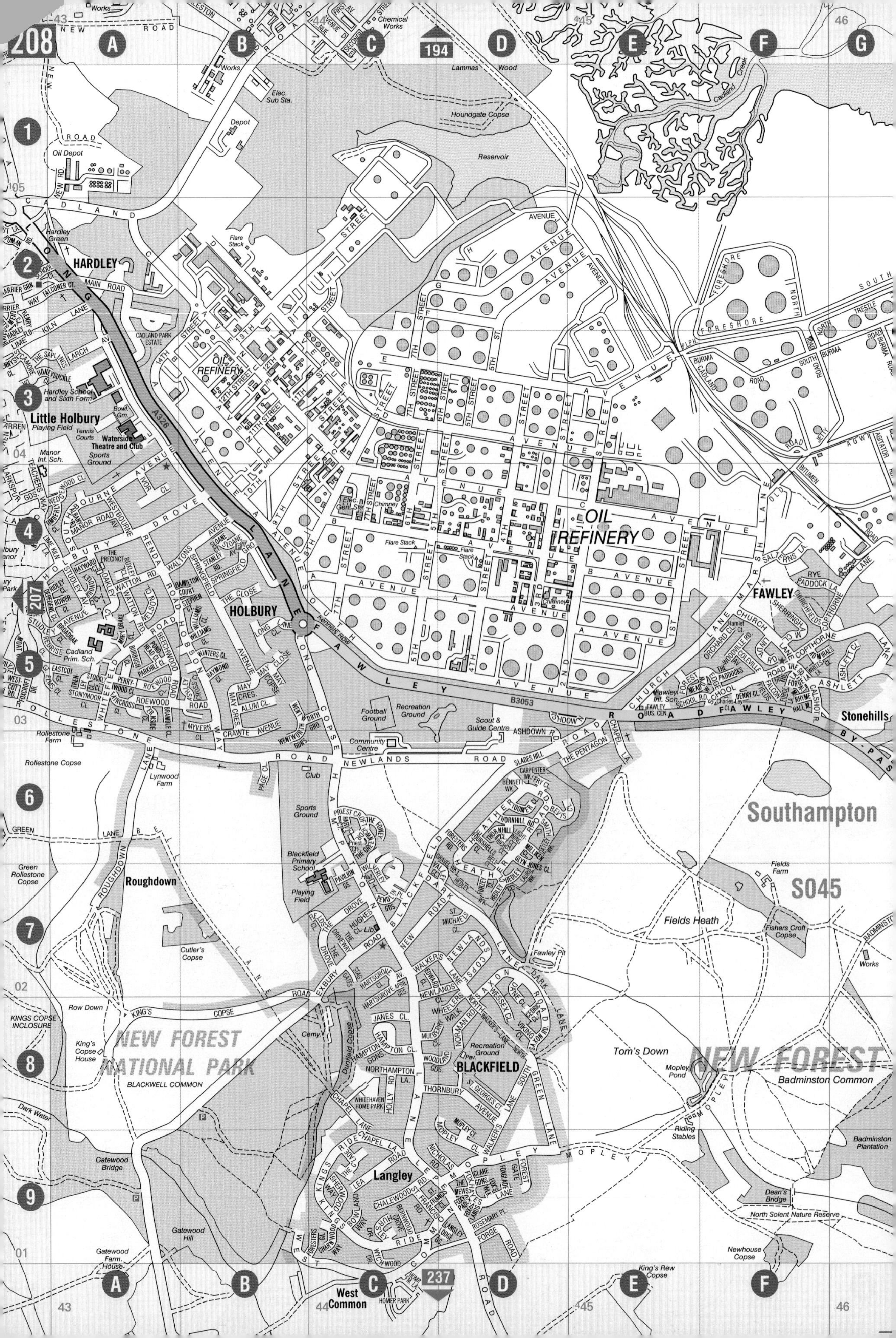
194
207
237
A
B
C
D
E
F
G
1
2
3
4
5
6
7
8
9
43
44
445
46
105
04
03
02
01
NEW ROAD
Works
Chemical Works
Lammas Wood
Elec. Sub Sta.
Depot
Houndgate Copse
Reservoir
Cadland Creek
Oil Depot
CADLAND ROAD
Hardley Green
HARDLEY
MAIN ROAD
CADLAND PARK ESTATE
LONG LANE
A326
OIL REFINERY
Flare Stack
Hardley School and Sixth Form
Little Holbury
Playing Field
Tennis Courts
Waterside Theatre and Club
Sports Ground
Manor Inf. Sch.
FORESHORE
BURMA ROAD
CADLAND ROAD
SOUTH BURMA
TRESTLE ROAD
AGWI
AGITATOR
BITUMEN
JETTY ROAD
Elec. Gen. Sta.
Chimney
HOLBURY
Kennels Row
FAWLEY ROAD
B3053
Cadland Prim. Sch.
ROLLESTONE ROAD
Rollestone Farm
Rollestone Copse
Lynwood Farm
Football Ground
Recreation Ground
Scout & Guide Centre
ASHDOWN RD.
Community Centre
NEWLANDS ROAD
Club
FAWLEY
Fawley Inf. Sch.
FAWLEY BUS. CEN.
FAWLEY BY-PASS
Stonehills
Southampton
S045
Fields Farm
Fields Heath
Fishers Croft Copse
Fawley Pit
Works
Sports Ground
Blackfield Primary School
Playing Field
Roughdown
Green Rollestone Copse
Cutler's Copse
Row Down
KINGS COPSE INCLOSURE
King's Copse House
NEW FOREST NATIONAL PARK
BLACKWELL COMMON
Cemy.
Recreation Ground
BLACKFIELD
Tom's Down
Mopley Pond
NEW FOREST
Badminston Common
Riding Stables
Badminston Plantation
Dark Water
Gatewood Bridge
Langley
Dean's Bridge
North Solent Nature Reserve
Gatewood Hill
Gatewood Farm House
Newhouse Copse
King's Rew Copse
West Common
HOMER PARK
MOPLEY
EXBURY ROAD
LEPE ROAD

SOUTHAMPTON WATER
Southampton Solent University (Warsash Maritime Centre)
Newtown
Hook Park
Hook Bird Sanctuary
Hook Lake
Hamble Spit
EASTLEIGH FAREHAM
Hook with Warsash Nature Reserve
Marine Terminal
Pier
Ashlett
Ashlett Creek
Ashlett Mill
Slipway
Seaclose Copse
Stonehill Farm
Badminston Farm
Chambers Copse
FAWLEY POWER STATION
Swing Bridge
Landing Stage
Landing Pad
Calshot Marshes Bird Sanctuary
Calshot Castle
Calshot Activities Centre
Castle Pier
Ower
Ower House
Ower Farm
NATIONAL PARK
CALSHOT
Sprat's Down
North Solent Nature Reserve
Ower Plantation
M'Lady's Piece
Waterside Youth Centre
Tennis Courts
Hillhead
Spratsdown Plantation
Floating Island
Eaglehurst
Stanswood Common
Little Stanswood Farm
Calshot Foreshore Country Pk.
Luttrells
JACK MAYNARD ROAD
B3053
SO31
195
210
237

Newtown
Hook Park
Hook Park Estate
Hook with Warsash Nature Reserve
Recreation Ground
Little Hook
Hook Farm Cottages
Football Ground
Dibles Bottom
Hook Lake
Mellows
Lane Rec. Ground
HOOK
Nursery
Abshot Manor Country Club
Little Abshot Farm Cottages
Hookhead Coppice
Hookgate Coppice
Nurseries
Holmepond Row
Solent Court Farm
Solent Court
Fish House
Southampton
SO31
Solent Court Cottage
Little Chilling Farm
Beam Cottage
Chilling
Chilling Copse
Tennis Courts
SOLENT BREEZES HOLIDAY VILLAGE
Slipway
Solent Breezes
Outfall
North Heath Coppice
Chilling Moor Coppice
South Leigh Farm
Brownwich Farm
Little Brownwich
Upper Brownwich Farm
Brownwich Pond
Lower Brownwich Farm
Brownwich Farm House
Sea House
HOOK PARK ROAD
HOOK ROAD
HOOK LANE
FLEET END ROAD
WORKMAN'S LANE
CHILLING LANE
COWES LANE
SOLENT DRIVE
BROWNWICH LANE
BROWNWICH
THE SOLENT
450
51
52
105
04
03
02
01
196
209

TITCHFIELD
Great Posbrook
Little Posbrook
Meon
Fareham
PO14
Crabthorn
STUBBINGTON
HILL HEAD
LEE-ON-THE-SOLENT
Lee-on-the-Solent
PO13
Bellfield
Cemetery
Heath Nursery
Road Coppice
Great Posbrooke
Great Posbrooke Farm
Singledge House
The Beeches
Upper Farm
Posbrook Gardens
Meon Bye Farm
Bay Tree Cottage
Little Posbrooke Cottage
Lower Posbrook Farm
Meon Ho.
Thatchers Coppice
Churchers Row
Fouracres Nursery
Elmstead
Cliff Cottage
Meon Marsh
Meon Shore Huts
Titchfield Haven Bird Sanctuary
Titchfield Haven Nature Reserve
Titchfield Haven Nature Reserve Visitor Centre
TITCHFIELD HAVEN
Hillhead Harbour
Hollam Farm
Bowling Green
Hollam House
Hollam Hill Farm
Nursery
RIVER MEON
RSPCA Animal Shelter
Crofton Manor Farm
Meon View Farm
Oxleys Coppice
Peak Lodge
Newlands Farm
Recreation Ground
Meoncross School
Tips Copse
Hellyers Copse
Bay Tree Lodge
Hangar West
Melvin Jones Ho.
Marchesi Ct.
Glamis Ct.
Crofton Anne Dale Inf. & Jun. Schs.
Sea Kings
Rec. Grd.
Comm. Cen.
Crofton Hammond Inf. & Jun. Schs.
Albany Caravan Site
Hammond Industrial Estate
Seafield Park Playing Field
Playing Field
Stubbington Study Centre
Hill Head Sailing Club
Slipway
Crofton Salterns Park
LEE-ON-SOLENT AERODROME
FAREHAM
GOSPORT
HMS DAEDALUS
Solent Vw.
West Lodge
War Memorial
Ten. Cts.
Mus.
Swimming Baths
Southwater
B3334
197
212
COMMON LANE
OCCUPATION LANE
HEATH LA.
POSBROOK LANE
TRIANGLE
MEON ROAD
CLIFF ROAD
COACH HILL
BRIDGE STREET
TITCHFIELD ROAD
RANVILLES LANE
PEAK LANE
LONGFIELD AVENUE
OAKCROFT LANE
MARKS LEY
ST. MARY'S ROAD
MAYS LANE
BURNT HOUSE LANE
STROUD GREEN LANE
GREEN ROAD
CUCKOO LANE
OLD STREET
MARSH LANE
BELLS LANE
THE GROVE
AVENUE ROAD
GOSPORT ROAD
STUBBINGTON LANE
STUBBINGTON GREEN
CRESCENT ROAD
EAST HOUSE AV.
SOUTHWAYS
HILL HEAD ROAD
SALTERN'S LANE
CROFTON LANE
CROFTON AV.
SEA LANE
MARINE PARADE
MONKS WAY
SEAFIELD PARK RD.
OLD FARM LANE
CUTLERS LANE
ERIC ROAD
STUART LANE
MARTIN AV.
IMPLACABLE RD.
EAGLE RD.
RICHMOND RD.
LONGMYND DR.
PROMENADE
Lee Cliffards
G
H
J
K
L
M
N
1
2
3
4
5
6
7
8
9
53
54
455
56
105
04
03
02
01

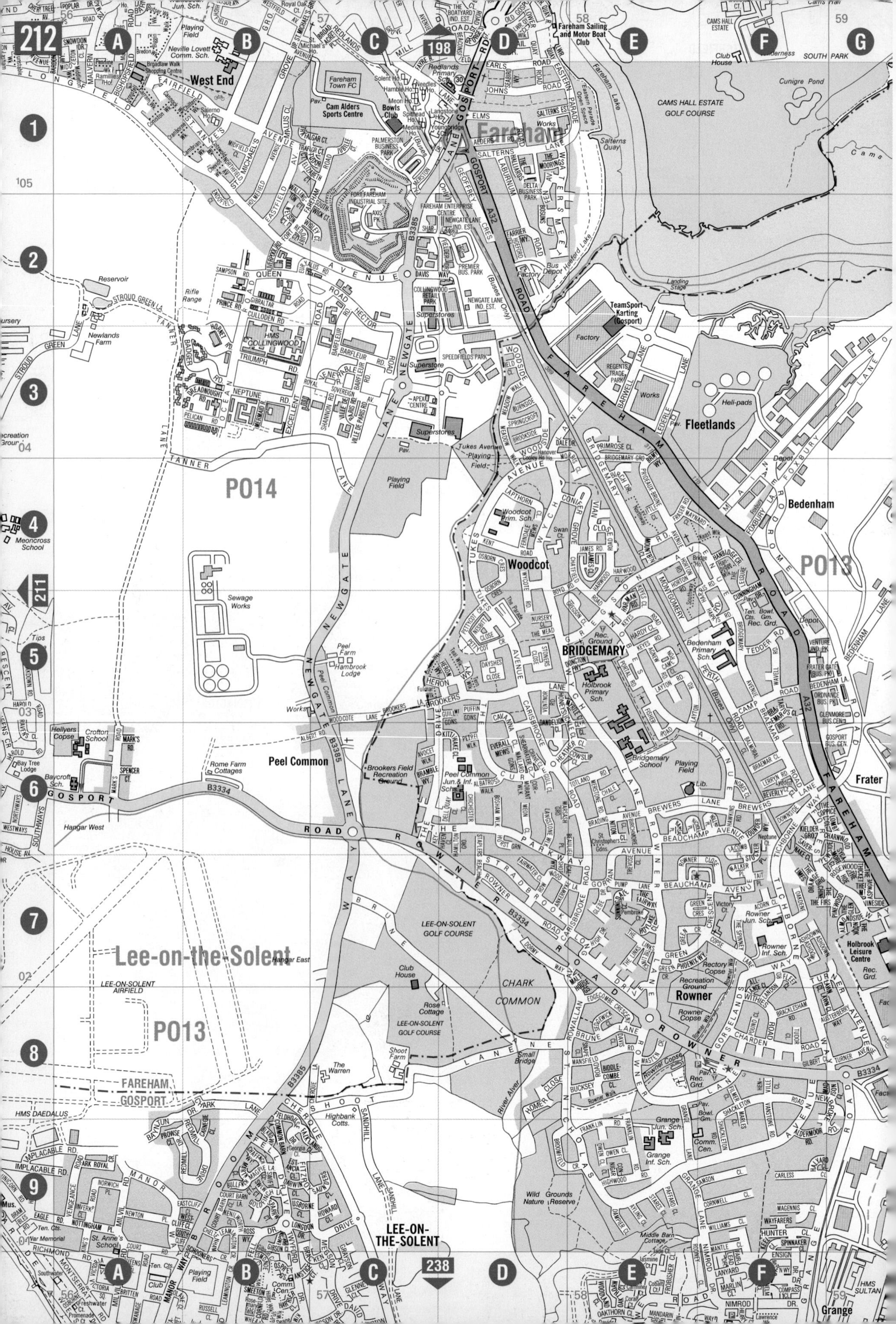

A
B
C
D
E
F
G
1
2
3
4
5
6
7
8
9
56
57
58
59
105
04
03
02
01
198
211
238
West End
Fareham
Fareham Sailing and Motor Boat Club
Cams Hall Estate
Cams Hall Estate Golf Course
Cunigre Pond
South Park
Fareham Lake
Fareham Town FC
Cam Alders Sports Centre
Bowls Club
Palmerston Business Park
Fort Fareham Industrial Site
Fareham Enterprise Centre
Newgate Lane Ind. Est.
Premier Bus. Park
Collingwood Retail Park
Superstores
Superstore
Speedfields Park
Apex Centre
Delta Business Park
Bus Depot
Factory
TeamSport Karting (Gosport)
Regents Trade Park
Works
Heli-pads
Fleetlands
Landing Stage
Reservoir
Rifle Range
Newlands Farm
HMS Collingwood
Queen Avenue
Hector Road
Newgate Lane
Tanner Lane
Stroud Green Lane
Playing Field
Tukes Avenue Playing Field
PO14
PO13
Woodcot
Woodcot Prim. Sch.
Bedenham
Bedenham Primary Sch.
Sewage Works
Meoncross School
Tips
Peel Farm
Hambrook Lodge
Peel Common
Brookers Field Recreation Ground
Peel Common Jun. & Inf. Sch.
BRIDGEMARY
Holbrook Primary Sch.
Bridgemary School
Rec. Ground
Lib.
Frater
Depot
Crofton School
Hellyers Copse
Rome Farm Cottages
Gosport Road
Bay Tree Lodge
Baycroft Sch.
Hangar West
Hangar East
Lee-on-the-Solent
Lee-on-Solent Airfield
Lee-on-Solent Golf Course
Club House
Rose Cottage
Chark Common
Shoot Farm
The Warren
Small Bridge
River Alver
Highbank Cotts.
Fareham
Gosport
HMS Daedalus
Rowner
Rowner Jun. Sch.
Rowner Inf. Sch.
Rectory Copse
Recreation Ground
Rowner Copse
Holbrook Leisure Centre
Grange Jun. Sch.
Grange Inf. Sch.
Comm. Cen.
Wild Grounds Nature Reserve
Middle Barn Cottage
St. Anne's School
War Memorial
Mus.
Lee-on-the-Solent
HMS Sultan
Grange
A32
B3385
B3334
B3333

213
PORTCHESTER
WEST STREET
EAST STREET
SOUTHAMPTON RD.
A27
PO16
Wicor Prim. School
Playing Field
Sports Ground
Pavilion
Birdwood Grove Open Space
CAMS BAY
Cams Lake
Wicor Farm
Seaview Farm
Wicor Lake
Boatyard
Slipway
FAREHAM
PORTSMOUTH
Portchester Comm. Sch.
Playing Fields
Castle Prim. Sch.
Castle Shore Open Space
Recreation Ground
Roman Grove Cemetery
Portchester House
Portchester Castle
Roman Fort (rems.)
Foxbury Point
Tidal Pond
Pewit Island
Spider Lake
Royal Naval Armaments Depot Gosport
Frater Lake
Frater Pier
Elson Wood
GOSPORT
PORTSMOUTH HARBOUR
BOMBKETCH LAKE
FAREHAM LAKE
PORTCHESTER LAKE
FORT ELSON
Gosport
Don Styler Physical Training Centre
HERITAGE WAY
Heritage Business Pk.
Shamrock Enterprise Cen.
Fort Brockhurst
Planet Ice (Gosport)
Brockhurst Ind. Estate
Hardway Sailing Club
Elson
Elson Inf. Sch.
Elson Jun. Sch.
Red Cross HQ
Rec. Grd.
PO12
Hardway
Playing Field
Brune Park Community College
Suncourt Villas
Brockhurst Inf. Sch.
Brockhurst Jun. Sch.
Brockhurst
Prim. Sch.
Camber Basin
Explosion ! The Mus. of Naval Firepower
Priddy's Hard
Reservoir
Waterbus Terminal
Shell Pier
Forton Lake
Rolling Bri.
Burrow Island (site of Fort James)
North Corner
North Railway Jetty
199
214
239
A32

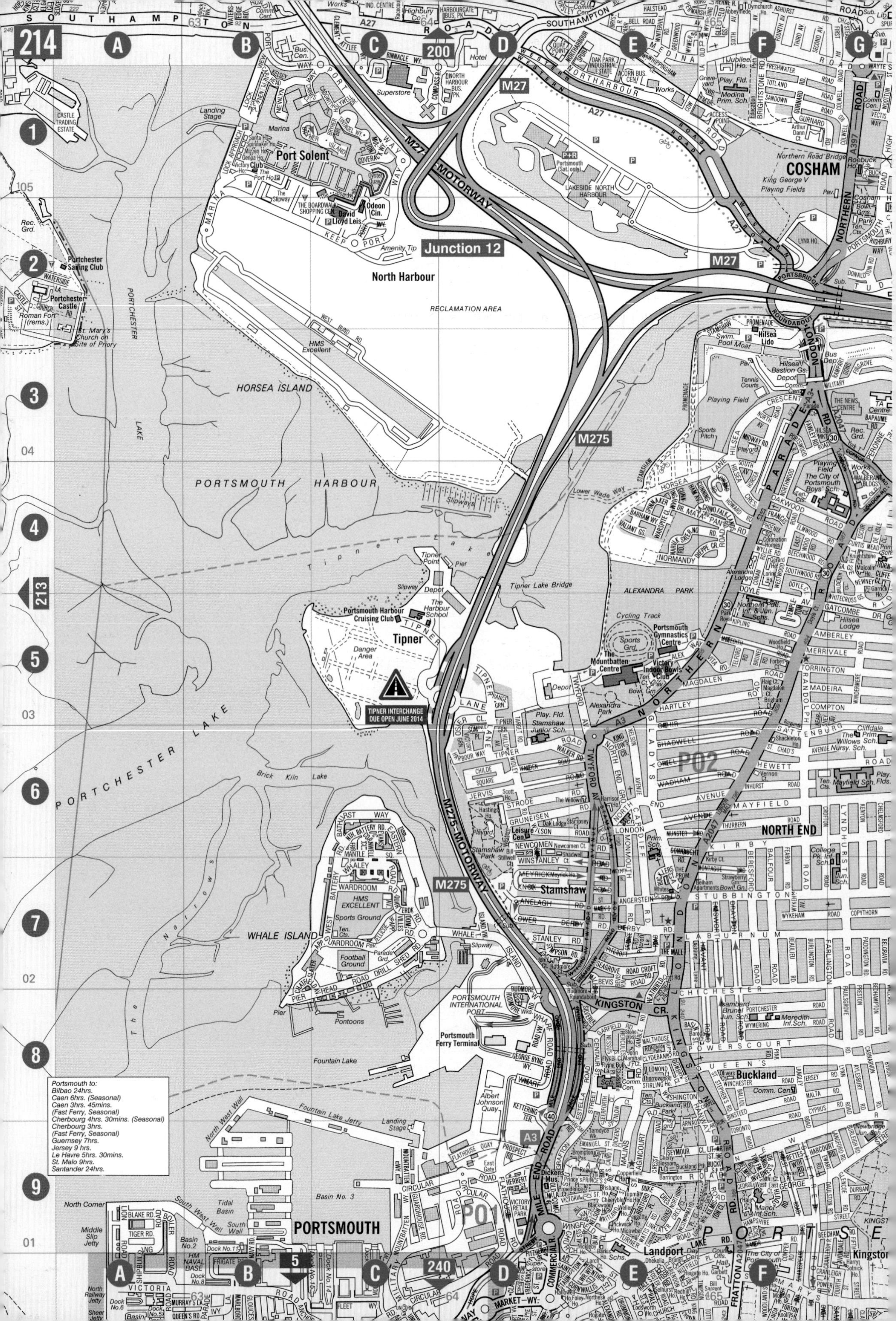
SOUTHAMPTON ROAD
A27
WESTERN ROAD
NORTHARBOUR
M27
M275
M27 MOTORWAY
Junction 12
Port Solent
Marina
Odeon Cin.
David Lloyd Leis.
THE BOARDWALK SHOPPING CEN.
Superstore
Hotel
North Harbour
RECLAMATION AREA
LAKESIDE NORTH HARBOUR
Portsmouth (Sat. only)
COSHAM
King George V Playing Fields
Northern Road Bridge
PORTSBRIDGE ROUNDABOUT
Hilsea Lido
Hilsea Bastion Gs. Depot
Castle Trading Estate
Portchester Sailing Club
Portchester Castle
Roman Fort (rems.)
St. Mary's Church on Site of Priory
PORTCHESTER LAKE
HORSEA ISLAND
HMS Excellent
PORTSMOUTH HARBOUR
Tipner Lake
Tipner Point
Portsmouth Harbour Cruising Club
The Harbour School
Tipner
Danger Area
TIPNER INTERCHANGE DUE OPEN JUNE 2014
Tipner Lake Bridge
ALEXANDRA PARK
Cycling Track
Portsmouth Gymnastics Centre
The Mountbatten Centre
Victory Indoor Bowls Club
Brick Kiln Lake
The Narrows
WHALE ISLAND
HMS EXCELLENT
Sports Ground
Football Ground
Stamshaw
Stamshaw Park
Leisure Cen.
NORTHERN ROAD
LONDON ROAD
KINGSTON ROAD
P02
NORTH END
PORTSMOUTH INTERNATIONAL PORT
Portsmouth Ferry Terminal
Fountain Lake
Fountain Lake Jetty
Albert Johnson Quay
North West Wall
South West Wall
Tidal Basin
Basin No. 3
HM NAVAL BASE
PORTSMOUTH
P01
Buckland
Landport
MILE END ROAD
COMMERCIAL R.
PORTSEA
Kingston
Portsmouth to:
Bilbao 24hrs.
Caen 6hrs. (Seasonal)
Caen 3hrs. 45mins.
(Fast Ferry, Seasonal)
Cherbourg 4hrs. 30mins. (Seasonal)
Cherbourg 3hrs.
(Fast Ferry, Seasonal)
Guernsey 7hrs.
Jersey 9hrs.
Le Havre 5hrs. 30mins.
St. Malo 9hrs.
Santander 24hrs.
200
213
240
5

201
216
241
Cosham
Drayton
Farlington
Hilsea
Hilsea Lines
Portsmouth
Copnor
Baffins
P06
P03
A27
A2030
A288
HAVANT BY PASS
EASTERN ROAD
FARLINGTON MARSHES
(Nature Reserve)
LANGSTONE HARBOUR
MALLARD SANDS
Sword Sands
Sword Point
Farlington Sports Ground
St. John's College Playing Fields
GREAT SALTERNS GOLF COURSE
GREAT SALTERNS RECREATION GROUND
Great Salterns Quay
Great Salterns Mansion
Great Salterns Lake
Tudor Sailing Club
Kendalls Wharf
New Milton Fishery
Seamus Pond
Lincolns Pond
Broom Channel
Mallard Lake
Salterns Lake
Shut Lake
Sluice Lake
Russell's Lake
Frog Lake
Duck Lake
Milton Lake
Milton Common
Baffins Pond
Rugby Camp Playing Field
Roko Health & Fitness
Admiral Lord Nelson School
Portsmouth College
Goals Soccer Cen.
Dundas Meadow Recreation Ground
Burrfields Retail Park
Highbury Prim. Sch.
Highbury College
Redwood Park School
Springfield School
Court Lane Inf. & Jun. Schs.
Copnor Inf. & Jun. Schs.
Langstone Jun. Sch.
Westover Prim. Sch.
Cosham Junc.
Drayton Park
Farlington Junction
Portcreek Junction
LivingWell Fitness Club
Superstores
Superstore
HMP Kingston
PORTSMOUTH HAVANT
HAYLING ISLAND
Cemetery
G H J K L M N
1 2 3 4 5 6 7 8 9
67 68 69
05 04 03 02 01

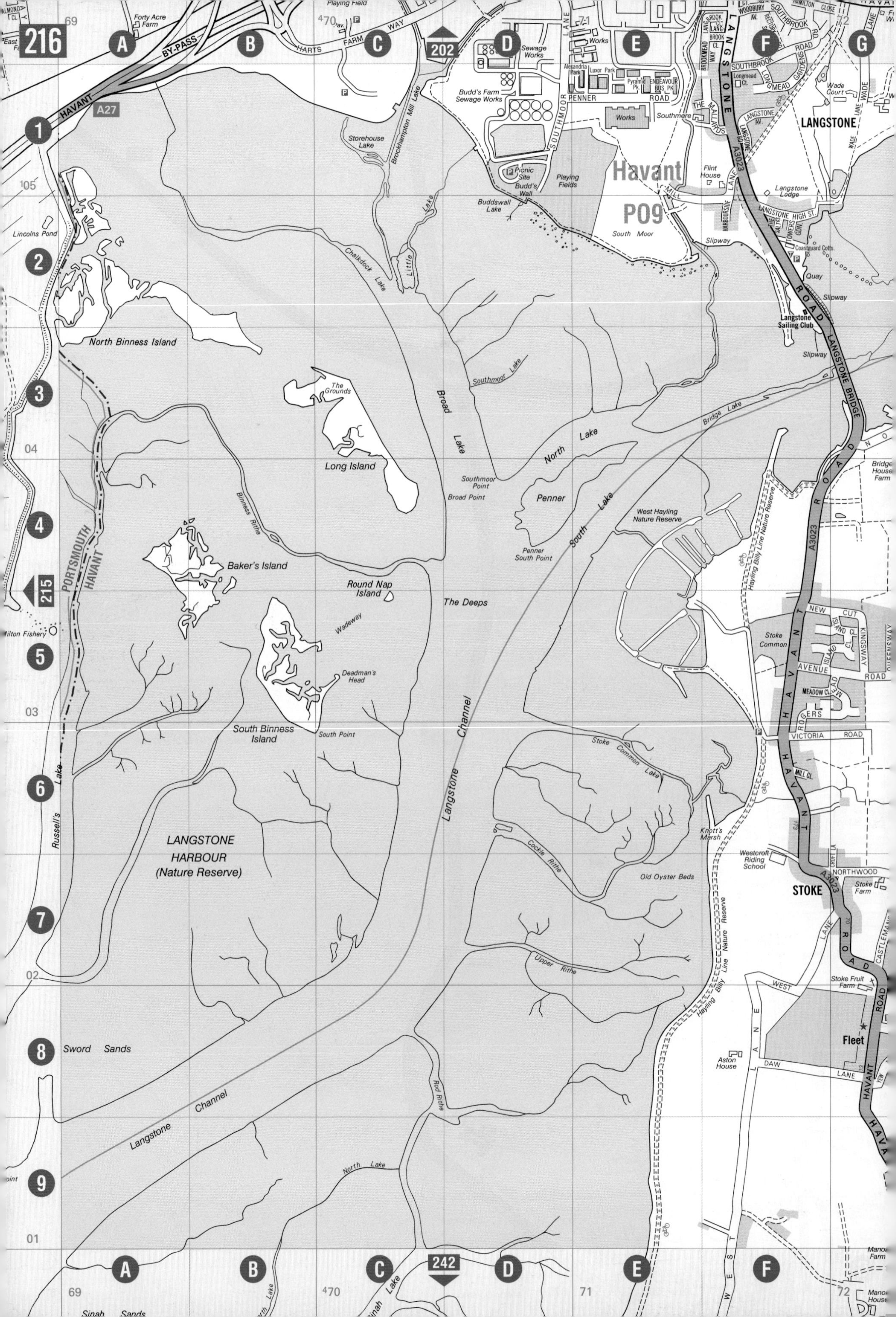
HAVANT BY-PASS
A27
HARTS FARM WAY
Forty Acre Farm
Playing Field
Sewage Works
Budd's Farm Sewage Works
Alexandra Park
Luxor Park
Pyramid Pk.
ENDEAVOUR BUS. PK.
PENNER ROAD
SOUTHMOOR LANE
Works
Southmere
THE MALLARDS
LANGSTONE
Havant
PO9
Playing Fields
Picnic Site
Budd's Wall
Buddswall Lake
Storehouse Lake
Brockhampton Mill Lake
Little Lake
Chalkdock Lake
South Moor
Flint House
MILL LANE
HARBOURSIDE
SOUTHBROOK
WOODBURY AV.
LONGMEAD GARDENS
Wade Court
WADE LANE
LANGSTONE AV.
Langstone Lodge
LANGSTONE HIGH ST.
Coastguard Cotts.
Quay
Slipway
Langstone Sailing Club
LANGSTONE ROAD
A3023
LANGSTONE BRIDGE
Lincolns Pond
North Binness Island
The Grounds
Long Island
Broad Lake
Southmoor Lake
North Lake
Bridge Lake
Southmoor Point
Broad Point
Penner
Penner South Point
South Lake
West Hayling Nature Reserve
Hayling Billy Line Nature Reserve
Bridge House Farm
Binness Rithe
Baker's Island
PORTSMOUTH HAVANT
Milton Fishery
Round Nap Island
The Deeps
Wadeway
Deadman's Head
South Binness Island
South Point
Langstone Channel
Stoke Common
NEW CUT
ISLAND CL.
KINGSWAY
QUEENSWAY
AVENUE ROAD
MEADOW CL.
ROGERS
VICTORIA ROAD
MILL CL.
Stoke Common Lake
Russell's Lake
LANGSTONE HARBOUR (Nature Reserve)
Knott's Marsh
Cockle Rithe
Old Oyster Beds
Westcroft Riding School
STOKE
NORTHWOOD
Stoke Farm
HAVANT ROAD
Upper Rithe
WEST LANE
Stoke Fruit Farm
CASTLEMAN
Fleet
DAW LANE
Aston House
Sword Sands
Rod Rithe
North Lake
Manor Farm
Sinah Sands
Sinah Lake
215
202
242
A B C D E F G
1 2 3 4 5 6 7 8 9
69 470 71 72
05 04 03 02 01

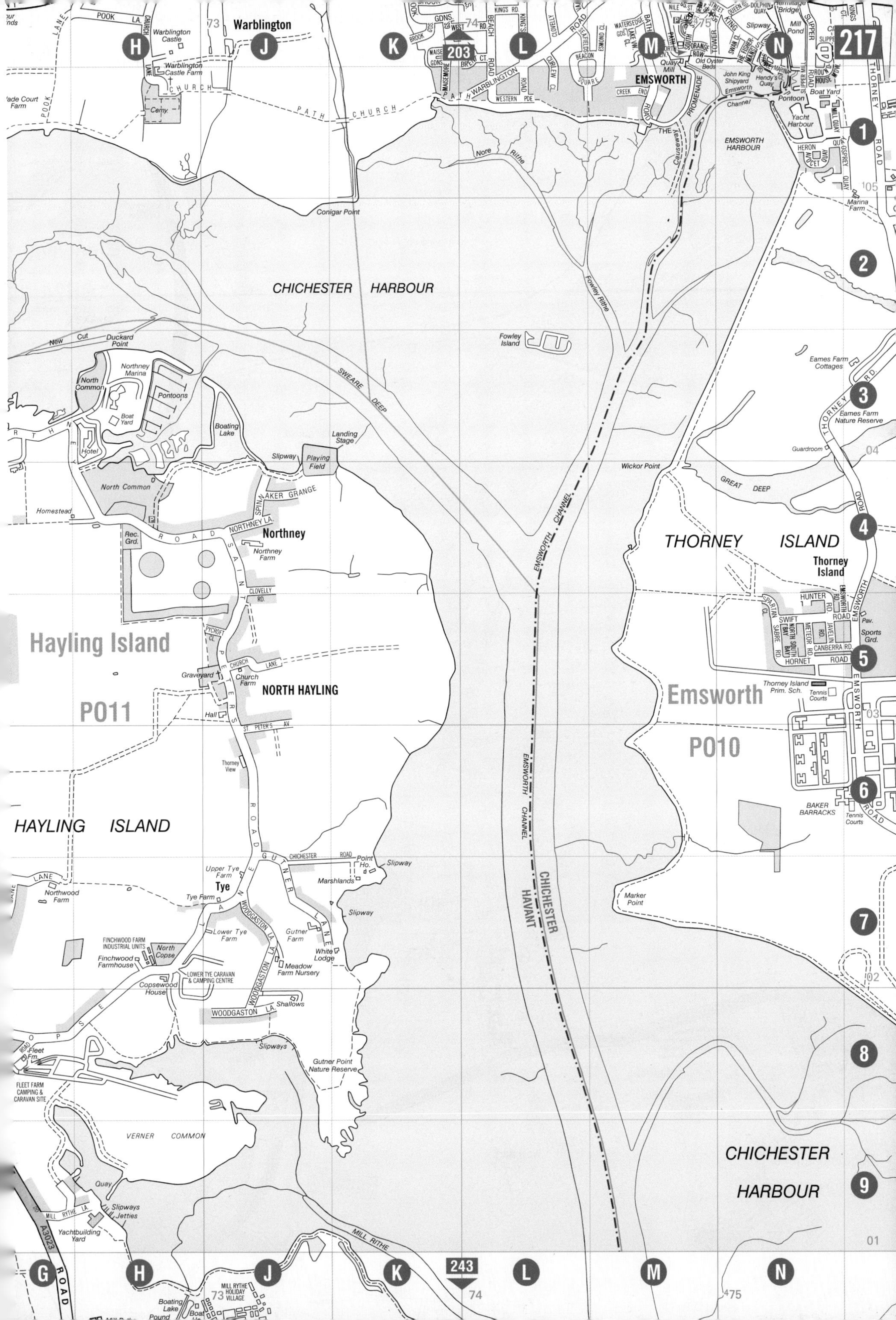

Warblington
Warblington Castle
Warblington Castle Farm
Cemy.
POOK LA.
CHURCH PATH
WARBLINGTON
EMSWORTH
Emsworth Channel
EMSWORTH HARBOUR
Yacht Harbour
Pontoon
Boat Yard
Slipway
Mill Pond
Hermitage Bridge
Quay Mill
Old Oyster Beds
John King Shipyard
Hendy's Quay
Marina Farm
THORNEY ROAD
Conigar Point
Nore Rithe
CHICHESTER HARBOUR
Fowley Rithe
Fowley Island
New Cut
Duckard Point
SWEARE DEEP
Northney Marina
North Common
Pontoons
Boat Yard
Hotel
Boating Lake
Landing Stage
Playing Field
Slipway
Homestead
SPINNAKER GRANGE
NORTHNEY LA.
Northney
Northney Farm
Rec. Grd.
CLOVELLY RD.
PYCROFT CL.
Hayling Island
Graveyard
Church Farm
CHURCH LANE
NORTH HAYLING
Hall
ST PETER'S AV
PO11
Thorney View
SAINT PETERS ROAD
HAYLING ISLAND
Eames Farm Cottages
Eames Farm Nature Reserve
Guardroom
Wickor Point
GREAT DEEP
EMSWORTH CHANNEL
THORNEY ISLAND
Thorney Island
HUNTER RD.
SWIFT
CANBERRA RD.
HORNET ROAD
Pav.
Sports Grd.
Thorney Island Prim. Sch.
Tennis Courts
Emsworth
PO10
BAKER BARRACKS
Tennis Courts
Marker Point
CHICHESTER HAVANT
CHICHESTER ROAD
Point Ho.
Slipway
Marshlands
Upper Tye Farm
Tye
Tye Farm
Northwood Farm
GUTNER LANE
Gutner Farm
White Lodge
Lower Tye Farm
FINCHWOOD FARM INDUSTRIAL UNITS
North Copse
Finchwood Farmhouse
LOWER TYE CARAVAN & CAMPING CENTRE
Copsewood House
Meadow Farm Nursery
WOODGASTON LA.
Shallows
Fleet Fm.
FLEET FARM CAMPING & CARAVAN SITE
Slipways
Gutner Point Nature Reserve
VERNER COMMON
Quay
Slipways Jetties
MILL RYTHE LA
Yachtbuilding Yard
A3023 ROAD
MILL RITHE
MILL RYTHE HOLIDAY VILLAGE
Boating Lake
Pound
CHICHESTER HARBOUR
G H J K L M N
203
243

MATCHAM'S PARK
186
High Harbour
Ringwood Raceway
Matchams Karting
Matchams Leisure Park
FOXBURY
Test Track
Foxbury Hill
HEATH ROAD
BARNSFIELD HEATH
HURN FOREST
Fir Grove Farm
Fir Grove Copse
Moors River
Keys Copse
WEST HEATH ROAD
WATERMAIN
EAST DORSET
CHRISTCHURCH
Longfield
LONGFIELD CARAVAN SITE
Bostwick Farm
TALL TREES CARAVAN PARK
Ebley
Barnsfield Heath
Snowtrax Outdoor Activity Centre
Kellsacre
PLANTATION
Pumping Station
Week Wood
A338
Ringwood
BH24
WATTONS LANE
Week Farm
Week Common
HURN FOREST
PORT VIEW CARAVAN PARK
Avon Common
Ventura
The Mount
MOUNT PLEASANT CAMPING PARK
Fillybrook
Causeway
Tory's Firs
Pithouse Copse
HGV Training Centre
Works
Tank
Rifle Range
NORTH EAST SECTOR
AVIATION PARK
Flying Club
NORTH WEST INDUSTRIAL AREA
AVIATION PARK WEST
AVIATION BUS. PK.
ENTERPRISE WAY
ENTERPRISE WY.
East Parley
BOURNEMOUTH AIRPORT
Sewage Works
Control Tower
SOUTH EAST SECTOR
MCINTYRE RD.
BRACKLEY CL.
THEOBOLD RD.
River Ct.
PUSSEX
Airport Terminal
College of Air Traffic Control
Troublefield Nature Reserve
Troublefield Cottage
Troublefield Copse
Government Offices
MOORS CLOSE
MATCHAMS LANE
Sopley Common (Nature Reserve)
CAUSEWAY
PITTHOUSE
PARLEY LANE
B3073
PARLEY GOLF COURSE
Club House
Driving Range
Bounds Farm
Adventure Wonderland
Bournemouth Aviation Museum
MERRITOWN LANE
Merritown Farm
Merritown
Merritown Copse
DALES LANE
Dales House
HURN COURT LANE
Hillside Cotts
West Hurn
Hurn Court Farm
HURN
Greywell
Humbridge Farm
Hurn Br.
MILL LANE
AVON
Christchurch FC
Hurn Bridge Sports Club
The Dorset Cricket Centre
Brickfield Cottage
CHRISTCHURCH ROAD
Mill Copse
Home Farm
Ramsdown Plantation
Rams Down
Dudmoor Farm
CHRISTCHURCH
BOURNEMOUTH
RIVER STOUR
Bournemouth
BH8
Sewage Works
Berry Hill
Barry Hill
228
HURN COURT LANE
North Lodge
Park Cottages
Quomp Copse

NEW FOREST NATIONAL PARK
BISTERNE
The Parsonage
Parsonage Wood
Sports Ground
Alder Bed Copse
Three Corner Copse
Lockyer's Copse
Copse
187
The Warren
Lower Side Copse
Long Plantation
Bisterne Manor
Gardens Cottage
Broad Heath
The Old Kennels
Ripley Wood
Hain Hill
Lower Ring
Ringwood Lodge
B3347
Lower Bisterne
Lower Bisterne Farm
North End Copse
North End Farm
NORTH END LANE
Bunnybrook
Furzy Piece
Tyrrell's Ford
Summergates
Pigshoot Farm
Pigshoot Bri.
Reed Cottage
North Ripley
North Ripley Farm
Ball's Copse
RIVER AVON
NEW FOREST
EAST DORSET
Watermeadows
Slape Copse
Sabines Farm
The Cot
Sabines Cott.
Avon Tyrrell Farm
Ford
Tinker's Copse
Tinkers Farm
Ripley Plantations
Burnett's Wood
The Old Manor Fm. House
London Farm
LONDON LA
Avon
Salway's Plantation
Middle Ripley Farm
South Ripley Farm
Ripley
FISH STREET
Sopley Prim. Sch.
220
Furzy Copse
Hackthorn Plantation
Coronation Cottages
Long Acre Plantation
Twobridges Plantation
Parsonage Farm
Pithouse Farm
PITHOUSE LANE
Ford
Dairyfarm House
Valley Farm
Christchurch
Pithouse Cottage
Lord's Piece
Court Farm
Whitcher's Plantation
Wright's Orchard
New Barn House
Avon Causeway Bri.
BH23
Dayman's Wood
AVON CAUSEWAY
RINGWOOD ROAD
Cemy.
LANE
Tole Cottage
Bramblewood
Watermeadows
PRIEST LANE
RIVER AVON
MEADOW CL
Priest Ho.
NEW FOREST
CHRISTCHURCH
Clockhouse Copse
SOPLEY
DERRITT LANE
Sopley Farm
Town Common
Mill Race
Sopley Farm Buildings
Morden
HARPWAY LANE
Lower Clockhouse Farm
ROAD
SALISBURY ROAD B3347
Sopley Park
Moorlands College
Sopley Mill
Ford
229
Winkton Acre
BURLEY
Holfleet
BOCKHAMPTON RD.
H J K L M N
G H J K L M N
1 2 3 4 5 6 7 8 9
14 415 16 17
01 100 99 98 097

BISTERNE COMMON
188
Dur Hill Inclosure
DUR HILL DOWN
LUGDEN BOTTOM
Hain Hill
Lower Ring
Ringwood Lodge
Whitefield Hill
Fortune Centre
Hillside Farm
Avon Tyrrell Activity Centre
Tennis Courts
Tyrells Farmhouse
Snag Grounds
White Lodge
Cross Ways
Vernon Dene
North Ripley
Blackberry Farm
Sunny Croft
Brookfield Farm
Stignall's Copse
Martins View
Black Firs
Fish Pond
Whistlers Copse
New Whistlers Copse
Scout Camp
Shirley Common
Christchurch
BH23
THORNEY HILL
Bungalow Farm
Lane End Farm
North Braggers
Kings Braggers
Purlieu
Shepherd's Crown
WILLOW LANE
NEW FOREST
Vatchers Farm
Burnett's Wood
Martin's Copse
Coules Farm
Shirley House
Shirley Farm
Holmy Copse
Hill Farm
Shirley
THATCHERS LANE
Legg's Row
Prink's Wood
Howen Copse
Stibb's Copse
DIAL CL.
Jopps Plantation
Elmers Copse
Burnt House Farm
BURNT HOUSE LANE
POORS COMMON
Nursery
MacPennys Woodland Garden
Playing Field
New Merryfield Farm
Bransgore House
Oaktree Pde.
RINGWOOD ROAD
Merryfield Farm
New Barn House
DERRITT LANE
BRANSGORE
Pavilion
War Meml.
Harrow Wood Farm
HARROW WOOD FARM CARAVAN PARK
Harrow Wood Pond
Harrow Wood
Barrett's Copse
Hall
Playing Field
River Mude
Bransgore C of E Prim. Sch.
Harrow Farm Cottage
Harrow Farm
Holmsley South
The Old Vicarage
Higher Clockhouse Farm
BURLEY ROAD
North Bockhampton
Bockhampton Corner
Waterhouse Farm
HARROW ROAD
Harrow House
COLBORNES
Clockhouse Copse
Marigold Cottage
Beehive Farm
At Last
Neacroft
Lower Clockhouse Farm
Ladbrook Villa
NEW FOREST
CHRISTCHURCH
Middle Bockhampton
Little Harrow
Bockhampton Farm
The Dairy House
CHISELS LA.
Godwinscroft
LYNDHURST ROAD
New Close Farm
230
New Close
219
BOCKHAMPTON ROAD
HAWTHORN RD.

Ringwood
BH24
BH25
New Milton
Ossemsley
Heathfield
Beckley
NATIONAL PARK
HOLMSLEY RIDGE
WHITTEN BOTTOM
Holmsley Lodge
Thorney Hill Holms
DEVILS DEN
Oakhanger
Thorneywood Farm
Thorneywood
PIGSTY HILL
Pigsty Hat
Great Hat
STONY MOORS
Bell's Hat
Black Slop
Holmsley Caravan & Camping Site
HOLMSLEY INCLOSURE
Avon Water
Hanging Shoot
Holmsley Toll House
Saw Mill
STATION ROAD
A35
PLAIN HEATH
FOREST ROAD
Nature Reserve
Tothill
Tothill Cottages
Hill Farm House
Heathfield Caravan Park
Heathfield Farm Cottage
Heathfield Farm
Waverley House
Forest Lodge
BROWNHILL INCLOSURE
Brownhill Lodge
Copper Mead Farm
Wootton Old Farm
Lobbs Hole Farm
Lobbs Hole Copse
BROWNHILL ROAD
Treetops
Rhinefield Farm
RHINEFIELD ROAD
WOOTTON FARM ROAD
WILVERLEY ROAD
HOLMSLEY ROAD
B3058
LITTLE WOOTTON INCLOSURE
Forest Mead
Wattons Farm
Manor Farm
Irongate
DRIVE
Big Rough
Oaklands
Badgers
Poultry Houses
Portnalls Farm
Willie's Holms
Scroy House
GREEN LANE
OSSEMSLEY BRAKE
HOLE COPSE
Walkford
Jone's Covert
OSSEMSLEY SOUTH DR.
NORTH DRIVE
Forest
THE LEG
BEECH CLOSE
NEW CROFT COPSE
BRAMBLE COPSE
HOME CLOSE
North Hinton Farm
HOLM HILL LANE
Brook
Two Acres
Locksbridge Copse
Blackstocks
Long Meadow
DRIVE
SOUTH DRIVE
Dairy Cottage
Stable Cottages
Ossemsley Fields
THE SHRUBBERY
Lynwood Farm
Estate Farm
Bashley Copse
WOOD
NORTH HINTON PARK
Shears
SHEARS WOOD
Keeper's Lodge
Eastclose Copse
East Close Farm
Ossemsley Manor House
Knightsholme
OSSEMSLEY COPSE
BECKLEY COMMON
Ames Cottage
Glen Cottage
The Dell House
White Cottage
Nursery Cottage
Stags Farm
Warwick Farm House
GLENDENE PARK
WESTWOODS PARK
Hobbs Plantation
White's Plantation
Hobbs Copse
GREEN LANE
BASHLEY
Beckley Bridge
CROSS B3055 ROAD
NEW LANE
STEM LA.
Bashley Wild Ground
188
231
222
H J K L M N G
1 2 3 4 5 6 7 8 9
21 22 23
01 100 99 98 097

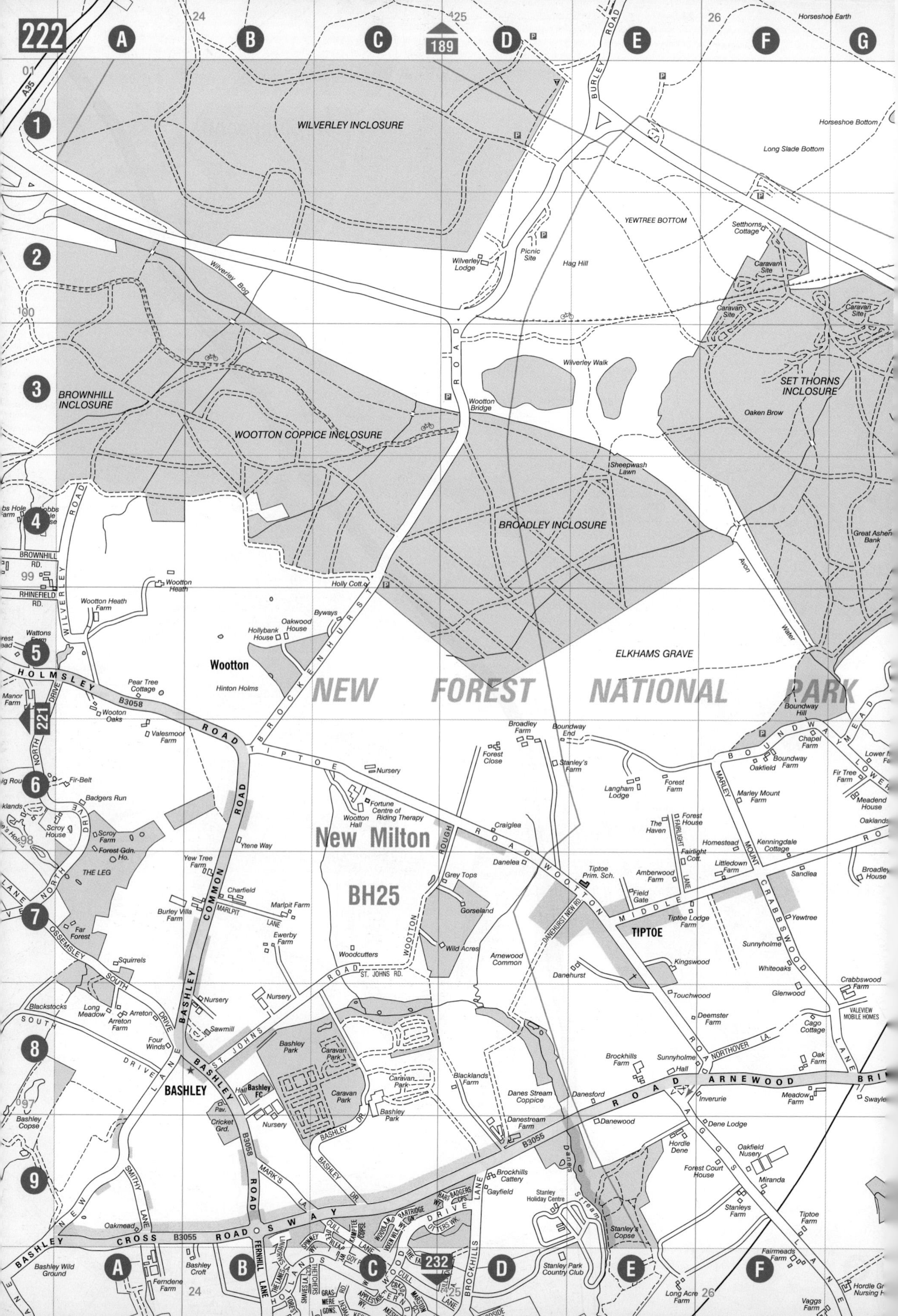
WILVERLEY INCLOSURE
BROWNHILL INCLOSURE
WOOTTON COPPICE INCLOSURE
BROADLEY INCLOSURE
SET THORNS INCLOSURE
YEWTREE BOTTOM
ELKHAMS GRAVE
NEW FOREST NATIONAL PARK
Wootton
New Milton
BH25
TIPTOE
BASHLEY
Horseshoe Earth
Horseshoe Bottom
Long Slade Bottom
Setthorns Cottage
Caravan Site
Hag Hill
Picnic Site
Wilverley Lodge
Wilverley Bog
Wilverley Walk
Wootton Bridge
Oaken Brow
Sheepwash Lawn
Great Ashen Bank
Avon Water
Holly Cott.
Byways
Oakwood House
Hollybank House
Wootton Heath
Wootton Heath Farm
Hinton Holms
Pear Tree Cottage
Wooton Oaks
Valesmoor Farm
Fir-Belt
Badgers Run
Scroy House
Scroy Farm
Forest Gdn. Ho.
THE LEG
Far Forest
Squirrels
Blackstocks
Long Meadow
Arreton
Arreton Farm
Four Winds
Bashley Copse
Bashley Wild Ground
Ferndene Farm
Bashley Croft
Oakmead
Nursery
Fortune Centre of Riding Therapy
Wootton Hall
Ytene Way
Yew Tree Farm
Charfield
Marlpit Farm
Burley Villa Farm
Ewerby Farm
Woodcutters
Sawmill
Bashley Park
Caravan Park
Bashley FC
Cricket Grd.
Pav.
Blacklands Farm
Grey Tops
Gorseland
Wild Acres
Arnewood Common
Danelea
Craiglea
Broadley Farm
Boundway End
Forest Close
Stanley's Farm
Langham Lodge
Forest Farm
The Haven
Forest House
Fairlight Cott.
Homestead
Amberwood Farm
Field Gate
Tiptoe Prim. Sch.
Tiptoe Lodge Farm
Littledown Farm
Kenningdale Cottage
Marley Mount Farm
Oakfield
Boundway Farm
Chapel Farm
Boundway Hill
Fir Tree Farm
Meadend House
Oaklands
Broadley House
Sandlea
Yewtree
Sunnyholme
Whiteoaks
Kingswood
Danehurst
Touchwood
Deemster Farm
Glenwood
Crabbswood Farm
VALEVIEW MOBILE HOMES
Cago Cottage
Oak Farm
Brockhills Farm
Hall
Inverurie
Meadow Farm
Swayle
Danesford
Danes Stream Coppice
Danestream Farm
Danewood
Dene Lodge
Hordle Dene
Oakfield Nusery
Forest Court House
Miranda
Stanleys Farm
Tiptoe Farm
Brockhills Cattery
Gayfield
Stanley Holiday Centre
Stanley's Copse
Stanley Park Country Club
Fairmeads Farm
Long Acre Farm
Vaggs Farm
Hordle Gr Nursing H
WILVERLEY ROAD
BROWNHILL RD.
RHINEFIELD RD.
HOLMSLEY ROAD
NORTH DRIVE
B3058
BROCKENHURST ROAD
TIPTOE ROAD
BASHLEY COMMON ROAD
MARLPIT LANE
OSSEMSLEY SOUTH DRIVE
SOUTH DRIVE
BASHLEY ROAD
ST. JOHNS RD.
WOOTTON ROUGH
WOOTTON ROAD
DANEHURST NEW RD.
MIDDLE ROAD
FAIRLIGHT LANE
MARLEY MOUNT
CRABBSWOOD LANE
BOUNDWAY
LOWER MEAD
NORTHOVER LA.
ARNEWOOD BRIDGE ROAD
VAGGS LANE
BASHLEY DR.
MARK'S LA.
B3055
SWAY ROAD
BASHLEY CROSS ROAD
NEW LANE
SMITHY LANE
FERNHILL LANE
BROCKHILLS LANE
BURLEY ROAD
A35
Danes Stream
Wootton
189
221
232

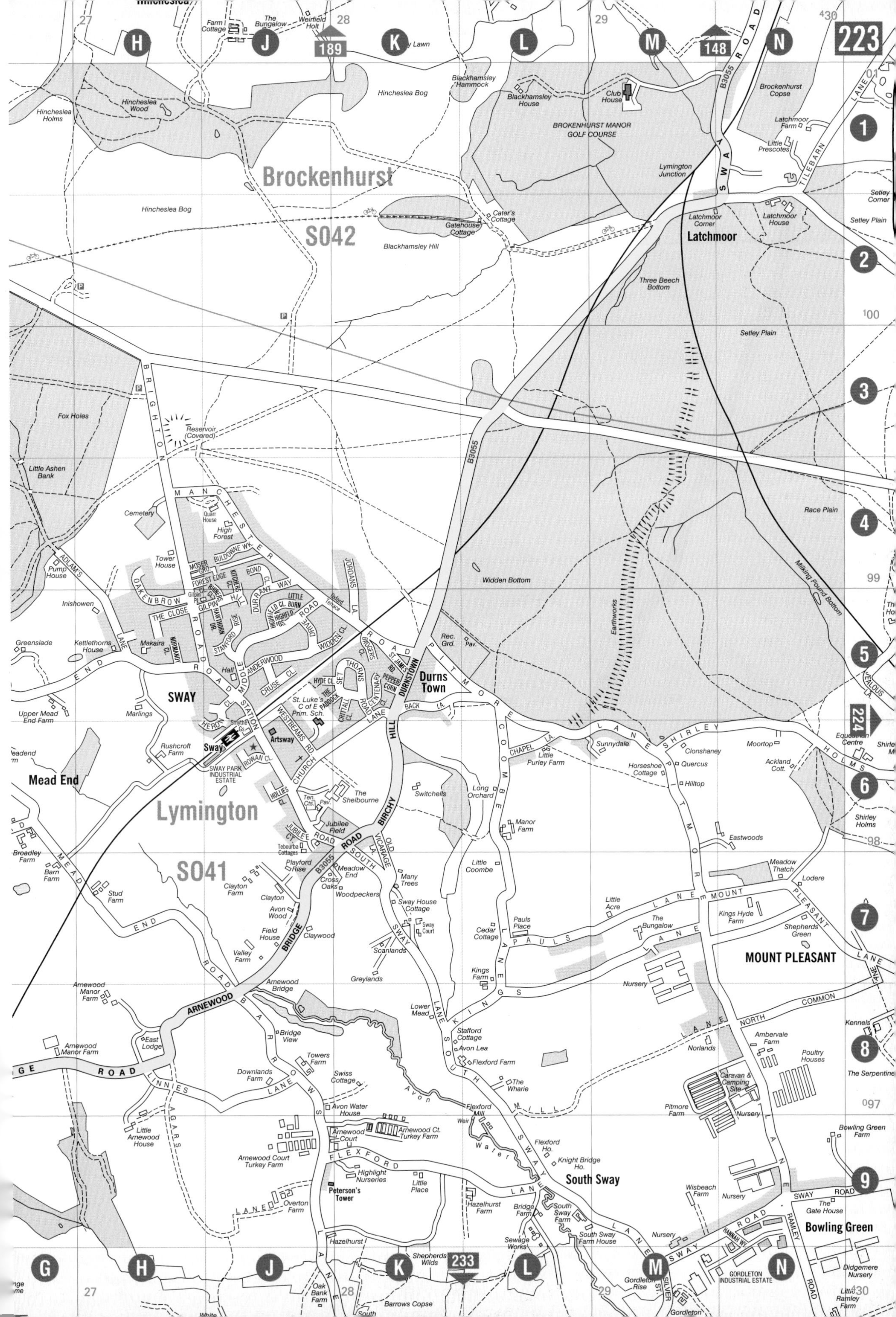
Brockenhurst
SO42
Latchmoor
Hinchesela Bog
Blackhamsley Hill
BROKENHURST MANOR GOLF COURSE
Club House
Blackhamsley House
Blackhamsley Hammock
Brockenhurst Copse
Latchmoor Farm
Little Prescotes
Lymington Junction
Latchmoor Corner
Latchmoor House
Setley Corner
Setley Plain
Three Beech Bottom
Hinchesela Wood
Hinchesela Holms
Cater's Cottage
Gatehouse Cottage
Farm Cottage
The Bungalow
Weirfield Holt
Fox Holes
Reservoir (Covered)
Little Ashen Bank
Cemetery
Race Plain
Milking Pound Bottom
Widden Bottom
Earthworks
SWAY
Durns Town
Mead End
Lymington
SO41
Arnewood Bridge
Arnewood Manor Farm
East Lodge
Little Arnewood House
Avon Water House
Arnewood Court
Arnewood Ct. Turkey Farm
Arnewood Court Turkey Farm
Peterson's Tower
Hazelhurst
Shepherds Wilds
Oak Bank Farm
Barrows Copse
Flexford Mill
Flexford Farm
South Sway
South Sway Farm
Gordleton Rise
GORDLETON INDUSTRIAL ESTATE
Bowling Green
Bowling Green Farm
Didgemere Nursery
Little Ramley Farm
MOUNT PLEASANT
Caravan & Camping Site
Pitmore Farm
Poultry Houses
Ambervale Farm
Kennels
The Serpentine
Shirley Holms
Ackland Cott.
Moortop
Equestrian Centre
Clonshaney
Quercus
Hilltop
Horseshoe Cottage
Sunnydale
Eastwoods
Meadow Thatch
Lodere
Kings Hyde Farm
Shepherds Green
Little Acre
The Bungalow
Nursery
Norlands
Pauls Place
Cedar Cottage
Kings Farm
Manor Farm
Little Coombe
Little Purley Farm
Long Orchard
Switchells
The Shelbourne
Jubilee Field
St. Luke's C of E Prim. Sch.
Artsway
SWAY PARK INDUSTRIAL ESTATE
Rushcroft Farm
Marlings
Upper Mead End Farm
Greenslade
Kettlethorns House
Inishowen
Pump House
Tower House
High Forest
Quarr House
Makaira
Hall
Broadley Farm
Barn Farm
Stud Farm
Clayton Farm
Clayton
Avon Wood
Field House
Valley Farm
Playford Rise
Meadow End
Cross Oaks
Woodpeckers
Many Trees
Sway House Cottage
Sway Court
Claywood
Scanlands
Greylands
Lower Mead
Stafford Cottage
Avon Lea
The Wharie
Flexford Ho.
Knight Bridge Ho.
Bridge View
Towers Farm
Swiss Cottage
Downlands Farm
Highlight Nurseries
Little Place
Hazelhurst Farm
Bridge Farm
Sewage Works
South Sway Farm House
Overton Farm
Wisbeach Farm
The Gate House
Tebourba Cottages
Rec. Grd.
B3055
MANCHESTER ROAD
BRIGHTON ROAD
STATION ROAD
BRIDGE ROAD
ARNEWOOD
BIRCHY HILL
DURNSTOWN
PITMORE ROAD
SHIRLEY HOLMS
MOUNT PLEASANT LANE
PAULS LANE
KINGS LANE
COOMBE LANE
NORTH COMMON
SWAY ROAD
FLEXFORD LANE
BARROWS LANE
AGARS LANE
MEAD END ROAD
ADAM'S LANE
CHURCH LANE
BACK LA.
CHAPEL LA.
SOUTH SWAY LANE
RAMLEY ROAD
SILVER ST.
HANNAH WY.
JEALOUS LA.
TILEBARN LANE
FINNIES LANE
Avon Water
189
148
233
224
H J K L M N G
1 2 3 4 5 6 7 8 9
27 28 29 430 01 100 99 98 097

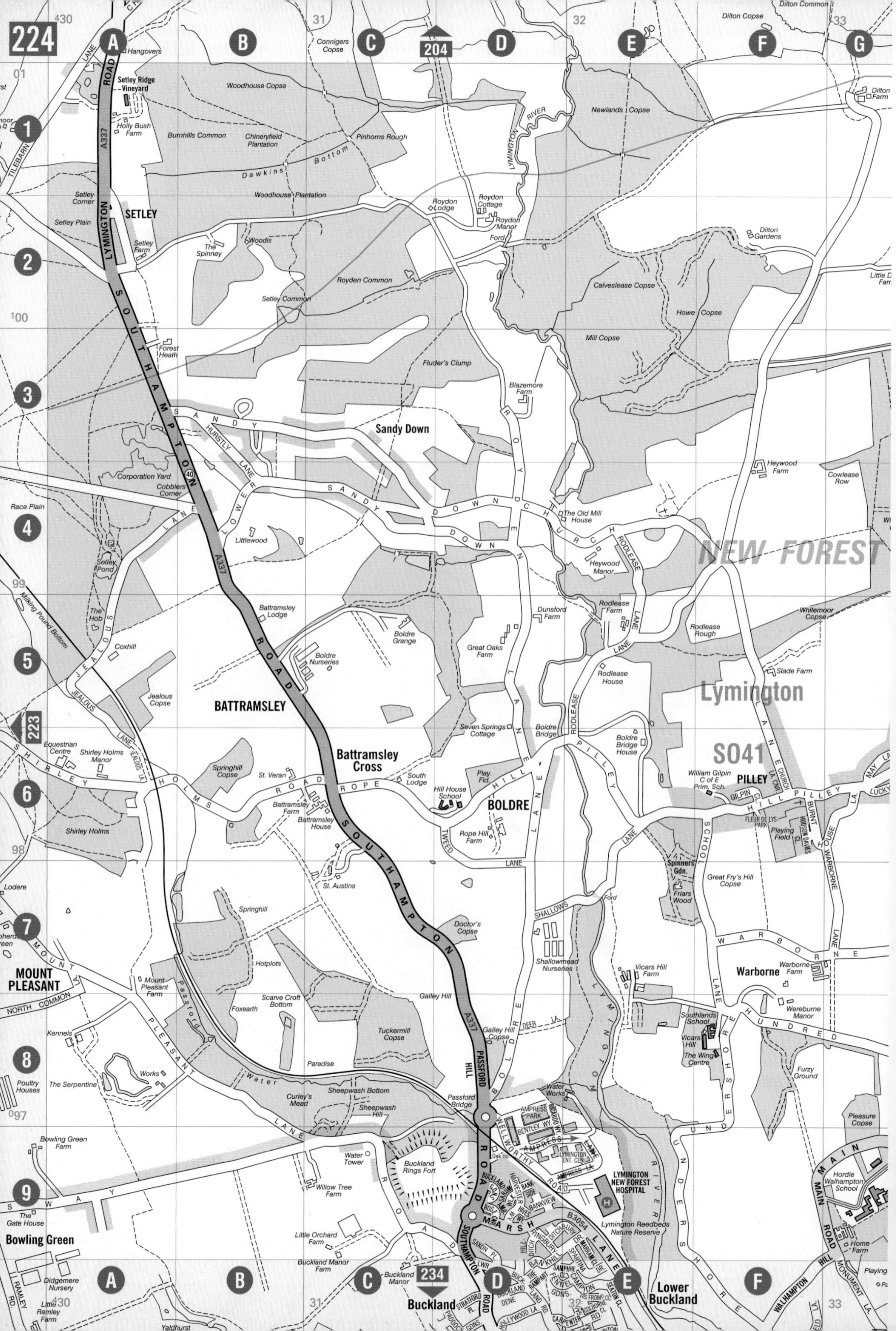
204
223
234
SETLEY
Setley Ridge Vineyard
Hangovers
Holly Bush Farm
Setley Corner
Setley Plain
Setley Farm
Woodhouse Copse
Burnhills Common
Chineryfield Plantation
Pinhorns Rough
Dawkins Bottom
Woodhouse Plantation
Conigers Copse
Roydon Lodge
Roydon Cottage
Roydon Manor
Ford
The Spinney
Woodis
Royden Common
Setley Common
Forest Heath
Fluder's Clump
Blazemore Farm
Newlands Copse
Dilton Copse
Dilton Common
Dilton Farm
Dilton Gardens
Calveslease Copse
Howe Copse
Mill Copse
Little Dilton Farm
LYMINGTON RIVER
Sandy Down
Corporation Yard
Cobblers Corner
Race Plain
Setley Pond
Littlewood
The Old Mill House
Heywood Manor
Heywood Farm
Cowlease Row
NEW FOREST
Whitemoor Copse
Rodlease Farm
Rodlease Rough
Rodlease House
Slade Farm
Lymington
Dunsford Farm
Great Oaks Farm
Battramsley Lodge
Boldre Grange
Boldre Nurseries
Milking Pound Bottom
The Hob
Coxhill
Jealous Copse
BATTRAMSLEY
Battramsley Cross
Seven Springs Cottage
Boldre Bridge
Boldre Bridge House
SO41
PILLEY
William Gilpin C of E Prim. Sch.
Equestrian Centre
Shirley Holms Manor
Shirley Holms
Springhill Copse
St. Veran
South Lodge
Hill House School
Play. Fld.
BOLDRE
Battramsley Farm
Battramsley House
Rope Hill Farm
Playing Field
FLEUR DE LYS PARK
Spinners Gdn.
Friars Wood
Great Fry's Hill Copse
St. Austins
Springhill
Doctor's Copse
Shallowmead Nurseries
Lodere
MOUNT PLEASANT
Mount Pleasant Farm
Hotplots
Foxearth
Scarve Croft Bottom
Galley Hill
Tuckermill Copse
Galley Hill Copse
Vicars Hill Farm
Warborne
Warborne Farm
Wereburne Manor
Southlands School
Vicars Hill
The Wing Centre
Furzy Ground
Kennels
Works
Poultry Houses
The Serpentine
Paradise
Curley's Mead
Sheepwash Bottom
Sheepwash Hill
Passford Bridge
Water Works
AMPRESS PARK
Oak Ho.
LYMINGTON ENT. CEN.
LYMINGTON NEW FOREST HOSPITAL
Lymington Reedbeds Nature Reserve
Pleasure Copse
Hordle Walhampton School
Home Farm
Bowling Green Farm
Water Tower
Buckland Rings Fort
Willow Tree Farm
The Gate House
Bowling Green
Little Orchard Farm
Buckland Manor Farm
Buckland Manor
Buckland
Lower Buckland
Didgemere Nursery
Little Ramley Farm
Yaldhurst
SOUTHAMPTON ROAD
LYMINGTON ROAD
SANDY LANE
HURSTLY
LOWER SANDY DOWN
SANDY DOWN
CHURCH LANE
ROYDEN LANE
RODLEASE LANE
JEALOUS LANE
SHIRLEY HOLMS ROAD
ROPE HILL
BOLDRE LANE
PILLEY HILL
PILLEY STREET
GILPIN CL.
HUDSON DAVIES CL.
BURNT HOUSE LANE
WARBORNE LANE
SCHOOL LANE
TWEED LANE
SHALLOWS LANE
DEER LA.
PASSFORD HILL
MOUNT PLEASANT LANE
NORTH COMMON
Passford Water
SWAY ROAD
WELLWORTHY ROAD
AMPRESS LANE
BENTLEY WY.
MARSH LANE
B3054
UNDERSHORE
MAIN ROAD
WALHAMPTON HILL
MONUMENT LA.
TILEBARN LANE
RAMLEY RD.
A337
40
Playing

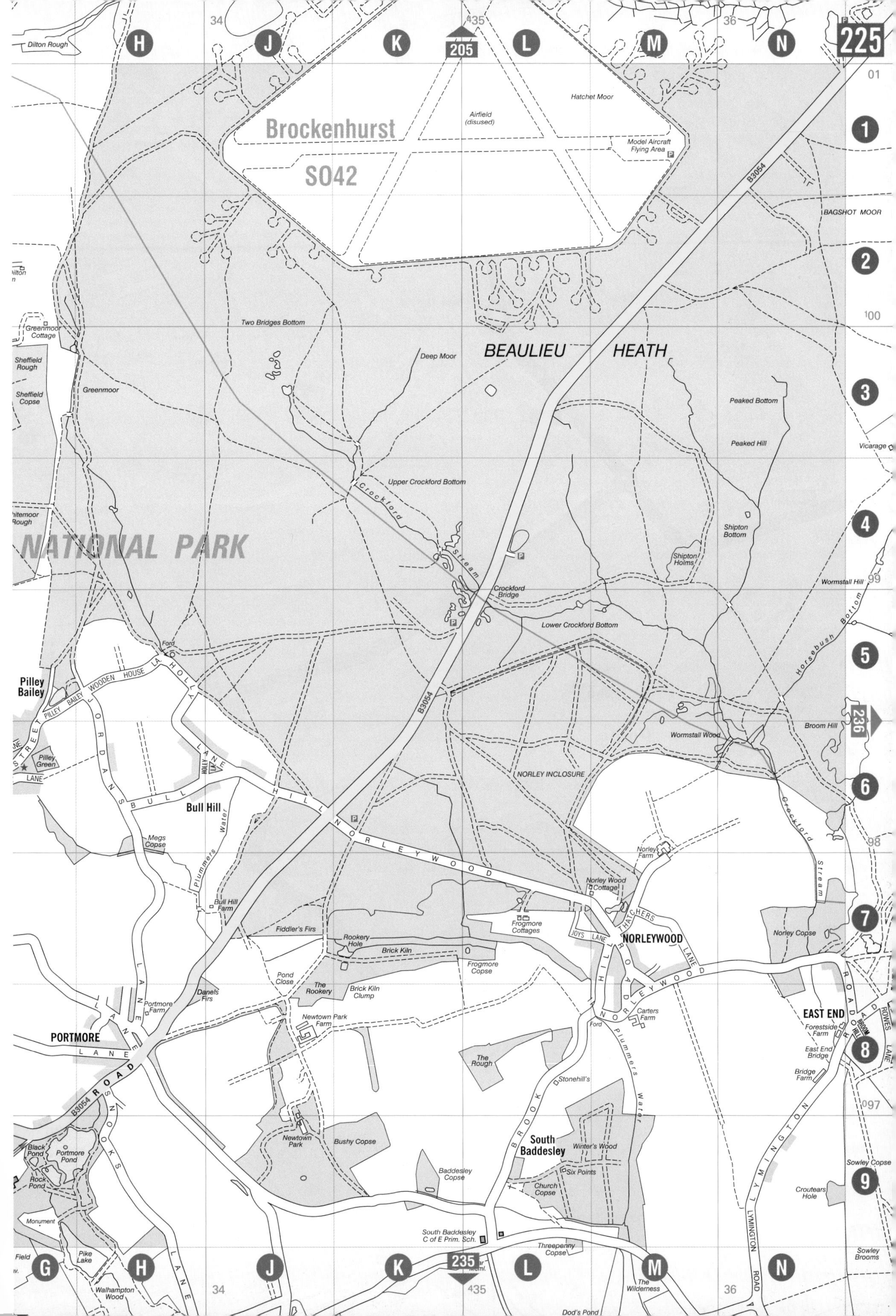

H J 205 K L M N

1

Brockenhurst

SO42

Airfield
(disused)

Hatchet Moor

Model Aircraft
Flying Area

BAGSHOT MOOR

2

100

Greenmoor
Cottage

Sheffield
Rough

Sheffield
Copse

Greenmoor

Two Bridges Bottom

Deep Moor

BEAULIEU   HEATH

3

Peaked Bottom

Peaked Hill

Vicarage

Whitemoor
Rough

NATIONAL PARK

Upper Crockford Bottom

Crockford Stream

Shipton
Bottom

Shipton
Holms

Wormstall Hill

4

99

Crockford
Bridge

Lower Crockford Bottom

5

Ford

Pilley
Bailey

Wooden House La

Pilley Bailey

Street Lane

Pilley
Green

Lane

Jordans

Bull

Plummers Water

Holly Hill Lane

Norley Farm

Wormstall Wood

Broom Hill

236

Horsebush Bottom

6

98

Bull Hill

Megs
Copse

NORLEYWOOD

Bull Hill
Farm

Fiddler's Firs

Rookery
Hole

Brick Kiln

NORLEY INCLOSURE

Norley Wood
Cottage

Frogmore
Cottages

Joys Lane

Thatchers Lane

NORLEYWOOD

Norley Copse

Crockford Stream

7

Portmore
Farm

Danels
Firs

Pond
Close

The
Rookery

Brick Kiln
Clump

Frogmore
Copse

Newtown Park
Farm

Norley Wood Road

Norley Wood

Carters
Farm

Ford

EAST END

Forestside
Farm

East End
Bridge

Bridge
Farm

Brook Lane

Rowes Lane

Lymington Road

8

97

PORTMORE

B3054 Road

Brooks Lane

Newtown
Park

Bushy Copse

The
Rough

Stonehill's

Plummers Water

South
Baddesley

Winter's Wood

Six Points

Sowley Copse

9

Black
Pond

Portmore
Pond

Rock
Pond

Baddesley
Copse

Church
Copse

Croutears
Hole

Monument

Pike
Lake

Walhampton
Wood

South Baddesley
C of E Prim. Sch.

Threepenny
Copse

The
Wilderness

Sowley
Brooms

G H J 235 K L M N

Dod's Pond

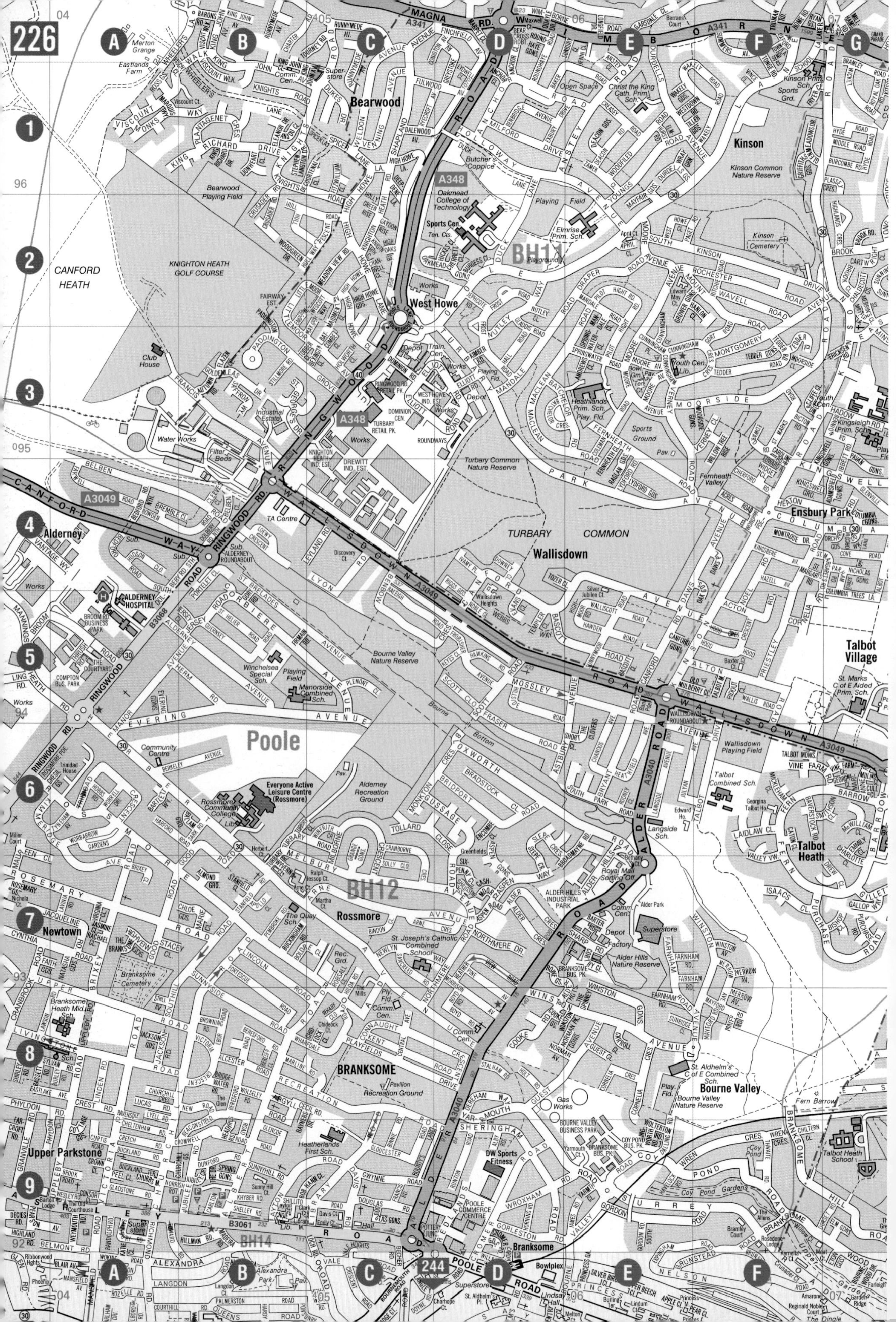

Merton Grange
Eastlands Farm
Bearwood
Bearwood Playing Field
CANFORD HEATH
KNIGHTON HEATH GOLF COURSE
Club House
Water Works
Filter Beds
Industrial Estate
West Howe
Oakmead College of Technology
Sports Cen.
Butcher's Coppice
Elmrise Prim. Sch.
BH11
Open Space
Christ the King Cath. Prim. Sch.
Kinson
Kinson Common Nature Reserve
Kinson Cemetery
Kinson Prim. Sch.
Sports Grd.
Heathlands Prim. Sch. Play. Fld.
Sports Ground
Turbary Common Nature Reserve
Fernheath Valley
TURBARY COMMON
Wallisdown
Wallisdown Heights
Ensbury Park
Kingsleigh Prim. Sch.
Alderney
ALDERNEY HOSPITAL
BROOM RD. BUSINESS PARK
COMPTON BUS. PARK
Winchelsea Special Sch.
Playing Field
Manorside Combined Sch.
Bourne Valley Nature Reserve
Talbot Village
St. Marks C of E Aided Prim. Sch.
Wallisdown Playing Field
Talbot Combined Sch.
Langside Sch.
Talbot Heath
Poole
Community Centre
Everyone Active Leisure Centre (Rossmore)
Rossmore Community College
Alderney Recreation Ground
BH12
Rossmore
Newtown
Branksome Cemetery
St. Joseph's Catholic Combined School
ALDER HILLS INDUSTRIAL PARK
Royal Mail Sorting Off.
Alder Park
Superstore
Alder Hills Nature Reserve
Branksome Heath Mid. Sch.
BRANKSOME
Pavilion
Recreation Ground
Heatherlands First Sch.
Gas Works
BOURNE VALLEY BUSINESS PARK
St. Aldhelm's C of E Combined Sch.
Bourne Valley
Bourne Valley Nature Reserve
DW Sports Fitness
POOLE COMMERCE CENTRE
Coy Pond Gardens
Talbot Heath School
Upper Parkstone
BH14
Alexandra Park
Branksome
Bowlplex
Superstore
A341
A348
A3049
A3040
B3068
B3061
244

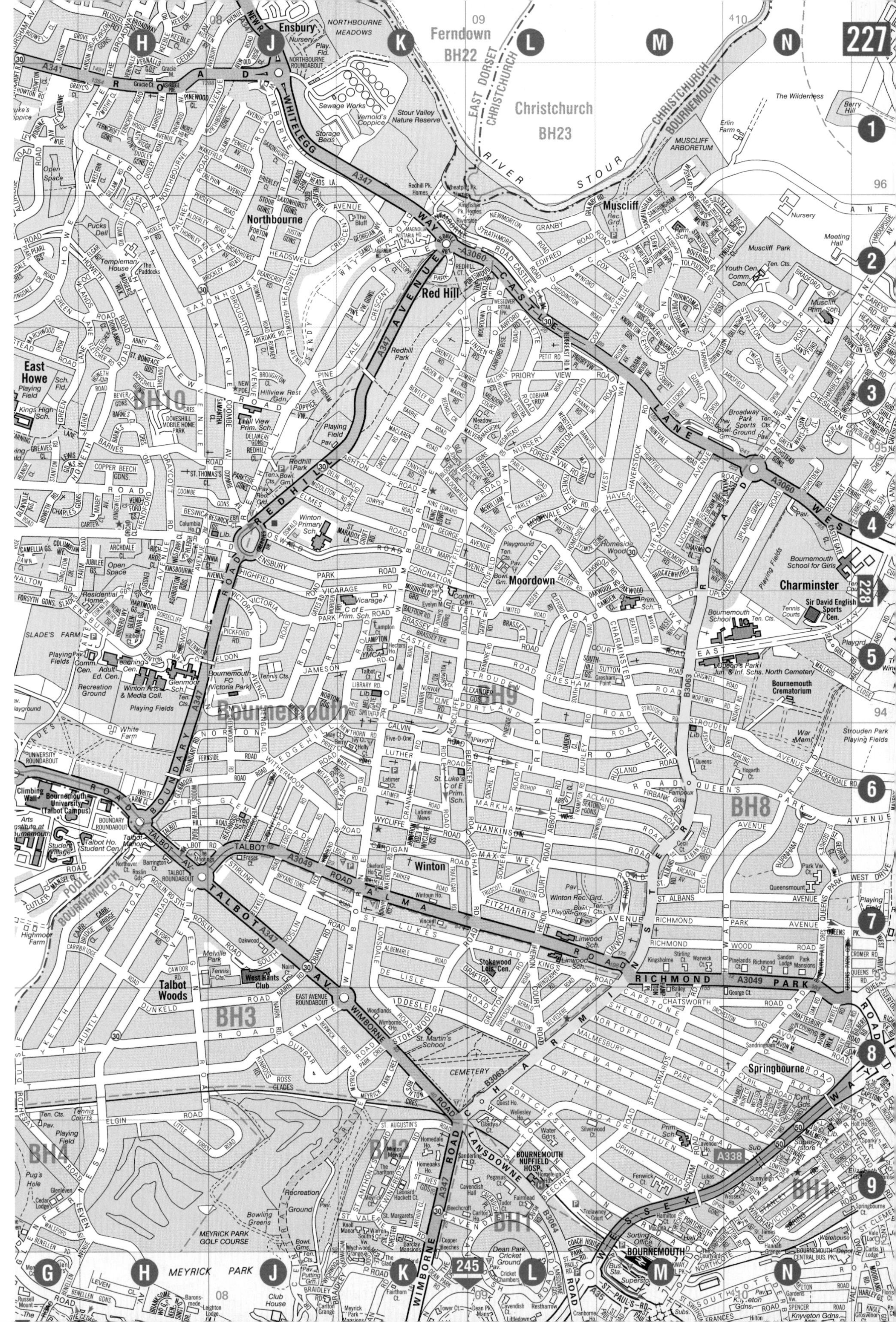
Ensbury
NORTHBOURNE MEADOWS
Ferndown
BH22
Christchurch
BH23
EAST DORSET
CHRISTCHURCH
BOURNEMOUTH
RIVER STOUR
The Wilderness
Berry Hill
Erlin Farm
MUSCLIFF ARBORETUM
Sewage Works
Vernold's Coppice
Stour Valley Nature Reserve
Storage Beds
NORTHBOURNE ROUNDABOUT
WHITELEGG WAY
A341
A347
A3060
Muscliff
Nursery
Meeting Hall
Muscliff Park
Youth Cen.
Comm. Cen.
Muscliff Prim. Sch.
Northbourne
Templeman House
The Paddocks
Red Hill
Redhill Park
East Howe
Playing Field
Kings High Sch.
BH10
Hill View Prim. Sch.
Hillview Rest Gdn.
Doveshill Mobile Home Park
Playing Field
Broadway Park Sports Ground
CASTLE LANE
Bournemouth School for Girls
Charminster
Sir David English Sports Cen.
Bournemouth School
Playing Fields
Moordown
Winton Primary Sch.
Open Space
Residential Home
SLADE'S FARM
Playing Fields
Adult Ed. Cen.
Winton Arts & Media Coll.
Glenmoor Sch.
Recreation Ground
Bournemouth FC (Victoria Park)
Bournemouth
BH9
Queen's Park Jun. & Inf. Schs.
North Cemetery
Bournemouth Crematorium
War Meml.
Strouden Park Playing Fields
BH8
UNIVERSITY ROUNDABOUT
Climbing Wall
Bournemouth University (Talbot Campus)
Arts Institute at Bournemouth
BOUNDARY ROUNDABOUT
Talbot Ho. Student Cen.
Student Village
TALBOT ROUNDABOUT
POOLE
BOURNEMOUTH
Highmoor Farm
Winton
St. Luke's C of E Prim. Sch.
Winton Rec. Grd.
Linwood Sch.
Stokewood Leis. Cen.
Talbot Woods
West Hants Club
Melville Park
EAST AVENUE ROUNDABOUT
BH3
St. Martin's School
CEMETERY
Springbourne
RICHMOND PARK
A3049
B3063
Ten. Cts.
Tennis Courts
Playing Field
BH4
Pug's Hole
Recreation Ground
Bowling Greens
MEYRICK PARK GOLF COURSE
BH2
BOURNEMOUTH NUFFIELD HOSP.
LANSDOWNE ROAD
BH1
Dean Park Cricket Ground
A338
WESSEX WAY
BOURNEMOUTH
Sorting Office
Bus Sta.
Superstore
BOURNEMOUTH CENTRAL BUS. PK.
MEYRICK PARK
Club House
245
228
G H J K L M N
1 2 3 4 5 6 7 8 9
08 09 410
96 95 94 93 92

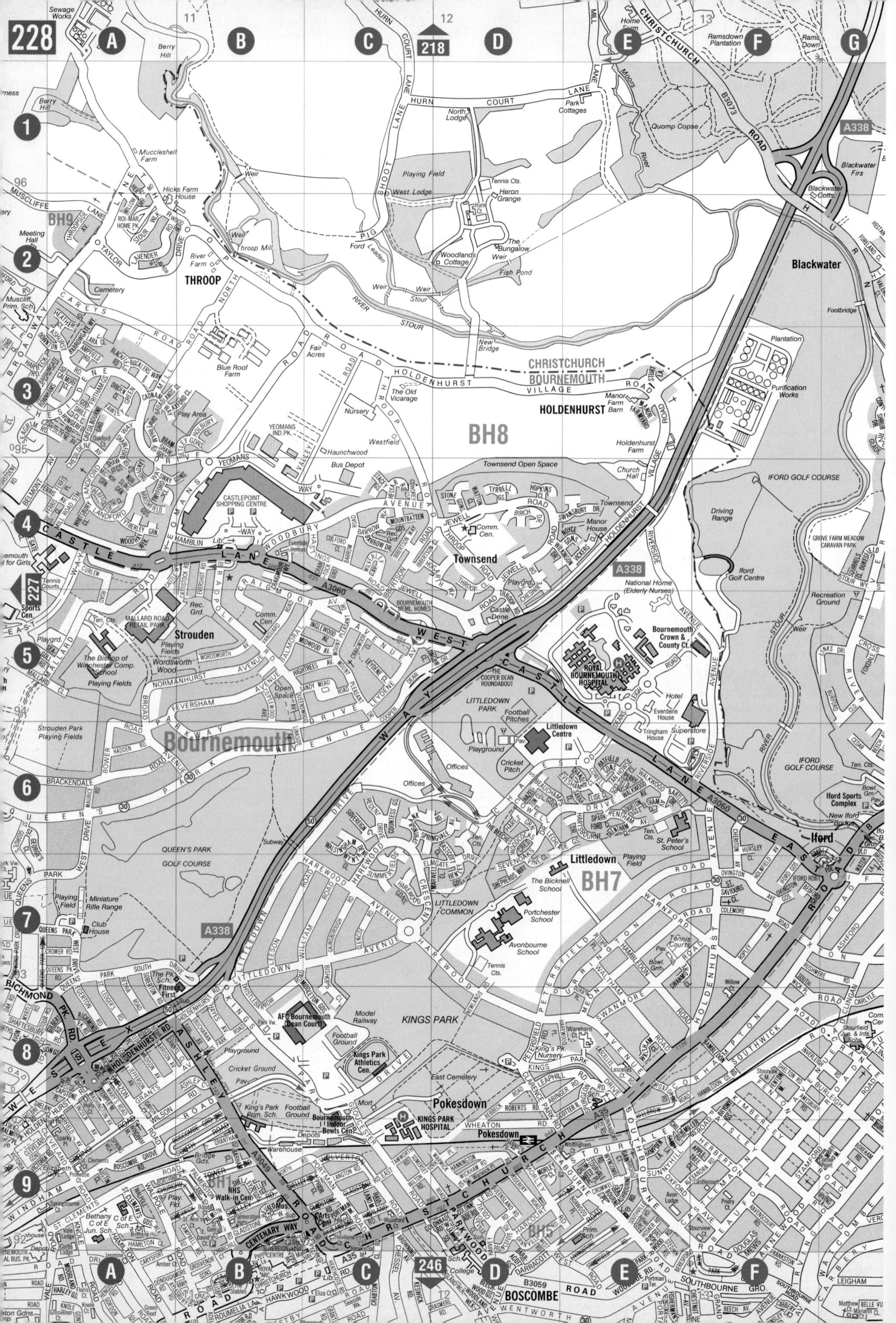
218
227
246
Sewage Works
Berry Hill
Muccleshell Farm
Hicks Farm House
MUSCLIFFE LANE
BH9
Meeting Hall
Throop Mill
River Farm
THROOP
Cemetery
Muscliff Prim. Sch.
Blue Roof Farm
Fair Acres
HURN COURT LANE
SHOOT LANE
North Lodge
Park Cottages
Playing Field
West Lodge
Tennis Cts.
Heron Grange
The Bungalow
Woodlands Cottage
Fish Pond
Weir
RIVER STOUR
New Bridge
Ramsdown Plantation
Rams Down
Quomp Copse
CHRISTCHURCH ROAD
B3073
A338
Blackwater Firs
Blackwater Cotts.
Blackwater
Footbridge
Plantation
Purification Works
CHRISTCHURCH
BOURNEMOUTH
HOLDENHURST VILLAGE ROAD
The Old Vicarage
Nursery
Manor Farm Barn
HOLDENHURST
BH8
Holdenhurst Farm
Church Hall
Westfield
Hauchwood
Bus Depot
YEOMANS IND.PK.
Play Area
Townsend Open Space
IFORD GOLF COURSE
Driving Range
Iford Golf Centre
GROVE FARM MEADOW CARAVAN PARK
Recreation Ground
CASTLEPOINT SHOPPING CENTRE
CASTLE LANE WEST
A3060
Comm. Cen.
Townsend
Manor House
National Home (Elderly Nurses)
Bournemouth Crown & County Ct.
ROYAL BOURNEMOUTH HOSPITAL
Eventide Homes
BOURNEMOUTH MEML. HOMES
Castle Dene
Tennis Courts
Sports Cen.
MALLARD ROAD RETAIL PARK
Strouden
Rec. Grd.
Playing Fields
Wordsworth Wood
The Bishop of Winchester Comp. School
Open Space
THE COOPER DEAN ROUNDABOUT
LITTLEDOWN PARK
Football Pitches
Littledown Centre
Hotel
Superstore
Tringham House
Strouden Park Playing Fields
Bournemouth
Playground
Cricket Pitch
Offices
CASTLE LANE EAST
IFORD GOLF COURSE
Iford Sports Complex
New Iford Bridge
Iford
QUEEN'S PARK GOLF COURSE
Subway
Littledown
St. Peter's School
Playing Field
The Bicknell School
BH7
Portchester School
Avonbourne School
LITTLEDOWN COMMON
Miniature Rifle Range
Club House
Playing Field
RICHMOND PK. RD.
The Pk. Sch.
Fitness First
AFC Bournemouth (Dean Court)
Model Railway
KINGS PARK
Football Ground
Kings Park Athletics Cen.
Playground
Cricket Ground
King's Pk. Nursery
East Cemetery
King's Park Prim. Sch.
Bournemouth Indoor Bowls Cen.
Pokesdown
KINGS PARK HOSPITAL
Depots
Warehouse
BOSCOMBE GROVE
BH1
NHS Walk-in Cen.
CENTENARY WAY
A3049
A35
CHRISTCHURCH ROAD
BH5
BOSCOMBE
B3059
ROAD
WINDHAM ROAD
ST. CLEMENTS ROAD
Bethany C of E Jun. Sch.
Stourfield Jun. & Infs. Schs.
SOUTHBOURNE GRO.
LEIGHAM

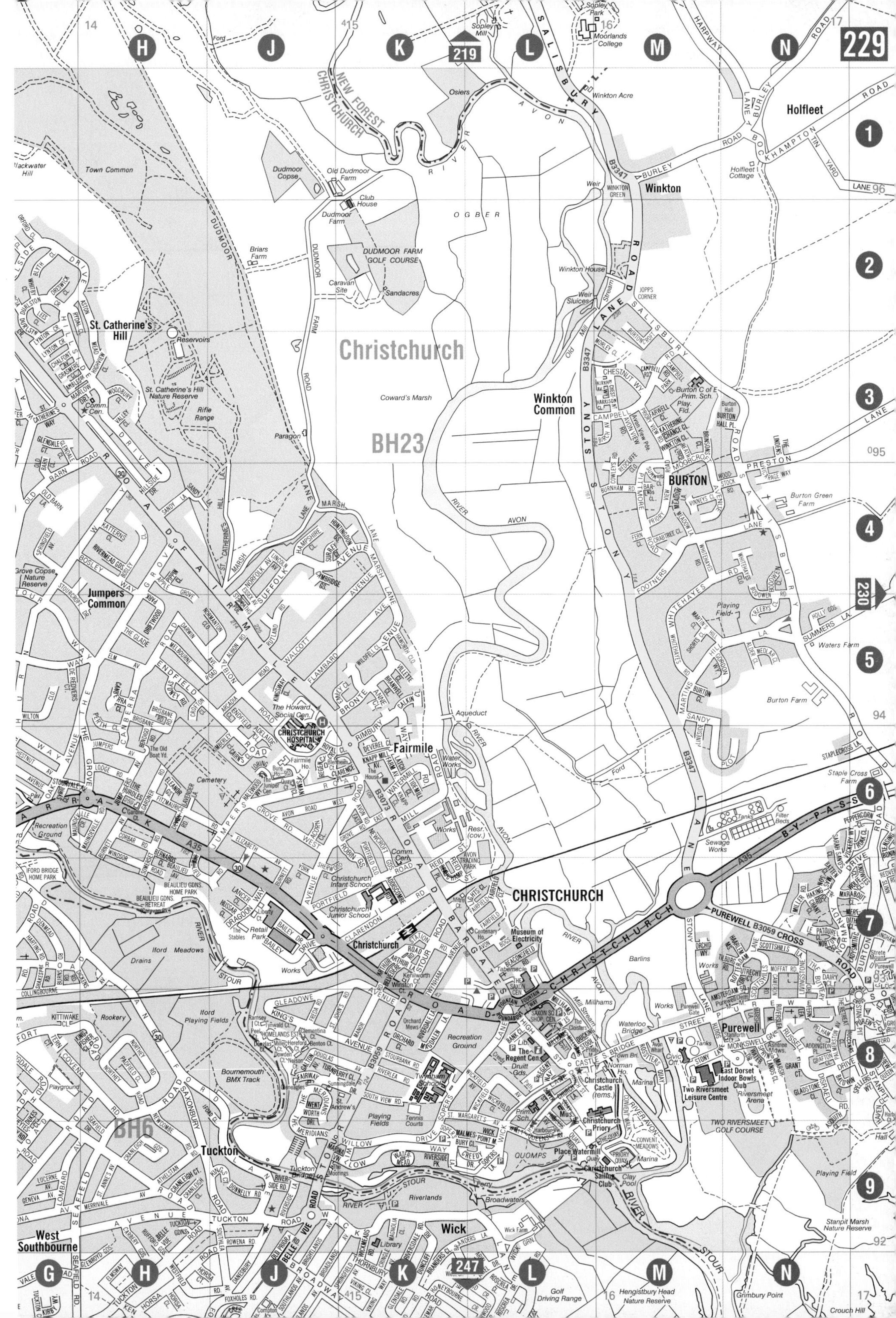

219
230
247
Christchurch
BH23
BH6
CHRISTCHURCH
BURTON
Winkton
Holfleet
Winkton Common
St. Catherine's Hill
Jumpers Common
Fairmile
Purewell
Tuckton
Wick
West Southbourne
Town Common
Dudmoor Copse
Old Dudmoor Farm
Dudmoor Farm
DUDMOOR FARM GOLF COURSE
Coward's Marsh
Osiers
Moorlands College
Winkton Acre
Winkton House
St. Catherine's Hill Nature Reserve
Rifle Range
Reservoirs
Grove Copse Nature Reserve
Burton Green Farm
Burton Farm
Waters Farm
Staple Cross Farm
Sewage Works
Christchurch Hospital
Cemetery
Recreation Ground
Iford Meadows
Iford Playing Fields
Bournemouth BMX Track
Christchurch Castle (rems.)
Christchurch Priory
Museum of Electricity
Place Watermill
Christchurch Sailing Club
Two Riversmeet Leisure Centre
East Dorset Indoor Bowls Club
TWO RIVERSMEET GOLF COURSE
Riverlands
Broadwaters
Stanpit Marsh Nature Reserve
Golf Driving Range
Hengistbury Head Nature Reserve
Grimbury Point
Crouch Hill
RIVER AVON
RIVER STOUR
A35
B3347
B3073
B3059

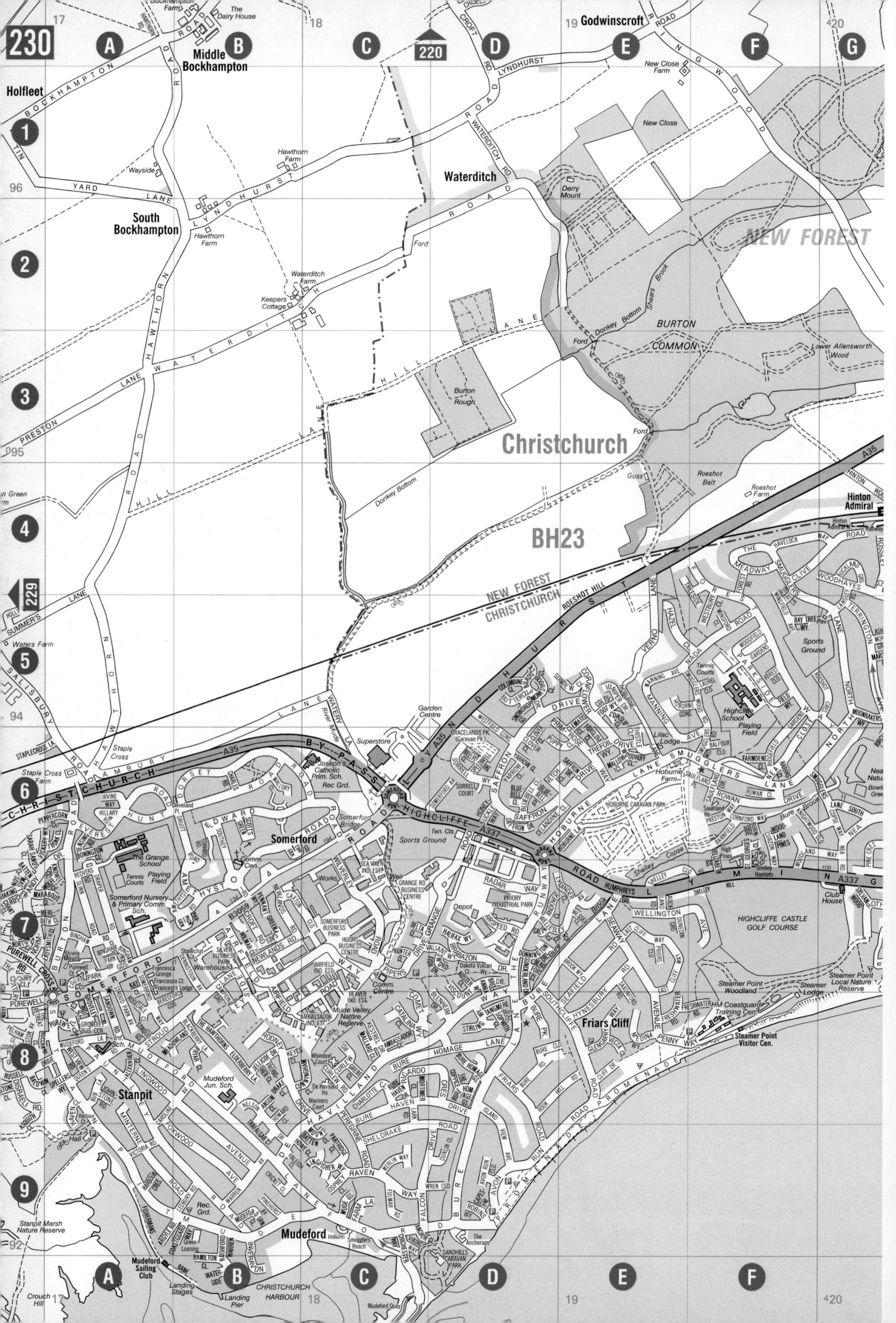

220
229
Middle Bockhampton
Holfleet
The Dairy House
Godwinscroft
New Close Farm
New Close
Waterditch
Derry Mount
South Bockhampton
Hawthorn Farm
Wayside
Waterditch Farm
Keepers Cottage
Ford
NEW FOREST
BURTON COMMON
Donkey Bottom
Shears Brook
Lower Allensworth Wood
Burton Rough
Christchurch
Roeshot Belt
Roeshot Farm
Hinton Admiral
BH23
NEW FOREST
CHRISTCHURCH
Waters Farm
Staple Cross
Staple Cross Farm
Garden Centre
Superstore
St. Joseph's Catholic Prim. Sch.
Rec Grd.
Somerford Bridge
Somerford
The Grange School
Playing Field
Tennis Courts
Comm. Cen.
Sports Ground
Somerford Nursery & Primary Comm. Sch.
Hoburne Farm
HOBURNE CARAVAN PARK
Highcliffe School
Playing Field
Sports Ground
Lilac Lodge
Priory Industrial Park
Depot
Somerford Business Park
Hughs Business Centre
Airfield Ind. Est.
Beaver Ind. Est.
Comm. Centre
Mude Valley Nature Reserve
Ambassador Ind. Est.
Stanpit
Mudeford Jun. Sch.
Friars Cliff
HIGHCLIFFE CASTLE GOLF COURSE
Club House
Steamer Point Woodland
Steamer Point Local Nature Reserve
Steamer Lodge
HM Coastguard Training Cen.
Steamer Point Visitor Cen.
Stanpit Marsh Nature Reserve
Mudeford
Mudeford Sailing Club
Landing Stages
Landing Pier
CHRISTCHURCH HARBOUR
Mudeford Quay
Crouch Hill
Sandhills Caravan Park
The Anchorage
Smugglers Reach
Rec. Grd.
A35
A337
B3059
CHRISTCHURCH BY-PASS
HIGHCLIFFE ROAD
LYMINGTON ROAD
SOMERFORD ROAD
MUDEFORD
STANPIT
HAWTHORN ROAD
WATERDITCH ROAD
LYNDHURST ROAD
BOCKHAMPTON ROAD
PRESTON LANE
HILL LANE
SALISBURY ROAD
SUMMER'S LANE
WATERY LANE
RINGWOOD ROAD
PROMENADE
SMUGGLERS LANE
HOBURNE LANE
BURE LANE
RUNWAY THE
HOMAGE LANE
HAVILLAND DRIVE
WELLINGTON AVE
A B C D E F G
1 2 3 4 5 6 7 8 9
17 18 19 420
96 95 94 93 92

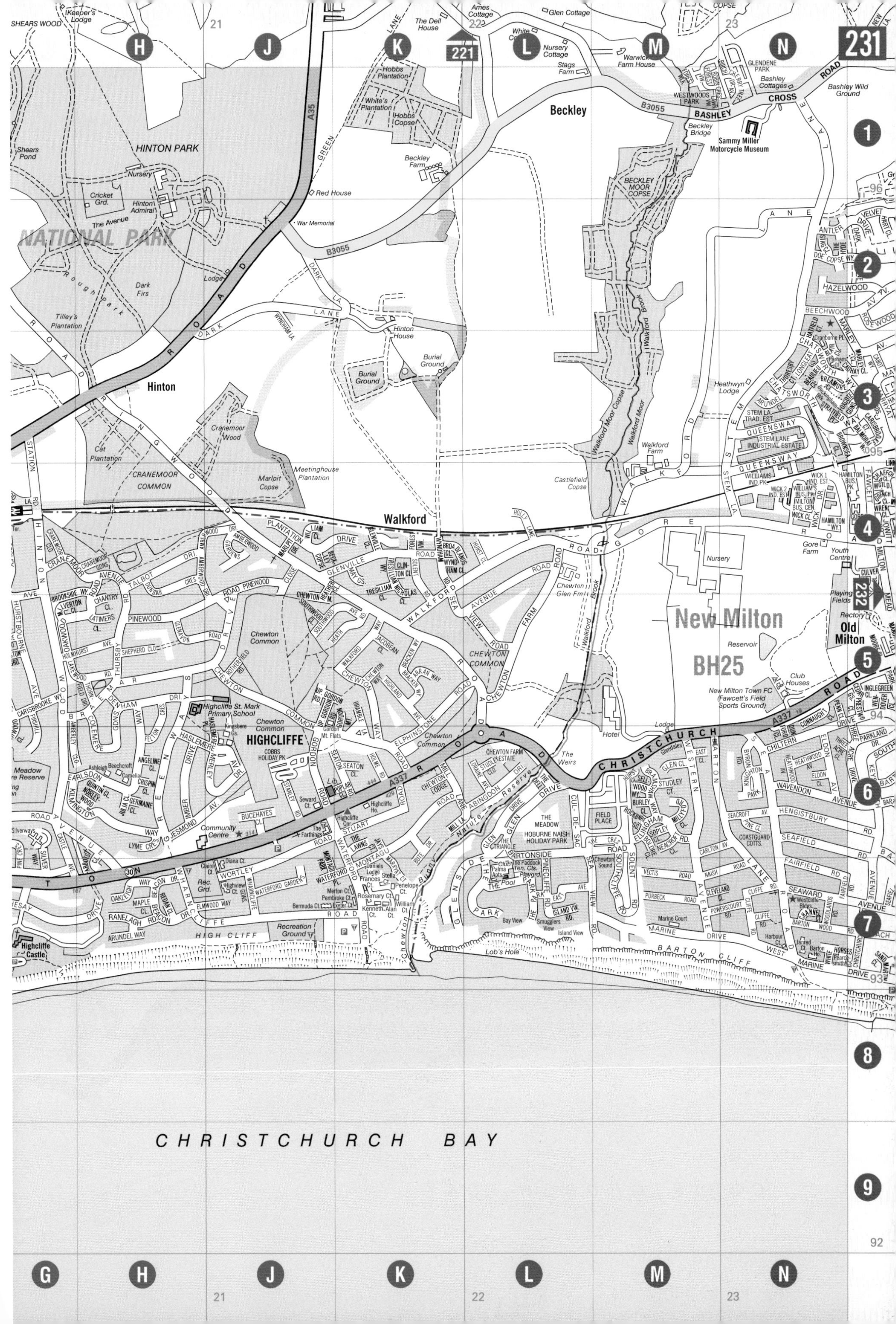

HINTON PARK
NATIONAL PARK
Shears Pond
Cricket Grd.
Hinton Admiral
The Avenue
Nursery
Rough Park
Dark Firs
Tilley's Plantation
Lodge
Hinton
Cat Plantation
CRANEMOOR COMMON
Cranemoor Wood
Marlpit Copse
Meetinghouse Plantation
Hobbs Plantation
White's Plantation
Hobbs Copse
Beckley Farm
Red House
War Memorial
B3055
A35
Hinton House
Burial Ground
Beckley
Glen Cottage
Nursery Cottage
Stags Farm
Warwick Farm House
The Dell House
Ames Cottage
WESTWOODS PARK
GLENDENE PARK
Bashley Cottages
Bashley Wild Ground
BASHLEY CROSS ROAD
B3055
Beckley Bridge
Sammy Miller Motorcycle Museum
BECKLEY MOOR COPSE
Walkford Brook
Walkford Moor
Walkford Moor Copse
Walkford Farm
Castlefield Copse
Heathwyn Lodge
STEM LANE INDUSTRIAL ESTATE
QUEENSWAY
WILLIAMS IND. PK.
HAZELWOOD
BEECHWOOD
CHATSWORTH WAY
Walkford
GORE ROAD
Gore Farm
Youth Centre
Nursery
Chewton Glen Fm.
New Milton
BH25
Reservoir
Playing Fields
Rectory
Old Milton
Club Houses
New Milton Town FC (Fawcett's Field Sports Ground)
Lodge
Hotel
The Weirs
CHRISTCHURCH ROAD
A337
Chewton Common
CHEWTON COMMON
HIGHCLIFFE
Highcliffe St. Mark Primary School
COBBS HOLIDAY PK.
CHEWTON FARM ESTATE
THE MEADOW
HOBURNE NAISH HOLIDAY PARK
FIELD PLACE
Community Centre
Rec. Grd.
HIGH CLIFF
Recreation Ground
Highcliffe Castle
Chewton Bunny
Nature Reserve
Lob's Hole
Bay View
Smugglers View
Island View
Marine Court
BARTON CLIFF
MARINE DRIVE
Westcliffe Bldgs.
COASTGUARD COTTS.
CHRISTCHURCH BAY
221
232
H J K L M N
G H J K L M N
1 2 3 4 5 6 7 8 9
21 22 23
96 95 94 93 92

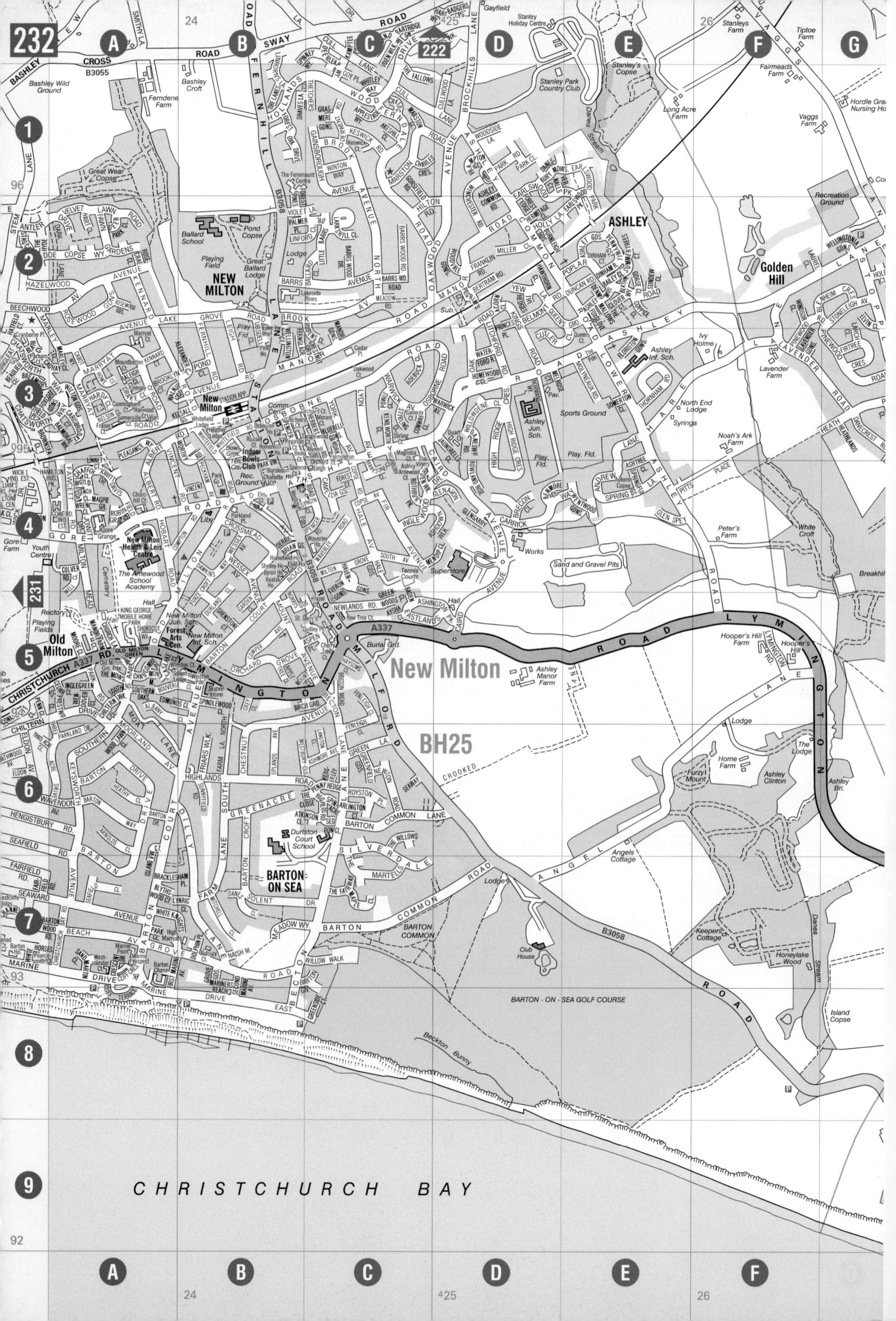

222
231
A
B
C
D
E
F
G
1
2
3
4
5
6
7
8
9
24
425
26
96
95
94
93
92
NEW MILTON
New Milton
ASHLEY
Golden Hill
Old Milton
BARTON ON SEA
BH25
CHRISTCHURCH BAY
BARTON - ON - SEA GOLF COURSE
BARTON COMMON
Bashley Wild Ground
Bashley Croft
Ferndene Farm
Great Wear Copse
Ballard School
Playing Field
Pond Copse
Great Ballard Lodge
The Fernmount Centre
Lakeside Pines
Stanley Holiday Centre
Stanley Park Country Club
Stanley's Copse
Stanleys Farm
Long Acre Farm
Tiptoe Farm
Fairmeads Farm
Vaggs Farm
Hordle Grange Nursing Home
Recreation Ground
Dane's Stream
Gayfield
Ashley Inf. Sch.
Ashley Jun. Sch.
Sports Ground
Play. Fld.
Ivy Holme
Lavender Farm
North End Lodge
Syringa
Noah's Ark Farm
Peter's Farm
White Croft
Breakhill
Sand and Gravel Pits
Works
Superstore
Tennis Courts
Indoor Bowls Club
Rec. Ground
New Milton Health & Leis Centre
The Arnewood School Academy
Cemetery
Gore Farm
Youth Centre
Rectory
Playing Fields
New Milton Jun. Sch.
Forest Arts Cen.
New Milton Inf. Sch.
Burial Grd.
Ashley Manor Farm
Hooper's Hill Farm
Hooper's Hill
Lodge
The Lodge
Home Farm
Furzy Mount
Ashley Clinton
Ashley Bri.
Angels Cottage
Durlston Court School
Club House
Keepers Cottage
Honeylake Wood
Island Copse
Beckton Bunny
BASHLEY CROSS ROAD
B3055
SWAY ROAD
FERNHILL LANE
B3058
STATION RD.
LYMINGTON ROAD
A337
CHRISTCHURCH RD.
MILFORD ROAD
ASHLEY ROAD
MANOR ROAD
LAKE GROVE ROAD
GORE ROAD
BARTON COMMON ROAD
BARTON COMMON LANE
ANGEL LANE
CROOKED LANE
MARINE DRIVE
MARINE DRIVE EAST
HIGHLANDS ROAD
OSBORNE ROAD
STEM LANE
VAGGS LANE
HARE LANE

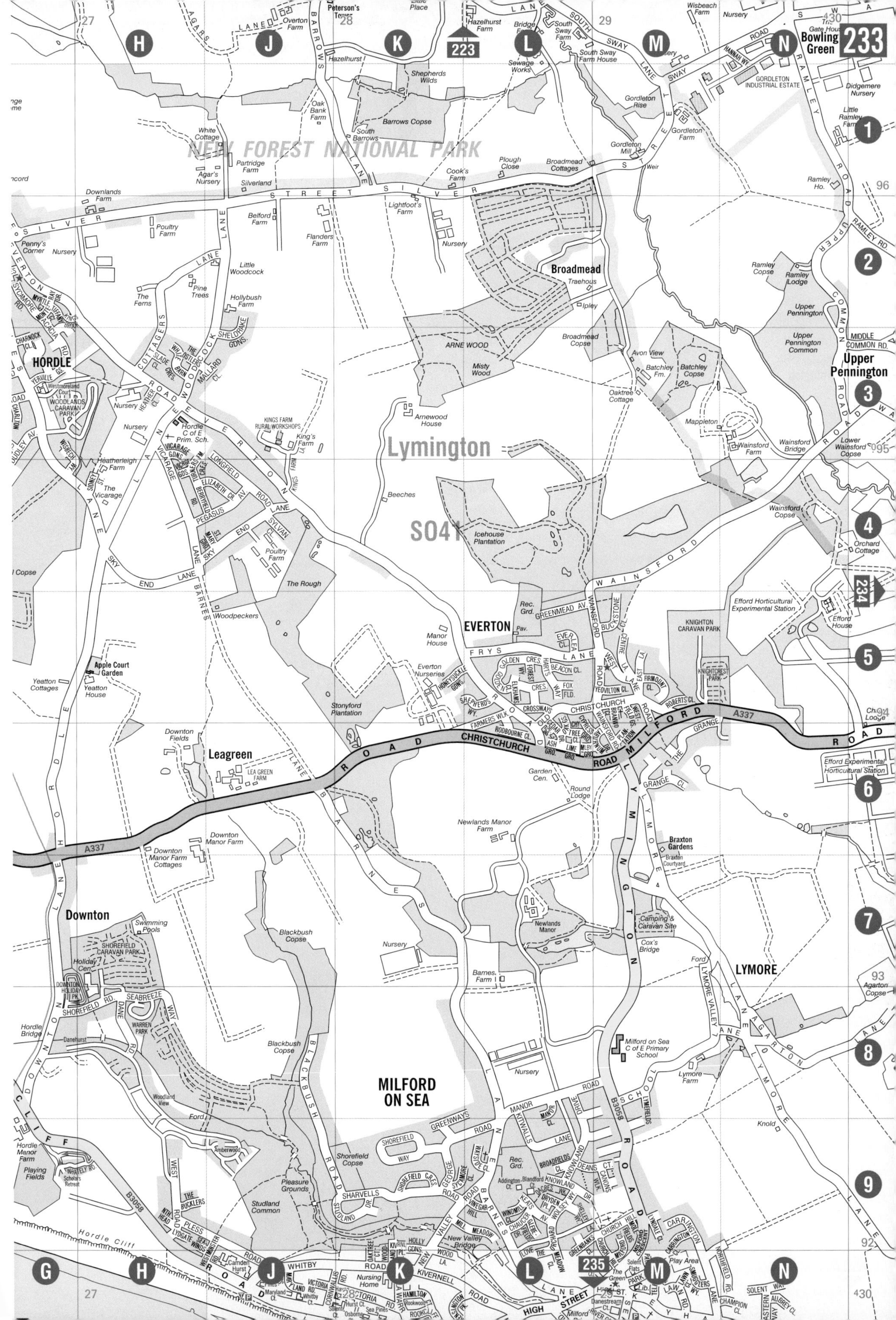
223
234
235
NEW FOREST NATIONAL PARK
Lymington
SO41
HORDLE
EVERTON
Broadmead
Upper Pennington
Leagreen
Downton
MILFORD ON SEA
LYMORE
Bowling Green
Peterson's Tower
Hazelhurst Farm
Overton Farm
South Sway Farm
South Sway Farm House
Sewage Works
Gordleton Rise
Gordleton Farm
Gordleton Mill
GORDLETON INDUSTRIAL ESTATE
Didgemere Nursery
Little Ramley Farm
Ramley Ho.
Shepherds Wilds
Barrows Copse
Oak Bank Farm
South Barrows
White Cottage
Partridge Farm
Agar's Nursery
Silverland
Cook's Farm
Plough Close
Broadmead Cottages
Downlands Farm
Belford Farm
Lightfoot's Farm
Flanders Farm
Poultry Farm
Penny's Corner
Little Woodcock
Pine Trees
The Ferns
Hollybush Farm
Traehous
Ipley
Broadmead Copse
ARNE WOOD
Misty Wood
Avon View
Batchley Fm.
Batchley Copse
Oaktree Cottage
Ramley Copse
Ramley Lodge
Upper Pennington Common
Mappleton
Wainsford Farm
Wainsford Bridge
Lower Wainsford Copse
Wainsford Copse
Orchard Cottage
Arnewood House
KINGS FARM RURAL WORKSHOPS
King's Farm
Hordle C of E Prim. Sch.
Heatherleigh Farm
The Vicarage
Beeches
Icehouse Plantation
Poultry Farm
The Rough
Woodpeckers
Rec. Grd.
Pav.
Manor House
Everton Nurseries
Stonyford Plantation
KNIGHTON CARAVAN PARK
KNIGHTCREST PARK
Efford Horticultural Experimental Station
Efford House
Apple Court Garden
Yeatton House
Yeatton Cottages
Downton Fields
LEA GREEN FARM
Garden Cen.
Round Lodge
Newlands Manor Farm
Braxton Gardens
Braxton Courtyard
Downton Manor Farm
Downton Manor Farm Cottages
Swimming Pools
SHOREFIELD CARAVAN PARK
Holiday Cen.
DOWNTON HOLIDAY PK
WARREN PARK
Blackbush Copse
Nursery
Newlands Manor
Camping & Caravan Site
Cox's Bridge
Barnes Farm
Ford
Agarton Copse
Hordle Bridge
Danehurst
Milford on Sea C of E Primary School
Lymore Farm
Knold
Woodland View
Amberwood
Hordle Manor Farm
Playing Fields
Scholars Retreat
Shorefield Copse
Pleasure Grounds
Studland Common
Addington
Blandford Ct.
Rec. Grd.
Hordle Cliff
Camden Hurst
Nursing Home
New Valley Bridge
Solent Flats
Play Area
The Green
Danestream
A337
B3058
CHRISTCHURCH ROAD
MILFORD ROAD
LYMINGTON ROAD
SILVER STREET
SWAY ROAD
RAMLEY ROAD
UPPER COMMON ROAD
MIDDLE COMMON RD.
EVERTON ROAD
HORDLE LANE
DOWNTON LANE
BARNES LANE
SKY END LANE
FRYS LANE
WAINSFORD ROAD
GREENMEAD AV.
LYMORE LANE
AGARTON LANE
LYMORE VALLEY
BLACKBUSH ROAD
SHOREFIELD ROAD
SEABREEZE WAY
CLIFF ROAD
WESTOVER ROAD
MANOR ROAD
SCHOOL LANE
HIGH STREET
KIVERNELL ROAD
WHITBY ROAD
GREENWAYS
SHOREFIELD WAY
STUDLAND DR.
SHARVELLS
NEW VALLEY ROAD
BARROWS LANE
AGARS LANE
COTTAGERS LANE
WOODCOCK LANE
VICARAGE LANE
PEGASUS AV.
LONGFIELD
SYLVAN CL.
GRANGE CL.
NORTHFIELD RD.
SOLENT WAY
HAMILTON
CARRINGTON
G H J K L M N
1 2 3 4 5 6 7 8 9
27 28 29 430
96 95 94 93 92

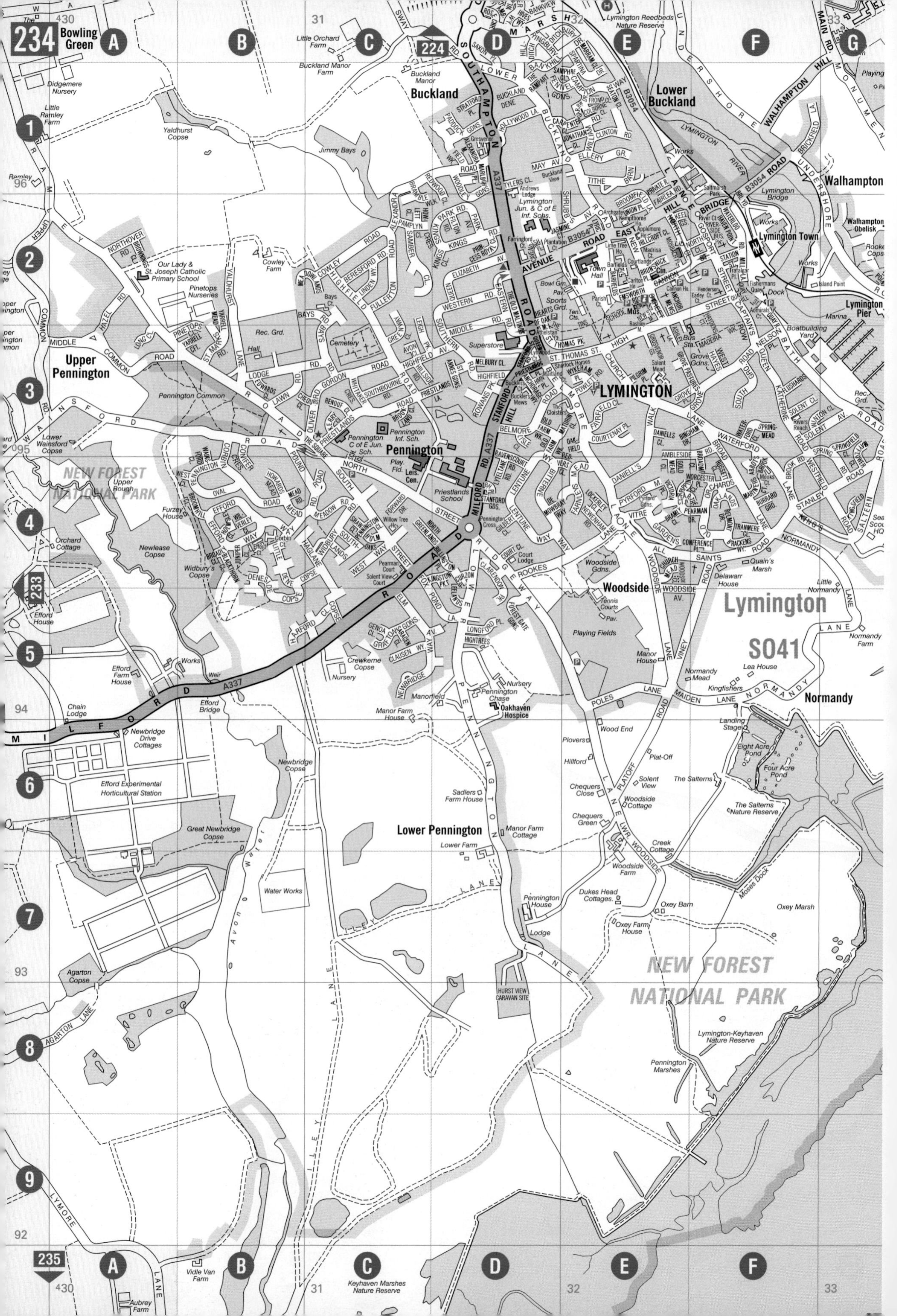
Bowling Green
A
B
C
D
E
F
G
224
233
235
430
31
32
33
96
95
94
93
92
1
2
3
4
5
6
7
8
9
Buckland
Lower Buckland
Walhampton
Upper Pennington
Pennington
LYMINGTON
Lymington Town
Lymington Pier
Woodside
Lymington
SO41
Normandy
Lower Pennington
NEW FOREST NATIONAL PARK
Lymington Reedbeds Nature Reserve
Little Orchard Farm
Buckland Manor Farm
Buckland Manor
Didgemere Nursery
Little Ramley Farm
Yaldhurst Copse
Jimmy Bays
Cowley Farm
Our Lady & St. Joseph Catholic Primary School
Pinetops Nurseries
Pennington Common
Lower Wainsford Copse
Upper Rough
Furzey House
Orchard Cottage
Newlease Copse
Widbury's Copse
Efford House
Efford Farm House
Chain Lodge
Efford Bridge
Newbridge Drive Cottages
Efford Experimental Horticultural Station
Newbridge Copse
Great Newbridge Copse
Water Works
Agarton Copse
Vidle Van Farm
Aubrey Farm
Keyhaven Marshes Nature Reserve
Crewkerne Copse
Manor Farm House
Manorfield
Pennington Chase
Oakhaven Hospice
Sadlers Farm House
Manor Farm Cottage
Lower Farm
Pennington House
Lodge
HURST VIEW CARAVAN SITE
Priestlands School
Pennington C of E Jun. Sch.
Pennington Inf. Sch.
Leis. Cen.
Play. Fld.
Superstore
Town Hall
Lymington Jun. & C of E Inf. Schs.
Lymington Bridge
Fishermans Quay
Dock
Marina
Boatbuilding Yard
Island Point
Walhampton Obelisk
Woodside Gdns.
Playing Fields
Manor House
Tennis Courts
Wood End
Plovers
Hillford
Plat-Off
Solent View
Chequers Close
Chequers Green
Woodside Cottage
Creek Cottage
Woodside Farm
Dukes Head Cottages
Oxey Barn
Oxey Farm House
Oxey Marsh
Moses Dock
The Salterns
The Salterns Nature Reserve
Eight Acre Pond
Four Acre Pond
Landing Stage
Kingfishers
Lea House
Normandy Mead
Normandy Farm
Delawarr House
Quain's Marsh
Lymington-Keyhaven Nature Reserve
Pennington Marshes
SOUTHAMPTON ROAD
MILFORD ROAD
STANFORD HILL
HIGH STREET
AVENUE ROAD
EAST HILL
GOSPORT STREET
WAINSFORD ROAD
MIDDLE COMMON ROAD
LYMINGTON RIVER
UNDERSHORE
WALHAMPTON HILL
A337
B3054
LYMORE LANE
AGARTON LANE
RIDGEWAY LANE
LOWER PENNINGTON LANE
LOWER WOODSIDE
PLATOFF ROAD
MAIDEN LANE
POLES LANE
NORMANDY LANE
ALL SAINTS ROAD
WATERFORD LANE
STANLEY ROAD
ROOKES LANE
NORTH STREET
SOUTH STREET
WEST WAY
ST. THOMAS ST.
BRIDGE ROAD
STATION ST.
QUAY HILL

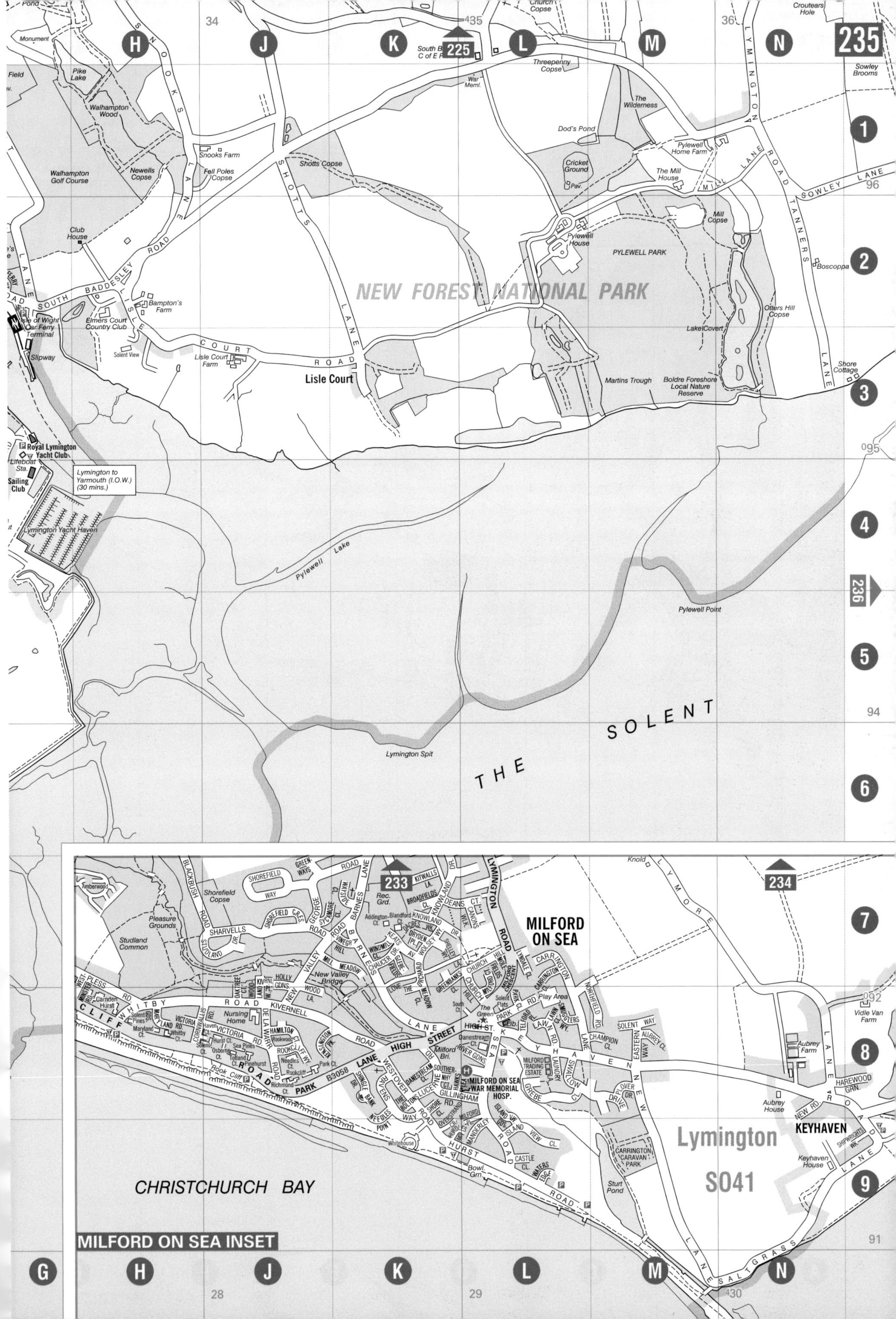

H **J** **K** **L** **M** **N**

1
2
3
4
5
6

225

235

236

NEW FOREST NATIONAL PARK

Monument

Pike Lake

Walhampton Wood

Walhampton Golf Course

Club House

Newells Copse

Snooks Farm

Fell Poles Copse

Shotts Copse

Shotts Copse

South B
C of E P

War Meml.

Threepenny Copse

Church Copse

Croutears Hole

Sowley Brooms

96

Dod's Pond

The Wilderness

Cricket Ground

Pav.

Pylewell Home Farm

The Mill House

Mill Copse

Mill Copse

Isle of Wight Car Ferry Terminal

Slipway

South BADDESLEY

ISLE

COURT

ROAD

ROAD

Elmers Court Country Club

Bampton's Farm

Lisle Court Farm

Solent View

Lisle Court

PYLEWELL PARK

Pylewell House

Lake Covert

Martins Trough

Boldre Foreshore Local Nature Reserve

Otters Hill Copse

Shore Cottage

Boscoppa

095

Royal Lymington Yacht Club

Lifeboat Sta.

Sailing Club

Lymington Yacht Haven

Lymington to Yarmouth (I.O.W.) (30 mins.)

Pylewell Lake

Pylewell Point

Lymington Spit

THE SOLENT

94

7
8
9

233

234

Knold

LYMINGTON ROAD

LYMORE

SALIGRASS

MILFORD ON SEA

Lymington

SO41

KEYHAVEN

Keyhaven House

Aubrey Farm

Aubrey House

Vidle Van Farm

HAREWOOD GRN.

092

NEW RD.

CHRISTCHURCH BAY

MILFORD ON SEA INSET

G **H** **J** **K** **L** **M** **N**

28
29
430
91

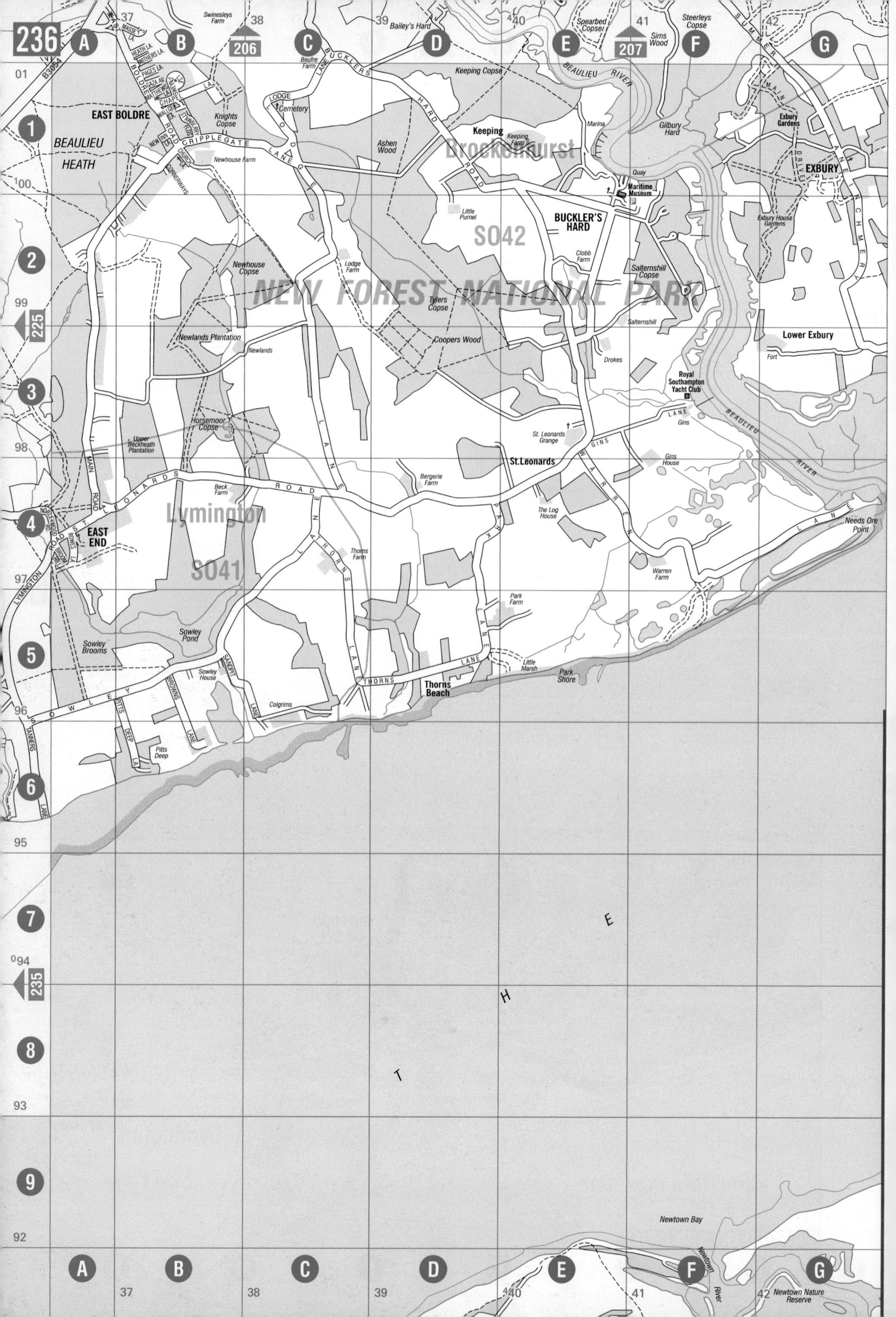

CALSHOT
Sprat's Down
Hillhead
Eaglehurst
LANGLEY
West Common
Horsemoor Copse
Southampton
SO45
North Solent Nature Reserve
Newhouse Copse
Stanswood Common
Calshot Foreshore Country Pk.
Stanswood
Stanswood Farm
Whitefield Farm
Nelson's Place
STANSWOOD BAY
East Wood
Dark Water
East Hill Farm
Cadland House
Stone
Stone Farm
Lepe Farm
The Moor
Exbury River
Lepe Point Nature Reserve
Lepe Country Park
LEPE
Inchmerry House
Stansore Point
Stone Point
Gull Island
SOLENT
COWES ROADS
West Cowes to Southampton 22 mins (Foot Ferry, Fast Ferry)
Egypt Point
QUEEN'S ROAD
Cowes Castle
PO31
COWES
Cowes High Sch.
Northwood Ho.
208
209
Winnall Moors Nature Reserve
Swift's Lake
Tumbling Bay
ITCHEN
River Park Leisure Cen.
Rec. Grd.
Dutton Bri.
St. Bede C of E Prim. Sch.
University of Southampton (Winchester Sch. of Art)
Textile Conservation Cen.
WINCHESTER
105
County Record Office
Theatre Royal
Disc. Cen. Lib.
Winchester
Oram's Arbour Recreation Grd.
Police HQ
HMP WINCHESTER
County Council Offices
Elizabeth II Ct.
Mottisfont Ct.
The Brooks Experience
Supermarket
Bus Sta.
Gt. Hall
Combined Courts
Royal Hampshire Regiment Mus.
Museums
Reservoir (covered)
SO22
SO23
City Museum
WINCHESTER
Winchester Cathedral
Guildhall
City Council Offs.
King Alfred's Statue
Abbey Grounds
Abbey Mill
City Mill
Youth Hostel
Chesil Theatre
ROYAL HAMPSHIRE COUNTY HOSPITAL
Marfield Ho.
St. James' Hall
St. Elizabeth's Hall
St. Grimbalds Ct.
West Hill
Cemetery
St. Thomas Cen.
Everyman Cinema
Visitor Cen.
The Deanery
The Close
Triforium Gallery
Priory Ga.
Kings Ga.
The Pilgrims Sch.
Wolvesey Castle
Wolvesey Palace
Meeting Ho.
Playing Field
University of Winchester (King Alfred Campus)
Playground
Medecroft
Milnthorpe
Tennis Court
Bowl. Grn.
Jane Austen Plaque
War Meml.
Winchester College
Play. Fld.
Wharf Hill
Millers Ho.
ROMSEY ROAD
B3040
HIGH STREET
JEWRY ST.
ST. GEORGE'S ST.
FRIARSGATE
EASTGATE ST.
CITY RD.
NORTH WALLS
B3330
SOUTHGATE ST.
ST. CROSS ROAD
B3335
CANON STREET
COLLEGE STREET
ST. SWITHUN STREET
CHESIL ST.
CLIFTON TER.
UPPER HIGH ST.
B3420
HYDE ST.
B3047
SUSSEX ST.
STAPLE GARDENS
ST. PETER ST.
PARCHMENT ST.
ST. PAUL'S HILL
ST. JAMES' LANE
CHRISTCHURCH ROAD
EDGAR ROAD
KINGSGATE
MILNTHORPE LANE
SPARKFORD ROAD
ERSKINE ROAD
PENINSULA ROAD
COMPTON ROAD
BEAUFORT ROAD
ST. MICHAEL'S RD.
ALEXANDRA TER.
CROWDER TER.
WEST END TER.
WEST HILL DRIVE
MILVERTON ROAD
FORDINGTON AVENUE
CHERITON ROAD
GREENHILL AV.
WESTERN ROAD
ELM ROAD
CLIFTON ROAD
MIDDLE ROAD
STOCKBRIDGE RD.
STATION HILL
GLADSTONE ST.
ANDOVER RD.
MARSTON GATE
ABBEY ROAD
GORDON ROAD
PARK AVENUE
DURNGATE
BROOK ST.
UNION ST.
BRIDGE STREET
WHARF HILL

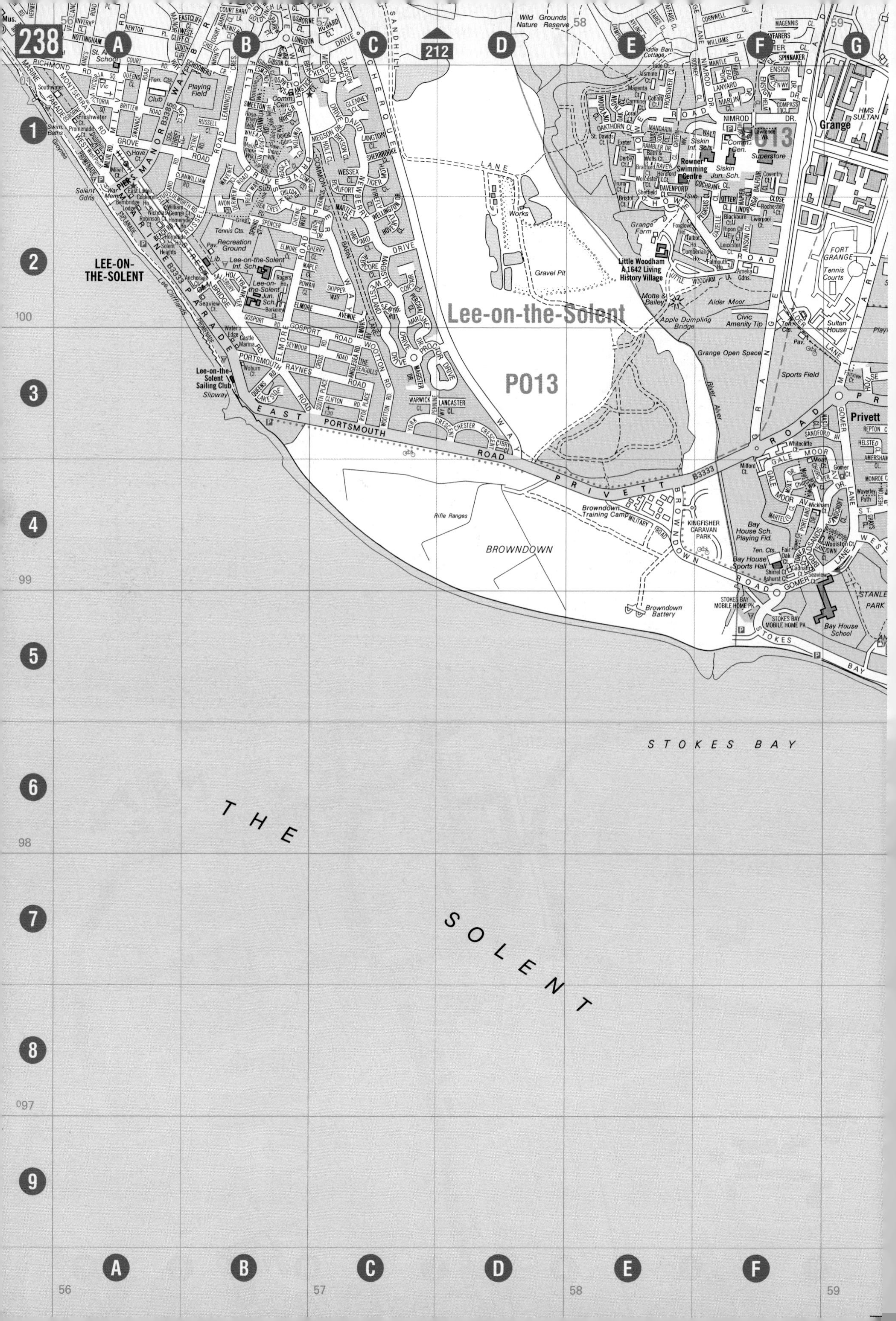
212
Lee-on-the-Solent
PO13
LEE-ON-THE-SOLENT
Wild Grounds Nature Reserve
Grange
HMS SULTAN
Privett
FORT GRANGE
Little Woodham A 1642 Living History Village
Gravel Pit
Works
Grange Farm
Motte & Bailey
Alder Moor
Apple Dumpling Bridge
Civic Amenity Tip
Grange Open Space
Sports Field
River Alver
Rowner Swimming Centre
Siskin Inf. Sch.
Siskin Jun. Sch.
Superstore
Comm. Cen.
Sultan House
Browndown Training Camp
KINGFISHER CARAVAN PARK
Rifle Ranges
BROWNDOWN
Browndown Battery
Bay House Sch. Playing Fld.
Bay House Sports Hall
Bay House School
STOKES BAY MOBILE HOME PK
Lee-on-the-Solent Sailing Club
Slipway
Recreation Ground
Tennis Cts.
Playing Field
Lee-on-the-Solent Inf. Sch.
Lee-on-the-Solent Jun. Sch.
Swim. Baths
Groynes
Solent Gdns
War Mem.
EAST PORTSMOUTH ROAD
PRIVETT ROAD
B3333
B3385
MARINE PARADE
CHEREQUE WAY
SANDHILL
GRANGE LANE
BROWNDOWN ROAD
MILITARY ROAD
STOKES BAY
THE SOLENT
A B C D E F G
1 2 3 4 5 6 7 8 9
56 57 58 59
100 99 98 97

H
J
K
L
M
N
G
1
2
3
4
5
6
7
8
9
460
61
62
01
100
99
98
97
213
240
FORT ROWNER
Brockhurst
Brockhurst Jun. Sch.
BROCKHURST RD.
A32
FORTON ROAD
MUMBY ROAD
Gosport
GOSPORT
Camdentown
Ann's Hill
Ann's Hill Cemetery
Forton
Leesland Park
Newtown
Seafield
Clayhall
Anglesey
ALVERSTOKE
PO12
H.M.S. Sultan
St. Vincent Leisure Centre
St. Vincent College
Quayside Education Centre
Playing Field
Newtown C of E Prim. Sch.
GOSPORT WAR MEML. HOSP.
Thorngate Hall
Leesland C of E Jun. Sch.
Privett Park (Recreation Ground)
Gosport Borough FC
Gomer Jun. & Inf. Schs.
Privett Gdns.
Alverstoke Jun. Sch.
Alverstoke Sports Club
Northcott House
Gosport Gallery
Walpole Park
Boating Pond
Cockle Pond
Superstore
Gas Works
Workhouse Lake
Stoke Lake
GOSPORT PARK
The Dell
Ewer Common
Little Anglesey Viaduct
Haslar Royal Naval Cemetery
HM Immigration Removal Centre Haslar
Defence Research Agency
HMS Alliance
Royal Navy Submarine Mus.
HM Sub. Holland 1
Recreation Ground
Haslar Bridge
Gosport Marina
Royal Clarence Marina
Priddy's Hard
The Mus. of Naval Firepower
Forton Lake
Burrow Island (site of Fort James)
Weevil Lake
PORTSMOUTH HARBOUR
PORTSMOUTH GOSPORT
Waterbus
Gosport to Portsea 4mins. (Foot Ferry)
King Charles's Fort
Falklands Gds.
Landing Stage
South Wharf
North Bastion
West Demi Bastion
Stokes Bay Sailing Club
Stokes Bay Open Space
Gosport & District Angling Club
GOSPORT & STOKES BAY GOLF COURSE
FORT MONCKTON
FORT GILKICKER
Gilkicker Point
Groynes
Club House
Sports Ground
Moncktown Ho. Institute of Naval Medicine
Royal Naval Physiological Laboratory
SPITHEAD
STOKES BAY ROAD
PROMENADE
HASLAR SEA WALL
DOLPHIN WAY
CLAYHALL ROAD
SOUTH STREET
STOKE ROAD
BURY ROAD
B3333
HIGH STREET
HASLAR ROAD
MILITARY ROAD
FORT ROAD
ANGLESEY ROAD
JELLICOE AVENUE
PALMERSTON WAY
SOLENT WAY
LEESLAND ROAD
PRIVETT ROAD
CAMBRIDGE ROAD
ANN'S HILL ROAD
THE AVENUE
WALPOLE ROAD
DOCK ROAD
JAMAICA PL.
SPRING GARDEN LA.
FERROL ROAD
PARHAM ROAD
MILL LANE
THE CROSSWAYS
WHITWORTH ROAD
CARNARVON ROAD
RICHMOND RD.
ELMHURST ROAD
ST. ANDREWS RD.
ST. MARY'S AVENUE
LITTLE ANGLESEY ROAD
CLAYHALL
ADMIRALTY ROAD
THE ESPLANADE
TRINITY GREEN
CLARENCE WHARF
ROPE QUAYS
Harlequin Ct.
The Officers Quarters

PORTSMOUTH
Portsea
Old Portsmouth
SOUTHSEA
Southsea
Somers Town
Fratton
Landport
Kingston
PORTSMOUTH HARBOUR
GUNWHARF QUAYS
HM NAVAL BASE
Historic Dockyard
HMS Victory
Mary Rose Mus.
Royal Naval Mus.
HMS Warrior 1860
Spinnaker Tower
I.O.W. Ferry Terminal (Vehicular)
The Round Tower
Point Battery
The Square Tower
Cathedral
Clarence Pier Amusement Park
I.O.W. Hovercraft Terminal
SOUTHSEA Royal Naval War Meml.
SOUTHSEA COMMON
Blue Reef Aquarium
D-Day Mus.
Southsea Castle & Mus.
The Pyramids Leisure Cen.
The Rock Gardens
South Parade Pier
Canoe Lake
Natural History Mus.
Southsea Model Village
University of Portsmouth
PORTSMOUTH & SOUTHSEA
City Mus. & Art Gall.
HMS NELSON
HMS Temeraire
Gosport to Portsea 4mins. (Foot Ferry)
Portsmouth to Fishbourne 40mins.
Portsmouth to Ryde 22mins. (Foot Ferry, Fast Ferry)
Portsmouth to Ryde 10mins. (Foot Ferry, Hovercraft)
WINSTON CHURCHILL AV.
GOLDSMITH
ANGLESEA RD.
HIGH STREET
CLARENCE PARADE
SOUTH PARADE
ESPLANADE
A3
A228
A2030
A288
B2154
B2151
A2047
SPITHEAD
ENGLISH
214
239
5
63
64
465
01
100
99
98
97
A B C D E F G
1 2 3 4 5 6 7 8 9

LANGSTONE HARBOUR
CHANNEL
Milton Common
Milton
Eastney
Fort Cumberland
Langstone Channel
University of Portsmouth (Langstone Campus)
University of Portsmouth (Marine Sciences)
St. James' Hospital
St. Mary's Hospital (West Wing)
Portsmouth FC (Fratton Park)
Eastney Beam Engine House
Royal Marines Mus.
Eastney Swimming Pool
Locks Sailing Club
Fraser Range
Eastney Sports Ground
Bransbury Park
Highland Road Cemetery
Milton Cemetery
Miniature Golf Course
West Winner
PO3
PO4
PO11
A2030
A288
B2154
215
242

LANGSTONE HARBOUR

Sinah Sands

Sinah Lake

North Lake

Sinah Lake

Golding Lake

Rabbit Lake

Boathouse Lake

Jetty

Jetty

Jetty

ing Stages

Slipway

THE KENCH

The Kench
(Nature Reserve)

Sinah Farm

Sinah Warren
HOLIDAY &
LEISURE CLUB

Pier

Playing Field

Sinah Warren

SINAH COMMON

Gunner Point

HAYLING GOLF COURSE

Club House

Miniature Golf Links

Pavilion

Beachcot

SOUTH HAYLING

East Winner

HAYLING BAY

ENGLISH

SHORE ROAD

NORTH ROAD

STATION ROAD

SINAH LANE

HARBOUR RD.

LIME GRO.

WARREN CL.

PARK

SINAH

ST. CATHERINES

ST. AUBIN

ST. THOMAS

ST. THOMAS

AVENUE

AVENUE

AVENUE

RICHMOND DR.

Maple Ct.

Milliam

Fountain Square

Tennis Courts

Bowling Green

Comm. Cen.

Hayling Park Recreation Ground

St. Catherines Court

ST. HELENS ROAD

ST. GEORGE RD.

STAUNTON

BACON

CLOSE

FERNHURST

The Gorseway

The Gate Ho.

BAY VIEW

NORFOLK CRES.

Norfolk

WEST CL.

BATHURST

R Ward

Royal Apartments

Reading
Rooms

Funland

HAYLING ISLAND

Newtown

Hayling Billy Line Nature Reserve

Station Theatre

HAYLING BILLY BUSINESS CENTRE

WOODLANDS

SALTMARSH LANE

BRIGHTS LANE

GLEBE RD.

CHARLE CL.

DANGE WAY

NEWTOWN LA.

Nursery

The OVEN CAMP SITE

Higworth Farm

HAYLING ISLAND HOLIDAY PARK

War Meml.

Gable Head

PO11

Manor Farm

Manor House

Pound Copse

Honeyrings Copse

HIGHFIELD

DOVER MANOR CT. RD.

KENSINGTON

SPINNAKER

SOUTH

FATHOMS

MAIN ROAD

BEACH ROAD

MENGHAM LANE

ST. MARYS ROAD

SYCAMORE DR.

GARDEN M.

SILVER SANDS CL.

WESTFIELD AV.

Westfield

OAKWOOD

ELM CLOSE

ELM CLOSE

ESTATE

WALNUT TREE

CHERRYWOOD GDNS.

ROOK FARM WY.

Mengham Inf. Sch.

WEST TOWN

West Town

Westfield

SEACOURT

Seacourt Tennis Club

VICTORIA RD.

ALEXANDRA

CHICHESTER AVE.

MANOR

SEA WAY

WEBB LA.

GROVE ROAD

RAMSEY AVE.

CHURCH ROAD

KATRINA GDNS.

LULWORTH CL.

GROVE

East Hayling Light Rly.

The Beach

241

CHICHESTER HARBOUR

Pilsey Sand

STOCKER'S LAKE

Slipways Jetties
Yachtbuilding Yard

Mill Rythe Jun. & Inf. Schools

MILL RYTHE

Boating Lake Pound Marsh
Boat Ho.

Mill Rythe Holiday Village

Middle Marsh

Harvey Brown House
Play ground

L A N D

TOURNERBURY GOLF COURSE

Pepper Cl.
The Hayling College

Driving Range

Club Ho.

Tourner Bury Farm

Tournerbury Marsh

Dip Rithe

Menghan Rithe

EASTWARD

Tourner Bury

Tourner Bury Wood

Rec. Grd.

Mengham Junior School

Tourner Bury Plantations

Mengham Court
Mengham House

Slipway

Jetty

My Lord's Pond

Mengham Rythe Sailing Club

Mengham Salterns

Mengham

Pond Head Ho.

Jetty

Salterns Quay

Cockle Point

CHICHESTER HAVANT EMSWORTH CHANNEL

Landing Stage   Black Point

Jetty

Selsmore

MARINE WALK

SEA VIEW ROAD

North's Salterns

Yacht Harbour

Boat Yard

Slipway

Hayling Island Sailing Club

Sea View

Mengham Pk. Rec. Grd.

CHAND-LERS CL.
BURDA

WOODCOTT CVN. PK.

Lakeside Holiday Village

Quay

FISHERS CVN. PK.

The Sanderlings

Dikusha

St. Herman's Caravan Estate

Boating Lake

Fishery Creek Caravan & Camping Pk.

The Triangle CVN. PK.
WATERS EDGE
THE RETREAT
TWO ACRES CVN. PK.
THE BINNACLE CVN. PK.

CAMARON CVN. PK.
BEVERLEY CVN. PK.

THE HOLLIES CARAVAN PK.

EARNLEY RING

WITTERING ROAD

SANDY POINT

Hayling Island Lifeboat Station & Museum

Coastguard Lookout

Eastoke

St. Herman's

Slipway Jetty

GOOSE GRN CVN. PK.

THE GLADE HOLIDAY HOME PK.
CHERRY TREE HOLIDAY CVN. PK.
ELLIOTS CVN. EST.

SEAFARERS

Sandy Point Nature Reserve

GREENHAVEN CARAVAN PK.

HAVEN ROAD

WEST HAYE RD.

Comm. Cen.

WHEATLANDS

SANDY POINT

AVENUE

BEACH ESTATE

Maloney M.

Chardan Ct.

Beach Ct.

Eastoke Point

C H A N N E L

244
226
ASHLEY
BRANKSOME
PARKSTONE
Poole
BH12
BH13
BH14
Branksome Park
Lilliput
Canford Cliffs
Compton Acres
SANDBANKS
POOLE HARBOUR
Branksome
Bowlplex
Lindsay Hall
Victoria Sch.
Convent
Monastery
Alexandra Park
Courthill First Sch.
Uplands School
Club House
Overlinks Viewpoint
Luscombe Valley
Luscombe Valley Nature Reserve
Lilliput C of E First Sch.
Lewis Manning Hospice
East Dorset Sailing Club
ST. ANN'S HOSPITAL
North Haven Yacht Club
Royal Motor Yacht Club
Sandbanks Pav.
Branksome Chine Pleasure Gds.
Canford Cliffs Chine Gardens
Pleasure Gardens
49 Alumhurst Road
Library
A35
A338
B3065
B3369
BOURNEMOUTH ROAD
POOLE ROAD
WESSEX WAY
POOLE BOURNEMOUTH
A
B
C
D
E
F
G
1
2
3
4
5
6
7
8
9
405
06
07
88
89
90
91
92

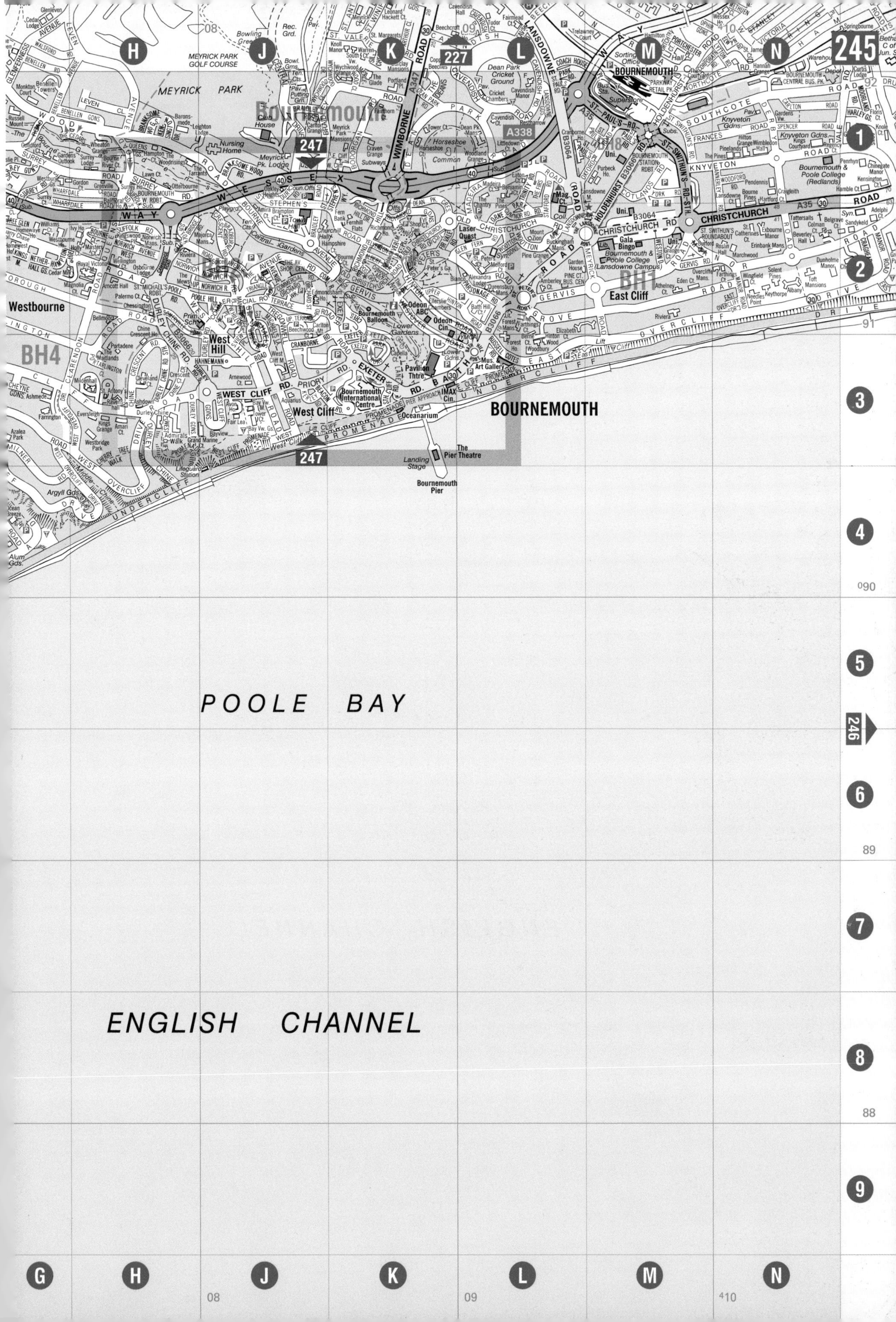
MEYRICK PARK GOLF COURSE
MEYRICK PARK
Bournemouth
WESSEX WAY
WIMBORNE ROAD
LANSDOWNE
BOURNEMOUTH
CHRISTCHURCH ROAD
Westbourne
BH4
BH1
East Cliff
West Hill
WEST CLIFF
West Cliff
Bournemouth International Centre
Pavilion Thtre.
BOURNEMOUTH
The Pier Theatre
Bournemouth Pier
OVERCLIFF DRIVE
UNDERCLIFF
POOLE BAY
ENGLISH CHANNEL
227
247
246
H
J
K
L
M
N
G
1
2
3
4
5
6
7
8
9

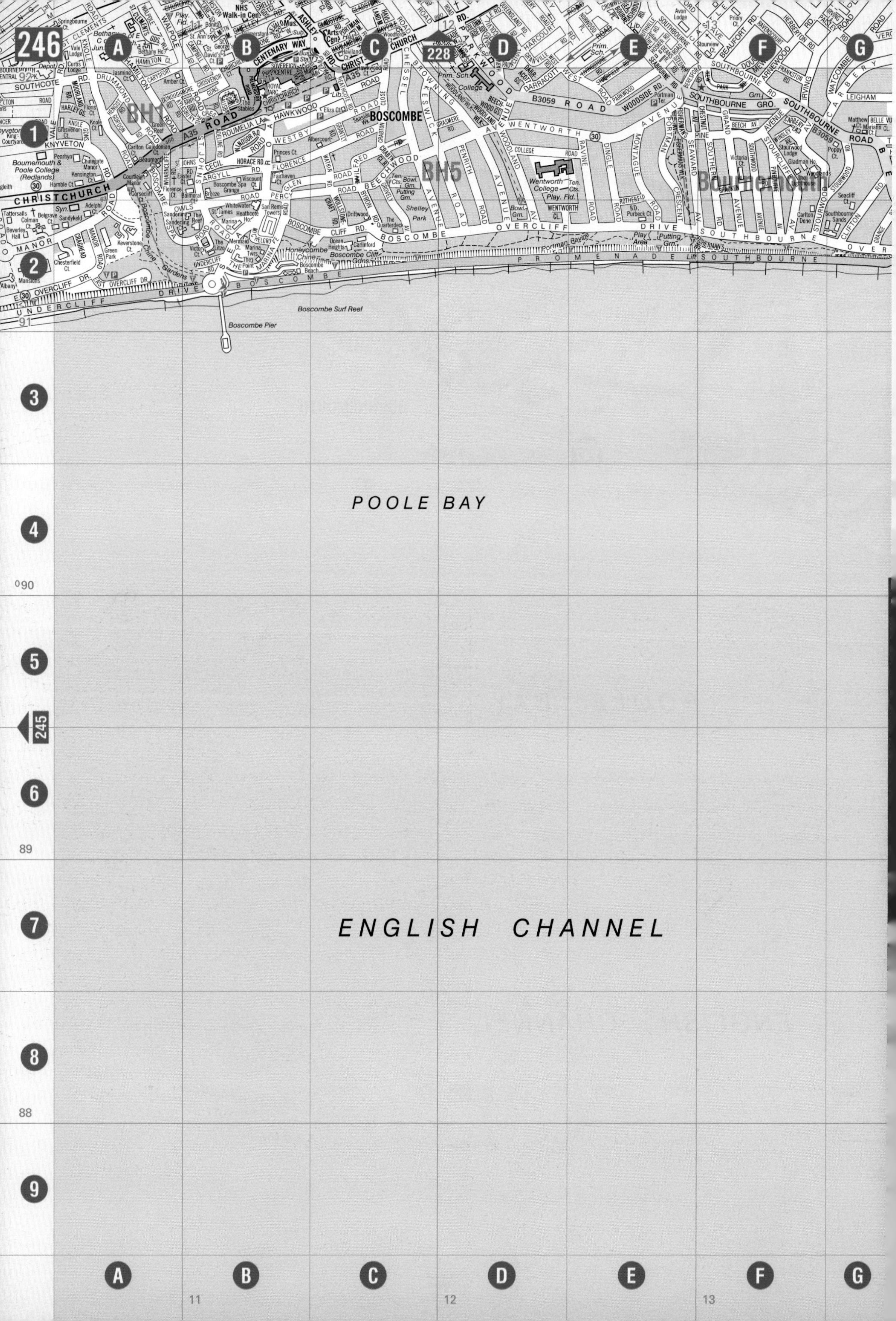

POOLE BAY

ENGLISH CHANNEL

Boscombe Surf Reef

Boscombe Pier

BOSCOMBE

Bournemouth

CHRISTCHURCH

CENTENARY WAY

BH1

BH5

245

228

229
West Southbourne
WICK
Golf Driving Range
Christchurch
BH23
Grimbury Point
Grimbury Marsh
Crouch Hill
Hengistbury Head Nature Reserve
St. Peter's School
BH6
SOLENT MEADS GOLF COURSE
SOLENT MEADS
Field Studies Cen.
Wick Hams
CHRISTCHURCH
BOURNEMOUTH
Pitch & Putt Course
SOUTHBOURNE
White Pits
Double Dykes
HENGISTBURY
HEAD
Coastguard Lookout Station
245
MEYRICK PARK GOLF COURSE
Horseshoe Common
A338
WESSEX WAY
A347
WIMBORNE R.
Central Gardens
BH2
Upper Gardens
Bournemouth Register Off.
Town Hall
Council Offices
THE AVENUE SHOPPING CENTRE
BH1
Laser Quest
Synagogue
St. Michael's C of E Prim.Sch.
BH4
West Hill
Bournemouth
Bournemouth Balloon
Lower Gardens
Odeon ABC Cin.
Odeon Cinema
Bandstand
YMCA
Pavilion Theatre
Russell-Cotes Art Gallery & Mus.
East Cliff
IMAX Cinema
Bournemouth International Centre
West Cliff
Oceanarium
BOURNEMOUTH
POOLE BAY
The Pier Theatre
Bournemouth Pier
Landing Stage
Lifeguard Station
B3066

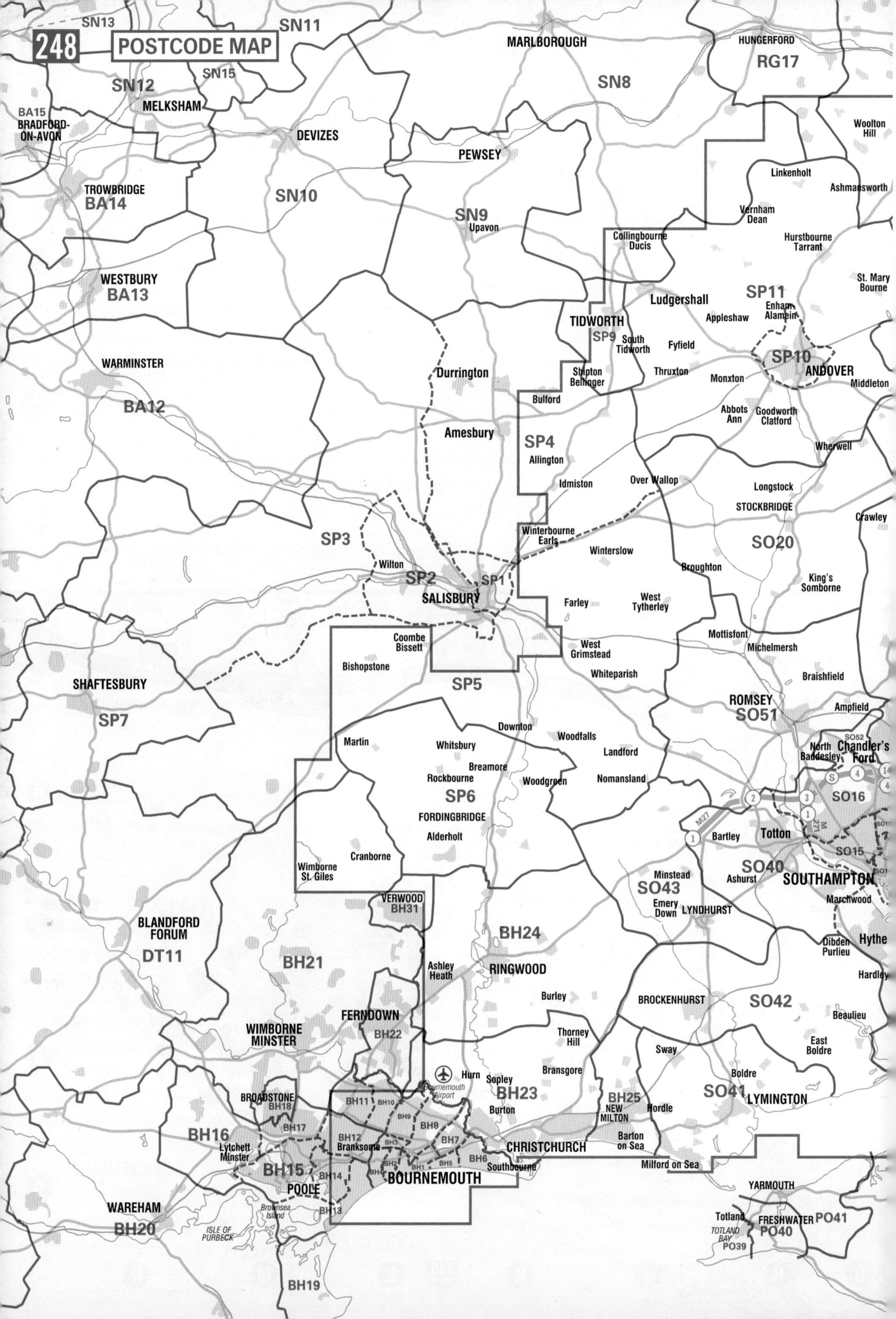

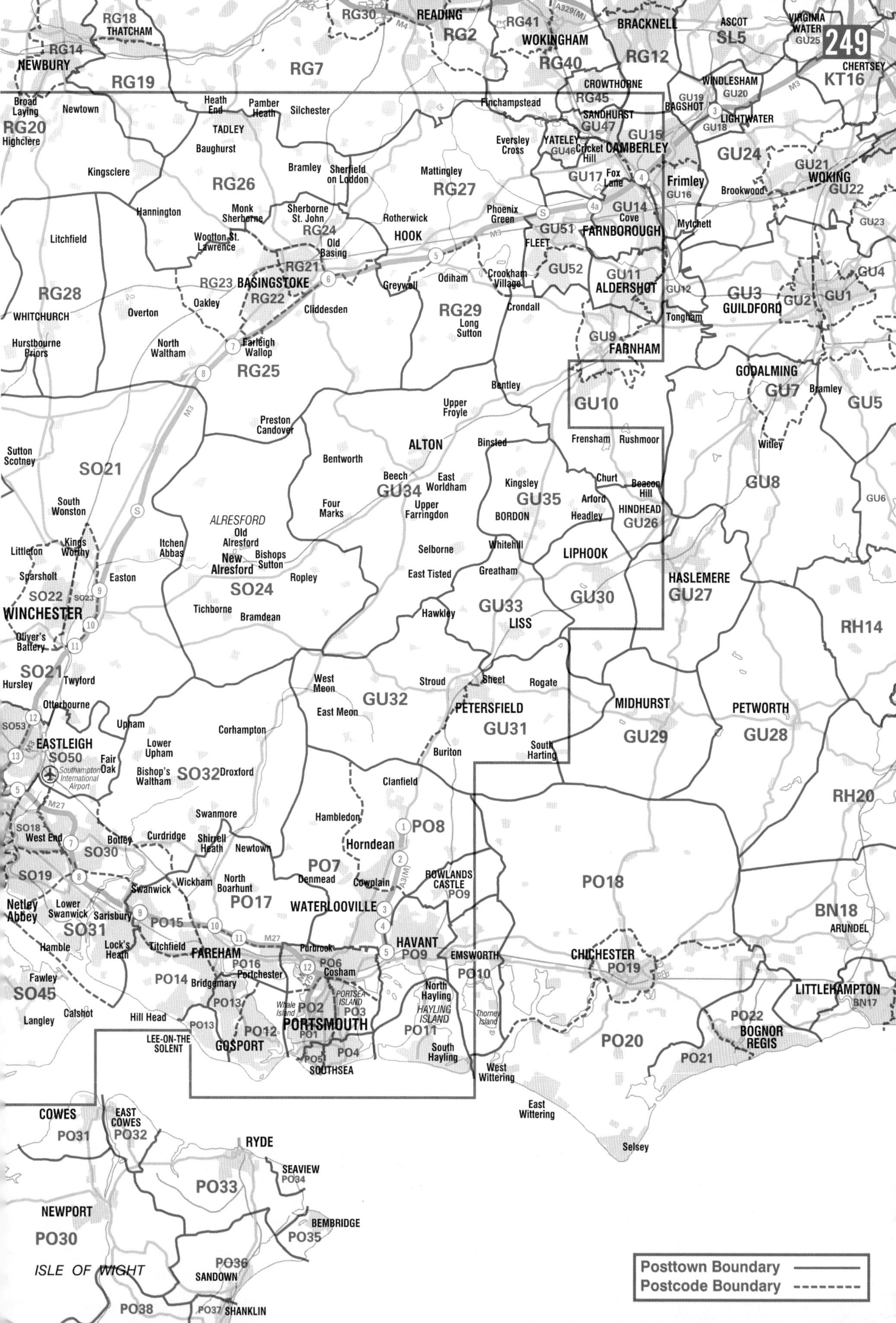
RG18
THATCHAM
RG30
READING
RG2
RG41
WOKINGHAM
BRACKNELL
ASCOT
SL5
VIRGINIA WATER
GU25
RG14
NEWBURY
RG7
RG40
RG12
CHERTSEY
KT16
RG19
CROWTHORNE
WINDLESHAM
GU20
Broad Laying
Newtown
Heath End
Pamber Heath
Silchester
Finchampstead
RG45
GU19
BAGSHOT
LIGHTWATER
GU18
RG20
Highclere
TADLEY
SANDHURST
GU47
Baughurst
Eversley Cross
YATELEY
GU46
Cricket Hill
GU15
CAMBERLEY
GU24
Kingsclere
RG26
Bramley
Sherfield on Loddon
Mattingley
RG27
GU17
Fox Lane
Frimley
GU16
GU21
WOKING
GU22
Brookwood
Hannington
Monk Sherborne
Sherborne St. John
RG24
Rotherwick
Phoenix Green
GU14
Cove
FARNBOROUGH
Mytchett
GU23
Litchfield
Wootton St. Lawrence
Old Basing
HOOK
GU51
FLEET
M3
RG21
RG23
BASINGSTOKE
RG22
Greywell
Odiham
Crookham Village
GU52
GU11
ALDERSHOT
GU12
GU4
RG28
WHITCHURCH
Overton
Oakley
Cliddesden
RG29
Long Sutton
Crondall
Tongham
GU3
GUILDFORD
GU2
GU1
Hurstbourne Priors
North Waltham
Farleigh Wallop
RG25
GU9
FARNHAM
GODALMING
GU7
Bramley
GU5
Bentley
GU10
Upper Froyle
Preston Candover
ALTON
Binsted
Frensham
Rushmoor
Witley
Sutton Scotney
SO21
Bentworth
Beech
East Worldham
GU34
Kingsley
GU35
Churt
Beacon Hill
GU8
South Wonston
Four Marks
Upper Farringdon
BORDON
Arford
Headley
HINDHEAD
GU26
GU6
ALRESFORD
Old Alresford
Itchen Abbas
New Alresford
Bishops Sutton
Littleton
Kings Worthy
Selborne
Whitehill
LIPHOOK
Sparsholt
Easton
Ropley
East Tisted
Greatham
HASLEMERE
GU27
SO22
SO23
SO24
GU30
WINCHESTER
Tichborne
Bramdean
Hawkley
GU33
LISS
RH14
Oliver's Battery
SO21
Hursley
Twyford
West Meon
Stroud
Sheet
Rogate
GU32
Otterbourne
East Meon
PETERSFIELD
GU31
MIDHURST
PETWORTH
GU29
GU28
SO53
Upham
Corhampton
EASTLEIGH
Lower Upham
Buriton
South Harting
SO50
Fair Oak
Southampton International Airport
Bishop's Waltham
SO32
Droxford
Clanfield
RH20
M27
Swanmore
Hambledon
PO8
SO18
West End
Botley
Curdridge
Shirrell Heath
Newtown
Horndean
SO30
PO7
PO18
SO19
Swanwick
Wickham
North Boarhunt
Denmead
Cowplain
A3(M)
ROWLANDS CASTLE
PO9
PO17
Netley Abbey
Lower Swanwick
Sarisbury
WATERLOOVILLE
BN18
SO31
PO15
ARUNDEL
Hamble
Lock's Heath
Titchfield
FAREHAM
M27
Purbrook
HAVANT
PO9
EMSWORTH
CHICHESTER
PO19
Fawley
PO16
Portchester
PO6
Cosham
PO10
SO45
PO14
Bridgemary
North Hayling
LITTLEHAMPTON
BN17
PO13
Whale Island
PO2
PORTSEA ISLAND
PO3
HAYLING ISLAND
Thorney Island
Langley
Calshot
Hill Head
PO13
PORTSMOUTH
PO22
BOGNOR REGIS
PO12
PO1
PO11
LEE-ON-THE SOLENT
GOSPORT
PO4
South Hayling
PO20
PO5
SOUTHSEA
PO21
West Wittering
East Wittering
COWES
EAST COWES
PO31
PO32
Selsey
RYDE
SEAVIEW
PO34
PO33
NEWPORT
BEMBRIDGE
PO30
PO35
ISLE OF WIGHT
PO36
SANDOWN
Posttown Boundary
Postcode Boundary
PO38
PO37
SHANKLIN

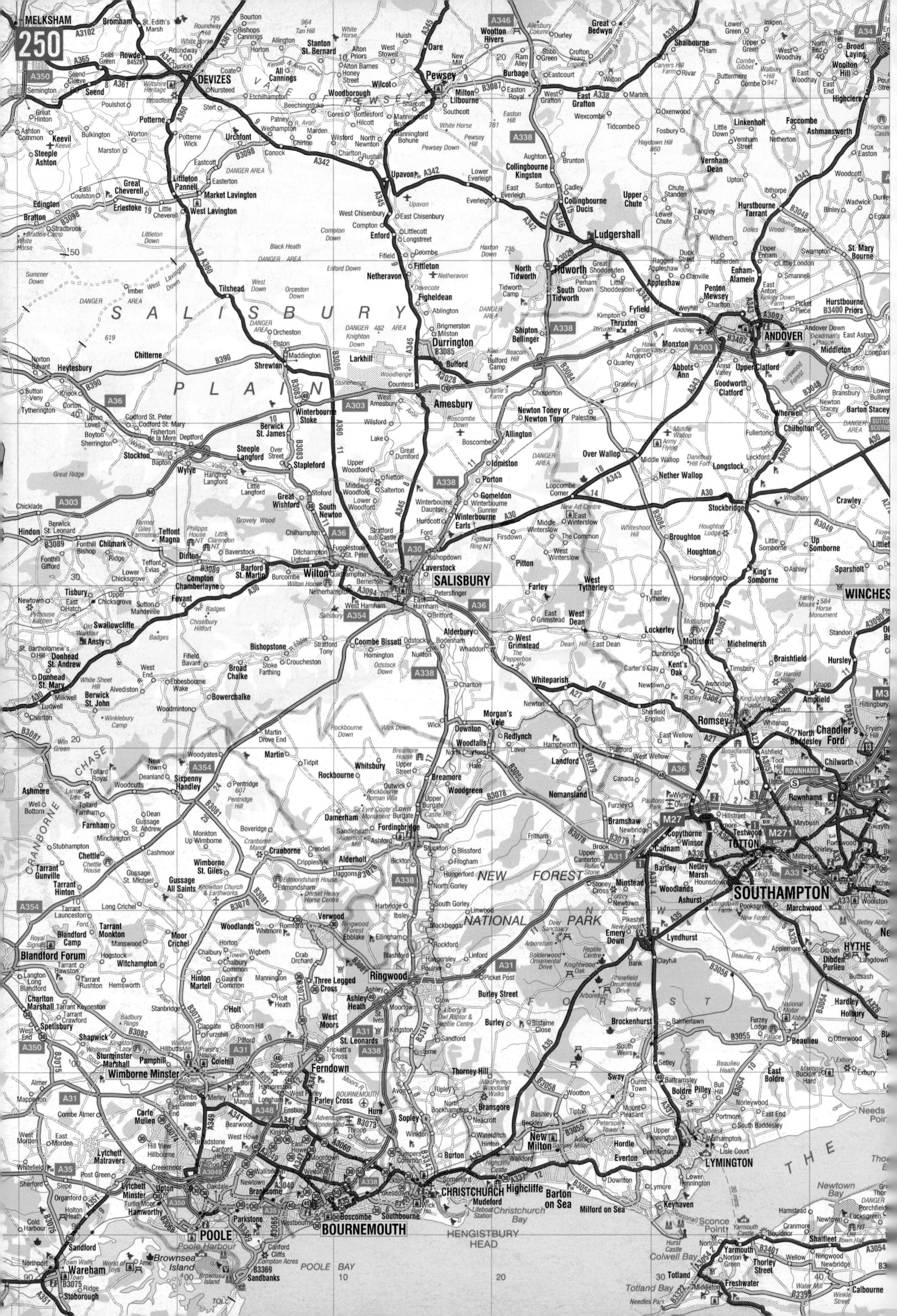
MELKSHAM
DEVIZES
VALE OF PEWSEY
Pewsey
Upavon
Ludgershall
Tidworth
Andover
ANDOVER
SALISBURY PLAIN
Tilshead
Shrewton
Larkhill
Durrington
Bulford
Amesbury
Stonehenge
Heytesbury
Wylye
Wilton
SALISBURY
Stockbridge
King's Somborne
WINCHES
Romsey
Chandler's Ford
Fordingbridge
Ringwood
Verwood
Ferndown
Wimborne Minster
Blandford Forum
CRANBORNE CHASE
NEW FOREST
NATIONAL PARK
Lyndhurst
Brockenhurst
Totton
SOUTHAMPTON
HYTHE
Beaulieu
Lymington
LYMINGTON
New Milton
Barton on Sea
Highcliffe
CHRISTCHURCH
Christchurch Bay
HENGISTBURY HEAD
BOURNEMOUTH
POOLE
Poole Harbour
POOLE BAY
Brownsea Island
Sandbanks
Wareham
Swanage
Yarmouth
Totland
Freshwater
THE SOLENT
Colwell Bay
Totland Bay
Needles Park
Keyhaven
Milford on Sea
M27
M271
A303
A338
A36
A30
A31
A35
A354
A350
A345
A342
A346
A343
A3057
A34

Brimpton
Aldermaston
Mortimer
Stratfield Mortimer
Swallowfield
Finchampstead
Crowthorne
Windlesham
Bagshot
Newtown
Crookham
Heath End
Pamber Heath
Silchester
Tadley
Eversley
Eversley Centre
Eversley Cross
Sandhurst
Little Sandhurst
Owlsmoor
CAMBERLEY
Lightwater
Chobham
Burghclere
Baughurst
Bramley
Bramley Green
Sherfield on Loddon
Yateley
Cricket Hill
Frogmore
Blackwater
Frimley
West End
Bisley
Horsell
Kingsclere
Hawley
Fox Lane
Frimley Green
Deepcut
Brookwood
Knaphill
Mayford
Sydmonton
Hartley Wintney
Phoenix Green
FLEET
Monk Sherborne
Sherborne St. John
Rotherwick
Mattingley
Hannington
Cove
FARNBOROUGH
Mytchett
Pirbright
Litchfield
Newnham
Hook
Fleet
Ash Vale
Worplesdon
Upper Wootton
Wootton St. Lawrence
Old Basing
North Warnborough
Greywell
Crookham Village
ALDERSHOT
Normandy
BASINGSTOKE
Odiham
GUILDFORD
Oakley
Overton
Cliddesden
Crondall
Ash
Flexford
Tongham
Whitchurch
Upton Grey
Long Sutton
South Warnborough
FARNHAM
Puttenham
Compton
North Waltham
Farleigh Wallop
Ellisfield
Shackleford
Bramley
GODALMING
Dummer
Peper Harow
Tilford
Elstead
Milford
Lower Froyle
Bentley
Upper Froyle
Preston Candover
Bradley
Holybourne
Millbridge
Frensham
Rushmoor
Witley
Hascombe
Alton
Binsted
Thursley
Micheldever
Sutton Scotney
Bentworth
Beech
Medstead
Chawton
East Worldham
Kingsley
Churt
Beacon Hill
Hambledon
South Wonston
Upper Farringdon
Four Marks
Lindford
Arford
Headley
Headley Down
Hindhead
Grayshott
Chiddingfold
Kings Worthy
Itchen Abbas
Old Alresford
Bighton
Selborne
Bordon
Whitehill
Bramshott
Haslemere
Headbourne Worthy
Easton
New Alresford
Bishops Sutton
Ropley
East Tisted
Greatham
Liphook
Linchmere
Tichborne
Cheriton
Bramdean
Hawkley
Liss Forest
Liss
Rake
Hill Brow
Fernhurst
Northchapel
Twyford
Steep
Sheet
PETERSFIELD
Stroud
West Meon
East Meon
Owslebury
Colden Common
Otterbourne
Rogate
Trotton
Dumpford
Minsted
Stedham
Midhurst
West Lavington
Easebourne
Lodsworth
Petworth
Tillington
Byworth
Upham
Lower Upham
Exton
Corhampton
Meonstoke
Buriton
South Harting
Cocking Causeway
EASTLEIGH
Fair Oak
Durley
Droxford
Bishop's Waltham
Swanmore
Clanfield
Cocking
Graffham
Duncton
Horton Heath
Waltham Chase
Shirrell Heath
Soberton Heath
Hambledon
HORNDEAN
Chilgrove
Compton
Singleton
West Dean
Sutton
Hedge End
Botley
Curdridge
Shedfield
Newtown
Denmead
Lovedean
Cowplain
Foreststide
Rowland's Castle
Wickham
North Boarhunt
WATERLOOVILLE
Bursledon
Lower Swanwick
Swanwick
Sarisbury
Park Gate
Locks Heath
Purbrook
HAVANT
Westbourne
Emsworth
Southbourne
Hambrook
East Ashling
West Ashling
CHICHESTER
Mid Lavant
East Lavant
Westhampnett
Boxgrove
Tangmere
Fontwell
Slindon
Walberton
Eastergate
Westergate
Barnham
Yapton
Hamble-le-Rice
Warsash
Titchfield
FAREHAM
Portchester
Cosham
Stubbington
Bridgemary
Hill Head
Lee-on-the-Solent
GOSPORT
PORTSMOUTH
Whale Island
Stoke
North Hayling
West Thorney
Thorney Island
Chidham
Nutbourne
Bosham
Fishbourne
Runcton
Merston
North Mundham
Hunston
SOUTH HAYLING
HAYLING ISLAND
Hayling Bay
West Itchenor
Birdham
Shipton Green
West Wittering
East Wittering
Bracklesham
Sidlesham
Pagham
Selsey
SELSEY BILL
BOGNOR REGIS
Felpham
Middleton-on-Sea
Fawley
Calshot
SOLENT
COWES
Cowes Roads
East Cowes
Osborne Bay
Gurnard
Northwood
Whippingham
Wootton
Wootton Bridge
Fishbourne
Ryde Roads
RYDE
SPITHEAD
Seaview
Nettlestone
Havenstreet
St. Helens
Bembridge
Brading
FORELAND
NEWPORT
Arreton
SOUTH DOWNS NATIONAL PARK
SOUTH DOWNS
M3
M27
M275
A3(M)
A3
A31
A27
A272
A339
A33
A34
A303
A32
A325
A331
A29
A259
A286
A283
A285
SCALE
1: 307,865
5 miles to 1"
0 1 2 3 Miles
0 1 2 3 4 5 Kilometres
Portsmouth to:
Bilbao 24hrs.
Caen 3hrs. 45mins. (Fast Ferry, Seasonal)
Caen 6hrs. (Seasonal)
Cherbourg 4hrs. 30mins. (Seasonal)
Cherbourg 3hrs. (Fast Ferry, Seasonal)
Guernsey 7hrs.
Jersey 9hrs.
Le Havre 5hrs. 30mins.
St. Malo 9hrs.
Santander 24hrs.
70
80
90

INDEX

Including Streets, Places & Areas, Industrial Estates,
Selected Flats & Walkways, Service Areas, Stations and Selected Places of Interest.

HOW TO USE THIS INDEX

1. Each street name is followed by its Postcode District, then by its Locality abbreviation(s) and then by its map reference; e.g. **Abbey Rd.** RG24: B'toke . . . .2B **42** is in the RG24 Postcode District and the Basingstoke Locality and is to be found in square 2B on page **42**. The page number is shown in bold type.

2. A strict alphabetical order is followed in which Av., Rd., St., etc. (though abbreviated) are read in full and as part of the street name;
e.g. **Avoncliffe Rd.** appears after **Avon Causeway** but before **Avon Cl.**

3. Streets and a selection of flats and walkways that cannot be shown on the mapping, appear in the index with the thoroughfare to which they are connected shown in brackets;
e.g. **Abbey Ter.** SP11: Stoke . . . .7H **35** (off Chapel La.)

4. Addresses that are in more than one part are referred to as not continuous.

5. Places and areas are shown in the index in BLUE TYPE and the map reference is to the actual map square in which the town centre or area is located and not to the place name shown on the map;
e.g. **ALDERSHOT** 9J **49**

6. An example of a selected place of interest is Aldershot Military Mus. 5L **49**

7. An example of a station is **Aldershot Station (Rail)** . . . .1K **65**, also included is Park & Ride
e.g. **East Winchester (Barfield) (Park & Ride)** 8M **105**

8. Service Areas are shown in the index in BOLD CAPITAL TYPE; e.g. **FLEET SERVICE AREA** 8J **27**

9. Map references for entries that appear on large scale pages **4-5**, **237** & **247** are shown first, with small scale map references shown in brackets; e.g. **Albert Rd.** BH1: Bour 6L **247** (2K **245**)

GENERAL ABBREVIATIONS

All. : Alley	**Ct.** : Court	**Info.** : Information	**Prom.** : Promenade
App. : Approach	**Cres.** : Crescent	**Intl.** : International	**Ri.** : Rise
Arc. : Arcade	**Cft.** : Croft	**Junc.** : Junction	**Rd.** : Road
Av. : Avenue	**Dr.** : Drive	**La.** : Lane	**Rdbt.** : Roundabout
Blvd. : Boulevard	**E.** : East	**Lit.** : Little	**Shop.** : Shopping
Bri. : Bridge	**Ent.** : Enterprise	**Lwr.** : Lower	**Sth.** : South
B'way. : Broadway	**Est.** : Estate	**Mnr.** : Manor	**Sq.** : Square
Bldg. : Building	**Fld.** : Field	**Mans.** : Mansions	**Sta.** : Station
Bldgs. : Buildings	**Flds.** : Fields	**Mkt.** : Market	**St.** : Street
Bungs. : Bungalows	**Gdn.** : Garden	**Mdw.** : Meadow	**Ter.** : Terrace
Bus. : Business	**Gdns.** : Gardens	**Mdws.** : Meadows	**Twr.** : Tower
C'way. : Causeway	**Gth.** : Garth	**M.** : Mews	**Trad.** : Trading
Cen. : Centre	**Ga.** : Gate	**Mt.** : Mount	**Up.** : Upper
Chu. : Church	**Gt.** : Great	**Mus.** : Museum	**Va.** : Vale
Circ. : Circle	**Grn.** : Green	**Nth.** : North	**Vw.** : View
Cl. : Close	**Gro.** : Grove	**Pde.** : Parade	**Vs.** : Villas
Comn. : Common	**Hgts.** : Heights	**Pk.** : Park	**Vis.** : Visitors
Cnr. : Corner	**Ho.** : House	**Pas.** : Passage	**Wlk.** : Walk
Cott. : Cottage	**Ho's.** : Houses	**Pl.** : Place	**W.** : West
Cotts. : Cottages	**Ind.** : Industrial	**Pct.** : Precinct	**Yd.** : Yard

POSTTOWN AND POSTAL LOCALITY ABBREVIATIONS

Abb W : **Abbots Worthy**	Blen : **Blendworth**	C'vle : **Clanville**	Edmo : **Edmondsham**
Abb A : **Abbotts Ann**	Blis : **Blissford**	Clid : **Cliddesden**	Elin : **Eling**
Abs : **Abshot**	Boar : **Boarhunt**	Col C : **Colden Common**	Ell : **Ellingham**
Alder : **Alderbury**	Bock : **Bockhampton**	Col H : **Cole Henley**	Elli : **Ellisfield**
Ald : **Alderholt**	Bold : **Boldre**	C'more : **Colemore**	Els : **Elsted**
A'mas : **Aldermaston**	Bor : **Bordon**	Coll : **College Town**	Elve : **Elvetham**
Alders : **Aldershot**	Bosc : **Boscombe**	Co Du : **Collingbourne Ducis**	Em D : **Emery Down**
All : **Allington**	Botl : **Botley**	Co Ki : **Collingbourne Kingston**	Emp : **Empshott**
Alt : **Alton**	Bour : **Bournemouth**	Comb : **Combe**	Ems : **Emsworth**
Ames : **Amesbury**	Bour A : **Bournemouth International Airport**	Comp : **Compton**	Enbo : **Enborne**
Ampf : **Ampfield**	Brac : **Bracknell**	Conh : **Conholt**	Enbo R : **Enborne Row**
Amp : **Amport**	Brad : **Bradley**	Com B : **Coombe Bissett**	Enh A : **Enham Alamein**
A'ver : **Andover**	Brai : **Braishfeld**	Copy : **Copythorne**	Eve : **Eversley**
And D : **Andover Down**	B'dge : **Brambridge**	Corh : **Corhampton**	Ever : **Everton**
A'ell : **Andwell**	Bram : **Bramdean**	Cosh : **Cosham**	Ews : **Ewshot**
An V : **Anna Valley**	B'ley : **Bramley**	Cott : **Cottonworth**	Exb : **Exbury**
Apple : **Appleshaw**	B'haw : **Bramshaw**	Cov : **Cove**	Ext : **Exton**
Ash : **Ash**	Brams : **Bramshill**	Cowes : **Cowes**	Fabe : **Faberstown**
Ashe : **Ashe**	B'sht : **Bramshott**	Cowp : **Cowplain**	Facc : **Faccombe**
A'field : **Ashfield**	Bran : **Bransgore**	Cram : **Crampmoor**	Fair O : **Fair Oak**
Ashf H : **Ashford Hill**	Brea : **Breamore**	Cran : **Cranborne**	Fare : **Fareham**
A'ley : **Ashley**	Brim : **Brimpton**	Craw : **Crawley**	Far W : **Farleigh Wallop**
Ashl H : **Ashley Heath**	Brim C : **Brimpton Common**	Crip : **Cripplestyle**	Far : **Farley**
Ashm : **Ashmansworth**	Br Ch : **Broad Chalke**	Croc H : **Crockham Heath**	Fa H : **Farley Hill**
Ashu : **Ashurst**	Broc : **Brockenhurst**	Cron : **Crondall**	Farl : **Farlington**
Ash V : **Ash Vale**	Broo : **Brook**	C Cmn : **Crookham Common**	Farn : **Farnborough**
Avin : **Avington**	Brou : **Broughton**	Cr V : **Crookham Village**	Farnh : **Farnham**
Avon : **Avon**	B Can : **Brown Candover**	Crow : **Crow**	Fawl : **Fawley**
Awb : **Awbridge**	B Oak : **Bucks Horn Oak**	Cr'tne : **Crowthorne**	F'std : **Finchampstead**
Axf : **Axford**	Bul : **Bulford**	C Eas : **Crux Easton**	Finch : **Finchdean**
Axm : **Axmansford**	Bul C : **Bulford Camp**	Curd : **Curdridge**	Firs : **Firsdown**
Bad L : **Badshot Lea**	B'gte : **Burgate**	Dame : **Damerham**	Fis P : **Fisher's Pond**
Bal H : **Ball Hill**	Burgh : **Burghclere**	Dea : **Deane**	Fleet : **Fleet**
Bart : **Bartley**	Buri : **Buriton**	Den : **Denmead**	Fob : **Fobdown**
B Sea : **Barton on Sea**	Bur : **Burley**	Dib : **Dibden**	Ford : **Ford**
Bar S : **Barton Stacey**	Burr : **Burridge**	Dib P : **Dibden Purlieu**	F'dge : **Fordingbridge**
Bash : **Bashley**	Burs : **Bursledon**	Dipp : **Dippenhall**	Fort : **Forton**
B'toke : **Basingstoke**	Burt : **Burton**	Dock : **Dockenfield**	Fos : **Fosbury**
Bass : **Bassett**	B'mre : **Buttermere**	Dogm : **Dogmersfield**	Four M : **Four Marks**
Bau : **Baughurst**	Cad : **Cadnam**	Down : **Downton**	Free : **Freefolk**
Beau : **Beaulieu**	Calm : **Calmore**	Dray : **Drayton**	Fren : **Frensham**
B'wth : **Beauworth**	Cals : **Calshot**	Drox : **Droxford**	Fri C : **Friars Cliff**
Bed : **Bedhampton**	Camb : **Camberley**	Dumm : **Dummer**	Frim : **Frimley**
Bee : **Beech**	Cath : **Catherington**	Dun : **Dunbridge**	Frim G : **Frimley Green**
Bee H : **Beech Hill**	Chal : **Chalton**	Durl : **Durley**	Frog : **Frogham**
Ben'ly : **Bentley**	Cha F : **Chandler's Ford**	E Ant : **East Anton**	Frox : **Froxfield**
Bent : **Bentworth**	Charl : **Charlton**	E Ch : **East Cholderton**	Full : **Fullerton**
Bick : **Bickton**	Ch St : **Charlton-All-Saints**	E Dean : **East Dean**	F'ley : **Funtley**
Bidd : **Biddesden**	Cha A : **Charter Alley**	E End : **East End**	Fyf : **Fyfield**
Bigh : **Bighton**	Cher : **Cheriton**	E Gri : **East Grimstead**	Gods : **Godshill**
Binl : **Binley**	Chil : **Chilbolton**	E Har : **East Harting**	Gome : **Gomeldon**
Bins : **Binsted**	Chilc : **Chilcomb**	E Meon : **East Meon**	G Cla : **Goodworth Clatford**
Bis G : **Bishop's Green**	Ch Can : **Chilton Candover**	E Par : **East Parley**	Gor E : **Gore End**
Bis S : **Bishop's Sutton**	Chilw : **Chilworth**	E Str : **East Stratton**	Gos : **Gosport**
B'stke : **Bishopstoke**	Chin : **Chineham**	E Tis : **East Tisted**	Grat : **Grateley**
Bish : **Bishopstone**	Chol : **Cholderton**	E Tyt : **East Tytherley**	Gray : **Grayshott**
Bis W : **Bishop's Waltham**	Chri : **Christchurch**	E Wel : **East Wellow**	G'ham : **Greatham**
Bist : **Bisterne**	Ch Cr : **Church Crookham**	E Win : **East Winterslow**	Gt S : **Great Shoddesden**
Blac : **Blackfield**	Chur : **Churt**	E Woo : **East Woodhay**	Green : **Greenham**
Blackm : **Blackmoor**	Chu C : **Chute Cadley**	E Wor : **East Worldham**	Grey : **Greywell**
Blackn : **Blacknest**	Chu F : **Chute Forest**	E'leigh : **Eastleigh**	Gund : **Gundleton**
Blackw : **Blackwater**	Chu S : **Chute Standen**	E'ton : **Easton**	Gus S : **Gussage All Saints**
Blas : **Blashford**	Clan : **Clanfield**	Ecc : **Ecchinswell**	Hale : **Hale**

Ham : **Ham**
H'don : **Hambledon**
Hamb : **Hamble-le-Rice**
H'twth : **Hamptworth**
Ham M : **Hamstead Marshall**
Hang : **Hangersley**
Hann : **Hannington**
Har : **Harbridge**
Hard : **Hardley**
H Wes : **Hartley Wespall**
H Win : **Hartley Wintney**
Hasl : **Haslemere**
Hath : **Hatherden**
Hav : **Havant**
Hawk : **Hawkley**
Haw : **Hawley**
H Isl : **Hayling Island**
Haze : **Hazeley**
Head : **Headley**
Head D : **Headley Down**
H End : **Heath End**
Heck : **Heckfield**
Hed E : **Hedge End**
Hen : **Henley**
Hens : **Hensting**
Herr : **Herriard**
Highb : **Highbridge**
High : **Highclere**
Highc : **Highcliffe**
Hight : **Hightown**
Highw : **Highwood**
Hi Br : **Hill Brow**
Hind : **Hindhead**
Hin : **Hinton**
Hin A : **Hinton Ampner**
Holb : **Holbury**
Hol P : **Holt Pound**
Holy : **Holybourne**
Hom : **Homington**
Hoo : **Hook**
Hor : **Hordle**
Horn : **Horndean**
Hor H : **Horton Heath**
Houg : **Houghton**
Hou : **Hound**
Hou G : **Hounds Green**
Hung : **Hungerford**
Hunt : **Hunton**
Hurd : **Hurdcott**
Hurn : **Hurn**
Hurs : **Hursley**
Hur P : **Hurstbourne Priors**
Hur T : **Hurstbourne Tarrant**
Hyde : **Hyde**
Hythe : **Hythe**
Ibsl : **Ibsley**
Ibt : **Ibthorpe**
Ibw : **Ibworth**
Idm : **Idmiston**
Ids : **Idsworth**
Ink : **Inkpen**
Isin : **Isington**
Itc A : **Itchen Abbas**
Itc S : **Itchen Stoke**
Key : **Keyhaven**
Kilm : **Kilmeston**
Kimb : **Kimbridge**
Kimp : **Kimpton**
Kings : **Kingsclere**
K'ly : **Kingsley**
K'ly G : **Kingsley Green**
Ki S : **King's Somborne**
King : **Kingston**
Kin W : **Kings Worthy**
K Enh : **Knights Enham**
K Vil : **Knowle Village**
Know : **Knowlton**
L'ford : **Landford**
Land : **Landfordwood**
Lang : **Langrish**
Langs : **Langstone**
Las : **Lasham**
Lave : **Laverstock**
L'stoke : **Laverstoke**
Leck : **Leckford**
Lee : **Lee**
Lee S : **Lee-on-the-Solent**
Lepe : **Lepe**
Linc : **Linchmere**
Lind : **Lindford**
Linf : **Linford**
Link : **Linkenholt**
Lin : **Linwood**
Lip : **Liphook**
Liss : **Liss**
Litc : **Litchfield**
Litt : **Littledown**
Lit L : **Little London**
Lit Shod : **Little Shoddesden**
Lit Som : **Little Somborne**
Lit : **Littleton**
Lock : **Lockerley**
Loc H : **Locks Heath**
Longc : **Longmoor Camp**
Longp : **Longparish**
Longs : **Longstock**
L Sut : **Long Sutton**
Lo Cnr : **Lopcombe Corner**
Love : **Lovedean**
Lover : **Lover**
Lwr B : **Lower Bullington**
Lwr C : **Lower Chute**
Lwr D : **Lower Draggons**
Lwr Farr : **Lower Farringdon**
Lwr Froy : **Lower Froyle**
Lwr Slac : **Lower Slackstead**
Lwr Swan : **Lower Swanwick**
Lwr U : **Lower Upham**
Lwr W : **Lower Wield**
Ludg : **Ludgershall**
Lych : **Lychpit**
Lymi : **Lymington**
Lymo : **Lymore**
Lyn : **Lyndhurst**
Mapl : **Mapledurwell**
March : **Marchwood**
Mart : **Martin**
Mar W : **Martyr Worthy**
Match : **Matchams**
Matt : **Mattingley**
Meds : **Medstead**
Meon : **Meonstoke**
M'dvr : **Micheldever**
Mich S : **Micheldever Station**
Mich : **Michelmersh**
Mid Wa : **Middle Wallop**
Mid W : **Middle Winterslow**
M Sea : **Milford on Sea**
Mill : **Milland**
Min : **Minley**
Mins : **Minstead**
Mis : **Mislingford**
Mock : **Mockbeggar**
M She : **Monk Sherborne**
Monk : **Monkwood**
Monx : **Monxton**
More : **Morestead**
M Val : **Morgan's Vale**
Mort : **Mortimer**
Mor W : **Mortimer West End**
Mott : **Mottisfont**
Mude : **Mudeford**
Mytc : **Mytchett**
Nat S : **Nately Scures**
Nea : **Neacroft**
Neat : **Neatham**
Nethe : **Netherhampton**
Net : **Netherton**
N Wal : **Nether Wallop**
Net A : **Netley Abbey**
Net M : **Netley Marsh**
New A : **New Alresford**
New : **Newbury**
Newf : **Newfound**
New M : **New Milton**
Newn : **Newnham**
New T : **Newton Tony**
New V : **Newton Valence**
Newt : **Newtown**
Nom : **Nomansland**
Norl : **Norleywood**
N Bad : **North Baddesley**
N Boa : **North Boarhunt**
Nth E : **North End**
N Gor : **North Gorley**
Nort : **Northington**
N Oak : **North Oakley**
N Rip : **North Ripley**
Nth S : **North Sydmonton**
Nth W : **North Waltham**
N War : **North Warnborough**
Nun : **Nunton**
Nur : **Nursling**
Nye : **Nyewood**
Oakh : **Oakhanger**
Oak : **Oakley**
Odi : **Odiham**
Ods : **Odstock**
Ogd : **Ogdens**
Old A : **Old Alresford**
Old Bas : **Old Basing**
Old Bur : **Old Burghclere**
Old D : **Old Ditcham**
Old N : **Old Netley**
Oli B : **Oliver's Battery**
Oss : **Ossemsley**
Ott : **Otterbourne**
Over : **Overton**
Ov Wa : **Over Wallop**
Ovin : **Ovington**
Ower : **Ower**
Owl : **Owlsmoor**
Owls : **Owslebury**
Oxen : **Oxenwood**
Pad C : **Padworth Common**
Pale : **Palestine**
Pam E : **Pamber End**
Pam G : **Pamber Green**
Pam H : **Pamber Heath**
P Ga : **Park Gate**
Pass : **Passfield**
Penn : **Pennington**
Pen C : **Penton Corner**
Pen G : **Penton Grafton**
Pen H : **Penton Harroway**
Pen M : **Penton Mewsey**
Pent : **Pentridge**
Pen : **Penwood**
Per D : **Perham Down**
Pet : **Petersfield**
Pic H : **Picket Hill**
Pic P : **Picket Piece**
Pil : **Pilley**
Pitt : **Pitt**
P'tn : **Pitton**
Plai : **Plaitford**
Poole : **Poole**
Portc : **Portchester**
Portm : **Portmore**
Port : **Porton**
Ports : **Portsmouth**
P Sol : **Port Solent**
Poul : **Poulner**
Pres C : **Preston Candover**
Pr De : **Priors Dean**
Priv : **Privett**
Purb : **Purbrook**
Quar : **Quarley**
Rag A : **Ragged Appleshaw**
Rake : **Rake**
R'dean : **Ramsdean**
Rams : **Ramsdell**
Rede : **Redenham**
Redl : **Redlynch**
Red R : **Red Rice**
Ring : **Ringwood**
Rip : **Ripley**
Rise : **Riseley**
R'bne : **Rockbourne**
Rock : **Rockford**
Rog : **Rogate**
Rom : **Romsey**
Rop : **Ropley**
Roth : **Rotherwick**
R Cas : **Rowland's Castle**
Rowl : **Rowledge**
Rown : **Rownhams**
Run : **Runfold**
Rush : **Rushmoor**
St I : **St Ives**
St L : **St Leonards**
S M Bo : **St Mary Bourne**
S'bks : **Sandbanks**
Sandf : **Sandford**
Sandh : **Sandhurst**
Sand : **Sandleheath**
Sar G : **Sarisbury Green**
Seal : **Seale**
Seg : **Segensworth**
Selb : **Selborne**
Shal : **Shalden**
Shaw : **Shawford**
Shed : **Shedfield**
Sher J : **Sherborne St John**
Sher E : **Sherfield English**
Sher L : **Sherfield on Loddon**
Shi B : **Shipton Bellinger**
Shir : **Shirley**
Shi H : **Shirrell Heath**
Shoo : **Shootash**
Sil : **Silchester**
Slea : **Sleaford**
Sman : **Smannell**
Sob : **Soberton**
Sob H : **Soberton Heath**
Sop : **Sopley**
South : **Southampton**
S'ton A : **Southampton International Airport**
S Badd : **South Baddesley**
S'brne : **Southbourne**
S Gor : **South Gorley**
S Hart : **South Harting**
S'sea : **Southsea**
S War : **South Warnborough**
S'wick : **Southwick**
Sth W : **South Wonston**
Spar : **Sparsholt**
Stan : **Standford**
Ste : **Steep**
Stev : **Steventon**
S Bri : **Stockbridge**
Stoke : **Stoke**
Stoke C : **Stoke Charity**
St Cr : **Stoney Cross**
Stra S : **Stratfield Saye**
Stra T : **Stratfield Turgis**
Stro : **Stroud**
Stub : **Stubbington**
Stuc : **Stuckton**
Sut : **Sutton**
Sut S : **Sutton Scotney**
Swal : **Swallowfield**
Swanm : **Swanmore**
Swanw : **Swanwick**
Sway : **Sway**
S'ing : **Swaythling**
Tadl : **Tadley**
Tang : **Tangley**
Thorn : **Thorney Hill**
T Isl : **Thorney Island**
Thru : **Thruxton**
Thur : **Thursley**
Tich : **Tichborne**
Tidw : **Tidworth**
Tilf : **Tilford**
Tims : **Timsbury**
Tip : **Tiptoe**
Titch : **Titchfield**
Titch C : **Titchfield Common**
Tong : **Tongham**
Toot : **Toothill**
Tott : **Totton**
Trot : **Trotton**
Tuft : **Tufton**
Tun : **Tunworth**
Twyf : **Twyford**
Uph : **Upham**
Up N : **Up Nately**
Up B : **Upper Bullington**
Up C : **Upper Clatford**
Up Farr : **Upper Farringdon**
Up Froy : **Upper Froyle**
Up H : **Upper Hale**
Up Sla : **Upper Slackstead**
Up Wield : **Upper Wield**
Up Woott : **Upper Wootton**
Up S : **Up Somborne**
Upt : **Upton**
Up G : **Upton Grey**
Ver D : **Vernham Dean**
Ver S : **Vernham Street**
Ver : **Verwood**
Wad : **Wadwick**
Wal : **Walhampton**
Walk : **Walkford**
Wal C : **Waltham Chase**
Warb : **Warblington**
Warn : **Warnford**
Wars : **Warsash**
Wa W : **Wash Water**
Wat : **Waterditch**
W'lle : **Waterlooville**
Wel : **Well**
W Dean : **West Dean**
Wes E : **West End**
W Gri : **West Grimstead**
W Meo : **West Meon**
W Str : **West Stratton**
W Tis : **West Tisted**
W Tyt : **West Tytherley**
W Wel : **West Wellow**
W Win : **West Winterslow**
W Wo : **West Woodhay**
W Wor : **West Worldham**
Westb : **Westbourne**
W'ton : **Weston**
We Co : **Weston Colley**
W Cor : **Weston Corbett**
Wes P : **Weston Patrick**
Weyb : **Weybourne**
Weyh : **Weyhill**
Whad : **Whaddon**
Wher : **Wherwell**
Whit : **Whitchurch**
W'hil : **Whitehill**
White : **Whiteley**
W'psh : **Whiteparish**
W'bry : **Whitsbury**
W'way : **Whitway**
Wick : **Wickham**
Wid : **Widley**
Wild : **Wildhern**
Wim G : **Wimborne St Giles**
Winche : **Winchester**
Winchf : **Winchfield**
Wink : **Winkton**
Winsl : **Winslade**
Wins : **Winsor**
Win D : **Winterbourne Dauntsey**
Win E : **Winterbourne Earls**
Win G : **Winterbourne Gunner**
Wive : **Wivelrod**
Wolve : **Wolverton**
Wolv C : **Wolverton Common**
Wons : **Wonston**
Wood : **Woodcott**
Woodf : **Woodfalls**
Woodg : **Woodgreen**
Woodl : **Woodlands**
W'cott : **Woodmancott**
W'ytes : **Woodyates**
Wol H : **Woolton Hill**
Woot : **Wootton**
W Law : **Wootton St Lawrence**
Wor E : **Worlds End**
Wor D : **Worthy Down**
Wort : **Worting**
Wrec : **Wrecclesham**
Wyck : **Wyck**
Yat : **Yateley**

A

Abbeyfield Dr.—Alexandra Ter.

Abbeyfield Dr. PO15: Fare 7M 197
Abbeyfield Ho. SO18: South 2C 174
Abbeyfields Cl. SO31: Net A 3H 195
Abbey Fruit Pk. Ind. Est. SO31: Net A 2F 194
Abbey Hill SO31: Net A 2D 194
Abbey Hill Cl. SO23: Winche 4L 105
Abbey Hill Rd. SO23: Winche 4K 105
Abbeymede PO6: Cosh 9F 200
Abbey M. SO31: Net A 3F 194
Abbey Pk. Ind. Est. SO51: Rom 6C 130
Abbey Pas. SO23: Winche 9N 237 (7L 105)
Abbey Rd. GU34: Bee, Meds 9L 79
PO15: Fare 7N 197
RG24: B'toke 2B 42
Abbey St. GU9: Farnh 8E 64
Abbey Ter. *SP11: Stoke* 7H 35
(off Chapel La.)
Abbey Wlk. *SO51: Rom* 5L 129
(off Church St.)
Abbey Water SO51: Rom 5L 129
Abbey Way GU14: Farn 8L 29
Abbots Brook SO41: Lymi 4F 234
Abbotsbury Rd. SO50: B'stke 1K 161
Abbots Cl. BH23: Highc 7H 231
GU51: Fleet 2M 47
PO7: Purb 5K 201
Abbotsfield SO40: Tott 3L 171
Abbotsfield Cl. SO16: South 6H 159
Abbotsford SO40: Bart 4B 170
Abbot's Ride GU9: Farnh 9G 65
ABBOTSTONE 5B 94
Abbotstone Av. PO9: Hav 5G 202
Abbotstone Rd. SO24: Fob 7C 94
Abbots Way PO15: Fare 8N 197
SO31: Net A 3H 195
Abbotswell Rd. SP6: Blis, Frog, Ogd 6A 154
ABBOTSWOOD 1N 129
Abbotswood Cl. RG26: Tadl 6H 11
SO51: Rom 3B 130
ABBOTS WORTHY 9A 92
Abbott Cl. BH9: Bour 6L 227
RG22: B'toke 9L 41
Abbott Rd. BH9: Bour 6L 227
ABBOTTS ANN 6F 68
Abbotts Ann Rd. SO22: Winche 3H 105
SP11: Abb A, Amp, Monx 4B 68
ABBOTTS BARTON 4L 105
Abbotts Cl. SO23: Winche 4L 105
SP9: Tidw 7C 30 (6G 30)
SP11: Abb A 5G 69
Abbotts Cotts. GU10: Dock 3A 84
Abbotts Ct. SO23: Winche 4K 105
Abbotts Drove SO51: W Wel 1N 155
Abbotts Hill SP11: Abb A 6G 69
Abbotts Ho. SO17: South 1M 173
Abbotts Rd. SO23: Winche 4L 105
SO50: E'leigh 2C 160
SP9: Tidw 7C 30 (6G 30)
Abbotts Way SO17: South 1N 173
A'Becket Ct. PO1: Ports 6K 5 (3B 240)
Abercorn Ho. GU17: Haw 3G 28
Abercrombie Gdns. SO16: South 7F 158
Aberdare Av. PO6: Dray 8J 201
Aberdare Rd. BH10: Bour 3J 227
Aberdeen Cl. PO15: Fare 6A 198
Aberdeen Rd. SO17: South 1A 174
Aberdeen Ter. GU26: Gray 3M 103
Aberdour Cl. SO18: South 2F 174
Abingdon Cl. PO12: Gos 3K 239
Abingdon Dr. BH23: Highc 6L 231
Abingdon Gdns. SO16: Bass 8K 159
Abingdon Rd. GU47: Sandh 5E 18
Abinger Rd. BH7: Bour 8D 228
Abney Rd. BH10: Bour 3H 227
Above Bar St. SO14: South 3C 4 (5L 173)
(not continuous)
Above Hedges SP5: P'tn 6E 86
Above Town SP11: Up C 5L 69
Abraham Cl. SO30: Botl 5B 176
Abro Ind. Est. GU11: Alders 7M 49
ABSHOT 9E 196
Abshot Cl. PO14: Titch C 8E 196
Abshot Rd. PO14: Titch C 8E 196
Acacia Av. GU47: Owl 4F 18
Acacia Gdns. PO8: Horn 5B 182
Acacia Lodge PO16: Fare 8D 198
Acacia Rd. SO19: South 5D 174
SO41: Hor 2G 233
Academy Cl. GU15: Camb 5N 19
Academy Ga. GU15: Camb 7K 19
Academy Pl. GU47: Coll 6G 19
Acanthus Ct. PO15: White 9G 177
Accentors Cl. GU34: Alt 2F 80
Access Point PO6: Cosh 1G 214
Acer Way PO9: Hav 5H 203
Achilles Cl. RG24: Chin 8G 22
Ackender Rd. GU34: Alt 5E 80
Ackrells Mead GU47: Sandh 4B 18
Ackworth Rd. PO3: Ports 3H 215
Acland Rd. BH9: Bour 6M 227
Acolade Health & Fitness 3A 174
Acorn Bus. Cen. PO6: Cosh 1E 214
Acorn Cl. BH23: Chri 6J 229
BH24: St L 5B 186
BH25: A'ley 2D 232
PO6: Farl 9N 201
PO13: Gos 7F 212
RG21: B'toke 6F 42
SO22: Winche 4H 105
SO40: March 9F 172
Acorn Ct. SO31: Hamb 6K 195
Acorn Dr. SO16: Rown 4D 158
SO53: Cha F 4A 132
Acorn Gdns. PO8: Horn 4B 182
Acorn Gro. SO53: Cha F 8L 131
Acorn Ind. Est. SO16: South 9G 158
Acorn Keep GU9: H End 2F 64
Acorn M. GU14: Farn 5J 29
Acorn Rd. GU17: Blackw 8D 18
Acorns, The PO7: Den 6H 181
SO31: Burs 1K 195
Acorn Workshops SO14: South 3N 173
Acre Ct. SP10: A'ver 1A 70
Acre La. PO7: W'lle 9C 182
Acre Path SP10: A'ver 1A 70
Acres Rd. BH11: Bour 4F 226
Action Stations Exhibition Mus. 3J 5 (2B 240)
Active Life Cen. 5N 41
Acton Ho. RG22: B'toke 7N 41
Acton Rd. BH10: Bour 5F 226
Adair Rd. PO4: S'sea 5H 241
Adam Cl. RG26: Bau 4E 10
Adames Rd. PO1: Ports 1F 240
Adampur Rd. SP9: Tidw 9A 30 (7F 30)
(not continuous)
Adams Cl. RG29: N War 8H 45
SO30: Hed E 8M 161
SP11: Per D 5B 30
Adams Ct. *BH5: Bour* 1C 246
(off Hawkwood Rd.)
Adams Dr. GU51: Fleet 2N 47
Adamsfield Gdns. BH10: Bour 4G 226
Adams Ho. GU34: Alt 4G 81
Adams La. GU34: Selb 8L 99
Adams M. GU30: Lip 4D 116
Adamson Cl. SO53: Cha F 4B 132
Adams Pk. Rd. GU9: Farnh 6F 64
Adams Rd. SO45: Hythe 7M 193
Adams Way GU34: Alt 4G 81
PO15: Seg 4F 196
Adams Wood Dr. SO40: March 9E 172
Adanac Dr. SO16: Nur 7B 158
Adanac Pk. SO16: Nur 7B 158
Adbury Holt RG20: Newt 2E 8
Adcock Ct. SO16: Rown 4D 158
Adderbury Av. PO10: Ems 6M 203
Addington Ct. SO41: M Sea 7K 235
Addington Pl. BH23: Chri 8N 229
Addiscombe Rd. BH23: Chri 7K 229
RG45: Cr'tne 1E 18
Addison Cl. SO22: Winche 9G 105
SO51: Rom 3A 130
Addison Gdns. RG29: Odi 8L 45
Addison Rd. GU16: Frim 4N 29
PO4: S'sea 4F 240
SO31: Sar G 3C 196
SO42: Broc 8C 148 (9N 189)
SO50: E'leigh 7F 132
Addison Sq. BH24: Ring 1L 187
Addis Sq. SO17: South 1N 173
(not continuous)
Adelaide Cl. BH23: Chri 6J 229
SP4: Bul C 3C 66
Adelaide La. BH1: Bour 6M 247 (2K 245)
Adelaide Pl. PO16: Fare 8E 198
Adelaide Rd. SO17: South 2A 174
SP10: A'ver 1A 70
Adela Verne Cl. SO19: South 7J 175
Adeline Rd. BH5: Bour 1B 246
Adelphi Ct. BH1: Bour 2A 246
Adey Cl. SO19: South 8F 174
Adhurst Rd. PO9: Hav 5G 202
Adlam's La. SO41: Sway 4G 223
Adlington Pl. GU14: Farn 1N 49
Admers Cres. GU30: Lip 4E 116
Admiral Ho. PO12: Gos 2M 239
Admiral Park, The PO3: Ports 5H 215
Admirals Cl. SO45: Fawl 5F 208
Admiral's Cnr. *PO5: S'sea* 5E 240
(off Victoria Rd. Sth.)
Admirals Ct. PO5: S'sea 5D 240
SO31: Hamb 7L 195
SO41: Lymi 2F 234
Admirals Ho. PO4: S'sea 3J 241
Admirals Pl. PO6: Cosh 9G 201
Admirals Point BH6: Bour 2H 247
Admiral Sq. *PO5: S'sea* 4D 240
(off Nelson Rd.)
Admiral's Rd. SO31: Loc H 5E 196
Admirals Wlk. BH2: Bour 9H 247 (3H 245)
PO1: Ports 2H 5 (1A 240)
PO12: Gos 4H 239
Admirals Way SO45: Hythe 4M 193
SP10: A'ver 1C 70
Admirals Wharf SO14: South 8D 4
Admiralty Cl. PO12: Gos 9L 213
Admiralty Ho. SO14: South 9E 4 (8M 173)
Admiralty Rd. BH6: Bour 2J 247
PO1: Ports 3J 5 (2B 240)
PO12: Gos 5N 239
Admiralty Twr. PO1: Ports 3J 5 (2B 240)
Admiralty Way GU15: Camb 9H 19
SO40: March 7E 172
Adrian Cl. RG27: H Win 7C 26
Adsdean Cl. PO9: Hav 5E 202
Adstone La. PO3: Ports 4K 215
Adur Cl. PO12: Gos 9H 213
SO18: Wes E 1F 174
Adventure Wonderland 8A 218
Aerial Rd. PO17: S'wick 7C 200
Aerodrome Rd. PO13: Gos 4F 212
Aerospace Blvd. GU14: Farn 4H 49
AFC Bournemouth 8B 228
AFC Totton 8K 157
Africa Dr. SO40: March 9E 172
Agars La. SO41: Sway 9H 223
Agarton La. SO41: Lymo 8N 233
AGC Museum, The 7K 237
Agevin Ct. GU51: Fleet 9L 27
Aghemund Cl. RG24: Chin 9F 22
Agincourt Rd. PO2: Ports 9E 214
Agitator Rd. SO45: Fawl 3G 208
Agnew Ho. PO12: Gos 1K 239
Agnew Rd. PO13: Gos 5E 212
Agra Rd. SP9: Tidw 9A 30 (8F 30)
Agricola Wlk. SP10: A'ver 7A 52
Agwi Rd. SO45: Fawl 3G 208
Aikman La. SO40: Tott 3H 171
Ailsa La. SO19: South 6B 174
Ainger Cl. GU12: Alders 8M 49
Ainsdale Rd. PO6: Dray 8L 201
Ainsley Gdns. SO50: E'leigh 7E 132
Aintree Cl. SO50: Hor H 4A 162
Aintree Ct. PO15: White 1E 196
Aintree Dr. PO7: W'lle 9B 182
Aintree Rd. SO40: Calm 1J 171
Aircraft Esplanade GU14: Farn 2L 49
Aird Cl. RG20: Wol H 3A 8
Airfield Ind. Est. BH23: Chri 7C 230
Airfield Rd. BH23: Chri 8B 230
Airfield Way BH23: Chri 7B 230
Airlie Cnr. SO22: Winche 8J 105
Airlie La. SO22: Winche 8J 105
Airlie Rd. SO22: Winche 8J 105
Airport Ind. Est. PO3: Ports 5J 215
Airport Service Rd. PO3: Ports 4H 215
Airspeed Rd. BH23: Chri 7D 230
PO3: Ports 6K 215
Airways Distribution Pk.
SO18: S'ing 5D 160
Ajax Cl. PO14: Stub 7N 211
RG24: Chin 8G 23
Akeshill Cl. BH25: New M 1C 232
Alameda Rd. PO7: Purb 5L 201
Alameda Way PO7: Purb 5L 201
Alamein Rd. GU11: Alders 9K 49
SP11: Enh A 3A 52
Alanbrooke Cl. RG27: H Win 6B 26
Alanbrooke Rd. GU11: Alders 5M 49
Alan Chun Ho. SO31: Net A 2G 194
Alan Ct. BH23: Highc 7K 231
Alandale Rd. SO19: South 6H 175
Alan Drayton Way SO50: B'stke 1J 161
(not continuous)
Alan Gro. PO15: Fare 7A 198
Albacore Av. SO31: Wars 8B 196
Albacore Ct. PO13: Lee S 2C 238
Albany BH1: Bour 2N 245
Albany Bus. Cen. PO17: Fare 2D 198
Albany Caravan Site PO14: Stub 7N 211
Albany Cl. BH25: B Sea 5A 232
GU51: Fleet 3N 47
Albany Ct. BH2: Bour 5M 247
GU16: Camb 3L 29
GU51: Fleet 2N 47
PO12: Gos 3K 239
SO32: Bis W 3K 163
Albany Dr. SO32: Bis W 3K 163
Albany Pk. GU16: Camb 3K 29
Albany Pk. Ct. SO17: South 2L 173
Albany Pk. Ind. Est. GU16: Camb 3L 29
Albany Rd. GU51: Fleet 3M 47
PO5: S'sea 4E 240
SO15: South 4H 173
SO32: Bis W 3K 163
SO45: Holb 4A 208
SO51: Rom 5M 129
SP10: A'ver 1L 69
Albatross Wlk. PO13: Gos 6D 212
Albemarle Av. PO12: Gos 9K 213
Albemarle Ct. SO17: South 8A 160
Albemarle Rd. BH3: Bour 7K 227
Albercourt BH5: Bour 1C 246
Albert Cl. SO31: Net A 4G 194
(not continuous)
Albert Ct. SO23: Winche 5K 105
Albert Gro. PO5: S'sea 4E 240
Albert Rd. BH1: Bour 6L 247 (2K 245)
BH12: Poole 9B 226
BH25: New M 3A 232
GU11: Alders 9K 49
GU14: Farn 1L 49
GU15: Camb 8L 19
GU34: Alt 6E 80
PO4: S'sea 4E 240
PO5: S'sea 4E 240
PO6: Cosh 1G 215
PO14: Fare 6B 212
RG45: Cr'tne 1D 18
SO30: Hed E 5M 175
SO32: Bis W 4L 163
SO50: E'leigh 7F 132
Albert Rd. Nth. SO14: South 7N 173
Albert Rd. Sth. SO14: South 8G 4 (7N 173)
Albert St. GU51: Fleet 3L 47
PO12: Gos 2L 239
Albert Wlk. RG45: Cr'tne 1D 18
Albert Yd. RG21: B'toke 7C 42
Albion Cl. PO16: Portc 2K 213
Albion Pl. RG27: H Win 6B 26
SO14: South 6C 4 (6L 173)
(not continuous)
SO23: Winche 7M 237 (6L 105)
Albion Rd. BH23: Chri 5J 229
GU47: Sandh 6D 18
SP6: F'dge 9J 151
Albion Towers SO14: South 5F 4 (6N 173)
Albretia Av. PO8: Cowp 7L 181
Albury Pl. SO53: Cha F 3N 131
Albury Way RG19: Green 1G 9
Alby Rd. BH12: Poole 9D 226
Alcantara Cres. SO14: South 7A 174
Alcester Rd. BH12: Poole 8B 226
Alchorne Pl. PO3: Ports 5J 215
Alcot Cl. RG45: Cr'tne 1D 18
Aldbury Ct. BH25: B Sea 7B 232
Alderbrook Cl. RG45: Cr'tne 1A 18
Alder Cl. BH23: Burt 5N 229
GU34: Alt 3E 80
SO21: Col C 4L 133
SO40: March 8E 172
SO45: Dib P 6H 193
SO51: Rom 6C 130
Alder Ct. GU51: Fleet 2H 47
Alder Cres. BH12: Poole 7D 226
Alder Dr. SP6: Ald 5C 152
Alderfield GU32: Pet 1L 145
Alder Gro. GU46: Yat 8M 17
Alder Hgts. BH12: Poole 8E 226
Alder Hill Dr. SO40: Tott 2H 171
Alder Hills BH12: Poole 7E 226
Alder Hills Ind. Pk. BH12: Poole 7D 226
Alder Hills Nature Reserve 7E 226
ALDERHOLT 5C 152
Alderholt Mill 1C 152
Alderholt Rd. SP6: Sand 1D 152
Alder La. PO12: Gos 2F 238
Alderley Rd. BH10: Bour 2H 227
Alderman Gdns. PO3: Ports 1H 241
Alderman Ho. *GU11: Alders* 1J 65
(off Grosvenor Rd.)
Aldermaston Rd.
RG24: B'toke, Sher J 9M 21
RG26: M She, Pam E, Pam G 1K 21
RG26: Tadl 3H 11
Aldermaston Rd. Rdbt. RG24: B'toke 3A 42
Aldermaston Rd. Sth. RG21: B'toke 4A 42
ALDERMASTON SOKE 2M 11
ALDERMOOR 8E 158
Aldermoor Av. SO16: South 7F 158
Aldermoor Cl. SO16: South 7H 159
Aldermoor Rd. PO7: Purb 5L 201
PO13: Gos 9F 212
SO16: South 7F 158
Aldermoor Rd. E. PO7: Purb 4L 201
ALDERNEY 4A 226
Alderney Av. BH12: Poole 5A 226
RG22: B'toke 3K 59
Alderney Cl. SO16: South 7D 158
Alderney Rdbt. BH12: Poole 4B 226
Alder Pk. BH12: Poole 7E 226
Alder Rd. BH12: Poole 9C 226
GU35: Head D 1D 102
SO16: South 7E 158
Alders, The GU9: Bad L 4K 65
GU52: Ch Cr 6K 47
Alders Cl. *RG21: B'toke* 6E 42
(off The Moorings)
Alders Ct. SO24: New A 9F 94
Aldersey Flds. GU34: Alt 3F 80
ALDERSHOT 9J 49
Aldershot Ho. PO9: Hav 4H 203
Aldershot Lodge
GU11: Alders 2L 65
Aldershot Military Mus. 5L 49
Aldershot Pk. 3M 65
Aldershot Pools & Lido 3M 65
Aldershot Rd. GU12: Ash 1N 65
GU51: Fleet 3M 47
GU52: Ch Cr 8L 47
Aldershot Station (Rail) 1K 65
Aldershot Town FC 9K 49
Alders Rd. PO16: Fare 1D 212
Alderwood RG24: Chin 9G 22
Alderwood Av. SO53: Cha F 6M 131
Alderwood Cl. PO9: Bed 6B 202
Alderwood Dr. RG27: Hoo 1H 45
Aldrich Rd. PO1: Ports 1K 5 (1B 240)
Aldridge Cl. PO8: Clan 6C 168
Aldridge Rd. BH10: Bour 2G 227
Aldrin Cl. SP10: Charl 7L 51
Aldrin Pl. GU14: Cov 8F 28
Aldroke St. PO6: Cosh 1G 215
Aldsworth Cl. PO6: Dray 9K 201
Aldsworth Gdns. PO6: Dray 9K 201
Aldsworth Path PO6: Dray 9K 201
Aldwell St. PO5: S'sea 3E 240
Aldwick Cl. GU14: Farn 6J 29
Aldworth Cres. RG22: B'toke 7N 41
Alec Rose Ho. PO12: Gos 3L 239
Alec Rose La. PO1: Ports 4N 5 (2D 240)
Alecto Rd. PO12: Gos 4K 239
Alencon Cl. PO12: Gos 8L 213
Alencon Ho. *RG21: B'toke* 6C 42
(off Alencon Link)
Alencon Link RG21: B'toke 6B 42
Alexander Bell Cen. SP10: A'ver 9H 51
Alexander Cl. BH23: Chri 8A 230
BH25: New M 3B 232
PO7: W'lle 3L 201
SO20: Houg 5D 88
SO40: Tott 2K 171
Alexander Ct. SO15: South 4J 173
Alexander Gdns. BH9: Bour 5L 227
Alexander Gro. PO16: Fare 9C 198
Alexander Ho. *GU11: Alders* 9K 49
(off Station Rd.)
SP9: Tidw 6C 30
(off Sidbury Circular Rd.)
Alexander Rd. GU11: Alders 9H 49
RG25: Over 3E 56
Alexanders La. GU34: Priv 1C 138
Alexander Sq. SO50: E'leigh 8F 132
Alexandra Av. GU15: Camb 8J 19
PO11: H Isl 5F 242
Alexandra Cl. GU47: Coll 6G 19
SO45: Hythe 5M 193
Alexandra Ct. GU14: Farn 2L 49
GU35: Bor 4K 101
PO4: S'sea 6F 240
(off Sth. Pde.)
Alexandra Lodge BH1: Bour 7N 247 (2L 245)
Alexandra M. BH14: Poole 1B 244
SO41: Lymi 1D 234
Alexandra Pk. PO9: Hav 1D 216
Alexandra Rd. BH6: Bour 9F 228
BH14: Poole 1A 244
GU11: Alders 9G 48
(not continuous)
GU14: Farn 1L 49
GU34: Alt 3F 80
PO1: Ports 1E 240
RG21: B'toke 6A 42
SO15: South 4J 173
SO30: Hed E 5M 175
SO41: Lymi 2C 234
SO45: Hythe 5M 193
SO53: Cha F 4C 132
SP6: F'dge 9J 151
SP10: A'ver 1M 69
Alexandra St. PO12: Gos 1J 239
Alexandra Ter. *GU11: Alders* 9J 49
(off Alexandra Rd.)
RG27: Sher L 3L 23

Alexandra Ter.—Anton La.

Alexandra Ter. *RG29: N War* 7J 45
(off Bridge Rd.)
SO23: Winche 9K 237 (7K 105)
Alexandra Way SO30: Botl 3D 176
Alexandria Rd. SO21: Sut S 6D 76
Alex Way PO2: Ports 5E 214
Alfonso Cl. GU12: Alders 2L 65
Alford Cl. GU47: Sandh 6C 18
Alford Rd. BH3: Bour 7H 227
Alfred Cl. GU51: Fleet 9J 27
SO40: Tott 3J 171
Alfred Gdns. SP10: A'ver 8M 51
Alfred Rd. GU9: Farnh 9E 64
PO1: Ports 3M 5 (2C 240)
PO14: Stub 5N 211
Alfred Rose Ct. SO18: S'ing 7C 160
Alfred St. SO14: South 1F 4 (4N 173)
Alfriston Gdns. SO19: South 6F 174
Algiers Rd. PO3: Ports 8J 215
Alhambra Rd. PO4: S'sea 6F 240
Alice Holt GU10: Hol P 9M 63
Alice Holt Cotts. GU10: Hol P 9M 63
Alice Holt Forest Cen. 10N 63
Alice Rd. GU11: Alders 9K 49
Alington Cl. BH14: Poole 6A 244
Alington Rd. BH3: Bour 8L 227
BH14: Poole 6A 244
Alipore Cl. BH14: Poole 2B 244
Alison Cl. GU14: Cov 9H 29
Alison's Rd. GU11: Alders 6J 49
Alison Way GU11: Alders 9H 49
SO22: Winche 6K 237 (6K 105)
Allan Gro. SO51: Rom 5A 130
Allaway Av. PO6: Cosh 9A 200
ALLBROOK 5F 132
Allbrook Ct. PO9: Hav 3D 202
Allbrook Hill SO50: E'leigh 5F 132
Allbrook Knoll SO50: E'leigh 5E 132
Allbrook Way SO50: E'leigh 4E 132
Allcot Rd. PO3: Ports 6G 215
Allden Av. GU12: Alders 3M 65
Allden Gdns. GU12: Alders 3M 65
Allee Dr. GU30: Lip 1D 116
Allenby Gro. PO16: Portc 1L 213
Allenby Rd. GU15: Camb 7J 19
PO12: Gos 1G 239
SP4: Win G 3B 86
Allen Cl. GU34: Alt 3G 81
RG21: B'toke 8A 42
Allendale Av. PO10: Ems 6L 203
Allendale Cl. GU47: Sandh 3C 18
Allen Gallery 5F 80
Allenmoor La. RG27: Roth 4E 24
Allen Rd. SO30: Hed E 3N 175
Allens, The BH12: Poole 9F 226
Allens Farm La. SO32: Ext 8M 135
Allens La. SO32: Corh, Ext 8L 135
SO32: Meon 8N 135
Allen's Rd. PO4: S'sea 5F 240
Allen Water Dr. SP6: F'dge 9H 151
Allerton Cl. SO40: Tott 1K 171
Alley, The SP5: Bish 3C 118
SP6: Woodg 2A 154
(off High St.)
Alley La. RG25: Elli 1J 79
ALL HALLOWS 7F 148
Alliance Cl. PO13: Gos 7F 212
Alliance Ho. PO1: Ports 1F 240
ALLINGTON 7D 66
Allington *BH4: Bour* 2G 245
(off Marlborough Rd.)
Allington Cl. GU9: Farnh 7G 64
Allington La. SO30: Wes E 8F 160
SO50: Fair O 4L 161
Allington Mnr. Farm Bus. Cen.
SO50: Fair O 4J 161
Allington Ri. RG27: Sher L 7H 23
Allington Rd. SO15: South 3C 172
Allington Track SP4: All, Ames 4B 66
Allington Way SP4: Ames 6A 66
Allison Ho. SO30: Hed E 2N 175
Alliston Way RG22: B'toke 8K 41
RG28: Whit 6G 55
Allmara Dr. PO7: W'lle 5N 201
Allnutt Av. RG21: B'toke 6D 42
Allotment Rd. SO30: Hed E 4M 175
SO31: Sar G 4B 196
All Saints Cl. SO16: South 1C 172
All Saints Cres. GU14: Cov 4G 29
All Saints Ho. SO14: South 7E 4
All Saints Rd. PO1: Ports 9E 214
SO41: Lymi 4E 234
All Saints St. PO1: Ports 1D 240
Allyn Ct. SO50: E'leigh 7F 132
Alma Cl. GU12: Alders 9M 49
Alma Cotts. GU14: Farn 3L 49
Alma Ho. GU12: Alders 9M 49
Alma La. GU9: H End, Up H 3D 64
SO32: Lwr U 2E 162
Alma Rd. BH9: Bour 7K 227
GU35: Bor 4K 101
GU35: Head D 2E 102
SO14: South 2M 173
SO51: Rom 5M 129
Alma Sq. GU14: Farn 3L 49
Alma St. PO12: Gos 1J 239
Almatade Rd. SO18: South 3E 174
Alma Ter. PO4: S'sea 4H 241
Alma Way GU9: H End 3F 64
Almerston Rd. RG24: Sher J 1K 21
Almond Cl. GU14: Farn 5J 29
PO8: Horn 6C 182
PO9: Bed 9N 201
RG24: Old Bas 5H 43
Almond Ct. GU15: Camb 6M 19
GU52: Ch Cr 5N 47
(off Pine Gro.)
SO15: South 4H 173
Almond Gro. BH12: Poole 7B 226
Almond Ho. SO14: South 8F 4
Almond Rd. SO15: South 4H 173
Almondsbury Rd. PO6: Cosh 7A 200
Almondside PO13: Gos 7G 212
Almswood Rd. RG26: Tadl 3G 10
Aloes, The GU51: Fleet 3N 47
Alpha Bus. Pk. SO14: South 3N 173
Alphage Rd. PO12: Gos 7H 213
Alpha Ho. SO16: Chilw 2H 159
Alpha Rd. GU12: Alders 1M 65
Alphington Av. GU16: Frim 3N 29
Alphington Grn. GU16: Frim 3N 29
Alpine Cl. GU14: Cov 9F 28
SO18: South 2F 174
Alpine Ct. RG22: B'toke 8J 41
Alpine Rd. BH24: Match 7F 186
GU35: W'hil 6J 101
SO40: Ashu 7F 170
Alpine Snowsports Cen. 7L 49
Alresford Drove
SO21: Kin W, Mar W, Sth W 2J 91
Alresford Golf Course 3E 108
Alresford La. SO24: Bram 8J 109
Alresford Rd. PO9: Hav 5E 202
RG25: Pres C 5E 78
SO21: Winche 7F 106
SO23: Winche 7M 105
SO24: New A, Ovin 2C 108
Alresford Station
Watercress Line (Mid-Hants Railway)
1F 108
Alsace Wlk. GU15: Camb 3K 29
Alsafa Hgts. *BH4: Bour* 4G 245
(off Alumhurst Rd.)
Alsford Rd. PO7: Purb 4L 201
Alswitha Ter. SO23: Winche 1L 105
Alten Rd. PO7: W'lle 8K 181
Althorpe Dr. PO3: Ports 4K 215
ALTON 5F 80
Altona Gdns. SP10: A'ver 7M 51
Alton Brewery (Coors Vis. Cen.) 5F 80
Alton Bus. Cen. GU34: Alt 5H 81
Alton Cl. SO50: Fair O 1M 161
Alton Ct. *SO23: Winche* 1L 105
(off Northlands Dr.)
Alton Golf Course 9C 62
Alton Gro. PO16: Portc 2L 213
Alton La. GU34: Four M 7J 97
Alton Ride GU17: Blackw 7E 18
Alton Rd. BH10: Bour 5F 226
BH14: Poole 2A 244
GU10: Farnh 9B 64 (7N 63)
GU51: Fleet 2A 48
RG25: B'toke, Winsl 1D 60
RG29: Odi, S War 4D 62
Alton Rd. Cotts. RG29: S War 5C 62
Alton Rd. E. BH14: Poole 3B 244
Alton Sports Cen. 7D 80
Alton Station (Rail) 4G 81
Alum Chine 4G 244
Alum Chine Rd. BH4: Bour 2F 244
Alum Cl. SO45: Holb 5B 208
Alumdale Rd. BH4: Bour 3F 244
Alumhurst Rd. BH4: Bour 2F 244
Alum Way PO16: Fare 8G 199
SO18: South 3F 174
Alvandi Gdns. BH25: New M 3C 232
Alvara Rd. PO12: Gos 5J 239
Alver Bri. Vw. PO12: Gos 4K 239
Alvercliffe Dr. PO12: Gos 5H 239
Alver Quay PO12: Gos 4K 239
Alver Rd. PO1: Ports 1F 240
PO12: Gos 3K 239
(not continuous)
ALVERSTOKE 5J 239
Alverstoke Ct. PO12: Gos 5J 239
Alverstoke Gdns. GU11: Alders 1G 65
Alverstoke Lawn Tennis, Squash & Badminton Club 4J 239
(within Alverstoke Sports Club)
Alverstoke Sports Club 4J 239
Alverstone Rd. PO4: S'sea 2H 241
Alverton Ct. *BH2: Bour* 9K 227
(off Wimborne Rd.)
Alverton Hall *BH4: Bour* 3G 245
(off West Cliff Rd.)
Alveston Av. PO14: Fare 9N 197
Alwin Pl. GU9: Up H 3D 64
Alwyn Hall SO22: Winche 9H 237 (7H 105)
Alyne Ho. SO15: South 2L 173
Alyth Rd. BH3: Bour 8G 226
Amari Ct. BH4: Bour 9G 247 (3H 245)
Amarone BH4: Bour 2F 244
Amarylis Cl. PO15: Seg 5H 197
Amazon Cl. RG21: B'toke 7A 42
Ambarrow Court Local Nature Reserve 3B 18
Ambarrow Cres. GU47: Sandh 4B 18
Ambarrow Farm Courtyard GU47: Sandh 3A 18
Ambarrow La. GU47: Sandh 3N 17
Ambassador Cl. BH23: Mude 8C 230
Ambassador Ind. Est. BH23: Chri 8C 230
Amber Cl. GU35: Bor 5K 101
Amber Ct. BH1: Bour 1A 246
GU12: Alders 9L 49
Amber Gdns. GU14: Farn 8J 29
SP10: A'ver 1K 69
Amberley Cl. BH23: Highc 6G 231
SO30: Botl 3D 176
SO52: N Bad 7D 130
Amberley Ct. BH1: Bour 7N 247 (2L 245)
PO14: Stub 7N 211
PO17: K Vil 2A 198
(off Knowle Av.)
SO40: Tott 4L 171
Amberley Grange GU11: Alders 2H 65
Amberley M. *GU34: Alt* 4F 80
(off Amery Hill)
Amberley Rd. PO2: Ports 5G 214
PO8: Clan 6D 168
PO12: Gos 8J 213
Amberslade Wlk. SO45: Dib P 8L 193
Amberwood SO41: Down 7H 235
Amberwood Cl. SO40: Calm 9J 157
Amberwood Dr. BH23: Walk 4H 231
GU15: Camb 6N 19
Amberwood Gdns. BH23: Walk 4J 231
Ambledale SO31: Sar G 5B 196
Ambleside BH23: Chri 3G 229
RG45: Cr'tne 1E 18
SO30: Botl 5A 176
SO32: Bis W 3K 163
Ambleside Cl. GU14: Cov 8G 28
Ambleside Ct. PO12: Gos 6J 239
Ambleside Cres. GU9: Up H 4C 64
Ambleside Gdns. SO19: South 7E 174
Ambleside Rd. SO41: Lymi 3E 234
Ambrose Cnr. SO41: Lymi 9D 224
Ambrose Rd. RG26: Tadl 5H 11
Ambury La. BH23: Chri 6A 230
Amelia Gdns. PO13: Gos 2F 238
American Wharf SO14: South 6A 174
Amersham Cl. PO12: Gos 3G 238
Amersham Ct. *BH4: Bour* 2G 244
(off Marlborough Rd.)
Amery Hill GU34: Alt 4F 80
Amery St. GU34: Alt 5F 80
AMESBURY 6A 66
Amesbury Ho. *SP9: Tidw* 8E 30
(off Kennet Rd.)
Amesbury Rd. BH6: Bour 8F 228
SP4: Ames, Bul, Bul C 5A 66
SP4: Chol 4D 66
SP4: New T 6D 66
SP11: Weyh 1N 67
Amethyst Gro. PO7: W'lle 1B 202
Amethyst Rd. BH23: Chri 7B 230
Amey Gdns. SO40: Calm 1H 171
Amey Ind. Est. GU32: Pet 1L 145
AMF Bowling
Eastleigh 1F 160
Havant 8B 202
Amherst Rd. GU35: Bor 1H 101
Amira Ct. BH2: Bour 6J 247 (2J 245)
Amity Way GU15: Camb 8N 19
Amoy St. SO15: South 1C 4 (4L 173)
AMPFIELD 1H 131
Ampfield Cl. PO9: Hav 5B 202
Ampfield Golf Course 1H 131
AMPFIELD HILL 9E 124
Ampfield Rd. BH8: Bour 3A 228
AMPORT 4A 68
Amport Cl. RG24: Lych 3H 43
SO22: Winche 3G 105
Amport Ct. PO9: Hav 3D 202
Amport Rd. RG26: Sher L 7H 23
Ampress La. SO41: Bold 9D 224
Ampress Pk. SO41: Bold 8D 224
Ampthill Rd. SO15: South 3G 172
Amsterdam Sq. BH23: Chri 8M 229
Amyas Ct. PO4: S'sea 3K 241
Ancasta Rd. SO14: South 3N 173
Ancells Bus. Pk. GU51: Fleet 7A 28
Ancells Farm Nature Reserve 8A 28
Ancells Rd. GU51: Fleet 7N 27
Anchorage, The BH23: Mude 9D 230
PO12: Gos 3L 239
Anchorage Ct. PO13: Lee S 2B 238
Anchorage Pk. PO3: Ports 5K 215
Anchorage Rd. PO3: Ports 4J 215
Anchorage Way SO41: Lymi 3D 234
Anchor Bus. Cen. SO53: Cha F 7N 131
Anchor Cl. BH11: Bour 1D 226
(not continuous)
BH23: Mude 9C 230
Anchor Ct. PO11: H Isl 6K 243
RG21: B'toke 7C 42
(off London St.)
Anchor Ga. Rd. PO1: Ports 1K 5 (1B 240)
Anchor La. PO1: Ports 3H 5 (2A 240)
Anchor Mdw. GU14: Cov 8H 29
Anchor M. SO41: Lymi 2E 234
Anchor Rd. BH11: Bour 1D 226
RG20: Kings 2B 6
Anchor Vw. SP11: Up C 5L 69
Anchor Yd. *RG20: Kings* 2B 6
(off Anchor Rd.)
RG21: B'toke 7C 42
Ancient La. SP11: Weyh 8D 50
Ancient Technology Centre, The 6D 149
Ancrum Lodge BH13: Poole 2F 244
Andalusian Gdns. PO15: White 1E 196
Andbourne Ct. BH6: Bour 2J 247
Andeferas Rd. SP10: A'ver 7M 51
Anderby Rd. SO16: South 9C 158
Andersen Cl. PO15: White 1F 196
Anderson Cl. PO9: Hav 6G 202
SO51: Rom 2B 130
Anderson Gdns. RG26: Tadl 4H 11
Anderson's Rd. SO14: South 7G 4 (7N 173)
Anders Rd. SO21: Sth W 3J 91
Anderwood Dr. SO41: Sway 5J 223
Andes Cl. SO14: South 7A 174
Andes Rd. SO16: Nur 8A 158
Andlers Ash Rd. GU33: Liss 3D 140
ANDOVER 2N 69
Andover Cl. BH23: Chri 7D 230
ANDOVER DOWN 9G 53
Andover Down Rdbt. SP10: A'ver 1D 70
Andover Dr. GU51: Fleet 9J 27
Andover Drove RG20: Enbo R 1B 8
Andover Golf Course 3N 69
Andover Ho. PO9: Hav 4G 202
Andover La. SP11: Gt S 4E 30 (6L 31)
Andover Leisure Cen. 1N 69
Andover Mus. 1A 70
Andover Rd. GU17: Blackw 7E 18
PO4: S'sea 5G 241
RG14: New 1C 8
RG20: Wa W 2B 8
RG23: Newf, Oak 2K 57
RG25: Dea, Oak 2K 57
RG28: Whit 6F 54
SO15: South 4J 173
SO21: Mich S 4J 77
Andover Rd. SO22: Winche 6L 237 (3J 105)
SO23: Winche 3J 105
SP11: A'ver, Monx 3D 68
SP11: Fabe, Ludg, Rede, Weyh 1C 30 (5K 31)
Andover Rd. Nth. SO22: Winche 9H 91
Andover Rd. Retail Pk. SO23: Winche 5K 105
Andover Station (Rail) 1M 69
Andover Way GU11: Alders 3K 65
Andrewartha Rd. GU14: Farn 1N 49
Andrew Bell St. PO1: Ports 1D 240
Andrew Cl. PO3: Ports 1G 241
RG29: N War 8H 45
SO40: Tott 3K 171
SO45: Dib P 8M 193
Andrew Cres. PO7: W'lle 8L 181
Andrewes Cl. SO32: Bis W 3M 163
Andrew La. BH25: A'ley 4E 232
Andrew Pl. PO14: Stub 6L 211
Andrews Cl. BH11: Bour 3E 226
GU52: Ch Cr 5M 47
Andrew's La. RG29: L Sut 4F 62
SO24: Rop 9F 96
Andrews Lodge SO41: Lymi 1D 234
Andrews Rd. GU14: Cov 7G 28
Andromeda Rd. SO16: South 7D 158
Androse Gdns. BH24: Ring 2J 187
ANDWELL 5N 43
Andwell Drove RG27: A'ell 6A 44
Andwell La. RG27: A'ell 6A 44
Anfield Cl. SO50: Fair O 2N 161
Anfield Ct. SO50: Fair O 2M 161
Angela Ct. PO9: Hav 5F 202
Angel Cres. SO18: South 3E 174
Angelica Ct. PO7: W'lle 3A 202
Angelica Gdns. SO50: Hor H 4N 161
Angelica Way PO15: White 1H 197
Angeline Cl. BH23: Highc 6H 231
Angel La. BH25: New M 7D 232
Angel Mdws. RG29: Odi 8L 45
Angelo Cl. PO7: W'lle 1A 202
Angels' La. SP6: Mart 9D 118
Angelus Cl. PO14: Stub 6M 211
Angerstein Rd. PO2: Ports 7E 214
Anglers Pl. *RG21: B'toke* 6E 42
(off The Moorings)
Anglers Way SO31: Lwr Swan 1A 196
Anglesea Ct. SO15: South 1G 173
Anglesea Rd. PO1: Ports 3M 5 (2C 240)
PO13: Lee S 3C 238
SO15: South 1G 173
Anglesea Ter.
SO14: South 7G 4 (7N 173)
ANGLESEY 6K 239
Anglesey Arms Rd. PO12: Gos 5J 239
Anglesey Av. GU14: Cov 5H 29
Anglesey Cl. RG24: B'toke 1D 42
SP10: A'ver 4N 69
Anglesey Rd. GU12: Alders 1M 65
PO12: Gos 6J 239
Anglesey Vw. PO12: Gos 4K 239
Anglia Ct. BH2: Bour 7J 247
Angmering Ho. PO1: Ports 2D 240
Angora Way GU51: Fleet 8N 27
Angus Cl. PO15: Fare 6A 198
Anjou Cl. BH11: Bour 1B 226
Anjou Cres. PO15: Fare 7N 197
Anker La. PO14: Stub 4M 211
Ankerwyke PO13: Gos 7D 212
ANMORE 6J 181
Anmore Cl. PO9: Hav 5D 202
Anmore Dr. PO7: W'lle 8L 181
Anmore La. PO7: Den 6J 181
Anmore Rd. PO7: Den 6H 181
Anna La. BH23: Avon, N Rip 3K 219
ANNA VALLEY 5J 69
Anne Armstrong Cl. GU11: Alders 6M 49
Anne Cl. BH23: Chri 5K 229
Anne Cres. PO7: W'lle 3M 201
Annerley Rd. BH1: Bour 1N 245
Annes Ct. PO11: H Isl 5E 242
Annes Way GU52: Ch Cr 5N 47
Annettes Cft. GU52: Ch Cr 7K 47
ANN'S HILL 3J 239
Ann's Hill Rd. PO12: Gos 1J 239
Ansell Rd. GU16: Frim 4N 29
Anson Cl. BH23: Mude 8B 230
BH24: Poul 9M 185
GU11: Alders 8H 49
PO13: Gos 2F 238
Anson Ct. PO1: Ports 5J 5 (3B 240)
Anson Dr. SO19: South 6G 175
Anson Gro. PO16: Portc 8M 199
Anson Ho. SO14: South 8F 4
Anson Rd. PO4: S'sea 2H 241
SO50: Hor H 4N 161
ANSTEY 3H 81
Anstey Cl. BH11: Bour 1E 226
RG21: B'toke 9B 42
Anstey La. GU34: Alt 1F 80
Anstey Mill Cl. GU34: Alt 3H 81
Anstey Mill La. GU34: Alt 3H 81
Anstey Rd. BH11: Bour 1E 226
GU9: Farnh 7G 64
GU34: Alt 4G 80
SO51: Rom 3A 130
Anstice Ct. PO13: Lee S 1B 238
Antar Cl. RG21: B'toke 7A 42
Antell's Way SP6: Ald 4D 152
Antelope Pk. SO19: South 5H 175
Anthill Cl. PO7: Den 4D 180
ANTHILL COMMON 5D 180
Anthony Gro. PO12: Gos 7H 213
Anthony's Av. BH14: Poole 5A 244
Anthony Way PO10: Ems 6M 203
Antigua Ho. PO6: Cosh 7A 200
Antler Dr. BH25: New M 2N 231
Anton Cl. RG23: Oak 1D 58
SO51: Rom 5B 130
Anton Lakes Nature Reserve 8M 51
Anton La. SP11: Enh A 3A 52

Anton Mill Rd.—Ashton Pl.

Anton Mill Rd. SP10: A'ver . . . 2N 69
Anton Rd. SP10: A'ver . . . 3N 69
Anton Trad. Est. SP10: A'ver . . . 2N 69
Antrim Cl. RG22: B'toke . . . 8K 41
Anvil Cl. GU32: E Meon . . . 4M 143
PO7: W'lle . . . 9C 182
SO30: Wes E . . . 9G 161
Anvil Ct. PO4: S'sea . . . 3J 241
Anvil Theatre, The . . . 6C 42
Anvil Way RG26: B'ley . . . 1G 23
Anzac Cl. PO14: Stub . . . 4M 211
Anzio Cl. GU11: Alders . . . 9J 49
Apex Cen. PO14: Fare . . . 3C 212
SO21: Col C . . . 4L 133
Apex Dr. GU16: Frim . . . 3M 29
Apless La. PO7: Wor E . . . 6A 180
Apollo Cinema
Fareham . . . 8D 198
(off Market Quay)
Apollo Cl. BH12: Poole . . . 7B 226
Apollo Ct. PO5: S'sea . . . 3E 240
Apollo Dr. GU35: Bor . . . 5K 101
PO7: Purb . . . 6N 201
Apollonia Ho. SP10: A'ver . . . 2N 69
(off Winchester Rd.)
Apollo Pl. SO18: South . . . 2E 174
Apollo Ri. GU14: Cov . . . 8E 28
Apollo Rd. SO53: Cha F . . . 5D 132
Apple Cl. BH12: Poole . . . 1E 244
Apple Court Garden . . . 5H 233
Apple Dene RG26: B'ley . . . 2G 22
Appledore M. GU14: Farn . . . 5J 29
Appledown Cl. SO24: New A . . . 2F 108
Appledown La. SO24: Cher, Tich . . . 3G 108
Applegarth Cl. RG21: B'toke . . . 8D 42
Applegate SP11: S M Bo . . . 1M 53
Applegate Pl. PO8: Horn . . . 4A 182
Apple Gro. BH23: Chri . . . 4H 229
Apple Ind. Est. PO15: Seg . . . 4F 196
APPLEMORE . . . 6H 193
Applemore Health & Leisure Cen. . . . 6H 193
Applemore Ho. SO41: Lymi . . . 2E 234
APPLESHAW . . . 4B 50
Appleshaw Cl. RG26: Tadl . . . 6H 11
SO22: Winche . . . 2H 105
Appleshaw Dene SP11: Rag A . . . 4B 50
Appleshaw Grn. PO9: Hav . . . 5C 202
Appleshaw Way SP11: Per D . . . 5B 30 (7J 31)
Appleslade Way BH25: New M . . . 1C 232
Appleton Cl. SO20: Ov Wa . . . 8M 67
Appleton Dr. RG24: B'toke, Sher J . . . 1B 42
Appleton M. SP10: A'ver . . . 3A 70
Appleton Rd. PO15: Fare . . . 8M 197
SO18: South . . . 1C 174
Appleton Vw. GU34: E Tis . . . 1D 112
Appletree Cl. BH6: Bour . . . 9F 228
BH25: New M . . . 5B 232
RG23: Oak . . . 2D 58
SO40: Calm . . . 1J 171
SP5: M Val . . . 1M 119 (7C 120)
Appletree Ct. SO30: Botl . . . 3D 176
SO43: Lyn . . . 3C 148
Apple Tree Gro. SP10: A'ver . . . 9K 51
Appletree Ho. PO7: W'lle . . . 2M 201
(off Hambledon Rd.)
Appletree Mead RG27: Hoo . . . 2J 45
Apple Tree Rd. SP6: Ald . . . 5C 152
Appletree Rd. SP5: M Val . . . 1M 119 (7C 120)
Appletree Way GU47: Owl . . . 4F 18
Apple Way RG24: Old Bas . . . 6J 43
Applewood SO31: P Ga . . . 4D 196
Applewood Gdns. SO19: South . . . 7E 174
Applewood Gro. PO7: Wid . . . 6K 201
Applewood Pl. SO40: Tott . . . 4J 171
Applewood Rd. PO9: Bed . . . 6C 202
Appley Ct. GU15: Camb . . . 8K 19
Appley Dr. GU15: Camb . . . 7K 19
Approach, The PO3: Ports . . . 7H 215
Approach Rd. GU9: Farnh . . . 9E 64
April Cl. BH11: Bour . . . 2E 226
GU15: Camb . . . 2L 29
SO18: South . . . 3F 174
April Ct. BH11: Bour . . . 2E 226
April Gdns. SO45: Blac . . . 7C 208
April Gro. SO31: Sar G . . . 6B 196
April Sq. PO1: Ports . . . 1E 240
Apsley Cl. SP10: A'ver . . . 4M 69
Apsley Ct BH8: Bour . . . 9L 227
(off Wellington Rd.)
Apsley Pl. SO53: Cha F . . . 3N 131
Apsley Rd. PO4: S'sea . . . 3H 241
Aquadrome . . . 6L 41
Aquarius BH2: Bour . . . 8K 247 (3J 245)
Aquarius Cl. GU10: Cron . . . 1K 63
Aquila Way SO31: Hamb . . . 7K 195
Aquitania Ho. SO14: South . . . 5A 174
Arabian Gdns. PO15: White . . . 2F 196
Aragon Rd. GU46: Yat . . . 9M 17
Aragon Way BH9: Bour . . . 2M 227
Arakan Cres. SO40: March . . . 9E 172
Arboretum, The RG25: Up G . . . 3A 62
Arbour Ct. PO15: White . . . 9H 177
SO22: Winche . . . 7K 237
Arcade, The BH1: Bour . . . 7M 247 (2K 245)
GU11: Alders . . . 9J 49
GU33: Liss . . . 9D 114
PO31: Cowes . . . 5P 237
Arcadia Av. BH8: Bour . . . 7M 227
Arcadia Cl. RG22: B'toke . . . 6J 59
SO16: South . . . 8H 159
Arcadia Pl. SO17: South . . . 1B 174
Arcadia Rd. BH23: Chri . . . 5J 229
Archdale Cl. BH10: Bour . . . 4H 227
Archer Ho. PO12: Gos . . . 6L 239
Archers SO15: South . . . 1A 4 (4K 173)
Archers Cl. SO40: Calm . . . 1J 171
Archers Rd. SO15: South . . . 1A 4 (3K 173)
SO50: E'leigh . . . 8E 132
Archery Flds. RG29: Odi . . . 8M 45
Archery Gdns. SO19: South . . . 8D 174
Archery Gro. SO19: South . . . 9C 174
Archery La. PO16: Fare . . . 7E 198
SO23: Winche . . . 8K 237 (7K 105)
Archery Ri. GU34: Alt . . . 6E 80
Archery Rd. SO19: South . . . 9C 174
Arch Farm Ind. Est. SP6: F'dge . . . 8H 151
Archgate SO41: Lymi . . . 2E 234
Archway Rd. BH14: Poole . . . 1C 244
Arcot Rd. SP9: Tidw . . . 8F 30
Arden Cl. PO12: Gos . . . 3H 239
SO18: South . . . 1F 174
Arden Rd. BH9: Bour . . . 3K 227
Arden Wlk. BH25: New M . . . 4C 232
Ardglen Rd. RG28: Whit . . . 5F 54
Ardingly Cres. SO30: Hed E . . . 9A 162
Ardington Ri. PO7: Purb . . . 6M 201
Ardnave Cres. SO16: Bass . . . 6L 159
Ardwell Cl. RG45: Cr'tne . . . 1A 18
Ardwick Ct. GU14: Farn . . . 1L 49
(off Sycamore Rd.)
Arena La. GU11: Alders . . . 7F 48
Arenal Dr. RG45: Cr'tne . . . 2D 18
Arena Leisure Cen. . . . 7L 19
Arethusa Ho. PO1: Ports . . . 6J 5 (3B 240)
ARFORD . . . 1B 102
Arford Comn. GU35: Head . . . 1B 102
Arford Rd. GU35: Head . . . 2B 102
Argente Cl. GU51: Fleet . . . 8N 27
Argent Ter. GU47: Coll . . . 5G 18
Argosy Cl. SO31: Wars . . . 8C 196
Argosy Cres. SO50: E'leigh . . . 3D 160
Argyle Cl. GU35: W'hil . . . 5J 101
Argyle Cres. PO15: Fare . . . 7A 198
Argyle Rd. BH23: Mude . . . 9A 230
SO14: South . . . 3E 4 (5M 173)
Argyll Ct. GU51: Fleet . . . 2M 47
SO23: Winche . . . 1J 127
Argyll Rd. BH5: Bour . . . 1B 246
BH12: Poole . . . 8B 226
Ariel Cl. BH6: Bour . . . 1L 247
Ariel Dr. BH6: Bour . . . 1L 247
Ariel Rd. PO1: Ports . . . 2F 240
Arismore Ct. PO13: Lee S . . . 9N 211
Ark Royal Cres. PO13: Lee S . . . 9A 212
Arkwright Cl. RG20: High . . . 4A 8
Arkwright Gate SP10: A'ver . . . 8H 51
Arlebury Pk. SO24: New A . . . 9D 94
Arle Cl. PO8: Clan . . . 7C 168
SO24: New A . . . 9E 94
Arle Gdns. SO24: New A . . . 9F 94
Arlington Ct. BH25: B Sea . . . 6C 232
Arlington Ho. BH4: Bour . . . 2H 245
(off Clarendon Rd.)
Arlington Pl. SO23: Winche . . . 6M 237
Arlington Ter. GU11: Alders . . . 9H 49
Arliss Rd. SO16: South . . . 1F 172
Arlott Cl. RG27: Eve . . . 5H 17
Arlott Ct. SO15: South . . . 2K 173
Arlott Dr. RG21: B'toke . . . 4C 42
Arlowe Dr. SO16: South . . . 9J 159
Armada Cl. SO16: Rown . . . 4D 158
Armada Dr. SO45: Hythe . . . 7L 193
Armadale Ho. SO14: South . . . 4A 174
(off Kent St.)
Armfield Ho. SO17: South . . . 1M 173
(off Winn Rd.)
Arminers Cl. PO12: Gos . . . 6K 239
Armitage Av. SO45: Dib P . . . 8L 193
Armory La. PO1: Ports . . . 6K 5 (3B 240)
Armoury, The SO40: March . . . 7F 172
Armoury La. RG45: Cr'tne . . . 2C 18
Armstrong Cl. PO7: W'lle . . . 8L 181
PO12: Gos . . . 2L 239
SO21: Sth W . . . 3J 91
SO42: Broc . . . 7B 148 (8N 189)
Armstrong Ct. SO16: South . . . 6E 158
Armstrong La. SO42: Broc . . . 7B 148 (8N 189)
Armstrong Mall GU14: Cov . . . 8F 28
Armstrong Ri. SP10: Charl . . . 7L 51
Armstrong Rd. RG24: B'toke . . . 4F 42
SO42: Broc . . . 7B 148 (8N 189)
Armstrong Way GU14: Farn . . . 2D 48
Armsworth La. PO7: H'don . . . 8M 165
SO32: Sob . . . 8M 165
Armsworth Pk. SO24: Old A . . . 9E 78
Army Golf Course . . . 5G 49
Army Physical Training Corps Mus. . . . 6K 49
Arnaud Cl. PO2: Ports . . . 9E 214
Arncott Hall BH2: Bour . . . 7G 247 (2H 245)
Arne Av. BH12: Poole . . . 7C 226
Arne Cl. RG22: B'toke . . . 3M 59
Arne Ct. BH12: Poole . . . 7B 226
Arne Cres. BH12: Poole . . . 7C 226
Arnewood Av. RG26: Tadl . . . 4K 11
Arnewood Bri. Rd.
SO41: Sway, Tip . . . 8F 222
Arnewood Ct. BH2: Bour . . . 8J 247 (3J 245)
Arnewood Rd. BH6: Bour . . . 1F 246
Arnheim Cl. SO16: South . . . 7H 159
Arnheim Rd. SO16: South . . . 7J 159
Arnhem Cl. GU11: Alders . . . 9K 49
Arnold Rd. SO17: South . . . 9A 160
SO50: E'leigh . . . 3E 160
Arnolds Cl. BH25: B Sea . . . 6A 232
Arnott Cl. SP9: Tidw . . . 8D 30
Arnside Rd. PO7: W'lle . . . 1M 201
Arnwood Av. SO45: Dib P . . . 9L 193
Arragon Ct. PO7: W'lle . . . 1A 202
Arran Cl. PO6: Cosh . . . 8G 200
RG23: Oak . . . 9C 40
Arran Way BH23: Walk . . . 5K 231
Arras Ho. PO15: Fare . . . 7M 197
Arreton SO31: Net A . . . 3G 195
Arreton Ct. PO12: Gos . . . 2J 239
Arrow Cl. SO19: South . . . 9B 174
SO50: E'leigh . . . 7E 132
Arrow Ind. Est. GU14: Farn . . . 1H 49
Arrow La. RG27: H Win . . . 6A 26
Arrow Rd. GU14: Cov . . . 1H 49
Arters Lawn SO40: March . . . 2N 191
Arthur Cl. BH2: Bour . . . 9K 227
GU9: Farnh . . . 9D 64
Arthur Ct. RG21: B'toke . . . 6B 42
(off Solby's Rd.)
Arthur Dann Ct. PO6: Cosh . . . 1F 214
Arthur Kille Ho. PO7: W'lle . . . 3L 201
Arthur La. BH23: Chri . . . 7K 229
Arthur Pope Ho. PO5: S'sea . . . 3E 240
Arthur Rd. BH23: Chri . . . 7K 229
GU9: Farnh . . . 9D 64
(not continuous)
SO15: South . . . 3J 173
SO23: Winche . . . 5L 105
SO50: E'leigh . . . 8E 132
Arthurs Gdns. SO30: Hed E . . . 8M 161
Arthurs La. SP11: Facc . . . 6K 7
Arthur St. GU11: Alders . . . 9K 49
PO2: Ports . . . 9F 214
Artillery Cl. PO6: Cosh . . . 8D 200
Artillery Rd. GU11: Alders . . . 4M 49
(Harmes Way)
GU11: Alders . . . 9K 49
(High St.)
Artists Way SP10: A'ver . . . 8M 51
Artsway . . . 6J 223
Arun Cl. GU31: Pet . . . 2L 145
Arun Ct. RG21: B'toke . . . 6E 42
Arundel Cl. BH25: New M . . . 3N 231
GU30: Pass . . . 7N 101
GU51: Fleet . . . 3N 47
SO24: New A . . . 2E 108
Arundel Dr. PO16: Fare . . . 7C 198
Arundel Gdns. RG23: B'toke . . . 4L 41
Arundel Ho. SO14: South . . . 4A 174
SO15: South . . . 2L 173
Arundell Pl. GU9: Farnh . . . 8D 64
Arundel Rd. PO12: Gos . . . 2H 239
SO40: Tott . . . 2N 171
SO50: E'leigh . . . 6E 132
Arundel St. PO1: Ports . . . 3N 5 (2D 240)
Arundel Way BH23: Highc . . . 7H 231
Arundel Way (Shopping Arc.)
PO1: Ports . . . 3N 5 (2D 240)
Arun Rd. SO18: Wes E . . . 8F 160
Arun Way SO51: W Wel . . . 1A 120 (9M 121)
Ascension Cl. RG24: B'toke . . . 2E 42
Ascham Rd. BH8: Bour . . . 9M 227
Ascot Cl. GU34: Alt . . . 6G 80
PO14: Titch C . . . 7F 196
Ascot Ct. GU11: Alders . . . 1J 65
Ascot Pl. SO30: Hed E . . . 3M 175
Ascot Rd. PO3: Ports . . . 9H 215
SO50: Hor H . . . 4A 162
Ascupart Ho. SO17: South . . . 2N 173
Ascupart St. SO14: South . . . 5F 4 (6N 173)
(not continuous)
Asford Gro. SO50: B'stke . . . 8G 133
Ashbarn Cres. SO22: Winche . . . 9H 105
Ashbourne Ct. BH1: Bour . . . 6N 247
SO22: Winche . . . 4K 105
(off Winton Cl.)
Ashbourne Rd. BH5: Bour . . . 9E 228
Ash Bri. Caravan Pk. GU12: Ash . . . 2N 65
Ashbridge Ri. SO53: Cha F . . . 3M 131
Ashburn Gth. BH24: Hight . . . 2N 187
Ashburnham Cl. SO19: South . . . 5B 174
Ashburn Pl. SP6: F'dge . . . 1H 153
Ashburton Cl. SO24: New A . . . 1E 108
SO45: Dib . . . 6J 193
Ashburton Ct. PO5: S'sea . . . 8N 5
SO23: Winche . . . 6L 237
Ashburton Gdns. BH10: Bour . . . 5H 227
Ashburton Rd. PO5: S'sea . . . 9N 5 (5D 240)
PO12: Gos . . . 5H 239
SO24: New A . . . 1E 108
Ashbury Dr. GU17: Haw . . . 3J 29
Ashbury Rd. GU35: Bor . . . 5J 101
Ashby Cres. SO40: Tott . . . 3K 171
Ashby Pl. PO5: S'sea . . . 9N 5 (5D 240)
PO12: Gos . . . 3M 239
Ashby Rd. SO19: South . . . 7F 174
SO40: Tott . . . 3K 171
Ash Cl. GU17: Blackw . . . 8E 18
PO8: Cowp . . . 7M 181
PO12: Gos . . . 3K 239
PO14: Fare . . . 9A 198
SO19: South . . . 4G 175
SO21: Col C . . . 3K 133
SO31: Burs . . . 1K 195
SO45: Hythe . . . 9M 193
SO51: Rom . . . 6B 130
SO52: N Bad . . . 7E 130
SP6: Ald . . . 5D 152
SP9: Tidw . . . 7E 30
Ash Copse PO8: Cowp . . . 5N 181
Ash Ct. SO19: South . . . 7D 174
Ashcroft Arts Cen. . . . 7E 198
Ashcroft Ct. GU32: Pet . . . 9M 139
SO53: Cha F . . . 6B 132
Ashcroft La. PO8: Finch . . . 4K 183
Ashdell Rd. GU34: Alt . . . 5G 80
Ashdene SO15: South . . . 2G 172
Ashdene Rd. SO40: Ashu . . . 8H 171
Ashdown BH2: Bour . . . 9H 247 (3H 245)
PO13: Gos . . . 7F 212
SO45: Fawl . . . 5D 208
Ashdown Av. GU14: Farn . . . 9M 29
Ashdown Cl. SO53: Cha F . . . 2A 132
Ashdown Dr. SO53: Cha F . . . 2A 132
Ashdown Rd. SO45: Fawl . . . 6D 208
SO53: Cha F . . . 2A 132
Ashdown Ter. SP9: Tidw . . . 9D 30 (7G 31)
Ashdown Wlk. BH25: New M . . . 4D 232
Ashdown Way SO51: Rom . . . 5A 130
ASHE . . . 2H 57
Ashe Cl. RG23: W Law . . . 4G 41
Ashen Cl. SO53: Cha F . . . 4A 132
Ashe Rd. PO9: Hav . . . 4H 203
ASHFIELD . . . 8A 130
Ashfield RG24: Chin . . . 9G 23
Ashfield Grn. GU46: Yat . . . 8B 18
Ashfield Rd. SP10: A'ver . . . 1K 69
Ashfields SO21: Bar S . . . 6A 76
Ashfield Vw. SO52: N Bad . . . 7F 130
ASHFORD . . . 1G 152
Ashford Chace GU32: Ste . . . 4L 139
Ashford Chace Nature Reserve . . . 3J 139
Ashford Cl. PO6: Cosh . . . 8F 200
SP6: F'dge . . . 1G 153
Ashford Cres. SO45: Hythe . . . 6N 193
Ashford Hangers National Nature Reserve
. . . 9J 113
Ashford Hangers Nature Reserve . . . 3K 139
ASHFORD HILL . . . 2N 9
Ashford Hill Rd. RG19: Ashf H, Head . . . 2J 9
Ashford Rd. BH6: Bour . . . 7G 228
SP6: F'dge . . . 2F 152
Ashford Works Ind. Est. SP6: F'dge . . . 1G 152
Ash Gro. BH24: Ring . . . 1M 187
GU30: Lip . . . 3F 116
RG20: Kings . . . 2B 6 (6K 9)
RG24: Old Bas . . . 5K 43
SO40: Ashu . . . 7J 171
SO41: Ever . . . 6L 233
Ashington Cl. PO8: Cowp . . . 6A 182
Ashington Pk. BH25: New M . . . 5C 232
Ash La. RG7: Sil . . . 8B 12
RG26: Bau . . . 4E 10
RG26: Lit L . . . 8B 12
Ashlawn Gdns. SP10: A'ver . . . 3A 70
Ashlea RG27: Hoo . . . 1H 45
Ashlea Cl. SO50: Fair O . . . 1A 162
Ashleigh BH23: Highc . . . 6H 231
Ashleigh Cl. SO45: Hythe . . . 9M 193
Ashleigh Ri. BH10: Bour . . . 4H 227
Ashlet Gdns. BH25: A'ley . . . 2E 232
ASHLETT . . . 5G 209
Ashlett Cl. SO45: Fawl . . . 5G 208
Ashlett Lawn PO9: Hav . . . 3D 202
Ashlett M. SO45: Fawl . . . 5F 208
Ashlett Rd. SO45: Fawl . . . 5G 208
ASHLEY
BH24 . . . 2E 232
BH25 . . . 3G 186
SO20 . . . 6J 89
Ashley Arnewood Ct. BH25: New M . . . 4C 232
Ashley Cl. BH1: Bour . . . 8B 228
BH24: Hight . . . 2N 187
GU10: Cron . . . 2L 63
PO8: Love . . . 5N 181
PO9: Hav . . . 5D 202
SO22: Winche . . . 3G 105
SO31: Swanw . . . 2E 196
Ashley Comn. Rd. BH25: A'ley . . . 1D 232
Ashley Ct. GU35: Bor . . . 5J 101
PO12: Gos . . . 2J 239
SN8: Hen . . . 4C 6
SO31: Burs . . . 8L 175
Ashley Cres. SO19: South . . . 8G 174
Ashley Cross Cl. SO45: Holb . . . 5B 208
Ashley Down La. PO17: Boar . . . 3K 199
Ashley Dr. BH24: A'ley, Har . . . 5F 184
GU17: Blackw . . . 9E 18
Ashley Dr. Nth. BH24: Ashl H . . . 2C 186
(not continuous)
Ashley Dr. Sth. BH24: Ashl H . . . 3C 186
Ashley Dr. W. BH24: Ashl H . . . 3C 186
Ashley Drove SN8: Hen . . . 5C 6
Ashley Gdns. RG23: Oak . . . 9D 40
SO32: Wal C . . . 8A 164
SO53: Cha F . . . 7C 132
ASHLEY HEATH . . . 3B 186
Ashley Ho. SO51: Rom . . . 6L 129
Ashley La. BH25: A'ley . . . 3E 232
SO41: Hor . . . 3E 232
SO41: Lymi . . . 3E 234
Ashley Lodge RG21: B'toke . . . 8B 42
(off Winchester Rd.)
Ashley Mdws. SO51: Rom . . . 4N 129
Ashley Meads BH25: A'ley . . . 2E 232
Ashley Pk. BH24: Ashl H . . . 2D 186
Ashley Rd. BH1: Bour . . . 8B 228
BH14: Poole . . . 9A 226
BH25: A'ley, New M . . . 4C 232
GU14: Farn . . . 8M 29
GU34: Bent . . . 6L 79
Ashley Wlk. PO6: Cosh . . . 1H 215
SP4: Ames . . . 6A 66
Ashling Cl. BH8: Bour . . . 6N 227
PO7: Den . . . 6G 180
Ashling Cres. BH8: Bour . . . 6M 227
Ashling Gdns. PO7: Den . . . 6G 181
Ashling La. PO2: Ports . . . 7E 214
Ashling Pk. Rd. PO7: Den . . . 6G 180
Ashlyn Cl. PO15: Fare . . . 8M 197
ASHMANSWORTH . . . 7M 7
Ashmead GU35: Bor . . . 4J 101
Ashmead Rd. SO16: South . . . 8E 158
Ashmede BH4: Bour . . . 3G 245
Ashmoor La. RG24: Old Bas . . . 5L 43
Ashmore Av. BH25: B Sea . . . 6C 232
Ashmore Cl. SP5: W'psh . . . 5H 121
(off The Green)
Ashmore Gro. BH23: Chri . . . 5G 230
Ashmore La. SP5: W Dean, W'psh . . . 4H 121
Ashmore Rd. SO22: Winche . . . 5G 105
Ashridge GU14: Cov . . . 5H 29
Ashridge Av. BH10: Bour . . . 1H 227
Ashridge Cl. SO15: South . . . 2L 173
Ashridge Gdns. BH10: Bour . . . 1H 227
Ashridge Pde. BH10: Bour . . . 1H 227
Ash Rd. GU12: Alders . . . 1L 65
RG20: Bis G . . . 1H 9
SO40: Ashu . . . 8H 171
Ashstead Gdns. BH8: Bour . . . 3N 227
Ashtead Cl. PO16: Portc . . . 9J 199
ASHTON . . . 9G 134
Ashton Cl. SO32: Bis W . . . 2K 163
Ashton Ct. BH13: Poole . . . 3E 244
Ashton Cross SO51: E Wel . . . 1A 156
Ashton Ho. GU14: Farn . . . 1K 49
SO19: South . . . 9D 174
Ashton La. SO32: Bis W . . . 2K 163
Ashton Pl. SO53: Cha F . . . 3N 131

Ashton Rd.—Balfour Dr.

Ashton Rd. BH9: Bour 4K 227
Ashton Way PO14: Stub 8N 211
Ash Tree Cl. GU14: Cov 9E 28
RG23: Oak 2C 58
Ashtree Cl. BH25: A'ley 4E 232
Ashtree Ct. SO53: Cha F 9A 132
Ashtree Mdws. BH23: Chri 8N 229
Ash Tree Rd. SO18: South 1C 174
SP10: A'ver 1J 69
ASHURST 8H 171
ASHURST BRIDGE 5J 171
Ashurst Bri. Rd. SO40: Tott 4J 171
Ashurst Campsite SO40: Ashu 1G 190
Ashurst Cl. RG26: Tadl 5G 11
SO19: South 9E 174
SO22: Winche 3H 105
SO40: Ashu 8H 171
Ashurst Ct. PO12: Gos 4F 238
Ashurst New Forest Station (Rail) 9G 171
Ashurst Rd. BH8: Bour 3A 228
PO6: Cosh 9F 200
Ash Wlk. SO24: New A 1F 108
Ash Way PO15: White 1G 197
Ashwell Av. GU15: Camb 7N 19
Ashwood PO15: White 4H 197
RG24: Chin 1F 42
SO31: Loc H 7F 196
Ashwood Cl. PO9: Bed 5B 202
PO11: H Isl 4G 242
Ashwood Ct. SO22: Winche 5H 105
Ashwood Gdns. SO16: South 8K 159
SO40: Tott 4J 171
Ashwood Lodge *PO16: Fare* 7D 198
(off Southampton Rd.)
Ashwood Way RG23: B'toke 4M 41
Ashwood Way Rdbt. RG23: B'toke 4M 41
Ashworth Ho. *PO12: Gos* 9M 213
(off Searle Dr.)
Aspect *GU15: Camb* 7L 19
(off Charles St.)
Aspen Av. SO31: Wars 9A 196
Aspen Cl. GU35: W'hil 6J 101
SO21: Col C 4L 133
SO30: Hed E 3A 176
Aspen Gdns. BH12: Poole 6D 226
RG27: Hoo 1H 45
Aspen Gro. GU12: Alders 2N 65
Aspengrove PO13: Gos 7G 212
Aspen Holt SO16: Bass 6M 159
Aspen Ho. RG24: Old Bas 6L 43
Aspen Pl. BH25: New M 5C 232
Aspen Rd. BH12: Poole 7D 226
Aspen Wlk. SO40: Tott 2H 171
Aspen Way BH12: Poole 7D 226
PO8: Horn 5A 182
RG21: B'toke 4D 42
Aspex Art Gallery 5J 5 (3B 240)
Aspin Way GU17: Blackw 8D 18
Asquith Cl. BH23: Chri 9N 229
Assheton Ct. PO16: Portc 1M 213
SP9: Tidw 7D 30
Astbury Av. BH12: Poole 6D 226
Aster Ct. *SP10: A'ver* 3K 69
(off Floral Way)
Aster Rd. RG22: B'toke 3J 59
SO16: S'ing 7A 160
Astley St. PO5: S'sea 6M 5 (3D 240)
Aston Mead BH23: Chri 2H 229
Aston Rd. PO4: S'sea 4G 241
PO7: W'lle 9L 181
Astor Cres. SP11: Ludg 1C 30 (5K 31)
Astra Ct. SO45: Hythe 4M 193
Astral Gdns. SO31: Hamb 6K 195
Astra Wlk. PO12: Gos 3M 239
Astrid Cl. PO11: H Isl 4J 243
Asturias Way SO14: South 7A 174
Asylum Rd. SO15: South 2D 4 (4M 173)
Atalanta Cl. PO4: S'sea 2K 241
Atbara Rd. GU52: Ch Cr 7M 47
Atheling Rd. SO45: Hythe 5M 193
Athelney Ct. BH1: Bour 2M 245
Athelstan Ct. SO41: Lymi 3D 234
Athelstan Rd. BH6: Bour 9H 229
SO19: South 3C 174
SO23: Winche 5K 105
Athena Av. PO7: Purb 6N 201
Athena Cl. SO50: Fair O 9L 133
Atherfield Rd. SO16: South 8D 158
Atherley Bowling Club 2K 173
Atherley Ct. SO15: South 2K 173
Atherley Rd. PO11: H Isl 2E 242
SO15: South 4J 173
Atherstone Wlk. PO5: S'sea 6N 5 (3D 240)
Athlone Cl. SP11: Enh A 2A 52
Athoke Cft. RG27: Hoo 2K 45
Atholl Ct. SP10: A'ver 7N 51
Atholl Rd. GU35: W'hil 5J 101
Atkinson Cl. BH25: B Sea 6B 232
PO12: Gos 5J 239
Atkins Pl. PO15: Fare 6M 197
Atlantic Cl. SO14: South 8N 173
Atlantic Pk. Vw. SO18: Wes E 8E 160
Atlantic Way SO14: South 9E 4 (8M 173)
Atlantis Av. PO7: Purb 7M 201
Atrebatti Rd. GU47: Sandh 4E 18
Atrium, The GU15: Camb 7L 19
Attenborough Cl. GU51: Fleet 9N 27
Attlee Gdns. GU52: Ch Cr 7L 47
Attoll, The RG24: B'toke 2E 42
Attwood Cl. RG21: B'toke 7A 42
SP6: Ald 5C 152
Attwood Cl. Mobile Home Pk.
RG21: B'toke 7A 42
Attwoods Drove SO21: Comp 5G 127
Aubrey Cl. PO11: H Isl 3E 242
SO41: M Sea 8M 235
Auburn Mans. BH12: Poole 1F 244
Auchinleck Ho. *SP9: Tidw* 6C 30
(off Sidbury Circular Rd.)
Auchinleck Way GU11: Alders 9G 49
Auckland Av. SO42: Broc 7D 148
Auckland Pl. SO42: Broc 7C 148
Auckland Rd. BH23: Chri 7E 230
SO15: South 3E 172
Auckland Rd. E. PO5: S'sea 5D 240
Auckland Rd. W. PO5: S'sea 9N 5 (5D 240)
Audemer Ct. BH24: Poul 9M 185
Audley Ct. PO16: Fare 8H 199
Audley Pl. SO50: B'stke 1K 161
Audret Cl. PO16: Portc 2K 213
Auger Way PO7: W'lle 9K 181
Augusta Way Central SP11: E Ant 6B 52
Augusta Way East SP11: E Ant 6B 52
Augusta Way West SP11: E Ant 7B 52
Augustine Rd. PO6: Dray 8K 201
SO14: South 4N 173
Augustine Way SP10: Charl 7K 51
Augustus Cl. SO53: Cha F 5C 132
Augustus Dr. RG23: B'toke 4L 41
Augustus Wlk. SP10: A'ver 7A 52
Augustus Way SO53: Cha F 5C 132
Auklet Cl. RG22: B'toke 3H 59
Auriol Dr. PO9: Bed 9N 201
Aurora Dr. RG22: B'toke 6J 59
SP4: Ames 5A 66
Austen Av. BH10: Bour 1H 227
SO22: Oli B 1F 126
Austen Cl. SO23: Winche 4L 105
SO40: Tott 4K 171
Austen Gdns. PO15: White 1F 196
Austen Gro. RG22: B'toke 9N 41
Austen Ho. SO23: Winche 6M 237
Austen Rd. GU14: Farn 6J 29
Austerberry Way PO13: Gos 8G 212
Auster Cl. BH23: Mude 7D 230
Austin Av. BH14: Poole 4A 244
Austin Cl. BH1: Bour 9A 228
Austin Ct. PO6: Cosh 8C 200
Austins Cotts. GU9: Farnh 8D 64
Australia Cl. PO1: Ports 2E 240
Aust Rd. PO14: Fare 9N 197
Authie Grn. SO52: N Bad 8F 130
Autumn Copse BH25: A'ley 4E 232
Autumn Pl. SO17: South 1M 173
Autumn Rd. BH11: Bour 3B 226
SO40: March 9F 172
Avalon BH14: Poole 5A 244
Avalon Ct. PO10: Ems 7M 203
Avebury Av. BH10: Bour 1J 227
Avebury Gdns. SO53: Cha F 3M 131
Avenger Cl. SO53: Cha F 7N 131
Avens Cl. SO50: Hor H 5N 161
Avenue, The BH9: Bour 4K 227
BH13: Poole 5E 244
GU12: Alders 3L 65
GU15: Camb 9K 19
GU26: Gray 4M 103
GU30: Lip 2C 116
GU31: Pet 1M 145
GU32: Frox 7C 138
GU34: Las 3M 79
GU51: Fleet 2K 47
PO12: Gos 5J 239
PO14: Fare 9L 197
RG25: B'toke 2F 60
RG25: Far W 7M 59
RG25: Herr 3M 79
RG45: Cr'tne 1D 18
SO14: South 1D 4 (3M 173)
SO17: South 8L 159
SO20: Mid Wa 4B 72
SO21: Bar S 7N 71
SO21: Sut S 7D 76
(off Winchester Hill)
SO21: Twyf 7L 127
SO24: New A 1D 108
SO32: Bis W 3L 163
SP4: Port 9B 66
SP5: E Tyt 8N 87
SP9: Tidw 9C 30 (8G 30)
SP10: A'ver 1L 69
SP11: Wild 9L 33
Avenue C SO45: Hard 9C 194
Avenue Cl. GU30: Lip 2D 116
SP10: A'ver 1L 69
Avenue Ct. BH13: Poole 2E 244
PO12: Gos 5J 239
SO17: South 2L 173
Avenue D SO45: Hard 9C 194
Avenue De Caen PO5: S'sea 6D 240
Avenue E SO45: Hard 9C 194
Avenue La. BH2: Bour 7K 247 (2J 245)
Avenue Lawn Tennis & Squash Club 8H 203
Avenue Rd. BH2: Bour 7J 247 (2J 245)
BH23: Chri 7J 229
BH23: Walk 5L 231
BH25: New M 3B 232
GU14: Farn 8M 29
GU26: Gray 4L 103
GU51: Fleet 1L 47
PO11: H Isl 5F 216
PO12: Gos 2L 239
PO14: Fare 8B 198
SO14: South 2M 173
SO22: Winche 6J 237 (6J 105)
SO41: Lymi 2D 234
SO42: Broc 7C 148 (8N 189)
Avenue Shop. Centre, The
BH2: Bour 6K 247 (2J 245)
Avenue Sucy GU15: Camb 9J 19
Avery Ct. *GU11: Alders* 9K 49
(off Windsor Way)
Avery Flds. SO50: E'leigh 5F 132
Avery La. PO12: Gos 9H 213
Aviary Ct. RG24: B'toke 3F 42
Aviation Bus. Pk. BH23: Bour A 6A 218
Aviation Pk. BH23: Bour A 6C 218
Aviation Pk. West BH23: Bour A 6A 218
Aviemore Dr. RG23: Oak 1C 58
AVINGTON 1H 107
Avington Cl. SO50: B'stke 7J 133
Avington Ct. SO16: Bass 7L 159
Avington Grn. PO9: Hav 3H 203
Avington La. SO21: Avin, Itc A 9J 93
Avington Pk. Golf Course 1J 107
Avington Way RG27: Sher L 7H 23
Avlan Ct. SO23: Winche 9K 105
Avocet Cl. PO4: S'sea 2J 241
Avocet Cres. GU47: Coll 5F 18
Avocet Ho. PO4: S'sea 2J 241
Avocet Quay PO10: S'brne 1N 217
Avocet Wlk. PO13: Gos 6C 212
Avocet Way PO8: Horn 3A 182
AVON 5J 219
Avon Av. BH24: A'ley 5G 186
Avonborne Way SO53: Cha F 4N 131
Avon Bldgs. BH23: Chri 7L 229
AVON CASTLE 4G 187
Avon Castle Dr. BH24: A'ley 4G 186
Avon Causeway BH23: Avon, Hurn 8E 218
Avoncliffe Rd. BH6: Bour 2G 247
Avon Cl. BH8: Bour 8A 228
GU14: Cov 5G 29
GU31: Pet 3L 145
PO13: Lee S 2B 238
SO41: Lymi 3C 234
Avon Ct. BH12: Poole 1E 244
GU9: Farnh 9E 64
PO8: Cowp 6N 181
SO31: Net A 4F 194
SP6: F'dge 9J 151
SP10: A'ver 8B 52
Avon Courtyard BH8: Bour 8N 227
Avon Cres. SO51: Rom 5B 130
Avondale Ct. SO17: South 9N 159
Avondale Mobile Home Pk. SO21: Col C 3L 133
Avondale Rd. GU11: Alders 2K 65
GU51: Fleet 1M 47
PO1: Ports 1G 240
PO7: W'lle 1N 201
Avondyke SP5: Down 3K 119 (8A 120)
Avon Gdns. BH8: Bour 8N 227
BH23: Bran 6D 220
Avon Grn. SO53: Cha F 5L 131
Avon Heath Country Pk. (North Pk.) 4D 186
Avon Heath Country Pk. (South Pk.) 7E 186
Avon Heath Country Pk. Vis. Cen. 6D 186
Avon Ho. BH2: Bour 9J 247 (3J 245)
SO14: South 4A 174
Avon Lodge BH6: Bour 9E 228
Avon Meade SP6: F'dge 9H 151
Avon Mdw. SP5: Down 2K 119 (7A 120)
Avon M. BH8: Bour 8N 227
Avon Pk. BH24: A'ley 2G 186
Avon Rd. BH8: Bour 8N 227
GU9: Farnh 9E 64
RG23: Oak 1D 58
SO18: South 1D 174
SP4: Bul C 3B 66
SP9: Tidw 9C 30 (7G 30)
Avon Rd. E. BH23: Chri 6K 229
Avon Rd. W. BH23: Chri 6J 229
Avon Run Cl. BH23: Fri C 9D 230
Avon Run Rd. BH23: Fri C 9D 230
Avons, The *BH8: Bour* 8A 228
(off Avon Cl.)
Avonside Ct. BH24: Ring 3K 187
Avon Trad. Pk. BH23: Chri 6L 229
Avon Tyrrell Activity Cen. 2C 220
Avon Vw. SP6: Gods 1N 153
Avon Vw. Pde. BH23: Burt 3M 229
Avon Vw. Rd. BH23: Burt 3M 229
Avon Wlk. BH8: Bour 8N 227
PO16: Portc 9J 199
RG21: B'toke 6E 42
Avon Way SO30: Wes E 9J 161
Avon Wharf BH23: Chri 8M 229
Avro Cl. SO15: South 3F 172
Avro Ct. SO31: Hamb 7K 195
Award Rd. GU52: Ch Cr 6L 47
AWBRIDGE 9F 122
AWBRIDGE HILL 9G 123
Awbridge Rd. PO9: Hav 5C 202
AWE Aldermaston 1J 11
AXFORD 3F 78
Axford Cl. BH8: Bour 3B 228
Axford Rd. RG25: Pres C 2H 79
Axis Pk. PO14: Fare 2C 212
AXMANSFORD 6C 10
Ayerswood SO30: Hed E 6M 175
Ayesgarth GU52: Ch Cr 6N 47
Ayjay Cl. GU11: Alders 3K 65
Aylen Rd. PO3: Ports 6H 215
Aylesbury Rd. BH1: Bour 1A 246
PO2: Ports 8G 214
Aylesham Way GU46: Yat 7L 17
Ayliffe Ho. RG22: B'toke 7M 41
Ayling Cl. PO13: Gos 9E 212
Ayling Ct. GU9: Weyb 3H 65
Ayling Hill GU11: Alders 1H 65
Ayling La. GU11: Alders 2H 65
Aylings Cl. RG23: Wort 6K 41
Aylward's Dr. GU34: Lwr Farr 4C 98
Aylward St. PO1: Ports 3K 5 (2B 240)
Aylwards Way SO20: N Wal 1N 87
Aylwin Cl. RG21: B'toke 9B 42
Aynsley Ct. SO15: South 3J 173
Ayres La. RG20: Burgh 3D 8
Ayrshire Gdns. GU51: Fleet 8N 27
Aysgarth Rd. PO7: W'lle 1M 201
Aysha Cl. BH25: New M 5C 232
Azalea Av. GU35: Lind 2M 101
Azalea Cl. BH24: St I 3D 186
PO9: Hav 5J 203
Azalea Ct. SP10: A'ver 3K 69
Azalea Gdns. GU52: Ch Cr 6N 47
Azalea Pk. BH4: Bour 3G 245

B

Babbs Mead GU9: Farnh 9C 64
Babs Flds. GU10: Ben'ly 7K 63
Bach Cl. RG22: B'toke 3M 59
Back Dr. RG45: Cr'tne 2D 18
Back Drove SP5: Mid W 5F 86
Back La. BH24: Hight 5A 188
GU10: B Oak 10M 63
PO7: H'don 9E 166
PO17: S'wick 3N 199
RG7: Brim 2B 10
RG7: Mor W 1B 12
RG25: Herr 2M 79
SO41: Sway 5K 223
SO51: Mott 9B 88
SP11: C'vle, Rag A 3C 50
SP11: Ver D 8D 6
Back of the Walls SO14: South 9D 4 (7M 173)
(not continuous)
Back St. SO23: Winche 1K 127
Bacon Cl. GU47: Coll 6F 18
SO19: South 9D 174
Bacon La. GU10: Chur 4E 84
PO11: H Isl 4D 242
Badajos Rd. GU11: Alders 8H 49
Baddesley Cl. SO52: N Bad 7E 130
Baddesley Gdns. PO9: Hav 3D 202
Baddesley Pk. Ind. Est. SO52: N Bad 8G 130
Baddesley Rd. SO52: N Bad 4M 131
SO53: Cha F 4M 131
Baden Cl. BH25: New M 5C 232
Baden Gdns. RG23: B'toke 4M 41
Baden Powell Ho. *SO51: Rom* 5M 129
(off Baden Powell Way)
Baden Powell Rd. GU33: Longc 4J 115
Baden Powell Way SO51: Rom 5M 129
Bader Cl. SO30: Hed E 2N 175
Bader Ct. GU14: Cov 4H 29
Bader Way PO15: White 4J 197
Badger Brow PO7: W'lle 3A 202
Badger Cl. GU34: Four M 4K 97
PO15: Fare 7N 197
SO50: B'stke 1K 161
Badger Ct. SO50: B'stke 1K 161
BADGER FARM 1G 127
Badger Farm Rd. SO22: Winche 9F 104
SO23: Winche 9F 104
(not continuous)
Badger Rd. PO14: Fare 3B 212
Badgers, The SO31: Net A 3G 195
Badgers Bank RG24: Lych 3G 42
Badgers Cl. BH24: Ashl H 3C 186
GU52: Fleet 3L 47
SO41: Sway 5K 223
Badgers Copse BH25: New M 9D 222
GU15: Camb 1N 29
SO31: P Ga 4E 196
Badgers Holt GU46: Yat 8L 17
Badgers Ridge RG20: New 1C 8
Badgers Wlk. BH10: Bour 2H 227
SO45: Dib P 7L 193
Badger Way GU10: Ews 2N 63
GU12: Alders 8M 49
Badgerwood Dr. GU16: Frim 2M 29
Badger Wood Pl. SO18: South 1D 174
Badminston Drove SO45: Fawl 8G 209
Badminston La. SO45: Fawl 7G 208
Badshear La. SO24: Cher 7F 108
Badshot Farm La. GU9: Bad L 5J 65
BADSHOT LEA 5J 65
Badshot Lea Rd. GU9: Bad L 5H 65
Badshot Pk. GU9: Bad L 4J 65
Badsworth Gdns. *RG14: New* 1C 8
(off Andover Rd.)
BAFFINS 9H 215
Baffins Rd. PO3: Ports 1H 241
Bagber Rd. SO40: Tott 3M 171
BAGMORE 2L 79
Bagmore La. RG25: Elli, Herr 3J 79
BAGNUM 8A 188
Bagnum La. BH24: King 6N 187
Bagot Ho. PO12: Gos 9H 213
Bagshot M. SO19: South 7D 174
Bagwell La. RG27: Winchf 4B 46
RG29: Odi 6N 45
Baigent Cl. SO23: Winche 6N 105
Bailey Cl. BH25: A'ley 2E 232
GU16: Frim 4M 29
SO22: Winche 8H 105
SO30: Botl 4D 176
Bailey Ct. BH8: Bour 8M 227
Bailey Dr. BH23: Chri 7J 229
BAILEY GREEN 2K 137
Bailey Grn. SO18: South 9E 160
Bailey Ho. *SO24: New A* 9F 94
(off Station App.)
Baileys Cl. GU17: Blackw 9E 18
BAILEY'S DOWN 1D 124
Baileys Hill BH21: Gus S, Wim G 8E 148
Bailey's Rd. PO5: S'sea 3E 240
Baillie Pk. BH13: Poole 3E 244
Bain Av. GU15: Camb 2K 29
Baird Av. RG22: B'toke 9N 41
Baird Rd. GU14: Farn 6L 29
Bakehouse Gdns. GU52: Ch Cr 6N 47
Bakehouse M. GU11: Alders 9J 49
Bakehouse Yd. *SO24: New A* 9F 94
(off The Dean)
Baker Rd. BH11: Bour 1D 226
Bakers Drove SO16: Rown 6D 158
Bakers Fld. GU33: G'ham 4E 114
Baker St. PO1: Ports 9E 214
Bakers Wharf SO14: South 5A 174
Bakers Yd. RG23: Oak 2D 58
Balaclava Rd. SO18: South 3E 174
Balchin Ho. PO1: Ports 3K 5
Balcombe Rd. BH13: Poole 2E 244
Balderton Cl. PO2: Ports 4G 214
Baldwin Cl. BH23: Chri 8N 229
Baldwin's La. RG26: Wolve, Wolv C 9A 10
Baler La. PO7: W'lle 9K 181
Balfour Cl. BH23: Chri 6F 230
PO13: Gos 1F 238
Balfour Dr. GU33: Liss 1E 140

Balfour Mus. of Red Cross—Bayly Av.

Balfour Mus. of Red Cross 5N 105
Balfour Rd. BH9: Bour 5K 227
PO2: Ports 7F 214
SO19: South 5G 174
Balintore Ct. GU47: Coll 5F 18
Balksbury Hill SP11: Up C 3K 69
Balksbury Hill Ind. Est. SP11: Up C 4L 69
Balksbury Rd. SP11: Up C 4L 69
Ballam Gro. BH12: Poole 6B 226
Ball & Wicket La. GU9: Up H 3E 64
Ballantyne Rd. GU14: Farn 6J 29
Ballard Cl. BH25: New M 2C 232
RG22: B'toke 8L 41
SO16: South 1C 172
Ballard Ct. PO12: Gos 3K 239
Balldown Caravan & Camping Pk.
SO21: Spar 9A 90
BALL HILL 1N 7
Ballhill Cotts. RG20: Bal H 1N 7
Balliol Cl. PO14: Titch C 8F 196
Balliol Rd. PO2: Ports 8F 214
Balliol Way GU47: Owl 4G 19
Ball's La. SO24: B'wth 2H 135
BALMERLAWN 6B 204
Balmer Lawn Rd. SO42: Broc 5D 148
Balmoral Av. BH8: Bour 5B 228
Balmoral Cl. GU34: Alt 5D 80
PO13: Gos 6F 212
SO16: South 6H 159
SO53: Cha F 4N 131
Balmoral Ct. BH5: Bour 1B 246
RG22: B'toke 8L 41
SO15: South 4F 172
SP10: A'ver 1N 69
Balmoral Cres. GU9: Up H 4D 64
Balmoral Dr. GU16: Frim 4N 29
PO7: Purb 5K 201
Balmoral Ho. BH2: Bour 6G 247 (1H 245)
Balmoral Rd. BH14: Poole 2A 244
PO15: Fare 6A 198
SP10: A'ver 1N 69
Balmoral Wlk. BH25: New M 3A 232
Balmoral Way GU32: Pet 9M 139
RG22: B'toke 4J 59
SO16: Rown 5C 158
Balsan Cl. RG24: B'toke 3L 41
Baltic Rd. SO30: Wes E 1J 175
Bamber La. GU34: Lwr Froy 8G 62
Bampton Cl. SO16: South 2C 172
Bampton Ct. SO53: Cha F 6A 132
Banbury Av. SO19: South 6G 174
Banbury Way RG24: B'toke 2B 42
Bances Ct. RG20: Bal H 1M 7
Band Hall Pl. RG27: Hoo 2H 45
Bangor Rd. SO15: South 4G 173
Banister Gdns. SO15: South 3L 173
Banister Grange SO15: South 3L 173
Banister M. SO15: South 3L 173
BANISTER PARK 3K 173
Banister Pk. Bowling Club 4A 160
Banister Rd. SO15: South 3L 173
BANK 4M 189
Bank, The SP4: Win D 3A 86
Bank Chambers BH14: Poole 1C 244
(off Penn Hill Av.)
Bank Cl. BH23: Chri 8L 229
Bankhill Dr. SO41: Lymi 1D 234
Bank Pde. BH12: Poole 5E 226
Bank Rd. GU11: Alders 6M 49
Banks, The SO51: Lock, Sher E 8A 122
Banks Cl. SP10: A'ver 2L 69
Bankside GU9: Weyb 3H 65
PO12: Gos 5H 239
SO18: S'ing 7C 160
SO41: Lymi 9D 224
SP5: W Gri 1D 120
Bankside Ho. SO22: Winche 6J 237 (6J 105)
Bankside Rd. BH9: Bour 3L 227
Banks Rd. BH13: S'bks 9A 244
Bank St. SO32: Bis W 3M 163
Bankview SO41: Lymi 9D 224
Bannerman Rd. GU32: Pet 9M 139
Banning St. SO51: Rom 6L 129
Bannister Ct. SO40: Tott 3N 171
Bannister Gdns. GU46: Yat 8B 18
RG27: Eve 5H 17
Bapaume Rd. PO3: Ports 3G 214
Baptist Hill SP11: S M Bo 9L 35
Barbara Cl. GU52: Ch Cr 5N 47
Barbara Ct. SO32: Uph 5J 135
(off Preshaw Est.)
Barbastelle Wlk. PO17: K Vil 2N 197
Barbe Baker Av. SO30: Wes E 9G 161
Barbel Av. RG21: B'toke 6E 42
Barber Rd. RG22: B'toke 2M 59
Barberry Cl. GU52: Fleet 5M 47
Barberry Dr. SO40: Tott 1H 171
Barberry Way GU17: Haw 2H 29
Barbican M. PO16: Portc 1N 213
Barbour Cl. RG29: Odi 2E 62
(off Wooldridge Cres.)
Barcelona Cl. SP10: A'ver 9A 52
Barclay Ho. PO12: Gos 3N 239
(off Trinity Grn.)
Barclay Mans. BH2: Bour 9K 227
Barclay M. SO45: Hythe 9M 193
Bardon Way PO14: Fare 9N 197
Bardwell Cl. RG22: B'toke 7L 41
Baredown, The RG27: Nat S 4D 44
BAR END 8M 105
Bar End Ind. Est. SO23: Winche 9M 105
Bar End Rd. SO23: Winche 9P 237 (8M 105)
(not continuous)
Barentin Way GU31: Pet 8N 139
Barfield Cl. SO23: Winche 8M 105
Barfields SO41: Lymi 2E 234
Barfields Ct. SO41: Lymi 2E 234
Barfleur Cl. PO15: Fare 7N 197
Barfleur Rd. PO14: Fare 3C 212
Barfoot Rd. SO30: Hed E 1M 175
BARFORD 8G 85
Barford Cl. GU51: Fleet 3B 48
SO53: Cha F 4N 131
Barford La. GU10: Chur 7G 85
SP5: Down 1L 119 (7B 120)
Bargate, The 6D 4
Bargate Level SO14: South 6D 4
(off Bargate Shop. Cen.)
Bargates BH23: Chri 7K 229
Bargate Shop. Cen. SO14: South 6D 4 (6M 173)
Bargate St. SO14: South 6C 4 (6L 173)
Barge Cl. GU11: Alders 6N 49
Barge La. RG7: Swal 2D 14
Barham Cl. BH1: Bour 9B 228
PO12: Gos 1K 239
Barham Rd. GU32: Pet 1M 145
Barham Way PO2: Ports 4E 214
Baring Cl. SO21: E Str 7M 77
SO21: Itc A 8K 93
Baring Dr. PO31: Cowes 5N 237
(off Baring Rd.)
Baring Rd. BH6: Bour 1K 247
PO31: Cowes 5N 237
SO23: Winche 7M 105
Barker Mill Cl. SO16: Rown 5D 158
Barkis Ho. PO1: Ports 9E 214
Barkis Mead GU47: Owl 3G 18
Bark Mill M. SO51: Rom 6L 129
Barlands Cl. BH23: Burt 4M 229
Barle Cl. SO18: Wes E 9F 160
Barleycorn Wlk. SO40: Cad 6N 155
(off Romsey Rd.)
Barley Down Dr. SO22: Winche 1H 127
Barley Flds. SO50: Hor H 5N 161
Barley Hill SO51: Dun 4E 122
Barley Mow Cl. RG27: Winchf 3E 46
Barley Mow Hill GU35: Head D 1B 102
Barley Rd. SP11: E Ant 6B 52
Barley Vw. RG25: Nth W 9B 58
Barley Way GU51: Fleet 7N 27
Barlow Cl. PO14: Stub 6L 211
Barlow M. GU34: Alt 3G 80
Barlows La. SP10: A'ver 4M 69
Barlows Rd. RG26: Tadl 6H 11
Barnaby Cl. SP5: Down 2J 119
Barnard Way GU11: Alders 8H 49
Barnbrook Rd. SO31: Sar G 5B 196
Barn Cl. GU15: Camb 7N 19
PO10: Ems 9K 203
PO14: Titch 1J 211
Barn Cl. La. RG20: Ashm 7M 7
Barncroft GU9: Farnh 9E 64
(not continuous)
SP11: Apple 5A 50
Barncroft Way PO9: Hav 5D 202
Barnes Cl. BH10: Bour 3H 227
GU14: Farn 8M 29
SO18: South 4G 174
SO23: Winche 9J 105
SO31: Sar G 5A 196
SO51: W Wel 1B 120 (9N 121)
Barnes Cres. BH10: Bour 3H 227
Barnes La. SO31: Sar G 3B 196
SO41: Down, Hor, M Sea 5H 233 & 7K 235
Barnes Rd. BH10: Bour 3H 227
GU16: Frim 4N 29
PO1: Ports 1F 240
SO19: South 4G 174
Barnes Wallis Cl. SP4: Ames 5A 66
(off Raleigh Cres.)
Barnes Wallis Rd. PO15: Seg 5G 196
Barnes Way PO9: Bed 6D 202
BARNET SIDE 9D 112
Barnet Side La. GU32: Frox 1D 138
Barnetts Wood La. SO24: Bigh 6A 96
Barney Evans Cres. PO8: Cowp 7L 181
Barney Hayes La. SO40: Cad 3A 170
Barn Fld. GU46: Yat 8N 17
Barnfield BH23: Chri 6F 230
Barnfield Cl. GU34: Lwr Froy 7G 63
SO19: South 9C 174
Barnfield Ct. PO14: Fare 9A 198
SO19: South 9D 174
Barnfield Flats SO19: South 9D 174
Barnfield Ri. SP10: A'ver 3L 69
Barnfield Rd. GU31: Pet 1B 146
SO19: South 9D 174
Barnfield Way SO19: South 9D 174
Barn Fold PO7: W'lle 9B 182
Barn Grn. Cl. PO7: Den 6G 180
Barn La. GU34: Four M 6G 96
RG23: Oak 2C 58
Barn Mdw. Cl. GU52: Ch Cr 8K 47
Barn Piece SO53: Cha F 6L 131
Barns, The RG25: Dumm 1C 78
Barnsfield Cres. SO40: Tott 3J 171
BARNSFIELD HEATH 3E 218
Barnsfield Rd. BH24: Match 6D 186
Barnside Way GU33: Liss 2E 140
Barnsland SO30: Wes E 8G 160
Barnwells Ct. RG27: H Win 5C 26
Barnwood Rd. PO15: Fare 8N 197
Baroda Ct. PO2: Ports 8E 214
Baroda Rd. SP9: Tidw 9A 30 (8F 30)
Baron Rd. SO31: Hamb 6K 195
Barons Ct. BH12: Poole 1F 244
Barons Mead SO16: South 8D 158
Baronsmede BH2: Bour 1H 245
Baronsmere Ct. PO12: Gos 3J 239
Barons Rd. BH11: Bour 1B 226
Barossa Rd. GU15: Camb 6M 19
Barracane Dr. RG45: Cr'tne 1D 18
Barrack La. BH24: Crow 4M 187
Barrack Rd. BH23: Chri 6G 228
GU11: Alders 9J 49
Barracks, The RG27: Hoo 3D 44
SP5: M Val 2M 119
Barracks Rd. PO4: S'sea 5K 241
Barra Cl. RG23: Oak 9C 40
Barratt Ind. Pk. PO15: Seg 4F 196
Barrett Ct. RG21: B'toke 9D 42
Barrie Cl. PO15: White 1F 196
Barrie Rd. BH9: Bour 3K 227
GU9: Up H 3C 64
Barrington Cl. SO50: E'leigh 7D 132
Barrington Ct. BH3: Bour 7H 227
Barrington Dr. RG24: B'toke 1C 42
Barrington Ho. PO2: Ports 9E 214
Barrington Ter. PO5: S'sea 7N 5
Barrita Cl. PO12: Gos 2J 239
Barron Pl. RG24: B'toke 3K 41
Barrow Down Gdns. SO19: South 7J 175
Barrow Dr. BH8: Bour 4C 228
Barrowfield SP11: G Cla 8M 69
Barrowgate Rd. BH8: Bour 3N 227
Barrowgate Way BH8: Bour 3A 228
BARROW HILL
SO40 8D 156
SP11 9M 69
Barrow Hill SP11: G Cla 1K 73
Barrow Hill Rd. SO40: Copy 8C 156
Barrow Rd. BH8: Bour 4C 228
Barrows La. SO41: Sway 8J 223
SP5: L'ford 8H 121
Barrows M. BH24: Ring 2K 187
Barrow Way BH8: Bour 4C 228
Barrs Av. BH25: New M 2B 232
Barrs Wood Dr. BH25: New M 2C 232
Barrs Wood Rd. BH25: New M 2C 232
Barry Rd. SO19: South 4F 174
Barry Way RG22: B'toke 3M 59
Bars Hill PO31: Cowes 5P 237
Barter Rd. BH12: Poole 7E 226
Barters Cl. SO16: South 1E 172
Bartholomew Cl. SO23: Winche 5L 105
Bartlett Cl. PO15: Fare 6A 198
RG26: B'ley 2J 23
Bartlett Dr. BH7: Bour 6E 228
Bartletts, The SO31: Hamb 7L 195
Bartletts Comn. SP6: Frog 6A 154
Bartlett Way BH12: Poole 6A 226
BARTLEY 4B 170
Bartley Av. SO40: Tott 4L 171
Bartley Ct. RG27: Hoo 2H 45
Bartley Point RG27: Hoo 3H 45
Bartley Rd. SO40: Woodl 6C 170
Bartley Way RG27: Hoo 3J 45
Bartley Wood Bus. Pk. (East) RG27: Hoo 3J 45
Bartley Wood Bus. Pk. (West) RG27: Hoo 3H 45
Bartok Cl. RG22: B'toke 1N 59
Barton Chase BH25: B Sea 7A 232
Barton Cl. GU11: Alders 1G 64
SO51: Rom 4A 130
SP10: Charl 7K 51
Barton Comn. La. BH25: B Sea 6C 232
Barton Comn. Rd. BH25: B Sea 7C 232
Barton Ct. Av. BH25: B Sea 7A 232
Barton Ct. Rd. BH25: New M 5B 232
Barton Cres. SO18: South 1D 174
Barton Cft. BH25: B Sea 7B 232
Barton Cross PO8: Horn 3B 182
Barton Dr. BH25: B Sea 6A 232
SO30: Hed E 3A 176
SO31: Hamb 6K 195
Barton Drove SO21: Bar S, Sut S 6B 76
Barton End GU34: Alt 5E 80
Barton Grn. BH25: B Sea 7C 232
Barton Gro. PO3: Ports 5J 215
Barton Ho. BH25: B Sea 7N 231
Barton La. BH25: B Sea 6M 231
BARTON ON SEA 7N 231
Barton-on-Sea Golf Course 7D 232
Barton Pk. Ind. Est. SO50: E'leigh 1F 160
Barton Rd. SO50: E'leigh 9G 132
Bartons, The SO30: Hed E 4L 175
SP6: F'dge 1J 153
Barton's Ct. RG29: Odi 8K 45
Bartons Dr. GU46: Yat 9N 17
Bartonside Rd. BH25: New M 6L 231
Barton's La. RG24: Old Bas 4G 43
(not continuous)
Bartons Rd. PO9: Hav 4G 202
SP6: F'dge 1J 153
BARTON STACEY 5A 76
Bartons Way GU14: Cov 5F 28
Barton Way BH25: B Sea 6A 232
Barton Wood Rd. BH25: B Sea 7N 231
Bartram Rd. SO40: Elin, Tott 4N 171
Barwell Cl. RG45: Cr'tne 1B 18
Barwell Gro. PO10: Ems 6L 203
Barwell La. PO13: Gos 3E 212
Barwell Ter. SO30: Hed E 4A 176
Bascott Cl. BH11: Bour 5E 226
Bascott Rd. BH11: Bour 5D 226
Basepoint Business & Innovation Cen.
SP10: A'ver 8K 51
Basepoint Ent. Cen. RG24: B'toke 3F 42
SO14: South 7G 4 (7N 173)
BASHLEY 8B 222
Bashley Comn. Rd. BH25: Bash 8B 222
Bashley Cross Rd. BH25: Bash 1M 231
Bashley Dr. BH25: Bash 9C 222
Bashley FC 8B 222
Bashley Rd. BH25: Bash 8B 222
Basing Barns GU34: Priv 8L 111
Basingbourne Cl. GU52: Fleet 5M 47
Basingbourne Rd. GU52: Fleet 6L 47
Basing Dean La. GU32: Frox 1L 137
GU34: Priv 1L 137
Basing Dr. GU11: Alders 3K 65
Basingfield Cl. RG24: Old Bas 7J 43
Basing House
Barton's La. 4H 43
Musket Copse 5H 43
Basing Ho. SO15: South 3H 173
Basing M. SO32: Bis W 4M 163
(off Basingwell St.)
BASING PARK 9L 111
Basing Rd. PO9: Hav 4E 202
RG24: Old Bas 5F 42
BASINGSTOKE 6C 42
Basingstoke Bus. Cen. RG22: B'toke 9N 41
Basingstoke Crematorium RG25: Nth W 1N 77
Basingstoke Ent. Cen. RG22: Wort 7K 41
Basingstoke Golf Cen. 7L 41
Basingstoke Golf Course 5H 59
Basingstoke Leisure Pk. RG22: B'toke 6M 41
Basingstoke Rd. GU34: Alt, Bee 5B 80
RG7: Rise, Swal 1G 14
RG20: Kings 2B 6 (6K 9)
RG26: Rams, Up Woott 5G 20
RG26: Wolve 6K 9
RG27: Stra T, Heck 8B 14
SO21: Kin W, Mar W 9A 92
SO23: Kin W 9A 92
SO24: Old A 6F 94
Basingstoke Station (Rail) 5C 42
Basingstoke Town FC (The Camrose) 9N 41
Basing Vw. RG21: B'toke 6D 42
Basing Way SO53: Cha F 8M 131
Basingwell St. SO32: Bis W 4M 163
Basin St. PO2: Ports 8E 214
Bassenthwaite Gdns. GU35: Bor 2J 101
Basset Cl. GU16: Frim 4N 29
Basset Ct. GU14: Farn 3K 49
(off Honington M.)
BASSETT 6M 159
Bassett Av. SO16: Bass 8L 159
Bassett Cl. SO16: Bass 7L 159
Bassett Ct. SO16: Bass 7L 159
Bassett Cres. E. SO16: Bass 7L 159
Bassett Cres. W. SO16: Bass 8L 159
Bassett Dale SO16: Bass 5L 159
Bassett Gdns. SO16: Bass 7L 159
BASSETT GREEN 6N 159
Bassett Grn. Cl. SO16: Bass 6M 159
Bassett Grn. Ct. SO16: Bass 6N 159
Bassett Grn. Dr. SO16: Bass 5M 159
Bassett Grn. Rd. SO16: Bass, S'ing 4M 159
Bassett Grn. Village SO16: Bass 6N 159
Bassett Heath Av. SO16: Bass 4L 159
Bassett Ho. BH1: Bour 1A 246
(off Knyveton Rd.)
Bassett Lodge SO16: Bass 7L 159
Bassett Mdw. SO16: Bass 7L 159
Bassett M. SO16: Bass 6L 159
Bassett Rd. BH12: Poole 8A 226
Bassett Row SO16: Bass 5L 159
Bassett Wlk. PO9: Hav 3D 202
Bassett Wood Dr. SO16: Bass 5L 159
Bassett Wood M. SO16: Bass 7L 159
Bassett Wood Rd. SO16: Bass 5L 159
Basswood Dr. RG24: B'toke 3M 41
Bastins Cl. SO31: P Ga 3E 196
Batchelor Cres. BH11: Bour 3D 226
Batchelor Dr. RG24: Old Bas 6K 43
Batchelor Grn. SO31: Burs 1K 195
Batchelor Rd. BH11: Bour 3D 226
Batchelor's Barn Rd. SP10: A'ver 1B 70
Batcombe Cl. BH11: Bour 3C 226
Bateson Hall PO1: Ports 4N 5
Bath & Wells Ct. PO13: Gos 1E 238
Bath Cl. SO19: South 4F 174
Bath Hill Ct. BH1: Bour 7N 247 (2L 245)
Bath Hill Rdbt. BH1: Bour 8N 247 (3L 245)
Bathing La. PO1: Ports 6H 5 (4A 240)
Bath La. PO16: Fare 8E 198
Bath La. Cotts. PO16: Fare 9E 198
Bath La. Lwr. PO16: Fare 8E 198
Bath Pl. SO22: Winche 7H 105
Bath Rd. BH1: Bour 8M 247 (3K 245)
GU15: Camb 7M 19
PO4: S'sea 4G 240
PO10: Ems 1M 217
PO31: Cowes 5P 237
SO19: South 4F 174
SO41: Lymi 3F 234
Bath Sq. PO1: Ports 6H 5 (3A 240)
Bath St. SO14: South 1E 4 (3M 173)
Bathurst Cl. PO11: H Isl 4E 242
Bathurst Way PO2: Ports 6C 214
Batsford SP11: S M Bo 9L 35
Battenburg Av. PO2: Ports 6F 214
Battenburg Rd. PO12: Gos 2L 239
Batten Cl. BH23: Chri 7N 229
Battens Rd. SP5: Down 1J 119 (7A 120)
Battens Av. RG25: Over 2E 56
Battens Way PO9: Hav 5F 202
Batten Way SO18: S'ing 7C 160
Batterley Drove BH21: Cran 8M 149
Battery Cl. PO12: Gos 8H 213
Battery Hill SO22: Winche 8G 104
SO32: Bis W 1C 163
Battery Prom. PO1: Ports 7H 5 (4A 240)
Battery Rd. PO31: Cowes 5N 237
Battery Row PO1: Ports 8J 5 (4B 240)
Battle Cl. SO31: Sar G 5C 196
Battledown Cotts. RG23: Wort 1G 59
BATTRAMSLEY 5B 224
BATTRAMSLEY CROSS 6C 224
BATT'S CORNER 2N 83
BAUGHURST 8E 10
BAUGHURST COMMON 4D 10
Baughurst Rd. RG26: Bau 5E 10
RG26: Bau, Rams 3E 20
B Avenue SO45: Fawl 4C 208
(8th Street, not continuous)
SO45: Fawl 3A 208
(14th Street)
Baverstock Rd. BH12: Poole 6F 226
Baverstocks GU34: Alt 2G 80
Bawdsey Rd. SP4: Ames 6A 66
Baxter Ct. BH10: Bour 5F 226
Baxter Rd. SO19: South 5J 175
BAYBRIDGE 5D 134
Baybridge La. SO21: Owls 5D 134
SO32: Uph 5D 134
Baybridge Rd. PO9: Hav 4H 203
Bay Cl. SO19: South 7E 174
Bayeux M. SP9: Tidw 7C 30
Bayfield Av. GU16: Frim 2M 29
Bayfields PO5: S'sea 9N 5
Bayford Cl. GU17: Haw 3J 29
Bayly Av. PO16: Portc 2M 213

Belmont Pl.—Bishops Cl.

Belmont Pl. PO5: S'sea 4D 240
Belmont Rd. BH14: Poole 9A 226
BH25: A'ley 2D 232
GU15: Camb 9L 19
SO17: South 2N 173
SO53: Cha F 9A 132
SP10: A'ver 3A 70
Belmont St. PO5: S'sea 7N 5 (4D 240)
Belmore Cl. PO1: Ports 9F 214
Belmore La. SO21: Owls 4D 134
SO32: Uph 5F 134
SO41: Lymi 3D 234
Belmore Rd. SO41: Lymi 3D 234
Belmour Lodge BH4: Bour 2G 244
(off Marlborough Rd.)
Belney La. PO7: Den 2E 200
PO17: S'wick 2E 200
Belstone M. GU14: Farn 5J 29
Belstone Rd. SO40: Tott 3L 171
Belt, The SP6: R'bne 4A 150
Beltex Wlk. SP11: E Ant 6B 52
(off Romney Rd.)
Belton Rd. GU15: Camb 8N 19
SO19: South 7F 174
Belvedere Cl. GU51: Fleet 2H 47
Belvedere Ct. GU17: Haw 1F 28
Belvedere Gdns. RG24: Chin 8H 23
Belvedere Pl. GU32: Pet 9M 139
Belvedere Rd. BH3: Bour 8L 227
BH23: Chri 7K 229
GU14: Farn 1L 49
SO45: Dib P 7M 193
Belverdere Ho. RG21: B'toke 5E 42
BELVIDERE 5A 174
Belvidere Ho. SO14: South 4A 174
Belvidere Rd. SO14: South 6A 174
Belvidere Ter. SO14: South 5A 174
Belvoir Cl. PO16: Fare 8C 198
Belvoir Pk. BH13: Poole 2F 244
Bembridge SO31: Net A 3G 195
Bembridge Cl. SO16: S'ing 6A 160
Bembridge Ct. PO11: H Isl 6J 243
RG45: Cr'tne 1A 18
Bembridge Cres. PO4: S'sea 6F 240
Bembridge Dr. PO11: H Isl 6J 243
Bembridge Ho. PO11: H Isl 5H 243
Bembridge Lodge PO13: Lee S 2A 238
Bemister Rd. BH9: Bour 6L 227
Bemister's La. PO12: Gos 3N 239
Benbow Cl. PO8: Horn 3C 182
Benbow Ct. SP10: A'ver 1C 70
Benbow Cres. BH12: Poole 4C 226
Benbow Gdns. SO40: Calm 9J 157
Benbow Ho. PO1: Ports 3J 5
Benbow Pl. PO1: Ports 3J 5 (2B 240)
Benbridge Av. BH11: Bour 1D 226
BENCH, THE 3D 148
Bencraft Ct. SO16: Bass 6N 159
Bendeng Cl. GU51: Fleet 9J 27
Bendigo Rd. BH23: Chri 6H 229
Benedict Cl. SO51: Rom 5B 130
Benedict Way PO16: Portc 8N 199
Beneficial St. PO1: Ports 3J 5 (2B 240)
Benellen Av. BH4: Bour 1G 245
Benellen Gdns. BH4: Bour 1G 245
Benellen Rd. BH4: Bour 9G 227
Benellen Towers BH4: Bour 1G 245
Benenden Grn. SO24: New A 2F 108
Benford Ct. RG29: Odi 9L 45
(off Buryfields)
Bengal Rd. BH9: Bour 5J 227
Benger's La. SO51: Mott 3D 122
Benham Dr. PO3: Ports 4G 215
Benham Drove SO20: N Wal 1M 87
Benham Gro. PO16: Portc 2M 213
Benham La. RG7: Rise 2H 15
RG19: Ashf H 2N 9
Benham Rd. RG24: B'toke 1B 42
SO16: Chilw 2G 159
Benhams Farm Cl. SO18: South 1E 174
Benham's La. GU33: Blackm, G'ham 2E 114
Benhams Rd. SO18: South 9E 160
Benin Rd. SP11: Per D 5B 30 (7J 31)
Benjamin Ct. BH1: Bour 5N 247 (1L 245)
SO31: Net A 3G 194
Ben La. SP5: Far 8F 86
Benmore Cl. BH25: New M 4D 232
Benmore Gdns. SO53: Cha F 4N 131
Benmore Rd. BH9: Bour 5L 227
Bennet Cl. GU34: Alt 4E 80
RG21: B'toke 4D 42
Bennett Cl. SP5: M Val 2M 119 (8C 120)
Bennett Ct. GU15: Camb 8L 19
Bennett Ho. BH4: Bour 2G 244
(off Westbourne Cl.)
Bennett Rd. BH8: Bour 8M 227
Bennetts La. BH24: Bur 7F 188
Bennetts Ri. GU11: Alders 2L 65
Bennett Wlk. SO45: Fawl 6D 208
Bennion Rd. BH10: Bour 3G 226
Benny Hill Cl. SO50: E'leigh 9D 132
Bensgreen La. GU32: Frox 2E 138
Benson Cl. BH23: Bran 6D 220
Benson Rd. RG45: Cr'tne 1B 18
SO15: South 2G 173
Bentall Pl. SP10: A'ver 2N 69
Bentham Ct. SO16: Bass 7M 159
Bentham Rd. PO12: Gos 4K 239
Bentham Way SO31: Lwr Swan 1A 196
Bent La. PO7: H'don 4A 180
BENTLEY 7K 63
Bentley Cl. PO8: Horn 2C 182
SO23: Kin W 9M 91
Bentley Ct. PO9: Hav 4H 203
SO17: South 1M 173
Bentley Cres. PO16: Fare 7B 198
Bentley Dr. GU51: Fleet 9J 27
Bentley Grn. SO18: South 2G 175
Bentley Ind. Cen. GU10: Ben'ly 8K 63
Bentley Lodge GU51: Fleet 9J 27
(off Bentley Dr.)
Bentley Rd. BH9: Bour 3K 227
Bentley Station (Rail) 8L 63
Bentley Way SO41: Bold 9D 224
SP5: Mid W 5H 87
Benton Ct. BH23: Chri 8J 229
Bent St. SO20: N Wal 1N 87
BENTWORTH 6L 79
Bentworth Cl. PO9: Hav 5D 202
Benwell Cl. RG29: Odi 2E 62
(off Kersley Cres.)
Benyon Rd. RG7: A'mas 1L 11
Bepton Down GU31: Pet 1N 145
Berber Cl. PO15: White 3F 196
Berberis Ho. SO14: South 8F 4
Bercote Cl. SO22: Lit 1F 104
Bere Cl. SO22: Winche 4H 105
SO53: Cha F 4M 131
Bere Farm La. PO17: N Boa 2H 199
BERE HILL
RG28 4H 55
SP10 3A 70
Bere Hill RG28: Whit 4H 55
Bere Hill Cl. RG28: Whit 4H 55
Bere Hill Cres. SP10: A'ver 2B 70
Bere Hill Pk. (Caravan Pk.) RG28: Whit 4H 55
Berehurst GU34: Alt 6E 80
Bere La. PO17: K Vil 2A 198
Bere Rd. PO7: Den 6G 181
Beresford Centre, The RG24: B'toke 3F 42
Beresford Cl. BH12: Poole 8B 226
PO7: W'lle 3M 201
SO53: Cha F 7C 132
SP10: A'ver 4N 69
Beresford Gdns. BH23: Chri 8A 230
SO53: Cha F 7C 132
Beresford Ga. SP10: A'ver 9D 52
Beresford Rd. BH6: Bour 1E 246
BH12: Poole 8B 226
PO2: Ports 7F 214
PO14: Stub 5N 211
SO41: Lymi 2C 234
SO53: Cha F 7C 132
Bereweeke Av. SO22: Winche 3J 105
Bereweeke Cl. SO22: Winche 5J 105
Bereweeke M. SO22: Winche 4J 105
Bereweeke Rd. SO22: Winche 5J 105
Bereweeke Way SO22: Winche 4J 105
Berewyk Cl. RG22: B'toke 3J 59
Bergen Cres. SO30: Hed E 5N 175
Berkeley, The PO4: S'sea 6F 240
(off Sth. Pde.)
Berkeley Av. BH12: Poole 6A 226
Berkeley Cl. GU51: Fleet 2N 47
PO14: Stub 6L 211
SO15: South 1A 4 (3K 173)
Berkeley Ct. BH1: Bour 1L 245
(off Cavendish Rd.)
PO13: Lee S 2B 238
Berkeley Dr. RG22: B'toke 2A 60
Berkeley Gdns. SO30: Hed E 5N 175
Berkeley Mans. BH1: Bour 2N 245
(off Christchurch Rd.)
Berkeley Rd. BH3: Bour 7J 227
SO15: South 1B 4 (4L 173)
Berkeley Sq. PO9: Warb 8H 203
Berkley Mnr. BH13: Poole 1F 244
Berkshire Cl. PO1: Ports 2E 240
Berkshire Copse Rd. GU14: Farn 5G 48
Bermuda Cl. RG24: B'toke 1D 42
Bermuda Ct. BH23: Highc 7J 231
Bermuda Ho. PO6: Cosh 7A 200
Bernard Av. GU34: Four M 5J 97
PO6: Cosh 9H 201
Bernard Ct. GU15: Camb 9K 19
Bernard Powell Ho. PO9: Hav 8G 202
Bernards Cl. BH23: Chri 6H 229
Bernard St. SO14: South 7D 4 (7M 173)
Berne Ct. BH1: Bour 7N 247 (3L 245)
Bernersh Cl. GU47: Sandh 4E 18
Berney Rd. PO4: S'sea 3K 241
Bernie Tunstall Pl. SO50: E'leigh 9F 132
(off Romsey Rd.)
Bernina Av. PO7: W'lle 8K 181
Bernina Cl. PO7: W'lle 8K 181
Bernstein Rd. RG22: B'toke 3L 59
(not continuous)
Bernwood Gro. SO45: Blac 9C 208
Berrans Ct. BH11: Bour 1E 226
Berrington Way RG24: B'toke 3F 42
Berrybank GU47: Coll 7G 18
Berry Cl. SO30: Hed E 4A 176
Berry Ct. BH9: Bour 6K 227
RG26: Lit L 2N 21
RG27: Hoo 3G 45
BERRY DOWN 2G 125
Berrydown La. RG25: Axf, Pres C 3F 78
RG25: Over 3F 56
Berrydown Rd. PO9: Hav 2C 202
Berryfield Ct. SO30: Hed E 5M 175
Berryfield Rd. SO41: Hor 4H 233
Berry Hill SO24: Rop 1B 110
Berrylands GU33: Liss 7F 114
Berry La. PO14: Stub 6K 211
SO21: Twyf 6K 127
Berry Mdw. Cotts. PO17: S'wick 3N 199
Berrysfield Ct. SP11: Ludg 1C 30
Berry Theatre, The 2N 175
Berry Way SP10: A'ver 2J 69
Berrywood Bus. Village SO30: Hed E 8M 161
Berrywood Gdns. SO30: Hed E 3M 175
Berrywood La. SO24: Brad 5H 79
Bert Betts Way SO31: Burs 7L 175
Berthia Gate BH8: Bour 8A 228
(off Holdenhurst Rd.)
Berthon Ho. SO51: Rom 6L 129
Bertie Rd. PO4: S'sea 3J 241
Bertram Rd. BH25: A'ley 2D 232
Bertune Cl. SO21: Bar S 5A 76
Berwick Cl. SO16: South 6F 158
Berwick Rd. BH3: Bour 8J 227
Berwyn Cl. RG22: B'toke 8J 41
Berwyn Wlk. PO14: Fare 9A 198
Beryl Av. PO12: Gos 8H 213
Beryton Cl. PO12: Gos 1J 239
Beryton Rd. PO12: Gos 1J 239
Besom Ct. RG26: Tadl 6H 11
Besomer Drove SP5: Lover 9D 120
Bessborough Rd. BH13: Poole 6C 244
Bessemer Cl. BH31: Ver 5A 184
Bessemer Pk. RG22: B'toke 9A 42
Bessemer Rd. RG21: B'toke 9A 42
Beswick Av. BH10: Bour 4H 227
Beswick Gdns. BH10: Bour 4J 227
Beta Ho. SO16: Chilw 2H 159
Beta Rd. GU14: Cov 7H 29
Bethany Ct. BH12: Poole 7E 226
Bethany Ho. BH1: Bour 9A 228
Bethany Oaks RG26: Tadl 5K 11
Bethel Cl. GU9: Up H 4F 64
Bethel La. GU9: Up H 3E 64
Bethia Cl. BH8: Bour 8A 228
Bethia Rd. BH8: Bour 7A 228
Betjeman Wlk. GU46: Yat 9L 17
Betsy Cl. BH23: Bran 6D 220
Betsy La. BH23: Bran 6D 220
Betteridge Dr. SO16: Rown 5C 158
Bettesworth Rd. PO1: Ports 9F 214
Betula Cl. PO7: W'lle 3A 202
Beulah Rd. SO16: South 1F 172
Bevan Cl. SO19: South 9C 174
Bevan Rd. PO8: Cowp 5N 181
Beveren Cl. GU51: Fleet 8N 27
Beverley Caravan Pk. PO11: H Isl 5L 243
Beverley Cl. RG22: B'toke 1C 60
SO31: P Ga 5F 196
Beverley Cres. GU14: Cov 1H 49
Beverley Gdns. BH10: Bour 3H 227
SO31: Old N 9J 175
SO32: Swanm 6D 164
SO51: Rom 3A 130
Beverley Grange BH4: Bour 2G 244
(off Portarlington Rd.)
Beverley Gro. PO6: Farl 8N 201
Beverley Hall BH1: Bour 2N 245
Beverley Hgts. SO18: South 8D 160
Beverley Hills Pk. SP4: Ames 5A 66
(off Porton Rd.)
Beverley Rd. PO14: Stub 7M 211
SO45: Dib P 9L 193
Beverly Cl. PO13: Gos 6F 212
Beverly Ho. GU14: Farn 1L 49
(off Wallis Sq.)
Beverston Rd. PO6: Cosh 8B 200
Bevis Cl. SO31: Wars 9A 196
SO45: Fawl 6D 208
Bevis Rd. PO2: Ports 7E 214
PO12: Gos 2K 239
Bevis Rd. Nth. PO2: Ports 7E 214
Bevois Gdns. SO14: South 3M 173
Bevois Hill SO14: South 2N 173
Bevois Mans. SO14: South 2N 173
(off Bevios Hill)
Bevois M. SO14: South 3M 173
BEVOIS MOUNT 2M 173
BEVOIS TOWN 3M 173
BEVOIS VALLEY 3N 173
Bevois Valley Rd. SO14: South 3N 173
Bexington Cl. BH11: Bour 3C 226
Bexmoor RG24: Old Bas 5H 43
Bexmoor Way RG24: Old Bas 5H 43
Beyne Rd. SO22: Oli B 2F 126
Bianco BH1: Bour 7N 247 (2K 245)
Bible Flds. RG25: Dumm 1C 78
Bicester Cl. RG28: Whit 5G 54
Bickerley Gdns. BH24: Ring 2J 187
Bickerley Grn. BH24: Ring 2J 187
Bickerley Rd. BH24: Ring 1J 187
Bickerley Ter. BH24: Ring 1J 187
Bickley, The BH24: Ring 1J 187
(off Strides La.)
Bicknell Ct. BH4: Bour 2G 244
(off Westbourne Cl.)
Bicknell Rd. GU16: Frim 2N 29
BICKTON 4J 153
Bickton Wlk. PO9: Hav 3D 202
Bicton Rd. BH11: Bour 3F 226
Bidbury La. PO9: Bed 8C 202
BIDDEN 2B 62
Biddenfield La. PO17: Wick 6N 177
SO32: Shed 7M 177
Bidden Rd. RG25: Up G 3A 62
RG29: N War 2C 62
BIDDESDEN 5N 31
Biddesden La. SP11: Bidd, Ludg 1F 30 (5L 31)
Biddlecombe Cl. PO13: Gos 8E 212
Biddlesgate Ct. SO14: South 7C 4 (7L 173)
Bideford Cl. GU14: Farn 5J 29
SO16: South 1D 172
Bietigheim Way GU15: Camb 7L 19
Biggin Wlk. PO14: Fare 9A 198
BIGHTON 6L 95
Bighton Dean La. GU34: Meds 6B 96
SO24: Bigh 6M 95
Bighton Hill SO24: Rop 8B 96
Bighton La. SO24: Bigh, Bis S, Gund 6L 95
Bighton Rd. GU34: Meds 2C 96
Big Tree Cotts. SO32: Sob 5L 165
Bilbao Ct. SP10: A'ver 9C 52
Bilberry Cl. SO31: Loc H 7C 196
Bilberry Ct. SO23: Winche 7L 237 (6K 105)
Bilberry Dr. SO40: March 8D 172
Bilberry La. SO21: M'dvr 7J 77
Billett Av. PO7: W'lle 9N 181
Billing Cl. PO4: S'sea 4J 241
Billington Ct. PO1: Ports 2F 240
(off Walmer Rd.)
Billington Gdns. SO30: Hed E 9A 162
Billington Pl. SO41: Penn 4D 234
Bill Sargent Cres. PO1: Ports 1F 240
Bill Stillwell Ct. PO2: Ports 6D 214
Billy Lawn Av. PO9: Hav 4F 202
Billys Copse PO9: Hav 4E 202
Bilton Bus. Pk. PO3: Ports 5K 215
Bilton Ind. Est. RG24: B'toke 2F 42
Bilton Rd. RG24: B'toke 2F 42
Bilton Way PO3: Ports 6K 215
Bindon Cl. BH12: Poole 7C 226
SO16: South 9F 158
Bindon Ct. SO18: South 2C 174
Bindon Rd. SO16: South 9F 158
Binfields Cl. RG24: Chin 2G 43
Binfields Farm La. RG24: Old Bas 2H 43
Binfields Rdbt. RG24: Chin 2G 42
Bingham Av. BH14: Poole 6A 244
Bingham Cl. BH23: Chri 7A 230
Bingham Dr. SO41: Lymi 3E 234
Bingham Rd. BH9: Bour 6L 227
BH23: Chri 7A 230
Bingley Cl. GU34: Alt 4E 80
RG21: B'toke 4D 42
BINLEY 4M 35
Binley Bottom SP11: Binl, Stoke 7J 35
Binnacle Caravan Park, The PO11: H Isl 5L 243
Binnacle Way PO6: Cosh 9C 200
Binness Path PO6: Farl 1M 215
Binness Way PO6: Farl 1M 215
Binnie Rd. BH12: Poole 9C 226
Binsey Cl. SO16: South 2D 172
Binstead Cl. SO16: S'ing 6A 160
Binstead Copse GU52: Fleet 4L 47
BINSTED 1D 82
Binsted Dr. GU17: Blackw 8F 18
Binsted Rd. GU34: Bins, Neat 1M 81
GU34: Blackn 1H 83
Binsteed Rd. PO2: Ports 8F 214
Binswood Nature Reserve 9C 82
Binton La. GU10: Seal 8N 65
Birch Av. BH23: Burt 3M 229
BH25: Bash 9N 221
GU51: Fleet 2L 47
Birch Cl. BH14: Poole 2C 244
BH24: St L 5A 186
GU15: Camb 5N 19
GU33: Liss 1F 140
GU35: Bor 5K 101
PO8: Cowp 7M 181
SO16: South 9F 158
SO21: Col C 4K 133
SO51: Rom 6C 130
Birch Ct. SO22: Winche 8G 105
SP9: Tidw 7E 30
Birchdale SO45: Hythe 7N 193
Birchdale Cl. SO31: Wars 9A 196
Birch Dr. BH8: Bour 4D 228
GU17: Haw 1F 28
PO13: Gos 4E 212
Birchen Cl. SO31: P Ga 5F 196
Birchen Coppice SO20: Mid Wa 4B 72
Birchen Rd. SO31: P Ga 5F 196
Birches, The GU14: Cov 8F 28
GU17: Blackw 8D 18
SO18: South 2F 174
SO21: Col C 3K 133
Birches Close, The SO52: N Bad 7E 130
Birches Crest RG22: B'toke 4M 59
Birches Ho. GU51: Fleet 2H 47
Birchett Rd. GU11: Alders 9J 49
GU14: Cov 7G 29
Birchfields GU15: Camb 9L 19
Birchglade SO40: Calm 9J 157
Birch Gro. BH25: New M 5B 232
GU35: W'hil 6J 101
RG27: Hoo 1H 45
SO20: Chil 6G 75
SO50: E'leigh 6D 132
Birchlands SO40: Tott 5K 171
Birchlands Cl. GU47: Owl 3G 18
Birchmore Cl. PO13: Gos 6E 212
Bircholt Rd. GU30: Lip 2N 115
Birch Pde. GU51: Fleet 2L 47
Birch Rd. BH24: St I 4E 186
GU35: Head D 1C 102
RG26: Tadl 3E 10
SO16: Chilw 3L 159
SO16: South 8F 158
SO30: Hed E 3A 176
Birch Tree Cl. PO10: Ems 5M 203
Birch Tree Ct. GU27: Hasl 1L 117
Birch Tree Dr. PO10: Ems 5M 203
Birchview Cl. GU46: Yat 9M 17
Birch Wood SO19: South 5J 175
Birchwood RG24: Chin 9G 22
Birchwood Cl. BH23: Chri 6G 231
Birchwood Dr. SP6: Ald 5D 152
Birchwood Gdns. SO30: Hed E 7N 175
Birchwood Lodge PO16: Fare 7D 198
(off Southampton Rd.)
Birchwood M. BH14: Poole 2B 244
Birchwood Pl. BH24: St L 6A 186
Birchwood Rd. BH14: Poole 2B 244
Birchy Hill SO41: Sway 6K 223
Bird Fld. SO53: Cha F 5K 131
Birdham Rd. PO11: H Isl 5L 243
Birdlip Cl. PO8: Horn 4A 182
Birdlip Rd. PO6: Cosh 8C 200
Birdwood Gro. PO16: Portc 9H 199
Birdwood Rd. GU15: Camb 7G 19
Birdworld & Underwater World 8M 63
Birinus Rd. SO23: Winche 5L 105
Birkbeck Pl. GU47: Owl 4G 19
Birkdale Av. PO6: Dray 8K 201
Birkenholme Cl. GU35: Head D 3E 102
Biscay Cl. PO14: Stub 5L 211
Bishearne Gdns. GU33: Liss 9D 114
Bishop Cl. BH12: Poole 7G 226
Bishop Ct. BH24: Ring 1K 187
Bishop Crispian Way PO1: Ports 3M 5 (2C 240)
Bishop Rd. BH9: Bour 6L 227
Bishops Cl. BH7: Bour 7C 228
GU52: Fleet 5M 47
RG26: Tadl 4G 11
SO40: Tott 2L 171
SP9: Tidw 9D 30 (8G 31)

Bishops Ct.—Botany Bay

Bishops Ct. SO50: B'stke ... 7H 133
Bishops Cres. SO19: South ... 6D 174
Bishopsfield Rd. PO14: Fare ... 1A 212
Bishops Ga. PO14: Titch C ... 6F 196
BISHOP'S GREEN ... 1H 9
Bishops La. SO32: Bis W ... 4M 163
SO32: Shi H ... 1D 178
Bishops Mead GU9: Farnh ... 8D 64
Bishops Reach *SP4: All* ... *7D 66*
(off Wyndham La.)
Bishops Rd. GU9: Up H ... 4D 64
SO19: South ... 7C 174
BISHOP'S SUTTON ... 1K 109
Bishops Sutton Rd. SO24: New A ... 9G 94
BISHOPSTOKE ... 9H 133
Bishopstoke La. SO50: B'dge ... 6J 133
Bishopstoke Mnr. SO50: E'leigh ... 9G 133
Bishopstoke Rd. PO9: Hav ... 4E 202
SO50: E'leigh ... 9F 132
BISHOPSTONE ... 3C 118
Bishopstone Hollow SP5: Bish ... 4B 118
Bishop St. PO1: Ports ... 3K 5 (2B 240)
Bishop Sumner Dr. GU9: Up H ... 4E 64
Bishop's Vw. GU34: Four M ... 5G 96
BISHOP'S WALTHAM ... 4M 163
Bishop's Waltham Palace & Museum ... *4M 163*
(off Brook St.)
Bishop's Way SP10: A'ver ... 1M 69
Bishopswood Ct. RG26: Tadl ... 4F 10
Bishopswood Golf Course ... 6F 10
Bishopswood La. RG26: Bau, Tadl ... 4E 10
Bishop's Wood Rd. PO17: Mis ... 8D 164
SO32: Swanm ... 8D 164
Bishopswood Rd. RG26: Tadl ... 4F 10
Bisley Ct. SO19: South ... 7F 174
Bissingen Way GU15: Camb ... 7M 19
BISTERNE ... 9J 187
BISTERNE CLOSE ... 8F 188
Bisterne Cl. BH24: Bur ... 7F 188
Bitham La. RG17: Hung, Ink ... 1E 6
Bittern Cl. GU11: Alders ... 3J 65
GU47: Coll ... 5F 18
PO12: Gos ... 9K 213
RG22: B'toke ... 2H 59
BITTERNE ... 3E 174
Bitterne Cl. PO9: Hav ... 3F 202
Bitterne Cres. SO19: South ... 4E 174
Bitterne Leisure Cen. ... 3E 174
Bitterne Mnr. Ho. SO18: South ... 3A 174
BITTERNE PARK ... 1C 174
Bitterne Rd. SO18: South ... 4G 174
(Keats Rd.)
SO18: South ... 3D 174
(Maybray King Way, not continuous)
SO18: South ... 4E 174
(Milbury Cres.)
Bitterne Rd. E. SO18: South ... 3E 174
Bitterne Rd. W. SO18: South ... 3A 174
Bitterne Station (Rail) ... 3B 174
Bitterne Village SO18: South ... 3E 174
Bitterne Way SO19: South ... 4C 174
SO41: Lymi ... 4D 234
Blackbarn Rd. SP4: Port ... 1D 86
Blackberry Cl. GU34: Four M ... 4K 97
PO8: Clan ... 7D 168
Blackberry Ct. RG26: Bau ... 3E 10
Blackberry Dr. SO50: Fair O ... 2M 161
Blackberry La. BH23: Chri ... 8B 230
GU34: Four M ... 6J 97
Blackberry Ter. SO14: South ... 1F 4 (3N 173)
Blackberry Wlk. RG24: Lych ... 4F 42
Blackbird Cl. GU47: Coll ... 5F 18
PO8: Cowp ... 6N 181
RG22: B'toke ... 2H 59
Blackbird Ct. SP10: A'ver ... 7A 52
Blackbird Rd. SO50: E'leigh ... 2B 160
Blackbird Way BH23: Bran ... 7E 220
PO13: Lee S ... 9B 212
Blackbrook Bus. Pk. PO15: Fare ... 8A 198
Blackbrook Ho. Dr. PO14: Fare ... 8A 198
Blackbrook Pk. Av. PO15: Fare ... 8A 198
Blackbrook Rd. PO15: Fare ... 7M 197
Blackburn Ct. PO13: Gos ... 2F 238
Blackbushe Bus. Pk. GU46: Yat ... 9M 17
Blackbushe Cl. SO16: South ... 6E 158
Blackbushe Pk. GU46: Yat ... 8M 17
Blackbushes Rd. GU51: Fleet ... 3G 27
RG27: Elve ... 3G 27
Blackbush Rd. SO41: M Sea ... 8J 233 & 7H 235
Blackcap Cl. PO9: R Cas ... 9G 183
Blackcap Pl. GU47: Coll ... 5G 18
Black Cottage La. PO17: Wick ... 8E 178
BLACK DAM ... 8E 42
Black Dam Cen. RG21: B'toke ... 8E 42
Blackdam Nature Reserve ... 7G 42
Black Dam Rdbt. RG21: B'toke ... 7F 42
Black Dam Way RG21: B'toke ... 8E 42
Blackdown Cl. RG22: B'toke ... 8K 41
SO45: Dib P ... 7J 193
Blackdown Cres. PO9: Hav ... 5E 202
Blackdown La. SO32: Uph ... 6E 134
BLACKFIELD ... 7C 208
Blackfield Rd. BH8: Bour ... 3A 228
SO45: Blac, Fawl ... 7C 208
Blackfriars Cl. PO5: S'sea ... 3E 240
Blackfriars Rd. PO5: S'sea ... 2E 240
Blackheath Rd. GU9: Up H ... 3C 64
BLACKHILL ... 2A 156
Blackhill Rd. SO43: B'haw ... 3N 155
SO51: E Wel ... 3N 155
Black Horse La. SP4: Win E ... 4A 86
Blackhorse La. SO32: Shed ... 1A 178
Blackhouse La. PO17: N Boa ... 9J 179
Black La. SP5: Lover ... 8E 120
SP5: P'tn ... 6E 86
Blackman Gdns. GU11: Alders ... 2K 65
Blackmans Way SO32: Bis W ... 3L 163
BLACKMOOR ... 7F 100
Blackmoor Golf Course ... 6G 100
Black Moor Rd. BH31: Ver ... 5A 184
Blackmoor Rd. GU33: Blackm ... 8F 100
Blackmoor Wlk. PO9: Hav ... 4H 203
Blackmore La. GU32: Frox ... 1E 138
SN8: Co Du ... 4K 31
BLACKNEST ... 10L 63
Blacknest Golf Course ... 2J 83
Blacknest Ind. Pk. GU34: Blackn ... 10L 63
Blacknest Rd. GU34: Blackn ... 9K 63
Blacksmiths SP11: S M Bo ... 9L 35
Blacksmiths Rdbt. SP10: A'ver ... 9A 52
Blackstocks La.
RG27: Nat S, Up N ... 6B 44
Blackstone Cl. GU14: Cov ... 6F 28
Black Swan Bldgs. SO23: Winche ... 7L 237
Black Swan Yd. *SP10: A'ver* ... *1A 70*
(off East St.)
Blackthorn Cl. RG26: Bau ... 5E 10
SO19: South ... 5D 174
SO21: Sth W ... 3G 91
SO41: Penn ... 4B 234
SO51: Brai ... 6C 124
Blackthorn Cres. GU14: Cov ... 4H 29
Blackthorn Dr. PO11: H Isl ... 4J 243
PO12: Gos ... 7J 213
Blackthorne Cl. GU35: Bor ... 4K 101
Blackthorn Grn. SO21: Col C ... 4L 133
Blackthorn Rd. PO11: H Isl ... 4J 243
SO19: South ... 5C 174
Blackthorns GU51: Fleet ... 2H 47
Blackthorn Ter. PO1: Ports ... 2K 5 (1C 240)
Blackthorn Wlk. *PO7: W'lle* ... *9B 182*
(off Grassmere Way)
Blackthorn Way BH25: A'ley ... 2E 232
RG23: B'toke ... 5L 41
BLACKWATER
BH23 ... 2F 228
GU17 ... 9G 18
Blackwater SO43: Lyn ... 1A 148 (1N 189)
Blackwater & Hawley Leisure Cen. ... 1F 28
Blackwater Cl. PO6: Cosh ... 9E 200
RG21: B'toke ... 6D 42
RG23: Oak ... 1D 58
SP6: Ald ... 5B 152
Blackwater Dr. SO40: Tott ... 1K 171
Blackwater Gro. SP6: Ald ... 5B 152
Blackwater M. SO40: Tott ... 1K 171
BLACKWATER PARK ... 9H 19
Blackwater Pk. GU12: Alders ... 1N 65
Blackwater Shop. Pk. GU14: Farn ... 5L 29
Blackwater Station (Rail) ... 9G 19
Blackwater Trad. Est. GU12: Alders ... 2M 65
Blackwater Valley Golf Course ... 5M 17
Blackwater Valley Rd. GU15: Camb ... 9H 19
Blackwater Valley Route GU11: Alders ... 4N 49
GU12: Alders ... 4N 65
GU14: Farn ... 5M 29
GU16: Frim ... 5M 29
Blackwater Vw. RG40: F'std ... 3L 17
Blackwater Way GU12: Alders ... 2M 65
Blackwell Rd. SO21: Wor D ... 4G 90
Blackwood Ho. PO1: Ports ... 9E 214
Bladon Cl. PO9: Hav ... 6J 203
Bladon Rd. SO16: South ... 9H 159
Blaegrove La. RG27: Up N ... 7B 44
Blair Atholl Ri. PO15: Fare ... 7B 198
Blair Av. BH14: Poole ... 1A 244
Blair Cl. BH25: New M ... 3N 231
Blaire Pk. GU46: Yat ... 5L 17
Blair Rd. RG21: B'toke ... 8B 42
Blaise Cl. GU14: Farn ... 9M 29
Blake Cl. PO15: White ... 9E 176
RG29: Odi ... *2E 62*
(off Wooldridge Cres.)
RG45: Cr'tne ... 1E 18
SO16: Nur ... 6C 158
Blake Ct. PO12: Gos ... 3N 239
SP10: A'ver ... 9N 51
Blake Dene Rd. BH14: Poole ... 4A 244
Blake Gdns. SO19: South ... 7F 174
Blake Hill Av. BH14: Poole ... 4B 244
Blake Hill Cres. BH14: Poole ... 4A 244
Blake Ho. PO1: Ports ... 5H 5 (3A 240)
Blakemere Cres. PO6: Cosh ... 8D 200
Blakeney Rd. SO16: South ... 9C 158
Blake Rd. PO1: Ports ... 9A 214
PO6: Farl ... 8L 201
PO12: Gos ... 2L 239
Blake's La. RG26: Tadl ... 4H 11
Blakesley La. PO3: Ports ... 4K 215
Blakes Ride GU46: Yat ... 7L 17
Blanchard Rd. SO32: Bis W ... 3L 163
Blandford Ct. SO41: M Sea ... 7K 235
Blandford Ho. SO16: South ... 1E 172
Blandford Rd. SP5: Com B ... 7C 118
SP6: Mart ... 7C 118
Blandford Row SO20: S Bri ... 3F 88
Blanket St. GU34: E Wor ... 8M 81
Blankney Cl. PO14: Stub ... 6L 211
Blann Cl. SO16: Nur ... 6B 158
BLASHFORD ... 7K 185
Blaven Wlk. PO14: Fare ... 9A 198
Bleach's Yd. Ind. Est. GU30: Lip ... 4D 116
BLEAK HILL ... 7F 152
Bleaklow Cl. SO16: South ... 2E 172
BLECHYNDEN ... 4A 4 (5K 173)
Blechynden Ter. SO15: South ... 4A 4 (5K 173)
Blencowe Dr. SO53: Cha F ... 7K 131
Blendon Dr. SP10: A'ver ... 9K 51
BLENDWORTH ... 2E 182
Blendworth Cres. PO9: Hav ... 6E 202
Blendworth Ho. *PO1: Ports* ... *1E 240*
(off Lake Rd.)
Blendworth La. PO8: Blen ... 3D 182
SO18: South ... 3G 174
Blendworth Rd. PO4: S'sea ... 2J 241
Blenheim BH13: Poole ... 2E 244
Blenheim Av. SO17: South ... 1M 173
Blenheim Cl. GU10: Tong ... 3N 65
GU34: Alt ... 5G 80
GU34: Four M ... 4J 97
SO40: Tott ... 4K 171
SO53: Cha F ... 8L 131
Blenheim Ct. *BH4: Bour* ... *2G 244*
(off Marlborough Rd.)
BH23: Chri ... 6J 229
GU14: Farn ... 1M 49
PO4: S'sea ... 4H 241
RG21: B'toke ... 6A 42
SO17: South ... 1M 173
Blenheim Cres. GU9: Up H ... 5C 64
SO41: Hor ... 2F 232
Blenheim Dr. BH23: Mude ... 8D 230
Blenheim Gdns. PO9: Hav ... 7H 203
PO12: Gos ... 8K 213
SO17: South ... 9N 159
SO45: Dib P ... 7J 193
Blenheim Ho. SO50: E'leigh ... 1F 160
SO51: Rom ... *5A 130*
(off Chambers Av.)
Blenheim M. GU9: Farnh ... 8C 64
Blenheim Pk. GU11: Alders ... 4L 49
Blenheim Pl. GU15: Camb ... 1L 29
Blenheim Rd. GU11: Alders ... 4K 49
PO8: Horn ... 5A 182
RG24: Old Bas ... 6K 43
SO50: E'leigh ... 1E 160
Bleriot Cres. PO15: White ... 4H 197
Blighmont Av. SO15: South ... 4G 172
Blighmont Cres. SO15: South ... 4G 172
Blighton La. GU10: Run ... 6M 65
Blind La. PO17: Wick ... 5B 178
SO30: Wes E ... 6N 161
SO32: Curd ... 9H 163
SP6: S Gor ... 9L 153
Blindmans Ga. RG20: Wol H ... 3A 8
Bliss Cl. PO7: W'lle ... 4M 201
RG22: B'toke ... 1N 59
BLISSFORD ... 6A 154
Blissford Cl. PO9: Hav ... 3H 203
Blissford Cross SP6: Blis ... 6A 154
Blissford Hill SP6: Blis, Frog ... 7A 154
Blissford Rd. SP6: Blis ... 1N 153
Blissmore La. SP11: Weyh ... 8D 50
Bloomfield Av. BH9: Bour ... 4K 227
Bloomfield Pl. BH9: Bour ... 4K 227
Bloomsbury Wlk. SO19: South ... 8C 174
Bloomsbury Way GU17: Haw ... 1E 28
Blossom Cl. SO30: Botl ... 4B 176
SP10: A'ver ... 2J 69
Blossom Dr. PO7: Wid ... 6K 201
Blossom Sq. PO1: Ports ... 2K 5 (1B 240)
Bloswood Dr. RG28: Whit ... 5F 54
Bloswood La. RG28: Hur P, Whit ... 2D 54
Blount Rd. PO1: Ports ... 7L 5 (4C 240)
Bloxworth Rd. BH12: Poole ... 6D 226
Blue Anchor La. SO14: South ... 7C 4 (7L 173)
Blue Ball Cnr. SO23: Winche ... 7P 237
Blue Ball Hill SO23: Winche ... 7P 237 (6M 105)
Bluebell Cl. BH23: Chri ... 6D 230
PO7: W'lle ... 3N 201
SP10: A'ver ... 2J 69
Bluebell Copse SO31: Loc H ... 7C 196
Bluebell Ct. PO15: White ... 1G 196
Bluebell Gdns. BH25: New M ... 3C 232
GU34: Meds ... 3K 97
SO45: Hythe ... 7N 193
Bluebell M. GU15: Camb ... 6M 19
Bluebell Rd. GU35: Lind ... 2M 101
SO16: Bass, S'ing ... 7N 159
Bluebell Wlk. GU51: Fleet ... 1L 47
Bluebell Way PO15: White ... 9G 176
Blueberry Gdns. SP10: A'ver ... 2J 69
Blue Bldg. PO1: Ports ... 5K 5
Bluehaven Wlk. RG27: Hoo ... 2F 44
Blue Hayes Cl. SP10: A'ver ... 2N 69
Blue Mdw. RG20: Kings ... 2A 6
Blueprint Portfield Rd. PO3: Ports ... 6H 215
Blue Pryor Ct. GU52: Ch Cr ... 8K 47
Blue Reef Aquarium
Southsea ... 6D 240
Bluestar Gdns. SO30: Hed E ... 9N 161
Bluethroat Cl. GU47: Coll ... 5G 18
Blue Timbers Cl. GU35: Bor ... 5J 101
Blue Valley M. SP6: F'dge ... 1J 153
Bluff, The BH10: Bour ... 2K 227
Bluff Cove GU11: Alders ... 8L 49
Blundell La. SO31: Burs ... 8M 175
Blunden Cl. RG21: B'toke ... 1B 60
Blunden Rd. GU14: Cov ... 8H 29
Blunt Rd. RG22: B'toke ... 6H 59
Blyth Cl. BH23: Chri ... 2G 229
SO16: South ... 9C 158
Blythe Cl. SP11: Enh A ... 4A 52
Blythswood Ct. BH25: B Sea ... 7A 232
Blythwood Dr. GU16: Frim ... 2M 29
Boakes Pl. SO40: Ashu ... 8J 171
Boames La. RG20: Enbo ... 1A 8
Boardwalk, The PO6: P Sol ... 1C 214
Boardwalk Shop. Centre, The PO6: P Sol ... 2B 214
Boardwalk Way SO40: March ... 7F 172
BOARHUNT ... 4K 199
Boarhunt Cl. PO1: Ports ... 2E 240
Boarhunt Rd. PO17: Boar, Fare ... 6G 198
Boatyard Ind. Estate, The PO16: Fare ... 9D 198
Bob Hann Cl. BH12: Poole ... 9B 226
Bockhampton Rd. BH23: Bock, Wink ... 1N 229
Bodley Rd. BH13: Poole ... 6D 244
Bodmin Cl. RG22: B'toke ... 8K 41
Bodmin Rd. PO6: Cosh ... 9B 200
SO50: B'stke ... 9J 133
Bodorgan Rd. BH2: Bour ... 5L 247 (1K 245)
Bodowen Cl. BH23: Burt ... 4N 229
Bodowen Rd. BH23: Burt ... 4N 229
Bodycoats Rd. SO53: Cha F ... 6B 132
Bodysound Fitness Club ... 7N 131
Bogmoor Cl. GU34: Four M ... 5J 97
Bogs, The RG27: Winchf ... 1H 47
BOHEMIA ... 9D 120
Bohemia La. SP5: Redl ... 9D 120
SP6: Hale ... 9D 120
Bohunt Cen. ... 3D 116
Boiler Rd. PO1: Ports ... 1H 5 (9A 214)
SO45: Fawl ... 7J 209
Bolde Cl. PO3: Ports ... 5J 215
Boldens Rd. PO12: Gos ... 6K 239
Bolderwood Arboretum ... 3H 189
Bolderwood Cl. SO50: B'stke ... 1K 161
BOLDRE ... 6D 224
Boldre Cl. BH12: Poole ... 7B 226
BH25: New M ... 6M 231
PO9: Hav ... 5C 202
Boldre Foreshore Local Nature Reserve
... 3M 235
Boldre La. SO41: Bold ... 8D 224
Boldrewood Rd. SO16: Bass ... 7K 159
Boleyn Cres. BH9: Bour ... 2N 227
Bolhinton Av. SO40: March ... 9C 172
Bolinge Hill GU31: Buri ... 5K 145
Bolle Rd. GU34: Alt ... 6D 80
Bolley Av. GU35: Bor ... 1G 100
Bolton Cl. BH6: Bour ... 2H 247
Bolton Cres. RG22: B'toke ... 8N 41
Bolton Dr. PO12: Gos ... 9L 213
Bolton Rd. BH6: Bour ... 2H 247
Boltons, The PO7: Purb ... 6M 201
SO41: M Sea ... 8K 235
Bolton's Bench ... 2C 148
Bonchurch Cl. SO16: S'ing ... 6A 160
Bonchurch Rd. PO4: S'sea ... 2H 241
Bond Cl. RG24: B'toke ... 3F 42
RG26: Tadl ... 4G 10
SO41: Sway ... 4J 223
Bondfields Cres. PO9: Hav ... 3E 202
Bond Rd. SO18: South ... 1C 174
Bond St. SO14: South ... 4A 174
SP4: Bul C ... 3B 66
Bones La. GU31: Buri ... 7K 145
Bonfire Cnr. PO1: Ports ... 2J 5 (1B 240)
Bonham Rd. BH9: Bour ... 7K 227
Bonhams Cl. GU34: Holy ... 1L 81
Boniface Cl. SO40: Tott ... 2K 171
Boniface Cres. SO16: South ... 8C 158
Bonington Cl. BH23: Chri ... 6A 230
Bonita Ct. BH1: Bour ... 9B 228
Bonners Fld. GU10: Ben'ly ... 7K 63
Boon Way RG23: Oak ... 9C 40
BOORLEY GREEN ... 1C 176
Boothby Cl. SO40: Elin ... 4N 171
Bordean La. GU32: Frox ... 8C 138
Borden Gates SP10: A'ver ... 2N 69
Borden Trad. Est. GU35: Bor ... 2F 100
Borden Way SO52: N Bad ... 8F 130
Border Cl. GU33: Hi Br ... 4G 141
Border End GU27: Hasl ... 9M 103
Border Rd. GU27: Hasl ... 9M 103
Borderside GU46: Yat ... 7K 17
BORDON ... 4J 101
Bordon & Oakhanger Sports Club ... 1G 101
BORDON CAMP ... 2J 101
Bordon Cl. RG26: Tadl ... 5G 11
Bordon Rd. PO9: Hav ... 4F 202
Boreen, The GU35: Head D ... 2D 102
Boreham Rd. BH6: Bour ... 9G 228
Borelli M. GU9: Farnh ... 8E 64
Borelli Yd. GU9: Farnh ... 8E 64
Boreway Cl. SP11: E Ant ... 6C 52
Borkum Cl. SP10: A'ver ... 7M 51
Borman Way SO21: Sth W ... 3J 91
Borodin Cl. RG22: B'toke ... 2A 60
Borough, The GU9: Farnh ... 8D 64
GU10: Cron ... 3L 63
GU32: Pet ... *1L 145*
(off Borough Hill)
SP5: Down ... 2J 119 (7A 120)
Borough Ct. Rd. RG27: H Win ... 9L 25
Borough Gro. GU32: Pet ... 2L 145
Borough Hill GU32: Pet ... 1L 145
Borough Rd. GU32: Pet ... 2K 145
Borovere Cl. GU34: Alt ... 6E 80
Borovere Gdns. GU34: Alt ... 6E 80
Borovere La. GU34: Alt ... 6E 80
Borrowdale Rd. SO16: South ... 1D 172
Borsberry Cl. SP10: A'ver ... 1A 70
Borthwick La. BH1: Bour ... 9A 228
Borthwick Rd. BH1: Bour ... 9B 228
Boscobel Rd. SO22: Winche ... 5K 105
BOSCOMBE
BH5 ... 1B 246
SP4 ... 8D 66
Boscombe Beach BH5: Bour ... 2B 246
Boscombe Centre, The *SP4: Ames* ... *5A 66*
(off Porton Rd.)
Boscombe Cliff Rd. BH5: Bour ... 2B 246
Boscombe Gro. Rd. BH1: Bour ... 9A 228
(not continuous)
Boscombe Overcliff Dr. BH5: Bour ... 2C 246
Boscombe Prom. BH5: Bour ... 2B 246
Boscombe Rd. SP4: Ames ... 6A 66
Boscombe Spa Grange BH5: Bour ... 1B 246
Boscombe Spa Rd. BH5: Bour ... 1A 246
Boscombe Surf Reef ... 2B 246
Boscowen Cl. *SP10: A'ver* ... *1C 70*
(off Admirals Way)
Bosenhill La. SO32: Warn ... 3N 135
Bosham Rd. PO2: Ports ... 8G 215
Bosham Wlk. PO13: Gos ... 6D 212
Bosley Cl. BH23: Chri ... 4H 229
Bosley Way BH23: Chri ... 4H 229
Bosmere Gdns. PO10: Ems ... 8L 203
Bosmere Rd. PO11: H Isl ... 5L 243
BOSSINGTON ... 6D 88
Bossington Cl. SO16: Rown ... 6D 158
Bostock Cl. SO21: Spar ... 3B 104
Boston Rd. BH14: Poole ... 1A 244
Boston Ct. SO53: Cha F ... 5B 132
Boston Lodge *BH4: Bour* ... *2G 245*
(off Marlborough Rd.)
Boston Rd. PO6: Cosh ... 8F 200
Bosuns Cl. PO16: Fare ... 2D 212
Bosville SO50: E'leigh ... 6D 132
Boswell Cl. SO19: South ... 4G 175
SO30: Botl ... 3D 176
Bosworth M. BH9: Bour ... 2M 227
BOTANY BAY ... 8E 174

Botany Bay Rd.—Braxton Ho.

Botany Bay Rd. SO19: South 7F 174
Botany Hill GU10: Seal 9M 65
Botisdone Cl. SP11: Ver D 8E 6
BOTLEY 3D 176
Botley Dr. PO9: Hav 3D 202
Botley Gdns. SO19: South 7J 175
Botley Hill SO30: Botl 4E 176
Botley Mills Craft & Business Cen.
SO30: Botl 3D 176
Botley Park Hotel & Country Club Golf Course
9C 162
Botley Rd. SO16: Chilw 6D 130
SO19: South 8G 174
SO30: Hed E, Wes E 1J 175
SO31: Burr, Swanw 1D 196
SO32: Bis W, Curd 3F 176
SO32: Durl 2A 162
SO32: Shed 3K 177
SO50: Fair O, Hor H 2A 162
SO51: Rom 5N 129
SO52: N Bad 6D 130
Botley Station (Rail) 3F 176
Bottings Ind. Est. SO30: Curd 3F 176
Bottlebrush La. BH21: Cran, Wim G 7F 148
Bottle La. RG27: Matt 3G 24
Bottom La. SO51: W Wel 1A 120 (9M 121)
(not continuous)
Bottom Rd. SO20: N Wal 1M 87
Boughton Ct. PO3: Ports 4K 215
Boulnois Av. BH14: Poole 2C 244
Boulter Cres. SP11: A'ver 2E 70
Boulter La. PO17: S'wick 2B 200
Boulter Rd. SP11: A'ver 2E 70
Boulter's Rd. GU11: Alders 9K 49
Boulton Rd. PO5: S'sea 4F 240
Boundary Acre SO31: Burs 6M 175
Boundary Cl. SO15: South 3E 172
Boundary La. BH24: Match, St L 7A 186
Boundary Rd. BH9: Bour 6H 227
BH10: Bour 6H 227
GU10: Dock, Rowl 2N 83 (9N 63)
GU14: Farn 1L 49
GU26: Gray 4M 103
SO31: Burs 1K 195
(not continuous)
Boundary Rdbt. BH12: Poole 6H 227
Boundary Wlk. PO17: K Vil 2A 198
Boundary Way PO6: Cosh 7J 201
PO9: Hav 8E 202
Bound La. PO11: H Isl 5G 243
Boundstone SO45: Hythe 6L 193
Boundway SO41: Sway 6F 222
Bounty Ri. RG21: B'toke 7B 42
Bounty Rd. RG21: B'toke 7B 42
Bounty's La. BH12: Poole 9C 226
Bourdillon Gdns. RG24: B'toke 2D 42
Bourley La. GU10: Ews 9B 48
Bourley Rd. GU11: Alders 9D 48
GU52: Ch Cr 7A 48
Bourne, The BH4: Bour 5G 247
GU52: Fleet 5M 47
Bourne Av. BH2: Bour 5J 247 (2J 245)
SO15: South 1H 173
Bourne Cl. BH2: Bour 6G 247 (2H 245)
PO8: Horn 4B 182
SO21: Ott 9G 126
SO51: W Wel 1A 120 (9M 121)
SP4: Port 9B 66
Bourne Cotts. RG20: E Woo 1A 8
Bourne Ct. BH2: Bour 6L 247 (2K 245)
GU11: Alders 2J 65
RG21: B'toke 6E 42
SP10: A'ver 8B 52
(off River Way)
Bourne Fld. RG24: Sher J 8N 21
Bournefields SO21: Twyf 6M 127
Bourne Gdns. SP4: Port 9B 66
Bourne La. SO21: Twyf 6L 127
SO40: Woodl 4D 170
SP9: Shi B 2C 66 (1G 67)
Bourne Mead BH2: Bour 6J 247
Bourne Mdw. SP11: S M Bo 1M 53
Bourne Mill Bus. Pk. GU9: Farnh 7G 64
BOURNEMOUTH 6L 247 (2K 245)
BOURNEMOUTH AIRPORT 7C 218
Bournemouth Av. PO12: Gos 9J 213
Bournemouth Aviation Mus. 8B 218
Bournemouth Balloon 7L 247 (2K 245)
Bournemouth BMX Track 8J 229
Bournemouth Central Bus. Pk.
BH1: Bour 1N 245
Bournemouth Crematorium BH8: Bour 5N 227
Bournemouth Ho. PO9: Hav 4G 202
Bournemouth Indoor Bowls Cen. 8C 228
Bournemouth International Cen.
8L 247 (3K 245)
Bournemouth Intl. Cen. Rdbt. BH2: Bour 8L 247
Bournemouth Memorial Homes
BH8: Bour 5C 228
Bournemouth Pier 9M 247 (4K 245)
Bournemouth Rd. BH14: Poole 1A 244
SO43: Lyn 2A 148 (2N 189)
SO53: Cha F 1N 159
SP11: Pale 6K 67
Bournemouth Station (Rail) 1M 245
Bournemouth Sta. Rdbt. BH8: Bour 1M 245
Bournemouth University
Talbot Campus 6G 227
Bournemouth W. Rdbt.
BH2: Bour 6H 247 (1H 245)
Bourne Pines *BH1: Bour 1K 245*
(off Dean Pk. Rd.)
BH1: Bour 1N 245
(Christchurch Rd.)
Bourne Ri. SN8: Co Du 1H 31
Bourne River Ct. BH4: Bour 5G 247 (1H 245)
Bourne Rd. PO6: Cosh 9C 200
SO15: South 5J 173
SO40: Woodl 5C 170
SP9: Tidw 8D 30 (7G 31)
Bourneside Mnr. BH2: Bour 6H 247
BOURNE VALLEY 9E 226
Bourne Valley Bus. Pk. BH12: Poole 9E 226
Bourne Valley Nature Reserve
Bourne Valley 8E 226
Poole 5C 226
Bourne Valley Rd. BH12: Poole 1E 244
Bourne Vw. SP4: All 8D 66
Bournewood Dr. BH4: Bour 1G 244
Bourton Gdns. BH7: Bour 6E 228
Bouverie Cl. BH25: B Sea 5A 232
BOVERIDGE 5K 149
Boveridge Gdns. BH9: Bour 2M 227
Bowater Cl. SO40: Calm 1J 171
Bowater Way SO40: Calm 1J 171
Bowcombe SO31: Net A 2G 194
Bowcott Hill GU35: Head 2B 102
Bowden Ho. SO17: South 9A 160
Bowden La. SO17: South 9A 160
Bowden Rd. BH12: Poole 4A 226
Bow Dr. RG27: Sher L 4L 23
Bowenhurst Gdns. GU52: Ch Cr 7M 47
Bowenhurst Golf Course 9H 47
Bowenhurst La. GU10: Cron 1K 63
GU51: Cr V 8H 47
Bowenhurst Rd. GU52: Ch Cr 6M 47
Bowen La. GU31: Pet 1M 145
Bower Cl. SO19: South 9D 174
SO45: Holb 5A 208
Bower Rd. BH8: Bour 6A 228
Bowers Cl. PO8: Cowp 6A 182
Bowers Gro. La. SO24: Rop 8B 96
Bowers Hill SP5: Redl 1N 119 (7C 120)
Bowers La. SP11: Ver D 7D 6
Bowerwood Cotts. SP6: F'dge 2F 152
Bowerwood Rd. SP6: F'dge 2F 152
Bowes Hill PO9: R Cas 7J 183
Bowes-Lyon Ct. PO8: Horn 3B 182
Bow Fld. RG27: Hoo 2J 45
Bow Gdns. RG27: Sher L 4L 23
Bow Gro. RG27: Sher L 3L 23
Bowland Ri. BH25: New M 4D 232
SO53: Cha F 5M 131
Bowland Way SO45: Blac 9C 208
Bowler Av. PO3: Ports 1G 241
Bowler Ct. PO3: Ports 1G 241
BOWLING ALLEY 2L 63
Bowling All. GU10: Cron 1L 63
BOWLING GREEN 9N 223
Bowling Grn. Ct. GU16: Frim G 5N 29
Bowling Grn. Dr. RG27: Hoo 2F 44
Bowling Grn. La. SP5: Pent 1F 148
Bowlings, The GU15: Camb 7L 19
Bowlplex
Basingstoke 6L 41
Branksome 1D 244
Camberley 7L 19
Portsmouth 5J 5
Bowman Ct. RG45: Cr'tne 1B 18
SO19: South 7B 174
(Florence Rd.)
SO19: South 7F 174
(Range Gdns.)
Bowman Rd. RG24: Chin 8G 23
Bowmonts Rd. RG26: Tadl 5J 11
Bow St. GU34: Alt 6E 80
Bowyer Cl. RG21: B'toke 7B 42
BOWYER'S COMMON 4B 140
Boxall's Gro. GU11: Alders 3J 65
Boxall's La. GU11: Alders 3J 65
Boxgrove Ho. PO1: Ports 1E 240
Boxwood Cl. PO7: W'lle 3M 201
PO16: Portc 8K 199
Boyatt Cres. SO50: E'leigh 4E 132
Boyatt La. SO21: Ott 3E 132
SO50: E'leigh 4E 132
BOYATT WOOD 7E 132
Boyatt Wood Shop. Cen. SO50: E'leigh 7E 132
Boyce Cl. RG22: B'toke 2L 59
Boyd Cl. PO14: Stub 7L 211
Boyd Rd. BH12: Poole 8D 226
PO13: Gos 5D 212
Boyes La. PO8: Blen, Ids 2F 182
SO21: Col C 3L 133
Boyle Cres. PO7: W'lle 4L 201
Boyne Mead Rd. SO23: Kin W 8M 91
Boyne Ri. SO23: Kin W 7M 91
Boyneswood Cl. GU34: Meds 3K 97
Boyneswood La. GU34: Meds 3J 97
Boyneswood Rd. GU34: Meds 3K 97
Boynton Cl. SO53: Cha F 4N 131
Brabant Cl. PO15: White 2E 196
Brabazon Dr. BH23: Chri 7D 230
Brabazon Rd. PO15: Seg 4G 196
Brabon Rd. GU14: Cov 7H 29
Bracebridge GU15: Camb 8J 19
Bracenbury Gdns. GU34: Meds 3K 97
Bracher Cl. SP10: A'ver 1A 70
Bracken Bank RG24: Lych 3G 43
Brackenbury SP10: A'ver 9K 51
Bracken Cl. BH24: Ashl H 4A 186
PO13: Lee S 1B 238
SO52: N Bad 9F 130
Bracken Cres. SO50: B'stke 1K 161
Brackendale Cl. GU15: Camb 1N 29
Brackendale Rd. BH8: Bour 6N 227
GU15: Camb 8M 19
Bracken Hall SO16: Chilw 3N 159
Bracken Heath PO7: W'lle 9B 182
Brackenhill BH13: Poole 4E 244
Bracken La. GU35: W'hil 7F 100
GU46: Yat 7K 17
SO16: South 1F 172
Bracken Pl. SO16: Chilw 4M 159
Bracken Rd. BH6: Bour 1F 246
GU31: Pet 2B 146
SO52: N Bad 9F 130
Brackens, The RG22: B'toke 4L 59
SO31: Loc H 7E 196
SO45: Dib P 6J 193
Brackens Way BH13: Poole 5D 244
SO41: Lymi 4F 234
Bracken Way BH23: Walk 5K 231
Brackenway Rd. SO53: Cha F 4A 132
Brackenwood Dr. RG26: Tadl 4G 11
Bracklesham Cl. GU14: Farn 5J 29
SO19: South 7D 174
Bracklesham Pl. BH25: B Sea 7A 232
Bracklesham Rd. PO11: H Isl 6M 243
PO13: Gos 8F 212
Brackley Av. RG27: H Win 6A 26
SO50: Fair O 9M 133
Brackley Cl. BH23: Bour A 7D 218
Brackley Way RG22: B'toke 1L 59
SO40: Tott 2K 171
Bracknell La. RG27: H Win, Haze 4A 26
Bradburne Rd. BH2: Bour 6J 247 (2J 245)
Bradbury Cl. RG28: Whit 5F 54
Bradford Ct. PO13: Gos 1E 238
Bradford Junc. PO5: S'sea 3F 240
Bradford Rd. BH9: Bour 2N 227
PO5: S'sea 3E 240
Brading Av. PO4: S'sea 5H 241
PO13: Gos 6E 212
Brading Cl. SO16: S'ing 6A 160
BRADLEY 5H 79
Bradley Ct. PO9: Hav 3H 203
Bradley Grn. SO16: South 7G 159
Bradley Peak SO22: Winche 5G 104
Bradley Rd. SO22: Winche 3G 105
Bradly Rd. PO15: Fare 7M 197
Bradman Sq. *SP10: A'ver 7B 52*
(off Cricketers Way)
Bradpole Rd. BH8: Bour 4B 228
Bradshaw Cl. SO50: Fair O 1B 162
Bradstock Cl. BH12: Poole 6D 226
Bradwell Cl. SP10: Charl 7K 51
Braehead SO45: Hythe 7L 193
Braemar Av. BH6: Bour 1K 247
PO6: Cosh 1J 215
Braemar Cl. BH6: Bour 1K 247
PO13: Gos 6F 212
PO15: Fare 6A 198
Braemar Dr. BH23: Highc 5H 231
RG23: Oak 9C 40
Braemar Rd. PO13: Gos 5F 212
Braeside Cl. SO19: South 5C 174
SO22: Oli B 1F 126
Braeside Cres. SO19: South 5C 174
Braeside Rd. BH24: St L 4B 186
SO19: South 5C 174
Braganza Ho. PO1: Ports 6K 5
Braggers La. BH23: Bran, Shir 4C 220
Brahms Rd. RG22: B'toke 2N 59
Braidley Rd. BH2: Bour 6K 247 (2J 245)
Braine L'Alleud Rd. RG21: B'toke 5C 42
Braintree Rd. PO6: Cosh 8E 200
BRAISHFIELD 6C 124
Braishfield Cl. SO16: South 1E 172
Braishfield Gdns. BH8: Bour 4A 228
Braishfield Rd. PO9: Hav 5G 202
SO51: Brai, Rom 6B 124
Brakes Ri. GU47: Coll 5G 19
Bramber Rd. PO12: Gos 9J 213
Bramble Cl. PO9: Hav 6J 203
PO14: Stub 7K 211
SO45: Holb 5A 208
SO50: E'leigh 7F 132
SP6: Ald 5D 152
Bramble Ct. *GU31: Pet 1B 146*
(off Rival Moor Rd.)
Bramble Dr. SO51: Rom 3B 130
Bramblegate SO50: Fair O 2A 162
Bramble Hill SO24: New A 1F 108
SO53: Cha F 6N 131
Bramble La. BH23: Highc 5K 231
PO8: Clan 4B 168
SO31: Sar G 4B 196
Bramble M. SO18: South 2E 174
Bramble Rd. GU31: Pet 1B 146
PO4: S'sea 3F 240
Brambles, The SO40: Tott 9L 157
Brambles Bus. Centre, The PO7: W'lle 9K 181
Brambles Cl. GU34: Four M 5J 97
SO21: Col C 4L 133
Brambles Ent. Centre PO7: W'lle 9K 181
Brambles Farm Ind. Est. PO7: W'lle 1L 201
Brambles La. PO31: Cowes 5N 237
Brambles Rd. PO13: Lee S 9N 211
Bramble Wlk. SO41: Lymi 1C 234
SP11: E Ant 6B 52
Bramble Way BH23: Bran 6D 220
PO13: Gos 6C 212
RG24: Old Bas 5K 43
Bramblewood Pl. GU51: Fleet 2K 47
Brambling Cl. RG22: B'toke 3H 59
SO16: South 5G 158
Brambling Rd. PO9: R Cas 9H 183
Bramblings, The SO40: Tott 3J 171
Bramblings Cl. GU9: Farnh 8G 65
Bramblys Cl. RG21: B'toke 7B 42
Bramblys Dr. RG21: B'toke 7B 42
BRAMBRIDGE 4K 133
Brambridge SO50: B'dge 4J 133
Brambridge Pk. 3J 133
BRAMDEAN 9L 109 (1N 135)
Bramdean Cl. RG26: Tadl 6H 11
Bramdean Dr. PO9: Hav 4D 202
Bramdean La. SO24: Cher 6H 109
Bramdean M. SO19: South 5C 174
Bramdean Rd. SO18: South 2H 175
Bramdown Hgts. RG22: B'toke 4K 59
Bramham Moor PO14: Stub 6L 211
BRAMLEY 1G 22
Bramley Cl. GU34: Alt 5G 80
PO7: W'lle 1N 201
SO41: Lymi 4E 234
BRAMLEY CORNER 1C 22
Bramley Ct. BH12: Poole 9F 226
Bramley Cres. SO19: South 8F 174
Bramley Gdns. PO12: Gos 6J 239
SO50: Hor H 4N 161
BRAMLEY GREEN 2H 23
Bramley Grn. Rd. RG26: B'ley 2H 23
Bramley Ho. PO5: S'sea 3D 240
SO30: Hed E 4M 175
Bramley La. GU17: Blackw 8D 18
RG26: B'ley 1G 22
Bramley Rd. BH10: Bour 1G 226
GU15: Camb 2K 29
RG7: Sil 4A 12
RG26: B'ley 4D 22
RG26: Lit L, Pam E 3L 21
RG27: Sher L 3L 23
Bramleys, The SP5: W'psh 5H 121
Bramley Station (Rail) 1G 22
Bramley Wlk. GU35: W'hil 5G 100
Bramling Av. GU46: Yat 7L 17
Brampton Ct. BH2: Bour 6K 247 (2J 245)
Brampton Gdns. RG22: B'toke 5K 59
Brampton La. PO3: Ports 4K 215
Brampton Mnr. SO16: Bass 6L 159
Brampton Twr. SO16: Bass 6L 159
BRAMSHAW 4L 155
Bramshaw Cl. SO22: Winche 3G 105
Bramshaw Ct. PO9: Hav 4H 203
Bramshaw Forest Golf Course 5L 155
Bramshaw Gdns. BH8: Bour 3A 228
Bramshaw Golf Course 5L 155
Bramshaw Way BH25: New M 6M 231
BRAMSHILL 6M 15
Bramshill Council Ho's. RG27: Brams 6L 15
BRAMSHILL PARK 9A 16
Bramshill Rd. RG27: Brams, Eve, Heck 7J 15
Bramshot Dr. GU51: Fleet 1M 47
Bramshot La. GU14: Cov 6E 28
GU51: Fleet 8C 28
Bramshot Rd. GU14: Farn 1C 48
BRAMSHOTT 8E 102
BRAMSHOTT CHASE 7K 103
Bramshott Chase GU26: B'sht 6K 103
Bramshott Ct. GU30: B'sht 7C 102
Bramshott Dr. RG27: Hoo 2H 45
Bramshott Pl. GU51: Fleet 9M 27
Bramshott Rd. GU30: Pass 6B 102
PO4: S'sea 3G 241
SO19: South 1D 194
BRAMSHOTT VALE 9D 102
Bramston Rd. SO15: South 2H 173
Bramtoco Way SO40: Tott 3L 171
Bramwell Ct. SO19: South 4F 174
Brancaster Av. SP10: Charl 7K 51
Branches La. SO51: Sher E 6N 121
Branders Cl. BH6: Bour 1K 247
Branders La. BH6: Bour 9K 229
Brand Ho. GU14: Farn 8L 29
Brandon Cl. GU34: Alt 4E 80
Brandon Ct. *BH12: Poole 1F 244*
(off Poole Rd.)
PO5: S'sea 4F 240
Brandon Ho. PO5: S'sea 5F 240
Brandon Rd. GU52: Ch Cr 6K 47
PO5: S'sea 5E 240
Brandy Bottom GU46: Yat 9A 18
Brandy Mt. SO24: New A 9F 94
Branewick Cl. PO15: Seg 6G 197
Branksea Grange BH13: Poole 4F 244
BRANKSOME 8C 226
Branksome Av. SO15: South 1H 173
SO20: Chil 5F 74
Branksome Bldgs. BH2: Bour 7J 247
Branksome Bus. Pk. BH12: Poole 9E 226
(Bourne Valley Bus. Pk.)
BH12: Poole 7E 226
(Cortry Cl.)
Branksome Chine Pleasure Gdns. 5E 244
Branksome Cl. BH25: New M 4C 232
GU15: Camb 7N 19
SO20: Chil 5F 74
SO22: Winche 8F 104
Branksome Ct. BH13: Poole 5E 244
Branksome Dene Chine 4F 244
Branksome Dene Rd. BH4: Bour 3F 244
Branksome Dorset Provincial Masonic Mus.
9B 228
Branksome Ga. BH13: Poole 2F 244
Branksome Hill Rd. BH4: Bour 8F 226
GU47: Coll, Owl 6G 18
BRANKSOME PARK 3E 244
Branksome Pk. Rd. GU15: Camb 7N 19
Branksome Station (Rail) 1D 244
Branksome Towers BH13: Poole 5F 244
Branksome Wlk. *GU51: Fleet 2L 47*
(off Branksomewood Rd.)
Branksome Wood Gdns. BH2: Bour 1H 245
Branksome Wood Rd.
BH2: Bour 5H 247 (1J 245)
BH4: Bour 9F 226
BH12: Poole 9F 226
Branksomewood Rd. GU51: Fleet 1K 47
BRANSBURY 8M 71
Bransbury Cl. SO16: South 7H 159
Bransbury Gro. RG27: Sher L 7H 23
Bransbury Rd. PO4: S'sea 4J 241
BRANSGORE 7C 220
Bransgore Av. PO9: Hav 5C 202
Bransgore Gdns. BH23: Bran 6D 220
Bransley Cl. SO51: Rom 3A 130
Branson Rd. GU35: Bor 4K 101
Branton Cl. RG22: B'toke 8L 41
Branwell Cl. BH23: Chri 5K 229
Branwood Cl. SO41: Ever 5M 233
Brasenose Cl. PO14: Titch C 8F 196
Brasher Cl. SO50: B'stke 1L 161
Brassey Cl. BH9: Bour 5L 227
Brassey Rd. BH9: Bour 5K 227
SO22: Winche 5K 105
Brassey Ter. BH9: Bour 5K 227
Brasted Ct. PO4: S'sea 2K 241
Braunston Cl. PO6: Cosh 8B 200
Braxell Lawn PO9: Hav 3D 202
Braxton Courtyard SO41: Lymo 7M 233
Braxton Gdns. 6M 233
Braxton Ho. SO23: Winche 5N 105

Braye Cl.—Brookmead Way

Braye Cl. GU47: Sandh 4E 18
Brazenhead La. RG26: Wolve 7N 9
Breachfield RG20: Burgh 3D 8
Breach Gdns. RG27: Sher L 4M 23
Breach La. BH24: Hight, Poul 5A 188
RG27: Sher L 4M 23
SO50: B'stke 7H 133
SP11: Chu S 3B 32
Breadels Ct. RG22: B'toke 6K 59
Breadels Fld. RG22: B'toke 6J 59
BREAMORE 3L 151
Breamore Cl. BH25: New M 3N 231
SO50: E'leigh 6E 132
Breamore House 9M 119
Breamore House Countryside Mus. 1K 151
Breamore Rd. SO18: South 3H 175
SP5: Down 3H 119 (8N 119)
Brean Cl. SO16: South 9D 158
Brecon Av. PO6: Dray 8J 201
Brecon Cl. BH25: New M 4D 232
GU14: Cov 5F 28
PO14: Fare 9A 198
SO45: Dib P 6K 193
SO53: Cha F 9N 131
Brecon Ho. PO1: Ports 5J 5 (3B 240)
Brecon Rd. SO19: South 5G 174
Bredenbury Cres. PO6: Cosh 8D 200
Bredon Wlk. PO14: Fare 9A 198
Breech, The GU47: Coll 6G 19
Breech Cl. PO3: Ports 4G 215
Breeze BH5: Bour 1B 246
Bremble Cl. BH12: Poole 4A 226
Bremen Gdns. SP10: A'ver 8M 51
Brenchley Cl. PO16: Portc 1K 213
Brendon Cl. SO45: Dib P 7J 193
Brendon Grn. SO16: South 2E 172
Brendon Rd. GU14: Cov 5F 28
PO14: Fare 9N 197
Brent Ct. PO4: S'sea 2J 241
PO10: Ems 9L 203
Brent Ho. PO9: Hav 5D 202
Brentwood Cres. SO18: South 1E 174
Bresler Ho. PO6: Cosh 8C 200
Bret Harte Rd. GU16: Frim 3N 29
Breton Cl. PO15: White 2E 196
Brewells La. GU33: Liss, Rake 8K 115
Brewer Cl. RG22: B'toke 8L 41
SO31: Loc H 5E 196
Brewers Cl. GU14: Cov 7J 29
Brewers La. PO13: Gos 6E 212
SO21: Twyf 8K 127
SO24: W Tis 8J 111
Brewer St. PO1: Ports 2N 5 (1D 240)
Brewery Gdns. GU34: Alt 5F 80
Brewery La. SO51: Rom 4L 129
Brew Ho. La. RG27: H Win 6C 26
Brewhouse Yd. *SO24: New A 9F 94*
(off West St.)
Brewster Cl. PO8: Cowp 7A 182
Briar Cl. BH23: Chri 8B 230
PO8: Horn 5B 182
PO12: Gos 4G 239
Briardene Ct. SO40: Tott 3L 171
Briarfield *BH4: Bour 2G 244*
(off Portarlington Rd.)
Briarfield Gdns. PO8: Horn 4B 182
Briar Gdns. PO7: Purb 5M 201
Briar La. GU34: Four M 4K 97
Briarleas Ct. GU14: Farn 3M 49
Briars, The GU52: Ch Cr 5M 47
PO7: W'lle 1K 201
Briars Cl. GU14: Cov 9F 28
Briars Cft. SP10: A'ver 2N 69
Briarswood SO16: South 1G 173
Briarswood Ri. SO45: Dib P 7J 193
Briar Way RG26: Tadl 5J 11
SO51: Rom 3B 130
Briar Wood GU33: Liss 7F 114
Briarwood Cl. PO16: Fare 9D 198
Briarwood Gdns. PO11: H Isl 4F 242
Briarwood Rd. SO40: Tott 4J 171
Briary Ct. PO31: Cowes 5N 237
Brickfield Cotts. GU11: Alders 2F 64
RG45: Cr'tne 2B 18
Brickfield La. SO41: Wal 1F 234
SO53: Cha F 7N 131
Brickfield Rd. SO17: South 9A 160
Brickfields Cl. RG24: Lych 3G 43
Brickfields Country Pk. 2K 65
Brickfield Trad. Est. SO53: Cha F 7A 132
Brickhouse Hill RG27: Eve 7F 16
Brickiln Ind. Est. RG26: Tadl 4J 11
Brickiln La. GU34: Four M 1N 97
Brick Kiln La. GU34: Alt 3C 80
SO24: W Tis 7G 111
Brick La. BH23: Thorn 3G 220
GU51: Fleet 1L 47
Brickmakers Rd. SO21: Col C 4K 133
Bricksbury Hill GU9: Up H 3E 64
Brickwoods Cl. SO51: Rom 4A 130
Brickworth La. SP5: W'psh 5F 120
Brickworth Rd. SP5: W'psh 5F 120
Brickyard, The SO40: Wins 2B 170
Brickyard Rd. SO32: Swanm 8B 164
Brickyards Ind. Estate, The GU32: Ste 4N 139
Bricky Lake La. SO51: Ower 4C 156
Bridefield Cl. PO8: Cowp 7L 181
Bridefield Cres. PO8: Cowp 7L 181
Bridge Cl. SO31: Burs 9M 175
Bridge Cotts. GU33: Liss 7D 114
SO51: W Wel 1C 120 (9N 121)
Bridge Ct. RG26: Tadl 5J 11
SO51: Rom 6L 129
Bridge End GU15: Camb 9K 19
Bridgefield GU9: Farnh 8F 64
Bridgefoot Dr. PO16: Fare 8E 198
Bridgefoot Hill PO16: Fare 8F 198
Bridgefoot Path PO10: Ems 9M 203
Bridge Ho. PO13: Gos 4E 212
Bridge Industries PO16: Fare 6E 198
Bridge La. SO21: Shaw 6J 127
BRIDGEMARY 5E 212
Bridgemary Av. PO13: Gos 5F 212
Bridgemary Gro. PO13: Gos 3E 212
Bridgemary Rd. PO13: Gos 3E 212
Bridgemary Way PO13: Gos 3E 212
Bridge Mead SO32: Meon 8N 135
Bridgemead *GU16: Frim 4L 29*
(off Frimley High St.)
Bridge Mdws. GU33: Liss 1E 140
Bridge M. GU10: Tong 3N 65
Bridge Rd. GU11: Alders 2J 65
GU14: Cov 8H 29
GU15: Camb 1K 29
PO10: Ems 8M 203
RG29: N War 7J 45
SO19: South 7B 174
SO24: New A 1D 108
SO31: Burs 9M 175
SO31: Lwr Swan, P Ga, Sar G 3B 196
SO41: Lymi 2F 234
SO51: Rom 5N 129
SP5: Bish 3C 118
Bridgers Cl. SO16: Rown 6D 158
Bridges, The BH24: Ring 1H 187
RG7: Mor W 1B 12
Bridges Av. PO6: Cosh 8A 200
Bridges Cl. SO50: E'leigh 9D 132
Bridge Shop. Centre, The PO1: Ports 2F 240
Bridgeside Cl. PO1: Ports 2E 240
Bridge Sq. GU9: Farnh 8E 64
Bridge St. BH23: Chri 8M 229
PO14: Titch 9K 197
PO17: S'wick 7M 199
PO17: Wick 6C 178
RG25: Over 2D 56
SO23: Winche 8P 237 (7M 105)
SP6: F'dge 1J 153
SP10: A'ver 2N 69
Bridget Cl. PO8: Horn 3C 182
Bridge Ter. SO14: South 7N 173
SO21: Shaw 7J 127
Bridgetts La. SO21: Mar W 5C 92
Bridge Wlk. GU46: Yat 6N 17
Bridgewater Rd. BH12: Poole 8B 226
Bridge Yd. SO41: Lymi 2F 234
Bridgwater Ct. SO15: South 4H 173
Bridle Cl. GU26: Gray 4J 103
GU34: E Tis 1D 112
Bridle Ct. GU11: Alders 9G 49
Bridle Cres. BH7: Bour 6F 228
Bridle Path GU10: Ews 2N 63
PO8: Horn 2B 182
Bridlington Av. SO15: South 2J 173
Bridport Ct. SO15: South 5H 173
Bridport Ho. *PO12: Gos 9M 213*
(off Searle Dr.)
Bridport Rd. BH12: Poole 6D 226
Bridport St. PO1: Ports 2D 240
Brierley Cl. BH10: Bour 1J 227
Brierley Rd. BH10: Bour 2H 227
Brigantine Rd. SO31: Wars 8B 196
Brigham Cl. PO2: Ports 5F 214
Brighstone Cl. SO16: S'ing 6A 160
Brighstone Rd. PO6: Cosh 1F 214
Brightlands Av. BH6: Bour 1J 247
Brighton Av. PO12: Gos 8H 213
BRIGHTON HILL 2M 59
Brighton Hill Cen. RG22: B'toke 2M 59
Brighton Hill Pde. RG22: B'toke 2M 59
Brighton Hill Retail Pk. RG22: B'toke 9N 41
Brighton Hill Rdbt. RG22: B'toke 9N 41
Brighton Rd. GU12: Alders 2L 65
SO15: South 3L 173
SO41: Sway 3H 223
Brighton Way RG22: B'toke 2M 59
Brightside PO7: W'lle 3L 201
Brightside Rd. SO16: South 9E 158
Brights La. PO11: H Isl 2F 242
Brightstone La. GU34: Lwr Farr 6M 97
Brightwell Pk. 8E 64
Brightwells Rd. GU9: Farnh 8E 64
Bright Wire Cres. SO50: E'leigh 1D 160
Brill Cl. SO24: New A 1E 108
Brimley Hill Ct. RG20: Kings 2B 6
BRIMPTON COMMON 2B 10
Brimpton La. RG7: Brim, Brim C 1A 10
Brimpton Rd. RG7: Brim C 3C 10
RG26: Bau 3C 10
Brindle Cl. GU11: Alders 3K 65
SO16: Bass 6M 159
BRINKSWAY 2M 117
Brinksway GU51: Fleet 2M 47
Brinn's La. GU17: Blackw 8E 18
Brinsley Cl. SO19: South 5G 175
Brinsons Cl. BH23: Burt 3M 229
Brinton La. SO45: Hythe 4M 193
Brinton's Rd. SO14: South 3E 4 (5M 173)
Brinton's Ter. SO14: South 2E 4 (4M 173)
Brisbane Gdns. SP4: Bul C 3C 66
Brisbane Ho. PO1: Ports 9E 214
Brisbane Rd. BH23: Chri 5H 229
Brislands La. GU34: Four M, Rop 8D 96
SO24: Rop 8D 96
Bristol Ct. PO13: Gos 2E 238
Bristol Rd. PO4: S'sea 5G 241
Bristow Rd. GU15: Camb 1K 29
Britain St. PO1: Ports 4K 5 (2B 240)
Britannia Cl. GU35: Bor 4K 101
Britannia Ct. SO14: South 5A 174
Britannia Dr. RG22: B'toke 6J 59
Britannia Gdns. SO30: Hed E 8M 161
Britannia Rd. PO5: S'sea 3E 240
SO14: South 5N 173
Britannia Rd. Nth. PO5: S'sea 3E 240
Britannia St. GU31: Pet 8N 139
Britannia Way BH23: Mude 7D 230
PO12: Gos 9L 213
Britannia Wharf SO14: South 6A 174
Britannic Ho. *SO14: South 5A 174*
(off Kent St.)
Britnell Ho. GU32: Pet 9M 139
Briton St. SO14: South 8D 4 (7M 173)
Brittain Ct. GU47: Sandh 6E 18
Brittany Cl. SO40: March 9E 172
Britten Rd. PO13: Lee S 1A 238
RG22: B'toke 1N 59
Britten Way PO7: W'lle 5M 201
Brixey Cl. BH12: Poole 7A 226
Brixey Rd. BH12: Poole 7A 226
Brixworth Cl. PO6: Cosh 8B 200
Broadacre Pl. PO14: Fare 9C 198
Broadacres GU51: Fleet 3J 47
Broad Av. BH8: Bour 5A 228
Broadbent Cl. SO16: Rown 5C 158
BROAD CHALKE 3A 118
Broad Chalke Down SO22: Winche 1G 127
Broadchalk Rd. SP5: Bish 2D 118
Broadcroft PO9: R Cas 7J 183
Broadcut PO16: Fare 7E 198
Broadfields Cl. SO41: M Sea 7K 235
Broad Gdns. PO6: Farl 9M 201
Broad Grn. SO14: South 5E 4 (6M 173)
Broad Halfpenny La. RG26: Tadl 4J 11
Broadhill La. SP6: Blis 2N 153
Broadhurst GU14: Cov 8E 28
Broadhurst Av. BH10: Bour 2J 227
Broadhurst Gro. RG24: Lych 4G 42
Broadhurst M. GU12: Alders 1L 65
Broadlands 7L 129
Broadlands *BH4: Bour 2G 245*
(off Marlborough Rd.)
GU14: Farn 1N 49
Broadlands Av. BH6: Bour 1J 247
PO7: W'lle 3M 201
SO50: E'leigh 6E 132
Broadlands Cl. BH8: Bour 3A 228
BH23: Walk 4K 231
GU10: Ben'ly 7K 63
Broadlands Lake 6L 157
Broadlands La. SO42: Broc 7B 148 (8N 189)
Broadlands Rd. SO17: South 7N 159
SO42: Broc 6B 148 (8N 189)
Broad La. PO7: H'don 4C 180
SO24: Cher 7G 109
SO32: Swanm 6C 164
SO41: Lymi 3F 234
SO52: N Bad 7D 130
Broadlaw Walk Shop. Cen. PO14: Fare 1A 212
BROAD LAYING 2A 8
Broadleaf Cl. SO45: Dib P 8K 193
Broad Leaze RG27: Hoo 1G 45
Broadley Cl. SO45: Holb 4A 208
Broadly Cl. SO41: Penn 4B 234
Broadmarsh Bus. & Innovation Cen.
PO9: Hav 9C 202
Broadmayne Rd. BH12: Poole 7D 226
BROADMEAD 2L 233
Broadmead GU14: Cov 9F 28
Broadmead Cl. SO41: Lymi 4F 234
Broadmeadow Cl. SO40: Tott 3L 171
Broadmeadows La. PO7: W'lle 2A 202
Broadmead Rd. SO16: Nur 5C 158
BROADMERE 6N 59
Broadmere RG25: Far W 7N 59
Broadmere Av. PO9: Hav 4F 202
Broadmere Rd. RG22: B'toke 5J 59
Broadmoor Est. RG45: Cr'tne 1F 18
BROAD OAK 7N 45
BROADOAK 3C 176
Broad Oak SO30: Botl 3B 176
Broadoak RG26: Tadl 5K 11
Broad Oak Bus. Pk. PO3: Ports 4J 215
Broadoak Cl. SO45: Holb 5A 208
Broad Oak La. RG29: Odi 8N 45
Broad Rd. SP11: Monx 6B 68
Broadsands Dr. PO12: Gos 4F 238
Broadsands Wlk. PO12: Gos 4E 238
Broadshard Ct. BH24: Ring 8K 185
Broadshard La. BH24: Ring 8K 185
Broad St. PO1: Ports 6H 5 (3A 240)
SO24: New A 9F 94
Broadview Cl. GU34: Bins 1E 82
SO23: Kin W 8N 91
Broad Vw. La. SO22: Oli B 2E 126
Broad Wlk. GU16: Frim 2N 29
PO8: Horn 5E 182
RG25: B'toke 2F 60
Broadwater Av. BH14: Poole 3A 244
Broadwater Rd. SO18: South 8D 160
SO51: Rom 6L 129
Broad Way GU32: Frox, Ste 5C 138
RG7: Bee H 2B 14
Broadway BH6: Bour 1J 247
RG28: Whit 6H 55
SO31: Hamb 4J 195
Broadway, The BH10: Bour 1H 227
GU47: Sandh 6D 18
SO17: South 1N 173
SO18: South 3H 175
SO23: Winche 8N 237 (7L 105)
SP10: A'ver 2N 69
(off Western Rd.)
Broadway Gables BH14: Poole 1B 244
Broadway Gdns. BH10: Bour 1H 227
Broadway La. BH8: Bour 3N 227
PO8: Love 4L 181
Broadway Pk. GU31: Pet 3M 145
Broad Woods La. SO51: E Wel 7N 121
Brocas Dr. RG21: B'toke 4D 42
BROCKBRIDGE 1L 165
Brockbridge Rd. SO32: Drox, Meon 1L 165
BROCKENHURST 7C 148 (8N 189)
Brockenhurst Av. PO9: Hav 3D 202
Brockenhurst Dr. GU46: Yat 9N 17
Brockenhurst Rd. BH9: Bour 4M 227
BH25: Woot 6B 222
GU11: Alders 2K 65
Brockenhurst Station (Rail) 8D 148
Brocketts Bus. Pk. RG27: H Win 3C 26
Brockham Hill La.
GU34: Holy, Up Froy 8D 62
BROCKHAMPTON 8D 202
Brockhampton La. PO9: Hav 8E 202
Brockhampton Rd. PO9: Hav 9D 202
(not continuous)
Brockhills La. BH25: New M 1D 232
BROCKHURST 1J 239
Brockhurst Ind. Est. PO12: Gos 7H 213
Brockhurst Rd. PO12: Gos 8H 213
Brockington La.
BH21: Gus S, Know 9E 148
Brockishill Rd. SO40: Bart 8N 155
Brocklands GU46: Yat 9L 17
PO9: Hav 8D 202
Brockley Rd. BH10: Bour 2J 227
Brock M. SO20: Mid Wa 4B 72
Brocks Cl. SO45: Dib P 7J 193
BROCK'S GREEN 3H 9
Brocks Pine BH24: St L 5C 186
BROCKWOOD 3A 136
Brockwood BH24: St L 6A 186
Brodrick Av. PO12: Gos 4J 239
BROKENFORD 3L 171
Brokenford Av. SO40: Tott 3N 171
Brokenford Bus. Cen. SO40: Tott 3M 171
Brokenford La. SO40: Tott 3M 171
Brokenhurst Manor Golf Course 1M 223
Broken Way RG20: Newt 2F 8
Brokle Cl. GU52: Ch Cr 7K 47
Bromelia Cl. RG26: B'ley 9G 12
Bromfield Pl. GU51: Fleet 9K 27
Bromley Rd. SO18: South 1D 174
Brompton Pas. PO2: Ports 9E 214
Brompton Rd. PO4: S'sea 5G 241
Bromyard Cres. PO6: Cosh 8D 200
Bronte Av. BH23: Chri 5K 229
Bronte Cl. SO40: Tott 4K 171
Bronte Gdns. PO15: White 1F 196
Bronte Way SO19: South 4C 174
Bronze Cl. RG22: B'toke 6J 59
BROOK
SO20 9E 88
SO43 5L 155
Brook, The SO24: Old A 7F 94
Brook Av. BH25: New M 2B 232
GU9: Weyb 3H 65
SO31: Wars 6N 195
Brook Av. Nth. BH25: New M 1C 232
Brook Cl. BH10: Bour 2G 226
GU47: Owl 4G 18
GU51: Fleet 3M 47
SO31: Sar G 6A 196
SO52: N Bad 9F 130
SO53: Cha F 8A 132
Brook Cotts. GU46: Yat 7M 17
Brook Ct. *GU14: Cov 7E 28*
(off Melrose Av.)
SO15: South 5J 173
Brookdale Cl. PO7: W'lle 1N 201
Brooke Cl. SO23: Kin W 7M 91
Brooke Dr. SP10: A'ver 9L 51
Brooke Ho. *BH8: Bour 9N 227*
(off Lowther Rd.)
PO9: Hav 7F 202
Brookers La. PO13: Gos 5C 212
(not continuous)
BROOKE'S HILL 7H 157
Brookes Hill Ind. Est. SO40: Calm 7H 157
Brook Farm Av. PO15: Fare 7B 198
Brookfield Cl. PO9: Hav 7E 202
RG24: Chin 9H 23
Brookfield Gdns. SO31: Sar G 5C 196
Brookfield Pl. SO17: South 9N 159
Brookfield Rd. GU12: Alders 8N 49
PO1: Ports 1F 240
SO50: Fair O 1M 161
Brookfields SO51: W Wel 1A 120 (9M 121)
Brook Gdns. GU14: Cov 1H 49
PO10: Ems 9K 203
Brook Grn. RG26: Tadl 5K 11
Brookham Grange RG27: Sher L 7H 23
BROOK HILL
GU51 6H 47
SO43 5L 155
Brook Hill SO41: Norl, S Badd 9L 225
Brook Ho. *GU9: Hale 4F 64*
(off Farnborough Rd.)
GU51: Fleet 2L 47
(off Upper St.)
SO19: South 7E 174
Brookhouse Rd. GU14: Cov 9H 29
Brookland Cl. SO41: Penn 3C 234
Brooklands BH4: Bour 2F 244
GU11: Alders 1G 65
Brooklands Cl. GU9: H End 3F 64
Brooklands Ct. PO7: W'lle 9N 181
Brooklands Rd. GU9: H End 3G 64
PO9: Bed 7B 202
SO32: Bis W 3M 163
Brooklands Way GU9: H End 3G 64
Brook La. BH23: Nea 8D 220
PO7: H'don 5C 166
SO30: Botl 3C 176
SO31: Sar G, Wars 8N 195
SP6: Woodg 2A 154
Brookley Cl. GU10: Run 7L 65
Brookley Ct. *BH8: Bour 7N 227*
(off Richmond Pk. Rd.)
Brookley Lodge SO42: Broc 7C 148
Brookley Rd. SO42: Broc 7C 148 (8N 189)
Brookly Gdns. GU51: Fleet 1N 47
Brooklyn BH14: Poole 6B 244
Brooklyn Cl. SO21: Ott 1G 132
Brooklyn Ct. BH25: New M 3A 232
SO21: Ott 1G 132
(off Main Rd.)
Brooklyn Dr. PO7: W'lle 1N 201
Brooklynn Cl. SO32: Wal C 9A 164
Brookmead Ct. *GU9: Farnh 9D 64*
(off Pengilly Rd.)
Brookmeadow PO15: Fare 8B 198
Brook Meadow Nature Reserve 8N 203
Brookmead Way PO9: Langs 9F 202

Brook Rd.—Burns Pl.

Brook Rd. BH10: Bour 2G 226
BH12: Poole 9A 226
GU15: Camb 9K 19
SO18: South 3E 174
SO41: Lymi 4F 234
SO50: Fair O 1N 161
Brooksby Cl. GU17: Blackw 8D 18
Brooks Cl. BH24: Ring 2L 187
RG28: Whit 6H 55
Brooks Experience, The 7N 237
Brookside GU9: Hale 4E 64
GU47: Sandh 6E 18
PO13: Gos 3D 212
SO40: Tott 5M 171
SP5: L'ford 9J 121
SP6: S Gor 8M 153
Brookside Av. SO15: South 3E 172
Brookside Cen. SO15: South 3D 172
Brookside Cl. BH23: Bran 6C 220
PO7: Den 6G 181
Brookside Dr. SO31: Sar G 6A 196
Brookside Ho. SO18: S'ing 7C 160
Brookside Residential Pk. Homes
GU14: Farn 3J 29
Brookside Rd. BH23: Bran 6C 220
PO9: Bed 7C 202
PO9: Hav 9D 202
SO42: Broc 6C 148 (8N 189)
Brookside Wlk. RG26: Tadl 5J 11
Brookside Way BH23: Highc 5G 231
SO18: S'ing 7C 160
SO30: Wes E 9J 161
Brooks Ri. SP10: A'ver 9L 51
Brooks Shop. Centre, The
SO23: Winche 7N 237 (6L 105)
Brook St. SO32: Bis W 4M 163
Brooks Way SO21: Hurs 9N 125
Brook Ter. SP6: F'dge 2J 153
Brook Trad. Estate, The
GU12: Alders 9N 49
Brookvale Cl. RG21: B'toke 6B 42
Brookvale Ct. SO17: South 1M 173
Brookvale Rd. SO17: South 1M 173
Brookvale School RG21: B'toke 6A 42
Brook Valley SO16: South 9F 158
Brookview Cl. PO14: Fare 9L 197
Brook Wlk. SO40: Calm 1J 171
Brook Way BH23: Fri C 7E 230
SO51: Rom 3N 129
SP11: An V 5J 69
Brookwood Av. SO50: E'leigh 9D 132
Brookwood Ind. Est. SO50: E'leigh 9E 132
Brookwood Rd. GU14: Farn 8M 29
SO16: South 2C 172
Broom Acres GU47: Sandh 5D 18
GU52: Fleet 5L 47
Broom Cl. PO4: S'sea 2L 241
PO7: W'lle 4A 202
Broome Cl. GU46: Yat 6M 17
Broomfield Cres. PO13: Gos 9D 212
Broomfield Dr. SP6: Ald 5D 152
Broomfield La. SO41: Lymi 2E 234
Broomfield Rd. GU35: W'hil 5G 100
Broom Hill SO41: E End 4A 236
Broomhill GU10: Ews 2N 63
SP5: L'ford 1J 155
Broomhill Cl. SO41: Penn 4B 234
Broomhill Rd. GU14: Cov 7F 28
Broomhill Way SO50: E'leigh 5E 132
Broomhurst La. GU51: Fleet 9K 27
Broom La. *BH6: Bour 1E 246*
(off Pine Av.)
Broomleaf Cnr. GU9: Farnh 8F 64
Broomleaf Rd. GU9: Farnh 8F 64
Broomrigg Rd. GU51: Fleet 1J 47
Broom Rd. BH12: Poole 5A 226
GU31: Pet 2B 146
Broom Rd. Bus. Pk. BH12: Poole 5A 226
Brooms Gro. SO19: South 7H 175
Broom Sq. PO4: S'sea 2L 241
Broom Way GU17: Haw 9G 18
PO13: Lee S 9B 212
Broomy Cl. SO45: Dib 5H 193
Brougham La. PO12: Gos 1J 239
Brougham Pl. GU9: Up H 3D 64
Brougham Rd. PO5: S'sea 6N 5 (3D 240)
Brougham St. PO12: Gos 1J 239
BROUGHTON 1A 86 (5A 88)
Broughton Av. BH10: Bour 2J 227
Broughton Cl. BH10: Bour 3J 227
SO16: South 1F 172
Broughton Drove SO20: Brou 5B 88
Broughton Ho. SO18: South 2C 174
Broughton M. GU16: Frim 3N 29
Broughton Rd. SO20: S Bri 3C 88
SO43: Lyn 1B 148 (2N 189)
Brow, The PO7: Wid 7J 201
PO12: Gos 3N 239
BROWN CANDOVER 7B 78
Brown Cft. RG27: Hoo 2F 44
Browndown Rd. PO12: Gos 4E 238
PO13: Lee S 4E 238
Brownen Rd. BH9: Bour 6M 227
Brownfield Ho. GU32: Pet 9M 139
BROWN HEATH 6G 162
Brownhill Cl. SO53: Cha F 5A 132
Brownhill Ct. SO16: South 8D 158
Brownhill Gdns. SO53: Cha F 5A 132
Brownhill Ho. SO16: South 8D 158
Brownhill Rd. BH25: Woot 4M 221
SO52: N Bad 8F 130
(not continuous)
SO53: Cha F 5A 132
Brownhill Way SO16: Nur 8B 158
Browning Av. BH5: Bour 9C 228
PO6: Cosh 8N 199
SO19: South 4H 175
Browning Cl. PO15: White 9F 176
RG24: B'toke 3D 42
SO40: Tott 3K 171
SO50: E'leigh 9D 132
Browning Dr. SO22: Winche 6H 105
BROWNINGHILL GREEN 1E 20
Browning Rd. BH12: Poole 8B 226
GU52: Ch Cr 7K 47
Brownings Cl. SO41: Penn 2A 234
Brownlow Av. SO19: South 4D 174
Brownlow Cl. PO1: Ports 9E 214
Brownlow Ct. *BH4: Bour 2G 245*
(off Marlborough Rd.)
Brownlow Gdns. SO19: South 4E 174
Browns Cl. RG26: B'ley 9G 12
Brownsea Cl. BH25: New M 3N 231
Brownsea Ct. BH14: Poole 5A 244
Brownsea Vw. Av. BH14: Poole 5A 244
Brownsea Vw. Cl. BH14: Poole 4A 244
Browns La. SO41: E End 5B 236
SP6: Dame 3N 149
Brownsover Rd. GU14: Cov 8E 28
Brownwich La. PO14: Titch 4F 210
Brow Path PO7: Wid 7K 201
Browsholme Cl. SO50: E'leigh 6E 132
Broxburn Cl. SO53: Cha F 3C 132
Broxhead Common (Nature Reserve) 9K 83
Broxhead Farm Rd. GU35: Lind 8K 83
Broxhead Rd. PO9: Hav 3G 203
Broxhead Trad. Est. GU35: Lind 1L 101
Bruce Cl. PO16: Fare 6C 198
Bruce Rd. PO4: S'sea 5G 241
Brudenell Av. BH13: S'bks 6B 244
Brudenell Rd. BH13: S'bks 6B 244
Brue Cl. SO53: Cha F 5N 131
Brunei Ho. SO16: Bass 6M 159
Brune La. PO13: Lee S 7C 212
(not continuous)
Brunel Cl. BH31: Ver 5A 184
SO21: Mich S 4J 77
SO30: Hed E 1A 176
Brunel Ct. PO1: Ports 1E 240
Brunel Gate SP10: A'ver 8H 51
Brunel Rd. PO2: Ports 5F 214
RG21: B'toke 5N 41
SO15: South 2B 172
SO40: Tott 8K 157
Brunel Way PO15: Seg 4G 196
Brunstead Pl. BH12: Poole 1F 244
Brunstead Rd. BH12: Poole 1E 244
Brunswick PO1: Ports 3K 5
Brunswick Cl. SO50: Fair O 9M 133
Brunswick Gdns. PO9: Bed 7D 202
Brunswick Pl. RG21: B'toke 1A 60
SO15: South 2C 4 (4L 173)
SO41: Lymi 2E 234
Brunswick Rd. SO50: Fair O 9M 133
Brunswick Sq. SO14: South 8D 4 (7M 173)
Brunswick St. PO5: S'sea 6N 5 (3D 240)
Bruntile Cl. GU14: Farn 2M 49
Brushers BH23: Thorn 3G 220
Bruyn Ct. SP6: F'dge 9K 151
Bruyn Rd. SP6: F'dge 9K 151
Bryanstone Cl. GU52: Ch Cr 5M 47
Bryanstone Rd. BH3: Bour 7J 227
Bryanston Rd. SO19: South 5B 174
Bryant Rd. BH12: Poole 6E 226
Bryce Gdns. GU11: Alders 3L 65
Bryces La. SO24: B Can 7B 78
SO51: Sher E 5M 121
Brydges Rd. SP11: Ludg 1D 30 (5K 31)
Bryher Bri. PO6: P Sol 1C 214
Bryher Island PO6: P Sol 1B 214
Brympton Cl. SP6: F'dge 9G 150
Bryony Cl. SO31: Loc H 7C 196
Bryony Gdns. BH6: Bour 8F 228
SO50: Hor H 5N 161
Bryony Way PO7: W'lle 2A 202
Bryson Cl. PO13: Lee S 1C 238
Bryson Rd. PO6: Cosh 9E 200
Bubb La. SO30: Wes E 8M 161
Bub La. BH23: Chri 8A 230
Buccaneer Ct. GU14: Farn 1L 49
Buccaneers Ct. BH23: Chri 8N 229
Buccaneer Way GU14: Farn 3D 48
Buccleuch Rd. BH13: Poole 4E 244
Bucehayes Cl. BH23: Highc 6J 231
Buchanan Av. BH7: Bour 8B 228
Buchanan Rd. SO16: South 6E 158
Buchan Av. PO15: White 1F 196
Buchan Ct. SO45: Dib P 7H 193
Buckby La. PO3: Ports 4K 215
RG21: B'toke 6E 42
BUCKET CORNER 5H 131
Bucketts Farm Cl. SO32: Swanm 6D 164
Buckfast Cl. RG24: B'toke 2B 42
Buckholt Rd. SO20: Brou 2A 86 (5A 88)
Buckingham Cl. GU34: Alt 5D 80
Buckingham Ct. PO15: Fare 6N 197
RG22: B'toke 1J 59
SO17: South 2M 173
(off Westwood Rd.)
Buckingham Grn. PO1: Ports 9F 214
Buckingham Mans. BH1: Bour 2L 245
Buckingham Pde. RG22: B'toke 1J 59
Buckingham Rd. BH12: Poole 7B 226
GU32: Pet 1K 145
Buckingham St. PO1: Ports 1D 240
Buckingham Wlk. BH25: New M 3N 231
Buckingham Way GU16: Frim 3N 29
BUCKLAND
PO2 8E 214
SO41 1D 234
Buckland Av. RG22: B'toke 1M 59
Buckland Cl. GU14: Farn 5L 29
PO7: W'lle 7L 181
SO50: E'leigh 6E 132
Buckland Dene SO41: Lymi 1D 234
Buckland Gdns. SO40: Calm 9J 157
SO41: Lymi 9D 224
Buckland Gro. BH23: Chri 4G 230
Buckland Mill RG27: Hoo 3E 44
Buckland Pde. RG22: B'toke 9M 41
Buckland Path PO2: Ports 9E 214
Buckland Rd. BH12: Poole 9A 226
Buckland St. PO2: Ports 9F 214
(not continuous)
Buckland Ter. BH12: Poole 9A 226
RG27: Sher L 7H 23
Buckland Vw. SO41: Lymi 1D 234
Bucklers, The SO41: M Sea 9H 233
Bucklers Ct. PO2: Ports 7E 214
PO9: Hav 2D 202
SO41: Lymi 3D 234
BUCKLER'S HARD 2E 236
Buckler's Hard Maritime Mus. 1F 236
Bucklers Hard Rd. SO42: Beau 8E 206
Bucklers M. SO41: Lymi 3D 234
Bucklers Rd. PO12: Gos 8L 213
Bucklers Way BH8: Bour 3A 228
Buckley Ct. SO16: South 1G 172
Buckmore Av. GU32: Pet 8K 139
Bucksey Rd. PO13: Gos 8E 212
Bucks Head Hill SO32: Meon 8N 135
BUCKS HORN OAK 10M 63
BUCKSKIN 8J 41
Buckskin La. RG22: B'toke 9J 41
Buckstone Cl. SO41: Ever 5M 233
Buckthorn Cl. SO40: Tott 2H 171
Budden's La. PO17: Wick 2G 178
Buddens Rd. PO17: Wick 6C 178
Buddle Hill SP6: N Gor 6M 153
Buddlesgate SO21: Sut S 7D 76
Budds Cl. RG21: B'toke 7B 42
SO30: Hed E 9N 161
Budds La. GU35: Bor 2H 101
SO51: Rom 3L 129
Budds La. Ind. Est. SO51: Rom 3L 129
Bude Cl. PO6: Cosh 8A 200
Buffbeards La. GU27: Hasl 8N 103
Buffins Cnr. RG29: Odi 9J 45
Buffins Rd. RG29: Odi 9J 45
Bufton Fld. RG29: N War 8J 45
Bugle St. SO14: South 8C 4 (7L 173)
Bugmore La. SP5: E Gri 9F 86
Bulbarrow Wlk. PO14: Fare 9A 198
Bulbeck Rd. PO9: Hav 8F 202
Bulbery SP11: Abb A 6F 68
Buldowne Wlk. SO41: Sway 4J 223
BULFORD 3A 66
BULFORD CAMP 3B 66
Bulford Droveway SP4: Bul 3A 66
Bulford Rd. SP4: Bul, Bul C 3A 66
SP9: Shi B 1A 66 (1F 66)
SP9: Tidw 9B 30 (9F 30)
Bullar Rd. SO18: South 3C 174
Bullar St. SO14: South 2F 4 (4N 173)
Buller Ct. GU14: Farn 2L 49
Buller Pk. SP4: Port 1C 86
Bullers Rd. GU9: Weyb 4G 64
Bullfield La. GU34: Bent 6J 79
Bullfinch Cl. GU47: Coll 5G 18
SO40: Tott 3J 171
Bullfinch Ct. PO13: Lee S 9B 212
BULL HILL 6H 225
Bull Hill GU33: Rake 1K 141
SO41: Pil 6H 225
Bullington La. SO21: Sut S, Up B 5D 76
Bull La. RG7: Rise 2D 14
(Barge La.)
RG7: Rise 2F 14
(Sun La.)
SO32: Wal C 8N 163
SO43: Mins 8M 155
Bullrush Cl. SO45: Dib P 8L 193
Bulls Bushes RG27: Hoo 3F 44
Bulls Copse La. PO8: Horn 4A 182
Bulls Copse Rd. SO40: Tott 6M 171
Bullsdown Cl. RG27: Sher L 3K 23
Bulls Drove SP5: W Tyt 9L 87
SP11: Bidd 4M 31
Bulls La. SP5: Br Ch 3A 118
Bulpitts Hill SP11: Ver D 8E 6
Bulwark Rd. PO14: Stub 7L 211
Bungum La. SN8: Ham 2F 6
BUNKERS HILL 6E 180
Bunkers Hill PO7: Den 7E 180
Bunnian Pl. RG21: B'toke 5C 42
Bunns La. PO7: H'don 7N 179
Bunny La. SO51: Sher E 5L 121
SO51: Tims 8L 123
BUNSTEAD 7B 126
Bunstead La. SO21: Hurs 7B 126
Bunting Gdns. PO8: Cowp 6N 181
Bunting M. RG22: B'toke 3H 59
Buntings GU34: Alt 2F 80
Burberry Ho. RG27: Hoo 2G 44
Burbidge Gro. PO4: S'sea 5H 241
Burbury Woods GU15: Camb 7N 19
Burbush Cl. SO45: Holb 5A 208
Burcombe La. BH24: Hang 4A 188
Burcombe Rd. BH10: Bour 1G 226
Burcote Dr. PO3: Ports 4J 215
Burdale Dr. PO11: H Isl 4K 243
Burdock Cl. BH23: Chri 5D 230
SP11: G Cla 9M 69
Bure Cl. BH23: Fri C 8D 230
Bure Ct. BH23: Mude 8D 230
Bure Haven Dr. BH23: Mude 8C 230
(not continuous)
Bure Homage Gdns. BH23: Mude 8D 230
Bure Homage La. BH23: Mude 8C 230
Bure Ho. BH23: Chri 6J 229
Bure La. BH23: Fri C, Mude 9D 230
Bure Pk. BH23: Fri C 8D 230
Bure Rd. BH23: Fri C 8D 230
Burfield RG20: High 4A 8
Burford Cl. BH23: Chri 5G 228
Burford Ct. BH1: Bour 2M 245
Burford La. SO42: Broc 6D 148
Burford Rd. GU15: Camb 9K 19
Burgage Fld. RG28: Whit 4H 55
Burgate Cl. PO9: Bed 6D 202
Burgate Ct. SP6: B'gte 7K 151
Burgate Cres. RG27: Sher L 7J 23
Burgate Flds. SP6: F'dge 8J 151
BURGATES 8D 114
Burge Cl. GU14: Cov 8E 28
Burgesmede Ho. GU31: Pet 1M 145
Burgess Cl. BH11: Bour 2D 226
PO11: H Isl 6K 243
RG29: Odi 9J 45
Burgess Ct. SO16: Bass 7N 159
Burgess Gdns. SO16: South 8K 159
Burgess La. RG20: Ham M 1K 7
Burgess Rd. RG21: B'toke 5B 42
SO16: Bass, South 8J 159
(not continuous)
SO17: Bass, S'ing 7M 159
BURGHCLERE 3E 8
Burghclere Rd. PO9: Hav 3H 203
SO19: South 1D 194
Burghead Cl. GU47: Coll 6F 18
Burghfield Rd. RG26: Tadl 3G 11
Burghfield Wlk. RG23: Wort 8J 41
Burgh Hill Rd. GU30: B'sht 8B 102
Burghley Ho. GU30: Lip 1E 116
Burgoyne Rd. PO5: S'sea 6E 240
SO19: South 6J 175
Burgundy Cl. SO31: Loc H 7C 196
Burgundy Ter. PO2: Ports 5F 214
BURITON 7K 145
Buriton Bus. Pk. GU32: W'ton 5J 145
Buriton Cl. PO16: Portc 8M 199
Buriton Ho. *PO1: Ports 2E 240*
(off Buriton St.)
Buriton Rd. SO22: Winche 2H 105
Buriton St. PO1: Ports 1E 240
Burkal Dr. SP10: A'ver 6N 51
Burke Dr. SO19: South 4G 175
Burleigh Rd. BH6: Bour 8G 228
GU16: Frim 4M 29
PO1: Ports 9G 214
BURLEY 7E 188
Burley Cl. BH25: New M 6M 231
PO9: Hav 3H 203
SO40: Tott 3H 171
SO53: Cha F 8N 131
Burley Ct. SO17: South 9M 159
Burley Down SO53: Cha F 8N 131
Burley Golf Course 8E 188
Burley La. RG25: Ashe 6H 57
BURLEY LAWN 7E 188
Burley Lawn BH24: Bur 7E 188
Burley Rd. BH12: Poole 8A 226
BH23: Bock, Bran, Thorn 8C 220
BH23: Bock, Bran, Thorn, Wink 1M 229
SO22: Winche 2H 105
SO42: Broc 1E 222
BURLEY STREET 6D 188
Burley Way GU17: Blackw 7E 18
Burlingham Grange
RG29: N War 8J 45
Burling Ter. BH12: Poole 1E 244
Burlington Arc. BH1: Bour 6M 247
Burlington Ct. GU11: Alders 1J 65
GU17: Haw 1F 28
SO19: South 5F 174
Burlington Ho. SO30: Hed E 2A 176
Burlington Mans. SO15: South 3H 173
Burlington Rd. PO2: Ports 7F 214
SO15: South 1A 4 (4K 173)
Burlington Wlk. SP9: Tidw 8D 30
Burma Ho. SO18: S'ing 7C 160
Burma Rd. SO22: Winche 9H 237 (7J 105)
SO51: Rom 6M 129
Burma Rd. Nth. SO45: Fawl 3F 208
Burma Rd. Sth. SO45: Fawl 3F 208
Burma Way SO40: March 9E 172
Burmese Cl. PO15: White 2F 196
Burnaby Cl. RG22: B'toke 8L 41
Burnaby Ct. BH4: Bour 4F 244
Burnaby Rd. BH4: Bour 4F 244
PO1: Ports 4L 5 (2C 240)
Burnbank Gdns. SO40: Tott 3L 171
Burne Cl. SO21: Wor D 5H 91
Burne-Jones Dr. GU47: Coll 7F 18
Burnett Av. BH23: Chri 6H 229
Burnett Cl. SO18: South 1C 174
SO22: Winche 4G 105
SO45: Hythe 7N 193
Burnett Rd. BH23: Chri 7J 229
PO12: Gos 1H 239
Burnetts Flds. SO50: Hor H 4N 161
Burnetts Gdns. SO50: Hor H 4N 161
Burnetts La. SO30: Wes E 8L 161
SO50: Hor H 8L 161
Burney Bit RG26: Pam H 5L 11
Burney Ho. *PO12: Gos 3M 239*
(off South St.)
Burney Rd. PO12: Gos 4G 239
Burnham Beeches
SO53: Cha F 6N 131
Burnham Chase SO18: South 3F 174
Burnham Dr. BH8: Bour 7N 227
Burnham Rd. BH23: Burt 4M 229
GU34: Alt 7C 80
PO6: Dray 8L 201
RG26: Tadl 3F 10
SP6: F'dge 8J 151
Burnhams Cl. SP10: A'ver 7N 51
Burnham's Wlk. PO12: Gos 3M 239
Burnham Wood PO16: Fare 6C 198
Burnleigh Gdns. BH25: A'ley 2D 232
Burnley Cl. RG26: Tadl 6H 11
Burnmoor Mdw. RG40: F'std 3H 17
Burnsall Cl. GU14: Farn 6K 29
Burns Av. GU52: Ch Cr 5N 47
Burns Cl. GU14: Farn 6H 29
RG24: B'toke 3D 42
SO21: Sth W 3J 91
SO50: E'leigh 2C 160
Burnside BH23: Chri 6F 230
GU51: Fleet 2M 47
PO7: W'lle 9A 182
PO13: Gos 3D 212
Burns Pl. SO16: South 9F 158

Cellar La.—Chawton

Cellar La. GU32: Lang 1A 144
Cellars Farm Rd. BH6: Bour 2K 247
Celtic Dr. SP10: A'ver 3L 69
Cement Ter. SO14: South 7C 4 (7L 173)
Cemetery Hill RG29: Odi 9L 45
Cemetery La. PO7: Den 5G 180
RG25: Up G 3A 62
Cemetery Rd. GU51: Fleet 4K 47
SO15: South 2K 173
Centaur St. PO2: Ports 8E 214
Centaury Gdns. SO50: Hor H 4N 161
Centenary Cl. SO41: Sway 5K 223
Centenary Gdns. PO9: Hav 7F 202
Centenary Ho. BH23: Chri 7L 229
Centenary Way BH1: Bour 9B 228
Central Av. BH12: Poole 8C 226
Central Bri. SO14: South 7F 4 (7N 173)
Central Cres. SO40: March 7F 172
Central Dr. BH2: Bour 5K 247 (1J 245)
Central Point PO3: Ports 1J 241
Central Precinct, The SO53: Cha F 7A 132
Central Retail Pk. PO9: Hav 7E 202
Central Rd. GU35: Bor 1J 101
PO6: Dray 1K 215
PO16: Portc 1K 213
SO14: South 9E 4 (8M 173)
Central Sta. Bri. SO15: South 4A 4 (5K 173)
Central St. PO1: Ports 1E 240
SP11: Ludg 1D 30 (5K 31)
Central Studio (Theatre) 8C 42
Central Trad. Est. SO14: South 5G 4 (6N 173)
Central Way SP10: A'ver 9D 52
Central Way Nth. SO45: Fawl 6J 209
Centre 27 Retail Pk. SO30: Hed E 1L 175
Centre Cinema 2E 234
Centre Ct. SO15: South 2G 172
Centre Court Tennis Cen. 2G 43
Centre Dr. RG24: Chin 2G 43
Centre for Community Arts 9C 228
Centre La. SO41: Ever 5M 233
Centre Pl. BH24: Ring 1J 187
Centre Way SO31: Loc H 6C 196
Centro GU15: Camb 7L 19
Centrum Bus. Pk. GU9: Farnh 7E 64
Centurion PO1: Ports 2K 5
Centurion Cl. GU47: Coll 5F 18
Centurion Ct. PO1: Ports 5J 5 (3B 240)
Centurion Ga. PO4: S'sea 4L 241
Centurion Pk. SO18: South 3A 174
Centurion Way RG22: B'toke 3K 59
(not continuous)
Century Cl. RG25: Clid 3B 60
Century Ct. SO14: South 8D 4
Cerdic Mews SO31: Hamb 5L 195
Cerne Abbas BH13: Poole 4E 244
Cerne Cl. BH9: Bour 2M 227
SO18: Wes E 1F 174
SO52: N Bad 8E 130
Cessac Ho. PO12: Gos 6L 239
Chadderton Gdns. PO1: Ports 7L 5 (4C 240)
Chaddesley Glen BH13: S'bks 7B 244
Chaddesley Pines BH13: Poole 7C 244
Chaddesley Wood Rd. BH13: S'bks 8C 244
Chadswell Mdw. PO9: Bed 7D 202
Chadwell Av. SO19: South 6F 174
Chadwick Rd. SO50: E'leigh 1D 160
Chadwick Way SO31: Hamb 7K 195
Chafen Rd. SO18: South 2B 174
Chaffers Cl. RG29: L Sut 5E 62
Chaffey Cl. BH24: Poul 9M 185
Chaffinch Cl. BH25: New M 4A 232
GU47: Coll 5F 18
RG22: B'toke 2J 59
SO40: Tott 2J 171
Chaffinch Grn. PO8: Cowp 6M 181
Chaffinch Rd. GU34: Four M 6G 97
Chaffinch Way PO13: Lee S 9B 212
PO16: Portc 9H 199
Chalbury BH13: Poole 3E 244
Chalcraft Cl. GU30: Lip 2C 116
Chalcrafts GU34: Alt 3G 81
Chalcroft Distribution Pk. SO30: Wes E 6M 161
Chaldecott Gdns. BH10: Bour 2G 226
Chaldon Grn. RG24: Lych 3H 43
Chale Cl. PO13: Gos 6E 212
Chalet Ct. *GU35: Bor* *4J 101*
(off Ashmead)
Chalet Hill GU35: Bor 4J 101
Chalewood Rd. SO45: Blac 9C 208
Chalfont Av. BH23: Chri 3G 229
Chalfont Ct. SO16: South 1F 172
Chalfont Dr. GU14: Farn 1L 49
Chalford Grange PO15: Fare 8N 197
Chalice Ct. SO30: Hed E 4M 175
Chalk Cl. GU34: Four M 5J 97
Chalkcroft La. SP11: Pen M 7G 50
Chalk Down SP9: Tidw 7E 30 (6H 31)
Chalke Valley Sports Cen. 3A 118
Chalk Hill SO18: Wes E 2G 174
SO20: Lit Som, Up S 5J 89
SO32: Sob 6L 165
Chalk Hill Rd. PO8: Horn 2C 182
Chalk La. PO15: Fare 8L 197
PO17: Fare 2D 198
Chalk Pit La. SP5: W Tyt 7L 87
Chalkpit La. SP11: Monx 4D 68
Chalkpit Rd. PO6: Cosh 8C 200
Chalk Pyt La. SP5: Br Ch 3A 118
Chalk Ridge PO8: Cath 8D 168
SO23: Winche 7N 105
Chalkridge Rd. PO6: Cosh 8H 201
Chalk's Cl. SP5: M Val 1M 119 (7C 120)
Chalk Va. RG24: Old Bas 6K 43
SO20: A'ley, Up S 6J 89
Chalky Copse RG27: Hoo 1G 44
Chalky La. RG27: Dogm 9D 46
SO32: Bis W 3N 163
Chalky Wlk. PO16: Portc 1L 213
Challenge Ent. Centre, The PO3: Ports 5J 215
Challenger Dr. PO12: Gos 9L 213
Challenger Pl. SO45: Dib P 6J 193
Challenger Way SO45: Dib, Dib P 5J 193
Challis Cl. RG22: B'toke 9L 41
Challis Ct. SO14: South 7E 4 (7M 173)
SP11: Ludg 1E 30
Challoner Cl. RG22: B'toke 8L 41
Chalmers Way SO31: Hamb 6J 195
Chaloner Cres. SO45: Dib P 8M 193
CHALTON 7J 169
Chalton Cres. PO9: Hav 4D 202
Chalton Ho. PO1: Ports 1D 240
Chalton La. PO8: Chal 5F 168
PO8: Clan 5B 168
(not continuous)
Chalvington Rd. SO53: Cha F 7A 132
Chalybeate Cl. SO16: South 9G 159
Chamberlain Gro. PO14: Fare 9C 198
Chamberlain Rd. SO17: South 8M 159
Chamberlains Mdw. RG27: Heck 7H 15
Chamber La. GU10: Farnh 6N 63
Chamberlayne Ct. SO52: N Bad 7G 130
Chamberlayne Ho. SO31: Net A 3F 194
Chamberlayne Leisure Cen. 9E 174
Chamberlayne Rd. SO31: Burs 1K 195
(not continuous)
SO31: Net A 3F 194
SO50: E'leigh 2E 160
Chambers Av. SO51: Rom 5N 129
Chambers Cl. SO16: Nur 6B 158
Chamomile Gdns. GU14: Cov 7E 28
Champion Cl. SO41: M Sea 8M 235
Champion Way GU52: Ch Cr 6M 47
Champney Cl. GU35: W'hil 6H 101
(not continuous)
Champneys Gdns. PO16: Fare 8H 199
Chancellors La. SO32: Durl 7B 162
Chancel Rd. SO31: Loc H 6E 196
Chancery Gate Bus. Cen. SO15: South 4D 172
Chanctonbury Ho. PO5: S'sea 4D 240
Chandler Ct. SP9: Tidw 7C 30
Chandler Rd. RG21: B'toke 9B 42
Chandlers, The PO12: Gos 1M 239
Chandlers Cl. BH7: Bour 6E 228
PO11: H Isl 5J 243
Chandlers Ct. SO14: South 8D 4
CHANDLER'S FORD 5C 132
Chandler's Ford Golf Academy Driving Range 3A 160
Chandler's Ford Ind. Est. SO53: Cha F 7N 131
Chandler's Ford Station (Rail) 6A 132
Chandlers Gate SO53: Cha F 6A 132
CHANDLER'S GREEN 2D 24
Chandlers La. GU46: Yat 6M 17
Chandlers Pl. SO31: Net A 3F 194
Chandlers Way SO31: P Ga 3E 196
Chandos Av. BH12: Poole 6E 226
Chandos Ho. SO14: South 7E 4 (7M 173)
Chandos Ri. *PO1: Ports* *1D 240*
(off Buckingham St.)
Chandos St. SO14: South 7E 4 (7M 173)
Channel Ct. BH25: B Sea 7N 231
Channel Mouth Rd. SO45: Fawl 7K 209
Channels Farm Rd. SO16: S'ing 6B 160
Channel Way SO14: South 7N 173
Chant Cl. BH23: Chri 7N 229
SP11: Wher 2E 74
Chantrell Wlk. PO15: Fare 6N 197
Chantreys GU51: Fleet 3J 47
Chantry, The BH1: Bour 6N 247 (1L 245)
PO14: Titch C 6F 196
Chantry Centre, The SP10: A'ver 1N 69
Chantry Cl. BH23: Highc 5H 231
RG27: Hoo 3G 45
Chantry Ct. *GU16: Frim* *3M 29*
(off Church Rd.)
Chantry Hall SO14: South 6F 4
Chantry La. SP11: Co Du 1M 31
Chantry M. RG22: B'toke 3K 59
Chantry Rd. PO8: Horn 2B 182
PO12: Gos 9H 213
SO14: South 7G 4 (7N 173)
Chantrys, The GU9: Farnh 8B 64
Chantrys Ct. *GU9: Farnh* *8C 64*
(off The Chantrys)
Chantry St. SP10: A'ver 1N 69
Chantry Wlk. SO31: Net A 4G 195
Chantry Way SP10: A'ver 1N 69
CHAPEL 6F 4 (6N 173)
Chapel Av. SO21: M'dvr 7K 77
Chapel Cl. RG24: Old Bas 4J 43
RG25: Dumm 9F 58
SO20: Houg 6E 88
SO30: Wes E 9H 161
SO51: Brai 7B 124
SP11: Amp 3B 68
Chapel Ct. *PO1: Ports* *9E 214*
(off Victoria St.)
SO20: Brou 1A 86 (4A 88)
SP11: Wher 2F 74
Chapel Cres. SO19: South 6E 174
Chapel Drove SO30: Hed E 4M 175
SO50: Hor H 4N 161
Chapel Fld. SO21: E'ton 2C 106
Chapel Gdns. GU35: Lind 2L 101
Chapel Gro. SO21: Col C 3K 133
Chapel Haye BH24: Bur 6D 188
Chapel Hill RG21: B'toke 5B 42
SP5: W Gri 2D 120
Chapel La. BH23: Bran 7C 220
BH24: Bur 7E 188
GU14: Cov 4G 29
GU17: Haw 4G 29
PO7: W'lle 2M 201
RG7: Pad C 1M 11
RG7: Rise 2G 14
RG19: Ashf H 2N 9
RG26: Bau 6E 10
RG26: Wolv C 5N 9
SO20: Brou 1A 86 (4A 88)
SO21: E'ton 2D 106
SO21: Ott 3F 132
SO32: Curd 1H 177
Chapel La. SO40: Tott 5L 171
SO41: Sway 6L 223
SO42: Beau 1B 236
SO43: Lyn 2A 148 (3N 189)
SO45: Blac 8C 208
SO45: Fawl 5E 208
SO51: Lock 4N 121
SO51: Tims 5K 123
SP5: Bish 3C 118
SP5: Ch St 4A 120
SP5: Nom 2J 155
SP5: Redl 2N 119 (8D 120)
SP11: Enh A 4A 52
SP11: Grat 5L 67
SP11: Ludg 1C 30
SP11: Stoke 7H 35
Chapel Mead RG27: Eve 5H 17
Chapel Pond Dr. RG29: N War 8J 45
Chapel Ri. BH24: A'ley 6G 186
Chapel River Cl. SP10: A'ver 2L 69
Chapel Rd. GU15: Camb 8K 19
SO14: South 6F 4 (6N 173)
SO30: Wes E 9H 161
SO31: Sar G 3B 196
SO32: Meon 9N 135
SO32: Sob H 9K 165
SO32: Swanm 6D 164
Chapel Row RG27: H Win 5C 26
Chapelside PO14: Titch 9K 197
Chapel Sq. GU15: Camb 7H 19
PO12: Gos 9H 213
Chapel St. GU14: Farn 6M 29
GU32: E Meon 3L 143
GU32: Pet 9M 139
PO2: Ports 8F 214
PO5: S'sea 7M 5 (4D 240)
PO12: Gos 8K 213
RG25: Nth W 9A 58
SO14: South 6E 4 (6M 173)
Chapel Vw. PO4: S'sea 2K 241
Chapel Wlk. RG25: Clid 3B 60
Chaplains Av. PO8: Cowp 7L 181
Chaplains Cl. PO8: Cowp 7L 181
Chaplain's Hill RG45: Cr'tne 1F 18
Chappell Cl. GU30: Lip 2E 116
Chapter Ho. *GU14: Farn* *8L 29*
(off Jubilee Hall Rd.)
Chapter House, The *BH5: Bour* *1C 246*
(off Hawkwood Rd.)
Chapter Ter. RG27: H Win 5C 26
Chardan Ct. PO11: H Isl 6L 243
Charden Ct. SO18: South 3F 174
Charden Rd. PO13: Gos 8F 212
SO50: B'stke 1L 161
Charfield Cl. PO14: Fare 9N 197
SO22: Winche 9J 105
Charhope Ct. BH14: Poole 1D 244
Charing Cl. BH24: Ring 2K 187
CHARING CROSS 5B 152
Charity Vw. PO17: K Vil 2A 198
Chark La. PO13: Lee S 8B 212
Charlbury La. RG24: B'toke 2B 42
Charlcot RG28: Whit 7G 55
(not continuous)
Charlcot Lawn PO9: Hav 3D 202
Charlecote Cl. GU14: Farn 9M 29
Charlecote Dr. SO53: Cha F 4M 131
Charlecote Ho. *SO15: South* *5J 173*
(off Millbrook Rd. E.)
Charledown Cl. RG25: Over 3D 56
Charledown Rd. RG25: Over 3D 56
Charlemont Dr. PO16: Fare 8F 198
Charlesbury Av. PO12: Gos 3H 239
Charles Clark Ho. PO4: S'sea 3H 241
Charles Cl. PO7: W'lle 3L 201
RG27: Hoo 2G 45
SO23: Winche 4M 105
Charles Cres. BH25: New M 1C 232
Charles Dalton Ct. SP10: A'ver 2N 69
Charles Dickens Birthplace Mus. 9D 214
Charles Dickens St.
PO1: Ports 4N 5 (2D 240)
Charles Gdns. BH10: Bour 4G 227
Charles Ho. PO12: Gos 2N 239
Charles Knott Gdns. SO15: South 3L 173
Charles Ley Ct. SO45: Fawl 5F 208
Charles Miller Ct. SO15: South 2L 173
Charles Norton-Thomas Ct. *PO1: Ports* *4K 5*
(off St George's Way)
Charles Richards Cl. RG21: B'toke 8B 42
Charles Rd. BH23: Chri 6B 230
Charles's La. BH24: Crow, King 7A 188
Charles St. GU15: Camb 7L 19
GU32: Pet 1L 145
PO1: Ports 1E 240
RG22: B'toke 7M 41
SO14: South 7E 4 (7M 173)
Charleston Cl. PO11: H Isl 3E 242
Charleston Rd. SO45: Hard 9B 194
Charles Vesey Rd. SP9: Tidw 7C 30
Charles Watts Way SO30: Wes E 3J 175
Charlesworth Dr. PO7: W'lle 9K 181
Charlesworth Gdns. PO7: W'lle 9L 181
Charles Wyatt Ho. SO14: South 3M 173
Charlie Adams Ct. *SO45: Hythe* *6N 193*
(off Seward Grn.)
Charliejoy Gdns. SO14: South 4N 173
Charlie Soar Ct. SO50: E'leigh 1E 160
Charlotte Cl. BH12: Poole 6G 226
BH23: Mude 8C 230
GU9: H End 2F 64
SP10: A'ver 1C 70
Charlotte Ct. BH25: New M 4B 232
PO5: S'sea 8N 5 (4D 240)
SO19: South 8D 174
SO53: Cha F 5C 132
Charlotte Dr. PO12: Gos 9L 213
Charlotte M. GU14: Farn 7M 29
PO12: Gos 5J 239
SO23: Winche 7L 237
Charlotte Pl. SO14: South 2D 4 (4M 173)
Charlottes Ct. *GU14: Farn* *3L 49*
(off Camp Rd.)
Charlotte St. PO1: Ports 2N 5 (1D 240)
CHARLTON 8L 51
CHARLTON-ALL-SAINTS 4A 120
Charlton Cl. BH9: Bour 2N 227
SO41: Hor 3G 233
Charlton Ct. GU47: Owl 4F 18
Charlton Dr. GU31: Pet 8N 139
Charlton Pl. SP10: A'ver 9N 51
Charlton Rd. SO15: South 2J 173
SP10: A'ver 8L 51
(not continuous)
Charlton Rdbt. SP10: A'ver 8L 51
Charltons, The BH2: Bour 9K 227
Charlton Sports & Leisure Cen. 7J 51
CHARLWOOD 2K 111
Charlwood La. SO24: Monk 1L 111
CHARMINSTER 4M 227
Charminster *PO4: S'sea* *5F 240*
(off Craneswater Pk.)
Charminster Av. BH9: Bour 5M 227
Charminster Cl. BH8: Bour 4M 227
PO7: W'lle 1M 201
Charminster Pl. BH8: Bour 4M 227
Charminster Rd. BH8: Bour 8L 227
Charmus Rd. SO40: Calm 9H 157
Charmwen Cres. SO30: Wes E 9G 160
Charnock Cl. SO41: Hor 3G 233
Charnwood PO13: Gos 6G 212
Charnwood Av. BH9: Bour 3M 227
Charnwood Cl. RG22: B'toke 8K 41
SO40: Tott 1K 171
SO53: Cha F 2A 132
SP10: A'ver 3A 70
Charnwood Cres. SO53: Cha F 2A 132
Charnwood Dr. SP6: F'dge 8H 151
Charnwood Gdns. SO53: Cha F 2A 132
Charnwood Ho. BH6: Bour 2J 247
Charnwood Way SO45: Blac 9C 208
Chartcombe BH13: Poole 5C 244
CHARTER ALLEY 4H 21
Charter Ho. PO1: Ports 5M 5
SO14: South 9F 4 (8N 173)
Charterhouse Way
SO30: Hed E 1N 175
Charter Rd. BH11: Bour 1B 226
Charters Cl. GU34: Meds 3K 97
Charters Ho. *GU11: Alders* *9K 49*
(off Sebastopol Rd.)
Chartwell BH13: Poole 2F 244
GU16: Frim G 7N 29
Chartwell Cl. PO14: Titch C 8F 196
SO50: E'leigh 6F 132
Chartwell Dr. PO9: Hav 6J 203
Chartwell Gdns. GU11: Alders 4L 49
Chase, The *BH8: Bour* *7A 228*
(off Queens Pk. Sth. Dr.)
BH24: A'ley 3G 186
BH31: Ver 4A 184
GU14: Farn 6M 29
PO12: Gos 3H 239
PO14: Titch C 7G 196
Chase Cl. GU33: Liss 1F 140
Chase Farm Cl. SO32: Wal C 8A 164
Chase Gdns. PO7: W'lle 5M 201
SO32: Wal C 8A 164
Chase Gro. SO32: Wal C 8A 164
Chase Plain GU26: Hind 6L 103
Chase Rd. GU33: Liss 1F 140
GU35: Lind 2L 101
Chaseside BH7: Bour 6D 228
Chase Vw. GU34: Lwr Farr 4D 98
Chasewater Av. PO3: Ports 9H 215
Chasewater Ct. GU11: Alders 1J 65
Chatburn Av. PO8: Cowp 7M 181
Chatfield Av. PO2: Ports 7B 214
Chatfield Cl. GU14: Farn 1L 49
Chatfield Ho. *PO1: Ports* *1E 240*
(off Fyning St.)
Chatfield Rd. PO13: Gos 4E 212
Chatham Cl. PO6: Cosh 8F 200
PO12: Gos 9L 213
Chatham Dr. PO1: Ports 8L 5 (4C 240)
Chatham Rd. SO22: Winche 9G 105
Chatsworth BH13: Poole 5F 244
Chatsworth Av. PO6: Cosh 2G 215
Chatsworth Cl. PO15: Fare 8M 197
Chatsworth Ct. PO5: S'sea 4E 240
Chatsworth Dr. SP10: A'ver 2L 69
Chatsworth Grn. RG22: B'toke 4L 59
Chatsworth Gro. GU9: Up H 4D 64
Chatsworth Rd. BH8: Bour 8M 227
GU14: Farn 9N 29
SO19: South 4E 174
SO50: E'leigh 6F 132
Chatsworth Way BH25: New M 3N 231
CHATTER ALLEY 4F 46
Chatter All. RG27: Dogm, Winchf 3E 46
Chatter La. RG28: Whit 5G 55
Chattis Hill Stables SO20: S Bri 2C 88
Chaucer Av. PO6: Cosh 8N 199
SP10: A'ver 9K 51
Chaucer Cl. PO7: W'lle 8M 181
PO16: Fare 7B 198
RG24: B'toke 2D 42
SO21: Sth W 2J 91
Chaucer Dr. SO41: M Sea 7K 235
Chaucer Gro. GU15: Camb 8M 19
Chaucer Rd. BH13: Poole 5D 244
GU14: Farn 6H 29
RG45: Cr'tne 2D 18
SO19: South 4H 175
Chaucombe Pl. BH25: New M 5A 232
Chaundler Rd. SO23: Winche 4L 105
Chaundlers Cft. GU10: Cron 3L 63
Chauntsingers Rd. GU34: Alt 4F 80
Chavasse Way GU14: Cov 7F 28
Chaveney Cl. SO45: Dib P 8L 193
Chavywater SO51: Rom 6L 129
CHAWTON 8E 80

Chawton Cl.—Churchill Cl.

Chawton Cl. GU51: Fleet .9H 27
SO18: South .2H 175
SO22: Winche .2H 105
Chawton End Cl. GU34: Four M .3K 97
Chawton House Library & Study Cen. .1D 98
Chawton Pk. Indoor Bowls Club .7D 80
Chawton Pk. Rd. GU34: Alt .8B 80
Chayofa Pl. PO12: Gos .1J 239
Cheam Way SO40: Tott .1K 171
Cheater's La. SP6: Lwr D, Sand .6P 149
Cheavley Cl. SP10: A'ver .1J 69
Cheddar Cl. SO19: South .7C 174
Cheddington Rd. BH9: Bour .2L 227
Chedworth Cres. PO6: Cosh .8B 200
Cheeryble Ho. PO1: Ports .9E 214
Cheesecombe Farm La.
GU33: Hawk .7M 113
Chelmarsh Gdns. SO50: Fair O .3A 162
Chelmer Ct. *RG21: B'toke .6E 42*
(off Loddon Dr.)
Chelmsford Rd. PO2: Ports .6G 214
Chelsea Gdns. BH8: Bour .8N 227
Chelsea Ho. *RG21: B'toke .6C 42*
(off Festival Pl.)
Chelsea Rd. PO5: S'sea .4E 240
Cheltenham Ct. SO17: South .1M 173
Cheltenham Cres. PO13: Lee S .9B 212
Cheltenham Gdns. SO30: Hed E .8N 161
Cheltenham Rd. BH12: Poole .9A 226
PO6: Cosh .9D 200
Chelveston Cres. SO16: South .7F 158
Chelwood Dr. GU47: Sandh .4B 18
Chelwood Ga. SO16: Bass .6L 159
Cheping Gdns. SO30: Botl .4D 176
Chepstow Cl. SO40: Tott .2J 171
SO53: Cha F .6N 131
Chepstow Ct. PO7: W'lle .9B 182
Chequer La. RG7: Stra S .3B 14
Chequers, The GU31: Nye .4K 147
Chequers Cl. SO41: Penn .3B 234
Chequers La. RG27: Eve .7H 17
Chequers Quay *PO10: Ems .9N 203*
(off Queen St.)
Chequers Rd. RG21: B'toke .6D 42
Cherberry Cl. GU51: Fleet .8N 27
Cherbourg Rd. SO50: E'leigh .2D 160
Cherford Rd. BH11: Bour .4F 226
CHERITON .8E 108
Cheriton BH4: Bour .3G 244
Cheriton Av. BH7: Bour .6F 228
SO18: South .3G 175
Cheriton Cl. PO8: Horn .3B 182
PO9: Hav .4D 202
RG26: Tadl .6H 11
SO22: Winche .5H 105
Cheriton La. SO24: Bis S .5H 109
SO24: Hin A .9H 109
Cheriton Lodge GU51: Fleet .8H 27
Cheriton Rd. PO4: S'sea .3K 241
PO12: Gos .3H 239
SO22: Winche .6H 237 (5H 105)
SO50: E'leigh .3D 160
Cheriton Way GU17: Blackw .8F 18
Cherque La. PO13: Lee S .8C 212
Cherque Way PO13: Lee S .8B 212
Cherrett Cl. BH11: Bour .2D 226
Cherries Dr. BH9: Bour .4J 227
Cherrimans Orchard GU27: Hasl .9N 103
Cherry Blossom Ct. PO2: Ports .9E 214
Cherry Cl. PO13: Lee S .2C 238
RG27: Hoo .1H 45
SO21: Sth W .3H 91
Cherry Drove SO50: Hor H .5N 161
Cherry Gdns. SO32: Bis W .4N 163
Cherrygarth Rd. PO15: Fare .8M 197
Cherryhill Gro. GU11: Alders .1H 65
Cherry Lodge GU12: Alders .1K 65
Cherry Orchard RG28: Whit .7H 55
SP10: A'ver .1M 69
Cherryton Gdns. SO45: Holb .5N 207
Cherry Tree Apartments PO7: W'lle .9L 181
Cherry Tree Av. GU27: Hasl .8N 103
PO8: Cowp .7B 182
PO14: Fare .9N 197
SP9: Tidw .7E 30
Cherry Tree Cl. BH24: St L .5A 186
GU9: Farnh .7E 64
GU14: Cov .7E 28
SO41: Ever .6L 233
Cherrytree Cl. GU47: Owl .4F 18
Cherry Tree Ct. BH25: New M .5C 232
SO31: Wars .8N 195
SO50: E'leigh .9C 132
Cherry Tree Dr. BH25: Bash .1N 231
Cherry Tree Holiday Caravan Pk.
PO11: H Isl .5L 243
Cherry Tree Rd. GU10: Rowl .8N 63
SP10: A'ver .9L 51
Cherry Tree Wlk. BH4: Bour .9G 247 (3H 245)
RG21: B'toke .3D 42
Cherry Wlk. SO15: South .2H 173
SO31: Wars .9N 195
Cherry Way GU34: Alt .3E 80
Cherrywood RG24: Chin .9F 22
SO30: Hed E .4M 175
Cherrywood Gdns. PO11: H Isl .3G 242
SO40: Tott .3J 171
SO50: B'stke .1M 161
Cherrywood Rd. GU14: Farn .5J 29
Chertsey St. GU51: Fleet .9K 27
Chervil Cl. PO8: Horn .1C 182
SO53: Cha F .6L 131
Cherville Ct. SO51: Rom .5L 129
Cherville M. SO51: Rom .4L 129
Cherville St. SO51: Rom .5L 129
Cherwell Cres. SO16: South .2D 172
Cherwell Gdns. SO53: Cha F .7B 132
Cherwell Ho. SO16: South .1D 172
Cheshire Cl. PO15: White .4J 197
Cheshire Dr. BH8: Bour .5D 228
Chesilbourne Gro. BH8: Bour .3A 228
Chesildene Av. BH8: Bour .3A 228
(not continuous)
Chesildene Dr. BH8: Bour .3N 227
Chesil Gdns. BH12: Poole .6A 226
Chesil St. SO23: Winche .9P 237 (7M 105)
Chesil Ter. SO23: Winche .9P 237 (7M 105)
Chesil Theatre .9P 237 (7M 105)
Chesilton Cres. GU52: Ch Cr .6M 47
Chesil Wood SO23: Winche .7N 105
Cheslyn Rd. PO3: Ports .1J 241
Chessel Av. BH5: Bour .1C 246
SO19: South .3C 174
Chessel Cres. SO19: South .3C 174
Chessington Ct. BH2: Bour .7H 247 (2H 245)
Chester Cl. PO10: Ems .8K 203
Chester Ct. SO16: South .9H 159
Chester Courts PO12: Gos .3L 239
Chester Cres. PO13: Lee S .3D 238
Chesterfield Cl. BH13: Poole .5D 244
SP4: Ames .5A 66
Chesterfield Ct. BH1: Bour .2A 246
Chesterfield Rd. PO3: Ports .8H 215
RG21: B'toke .8D 42
Chester Pl. PO5: S'sea .5E 240
RG21: B'toke .7B 42
Chester Rd. BH13: Poole .3E 244
SO18: South .1E 174
SO23: Winche .7P 237 (6M 105)
Chesterton Gdns. PO8: Cowp .7M 181
Chesterton Pl. PO15: White .1F 196
Chester Way GU10: Tong .4N 65
Chestnut Av. BH6: Bour .1F 246
BH23: Chri .6G 229
BH24: Har .3E 184
BH25: B Sea .6B 232
GU12: Alders .3N 65
PO4: S'sea .3G 240
PO8: Horn .5C 182
PO9: Bed .6B 202
SO21: Col C .3K 133
SO22: Lit .2F 104
SO40: Ashu .7J 171
SO50: E'leigh .2B 160
SO53: Cha F .9A 132
SP9: Tidw .7D 30
SP10: A'ver .4M 69
Chestnut Bank RG24: Old Bas .4J 43
Chestnut Cl. GU17: Blackw .9G 18
GU26: Gray .4L 103
GU30: Lip .3F 116
GU34: Alt .3E 80
GU51: Fleet .8A 28
PO7: Den .6G 181
SO30: Wes E .8H 161
SO51: Rom .6C 130
SO53: Cha F .9A 132
Chestnut Ct. GU12: Alders .9M 49
GU35: Bor .5K 101
PO9: R Cas .1H 203
SO17: South .9N 159
Chestnut Dr. GU31: Pet .3M 145
SO40: Ashu .7J 171
Chestnut End GU35: Head .3C 102
Chestnut Gro. BH25: New M .3C 232
GU51: Fleet .1N 47
Chestnut Lodge SO16: Bass .8K 159
Chestnut Mead SO23: Winche .9K 105
Chestnut M. SO19: South .6G 174
Chestnut Pl. SO20: Mid Wa .4B 72
Chestnut Ri. SO32: Drox .2K 165
SO50: E'leigh .2B 160
Chestnut Rd. GU14: Farn .7J 29
SO16: South .9F 158
SO42: Broc .7D 148
Chestnuts, The SO31: Loc H .7D 196
SP5: Br Ch .3A 118
SP5: E Gri .1F 120
Chestnut Sq. SO20: Mid Wa .4B 72
Chestnut Tree Gro. GU14: Cov .7E 28
Chestnut Vw. *GU14: Farn .2L 49*
(off Alexandra Rd.)
Chestnut Wlk. PO12: Gos .7J 213
SO24: New A .1F 108
SO30: Botl .3C 176
Chestnut Way BH23: Burt .3M 229
PO14: Titch C .8F 196
Cheswell Gdns. GU51: Ch Cr .5K 47
Chettle Rd. SO19: South .5J 175
Chetwode Pl. GU12: Alders .3L 65
Chetwode Ter. GU11: Alders .1G 64
Chetwynd Dr. SO16: Bass .7L 159
Chetwynd Rd. PO4: S'sea .4F 240
SO16: Bass .7L 159
Chevening Ct. PO4: S'sea .2J 241
Cheviot Cl. GU14: Cov .5G 29
RG14: New .1C 8
RG22: B'toke .8K 41
Cheviot Cres. SO16: South .2D 172
Cheviot Dr. GU51: Fleet .8N 27
SO45: Dib .6J 193
Cheviot Grn. SO31: Wars .9A 196
Cheviot Rd. GU47: Sandh .3B 18
SO16: South .2D 172
SP11: E Ant .6B 52
Cheviots, The BH14: Poole .2A 244
Cheviot Wlk. PO14: Fare .1B 212
Chevron Bus. Pk. SO45: Holb .2N 207
Chewter Cl. PO4: S'sea .6F 240
Chewton Bunny Nature Reserve .7K 231
Chewton Comn. Rd. BH23: Highc .5J 231
Chewton Farm Est. BH23: Highc .6L 231
Chewton Farm Rd. BH23: Walk .5L 231
Chewton Lodge BH23: Highc .6K 231
Chewton M. BH23: Walk .5J 231
Chewton Sound BH25: New M .7M 231
Chewton Way BH23: Walk .5K 231
Cheyne Ct. *BH4: Bour .1G 244*
(off Surrey Rd.)
Cheyne Gdns. BH4: Bour .3G 245
Cheyne Way GU14: Cov .5H 29
PO13: Lee S .2B 238
Cheyney Ct. SO23: Winche .9M 237
Chicheley Ct. GU14: Farn .6J 29
Chichester Av. PO11: H Isl .5F 242
Chichester Cl. PO13: Gos .6D 212
SO30: Hed E .1N 175
SO31: Sar G .6B 196
SO51: E Wel .1B 156
SP10: A'ver .1K 69
Chichester Ho. PO9: Hav .6G 202
Chichester Pl. RG22: B'toke .9N 41
Chichester Rd. BH24: Poul .8M 185
PO2: Ports .8E 214
PO11: H Isl .7J 217
SO18: South .3E 174
Chichester Way BH23: Mude .9C 230
Chickenhall La. SO50: E'leigh .9G 132
Chickerell Cl. BH9: Bour .2M 227
Chicks La. SN8: Co Du .2G 31
CHIDDEN .3G 167
Chidden Cl. GU32: E Meon .3L 143
Chidden Holt SO53: Cha F .7M 131
Chideock Cl. BH12: Poole .8C 226
Chideock Ct. BH12: Poole .8C 226
Chidham Cl. PO9: Hav .7E 202
Chidham Dr. PO9: Hav .7E 202
Chidham Rd. PO6: Cosh .8H 201
Chidham Sq. PO9: Hav .7E 202
Chidham Wlk. PO9: Hav .7E 202
Chigwell Rd. BH8: Bour .5M 227
CHILBOLTON .4F 74
Chilbolton Av. SO22: Winche .6G 105
Chilbolton Ct. PO9: Hav .3H 203
CHILCOMB .9C 106
Chilcomb Cl. PO13: Lee S .1B 238
Chilcombe Cl. PO9: Hav .6F 202
Chilcombe Hgts. *SO23: Winche .7M 105*
(off Quarry Rd.)
Chilcombe Rd. BH6: Bour .9E 228
Chilcomb La. SO21: Chilc .9A 106
SO23: Winche .9M 105
Chilcomb Rd. SO18: South .2G 174
Chilcote Rd. PO3: Ports .9H 215
Chilcott Ct. SO52: N Bad .8F 130
Childerstone Cl. GU30: Lip .2D 116
Childe Sq. PO2: Ports .6D 214
Chilgrove Rd. PO6: Dray .9K 201
Chilham Cl. SO50: E'leigh .5E 132
CHILLAND .9F 92
Chillandham La.
SO21: Itc A, Mar W .2F 92
(not continuous)
Chilland La. SO21: Mar W .9F 92
Chillenden Ct. SO40: Tott .4J 171
Chillerton SO31: Net A .2G 195
Chillingham Way GU15: Camb .9L 19
Chilling La. SO31: Wars .3B 210
Chillington Gdns. SO53: Cha F .3N 131
Chilmark Ct. GU33: Liss .1E 140
Chilsdown Way PO7: W'lle .5M 201
Chiltern Av. GU14: Cov .8F 28
Chiltern Cl. BH4: Bour .9F 226
BH25: B Sea .5A 232
GU14: Cov .8E 28
GU52: Ch Cr .5N 47
RG14: New .1C 8
SO40: Tott .5K 171
Chiltern Ct. *BH23: Chri .6B 230*
(off Hunt Rd.)
PO5: S'sea .6E 240
PO12: Gos .2K 239
SO24: New A .1F 108
Chiltern Dr. BH25: B Sea .6N 231
Chiltern Grn. SO16: South .2D 172
Chiltern Rd. GU47: Sandh .4B 18
Chiltern Wlk. PO14: Fare .1B 212
Chiltern Way RG22: B'toke .8J 41
Chiltlee Cl. GU30: Lip .2E 116
Chiltlee Mnr. GU30: Lip .3E 116
Chiltley La. GU30: Lip .4F 116
Chiltley Way GU30: Lip .3E 116
CHILTON CANDOVER .6D 78
Chilton Farm Pk. GU14: Cov .8E 28
Chilton Ridge RG22: B'toke .5K 59
CHILWORTH .2K 159
Chilworth Cl. SO16: Chilw .2J 159
Chilworth Drove SO16: Chilw, South .5G 159
SO16: South .6G 158
Chilworth Gdns. PO8: Clan .7C 168
Chilworth Golf Course .9G 131
Chilworth Grange SO16: Chilw .3M 159
Chilworth Gro. PO12: Gos .2J 239
CHILWORTH OLD VILLAGE .1H 159
Chilworth Rd. SO16: Bass, Chilw .2K 159
Chilworth Way RG27: Sher L .7H 23
Chine, The PO13: Gos .7G 212
Chine Av. SO19: South .5C 174
(not continuous)
Chine Cl. SO31: Loc H .5D 196
Chine Ct. BH2: Bour .8H 247
Chine Cres. BH2: Bour .8H 247 (3H 245)
Chine Cres. Ho. BH2: Bour .7H 247 (2H 245)
Chine Cres. Rd. BH2: Bour .9H 247 (3H 245)
Chinegate Mnr. BH1: Bour .1A 246
Chine Grange BH2: Bour .8G 247
CHINEHAM .1G 43
Chineham Bus. Pk. RG24: Chin .8F 22
Chineham Cl. GU51: Fleet .9H 27
Chineham La. RG24: B'toke .3D 42
RG24: B'toke, Sher J .1A 42
Chineham Pk. Ct. RG24: B'toke .3E 42
Chineham Shop. Cen. RG24: Chin .2G 42
Chine Mans. BH2: Bour .8G 247
Chines, The BH4: Bour .2G 244
Chinewood Mnr. *BH1: Bour .2A 246*
(off Manor Rd.)
Chingford Av. GU14: Farn .7L 29
Chinham Rd. SO40: Bart .4B 170
Chinnock Cl. GU52: Fleet .4L 47
Chippendale Cl. GU17: Haw .9G 18
RG26: Bau .4E 10
Chippenham Cl. RG23: Wort .7J 41
Chipping Dene *BH2: Bour .1K 245*
(off Wimborne Rd.)
Chipstead Ho. PO6: Cosh .9G 200
Chipstead Rd. PO6: Cosh .9G 200
Chirk Pl. SO51: Rom .5N 129
Chisels La. BH23: Nea .9D 220
Chisholm Cl. SO16: South .6E 158
Chislehurst Flats BH4: Bour .2G 244
Chislett Gdns. GU47: Sandh .5B 18
Chitty Rd. PO4: S'sea .5H 241
Chive Ct. GU14: Cov .8E 28
Chivers Cl. PO5: S'sea .4D 240
RG22: B'toke .8L 41
Chloe Gdns. BH12: Poole .7B 226
Chobham Rd. GU16: Frim .3N 29
CHOLDERTON .4F 66
Cholderton Rd. SP4: Chol .4G 66
SP4: New T .5E 66
SP11: Grat .5J 67
SP11: Quar .4H 67
Cholseley Dr. GU51: Fleet .9K 27
Chopin Rd. RG22: B'toke .2M 59
Chrisalex Ct. PO8: Cowp .7A 182
Chrismas Av. GU12: Alders .1L 65
Chrismas Pl. GU12: Alders .1L 65
CHRISTCHURCH .8L 229
Christchurch Bay Rd.
BH25: B Sea .7A 232
Christchurch By-Pass BH23: Chri .7L 229
Christchurch Castle .8L 229
Christchurch Cl. GU52: Ch Cr .7L 47
Christchurch Dr. GU17: Blackw .7E 18
Christchurch Gdns. PO7: Wid .7J 201
SO23: Winche .9K 105
Christchurch Priory .8L 229
Christchurch Rd. BH1: Bour .2M 245
BH7: Bour .9C 228
BH23: Hurn .9E 218
BH24: King, Ring .1J 187
BH25: New M .6M 231
SO23: Winche .9K 237 (9J 105)
SO41: Ever .6L 233
Christchurch Sailing Club .9L 229
Christchurch Station (Rail) .7K 229
Christie Av. PO15: White .1F 196
Christie Wlk. GU46: Yat .9M 17
Christine Cl. GU12: Ash .1N 65
Christmas Hill SO21: Sth W, Sut S .9D 76
Christopher Ct. SP11: Quar .3L 67
Christopher Way PO10: Ems .7M 203
Christy Ct. RG26: Tadl .6J 11
Christy Est. GU12: Alders .9M 49
Christyne Ct. PO7: Purb .4L 201
Chubbs M. BH12: Poole .9A 226
Chudleigh Ct. GU14: Farn .8K 29
Church Av. GU14: Farn .8L 29
Church Bank Rd. SO21: E Str .7L 77
Church Barns SO21: E Str .7M 77
Church Brook RG26: Tadl .7G 10
Church Circ. GU14: Farn .1L 49
Church Cl. GU33: Liss .1D 140
PO8: Clan .5B 168
SO31: Loc H .6E 196
SO43: Mins .9M 155
SO50: B'stke .8H 133
SO52: N Bad .8F 130
SP10: A'ver .1A 70
SP11: Abb A .6G 68
CHURCH COMMON .5L 139
Church Cotts. GU9: Bad L .4J 65
GU33: Blackm .8E 100
Church Ct. GU51: Fleet .2K 47
(Church Gro.)
GU51: Fleet .2L 47
(St Nicholas Cl.)
CHURCH CROOKHAM .6M 47
CHURCH END .6K 23
Church End SO15: South .2H 173
Churcher Cl. PO12: Gos .4F 238
Churcher Wlk. PO12: Gos .4F 238
Church Farm SP6: F'dge .2J 153
Church Farm Caravan Site SO45: Dib .3G 192
Church Farm Cl. RG25: Nth W .8A 58
SO45: Dib .3G 192
Churchfield Ct. GU30: Lip .3D 116
Churchfield Rd. GU31: Pet .9A 140
Church Flds. GU35: Head .2N 101
Churchfields GU35: K'ly .7G 83
SO21: Twyf .7L 127
SO45: Fawl .5F 208
Churchfields La. BH24: Har .7H 153
Churchfields Rd. SO21: Twyf .7K 127
Church Ga. *SP11: Ludg .1C 30*
(off Chapel La.)
Church Grn. Cl. SO23: Kin W .1N 105
Church Gro. GU51: Fleet .2K 47
Church Hatch
SP5: Down .1L 119 (7B 120)
Church Hill GU12: Alders .2K 65
GU15: Camb .8N 19
SO20: N Wal .1A 88
SO30: Wes E .9G 160
SO41: M Sea .7L 235
SP5: Lover, Redl .2N 119 (8D 120)
Church Hill Ter. *GU10: Cron .3L 63*
(off Church St.)
Churchill Av. GU12: Alders .2L 65
RG29: Odi .1E 62
SO32: Bis W .2K 163
SP4: Bul .3A 66
Churchill Cl. GU14: Farn .4K 29
GU34: Alt .6F 80
GU34: Four M .4J 97
PO14: Titch C .8F 196
RG26: Tadl .6K 11
RG27: H Win .5A 26
RG29: Odi .2E 62
(off Churchill Av.)
SO23: Kin W .6M 91
SP6: Ald .5B 152
SP9: Tidw .6B 30 (6F 30)

Churchill Ct. BH1: Bour 1B 246
BH25: New M 4A 232
PO6: Farl 9M 201
PO8: Horn 4A 182
Churchill Cres. BH12: Poole 8A 226
GU14: Farn 4K 29
GU35: Head 3B 102
GU46: Yat 8N 17
Churchill Dr. PO10: Ems 5M 203
Churchill Drove BH21: Cran 6L 149
Churchill Gdns. BH12: Poole 9B 226
Churchill Ho. SO18: South 2G 175
Churchill M. *PO12: Gos 1J 239*
(off Forton Rd.)
Churchill Plaza RG21: B'toke 6D 42
Churchill Rd. BH1: Bour 9A 228
BH12: Poole 9A 226
Churchill Sq. PO4: S'sea 5J 241
Churchill Way RG21: B'toke 6C 42
SP10: A'ver 9A 52
Churchill Way E. RG21: B'toke 6D 42
Churchill Way W. RG21: B'toke 6N 41
RG22: B'toke 6M 41
SP10: A'ver 1H 69
Churchill Yd. Ind. Est. PO7: W'lle 9L 181
Church Lands RG26: B'ley 1E 22
Churchlands GU11: Alders 2K 65
Church La. BH23: Chri 8L 229
BH24: Bur 7E 188
BH25: New M 5A 232
GU10: Ben'ly 7K 63
GU10: Ews 1N 63
GU10: Rowl 8N 63
GU14: Cov 8G 28
GU26: Gray 4L 103
GU30: B'sht 9D 102
GU32: W Meo 8C 136
GU33: Emp 3N 113
GU33: G'ham 3C 114
GU34: Holy 1J 81
GU34: Meds 9K 79
GU34: Priv 2K 137
GU35: Head 1N 101
PO7: H'don 7D 166
PO9: Warb 9H 203
PO11: H Isl 5J 217
RG7: Sil 6C 12
RG17: Comb 4G 7
RG20: Burgh 3E 8
RG20: High 4A 8
(Star La.)
RG20: High 6A 8
(Highclere Castle)
RG20: Wol H 3N 7
RG21: B'toke 6C 42
RG23: Wort 7J 41
RG24: Old Bas 5J 43
RG25: Clid 3B 60
RG25: Elli 9C 60
RG26: Bau 9E 10
RG26: Wolve 6M 9
RG27: Dogm 7E 46
RG27: H Win 8C 26
RG27: Heck 7G 15
RG40: F'std 1H 17
SN8: B'mre 3E 6
SO14: South 7C 4 (7L 173)
SO16: Nur 5M 157
SO17: South 9N 159
SO20: Houg 5E 88
SO21: Col C 4K 133
SO21: E'ton 1C 106
SO21: Mar W 9E 92
SO21: Owls 3G 134
SO21: Spar 3A 104
SO21: Twyf 6L 127
SO22: Lit 9E 90
SO23: Kin W 9N 91
SO24: B Can 6B 78
SO24: Bis S 2K 109
SO24: Bram 1N 135
SO24: B'wth 3G 134
SO24: Rop 2D 110
SO30: Botl 5D 176
SO30: Hed E 5M 175
SO31: Burs 1M 195
SO32: Curd 2G 176
SO32: Durl 5C 162
SO32: Ext 8N 135
SO32: Swanm 5E 164
SO41: Bold, Pil 4D 224
SO41: Lymi 3E 234
SO41: Sway 6J 223
SO42: Beau 1B 236
SO42: Broc 9D 148
SO43: Lyn 2B 148 (2N 189)
SO45: Fawl 5E 208
SO51: Awb 9D 122
SO51: Brai 6B 124
SO51: Mott 4F 122
SO51: Plai 8L 121
SO51: Rom 5L 129
SO51: Sher E 5M 121
SP5: Bish 2E 118
SP5: Ch St 4A 120
SP5: P'tn 6E 86
(off High St.)
SP5: W Tyt 8L 87
SP6: Dame 7A 150
SP9: Tidw 9D 30 (8G 31)
SP11: Abb A 5F 68
SP11: G Cla 8N 69
SP11: Ludg 1C 30
SP11: Up C 6M 69
SP11: Ver D, Ver S 7D 6
Church La. Cnr. SO41: Pil 6F 224
Church La. E. GU11: Alders 1J 65
Church La. W. GU11: Alders 1H 65
Church Leat SP5: Down 1K 119 (7A 120)
Church Mead SO41: Lymi 4E 234
Churchmeadows SP9: Shi B 1B 66 (1G 66)

Church M. GU34: Alt 4F 80
GU46: Yat 6N 17
PO4: S'sea 5H 241
(off Priory Rd.)
SP11: An V 5J 69
Church Pas. GU9: Farnh 8D 64
Church Path GU14: Cov 8G 28
GU14: Farn 3L 49
(Queen's Rd.)
GU14: Farn 8L 29
(Rectory Rd.)
PO8: Horn 4D 182
PO9: Warb 1H 217
PO10: Ems 1K 217
(Maisemore Gdns.)
PO10: Ems 9M 203
(St James' Rd.)
PO12: Gos 3M 239
PO14: Titch 9K 197
PO16: Fare 8E 198
RG24: Sher J 8N 21
RG27: Hoo 3F 44
RG27: Newn 2C 44
SO17: South 9N 159
SO19: South 7E 174
Church Path Nth. PO1: Ports 1E 240
Church Pl. PO16: Fare 7E 198
SO51: Rom 5L 129
Church Rd. BH6: Bour 2J 247
GU11: Alders 3L 65
GU16: Frim 3M 29
GU30: B'sht 9E 102
GU32: Ste 6K 139
GU34: Up Farr 4E 98
GU47: Owl 4G 18
GU47: Sandh 4B 18
GU51: Fleet 1K 47
PO1: Ports 1E 240
(not continuous)
PO10: Westb 6N 203
PO11: H Isl 3G 242
PO12: Gos 5J 239
PO14: Titch C 6G 196
PO16: Portc 2N 213
PO17: Newt 2K 179
PO31: Cowes 5P 237
RG7: Mor W 1B 12
RG20: Wol H 3N 7
RG25: Nth W 9A 58
RG25: Over 2D 56
RG26: Pam H 4L 11
RG26: Tadl 6H 11
RG27: Eve 7E 16
SO19: South 9B 174
SO20: Ki S 9B 86 (7G 88)
SO20: Longs 8H 73
SO20: N Wal 1A 88
SO31: Loc H 6E 196
SO31: Wars 8A 196
SO32: Shed 3N 177
SO32: Swanm 5C 164
SO50: B'stke 9H 133
SO51: Mich 3K 123
SO51: Rom 5L 129
SP4: Idm 9C 66
SP5: Far 8F 86
Church Rd. E. GU14: Farn 2M 49
RG45: Cr'tne 1D 18
Church Rd. Rdbt. PO11: H Isl 1G 242
Church Rd. W. GU14: Farn 2L 49
RG45: Cr'tne 1D 18
Church Sq. RG21: B'toke 6C 42
Church St. *BH21: Cran 6J 149*
(off The Square)
BH23: Chri 8L 229
GU10: Cron 3L 63
GU11: Alders 9H 49
GU32: E Meon 3M 143
GU33: Liss 8D 114
GU34: Alt 4F 80
GU34: Bent 6L 79
PO1: Ports 9D 214
PO14: Titch 9K 197
RG21: B'toke 6C 42
(not continuous)
RG25: Up G 3A 62
RG28: Whit 6F 54
RG29: Odi 8K 45
(not continuous)
RG45: Cr'tne 1D 18
SN8: Co Du 2H 31
SO15: South 2G 173
SO21: M'dvr, Mich S 7H 77
SO24: Rop 2D 110
SO32: Uph 8E 134
SO51: Rom 5L 129
SP5: W Gri 2E 120
SP6: F'dge 2H 153
SP11: Hur T 4D 34
SP11: S M Bo 1M 53
SP11: Wher 2F 74
Church Vw. GU46: Yat 6N 17
PO4: S'sea 3H 241
PO10: Westb 6N 203
RG27: H Win 8B 26
RG27: Hoo 2H 45
RG29: S War 4C 62
SO32: Shed 3B 178
SO50: E'leigh 2E 160
SP11: Up C 5L 69
Churchview SO19: South 7E 174
Church Vw. Cl. SO19: South 7E 174
Church Wlk. SP5: Lover 8E 120
Churchward Gdns. SO30: Hed E 9N 161
Churchyard Cotts. SO24: New A 9F 94
Churn Cl. RG24: Old Bas 4J 43
Chur St. SP4: Bul C 3B 66
CHURT 7H 85
Churt Rd. GU10: Chur 7H 85
GU26: Hind 7H 85
GU35: Head D 1C 102

Churt Wynde GU26: Hind 9M 85
CHUTE CADLEY 4D 32
Chute Causeway
SP11: Chu S, Co Du, Conh 9A 6
Chute Cl. RG26: B'ley 9G 13
CHUTE FOREST 7B 32
Chute Hill SO21: Spar 6N 89
Chute Ho. *RG21: B'toke 6C 42*
(off Festival Pl.)
CHUTE STANDEN 3B 32
Cibbons Rd. RG24: Chin 9G 23
Cinderford Cl. PO6: Cosh 8D 200
Cineworld Cinema
Aldershot 9J 49
Southampton 9F 4 (8N 173)
Cinnamon Ct. SO15: South 1A 4 (4K 173)
SO18: South 2C 174
Circle, The BH9: Bour 2L 227
BH13: Poole 6D 244
PO5: S'sea 5E 240
PO17: Wick 6B 178
Circular Rd. PO1: Ports 2L 5 (9C 214)
Circus, The PO17: S'wick 7B 200
Cirrus Gdns. SO31: Hamb 7K 195
City Bus. Cen. SO23: Winche 6M 237 (6L 105)
City Commerce Cen. SO14: South 7F 4 (7N 173)
City Ct. SO14: South 8D 4
City Cruise Terminal 7A 4 (7K 173)
City Gym 2G 173
City Ind. Pk. SO15: South 5A 4 (6K 173)
City Mill 8P 237 (7M 105)
City Mus. 8M 237 (7L 105)
City Mus. & Art Gallery 7L 5 (4C 240)
City Records Office *4N 5*
(off Guildhall Sq.)
City Rd. SO23: Winche 6L 237 (6K 105)
City Wall Ho. RG21: B'toke 5E 42
Civic Cen. Rd. PO9: Hav 7F 202
SO14: South 5L 173
SO15: South 4B 4 (5L 173)
Civic Way PO16: Fare 8E 198
Clack La. SP6: R'bne 4D 150
Clacton Rd. PO6: Cosh 9E 200
Claire Ct. BH23: Highc 7J 231
Claire Gdns. PO8: Horn 9C 168
Clamp Grn. SO21: Col C 4K 133
Clandon Ct. GU14: Farn 9M 29
Clandon Dr. SO50: E'leigh 6D 132
CLANFIELD 5B 168
Clanfield Cl. SO53: Cha F 6B 132
Clanfield Dr. SO53: Cha F 6B 132
Clanfield Ho. PO1: Ports 1E 240
Clanfield Ride GU17: Blackw 8F 18
Clanfield Rd. SO18: South 3G 175
Clanfield Way SO53: Cha F 6B 132
CLANVILLE 3D 50
Clanville Ri. RG27: Sher L 7H 23
Clanwilliam Rd. PO13: Lee S 1B 238
Clappers Farm Rd. RG7: Sil 4E 12
Clappsgate Rd. RG26: Pam H 4L 11
Clare Cl. PO14: Titch C 7F 196
Clare Ct. GU51: Fleet 2M 47
Clare Gdns. GU31: Pet 1B 146
SO45: Blac 9D 208
Clare Ho. PO12: Gos 9H 213
Clare Lodge Cl. BH23: Bran 6C 220
Claremont Av. BH9: Bour 4M 227
Claremont Cl. SO50: E'leigh 6E 132
Claremont Cres. SO15: South 3F 172
Claremont Gdns. PO7: Purb 5M 201
Claremont Pl. GU17: Haw 1H 29
Claremont Rd. BH9: Bour 4M 227
PO1: Ports 2F 240
SO15: South 3F 172
Clarence Cl. GU12: Alders 9L 49
SP11: Ludg 1C 30
Clarence Ct. GU51: Fleet 2M 47
Clarence Esplanade PO5: S'sea 9L 5 (5C 240)
Clarence Ho. SO14: South 4A 174
Clarence Pde. PO5: S'sea 9M 5 (5C 240)
Clarence Pk. Rd. BH7: Bour 8D 228
Clarence Pier Amusement Pk. 9K 5 (5B 240)
Clarence Pl. BH23: Chri 6K 229
Clarence Rd. GU51: Fleet 3L 47
PO5: S'sea 5E 240
PO12: Gos 3M 239
SO43: Lyn 2B 148
Clarence St. PO1: Ports 1N 5 (1D 240)
Clarence Wharf PO12: Gos 2M 239
Clarendon Av. SP10: A'ver 3L 69
Clarendon Cl. PO7: Den 5G 180
SO51: Rom 3A 130
Clarendon Ct. *BH4: Bour 3H 245*
(off Clarendon Rd.)
GU17: Haw 1F 28
GU51: Fleet 2L 47
PO5: S'sea 6E 240
(off Clarendon Rd.)
SP9: Tidw 7D 30
Clarendon Cres. PO14: Titch C 8E 196
Clarendon Pk. SO41: Lymi 4D 234
Clarendon Pl. PO1: Ports 2D 240
(Arundel St.)
PO1: Ports 1E 240
(Clarendon St.)
Clarendon Rd. BH4: Bour 7G 247 (3H 245)
BH23: Chri 7K 229
PO4: S'sea 6F 240
PO5: S'sea 5D 240
SO16: South 2F 172
SP5: Alder, W Gri 9C 86 & 1D 120
Clarendon St. PO1: Ports 1E 240
Clarendon Way SO22: Winche 6E 104
Clarewood Dr. GU15: Camb 7N 19
Clark Ct. BH12: Poole 9B 226
Clarke Cres. GU15: Camb 6G 19
CLARKEN GREEN 9A 40
Clarke's La. SP11: Tang 5F 32
Clarke's Rd. PO1: Ports 1G 240
Clark M. RG28: Whit 6G 54
Clarks Cl. BH24: Ring 1K 187

Clarks Hill GU10: Dipp 5N 63
Clatford Mnr. SP11: Up C 5L 69
CLATFORD OAKCUTS 4G 73
Claude Ashby Cl. SO18: S'ing 7C 160
Claudeen Cl. SO18: S'ing 6C 160
Claudeen Ct. SO18: South 4J 175
Claudia Ct. PO12: Gos 1H 239
Claudius Cl. SO53: Cha F 5D 132
SP10: A'ver 6A 52
Claudius Dr. RG23: B'toke 4L 41
Claudius Gdns. SO53: Cha F 5D 132
Clausentum Cl. SO53: Cha F 5C 132
Clausentum Rd. SO14: South 3M 173
SO23: Winche 9K 105
Clausen Way SO41: Penn 5C 234
Claxton St. PO1: Ports 2E 240
Claybank Rd. PO3: Ports 7H 215
Claybank Spur PO3: Ports 7H 215
Claycart Rd. GU11: Alders 7F 48
Claydon Av. PO4: S'sea 3H 241
Claydon Gdns. GU17: Haw 3J 29
Clayfields Sports Cen. 5J 193
CLAYHALL 5L 239
Clayhall Rd. PO12: Gos 5J 239
CLAYHILL 4C 148
Clayhill Cl. SO32: Wal C 7N 163
Claylands Ct. SO32: Bis W 3L 163
Claylands Rd. SO32: Bis W 3L 163
Claylands Rd. Ind. Est.
SO32: Bis W 3L 163
Claypit La. GU32: Frox 8C 112
Claypit Rd. SO51: Ampf 6H 125
CLAYPITS 9M 175
Claypits La. SO45: Dib 6H 193
Clay's La. GU34: Bins 1N 81
GU34: E Wor 7L 81
Clay St. SP5: W'psh 5H 121
Claythorpe Rd. RG22: B'toke 8L 41
Clayton Cl. RG27: H Win 7B 26
Clayton Rd. GU14: Cov 3H 29
SP4: Bul 3A 66
Clearbury Vw. SP5: Down 2H 119
Clearwater Apartments
PO4: S'sea 6F 240
Cleasby Cl. SO16: South 3D 172
Cleasby Grange *BH5: Bour 2C 246*
(off Wollstonecraft Rd.)
Clease Way SO21: Comp 6G 127
Cleaver Rd. RG22: B'toke 8L 41
Clee Av. PO14: Fare 9N 197
Cleek Dr. SO16: Bass 6L 159
Cleethorpes Rd. SO19: South 6F 174
Cleeve Cl. PO6: Cosh 8C 200
Cleeve Rd. RG24: B'toke 1C 42
Cleeves, The SO40: Tott 4J 171
Cleeves Cl. BH12: Poole 4B 226
Clegg Rd. PO4: S'sea 4H 241
Clematis Cl. BH23: Chri 5E 230
Clement Attlee Way PO6: Cosh 9C 200
Clement Ct. GU34: Alt 8D 80
Clementina Ct. BH23: Chri 8J 229
Clement M. BH4: Bour 2F 244
Clements Cl. GU34: Bins 1D 82
Clements Gdns. RG28: Whit 5G 54
Clems Way SO51: Lock 4A 122
Clench St.
SO14: South 7F 4 (7N 173)
Clere Ct. RG20: Kings 2A 6
Clere Gdns. RG24: Chin 1G 43
Cleric Ct. PO14: Titch C 6G 196
Clevedge Way RG29: N War 7J 45
Clevedon Ct. GU14: Farn 9M 29
Cleveland Cl. BH25: B Sea 7M 231
RG22: B'toke 8K 41
Cleveland Ct. BH2: Bour 8H 247 (3H 245)
SO18: South 1E 174
Cleveland Dr. PO14: Fare 9N 197
SO45: Dib P 7J 193
Cleveland Gdns. BH1: Bour 9N 227
Cleveland Pl. BH23: Chri 6B 230
Cleveland Rd. BH1: Bour 9A 228
PO5: S'sea 3F 240
PO12: Gos 4K 239
SO18: South 9D 160
Clevelands Cl. SO53: Cha F 3N 131
Cleverley Ho. PO1: Ports 4J 5
Cleves La. RG25: Up G 3A 62
CLEWERS HILL 7A 164
Clewers Hill SO32: Wal C 7N 163
Clewers La. SO32: Wal C 7N 163
CLIDDESDEN 3B 60
Cliddesden Ct. RG21: B'toke 9C 42
Cliddesden La. RG22: B'toke 5K 59
Cliddesden Rd. RG21: B'toke 9C 42
(not continuous)
Cliff, The *SO19: South 7B 174*
(off Portsmouth Rd.)
Cliff Cres. BH25: B Sea 7A 232
Cliffdale Gdns. PO6: Cosh 8H 201
Cliff Dr. BH13: Poole 7C 244
BH23: Fri C 8E 230
Cliffe Av. SO31: Hamb 6J 195
Cliffe Rd. BH25: B Sea 7N 231
Clifford Dibben M.
SO14: South 2M 173
Clifford Pl. SO50: Fair O 1N 161
Clifford Rd. BH9: Bour 5L 227
Clifford St. SO14: South 4F 4 (5N 173)
Cliff Rd. PO14: Stub 7H 211
PO31: Cowes 5N 237
SO15: South 5J 173
SO41: M Sea 9G 233 & 8H 235
Cliff Ter. BH25: B Sea 8A 232
Cliff Wlk. *BH4: Bour 3G 244*
(off West Cliff Rd.)
Cliff Way SO21: Comp 7H 127
Clifton Cres. PO7: Den 6J 181
Clifton Gdns. SO15: South 2F 172
SO18: Wes E 1G 174
Clifton Hill SO22: Winche 7K 237 (6K 105)
Clifton M. PO16: Fare 7E 198

Clifton Rd.—Compton Sq.

Clifton Rd. BH6: Bour 2G 246
BH14: Poole 3B 244
PO5: S'sea 9N 5 (5D 240)
PO13: Lee S 3C 238
SO15: South 2F 172
SO22: Winche 6K 237 (6J 105)
Clifton St. PO1: Ports 1F 240
PO12: Gos 1H 239
Clifton Ter. PO5: S'sea 5D 240
RG21: B'toke 5C 42
SO22: Winche 7K 237 (6K 105)
Clifton Wlk. RG21: B'toke 6C 42
(off Festival Pl.)
Climaur Ct. PO5: S'sea 5E 240
Clingan Rd. BH6: Bour 8G 228
Clinkley Rd. SO24: W Tis 7D 110
Clinton Cl. BH23: Walk 4K 231
Clinton Rd. PO7: W'lle 7K 181
SO41: Lymi 1E 234
Clipper Cl. SO31: Wars 8B 196
Clipper Ho. SO14: South 6G 4
Clitheroe Rd. GU17: Min 3B 28
Clive Ct. BH4: Bour 2G 245
(off Marlborough Rd.)
Clive Gro. PO16: Portc 1L 213
Clive Rd. BH9: Bour 5K 227
BH23: Chri 4F 230
GU12: Alders 1M 65
PO1: Ports 1F 240
Clock Ho. PO7: W'lle 2M 201
Clock House, The SO40: Calm 9G 157
Clockhouse Rd. GU14: Farn 8K 29
Clockhouse Rdbt. GU14: Farn 8K 29
Clock St. PO1: Ports 4J 5 (2B 240)
Clocktower Dr. PO4: S'sea 5J 241
Cloisters, The BH23: Chri 8L 229
BH24: Hight 2M 187
GU16: Frim 3M 29
GU34: Alt 4E 80
PO15: Fare 7M 197
SO16: Bass 8M 159
SO41: Lymi 3D 234
SO51: Rom 3L 129
SP10: A'ver 1N 69
CLOSE, THE 9M 237 (7L 105)
Close, The BH24: A'ley 4G 186
BH24: Ring 1J 187
BH24: St I 4D 186
BH25: B Sea 6C 232
GU9: Farnh 9F 64
GU16: Frim 4L 29
GU30: Lip 4E 116
GU32: Lang 1C 144
GU47: Coll 5G 19
PO6: Cosh 1H 215
PO14: Titch 1J 211
PO16: Portc 9L 199
RG23: B'toke 4M 41
RG26: M She 6K 21
RG29: Odi 9K 45
SO18: South 3H 175
SO30: Hed E 4M 175
SO31: Hamb 5L 195
SO41: Sway 5H 223
SO45: Holb 5B 208
SO50: B'dge 3H 133
SP5: M Val 1M 119 (7C 120)
SP6: W'bry 9J 119
SP11: Hath 9J 33
Closewood Rd. PO7: Den 9H 181
Closeworth Rd. GU14: Farn 3N 49
Cloudbank SO21: Sth W 3G 91
Clough La. BH24: Bur 7D 188
SP5: Mid W 4G 87
Clough's Rd. BH24: Ring 1L 187
Clouston Rd. GU14: Cov 7H 29
Clovelly Dr. GU26: Hind 9L 85
Clovelly Pk. GU26: Hind 9L 85
Clovelly Rd. GU26: Hind 1L 103
PO4: S'sea 3H 241
PO10: Ems 9L 203
PO11: H Isl 4J 217
SO14: South 2E 4 (4M 173)
Cloverbank SO23: Kin W 5M 91
Clover Cl. BH23: Chri 6D 230
GU35: Lind 2M 101
PO13: Gos 6E 212
SO31: Loc H 7B 196
Clover Ct. BH25: A'ley 2E 232
PO7: W'lle 3A 202
Clover Fld. RG24: Lych 4G 42
Clover Gdns. SP11: Ludg 1D 30
Clover La. GU46: Yat 7K 17
Clover Leaf Way RG24: Old Bas 7J 43
Clover M. SP10: A'ver 2A 70
Clover Nooke SO15: South 2B 172
Clover Rd. PO9: Hav 3C 202
Clovers, The BH12: Poole 6E 226
Clover Way SO30: Hed E 4L 175
SO51: Rom 4B 130
Clowes Av. BH6: Bour 2L 247
Clubhouse La. SO32: Wal C 8N 163
Clubhouse Rd. GU11: Alders 6H 49
Club La. SP9: Tidw 9C 30 (8G 30)
Cluster Ind. Est. PO4: S'sea 2G 241
Clydebank Rd. PO2: Ports 8E 214
Clyde Ct. PO12: Gos 1H 239
SP10: A'ver 8B 52
Clyde Ho. SO14: South 5A 174
Clyde Rd. PO12: Gos 1H 239
Clydesdale Rd. PO15: White 2E 196
Clydesdale Way SO40: Tott 2H 171
Coach Hill PO14: Titch 9J 197
Coach Hill Cl. SO53: Cha F 5N 131
Coach Hill La. BH24: Bur 6D 188
Coach Ho. PO4: S'sea 3K 241
Coach Ho. Cl. GU16: Frim 1N 29
Coach Ho. Gdns. GU51: Fleet 9M 27
Coach Ho. Pl. BH1: Bour 9L 227
Coachmakers M. SO51: Rom 5L 129
Coachmans Copse SO18: South 9E 160
Coachmans Gro. GU47: Sandh 6D 18
Coachmans Halt PO7: H'don 9D 166
Coach Rd. BH21: Wim G 7E 148
SO31: Hamb 7J 195
Coach Road, The SP5: E Tyt, W Tyt 8L 87
Coachways SP10: A'ver 3N 69
Coal Pk. La. SO31: Lwr Swan 1A 196
Coalporters Amateur Rowing Club 4A 174
Coalville Rd. SO19: South 6F 174
Coal Yd. Rd. PO4: S'sea 2G 240
Coastguard Cl. PO12: Gos 5H 239
Coastguard Cotts. BH25: B Sea 6N 231
PO9: Langs 2F 216
Coastguard Way BH23: Mude 9B 230
Coastside BH4: Bour 4G 245
Coate Dr. SO21: Wor D 5G 91
Coates Cl. RG22: B'toke 1A 60
Coates Rd. SO19: South 6H 175
Coates Way PO7: W'lle 4M 201
Coat Gdns. SO45: Hythe 6M 193
Cobalt Ct. PO13: Gos 1E 238
Cobalt Quarter SO14: South 9G 4
Cobb Dr. SP11: E Ant 6B 52
Cobbett Cl. SO22: Winche 9G 105
SO32: Swanm 6D 164
Cobbett Ct. SO18: South 3C 174
Cobbett Grn. RG22: B'toke 9N 41
Cobbett Rd. SO18: South 3C 174
Cobbetts, The GU34: Alt 6E 80
Cobbett's La. GU17: Blackw 8B 18
GU46: Yat 8B 18
Cobbetts M. GU9: Farnh 8D 64
(off The Hart)
Cobbetts Ridge GU10: Farnh 9L 65
Cobbett's Vw. RG20: Burgh 3D 8
Cobbett Way SO30: Botl 3C 176
Cobb La. SP5: W Win 4F 86
Cobbles Cl. SO21: Sut S 7D 76
(off Stockbridge Rd.)
Cobblewood PO10: Ems 6M 203
Cobbs Holiday Pk. BH23: Highc 6J 231
Cobden Av. PO3: Ports 8H 215
SO18: South 1B 174
Cobden Bri. SO17: South 1B 174
SO18: South 1B 174
Cobden Ct. SO18: South 2C 174
Cobden Cres. SO18: South 2D 174
Cobden Gdns. SO18: South 1C 174
Cobden Hgts. SO18: South 1C 174
Cobden Ri. SO18: South 1C 174
Cobden St. PO12: Gos 2K 239
Cobham Gro. PO15: White 4H 197
Cobham Rd. BH9: Bour 3L 227
Coblands Av. SO40: Tott 3K 171
Cobley Cl. SP5: W'ytes 1F 148
Cob Mews SP11: Amp 3B 68
Coburg Ho. SO14: South 4A 174
Coburg St. PO1: Ports 2E 240
SO14: South 4A 174
Cochrane Cl. PO13: Gos 1F 238
Cochrane Ho. PO1: Ports 4J 5 (2B 240)
Cock-A-Dobby GU47: Sandh 4C 18
Cockerell Cl. PO15: Seg 4F 196
Cockerell Ho. PO13: Lee S 2A 238
Cocket's Mead SO21: E'ton 2D 106
Cockey Down Nature Reserve 6A 86
Cockleshell Cl. SO31: Wars 8B 196
Cockleshell Gdns. PO4: S'sea 4K 241
Cockleshell Sq. PO12: Gos 2M 239
Cocklydown La. SO40: Tott 6K 171
Cockshott La. GU32: Frox 3H 139
Codgoan Pl. GU30: Lip 4E 116
(off Station Rd.)
Codrington Ho. PO1: Ports 3J 5
Cody Ct. GU14: Farn 5L 29
Cody Rd. GU14: Cov 9H 29
Cody Technology Pk. GU14: Farn 3E 48
(Buccaneer Way)
GU14: Farn 2C 48
(The Romany)
Coe Cl. GU11: Alders 1J 65
Coghlan Cl. PO16: Fare 7D 198
Coker Cl.
SO22: Winche 6J 237 (6K 105)
Colbeck GU52: Ch Cr 7N 47
Colborne Cl. SO41: Lymi 1E 234
Colbourne Cl. BH23: Bran 7C 220
Colbourne Ct. SO23: Winche 4L 105
Colbred Cnr. GU51: Fleet 8A 28
Colbred Wlk. SP11: E Ant 6C 52
Colburn Cl. SO16: South 9C 158
COLBURY 8K 171
Colbury Gro. PO9: Hav 4C 202
Colchester Av. SO50: B'stke 8J 133
Colchester Rd. PO6: Cosh 8E 200
COLD ASH HILL 9F 102
Coldeast Cl. SO31: Sar G 4B 196
Coldeast Way SO31: Sar G 4C 196
COLDEN COMMON 4L 133
Colden La. SO24: Old A 6G 94
Coldharbour RG25: Nth W 9A 58
Cold Harbour Cl. PO17: Wick 6B 178
Cold Harbour Cotts. RG25: Clid 3A 60
Cold Harbour Ct. SP10: A'ver 2A 70
Coldharbour Farm Rd. PO10: Ems 8M 203
Cold Harbour La. GU14: Cov 4G 29
Coldharbour La. SO16: Nur 3N 157
Coldhill La. PO8: Love 3M 181
Coldridge Ride SP11: Chu F 3N 31
Cole Av. GU11: Alders 8H 49
Colebrook Av. PO3: Ports 8J 215
SO15: South 1H 173
Colebrook Pl. SO23: Winche 9P 237 (7M 105)
Colebrook St. SO23: Winche 8N 237 (7L 105)
Colebrook Way SP10: A'ver 2K 69
Cole Cl. SP10: A'ver 6N 51
Coleford Bri. Rd. GU16: Mytc 8M 29
COLE HENLEY 8H 37
Cole Hill SO32: Sob 6K 165
Colehill Cres. BH9: Bour 3M 227
Colehill Gdns. SO32: Bis W 3K 163
Coleman Cl. RG21: B'toke 4D 42
Coleman Rd. BH11: Bour 3E 226
GU12: Alders 1M 65
Coleman St. SO14: South 5F 4 (6N 173)
Colemere Gdns. BH23: Highc 5H 231
COLEMORE 4D 112
Colemore La. GU34: C'more 6E 112
Colemore Rd. BH7: Bour 7F 228
GU34: C'more 6A 112
Colemore Sq. PO9: Hav 5F 202
Colenso Rd. PO16: Fare 8C 198
Colenzo Dr. SP10: A'ver 9A 52
Coleridge Av. GU46: Yat 8A 18
Coleridge Cl. RG45: Cr'tne 1E 18
SO31: Wars 8A 196
Coleridge Ct. SO19: South 5H 175
Coleridge Dr. PO15: White 9F 176
Coleridge Gdns. PO8: Cowp 6N 181
Coleridge Grn. BH23: Chri 6B 230
Coleridge Rd. PO6: Cosh 8A 200
Colesbourne Rd. PO6: Cosh 8C 200
Coles Cl. SO21: Twyf 6L 127
SO50: E'leigh 9F 132
Cole's La. SP5: L'ford 8G 120
Coles Mede SO21: Ott 1F 132
(not continuous)
Coleson Rd. SO18: South 2C 174
Coleville Av. SO45: Fawl 5F 208
Coleville Rd. GU14: Cov 7H 29
Coley La. SO20: Chil 5D 74
Colinton Av. PO16: Portc 8M 199
Coliseum Bus. Cen. GU15: Camb 1J 29
Collard Way GU33: Liss 1E 140
College Cl. GU15: Camb 5M 19
PO9: R Cas 8J 183
SO31: Hamb 7K 195
College Cres. GU47: Coll 5G 19
College Farm Caravan Site SP5: Com B 5H 119
College Gdns. GU9: Farnh 8D 64
College La. PO1: Ports 4J 5 (2B 240)
RG25: Elli 2H 79
College M. SP10: A'ver 1N 69
College Pl.
SO15: South 1D 4 (4M 173)
College Ride GU15: Camb 6M 19
College Rd. BH5: Bour 1D 246
BH24: Ring 1K 187
GU47: Coll 6G 18
PO1: Ports 2J 5 (2B 240)
PO7: Purb 7M 201
RG21: B'toke 6A 42
SO19: South 8B 174
College St. GU31: Pet 1M 145
GU32: Pet 1M 145
PO1: Ports 4J 5 (2B 240)
SO14: South 7E 4 (7M 173)
SO23: Winche 9M 237 (7L 105)
COLLEGE TOWN 7G 18
College Wlk. SO23: Winche 9N 237 (8L 105)
Collett Cl. SO30: Hed E 9M 161
Colley Cl. SO23: Winche 3L 105
Colleywater La. GU32: Frox 3B 138
Collier Cl. GU14: Cov 7F 28
SO17: South 2A 174
Collingbourne Av. BH6: Bour 8G 229
Collingbourne Dr. SO53: Cha F 6M 131
COLLINGBOURNE DUCIS 2H 31
COLLINGBOURNE KINGSTON 1H 31
Collingbourne Rd. SP9: Tidw 4G 30
Collingdale Lodge BH8: Bour 7M 227
(off Richmond Pk. Rd.)
Collington Cres. PO6: Cosh 8C 200
Collingwood GU14: Farn 1N 49
Collingwood Ho. PO12: Gos 9L 213
PO15: Fare 7N 197
Collingwood Retail Pk. PO14: Fare 2C 212
Collingwood Rd. PO5: S'sea 5E 240
Collingwood Wlk. SP10: A'ver 1C 70
Collingwood Way GU31: Pet 8N 139
Collingworth Ri. SO31: P Ga 3E 196
Collins Cl. SO53: Cha F 6L 131
SP10: Charl 7L 51
Collins Ct. SP9: Tidw 6C 30 (6G 30)
Collins Ho. SO50: E'leigh 9G 132
SO53: Cha F 6B 132
Collins La. BH24: Ring 1K 187
GU31: S Hart 5E 146
SO21: Hurs 6N 125
Collins Pl. PO5: S'sea 2F 240
(off Victoria Rd. Nth.)
Collins Rd. PO4: S'sea 5H 241
Collis Rd. PO3: Ports 8H 215
Collis Ter. SP11: Ludg 1D 30
Collyers Cres. GU30: Lip 2G 116
Collyers Rd. SO42: Broc 9C 148 (9N 189)
Colman Ct. BH1: Bour 2N 245
Colne Av. SO16: South 8C 158
Colne Ct. SO16: South 9D 158
Colne Way RG21: B'toke 6E 42
Colombus Ho. SO14: South 6F 4
Colonel Crabbe M. SO16: Bass 6L 159
Colonnade, The SO19: South 7B 174
Colonnade Rd. BH5: Bour 9D 228
Colonnade Rd. W. BH5: Bour 9D 228
Colpoy St. PO5: S'sea 6M 5 (3C 240)
Colson Cl. SO23: Winche 6M 105
Colson Rd. SO23: Winche 6M 105
Colt Cl. SO16: Rown 6E 158
COLT HILL 8M 45
Colthouse La. GU34: Up Froy 9F 62
Colton Copse SO53: Cha F 6L 131
Coltsfoot Cl. SO30: Hed E 3M 175
Coltsfoot Dr. PO7: W'lle 4N 201
SO31: Loc H 7B 196
Coltsfoot Pl. RG27: Hoo 1J 45
Coltsfoot Rd. GU35: Lind 2M 101
Coltsfoot Wlk. SO51: Rom 3B 130
Coltsfoot Way BH23: Chri 5E 230
Coltsmead PO6: Cosh 9A 200
Colts Rd. SO16: Rown 4D 158
Columbia Gdns. BH10: Bour 4G 226
Columbia Ho. BH10: Bour 4H 227
Columbian Way BH10: Bour 4G 227
Columbia Rd. BH10: Bour 4F 226
Columbia Trees La. BH10: Bour 5G 226
Columbine Cl. BH23: Chri 5D 230
Columbine Rd. RG22: B'toke 3J 59
Columbine Wlk. SO40: Tott 5K 171
Columbus Dr. GU14: Cov 8E 28
SO31: Sar G 4C 196
Columbus Way SP10: A'ver 1D 70
Colvedene Cl. SO21: Col C 3K 133
Colville Cl. BH5: Bour 9D 228
Colville Dr. SO32: Bis W 3N 163
Colville Rd. BH5: Bour 9D 228
PO6: Cosh 9H 201
Colvin Cl. SP10: A'ver 2A 70
Colvin Gdns. SO53: Cha F 4N 131
Colwell Cl. SO16: South 2C 172
Colwell Rd. PO6: Cosh 1G 214
Colwyn Cl. GU46: Yat 7M 17
Colyer Cl. RG22: B'toke 8L 41
Combat Sports Cen. 5L 49
COMBE 4H 7
COMBE HILL 4J 7
Combe Hill Cl. GU31: Hi Br 4H 141
Combe La. GU14: Farn 6J 29
Comber Rd. BH9: Bour 3K 227
Combined Court
Southampton 1D 4 (4M 173)
Winchester 8L 237 (7K 105)
Combined Court Cen.
Portsmouth 5N 5 (3D 240)
Comet Rd. GU14: Farn 3D 48
Comet Way BH23: Mude 8C 230
Comfrey Cl. GU14: Cov 7E 28
PO8: Horn 1C 182
SO51: Rom 3B 130
Comilla Ct. BH13: Poole 3F 244
Comines Way SO30: Hed E 4J 175
Comley Hill PO9: R Cas 3J 203
Comley Rd. BH9: Bour 4K 227
Commercial Centre, The SP11: Pic P 7F 52
Commercial Pl. PO1: Ports 1D 240
Commercial Rd. BH2: Bour 7J 247 (2J 245)
GU12: Alders 2L 65
PO1: Ports 3N 5 (2D 240)
(not continuous)
SO15: South 3A 4 (5K 173)
(not continuous)
SO40: Tott 3N 171
Commercial St. SO18: South 3E 174
Commerical Rd. SO14: South 3B 4 (5L 173)
Commodore Ct. GU14: Farn 3L 49
SO14: South 8F 4 (7N 173)
Commodore Pl. PO12: Gos 1M 239
COMMON, THE 5H 87
Common, The RG26: Cha A 3F 20
SO15: South 1K 173
SP5: Mid W 5H 87
SP6: Woodg 2A 154
Common Barn La. PO13: Lee S 9B 212
(Fieldhouse Dr.)
PO13: Lee S 1C 238
(Holt Cl.)
Common Cl. SO53: Cha F 4A 132
Common Flds. SO30: Hed E 4K 175
Common Gdns. SO53: Cha F 4A 132
Common Hill GU34: Meds 1E 96
Common Hill Rd. SO51: Brai 7C 124
Common La. GU34: Selb 1K 113
PO14: Titch 9G 197
PO17: S'wick 9N 179
Common Rd. RG19: Head 3K 9
SO53: Cha F 4A 132
SP5: W'psh 5H 121
Common St. PO1: Ports 1E 240
Common Va. SP5: Mid W 5H 87
Communications Rd. RG19: Green 1G 9
Compass, The SO14: South 6F 4 (6N 173)
Compass Cl. PO13: Gos 1F 238
SO19: South 6E 174
Compass Ct. SO17: South 1M 173
Compass Fld. RG27: Hoo 2H 45
Compass Point PO16: Fare 9D 198
SO31: Hamb 7J 195
Compass Rd. PO6: Cosh 1C 214
Complins GU34: Holy 2J 81
COMPTON
GU9 8G 65
SO20 8E 88
SO21 5H 127
Compton Acres 5C 244
Compton Av. BH14: Poole 3B 244
Compton Beeches BH24: St I 3D 186
Compton Bus. Pk. BH12: Poole 5A 226
Compton Cl. GU47: Sandh 4E 18
GU52: Ch Cr 6N 47
PO9: Hav 6F 202
PO13: Lee S 1B 238
RG27: Hoo 2H 45
SO22: Oli B 2F 126
SO50: E'leigh 6D 132
Compton Ct. BH6: Bour 1J 247
PO9: Hav 7E 202
Compton Dr. BH14: Poole 3A 244
Compton Gdns. BH14: Poole 3A 244
Compton Ho. SO16: South 2G 173
SO40: Tott 1K 171
Compton Lodge BH4: Bour 2H 245
(off Marlborough Rd.)
Compton Pl. GU35: Bor 2J 101
Compton Pl. Bus. Cen. GU15: Camb 9J 19
(off Watchmoor Point)
Compton Rd. BH25: New M 4B 232
GU52: Ch Cr 6N 47
PO2: Ports 5F 214
SO23: Winche 9K 237 (7K 105)
SO40: Tott 2N 171
SP9: Tidw 8D 30
Compton's Dr. SO51: Plai 7K 121
Compton Sq. SP10: A'ver 7B 52

Compton St.—Courtmount Gro.

Compton St. SO21: Comp 5G 127
Compton Wlk. SO14: South 3E 4 (5M 173)
Compton Way GU10: Farnh 8J 65
RG27: Sher L 7J 23
SO22: Oli B 2F 126
Conan Rd. PO2: Ports 4F 214
Concept Ho. GU14: Farn 8L 29
Concorde Cl. PO15: Seg 4G 196
Concorde Rd. GU14: Farn 2E 48
Concorde Way PO15: Seg 4G 197
Conde Way GU35: Bor 5J 101
Condor Av. PO16: Portc 9H 199
Condor Cl. SO19: South 7B 174
Conel Ct. *BH9: Bour 6J 227*
(off Talbot Rd.)
Coney Grn. SO23: Winche 4L 105
Conference Dr. SO31: Loc H 6E 196
Conference Pl. SO41: Lymi 4F 234
CONFORD 8A 102
Conford Ct. PO9: Hav 3D 202
Congleton Cl. SO43: Mins 8M 155
CONHOLT 9C 6
Conholt Hill SP11: Conh, Ver D 9C 6
Conholt La. SP11: Conh, Ver D 9C 6
Conholt Rd. SP10: A'ver 4N 69
Conifer Av. BH14: Poole 3A 244
Conifer Cl. BH23: Chri 3G 228
BH24: St L 4A 186
GU35: W'hil 6H 101
GU52: Ch Cr 6L 47
PO8: Cowp 8A 182
RG26: Bau 3E 10
SO22: Winche 5J 105
SO45: Hythe 6K 193
Conifer Cres. SO41: Penn 3B 234
Conifer Crest RG14: New 1C 8
Conifer Gro. PO13: Gos 4D 212
Conifer M. PO16: Portc 8M 199
Conifer Rd. SO16: South 7F 158
Conifers BH13: Poole 2F 244
Conigar Rd. PO10: Ems 6M 203
Coniston Av. BH11: Bour 1C 226
PO3: Ports 8H 215
Coniston Cl. GU14: Cov 9G 29
SP4: Ames 5A 66
Coniston Ct. *GU12: Ash V 7N 49*
(off Lakeside Cl.)
Coniston Dr. GU9: Up H 4C 64
Coniston Gdns. SO30: Hed E 5M 175
Coniston Gro. SO24: New A 2F 108
Coniston Rd. BH24: Ring 2L 187
GU35: Bor 2J 101
RG22: B'toke 1J 59
SO16: South 2B 172
SO50: E'leigh 1D 160
Coniston Wlk. PO14: Fare 1A 212
Coniston Way GU52: Ch Cr 6K 47
Connaught Barracks GU11: Alders 5M 49
Connaught Cl. BH25: New M 5N 231
GU35: Bor 5J 101
GU46: Yat 7L 17
RG45: Cr'tne 2B 18
Connaught Cres. BH12: Poole 8C 226
Connaught La. PO6: Cosh 9A 200
Connaught Leisure Cen. 3N 65
Connaught Pl. *PO9: Hav 8G 203*
(off Oaklands Rd.)
Connaught Rd. BH7: Bour 9E 228
GU12: Alders 9L 49
GU51: Fleet 3L 47
PO2: Ports 6E 214
PO9: Hav 8G 202
SO21: Wor D 5G 90
SP9: Tidw 8D 30 (7G 31)
Connaught Way GU34: Alt 7D 80
Connemara Cres. PO15: White 2E 196
Connigar Cl. PO13: Gos 9E 212
Connors Keep PO8: Cowp 6L 181
Conqueror Way PO14: Stub 7N 211
Conrad Gdns. PO15: White 1F 196
Conservatory, The SO23: Winche 7M 105
Consort Cl. BH12: Poole 9A 226
SO50: E'leigh 7F 132
Consort Ct. PO16: Fare 8E 198
Consort Ho. *PO1: Ports 9E 214*
(off Princes St.)
Consort M. PO17: K Vil 2N 197
Consort Rd. SO50: E'leigh 7F 132
Constable Cl. PO12: Gos 6L 239
RG21: B'toke 8E 42
SO19: South 8G 174
Constable Ct. SP10: A'ver 9N 51
Constables Ga. SO23: Winche 8K 237
Constable Way GU47: Coll 7G 18
Constantine Av. SO53: Cha F 6C 132
Constantine Cl. SO53: Cha F 6D 132
Constantine Sq. *SP10: A'ver 7B 52*
(off Cricketers Way)
Constantine Way RG22: B'toke 4J 59
Constantius Ct. *GU52: Ch Cr 7K 47*
(off Brandon Rd.)
Constant Rd. GU14: Farn 1C 48
Consulate Ho. SO14: South 7N 173
Convent Ct. PO10: Ems 8L 203
Convent La. PO10: Ems 9M 203
(not continuous)
Convent Mdws. BH23: Chri 9M 229
Convent Wlk. BH23: Chri 8M 229
Conway Cl. BH25: New M 3C 232
GU16: Frim 3N 29
SO53: Cha F 9N 131
Conway Ct. BH25: New M 3C 232
Conway Dr. GU14: Cov 8F 28
Cook Cl. BH24: Poul 9M 185
Cooke Gdns. BH12: Poole 8D 226
Cooke Rd. BH12: Poole 8D 226
Cookham Cl. GU47: Sandh 4E 18
Cook Ho. SO14: South 8F 4
Cooks La. SO40: Calm 9H 157
SO51: Awb 9G 123
SO51: Lock 3M 121
Cook St. SO14: South 6E 4 (6M 173)
Coolers Farm SO20: Brou 2B 86 (5B 88)
Cooley Ho. PO13: Gos 3D 212
COOMBE 6H 143
Coombe Av. BH10: Bour 3J 227
COOMBE BISSETT 2G 119
Coombe Cl. GU16: Frim 4M 29
Coombe Cnr. RG20: High 4A 8
Coombedale SO31: Loc H 7E 196
Coombe Dr. GU51: Fleet 2A 48
Coombe Farm Av. PO16: Fare 9C 198
Coombe Gdns. BH10: Bour 4H 227
Coombehurst Dr. RG21: B'toke 9C 42
Coombe La. SO41: Sway 6L 223
SO51: Awb 1F 128
Coombe Nurseries Caravan Pk.
SP2: Nethe 1F 118
Coombe Rd. GU32: E Meon 4K 143
GU33: Hi Br 4H 141
GU46: Yat 6L 17
PO12: Gos 9K 213
Coombe Rd. Ter. *GU32: E Meon 4L 143*
(off Coombe Rd.)
Coombe Way GU14: Farn 8L 29
Coombs Cl. PO8: Horn 1C 182
Cooperage, The GU34: Alt 5E 80
Cooperage Grn. PO12: Gos 2M 239
Cooper Dean Dr. BH8: Bour 5C 228
Cooper Dean Roundabout, The
BH7: Bour 5D 228
Cooper Gro. PO16: Portc 2M 213
Cooper Rd. PO3: Ports 8J 215
SO40: Ashu 7J 171
Coopers Cl. SO18: Wes E 1G 174
SO21: Wor D 5H 91
SO51: E Wel 1B 156
Coopers Ct. RG26: B'ley 1G 22
SO14: South 8D 4
Cooper's Hill RG27: Eve 1G 27
Coopers La. BH31: Ver 9M 149
RG26: B'ley 1F 22
SO19: South 7B 174
SO43: B'haw 3N 155
SO51: Ower 5A 156
Coopers Ter. GU9: Farnh 7E 64
Coop La. RG27: A'ell 5A 44
Copeland Rd. SO16: South 1C 172
Copenhagen Towers SO19: South 1C 194
Copenhagen Wlk. RG45: Cr'tne 1D 18
Copes La. RG27: Brams 6L 15
Copinger Cl. SO40: Tott 4J 171
Copland Cl. RG22: B'toke 2L 59
COPNOR 7H 215
Copnor *RG20: Wol H 3N 7*
(off Trade St.)
Copnor Bri. Bus. Pk. PO3: Ports 9H 215
Copnor Cl. RG20: Wol H 3N 7
(not continuous)
Copnor Rd. PO3: Ports 3G 214
Copper Beech Cl. BH12: Poole 1E 244
Copper Beech Dr. PO6: Farl 9M 201
Copper Beeches BH2: Bour 9K 227
Copper Beech Gdns. BH10: Bour 4H 227
Copperbeech Pl. *RG14: New 1C 8*
(off Andover Rd.)
Copperfield Av. GU47: Owl 3G 18
Copperfield Ho. PO1: Ports 9E 214
Copperfield Rd. SO16: Bass 6M 159
Copperfields SO40: Tott 3H 171
Coppers Cl. SP6: Ald 4D 152
Copper St. PO5: S'sea 7M 5 (4C 240)
Copperwood Cl. GU30: Lip 2D 116
Coppice, The BH23: Mude 8D 230
GU52: Ch Cr 5M 47
PO8: Horn 4A 182
PO13: Gos 6F 212
SO42: Broc 6A 148 (8M 189)
Coppice Cl. BH24: St I 4C 186
BH25: A'ley 2E 232
GU9: Weyb 4G 65
RG26: Bau 5D 10
SO22: Winche 5G 104
Coppice Gdns. GU46: Yat 8M 17
RG45: Cr'tne 1B 18
Coppice Hill SO32: Bis W 4M 163
Coppice M. RG23: B'toke 5L 41
Coppice Pale RG24: Old Bas 1H 43
Coppice Rd. RG20: Kings 2C 6 (6L 9)
SO40: Calm 9J 157
Coppice Vw. BH10: Bour 3J 227
Coppice Way PO15: Fare 6N 197
Coppins Gro. PO16: Portc 2L 213
Copse, The GU14: Cov 9F 28
PO15: Fare 5N 197
RG23: Dumm 7F 58
RG26: Tadl 5G 11
SO51: Rom 3B 130
SO53: Cha F 7C 132
Copse Av. BH25: New M 4C 232
GU9: Weyb 3G 64
Copse Bus. Cen. SO40: Tott 6N 171
Copse Caravan Park, The
SO40: Woodl 5D 170
Copse Caravan Site, The
RG23: Dumm 7F 58
Copse Cl. GU31: Pet 9B 140
GU33: Liss 1F 140
PO7: Wid 7L 201
SO21: Ott 9G 126
SO40: Tott 4M 171
SO52: N Bad 8E 130
Copse End GU51: Fleet 3J 47
Copse Fld. RG24: Lych 3H 43
Copse La. GU46: Yat 5L 17
GU52: Ch Cr 6K 47
PO11: H Isl 8G 217
PO13: Gos 7F 212
RG29: L Sut 4E 62
SO16: Chilw 2L 159
SO24: B Can 7A 78
SO31: Hamb 7K 195
Copse Rd. BH24: Bur 8D 188
BH25: New M 4C 232
GU27: Hasl 1M 117
RG25: Over 9E 38
SO18: South 9D 160
Copse Vw. SO19: South 5J 175
SP11: Rede 6N 31
Copse Vw. Cl. RG24: Chin 9G 23
Copse Way BH23: Chri 6G 230
GU26: Hind 3N 103
Copsewood Av. BH8: Bour 5B 228
Copsewood Rd. SO18: South 9C 160
SO40: Ashu 7J 171
SO45: Hythe 6L 193
Copsey Cl. PO6: Dray 9L 201
Copsey Gro. PO6: Dray 1L 215
Copsey Path PO6: Farl 9L 201
Copthorne La. SO45: Fawl 5F 208
COPYTHORNE 1B 170
Copythorne Cl. BH8: Bour 4A 228
Copythorne Cres.
SO40: Copy 8C 156
Copythorn Rd. PO2: Ports 7G 214
Coracle Cl. SO31: Wars 8C 196
Coral Cl. PO16: Portc 2L 213
Coral Ct. PO13: Gos 1E 238
Coralin Gro. PO7: W'lle 9B 182
Coram Cl. SO23: Winche 4L 105
Corbar Rd. BH23: Chri 6H 229
Corbett Rd. PO7: W'lle 3L 201
Corbiere Av. BH12: Poole 5B 226
Corbiere Cl. SO16: South 8D 158
Corbin Ct. SO41: Penn 4B 234
Corbin Rd. SO41: Penn 3B 234
Corbould Rd. SO45: Dib P 8L 193
Corby Cres. PO3: Ports 4J 215
Cordale Rd. RG21: B'toke 8B 42
Cordelia Cl. SO45: Dib 6J 193
Corelli Rd. RG22: B'toke 2A 60
Corfe Cl. PO14: Stub 6K 211
SO24: New A 2E 108
Corfe Vw. Rd. BH14: Poole 2A 244
Corfe Wlk. RG23: B'toke 5L 41
Corfe Way GU14: Farn 2N 49
Corfield Cl. RG40: F'std 2H 17
CORHAMPTON 8N 135
Corhampton Cres. PO9: Hav 5D 202
Corhampton Golf Course 9L 135
Corhampton Ho. *PO1: Ports 1E 240*
(off Church Rd.)
Corhampton La. SO32: Corh 8K 135
Corhampton Rd. BH6: Bour 8E 228
Coriander Cl. GU14: Cov 7E 28
Coriander Dr. SO40: Tott 3J 171
Coriander Way PO15: White 1G 197
Corinna Gdns. SO45: Dib 6J 193
Corinthian Cl. RG22: B'toke 3K 59
SP10: A'ver 6A 52
Corinthian Rd. SO53: Cha F 5C 132
Cork La. SO40: March 8E 172
Cormorant Cl. PO16: Portc 9H 199
RG22: B'toke 2H 59
Cormorant Dr. SO45: Hythe 7A 194
Cormorant Pl. GU47: Coll 6F 18
Cormorant Wlk. PO13: Gos 6D 212
Cornaway La. PO16: Portc 1K 213
Cornbrook Gro. PO7: W'lle 9C 182
Cornbunting Cl. GU47: Coll 5F 18
Cornelia Cl. GU14: Cov 9F 28
Cornelia Cres. BH12: Poole 8E 226
Cornelia Rd. BH10: Bour 5F 226
Cornelius Dr. PO7: W'lle 9A 182
Cornel Rd. SO19: South 5D 174
Corner Mead PO7: Den 6G 180
Corner Point BH6: Bour 9G 228
Cornerways SO23: Kin W 9M 91
SO42: Beau 1B 236
Cornes Cl. SO22: Winche 7H 105
Cornfield PO16: Fare 5D 198
Cornfield Cl. SO53: Cha F 6L 131
Cornfield Rd. PO13: Lee S 1B 238
Cornfields GU46: Yat 9L 17
SP10: A'ver 3B 70
Cornfields, The RG22: B'toke 3L 59
Cornflower Cl. SO31: Loc H 6B 196
Cornflower Dr. BH23: Chri 5E 230
Cornflower Way
SP11: Ludg 2D 30 (5K 31)
Cornford Way BH23: Chri 6F 230
Cornforth Rd. SO40: Calm 1J 171
Cornish Cl. RG22: B'toke 8L 41
Cornish Gdns. BH10: Bour 5H 227
Cornmarket SO51: Rom 5L 129
Cornpits La. SP6: Dame 4N 149
Corn Store Cotts. SP6: N Gor 7L 153
Cornwall Cl. SO18: South 9E 160
Cornwall Cres. SO18: South 9D 160
Cornwallis Cres. PO1: Ports 1E 240
Cornwallis Ho. *PO1: Ports 1E 240*
(off Cornwallis Cres.)
Cornwallis Rd. SO41: M Sea 8H 235
Cornwall Rd. GU35: W'hil 6J 101
PO1: Ports 2F 240
SO18: South 9D 160
SO53: Cha F 9A 132
Cornwell Cl. PO2: Ports 6C 214
PO13: Gos 9F 212
Coronado Rd. PO12: Gos 9K 213
Coronation Av. BH9: Bour 4K 227
SO15: South 8K 159
Coronation Cl. RG20: Burgh 3D 8
RG29: Odi 8L 45
Coronation Cotts. RG23: W Law 4G 40
Coronation Homes PO2: Ports 4F 214
SO18: South 2N 175
Coronation Pde. *SO31: Hamb 6J 195*
(off Kings Av.)
Coronation Rd. GU11: Alders 3K 65
GU46: Yat 6A 18
PO7: W'lle 1M 201
PO11: H Isl 6L 243
Coronation Rd. RG21: B'toke 5D 42
SO32: Swanm 6D 164
SP9: Tidw 6C 30 (6G 30)
SP11: Ludg 1E 30 (5L 31)
Coronation Ter. SP6: Sand 9D 150
Corporation Rd. BH1: Bour 9M 227
Corringway GU52: Ch Cr 5N 47
Corry Rd. GU26: Hind 1L 103
Corsair Cl. PO13: Lee S 2C 238
Corsair Dr. SO45: Dib 6J 193
Cortina Way SO30: Hed E 5A 176
Cortmerron *BH4: Bour 3G 245*
(off West Cliff Rd.)
Cortry Cl. BH12: Poole 7E 226
Cort Way PO15: Fare 5M 197
Corunna Main SP10: A'ver 1A 70
Corvette Av. SO31: Wars 8C 196
Corylus Ct. SO40: Tott 1H 171
Cosford Cl. SO50: B'stke 1L 161
COSHAM 2G 214
Cosham Pk. Av. PO6: Cosh 1G 215
Cosham Station (Rail) 1G 215
Cossack Grn. SO14: South 5E 4 (6M 173)
Cossack La. SO23: Winche 7N 237 (6L 105)
Cossack La. Ho. SO23: Winche 7N 237
Cossaton Ri. SO20: Mid Wa 4B 72
Cosworth Dr. SO45: Dib 6J 193
Cotlands Rd. BH1: Bour 1M 245
Cotsalls SO50: Fair O 2N 161
Cotswold Cl. GU14: Cov 5G 29
PO9: Hav 3E 202
RG22: B'toke 7K 41
SO45: Dib P 6J 193
Cotswold Ct. *BH23: Chri 6B 230*
(off Hunt Rd.)
GU51: Fleet 2L 47
Cotswold Ho. PO6: Cosh 9D 200
Cotswold Rd. GU47: Sandh 4B 18
SO16: South 2E 172
Cotswold Wlk. PO14: Fare 1B 212
Cottage Cl. PO7: Den 7G 180
Cottage Gdns. BH12: Poole 9A 226
GU14: Cov 8H 29
Cottage Grn. RG27: H Win 7C 26
SP11: G Cla 9M 69
Cottage Gro. PO5: S'sea 3D 240
PO12: Gos 2K 239
Cottage La. GU33: Liss 1M 139
Cottage M. SP6: F'dge 9H 151
Cottage Rd. SO20: Mid Wa 9M 67
Cottagers La. SO41: Hor 3H 233
Cottage St. La. SO32: Swanm 7G 165
Cottage Vw. PO1: Ports 2E 240
Cotterell Ct. GU52: Ch Cr 7L 47
Cotteridge Ho. PO5: S'sea 2E 240
Cottesloe Ct. PO5: S'sea 5D 240
Cottesmore Pl. GU14: Farn 3K 49
Cottes Way PO14: Stub 7K 211
Cottes Way East PO14: Stub 7L 211
Cottington Cl. RG20: Kings 2C 6
COTTINGTON'S HILL 8K 9
Cott La. BH24: Bur 8E 188
Cottle Cl. RG21: B'toke 9B 42
Cotton Cl. GU11: Alders 8H 49
SO50: B'stke 9J 133
Cotton Dr. PO10: Ems 5L 203
(not continuous)
Cotton Rd. PO3: Ports 1H 241
COTTONWORTH 4D 74
Cottrell Flats GU14: Farn 3M 49
Cott St. SO32: Swanm 6E 164
Cotwell Av. PO8: Cowp 6B 182
COUCH GREEN 8F 92
Couch Grn. SO21: Mar W 8F 92
Coulmere Rd. PO12: Gos 1J 239
Coulsdon Rd. SO30: Hed E 4N 175
Coultas Rd. SO53: Cha F 2C 132
Coulter Rd. PO7: W'lle 9K 181
Council Rd. RG21: B'toke 7C 42
Countess Gdns. BH7: Bour 6C 228
Country Vw. PO14: Stub 4L 211
SO51: W Wel 1B 120 (9N 121)
County Court
Aldershot & Farnham 9K 49
Bournemouth 5E 228
County Gdns. PO14: Fare 9M 197
County Gates La. BH4: Bour 1F 244
County Hgts. BH1: Bour 8N 247
COURSE PARK 7F 196
Course Pk. Cres. PO14: Titch C 7F 196
Court Barn Cl. PO13: Lee S 9B 212
Court Barn La. PO13: Lee S 9B 212
Court Cl. BH23: Chri 7A 230
GU30: Lip 3D 116
PO6: Cosh 1J 215
SO18: South 4E 174
SO40: Calm 9K 157
SO41: Lymi 4D 234
COURT CORNER 1K 21
Court Dr. GU52: Fleet 5M 47
Court Drove RG25: Over 8C 38
Courtenay Cl. PO15: Seg 6G 197
Courtenay Pl. SO41: Lymi 3E 234
Courtenay Rd. GU9: Weyb 3G 64
SO23: Winche 4L 105
Court Gdns. GU15: Camb 8L 19
Court Hill SP6: Dame, Sand 7A 150
Courthill Rd. BH14: Poole 1A 244
Court Ho. Cl. SO45: Hythe 5M 193
Courtier Cl. SO45: Dib 6H 193
Courtland Gdns. SO16: Bass 6N 159
Courtlands SO41: Lymi 2E 234
Courtlands Ter. PO8: Cowp 6A 182
Court La. PO6: Cosh 1J 215
SO20: Up S 5K 89
SO24: Rop 8E 96
Courtleigh Mnr. BH5: Bour 1A 246
Court Lodge SO41: Lymi 4D 234
Court Mead PO6: Cosh 9J 201
Courtmoor Av. GU52: Fleet 4M 47
Courtmount Gro. PO6: Cosh 9H 201

Courtmount Path—Crookham Comn. Rd.

Courtmount Path PO6: Cosh 8H 201
Court Rd. BH9: Bour 5M 227
GU11: Alders 9J 49
PO13: Lee S 9A 212
SO15: South 3L 173
SO23: Kin W 1N 105
Court Royal M. SO15: South 2L 173
Court Vw. BH2: Bour 5J 247
Court Yard, The GU31: Pet 1M 145
Courtyard, The BH1: Bour 1M 245
BH4: Bour 5G 247
BH12: Poole 5A 226
GU15: Camb 8L 19
RG22: B'toke 5J 59
SO22: Lit 1F 104
Cousins Gro. PO4: S'sea 5H 241
COVE 7E 28
Cove Ct. GU14: Cov 7E 28
Covena Rd. BH6: Bour 8G 229
Coventry Cl. RG22: B'toke 2K 59
Coventry Ct. PO13: Gos 1F 238
SO23: Winche 4L 105
Coventry Rd. SO15: South 1B 4 (4L 173)
Coverack Way PO6: P Sol 1C 214
Cove Rd. BH10: Bour 4G 226
GU14: Cov 8G 29
GU51: Fleet 8N 27
Covers La. GU27: Lip 9L 103
Covert, The GU14: Cov 4G 29
SO51: Rom 6A 130
Covert Gro. PO7: W'lle 4A 202
Coverts, The RG26: Tadl 7H 11
Coverts Cl. GU9: Farnh 6G 64
Covey Cl. GU14: Farn 4J 29
Covey Way SO24: New A 2D 108
Covindale Ho. PO4: S'sea 4H 241
Cowan Rd. PO7: W'lle 4L 201
Coward Rd. PO12: Gos 5H 239
Cowden Cl. GU9: Farnh 6G 64
Cowdery Hgts. RG24: Old Bas 5F 42
COW DOWN 5E 70
Cowdown La. PO8: Comp 8N 169
SP11: A'ver, G Cla 6A 70
Cowdray Cl. SO16: South 7G 159
SO50: B'stke 1K 161
Cowdray Ho. *PO1: Ports* *2E 240*
(off Arundel St.)
Cowdray Pk. GU34: Alt 6F 80
PO14: Stub 6K 211
Cowdrey Gdns. BH8: Bour 4C 228
Cowdrey Sq. SP10: A'ver 7A 52
Cow Drove Hill SO20: Ki S 8B 86 (6F 88)
Cowell Dr. BH7: Bour 6D 228
COWES 5N 237
Cowes Ct. PO14: Fare 9M 197
COWESFIELD 5K 121
COWESFIELD GREEN 5J 121
Cowes La. SO31: Wars 3A 210
Cowfold La. RG27: Matt, Roth 6G 24
Cow La. GU31: S Hart 8F 146
PO6: Cosh 1E 214
PO16: Portc 1M 213
SP11: Kimp 5D 30 (7K 31)
Cowleas Cl. SO51: Awb 8E 122
Cowleas Cotts. SO51: Awb 8E 122
Cowley Cl. SO16: South 9D 158
Cowley Dr. SO21: Wor D 5H 91
Cowley Rd. SO41: Lymi 2C 234
Cowleys La. SO42: Beau 8K 207
Cowleys Rd. BH23: Burt 4M 229
Cowper Av. BH25: New M 5B 232
Cowper Rd. BH9: Bour 4K 227
PO1: Ports 1F 240
SO19: South 4H 175
Cowpitts La. BH24: Hang, Poul 7M 185
COWPLAIN 7A 182
Cowplain Activity Cen. 7B 182
Cowslad Dr. RG24: Old Bas 1H 43
Cowslip Bank RG24: Lych 3G 42
Cowslip Cl. BH23: Chri 5E 230
GU35: Lind 3M 101
PO13: Gos 6C 212
SO31: Loc H 7B 196
Cowslip Ct. PO7: W'lle 8K 181
Cowslip Wlk. SO40: Tott 5K 171
(Denbigh Cl.)
SO40: Tott 5L 171
(Trevone Cl.)
Cowslip Way SO51: Rom 3B 130
Cox Av. BH9: Bour 2M 227
Coxbridge Bus. Pk. GU10: Farnh 9A 64
Coxbridge Mdw. GU9: Farnh 9B 64
Cox Cl. BH9: Bour 2M 227
Cox Dale PO14: Titch C 8F 196
Coxes Mdw. GU32: Pet 8L 139
COXFORD 9F 158
Coxford Cl. SO16: South 9F 158
Coxford Drove SO16: South 8F 158
Coxford Rd. SO16: South 9E 158
Cox Grn. GU47: Coll 7F 18
Coxheath Rd. GU51: Ch Cr 5K 47
GU52: Ch Cr 5K 47
Coxmoor Cl. GU52: Ch Cr 6A 48
Cox Row SO53: Cha F 9A 132
Cox's Dr. SO19: South 8F 174
Cox's Hill SO21: Twyf 5L 127
Cox's La. SO19: South 8B 174
Coxstone La. BH24: Ring 2K 187
Coy Pond Bus. Pk. BH12: Poole 9E 226
Coy Pond Rd. BH12: Poole 9E 226
Cozens Cl. SO19: South 9C 174
Crabapple Cl. SO40: Tott 3J 171
Crabbe Ct. PO5: S'sea 3D 240
Crabbe La. SO16: Bass 6M 159
(not continuous)
Crabbs Way SO40: Tott 3H 171
Crabbswood La. SO41: Sway 7F 222
Crabden La. PO8: Blen 2E 182
Crableck La. SO31: Sar G 4N 195
Crabs Hill RG26: Wolve 6M 9
CRABTHORN 5L 211
Crabthorn Farm La. PO14: Stub 5L 211
Crabton Cl. Rd. BH5: Bour 1C 246
Crabtree SO16: South 1E 172
Crabtree Cl. BH23: Burt 4M 229
Crabtree Gdns. GU35: Head 2A 102
Crabtree La. GU10: Chur 6J 85
GU35: Head 2A 102
SP11: Stoke 7H 35
Crabtree Rd. GU15: Camb 2K 29
Crabtree Way RG24: Old Bas 7J 43
Crabwood Cl. SO16: South 9E 158
Crabwood Ct. PO9: Hav 2D 202
Crabwood Dr. SO30: Wes E 1J 175
Crab Wood (Nature Reserve) 6B 104
Crabwood Rd. SO16: South 9D 158
Cracknore Hard SO40: March 9F 172
Cracknore Hard La. SO40: March 8F 172
Cracknore Ind. Pk. SO40: March 8H 173
Cracknore Rd. SO15: South 5J 173
Craddock Ho. PO1: Ports 3J 5
SO23: Winche 5N 105
Cradle La. GU35: Head, Slea 4M 83
Cradle of Cricket Memorial 5K 167
Crafts La. GU31: Pet 8N 139
Crafts Study Cen. (Gallery) 8D 64
Craghead BH1: Bour 2A 246
Craigbank Ct. PO15: Fare 8B 198
Craig Ho. *PO5: S'sea* *5E 240*
(off Marmion Av.)
Craigleith BH1: Bour 1N 245
Craigmoor Av. BH8: Bour 4B 228
Craigmoor Cl. BH8: Bour 5C 228
Craigmoor Way BH8: Bour 4B 228
Craigside Rd. BH24: St L 5A 186
Craigwell Rd. PO7: Purb 5M 201
Crake Pl. GU47: Coll 5F 18
CRAMPMOOR 3D 130
Crampmoor La. SO51: Cram 3C 130
Cramptons GU34: Bee 6A 80
Cranberry Cl. SO40: March 9E 172
Cranberry Wlk. GU17: Haw 1H 29
CRANBORNE 6J 149
Cranborne Common (Nature Reserve) 8P 149
Cranborne Cres. BH12: Poole 6C 226
Cranborne Gdns. SO53: Cha F 3N 131
Cranborne Ho. BH8: Bour 1L 245
Cranborne Manor Garden 6J 149
Cranborne Pl. BH25: New M 3N 231
Cranborne Rd. BH2: Bour 8K 247 (3J 245)
PO6: Cosh 8H 201
SP6: Crip 7N 149
Cranborne Wlk. PO14: Fare 1A 212
CRANBOURNE 9B 42
Cranbourne Cl. SO15: South 1J 173
Cranbourne Ct. *BH9: Bour* *6M 227*
(off Rutland Rd.)
RG21: B'toke 9B 42
Cranbourne Dr. SO21: Ott 1F 132
Cranbourne La. RG21: B'toke 1A 60
Cranbourne Pk. SO30: Hed E 6N 175
Cranbourne Rd. PO12: Gos 4L 239
Cranbrook Ct. GU51: Fleet 9M 27
Cranbrook Rd. BH12: Poole 8A 226
Cranbury, The SO14: South 1D 4
Cranbury Av. SO14: South 1E 4 (4M 173)
Cranbury Cl. SO21: Ott 2F 132
SP5: Down 3K 119 (8A 120)
Cranbury Ct. *SO19: South* *7D 174*
(off Cranbury Rd.)
Cranbury Gdns. SO31: Old N 9K 175
Cranbury Pl. SO14: South 1D 4 (4M 173)
Cranbury Rd. SO19: South 7D 174
SO50: E'leigh 2E 160
(not continuous)
Cranbury Ter. SO14: South 1E 4 (4M 173)
Cranbury Towers SO14: South 1E 4
Crane Cl. PO13: Gos 6D 212
Crane Ct. GU47: Coll 5F 18
PO4: S'sea *2J 241*
(off Velder Av.)
Cranemoor Av. BH23: Chri 4G 231
Cranemoor Cl. BH23: Chri 4G 231
Cranemoor Gdns. BH23: Chri 4H 231
Cranesfield RG24: Sher J 8N 21
Cranes Rd. RG24: Sher J 8M 21
(not continuous)
Crane St. *BH21: Cran* *6J 149*
(off The Square)
Craneswater Av. PO4: S'sea 6F 240
Craneswater Ga. PO4: S'sea 6F 240
Craneswater M. *PO4: S'sea* *5F 240*
(off Craneswater Pk.)
Craneswater Pk. PO4: S'sea 5F 240
Cranford Av. GU52: Ch Cr 6K 47
Cranford Dr. GU34: Holy 2J 81
Cranford Gdns. SO53: Cha F 4N 131
Cranford Ho. SO17: South 9M 159
Cranford Pk. Dr. GU46: Yat 7N 17
Cranford Rd. GU32: Pet 2K 145
Cranford Way SO17: South 9M 159
Cranleigh Av. PO1: Ports 1F 240
Cranleigh Cl. BH6: Bour 9H 229
SP4: Ames *5A 66*
(off Raleigh Cres.)
Cranleigh Ct. BH6: Bour 9H 229
GU14: Cov 8H 29
SO17: South 2M 173
Cranleigh Gdns. BH6: Bour 9H 229
Cranleigh Paddock SO43: Lyn 1B 148
Cranleigh Rd. BH6: Bour 8G 228
PO1: Ports 1F 240
PO16: Portc 1J 213
SO30: Hed E 4N 175
Cranmer Dr. SO16: Nur 6B 158
Cranmer Rd. BH9: Bour 6K 227
Cranmore SO31: Net A 2G 194
Cranmore Cl. GU11: Alders 1G 64
Cranmore Gdns. GU11: Alders 1F 64
Cranmore La. GU11: Alders 2F 64
Cransley Ct. *BH4: Bour* *3G 245*
(off Portarlington Rd.)
Crantock Gro. BH8: Bour 4C 228
Cranwell Cl. BH11: Bour 2C 226
BH23: Bran 6D 220
Cranwell Ct. SO16: South 6E 158
Cranworth Ho. *SO22: Winche* *5K 105*
(off Cranworth Rd.)
Cranworth Rd. SO22: Winche 5K 105
Crasswell St. PO1: Ports 2N 5 (1D 240)
(not continuous)
Craven Ct. *BH1: Bour* *1M 245*
(off Knyveton Rd.)
PO15: Fare 6A 198
Craven Grange BH2: Bour 5L 247 (1K 245)
Craven Rd. RG17: Ink 1F 6
SO53: Cha F 6B 132
Craven St. SO14: South 4E 4 (5M 173)
Craven Wlk. SO14: South 4D 4 (5M 173)
Crawford Cl. SO16: Nur 6C 158
Crawford Dr. PO16: Fare 6B 198
Crawford Gdns. GU15: Camb 8K 19
Crawlboys La. SP11: Ludg 1F 30 (4L 31)
Crawlboys Rd. SP11: Ludg 1D 30 (5K 31)
CRAWLEY 3N 89
Crawley Av. PO9: Hav 3G 203
Crawley Ct. SO21: Craw 3N 89
Crawley Dr. GU15: Camb 7N 19
CRAWLEY HILL 8M 19
Crawley Hill GU15: Camb 8N 19
SO51: W Wel 2B 120 (1N 155)
Crawley Ridge GU15: Camb 7N 19
Crawshaw Rd. BH14: Poole 3A 244
Crawte Av. SO45: Holb 6B 208
Crawters La. *GU31: Pet* *1M 145*
(off College St.)
Crawts Rd. RG25: Over 3D 56
Craydown La. SO20: Ov Wa 7M 67
Cray Ho. PO12: Gos 3L 239
Creasey Rd. BH11: Bour 1E 226
Credenhill Rd. PO6: Cosh 8D 200
Credon Cl. GU14: Cov 7H 29
Creech Rd. BH12: Poole 9A 226
Creech Vw. PO7: Den 6F 180
Creedy Dr. BH23: Chri 9L 229
Creedy Gdns. SO18: Wes E 8E 160
Creedy Path BH23: Chri 8L 229
Creek End PO10: Ems 1M 217
Creek Rd. PO11: H Isl 5K 243
PO12: Gos 3M 239
Creighton Rd. SO15: South 4E 172
Cremer Mall PO16: Fare 8D 198
Cremorne Pl. GU32: Pet 9M 139
Cremyll Cl. PO14: Stub 6M 211
CRENDELL 6M 149
Crerar Cl. GU14: Cov 9F 28
Crescent, The BH1: Bour 1B 246
BH25: New M 6M 231
GU9: H End 3E 64
GU14: Farn 9L 29
GU17: Haw 9F 18
GU34: Meds 3J 97
GU46: Yat 6N 17
GU51: Cr V 5H 47
PO1: Ports 5K 5
PO7: Purb 5K 201
RG24: B'toke 3M 41
RG26: B'ley *1F 22*
(off The Street)
SO19: South 8E 174
SO21: Twyf 7L 127
SO31: Net A 3G 194
SO32: Lwr U 1F 162
SO40: Ashu 7E 170
SO40: March 9D 172
SO50: E'leigh 8E 132
SO51: Rom 4A 130
SP4: Ames 5A 66
SP10: A'ver 1J 69
SP11: G Cla 8M 69
SP11: Hur T 4D 34
SP11: Up C 5L 69
Crescent Cl. SO22: Oli B 1F 126
Crescent Ct. BH2: Bour 8H 247 (3H 245)
BH25: B Sea *7A 232*
(off Marine Dr.)
Crescent Dr. BH25: B Sea 7A 232
Crescent Gdns. PO16: Fare 8C 198
Crescent Grange BH2: Bour 6J 247
Crescent Rd. BH2: Bour 6J 247 (2J 245)
BH14: Poole 1C 244
PO12: Gos 6J 239
PO16: Fare 8C 198
SO31: Loc H 6C 196
SO52: N Bad 7E 130
SP4: Bul 3A 66
Cressey Rd. SO51: Rom 5M 129
Cress Gdns. SP10: A'ver 3M 69
Cressy Rd. PO2: Ports 9E 214
Crest, The PO7: Wid 7K 201
Cresta Ct. BH2: Bour 6J 247
PO4: S'sea 5G 241
Crest Cl. PO16: Fare 8F 198
Crestland Cl. PO8: Cowp 7A 182
Crest Rd. BH12: Poole 8A 226
Crest Way SO19: South 6G 175
Crestwood College Leisure Cen. 7D 132
Crestwood Vw. SO50: E'leigh 7D 132
Creswell RG27: Hoo 2K 45
Crete Cotts. SO45: Dib P 9K 193
Crete La. SO45: Dib P 8L 193
Crete Rd. SO45: Dib P 9L 193
Crichel Mt. Rd. BH14: Poole 6A 244
Crichel Rd. BH9: Bour 6L 227
Crichton Ho. SO31: Net A 3F 194
Cricket Chambers BH1: Bour 1L 245
Cricket Cl. BH23: Mude 9B 230
GU26: Hind 1M 103
SO21: Craw 3N 89
Cricket Dr. PO8: Cowp 5A 182
Cricketers Way SP10: A'ver 7A 52
Cricket Fld. Gro. RG45: Cr'tne 1F 18
Cricket Grn. RG27: H Win 6C 26
Cricket Grn. La. RG27: H Win 6C 26
CRICKET HILL 8A 18
Cricket Hill RG40: F'std 3J 17
Cricket Hill La. GU46: Yat 1N 27
(not continuous)
Cricket Lea GU35: Lind 2L 101
Cricklade Pl. SP10: A'ver 9L 51
Cricklemede SO32: Bis W 4N 163
Cricklewood Cl. SO32: Bis W 4N 163
CRIDDLESTYLE 1M 153
Crigdon Cl. SO16: South 2D 172
Crimea Rd. BH9: Bour 7K 227
GU11: Alders 9K 49
(not continuous)
Cringle Av. BH6: Bour 1K 247
Crinoline Gdns. PO4: S'sea 5H 241
Cripley Rd. GU14: Cov 6F 28
Cripplegate La. SO42: Beau 1B 236
CRIPPLESTYLE 7N 149
Cripstead La. SO23: Winche 9K 105
Crispin Cl. BH23: Highc 6H 231
SO31: Loc H 5E 196
SO50: Hor H 5N 161
Crisspyn Cl. PO8: Horn 4B 182
Criswick Cl. SP11: Abb A 7F 68
CRITCHELL'S GREEN 3N 121
CRITCHMERE 8N 103
Critchmere Hill GU27: Hasl 8N 103
Critchmere La. GU27: Hasl 9N 103
Critchmere Va. GU27: Hasl 9N 103
Criterion Arc. BH1: Bour 7L 247 (2K 245)
Critall Cl. SO41: Sway 5K 223
Croad Ct. PO16: Fare 8E 198
CROCKERHILL 1D 198
Crockers Mead RG20: Bal H 1M 7
Crockford Cl. BH25: New M 1C 232
Crockford La. RG24: B'toke, Chin 2E 42
(not continuous)
Crockford Rd. SP5: W Gri 2D 120
Croft, The GU46: Yat 6N 17
GU51: Fleet 3J 47
PO14: Stub 4M 211
SO40: Calm 9J 157
SO50: E'leigh 1E 160
SO53: Cha F 9A 132
SP4: New T 6E 66
SP5: Bish 3D 118
Croft Av. SP10: A'ver 3N 69
Crofters Cl. GU47: Sandh 5C 18
Crofters Mdw. RG24: Lych 3G 42
Croft Gdns. GU34: Alt 4E 80
SP10: A'ver 3N 69
Croft Hgts. SP5: W'psh 5H 121
Croftlands Av. PO14: Stub 5M 211
Croft La. GU10: Cron 3L 63
GU46: Yat 6M 17
PO11: H Isl 7G 216
Crofton Av. PO13: Lee S 8M 211
Crofton Cl. BH23: Chri 5H 229
PO7: Purb 4K 201
SO17: South 1M 173
Crofton Ct. PO14: Stub 6M 211
Crofton La. PO14: Stub 7L 211
Crofton Rd. PO2: Ports 6F 214
PO4: S'sea 2J 241
Crofton Sq. RG27: Sher L 7H 23
Crofton Way SO31: Wars 8N 195
SO32: Swanm 6C 164
Croft Rd. BH9: Bour 4K 227
BH23: Chri 7B 230
BH23: Nea 9D 220
BH24: Poul 8M 185
GU11: Alders 2K 65
PO2: Ports 7E 214
(not continuous)
RG23: Oak 9C 40
RG27: H Win 8A 26
Crofts, The RG22: B'toke 4L 59
Cromalt Cl. SO45: Dib P 7J 193
Cromarty Av. PO4: S'sea 3J 241
Cromarty Cl. PO14: Stub 5L 211
Cromarty Rd. SO16: South 6D 158
Crombie Cl. PO8: Cowp 6N 181
(not continuous)
Cromer Gdns. BH12: Poole 9D 226
Cromer Rd. BH8: Bour 7A 228
BH12: Poole 1D 244
PO6: Cosh 8F 200
SO16: South 1C 172
Cromhall Cl. PO14: Fare 9M 197
Crompton Way PO15: Seg 4F 196
Cromwell Cl. RG24: Old Bas 5J 43
Cromwell Gdns. GU34: Alt 4F 80
Cromwell Pl. BH5: Bour 9E 228
Cromwell Rd. BH5: Bour 9E 228
BH12: Poole 9B 226
GU15: Camb 6M 19
PO4: S'sea 5J 241
RG21: B'toke 5B 42
SO15: South 1B 4 (3L 173)
SO22: Winche 9H 105
Cromwell Way GU14: Farn 5K 29
CRONDALL 3L 63
Crondall Av. PO9: Hav 3E 202
Crondall Ct. GU15: Camb 9K 19
Crondall End GU46: Yat 6M 17
Crondall La. GU9: Farnh 8A 64
GU10: Dipp, Farnh 5N 63
Crondall Rd. GU10: Cron 6H 47
GU10: Farnh 6M 63
GU51: Cr V 6H 47
Crondall Ter. RG24: B'toke 3M 41
Crooked Hays Cl. SO40: March 9E 172
Crooked La. BH25: New M 6D 232
Crooked Wlk. La. PO17: S'wick 6N 199
CROOKHAM 1M 9
Crookham Cl. PO9: Hav 4C 202
RG26: Tadl 7H 11
CROOKHAM COMMON 1K 9
Crookham Comn. Rd. RG7: Brim 1L 9
RG19: C Cmn 1L 9

Crookham Reach—Dart Ho.

Crookham Reach GU52: Ch Cr 6K 47
Crookham Rd. GU51: Ch Cr, Fleet 6K 47
SO19: South 1D 194
CROOKHAM VILLAGE 5H 47
CROOK HILL 8B 124
CROOKHORN 6M 201
Crookhorn La. PO7: Purb 8M 201
SO32: Sob 3L 165
Crooksbury La. GU10: Seal 9N 65
Crooksbury Rd. GU10: Farnh, Run, Tilf 7K 65
Cropmark Way RG22: B'toke 3K 59
Crosby Gdns. GU46: Yat 6K 17
Crosby Rd. BH4: Bour 4G 244
Crosby Way GU9: Farnh 9C 64
Crosfield Cl. SO51: E Wel 1B 156
Cross, The BH24: Bur 7E 188
GU32: E Meon 3L 143
SO20: Ki S 9B 86 (7G 88)
SP5: Bish 3C 118
Cross & Pillory La. GU34: Alt 5F 80
Crossbill Cl. PO8: Horn 3A 182
Crossborough Gdns. RG21: B'toke 7D 42
Crossborough Hill RG21: B'toke 7D 42
Crossfell Wlk. PO14: Fare 1A 212
Crossfield Av. PO31: Cowes 5P 237
Cross Gdns. GU16: Frim G 6N 29
CROSSHOUSE 7N 173
Cross Ho. Cen. SO14: South 7A 174
Crosshouse Rd. SO14: South 7A 174
Cross Keys Pas. SO23: Winche 8N 237
Crossland Cl. PO12: Gos 4L 239
Crossland Dr. PO9: Hav 6F 202
Cross La. GU16: Frim G 6N 29
PO8: Horn 5A 182
RG20: Ashm 7M 7
SO32: Bis W 9E 134
SP10: A'ver 1M 69
Crossley Ct. SO15: South 4H 173
Crossley Pl. SO15: South 1A 4 (4K 173)
Crossmead Av. BH25: New M 4B 232
Cross Rd. PO13: Lee S 3C 238
SO19: South 3C 174
Cross St. GU11: Alders 9J 49
GU14: Farn 3L 49
PO1: Ports 3K 5 (2B 240)
PO5: S'sea 3E 240
RG21: B'toke 7C 42
SO23: Winche 7L 237 (6K 105)
SO32: Bis W 3M 163
Crosstrees SO31: Sar G 3C 196
CROSSWATER 4G 85
Crosswater La. GU10: Chur 4G 85
Cross Way BH23: Chri 5G 228
PO9: Hav 7E 202
SO21: Shaw 8H 127
Crossway, The PO16: Portc 9K 199
Crossways GU10: Chur 7G 85
GU12: Alders 1L 65
GU51: Cr V 5H 47
RG28: Whit 4G 55
SO41: Ever 5L 233
SP10: A'ver 9M 51
Crossways, The PO12: Gos 1K 239
SO53: Cha F 8A 132
Crossways Cl. GU10: Chur 7H 85
SP5: Down 2J 119
Crossways Rd. GU26: Gray, Hind 4L 103
Crosswell Cl. SO19: South 5G 174
Croucher's Cft. SO22: Winche 4G 104
CROUCHESTON 3C 118
Croucheston Drove SP5: Bish 3C 118
Croucheston Hollow SP5: Bish 3C 118
Crouch La. PO8: Horn 3A 182
CROW 4M 187
Crow Arch La. BH24: Crow, Ring 2L 187
Crow Arch La. Ind. Est. BH24: Ring 3L 187
Crowdale Dr. GU51: Fleet 9K 27
Crowders Grn. SO21: Col C 4K 133
Crowder Ter. SO22: Winche 8K 237 (7K 105)
CROWDHILL 7N 133
CROW HILL 7A 188
Crow La. BH24: Crow, Hight 2M 187
Crowley Dr. GU34: Alt 5G 80
Crowlin Ho. SO40: Tott 2J 171
Crown Bingo 4F 202
Crown Cl. BH12: Poole 9A 226
PO7: Purb 6M 201
Crown Cl. M. GU34: Alt 5F 80
Crown Court
Bournemouth 5E 228
Crown Ct. PO1: Ports 1E 240
(Crown St.)
PO1: Ports 7K 5
(Peacock La.)
PO31: Cowes 5P 237
(off Market Hill)
Crown Cres. RG24: Old Bas 5H 43
Crown Dr. GU9: Bad L 5J 65
Crownfields RG29: Odi 9K 45
Crown Gdns. GU51: Fleet 3N 47
Crown Hgts. RG21: B'toke 6C 42
Crown Ho. SP11: Ludg 1D 30
Crown La. GU9: Bad L 5H 65
RG24: Old Bas 5H 43
RG27: Nat S, Newn 4B 44
SP11: Ludg 1C 30
Crown M. PO12: Gos 3M 239
Crown Pl. GU47: Owl 4G 18
Crown St. PO1: Ports 1E 240
SO15: South 2G 173
Crown Vs. *SP11: Ludg 1C 30*
(off Crown La.)
Crown Wlk. BH1: Bour 1B 246
Crown Way SP10: A'ver 9C 52
Crown Wood GU34: Meds 4H 97
Crownwood Ga. GU9: Farnh 8C 64
Crowsbury Cl. PO10: Ems 6L 203
Crows La. GU34: Up Farr 4E 98
Crows Nest La. SO32: Botl 1C 176
CROWSPORT 6L 195
Crowsport SO31: Hamb 6L 195
Crowther Cl. SO19: South 6G 175
CROWTHORNE 1E 18
Crowthorne Rd. GU47: Sandh 5C 18
RG45: Cr'tne 5C 18
Crowthorne Station (Rail) 1A 18
Croxton Rd. PO1: Ports 8L 5 (4C 240)
Croyde Cl. GU14: Farn 6J 29
Croydon Cl. SO16: South 7F 158
Croye Cl. SP10: A'ver 1M 69
Cruikshank Lea GU47: Coll 7G 18
Crummock Rd. SO53: Cha F 4M 131
Crundles GU31: Pet 1N 145
Crundwell Ct. GU9: Farnh 7F 64
Crusader Ct. BH4: Bour 1F 244
PO12: Gos 9L 213
Crusader Rd. BH11: Bour 2B 226
SO30: Hed E 5A 176
Crusaders Way SO53: Cha F 6L 131
Cruse Cl. SO41: Sway 5J 223
CRUX EASTON 8A 8
Crystal Way PO7: W'lle 1A 202
Cucklington Gdns. BH9: Bour 2M 227
Cuckmere La. SO16: South 2B 172
CUCKOO BUSHES 4A 132
Cuckoo Bushes La. SO53: Cha F 4N 131
Cuckoo Cl. RG25: Nth W 9A 58
(not continuous)
Cuckoo Hill Railway 9M 153
Cuckoo Hill Way BH23: Bran 6E 220
Cuckoo La. PO14: Stub 5L 211
SO14: South 8C 4 (7L 173)
Cuckoo Leaze RG26: Cha A 4H 21
CUCKOO'S CORNER 1L 81
Cudbury Dr. GU51: Fleet 9K 27
Cudworth Mead SO30: Hed E 1A 176
CUFAUDE 5E 22
Cufaude La. RG24: Chin 8G 23
RG26: B'ley 3E 22
Cuffelle Cl. RG24: Chin 9H 23
Cuffnells Cl. BH24: Mock 1L 185
Cul-de-Sac BH25: New M 6L 231
Culdrose Ho. *GU11: Alders 9J 49*
(off Frederick St.)
Culford Av. SO40: Tott 4M 171
Culford Cl. BH8: Bour 4C 228
Culford Ct. *BH8: Bour 9L 227*
(off Wellington Rd.)
Culford Way SO40: Tott 4M 171
Cull Cl. BH12: Poole 6G 226
Cullen Cl. GU46: Yat 8M 17
Cullens M. GU11: Alders 1J 65
Culley Vw. SO24: New A 2F 108
Cull La. BH25: New M 9C 222
(not continuous)
Culloden Cl. PO15: Fare 7A 198
Culloden Rd. PO14: Fare 2B 212
Cullwood La. BH25: New M 1D 232
Culver SO31: Net A 2G 195
Culver Cl. SO16: South 9C 158
Culver Dr. PO11: H Isl 6J 243
Culverin Sq. PO3: Ports 4H 215
Culverlands Cl. SO32: Shed 4A 178
Culverley Cl. SO42: Broc 7C 148 (8N 189)
Culver M. SO23: Winche 9M 237 (7L 105)
Culver Rd. BH25: New M 4A 232
GU47: Owl 4F 18
PO4: S'sea 5H 241
RG21: B'toke 8B 42
SO23: Winche 9L 237 (8K 105)
Culvers GU31: S Hart 9G 147
(not continuous)
Culverwell Gdns.
SO23: Winche 9L 237 (7K 105)
Culvery Gdns. SO18: Wes E 1E 174
Cumberland Av. PO10: Ems 5L 203
RG22: B'toke 1N 59
SO53: Cha F 6C 132
Cumberland Bus. Cen. PO5: S'sea 2E 240
Cumberland Cl. SO53: Cha F 6C 132
Cumberland Ct. BH2: Bour 9J 247
PO4: S'sea 5G 240
Cumberland Ho. PO1: Ports 2K 5 (1B 240)
PO13: Gos 2E 238
Cumberland House Natural History Mus.
6G 240
Cumberland Pl. SO15: South 3B 4 (5L 173)
Cumberland Rd. PO5: S'sea 2E 240
Cumberland St. PO1: Ports 2K 5 (1B 240)
SO14: South 5F 4 (6N 173)
Cumberland Way SO45: Dib 6H 193
Cumber Rd. SO31: Loc H 6B 196
Cumber's La. GU32: E Meon 4B 144
Cumbria Ct. GU14: Farn 2N 49
Cumbrian Way SO16: South 2D 172
Cummins Cl. SP10: A'ver 2B 70
Cummins Grn. SO31: Burs 9L 175
Cumnor Rd. BH1: Bour 6N 247 (2L 245)
Cunard Av. SO15: South 2H 173
Cunard Rd. SO14: South 9E 4 (8M 173)
Cundell Way SO23: Kin W 6M 91
Cunningham Av. PO2: Ports 4F 214
SO32: Bis W 3K 163
Cunningham Cl. BH11: Bour 3E 226
BH23: Mude 8C 230
BH24: Poul 9M 185
PO2: Ports 4E 214
Cunningham Ct. BH25: New M 3A 232
PO5: S'sea 5E 240
(off Collingwood Rd.)
Cunningham Cres. BH11: Bour 3E 226
SO19: South 6F 174
Cunningham Dr. PO13: Gos 5F 212
SO31: Loc H 5E 196
Cunningham Gdns. SO31: Old N 1K 195
Cunningham Ho. SO32: Bis W 3L 163
SP9: Tidw 6C 30
(off Sidbury Circular Rd.)
Cunningham Pl. BH11: Bour 3E 226
Cunningham Rd. PO7: W'lle 4L 201
PO8: Horn 3C 182
Cunnington Rd. GU14: Farn 1N 49
CUPERNHAM 3A 130
Cupernham Cl. SO51: Rom 3N 129
Cupernham La. SO51: Rom 1N 129
Cupid Ho. SO17: South 8A 160
CURBRIDGE 6G 177
Curbridge Nature Reserve 6F 176
CURDRIDGE 2G 177
Curdridge Cl. PO9: Hav 4G 203
Curdridge La.
SO32: Curd, Wal C 9J 163
Curie Rd. PO6: Cosh 8G 200
Curlew Cl. PO10: Ems 9L 203
RG22: B'toke 1J 59
SO16: South 6G 159
SO45: Hythe 7N 193
Curlew Ct. *GU11: Alders 3J 65*
(off Boxhalls La.)
Curlew Dr. PO16: Portc 9H 199
SO45: Hythe 7N 193
Curlew Gdns. PO8: Cowp 6N 181
Curlew Path PO4: S'sea 2J 241
Curlew Rd. BH8: Bour 4A 228
BH23: Mude 8C 230
Curlews GU34: Alt 2F 80
Curlew Sq. SO50: E'leigh 1C 160
Curlew Wlk. PO13: Gos 5C 212
SO45: Hythe 7N 193
Curly Bri. Cl. GU14: Cov 4H 29
Curtis Cl. GU35: Head 1A 102
Curtis Ct. GU52: Ch Cr 6M 47
Curtis La. GU35: Head 1N 101
Curtis Lodge BH1: Bour 9A 228
Curtis Mead PO2: Ports 4G 214
Curtis Museum, The 5F 80
Curtis Rd. BH12: Poole 9A 226
GU34: Alt 6G 81
Curtiss Gdns. PO12: Gos 3H 239
Curve, The PO8: Love 4N 181
PO13: Gos 5D 212
Curzon Ct. *BH4: Bour 2G 245*
(off Portarlington Rd.)
SO16: South 7J 159
Curzon Dr. GU52: Ch Cr 6N 47
Curzon Howe Rd. PO1: Ports 3K 5 (2B 240)
Curzon Pl. SO41: Penn 4D 234
Curzon Rd. BH1: Bour 8A 228
PO7: W'lle 2M 201
(not continuous)
Curzon Way BH23: Chri 6F 230
Cusden Dr. SP10: A'ver 8N 51
CUSTARDS 1C 148
Custards, The SO43: Lyn 1C 148
Cutbush La. SO18: South 9E 160
(not continuous)
Cuthbert Rd. PO1: Ports 1G 240
Cutler Cl. BH12: Poole 7G 227
BH25: A'ley 3D 232
Cutlers La. PO14: Stub 5M 211
Cutter Av. SO31: Wars 8B 196
Cut Throat La. SO32: Drox 1K 165
SO32: Swanm 5E 164
Cutting Dr. RG24: B'toke 3M 41
Cutts Arch SO32: Drox, Sob 4K 165
Cutts Rd. GU11: Alders 4M 49
Cuxhaven Way SP10: A'ver 7M 51
Cygnet Ct. GU51: Fleet 9N 27
PO16: Portc 9H 199
Cygnet Ho. PO12: Gos 9K 213
Cygnet Rd. PO6: Farl 1N 215
Cygnus Gdns. SO45: Dib 6H 193
Cynthia Rd. BH12: Poole 7A 226
Cypress Av. SO19: South 5D 174
Cypress Cres. PO8: Horn 5A 182
Cypress Dr. GU51: Fleet 2B 48
Cypress Gdns. SO30: Botl 3D 176
SO40: Tott 3J 171
Cypress Gro. SO41: Ever 5L 233
SO53: Cha F 4A 132
SP10: A'ver 2J 69
Cypress Hill Ct. GU14: Cov 3H 29
Cypress Rd. GU35: W'hil 5F 100
Cypress Way GU17: Blackw 8D 18
GU26: Hind 5M 103
Cyprus Rd. PO2: Ports 8F 214
PO14: Titch C 8F 196
RG22: B'toke 5L 59
Cyril Rd. BH8: Bour 8N 227

D

Dacre Cl. SP10: Charl 7K 51
Dacres Wlk. SO41: M Sea 7K 235
Daffodil Cl. RG22: B'toke 2J 59
Daffodil Rd. SO16: S'ing 7A 160
DAGGONS 7P 149
Daggons Rd. SP6: Ald 7P 149
Dahlia Cl. RG22: B'toke 2K 59
Dahlia Ct. SP10: A'ver 3M 69
Dahlia Rd. SO16: Bass 7M 159
Daintree Cl. SO19: South 7H 175
Dairy Cl. BH23: Chri 7N 229
SP5: Woodf 3M 119 (8C 120)
Dairy La. SO16: Nur 7N 157
Dairymoor PO17: Wick 6C 178
Dairy Pl. SO21: M'dvr 6J 77
Dairy Wlk. RG27: H Win 6C 26
Daisy Flds. SO50: Fair O 3A 162
Daisy La. PO12: Gos 3J 239
SO31: Loc H 6E 196
Daisy Mead PO7: W'lle 3A 202
Daisy Rd. SO16: Bass 7N 159
Dakota Bus. Pk. PO9: Hav 5H 203
Dakota Cl. BH23: Chri 7D 230
Dakota Way SO50: E'leigh 3D 160
Dale, The PO7: Wid 7K 201
Dale Cl. SO22: Lit 1E 104
Dale Dr. PO13: Gos 3D 212
Dale Gdns. GU47: Sandh 5C 18
Dale Grn. SO53: Cha F 3N 131
Dale Pk. Ho. PO1: Ports 2D 240
Dale Rd. PO14: Stub 5N 211
SO16: South 9H 159
SO45: Hythe 6L 193
Dales La. BH23: Hurn 8B 218
Dale Sq. PO9: Hav 3C 202
Dales Way SO40: Tott 2H 171
Dale Valley Cl. SO16: South 9H 159
Dale Valley Gdns. SO16: South 9H 159
Dale Valley Rd. SO16: South 9H 159
Dalewood RG22: B'toke 9J 41
Dalewood Av. BH11: Bour 1C 226
Dalewood Rd. PO15: Fare 8N 197
Dalkeith La. BH1: Bour 6M 247 (2K 245)
Dalkeith Rd. BH13: Poole 4E 244
Dalkeith Steps BH1: Bour 6M 247
Dalley Ct. GU47: Coll 6F 18
Dalley Way GU33: Liss 1E 140
Dalling Rd. BH12: Poole 9E 226
Dallington Cl. PO14: Stub 7M 211
Dalmally Gdns. SO18: South 2D 174
Dalmeny Rd. BH6: Bour 2K 247
Damask Gdns. PO7: W'lle 9B 182
Dame Elizabeth Kelly Ct. *PO2: Ports 4F 214*
(off Phoenix Sq.)
Damen Cl. SO30: Hed E 5M 175
DAMERHAM 4P 149
Damerham Rd. BH8: Bour 3A 228
BH21: Cran 6J 149
Dampier Cl. PO13: Gos 9E 212
Damsel La. RG25: Pres C 4F 78
Damsel Path RG21: B'toke 6E 42
Damson Cres. SO50: Fair O 2L 161
Damson Dr. RG27: H Win 8B 26
Damson Hill SO32: Bis W, Swanm 2D 164
Danbury Ct. PO10: Ems 7N 203
Dancers Mdw. RG24: Sher J 9A 22
Dances Cl. SP10: A'ver 9A 52
Dance's La. RG28: Whit 4G 55
Dances Way PO11: H Isl 3E 242
Dandelion Cl. PO13: Gos 6D 212
Dando Rd. PO7: Den 6H 181
Dandy's Ford La. SO51: Sher E, W Wel 7N 121
DANEBURY 1B 88
Danebury Cl. PO9: Hav 3E 202
Danebury Gdns. SO53: Cha F 8M 131
Danebury Hill Fort 8E 72
Danebury Rd. RG22: B'toke 4K 59
Danebury Wlk. GU16: Frim 4N 29
Danebury Way SO16: Nur 8C 158
Dane Cl. SO45: Blac 7D 208
Danecrest Rd. SO41: Hor 3G 232
Danegeld Cl. SP10: A'ver 6A 52
Danehurst SO41: Down 8G 233
Danehurst New Rd. SO41: Tip 7D 222
Danehurst Pl. SO31: Loc H 7D 196
SP10: A'ver 1J 69
Danemark Ct. SO23: Winche 6N 237 (6L 105)
Dane Rd. SO41: Down 8H 233
Danes, The RG21: B'toke 6D 42
Danesbrook La. PO7: W'lle 2A 202
Danesbury Av. BH6: Bour 1J 247
Danesbury Mdws. BH25: A'ley 1D 232
Danes Cl. BH25: B Sea 7B 232
DANESHILL 3E 42
Daneshill Ct. RG24: Lych 2G 43
Daneshill Dr. RG24: Lych 3G 43
Daneshill E. Ind. Est. RG24: B'toke 4F 42
Daneshill Ind. Est. RG24: B'toke 4F 42
Daneshill Rdbt. RG24: B'toke 4F 42
Daneshill W. Ind. Est. RG24: B'toke 3E 42
Danes Rd. PO16: Portc 7K 199
SO23: Winche 5L 105
SO51: Awb, Shoo 1D 128
Danestream Cl. SO41: M Sea 8K 235
Danestream Ct. SO41: M Sea 8L 235
Daneswood Rd. BH25: A'ley 3D 232
Danielle Ct. *BH8: Bour 9N 227*
(off Lowther Gdns.)
Daniells Cl. SO41: Lymi 3E 234
Daniell's Wlk. SO41: Lymi 4E 234
Daniel Rd. RG28: Whit 6H 55
Daniels Cl. PO12: Gos 3G 239
Daniel's Ct. BH24: Ring 1H 187
Daniels Lodge BH23: Highc 7K 231
Daniels Wlk. SO40: Calm 1H 171
Dankworth Rd. RG22: B'toke 2L 59
(not continuous)
Danley La. GU27: Linc 3J 117
Danvers Dr. GU52: Ch Cr 7K 47
Daphne Dr. GU52: Ch Cr 8K 47
Dapple Pl. SO40: March 9F 172
DARBY GREEN 8D 18
Darby Grn. La. GU17: Blackw 8C 18
Darby Grn. Rd. GU17: Blackw 8C 18
Darcy Cl. RG21: B'toke 4D 42
D'arcy Ho. RG22: B'toke 9L 41
Darent Ct. *RG21: B'toke 6E 42*
(off Loddon Dr.)
Dare's La. GU10: Ews 1M 63
Dark Hollow GU32: Pet 9L 139
Dark La. BH23: Hin 2J 231
BH25: New M 2A 232
RG24: Sher J 9N 21
SO24: Bis S 4H 109
SO24: Cher 9F 108
SO32: Warn 6A 136
SO45: Blac 7C 208
Darlee Ga. SO31: Old N 9K 175
Darleydale Cl. GU47: Owl 3F 18
Darlington Gdns. SO15: South 1J 173
Darlington Rd. PO4: S'sea 4F 240
RG21: B'toke 4B 42
Darnel Cres. PO7: W'lle 8K 181
Darracott Gdns. BH5: Bour 1D 246
Darracott Rd. BH5: Bour 1D 246
Darren Cl. PO14: Stub 4N 211
Darren Ct. PO16: Fare 7D 198
Darset Av. GU51: Fleet 1M 47
Dart Ct. *SP10: A'ver 8B 52*
(off River Way)
Dart Ho. SO18: South 2D 174

Dartington Rd.—District Vs.

Dartington Rd. SO50: B'stke 7H 133
Dartmouth Cl. PO12: Gos 9L 213
Dartmouth Ct. *PO12: Gos* 9L 213
(off Dartmouth Cl.)
Dartmouth M. PO5: S'sea 8M 5 (4C 240)
Dartmouth Rd. PO3: Ports 6H 215
Dartmouth Wlk. RG22: B'toke 8L 41
Dartmouth Way RG22: B'toke 8L 41
Dart Rd. GU14: Cov 6F 28
SO18: Wes E 8F 160
Darvill Rd. SO24: Rop 1B 110
Darvills La. GU9: Farnh 8E 64
Darwell Ho. *RG21: B'toke* 6B 42
(off Essex Rd.)
Darwin Av. BH23: Chri 5H 229
Darwin Cl. PO13: Lee S 9B 212
SP4: Bul C 3C 66
Darwin Ct. BH12: Poole 1E 244
GU15: Camb 1K 29
(off Watchetts Rd.)
Darwin Gro. GU11: Alders 8L 49
Darwin Ho. *PO1: Ports* 2E 240
(off Australia Cl.)
Darwin Rd. SO15: South 3J 173
SO50: E'leigh 8F 132
Dashwood Cl. GU34: Alt 6D 80
Dasna Rd. SP9: Tidw 9B 30 (7F 30)
Daubney Gdns. PO9: Hav 3D 202
Daulston Rd. PO1: Ports 9G 214
Daunch Cl. SP9: Tidw 7B 30 (6F 30)
Dauntsey Drove SP11: Weyh 8A 50
Dauntsey La. SP11: Weyh 9A 50
Davenport Cl. PO13: Gos 1E 238
Davenport Ga. SP10: A'ver 9J 51
Daventry La. PO3: Ports 4K 215
D Avenue SO45: Fawl 2B 208
David Ct. SO51: Rom 6N 129
David Cowan Ho. SO23: Winche 7L 237
David Hart Bus. Cen. SP5: Down 1J 119 (7A 120)
Davidia Ct. PO7: W'lle 3A 202
David Lloyd Leisure
Port Solent 2C 214
Ringwood 3K 187
Southampton 8C 158
David Lockhart Ct. SO17: South 1N 173
David Moxon Annexe SO14: South 6F 4
David Newberry Dr. PO13: Lee S 1C 238
David's Gdn. *SP5: P'tn* 6E 86
(off Black La.)
David's La. BH24: A'ley 3F 186
Davidson Cl. SO45: Hythe 5N 193
Davidson Ct. PO1: Ports 4K 5
David Trenchard Ho. *BH1: Bour* 9L 227
(off Lansdowne Rd.)
Davies Ct. BH12: Poole 9C 226
Davis Cl. PO13: Gos 8E 212
Davis Fld. BH25: New M 4A 232
Davis Gdns. GU47: Coll 6G 18
Davis Rd. BH12: Poole 9C 226
Davis Way PO14: Fare 2C 212
Davy Cl. RG22: B'toke 7N 41
Dawkins Way BH25: New M 4B 232
Daw La. PO11: H Isl 8F 216
Dawlish Av. SO15: South 2J 173
Dawnay Cl. SO16: S'ing 6B 160
Dawnay Rd. GU15: Camb 5K 19
(not continuous)
Dawn Cl. BH10: Bour 4G 227
Dawn Gdns. SO22: Winche 8G 105
Daws Av. BH11: Bour 5E 226
Dawson Lodge SO30: Wes E 1K 175
Dawson Rd. SO19: South 8G 174
SO21: Bar S 3A 76
Daws Pl. BH11: Bour 4F 226
Dawtrey Ct. SO17: South 9A 160
Day La. PO8: Love 3L 181
Dayrell Cl. SO40: Calm 1H 171
Dayshes Cl. PO13: Gos 5D 212
Dayslondon Rd. PO7: Purb 4L 201
Days Mdw. RG20: Wol H 3N 7
D-Day Mus. & Overlord Embroidery 6D 240
Deacon Cl. SO19: South 5E 174
Deacon Cres. SO19: South 5E 174
Deacon Gdns. BH11: Bour 1E 226
Deacon Rd. BH11: Bour 1E 226
SO19: South 5E 174
SO31: Loc H 7E 196
SP11: Kimp, Lit Shod 7M 31
Deacon Trad. Est. SO50: E'leigh 1G 160
Deadbrook La. GU12: Alders 7N 49
Deadman's Plack Monument 3H 71
Deadmoor La.
RG20: Burgh, Newt 2D 8
DEADWATER 3L 101
Deadwater Valley Local Nature Reserve 5K 101
Deakin Ct. SO53: Cha F 7A 132
Deal Cl. PO14: Stub 4M 211
Deal Rd. PO6: Cosh 8F 200
DEAN
SO21 3C 104
SO32 9H 135
Dean, The SO24: New A 9E 94
Dean Cl. SO22: Winche 4G 104
Dean Court 8B 228
Dean Ct. SO18: South 2C 174
SO30: Hed E 3M 175
DEANE 1L 57
Deane Cotts. RG25: Dea 1L 57
Deane Ct. PO9: Hav 4H 203
Deane Down Drove SO22: Lit 2F 104
Deane Gdns. PO13: Lee S 1B 238
Deanery, The 9M 237 (7L 105)
Deanery, The SO53: Cha F 3N 131
Deanery Halls SO14: South 7F 4
Deanes Cl. RG21: B'toke 5D 42
Deane's Pk. Rd. PO16: Fare 8F 198
Dean Farm Est. PO17: Fare 4C 198
Dean Farm Golf Course 8F 82
Deanfield Cl. SO31: Hamb 7K 195
Deanfields Ct. SO18: South 2F 174
Dean La. PO8: Finch, R Cas 4K 183
PO9: R Cas 4K 183
SO21: Spar 3B 104
SO22: Spar, Winche 4F 104
SO32: Bis W 8H 135
SP5: W'psh 5H 121
DEANLANE END 5L 183
Dean M. SO18: South 3E 174
Dean Pk. Cres. BH1: Bour 5M 247 (1K 245)
Dean Pk. Lodge *BH1: Bour* 1L 245
(off Cavendish Rd.)
Dean Pk. Mans. BH1: Bour 5N 247 (1L 245)
Dean Pk. Rd. BH1: Bour 5M 247 (1K 245)
Dean Pl. SO53: Cha F 6A 132
Dean Ri. SP11: Hur T 4E 34
Dean Rd. PO6: Cosh 9H 201
SO18: South 2E 174
SO50: Fair O 2M 161
SP5: E Gri, W Dean 1F 120
SP5: W Dean, W Tyt 1J 121
Deans, The BH1: Bour 1K 245
Deans Cl. SP9: Tidw 9D 30 (8G 31)
Deans Ct. SO41: M Sea 7K 235
Deanscroft Rd. BH10: Bour 2J 227
Deans Dell GU32: Frox 4E 138
Deansfield Cl. SO51: Rom 4A 130
Deans Ga. PO14: Stub 7M 211
Deans La. RG26: Cha A 2G 20
Deansleigh Rd. BH7: Bour 5E 228
Deans Rd. BH5: Bour 9E 228
Dean Station (Rail) 1J 121
Dean St. PO1: Ports 4K 5 (2B 240)
Deansway Ct. BH1: Bour 5N 247
Dean Swift Cres. BH14: Poole 5A 244
Deanswood Dr. PO7: W'lle 9M 181
Deanswood Rd. RG26: Tadl 5G 10
Dean Ter. SP11: Ver D 8E 6
Dean Vs. PO17: K Vil 3A 198
Dearing Cl. SO43: Lyn 2B 148 (2N 189)
Dearly Cft. SP6: Woodg 2A 154
Debney Lodge PO7: W'lle 2N 201
Decies Rd. BH14: Poole 9A 226
De Courtenai Cl. BH11: Bour 1B 226
Decouttere Cl. GU52: Ch Cr 6K 47
Dee Cl. SO53: Cha F 7N 131
Deep Dell PO8: Horn 5B 182
Deepdene GU27: Hasl 9N 103
Deepdene, The SO18: South 2C 174
Deepdene La. BH11: Bour 1C 226
Deeping Cl. SO19: South 9D 174
Deeping Ga. PO7: W'lle 2A 202
Deep La. RG21: B'toke 6A 42
Deep Well Dr. GU15: Camb 8N 19
Deerbrook Cl. SO31: Sar G 4C 196
Deerfield Cl. RG26: B'ley 2J 23
Deergrass Wlk. PO17: K Vil 2N 197
Deerhurst Cl. SO40: Tott 4K 171
Deerhurst Cres. PO6: Cosh 8B 200
Deer La. SO41: Bold 8D 224
Deer Leap PO15: F'ley 4N 197
Deerleap GU35: Head D 3E 102
Deerleap Cl. SO45: Hythe 6M 193
Deerleap La. SO40: March, Tott 7K 171
Deerleap Way BH25: New M 9C 222
SO45: Hythe 6M 193
Deer Pk. Cl. BH25: New M 2A 232
Deer Pk. Farm Ind. Est.
SO50: Fair O 2B 162
Deer Pk. Vw. RG29: Odi 8L 45
Deer Rock Rd. GU15: Camb 6N 19
Deer Sanctuary 2G 189
Deers Leap Caravan Pk.
BH24: Lin 1B 188
Deer Wlk. SO30: Hed E 2A 176
Defender Rd. SO19: South 7B 174
Defender Wlk. SO19: South 7B 174
Defiance Way SP11: A'ver 2E 70
Defiant Rd. GU14: Farn 3H 49
Defoe Cl. PO15: White 1F 196
De Grouchy La. SO17: South 1M 173
De Haviland Ho. BH23: Mude 8C 230
De Havilland Way BH23: Mude 9B 230
Delamere Gdns. BH10: Bour 3J 227
Delamere Rd. PO4: S'sea 4F 240
De La Rue Ho. RG21: B'toke 5E 42
De La Warr Rd. SO41: M Sea 8J 235
Delft Cl. SO31: Loc H 6C 196
Delft Gdns. PO8: Cowp 8L 181
Delft M. BH23: Chri 8N 229
Delhi Cl. BH14: Poole 2B 244
Delhi Rd. BH9: Bour 4J 227
Delibes Rd. RG22: B'toke 2A 60
De Lisle Cl. PO2: Ports 4G 214
De Lisle Rd. BH3: Bour 7K 227
Delius Av. SO19: South 7H 175
Delius Cl. RG22: B'toke 1N 59
Delius Wlk. PO7: W'lle 4M 201
Dell, The BH25: New M 6L 231
GU9: H End 3F 64
GU46: Yat 8M 17
PO9: Bed 7B 202
PO16: Fare 8F 198
RG20: Kings 3B 6 (6K 9)
RG24: Old Bas 6K 43
SO15: South 1A 4 (4K 173)
SP11: Grat 4L 67
SP11: Ver D 8E 6
Dellands RG25: Over 3D 56
Dellands La. RG25: Over 3C 56
Dell Cl. PO7: Wid 7J 201
SO50: Fair O 2N 161
Dellcrest Path PO6: Cosh 8J 201
(not continuous)
PO7: Wid 7J 201
Dellfield GU32: Frox 3E 138
(not continuous)
RG23: Oak 8D 40
Dellfield Cl. PO6: Cosh 8B 200
Dell Piece E. PO8: Horn 5D 182
Dell Piece W. PO8: Horn 4B 182
Dell Quay Cl. PO13: Gos 6D 212
Dell Rd. RG40: F'std 1K 17
SO18: South 9D 160
SO23: Winche 8N 105
SP10: A'ver 9M 51
Delme Ct. PO16: Fare 8C 198
Delme Dr. PO16: Fare 7F 198
Delme Sq. PO16: Fare 8D 198
Delphina Chase BH13: Poole 6C 244
Delphi Way PO7: Purb 7N 201
Delta Bus. Pk. GU34: Alt 5H 81
PO16: Fare 1D 212
Delta Cl. BH23: Chri 7C 230
Delta Ho. SO16: Chilw 2H 159
De-Lucy Av. SO24: New A 1D 108
De Lunn Bldgs. SO23: Winche 6M 237
Delville Cl. GU14: Cov 9F 28
De Mauley Rd. BH13: Poole 5C 244
De Mowbray Way SO41: Lymi 4D 234
Dempsey Cl. SO19: South 6F 174
Denbigh Cl. SO40: Tott 5K 171
SO50: E'leigh 7D 132
Denbigh Dr. PO16: Fare 7B 198
Denbigh Gdns. SO16: Bass 7L 159
DENE, THE 3E 34
Dene, The BH13: Poole 3E 244
SO24: Rop 1B 110
SP11: Hur T 4D 34
Dene Cl. BH24: Poul 8M 185
GU35: Bor 5J 101
SO16: Chilw 4L 159
SO24: Rop 1B 110
SO31: Sar G 5B 196
Dene Ct. SP10: A'ver 2A 70
Dene Hollow PO6: Dray 9L 201
Dene Path SP10: A'ver 2A 70
Dene Rd. GU14: Cov 9H 29
SO40: Ashu 8J 171
SP10: A'ver 2A 70
Deneside Copse SO41: Penn 4B 234
Dene Way SO40: Ashu 7J 171
Denewood Rd. BH4: Bour 3F 244
Denewulf Cl. SO32: Bis W 3M 163
Denham Cl. PO14: Stub 6L 211
SO23: Winche 4K 105
Denham Ct. SO23: Winche 4L 105
Denham Dr. BH23: Highc 5H 231
GU46: Yat 8N 17
RG22: B'toke 9L 41
Denham Flds. SO50: Fair O 9N 133
Denham Gdns. SO31: Net A 4F 194
Denham Ter. SP11: S M Bo 9L 35
Denhill Cl. PO11: H Isl 2E 242
Denholm Cl. BH24: Poul 8N 185
Denman Cl. GU51: Fleet 2A 48
Denmark Rd. BH9: Bour 5K 227
Denmark Sq. GU12: Alders 9M 49
Denmark St. GU12: Alders 9M 49
DENMEAD 5G 181
Denmead BH25: A'ley 2E 232
Denmead Ho. PO1: Ports 1E 240
Denmead La. PO7: Den 4J 181
Denmead Pk. PO7: Den 6H 181
Denmead Rd. BH6: Bour 7G 229
RG26: Tadl 5H 11
SO18: South 2G 174
Dennett Ho. SO23: Winche 5A 106
Denning Cl. GU52: Fleet 4K 47
Denning Mead SP10: A'ver 2M 69
Denning M. PO5: S'sea 2D 240
Dennison Ct. SO15: South 2G 172
Dennistoun Av. BH23: Chri 7B 230
Dennistoun Cl. GU15: Camb 8M 19
Dennis Way GU33: Liss 2F 140
Denny Cl. SO45: Fawl 5F 208
Denton Way GU16: Frim 2M 29
Denvale Trade Pk. RG21: B'toke 4A 42
Denville Av. PO16: Portc 2M 213
Denville Cl. PO6: Farl 9N 201
Denville Cl. Path PO6: Farl 9N 201
DENVILLES 7H 203
Denvilles Cl. PO9: Hav 7H 203
Denzil Av. SO14: South 1E 4 (4M 173)
SO31: Net A 3G 194
Depden Gdns. SO45: Dib P 8J 193
Depedene Cl. SO45: Holb 4N 207
De Port Gdns. RG24: Old Bas 1H 43
De Port Hgts. SO32: Corh 8N 135
Deptford La. RG29: Grey 8F 44
Derby Ct. PO13: Gos 1E 238
Derbyfields RG29: N War 5J 45
Derby Rd. BH1: Bour 1N 245
PO2: Ports 7E 214
SO14: South 3F 4 (5N 173)
SO50: E'leigh 1C 160
De Redvers Ct. BH23: Chri 5G 229
De Redvers Rd. BH14: Poole 3A 244
Dereham Way BH12: Poole 8D 226
Derek Horn Ct. GU15: Camb 7K 19
Deridene Ct. SO40: Tott 4K 171
Derlyn Rd. PO16: Fare 8C 198
Derritt La. BH23: Bran, Sop 4N 219
Derrybrian Gdns. BH25: New M 4B 232
DERRY DOWN 2M 53
Derry Rd. GU14: Cov 4N 29
Dersingham Cl. PO6: Cosh 8F 200
Derwent Cl. BH9: Bour 4L 227
GU9: Up H 4C 64
GU14: Cov 8G 28
GU35: Bor 2J 101
PO8: Horn 9C 168
PO14: Stub 4N 211
SO18: Wes E 1F 174
Derwent Ct. *SP10: A'ver* 8B 52
(off Clyde Ct.)
Derwent Dr. SO40: Tott 2H 171
Derwent Gdns. SO24: New A 2F 108
Derwent Rd. BH25: New M 1C 232
PO13: Lee S 2B 238
RG22: B'toke 1J 59
SO16: South 1D 172
Desborough Cl. PO6: Cosh 8B 200
Desborough Rd. SO50: E'leigh 2E 160
Devenish Rd. SO22: Winche 3H 105
Dever Cl. SO21: M'dvr 7J 77
Deverel Cl. BH23: Chri 6K 229
Deverell Pl. PO7: Wid 6K 201
Dever Ho. GU14: Farn 8L 29
Dever Way RG23: Oak 1D 58
Devil's Highway, The RG7: Rise 2J 15
Devil's Jumps, The 4K 85
Devils La. GU30: Lip 2G 116
Devine Gdns. SO50: B'stke 1J 161
Devizes Cl. RG23: Wort 8J 41
Devizes Ho. SP9: Tidw 7D 30
Devon Cl. GU47: Coll 6F 18
GU51: Fleet 8N 27
SO53: Cha F 9A 132
Devon Dr. SO53: Cha F 9A 132
Devon M. *SO15: South* 5K 173
(off Mandela Way)
Devon Rd. BH23: Chri 6H 229
GU35: Bor 4J 101
PO3: Ports 5H 215
Devonshire Av. PO4: S'sea 3G 241
Devonshire Bus. Pk. RG21: B'toke 4A 42
Devonshire Gdns. SO31: Burs 8L 175
SO45: Hythe 9M 193
Devonshire Mans. SO15: South 2B 4
Devonshire Pl. GU11: Alders 1H 65
RG21: B'toke 7B 42
Devonshire Rd. SO15: South 1B 4 (4L 173)
Devonshire Sq. PO4: S'sea 3G 240
Devonshire Way PO14: Fare 9M 197
Dewar Cl. PO15: Seg 4F 196
Deweys La. BH24: Ring 1J 187
SP11: Ludg 1D 30 (5K 31)
Dew La. SO50: E'leigh 9D 132
Dewpond Wlk. RG24: Lych 3G 42
Dewsbury Ct. SO18: South 9E 160
Dexter Sq. SP10: A'ver 7B 52
Dexter Way GU51: Fleet 8N 27
Dhekelia Ct. PO1: Ports 1E 240
Dial Cl. BH23: Bran 5F 220
Diamond Cl. SP6: F'dge 2H 153
Diamond Ct. SP6: F'dge 2H 153
Diamond Hill GU15: Camb 6N 19
Diamond Ridge GU15: Camb 6M 19
Diamond St. PO5: S'sea 7M 5 (4C 240)
Diana Cl. PO10: Ems 5L 203
PO12: Gos 3G 239
RG22: B'toke 8N 41
Diana Ct. BH23: Highc 7J 231
Dibben Wlk. SO51: Rom 3B 130
Dibber Rd. PO7: W'lle 9K 181
Dibble Dr. SO52: N Bad 9E 130
DIBDEN 4H 193
Dibden Cl. BH8: Bour 3A 228
PO9: Hav 5C 202
Dibden Golf Course 4H 193
Dibden Lodge Cl. SO45: Hythe 4L 193
DIBDEN PURLIEU 8K 193
Dibles Pk. Caravan Site SO31: Wars 8B 196
Dibles Rd. SO31: Wars 8A 196
(not continuous)
Dibles Wharf SO14: South 5A 174
Dibley Cl. RG22: B'toke 8L 41
Dickens Cl. PO2: Ports 9E 214
Dickens Dell SO40: Tott 3H 171
Dickens Dr. PO15: White 9F 176
Dickens Ho. PO4: S'sea 3J 241
Dicken's La. RG24: Old Bas 7H 43
RG25: Tun 9G 43
Dickenson Wlk. SO24: New A 2F 108
Dickens Rd. BH6: Bour 7H 229
Dickens Way GU46: Yat 8M 17
Dicker's La. GU34: Alt 4G 81
Dickins La. GU31: Pet 8N 139
Dickinson Ho. SP9: Tidw 9D 30
Dickinson Rd. PO4: S'sea 2G 240
Dickson Pk. PO17: Wick 6C 178
Dickson Rd. SP11: A'ver 2G 68
Didcot Rd. SO15: South 1H 173
Dieppe Cres. PO2: Ports 4F 214
Dieppe Gdns. PO12: Gos 3H 239
Digby Ho. BH2: Bour 6H 247
Digby Way GU33: G'ham 2F 114
Dight Rd. PO12: Gos 5L 239
Diligence Cl. SO31: Burs 9L 175
Dilkusha Ct. PO11: H Isl 5G 243
Dilly La. BH25: B Sea 6B 232
RG27: H Win 8B 26
DILTON 9F 204
Dimond Cl. SO18: South 1C 174
Dimond Hill SO18: South 1C 174
Dimond Rd. SO18: South 9C 160
Dines Cl. SP11: Hur T 4D 34
Dines Mdw. SP11: Hur T 4D 34
Dingle Rd. BH5: Bour 1E 246
Dingle Way SO31: Loc H 5D 196
Dingley Way GU14: Farn 3J 49
Dinham Ct. BH25: A'ley 2E 232
Dinham Rd. BH25: A'ley 2E 232
Dinorben Av. GU52: Fleet 4K 47
Dinorben Beeches GU52: Fleet 4K 47
Dinorben Cl. GU52: Fleet 4K 47
Dinwoodie Dr. RG24: B'toke 3N 41
DIPLEY 5L 25
Dipley Rd. RG27: H Win, Matt 4J 25
DIPPENHALL 5N 63
Dippenhall Rd. GU10: Dipp 5N 63
Dippenhall St. GU10: Cron 3L 63
Dirty Dr. SO52: N Bad 7J 131
Dirty La. GU34: Bent 7J 79
Disa Ho. SO15: South 2A 4 (4K 173)
Discovery Cen.
Gosport 3M 239
(off High St.)
Discovery Cl. PO14: Stub 3M 211
Discovery Ct. BH12: Poole 4C 226
Disraeli Rd. BH23: Chri 8N 229
District Vs. SP11: Longp 2B 76

Ditcham Cres.—Dummer Golf Course

Ditcham Cres. PO9: Hav 5E 202
Ditchbury SO41: Lymi 9D 224
Ditton Cl. PO14: Stub 5M 211
Divers Cl. GU34: Alt 2F 80
Dix Hill RG26: Pam G, Tadl 7K 11
Dixon Rd. RG26: B'ley 3H 23
Dixons La. SO20: Brou 1A 86 (4A 88)
DOCKENFIELD 2A 84
Dockenfield Cl. PO9: Hav 5C 202
Dockenfield St. GU10: Dock 10M 63
Dock La. SO42: Beau 7F 206
Dock Mill Cotts. PO5: S'sea 5E 240
Dock Rd. PO12: Gos 3L 239
Dockyard Apprentice Exhibition Mus. 3H 5 (2A 240)
Doctors Acre RG27: Hoo 1K 45
Doctors Drove SP11: Hur T 4C 34
DOCTOR'S HILL 1A 128
Doctor's Hill SO51: Sher E 5N 121
Doctors La. GU32: W Meo 8D 136
Dodds La. SO32: Swanm 6D 164
Dodgson Cl. SP6: Woodg 2A 154
Dodwell La. SO31: Burs 9M 175
Dodwell Ter. SO31: Burs 9M 175
Doe Copse Way BH25: New M 2N 231
Doe Wlk. SO30: Hed E 2A 176
Dogflud Way GU9: Farnh 7E 64
Dogkennel La. PO7: H'don 7G 166
DOGMERSFIELD 5F 46
Dogwood Dell PO7: W'lle 4N 201
Doiley Bottom SP11: Binl, Hur T 3J 35
Doiley Hill SP11: Hur T 2F 34
Dolbery Rd. Nth. BH12: Poole 4B 226
Dolbery Rd. Sth. BH12: Poole 5A 226
Dollis Dr. GU9: Farnh 7F 64
Dollis Grn. RG26: B'ley 1G 23
DOLLY'S HILL 9G 49
Dolman Rd. PO12: Gos 4L 239
Dolomans La. SP11: Ibt 4B 34
Dolphin Av. BH10: Bour 1J 227
Dolphin Cl. GU27: Hasl 9N 103
  SO50: B'stke 1K 161
Dolphin Ct. BH13: Poole 3F 244
  PO4: S'sea 6G 240
  PO13: Lee S 1A 238
  PO14: Stub 4L 211
Dolphin Cres. PO12: Gos 4L 239
Dolphin Hill SO21: Twyf 7L 127
Dolphin M. *BH5: Bour* 9E 228
  (off Seabourne Rd.)
Dolphin Pl. BH25: B Sea 7B 232
Dolphin Quay PO10: Ems 9N 203
Dolphin Way PO12: Gos 6M 239
Dolton Rd. SO16: South 8E 158
Doman Rd. GU15: Camb 9L 19
Dome All. SO23: Winche 9M 237 (7L 105)
Dominica Cl. RG24: B'toke 1D 42
Dominie Wlk. PO13: Lee S 1B 238
Dominion Cen. BH11: Bour 3C 226
Dominion Rd. BH11: Bour 3C 226
Dominy Cl. SO45: Hythe 5N 193
Domitian Gdns. RG24: B'toke 3L 41
Domum Rd. PO2: Ports 6G 215
  SO23: Winche 8M 105
Domvilles App. PO2: Ports 7C 214
Donaldson Rd. PO6: Cosh 2G 214
Doncaster Drove SO50: E'leigh 4C 160
Doncaster Rd. SO50: E'leigh 3E 160
Donigers Cl. SO32: Swanm 5C 164
Donigers Dell SO32: Swanm 5C 164
Donkey La. SO30: Botl 3D 176
Donnelly Rd. BH6: Bour 9J 229
Donnelly St. PO12: Gos 1J 239
Donnington Cl. GU15: Camb 9K 19
Donnington Ct. SO23: Winche 5L 105
Donnington Dr. BH23: Chri 7D 230
  SO53: Cha F 9M 131
Donnington Gro. SO17: South 9N 159
Donoughmore Rd. BH1: Bour 1A 246
Don Styler Physical Training Cen. 6J 213
DORA'S GREEN 3N 63
Dora's Grn. La. GU10: Dipp, Ews 5N 63
Dora's Grn. Rd. GU10: Dipp 5M 63
Dorcas Cl. PO7: W'lle 9A 182
Dorcas Ct. GU15: Camb 1K 29
Dorchester Cl. RG23: B'toke 6K 41
Dorchester Ct. GU15: Camb 7K 19
  SO15: South 2L 173
Dorchester Ho. *SO41: Lymi* 2E 234
  (off Hillcroft Cl.)
Dorchester Mans. *BH1: Bour* 2A 246
  (off Manor Rd.)
Dorchester Rd. RG27: Hoo 2G 44
Dorchester Way RG29: Grey 7G 44
Dore Av. PO16: Portc 9K 199
Doreen Cl. GU14: Cov 5G 28
Dores La. SO51: Brai, Lwr Slac 6D 124
  (Dummers Rd.)
  SO51: Brai, Lwr Slac 3G 124
  (Farley La.)
Dorian Gro. SO24: New A 2D 108
Doric Cl. SO53: Cha F 5D 132
Dorking Cres. PO6: Cosh 1G 215
Dorland Gdns. SO40: Tott 4K 171
Dormer Cl. RG45: Cr'tne 1C 18
Dormington Rd. PO6: Cosh 8D 200
Dormy Cl. SO31: Sar G 6A 196
Dormy Way PO13: Gos 7D 212
Dornan Ho. SO14: South 1D 4 (3M 173)
Dorney Ct. PO6: Cosh 1H 215
Dornie Rd. BH13: Poole 6C 244
Dornmere La. PO7: W'lle 2A 202
Dorothy Ct. PO5: S'sea 4E 240
Dorothy Dymond St. PO1: Ports 4N 5 (2D 240)
Dorrel Cl. RG22: B'toke 4K 59
Dorrick Ct. SO15: South 3L 173
Dorrien Rd. PO12: Gos 9K 213
Dorrita Av. PO8: Cowp 6A 182
Dorrita Cl. PO4: S'sea 5G 240
Dorrits, The SO40: Tott 3H 171
Dorset Cl. PO8: Horn 4B 182
Dorset Ct. *BH4: Bour* 1G 244
  (off Branksome Wood Rd.)
Dorset Cres. RG23: Wort 8J 41
Dorset Cricket Centre, The 9E 218
Dorset Heavy Horse Cen. 9L 149
Dorset Ho. BH13: Poole 3E 244
Dorset Lake Av. BH14: Poole 5A 244
Dorset Rd. BH4: Bour 9G 226
  BH23: Chri 6B 230
  SO53: Cha F 9A 132
Dorset St. SO15: South 1D 4 (4M 173)
Dorstone Rd. PO6: Cosh 8D 200
Dorval Ho. SO15: South 3K 173
Dorval Mnr. SO15: South 3K 173
Doswell Way RG21: B'toke 5D 42
Douai Cl. GU14: Farn 8L 29
Double Hedges SP4: Bul 3A 66
Doughty Way SP10: A'ver 9D 52
Douglas Av. BH23: Chri 8J 229
Douglas Ct. BH23: Chri 8J 229
  GU51: Fleet 9M 27
  (off Fleet Rd.)
Douglas Cres. SO19: South 4G 175
Douglas Gdns. BH12: Poole 9C 226
  PO9: Hav 5G 203
Douglas M. BH6: Bour 9F 228
Douglas Pl. GU14: Cov 7J 29
Douglas Ride RG20: Wol H 3A 8
Douglas Rd. BH6: Bour 1H 247
  BH12: Poole 9C 226
  PO3: Ports 9H 215
  SP11: A'ver 1H 69
Douglas Way SO45: Hythe 5L 193
Douro Cl. RG26: Bau 4D 10
Dove Cl. PO8: Cowp 6N 181
  RG22: B'toke 1H 59
  SP10: A'ver 8A 52
Dove Ct. GU34: Alt 2G 80
Dove Dale SO50: E'leigh 1B 160
Dovedale Cl. GU47: Owl 3F 18
Dove Gdns. SO31: P Ga 4E 196
Dove La. SO51: Lwr Slac 6G 125
Dover Cl. BH13: Poole 2E 244
  PO14: Stub 5L 211
  RG23: B'toke 5M 41
  SO24: New A 2F 108
Dover Ct. PO11: H Isl 2E 242
Dovercourt Rd. PO6: Cosh 2H 215
Dover Rd. BH13: Poole 2E 244
  PO3: Ports 8H 215
Dover St. SO14: South 1E 4 (3M 173)
Doveshill Cres. BH10: Bour 3H 227
Doveshill Gdns. BH10: Bour 3H 227
Doveshill Mobile Home Pk. BH10: Bour 3H 227
Doveys Cl. *BH24: Bur* 7E 188
  (off Ringwood Rd.)
Dowden Ct. BH23: Chri 8J 229
Dowden Gro. GU34: Alt 3F 80
Dowds Cl. SO30: Hed E 2M 175
Dowlands Cl. BH10: Bour 2H 227
Dowlands Rd. BH10: Bour 2H 227
Dowley Ct. PO14: Titch 9J 197
DOWNEND 8G 199
Down End PO6: Dray 8K 201
Down End Rd. PO6: Dray 8K 201
  PO16: Fare 8H 199
  PO17: Fare 8H 199
Downey Cl. BH11: Bour 4D 226
Down Farm La. SO22: Winche 7G 91
  SO23: Winche 7G 91
Down Farm Pl. PO8: Horn 1C 182
Down Ga. SO24: New A 2E 108
Downham Cl. PO8: Cowp 7N 181
Downhouse Rd. PO8: Cath, Clan 7A 168
Downing Ct. PO14: Titch C 8F 196
Downing St. GU9: Farnh 8D 64
Downland Cl. SO30: Botl 3C 176
  SO31: Loc H 5D 196
Downland Pl. SO30: Hed E 5M 175
Downlands Cl. SP5: Down 3K 119 (8A 120)
Downlands Rd. SO22: Oli B 1F 126
Downlands Way SO21: Sth W 3G 91
  (not continuous)
Down La. RG25: Mapl 8N 43
  RG25: Pres C 5G 78
  SO51: Rom 4A 130
Downley Point PO9: Hav 5H 203
Downley Rd. PO9: Hav 6H 203
Down Lodge Cl. SP6: Ald 4D 152
Down Rd. PO8: Horn 1C 182
  SP11: Kimp 8K 31
Downs Cl. GU14: Cov 5G 28
  PO7: Purb 6N 201
Downscroft Gdns. SO30: Hed E 3M 175
Downside GU26: Hind 9M 85
  PO13: Gos 6F 212
Downside Av. SO19: South 4E 174
Downside Cl. RG24: B'toke 4M 41
Downside Rd. PO7: Wid 6K 201
  SO22: Winche 4F 104
Downsland Ct. *RG21: B'toke* 7A 42
  (off Downsland Rd.)
Downsland Pde. RG21: B'toke 7A 42
Downsland Rd. RG21: B'toke 7A 42
  (not continuous)
Downs Pk. Av. SO40: Elin 4N 171
Downs Pk. Cres. SO40: Elin 4N 171
Downs Pk. Rd. SO40: Elin 4N 171
Downs Rd. SO20: Ov Wa 7M 67
  SO21: Sth W 3G 90
Down St. RG25: Dumm 9F 58
Downs Vw. GU34: Holy 1L 81
Downsview Rd. GU35: Head D 2E 102
Downsview Way SP11: Per D 5B 30 (7J 31)
Downsway GU34: Alt 6D 80
Downsway, The PO16: Portc 9L 199
DOWNTON
  SO41 8H 233
  SP5 2L 119 (7B 120)
Downton Bus. Cen. SP5: Down 1J 119
Downton Cl. BH8: Bour 3N 227
Downton Hill SP5: M Val 1M 119 (7C 120)
Downton Holiday Pk.
  SO41: Down 7G 233
Downton Ho. PO6: Cosh 8D 200
Downton La. SO41: Down 8G 233
Downton Leisure Cen. 1H 119 (7N 119)
Downton Rd. SO18: South 9D 160
Downview Cl. GU26: Hind 1M 103
Down Vw. Rd. SP6: Mart 9C 118
Downwood Cl. SO45: Dib P 7H 193
  SP6: F'dge 9G 150
Downwood Way PO8: Horn 1C 182
Downy Ct. *BH14: Poole* 1B 244
  (off Bournemouth Rd.)
Doyle Av. PO2: Ports 4F 214
Doyle Cl. PO2: Ports 4F 214
Doyle Ct. PO2: Ports 5F 214
  SO19: South 9D 174
Doyle Gdns. GU46: Yat 9M 17
Doyle Ho. PO9: Bed 6B 202
Doyne Rd. BH14: Poole 1C 244
Dradfield La. SO32: Sob H 2K 179
Dragon Est. PO6: Farl 1M 215
Dragonfly Dr. RG24: Lych 3G 43
Dragon La. BH24: Bist, Sandf 8J 187
Dragon St. GU31: Pet 1M 145
Dragoon Cl. SO19: South 6G 174
Dragoon Ct. GU11: Alders 9G 49
Dragoon Ho. PO7: W'lle 9K 181
Dragoon Way BH23: Chri 7J 229
Drake Cl. BH23: Mude 8B 230
  BH24: Poul 8N 185
  BH25: New M 3A 232
  SO31: Loc H 4E 196
  SO40: March 8F 172
Drake Ct. SP10: A'ver 9C 52
Drake Ho. PO1: Ports 3J 5 (2B 240)
  SO14: South 8F 4
Drake Rd. PO13: Lee S 9N 211
  SO50: B'stke 8J 133
Drakes Cl. SO45: Hythe 7L 193
Drakes Ct. SO40: March 7E 172
Draper Rd. BH11: Bour 2E 226
  BH23: Chri 7A 230
Drapers Copse Residential Pk.
  SO45: Dib 5J 193
Draycote Rd. PO8: Cath 8C 168
Draycott Rd. BH10: Bour 4H 227
Draymans Way GU34: Alt 5F 80
DRAYTON
  GU32 1K 143
  PO6 1K 215
  SO21 3A 76
Drayton Cl. SO19: South 1D 194
Drayton Farm La.
  SO24: Bigh, Old A 7J 95
Drayton La. PO6: Dray 8J 201
Drayton Pl. SO40: Tott 3K 171
Drayton Rd. PO2: Ports 7F 214
Drayton St. SO22: Winche 8G 104
Dreadnought Ho. PO12: Gos 9L 213
Dreadnought Rd. PO14: Fare 3B 212
Dresden Dr. PO8: Cowp 7L 181
Dreswick Cl. BH23: Chri 2G 229
Drew Cl. BH12: Poole 7G 226
Drewitt Ind. Est. BH11: Bour 4C 226
Drift, The GU10: Ben'ly 8K 63
  PO9: R Cas 9H 183
Drift Rd. GU33: Blackm 8F 100
  GU35: W'hil 8F 100
  PO8: Clan 6B 168
  PO16: Fare 7F 198
  SO20: Chil 6L 75
Driftway, The SO32: Drox 3M 165
Driftway Rd. RG27: Hoo 2J 45
Driftways *GU46: Yat* 6N 17
  (off White Lion Way)
Driftwood BH5: Bour 2C 246
Driftwood Gdns. PO4: S'sea 5K 241
  SO40: Tott 4J 171
Driftwood Pk. BH23: Chri 5H 229
Drill Shed Rd. PO2: Ports 7C 214
Drinkwater Cl. SO50: E'leigh 9D 132
Drive, The BH12: Poole 9B 226
  BH13: S'bks 6B 244
  PO9: Hav 6F 202
  PO13: Gos 6C 212
  PO16: Fare 8C 198
  RG23: Oak 2D 58
  SO30: Wes E 8F 160
  SO40: Tott 5M 171
  SO51: E Wel 1A 156
  SO51: Sher E 6L 121
Driveway, The PO4: S'sea 2K 241
  SO45: Blac 7C 208
Driving Test Cen.
  Farnborough 4J 29
Droffatts Ho. SO15: South 3J 173
Droke, The PO6: Cosh 1G 215
  (not continuous)
Drove, The RG7: Sil 3C 12
  RG17: Ink 1F 6
  RG19: Ashf H 2L 9
  SO18: South 3E 174
  SO21: Twyf 8K 127
  SO30: Wes E 8K 161
  SO32: Durl 3G 163
  SO32: Swanm 6D 164
  SO40: Calm 1H 171
  SO45: Blac 7C 208
  SO50: Hor H 5A 162
  SO51: W Wel 1B 120 (9N 121)
  SP5: M Val 2M 119
  SP5: Woodf 3M 119
  SP10: A'ver 1K 69
Drove Cl. SO21: Twyf 8K 127
  SP5: Com B 2G 119
Drove Cotts. GU34: E Wor 8M 81
Drove Hill SO20: Chil 5F 74
Drove La. SO24: New A, Old A 9C 94
  SP5: Com B 1G 118
Drove Rd. PO17: S'wick 5B 200
  SO19: South 5F 174
  SO20: Chil 4F 74
Drovers End GU51: Fleet 8A 28
Drovers Vw. SP11: Ludg 2C 30 (5K 31)
Drovers Way GU9: Up H 4C 64
DROXFORD 2K 165
Droxford Cl. PO12: Gos 3H 239
Droxford Cres. RG26: Tadl 6G 11
Droxford Rd. BH6: Bour 8E 228
  GU32: E Meon 9L 143
  PO17: Wick 6D 178
  SO32: Swanm 7D 164
Druitt Rd. BH23: Chri 6B 230
Drum La. GU32: Pet 9M 139
Drum Mead GU32: Pet 1L 145
Drummer La. SP9: Tidw 9D 30 (7G 31)
Drummond Cl. GU34: Four M 5G 97
  SO22: Winche 9J 105
Drummond Ct. SO19: South 7C 174
  SO50: E'leigh 7F 132
Drummond Dr. SO14: South 2A 174
Drummond Rd. BH1: Bour 1A 246
  PO1: Ports 1E 240
  PO15: Seg 5G 197
  SO30: Hed E 1N 175
  SO45: Hythe 5M 193
Drummond Way SO53: Cha F 4N 131
Drum Rd. SO50: E'leigh 1D 160
Drury Cl. RG28: Hur P 1A 76
Drury La. GU34: Bent 6L 79
  RG7: Mort 1F 12
Drury Rd. BH4: Bour 3F 244
Dryden Av. PO6: Cosh 8N 199
Dryden Cl. BH24: Ashl H 3B 186
  PO7: W'lle 8M 181
  PO16: Fare 7B 198
  RG24: B'toke 2D 42
Dryden Pl. SO41: M Sea 7K 235
Dryden Rd. GU14: Farn 6H 29
  SO19: South 5J 175
Dryden Way GU30: Lip 1C 116
Drysdale M. PO4: S'sea 5J 241
Duart Ct. BH25: New M 3D 232
Duchess Cl. GU34: Alt 5E 80
Ducking Stool La. BH23: Chri 8L 229
Ducking Stool Wlk. *BH23: Chri* 8L 229
  (off Ducking Stool La.)
Duck Island La. BH24: Ring 2J 187
Ducklands GU35: Bor 5K 101
Duck La. BH11: Bour 1D 226
Duckmead La. GU33: Liss 8G 115
Duckpond La. PO8: Blen 2E 182
Ducks La. SO20: N Wal 1N 87
Duck Stile La. PO8: Blen 2E 182
Duck St. SP11: Abb A 5F 68
Duckworth Ho. PO1: Ports 4K 5 (2B 240)
Duddon Cl. SO18: Wes E 1F 174
Duddon Way RG21: B'toke 6E 42
Dudleston Heath Dr. PO8: Cowp 8B 182
Dudley Av. SO41: Hor 3G 233
  SP6: F'dge 8J 151
Dudley Cl. GU35: W'hil 6H 101
  RG23: B'toke 6K 41
Dudley Ct. GU52: Ch Cr 5M 47
Dudley Gdns. BH10: Bour 1H 227
Dudley Pl. BH25: New M 5C 232
Dudley Rd. BH10: Bour 1H 227
  PO3: Ports 9H 215
Dudmoor Farm Golf Course 2K 229
Dudmoor Farm Rd. BH23: Chri 2J 229
Dudmoor La. BH23: Chri 2J 229
  BH23: Hurn 8G 218
Dugald Drummond St.
  PO1: Ports 4N 5 (2D 240)
Duisburg Way PO5: S'sea 8L 5 (4C 240)
Duke Cl. SP10: A'ver 9C 52
Duke Cres. PO1: Ports 9E 214
Duke of Cornwall Av. GU15: Camb 4M 19
Duke of Edinburgh Ho. PO1: Ports 2L 5
Duke of Wellington Commemorative Column 5F 14
Duke Rd. SO30: Hed E 5A 176
Dukes Cl. BH6: Bour 8G 229
  GU9: Up H 4C 64
  GU32: Pet 9K 139
  GU34: Alt 6D 80
Dukes Ct. *SO32: Bis W* 3M 163
  (off St Bonnet Dr.)
Dukes Dr. BH11: Bour 1C 226
  SO21: Avin, Winche 3G 106
Dukesfield BH23: Chri 4G 228
Dukes Keeps SO14: South 7F 4
Dukes Mead GU51: Fleet 2J 47
Dukes Mill Cen. SO51: Rom 5L 129
Dukes Pk. GU11: Alders 5M 49
Dukes Ride RG7: Sil 5N 11
  RG45: Cr'tne 1A 18
Dukes Rd. PO12: Gos 1J 239
  SO14: South 2N 173
Dukes Ter. GU11: Alders 8K 49
Duke St. SO14: South 7F 4 (7N 173)
  SO21: M'dvr 7J 77
Dukes Wlk. GU9: Up H 4C 64
  PO7: W'lle 2M 201
Dukes Way *SP4: Bul* 3A 66
  (off Churchill Av.)
Dukeswood Dr. SO45: Dib P 8L 193
Duke Ter. PO9: Hav 5D 202
Dulsie Rd. BH3: Bour 8G 227
Dumas Cl. GU46: Yat 8M 17
Dumas Dr. PO15: White 9F 176
Du Maurier Cl. GU52: Ch Cr 8K 47
Dumbarton Cl. PO2: Ports 8E 214
Dumbleton Cl. SO19: South 5K 175
Dumbleton's Towers SO19: South 6J 175
DUMMER 9F 58 (1C 78)
DUMMER CLUMP 9H 59
Dummer Ct. PO9: Hav 3D 202
Dummer Down La. RG25: Dumm 1B 78
Dummer Golf Course 8G 58

Dummer La.—Edneys La.

Dummer La. SP11: Chu S, Lwr C 9A 6
Dummer M. SO23: Winche 9L 237
Dummer Rd. RG25: Axf 3E 78
Dummers Rd. SO51: Brai 6C 124
Dumpers Drove SO50: Hor H 4A 162
Dumpford La. GU31: Nye, Trot 4L 147
Dump Rd. GU14: Farn 2G 48
Dunbar Cl. SO16: South 6E 158
Dunbar Cres. BH23: Chri 4H 231
Dunbar Rd. BH3: Bour 8J 227
PO4: S'sea 3J 241
DUNBRIDGE 4D 122
Dunbridge La.
SO51: Awb, Dun 4D 122
Dunbridge Rd. SO51: Lock 4A 122
Dunbridge Station (Rail) 4D 122
Duncan Cl. SO19: South 9C 174
Duncan Cooper Ho. PO7: W'lle 2L 201
Duncan Ct. SO19: South 5G 175
SP10: A'ver 1C 70
Duncan Hood Ct. SO17: South 8A 160
Duncan Rd. BH25: A'ley 2E 232
PO5: S'sea 5E 240
SO31: P Ga 3E 196
Duncan's Cl. SP11: Fyf 9N 31
Duncans Dr. PO14: Fare 9L 197
Duncliff Rd. BH6: Bour 1K 247
Duncombe Dr. BH24: Har 7E 184
Duncombe Rd. GU32: E Meon 4L 143
Duncton Rd. PO8: Clan 6D 168
Duncton Way PO13: Gos 5E 212
Dundas Cl. PO3: Ports 6J 215
Dundas La. PO3: Ports 7J 215
Dundas Spur PO3: Ports 6J 215
Dundee Cl. PO15: Fare 6A 198
Dundee Gdns. RG22: B'toke 7K 41
Dundee Rd. SO17: South 1A 174
Dundonald Cl. PO11: H Isl 2G 243
SO19: South 9B 174
DUNDRIDGE 2D 164
Dundridge La. SO24: Ch Can 6C 78
SO32: Bis W 2N 163
Dundry Way SO30: Hed E 3N 175
Dune Crest BH13: S'bks 9A 244
Dunedin Gro. BH23: Chri 7E 230
Dunford Cl. BH25: New M 6N 231
Dunford Rd. BH12: Poole 9B 226
Dungells Farm Cl. GU46: Yat 9N 17
Dungells La. GU46: Yat 9M 17
Dunhills La. SP11: Enh A 3A 52
Dunholme Mnr. BH1: Bour 2N 245
Dunhurst Cl. PO9: Hav 6G 202
Dunkeld Rd. BH3: Bour 8H 227
PO12: Gos 9H 213
Dunketts La. RG26: Bau 8B 10
Dunkirk Cl. SO16: South 7J 159
Dunkirk Rd. SO16: South 7H 159
Dunkirt La. SP11: Abb A 8D 68
DUNLEY 3E 36
Dunley Dr. GU51: Fleet 9H 27
Dunley's Hill RG29: N War, Odi 7J 45
Dunlin Cl. BH23: Mude 9D 230
PO4: S'sea 2L 241
Dunmow Hill GU51: Fleet 1M 47
Dunmow Rd. SP10: A'ver 3A 70
Dunn Cl. PO4: S'sea 4J 241
Dunnings La. SO52: N Bad 7D 130
Dunnock Cl. PO9: R Cas 9H 183
Dunsbury Way PO9: Hav 3E 202
Dunsells Cl. SO24: Rop 1E 110
Dunsell's La. SO24: Rop 1E 110
Dunsford Cres. RG23: B'toke 4L 41
Dunsmore Cl. PO5: S'sea 6N 5 (3D 240)
Dunsmore Gdns. GU46: Yat 8K 17
Dunstable Wlk. PO14: Fare 9N 197
Dunstall Pk. GU14: Farn 5J 29
Dunstan's Drove SP11: Ibt 2A 34
Dunster Cl. SO16: South 6H 159
Dunvegan Dr. SO16: South 6H 159
DUNWOOD HILL 3D 128
Dunwood Manor Golf Course 1D 128
Dupree Dr. PO4: S'sea 4H 241
Durban Cl. SO51: Rom 3N 129
Durban Homes PO1: Ports 1E 240
Durban Rd. PO1: Ports 9G 214
Durbidges RG19: Head 3K 9
Durdells Av. BH11: Bour 1E 226
Durdells Gdns. BH11: Bour 1E 226
Durford Ct. PO9: Hav 3D 202
Durford Rd. GU31: Pet 1A 146
DURFORD WOOD 6E 140
Durham Gdns. PO7: W'lle 4N 201
Durham Rd. GU47: Owl 3G 18
Durham St. PO1: Ports 2D 240
PO12: Gos 1J 239
Durham Way RG22: B'toke 2K 59
Durland Cl. BH25: New M 5B 232
Durlands Ct. PO8: Horn 2C 182
Durlands Rd. PO8: Horn 2C 182
DURLEIGHMARSH 9F 140
DURLEY 5E 162
Durley Av. PO8: Cowp 7M 181
Durley Brook Rd. SO32: Durl 5C 162
Durley Chine BH2: Bour 9H 247 (3H 245)
Durley Chine Ct. BH2: Bour 9H 247 (3H 245)
Durley Chine Rd.
BH2: Bour 7H 247 (2H 245)
Durley Chine Rd. Sth.
BH2: Bour 8H 247 (3H 245)
Durley Cl. SP10: A'ver 2L 69
Durley Cres. SO40: Tott 5K 171
Durley Gdns. BH2: Bour 9H 247 (3H 245)
Durley Hall La. SO32: Durl 2E 162
Durley Mews SO32: Durl 5E 162
Durley Rd. BH2: Bour 8J 247 (3J 245)
PO12: Gos 1H 239
SO50: Hor H 3A 162
Durley Rd. Sth. BH2: Bour 8J 247 (3H 245)
DURLEY STREET 3G 163
Durley St. SO32: Durl 5E 162
Durlston Cres. BH23: Chri 2G 229
Durlston Rd. BH14: Poole 3A 244
SO16: South 1C 172
Durnford Cl. SO20: Chil 4F 74
Durnford Rd. SO14: South 2F 4 (4N 173)
Durngate Pl.
SO23: Winche 7P 237 (6M 105)
Durngate Ter.
SO23: Winche 7P 237 (6M 105)
Durnsford Av. GU52: Fleet 4M 47
DURNS TOWN 5K 223
Durnstown SO41: Sway 5K 223
Durrant Ho. BH2: Bour 6J 247
Durrant Rd. BH2: Bour 5K 247 (1J 245)
BH14: Poole 2A 244
DURRANTS 1H 203
Durrants Gdns. PO9: R Cas 1H 203
Durrants Rd. PO9: R Cas 2H 203
Durrant Way SO41: Sway 5J 223
Durrington Pl. BH7: Bour 8E 228
Durrington Rd. BH7: Bour 7E 228
Dursley Cres. PO6: Cosh 9D 200
Durweston Cl. BH9: Bour 3M 227
Dutton La. SO50: E'leigh 8F 132
Duttons Rd. SO51: Rom 4L 129
Duxford Way GU14: Farn 3K 49
DW Sports Fitness
Branksome 9D 226
Dyer Rd. SO15: South 3H 173
Dymchurch Ho. PO6: Cosh 9F 200
Dymoke St. PO10: Ems 5L 203
Dymond Ho. PO4: S'sea 3J 241
Dymott Cl. SO15: South 5J 173
Dyneley Grn. SO18: South 1E 174
Dyram Cl. SO50: E'leigh 7D 132
Dysart Av. PO6: Cosh 1J 215
Dyserth Cl. SO19: South 9F 174
Dyson Dr. SO23: Winche 4L 105

E

Eadens La. SO40: Bart 2D 170
Eagle Av. PO8: Cowp 6L 181
Eagle Cl. GU34: Alt 2F 80
PO16: Portc 9H 199
RG22: B'toke 2H 59
SO53: Cha F 8N 131
Eagle Ct. RG24: B'toke 5G 42
SO23: Winche 6L 237
Eagle Cft. SO20: Mid Wa 3A 72
Eagle Dean SO20: Mid Wa 4A 72
Eaglehurst *BH12: Poole* *1E 244*
(off Eagle Rd.)
Eagle Rd. BH12: Poole 1E 244
PO13: Lee S 9N 211
RG20: Bis G 2H 9
Eagles Nest GU47: Sandh 4C 18
Eames La. GU33: Hawk 6M 113
Eardley Av. SP10: A'ver 9K 51
Earle Ho. SO23: Winche 6A 106
Earle Rd. BH4: Bour 4G 244
Earley Ct. SO41: Lymi 2F 234
Earl Godwin Cl. PO16: Fare 8F 198
Earlham Dr. BH14: Poole 1A 244
Earlsbourne GU52: Ch Cr 7N 47
Earls Cl. SO50: B'stke 1L 161
SP4: Ames 6A 66
Earlsdon Lodge BH2: Bour 5H 247
Earlsdon St. PO5: S'sea 5N 5 (3D 240)
Earlsdon Way BH23: Highc 6G 231
Earls Gro. GU15: Camb 7N 19
Earls Mnr. Ct. SP4: Win E 3A 86
Earls Rd. PO16: Fare 1D 212
SO14: South 2M 173
Earlswood *BH4: Bour* *3G 245*
(off Clarendon Rd.)
Earlswood Dr. SP6: Ald 5C 152
Earlswood Pk. BH25: A'ley 1D 232
Early Lands RG7: Sil 6N 11
Earnley Rd. PO11: H Isl 5M 243
Earthpits La. SP5: Pent 2G 148
Eastacre SO22: Winche 5J 105
EAST ACTON 1A 76
EAST ANTON 6B 52
East Av. BH3: Bour 8G 226
BH25: New M 7L 231
GU9: H End 4F 64
East Av. Rdbt. BH3: Bour 8J 227
E. Bank Rd. SO42: Broc 8D 148
East Bargate
SO14: South 6D 4 (6M 173)
EAST BOLDRE 1B 236
E. Boldre Rd. SO42: Beau 9A 206
Eastbourne Av. PO12: Gos 8H 213
SO15: South 2J 173
Eastbourne Rd. PO3: Ports 8H 215
Eastbrook Cl. PO12: Gos 8H 213
SO31: P Ga 4D 196
Eastbrooke Rd. GU34: Alt 4G 80
East Cams Cl. PO16: Fare 8H 199
EAST CHOLDERTON 2A 68
Eastchurch Cl. SO16: South 7E 158
EAST CLIFF 7N 247 (2L 245)
East Cliff BH2: Bour 5L 247 (1K 245)
Eastcliff Cl. PO13: Lee S 9B 212
East Cliff Grange *BH1: Bour* *1A 246*
(off Knyveton Rd.)
East Cliff Prom. BH1: Bour 8M 247 (3L 245)
East Cliff Way BH23: Fri C 7E 230
East Cl. BH25: B Sea 6M 231
E. Copsey Path PO6: Dray 9L 201
E. Cosham Rd. PO6: Cosh 8J 201
Eastcot Cl. SO45: Holb 5A 208
Eastcott Cl. BH7: Bour 6D 228
East Ct. PO1: Ports 9F 214
PO6: Cosh 9J 201
Eastcroft Rd. PO12: Gos 2H 239
EAST DEAN 2L 121
E. Dean Rd. SO51: Lock 2M 121
East Dorset Indoor Bowls Club 8N 229
East Dorset Sailing Club 6A 244
East Dr. SO50: B'stke 8H 133
EAST END
GU32 .... 8E 136
RG20 .... 3M 7
SO41 .... 8N 225 (4A 236)
SP6 .... 6A 150
Easter Ct. BH5: Bour 1B 246
Eastern Av. PO4: S'sea 1J 241
SP10: A'ver 2A 70
Eastern Ind. Cen. PO6: Farl 2K 215
Eastern La. RG45: Cr'tne 1H 19
Eastern Pde. PO4: S'sea 6G 240
PO16: Fare 1D 212
Eastern Rd. GU12: Alders 9M 49
GU35: Bor 1J 101
PO2: Ports 6C 214
PO3: Ports 2J 241
PO6: Farl 2L 215
PO9: Hav 7F 202
SO30: Wes E 1H 175
SO41: Lymi 2D 234
SO45: Fawl 6J 209
Eastern Vs. Rd. PO4: S'sea 6E 240
Eastern Way PO16: Fare 8E 198
SO41: M Sea 8M 235
Easter Pk. RG7: Sil 1L 11
Easter Rd. BH9: Bour 4L 227
Easter Sq. RG24: B'toke 3M 41
Eastfield Av. PO14: Fare 2B 212
RG21: B'toke 6D 42
Eastfield Cl. SP10: A'ver 1B 70
Eastfield Ct. BH24: Ring 1M 187
Eastfield La. BH24: Poul 9M 185
BH24: Ring 1M 187
GU31: E Har 8K 147
Eastfield Lodge *SP10: A'ver* *1A 70*
(off Eastfield Rd.)
Eastfield Rd. PO4: S'sea 4H 241
PO17: S'wick 7C 200
SO17: South 2A 174
SP10: A'ver 1A 70
East Ga. PO1: Ports 9D 214
Eastgate St. SO14: South 7D 4 (7M 173)
SO23: Winche 8P 237 (7M 105)
E. Gomeldon Rd. SP4: Gome 2C 86
East Grn. GU17: Blackw 9E 18
EAST GRIMSTEAD 1F 120
EAST HARTING 8J 147
E. Harting St. GU31: E Har 9J 147
East Hayling Light Railway 5G 242
East Hill SO23: Winche 8M 105
SO41: Lymi 2E 234
East Hill Cl. PO16: Fare 7F 198
East Hill Dr. GU33: Liss 2F 140
East Hoe Rd. PO7: H'don 9B 166
East Horton Golf Cen. 2C 162
East Horton Golf Course 2C 162 (9C 134)
East Ho. Av. PO14: Stub 6N 211
EAST HOWE 2G 227
E. Howe La. BH10: Bour 3G 226
East Hundreds GU51: Fleet 9K 27
Eastlake Av. BH12: Poole 8A 226
Eastlake Cl. GU31: Pet 1B 146
Eastlake Hgts. PO4: S'sea 4L 241
EASTLAND GATE 5L 181
Eastland Ga. Cotts. PO8: Love 4L 181
Eastlands BH25: New M 5C 232
Eastlands Boatyard SO31: Lwr Swan 9A 176
East La. SO24: Ovin 2A 108
SO41: Ever 5M 233
EASTLEIGH 1F 160
Eastleigh FC 4C 160
Eastleigh Lakeside Steam Railway 3D 160
Eastleigh Mus. 1E 160
Eastleigh Rd. PO9: Hav 6J 203
SO50: Fair O 2N 161
Eastleigh Station (Rail) 9F 132
EAST LISS 1F 140
East Lodge PO13: Lee S 1A 238
PO15: Fare 8M 197
E. Lodge Pk. PO6: Farl 9N 201
Eastlyn Rd. RG26: Pam H 4L 11
Eastman Cl. SP5: Down 3L 119 (8B 120)
Eastman's Fld. SO20: Chil 5F 74
EAST MARTIN 9D 118
Eastmead GU14: Farn 8K 29
Eastmeare Ct. SO40: Tott 4J 171
EAST MEON 3M 143
E. Meon Rd. PO8: Clan 4A 168
East M. PO17: K Vil 2A 198
EASTNEY 4J 241
Eastney Beam Engine House 4K 241
Eastney Esplanade PO4: S'sea 5H 241
Eastney Farm Rd. PO4: S'sea 4K 241
Eastney Rd. PO4: S'sea 3J 241
Eastney St. PO4: S'sea 5J 241
Eastney Swimming Pool 5K 241
EAST OAKLEY 1D 58
EASTOKE 5J 243
Eastoke Av. PO11: H Isl 6K 243
EASTON 1D 106
Easton Comn. Hill SP5: Mid W 5J 87
Easton La. SO21: E'ton, Mar W, Winche 9D 92
SO21: E'ton, Winche 4A 106
SO23: Winche 6M 105
Easton La. Bus. Pk. SO23: Winche 6M 105
E. Overcliff Dr. BH1: Bour 3L 245
Eastover Ct. PO9: Hav 3D 202
East Pallant PO9: Hav 8F 202
East Pk. Ter. SO14: South 3D 4 (5M 173)
EAST PARLEY 7A 218
Eastpoint Cen. SO19: South 6J 175
East Portway SP10: A'ver 1J 69
East Rd. PO17: S'wick 3B 200
SO21: Bar S 5B 76
SO40: March 7F 172
SO45: Hard 9B 194
EASTROP 7E 42
Eastrop La. RG21: B'toke 6D 42
Eastrop Rdbt. RG21: B'toke 6D 42
Eastrop Way RG21: B'toke 6D 42
E. Shore Way PO3: Ports 1J 241
East Sta. Rd. GU12: Alders 1K 65
EAST STRATTON 7M 77
East St. GU9: Farnh 7E 64
GU31: Rog 9L 141
PO1: Ports 6H 5 (4A 240)
PO7: H'don 8E 166
PO9: Hav 8F 202
PO14: Titch 9K 197
PO16: Fare 8E 198
PO16: Portc 9M 199
SO14: South 6D 4 (6M 173)
SO24: New A 9F 94
SP10: A'ver 1A 70
East St. Shopping Cen.
SO14: South 6E 4 (6M 173)
E. Surrey St. PO1: Ports 2D 240
EAST TISTED 1D 112
EAST TYTHERLEY 8N 87
E. Tytherley Rd. SO51: Lock 9N 87
Eastview Gdns. GU34: Up Farr 4E 98
East Vw. Rd. BH24: Ring 1L 187
Eastville SP11: Rag A 3B 50
Eastville Rd. SO50: Fair O 2N 161
East Way BH8: Bour 5M 227
Eastways SO32: Bis W 4M 163
EAST WELLOW 7A 128
East Winchester (Barfield)
(Park & Ride) 8M 105
East Winchester (St Catherine's)
(Park & Ride) 9M 105
EAST WINTERSLOW 4H 87
Eastwood SO51: Sher E 6M 121
Eastwood Cl. PO11: H Isl 3H 243
Eastwood Ct. SO51: Rom 5L 129
EAST WOODHAY 3L 7
E. Woodhay Rd. SO22: Winche 2H 105
Eastwood Rd. PO2: Ports 4F 214
EAST WORLDHAM 7M 81
Eaton Ct. BH1: Bour 5N 247 (1L 245)
Eaton Rd. BH13: Poole 3E 244
GU15: Camb 9K 19
E Avenue SO45: Fawl 3C 208
EBBLAKE 4A 184
Ebblake Cl. BH31: Ver 6A 184
Ebblake Ent. Pk. BH31: Ver 5A 184
Ebblake Ind. Est. BH31: Ver 5A 184
Ebble Cl. SP9: Tidw 7D 30
EBB Stadium, The 9K 49
Ebden Rd. SO23: Winche 6M 105
Ebenezer La. BH24: Ring 1J 187
Ebery Gro. PO3: Ports 1J 241
Ebor Rd. BH12: Poole 8B 226
ECCHINSWELL 5H 9
Ecchinswell Rd. RG20: Ecc, Kings 2A 6 (5G 9)
Echo Barn La. GU10: Wrec 7N 63
Ecton La. PO3: Ports 5K 215
Eddeys Cl. GU35: Head D 1D 102
Eddeys La. GU35: Head D 1D 102
Eddy Rd. GU12: Alders 1L 65
Eddystone Ct. GU10: Chur 7H 85
Eddystone Rd. SO40: Tott 9K 157
Edelvale Rd. SO18: South 1F 174
Edelweiss Cl. SP11: Ludg 2D 30 (5K 31)
Edenbridge Rd. PO4: S'sea 2J 241
Edenbridge Way SO31: Sar G 3C 196
Edenbrook GU17: Haw 2H 29
Eden Ct. BH1: Bour 2M 245
BH4: Bour *3G 245*
(off West Cliff Rd.)
Eden Path PO6: Dray 8K 201
Eden Ri. PO16: Fare 9D 198
Eden Rd. SO18: Wes E 8F 160
Eden St. PO1: Ports 2N 5 (1D 240)
Eden Wlk. SO53: Cha F 7N 131
Edgar Cl. SP10: A'ver 6A 52
Edgar Cres. PO16: Portc 2M 213
Edgar Rd. SO23: Winche 9L 237 (9K 105)
Edgar Vs. SO23: Winche 9K 237 (7K 105)
Edgbarrow Ct. RG45: Cr'tne 2C 18
Edgbarrow Ri. GU47: Sandh 3C 18
Edgbarrow Sports Cen. 2E 18
Edgbarrow Woods Local Nature Reserve 3C 18
Edgbaston Ho. PO5: S'sea 3D 240
Edgcumbe Pk. Dr. RG45: Cr'tne 1C 18
Edge, The PO6: Cosh 9A 200
Edgecombe Cres. PO13: Gos 8E 212
Edgedale Cl. RG45: Cr'tne 1D 18
Edgefield Gro. PO7: W'lle 9C 182
Edgehill Cl. RG22: B'toke 8K 41
Edgehill Rd. BH9: Bour 6J 227
SO18: South 1D 174
Edgehurst SO31: Loc H 7C 196
Edge Leisure Centre, The 7M 103
Edgerly Gdns. PO6: Cosh 2G 215
Edgeware Rd. PO4: S'sea 2H 241
Edgifred Rd. BH9: Bour 2L 227
Edinburgh Ct. *GU11: Alders* *9H 49*
(off Queen Elizabeth Dr.)
SO15: South *4F 172*
(off Regent's Pk. Rd.)
Edinburgh Ho.
SO22: Winche 6K 237 (6K 105)
Edinburgh Rd. PO1: Ports 3M 5 (2D 240)
SO23: Kin W 6M 91
Edington Cl. SO32: Bis W 3L 163
Edington Rd. SO23: Winche 4L 105
Edison Gate SP10: A'ver 8H 51
Edison Rd. RG21: B'toke 4N 41
Edith Haisman Cl. SO15: South 5J 173
EDMONDSHAM 8K 149
Edmondsham Ho.
BH2: Bour 7K 247 (2J 245)
Edmondsham Rd. BH31: Ver 9M 149
Edmund Ct. RG24: B'toke 2D 42
Edmund Rd. PO4: S'sea 4F 240
Edmunds Cl. BH25: B Sea 5A 232
SO30: Botl 5A 176
Edney Cl. GU52: Ch Cr 5N 47
Edney Path SO31: Sar G 3A 196
Edneys La. PO7: Den 6J 181

Enterprise Ct.—Farm Rd.

Enterprise Ct. RG24: B'toke 4E **42**
Enterprise Ho. PO1: Ports 4N **5**
Enterprise Ind. Est. PO8: Horn 2C **182**
Enterprise Rd. PO8: Horn 2C **182**
SO16: Chilw 2H **159**
Enterprise Way BH23: Bour A 6A **218**
Eperston Rd. PO8: Horn 4A **182**
Epping Cl. SO18: South 1F **174**
Epsilon Ho. SO16: Chilw 2J **159**
Epsom Cl. GU15: Camb 5L **19**
SO50: Hor H 4A **162**
Epsom Ct. *PO15: White* 1F *196*
(off Timor Cl.)
Epsom Down GU34: Alt 6F **80**
Epworth Rd. PO2: Ports 7G **215**
Equinox Dr. SP4: Ames 5A **66**
Equinox Pl. GU14: Farn 8K **29**
Erasmus Pk. SO23: Winche 5N **105**
Erica Cl. PO8: Cowp 7B **182**
SO31: Loc H 6C **196**
Erica Way PO8: Cowp 6B **182**
Ericksen Rd. BH11: Bour 3G **226**
Eric Meadus Cl. SO18: S'ing 7B **160**
Eric Rd. PO14: Stub 6M **211**
Eric Taplin Ct. PO4: S'sea 4F **240**
Erinbank Mans. BH1: Bour 2N **245**
Erles Rd. GU30: Lip 2E **116**
Ernest Cl. PO10: Ems 8M **203**
Ernest Rd. PO1: Ports 9F **214**
PO9: Bed 6C **202**
Erpingham Rd. BH12: Poole 1E **244**
Erskine Cl. RG26: Pam H 4M **11**
Erskine Ct. SO16: South 6E **158**
Erskine Rd. SO22: Winche 9J **237** (7J **105**)
Escombe Rd. SO50: B'stke 9H **133**
Escur Cl. PO2: Ports 4G **214**
Esdaile La. *BH24: Bur* 7D *188*
(off Ringwood Rd.)
Esher Cl. RG22: B'toke 1M **59**
Esher Gro. PO7: W'lle 8K **181**
Eskdale Cl. PO8: Horn 9C **168**
Eskdale Ct. *GU12: Ash V* 6N *49*
(off Lakeside Cl.)
Esmond Cl. PO10: Ems 9M **203**
Esmonde Cl. PO13: Lee S 1B **238**
Esplanade BH13: Poole 6D **244**
PO13: Lee S 2A **238**
PO31: Cowes 5P **237**
Esplanade, The PO12: Gos 3N **239**
Esplanade Gdns. PO4: S'sea 5K **241**
Essex Av. BH23: Chri 4J **229**
Essex Cl. GU35: Bor 3J **101**
Essex Grn. SO53: Cha F 1A **160**
Essex Rd. GU35: Bor 3J **101**
PO4: S'sea 3H **241**
RG21: B'toke 6B **42**
Esslemont Rd. PO4: S'sea 4G **240**
Estancia Cl. PO13: Lee S 9B **212**
Estella Rd. PO2: Ports 8E **214**
Estridge Cl. SO31: Burs 9L **175**
Etches Cl. BH10: Bour 2H **227**
Ethelbert Dr. SP10: Charl 7K **51**
Ethelburt Av. SO16: S'ing 6A **160**
Ethelred Gdns. SO40: Tott 4J **171**
Ethel Rd. PO1: Ports 1F **240**
Eton Cl. RG22: B'toke 4J **59**
Eton Gdns. BH4: Bour 1G **244**
Eton Pl. GU9: Up H 3D **64**
Eton Rd. PO5: S'sea 3F **240**
ETPS Rd. GU14: Farn 3K **49**
Ettrick Rd. BH13: Poole 4E **244**
Etwall SP11: Quar 3L **67**
Eucalyptus Av. BH24: Match 6D **186**
Eulalia Ct. *BH9: Bour* 7K *227*
(off Alma Rd.)
Europa Cl. RG26: B'ley 1G **22**
European Way SO14: South 9E **4** (8N **173**)
Euryalus Rd. PO14: Fare 2B **212**
Euskirchen Way RG22: B'toke 6L **41**
Euston Gro. BH24: Ring 2K **187**
Euston Rd. PO4: S'sea 2J **241**
Eva Allaway Ct. PO1: Ports 4K **5**
Evans Cl. BH11: Bour 5D **226**
BH24: Ashl H 2B **186**
PO2: Ports 6C **214**
SO20: Ov Wa 8L **67**
Evans Rd. PO4: S'sea 3H **241**
Evans St. SO14: South 6E **4** (6M **173**)
Evelegh Rd. PO6: Farl 9L **201**
Eveley Cl. GU35: W'hil 6G **100**
Eveley La. GU33: Blackm 7E **100**
GU35: W'hil 7E **100**
Evelyn Av. GU11: Alders 2K **65**
Evelyn Cl. SO32: Wal C 7A **164**
Evelyn Cres. SO15: South 2J **173**
Evelyn M. BH9: Bour 5K **227**
SO24: New A 9F **94**
Evelyn Rd. BH9: Bour 5K **227**
Evelyn Woods Rd. GU11: Alders 4L **49**
Evenlode Rd. SO16: South 1D **172**
Evenlode Way GU47: Sandh 5E **18**
Eventide Homes BH8: Bour 4B **228**
Everdene Ho. BH7: Bour 5E **228**
Everdon La. PO3: Ports 4J **215**
Everell Ct. PO4: S'sea 6E **240**
Everest Rd. BH23: Chri 6A **230**
GU15: Camb 5M **19**
Everglades Av. PO8: Cowp 7N **181**
Evergreen RG19: Head 2J **9**
Evergreen Cl. PO7: W'lle 2L **201**
SO40: March 9E **172**
Evergreens BH24: Ashl H 3B **186**
SO40: Elin 4N **171**
Evering Av. BH12: Poole 5A **226**
Evering Gdns. BH12: Poole 5A **226**
Everlea Cl. SO41: Ever 5L **233**
Everleigh Rd. SN8: Co Du 2G **31**
Everon Gdns. BH25: New M 4C **232**
Eversfield Cl. SP10: A'ver 1M **69**
Evershot Rd. BH8: Bour 4B **228**
Eversleigh BH4: Bour 3H **245**
EVERSLEY 4D **16**
EVERSLEY CENTRE 5G **17**
Eversley Cres. PO9: Hav 5E **202**
EVERSLEY CROSS 5H **17**
Eversley Dr. GU51: Fleet 9H **27**
Eversley Pl. SO22: Winche 9H **105**
Eversley Rd. GU46: Yat 6K **17**
EVERTON 5M **233**
Everton Rd. SO41: Ever, Hor 2G **233**
Everyman Cinema 8L **237** (7K **105**)
Everyone Active Leisure Cen.
Rossmore 6B **226**
Evesham Cl. BH7: Bour 6E **228**
SO16: Bass 6N **159**
Evesham Ct. BH13: Poole 3E **244**
Evesham Wlk. GU47: Owl 4F **18**
RG24: B'toke 2C **42**
Evingar Gdns. RG28: Whit 4G **54**
Evingar Ind. Est. RG28: Whit 5G **54**
Evingar Rd. RG28: Whit 5G **54**
Ewart Ct. SO45: Hythe 4M **193**
Ewart Rd. PO1: Ports 9F **214**
Ewell Way SO40: Tott 1K **171**
Ewer Common PO12: Gos 5K **239**
Ewhurst Cl. PO9: Hav 5D **202**
Ewhurst Rd. RG26: Rams 8C **20**
EWSHOT 2N **63**
Ewshot Hill Cross GU10: Ews 2N **63**
Ewshot La. GU10: Ews 8L **47**
GU52: Ch Cr 8L **47**
Exbourne Mnr. BH1: Bour 2N **245**
EXBURY 1G **236**
Exbury Cl. SO50: B'stke 1K **161**
Exbury Dr. BH11: Bour 1D **226**
Exbury Gdns. 1G **236**
Exbury Rd. PO9: Hav 4G **202**
SO42: Beau 5H **207**
SO45: Blac 7C **208**
Exbury Way SP10: A'ver 2L **69**
Excellent Rd. PO14: Fare 3B **212**
Excelsior Rd. BH14: Poole 2A **244**
Exchange Bldg. BH1: Bour 7M **247**
Exchange Rd. PO1: Ports 4M **5** (2C **240**)
Exchange Sq. SO23: Winche 7M **237**
Exeter Cl. PO10: Ems 6M **203**
RG22: B'toke 3K **59**
SO18: South 1E **174**
SO31: Loc H 6C **196**
SO50: E'leigh 7D **132**
Exeter Ct. BH23: Highc 7K **231**
PO13: Gos 1E **238**
Exeter Cres. BH2: Bour 7L **247** (3K **245**)
Exeter Gdns. GU46: Yat 6L **17**
Exeter Grange BH2: Bour 8L **247**
Exeter La. BH2: Bour 7L **247** (2K **245**)
Exeter Pk. Mans. BH2: Bour 8L **247**
Exeter Pk. Rd. BH2: Bour 8L **247** (3K **245**)
Exeter Rd. BH2: Bour 7L **247** (2K **245**)
PO4: S'sea 5G **240**
SO18: South 2E **174**
Exford Av. SO18: South 3G **174**
Exford Dr. SO18: South 3G **174**
Exleigh Cl. SO18: South 4F **174**
Exmoor Cl. PO15: White 2E **196**
RG22: B'toke 8K **41**
SO40: Tott 3H **171**
Exmoor Rd. SO14: South 2E **4** (4N **173**)
Exmouth Gdns. SO50: Hor H 4N **161**
Exmouth Rd. PO5: S'sea 5E **240**
PO12: Gos 8J **213**
Exmouth St. SO14: South 4D **4** (5M **173**)
Explosion!
(The Mus. of Naval Firepower) 9M **213**
EXTON 8N **135**
Exton Gdns. PO16: Portc 7L **199**
Exton Rd. BH6: Bour 7F **228**
PO9: Hav 4H **203**
Eyebright Cl. SO50: Hor H 5N **161**
Eyeworth Wlk. SO45: Dib 5H **193**
Eynham Av. SO19: South 4G **174**
Eynham Cl. SO19: South 4G **174**
Eynham Gdns. SO19: South 4F **174**
Eynon M. BH24: Ring 2J **187**
Eyre Cl. SO40: Tott 4K **171**

F

Faber Cl. PO9: Hav 5G **203**
Faber M. SO51: Rom 4A **130**
FABERSTOWN 1F **30** (5L **31**)
Fabers Yd. SO23: Winche 7L **237** (6K **105**)
Fabian Cl. PO7: W'lle 1A **202**
RG21: B'toke 7B **42**
FACCOMBE 6K **7**
Factory Rd. SO50: E'leigh 1E **160**
Fairacre RG20: Wol H 3A **8**
Fairacre Ri. PO14: Fare 9L **197**
Fairacre Wlk. PO14: Fare 1L **211**
Fairbairn Wlk. SO53: Cha F 6L **131**
Fairbourne Cl. PO8: Cowp 8M **181**
Fairclose RG28: Whit 6F **54**
(not continuous)
Fairclose Dr. SO22: Lit 1F **104**
Fairclose Ter. *RG28: Whit* 5G *54*
(off Fairclose)
FAIR CROSS 3B **14**
Faircross Cl. SO45: Holb 5A **208**
FAIRDOWN 7N **105**
Fairdown Cl. SO23: Winche 7N **105**
Fairfax Cl. SO22: Winche 9F **104**
Fairfax Ct. SO19: South 4J **175**
Fairfax Ind. Est. GU12: Alders 9N **49**
Fairfax M. GU14: Farn 1M **49**
SO19: South 4J **175**
Fairfax Rd. GU14: Farn 5K **29**
Fair Fld. SO51: Rom 3N **129**
Fairfield BH23: Chri 7L **229**
RG28: Whit 4G **55**
Fairfield, The GU9: Farnh 8E **64**
Fairfield Av. PO14: Fare 1A **212**
Fairfield Cl. BH23: Chri 7L **229**
PO10: Ems 7M **203**
SO41: Lymi 3E **234**
SO45: Hythe 5L **193**
Fairfield Ct. *BH8: Bour* 8N *227*
(off Richmond Pk. Rd.)
Fairfield Dr. GU16: Frim 1N **29**
Fairfield Grn. GU34: Four M 4K **97**
Fairfield Lodge SO16: South 7H **159**
Fairfield Rd. BH25: B Sea 7N **231**
PO9: Hav 8F **202**
SO21: Shaw 8H **127**
SO22: Winche 5J **105**
Fairfields Arts Cen. 7C **42**
Fairfield Sq. PO6: Cosh 9F **200**
Fairfields Rd. RG21: B'toke 8C **42**
Fairfield Ter. *PO9: Hav* 8F *202*
(off Fairfield Rd.)
Fairgate Centre, The SP6: B'gte 7K **151**
Fair Grn. SO19: South 5F **174**
Fairground, The SP11: Weyh 8C **50**
Fairground Craft, The and Design Cen. 8D **50**
Fairground Ind. Pk.
SP11: Weyh 8C **50**
Fairhaven Ct. BH5: Bour 1B **246**
Fairholme Ct. SO50: B'stke 9E **132**
Fairholme Gdns. GU9: Farnh 9E **64**
Fairholme Pde. RG27: Hoo 2G **45**
Fairhome Cl. PO12: Gos 9J **213**
Fairings, The *SP6: F'dge* 1J *153*
(off Market Pl.)
Fair Isle Cl. PO14: Stub 5L **211**
Fairisle Rd. SO16: South 7D **158**
Fairland Cl. GU52: Fleet 3N **47**
Fairlands GU35: Head D 2F **102**
Fair La. SO21: Winche 6C **106**
Fairlawn Cl. SO16: Rown 5E **158**
Fairlawn Ho. SO23: Winche 9K **237** (7K **105**)
Fairlawn Rd. RG26: Tadl 6K **11**
Fairlawns SO31: Burr 9E **176**
Fair Lea BH2: Bour 9J **247** (3J **245**)
Fairlead Dr. PO13: Gos 1F **238**
Fairlea Grange SO16: Bass 7L **159**
Fairlea Rd. PO10: Ems 6M **203**
SO41: Lymi 2E **234**
Fairlie BH24: Poul 8M **185**
Fairlie Cl. SO30: Hed E 8N **161**
Fairlie Pk. BH24: Poul 8L **185**
Fairlight Chalets PO11: H Isl 4H **243**
Fairlight Gdns. GU34: Four M 4K **97**
Fairlight La. SO41: Tip 6E **222**
Fairmead Cl. GU47: Coll 6G **19**
Fairmead Ct. BH1: Bour 9L **227**
PO11: H Isl 4E **242**
Fairmead Wlk. PO8: Cowp 7A **182**
Fairmead Way SO40: Tott 5L **171**
FAIRMILE 6K **229**
Fairmile GU52: Fleet 5L **47**
Fairmile Ho. BH23: Chri 6J **229**
Fairmile Rd. BH23: Chri 4H **229**
FAIR OAK
RG19 3N **9**
SO50 1M **161**
Fair Oak Ct. PO12: Gos 4F **238**
SO50: Fair O 1N **161**
Fair Oak Dr. PO9: Hav 6F **202**
FAIR OAK GREEN 7J **13**
Fair Oak La. RG7: Stra S 7J **13**
Fair Oak Rd. PO4: S'sea 3K **241**
SO50: B'stke, Fair O 9H **133**
Fair Oak Squash Club 1N **161**
Fairoak Way RG26: Bau 4D **10**
Fair Piece SP11: Wher 2E **74**
Fairthorn Ct. BH2: Bour 1K **245**
Fairthorne Gdns. PO12: Gos 3J **239**
Fairthorne Ho. RG22: B'toke 8N **41**
Fairthorne Manor Golf Course 4F **176**
Fairthorne Ri. RG24: Old Bas 6K **43**
Fair Vw. SO24: New A 2E **108**
Fairview Cl. SO45: Hythe 6M **193**
SO51: Rom 3A **130**
Fairview Ct. PO12: Gos 3G **238**
Fairview Dr. SO45: Hythe 7L **193**
SO51: Rom 3A **130**
Fairview Gdns. GU9: Hale 4F **64**
Fairview Mdw. RG23: Oak 2D **58**
Fairview Pde. SO45: Hythe 7M **193**
Fairview Pk. BH14: Poole 2A **244**
Fairview Rd. GU35: Head D 2D **102**
SP11: Weyh 8C **50**
Fairview Ter. GU35: Head 1C **102**
Fairwater Cl. PO13: Gos 7D **212**
Fairway, The BH25: B Sea 7C **232**
GU9: H End 3F **64**
GU14: Farn 3D **48**
(Armstrong Way)
GU14: Farn 2C **48**
(The Romany)
GU35: W'hil 6G **100**
PO9: R Cas 8H **183**
PO13: Gos 7E **212**
PO16: Portc 9L **199**
SO31: Wars 8C **196**
Fairway Bus. Cen. PO3: Ports 6J **215**
Fairway Cl. GU30: Lip 3N **115**
Fairway Dr. BH23: Chri 8J **229**
SO22: Oli B 2E **126**
Fairway Est. BH11: Bour 2B **226**
Fairway Gdns. SO16: Rown 6D **158**
Fairway Rd. BH14: Poole 5A **244**
SO45: Hythe 5L **193**
FAIRWAYS 8B **50**
Fairways *BH8: Bour* 7N *227*
(off Richmond Pk. Rd.)
GU26: Hind 1K **103**
SP11: Weyh 8B **50**
Fairways, The PO6: Farl 1M **215**
Fairy Cross Way PO8: Cowp 7B **182**
Faithfulls Drove SO20: Houg 6D **88**
Faith Gdns. BH12: Poole 7A **226**
Fakenham Way GU47: Owl 4F **18**
Falaise Cl. GU11: Alders 9K **49**
SO16: South 7H **159**
Falaise Rd. SO20: Mid Wa 4A **72**
Falcon Cl. PO12: Gos 9L **213**
PO16: Portc 9H **199**
RG22: B'toke 1H **59**
Falcon Coppice RG20: Wol H 3A **8**
Falcon Ct. GU16: Frim 3M **29**
GU34: Alt 2F **80**
Falcon Dr. BH23: Mude 9C **230**
Falconer Ct. SO45: Hard 2A **208**
Falconer Ho. PO3: Ports 1H **241**
Falconer Rd. GU51: Fleet 9K **27**
Falcon Flds. RG26: Tadl 3H **11**
SO45: Fawl 5F **208**
Falcon Grn. PO6: Farl 1N **215**
Falcon Ho. Gdns. RG20: Wol H 3A **8**
Falcon Rd. PO8: Horn 3A **182**
Falcon Sq. SO50: E'leigh 2C **160**
Falcon Vw. SO22: Winche 1G **127**
Falcon Way GU46: Yat 7L **17**
SO32: Botl 1C **176**
Falconwood Cl. SP6: F'dge 1G **152**
Falkland Ct. GU14: Farn 3N **49**
SO53: Cha F 9A **132**
Falkland Rd. RG24: B'toke 1D **42**
SO15: South 2F **172**
SO53: Cha F 1A **160**
Falklands Cl. PO13: Lee S 9B **212**
Falklands Rd. PO2: Ports 4F **214**
Falkner Ct. GU9: Farnh 8E **64**
Falkner Ho. GU51: Fleet 8A **28**
Falkner Rd. GU9: Farnh 8D **64**
Falkners Cl. GU51: Fleet 8A **28**
Fallow Cres. SO30: Hed E 2A **176**
Fallow Fld. SO22: Winche 1G **127**
Fallowfield GU46: Yat 6L **17**
GU51: Fleet 8A **28**
Fallows, The BH25: New M 1C **232**
Falmouth Ho. PO13: Gos 2F **238**
Falmouth Rd. PO6: Cosh 8A **200**
Falstaff Way SO40: Tott 5K **171**
Fanshawe St. SO14: South 1E **4** (4M **173**)
Fantails GU34: Alt 2F **80**
Fanum Ho. RG21: B'toke 5E **42**
Faraday Ct. RG24: B'toke 3E **42**
Faraday Office Pk. RG24: B'toke 3E **42**
Faraday Pk. SP10: A'ver 9H **51**
Faraday Rd. GU14: Farn 6L **29**
RG24: B'toke 3E **42**
Farcroft Rd. BH12: Poole 9A **226**
Farcrosse Cl. GU47: Sandh 5E **18**
FAREHAM 8D **198**
Fareham Dr. GU46: Yat 6L **17**
Fareham Ent. Cen. PO14: Fare 2C **212**
Fareham Hgts. PO16: Fare 6F **198**
Fareham Ind. Pk. PO16: Fare 6F **198**
Fareham Leisure Cen. 7C **198**
Fareham Pk. Rd. PO15: Fare 5M **197**
Fareham Rd. PO7: H'don 3C **180**
PO13: Gos 3D **212**
PO17: S'wick 4N **199**
PO17: Wick 7C **178**
Fareham Sailing and Motor Boat Club 9D **198**
Fareham Shop. Cen. PO16: Fare 8D **198**
Fareham Station (Rail) 8B **198**
Faringdon Cl. GU47: Sandh 4E **18**
Faringdon Ct. RG24: B'toke 2B **42**
SO23: Winche 4L **105**
Faringdon Rd. SO18: South 3H **175**
Farleigh BH4: Bour 1G **244**
Farleigh Cl. PO9: Hav 4D **202**
Farleigh La. RG25: Dumm, Far W 9F **58**
Farleigh Ri. RG21: B'toke 9D **42**
Farleigh Rd. RG25: Clid 3B **60**
RG25: Clid, Far W 7M **59**
FARLEIGH WALLOP 8N **59**
Farleigh Wallop Dr. GU51: Fleet 9H **27**
FARLEY 8F **86**
Farley Cl. SO22: Oli B 1F **126**
SO50: Fair O 2A **162**
Farley Ct. GU14: Farn 1M **49**
SO16: South 9J **159**
Farley La. SO51: Brai 4C **124**
SO51: Lwr Slac, Up Sla 6F **124**
Farley Lodge BH14: Poole 1A **244**
Farley Mount Country Pk. 6A **104** (8M **89**)
Farley Mt. Rd. SO21: Hurs, Spar 9N **89**
Farley St. SO20: N Wal 9N **67**
FARLINGTON 9M **201**
Farlington Av. PO6: Dray 8K **201**
Farlington Marshes (Nature Reserve) 3M **215**
Farlington Rd. PO2: Ports 7G **214**
Farm Cl. BH24: Ring 9K **185**
GU46: Yat 8N **17**
SO31: Hamb 7L **195**
Farm Cotts. RG24: B'toke 3M **41**
Farmdene Cl. BH23: Chri 6F **230**
Farm Dr. GU51: Fleet 8N **27**
Far Mdw. Way PO10: Ems 9K **203**
Farm Edge Rd. PO14: Stub 7M **211**
Farmers Wlk. SO41: Ever 6L **233**
Farmery Way PO8: Horn 2C **182**
Farmery Cl. SO18: S'ing 7B **160**
Farm Ground Cl. RG27: Hoo 2J **45**
Farm Ho. Cl. PO14: Stub 3M **211**
Farmhouse Way PO8: Horn 5A **182**
Farm La. BH23: Mude 9C **230**
GU10: Cron 3L **63**
RG7: Mor W 1C **12**
RG45: Cr'tne 3A **18**
SO40: Ashu 8H **171**
Farm La. Cl. PO7: W'lle 3L **201**
Farm La. Nth. BH25: B Sea 6B **232**
Farm La. Sth. BH25: B Sea 7B **232**
Farmlea Rd. PO6: Cosh 9B **200**
Farm Rd. GU12: Alders 8N **49**
GU16: Frim 2N **29**
PO14: Titch 7H **197**
SO21: Spar 5N **89**
SP11: A'ver 3F **68**

Fitzwilliam Av.—Fox's Furlong

Fitzwilliam Av. PO14: Stub .6K 211
Fitzwilliam Cl. BH11: Bour .1C 226
Fitzwygram Cres. PO9: Hav .6F 202
Five Acres Cl. GU35: Lind .2L 101
Five Ash Rd. GU34: Meds .3H 97
Five Bells La. SO20: N Wal .1N 87
Five Bridges Rd. SO23: Winche .2J 127
Five Elms Dr. SO51: Rom .6A 130
Fivefields Cl. SO23: Winche .7N 105
Fivefields Rd. SO23: Winche .7N 105
Five Heads M. PO8: Horn .2C 182
Five Heads Rd. PO8: Cath, Horn .2A 182
Five Lanes SP11: S M Bo .1K 53
Five-O-One BH9: Bour .6K 227
Five Post La. PO12: Gos .1K 239
Flag Farm BH13: S'bks .6B 244
Flaghead Chine Rd.
BH13: Poole .7C 244
Flaghead Rd. BH13: Poole .6C 244
Flag Staff Grn. PO12: Gos .1M 239
Flag Wlk. PO8: Cowp .5N 181
Flambard Av. BH23: Chri .5J 229
Flambard Rd. BH14: Poole .3A 244
Flamborough Cl. SO16: South .8C 158
Flamingo Ct. PO16: Portc .9H 199
Flamstone St. SP5: Bish .3C 118
Flanders Ho. PO14: Fare .9A 198
Flanders Ind. Pk. SO30: Hed E .2M 175
Flanders Rd. SO30: Hed E .2M 175
Flashes, The (Nature Reserve) .4J 85
Flashett, The SP5: Mid W .5H 87
FLAT FIRS .9K 21
Flathouse Quay PO2: Ports .9D 214
Flathouse Rd. PO1: Ports .2L 5 (1C 240)
(Circular Rd.)
PO1: Ports .9D 214
(Regent St.)
Flats, The GU17: Blackw .9D 18
Flaxfield Ct. RG21: B'toke .6B 42
Flaxfield Rd. RG21: B'toke .6B 42
Flaxfields End SP6: F'dge .1H 153
Flazen Cl. BH11: Bour .3B 226
FLEET
GU51 .2L 47
PO11 .8G 216
Fleet Bus. Pk. GU52: Ch Cr .7N 47
Fleet Cl. PO13: Gos .7F 212
FLEETEND .8C 196
Fleet End Bottom SO31: Wars .9C 196
Fleet End Cl. PO9: Hav .3E 202
Fleet End Rd. SO31: Wars .8C 196
Fleet Farm Camping & Caravan Site
PO11: H Isl .8G 217
Fleet Hill RG27: Eve .3E 16
RG40: F'std .3E 16
FLEETLANDS .3E 212
Fleet La. RG40: F'std .3E 16
Fleet Mill GU51: Fleet .8N 27
Fleet Pond (Nature Reserve) .9N 27
Fleet Rd. GU11: Alders .4C 48
GU14: Cov .8C 28
GU51: Fleet .3L 47
(Reading Rd. Sth.)
GU51: Fleet .9B 28
(Sankey La.)
GU51: Winchf .6C 26
RG27: Elve, H Win, Winchf .6C 26
FLEET SERVICE AREA .8J 27
Fleet Station (Rail) .9N 27
Fleet Ter. SO21: Ott .3E 132
Fleet Way PO1: Ports .1L 5 (1C 240)
Fleming Av. SO52: N Bad .8G 130
Fleming Cl. GU14: Farn .6M 29
PO15: Seg .5G 197
SP11: Ludg .1D 30
Fleming Ct. SO52: N Bad .8G 130
Fleming Ho. SO50: E'leigh .1C 160
Fleming Pk. Leisure Cen. .9C 132
Fleming Pl. SO21: Col C .3K 133
SO51: Rom .4M 129
Fleming Rd. SO16: S'ing .7B 160
SO22: Winche .3G 105
Flensburg Cl. SP10: A'ver .7M 51
Fletcher Cl. BH10: Bour .3H 227
RG21: B'toke .7A 42
SO45: Dib .6J 193
Fletcher Rd. BH10: Bour .3H 227
Fletchers Fld. GU30: Lip .3E 116
Fletchers Ho. GU30: Lip .3D 116
Fletchwood La. SO40: Ashu, Tott .8F 170
(not continuous)
Fletchwood Meadows Nature Reserve .7H 171
Fletchwood Rd. SO40: Tott .4H 171
Fleur De Lys Pk. SO41: Pil .6F 224
Fleuret Cl. SO45: Hythe .8M 193
FLEXFORD .4M 131
Flexford Cl. RG20: High .4A 8
SO53: Cha F .3M 131
Flexford Gdns. PO9: Hav .6G 203
(not continuous)
Flexford La. SO41: Sway .9K 223
Flexford Nature Reserve .3M 131
Flexford Rd. SO52: N Bad .6H 131
Flinders Cl. SP10: A'ver .9E 52
Flinders Ct. PO4: S'sea .5J 241
Flint Cl. SO19: South .6J 175
SP10: A'ver .3L 69
Flint Ho. Path PO6: Dray .2K 215
Flint La. SP11: C'vle .2E 50
Flint St. PO5: S'sea .7M 5 (4C 240)
Floating Bri. Rd. SO14: South .7A 174
Flood, The SP5: Mid W .4G 87
FLOOD STREET .4K 151
Floral Way SP10: A'ver .3K 69
Flora Twort Gallery .1M 145
Florence Cl. GU46: Yat .7M 17
SO51: E Wel .1B 156
Florence Ct. BH5: Bour .1A 246
SP10: A'ver .7A 52
(not continuous)
Florence Portal Cl. RG28: L'stoke .5N 55
Florence Rd. BH5: Bour .1B 246
BH14: Poole .1A 244
GU47: Coll .6F 18
GU52: Fleet .5M 47
PO5: S'sea .6E 240
SO19: South .8B 174
Florence Way GU34: Alt .7D 80
RG24: B'toke .3L 41
Florentine Way PO7: W'lle .1A 202
Florin Mall BH1: Bour .1B 246
Florins, The PO7: Purb .6M 201
PO14: Titch C .8D 196
Floris Ct. BH1: Bour .1A 246
Floriston Gdns. BH25: A'ley .3E 232
Florrie Pl. GU34: Lwr Farr .4D 98
Floud La. GU32: W Meo .8C 136
Flowerdew Ct. SP10: A'ver .3A 70
Flowerdown Barrows .2G 104
Flowerdown Cl. SO40: Calm .2J 171
Flowerdown Mobile Home Pk. SO22: Lit .1G 104
Flowers Cl. SO31: Hamb .6J 195
Flowers La. SO51: Plai .7M 121
Flume Rd. SO45: Fawl .4G 209
Flushards SO41: Lymi .3F 234
Flying Bull Cl. PO2: Ports .8E 214
Flying Bull La. PO2: Ports .8E 214
FOBDOWN .7C 94
Focus 303 Bus. Cen. SP10: A'ver .9D 52
Focus Way SP10: A'ver .9C 52
Foden Rd. GU11: Alders .1J 65
Foldsgate Cl. SO43: Lyn .1B 148
Foley Estate GU30: Lip .4B 116
Foley Ho. PO1: Ports .1E 240
Folkestone Rd. PO3: Ports .9H 215
Folland Cl. SO52: N Bad .8F 130
Folly Cl. GU52: Fleet .4M 47
Folly Drove SP6: Hale .1B 154
Folly Farm La. BH24: A'ley .2F 186
Folly Fld. SO32: Bis W .4N 163
Folly Hill GU9: Farnh, Up H .4C 64
Folly La. GU31: Pet .1M 145
RG7: Stra S .1H 23
RG26: B'ley .1H 23
RG26: Rams .9N 9
Folly La. Nth. GU9: Up H .3D 64
Folly La. Sth. GU9: Up H .4C 64
Folly Roundabout, The SP10: A'ver .9M 51
Font Cl. PO14: Titch C .6F 196
Fontley La. PO15: Titch .6K 197
Fontley Rd. PO15: F'ley, Titch .5K 197
Fontwell Cl. GU12: Alders .9M 49
SO40: Calm .1J 171
Fontwell Dr. GU34: Alt .6F 80
Fontwell Gdns. SO50: Hor H .4A 162
Fontwell M. PO7: W'lle .9B 182
Fontwell Rd. PO5: S'sea .5E 240
Foord Rd. SO30: Hed E .5L 175
Football Grn. SO43: Mins .8M 155
Footner Cl. SO51: Rom .2B 130
Footners La. BH23: Burt .4M 229
Forbes Chase GU47: Coll .6F 18
Forbes Cl. SO16: South .5E 158
Forbes Ct. PO2: Ports .5F 214
Forbes Rd. SO23: Kin W .7M 91
Forbury Rd. PO5: S'sea .3E 240
Ford Av. SO53: Cha F .8B 132
Forder's Cl. SP5: Woodf .3M 119 (8C 120)
FORDINGBRIDGE .1J 153
Fordingbridge Bus. Pk. SP6: F'dge .1F 152
Fordingbridge Mus. .1J 153
Fordingbridge Rd. PO4: S'sea .4J 241
SP6: Ald, F'dge .3D 152
Fordington Av. SO22: Winche .6H 237 (6H 105)
Fordington Rd. SO22: Winche .6H 237 (6J 105)
Fordington Vs. SO53: Cha F .6A 132
Ford La. RG7: Swal .1L 15
RG25: Up G .2C 62
RG27: Brams .2L 15
RG29: S War .2C 62
Ford Rd. PO12: Gos .1H 239
Forehead, The RG7: Mort .1L 13
Foreland Cl. BH23: Chri .2G 228
Foreland Ct. PO11: H Isl .5J 243
Forelle Centre, The BH31: Ver .5A 184
Foremans Cotts. PO12: Gos .5M 239
Foreshore Nth. SO45: Fawl .2F 208
Foreshore Sth. SO45: Fawl .3F 208
Forest Arts Cen. .5A 232
Forest Av. PO8: Cowp .7N 181
Forest Cen. GU35: Bor .4K 101
Forest Cl. BH23: Chri .5F 230
BH31: Ver .5A 184
PO8: Cowp .7N 181
RG26: Bau .3E 10
SO32: Wal C .8A 164
SO52: N Bad .7D 130
SO53: Cha F .4A 132
Forest Cnr. GU33: Liss .7F 114
Forest Ct. BH25: New M .4C 232
SP6: F'dge .1J 153
SP9: Tidw .7E 30
Forestdale GU26: Hind .4M 103
Forest Dean GU51: Fleet .8A 28
Forest Dr. RG24: Chin .8G 23
SP9: Tidw .8E 30 (7H 31)
Forest Edge BH25: A'ley .2D 232
SO45: Fawl .5E 208
SP5: Down .9A 120
Forest Edge Cl. BH24: Ashl H .3A 186
SO41: Sway .4H 223
Forest Edge Dr. BH24: Ashl H .3A 186
Forest Edge Pk. SO51: E Wel .6F 128
Forest Edge Rd. BH24: Crow .6A 188
Forest End GU47: Sandh .4B 18
GU52: Fleet .5L 47
PO7: W'lle .2L 201
Forest End Rd. GU47: Sandh .4B 18
Forest End Rdbt. PO7: W'lle .2M 201
Forester Rd. SO32: Sob H .1J 179
Foresters Ga. SO45: Blac .9C 208
Foresters Rd. SO45: Fawl .6D 208
Foresters Way RG45: Cr'tne .2H 19
Forest Front SO45: Hythe .9L 193
Forest Gdns. SO32: Wal C .8A 164
SO43: Lyn .2B 148 (2N 189)
FOREST GATE .3F 180
Forest Ga. SO45: Blac .9D 208
Forest Gate Ct. BH24: Ring .1J 187
Forest Gate Gdns. SO41: Lymi .5D 234
Forest Glade GU10: Rowl .8N 63
Forest Glade Cl. SO42: Broc .7A 148 (8M 189)
Forest Hall SO42: Broc .7D 148
Forest Hills GU15: Camb .9K 19
Forest Hills Ct. BH24: Hight .2N 187
Forest Hills Dr. SO18: South .8C 160
Forest Hill Way SO45: Dib P .7L 193
Forest Ho. BH1: Bour .7N 247 (3L 245)
Forestlake Av. BH24: Hight .2N 187
Forest La. BH24: Hight .6A 188
GU35: Lind .1M 101
PO17: Fare .2D 198
RG26: Tadl .7K 11
SO45: Hard .2N 207
SP11: A'ver, And D .3E 70
SP11: Co Du .2N 31
Forest La. Cl. GU30: Lip .2C 116
Forest Mead PO7: Den .7G 181
Forest Mdw. SO45: Hythe .9M 193
FOREST MERE .5N 115
Forest M. SO40: Tott .9K 157
Forest Oak Dr. BH25: New M .1B 232
FOREST PARK .6B 148 (8N 189)
Forest Pk. Rd. SO42: Broc .6B 148 (8N 189)
Forest Pines BH25: New M .2B 232
Forest Ri. BH23: Chri .4F 230
GU33: Liss .8F 114
Forest Rd. BH13: Poole .4E 244
BH23: Bran, Thorn .2G 220
BH24: Bur .6D 188
GU33: G'ham, Liss .4B 132
GU35: Bor, W'hil .6J 101
(not continuous)
PO7: Den, Wor E .6B 180
RG45: Cr'tne .1E 18
SO32: Swanm, Wal C .8A 164
SO53: Cha F .4B 132
SP5: Hale .9C 120
SP5: Nom .4H 155
SP5: Redl .9C 120
SP6: Hale .9C 120
FORESTSIDE .4N 183
Forest Side SO45: Hythe .9L 193
Forestside, The BH31: Ver .4A 184
Forestside Av. PO9: Hav .4G 203
Forestside Gdns. BH24: Poul .8M 185
Forest Vw. BH23: Walk .4K 231
BH25: Bash .1M 231
GU10: B Oak .10M 63
SO14: South .7C 4 (6L 173)
SO42: Broc .7A 148 (8M 189)
Forest Vw. Cl. BH9: Bour .4L 227
Forest Vw. Rd. BH9: Bour .3L 227
Forest Wlk. BH25: Bash .1M 231
Forest Way BH23: Chri .4F 230
PO13: Gos .6F 212
SO40: Calm .9G 156
SO41: Ever .5L 233
Forfield Dr. RG22: B'toke .5J 59
Forge Cl. GU9: Farnh .7F 64
RG26: B'ley .2H 23
SO20: Ki S .9B 86
SO31: Burs .9L 175
Forge Fld. SP10: A'ver .9A 52
Forge La. GU11: Alders .5H 49
SO45: Fawl .5F 208
Forge Rd. GU35: K'ly .8E 82
GU35: Slea .7K 83
SO45: Blac .9D 208
Forges La. RG27: Eve .2N 15
Forneth Gdns. PO15: Fare .9L 197
Forrest Mnr. BH5: Bour .9E 228
(off Seabourne Rd.)
Forster Rd. SO14: South .3M 173
Forsyte Shades BH14: Poole .5C 244
Forsyth Gdns. BH10: Bour .5G 227
Forsythia Cl. PO9: Hav .5H 203
SO30: Hed E .2M 175
SO45: Hythe .1M 207
Forsythia Pl. SO19: South .5D 174
Forsythia Wlk. RG21: B'toke .3D 42
Fort Brockhurst .7H 213
Fort Cumberland Rd. PO4: S'sea .4L 241
Fortescue Rd. BH3: Bour .8L 227
BH12: Poole .7B 226
Fort Fareham Ind. Site PO14: Fare .2C 212
Fort Fareham Rd. PO14: Fare .2B 212
Forth Cl. GU14: Cov .6F 28
PO14: Stub .5L 211
SO53: Cha F .7N 131
Forth Ct. SP10: A'ver .8B 52
Forth Ho. SO14: South .4A 174
Fort Hill Dr. RG23: B'toke .5L 41
Forthill Rd. SO20: Mid Wa .3A 72
Forties Cl. PO14: Stub .4L 211
Fort Narrien GU15: Camb .7G 19
Fort Nelson (Royal Armouries) .6K 199
Fort Nelson Vis. Cen. .6K 199
FORTON
PO12 .2K 239
SP11 .5L 71
Forton Cl. BH10: Bour .2J 227
Forton Lodge PO12: Gos .2L 239
(off Forton Rd.)
Forton Rd. PO1: Ports .1F 240
PO12: Gos .1J 239
Fort Purbrook .7L 201
Fort Rd. PO12: Gos .6J 239
SO19: South .7C 174
Fortrose Cl. GU47: Coll .6F 18
Fortune Ct. SO53: Cha F .6A 132
Fortune Ho. PO12: Gos .2J 239
Fortunes Way PO9: Bed .8N 201
Fort Wallington Ind. Est. PO16: Fare .7F 198
Forty Acre La. GU31: Old D, S Hart .9B 146
Forum, The PO9: Hav .7E 202
Forum Cl. RG23: B'toke .6K 41
Forward Dr. SO41: Penn .4C 234
FOSBURY .7C 6
Fosseway RG45: Cr'tne .1B 18
Fossewood Dr. GU15: Camb .5M 19
Foster Cl. PO14: Stub .4M 211
Foster Rd. PO1: Ports .1E 240
PO12: Gos .4J 239
Fosters Bus. Pk. RG27: Hoo .3E 44
Foul La. GU34: Meds .9K 79
Foundary Rd. SP5: M Val .1M 119
Founders Way PO13: Gos .6F 212
Foundry Cl. RG27: Hoo .2G 45
Foundry Ct. PO1: Ports .3K 5 (2B 240)
SO19: South .8B 174
Foundry Cres. SO31: Burs .1K 195
Foundry La. SO15: South .2G 173
Foundry Rd. SP11: An V .5J 69
Fountain Ct. BH13: Poole .3F 244
SO21: Col C .3K 133
SO30: Hed E .4M 175
Fountain Rd. GU34: Selb .8L 99
Fountain Rdbt. BH23: Chri .8L 229
Fountains Cl. RG24: B'toke .2B 42
Fountain's Mall RG29: Odi .8L 45
Fountains Pk. SO31: Net A .2E 194
Fountain Sq. PO11: H Isl .3E 242
Fountain St. PO1: Ports .3N 5 (2D 240)
Fountain Way BH23: Chri .8L 229
Four Acre Coppice RG27: Hoo .1J 45
Four Acres SO30: Botl .4D 176
Fourhomes SP11: Stoke .7H 35
Four Lanes Cl. RG24: Chin .9H 23
FOUR MARKS .4K 97
Four Marks Golf Course .6M 97
Four Marks Grn. PO9: Hav .3H 203
Four Oaks RG20: High .4A 8
FOURPOSTS .5K 173
Fourposts Hill SO15: South .3A 4 (5K 173)
Fourshells Cl. SO45: Fawl .6D 208
Fourth Av. PO6: Cosh .9F 200
PO9: Hav .7H 203
Fourth St. PO1: Ports .1G 240
RG19: Green .1G 9
(off Warehouse Rd.)
Fowey, The SO45: Blac .6C 208
Fowey Cl. SO53: Cha F .5N 131
Fowey Ct. PO12: Gos .8L 213
(off Hayling Cl.)
Fowler Av. GU14: Farn .1K 49
Fowler Rd. GU14: Cov .9H 29
Fowlers Rd. GU11: Alders .5L 49
SO30: Hed E .2M 175
Fowlers Wlk. SO16: Chilw .1J 159
Foxbury PO13: Gos .4F 212
Foxbury Cl. SO45: Hythe .7M 193
Foxbury Gro. PO16: Portc .1K 213
Foxbury La. PO13: Gos .4F 212
(not continuous)
Foxbury Rd. BH24: Match, St L .7C 186 & 1B 218
(not continuous)
Fox Cl. SO50: B'stke .1K 161
Foxcombe Cl. SO32: Swanm .5C 164
Fox Cnr. SP11: Amp .3N 67
Foxcote Gdns. BH25: New M .3N 231
Foxcote Ho. PO6: Cosh .7A 200
Foxcott Cl. SO19: South .1D 194
FOXCOTTE .7J 51
Foxcotte Cl. SP10: Charl .8K 51
Foxcotte La. SP10: Charl .7J 51
SP11: Charl .7J 51
Foxcotte Rd. SP10: Charl .7G 50
SP11: Pen M .7G 50
Foxcott Gro. PO9: Hav .4F 202
Fox Ct. GU12: Alders .8N 49
Fox Cover, The SO20: Mid Wa .4B 72
Foxcroft GU52: Ch Cr .6M 47
Foxcroft Dr. SO45: Holb .5N 207
Foxdale BH23: Chri .5G 228
Foxdale Ct. BH2: Bour .7K 247
FOXDOWN .9E 38
Foxdown RG25: Over .9E 38
Foxdown Cl. GU15: Camb .8L 19
Fox Dr. GU46: Yat .6N 17
Foxes Cl. PO7: W'lle .3M 201
Foxes La. SO51: W Wel .1C 120 (7N 121)
Fox Farm SP11: Amp .3N 67
Fox Fld. SO41: Ever .5L 233
Foxglade SO45: Blac .9D 208
Foxglove Cl. BH23: Chri .6E 230
RG22: B'toke .3J 59
Foxglove Dr. GU35: Bor .5K 101
Foxglove Ho. PO13: Gos .2E 238
Foxglove Pl. BH25: A'ley .2E 232
Foxgloves BH23: Bran .7B 220
PO16: Fare .6E 198
Foxgloves, The SO30: Hed E .5A 176
FOXHALL .8L 59
Foxhayes La. SO45: Blac .9D 208
Fox Heath GU14: Cov .9E 28
FOXHILLS .6J 171
Foxhills SO40: Ashu .6J 171
Foxhills Cl. SO40: Ashu .7J 171
Foxholes BH6: Bour .1J 247
Foxholes Rd. BH6: Bour .1J 247
Foxlands SO45: Blac .9D 208
FOX LANE .4G 28
Fox La. RG23: Oak .8E 40
RG27: Eve .5J 17
SO22: Winche .9G 104
SO24: Bram .1N 135
Foxlea Gdns. PO12: Gos .9K 213
Foxley Cl. GU17: Blackw .8E 18
Foxley Dr. PO3: Ports .4J 215
Foxmoor Cl. RG23: Oak .8D 40
Fox Pond La. SO41: Penn .4C 234
Fox Rd. GU27: Hasl .9N 103
Fox's Furlong RG24: Chin .8J 23

Garden La.—Godiva Lawn

Garden La. BH24: St L .5B 186
PO5: S'sea .8N 5 (4D 240)
SO23: Winche .7N 237 (6L 105)
Garden M. GU31: Pet .1M 145
SO31: Wars .8N 195
Garden Ridge BH4: Bour .1G 244
Garden Rd. BH24: Bur .7D 188
Gardens, The PO7: H'don .8E 166
PO9: Warb .8H 203
PO16: Fare .6E 198
SO20: Brou .1A 86 (4A 88)
SO32: Bis W .4A 164
Gardens Cres. BH14: Poole .5A 244
Gardens Outlook BH4: Bour .1G 245
Gardens Rd. BH14: Poole .5A 244
Gardens Vw. BH1: Bour .1N 245
Garden Ter. PO5: S'sea .5E 240
Garden Vw. BH4: Bour .1G 244
(off Branksome Wood Rd.)
PO5: S'sea .5E 240
(off St Vincent Rd.)
Gardiner Cl. SO40: March .8F 172
Gardiner Rd. RG24: B'toke .1C 42
Gardner Ct. BH23: Chri .6H 229
Gardner Rd. BH23: Chri .6H 229
BH24: Ring .2L 187
PO14: Titch .1J 211
Gardner Way SO53: Cha F .4N 131
Garendon Ct. SP6: F'dge .9H 151
Garfield Av. BH1: Bour .9A 228
Garfield Cl. SO32: Bis W .3M 163
Garfield Rd. GU15: Camb .8L 19
PO2: Ports .8E 214
SO19: South .3C 174
SO31: Net A .3E 194
SO32: Bis W .3M 163
Garland Av. PO10: Ems .6M 203
Garland Ct. PO12: Gos .2K 239
Garland Way SO40: Tott .2H 171
Garnet Fld. GU46: Yat .8K 17
Garnet Rd. GU35: Bor .5K 101
Garnett Cl. PO14: Stub .4M 211
Garnier Pk. PO17: Wick .6C 178
Garnier Rd. SO23: Winche .9K 105
Garnier St. PO1: Ports .2E 240
Garnock Rd. SO19: South .8B 174
Garratt Cl. SO30: Hed E .9N 161
Garrett Cl. RG20: Kings .1A 6 (5K 9)
Garrett Ct. RG23: Oak .1C 58
Garrett M. GU11: Alders .1J 65
Garretts Cl. SO19: South .9E 174
Garrick Gdns. SO19: South .8E 174
Garrick Ho. PO2: Ports .4G 214
Garrick Way GU16: Frim G .5N 29
Garrison Hill SO32: Drox .1K 165
Garrison Sports Cen.
Aldershot .5L 49
Garrow Dr. SO41: Lymi .1E 234
Garsdale Cl. BH11: Bour .1E 226
Garside Cl. RG26: B'ley .3G 23
Garston Cl. GU32: E Meon .4L 143
Garston Mede SO20: Chil .4F 74
Garstons Cl. PO14: Titch .9J 197
Garstons Rd. PO14: Titch .9J 197
Garstons Track SO21: Spar .5N 89
Gar St. SO23: Winche .8L 237 (7K 105)
Garth, The GU12: Ash .1N 65
GU14: Farn .8M 29
GU34: Alt .4G 80
SO45: Dib P .7L 193
Garth Cl. BH24: St L .4A 186
GU35: Bor .3J 101
Garth Rd. BH9: Bour .5L 227
Garton Rd. SO19: South .7C 174
Gascoigne La. SO24: Rop .1C 110
Gashouse Hill SO31: Net A .4G 195
Gaskell Cl. GU34: Holy .2J 81
Gason Hill Rd. SP9: Tidw .6C 30 (6G 30)
Gaston Gdns. SO51: Rom .4M 129
Gaston La. GU34: Up Farr .4E 98
RG29: S War .3C 62
Gastons Wood RG24: Chin .2E 42
Gatcombe SO31: Net A .2G 195
Gatcombe Av. PO3: Ports .6G 215
Gatcombe Dr. PO2: Ports .5G 214
Gatcombe Gdns. PO14: Fare .9L 197
SO18: Wes E .9E 160
Gate House, The PO11: H Isl .4D 242
Gatehouse, The SO18: South .2C 174
SO30: Wes E .9G 160
Gate Ho. Rd. PO16: Portc .1J 213
Gatekeeper Cl. SO23: Winche .6N 105
Gateley Hall SO15: South .3L 173
Gaters Hill SO18: Wes E .8E 160
Gaters La. SP4: Win D .3A 86
Gates, The GU51: Fleet .8A 28
Gateswood RG27: Sher L .7J 23
Gateway, The BH13: Poole .1D 244
Gatwick Cl. SO16: South .7F 158
Gauldy La. RG26: Bau .3E 20
Gaulter Cl. PO9: Hav .6G 202
Gauvain Cl. GU34: Alt .6G 80
Gavan St. SO19: South .5H 175
G Avenue SO45: Fawl .2D 208
Gawaine Cl. SP10: A'ver .6N 51
Gawn Pl. PO12: Gos .5L 239
Gaydon Ri. BH11: Bour .2C 226
Gaylyn Way PO14: Fare .9L 197
Gaza Av. SO42: Beau .1B 236
Gaza Ho. PO15: Fare .6M 197
Gazebo Garden .8F 202
Gazelle Cl. PO13: Gos .2F 238
Gazing La. SO51: W Wel .1B 120 (9N 121)
Gazings, The SO51: W Wel .1B 120 (9N 121)
Geale's Ct. GU34: Alt .3G 81
Geale's Cres. GU34: Alt .3G 80
Geddes Way GU31: Pet .9B 140
Geffery's Flds. RG21: B'toke .7D 42
Geffery's Ho. RG27: Hoo .1H 45
Gemini Cl. SO16: South .7E 158
General Johnson Ct. SO22: Winche .8G 105
Geneva Av. BH6: Bour .9G 229
Genoa Cl. SO41: Penn .5C 234
Genoa Ct. SP10: A'ver .6A 52
(not continuous)
Genoa Ho. PO6: P Sol .1B 214
Gentles La. GU30: Pass .6C 102
GU35: Head .4C 102
Gento Cl. SO30: Botl .4B 176
Geoffrey Av. PO7: Wid .7J 201
Geoffrey Cres. PO16: Fare .1D 212
George VI Rd. SP9: Tidw .6C 30
George Byng Way PO2: Ports .8D 214
George Ct. BH8: Bour .8N 227
George Court, The PO1: Ports .7K 5
George Curl Way SO18: S'ton A .5D 160
George Eyston Dr. SO22: Winche .8H 105
George Gdns. GU11: Alders .3L 65
GU51: Fleet .2N 47
Georgeham Rd. GU47: Owl .3F 18
George Mews, The BH24: Ring .1J 187
George Perrett Way SO53: Cha F .8L 131
George Raymond Rd.
SO50: E'leigh .1D 160
George Rd. GU51: Fleet .2N 47
SO41: M Sea .7J 235
George St. PO1: Ports .9F 214
PO2: Ports .9F 214
PO12: Gos .2L 239
RG20: Kings .2B 6 (6K 9)
RG21: B'toke .6A 42
SO50: E'leigh .9F 132
Georges Way SO50: E'leigh .9C 132
George Wright Cl. SO50: E'leigh .1D 160
George Yd. SP10: A'ver .2A 70
George Yard, The SO24: New A .9F 94
Georgia Cl. PO9: Hav .6E 202
PO13: Lee S .9B 212
SP10: A'ver .3K 69
Georgia La. SO20: Ov Wa .6N 67
SP11: Amp, Grat, Ov Wa .3N 67
Georgian Cl. BH24: Ring .9K 185
GU15: Camb .6N 19
Georgian Way BH10: Bour .2K 227
Georgina Cl. BH12: Poole .6G 226
SO40: Tott .1H 171
Georgina Ct. GU51: Fleet .2M 47
Georgina Gdns. RG26: Pam H .5L 11
Georgina Talbot Ho. BH12: Poole .6F 226
Gerald Rd. BH3: Bour .8L 227
Gerald Sq. GU34: Alt .2G 80
Geranium Gdns. PO7: Den .6H 181
Gerard Cres. SO19: South .4H 175
Gerard Ho. PO2: Ports .4F 214
Germaine Cl. BH23: Highc .6H 231
German Rd. RG26: B'ley .2H 23
Gershwin Ct. RG22: B'toke .2L 59
Gershwin Rd. RG22: B'toke .2L 59
Gervis Pl. BH1: Bour .7L 247 (2K 245)
Gervis Rd. BH1: Bour .2L 245
Gibbons Cl. GU47: Sandh .5E 18
Gibbons Pl. RG24: B'toke .1B 42
Gibbs Cl. SO45: Hythe .9M 193
Gibb's La. GU35: Bor, Oakh .1F 100
Gibbs Rd. SO14: South .4C 4 (5L 173)
Gibbs Way GU46: Yat .9L 17
Gibraltar Cl. PO15: Fare .7N 197
Gibraltar Rd. PO4: S'sea .4L 241
PO14: Fare .2B 212
Gibson Cl. PO13: Lee S .9B 212
(not continuous)
PO15: White .3H 197
Gid La. GU34: Up Froy .8G 63
Giffard Dr. GU14: Cov, Farn .7H 29
Giffard La. GU51: Fleet .9K 27
Giffards Mdw. GU9: Farnh .9G 64
Gifford Cl. PO15: Fare .6A 198
Gilbard Ct. RG24: Chin .9H 23
Gilbert Cl. PO13: Gos .8F 212
RG24: B'toke .2D 42
SO41: Lymi .4D 234
SP6: Ald .4E 152
Gilbert Mead PO11: H Isl .3E 242
Gilbert Rd. BH8: Bour .8A 228
GU16: Camb .3L 29
Gilbert's Grn. SP9: Shi B .2B 66
Gilberts Mead Cl. SP11: An V .5J 69
Gilberts Piece SN8: Co Du .2H 31
GILBERT STREET .9F 96
Gilbert St. SO24: Rop .1E 110
Gilbert Way PO7: W'lle .4M 201
Gilbert White's House & Garden
(& The Oates Collection) .7K 99
Gilbert White Way GU34: Alt .3L 173
Gilbury Cl. SO18: S'ing .7C 160
Gilchrist Gdns. SO31: Wars .1N 209
Giles Cl. PO12: Gos .1J 239
PO16: Fare .6D 198
SO30: Hed E .1A 176
Giles Ct. RG26: Tadl .5J 11
Giles La. SP5: L'ford .9L 121
Giles Rd. RG26: Tadl .5J 11
Gilkicker Rd. PO12: Gos .6L 239
Gillam Rd. BH10: Bour .1H 227
Gillcrest PO14: Titch C .5F 196
Gillett Rd. BH12: Poole .7G 226
Gillham's La. GU27: Hasl .2H 117
Gillian Av. GU12: Alders .2L 65
Gillian Cl. GU12: Alders .2M 65
Gillies, The PO16: Fare .8C 198
Gillies Dr. RG24: B'toke .3L 41
Gillingham Cl. BH9: Bour .3N 227
SO23: Kin W .8N 91
Gillingham Rd. SO41: M Sea .8K 235
Gillman Rd. PO6: Farl .8M 201
Gilmour Gdns. GU34: Alt .2G 80
Gilpin Cl. SO19: South .5J 175
SO41: Pil .6F 224
Gilpin Hill SO41: Sway .5J 223
Gilpin Pl. SO41: Sway .5H 223
Gins La. SO42: Beau .3E 236
Gipsy Gro. SO15: South .3H 173
Girton Cl. GU47: Owl .4G 19
PO14: Titch C .8F 196
Gisors Rd. PO4: S'sea .3J 241
Gitsham Gdns. PO7: Wid .6K 201
Gladdis Rd. BH11: Bour .2D 226
Glade, The BH2: Bour .1K 245
BH23: Chri .5H 229
BH24: Ashl H .3B 186
GU9: H End .3F 64
GU10: B Oak .9M 63
PO7: W'lle .1A 202
PO11: H Isl .5J 243
PO15: Fare .5N 197
SO45: Blac .9C 208
SO53: Cha F .3D 132
Glade Cl. RG24: Chin .1G 42
Glade Holiday Home Park, The
PO11: H Isl .5L 243
Glades, The SO31: Loc H .5D 196
Gladiator Way GU14: Farn .3J 49
Gladman Ho. BH6: Bour .1F 246
Gladstone Cl. BH23: Chri .8N 229
Gladstone Gdns. PO16: Portc .1L 213
Gladstone Ho. SO14: South .4F 4
Gladstone Pl. PO2: Ports .8E 214
Gladstone Rd. BH7: Bour .9C 228
BH12: Poole .9A 226
PO12: Gos .9J 213
SO19: South .5F 174
Gladstone Rd. E. BH7: Bour .9C 228
Gladstone Rd. W. BH1: Bour .9B 228
Gladstone St. SO23: Winche .6L 237 (6K 105)
Gladstone Ter. SP11: Longp .4N 71
Gladys Av. PO2: Ports .6E 214
PO8: Cowp .6A 182
Gladys Ct. BH8: Bour .9L 227
Glamis Av. BH10: Bour .1J 227
Glamis Cl. PO7: W'lle .1A 202
RG23: Oak .9D 40
Glamis Ct. PO14: Stub .5M 211
Glamorgan Rd. PO8: Cath .9B 168
Glasgow Rd. PO4: S'sea .4J 241
Glasslaw Rd. SO18: South .2E 174
Glasspool PO7: Den .5F 180
Glastonbury Cl. RG24: B'toke .3B 42
Glaston Hill Rd. RG27: Eve .5F 16
Glayshers Hill GU35: Head D .1C 102
Gleadowe Av. BH23: Chri .8J 229
GLEBE .7M 163
Glebe, The GU17: Haw .9G 18
PO14: Stub .7M 211
Glebe Cl. GU11: Alders .3J 65
GU34: Bent .6L 79
PO11: H Isl .2E 242
RG25: Dumm .9F 58
RG26: Tadl .6J 11
SP5: P'tn .6E 86
Glebe Cnr. PO17: Wick .7D 178
Glebe Ct. GU51: Fleet .2L 47
SO17: South .9M 159
SO30: Botl .2D 176
SO50: Fair O .1A 162
Glebe Dr. PO13: Gos .7E 212
Glebefield Gdns. PO6: Cosh .9F 200
Glebe Flds. GU34: Bent .6L 79
Glebefields SO41: M Sea .7K 235
Glebe Gdns. PO9: Warb .8H 203
Glebe Ho. RG21: B'toke .5C 42
(off Vyne Rd.)
Glebeland Rd. GU15: Camb .9H 19
Glebelands SP11: G Cla .8A 70
Glebe La. GU10: Rush .3L 85
RG23: Wort .7J 41
RG27: H Win .7C 26
SP5: L'ford .9J 121
Glebe Mdw. RG25: Over .2D 56
Glebe Pk. SO32: E Dean .2L 121
Glebe Pk. Av. PO9: Bed .8A 202
Glebe Rd. GU10: Cron .3L 63
GU14: Cov .7H 29
GU31: Buri .7K 145
GU35: Head .2A 102
SO14: South .7G 4 (7N 173)
Glen, The BH12: Poole .8B 226
BH13: Poole .5C 244
GU9: Up H .4E 64
PO13: Gos .7G 212
RG26: Pam H .4L 11
SO50: E'leigh .1E 160
(off Grantham Rd.)
Glenavon BH25: New M .4D 232
Glenavon Gdns. GU46: Yat .9N 17
Glenavon Rd. BH23: Highc .5H 231
Glenbrook Wlk. PO14: Fare .9M 197
Glencarron Way SO16: Bass .8K 159
Glen Cl. BH25: B Sea .6M 231
GU26: Hind .1L 103
SP10: A'ver .1L 69
Glencoe Rd. BH7: Bour .7C 228
BH12: Poole .9B 226
PO1: Ports .9G 214
Glen Ct. GU26: Hind .1L 103
Glencoyne Gdns. SO16: South .9E 158
Glenda Cl. SO31: Wars .9A 196
Glen Dale PO9: R Cas .8J 183
Glendale SO31: Loc H .7D 196
SO32: Swanm .7D 164
Glendale Cl. BH23: Chri .3G 229
Glendale Ct. BH23: Chri .3G 229
Glendale Pk. GU51: Fleet .1H 47
Glendale Rd. BH6: Bour .1K 247
RG26: Tadl .4G 11
Glendales BH25: New M .6M 231
Glendeep Cl. SO23: Kin W .9M 91
Glendene Pk. BH25: Bash .9N 221
Glendowan Rd. SO53: Cha F .5M 131
Glen Dr. BH25: New M .6L 231
Gleneagles BH13: Poole .3F 244
BH23: Chri .8J 229
Gleneagles Av. BH14: Poole .3B 244
Gleneagles Cl. RG22: B'toke .5J 59
Gleneagles Dr. GU14: Cov .9E 28
PO7: W'lle .8B 182
Gleneagles Equestrian Cen. .6H 161
Glenelg PO15: Fare .7B 198
Glenesha Gdns. PO15: Fare .7N 197
Glen Eyre Cl. SO16: Bass .7M 159
Glen Eyre Dr. SO16: Bass .6M 159
Glen Eyre Halls SO16: Bass .6M 159
Glen Eyre Rd. SO16: Bass .6L 159
Glen Eyre Way SO16: Bass .7M 159
Glenferness Av. BH3: Bour .9G 227
BH4: Bour .9G 227
Glenfern Hall BH4: Bour .9G 227
(off Glenferness Av.)
Glen Fern Rd. BH1: Bour .6N 247 (2L 245)
Glenfield Av. SO18: South .3D 174
Glenfield Cl. SP5: Mid W .5H 87
Glenfield Cres. SO18: South .3D 174
Glenfield Way SO18: South .3D 174
Glengariff Rd. BH14: Poole .3A 244
Glengarry BH25: New M .4D 232
Glengarry Way BH23: Fri C .8E 230
Glenhurst Cl. GU17: Haw .9G 19
Glen Innes GU47: Coll .4H 19
Glenives Cl. BH24: St I .4D 186
Glen Lea GU26: Hind .6N 103
Glenlea Cl. SO30: Wes E .1H 175
Glenlea Dr. SO30: Wes E .1H 175
Glenlea Hollow GU26: Hind .7N 103
Glen Lee SO18: South .2E 174
Glenleigh Av. PO6: Cosh .1G 215
Glenleigh Pk. PO9: Warb .7H 203
Glenleven BH4: Bour .9G 227
Glenmeadows Dr. BH10: Bour .1F 226
Glenmoor Cl. BH10: Bour .5H 227
Glenmoor Gdns. BH10: Bour .5H 227
Glenmoor Rd. BH9: Bour .6H 227
Glenmore Bus. Cen. PO13: Gos .5F 212
Glenmore Bus. Pk. SP10: A'ver .2K 69
Glenmore Ct. SO17: South .2M 173
Glenmore Gdns. PO8: Cowp .8N 181
Glenney Cl. PO13: Lee S .1C 238
Glenn Rd. SO30: Wes E .9H 161
Glen Pk. Mobile Home Pk. SO21: Col C .3L 133
Glen Rd. BH5: Bour .1B 246
GU26: Gray .4M 103
GU26: Hind .1M 103
GU51: Fleet .3L 47
SO19: South .9B 174
SO31: Sar G, Swanw .2B 196
(not continuous)
Glenroyd Gdns. BH6: Bour .1H 247
Glenside BH25: New M .7K 231
SO30: Wes E .1H 175
SO45: Hythe .6L 193
Glenside Av. SO19: South .6H 175
Glen Spey BH25: New M .4E 232
Glenthorne Cl. PO14: Stub .7N 211
Glenthorne Mdw. GU32: E Meon .4M 143
Glenthorne Rd. PO3: Ports .7H 215
Glenville Cl. BH23: Walk .4K 231
Glenville Gdns. BH10: Bour .4G 227
GU26: Hind .3N 103
Glenville Rd. BH10: Bour .4G 226
BH23: Walk .4K 231
Glenwood GU9: Up H .4E 64
Glenwood Av. SO16: Bass .6M 159
Glenwood Ct. GU14: Farn .8J 29
SO50: Fair O .1B 162
Glenwood Gdns. PO8: Cowp .7N 181
Glidden Cl. PO1: Ports .2E 240
Glidden La. PO7: H'don .8F 166
Globe Farm La. GU17: Blackw .8D 18
Glorney Mead GU9: Bad L .4J 65
Gloster Cl. GU14: Farn .8K 29
Gloster Ct. PO15: Seg .4F 196
Gloucester PO1: Ports .3K 5
Gloucester Cl. GU16: Frim G .6N 29
GU32: Pet .1K 145
GU34: Four M .5H 97
Gloucester Ct. GU32: Pet .9M 139
Gloucester Dr. RG22: B'toke .2K 59
Gloucester Ho. PO12: Gos .3L 239
(off Holly St.)
Gloucester M. PO5: S'sea .6N 5 (3D 240)
Gloucester Pl. PO5: S'sea .7N 5 (4D 240)
Gloucester Rd. BH7: Bour .8C 228
BH12: Poole .9C 226
GU11: Alders .3L 65
PO1: Ports .1J 5 (1B 240)
PO7: W'lle .3N 201
Gloucester Sq. SO14: South .8D 4
Gloucester Ter. PO5: S'sea .7N 5 (4D 240)
Gloucester Vw. PO5: S'sea .6N 5 (4D 240)
Glovers Fld. GU27: Hasl .9N 103
Glyn Dr. PO14: Stub .6M 211
Glyn Jones Cl. SO45: Fawl .6D 208
Glynswood GU15: Camb .1N 29
Glyn Way PO14: Stub .6M 211
Goals Soccer Cen.
Portsmouth .9K 215
Southampton .4F 172
Go Ape
Moors Valley Country Pk. .9A 184
Goatacre Rd. GU34: Meds .2E 96
Goathouse La. PO17: Newt .6K 179
Goat La. RG21: B'toke .6D 42
Goch Way SP10: A'ver, Charl .8L 51
Goddard Cl. SO51: W Wel .1B 120 (9N 121)
Goddards Cl. GU14: Cov .5F 28
RG27: Sher L .4L 23
Goddards Firs RG23: Oak .2E 58
Goddards La. GU15: Camb .1K 29
RG27: Sher L .4K 23
Goddards Mead SP10: A'ver .2L 69
Goddard Sq. SP10: A'ver .8B 52
(off Cricketers Way)
Godfrey Cl. GU47: Coll .5F 18
Godfrey Olson Ho. SO50: E'leigh .9F 132
Godfrey Pink Way SO32: Bis W .4N 163
Godiva Lawn PO4: S'sea .4K 241

Godshill—Green Cl.

GODSHILL 5A 154
Godshill Cl. BH8: Bour 3A 228
Godson Ho. SO23: Winche 7N 237
Godwin Cl. PO10: Ems 6L 203
SO22: Winche 3G 104
Godwin Cres. PO8: Cath 7C 168
GODWINSCROFT 9E 220
Godwins Fld. SO21: Comp 5G 127
Godwit Cl. PO12: Gos 8K 213
Godwit Rd. PO4: S'sea 1K 241
Gofton Av. PO6: Cosh 1J 215
Goggs La. SP5: Redl 2N 119 (8D 120)
Goldcrest Cl. GU46: Yat 7L 17
PO8: Horn 3A 182
PO16: Portc 9G 199
Goldcrest Gdns. SO16: South 6F 158
Goldcrest La. SO40: Tott 2J 171
Goldcrest Way GU34: Four M 5H 97
Golden Ct. PO7: W'lle 2M 201
SO30: Wes E 8K 161
Golden Cres. SO41: Ever 5L 233
Goldenfields GU30: Lip 3F 116
Goldenfields Cl. GU30: Lip 3F 116
Golden Gro. SO14: South 4F 4 (5N 173)
GOLDEN HILL 2G 233
Golden Hind Pk. SO45: Hythe 7L 193
Goldenleas Ct. *BH11: Bour 3B 226*
(off Goldenleas Dr.)
Goldenleas Dr. BH11: Bour 3B 226
Golden Lion Rdbt. RG21: B'toke 9C 42
GOLDEN POT 8B 62
GOLDFINCH BOTTOM 1H 9
Goldfinch Cl. BH25: New M 4A 232
GU11: Alders 2H 65
Goldfinch Gdns. RG22: B'toke 4H 59
Goldfinch La. PO13: Lee S 9B 212
Goldfinch Way SO21: Sth W 2J 91
Gold Hill GU35: K'ly 7H 83
Gold La. GU11: Alders 7N 49
GU12: Alders 7N 49
Gold Mead Cl. SO41: Lymi 4E 234
Goldring Cl. PO11: H Isl 4G 243
Golds Gym 8L 19
Goldsmith Av. PO4: S'sea 3F 240
Goldsmith Cl. SO40: Tott 3K 171
Goldsmith Rd. SO50: E'leigh 2D 160
Goldsmiths Ct. SO14: South 8D 4
Goldsmith Way RG45: Cr'tne 1D 18
Gold St. PO5: S'sea 7M 5 (4C 240)
Gold Valley Lakes 7N 49
Goldwire Dr. SO53: Cha F 7L 131
Golf Course Rd. SO16: Bass 6K 159
Golf La. GU35: W'hil 5F 100
Golf Links Av. GU26: Hind 1K 103
GOMELDON 2C 86
Gomer Ct. PO12: Gos 4G 238
Gomer La. PO12: Gos 3G 238
Gondreville Gdns. GU52: Ch Cr 7K 47
Goodacre Dr. SO53: Cha F 7L 131
Goodalls La. SO30: Hed E 3M 175
Goodchilds Hill RG7: Stra S 6J 13
Goodden Cres. GU14: Cov 9H 29
Goodens, The SO24: Cher 9E 108
Goodison Cl. SO50: Fair O 2M 161
Goodlands Va. SO30: Hed E 3L 175
Goodman Cl. RG21: B'toke 7A 42
Good Rd. BH12: Poole 7A 226
Goodsell Cl. PO14: Stub 6L 211
Goodwin Cl. SO16: South 9C 158
Goodwood Cl. GU15: Camb 5L 19
GU34: Alt 6F 80
PO8: Cowp 9B 182
PO12: Gos 8K 213
PO14: Titch C 7G 196
Goodwood Ct. SO50: Hor H 4A 162
Goodwood Gdns. SO40: Tott 2J 171
Goodwood Pl. GU14: Farn 9N 29
Goodwood Rd. PO5: S'sea 4F 240
PO12: Gos 8K 213
SO50: E'leigh 7C 132
GOODWORTH CLATFORD 8N 69
Goodworth Vw. SP11: G Cla 8N 69
Goodwyns Cl. SP9: Shi B 2A 66 (1F 66)
Goodwyns Grn. GU34: Alt 2G 80
Goodyer Cl. GU32: Pet 2L 145
Goodyers GU34: Alt 5G 81
Gooseberry La. BH24: Ring 1J 187
GOOSE GREEN
GU31 4D 146
SO43 3C 148
Goose Grn. RG27: Hoo 1F 44
SO43: Lyn 3B 148
Goose Grn. Caravan Pk. PO11: H Isl 5L 243
GOOSE HILL 1L 9
Goose La. RG27: Hoo 1G 45
Goose Rye Ct. GU30: Lip 3D 116
Gordleton Ind. Est. SO41: Penn 1N 233
Gordon Av. GU15: Camb 9K 19
GU52: Ch Cr 5N 47
SO14: South 2M 173
SO23: Winche 8N 105
Gordon Brown Outdoor Education Centre, The 1D 44
Gordon Cl. RG21: B'toke 5D 42
Gordon Ct. BH4: Bour 1H 245
GU15: Camb 8L 19
Gordon Cres. GU15: Camb 9L 19
Gordon Mt. BH23: Highc 5K 231
Gordon Mt. Flats BH23: Highc 6J 231
Gordon Rd. BH1: Bour 1A 246
BH12: Poole 9E 226
BH23: Highc 6J 231
GU11: Alders 1J 65
GU14: Farn 3M 49
(not continuous)
GU15: Camb 9L 19
PO1: Ports 8L 5 (4C 240)
PO7: W'lle 3L 201
PO12: Gos 3J 239
PO16: Fare 8C 198
RG45: Cr'tne 2F 18
Gordon Rd. SO23: Winche 6N 237 (6L 105)
SO32: Curd 1J 177
SO41: Lymi, Penn 3C 234
SO53: Cha F 3B 132
Gordon Rd. Sth. BH12: Poole 9E 226
Gordon Ter. SO19: South 8E 174
Gordon Wlk. GU46: Yat 8A 18
Gordon Watson Ho. SO23: Winche 9K 105
Gordon Way BH23: Burt 5M 229
GORE END 1M 7
Gore End Rd. RG20: Bal H, Gor E 1M 7
Gore End Vs. RG20: Gor E 1M 7
Gore Grange BH25: New M 4A 232
Gore Rd. BH25: New M 4M 231
Gore Rd. Ind. Est. BH25: New M 4A 232
Gorey Rd. BH12: Poole 5B 226
Goring Av. PO8: Clan 6D 168
Goring Fld. SO22: Winche 5G 104
Gorleston Rd. BH12: Poole 9D 226
Gorley Ct. PO9: Hav 3D 202
Gorley Lynch SP6: Hyde 5N 153
Gorley Rd. BH24: Poul 9M 185
Gorran Av. PO13: Gos 7E 212
Gorrings, The SO20: Ki S 9B 86 (7G 88)
Gorsecliff Ct. BH5: Bour 1A 246
Gorsecliff Rd. BH10: Bour 5H 227
Gorse Cl. BH24: St L 4A 186
BH25: A'ley 2E 232
SO31: Loc H 7C 196
Gorse Down SO21: Owls 5C 134
Gorsedown Cl. GU35: W'hil 6G 100
Gorsefield Rd. BH25: New M 1C 232
Gorselands GU9: Up H 3E 64
GU46: Yat 9M 17
RG26: Tadl 5J 11
Gorselands Cl. GU35: Head D 3E 102
Gorselands Rd. SO18: South 1F 174
Gorselands Way PO13: Gos 8F 212
Gorse Rd. GU16: Frim 2N 29
GU31: Pet 1B 146
Gorseway GU52: Fleet 4M 47
Gorseway, The PO11: H Isl 4D 242
Gort Cl. GU11: Alders 4N 49
Gort Cres. SO19: South 6F 174
Gort Rd. BH11: Bour 3F 226
Goscombe La. SO24: Bigh, Gund 8M 95
Goshawk Rd. *RG20: Bis G 1G 9*
(off Peregrine Rd.)
Goslings Cft. GU34: Selb 6L 99
GOSPORT 3M 239
Gosport & District Angling Club 6J 239
Gosport & Stokes Bay Golf Course 6L 239
Gosport Bus. Cen. PO13: Gos 6G 212
Gosport Gallery 3M 239
Gosport Ho. PO9: Hav 4H 203
Gosport La. SO43: Lyn 2C 148
Gosport Rd. GU34: Alt 1D 98
PO13: Lee S 2B 238
PO14: Stub 5N 211
PO16: Fare 1D 212
Gosport Shop. Precinct PO12: Gos 3M 239
Gosport St. SO41: Lymi 2F 234
GOTHAM 8M 149
Gothic Bldgs. PO5: S'sea 4E 240
Gough Rd. GU51: Fleet 1K 47
Gough's Mdw. GU47: Sandh 6D 18
Gould Cl. SP11: Ludg 1C 30
Government Ho. Rd. GU11: Alders 3J 49
Government Rd. GU11: Alders 7M 49
Governor's Rd. GU15: Camb 7H 19
Gover Rd. SO16: South 1B 172
Gower Cl. RG21: B'toke 4C 42
Gower Cres. RG27: Hoo 2H 45
Gower Pk. GU47: Coll 6F 18
Goyda Ho. PO12: Gos 1H 239
Grace Bennett Cl. GU14: Farn 5J 29
Grace Dieu Gdns. SO31: Burs 9K 175
Grace Gdns. GU51: Fleet 3K 47
Gracelands Pk. (Caravan Pk.)
BH23: Chri 6D 230
Grace La. SP6: Woodg 2A 154
Gracemere Cres. RG22: B'toke 3H 59
Grace Reynolds Wlk. GU15: Camb 7L 19
Grace Sq. SP10: A'ver 8B 52
Gracie Ct. BH10: Bour 1H 227
Gracie M. BH10: Bour 1H 227
Gracious St. GU34: Selb 7K 99
Graddidge Way SO40: Tott 3K 171
Graduate Ct. PO6: Cosh 2H 215
Gradwell La. GU34: Four M 7H 97
Graemar La. SO51: Sher E 6M 121
Grafton Cl. BH3: Bour 7L 227
BH23: Chri 8N 229
GU35: W'hil 5K 101
PO12: Gos 9L 213
Grafton Gdns. SO16: South 6H 159
SO41: Penn 5C 234
Grafton Pl. SP11: Pen G 7F 50
Grafton Rd. BH3: Bour 8L 227
SO23: Winche 8K 105
Grafton St. PO2: Ports 9D 214
Grafton Way RG22: B'toke 7M 41
Graham Ct. SO19: South 4E 174
Graham Ho. SO14: South 4A 174
Graham Rd. PO4: S'sea 4F 240
PO12: Gos 1J 239
SO14: South 2E 4 (4M 173)
Graham St. SO14: South 4A 174
Grainger Cl. RG22: B'toke 1N 59
Grainger Gdns. SO19: South 7G 175
Grain Wlk. SP11: E Ant 6B 52
Grammarsham La. RG25: Elli, Far W 8N 59
Grampian Rd. GU47: Sandh 3B 18
Grampian Way RG22: B'toke 8K 41
Granada Cl. PO8: Cowp 7A 182
Granada Pl. SP10: A'ver 9B 52
Granada Rd. PO4: S'sea 6F 240
SO30: Hed E 5L 175
Granary & Bakery, The PO12: Gos 1M 239
Granby Gro. SO17: South 8N 159
Granby Rd. BH9: Bour 2L 227
Grand Av. BH6: Bour 1F 246
GU15: Camb 7L 19
Grand Division Row PO4: S'sea 4J 241
Grand Marine Ct.
BH2: Bour 9J 247 (3H 245)
Grand Pde. BH10: Bour 1G 226
PO1: Ports 8J 5 (4B 240)
PO11: H Isl 5G 243
RG27: Hoo 2G 45
Grand Trunk Rd. SP9: Tidw 9A 30 (8F 30)
GRANGE 1F 238
Grange, The BH2: Bour 5J 247
GU10: Fren 1F 84
PO10: Ems 7M 203
(off New Brighton Rd.)
RG14: Enbo 1C 8
(off Enborne St.)
SO41: Ever 6M 233
Grange Cl. PO9: Hav 7H 203
PO12: Gos 1H 239
SO18: S'ing 7C 160
SO23: Winche 1J 127
SO24: New A 1E 108
SO41: Ever 6M 233
SP11: Fyf 9N 31
Grange Ct. BH1: Bour 2M 245
GU10: Tong 4N 65
SO18: S'ing 6C 160
SO31: Net A 3F 194
Grange Cres. PO12: Gos 1H 239
Grange Dr. SO30: Hed E 2A 176
GRANGE ESTATE 8C 186
Grange Est. GU52: Ch Cr 6L 47
Grange Farm SO31: Net A 2F 194
Grange Gdns. BH12: Poole 6C 226
Grange La. PO13: Gos 8E 212
(not continuous)
RG27: H Win 6A 26
Grange M. SO51: Rom 3B 130
Grange, The (Northington) 2A 94
Grange Pk. SO30: Hed E 1N 175
Grange Rd. BH6: Bour 2G 246
BH23: Chri 7D 230
BH24: St L 6A 186
GU10: Tilf 1K 85
GU10: Tong 4N 65
GU14: Farn 5K 29
GU15: Camb 8N 19
GU32: Pet 2L 145
GU52: Ch Cr 6L 47
PO2: Ports 7E 214
PO13: Gos 3F 238
SO16: South 1G 172
SO23: Winche 2J 127
SO24: New A 1E 108
SO30: Botl, Hed E 2N 175
SO31: Net A 3E 194
Grange Rd. Bus. Cen. BH23: Chri 7C 230
Grangewood Ct. SO50: Fair O 1M 161
Grangewood Gdns. SO50: Fair O 1M 161
Grantham Av. SO31: Hamb 6J 195
Grantham Cl. GU47: Owl 4G 18
Grantham Dr. GU14: Cov 7F 28
Grantham Rd. BH1: Bour 9B 228
SO19: South 4D 174
SO50: E'leigh 1D 160
Grantley Dr. GU52: Fleet 4L 47
Grantley Rd. BH5: Bour 1C 246
Grant Rd. PO6: Farl 9L 201
RG45: Cr'tne 2E 18
Grants Av. BH1: Bour 8A 228
Grants Cl. BH1: Bour 8A 228
Granville *BH4: Bour 1G 244*
(off Branksome Wood Rd.)
Granville Cl. PO9: Warb 8G 203
Granville Pl. BH1: Bour 6M 247
SO23: Winche 8M 105
Granville Rd. BH5: Bour 9D 228
BH12: Poole 9A 226
Granville St. SO14: South 6N 173
Grasdean Cl. SO18: South 1E 174
Grasmere SO50: E'leigh 1D 160
Grasmere Cl. BH23: Chri 3G 229
GU35: Bor 2J 101
SO18: Wes E 1F 174
Grasmere Ct. SO16: South 9D 158
Grasmere Gdns. BH25: New M 1C 232
Grasmere Ho. PO6: Cosh 8C 200
Grasmere Rd. BH5: Bour 1D 246
BH13: S'bks 9A 244
GU9: Up H 4C 64
GU14: Cov 9G 28
Grasmere Way PO14: Stub 4N 211
Grason BH13: Poole 5F 244
Graspan Rd. SP11: Fabe 2F 30 (5L 31)
Grassmere Way PO7: W'lle 9B 182
Grassymead PO14: Titch C 5F 196
GRATELEY 5L 67
Grateley Bus. Pk. SP11: Grat 5K 67
Grateley Cl. SO19: South 1D 194
Grateley Cres. PO9: Hav 5C 202
Grateley Drove SP11: Grat 5K 67
(not continuous)
Grateley Rd. SP4: Chol 4F 66
Grateley Station (Rail) 5K 67
Gratton Cl. SO21: Sut S 7D 76
Gravel Cl. SO24: Ch Can 7C 78
SP5: Down 1J 119 (7A 120)
GRAVEL HILL 2F 168
Gravel Hill SO32: Shi H, Swanm 1C 178
Gravel Hill Rd. GU10: Ben'ly, Hol P 8L 63
Gravel La. BH24: Ring 9K 185
(Regency Pl.)
BH24: Ring 1J 187
(The Sweep)
GU32: E Meon 3N 143
GU34: Four M 6F 96
SO21: Bar S 6A 76
Gravelly Cl. RG20: Nth E 1M 7
RG26: Tadl 7J 11
Gravelly La. SN8: Co Du 2K 31
Gravel Rd. GU9: Up H 3D 64
GU14: Farn 3M 49
GU52: Ch Cr 5N 47
Gravel Wlk. SO45: Fawl 6D 208
Graveney Sq. *SP10: A'ver 8A 52*
(off Cricketers Way)
Gray Cl. SO31: Wars 7C 196
Graycot Cl. BH10: Bour 1G 227
Grayland Cl. PO11: H Isl 3E 242
Grayling Mead SO51: Rom 3M 129
Graylings SO15: South 2F 172
Grays Av. SO45: Hythe 6N 193
Grays Cl. PO12: Gos 4G 238
SO21: Col C 4K 133
SO51: Rom 5N 129
Grays Ct. PO1: Ports 6K 5 (3B 240)
Grayshot Dr. GU17: Blackw 8E 18
GRAYSHOTT 4L 103
Grayshott Cl. SO22: Winche 2H 105
Grayshott Laurels GU35: Lind 2M 101
Grayshott Rd. GU35: Head D 1D 102
PO4: S'sea 3G 241
PO12: Gos 3H 239
Grayson Cl. PO13: Lee S 1C 238
Great Austins GU9: Farnh 9F 64
Gt. Austins Ho. GU9: Farnh 9F 64
Gt. Binfields Cres. RG24: Lych 3G 43
Gt. Binfields Rd. RG24: Chin, Lych 2G 42
Greatbridge Rd. SO51: Rom 1L 129
Gt. Copse Dr. PO9: Hav 3E 202
Great Cft. SP5: Firs 4E 86
Gt. Elms Cl. SO45: Holb 5N 207
Greater Horseshoe Way
PO17: K Vil 1A 198
Gt. Farm Rd. SO50: E'leigh 9D 132
Greatfield Cl. GU14: Farn 4K 29
Greatfield Rd. GU14: Farn 4J 29
SO22: Winche 3H 105
Greatfield Way PO9: R Cas 7H 183
Great Gays PO14: Stub 7K 211
GREATHAM 3E 114
Greatham Mill Garden 5B 114
Great Hanger GU31: Pet 1A 146
Great Marlow RG27: Hoo 2K 45
Great Mead PO7: Den 7H 181
SO43: Lyn 3B 148 (3N 189)
Great Mead Pk. SO43: Lyn 2C 148
Gt. Minster St. SO23: Winche 8M 237 (7L 105)
Great Oaks Chase RG24: Chin 1F 42
GREAT POSBROOK 1J 211
Great Salterns Golf Course 7J 215
Gt. Sheldons Coppice RG27: Hoo 2F 44
GREAT SHODDESDEN 5F 30 (7L 31)
Gt. Southsea St. PO5: S'sea 7N 5 (4D 240)
Great Weir SO24: New A 8F 94
Gt. Well Dr. SO51: Rom 4N 129
Gt. Western Cotts. RG21: B'toke 5C 42
Greatwood Cl. SO45: Hythe 7M 193
Greaves Cl. BH10: Bour 3G 227
Grebe Cl. BH23: Mude 8C 230
GU34: Alt 2E 80
PO8: Cowp 6M 181
PO16: Portc 9H 199
RG22: B'toke 3H 59
SO41: M Sea 8L 235
GREEN, THE 8L 87
Green, The BH4: Bour 9G 227
GU9: Bad L 5J 65
GU9: Up H 4E 64
GU10: Seal 9N 65
GU17: Blackw 9E 18
GU32: E Meon 3L 143
GU33: Liss 9D 114
GU46: Yat 7L 17
PO7: Den 5F 180
PO9: R Cas 8J 183
RG25: Elli 9C 60
RG25: Over 2E 56
RG26: Tadl 7J 11
RG28: Whit 5H 55
RG29: N War 6H 45
SO20: Mid Wa 4B 72
SO21: Bar S 5B 76
SO22: Pitt 2D 126
SO31: Sar G 3B 196
SO51: Rom 3B 130
SP5: P'tn 6E 86
SP5: W'psh 5H 121
SP10: Charl 7L 51
SP11: Kimp 9M 31
SP11: Up C 5L 69
Green Acre GU11: Alders 1H 65
Greenacre BH25: B Sea 6B 232
RG20: Kings 2B 6
SO20: Brou 2A 86 (5A 88)
Greenacre Gdns. PO7: Purb 5L 201
Green Acres *BH4: Bour 2G 245*
(off Marlborough Rd.)
Greenacres BH13: Poole 2E 244
BH23: Chri 7B 230
GU10: Run 8L 65
GU35: Bor 3L 101
RG20: Wol H 3A 8
SO21: Bar S 6A 76
SP5: Down 1H 119 (7N 119)
Greenacres Cl. BH24: A'ley 3G 186
Greenacres Dr. SO21: Ott 1G 133
Greenaway La. SO31: Wars 7A 196
Greenaways, The RG23: Oak 9D 40
Greenbank Cres. SO16: Bass 6L 159
Greenbanks Cl. SO41: M Sea 7K 235
Greenbanks Gdns. PO16: Fare 7F 198
Greenbank Way GU15: Camb 2M 29
Greenbirch Cl. RG22: B'toke 3H 59
Greenbury Cl. RG23: B'toke 6L 41
Green Cl. SO21: Sth W 3J 91
SO23: Winche 1L 105
SO24: Old A 6F 94
SO40: Woodl 6F 170
SO45: Hythe 5M 193
SP5: W'psh 5H 121

Green Cres.—Hadleigh Gdns.

Green Cres. PO13: Gos 7E 212
Green Cft. GU9: Bad L 4K 65
Greencroft GU14: Farn 8K 29
GREEN CROSS 7J 85
Green Cross La. GU10: Chur 7J 85
Greendale, The PO15: Fare 5N 197
Greendale Cl. PO15: Fare 5N 197
SO53: Cha F 6C 132
Green Dr. SP6: Ald 4E 152
Green Drove SP5: W Gri 1D 120
SP11: Grat 4M 67
SP11: Lit L 9A 34
Green End GU46: Yat 6N 17
Green Farm Gdns. PO3: Ports 4G 215
Greenfield GU33: Hawk 6M 113
Greenfield Cl. GU30: Lip 1E 116
SO30: Hed E 6M 175
Greenfield Cres. PO8: Cowp 7B 182
PO8: Horn 5C 182
Greenfield Gdns. BH25: B Sea 6C 232
Greenfield Ri. PO8: Cowp 7B 182
Green Flds. SP11: Enh A 2B 52
Greenfields BH12: Poole 6D 226
GU31: Nye 5K 147
GU33: Liss 1F 140
SP5: W Gri 2E 120
Greenfields Av. GU34: Alt 4D 80
SO40: Tott 1L 171
Greenfields Cl. GU31: Nye 4K 147
SO40: Tott 1L 171
Greenfinch Cl. GU47: Owl 5F 18
SO50: E'leigh 2B 160
Greenfinch Wlk. BH24: Hight 2M 187
Green Gables GU14: Cov 4H 29
Green Glades GU52: Ch Cr 6L 47
Greenhanger GU10: Chur 8J 85
Greenhaven GU46: Yat 8L 17
Greenhaven Caravan Pk. PO11: H Isl 6L 243
Greenhaven Cl. SP10: A'ver 2B 70
Green Haven Ct. PO8: Cowp 7A 182
Greenhill Av. SO22: Winche 7H 237 (6J 105)
Greenhill Cl. SO22: Winche 7H 237 (6H 105)
Greenhill La. SO16: Rown 3D 158
SO32: Uph 7D 134
Greenhill Rd. GU9: Farnh 9G 64
SO22: Winche 7H 237 (7H 105)
Greenhills GU9: Farnh 9G 64
Greenhill Ter. SO22: Winche 7H 237 (6J 105)
SO51: Rom 6K 129
Greenhill Vw. SO51: Rom 5K 129
Green Hollow Cl. PO16: Fare 5B 198
Green Jacket Cl. SO22: Winche 9J 105
Greenlands RG20: Wol H 2A 8
Greenlands Rd. GU15: Camb 3K 29
RG20: Kings 2B 6 (6K 9)
RG24: B'toke 3M 41
Greenlands Vw. SO30: Botl 3B 176
Green La. BH10: Bour 2G 227
BH23: Hin 1J 231
BH24: Crow 5L 187
BH24: Ring 1K 187
BH25: B Sea 6C 232
BH25: Oss 5M 221
GU9: Bad L, Weyb 4H 65
GU10: Chur 8H 85
GU10: Dock 2A 84
GU17: Blackw 9D 18
GU17: Haw 9G 18
GU32: Frox 9E 112
GU34: Four M 6G 97
GU34: New V 1H 113
GU46: Yat 7L 17
GU47: Sandh 6E 18
PO3: Ports 5G 215
PO7: Den 5F 180
PO7: H'don 5C 166
PO8: Clan 7C 168
PO11: H Isl 4E 242
PO12: Gos 8L 213
(Bucklers Rd.)
PO12: Gos 5J 239
(Little Green)
RG7: Stra S 5J 13
RG25: Elli 2H 79
RG26: Pam G 9L 11
RG27: H Win 7B 26
RG27: Roth 8E 24
SO16: Chilw 2L 159
SO16: South 9D 158
SO24: Bis S 1L 109
SO24: Monk 2K 111
SO24: W Tis 7E 110
SO31: Burr 9D 176
SO31: Burs, Old N 8K 175
SO31: Hamb 7L 195
SO31: Lwr Swan 1A 196
SO31: Wars 8C 196
SO32: Bis W 4N 163
SO32: Drox, Swanm 6J 165
SO32: Swanm 4E 164
SO32: Warn 3N 135
SO40: Calm 7H 157
SO45: Blac 6N 207
(Roughdown La.)
SO45: Blac 8D 208
(Walker's La. Nth.)
SO51: Ampf, Rom 4D 130
SP5: Down 1K 119 (7A 120)
SP6: F'dge 9J 151
SP6: F'dge, W'bry 3F 150
SP11: Facc 7J 7
SP11: Monx 4B 68
SP11: Stoke 6G 35
Green La. Cl. GU15: Camb 6L 19
Green La. Cotts. GU9: Bad L 5H 65
GU10: Chur 7H 85
Green La. Gdns. RG27: H Win 8B 26
Greenlea Cl. PO7: Wid 7J 201
Greenlea Cres. SO16: S'ing 6B 160
Greenlea Gro. PO12: Gos 9H 213
Greenleas GU16: Frim 2N 29
Greenleas Cl. GU46: Yat 6M 17
Green Leys GU52: Ch Cr 7L 47
Green Link PO13: Lee S 2B 238
Green Loaning BH23: Mude 9B 230
Greenly Ct. SP10: A'ver 2M 69
Greenmead Av. SO41: Ever 5L 233
Green Mdw. La. SP11: G Cla 7N 69
Green Pk. BH1: Bour 2A 246
Green Pk. Cl. SO23: Winche 4M 105
Green Pk. Rd. SO16: South 3D 172
Green Pond Cnr. PO9: Warb 8H 203
Green Pond La. SO51: Ampf 1H 131
Green Reef BH1: Bour 1A 246
Green Ride Cl. RG27: Brams 9A 16
Greenridge Ct. *SO15: South* 2L 173
(off Marshall Sq.)
Green Rd. BH9: Bour 6L 227
PO5: S'sea 7N 5 (4D 240)
PO12: Gos 5J 239
PO14: Stub 4M 211
Greens Cl. SO32: Bis W 3L 163
SO50: B'stke 2L 161
Greensey SP11: Rag A 4B 50
Greenside Ct. BH25: B Sea 8C 232
Greens Meade
SP5: Woodf 2M 119 (8C 120)
Green Springs GU10: Cron 2L 63
Green's School La. GU14: Farn 8J 29
Green Stile GU34: Meds 9K 79
Green St. GU34: E Wor 7B 82
GU35: K'ly 7B 82
Green Wlk. PO15: Fare 6A 198
Green Way GU12: Alders 8N 49
RG22: B'toke 6L 41
RG23: B'toke 5L 41
Greenway GU32: E Meon 4N 143
RG27: Sher L 4L 23
Greenway, The PO10: Ems 6M 203
Greenway Cl. SO41: Lymi 3C 234
Greenway Ct. SO16: South 9H 159
Greenway La. GU31: Buri 6J 145
Greenway Rd. PO12: Gos 1K 239
Greenways BH23: Highc 6H 231
GU47: Sandh 4D 18
GU52: Fleet 5L 47
RG20: Wol H 2A 8
SO16: S'ing 6B 160
SO32: Swanm 6D 164
SO41: M Sea 7J 235
SO53: Cha F 6C 132
Greenways Av. BH8: Bour 3N 227
Greenways Rd. SO42: Broc 7D 148
Greenwich, The SO14: South 8D 4
SO45: Blac 6C 208
Greenwich Way SP10: A'ver 8N 51
Greenwood Av. BH14: Poole 4A 244
PO6: Cosh 9E 200
SO16: Rown 5C 158
Greenwood Cl. PO16: Fare 5C 198
SO50: E'leigh 2D 160
SO51: Rom 4N 129
Greenwood Copse BH24: St I 4C 186
Greenwood Dr. RG24: Chin 8G 23
Greenwood La. SO32: Durl 5C 162
Greenwood Rd. BH9: Bour 5J 227
Greenwoods BH25: New M 5C 232
RG28: Whit 4G 54
Greenwood Way BH24: St I 4D 186
Greetham St. PO5: S'sea 4N 5 (2D 240)
Gregory Cl. RG21: B'toke 4D 42
Gregory Gdns. SO40: Calm 1J 171
Gregory Ho. RG27: Hoo 2G 45
Gregory La. SO32: Durl 6E 162
Gregson Av. PO13: Gos 5E 212
Gregson Cl. PO13: Gos 5E 212
Grenadier Cl. SO31: Loc H 7E 196
Grenadiers Way GU14: Cov 9E 28
Grendon Cl. SO16: Bass 6N 159
Grenehurst Way GU31: Pet 1M 145
Grenfell Rd. BH9: Bour 3K 227
Grenfield Ct. PO10: Ems 6M 203
Grensell Cl. RG27: Eve 5H 17
Grenville Cl. BH24: Poul 8N 185
GU30: Lip 2E 116
Grenville Ct. BH4: Bour 5G 247 (1H 245)
SO15: South 3K 173
SO18: South 8D 160
Grenville Dr. GU51: Ch Cr 5K 47
Grenville Gdns. GU16: Frim G 6N 29
SO45: Dib P 8M 193
Grenville Ho. PO1: Ports 4K 5
Grenville Rd. PO4: S'sea 4F 240
Gresham Ind. Est.
GU12: Alders 9N 49
Gresham Point BH9: Bour 5M 227
Gresham Rd. BH9: Bour 5L 227
Gresham Way GU16: Frim G 6N 29
Gresley Gdns. SO30: Hed E 9N 161
Gresley Rd. RG21: B'toke 5D 42
RG24: B'toke 5D 42
Grevillea Av. PO15: Seg 6H 197
Greville Cl. GU11: Alders 8J 49
Greville Grn. PO10: Ems 5L 203
Greville Rd. SO15: South 3J 173
Greyfriars SO23: Winche 7P 237
Greyfriars Ct. PO5: S'sea 4D 240
Greyfriars Rd. PO15: Fare 7M 197
Greyhound Cl. SO30: Hed E 8M 161
Greyhound La. RG25: Over 3D 56
Greys Ct. GU11: Alders 9G 48
Greys Farm Cl. SO24: Cher 1K 135
Greyshott Av. PO14: Fare 9M 197
Greystoke Av. BH11: Bour 1D 226
Greystoke Ct. RG45: Cr'tne 1C 18
GREYWELL 8F 44
Greywell BH23: Hurn 8E 218
Greywell Av. SO16: South 7H 159
Greywell Cl. RG26: Tadl 5G 11
Greywell Ct. SO16: South 7H 159
Greywell Hgts. *PO9: Hav* 5E 202
(off Dunsbury Way)
Greywell Rd. PO9: Hav 4F 202
RG24: Mapl, Old Bas 6L 43
RG25: Mapl 6L 43
RG27: A'ell, Up N 6B 44
Greywell Shop. Cen. PO9: Hav 4F 202
Greywell Sq. PO9: Hav 4F 202
Grieg Cl. RG22: B'toke 1N 59
Grieve Cl. GU10: Tong 3N 65
Griffen Cl. SO50: B'stke 1J 161
Griffin Ct. SO17: South 2A 174
Griffin Ind. Pk. SO40: Tott 8L 157
Griffin Wlk. PO13: Gos 1E 238
Griffin Way Nth. RG27: Hoo 9H 25
Griffin Way Sth. RG27: Hoo 1J 45
Griffiths Gdns. BH10: Bour 1F 226
Griffon Cl. GU14: Cov 9F 28
SO31: Burs 9L 175
Grigg La. SO42: Broc 7C 148 (8N 189)
GRIGGS GREEN 2A 116
Grimstead Rd. SP5: E Gri, Far 8E 86
SP5: W Gri, Whad 2D 120
(not continuous)
Grindle Cl. PO16: Portc 8L 199
Gritanwood Rd. PO4: S'sea 4J 241
Grosvenor Cl. BH24: Ashl H 3A 186
RG22: B'toke 5K 59
SO17: South 9A 160
SP9: Tidw 8E 30
Grosvenor Ct. BH1: Bour 1A 246
BH2: Bour 6J 247
GU17: Haw 1F 28
PO9: Hav 8F 202
(off East St.)
PO14: Stub 6N 211
SO17: South 1A 174
(off Grosvenor Rd.)
SO51: Rom 5B 130
Grosvenor Dr. SO23: Winche 4M 105
Grosvenor Gdns. BH1: Bour 1B 246
SO17: South 9A 160
SO30: Wes E 2H 175
SO41: Lymi 3E 234
Grosvenor Ho. PO5: S'sea 3D 240
RG21: B'toke 6D 42
Grosvenor Mans. SO15: South 2B 4
Grosvenor M. PO12: Gos 2L 239
SO17: South 9A 160
SO41: Lymi 1D 234
Grosvenor Rd. BH4: Bour 2G 244
GU11: Alders 9J 49
GU34: Meds 4F 96
SO17: South 9A 160
SO53: Cha F 3C 132
Grosvenor Sq. SO15: South 2C 4 (4L 173)
Grosvenor St. PO5: S'sea 3D 240
GROUSE GREEN 7K 15
Grove, The BH9: Bour 3K 227
BH23: Chri 5H 229
GU9: Farnh 8D 64
GU11: Alders 1J 65
GU14: Farn 2M 49
GU16: Frim 3M 29
GU26: Gray 4L 103
GU30: Lip 2D 116
PO10: Westb 6N 203
PO14: Stub 6L 211
PO31: Cowes 5P 237
SO19: South 9F 174
SO31: Burs 9L 175
SO31: Net A 2H 195
SO43: Mins 9L 155
SP11: Pen G 6F 50
Grove Av. PO12: Gos 2L 239
PO16: Portc 2L 213
Grove Bldgs. PO12: Gos 3L 239
Grovebury SO31: Loc H 7D 196
Grove Cl. RG21: B'toke 8D 42
Grove Copse SO19: South 9G 174
Grove Copse Nature Reserve 4G 229
Grove Ct. PO9: Hav 8F 202
Grove Cross Rd. GU16: Frim 3M 29
Grove Farm Mdw. Caravan Pk.
BH23: Chri 4G 228
Grovefields Av. GU16: Frim 3M 29
Grove Gdns. BH25: B Sea 7B 232
SO19: South 9F 174
Grove Ho. *BH5: Bour* 2C 246
(off Wollstonecraft Rd.)
PO5: S'sea 4E 240
(off Grove Rd. Sth.)
PO5: S'sea 4E 240
(Homegrove Ho.)
RG24: Lych 2G 42
Grovelands Rd.
SO22: Winche 5F 104
Grove La. SP5: Redl 1N 119 (7D 120)
Groveley Bus. Cen.
BH23: Chri 8A 230
Groveley Rd. BH4: Bour 3F 244
BH23: Chri 8A 230
Grovely Av. BH5: Bour 1C 246
Grovely Way SO51: Cram 3D 130
Grove M. SO19: South 8F 174
Grove Pk. BH13: Poole 1D 244
Grove Pk. Ind. Est. GU34: Alt 4H 81
Grove Pastures SO41: Lymi 3E 234
Grove Pl. SO19: South 8F 174
SO22: Winche 3J 105
SO41: Lymi 3E 234
Grove Rd. BH1: Bour 7N 247 (2L 245)
BH25: B Sea 7A 232
GU15: Camb 8N 19
GU26: Hind 1K 103
GU34: Alt 6F 80
GU52: Ch Cr 6N 47
PO6: Dray 1K 215
PO9: Hav 8F 202
PO12: Gos 1K 239
PO13: Lee S 1A 238
PO16: Fare 8C 198
RG21: B'toke 9C 42
Grove Rd. SO15: South 3H 173
SO21: Shaw 8G 127
SO41: Lymi 3F 234
Grove Rd. E. BH23: Chri 6K 229
Grove Rd. Nth. PO5: S'sea 4E 240
Grove Rd. Sth. PO5: S'sea 5D 240
Grove Rd. W. BH23: Chri 6J 229
Grovers Gdns. GU26: Hind 1M 103
Grover's Mnr. GU26: Hind 1M 103
Groves Cl. SO21: Sth W 3G 91
Groves Down SO51: W Wel 9N 121
Groves Orchard RG28: Whit 5F 54
Grove St. SO14: South 6F 4 (6N 173)
Grower Gdns. BH11: Bour 2E 226
Grugs La. BH21: Cran 6J 149
Gruneisen Rd. PO2: Ports 6D 214
Guardhouse Rd. PO1: Ports 1M 5 (9C 214)
Guardian Ct. SO17: South 1M 173
Guardroom Museum, The 7K 237 (6K 105)
Guardroom Rd. PO2: Ports 7C 214
Gudge Heath La. PO15: Fare 6N 197
Guelders, The PO7: Purb 6M 201
Guernsey Cl. RG24: B'toke 1D 42
SO16: South 8D 158
Guernsey Dr. GU51: Fleet 8N 27
Guernsey Rd. BH12: Poole 5B 226
Guessens La. PO14: Titch 9J 197
Guest Av. BH12: Poole 8D 226
Guest Cl. BH12: Poole 8E 226
Guest Rd. SO50: B'stke 9H 133
Guildford Ct. BH4: Bour 1G 245
Guildford Dr. SO53: Cha F 9N 131
Guildford Rd. GU9: Farnh 7F 64
GU10: Farnh, Run 6H 65
GU12: Alders 3M 65
GU51: Fleet 3A 48
PO1: Ports 1F 240
(not continuous)
Guildford Rd. E. GU14: Farn 2L 49
Guildford Rd. Trad. Est. GU9: Farnh 7F 64
Guildford Rd. W. GU14: Farn 2L 49
Guildford St. SO14: South 5N 173
Guildhall Sq. PO1: Ports 4N 5 (2D 240)
Guildhall Wlk. PO1: Ports 5M 5 (3D 240)
Guildhill Rd. BH6: Bour 1H 247
Guild Ho. SO14: South 8D 4
Guillemont Flds. GU14: Cov 7F 28
Guillemont Pk. GU17: Min 6E 28
Guillemot Cl. SO45: Hythe 6N 193
Guillemot Gdns. PO13: Gos 5D 212
Guillemot Pl. PO11: H Isl 6K 243
Guinea Ct. RG24: Chin 8H 23
Gull Cl. PO13: Gos 6D 212
Gull Coppice PO15: White 2F 196
Gullet La. GU34: Meds 6B 96
Gulliver Cl. BH14: Poole 5A 244
Gulls, The SO40: March 8E 172
Gullycroft Mead SO30: Hed E 3M 175
GUNDLETON 8M 95
Gun Hill GU11: Alders 8K 49
Gunners Bldgs. PO3: Ports 4G 215
Gunners La. SO24: B Can 6B 78
Gunners M. SO32: Bis W 3N 163
Gunners Pk. SO32: Bis W 3A 164
Gunners Row PO4: S'sea 5J 241
Gunner St. SP4: Bul C 3B 66
Gunners Way PO12: Gos 8H 213
Gunns Farm GU30: Lip 4E 116
Gunstore Rd. PO3: Ports 4H 215
GUNVILLE 6M 153
Gunville Cres. BH9: Bour 3M 227
Gunville Hill SP5: Mid W 5H 87
Gunville Rd. SP5: Mid W 5H 87
Gunwharf Quays PO1: Ports 5J 5 (3B 240)
Gunwharf Rd. PO1: Ports 6J 5 (3B 240)
Gurdons GU34: Alt 7D 80
Gurkha Museum, The 8K 237 (7K 105)
Gurnard Rd. PO6: Cosh 1F 214
Gurnays Mead SO51: W Wel 1A 120 (9M 121)
Gurney Ct. RG29: Odi 9K 45
Gurney Rd. PO4: S'sea 3J 241
SO15: South 2H 173
Gussage Rd. BH12: Poole 6C 226
Gutner La. PO11: H Isl 7J 217
Gutner Point Nature Reserve 8J 217
Guttridge La. RG26: Tadl 5G 11
Guy's Cl. BH24: Ring 1L 187
Gwatkin Cl. PO9: Bed 6C 202
Gwelo Dr. SO30: Hed E 6M 175
Gwynne Rd. BH12: Poole 9C 226
Gwynn Way PO17: Wick 6C 178
Gypsy La. BH24: Ring 9L 185
PO8: Cowp 5N 181
SO21: Chilc 9E 106
SP5: Com B 3G 119

H

Haarlem M. BH23: Chri 7N 229
Habens La. PO7: H'don 2B 180
HABIN 2L 147
Habin Hill GU31: Rog 9L 141
Haccups La. SO51: Mich 4K 123
Hack Dr. SO21: Col C 4K 133
Hacketts La. SO32: Drox 9L 135
Hackett Way *PO14: Fare* 2C 212
(off Sharlands Rd.)
Hackleys La. SO51: E Wel 7A 128
Hacks La. SO21: Craw 3N 89
Hackwood Cl. SP10: A'ver 2K 69
Hackwood Cotts. RG21: B'toke 9D 42
Hackwood La. RG25: Clid 4B 60
Hackwood Rd. RG21: B'toke 7C 42
Hackwood Rd. Rdbt. RG21: B'toke 8D 42
Hackworth Gdns. SO30: Hed E 8N 161
Hadden Rd. BH8: Bour 6A 228
Haddon Cl. PO14: Fare 8A 198
Haddon Dr. SO50: E'leigh 7E 132
Hadleigh Gdns. GU16: Frim G 6N 29
SO50: E'leigh 7E 132

Hadleigh Pl.—Harper Way

Hadleigh Pl. RG21: B'toke 6B 42
Hadleigh Rd. PO6: Cosh 9E 200
Hadley Fld. SO45: Hard 3N 207
Hadow Rd. BH10: Bour 3G 226
Hadrian Rd. SP10: A'ver 7A 52
Hadrians GU9: Farnh 6G 64
Hadrians Cl. SO53: Cha F 5C 132
Hadrians Way RG23: B'toke 4L 41
Hadrian Way SO16: Chilw 4K 159
Haflinger Dr. PO15: White 1E 196
Haglane Copse SO41: Penn 4C 234
Hagley Rd. GU51: Fleet 1K 47
Hahnemann Rd.
BH2: Bour 8J 247 (3J 245)
Haig Av. BH13: Poole 4C 244
Haig Ct. PO2: Ports 5F 214
Haig La. GU52: Ch Cr 6N 47
Haig Rd. GU12: Alders 1L 65
GU15: Camb 7H 19
SO24: New A 9F 94
SO50: B'stke 1L 161
SP4: Bul C 3B 66
SP10: A'ver 1L 69
Haileybury Gdns. SO30: Hed E 1N 175
Hailsham Cl. GU47: Owl 4F 18
Hailstone Rd. RG21: B'toke 3C 42
Haking Rd. BH23: Chri 7N 229
Halcyon *GU9: Up H 3C 64*
(off Lawday Link)
Halcyon Dr. SP11: Thru 1N 67
Halden Cl. SO51: Rom 3A 130
HALE
GU9 5F 64
SP6 9C 120
Hale Av. BH25: New M 4C 232
Hale Barn Ct. SP4: Idm 9C 66
Halebrose Ct. BH6: Bour 2H 247
Hale Cl. SO24: Rop 1D 110
HALECOMMON 8K 141
Hale Ct. PO1: Ports 9F 214
Hale Gdns. BH25: New M 4C 232
Hale Ho. *GU9: Farnh 6F 64*
(off Hale Rd.)
Hale Ho. Cl. GU10: Chur 7H 85
Hale Ho. La. GU10: Chur 7H 85
Hale La. SP6: Hale 1A 154
Hale Pl. GU9: Hale 5G 64
Hale Reeds GU9: H End 4F 64
Hale Rd. GU9: Farnh, Hale 5F 64
SP6: Woodg 2A 154
Hales Dr. SO30: Hed E 5L 175
Halesowen Ho. PO5: S'sea 6N 5
Hale St. Nth. PO1: Ports 1E 240
Hale St. Sth. PO1: Ports 1E 240
Hale Way GU16: Frim 4M 29
Halewood Way BH23: Chri 6J 229
Haley La. GU34: Bent 5L 79
Half Moon St. PO1: Ports 3J 5 (2B 240)
Halfpenny La. PO1: Ports 7K 5 (4B 240)
Halfway Rd. SO45: Fawl 7J 209
Halifax Cl. GU14: Cov 9H 29
SP10: A'ver 9M 51
Halifax Ct. SO30: Wes E 9G 160
Halifax Ri. PO7: W'lle 2N 201
Halifax Way BH23: Chri 7D 230
Halimote Rd. GU11: Alders 1J 65
Hall Cl. GU15: Camb 7N 19
SO32: Bis W 3N 163
Hall Dr. GU52: Fleet 5N 47
Hallett Cl. SO18: South 9E 160
Hallett Rd. PO9: Hav 7H 203
Halletts Cl. PO14: Stub 5M 211
Hall Farm Cres. GU46: Yat 8N 17
Halliards, The PO16: Fare 1D 212
Halliday Cl. PO12: Gos 2K 239
RG21: B'toke 9B 42
Halliday Cres. PO4: S'sea 4K 241
Hall Lands La. SO50: Fair O 1A 162
Hall La. GU34: Selb, Up Farr 5F 98
GU46: Yat 8M 17
Hallmark Cl. GU47: Coll 5G 18
Hallowell Ho. PO1: Ports 1D 240
Hall Rd. BH11: Bour 3D 226
GU34: Alt 2G 81
Halls Farm Cl. SO22: Winche 3J 105
Halls La. RG27: Matt 4E 24
Hall Way, The SO22: Lit 1F 104
Halnaker La. GU32: E Meon 3J 143
Halsey Cl. PO12: Gos 4H 239
Halstead Rd. PO6: Cosh 9E 200
SO18: South 9D 160
Halters End GU26: Gray 4J 103
HALTERWORTH 5B 130
Halterworth Cl. SO51: Rom 5A 130
Halterworth La. SO51: Cram, Rom 5B 130
Halton Cl. BH23: Bran 7D 220
Halton Rd. SP11: Per D 4B 30 (6J 31)
Haltons Cl. SO40: Tott 1K 171
Halyard Cl. PO13: Gos 9F 212
Halyards SO31: Hamb 5L 195
Hambert Way SO40: Tott 5L 171
Hamble Av. GU17: Blackw 8F 18
HAMBLE CLIFF 6H 195
Hamblecliff Ho. SO31: Hamb 6H 195
Hamble Cliff Stables SO31: Hamb 6H 195
Hamble Cl. RG23: Oak 1D 58
SO31: Wars 8N 195
Hamble Ct. BH1: Bour 1A 246
PO8: Cowp 6N 181
PO14: Stub 5L 211
RG21: B'toke 6E 42
SO53: Cha F 7B 132
SP10: A'ver 8B 52
Hamble Ct. Business Pk.
SO31: Hamb 6J 195
HAMBLEDON 8E 166
Hambledon Cl. SO22: Winche 2H 105
Hambledon Gdns. BH6: Bour 8F 228
Hambledon La. PO7: H'don 9L 165
SO32: Sob 9L 165
Hambledon Pde. PO7: W'lle 8K 181
Hambledon Rd. BH6: Bour 8F 228
BH7: Bour 7E 228
PO7: Den, H'don 1D 180
PO7: W'lle 8K 181
(not continuous)
PO8: Clan 5A 168
Hambledon Way RG27: Sher L 7J 23
Hamble Dr. RG26: Tadl 5K 11
Hamble Ho. PO16: Fare 1C 212
Hamble Ho. Gdns. SO31: Hamb 7L 195
Hamble La. PO7: W'lle 4M 201
SO31: Burs, Hamb, Hou, Old N 2K 195
HAMBLE-LE-RICE 7L 195
Hamble Mnr. Ct. SO31: Hamb 7L 195
Hamble Pk. Caravan Site SO31: Wars 8C 196
Hamble Rd. PO12: Gos 3H 239
Hambleside Ct. SO31: Hamb 7K 195
Hamble Sports Complex 4K 195
Hamble Springs SO32: Bis W 4N 163
Hamble Station (Rail) 4J 195
Hamble Wood SO30: Botl 4D 176
Hamblewood Ct. SO30: Botl 4E 176
Hamblin Way BH8: Bour 4B 228
Hambrook Ho. *PO3: Ports 1H 241*
(off Cotton Rd.)
Hambrook Rd. PO12: Gos 1J 239
Hambrook St. PO5: S'sea 8M 5 (4C 240)
Hamburg PO1: Ports 2K 5
Hamburg Cl. SP10: A'ver 7M 51
HAM DOWN 1B 156
Hamdown Cres. SO51: E Wel 1B 156
Hameldon Cl. SO16: South 3E 172
Hamelyn Cl. RG21: B'toke 7B 42
Hamelyn Rd. RG21: B'toke 7B 42
Hamesmoor Rd. GU16: Mytc 8N 29
Hamesmoor Way GU16: Mytc 8N 29
Hamfield Dr. PO11: H Isl 3E 242
Hamilton Bus. Pk. BH25: New M 4N 231
SO30: Hed E 1M 175
Hamilton Cl. BH1: Bour 9A 228
BH23: Mude 9B 230
GU35: Bor 3L 101
PO8: Horn 4B 182
PO9: Langs 9F 202
RG21: B'toke 4N 41
SP4: Ames 5A 66
(off Raleigh Cres.)
Hamilton Ct. BH8: Bour 9M 227
PO5: S'sea 9N 5 (5D 240)
SO17: South 1M 173
(off Winn Rd.)
SO41: M Sea 8J 235
SO45: Holb 4B 208
SP9: Tidw 9C 30
Hamilton Ent. Cen. PO6: Farl 1M 215
Hamilton Gdns. GU14: Cov 7E 28
Hamilton Grn. SP9: Tidw 9C 30
Hamilton Gro. PO13: Gos 6D 212
Hamilton Ho. *PO1: Ports 1F 240*
(off Clive Rd.)
Hamilton M. SO45: Hythe 8N 193
Hamilton Pk. SP5: Down 1L 119 (7B 120)
Hamilton Pl. GU11: Alders 1H 65
SO41: Lymi 3D 234
Hamilton Rd. BH1: Bour 9A 228
GU33: Longc 4J 115
GU52: Ch Cr 5N 47
PO5: S'sea 5E 240
PO6: Cosh 9N 199
SO31: Sar G 4C 196
SO45: Hythe 9N 193
SO50: B'stke 9H 133
Hamilton Way BH25: New M 4N 231
Ham La. PO8: Cath 2N 181
PO12: Gos 8J 213
RG26: Bau 7B 10
Hamlet Ct. SO45: Fawl 5F 208
Hamlet Gdns. SP11: Enh A 4A 52
Hamlet Way PO12: Gos 7J 213
HAMMER 1M 117
HAMMER BOTTOM 9L 103
Hammer Hill GU27: Hasl 2L 117
Hammer La. GU10: Chur 8G 84
GU26: Gray 8G 84
GU26: Hasl 7L 103
GU27: Lip 1J 117
Hammersley Rd. GU11: Alders 4K 49
Hammer Va. GU27: Lip 9L 103
Hammerwood Copse GU27: Hasl 1M 117
Hammond Ct. PO12: Gos 3N 239
Hammond Ind. Est. PO14: Stub 7N 211
Hammond Rd. PO15: Fare 7N 197
RG21: B'toke 8B 42
Hammonds Cl. SO40: Tott 2L 171
HAMMOND'S GREEN 2K 171
Hammond's Grn. SO40: Tott 1K 171
Hammonds La. SO24: Rop 2D 110
SO40: Tott 2L 171
Hammond's Pas. SO23: Winche 8L 237
Hammond Sq. *SP10: A'ver 8A 52*
(off Cricketers Way)
Hammonds Way SO40: Tott 2L 171
Hampage Grn. PO9: Hav 2D 202
Hampden La. BH6: Bour 9E 228
Hampshire Cl. BH23: Chri 4J 229
GU12: Alders 3M 65
RG22: Wort 8J 41
SP4: Bul 3A 66
(off Churchill Av.)
Hampshire Corporate Pk. SO53: Cha F 9N 131
Hampshire County Cricket Club 1K 175
Hampshire Ct. BH2: Bour 6L 247 (2K 245)
SO53: Cha F 9A 132
Hampshire Cross SP9: Tidw 8D 30 (7G 30)
Hampshire Golf Course, The 7A 70
Hampshire Hatches La. BH24: Ring 5J 187
Hampshire Ho. BH2: Bour 6L 247
Hampshire Intl. Bus. Pk. RG24: Chin 8F 22
Hampshire Rd. GU35: Bor 3J 101
Hampshire Rose Bowl, The 1K 175
Hampshire St. PO1: Ports 9F 214
Hampshire Tennis & Health Club 1K 175
Hampshire Ter. PO1: Ports 6M 5 (3C 240)
Hampstead Ho. *RG21: B'toke 6C 42*
(off Festival Pl.)
Hampton Cl. GU52: Ch Cr 7M 47
PO7: W'lle 2A 202
SO45: Blac 8C 208
Hampton Ct. BH2: Bour 5H 247 (1H 245)
RG23: B'toke 5M 41
Hampton Dr. BH24: Poul 8L 185
Hampton Farm La. SO32: Swanm 5C 164
Hampton Gdns. SO45: Blac 8C 208
Hampton Gro. PO15: Fare 8L 197
Hampton Hill SO32: Swanm 5G 164
Hampton La. SO22: Winche 5G 105
SO45: Blac 6C 208
Hampton Lodge BH4: Bour 2G 245
HAMPTON PARK 8N 159
Hampton Pl. BH8: Bour 7M 227
Hampton Rd. GU9: Up H 4C 64
Hamptons, The BH14: Poole 5C 244
Hampton Towers SO19: South 1C 194
HAMPTWORTH 9H 121
Hamptworth Golf Course 9H 121
Hamptworth Rd.
SP5: H'twth, L'ford, Redl 8E 120
Ham Rd. PO17: Boar 3L 199
Hams Cnr. RG27: Sher L 5M 23
Hamtun Cres. SO40: Tott 1L 171
Hamtun Gdns. SO40: Tott 1L 171
Hamtun Rd. SO19: South 7G 174
Hamtun St. SO14: South 7C 4 (7L 173)
Hamwic Hall SO14: South 6E 4
Hanbidge Cres. PO13: Gos 4F 212
Hanbidge Wlk. PO13: Gos 4F 212
Hanbury Sq. GU31: Pet 8N 139
Hanbury Way GU15: Camb 1L 29
Hancombe Rd. GU47: Sandh 4C 18
Handcroft Cl. GU10: Cron 2L 63
Handel Cl. RG22: B'toke 1N 59
Handel Rd. SO15: South 3B 4 (4L 173)
Handel Ter. SO15: South 3A 4 (5K 173)
Handford La. GU46: Yat 8M 17
Handford Pl. SO15: South 1C 4 (4L 173)
Handley Ct. BH24: Ring 1J 187
Handley Rd. PO12: Gos 1H 239
Handsworth Ho. PO5: S'sea 3E 240
Handyside Pl. GU34: Four M 3L 97
Handy Vs. *SO23: Winche 6N 237*
(off Park Av.)
Hangar Rd. RG26: Tadl 4F 10
Hanger, The GU35: Head 9A 84
Hanger Farm Arts Cen. 2H 171
Hangerfield Cl. GU46: Yat 8M 17
Hangers, The SO32: Bis W 2N 163
HANGERSLEY 4A 188
HANGERSLEY HILL 4A 188
Hanger Way GU31: Pet 1A 146
Hanging Bushes La. SP11: Pen G 8F 50
Hankins Ct. GU52: Fleet 4M 47
Hankinson Rd. BH9: Bour 6L 227
Hanley Rd. SO15: South 2J 173
Hanlon Cl. BH11: Bour 2F 226
Hanmore Rd. RG24: Chin 1F 42
Hannah Gdns. PO7: W'lle 1N 201
Hannah Grange BH1: Bour 9N 227
Hannah Way SO41: Penn 9N 223
Hannam's Farm Cl. GU10: Cron 3L 63
Hannay Ri. SO19: South 5H 175
HANNINGTON 9L 9
Hannington Gro. *BH7: Bour 9D 228*
(off Hannington Pl.)
Hannington Pl. BH7: Bour 9D 228
Hannington Rd. BH7: Bour 9D 228
PO9: Hav 2D 202
RG26: Hann, N Oak 2K 39
Hann Rd. SO16: Rown 5D 158
Hanns Way SO50: E'leigh 9E 132
Hanover Bldgs. SO14: South 6D 4 (6M 173)
Hanover Cl. GU16: Frim 3N 29
GU46: Yat 6N 17
SO51: Rom 5L 129
SP10: A'ver 3K 69
Hanover Ct. GU30: Lip 1D 116
PO1: Ports 6K 5 (4B 240)
SO45: Hythe 5M 193
Hanover Dr. GU51: Fleet 8A 28
Hanover Gables *SO17: South 2M 173*
(off Westwood Rd.)
Hanover Gdns. GU14: Cov 6G 29
PO16: Fare 6D 198
RG21: B'toke 9B 42
Hanover Ho. PO13: Gos 3D 212
SO40: Tott 2N 171
SP10: A'ver 2A 70
(off Kings Mdw.)
Hanoverian Way PO15: White 2F 196
Hanover Lodge SO23: Winche 8K 105
Hanover St. PO1: Ports 3J 5 (2B 240)
Hansen Gdns. SO30: Hed E 1M 175
Hanson Rd. SP10: A'ver 9L 51
Hanway Rd. PO1: Ports 9F 214
PO2: Ports 8F 214
Ha'penny Dell PO7: Purb 6M 201
Harbeck Rd. BH8: Bour 3N 227
Harborough Rd. SO15: South 1B 4 (4L 173)
Harbour Cl. BH13: S'bks 7B 244
GU14: Farn 4J 29
SO40: March 8H 173
Harbour Ct. BH23: Chri 8A 230
BH25: B Sea 7N 231
Harbour Cres. BH23: Chri 9A 230
Harbourgate Bus. Pk. PO6: Cosh 9D 200
Harbour Lights Picturehouse 9G 4 (8N 173)
Harbourne Gdns. SO18: Wes E 9F 160
Harbour Pde. SO15: South 5A 4 (6K 173)
Harbour Prospect BH14: Poole 5A 244
Harbour Ridge PO1: Ports 3K 5
Harbour Rd. BH6: Bour 2K 247
PO11: H Isl 3C 242
PO12: Gos 2M 239
Harbourside PO9: Langs 2F 216
Harbour Side Caravan & Camping Site
PO3: Ports 7L 215
Harbour Tours
Portsmouth 3H 5 (2A 240)
Harbour Twr. PO12: Gos 3N 239
Harbour Vw. PO16: Portc 2L 213
Harbour Vw. Ct. BH23: Chri 9L 229
Harbour Watch BH14: Poole 6A 244
Harbour Way PO2: Ports 6D 214
PO10: Ems 9N 203
HARBRIDGE 9H 153
Harbridge Ct. BH24: Har 3D 184
PO9: Hav 2D 202
Harbridge Drove BH24: Har 6F 152
HARBRIDGE GREEN 8H 153
Harcourt *BH1: Bour 2N 245*
(off Derby Rd.)
Harcourt Cl. PO8: Cowp 6A 182
Harcourt Rd. BH5: Bour 9D 228
GU15: Camb 8J 19
PO1: Ports 9F 214
PO12: Gos 2J 239
PO14: Fare 1L 211
SO18: South 2B 174
Hard, The PO1: Ports 3J 5 (2B 240)
Harding Rd. PO12: Gos 1H 239
Hardings La. RG27: H Win 6C 26
SO50: Fair O 9M 133
Hardings Rd. GU10: B Oak 10M 63
Hard Interchange, The PO1: Ports 4J 5 (2B 240)
HARDLEY 2A 208
Hardley Ind. Est. SO45: Hard 2M 207
Hardley La. SO45: Hard, Hythe 1M 207
(not continuous)
Hardman Ct. PO3: Ports 4J 215
HARDWAY 8K 213
Hardway Sailing Club 8L 213
Hardwicke Cl. SO16: South 9E 158
Hardwicke Way SO31: Hamb 7H 195
Hardwick Rd. SO53: Cha F 6B 132
Hardy Av. GU31: Pet 8N 139
GU46: Yat 9M 17
Hardy Cl. BH25: New M 3A 232
PO13: Gos 5E 212
SO15: South 4G 173
SO31: Loc H 5E 196
Hardy Dr. SO45: Hythe 7N 193
Hardyfair Cl. SP11: Weyh 8D 50
Hardy Grn. RG45: Cr'tne 1D 18
Hardy La. RG21: B'toke 7B 42
Hardy Rd. BH14: Poole 1B 244
PO6: Farl 9M 201
SO50: E'leigh 2E 160
Hardy's Fld. RG20: Kings 1A 6 (5K 9)
Harebell Cl. PO16: Fare 6E 198
RG27: H Win 5C 26
Harebell Gdns. RG27: H Win 5C 26
HAREFIELD
SO18 3G 174
SO51 4B 130
Harefield Ct. SO51: Rom 4A 130
Harefield Rd. SO17: South 7A 160
Hare La. BH21: Cran 7L 149
BH25: A'ley 3E 232
SO21: Twyf 9L 127
SO41: Hor 3E 232
Hares Grn. BH7: Bour 6D 228
Hare's La. RG27: H Win 4D 26
HARESTOCK 3G 105
Harestock Cl. SO22: Winche 1H 105
Harestock Rd. PO9: Bed 6D 202
SO22: Winche 3G 104
Harewood Av. BH7: Bour 7C 228
Harewood Cl. SO50: E'leigh 6E 132
Harewood Cres. BH7: Bour 7C 228
Harewood Forest Ind. Est.
SP11: Longp 6K 71
Harewood Gdns. BH7: Bour 7C 228
Harewood Grn. SO41: Key 8N 235
Harewood Mobile Home Pk.
SP11: And D 9E 52
Harewood Pl. BH7: Bour 8E 228
Harfield Cl. RG27: Hoo 2G 44
Harford Cl. SO41: Penn 5B 234
Harford Rd. BH12: Poole 6A 226
Hargreaves Cl. RG24: B'toke 2D 42
Harkness Dr. PO7: W'lle 1B 202
Harland Cres. SO15: South 1J 173
Harland Rd. BH6: Bour 1K 247
Harlaxton Cl. SO50: E'leigh 7D 132
Harlech Cl. RG23: B'toke 6L 41
Harlech Dr. SO53: Cha F 8M 131
Harlech Rd. GU17: Haw 9F 18
Harlequin Ct. PO12: Gos 2M 239
Harlequin Gro. PO15: Fare 8B 198
Harleston Rd. PO6: Cosh 8E 200
Harley Ct. *PO1: Ports 1E 240*
(off Lords St.)
SO31: Wars 8A 196
Harley Gdns. BH1: Bour 1A 246
Harley La. SO43: B'haw 3L 155
Harley Wlk. PO1: Ports 1E 240
Harling Ho. *BH6: Bour 1F 246*
(off Stourwood Av.)
Harlington Centre, The 2L 47
Harlington Way GU51: Fleet 2L 47
Harlyn Rd. SO16: South 1E 172
Harman Rd. PO13: Gos 5E 212
Harmes Way GU11: Alders 4M 49
Harmsworth Rd. RG26: Tadl 5H 11
Harness Ct. RG24: B'toke 3M 41
Harold Cl. SO40: Tott 4K 171
Harold Gdns. GU34: Alt 3G 80
Harold Jackson Ter. RG21: B'toke 7D 42
Harold Rd. PO4: S'sea 4F 240
PO11: H Isl 5H 243
PO14: Stub 5N 211
SO15: South 3H 173
Harold Ter. PO10: Ems 8M 203
Harper Way PO16: Fare 8D 198

A-Z Hampshire 285

Harpton Cl. GU46: Yat 6N 17
Harpton Pde. GU46: Yat 6N 17
Harpway La. BH23: Sop, Wink 8M 219
Harrage, The SO51: Rom 5M 129
Harrier Cl. PO8: Horn 3A 182
PO13: Lee S 1B 238
SO16: South 5G 158
Harrier Grn. SO45: Hard 2N 207
Harrier M. SO31: Hamb 6J 195
Harrier Rd. GU14: Farn 2E 48
RG20: Bis G 1G 9
Harriers Cl. BH23: Chri 6F 230
Harrier Way GU31: Pet 2B 146
SO45: Hard 2N 207
Harriet Cl. PO14: Stub 6L 211
Harrington Dr. SP4: Bul C 3B 66
Harris Av. SO30: Hed E 2N 175
Harris Ct. GU30: Lip 4D 116
Harris Hill RG22: B'toke 3K 59
Harris La. PO8: Chal 6K 169
Harrison Av. BH1: Bour 8A 228
Harrison Cl. BH23: Burt 3M 229
Harrison Ho. PO2: Ports 6E 214
Harrison Pl. RG21: B'toke 6B 42
Harrison Rd. PO16: Fare 7D 198
SO17: South 8A 160
Harrisons Cut SO14: South 6E **4** (6N 173)
SO15: South 1G 173
Harris Rd. PO13: Gos 5F 212
Harris Way BH25: New M 9D 222
SO52: N Bad 8F 130
Harroway RG28: Hur P, Whit 5M 53
Harroway La. SP11: Pen H, Pen M 7G 50
Harrow Cl. BH23: Nea 8D 220
Harrow Ct. *PO7: W'lle 9K 181*
(off Harrow Way)
Harrow Down SO22: Winche 1H 127
Harrowgate La. PO7: H'don 2H 181
Harrow La. GU32: Pet 7M 139
Harrow Rd. BH23: Bock, Bran, Nea 8C 220
GU51: Fleet 9L 27
PO5: S'sea 3F 240
Harrow Way PO7: W'lle 9J 181
RG23: Oak 8M 39
RG25: Over 7E 38
SP10: A'ver 9K 51
SP10: A'ver, Pen H 8G 50
Harrow Way, The RG22: B'toke 1N 59
RG28: Whit 2H 55
Harrow Wood Farm Caravan Pk.
BH23: Bran 7E 220
Harry Barrows Cl. BH24: Ring 2K 187
Harry Law Cotts. *BH24: Bur 8D 188*
(off Wares La.)
Harry Law Hall PO1: Ports 4N **5** (2D 240)
Harry Sotnick Ho. PO1: Ports 1G 240
Hart, The GU9: Farnh 8D 64
Hart Centre, The GU51: Fleet 2L 47
Hart Cl. BH25: New M 2A 232
GU14: Cov 4G 28
Hart Ct. SO19: South 7D 174
HARTFORDBRIDGE 4E 26
Hartford Ct. BH1: Bour 1N 245
RG27: H Win 6B 26
Hartford Ho. PO1: Ports 7M **5** (4C 240)
Hartford Ri. GU15: Camb 7M 19
Hartford Rd. GU51: Fleet 9L 27
RG27: H Win 6B 26
Hartford Ter. RG27: H Win 6C 26
Hart Hill SO45: Hythe 8A 194
Harthill Drove SP5: Redl 3N 119 (8D 120)
Hart Ho. Ct. RG27: H Win 6C 26
Harting Cl. PO8: Clan 7D 168
Harting Down GU31: Pet 1A 146
Harting Gdns. PO16: Portc 8L 199
Harting Rd. BH6: Bour 7G 229
Hartington Rd. PO12: Gos 1H 239
SO14: South 3G **4** (5N 173)
Hartland Pl. GU14: Farn 6J 29
Hartland's Rd. PO16: Fare 8D 198
Hart Leisure Cen. 3H 47
Hartley Av. SO17: South 9N 159
Hartley Cl. GU17: Blackw 8D 18
SO45: Dib P 8M 193
SO50: B'stke 2L 161
Hartley Ct. *SO17: South 2M 173*
(off Winn Rd.)
Hartley Gdns. RG26: Tadl 6H 11
Hartley Gro. SO16: Bass 7M 159
Hartley La. RG27: H Wes 2N 23
HARTLEY MAUDITT 1L 99
Hartley Mdw. RG28: Whit 5F 54
Hartley M. RG27: H Win 5C 26
Hartley Pk. Farm Bus. Cen. GU34: Alt 3J 99
Hartley Rd. PO2: Ports 5E 214
SO50: B'stke 2L 161
Hartleys RG7: Sil 5A 12
Hartley Wlk. SO45: Dib P 8M 193
HARTLEY WESPALL 4B 24
HARTLEY WINTNEY 6C 26
Hartley Wintney Golf Course 5D 26
Hart M. GU46: Yat 7L 17
Hartmoor Gdns. BH10: Bour 5H 227
Hart Plain Av. PO8: Cowp 6L 181
(not continuous)
Hart Plain Ho. PO7: W'lle 8M 181
Hartsbourne Dr. BH7: Bour 6E 228
Harts Farm Way PO9: Hav 9C 202
Hartsgrove Av. SO45: Blac 8C 208
Hartsgrove Cl. SO45: Blac 7C 208
Hartshill Rd. RG26: Tadl 5F 10
Harts La. RG20: Burgh 4D 8
Hartsleaf Cl. GU51: Fleet 3L 47
Harts Leap Cl. GU47: Sandh 4D 18
Harts Leap Rd. GU47: Sandh 5C 18
Harts Ri. SP6: Ald 5B 152
Harts Way SO41: Ever 5L 233
Hartswood RG24: Chin 1F 42
Harts Yd. GU9: Farnh 8D 64
Hartwell Rd. PO3: Ports 4J 215
Hartwood Gdns. PO8: Cowp 8M 181

Harvard Cl. PO13: Lee S 2C 238
Harvard Rd. GU47: Owl 4G 19
Harvest Cl. GU46: Yat 9L 17
SO22: Winche 1H 127
Harvest Cres. GU51: Fleet 7N 27
Harvester Dr. PO15: Fare 8L 197
Harvester Way SO41: Lymi 9D 224
Harvestgate Wlk. PO9: Hav 3D 202
Harvesting La. GU32: E Meon 5A 144
Harvest La. SP5: Bish 3D 118
Harvest Rd. PO7: Den 5F 180
SO53: Cha F 6L 131
Harvest Way RG24: Lych 4G 42
SO20: Mid Wa 4B 72
Harvey Brown Ho. PO11: H Isl 2G 243
Harvey Ct. SO45: Blac 6C 208
Harvey Cres. SO31: Wars 8C 196
Harvey Gdns. SO45: Hythe 6N 193
Harvey Pl. SP10: A'ver 1C 70
Harvey Rd. BH5: Bour 9D 228
GU14: Cov 7E 28
PO6: Cosh 8F 200
SO50: B'stke 9J 133
Harveys Fld. RG25: Over 2D 56
Harwich Rd. PO6: Cosh 8E 200
Harwood Cl. PO13: Gos 4E 212
SO40: Tott 2L 171
Harwood Ct. BH25: New M 3A 232
Harwood Pl. SO23: Kin W 7N 91
Harwood Ri. RG20: Wol H 2A 8
(not continuous)
Harwood Rd. PO13: Gos 4E 212
Haselbury Rd. SO40: Tott 3M 171
Haselfoot Gdns. SO30: Wes E 3J 175
Haselworth Dr. PO12: Gos 6K 239
Haskells Cl. SO43: Lyn 3A **148** (3N 189)
Haskins Dr. GU14: Cov 7F 28
Haskins Gdns. GU14: Cov 7F 28
Haslar Cres. PO7: W'lle 8K 181
Haslar Jetty Rd. PO12: Gos 5M 239
Haslar Marine Technology Pk.
PO12: Gos 5L 239
Haslar Rd. PO12: Gos 3N 239
(not continuous)
Haslar Sea Wall PO12: Gos 6M 239
Haslar Ter. PO12: Gos 5M 239
Haslegrave Ho. *PO2: Ports 8E 214*
(off Nessus St.)
Haslemere Av. BH23: Highc 6H 231
Haslemere Gdns. PO11: H Isl 5M 243
Haslemere Pl. BH23: Highc 5J 231
Haslemere Rd. GU30: Lip 2E 116
PO4: S'sea 4G 241
Hassocks, The PO7: W'lle 2A 202
Hassocks Workshops RG24: B'toke 4F 42
Hastards La. GU34: Selb 7L 99
Hasted Dr. SO24: New A 2E 108
Hastings Av. PO12: Gos 8H 213
Hastings Cl. RG23: B'toke 6K 41
Hastings Ho. PO2: Ports 6D 214
Hastings Rd. BH8: Bour 4C 228
HATCH 6L 43
HATCH BOTTOM 9J 161
Hatchbury La. SP11: Ver D 8E 6
Hatch Caravan Pk. RG24: Old Bas 6K 43
Hatch Ct. PO9: Hav 2C 202
Hatchers La. SO21: Owls 4B 134
Hatchery Hill SO21: Spar 5N 89
Hatches, The GU16: Frim G 6M 29
Hatchet Cl. SP6: Hale 9C 120
HATCHET GREEN 9C 120
Hatchet La. SO42: Beau 8B 206
SP11: C'vle, Hath 1G 50
Hatchett Hill SP11: Chu F, Lwr C 5A 32
Hatchetts Dr. GU27: Hasl 9L 103
Hatchlands Dr. GU26: Hind 3N 103
Hatch La. GU33: Liss 1G 140
RG24: Old Bas 5J 43
SP11: Ver D 7E 6
Hatchley La. SO32: Lwr U 8C 134
Hatch Mead SO30: Wes E 9G 161
Hatchmore Rd. PO7: Den 6F 180
HATCH WARREN 3K 59
Hatch Warren Cotts. RG22: B'toke 3L 59
Hatchwarren Gdns. RG22: B'toke 3N 59
Hatch Warren La. RG22: B'toke 3K 59
Hatch Warren Retail Pk. RG22: B'toke 4J 59
Hatch Warren Way RG22: B'toke 3N 59
Hatfield Ct. BH25: New M 3N 231
Hatfield Gdns. BH7: Bour 6E 228
GU14: Farn 9N 29
Hatfield Rd. PO4: S'sea 4H 241
Hathaway Cl. SO50: E'leigh 8F 132
Hathaway Gdns. PO7: W'lle 9B 182
RG24: B'toke 3E 42
Hathaway Rd. BH6: Bour 1G 247
HATHERDEN 1J 51
Hatherden Ct. *SP10: A'ver 1A 70*
(off Eastfield Rd.)
Hatherell Cl. SO30: Wes E 1H 175
Hatherley Cres. PO16: Portc 9J 199
Hatherley Dr. PO16: Portc 9K 199
Hatherley Mans. SO15: South 3H 173
Hatherley Rd. PO6: Cosh 8B 200
SO22: Winche 5J 105
Hatherwood GU46: Yat 8B 18
Hatley Rd. SO18: South 2E 174
Hattem Pl. SP10: A'ver 7M 51
HATT HILL 3D 122
HATTINGLEY 9J 79
Hattingley Rd. GU34: Meds 9H 79
Hatt La. SO51: Mott 3D 122
HAUGHURST HILL 4C 10
Haughurst Hill RG26: Bau 5B 10
HAVANT 8F 202
Havant & Waterlooville FC 4G 203
Havant Bus. Cen. PO9: Hav 9D 202
Havant By-Pass PO6: Cosh, Farl 2H 215
PO9: Hav 1A 216
PO9: Hav, Warb 9G 202
Havant Farm Cl. PO9: Hav 6F 202

Havant Leisure Cen. 7F 202
Havant Retail Pk. PO9: Bed 8B 202
Havant Rd. PO2: Ports 7F 214
PO6: Cosh, Dray, Farl 9G 201
PO8: Horn 3D 182
PO9: Bed 9L 201
PO9: R Cas 5D 182
PO10: Ems 9J 203
PO11: H Isl 5F 216
Havant Station (Rail) 7F 202
Havant St. PO1: Ports 3J **5** (2B 240)
Havelock Ct. SO31: Wars 8N 195
Havelock Mans. PO5: S'sea 3F 240
Havelock Rd. BH12: Poole 9E 226
PO5: S'sea 3E 240
SO14: South 3B **4** (5L 173)
SO31: Wars 8N 195
Havelock Way BH23: Chri 4F 230
Haven, The PO4: S'sea 2J 241
PO12: Gos 5K 239
SO16: Bass 5M 159
SO30: Hed E 6M 175
SO31: Loc H 5F 196
SO50: E'leigh 6F 132
Haven Cl. BH23: Chri 8A 230
Haven Ct. SO41: M Sea 8J 235
Haven Cres. PO14: Stub 7J 211
Havendale SO30: Hed E 5A 176
(not continuous)
Haven Gdns. BH25: New M 4C 232
Haven Hgts. BH13: Poole 6D 244
Haven Point SO41: Lymi 2F 234
Haven Rd. BH13: Poole, S'bks 7B 244
PO11: H Isl 6L 243
Havenstone Way SO18: S'ing 7C 160
H Avenue SO45: Fawl 2D 208
Haven Way GU9: Farnh 6F 64
Haverstock Rd. BH9: Bour 4M 227
Haviland Ct. BH7: Bour 9C 228
Haviland M. BH7: Bour 9C 228
Haviland Rd. BH7: Bour 9C 228
Haviland Rd. E. BH7: Bour 9C 228
Haviland Rd. W. BH1: Bour 1C 246
Havisham Rd. PO2: Ports 9E 214
Havre Towers SO19: South 1C 194
Hawden Rd. BH11: Bour 5E 226
Haweswater Cl. GU35: Bor 2J 101
SO16: South 1E 172
Haweswater Ct. *GU12: Ash V 6N 49*
(off Lakeside Cl.)
Hawfinch Cl. SO16: South 5G 158
Hawk Cl. PO14: Stub 6L 211
RG22: B'toke 2H 59
Hawk Conservancy, The 1B 68
Hawke Cl. SP10: A'ver 9C 52
Hawkers Cl. SO40: Tott 1L 171
Hawkes Cl. RG27: H Win 5B 26
Hawkes Ho. SO14: South 7F 4
Hawke St. PO1: Ports 3J **5** (2B 240)
Hawkeswood Rd. SO18: South 3A 174
Hawkewood Av. PO7: W'lle 8L 181
Hawkfield La. RG21: B'toke 7B 42
Hawkhill SO45: Dib 6H 193
Hawkhurst Cl. SO19: South 9E 174
Hawkins Cl. BH24: Poul 8M 185
GU46: Yat 8L 17
Hawkins Ct. SO24: New A 9F 94
SO40: March 7E 172
Hawkins Gro. GU51: Ch Cr 5J 47
Hawkins Rd. BH12: Poole 5D 226
PO13: Gos 6F 212
Hawkins Way GU52: Fleet 3A 48
HAWKLEY 7M 113
Hawkley Cl. PO9: Hav 3E 202
Hawkley Dr. RG26: Tadl 6J 11
Hawkley Grn. SO19: South 9D 174
Hawkley Rd.
GU33: Hawk, Liss 7M 113
Hawkley Way GU51: Fleet 9H 27
Hawkshaw Cl. GU30: Lip 2F 116
Hawks Lea SO41: M Sea 8K 235
Hawks Mead GU33: Liss 9D 114
Hawkswood Av. GU16: Frim 2N 29
Hawkwell GU52: Ch Cr 7N 47
PO16: Portc 8H 199
Hawkwood M. BH5: Bour 9C 228
Hawkwood Rd. BH5: Bour 1B 246
HAWLEY 1G 29
Hawley Ct. GU14: Cov 4G 29
Hawley Grn. GU17: Haw 1G 28
(not continuous)
Hawley Gro. GU17: Haw 2G 28
HAWLEY LANE 5J 29
Hawley La. GU14: Farn 3J 29
(not continuous)
Hawley La. Ind. Est. GU14: Farn 4K 29
Hawley Lodge GU17: Haw 2H 29
Hawley Rd. GU17: Haw 9F 18
Haworth Cl. BH23: Chri 5K 229
Hawstead Grn. PO9: Hav 3D 202
HAWTHORN 7K 97
Hawthorn Cl. BH25: A'ley 2D 232
GU12: Alders 2N 65
PO16: Portc 8K 199
SO21: Col C 4L 133
SO21: M'dvr 8J 77
SO24: New A 1F 108
SO30: Hed E 4A 176
SO50: Fair O 1N 161
Hawthorn Ct. GU14: Farn 3L 49
GU31: Pet 1B 146
Hawthorn Cres. PO6: Cosh 2G 215
Hawthorn Dr. SO41: Sway 5J 223
Hawthorne Cl. SP11: Grat 4L 67
Hawthorne Ct. SO31: Sar G 4D 196
Hawthorne Cres. GU17: Haw 9G 19
Hawthorne Gro. PO11: H Isl 3G 243
Hawthorne Rd. SO40: Tott 2K 171
Hawthorn La. GU34: Four M 7L 97
SO31: Sar G 4B 196
Hawthorn Ri. RG27: Hoo 1H 45

Hawthorn Rd. BH9: Bour 6K 227
BH23: Bock, Burt 8A 220
GU14: Farn 8K 29
GU34: Four M 7J 97
PO7: Den 6F 180
PO8: Horn 9C 168
(not continuous)
SO17: South 9M 159
SO45: Hythe 6L 193
SP9: Tidw 7E 30
Hawthorns GU34: Alt 3E 80
Hawthorns, The BH23: Chri 8B 230
RG26: Bau 5E 10
SO32: Bis W 2K 163
SO40: March 9E 172
(Baytree Gdns.)
SO40: March 9F 172
(The Limes)
SO50: E'leigh 2C 160
Hawthorns Urban Wildlife Centre, The 2L 173
Hawthorn Wlk. PO13: Lee S 1B 238
Hawthorn Way GU35: Lind 3K 101
RG23: B'toke 5L 41
Hayburn Rd. SO16: South 9C 158
Hayden La. GU32: W Meo 2C 142
Hayden Rd. GU32: W Meo 2B 142
SO32: Warn 1A 142
Haydens Ct. SO41: Lymi 2F 234
Haydn Cl. SO23: Kin W 7M 91
Haydn Rd. RG22: B'toke 2M 59
Haydock Cl. GU34: Alt 6F 80
SO40: Tott 2J 171
Haydock M. PO7: W'lle 9B 182
Haydon Pl. GU14: Cov 4J 29
GU46: Yat 7A 18
Haydon Rd. BH13: Poole 4F 244
Hay Down La. SP11: Amp 2N 67
Haydown Leas SP11: Ver D 8E 6
Hayes Av. BH7: Bour 8B 228
Hayes Cl. PO15: Fare 6N 197
SO20: Ki S 9A **86** (7F 88)
Hayes Ct. PO5: S'sea 4E 240
Hayes Mead SO45: Hard 3N 207
Hayle Ct. SP10: A'ver 8B 52
Hayle Rd. PO6: Cosh 8A 200
SO18: Wes E 9F 160
Hayley Cl. SO45: Hythe 9L 193
Hayley La. RG29: L Sut 3D 62
Hayling Av. PO3: Ports 9H 215
Hayling Billy Bus. Cen. PO11: H Isl 3D 242
Hayling Billy Line Nature Reserve 4F 216
Hayling Cl. PO12: Gos 8L 213
PO14: Fare 9N 197
Hayling Golf Course 4C 242
HAYLING ISLAND 2G 242
Hayling Island Holiday Pk. PO11: H Isl 2F 242
Hayling Island Lifeboat Station & Mus. 5N 243
Hayling Island Sailing Club 4M 243
Haymarket Theatre 7C 42
Haynes Rd. SO18: South 3E 174
Haynes Way SO45: Dib P 8K 193
Hay Place La. GU34: Bins 2D 82
Hays Cotts. GU32: Ste 6K 139
Haysoms Cl. BH25: New M 5C 232
Hayter Gdns. SO51: Rom 4N 129
Hayters Way SP6: Ald 4D 152
Hayton Ct. SO40: Tott 3M 171
Hayward Bus. Cen. PO9: Hav 6H 203
Hayward Cl. SO40: Tott 3K 171
Hayward Ct. SO45: Holb 4A 208
Haywarden Pl. RG27: H Win 5C 26
Haywards Cotts. PO1: Ports 6K **5** (3B 240)
Haywood Dr. GU52: Fleet 4M 47
Hazel Av. GU14: Cov 9H 29
Hazelbank Cl. GU30: Lip 2F 116
GU31: Pet 9A 140
Hazelbank M. GU30: Lip 2F 116
Hazelby Cotts. RG20: Nth E 1M 7
Hazel Cl. BH23: Chri 5E 230
RG23: Oak 1D 58
SO21: Col C 3L 133
SO53: Cha F 2A 132
SP6: Ald 5D 152
SP10: A'ver 3K 69
Hazelcombe RG25: Over 3E 56
Hazel Coppice RG27: Hoo 1H 45
Hazel Ct. BH25: New M 5C 232
PO4: S'sea 3G 241
SO22: Winche 4G 105
Hazeldean Ct. PO9: R Cas 9H 183
Hazeldean Dr. PO9: R Cas 9H 183
Hazeldene RG24: Chin 1G 43
Hazeldene Ct. *BH8: Bour 7M 227*
(off Richmond Pk. Rd.)
Hazeldene Gdns. SO21: Itc A 8H 93
Hazeldene Rd. GU30: Lip 2N 115
Hazeldown Rd. SO16: Rown 6D 158
Hazeleigh Av. SO19: South 8C 174
HAZELEY
RG27 1L 25
SO21 3B 134
HAZELEY BOTTOM 4N 25
Hazeley Bottom RG27: H Win, Haze 3L 25
Hazeley Cl. RG27: H Win 5B 26
HAZELEY DOWN 3B 134
Hazeley Dr. GU51: Fleet 9H 27
Hazeley Enterprise Pk. SO21: Twyf 6M 127
Hazeley Grn. *PO9: Hav 4H 203*
(off Sharps Rd.)
HAZELEY HEATH 2M 25
HAZELEY LEA 9M 15
Hazeley Lea RG27: Haze 9M 15
Hazeley Rd. SO21: More, Twyf 7L 127
Hazel Farm Rd. SO40: Tott 3J 171
Hazel Grn. RG26: Bau 4D 10
Hazel Gro. GU26: Hind 6N 103
PO8: Clan 6C 168
SO22: Winche 9H 105
SO31: Loc H 7E 196
SO32: Bis W 3A 164
SO40: Ashu 7F 170

Hazelholt Dr.—Highclere Castle

Hazelholt Dr. PO9: Bed 6D **202**
Hazell Av. BH10: Bour 4F **226**
Hazell Rd. GU9: Farnh 8B **64**
Hazel Rd. GU34: Four M 4K **97**
PO8: Clan 6C **168**
SO19: South 6B **174**
SO41: Penn 2A **234**
Hazelton Cl. BH7: Bour 6D **228**
Hazel Wlk. GU31: Pet 3M **145**
Hazelwood PO14: Stub 3L **211**
RG24: Chin 8F **22**
Hazelwood Av. BH25: New M 2N **231**
PO9: Bed 6B **202**
Hazelwood Cl. RG23: B'toke 4M **41**
Hazelwood Ct. GU14: Cov 4G **29**
Hazelwood Dr. RG23: B'toke 4M **41**
Hazelwood Rd. SO18: South 1E **174**
Hazlemere Dr. BH24: St L 5B **186**
Hazleton Interchange PO8: Horn 4C **182**
Hazleton Way PO8: Cowp, Horn 7B **182**
PO8: Horn 5B **182**
HEADBOURNE WORTHY 9L **91**
Headbourne Worthy Ho. SO23: Winche 1M **105**
Head Down GU31: Pet 1A **146**
Headington Cl. RG22: B'toke 2M **59**
Headland Dr. SO31: Loc H 5D **196**
Headlands, The SP5: Down 1J **119** (7A **120**)
Headlands Adventure Cen. 7K **185**
Headlands Bus. Pk. BH24: Blas 7K **185**
HEADLEY
GU35 2A **102**
RG19 2J **9**
Headley Cl. PO13: Lee S 1B **238**
SO24: New A 2F **108**
HEADLEY DOWN 2D **102**
Headley Flds. GU35: Head 2A **102**
Headley Hill Rd. GU35: Head 2B **102**
Headley La. GU30: Pass 6A **102**
Headley Mill 3M **101**
Headley Pk. Cotts. GU35: Head 7M **83**
Headley Rd. GU26: Gray, Hind 3G **102**
GU30: Lip 1D **116**
GU35: Lind 2M **101**
Headlinglea BH13: Poole 2F **244**
Headmore La. GU34: Four M 6M **97**
Headon Ct. GU9: Farnh 9F **64**
Headon Vw. GU32: W Meo 8D **136**
Headquarters Rd. SP4: Bul C 3C **66**
Heads Farm Cl. BH10: Bour 1J **227**
Heads La. BH10: Bour 1J **227**
RG17: Ink 1J **7**
Headswell Av. BH10: Bour 2J **227**
Headswell Cres. BH10: Bour 2J **227**
Headswell Gdns. BH10: Bour 1J **227**
Heanor Cl. BH10: Bour 4G **227**
Hearmon Cl. GU46: Yat 7A **18**
HEARN 9D **84**
Hearne Gdns. SO32: Shi H 1C **178**
Hearn Va. GU35: Head D 9C **84**
Hearsey Gdns. GU17: Blackw 7D **18**
(not continuous)
Hearts of Oak M. SO41: Lymi 2D **234**
Heath, The PO7: Den 6H **181**
Heath Cl. GU9: Up H 3E **64**
GU12: Alders 1M **65**
GU26: Hind 9L **85**
PO8: Horn 3B **182**
SO50: Fair O 2A **162**
Heathcote Ct. *BH5: Bour* *1C **246***
(off Heathcote Rd.)
Heathcote Ho. BH5: Bour 2B **246**
Heathcote Pl. SO21: Hurs 6N **125**
Heathcote Rd. BH5: Bour 1C **246**
GU15: Camb 8M **19**
GU35: Bor 4J **101**
PO2: Ports 7G **215**
SO53: Cha F 6B **132**
Heath Cotts. GU26: Hind 1L **103**
Heath Ct. GU31: Pet 2M **145**
RG26: Bau 3E **10**
HEATH END
GU9 3E **64**
RG20 2M **7**
RG26 4F **10**
Heath End Farm RG26: Bau 4E **10**
Heath End Rd. RG26: Bau 5D **10**
Heathen St. SO32: Durl 7D **162**
Heatherbank Rd. BH4: Bour 2G **244**
Heatherbrae Gdns. SO52: N Bad 8E **130**
Heather Chase SO50: B'stke 1L **161**
Heather Cl. BH8: Bour 2A **228**
BH23: Walk 4J **231**
BH24: St L 5B **186**
GU11: Alders 1G **64**
GU35: W'hil 6G **101**
PO7: W'lle 3N **201**
PO13: Gos 6D **212**
SO40: Tott 3L **171**
SO41: Hor 3H **233**
Heather Cotts. GU26: Hind 8M **85**
Heather Ct. SO18: South 3G **175**
SO19: South 7C **174**
Heatherdale Rd. GU15: Camb 9L **19**
Heatherdeane Rd. SO17: South 9M **159**
Heatherdene Av. RG45: Cr'tne 1A **18**
Heatherdene Rd. SO53: Cha F 3C **132**
Heatherdown SO45: Dib P 9L **193**
Heather Dr. GU35: Lind 2L **101**
GU52: Ch Cr 6L **47**
RG26: Tadl 3F **10**
SP10: A'ver 9M **51**
Heatherfield GU31: Buri 7K **145**
Heather Gdns. GU14: Cov 1F **48**
PO15: Fare 6N **197**
Heather Grange BH24: Ashl H 3B **186**
Heather Gro. RG27: H Win 5B **26**
Heatherlands Ri. BH12: Poole 9B **226**
Heatherlands Rd. SO16: Chilw 3L **159**
Heather La. RG27: Up N 6C **44**
Heatherlea Rd. BH6: Bour 1G **247**
Heatherley Cl. GU15: Camb 8K **19**
Heatherley Ct. PO5: S'sea 4E **240**
Heatherley Rd. GU15: Camb 8K **19**
Heather Lodge BH25: New M 3B **232**
Heather Rd. BH10: Bour 3H **227**
GU31: Pet 1B **146**
SO45: Fawl 6D **208**
HEATHER ROW 5E **44**
Heather Row La. RG27: Nat S, Up N 4E **44**
Heathers, The SO50: E'leigh 1C **160**
Heatherstone Av. SO45: Dib P 9L **193**
Heatherton M. PO10: Ems 6M **203**
Heatherview Cl. SO52: N Bad 7E **130**
Heather Vw. Rd. BH12: Poole 7D **226**
Heather Way RG22: B'toke 3J **59**
HEATHFIELD
BH23 6H **221**
PO15 8N **197**
Heathfield RG22: B'toke 3M **59**
SO45: Hythe 7L **193**
Heathfield Av. BH12: Poole 8E **226**
PO15: Fare 8N **197**
Heathfield Caravan Pk. BH23: Bran 5H **221**
Heathfield Cl. SO19: South 7G **174**
SO53: Cha F 2A **132**
Heathfield Ct. GU51: Fleet 4K **47**
Heathfield Rd. GU31: Pet 1B **146**
PO2: Ports 8E **214**
SO19: South 7F **174**
SO53: Cha F 2A **132**
Heath Gdns. SO31: Net A 2H **195**
HEATH GREEN 9H **79**
Heath Grn. La. GU34: Meds 9H **79**
Heath Hill GU10: Dock 5A **84**
Heath Hill Rd. Nth. RG45: Cr'tne 1D **18**
Heath Hill Rd. Sth. RG45: Cr'tne 1D **18**
Heath Ho. Cl. SO30: Hed E 6M **175**
Heath Ho. Gdns. SO30: Hed E 6M **175**
Heath Ho. La. SO30: Hed E 6M **175**
Heathland Cl. GU51: Fleet 2A **48**
Heathlands RG20: Pen 3B **8**
RG26: Bau 4E **10**
SO32: Shed 3A **178**
SO41: Hor 3G **232**
Heathlands Cl. BH23: Burt 3M **229**
SO53: Cha F 4A **132**
Heathlands Ct. GU46: Yat 9A **18**
SO45: Dib P 9K **193**
Heathlands Rd. SO53: Cha F 4A **132**
Heathland St. GU11: Alders 9J **49**
Heath La. GU9: Up H 3E **64**
GU10: Cron, Ews 3L **63**
PO14: Titch 1H **211**
SN8: B'mre, Litt 3E **6**
SO42: Beau 9B **206**
SP11: Litt 4E **6**
Heath Lawns PO15: Fare 8N **197**
Heathman Rd. SO20: N Wal 1A **88**
Heath Ride RG45: Cr'tne 1M **17**
Heath Ri. GU15: Camb 8M **19**
Heath Rd. BH23: Walk 5K **231**
BH24: St L 4A **186**
GU27: Hasl 1M **117**
GU31: Pet 1M **145**
PO17: Wick 2H **179**
RG26: Pam H 4L **11**
SO19: South 5E **174**
SO31: Loc H 6C **196**
SO32: Sob H 2H **179**
SO41: Hor 3G **232**
SO52: N Bad 9F **130**
Heath Rd. E. BH23: Hurn 3C **218**
GU31: Pet 2A **146**
Heath Rd. Nth. SO31: Loc H 6C **196**
Heath Rd. Sth. SO31: Loc H 6C **196**
Heath Rd. W. BH24: Match 1B **218**
GU31: Pet 2N **145**
Heathrow Copse RG26: Bau 5D **10**
Heathside La. GU26: Hind 1M **103**
Heathside Way RG27: H Win 5B **26**
Heath Va. SP10: A'ver 2A **70**
Heathview RG27: Hoo 1J **45**
Heathway GU15: Camb 8M **19**
Heathway Cl. GU15: Camb 8M **19**
Heathwood Av. BH25: B Sea 6N **231**
Heathwood Cl. GU46: Yat 6N **17**
Heathwood Rd. BH9: Bour 6J **227**
Heathy Cl. BH25: B Sea 6A **232**
Heathyfields Rd. GU9: Up H 4B **64**
Heaton Rd. BH10: Bour 4F **226**
PO12: Gos 9H **213**
Heavytree Rd. BH14: Poole 1A **244**
Hebrides Cl. PO14: Stub 5L **211**
Hebron Ct. SO15: South 2A **4** (4K **173**)
HECKFIELD 7H **15**
Heckfield Cl. PO9: Hav 4H **203**
Heckfield Dr. GU51: Fleet 9H **27**
Hector Cl. PO7: Purb 7M **201**
Hector Rd. PO14: Fare 2C **212**
Hectors Ho. BH9: Bour 5K **227**
Heddon Wlk. GU14: Farn 5J **29**
Hedera Rd. SO31: Loc H 6C **196**
(not continuous)
Hedge Cft. GU46: Yat 7L **17**
HEDGE END 4N **175**
Hedge End *RG26: Tadl* *6J **11***
(off Mortimer Gdns.)
Hedge End Bus. Cen. SO30: Hed E 1M **175**
Hedge End Golf Cen. 4L **175**
Hedge End Retail Pk. SO30: Hed E 3L **175**
Hedge End Rd. SP10: A'ver 3A **70**
Hedge End Station (Rail) 8A **162**
Hedge End Trade Pk. SO30: Hed E 1L **175**
Hedge End Wlk. PO9: Hav 3J **203**
Hedgerley BH25: B Sea 6C **232**
Hedge Row *RG20: Bal H* *1M **7***
(off Gore End Rd.)
Hedgerow Cl. SO16: Rown 4D **158**
Hedgerow Dr. SO18: South 1F **174**
Hedgerow Gdns. PO10: Ems 6M **203**
Hedgerows, The RG24: Lych 3H **43**
Hedgerow Way SP11: E Ant 7B **52**
Hedges, The BH25: A'ley 2D **232**
SO50: E'leigh *1E **160***
(off Grantham Rd.)
Hedges Cl. SP9: Shi B 2A **66** (1F **66**)
Hedges Footpath SP10: A'ver 2M **69**
Hedley Cl. SO45: Fawl 7D **208**
Hedley Gdns. SO30: Hed E 9M **161**
Hedley Wlk. SO45: Fawl 7D **208**
Heenan Cl. GU16: Frim G 5N **29**
Heidelberg Rd. PO4: S'sea 3G **240**
Heidi Cl. PO12: Gos 1K **239**
Heights, The PO16: Fare 7F **198**
SO30: Hed E 4L **175**
Hei-Lin Way SP11: Ludg 1C **30**
Heinz Burt Cl. SO50: E'leigh 9D **132**
Hele Cl. RG21: B'toke 9B **42**
Helena Rd. PO4: S'sea 5G **240**
Helen Ct. GU14: Farn 8K **29**
Helen's Cl. GU34: Alt 6E **80**
Helford Ct. SP10: A'ver 8B **52**
Helford Gdns. SO18: Wes E 9F **160**
Helica Trade Cen. SO15: South 3D **172**
Helix Bus. Pk. GU15: Camb 1K **29**
HELL CORNER 1J **7**
Hellyer Rd. PO4: S'sea 4H **241**
Helm Cl. PO13: Gos 1F **238**
Helsby Cl. PO14: Fare 9A **198**
Helsted Cl. PO12: Gos 3G **238**
Helston Dr. PO10: Ems 6L **203**
Helston Rd. PO6: Cosh 8A **200**
Helvellyn Rd. SO16: South 2E **172**
Helyar Rd. BH8: Bour 4C **228**
Hemdean Gdns. SO30: Wes E 1H **175**
Hemingway Gdns. PO15: White 1F **196**
Hemlock Rd. PO8: Cowp 6L **181**
Hemlock Way SO53: Cha F 7L **131**
Hemming Cl. SO40: Tott 4L **171**
Hempland La. GU34: Priv 1K **137**
Hempsted Path PO6: Cosh 8C **200**
Hempsted Rd. PO6: Cosh 8C **200**
Hemsley Wlk. PO8: Cowp 6A **182**
Henderson Ct. SO41: Lymi 2F **234**
Henderson Mobile Home Pk. PO4: S'sea 4K **241**
Henderson Rd. PO4: S'sea 4J **241**
Hendford Gdns. BH10: Bour 4H **227**
Hendford Rd. BH10: Bour 4H **227**
Hendon Rd. GU35: Bor 5J **101**
Hendren Sq. SP10: A'ver 8B **52**
Hendy Cl. PO5: S'sea 4D **240**
Hengest Cl. SP10: Charl 7K **51**
Hengistbury Head Nature Reserve 1M **247**
Hengistbury Ho. *BH23: Chri* *8N **229***
(off Purewell)
Hengistbury Rd. BH6: Bour 1J **247**
BH25: B Sea 6N **231**
Hengist Pk. (Caravan Pk.) BH6: Bour 1L **247**
Hengist Rd. BH1: Bour 1A **246**
HENLEY 5C **6**
Henley Cl. GU14: Cov 4G **28**
Henley Dr. GU16: Frim G 5N **29**
Henley Gdns. BH7: Bour 7D **228**
GU46: Yat 8N **17**
PO15: Fare 5N **197**
Henley Rd. PO4: S'sea 5G **240**
Henry Cl. SO45: Hard 2N **207**
Henry Cort Dr. PO15: Fare 6M **197**
Henry Player Av. PO12: Gos 2M **239**
Henry Rd. SO15: South 3G **173**
SO50: B'stke 8H **133**
Henry St. PO12: Gos 3L **239**
SO15: South 1B **4** (4L **173**)
Henstead Ct. SO15: South 2B **4** (4L **173**)
Henstead Rd. SO15: South 2B **4** (4L **173**)
HENSTING 6A **134**
Hensting La. SO21: Owls 6A **134**
SO50: Fis P, Hens 5M **133**
Henty Rd. SO16: South 2G **172**
Henville Cl. PO13: Gos 8F **212**
Henville Rd. BH8: Bour 9N **227**
Henwood Down GU31: Pet 1N **145**
Hepburn Ct. *BH23: Chri* *8J **229***
(off King's Av.)
Hepplewhite Cl. RG26: Bau 4E **10**
Hepplewhite Dr. RG22: B'toke 3J **59**
Hepworth Cl. SO19: South 8G **174**
SP10: A'ver 9N **51**
Hepworth Cft. GU47: Coll 7G **18**
Herald Ct. GU12: Alders 1M **65**
Herald Ind. Est. SO30: Hed E 1M **175**
Herald Rd. SO30: Hed E 1M **175**
Herbert Av. BH12: Poole 6A **226**
Herbert Ct. BH12: Poole 6B **226**
Herberton Rd. BH6: Bour 9F **228**
Herbert Rd. BH4: Bour 3F **244**
BH25: New M 3C **232**
GU51: Fleet 2K **47**
PO4: S'sea 5F **240**
PO12: Gos 2H **239**
SP5: Woodf 2M **119** (8C **120**)
Herbert St. PO1: Ports 9D **214**
Herbert Walker Av. SO15: South 7A **4** (5F **172**)
(not continuous)
Herbs End GU14: Cov 7E **28**
Hercules St. PO2: Ports 8E **214**
Hercules Way GU14: Farn 4H **49**
Herdman Ho. *GU34: Alt* *4G **80***
(off York M.)
Herdwick Rd. SP11: E Ant 6C **52**
Hereford Cl. RG29: Odi 9J **45**
Hereford Ct. BH23: Chri 8J **229**
PO5: S'sea *4E **240***
(off Hereford Rd.)
PO13: Gos 1E **238**
Hereford La. GU9: Up H 4D **64**
Hereford Mead GU51: Fleet 8N **27**
Hereford Rd. PO5: S'sea 4E **240**
RG23: B'toke 6L **41**
Hereward Cl. SO51: Rom 5A **130**
Heritage Bus. Pk. PO12: Gos 7H **213**
Heritage Gdns. PO16: Portc 1J **213**
Heritage Pk. RG22: B'toke 5K **59**
Heritage Vw. RG22: B'toke 5K **59**
Heritage Way PO12: Gos 7J **213**
PO13: Gos 7G **213**
Hermes Cl. GU51: Fleet 2A **48**
Hermes Ct. PO12: Gos 8L **213**
Hermes Rd. PO13: Lee S 9N **211**
HERMITAGE 8N **203**
Hermitage, The PO10: S'brne 8N **203**
Hermitage Cl. BH25: A'ley 2D **232**
GU14: Farn 2M **49**
GU34: Alt 6E **80**
PO9: Hav 5E **202**
SO32: Bis W 3K **163**
Hermitage Gdns. PO7: W'lle 1N **201**
Herm Rd. BH12: Poole 5B **226**
Herne Farm Leisure Centre, The 1N **145**
Herne Rd. GU31: Pet 1N **145**
PO6: Cosh 9F **200**
Hern La. SP6: Stuc 4K **153**
Heron Cl. GU34: Alt 2F **80**
GU52: Ch Cr 5A **48**
PO4: S'sea 2J **241**
SO41: Sway 6J **223**
Heron Ct. GU47: Sandh 6E **18**
Heron Ct. Rd. BH3: Bour 7L **227**
BH9: Bour 7L **227**
Herondale GU27: Hasl 9N **103**
Heron Ho. PO5: S'sea 5F **240**
Heron La. SO51: Tims 7K **123**
Heron Pk. RG24: Lych 2G **43**
Heron Quay PO10: S'brne 1N **217**
Herons Cl. PO14: Stub 4M **211**
Herons Mead BH8: Bour 1A **228**
Heron Sq. SO50: E'leigh 1C **160**
Herons Ri. SP10: A'ver 3A **70**
Herons Wood SO40: Calm 9K **157**
Heronswood RG29: Odi 7M **45**
Heron Way PO13: Gos 5D **212**
RG22: B'toke 2H **59**
Heron Wood Rd. GU12: Alders 2M **65**
Herretts Gdns. GU12: Alders 1M **65**
Herrett St. GU12: Alders 2M **65**
HERRIARD 9H **61**
Herriard Grn. RG25: Herr 1M **79**
Herriard Pl. RG22: B'toke 5J **59**
Herriard Way RG26: Tadl 6J **11**
Herrick Cl. SO19: South 6H **175**
Herridge Cl. RG26: B'ley 2J **23**
Herriot Ct. GU46: Yat 9M **17**
Herriot Ho. PO8: Cowp 7A **182**
Herriott Cl. PO8: Cowp 5A **182**
Hertford Cl. SP6: F'dge 8J **151**
Hertford Pl. PO1: Ports 9E **214**
Hertsfield PO14: Titch C 6F **196**
Hesketh Cl. BH24: St I 3D **186**
Hesketh Ho. SO15: South 4H **173**
Hestan Cl. BH23: Chri 2G **229**
Hester Rd. PO4: S'sea 3J **241**
Hesters Vw. RG29: L Sut 5E **62**
Hestia Cl. SO51: Rom 4B **130**
Heston Wlk. PO12: Gos 4G **238**
Hevalo Cl. BH1: Bour 9B **228**
Hewett Cl. PO14: Titch 1J **211**
Hewett Ho. PO14: Titch 1J **211**
Hewett Rd. PO2: Ports 6F **214**
PO14: Titch 1J **211**
Hewetts Ri. SO31: Wars 9N **195**
Hewitt Cl. PO12: Gos 1J **239**
Hewitt Rd. RG24: B'toke 1C **42**
Hewitt's Rd. SO15: South 5J **173**
Hewlett Ct. PO16: Fare 8E **198**
Hewshott Gro. GU30: Lip 1G **117**
Hewshott La. GU30: Lip 1E **116**
Hexagon, The SP10: A'ver 3K **69**
Hexagon Centre, The SO53: Cha F 1A **160**
Hexham Cl. GU47: Owl 3F **18**
Heye's Dr. SO19: South 7G **174**
Heyford Cl. *SP4: Ames* *5A **66***
(off Raleigh Cres.)
Heysham Rd. SO15: South 2G **173**
Heyshott Gdns. PO8: Clan 7D **168**
Heyshott Rd. PO4: S'sea 3G **241**
Heytesbury Rd. BH6: Bour 9G **229**
Heyward Rd. PO4: S'sea 4F **240**
Heywood Gdns. PO9: Hav 3D **202**
Heywood Grn. SO19: South 5J **175**
Hibberd Ct. BH10: Bour 5H **227**
Hibberd Ri. SO30: Hed E 9M **161**
Hibberds Fld. BH21: Cran 6J **149**
Hibberd Way BH10: Bour 5H **227**
Hibiscus Cres. SP10: A'ver 2J **69**
Hibiscus Gro. GU35: Bor 5K **101**
Hickes Cl. BH11: Bour 2D **226**
Hickley Path PO16: Fare 7E **198**
Hickory Dr. SO22: Winche 2H **105**
Hickory Gdns. SO30: Wes E 8G **161**
Hicks Cl. RG26: Tadl 5J **11**
Hicks La. GU17: Blackw 8D **18**
Hides Cl. RG28: Whit 6G **55**
Hides Hill La. SO42: Beau 4D **206**
Highams Cl. RG20: Kings 2C **6**
Highbank Av. PO7: Wid 6J **201**
Highbank Gdns. SP6: F'dge 1J **153**
High Beeches GU16: Frim 2M **29**
High Beech Gdns. SP10: A'ver 2B **70**
HIGHBRIDGE 5H **133**
Highbridge Rd. BH14: Poole 2A **244**
SO21: Twyf 4J **133**
SO50: B'dge, Highb 5G **132**
Highbury Bldgs. PO6: Cosh 2G **215**
Highbury Cl. BH25: New M 3C **232**
SO50: Fair O 2N **161**
Highbury College Community Sports Cen. 2H **215**
Highbury Gro. PO6: Cosh 2G **215**
Highbury Rd. SP11: An V 5K **69**
Highbury St. PO1: Ports 6K **5** (3B **240**)
Highbury Way PO6: Cosh 2G **214**
HIGHCLERE 4A **8**
Highclere Av. PO9: Hav 5D **202**
Highclere Castle 6B **8**

Highclere Hall—Hinwood Cl.

Highclere Hall *BH1: Bour* . . . 1A 246 *(off Manor Rd.)*
Highclere Rd. GU12: Alders . . . 2M 65
SO16: South . . . 8J 159
HIGHCLERE STREET . . . 5A 8
Highclere Way SO53: Cha F . . . 9M 131
Highcliff Av. SO14: South . . . 2M 173
HIGHCLIFFE
BH23 . . . 6J 231
SO23 . . . 8N 105
Highcliffe Castle . . . 7G 231
Highcliffe Castle Golf Course . . . 7G 230
Highcliffe Cnr. BH23: Highc . . . 6K 231
Highcliffe Dr. SO50: E'leigh . . . 5E 132
Highcliffe Ho. BH23: Highc . . . 6K 231
Highcliffe Rd. BH23: Chri . . . 6C 230
PO12: Gos . . . 3H 239
SO23: Winche . . . 8M 105
High Common Nature Reserve . . . 2L 113
High Copse GU9: Up H . . . 4C 64
High Ct. PO4: S'sea . . . 4H 241
Highcroft Ind. Est. PO8: Horn . . . 2C 182
Highcroft La. PO8: Horn . . . 2C 182
Highcroft Rd. SO22: Winche . . . 7G 105
HIGH CROSS . . . 3F 138
High Cross GU32: Frox . . . 3E 138
High Cross La. GU32: Frox . . . 5B 138
Highcrown M. SO17: South . . . 9M 159
Highcrown St. SO17: South . . . 9M 159
Highdown GU51: Fleet . . . 1M 47
Highdowns RG22: B'toke . . . 4L 59
High Dr. PO13: Gos . . . 7E 212
RG22: B'toke . . . 9L 41
Higher End La. SP6: Hale . . . 1A 154
Higher Mead RG24: Lych . . . 3G 43
HIGHFIELD . . . 9M 159
Highfield RG20: Ashm . . . 7M 7
SO21: Twyf . . . 8L 127
SO41: Lymi . . . 3D 234
Highfield Av. BH24: Ring . . . 9K 185
GU11: Alders . . . 3J 65
PO7: W'lle . . . 9N 181
PO14: Fare . . . 9B 198
SO17: South . . . 8L 159
SO21: Twyf . . . 8L 127
SO41: Lymi . . . 3C 234
Highfield Chase RG21: B'toke . . . 6A 42
Highfield Cl. GU11: Alders . . . 2K 65
GU14: Cov . . . 8H 29
PO7: W'lle . . . 9N 181
SO17: South . . . 9M 159
SO41: Sway . . . 5J 223
SO53: Cha F . . . 6C 132
Highfield Ct. SO32: Bis W . . . 3K 163
Highfield Cres. GU26: Hind . . . 3N 103
SO17: South . . . 9N 159
SP5: Mid W . . . 5G 87
Highfield Dr. BH24: Ring . . . 8K 185
Highfield Gdns. GU11: Alders . . . 2J 65
GU33: Liss . . . 1G 140
SO41: Sway . . . 5J 223
Highfield Hall SO17: South . . . 9M 159
Highfield La. GU30: Lip . . . 4F 116
SO17: South . . . 9M 159
SP5: Woodf . . . 3M 119 (8C 120)
Highfield Pde. PO7: W'lle . . . 9A 182
Highfield Path GU14: Cov . . . 8H 29
Highfield Rd. BH9: Bour . . . 4J 227
BH24: Ring . . . 9K 185
GU14: Cov . . . 8H 29
GU32: Pet . . . 9M 139
PO1: Ports . . . 2E 240
PO12: Gos . . . 1H 239
SO17: South . . . 1L 173
SO41: Lymi . . . 2C 234
SO53: Cha F . . . 6C 132
Highfields RG25: Over . . . 3E 56
SO17: South . . . 1N 173
SO31: Wars . . . 8C 196
Highfield Ter. SO22: Winche . . . 8K 237 (7J 105)
High Firs Gdns. SO51: Rom . . . 5B 130
High Firs Rd. SO19: South . . . 5F 174
SO51: Rom . . . 4B 130
Highgate La. GU14: Farn . . . 7L 29
Highgate Rd. PO3: Ports . . . 7H 215
Highgrove GU14: Farn . . . 5K 29
Highgrove Cl. SO40: Tott . . . 5K 171
Highgrove Ind. Pk. PO3: Ports . . . 5J 215
Highgrove Rd. PO3: Ports . . . 8J 215
High Howe Cl. BH11: Bour . . . 2C 226
High Howe Gdns. BH11: Bour . . . 2C 226
High Howe La. BH11: Bour . . . 2C 226
Highland Av. BH23: Highc . . . 5K 231
Highland Cl. PO10: Ems . . . 9L 203
Highland Dr. GU51: Fleet . . . 8N 27
RG23: Oak . . . 9C 40
Highland Rd. BH14: Poole . . . 9A 226
GU12: Alders . . . 9M 49
GU15: Camb . . . 5N 19
PO4: S'sea . . . 5G 240
PO10: Ems . . . 8L 203
Highlands Cl. SO45: Dib P . . . 7M 193
SO52: N Bad . . . 7D 130
Highlands Cres. BH10: Bour . . . 2G 226
Highlands Ho. SO19: South . . . 7B 174
Highlands Rd. BH25: B Sea . . . 6B 232
GU9: H End . . . 3E 64
PO6: Dray . . . 9L 201
PO15: Fare . . . 9L 197
PO16: Fare . . . 6A 198
RG22: Wort . . . 8J 41
SP10: A'ver . . . 2B 70
Highland St. PO4: S'sea . . . 5H 241
Highlands Way SO45: Dib P . . . 7L 193
SP5: W'psh . . . 5H 121
Highland Ter. PO4: S'sea . . . 4G 241
High La. SP5: Br Ch . . . 3A 118
High Lawn Way PO9: Hav . . . 4E 202
High Marryats BH25: B Sea . . . 7A 232
High Mead PO15: Fare . . . 6A 198
High Mdw. SO19: South . . . 4G 174
Highmoor Cl. BH14: Poole . . . 2A 244
Highmoor Rd. BH11: Bour . . . 5E 226
BH14: Poole . . . 2A 244
Highmoors RG24: Chin . . . 9G 22
Highmount Cl. SO23: Winche . . . 7M 105
Highnam Gdns. SO31: Sar G . . . 5C 196
High Oaks Cl. SO31: Loc H . . . 6D 196
High Oaks Gdns. BH11: Bour . . . 2C 226
High Pk. Rd. GU9: Farnh . . . 7D 64
Highpath Ct. RG24: B'toke . . . 4M 41
Highpath M. RG24: B'toke . . . 4M 41
Highpath Way RG24: B'toke . . . 3L 41
High Pines BH23: Chri . . . 6F 230
High Pitfold GU26: Hind . . . 6M 103
High Point BH14: Poole . . . 1A 244
Highridge GU34: Alt . . . 5D 80
High Ridge Cres. BH25: A'ley . . . 3D 232
High Rd. SO16: S'ing . . . 8B 160
SP5: Bish, Br Ch . . . 3A 118
High St. BH21: Cran . . . 6J 149
BH23: Chri . . . 8L 229
BH24: Ashl H . . . 2B 186
BH24: Ring . . . 1J 187
GU10: Rowl . . . 8N 63
GU11: Alders . . . 9J 49
GU12: Alders . . . 1L 65
GU14: Farn . . . 3M 49
GU15: Camb . . . 7M 19
GU31: Buri . . . 7K 145
GU31: Pet . . . 1M 145
GU32: E Meon . . . 3L 143
GU32: Pet . . . 1M 145
GU32: W Meo . . . 8D 136
GU34: Alt . . . 5F 80
GU34: Meds . . . 9K 79
GU34: Selb . . . 7L 99
GU35: Bor . . . 5J 101
GU35: Head . . . 2A 102
GU47: Sandh . . . 4B 18 (Church Rd.)
GU47: Sandh . . . 4B 18 (Mountbatten Ri.)
PO1: Ports . . . 7J 5 (4B 240)
PO6: Cosh . . . 1G 214
PO7: H'don . . . 8E 166
PO10: Ems . . . 9M 203
PO12: Gos . . . 3M 239
PO13: Lee S . . . 1A 238
PO14: Titch . . . 9J 197
PO16: Fare . . . 8E 198
PO17: S'wick . . . 3A 200
PO31: Cowes . . . 5P 237
RG25: Over . . . 2D 56
RG27: H Win . . . 6C 26
RG29: Odi . . . 8K 45
RG45: Cr'tne . . . 1E 18
SN8: Co Du . . . 2H 31
SO14: South . . . 6C 4 (6M 173)
SO20: Brou . . . 1A 86 (4A 88)
SO20: N Wal . . . 1A 88
SO20: S Bri . . . 2F 88
SO21: Twyf . . . 8L 127
SO23: Winche . . . 8P 237 (7M 105) (Bridge St.)
SO23: Winche . . . 7L 237 (6K 105) (Tower St., not continuous)
SO30: Botl . . . 3C 176
SO30: Wes E . . . 9G 161
SO31: Burs . . . 2L 195
SO31: Hamb . . . 7L 195
SO32: Bis W . . . 4M 163
SO32: Drox . . . 2K 165
SO32: Meon . . . 8N 135
SO32: Shi H . . . 3B 178
SO32: Sob . . . 8K 165
SO40: Tott . . . 3N 171
SO41: Lymi . . . 3E 234
SO41: M Sea . . . 8K 235
SO42: Beau . . . 8E 206
SO43: Lyn . . . 2B 148 (2N 189)
SO45: Hythe . . . 4M 193
SO50: E'leigh . . . 2E 160 (Desborough Rd., not continuous)
SO50: E'leigh . . . 1E 160 (Wells Pl., not continuous)
SP4: Bul . . . 3A 66
SP5: Down . . . 2L 119 (7B 120)
SP5: P'tn . . . 6E 86
SP6: Dame . . . 3P 149
SP6: F'dge . . . 1J 153
SP6: Woodg . . . 2A 154
SP9: Shi B . . . 1B 66 (1G 66)
SP10: A'ver . . . 2N 69
SP11: Grat . . . 4L 67
SP11: Ludg . . . 1C 30 (5K 31)
SP11: Monx . . . 4C 68
SP11: Wher . . . 2E 74
High Thicket Rd. GU10: Dock . . . 4N 83
HIGHTOWN
BH24 . . . 2N 187
SO19 . . . 7H 175
Hightown Gdns. BH24: Ring . . . 2L 187
Hightown Hill BH24: Hight, Pic H . . . 2N 187
Hightown Ind. Est. BH24: Ring . . . 2L 187
Hightown Rd. BH24: Hight, Ring . . . 2K 187
Hightown Towers SO19: South . . . 6J 175
High Trees BH13: Poole . . . 5E 244
PO7: W'lle . . . 1N 201
SO50: Fair O . . . 1B 162
Hightrees SO41: Penn . . . 5D 234
Hightrees Av. BH8: Bour . . . 5B 228
High Trees Dr. SO22: Winche . . . 4J 105
High Vw. GU32: Pet . . . 9M 139
PO16: Portc . . . 8L 199
Highview Bus. Cen. GU35: Bor . . . 4H 101
Highview Bus. Pk. RG27: Hoo . . . 3D 44
High Vw. Cl. GU14: Farn . . . 8J 29
Highview Cl. BH23: Chri . . . 3H 229
Highview Ct. BH23: Highc . . . 7J 231
Highview Gdns. BH12: Poole . . . 7A 226
High Vw. Lodge GU11: Alders . . . 9J 49
High Vw. Rd. GU14: Farn . . . 8J 29
High Vw. Way SO18: South . . . 2D 174
High Wlk. PO15: Fare . . . 6A 198
Highway, The SP5: Ch St . . . 4N 119
Highways Rd. SO21: Comp . . . 8G 127
HIGHWOOD . . . 3A 188
Highwood Cl. GU46: Yat . . . 9M 17
SP6: Ald . . . 4A 152
Highwood La. BH24: Highw . . . 7M 185
SO51: Rom . . . 4B 130
Highwood Lawn PO9: Hav . . . 2D 202
Highwood Ridge RG22: B'toke . . . 4K 59
Highwood Rd. BH14: Poole . . . 1C 244
PO13: Gos . . . 9E 212
SO42: Broc . . . 8C 148 (9N 189)
Highworth Cotts. RG26: Bau . . . 4C 10
Higworth La. PO11: H Isl . . . 2F 242
Hilary Av. PO6: Cosh . . . 1H 215
Hilary Ct. PO13: Gos . . . 1F 238
Hilda Gdns. PO7: Den . . . 7H 181
Hilda Pl. *SO14: South* . . . 5A 174 *(off Kent St.)*
Hilda Rd. BH12: Poole . . . 8C 226
Hilden Way SO22: Lit . . . 1E 104
Hilder Gdns. GU14: Farn . . . 9M 29
Hilfield GU46: Yat . . . 8B 18
HILL . . . 4K 173
Hilland Ri. GU35: Head . . . 3B 102
Hillary Cl. PO16: Fare . . . 7B 198
SO43: Lyn . . . 4C 148
Hillary Rd. BH23: Chri . . . 6A 230
RG21: B'toke . . . 4A 42
Hill Barn La. SO21: Lwr B, Sut S . . . 6C 76
Hillborough Ct. PO5: S'sea . . . 4E 240
Hillborough Cres. PO5: S'sea . . . 4E 240
Hillbrook Ri. GU9: Up H . . . 4D 64
HILL BROW . . . 3G 141
Hill Brow Cl. PO9: R Cas . . . 9H 183
Hillbrow Cl. PO15: Fare . . . 6N 197
Hill Brow Rd. GU33: Hi Br, Liss . . . 1E 140
Hillbrow Rd. BH6: Bour . . . 8E 228
Hillbury Av. SP10: A'ver . . . 3L 69
Hillbury Pk. (Mobile Home Pk.) SP6: Ald . . . 5D 152
Hillbury Rd. SP6: Ald . . . 4D 152
Hill Cl. BH23: Bran . . . 7C 220
SO50: Fair O . . . 7N 133
SP6: Woodg . . . 2A 154
Hill Coppice Rd. PO15: White . . . 3G 197
Hill Corner Farm Caravan Pk. GU14: Cov . . . 5F 28
Hill Cottage Farm Caravan Pk. SP6: Ald . . . 3C 152
Hill Cottage Gdns. SO18: Wes E . . . 8E 160
Hillcrest *GU9: H End* . . . 2F 64 *(off Up. Weybourne La.)*
GU51: Fleet . . . 9M 27
RG26: Tadl . . . 4H 11
Hillcrest Av. SO53: Cha F . . . 6B 132
Hillcrest Cl. BH9: Bour . . . 3L 227
SO52: N Bad . . . 7E 130
Hillcrest Ct. RG23: B'toke . . . 5K 41
Hillcrest Dr. SO53: Cha F . . . 6B 132
Hillcrest Gdns. SO32: Wal C . . . 7N 163
Hillcrest Mobile Home Pk.
SP4: Ames . . . 5A 66 *(off Porton Rd.)*
Hillcrest Rd. BH9: Bour . . . 3L 227
Hillcrest Wlk. RG23: B'toke . . . 6K 41
Hill Cft. PO15: Seg . . . 6G 197
Hillcroft SP5: Woodf . . . 2M 119 (8C 120)
Hillcroft Cl. SO41: Lymi . . . 2E 234
Hilldene Way SO30: Wes E . . . 1H 175
Hillditch SO41: Lymi . . . 9D 224
Hilldown Rd. SO17: South . . . 9N 159
Hilldowns Av. PO2: Ports . . . 6D 214
Hill Dr. PO15: Fare . . . 6N 197
Hill End Rd. RG26: M She . . . 4M 21
Hiller Wlk. PO13: Lee S . . . 1B 238
Hill Farm Rd. SO15: South . . . 4K 173
SO24: Monk . . . 5J 111
Hillgarth GU26: Hind . . . 2M 103
HILL GROVE . . . 6E 164
Hill Gro. La. SO32: Swanm . . . 6E 164
Hillgrove Rd. SO18: South . . . 8D 160
HILL HEAD . . . 6L 211
HILLHEAD . . . 9K 209
Hill Head Rd. PO14: Stub . . . 7K 211
Hill Head Sailing Club . . . 8L 211
Hill Ho. Hill GU30: Lip . . . 8B 102
Hillhouse La.
RG19: Ashf H, Head . . . 3K 9
HILL HOUSES . . . 9D 108
Hill Houses La. SO24: Cher . . . 9D 108
Hillier Way SO23: Winche . . . 4L 105
Hill La. BH23: Bran . . . 7C 220
BH23: Wat . . . 4A 230
GU31: E Har, S Hart . . . 9H 147
SO15: South . . . 1A 4 (8J 159)
SO16: South . . . 8J 159
SO21: Col C . . . 3K 133
Hillman Rd. BH14: Poole . . . 9B 226
Hillmead Gdns. PO9: Bed . . . 7B 202
Hill Meadow RG25: Over . . . 9D 38
Hillmorton Ct. *BH8: Bour* . . . 9L 227 *(off Wellington Rd.)*
HILL PARK . . . 6N 197
Hill Pk. Rd. PO12: Gos . . . 1H 239
PO15: Fare . . . 5N 197
Hill Pl. SO31: Burs . . . 1M 195
HILLPOUND . . . 7E 164
Hill Ri. SO21: Twyf . . . 7L 127
SO32: Meon . . . 8N 135
Hill Rd. BH24: Match . . . 1D 218
GU9: H End . . . 3E 64
GU26: Gray . . . 4L 103
GU26: Hind . . . 1L 103
PO16: Portc . . . 8M 199
RG23: Oak . . . 1C 58
SO21: Bar S . . . 7N 71
Hillsborough Ct. GU14: Cov . . . 4G 29
HILL SIDE
GU33 . . . 3G 140
RG29 . . . 9N 45
Hillside GU15: Camb . . . 6H 19
RG26: Bau . . . 9D 10
RG28: Whit . . . 5J 55
SO22: Lit . . . 1F 104
SO32: Curd . . . 2J 177
SP11: Abb A . . . 5F 68
SP11: Upt . . . 1M 33
Hillside Av. PO7: Wid . . . 7J 201
SO18: South . . . 1C 174
SO51: Rom . . . 5N 129
Hillside Camping & Caravan Site
BH21: Cran . . . 9M 149
Hillside Cl. GU34: Alt . . . 3F 80
GU35: Head D . . . 1C 102
GU51: Cr V . . . 5H 47
PO8: Cath . . . 8C 168
SO22: Winche . . . 4G 105
SO53: Cha F . . . 6B 132
SP5: W Dean . . . 2J 121
Hillside Ct. SP10: A'ver . . . 2M 69
Hillside Cres. GU16: Frim . . . 5N 29
PO6: Cosh . . . 8A 200
Hillside Dr. BH23: Chri . . . 2G 228
Hillside Ind. Est. PO8: Horn . . . 2C 182
Hill Side La. GU33: Hi Br . . . 3G 141
Hillside La. GU9: H End . . . 2F 64
Hillside M. SO31: Sar G . . . 3A 196
Hillside Rd. BH12: Poole . . . 5D 226
GU9: Weyb . . . 3G 65
GU11: Alders . . . 2H 65
GU27: Hasl . . . 1N 117
RG29: Odi . . . 1F 62
SO21: Spar . . . 5N 89
SO22: Winche . . . 5G 104
SO41: Lymi . . . 3C 234
Hillside Vs. SP10: Charl . . . 8L 51
Hillsley Rd. PO6: Cosh . . . 7A 200
Hillson Dr. PO15: Fare . . . 6M 197
Hillson Ho. PO15: Fare . . . 6N 197
Hillsons Rd. SO30: Curd . . . 3E 176
Hill Sq. RG24: Lych . . . 2H 43
Hillstead Ct. RG21: B'toke . . . 7D 42
HILLSTREET . . . 6J 157
Hill St. SO19: South . . . 7B 174
SO40: Calm . . . 5J 157
Hills Way RG26: B'ley . . . 2G 23
Hill Ter. SO24: New A . . . 9F 94
SO50: Fair O . . . 7N 133
HILL TOP . . . 5H 207
Hilltop SO22: Lit . . . 1G 104
Hill Top Av. SP9: Tidw . . . 6C 30 (6G 30)
Hilltop Cres. PO6: Cosh . . . 7K 201
Hilltop Dr. SO19: South . . . 6H 175
Hilltop Gdns. PO8: Horn . . . 8D 168
Hilltop Rd. PO17: S'wick . . . 7B 200
RG25: Over . . . 9E 38
SO42: Beau . . . 5G 206
Hilltop Vw. GU46: Yat . . . 8L 17
Hill Vw. GU32: E Meon . . . 3L 143
Hillview GU29: Els . . . 8N 147
PO8: Horn . . . 5C 182
Hillview Manor Pk. Homes SO50: Fair O . . . 7M 133
Hill Vw. Rd. BH10: Bour . . . 2H 227
GU9: Farnh . . . 8B 64
PO16: Portc . . . 8L 199
RG22: B'toke . . . 8N 41
SO51: Brai . . . 7B 124
SO51: Mich . . . 5H 123
Hillview Rd. SO45: Hythe . . . 6L 193
Hill Wlk. PO15: Fare . . . 6N 197
Hill Way BH24: Ashl H . . . 3C 186
Hillway, The PO16: Portc . . . 9L 199
SO53: Cha F . . . 5B 132
Hilly Cl. SO21: Owls . . . 5C 134
HILLYFIELDS . . . 8C 158
Hillyfields SO16: Nur . . . 7C 158
HILSEA . . . 3F 214
Hilsea Cres. PO2: Ports . . . 3F 214
Hilsea Lido . . . 3F 214
HILSEA LINES . . . 3H 215
Hilsea Mkt. PO2: Ports . . . 3F 214
Hilsea Station (Rail) . . . 4H 215
HILTINGBURY . . . 3B 132
Hiltingbury Cl. SO53: Cha F . . . 3B 132
Hiltingbury Ct. SO53: Cha F . . . 3N 131
Hiltingbury Rd. PO9: Hav . . . 4G 203
SO53: Cha F . . . 3N 131
Hiltom Rd. BH24: Ring . . . 1L 187
Hilton Grange BH1: Bour . . . 1N 245
Hilton Rd. BH25: New M . . . 2C 232
PO12: Gos . . . 4L 239
SO30: Hed E . . . 3N 175
HINCHESLEA . . . 9L 189
Hindell Cl. GU14: Farn . . . 4J 29
HINDHEAD . . . 3N 103
Hindhead Golf Course . . . 1K 103
Hindhead Rd. GU26: Hind . . . 8N 103
GU27: Hasl, Hind . . . 8N 103
Hines Ct. RG24: B'toke . . . 3M 41
Hinkler Ct. SO19: South . . . 6H 175
Hinkler Rd. SO19: South . . . 4J 175
Hinstock Cl. GU14: Cov . . . 9J 29
HINTON . . . 3H 231
Hinton Admiral M. BH23: Hin . . . 4G 230
Hinton Admiral Station (Rail) . . . 4G 231
HINTON AMPNER . . . 1L 135
Hinton Ampner House & Gardens . . . 1L 135
Hinton Broad La. SO24: Cher, Hin A, Tich . . . 5E 108
Hinton Cl. PO9: Hav . . . 5C 202
RG26: Tadl . . . 6H 11
Hinton Cres. SO19: South . . . 5J 175
Hinton Flds. SO23: Kin W . . . 9N 91
Hinton Hill SO24: Hin A . . . 1L 135
Hinton Ho. Dr. SO23: Kin W . . . 9N 91
Hinton Mnr. La. PO8: Cath, Clan, Love . . . 9M 167
Hinton Rd. BH1: Bour . . . 7M 247 (2K 245)
Hinton Va. SO24: Cher . . . 1K 135
Hinton Wood BH1: Bour . . . 8N 247 (3L 245)
Hinton Wood Av. BH23: Chri . . . 4G 231
Hinton Wood La. BH23: Hin . . . 4G 230
Hinwood Cl. SO20: Brou . . . 1A 86

Hipley—Hopfield Rd.

HIPLEY .6N 179
Hipley Rd. PO9: Hav .6G 202
HIPPENSCOMBE .8B 6
Hipple La. RG20: Ashm .7M 7
Hirst Copse SP11: S M Bo .9M 35
Hirst Rd. SO45: Hythe .6N 193
Hispano Av. PO15: White .2F 196
Historic Dockyard
Portsmouth .3H 5 (2A 240)
Hitches La. GU51: Cr V, Fleet .5H 47
Hitherwood Cl. PO7: W'lle .9B 182
Hive Gdns. BH13: S'bks .7B 244
Hives Way SO41: Lymi .9D 224
H Jones Cres. GU11: Alders .8L 49
HM Immigration Removal Cen. Haslar
PO12: Gos .6L 239
HMP Kingston PO3: Ports .1G 241
HMP Winchester SO22: Winche .7H 237 (6J 105)
HMS Alliance .4N 239
HM Sub Holland 1 .4N 239
HMS Victory .2H 5 (1A 240)
HMS Warrior 1860 .4H 5 (2A 240)
Hoadlands GU31: Pet .9N 139
Hoads Hill PO17: Wick .8D 178
Hobart Dr. SO45: Hythe .6M 193
Hobart Rd. BH25: New M .4A 232
Hobb La. SO30: Hed E .5A 176
Hobbs Cl. SO24: Bis S .2L 109
Hobbs Ct. RG24: B'toke .2M 41
SO50: Fair O .9M 133
Hobbs Pk. BH24: St L .4C 186
Hobbs Pas. PO12: Gos .3N 239
Hobbs Rd. BH12: Poole .6A 226
Hobbs Sq. GU31: Pet .8N 139
SP10: A'ver .8B 52
(off Cricketers Way)
Hobby Cl. PO3: Ports .4H 215
PO8: Cowp .6M 181
Hobley La. RG20: Wol H .2N 7
Hobson Way SO45: Holb .5B 208
Hoburne Caravan Pk. BH23: Chri .6E 230
Hoburne Gdns. BH23: Chri .5E 230
Hoburne La. BH23: Chri .5E 230
Hoburne Naish Holiday Pk.
BH25: New M .6L 231
Hoburne Rdbt. BH23: Chri .6D 230
Hockford La. RG7: Brim C .1N 9
Hockham Ct. PO9: Hav .2C 202
Hockley Cl. PO6: Cosh .9E 200
Hockley Cotts. SO24: Cher .1H 135
Hockley Golf Course .4L 127
Hockley Link SO21: Winche .3J 127
Hockley Path PO6: Cosh .9F 200
Hockleys La. RG25: Herr .1M 79
Hockney Grn. SP10: A'ver .9N 51
HOCOMBE .2N 131
Hocombe Dr. SO53: Cha F .2N 131
Hocombe Mead Nature Reserve .2N 131
Hocombe Pk. Cl. SO53: Cha F .2N 131
Hocombe Rd. SO53: Cha F .2N 131
Hocombe Wood Rd.
SO53: Cha F .2M 131
Hodder Cl. SO53: Cha F .7N 131
HODDINGTON .3B 62
Hoddinott Rd. SO50: E'leigh .1D 160
Hodges Cl. PO9: Hav .6G 202
HOE .4B 164
Hoe, The PO13: Gos .7G 212
Hoeford Cl. PO16: Fare .2D 212
HOE GATE .3A 180
Hoe La. SO51: Toot .1A 158
SO52: N Bad .9E 130
Hoe Rd. SO32: Bis W .3N 163
Hoe St. PO7: H'don .4A 180
Hogarth Cl. GU47: Coll .7G 19
RG21: B'toke .7F 42
SO19: South .8G 174
SO51: Rom .3A 130
Hogarth Ct. BH8: Bour .6N 227
SP10: A'ver .8M 51
Hogarth Way BH8: Bour .4D 228
Hoggarth Cl. GU31: Pet .9N 139
HOG HATCH .4C 64
Hog Hatch *GU9: Up H .3C 64*
(off Newmans Ct.)
Hoghatch La. GU9: Up H .4C 64
Hogmoor Rd. GU35: W'hil .6G 100
Hog's Back GU10: Seal .6M 65
Hogs Back Brewery .5N 65
Hogs Lodge La. PO8: Clan .9D 144
Hogue Av. BH10: Bour .1H 227
Hogwood La. SO30: Wes E .5H 161
Holbeach Cl. PO6: Cosh .8F 200
Holbeche Cl. GU46: Yat .7K 17
Holbein Cl. RG21: B'toke .8E 42
Holbrook Cl. GU9: Weyb .2H 65
Holbrook Leisure Cen. .7G 212
Holbrook Rd. PO1: Ports .1E 240
PO5: S'sea .1E 240
PO16: Fare .9D 198
Holbrook Way GU11: Alders .3K 65
HOLBURY .4B 208
Holbury Cl. BH8: Bour .3B 228
Holbury Ct. PO9: Hav .4H 203
Holbury Drove SO45: Holb .5N 207
Holbury La. SO51: Lock .1M 121
Holcot La. PO3: Ports .4K 215
Holcroft Ho. SO19: South .4J 175
Holcroft Rd. SO19: South .5J 175
Holdaway Cl. SO23: Kin W .8N 91
Holdenbury Ho. *GU30: Lip .1E 116*
(off King George's Dr.)
Holdenby Ct. PO3: Ports .3K 215
HOLDENHURST .3D 228
Holdenhurst Av. BH7: Bour .8F 228
Holdenhurst Cl. PO8: Horn .1C 182
Holdenhurst Rd. BH8: Bour .2M 245
Holdenhurst Village Rd.
BH8: Bour .3C 228
Holden La. SO24: B'wth, Cher .2H 135
Holder Rd. GU12: Alders .1N 65
Hole La. GU10: Ben'ly .7K 63
GU10: Farnh .5K 63
PO7: H'don .2A 180
SO32: Curd .1J 177
Holes Cl. SO41: Hor .2G 232
HOLFLEET .1N 229
Holkham Cl. SO16: South .8D 158
Hollam Cl. PO14: Fare .9L 197
Hollam Cres. PO14: Fare .9L 197
Hollam Dr. PO14: Fare .9L 197
Hollam Rd. PO4: S'sea .2J 241
Holland Cl. GU9: Farnh .9G 64
SO53: Cha F .9A 132
Holland Dr. SP10: A'ver .7M 51
Holland Gdns. GU51: Fleet .3M 47
Holland Pk. SO31: Loc H .6C 196
Holland Pl. PO13: Gos .6F 212
SO16: South .1G 172
Holland Rd. PO4: S'sea .3F 240
SO19: South .8B 174
SO40: Tott .3J 171
Hollands Cl. SO22: Lit .1F 104
Hollands Wood Dr. BH25: New M .1B 232
Hollenden *BH12: Poole .1E 244*
(off Poole Rd.)
Hollies, The GU17: Haw .3J 29
PO8: Horn .9C 168
RG24: Old Bas .6L 43
RG27: H Win .8B 26
SO51: W Wel .1B 120
Hollies Caravan Park, The PO11: H Isl .5L 243
Hollies Cl. SO41: Sway .6J 223
Hollies Ct. RG24: B'toke .3M 41
Hollies Ind. Estate, The RG24: Old Bas .6L 43
Hollingbourne Cl. SO18: South .2B 174
HOLLINGTON .4N 7
HOLLINGTON CROSS .6N 7
Hollington Herb Garden .3N 7
Hollington La. RG20: High, Wol H .4N 7
Hollin's Wlk. *RG21: B'toke .6C 42*
(off Festival Pl.)
Hollist La. GU31: E Har .8J 147
Hollman Dr. SO51: Rom .4K 129
Hollow, The GU10: Ews .2M 63
RG20: Kings .2A 6
SO20: Brou .5B 88
Holloway Av. BH11: Bour .1D 226
Hollow La. GU35: Head .1A 102
PO11: H Isl .4F 242
Hollowshot La. RG20: Kings .3A 6 (6K 9)
RG26: Wolve .7L 9
Hollow Way GU26: Gray .3L 103
Holly Acre GU46: Yat .8N 17
Hollybank PO13: Lee S .2B 238
Hollybank Cl. PO8: Horn .5C 182
SO45: Hythe .6M 193
Hollybank Cres. SO45: Hythe .5L 193
Hollybank La. PO10: Ems .5M 203
Hollybank Rd. SO45: Hythe .5L 193
Hollybrook Av. SO16: South .8H 159
Hollybrook Cl. SO16: South .9G 159
Hollybrook Gdns. SO31: Loc H .4D 196
Hollybrook Pk. GU35: Bor .4K 101
Hollybrook Rd. SO16: South .9H 159
Holly Bush RG19: Head .2J 9
Hollybush Ho. *BH5: Bour .2C 246*
(off Wollstonecraft Rd.)
Hollybush Ind. Est. GU11: Alders .6N 49
Hollybush La. GU11: Alders .6N 49
RG26: Bau .2F 20
RG27: Eve .5H 17
Hollybush Ride RG45: Cr'tne .1M 17
Holly Cl. BH24: St L .4A 186
GU12: Alders .9L 49
GU14: Cov .8J 29
GU35: Head D .2E 102
RG26: B'ley .2H 23
RG27: Eve .6H 17
SO31: Sar G .6B 196
SO45: Hythe .1M 207
HOLLYCOMBE .6F 116
Hollycombe Cl. GU30: Lip .4E 116
Hollycombe Gdns. .7G 117
Hollycombe Steam Collection .7G 117
Holly Ct. BH1: Bour .8A 228
BH2: Bour .2H 245
BH5: Bour .1C 246
(off Florence Rd.)
BH9: Bour .6K 227
PO15: White .1G 197
RG45: Cr'tne .1A 18
Hollycroft RG19: Ashf H .2N 9
HOLLY CROSS .8H 13
Holly Dell SO16: Bass .6K 159
Hollydene Vs. SO45: Hythe .5M 193
Holly Dr. PO7: W'lle .3A 202
RG24: Old Bas .5K 43
Hollyfields Cl. GU15: Camb .8K 19
Holly Gdns. BH23: Burt .5N 229
SO30: Wes E .8H 161
SO41: M Sea .7J 235
Holly Grn. Ri. BH11: Bour .2C 226
Holly Gro. PO16: Fare .5A 198
Holly Hatch Rd. SO40: Tott .4L 171
Holly Hedge Cl. GU16: Frim .2N 29
Holly Hedge Rd. GU16: Frim .2N 29
Holly Hill SO16: Bass .6K 159
Holly Hill Cl. SO16: Bass .6K 159
Holly Hill La. SO31: Sar G .5N 195
Holly Hill Mans. SO31: Sar G .5B 196
Holly Hill Woodland Pk. .5A 196
Hollyhock Cl. RG22: B'toke .2J 59
Holly Ho. RG24: Old Bas .6L 43
Holly La. BH23: Walk .4L 231
BH25: A'ley .2D 232
RG7: Sil .5A 12
RG20: W Wo .1K 7
SO41: Pil .5H 225
Holly Lodge BH13: Poole .1E 244
SO17: South .1N 173
SO53: Cha F .9A 132
Holly Mdws. SO22: Winche .4G 104
Holly M. SO16: Bass .7L 159
Hollyoak Ct. SO16: South .7F 158
Holly Oak Rd. SO16: South .8F 158
(not continuous)
Holly Pl. SO16: South .8J 159
Holly Rd. GU12: Alders .9L 49
GU14: Cov .8H 29
SO40: Ashu .8H 171
SO45: Blac .8C 208
Holly St. PO12: Gos .3L 239
Hollythorns, The SO32: Swanm .6C 164
Hollytree Gdns. GU16: Frim .4M 29
Holly Tree Pk. *SO21: Sut S .7D 76*
(off Sutton Pk. Cl.)
Hollytrees GU51: Ch Cr .5K 47
Holly Vs. SP6: Sand .9D 150
Holly Wlk. SP10: A'ver .3K 69
HOLLYWATER .6L 101
Hollywater Rd. GU30: Pass .7L 101
GU35: Bor, W'hil .6L 101
Holly Way GU17: Blackw .9F 18
Hollywood Cl. SO52: N Bad .8E 130
Hollywood La. SO41: Lymi .1D 234
Holman Cl. PO8: Cowp .8A 182
RG26: B'ley .2J 23
Holmbrook Cl. GU14: Cov .8E 28
Holmbrook Gdns. GU14: Cov .8E 28
Holmbush Ct. PO5: S'sea .4D 240
Holm Cl. BH24: Poul .8M 185
Holm Ct. PO11: H Isl .5F 242
Holmdale Rd. PO12: Gos .9H 213
Holmdene Ct. BH2: Bour .7H 247
Holmefield Av. PO14: Fare .2B 212
Holme Rd. BH23: Highc .6K 231
Holmes Cl. RG22: B'toke .4L 59
SO31: Net A .3F 194
Holmes Ct. *GU26: Gray .4M 103*
(off Boundary Rd.)
SP10: A'ver .2L 69
Holmesland Dr. SO30: Botl .3C 176
Holmesland La. SO30: Botl .3C 176
Holmesland Wlk. SO30: Botl .3C 176
Holmfield Av. BH7: Bour .7F 228
Holmgrove PO14: Titch C .6F 196
Holm Hill La. BH23: Hin, Oss .8K 221
Holmhurst Av. BH23: Highc .5G 231
Holm Oak Cl. SO22: Lit .1E 104
Holm Oaks SO41: Penn .4C 234
Holmsley Caravan & Camping Site
BH23: Bran .4K 221
Holmsley Cl. SO18: South .3G 175
SO41: Penn .4B 234
Holmsley Ct. SO40: Tott .2H 171
Holmsley Pas. BH24: Bur .9F 188
Holmsley Rd. BH25: Woot .4M 221
Holmwood Gth. BH24: Hight .2N 187
Holne Ct. PO4: S'sea .4K 241
Holst Cl. RG22: B'toke .3N 59
Holst Way PO7: W'lle .4M 201
Holt Cl. GU14: Farn .5L 29
PO13: Lee S .1C 238
PO17: Wick .6B 178
Holt Cotts. RG19: Ashf H .3N 9
Holt Ct. SO19: South .1C 194
Holt Down GU31: Pet .1A 146
Holt End La. GU34: Bent .8K 79
Holt Gdns. PO9: R Cas .7H 183
Holtham La. GU34: E Tis, Selb .2G 113
Holt Ho. BH1: Bour .9A 228
Holt La. RG26: Wolv C .5N 9
RG27: Hoo .4J 45
SP11: Tang .5H 33
HOLT POUND .7N 63
Holt Pound Cotts. GU10: Hol P .8N 63
Holt Pound La. GU10: Hol P .7N 63
Holt Rd. BH12: Poole .8D 226
SO15: South .1B 4 (3L 173)
Holt Vw. SO50: B'stke .1K 161
Holt Way RG27: Hoo .1J 45
HOLTWOOD .1M 7
HOLWELL .6K 149
Holworth Cl. BH11: Bour .3C 226
Holy Barn Cl. RG22: B'toke .1J 59
Holyborne Rd. SO51: Rom .5A 130
HOLYBOURNE .1K 81
Holybourne Rd. PO9: Hav .6F 202
Holybourne Theatre .2J 81
Holyrood Av. SO17: South .9N 159
Holyrood Cl. PO7: W'lle .2A 202
Holyrood Ct. RG22: B'toke .8K 41
Holy Rood Est. SO14: South .7E 4
Holyrood Ho. SO14: South .7D 4 (7M 173)
Holyrood Pl. SO14: South .7D 4 (7M 173)
Holywell Cl. GU14: Farn .5J 29
Holywell Dr. PO6: P Sol .1C 214
Holywell Rd. SO32: Swanm .9F 164
Homeborough Ho. SO45: Hythe .4M 193
Homebridge Ho. SP6: F'dge .9J 151
Homechurch Ho. *BH23: Chri .8N 229*
(off Purewell)
Home Cl. SO24: Up Wield .8H 79
Homedale Ho. BH2: Bour .9K 227
Home Farm Bus. Cen. SO51: Lock .9N 87
Home Farm Cl. GU14: Farn .6M 29
SO45: Hythe .6N 193
Home Farm Gdns. SP10: Charl .7K 51
Home Farm Rd. RG27: Elve .5G 26
Homefayre Ho. PO16: Fare .8D 198
Homefield SO51: Rom .3N 129
SP11: S M Bo .9L 35
Home Fld. Cotts. GU34: E Tis .1D 112
Home Fld. Dr. SO16: Nur .6B 158
Homefield Ho. BH25: New M .4B 232
Homefield Path PO6: Dray .1K 215
Homefield Rd. PO6: Dray .1K 215
Homefield Way PO8: Clan .5B 168
RG24: B'toke .2L 41
Homeforde Ho. SO42: Broc .7D 148
Homefort Ho. *PO12: Gos .3K 239*
(off Stoke Rd.)
Homegrove Ho. PO5: S'sea .4E 240
Homeheights PO5: S'sea .9N 5 (5D 240)
Homelands Est. BH23: Chri .8J 229
Home La. SO21: Spar .3A 104
Homelea Cl. GU14: Farn .4K 29
Homeleigh Ho. BH8: Bour .9L 227
Home Mead PO7: Den .7G 180
RG25: Nth W .9B 58
Homemead Ho. SO51: Rom .6L 129
Homemill Ho. BH25: New M .3B 232
Homeoaks Ho. BH2: Bour .9K 227
Homepark Ho. GU9: Farnh .8E 64
Home Pk. Rd. GU46: Yat .7N 17
Homepoint Ho. SO18: South .3E 174
Homer Cl. PO8: Cowp .8M 181
PO13: Gos .8D 212
Homer Farm La. SO45: Blac .1J 237
Homerise Ho. SO23: Winche .6M 237
Home Rd. BH11: Bour .1F 226
Homerose Ho. PO5: S'sea .3D 240
Homer Pk. SO45: Blac .1J 237
Home Rule Rd. SO31: Loc H .5E 196
Homeryde Ho. PO13: Lee S .2A 238
Homesea Ho. PO5: S'sea .6N 5 (4D 240)
Homeside Rd. BH9: Bour .4L 227
Homespinney Ho. SO18: South .9B 160
Homestead Rd. GU34: Meds .2E 96
Homesteads Rd. RG22: B'toke .1J 59
HOME STREET .1N 187
Homewater Ho. PO7: W'lle .1M 201
Home Way GU31: Pet .1B 146
Homewaye Ho. BH4: Bour .2G 245
Homewell PO9: Hav .8F 202
Homewest Ho. BH4: Bour .2G 245
Homewood Cl. BH25: A'ley .3D 232
Homington Rd. SP5: Com B, Hom .2G 119
(not continuous)
SP5: Hom .4J 119
Hone Hill GU47: Sandh .5D 18
Hones Yd. Business Pk. GU9: Farnh .8F 64
Honeybottom Rd. RG26: Tadl .4H 11
Honeybourne Cres. BH6: Bour .1K 247
Honeycritch La. GU32: Frox .2H 139
Honey La. BH24: Bur .8D 188
GU33: Blackm .8M 99
GU34: Selb .8M 99
PO15: F'ley .4N 197
SO24: Cher .1H 135
Honeyleaze RG22: B'toke .5J 59
Honeyman La. SO21: More, Owls .4D 134
Honeysuckle Cl. GU46: Yat .7K 17
PO13: Gos .5D 212
RG22: B'toke .2J 59
SO22: Winche .1H 127
SO31: Loc H .4D 196
Honeysuckle Cotts. SO16: S'ing .7A 160
Honeysuckle Ct. PO7: W'lle .4N 201
SO22: Winche .3G 104
Honeysuckle Gdns. SO41: Ever .5K 233
SP10: A'ver .2J 69
Honeysuckle La. GU35: Head D .2D 102
Honeysuckle Rd. SO16: Bass, S'ing .7M 159
Honeysuckle Way BH23: Chri .6D 230
SO53: Cha F .6M 131
Honeywood Cl. PO3: Ports .4G 215
SO40: Tott .1K 171
Honington M. GU14: Farn .3K 49
Honister Cl. SO16: South .2D 172
Honister Gdns. GU51: Fleet .1A 48
Hood Cl. BH10: Bour .5F 226
SO31: Loc H .5E 196
SP10: A'ver .1C 70
Hood Cres. BH10: Bour .5F 226
Hood Rd. SO18: South .2E 174
HOOK
RG27 .2G 45
SO31 .1D 210
Hook Cl. SO51: Ampf .2M 131
HOOK COMMON .4F 44
Hook Cres. SO51: Ampf .2M 131
Hooke Ct. GU30: Lip .1F 116
Hook La. PO14: Abs .1D 210
RG23: Oak .5A 40
RG26: Axm .7B 10
RG26: Up Woott .5A 40
SO24: Rop .2A 110
SO31: Wars .1D 210
SP11: Monx .6B 68
HOOK PARK .2A 210
Hook Pk. Est. SO31: Wars .2A 210
Hook Pk. Rd. SO31: Wars .1N 209
Hookpit Farm La. SO23: Kin W .7M 91
Hook Rd. RG20: Kings .2C 6 (6L 9)
RG27: Hoo .4G 45
RG27: Roth .7F 24
RG29: Grey, N War .7F 44
RG29: N War .6J 45
SO51: Ampf .1K 131
Hook's Farm Way PO9: Bed .6D 202
Hook's La. PO9: Bed .6C 202
(not continuous)
Hook Station (Rail) .3H 45
Hookstile La. GU9: Farnh .9E 64
Hookwater Cl. SO53: Cha F .2N 131
Hookwater Rd. SO53: Cha F .2N 131
Hook with Warsash Nature Reserve .2N 209
Hookwood La. SO51: Ampf .2L 131
SP11: Co Du .4A 32
Hoopersmead RG25: Clid .3B 60
Hoopers Way RG23: Oak .1D 58
Hope Grant's Rd. GU11: Alders .7J 49
(not continuous)
Hope La. GU9: Up H .4D 64
Hopeman Cl. GU47: Coll .5F 18
Hope Rd. SO30: Wes E .9J 161
Hope St. PO1: Ports .1N 5 (1D 240)
Hopeswood GU33: G'ham .3F 114
Hope Way GU11: Alders .8H 49
Hopfield Cl. PO7: W'lle .2M 201
Hopfield Ho. PO7: W'lle .3M 201
Hopfield Rd. RG27: H Win .7B 26

Hop Garden—Ideal Pk. Homes Caravan Site

Hop Garden GU52: Ch Cr 7K 47
Hop Garden, The GU31: S Hart 9G 146
Hop Garden Rd. RG27: Hoo 2F 44
Hop Gdns. SP5: W'psh 5H 121
Hopkins Cl. BH8: Bour 4D 228
PO6: Cosh 9N 199
Hopkins Ct. PO4: S'sea 5J 241
Hopkinson Way SP10: A'ver 9H 51
Hopton Gth. RG24: Lych 2H 43
Hoptons Retreat SO24: Cher 1K 135
Horace Rd. BH5: Bour 1B 246
Horatia Ho. PO5: S'sea 5M 5 (3C 240)
Horder Cl. SO16: Bass 8L 159
HORDLE 3G 233
Hordle La. SO41: Down, Hor 6G 233
Hordle Rd. PO9: Hav 5B 202
Horefield SP4: Port 9C 66
Horlock Rd. SO42: Broc 6D 148
Hormer Cl. GU47: Owl 4F 18
Hornbeam Cl. GU14: Cov 7E 28
GU47: Owl 4F 18
SO21: Sth W 3J 91
SO30: Hed E 4A 176
Hornbeam Gdns. SO30: Wes E 8H 161
Hornbeam Pl. RG27: Hoo 1H 45
Hornbeam Rd. PO9: Hav 6H 203
SO53: Cha F 6K 131
Hornby Ii BH23: Chri 7K 229
(off Arthur Rd.)
Hornby Cl. SO31: Wars 9A 196
Hornchurch Rd. SO16: South 6E 158
HORNDEAN 3C 182
Horndean Caravan Site PO8: Horn 1C 182
Horndean Cen. 3B 182
(off Barton Cross)
Horndean Ho. PO1: Ports 1E 240
Horndean Pct. PO8: Horn 3D 182
Horndean Rd. PO8: Blen 2E 182
PO10: Ems 5K 203
Horne Cl. SO18: Wes E 9F 160
Hornes Fld. Ct. GU52: Ch Cr 7K 47
Hornet Cl. PO12: Gos 4L 239
PO15: Fare 7N 197
Hornetide Ho. PO13: Lee S 2A 238
Hornet Rd. PO10: T Isl 5N 217
PO14: Fare 3B 212
Hornet Sailing Club 4M 239
(off Haslar Rd.)
Horning Rd. BH12: Poole 9D 226
Horn Rd. GU14: Cov 7G 29
Horns Drove SO16: Rown 6C 158
Horns Hill SO16: Nur 5C 158
SO32: Sob H 9K 165
Horns Hill Cl. SO16: Nur 5C 158
HORRIS HILL 1D 8
Horsa Cl. BH6: Bour 1H 247
Horsa Ct. BH6: Bour 1H 247
Horsa Rd. BH6: Bour 1H 247
Horsea La. PO2: Ports 4E 214
Horsea Rd. PO2: Ports 4F 214
HORSEBRIDGE 7E 88
Horsebridge Rd. PO9: Hav 5G 203
SO20: Brou 2B 86 (5B 88)
SO20: Houg, Ki S 9A 86 (6D 88)
Horsebridge Way SO16: Rown 6D 158
Horsecroft SO51: Rom 4M 129
Horsefair, The SO51: Rom 5L 129
Horsefair Ct. SO51: Rom 5L 129
Horsefair M. SO51: Rom 5L 129
Horse La. SO24: Rop 7E 96
HORSEPORT 1K 153
Horsepost La. PO7: H'don 8H 167
HorsePower -
The Museum of the King's Royal Hussars
. . . . . 8K 237 (7K 105)
Horse Sands Cl. PO4: S'sea 4L 241
Horseshoe, The BH13: S'bks 9A 244
Horseshoe Apartments
PO5: S'sea 6M 5
Horseshoe Bend GU26: Gray 4J 103
Horseshoe Bri. SO17: South 2N 173
Horseshoe Cl. PO14: Titch C 7G 196
Horseshoe Comn. Rdbt. BH1: Bour 6M 247
Horseshoe Ct. BH1: Bour 5M 247 (1K 245)
SP5: Down 1K 119 (7A 120)
Horseshoe Cres. GU35: Bor 4K 101
Horseshoe Dr. SO40: Calm 9G 156
SO51: Rom 2A 130
Horseshoe Lake Watersports Cen. 4N 17
Horseshoe La. SP11: Ibt 3C 34
Horseshoe Lodge SO31: Wars 8B 196
Horseshoe Paddocks Bus. Cen.
PO15: F'ley 3L 197
Horsham Av. BH10: Bour 1G 227
Horsham Rd. GU47: Owl 4F 18
Horshells Drove SO20: Ov Wa 8M 67
Horton Cl. BH9: Bour 3N 227
HORTON HEATH 4A 162
Horton Rd. BH21: Woodl 9H 149
BH24: A'ley, Ashl H 2A 186
PO13: Gos 4E 212
Horton Way SO50: B'stke 1K 161
Horwood Gdns. RG21: B'toke 9A 42
Hosker Rd. BH5: Bour 9E 228
Hosketts La. SO20: N Wal 1N 87
Hoskins Ho. PO1: Ports 2L 5
Hoskins Pl. Ind. Est. GU15: Camb 1K 29
Hospital Hill GU11: Alders 8J 49
Hospital La. PO16: Portc 2N 213
Hospital Rd. GU11: Alders 8J 49
SO32: Shi H 1C 178
Hot Rocks Indoor Climbing 6G 227
Hotspur Cl. SO45: Hythe 4L 193
Houchin St. SO32: Bis W 4M 163
HOUGHTON 5E 88
Houghton Cl. PO9: Hav 3H 203
HOUGHTON DRAYTON 6D 88
Houghton Lodge & Gardens 4E 88
Houghton Rd. SO20: S Bri 3F 88
Houghton Sq. RG27: Sher L 7J 23
HOUND 3J 195
Hound Cl. SO31: Net A 4H 195
HOUND GREEN 1H 25
Hound Grn. Cl. RG27: Hou G 1H 25
HOUNDMILLS 5N 41
Houndmills Rd. RG21: B'toke 5N 41
Houndmills Rdbt. RG21: B'toke 4A 42
Hound Rd. SO31: Hou, Net A 4G 195
Hound Rd. Gdns.
SO31: Net A 3H 195
Hound Way SO31: Net A 3G 195
Houndwell Pl. SO14: South 6E 4 (6M 173)
HOUNSDOWN 5M 171
Hounsdown Av. SO40: Tott 5M 171
Hounsdown Bus. Pk. SO40: Tott 6M 171
Hounsdown Cl. SO40: Tott 5M 171
Hoursome Cl. RG22: B'toke 6K 59
House, The BH23: Chri 6K 229
House Farm Rd. PO12: Gos 3G 238
Houseman Rd. GU14: Farn 6H 29
House Plat Ct. GU52: Ch Cr 7K 47
(off Brandon Rd.)
Hove Ct. PO13: Lee S 1A 238
Hovercraft Museum, The 9N 211
Hoverfly Cl. PO13: Lee S 2C 238
Hoveton Gro. SO53: Cha F 4N 131
Howard Cl. BH23: Mude 8B 230
BH24: Bur 7E 188
(off Ringwood Rd.)
GU51: Fleet 2A 48
PO13: Lee S 9C 212
SO18: S'ing 7C 160
SO50: Fair O 1N 161
SO53: Cha F 8B 132
Howard Cole Way GU11: Alders 9G 49
Howard Dr. GU14: Cov 8D 28
Howard Lodge PO5: S'sea 5D 240
Howard Oliver Ho. SO45: Hythe 6N 193
Howard Rd. BH8: Bour 7N 227
PO2: Ports 4F 214
RG21: B'toke 8D 42
SO15: South 4J 173
Howard's Gro. SO15: South 2H 173
Howards La. GU34: Holy 10D 62
Howards Mead SO41: Penn 4B 234
Howard Vw. RG22: B'toke 8M 41
Howe, The GU14: Farn 2C 48
Howe Cl. BH23: Mude 9C 230
BH25: New M 3A 232
Howell Cl. SO14: South 5A 174
Howe Rd. PO13: Gos 1E 238
Howerts Cl. SO31: Wars 1A 210
Howes Gdns. GU52: Ch Cr 5K 47
Howeth Cl. BH10: Bour 3H 227
Howeth Rd. BH10: Bour 2H 227
Howgare Rd. SP5: Br Ch . . . . . 4A 118 & 7A 118
Howlett Cl. SO41: Lymi 2C 234
Howton Cl. BH10: Bour 1G 227
Howton Rd. BH10: Bour 1G 227
Hoxley Rd. BH10: Bour 2H 227
Hoylake Cl. PO13: Gos 7E 212
Hoylake Rd. PO6: Dray 8K 201
Hoyle Cl. SO32: Lwr U 9D 134
Hoylecroft Cl. PO15: Fare 6A 198
Hub, The
Eastleigh 9G 133
Hubbard Rd. RG21: B'toke 4A 42
Hubert Hamilton Rd. SP4: Bul C 3B 66
(not continuous)
Hubert Rd. SO23: Winche 1J 127
Hubert Rd. Rdbt. PO7: W'lle 1M 201
Huckers La. GU34: Selb 7L 99
Huckswood La. PO8: Chal, Ids 7L 169
Huddington Glade GU46: Yat 8K 17
Hudson Cl. BH12: Poole 4A 226
BH24: Poul 9M 185
GU30: Lip 3E 116
PO13: Gos 1E 238
Hudson Ct. SO40: Tott 4K 171
Hudson Davies Cl. SO41: Pil 6F 224
Hudson Ho. SO14: South 8F 4
Hudson Rd. PO5: S'sea 3E 240
Hudsons Mdw. RG27: Hou G 1H 25
Hugh De Port La. GU51: Fleet 9L 27
Hughes Cl. SO45: Blac 7C 208
Hughs Bus. Cen. BH23: Chri 7C 230
Hugo Platt GU31: Rog 9K 141
Huish La. RG24: Old Bas 7J 43
RG25: Tun 7J 43
Hulbert Rd. PO7: Hav, W'lle 1M 201
(not continuous)
PO9: Bed, Hav 5B 202
Hulbert Way RG22: B'toke 9L 41
Hulfords La. RG27: H Win 3C 26
Hullam La. GU34: New V 9G 99
Hull Cres. BH11: Bour 2B 226
Huller Ct. PO7: W'lle 9K 181
Hulles Way SO52: N Bad 8E 130
Hull Rd. BH11: Bour 2B 226
Hull Way BH11: Bour 2C 226
Hulse Lodge SO15: South 2L 173
Hulse Rd. SO15: South 2L 173
Hulton Cl. SO19: South 9B 174
Humber Cl. GU47: Sandh 5F 18
PO14: Stub 5L 211
Humber Ct. SP10: A'ver 8B 52
(off Itchen Ct.)
Humber Gdns. SO31: Burs 9L 175
Humber La. SP9: Tidw 9C 30 (8F 30)
Humberstone Rd. SP10: A'ver 3N 69
Humbers Vw. SO20: Ki S 9B 86 (7G 88)
Humber Way GU47: Sandh 5F 18
HUMBLY GROVE 6B 62
Hummicks, The SO42: Beau 8H 207
Humming Bird Ct. RG22: B'toke 2H 59
(off Heron Way)
Humphrey Pk. GU52: Ch Cr 8L 47
(not continuous)
Humphrey's Bri. BH23: Chri 7E 230
Hundred, The PO7: W'lle 9L 181
SO51: Rom 5L 129
SP6: F'dge 1J 153
Hundred Acre Rdbt. SP10: A'ver 1J 69
HUNDRED ACRES 6H 179
Hundred Acres Rd. PO17: Wick 8G 178
Hundred La. SO41: Lymi, Portm 8F 224
Hungerfield Cl. BH23: Bran 6C 220
HUNGERFORD 5N 153
Hungerford SO31: Burs 2K 195
Hungerford Cl. GU47: Sandh 5E 18
RG23: Wort 7J 41
Hungerford Hill SP6: Hung 5N 153
Hungerford La. SP10: K Enh 3M 51
SP11: Conh, Hath, Tang, Wild 9C 6
(not continuous)
Hungerford Rd. BH8: Bour 3A 228
SN8: B'mre 4D 6
Hunnels Cl. GU52: Ch Cr 8K 47
Hunt Av. SO31: Net A 3G 194
Hunt Cl. SO21: Sth W 3J 91
Hunter Cl. BH23: Chri 7C 230
PO13: Gos 9F 212
SO20: Ki S 9B 86 (7G 88)
SO45: Hard 2N 207
Hunter Ct. SO15: South 1G 172
Hunter Rd. GU14: Cov 9H 29
PO4: S'sea 4G 241
PO6: Cosh 8G 200
PO10: T Isl 5N 217
Hunters Chase GU30: Lip 1D 116
SO32: Swanm 8E 164
Hunters Cl. BH31: Ver 4A 184
RG23: Oak 8D 40
Hunters Ct. SO31: Burs 6M 175
Hunters Cres. SO40: Tott 4H 171
SO51: Rom 2B 130
Hunters Hill SO40: Tott 7K 171
Hunters Lodge PO15: Fare 8L 197
Hunters Ride PO7: W'lle 3M 201
SO21: Hurs 9K 125
Hunters Rd. GU33: Longc 4J 115
Hunters Way SO50: B'stke 1L 161
Huntfield Rd. BH9: Bour 3M 227
Huntingdon Cl. PO14: Titch C 8F 196
SO40: Tott 1L 171
Huntingdon Gdns. BH23: Chri 4K 229
SO50: Hor H 5A 162
Huntingdon Ho. Dr.
GU26: Hind 3N 103
Huntingford Cl. GU26: Hind 9L 85
Hunting Ga. SP10: A'ver 1J 69
Huntley Cl. PO6: Cosh 8C 200
Huntly Mans. BH7: Bour 8E 228
(off Christchurch Rd.)
Huntly Rd. BH3: Bour 8H 227
Huntly Way SO18: South 3D 174
HUNTON 7F 76
Hunton Cl. SO16: South 8J 159
Hunton Down La. SO21: Hunt, Sut S 7F 76
Hunton La. SO21: Hunt, Wons 7E 76
Hunt Rd. BH23: Chri 6A 230
Huntsbottom La. GU33: Hi Br, Liss 1F 140
Hunts Cl. RG27: Hoo 2J 45
SO21: Col C 3L 133
Hunts Comn. RG27: H Win 5C 26
Hunts Cotts. RG27: H Win 5C 26
Hunt's La. SP11: E Ch 3A 68
Huntsman Cl. PO8: Cowp 5N 181
Huntsman's M. GU16: Mytc 9N 29
Huntsmead GU34: Alt 5G 81
Huntsmoor Rd. RG26: Tadl 5F 10
Hunts Pond Rd. PO14: Titch C 7F 196
SO31: P Ga 4E 196
Huntvale Rd. BH9: Bour 3M 227
HURDCOTT 4A 86
Hurdcott La. SP4: Hurd, Win E 4A 86
Hurdles, The BH23: Chri 6H 229
PO14: Titch C 7G 196
Hurdles Mead SO41: M Sea 9K 235
Hurdle Way SO21: Comp 5G 126
Hurland La. GU35: Head 3B 102
Hurlands Bus. Cen. GU9: Farnh 6H 65
Hurlands Cl. GU9: Farnh 6H 65
Hurlands Pl. GU9: Farnh 6H 65
Hurley Cl. SP4: Ames 5A 66
Hurlingham Gdns. SO16: Bass 6M 159
Hurlingham Ho. BH1: Bour 2N 245
(off Manor Rd.)
HURN 8E 218
Hurn Bridge Sports Club 8E 218
Hurn Cl. BH24: A'ley 2G 186
Hurn Ct. BH23: Hurn 2D 228
PO9: Hav 3H 203
Hurn Ct. La. BH23: Hurn 9C 218
Hurne Ct. RG21: B'toke 6E 42
(off Lytton Rd.)
Hurn Ho. BH1: Bour 2M 245
(off Christchurch Rd.)
Hurn La. BH24: A'ley 2G 187
Hurn Rd. BH23: Chri 2G 228
BH24: A'ley, Match 7F 186
Hurn Way BH23: Chri 5G 229
Hurnwood Pk. BH23: Hurn 8G 218
Huron Dr. GU30: Lip 3E 116
Hurricane Dr. SO16: Rown 5D 158
HURSLEY 6N 125
Hursley Cl. BH7: Bour 6F 228
Hursley Ct. SO53: Cha F 3N 131
Hursley Dr. GU51: Fleet 9H 27
SO45: Blac 9C 208
Hursley Pk. SO21: Hurs 6M 125
Hursley Pk. Rd. SO21: Hurs 6L 125
Hursley Rd. PO9: Hav 4D 202
SO21: Hurs 1N 131
SO53: Cha F 1N 131
Hurst, The RG27: Winchf 2E 46
Hurstbourne Av. BH23: Chri 5G 231
Hurstbourne Cl. PO9: Hav 3D 202
Hurstbourne Ho. PO3: Ports 1H 241
(off Cotton Rd.)
Hurstbourne Pl. SO19: South 1D 194
HURSTBOURNE PRIORS 8B 54
HURSTBOURNE TARRANT 4D 34
Hurst Cl. BH23: Walk 4L 231
BH25: New M 6M 231
GU30: Lip 1C 116
PO14: Stub 7K 211
SO40: Tott 2M 171
SO53: Cha F 8M 131
Hurst Ct. SO41: M Sea 8J 235
Hurstdene Rd. BH8: Bour 4N 227
Hurst Grn. PO13: Gos 6D 212
Hurst Grn. Cl. PO8: Cowp 8B 182
SO19: South 9E 174
Hurst Hill BH14: Poole 5A 244
Hurst La. GU34: Priv 2A 138
SO21: Owls 6C 134
Hurst Leisure Centre, The 4D 10
Hurstly La. SO41: Bold 3B 224
Hurstmere Cl. GU26: Gray 4M 103
Hurst Rd. BH24: Ring 8K 185
GU11: Alders 7L 49
GU14: Farn 4K 29
SO41: M Sea 9K 235
Hurst Vw. Caravan Site SO41: Penn 8D 234
Hurstville Dr. PO7: W'lle 3N 201
(not continuous)
Hussar Cl. BH23: Chri 7J 229
Hussar Ct. GU11: Alders 9G 48
PO7: W'lle 9K 181
Hussell La. GU34: Meds 9K 79
Hussey Cl. SO23: Winche 4L 105
Husseys La. GU34: Lwr Froy 7H 63
Hutchins Way RG24: B'toke 1C 42
Hut Farm Pl. SO53: Cha F 7A 132
Hutfield Ct. PO12: Gos 2K 239
(off Lees La.)
Hutton Sq. SP10: A'ver 8B 52
Hutwood Rd. SO16: Chilw 3M 159
Huxley Cl. SO31: Loc H 7E 196
Huxley Ct. SO45: Dib P 7H 193
Hyacinth Cl. RG22: B'toke 2J 59
HYDE
SO23 . . . . . 5L 105
SP6 . . . . . 4N 153
Hyde, The BH25: New M 2N 231
Hyde Abbey Gatehouse 5L 105
(off King Alfred Pl.)
Hyde Abbey Rd. SO23: Winche . . 6M 237 (6L 105)
Hyde Church La. SO23: Winche 5L 105
Hyde Church Path SO23: Winche 5L 105
(off Hyde St.)
Hyde Cl. SO15: South 1H 173
SO23: Winche 5K 105
SO40: Tott 3H 171
SO41: Sway 5J 223
HYDE END 1N 9
Hyde End La. RG7: Brim 1M 9
Hyde Gate SO23: Winche 5L 105
Hyde Ho. Gdns. SO23: Winche 5L 105
Hyde La. GU8: Thur 7M 85
GU10: Chur 7M 85
GU10: Cron 2K 63
RG20: Ecc 2H 9
SP5: Down 2H 119
SP6: Stuc 5M 153
Hyde Lodge SO23: Winche 5K 105
Hyden Farm La. GU32: E Meon 5L 167
PO8: Clan 5L 167
Hyden Wood GU32: E Meon 1M 167
Hyde Pk. Ho. PO5: S'sea 3D 240
Hyde Pk. Rd. PO5: S'sea 3D 240
Hyde Rd. BH10: Bour 1G 226
RG29: L Sut 4F 62
Hydes Platt RG7: Sil 5A 12
Hyde St. PO5: S'sea 7N 5 (4D 240)
SO23: Winche 6M 237 (6L 105)
Hylton Ct. RG26: Tadl 5K 11
Hylton Rd. GU32: Pet 1M 145
Hymans Way SO40: Tott 3M 171
Hynesbury Rd. BH23: Fri C 8E 230
Hynes Ct. SP11: Ludg 1C 30
Hyson Cres. SP11: Ludg 1F 30
Hyssop Cl. PO15: White 2G 196
HYTHE 4M 193
Hythe By-Pass
SO45: Dib, Dib P, Hard, Hythe 4G 192
Hythe Cl. RG26: Tadl 6H 11
Hythe Marine Pk. SO45: Hythe 5N 193
Hythe Rd. PO6: Cosh 8F 200
SO40: March 1D 192
Hythe Sailing Club 6A 194
Hythe Spartina Marsh Nature Reserve 6A 194

I

Iachino Av. PO2: Ports 4F 214
Ian Gibson Ct. PO5: S'sea 2E 240
(off Carlisle Rd.)
Ibbertson Cl. BH8: Bour 4C 228
Ibbertson Rd. BH8: Bour 5C 228
Ibbertson Way BH8: Bour 4C 228
Ibbett Rd. BH10: Bour 4G 226
Ibbotson Way SO40: Tott 5K 171
Ibsen Cl. PO15: White 1F 196
IBSLEY 2K 185
Ibsley Cl. BH8: Bour 8N 227
Ibsley Drove BH24: Ibsl 9K 153
Ibsley Gro. PO9: Bed 6D 202
IBTHORPE 3C 34
IBWORTH 1B 40
Ibworth La. GU51: Fleet 9H 27
RG26: Hann, Ibw 9M 9
Ibworth Rd. RG26: Hann, Ibw 4N 39
Icarus Pl. PO7: Purb 7N 201
Icknield Ho. SP10: A'ver 8B 52
Icknield Wlk. SP11: E Ant 6B 52
(off Augusta Way West)
Icknield Way SP10: A'ver 5A 52
Ida Ct. SO19: South 8D 174
Iddesleigh Rd. BH3: Bour 8K 227
Ideal Pk. Homes Caravan Site
SO50: B'dge 6J 133

Idmiston—Jubilee Cres.

IDMISTON 9C 66
Idmiston Rd. SP4: Port 1C 86
Idsworth Cl. PO8: Horn 4D 182
Idsworth Ct. RG24: B'toke 3M 41
Idsworth Down GU31: Pet 1N 145
Idsworth Ho. *PO1: Ports* *1D 240*
(off Crasswell St.)
Idsworth Rd. PO3: Ports 8H 215
PO8: Cowp 8B 182
IFORD 7F 228
Iford Bri. Home Pk. BH6: Bour 7G 229
Iford Cl. BH6: Bour 8H 229
Iford Ct. PO9: Hav 3H 203
Iford Gdns. BH7: Bour 7F 228
Iford Golf Cen. 4F 228
Iford Golf Course 4F 228
Iford La. BH6: Bour 7G 228
Iford Rdbt. BH7: Bour 7F 228
Iford Sports Complex 6G 228
Ilex Cl. GU46: Yat 7L 17
RG26: Pam H 4L 11
SO23: Kin W 7M 91
Ilex Cres. SO31: Loc H 6C 196
Ilex Wlk. PO11: H Isl 4J 243
Iley La. SO41: Penn 9C 234
Illingworth Cl. *RG26: B'ley* *2J 23*
(off St Mary's Av.)
Illustrious Rd. PO14: Stub 7L 211
Ilynton Av. SP5: Firs 4E 86
Imadene Cl. GU35: Lind 3L 101
Imadene Cres. GU35: Lind 3L 101
IMAX Cinema
Bournemouth 8M 247 (3K 245)
Imber Av. SP4: Ames 6A 66
Imber Dr. BH23: Highc 6H 231
Imber Rd. SO23: Winche 6N 105
Imber Way SO19: South 6G 174
Imbrecourt BH13: Poole 6C 244
Imjin Cl. GU11: Alders 8K 49
Imperial Av. SO15: South 2G 173
Imperial Ct. SP10: A'ver 9D 52
Imperial Pk. Ind. Est.
SO14: South 3N 173
Imperial Rd. SO14: South 1G 4 (3N 173)
Imperial Way SO15: South 5H 173
Implacable Rd. PO13: Lee S 9N 211
Impstone Rd. RG26: Pam H 4M 11
Imran Ct. GU12: Alders 1L 65
Inchmery La. SO45: Exb 2G 236
Ingersley Ri. SO30: Wes E 1J 175
Ingle Dell GU15: Camb 9M 19
Ingledene Cl. PO9: Bed 7D 202
PO12: Gos 3K 239
Ingle Glen SO45: Dib P 8M 193
Ingle Grn. SO40: Calm 1H 171
Inglegreen Cl. BH25: New M 5A 232
Ingles Edge RG17: Ink 1G 7
Ingleside SO31: Net A 2G 195
Ingleside Cl. PO14: Fare 9L 197
Ingleton Rd. SO16: South 1C 172
Inglewood Av. BH8: Bour 5C 228
Inglewood Dr. BH25: New M 4C 232
RG22: B'toke 4K 59
Inglewood Gdns. SO50: Fair O 9N 133
Inglis Rd. PO5: S'sea 4F 240
Ingoldfield La. PO17: Newt, Sob H 3L 179
SO32: Sob H 9L 165
Ingram Ct. SO17: South 2A 174
Ings Cl. GU34: Alt 6F 80
Ingworth Rd. BH12: Poole 9E 226
Inhams La. PO7: Den 6E 180
Inhams Rd. GU34: Holy 2K 81
Inhams Row SO24: Old A 6F 94
Inhams Way RG7: Sil 5N 11
Inholmes Dr. GU51: Fleet 9K 27
INHURST 5C 10
Inhurst Av. PO7: W'lle 9A 182
Inhurst La. RG26: Bau 4C 10
Inhurst Rd. PO2: Ports 6F 214
Inhurst Way RG26: Tadl 4F 10
Inkerman Rd. SO19: South 7B 174
INKPEN 1H 7
Inkpen Common Nature Reserve 1J 7
Inkpen Gdns. RG24: Lych 3H 43
Inkpen Wlk. PO9: Hav 2D 202
Inmans La. GU32: Pet 8A 140
Innisfail Gdns. GU11: Alders 2H 65
Institute Rd. GU11: Alders 4L 49
GU12: Alders 1M 65
Instow Gdns. GU14: Farn 5J 29
Intec Bus. Cen. RG24: B'toke 3F 42
Intech Science Centre & Planetarium 7E 106
Interchange Pk. PO3: Ports 5K 215
International Way SO19: South 1C 194
Inveravon BH23: Mude 9B 230
Inverclyde Rd. BH14: Poole 1A 244
Invergordon Av. PO6: Cosh 1J 215
Inverkip Cl. PO13: Lee S 9A 212
Inverleigh Rd. BH6: Bour 8F 228
Inverness Av. PO15: Fare 6A 198
Inverness Rd. BH13: Poole 6C 244
PO1: Ports 9F 214
PO12: Gos 1J 239
Inverness Way GU47: Coll 6F 18
Invincible Rd. GU14: Farn 1J 49
PO14: Stub 7L 211
Invincible Rd. Ind. Est. GU14: Farn 9J 29
Inwood Ct. GU34: Alt 5F 80
Inwood Rd. GU33: Liss 2F 140
Iona Ho. *GU11: Alders* *9J 49*
(off Nelson St.)
Ionic Cl. SO53: Cha F 5D 132
Iping Av. PO9: Hav 4E 202
Ipley Way SO45: Hythe 7M 193
Ipswich Rd. BH4: Bour 1F 244
BH12: Poole 1F 244
IQ Farnborough GU14: Farn 1J 49
Ireland Way PO7: W'lle 4M 201
Irene Ct. SO16: South 9G 158
Iridiuim BH23: Mude 9C 230
Iris Cl. RG22: B'toke 3J 59
Iris Rd. BH9: Bour 5K 227
SO16: Bass 7N 159
Ironbridge Cres. SO31: P Ga 3D 196
Ironbridge La. PO4: S'sea 3K 241
Iron Mill PO15: Titch 4L 197
Iron Mill Cl. PO15: Fare 6N 197
Ironside Ct. SO14: South 7C 4
Irvine Cl. PO16: Fare 6C 198
Irvine Cres. RG24: B'toke 2D 42
Irvine Dr. GU14: Cov 4G 28
Irvine Way BH23: Chri 6A 230
Irving La. BH6: Bour 9G 228
Irving Rd. BH6: Bour 1F 246
SO16: South 1E 172
Irwell Cl. RG21: B'toke 6E 42
SO53: Cha F 7M 131
Irwin Hgts. PO12: Gos 8J 213
Isaacs Cl. BH12: Poole 7F 226
Isambard Brunel Rd. PO1: Ports 4N 5 (2D 240)
ISINGTON 9J 63
Isington La. GU34: Isin 8J 63
Isington Rd. GU34: Bins, Isin 1D 82
Isis Cl. SO16: South 2D 172
Isis Way GU47: Sandh 5F 18
ISLAND 5K 139
Island Cl. PO11: H Isl 5G 216
Islander Wlk. SO50: E'leigh 3D 160
Island Farm La. GU32: Ste 5K 139
Island Point SO41: Wal 2G 234
Island Vw. BH25: New M 7L 231
Island Vw. Av. BH23: Fri C 8D 230
Island Vw. Cl. SO41: M Sea 9L 235
Island Vw. Ct. BH25: B Sea 7A 232
Island Vw. Gdns. SO41: M Sea 8L 235
Island Vw. Rd. BH25: New M 7L 231
Island Vw. Ter. PO2: Ports 7D 214
Island Vw. Wlk. PO16: Portc 8L 199
Islay Gdns. PO6: Cosh 8G 201
Isle of Wight Car Ferry 9C 4 (8L 173)
Isle of Wight Ferry Terminal (Vehicular)
6J 5 (3B 240)
Isle of Wight Hovercraft Terminal 9K 5 (5B 240)
Isley Rd. RG24: B'toke 1C 42
Issac Ho. PO12: Gos 9M 213
Itchel La. GU10: Cron 2K 63
Itchell Dr. GU51: Fleet 9K 27
ITCHEN 7B 174
ITCHEN ABBAS 8H 93
Itchen Av. SO50: B'stke 1K 161
Itchen Bridge, The SO14: South 7N 173
SO19: South 7N 173
Itchen Bus. Pk. SO17: South 9A 160
Itchen Cl. GU31: Pet 2L 145
RG23: Oak 1D 58
SO51: W Wel 1A 120 (9M 121)
Itchen College Sports Cen. 5E 174
Itchen Ct. PO8: Cowp 6N 181
SO23: Winche 8P 237
SP10: A'ver 8B 52
Itchen Grange SO50: E'leigh 9H 133
Itchenor Rd. PO11: H Isl 5M 243
Itchen Rd. PO9: Hav 3H 203
Itchenside Cl. SO18: S'ing 7D 160
ITCHEN STOKE 9A 94
Itchen Valley Country Pk. 6G 161
Itchen Valley Country Pk. Visitor Cen. 6F 160
Itchen Valley Nature Reserve 7E 160
Itchen Vw. SO18: S'ing 7D 160
SO24: Itc S 1N 107
Itchin Cl. SO40: Tott 4K 171
Ithica Cl. PO11: H Isl 3G 243
Ivamy Pl. BH11: Bour 4D 226
Ivanhoe Rd. SO15: South 1J 173
Ivar Gdns. RG24: Lych 2H 43
Ively Rd. GU14: Cov, Farn 9G 28
GU14: Farn 3C 48
Ives Cl. GU46: Yat 6L 17
Ivor Cl. SO45: Holb 4A 208
Ivy Cl. BH24: St L 4A 186
SO22: Winche 9J 105
SO40: Tott 9L 157
Ivy Ct. BH9: Bour 6K 227
PO7: Purb 5L 201
Ivy Dene SO19: South 6H 175
Ivydene Gdns. PO8: Cowp 6A 182
Ivy Down La. RG23: Oak 7A 40
Ivyhole Hill RG27: Elve 5G 26
Ivy Ho. BH2: Bour 2H 245
PO12: Gos 3L 239
Ivyhouse La. GU32: Frox 3D 138
Ivy La. BH24: Blas, Rock 6K 185
GU9: Farnh 8D 64
PO1: Ports 1J 5 (1B 240)
SO18: Wes E 9F 160
SO30: Wes E 9G 160
Ivy Orchard PO8: Clan 5B 168
Ivy Rd. GU12: Alders 9M 49
SO17: South 2A 174
Ivy Ter. SO30: Hed E 4M 175
Iwerne Cl. BH9: Bour 2M 227

J

Jacana Ct. PO12: Gos 2M 239
Jacaranda Cl. PO15: Seg 5H 197
Jacaranda Rd. GU35: Bor 4J 101
Jack Cl. SO53: Cha F 6K 131
Jack Cockerill Way PO5: S'sea 6E 240
Jackdaw Cl. PO8: Cowp 6M 181
RG22: B'toke 2H 59
Jackdaw Ri. SO50: E'leigh 2B 160
Jackie Wigg Gdns. SO40: Tott 3N 171
Jacklyns Cl. SO24: New A 2E 108
Jacklyns La. SO24: New A 9F 94
Jackman's Cl. SO19: South 7B 174
Jackman's Hill SO21: More 3C 134
Jack Maynard Rd. SO45: Cals 9L 209
Jackson Cl. PO6: Farl 2K 215
Jackson Gdns. BH12: Poole 8A 226
Jackson Rd. BH12: Poole 8A 226
Jacksons Rd. SO30: Hed E 9N 161
Jacobean Cl. BH23: Walk 5K 231
Jacob Ho. PO1: Ports 3K 5 (2B 240)
Jacob Rd. GU15: Camb 6J 19
Jacob's All. RG21: B'toke 7C 42
Jacobs Cl. PO8: Clan 6C 168
SO51: Rom 5N 129
SP11: E Ant 6C 52
Jacobs Ct. PO9: Hav 8E 202
Jacob's Gutter La. SO40: Elin, Tott 5M 171
(not continuous)
Jacob's St. PO1: Ports 1D 240
Jacob's Wlk. SO40: Tott 6L 171
Jacob's Yd. RG21: B'toke 7C 42
Jacomb Pl. PO13: Gos 6F 212
Jacqueline Av. PO7: Purb 5L 201
Jacqueline Rd. BH12: Poole 7A 226
Jade Ct. PO7: W'lle 1M 201
PO13: Gos 1E 238
Jagdalik Rd. SP9: Tidw 8G 30
Jago Rd. PO1: Ports 2H 5 (1A 240)
Jaguar Rd. GU14: Farn 1K 49
Jamaica Pl. PO12: Gos 3L 239
Jamaica Rd. PO12: Gos 2M 239
James Butcher Ct. *PO5: S'sea* *6E 240*
(off Eastern Villas Rd.)
James Callaghan Dr. PO6: Cosh 7A 200
PO17: S'wick 7A 200
James Cl. PO11: H Isl 3E 242
PO13: Gos 4E 212
James Copse Rd. PO8: Love 5N 181
James Ct. *BH8: Bour* *7M 227*
(off Richmond Pk. Rd.)
SO51: Rom 6N 129
James Grieve Av. SO31: Loc H 7D 196
James Hockey & Foyer Galleries 8D 64
James Howell Ct. PO7: Den 6G 181
James Michael Ho. *BH2: Bour* *7H 247*
(off Norwich Av.)
Jameson Ho. RG24: Lych 2G 42
Jameson Rd. BH9: Bour 5J 227
SO19: South 7D 174
James Pl. RG26: Tadl 5J 11
James Rd. BH12: Poole 9E 226
GU15: Camb 2K 29
PO3: Ports 1H 241
PO9: Bed 7E 202
PO13: Gos 4E 212
James St. SO14: South 5F 4 (6N 173)
James Watson Hall PO1: Ports 4M 5
James Way GU15: Camb 2K 29
James Weld Cl. SO15: South 1C 4 (3L 173)
Jamrud Rd. SP9: Tidw 9B 30 (7F 30)
Janaway Gdns. SO17: South 2B 174
Jane Austen Plaque 9M 237
Jane Austen's House Mus. 8D 80
Janes Cl. SO45: Blac 8C 208
Janred Ct. BH25: B Sea 7N 231
Jan Smuts Cl. GU33: Longc 5J 115
Janson Rd. SO15: South 3H 173
Japonica Way PO9: Hav 6J 203
Jardine Sq. *SP10: A'ver* *8B 52*
(off Cricketers Way)
Jarndyce Wlk. PO2: Ports 9E 214
Jarvis Cl. RG27: Eve 5H 17
Jarvis Flds. SO31: Burs 1M 195
Jasmine Cl. BH12: Poole 7A 226
Jasmine Ct. BH1: Bour 1A 246
BH25: New M *3B 232*
(off Whitefield Rd.)
PO13: Gos 1E 238
PO15: White 9G 177
SO17: South *2L 173*
(off Westwood Rd.)
SO41: Lymi 2D 234
SP10: A'ver *3L 69*
(off Floral Way)
Jasmine Gro. PO7: W'lle 3A 202
Jasmine Rd. RG22: B'toke 2K 59
SO30: Hed E 2M 175
Jasmine Wlk. PO14: Fare 9A 198
Jasmine Way GU35: Bor 5K 101
PO8: Clan 6C 168
Jasmond Rd. PO6: Cosh 2G 215
Jason Pl. PO7: Purb 7M 201
Jason Way PO12: Gos 8H 213
Jaundrells Cl. BH25: New M 3D 232
Java Dr. PO15: White 2F 196
Java Ho. GU17: Min 6E 28
Javelin Cl. *SP4: Ames* *5A 66*
(off Porton Rd.)
Javelin Rd. PO10: T Isl 5N 217
J Avenue SO45: Fawl 2D 208
Jay Cl. PO8: Horn 3A 182
PO14: Stub 3L 211
Jays Cl. RG22: B'toke 1B 60
Jays Ct. BH23: Highc 6K 231
Jays Nest Cl. GU17: Blackw 9F 18
Jazmine Ct. SO31: Net A 3G 194
Jealous La. SO41: Bold, Lymi 5A 224
Jean Orr Ct. GU52: Ch Cr 6M 47
Jefferson Av. BH1: Bour 8A 228
Jefferson Rd. RG21: B'toke 4C 42
Jeffries Cl. SO16: Rown 6D 158
Jelico Ct. SO16: Bass 6M 159
Jellicoe Av. PO12: Gos 5H 239
Jellicoe Ct. *SP10: A'ver* *9C 52*
(off Admirals Way)
Jellicoe Dr. BH23: Mude 8B 230
Jellicoe Ho. *PO1: Ports* *1E 240*
(off Fyning St.)
SO30: Hed E 2A 176
Jellicoe Way PO2: Ports 7C 214
Jenkins Gro. PO3: Ports 9J 215
Jenkins Pl. GU14: Farn 3M 49
Jenkyns Cl. SO30: Botl 3D 176
Jenner Rd. PO6: Cosh 8G 200
Jenner Way GU34: Alt 2G 80
SO51: Rom 4B 130
Jenni Cl. BH11: Bour 1E 226
Jennie Grn. La. GU34: Meds 7J 79
Jennings Rd. BH14: Poole 3A 244
SO40: Tott 2N 171
Jennys Wlk. GU46: Yat 7A 18
Jensen Ct. SO15: South 2L 173
Jenson Gdns. SP10: A'ver 2L 69
Jephcote Rd. BH11: Bour 2D 226
Jermyns La. SO51: Ampf 1B 130
Jerome Cnr. RG45: Cr'tne 2E 18
Jerome Ct. SO19: South 4H 175
Jerome St. PO15: White 9F 176
Jerram Cl. PO12: Gos 4H 239
Jerrems Hill SO51: Mott 9B 88
Jerrett's La. SO16: Nur 8C 158
Jersey Cl. BH12: Poole 5B 226
GU51: Fleet 8N 27
PO14: Stub 7N 211
RG24: B'toke 1D 42
SO16: South 8D 158
Jersey Rd. BH12: Poole 5B 226
PO2: Ports 8F 214
Jervis Ct. SP10: A'ver 9C 52
Jervis Ct. La. SO32: Bis W, Swanm 3B 164
Jervis Dr. PO12: Gos 1K 239
Jervis Rd. PO2: Ports 6D 214
Jesmond Av. BH23: Highc 6H 231
Jesmond Gro. SO31: Loc H 8D 196
Jessamine Rd. SO16: South 9G 158
Jesse Cl. GU46: Yat 8B 18
Jessett Dr. GU52: Ch Cr 7K 47
Jessica Cl. PO7: W'lle 9B 182
Jessica Cres. SO40: Tott 1H 171
Jessie Rd. PO4: S'sea 3F 240
PO9: Bed 6C 202
PO12: Gos 3J 239
Jessie Ter. SO14: South 8E 4 (7M 173)
Jessop Cl. SO45: Hythe 4L 193
Jessopp Cl. BH10: Bour 2K 227
Jessop Wlk. *SO45: Hythe* *4L 193*
(off Waterside Sq.)
Jesty Rd. SO24: New A 2D 108
Jetty Rd. SO45: Fawl 3F 208
Jewell Rd. BH8: Bour 4D 228
Jewry St. SO23: Winche 7L 237 (6L 105)
Jex Blake Cl. SO16: South 7G 159
Jibbs Mdw. RG26: B'ley 1G 22
Jinny La. SO51: Rom 8L 123
Joanna Cl. SP5: Down 2H 119 (7N 119)
JOB'S CORNER 2E 162
Jobson Cl. RG28: Whit 5G 55
Jocelyn Ct. *PO4: S'sea* *5G 240*
(off Eastern Pde.)
Jockey La. SO50: B'stke 7J 133
Jodrell Cl. PO8: Horn 3C 182
Joe Bigwood Cl. SO16: Nur 6C 158
John Arlott Ct. SO24: New A 1E 108
John Bunyan Cl. PO15: White 1F 196
John Cl. GU11: Alders 2G 64
John Darling Mall SO50: E'leigh 8E 132
John Eddie Ct. RG22: B'toke 8L 41
John Eggar's Sq. GU34: Alt 3H 81
John French Way SP4: Bul 3A 66
John Hansard Gallery 8M 159
John Hunt Dr. RG24: B'toke 2C 42
John Marshall Ct. PO2: Ports 8E 214
John Morgan Cl. RG27: Hoo 1G 45
Johnson St. SO14: South 5E 4 (6M 173)
(not continuous)
Johnson Vw. PO15: White 3H 197
Johnson Way GU52: Ch Cr 6M 47
SP11: Ludg 2C 30 (5K 31)
Johns Rd. PO16: Fare 1D 212
SO19: South 8B 174
Johnstone Rd. BH23: Chri 8A 230
John St. SO14: South 8E 4 (7M 173)
John Thornycroft Rd. SO19: South 8A 174
Joices Yd. RG21: B'toke 7C 42
Joiners M. SO19: South 8B 174
Jo Jo's Health & Fitness 2M 173
Jollies, The GU10: Cron 3L 63
Jolliffe Ct. *GU32: Pet* *1M 145*
(off Hylton Rd.)
Jonas Nichols Sq. SO14: South 5F 4 (6N 173)
Jonathan Cl. SO41: Lymi 1E 234
Jonathan Hill RG20: Newt 1E 8
(not continuous)
Jonathan Rd. PO15: Fare 8A 198
Jones Dr. RG19: Green 1G 9
Jones La. SO45: Hythe 5L 193
Jopps Cnr. BH23: Wink 2M 229
Jordan Ho. SO15: South 5H 173
Jordans La. SO41: Pil, Portm 5H 225
SO41: Sway 4K 223
Joseph Ct. PO3: Ports 1H 241
Joseph Nye Ct. PO1: Ports 4K 5
Joseph St. PO12: Gos 3L 239
Josian Wlk. SO14: South 4F 4 (5N 173)
Joslin Cl. PO12: Gos 1M 239
Jouldings La. RG7: Fa H 1N 15
Joule Rd. RG21: B'toke 4A 42
SP10: A'ver 9H 51
Jowitt Dr. BH25: New M 4A 232
Joyce Dickson Cl. BH24: Ring 2L 187
Joys La. SO20: Chil 4F 74
SO41: Norl 7L 225
J Ten Trade Pk. PO16: Fare 6D 198
Jubilee Av. PO6: Cosh 8N 199
SO21: Owls 7B 134
Jubilee Bus. Cen. PO7: W'lle 1L 201
Jubilee Cl. BH24: Poul 9M 185
GU14: Cov 8F 28
RG26: Pam H 4L 11
RG28: Litc 2G 36
SO50: E'leigh 2D 160
SP6: F'dge 1F 152
Jubilee Ct. PO14: Fare 1C 212
SO30: Hed E 5M 175
SO41: Sway 6J 223
SP6: Ald 5B 152
SP9: Tidw 7D 30
Jubilee Cres. BH12: Poole 9B 226
SP6: F'dge 1G 152

Jubilee Gdns.—Kingfisher Rd.

Jubilee Gdns. BH10: Bour 4H 227
SO18: South 3F 174
Jubilee Hall Rd. GU14: Farn 8L 29
Jubilee Ho. PO10: Ems 8L 203
Jubilee La. GU26: Gray 4L 103
Jubilee M. SO31: Net A 3E 194
Jubilee Path PO9: Bed 8D 202
Jubilee Rd. BH12: Poole 9B 226
GU11: Alders 3K 65
PO4: S'sea 4G 240
PO7: W'lle 9L 181
PO12: Gos 2K 239
PO16: Portc 9M 199
RG21: B'toke 7C 42
RG40: F'std 1J 17
SO51: Rom 4L 129
SP6: F'dge 1F 152
Jubilee Sports Cen.
Southampton 8M 159
Jubilee Ter. PO5: S'sea 7M 5 (4C 240)
Judd Cl. SO50: E'leigh 8C 132
Jukes Wlk. SO30: Wes E 9K 161
Julia Cl. BH23: Highc 6H 231
Julian Cl. SO16: Chilw 5K 159
Julian Ct. SO18: South 9C 160
Julian Rd. SO19: South 7F 174
Julian Ter. BH5: Bour 9E 228
Julie Av. PO15: Fare 8A 198
Juliet Ct. PO7: W'lle 1A 202
Julius Cl. RG24: B'toke 3L 41
SO53: Cha F 6C 132
Julyan Av. BH12: Poole 6E 226
Jumar Cl. SO31: Wars 1A 210
Jumpers Av. BH23: Chri 6H 229
JUMPERS COMMON 5H 229
Jumpers Rd. BH23: Chri 6J 229
Jumps Rd. GU10: Chur 5G 84
Junction Rd. BH9: Bour 6K 227
SO40: Tott 3N 171
SP10: A'ver 9M 51
June Dr. RG23: B'toke 6K 41
Juniper Centre, The BH23: Chri 6J 229
Juniper Cl. GU35: W'hil 5F 100
RG24: Chin 8H 23
SO22: Winche 9H 105
SO41: Penn 4B 234
SO52: N Bad 7E 130
SP10: A'ver 2K 69
Juniper Ct. SO18: South 3C 174
SP9: Tidw 7E 30
Juniper Dr. BH23: Chri 5E 230
Juniper Rd. GU14: Cov 7E 28
PO8: Horn 1C 182
SO18: South 3D 174
SP5: Firs 4E 86
Juniper Sq. PO9: Hav 9F 202
Jupiter Cl. GU14: Farn 1K 49
PO1: Ports 5J 5 (3B 240)
SO16: South 8E 158
Jura Cl. PO6: Cosh 8H 201
Jurds Lake Way SO19: South 9B 174
Jurd Way SO31: Burs 9K 175
Justin Cl. PO14: Fare 9A 198
Justin Gdns. BH10: Bour 2J 227
Justinian Cl. SO53: Cha F 5D 132
Jute Cl. PO16: Portc 8K 199
Jutland Cl. PO15: White 2E 196
Jutland Cres. SP10: A'ver 7M 51
Juventu Cl. PO9: Hav 5G 202

K

Kamptee Copse BH25: New M 9C 222
Kamran Ct. GU11: Alders 3J 65
(off Boxhalls La.)
Kanes Hill SO19: South 4J 175
Kanes Hill Caravan Site
SO19: South 6K 175
Karachi Cl. SP9: Tidw 7C 30 (6G 30)
Karen Av. PO6: Dray 2K 215
Kashmir Ct. GU14: Farn 2L 49
Kassassin St. PO4: S'sea 5H 241
Kassel Cl. PO7: W'lle 1B 202
Katherine Chance Cl. BH23: Burt 3M 229
Katherine Cl. RG22: B'toke 9J 41
Katherine Ct. GU15: Camb 8M 19
(off Up. Gordon Rd.)
Kathleen Cl. RG21: B'toke 9B 42
Kathleen Rd. SO19: South 7E 174
Kathryn Cl. SO40: Calm 1H 171
Katie Cl. BH14: Poole 9A 226
Katrina Gdns. PO11: H Isl 2G 242
Katrine Cres. SO53: Cha F 4M 131
Katterns Cl. BH23: Chri 4H 229
Kayak Cl. SO31: Wars 8B 196
Kay Cl. BH23: Chri 7A 230
Kay Cres. GU35: Head D 1C 102
Kayleigh Cl. SO40: Tott 4K 171
Kealy Rd. PO12: Gos 1J 239
Kearsney Av. PO2: Ports 5F 214
Keast Wlk. PO13: Gos 4F 212
Keats Av. PO6: Cosh 8N 199
SO41: M Sea 7K 235
Keats Cl. PO8: Cowp 6N 181
PO15: White 9E 176
RG24: B'toke 2D 42
SO21: Sth W 3H 91
SO22: Oli B 1G 126
Keats Gdns. GU51: Fleet 2N 47
Keats Ho. BH25: New M 4B 232
PO9: Hav 5E 202
Keats Rd. SO19: South 4G 174
Keats Way GU46: Yat 9L 17
Keble Cl. SO21: Hurs 6N 125
SO53: Cha F 7A 132
Keble Rd. SO53: Cha F 8A 132
Keble St. SO22: Winche 8G 105
Keble Way GU47: Owl 3G 19
Keeble Cl. BH10: Bour 1H 227
Keeble Cres. BH10: Bour 1H 227
Keeble Rd. BH10: Bour 1H 227
Keelan Ct. PO5: S'sea 5E 240
Keel Cl. PO3: Ports 5K 215
PO13: Gos 9F 212
Keel Gdns. SO41: Lymi 2E 234
Keep, The PO16: Portc 9M 199
Keepers Cl. SO53: Cha F 6N 131
Keeper's Hill SP11: Amp 4A 68
Keeper's La. SO51: Mott 3C 122
KEEPING 1D 236
Keeps Mead RG20: Kings 1A 6 (5K 9)
Kefford Cl. PO8: Horn 4B 182
Keith Cl. PO12: Gos 1K 239
Keith Ho. PO1: Ports 3K 5
Keith Lucas Rd. GU14: Cov 1H 49
Keith Rd. BH3: Bour 8G 227
Kelburn Cl. SO53: Cha F 5N 131
Kellett Rd. SO15: South 2K 173
Kelly Ct. PO4: S'sea 4F 240
PO16: Fare 7D 198
Kelly Ho. SO18: S'ing 7C 160
Kellynch Cl. GU34: Alt 4E 80
Kelly Rd. PO7: W'lle 4M 201
Kellys Wlk. SP10: A'ver 2L 69
Kelmscott Gdns. SO53: Cha F 3N 131
Kelsall Gdns. BH25: New M 3B 232
Kelsey Cl. GU33: Liss 9F 114
PO14: Titch C 8E 196
Kelsey Gro. GU46: Yat 8A 18
Kelsey Head PO6: P Sol 1B 214
Kelston Cl. SO15: South 3F 172
Kelvin Cl. SO45: Hythe 6M 193
Kelvin Gro. PO16: Portc 9M 199
SO31: Net A 3G 194
Kelvin Hill RG22: B'toke 8N 41
Kelvin Rd. SO50: E'leigh 1D 160
Kembers La. RG25: Mapl 7M 43
Kemmel Rd. SP11: Per D 4A 30 (6J 31)
Kemmitt Way SP10: A'ver 3L 69
Kempenfelt Ho. PO1: Ports 3K 5
Kemp Rd. BH9: Bour 6K 227
KEMPSHOTT 1J 59
Kempshott Gdns. RG22: B'toke 2J 59
Kempshott Gro. RG22: Wort 7J 41
Kempshott La. RG22: B'toke 3J 59
Kempshott Pk. Ind. Est. RG23: B'toke 7H 59
Kempshott Rdbt. RG22: B'toke 3K 59
Kemps Quay Ind. Pk. SO18: South 3B 174
Kempthorne Ho. SO22: Winche 6K 237
SO41: Lymi 2E 234
Kempton Cl. GU34: Alt 6F 80
Kempton Ct. GU14: Cov 1H 49
PO15: White 1F 196
(off Timor Cl.)
Kempton Pk. PO7: W'lle 9B 182
Kemshott Ct. PO9: Hav 3D 202
Kemys Gdns. SP10: A'ver 1M 69
Ken Berry Ct. PO9: Hav 3H 203
Kench, The PO11: H Isl 3N 241
Kenchester Cl. PO6: Cosh 9D 200
Kench, The (Nature Reserve) 3A 242
Kendal Av. PO3: Ports 7H 215
SO16: South 1C 172
Kendal Cl. GU14: Cov 8G 28
PO8: Cowp 6A 182
SO53: Cha F 5C 132
Kendal Ct. SO16: South 1C 172
Kendal Gdns. RG22: B'toke 9K 41
Kendrick Rd. RG14: New 1C 8
Kenilworth Cl. BH25: New M 3C 232
PO13: Lee S 9B 212
Kenilworth Ct. BH13: Poole 5D 244
BH23: Chri 7K 229
SO23: Winche 4L 105
(off Northlands Dr.)
Kenilworth Cres. GU51: Fleet 1A 48
Kenilworth Dr. SO50: E'leigh 6E 132
Kenilworth Gdns. SO30: Wes E 1J 175
Kenilworth Ho. SO14: South 4A 174
(off Kent St.)
SO30: Wes E 1J 175
Kenilworth Rd. GU14: Cov 7E 28
GU51: Fleet 2N 47
PO5: S'sea 6E 240
RG23: B'toke 5K 41
SO15: South 2B 4 (4L 173)
Kenley Pl. GU14: Farn 3K 49
Kenley Rd. GU35: Head D 2D 102
Kenmore Cl. GU16: Frim 4M 29
GU52: Ch Cr 6N 47
SO40: Tott 6L 171
Kennard Ct. BH25: New M 3A 232
Kennard Pl. BH25: New M 3B 232
(off Kennard Rd.)
Kennard Rd. BH25: New M 2A 232
Kennedy Av. PO15: Fare 6A 198
Kennedy Cl. PO7: Purb 5L 201
Kennedy Cres. PO12: Gos 5G 239
Kennedy Rd. SO16: South 8E 158
Kennel La. SO22: Lit 2F 104
Kennels La. GU14: Cov, Farn 9D 28
(not continuous)
Kennet Cl. GU14: Cov 6G 28
PO12: Gos 6K 239
RG21: B'toke 6E 42
SO18: Wes E 8F 160
Kennet Ct. SP10: A'ver 8B 52
Kenneth Ct. BH23: Highc 7K 231
Kennet Rd. GU31: Pet 2L 145
SP9: Tidw 7D 30 (6G 31)
Kennett Cl. SO51: Rom 4B 130
Kennett Rd. SO51: Rom 4B 130
Kennet Way RG23: Oak 1D 58
Kennington La. SO40: Cad 3B 170
Ken Rd. BH6: Bour 1H 247
Kensington Cl. SO50: B'stke 7H 133
Kensington Ct. BH1: Bour 1A 246
GU51: Fleet 8J 27
Kensington Dr. BH2: Bour 5H 247 (1H 245)
Kensington Flds. SO45: Dib P 7J 193
Kensington Gdns. PO14: Titch C 7F 196
Kensington Ho. PO11: H Isl 3E 242
RG21: B'toke 6C 42
(off Festival Pl.)
Kensington Pk. SO41: M Sea 8J 235
Kensington Rd. PO2: Ports 6G 215
PO12: Gos 4L 239
Kenson Gdns. SO19: South 6E 174
Kent Gdns. SO40: Tott 5K 171
Kent Gro. PO16: Portc 2L 213
Kent Ho. BH4: Bour 2G 245
(off Marlborough Rd.)
SO14: South 4A 174
Kentidge Rd. PO7: Purb 4L 201
Kentigern Dr. RG45: Cr'tne 1G 19
Kentish Rd. SO15: South 3H 173
Kent La. BH24: Har 8F 152
Kent Rd. BH12: Poole 8C 226
GU35: W'hil 5J 101
GU51: Fleet 2N 47
PO5: S'sea 8M 5 (4C 240)
PO13: Gos 4D 212
SO17: South 1A 174
SO53: Cha F 9A 132
KENTSBORO 4B 72
KENT'S OAK 8E 122
Kent St. PO1: Ports 4K 5 (2B 240)
SO14: South 5A 174
Kenwith Av. GU51: Fleet 2A 48
Kenwood Bus. Pk. PO9: Hav 7G 203
Kenwood Rd. PO16: Portc 2M 213
Kenwyn Cl. SO18: Wes E 9F 160
Kenya Rd. PO16: Portc 1K 213
Kenyon Rd. PO2: Ports 6G 214
Kenyons Yd. SP10: A'ver 1L 69
Keppel PO1: Ports 2K 5
Keppel Cl. BH24: Ring 1L 187
Kerchers Fld. RG25: Over 3D 56
Kerfield Way RG27: Hoo 2H 45
Kerley Rd. BH2: Bour 8K 247 (3J 245)
Kern Cl. SO16: South 8E 158
Kernella Ct. BH4: Bour 1F 244
Kerrfield SO22: Winche 7H 105
Kerrfield M. SO22: Winche 7H 105
Kerridge Ind. Est. GU34: Alt 4G 81
Kerrigan Ct. SO17: South 2M 173
Kerry Cl. GU51: Fleet 7N 27
SO41: Penn 3C 234
SO53: Cha F 6A 132
Kerry Gdns. SP6: Sand 9E 150
Kersley Cres. RG29: Odi 2E 62
Kersley Gdns. SO19: South 6E 174
Kesteven Way SO18: South 2E 174
Kestrel Cl. GU10: Ews 2N 63
PO8: Clan 7C 168
PO14: Stub 4L 211
SO16: South 6G 158
SO22: Winche 1H 127
SO32: Bis W 3K 163
SO32: Botl 1C 176
SO40: March 9D 172
Kestrel Ct. BH24: Ring 9K 185
GU34: Alt 3F 80
Kestrel Dr. BH23: Mude 8C 230
Kestrel Gdns. RG20: Bis G 2G 9
Kestrel Ho. GU9: Farnh 9C 64
Kestrel Pl. PO6: Farl 1N 215
Kestrel Rd. GU14: Farn 1K 49
PO3: Ports 4H 215
RG22: B'toke 1H 59
SO50: E'leigh 1B 160
Kestrels, The SO31: Burs 1K 195
Kestrels Mead RG26: Tadl 3H 11
Kestrel Way SP6: Ald 5E 152
Keswick Av. PO3: Ports 8H 215
Keswick Ct. BH25: New M 1C 232
Keswick Rd. BH5: Bour 1C 246
BH25: New M 1C 232
SO19: South 7B 174
Ketchers Fld. GU34: Selb 9M 99
Ketelbey Ri. RG22: B'toke 3A 60
Kettering Ter. PO2: Ports 8D 214
Keverstone Ct. BH1: Bour 2A 246
Kevins Cl. RG20: Kings 2D 6
Kevins Dr. GU46: Yat 6A 18
Kevins Gro. GU51: Fleet 2N 47
Kevlyn Cres. SO31: Old N 9J 175
Kew Cl. RG24: B'toke 1C 42
Kewlake La. SO40: Cad 5M 155
Kew La. SO31: Burs 2L 195
Kew Wlk. SP10: A'ver 2L 69
Key, The GU51: Fleet 9J 27
Keydell Av. PO8: Horn 5A 182
Keydell Cl. PO8: Horn 5A 182
Keyes Cl. BH12: Poole 5D 226
BH23: Mude 8B 230
PO13: Gos 5E 212
Keyes Ct. PO5: S'sea 5E 240
(off Albert Rd.)
Keyes Rd. PO13: Gos 5E 212
KEYHAVEN 8N 235
Keyhaven Cl. PO13: Gos 6C 212
Keyhaven Dr. PO9: Hav 4C 202
Keyhaven Marshes Nature Reserve 9C 234
Keyhaven Rd. SO41: Key, M Sea 8L 235
Keynes Cl. GU52: Ch Cr 7N 47
Keynsham Rd. SO19: South 4F 174
Keynsham Way GU47: Owl 3F 18
Keysworth Av. BH25: B Sea 6A 232
Keytech Cen. RG23: B'toke 4M 41
Keythorpe BH1: Bour 2N 245
Khandala Gdns. PO7: Purb 5N 201
Khartoum Rd. SO17: South 9M 159
Khyber Rd. BH12: Poole 9B 226
Kidlington Rd. RG24: B'toke 2B 42
Kidmore La. PO7: Den 3G 181
Kielder Cl. SO53: Cha F 5M 131
Kielder Gro. PO13: Gos 6F 212
Kiel Dr. SP10: A'ver 7M 51
Kilbride BH13: Poole 1E 244
Kilbride Path PO2: Ports 8E 214
Kildare Cl. GU35: Bor 3J 101
Kildare Rd. GU35: Bor 3J 101
Kilderkin Dr. PO8: Horn 3D 182
Kilford Ct. SO30: Botl 4D 176
Kilham La. SO22: Winche 7E 104
Killarney Cl. SO19: South 7J 175
Kilmarnock Rd. BH9: Bour 5K 227
KILMESTON 2L 135
Kilmeston Cl. PO9: Hav 3F 202
Kilmeston Rd. SO24: Cher, Kilm 1K 135
Kilmington Way BH23: Highc 6G 231
Kilmiston Cl. PO1: Ports 9F 214
Kilmiston Dr. PO16: Portc 8K 199
Kilmuir Cl. GU47: Coll 6F 18
Kiln, The GU34: Selb 8A 100
Kiln Acres Bus. Pk.
PO16: Fare 6D 198
Kiln Cl. SO45: Dib P 6K 193
Kiln Fld. GU33: Liss 9D 114
Kiln Gdns. RG27: H Win 6B 26
Kiln Grn. SO21: Col C 4L 133
Kiln Hill SO32: Sob H 2K 179
Kiln La. GU31: Buri 8J 145
PO7: H'don 7M 179
RG7: Mort 1H 13
RG26: M She 7J 21
SO21: Ott 2F 132
SO24: Old A 6F 94
SO50: B'dge 3H 133
SO51: Brai 7A 124
Kiln Pl. GU14: Cov 9J 29
Kiln Rd. PO3: Ports 7H 215
PO16: Fare 5B 198
RG24: Sher J 9N 21
SP5: Redl 1N 119 (7D 120)
Kilns, The GU34: Alt 5H 81
GU35: Slea 3K 83
Kilnside PO7: Den 7G 180
Kiln Way GU11: Alders 3K 65
GU26: Gray 2G 103
Kilnyard Cl. SO40: Tott 1K 171
Kilometre, The RG45: Cr'tne 1B 18
Kilpatrick Cl. PO2: Ports 8E 214
Kilwich Way PO16: Portc 2K 213
Kimbell Rd. RG22: B'toke 9A 42
Kimber Cl. RG24: Chin 1G 42
SP9: Tidw 7C 30
Kimber Hall SO14: South 6E 4
Kimber Ho. SO14: South 8C 4
Kimberley GU52: Ch Cr 7N 47
Kimberley Cl. BH23: Chri 6J 229
SO30: Hed E 5M 175
SO50: Fair O 1A 162
SP10: Charl 8L 51
Kimberley Ct. SO19: South 8C 174
Kimberley Rd. BH6: Bour 8F 228
BH14: Poole 2A 244
GU33: Longc 4H 115
PO4: S'sea 5H 241
RG22: B'toke 8N 41
Kimber Rd. BH11: Bour 3D 226
Kimbers GU32: Pet 9L 139
Kimbers La. GU9: Farnh 7F 64
RG26: Pam G 9K 11
Kimbolton Rd. PO3: Ports 1H 241
KIMBRIDGE 6F 122
Kimbridge Cl. SO16: Rown 6D 158
Kimbridge Cres. PO9: Hav 3G 203
Kimbridge La. SO51: Kimb 6F 122
Kimmeridge Av. BH12: Poole 6A 226
KIMPTON 9M 31
Kimpton Cl. PO13: Lee S 1B 238
Kimpton Ct. PO9: Hav 3H 203
Kimpton Dr. GU51: Fleet 9H 27
Kindersley Pk. Homes SP11: Abb A 6H 69
Kineton Rd. SO15: South 1K 173
King Albert Ct. PO1: Ports 1F 240
King Albert St. PO1: Ports 1E 240
King Alfred Pl. SO23: Winche 5L 105
King Alfred's Statue 8N 237
King Alfred Ter. RG20: Kings 2B 6
SO23: Winche 5L 105
King Arthurs Ct. PO6: Dray 9L 201
King Arthur's Way SP10: A'ver 7N 51
King Arthur's Way Rdbt. SP10: A'ver 6A 52
King Charles St. PO1: Ports 6J 5 (3B 240)
King Cl. BH24: St I 4C 186
Kingcome Ho. PO1: Ports 1E 240
(off Staunton St.)
King Ct. BH13: Poole 3F 244
King Cup Av. SO31: Loc H 6C 196
Kingdom Cl. PO15: Seg 4G 196
Kingdom's M. GU34: Alt 5F 80
King Edward Av. BH9: Bour 4K 227
SO16: South 2F 172
King Edward Ct. BH9: Bour 4K 227
King Edward Pk. SO52: N Bad 3L 131
King Edward's Cres. PO2: Ports 6E 214
Kingfisher Caravan Pk. PO13: Lee S 4E 238
Kingfisher Cl. BH6: Bour 8H 229
GU14: Cov 6E 28
GU35: Bor 5K 101
GU52: Ch Cr 6M 47
PO8: Cowp 6M 181
PO9: R Cas 9H 183
PO11: H Isl 5J 243
RG22: B'toke 1H 59
RG28: Whit 5G 55
SO31: Hamb 5L 195
Kingfisher Copse SO31: Loc H 6E 196
Kingfisher Ct. BH1: Bour 2N 245
(off Christchurch Rd.)
GU34: Alt 2F 80
GU51: Fleet 3L 47
(off Connaught Rd.)
PO3: Ports 4H 215
PO9: Hav 6H 203
RG21: B'toke 5B 42
Kingfisher Dr. GU46: Yat 7L 17
Kingfisher Pk. BH24: Blas 7K 185
Kingfisher Pk. Homes BH10: Bour 2K 227
Kingfisher Rd. SO50: E'leigh 1B 160

Kingfishers—Krooner Rd.

Kingfishers PO16: Portc .9H 199
SP9: Shi B .2B 66
Kingfisher Way BH23: Mude .9C 230
BH24: Poul .7L 185
SO40: March .9D 172
SO51: Rom .4M 129
King George Av. BH9: Bour .4K 227
GU32: Pet .9M 139
King George Cl. GU14: Farn .1M 49
King George M. *GU32: Pet .9M 139*
(off King George Av.)
King George Mobile Home Pk.
BH25: New M .5A 232
King George Rd. PO16: Portc .1L 213
SP10: A'ver .1K 69
King George's Av. SO15: South .4E 172
King George's Dr. GU30: Lip .1F 116
Kingham Pl. *GU9: Farnh .8D 64*
(off West St.)
King Harold Ct. SO23: Winche .8J 105
King Henry I St. PO1: Ports .4M 5 (2C 240)
King Henry Rd. GU51: Fleet .9L 27
King James's Gate .5L 5 (3C 240)
King James Ter. PO1: Ports .7J 5
King John Av. BH11: Bour .1B 226
PO16: Portc .1K 213
King John Cl. BH11: Bour .1B 226
King John Ct. RG20: Kings .2B 6
King John Rd. RG20: Kings .2B 6 (6K 9)
King John's House & Heritage Cen. .5L 129
King Johns Rd. RG29: N War .7J 45
King John St. GU51: Fleet .9L 27
King La. GU32: Frox .5E 138
SO20: Ov Wa .6L 67
King La. Cotts. SO20: Ov Wa .8M 67
King Richard I Rd. PO1: Ports .4M 5 (2C 240)
King Richard Cl. PO6: Cosh .9E 200
King Richard Dr. BH11: Bour .1B 226
Kings Acre SO20: Ki S .8B 86 (6G 88)
Kings Apartments GU15: Camb .9L 19
King's Arms La. BH24: Ring .1J 187
Kings Arms Row BH24: Ring .1J 187
Kings Av. BH14: Poole .3B 244
BH23: Chri .8J 229
GU10: Tong .2N 65
SO22: Winche .9J 105
SO31: Hamb .6J 195
Kings Bench All. PO1: Ports .3K 5 (2B 240)
Kingsbere Av. BH10: Bour .4F 226
Kingsbere Gdns. BH23: Highc .5J 231
Kingsbourne Cl. SP4: Win D .3A 86
Kingsbridge Copse RG27: Newn .3E 44
Kingsbridge End *RG27: Hoo .3E 44*
(off Old School Rd.)
Kingsbridge La. SO15: South .4B 4 (5L 173)
Kingsbridge Rd. BH14: Poole .2A 244
Kingsbrook SO41: Hor .2G 233
Kingsbury Ct. PO8: Clan .5B 168
Kingsbury Rd. SO14: South .3N 173
Kingsbury's La. BH24: Ring .1J 187
Kings Chase SP10: A'ver .2L 69
Kingsclear Pk. GU15: Camb .9M 19
KINGSCLERE .2B 6 (6K 9)
Kingsclere Av. PO9: Hav .3D 202
SO19: South .9D 174
Kingsclere Bowling Club .2B 6
Kingsclere By-Pass RG20: Kings .1A 6 (5K 9)
Kingsclere Cl. SO19: South .9D 174
Kingsclere Pk. RG20: Kings .1A 6 (5K 9)
Kingsclere Rd. RG21: B'toke .4A 42
RG23: W Law .1E 40
RG25: Over .7D 38
RG26: Rams, Up Woott .7B 20
RG28: Whit .2H 55
Kings Cl. PO9: R Cas .8G 183
SO21: Twyf .6L 127
SO23: Kin W .6M 91
SO41: Lymi .2D 234
SO43: Lyn .2B 148 (2N 189)
SO53: Cha F .5B 132
Kings Copse Av. SO30: Botl, Hed E .6A 176
Kings Copse Rd. SO30: Hed E .6A 176
SO45: Blac .8A 208
Kingscote Ho. PO6: Cosh .7A 200
Kingscote Rd. PO6: Cosh .7A 200
PO8: Cowp .7L 181
Kings Ct. BH6: Bour .9J 229
GU10: Tong .2N 65
PO10: S'brne .9N 203
SP6: F'dge .1J 153
Kings Courtyard BH1: Bour .1N 245
Kings Cres. BH14: Poole .3C 244
GU15: Camb .5L 19
SO22: Winche .8H 105
SO41: Lymi .2D 234
Kingscroft GU51: Fleet .3M 47
Kingscroft Cnr. PO9: Hav .8D 202
Kingscroft Ct. PO9: Hav .8D 202
Kingscroft La. PO9: Bed .8C 202
Kingsdale Ct. SO23: Winche .6L 237 (6K 105)
Kingsdown Pl. PO1: Ports .2F 240
Kingsdown Rd. PO7: W'lle .8K 181
Kingsdown Way SO18: South .9D 160
King's Elms SO21: Bar S .5A 76
Kingsey Av. PO10: Ems .9L 203
Kings Farm La. SO41: Hor .4J 233
Kings Farm Rural Workshops SO41: Hor .3J 233
Kingsfernsden La. GU32: Pet .8N 139
Kingsfield BH24: Ring .2K 187
SO31: Burs .9L 175
SO41: Lymi .4G 234
Kingsfield Gdns. SO31: Burs .9L 175
Kingsfold Av. SO18: South .8D 160
Kingsford Cl. SP5: Woodf .3M 119 (8C 120)
KING'S FURLONG .8B 42
Kings Furlong Cen. RG21: B'toke .8B 42
King's Furlong Dr. RG21: B'toke .8A 42
Kings Gate .9M 237 (7L 105)
Kingsgate BH13: Poole .2F 244
Kingsgate Rd. SO23: Winche .9K 105
Kingsgate St. SO23: Winche .9M 237 (8L 105)
Kings Glade GU46: Yat .7B 18
Kings Grange BH4: Bour .9G 247 (3H 245)
Kingsgrove Ind. Est. GU14: Cov .9J 29
Kings Head Yd. SO23: Winche .8M 237 (7L 105)
King's Hill GU34: Bee .9M 79
Kingsholme BH8: Bour .7M 227
Kings Ho. SO14: South .7E 4 (7M 173)
Kings Keep GU47: Sandh .4D 18
GU52: Fleet .5M 47
Kingsland Bus. Pk. RG24: B'toke .2F 42
Kingsland Cl. PO6: Cosh .8D 200
Kingsland Ct. SO14: South .5E 4 (6M 173)
Kingsland Ho. SO14: South .4D 4
KINGSLAND PLACE .4E 4
Kingsland Rd. GU34: Alt .5E 80
Kingsland Sq. SO14: South .5E 4 (6M 173)
Kings La. GU32: Frox .3C 138
SO21: Chilc .7B 106
SO41: Sway .8L 223
KINGSLEY .7G 83
Kingsley Av. BH6: Bour .1K 247
GU15: Camb .9L 19
Kingsley Bungs. SO24: New A .2D 108
Kingsley Bus. Pk. GU35: K'ly .7H 83
Kingsley Cl. BH6: Bour .1K 247
RG45: Cr'tne .2D 18
Kingsley Ct. *GU11: Alders .9K 49*
(off Windsor Way)
Kingsley Gdns. SO40: Tott .3H 171
Kingsley Grn. PO9: Hav .3E 202
Kingsley Ho. BH9: Bour .4K 227
PO10: Ems .9L 203
Kingsley Pk. RG28: Whit .4G 54
Kingsley Pl. SO22: Winche .9J 105
Kingsley Rd. GU14: Farn .6H 29
PO4: S'sea .4J 241
PO12: Gos .9H 213
RG27: Eve .6F 16
SO15: South .3G 172
Kingsley Sq. GU51: Fleet .8H 27
Kingsley Tennis Cen. .7G 82
Kingsley Way PO15: White .9E 176
Kings Lodge *SO22: Winche .7H 105*
(off Highcroft Rd.)
KINGSMEAD .2E 178
Kingsmead GU14: Farn .8K 29
GU16: Frim G .5N 29
GU34: Alt .5G 80
PO17: Wick .2F 178
SO51: W Wel .1B 120 (9N 121)
SP11: An V .5J 69
Kingsmead Av. PO14: Stub .7N 211
Kingsmead Ct. SO15: South .1G 173
SO23: Winche .8K 105
Kings Mdw. RG25: Over .2D 56
SP10: A'ver .2A 70
Kingsmead Shop. Cen. GU14: Farn .8K 29
Kings Mede PO8: Horn .5A 182
Kingsmere Station
Moors Valley Railway .8A 184
Kings M. BH4: Bour .2G 245
PO5: S'sea .5E 240
Kingsmill Cl. PO12: Gos .4H 239
Kingsmill Rd. RG21: B'toke .9B 42
Kings Orchard RG23: Oak .2D 58
Kings Paddock SP5: W Win .5G 86
Kings Pde. GU51: Fleet .1M 47
Kings Pk. Athletics Cen. .8C 228
Kings Pk. Dr. BH7: Bour .8D 228
(Petersfield Rd.)
BH7: Bour .8B 228
(Thistlebarrow Rd.)
Kings Pk. Rd. BH7: Bour .8B 228
SO15: South .2D 4 (4M 173)
Kings Peace, The
GU26: Gray .4M 103
Kings Pightle RG24: Chin .9G 23
King's Pond Nature Reserve .5G 80
Kings Ride GU15: Camb .4M 19
SO45: Blac .9C 208
Kings Rd. BH3: Bour .7L 227
BH25: A'ley .2D 232
GU11: Alders .1G 65
GU32: Pet .9K 139
GU34: Alt .6D 80
GU51: Fleet .1M 47
PO5: S'sea .7M 5 (4C 240)
PO8: Cowp .7N 181
PO10: Ems .9L 203
PO11: H Isl .1G 243
PO12: Gos .3K 239
PO13: Lee S .9A 212
PO16: Fare .8D 198
RG7: Sil .4N 11
RG22: B'toke .8N 41
RG45: Cr'tne .1D 18
SO22: Winche .8G 104
SO41: Lymi .2D 234
SO53: Cha F .6A 132
SP11: Enh A .3A 52
King's Saltern Rd. SO41: Lymi .4F 234
KING'S SOMBORNE .9B 86 (7G 88)
King's Somborne Rd.
SO51: Brai .4C 124
King's Stone .9H 183
King's Ter. PO5: S'sea .7M 5 (4C 240)
PO10: Ems .9M 203
King's Theatre .5E 240
KINGSTON
BH24 .6K 187
PO1 .1G 240
Kingston SO31: Net A .2G 195
Kingston Cl. SP10: A'ver .3L 69
Kingston Cres. PO2: Ports .8E 214
Kingston Gdns. PO15: Fare .5N 197
Kingston Pk. SO41: Penn .4D 234
Kingston Rd. PO1: Ports .8E 214
PO2: Ports .8E 214
PO12: Gos .2H 239
SO15: South .4J 173
Kingstons Ind. Est. GU12: Ash .9N 49
King St. PO5: S'sea .6M 5 (3C 240)
(not continuous)
PO10: Ems .9N 203
PO10: Westb .6N 203
PO12: Gos .2M 239
RG29: Odi .9L 45
(Cemetery Hill)
RG29: Odi .8L 45
(Red Lion M.)
SO14: South .7E 4 (7M 173)
Kingsvale Ct. RG21: B'toke .7A 42
(not continuous)
Kings Vw. GU34: Alt .5G 81
Kings Wlk. GU15: Camb .7H 19
RG28: Whit .5G 55
Kings Way PO9: R Cas .9G 183
SO32: Swanm .6H 165
SO32: Uph .7E 134
Kingsway GU11: Alders .1G 65
GU17: Blackw .8F 18
PO11: H Isl .5G 216
SO14: South .4E 4 (5M 173)
SO53: Cha F .5B 132
SP10: A'ver .8D 52
Kingsway, The PO16: Portc .9L 199
Kingsway Cl. BH23: Chri .5J 229
Kingsway Ct. SO53: Cha F .4C 132
Kingsway Gdns. SO53: Cha F .4C 132
SP10: A'ver .7N 51
Kingswell Cl. BH10: Bour .4H 227
Kingswell Gdns. BH10: Bour .3F 226
Kingswell Gro. BH10: Bour .4F 226
Kingswell Path PO1: Ports .2N 5 (1D 240)
Kingswell Rd. BH10: Bour .4F 226
Kingswell St. PO1: Ports .3N 5 (2D 240)
Kingswood *BH4: Bour .3G 245*
(off West Cliff Rd.)
SO40: March .9F 172
Kingswood Cl. PO15: White .1G 196
Kingswood Ct. GU51: Fleet .2M 47
Kingswood Firs GU26: Gray .5K 103
Kingswood La. GU26: Gray .5L 103
Kingswood Pl. BH2: Bour .6G 247 (2H 245)
PO17: K Vil .2A 198
Kingswood Ri. GU34: Four M .5G 97
KINGS WORTHY .9N 91
Kings Worthy Ct. SO23: Kin W .1N 105
Kings Worthy Rd. GU51: Fleet .8H 27
Kingsworthy Rd. PO9: Hav .6F 202
Kings Yd. *SP6: F'dge .1J 153*
(off Salisbury St.)
SP10: A'ver .1A 70
King William St. PO1: Ports .2K 5 (1B 240)
Kinloss Ct. SO16: South .6F 158
Kinnell Cl. PO10: Ems .9M 203
Kinross Cres. PO6: Cosh .1J 215
Kinross Rd. BH3: Bour .8J 227
SO40: Tott .3M 171
Kinsbourne Av. BH10: Bour .4H 227
Kinsbourne Cl. SO19: South .4J 175
Kinsbourne Ri. SO19: South .4K 175
Kinsbourne Way SO19: South .4J 175
KINSON .1F 226
Kinson Common Nature Reserve .1F 226
Kinson Gro. BH10: Bour .1G 227
Kinson Rd. BH10: Bour .5E 226
Kintbury Cl. GU51: Fleet .9H 27
Kinterbury Ct. SO17: South .2M 173
Kintyre Cl. RG23: Oak .9C 40
Kintyre Rd. PO6: Cosh .8G 201
Kinver Cl. SO51: Rom .3A 130
Kipling Cl. GU46: Yat .9M 17
PO15: White .9E 176
Kipling Ct. SO19: South .9D 174
Kipling Hall RG45: Cr'tne .1D 18
Kipling Rd. GU34: Alt .7D 80
PO2: Ports .5F 214
SO50: E'leigh .9D 132
Kipling Wlk. RG22: B'toke .8N 41
Kirby Ct. PO2: Ports .6F 214
Kirby Dr. RG26: B'ley .2G 23
Kirby Rd. PO2: Ports .6F 214
Kirby Way BH6: Bour .1G 247
Kirkby Ct. GU16: Frim .3N 29
Kirkee Rd. SP9: Tidw .9C 30 (7G 30)
Kirk Gdns. SO40: Tott .5M 171
Kirkham Av. BH23: Burt .3M 229
Kirkham Cl. GU47: Owl .3F 18
Kirk Knoll GU35: Head .2B 102
Kirkstall Rd. PO4: S'sea .6F 240
Kirpal Rd. PO3: Ports .1J 241
Kirtle Dr. GU34: Four M .5H 97
Kirtley Cl. PO6: Dray .2K 215
Kirtling Pl. SO22: Winche .5H 105
Kirton Rd. PO6: Dray .1K 215
Kisbys La. RG20: Ecc .4H 9
Kitchener Rd. GU11: Alders .5M 49
(not continuous)
GU33: Longc .4H 115
SO17: South .8A 160
Kitchers Cl. SO41: Sway .4J 223
Kitcombe La. GU34: Lwr Farr, New V .6N 97
Kite Cl. PO8: Cowp .6M 181
Kite Hill Cotts. RG22: Wort .8J 41
Kite's Croft Bus. Pk. PO14: Titch .8H 197
Kites Croft Cl. PO14: Titch C .8F 196
Kit La. RG25: Elli .2J 79
KITNOCKS .2H 177
Kitnocks Hill SO32: Curd .2H 177
Kitscroft Rd. BH10: Bour .1G 226
Kittiwake Cl. BH6: Bour .8G 229
PO13: Gos .6D 212
Kitts La. GU10: Chur .7G 85
SO24: Bram .3C 136
Kitwalls La. SO41: M Sea .7K 235
KITWOOD .8J 97
Kitwood Grn. PO9: Hav .4H 203
Kitwood La. SO24: Rop .8J 97
Kitwood Rd. GU34: Four M .8J 97
Kivernell Pl. SO41: M Sea .7J 235
Kivernell Rd. SO41: M Sea .8J 235
Kleves Ct. SO19: South .4F 174
KNAPP .9J 125
Knapp Cl. BH23: Chri .6K 229
Knapp Close, The SN8: Co Du .2G 31
KNAPP HILL .9J 125
Knapp La. GU34: Meds .3G 97
RG26: Tadl .7K 11
SO51: Ampf .1H 131
Knapp Mill Av. BH23: Chri .6K 229
Knapps Hard GU32: W Meo .8C 136
Knatchbull Cl. SO51: Rom .5M 129
Knellers La. SO40: Tott .6K 171
Knight Cl. GU51: Cr V .5H 47
SO23: Winche .4L 105
Knightcrest Pk. SO41: Ever .5M 233
Knight Gdns. PO6: Farl .1M 215
Knighton Caravan Pk. SO41: Ever .5M 233
Knighton Cnr. PO8: Horn .3C 182
Knighton Heath Cl. BH11: Bour .2C 226
Knighton Heath Golf Course .3A 226
Knighton Heath Ind. Est. BH11: Bour .3C 226
Knighton Heath Rd. BH11: Bour .2C 226
Knighton Pk. BH25: B Sea .6N 231
Knighton Rd. SO19: South .6D 174
SP5: Br Ch .3A 118
Knights Bank Rd. PO14: Stub .7J 211
Knightsbridge Ct. BH2: Bour .8K 247
Knightsbridge Dr. RG19: Head .1H 9
Knightsbridge Gro. GU15: Camb .6N 19
Knightsbridge Rd. GU15: Camb .6N 19
SP11: Enh A .3B 52
Knights Cl. SO31: Wars .8B 196
SP5: Mid W .4G 87
(off Middleton)
Knights Ct. SP10: A'ver .9D 52
KNIGHTS ENHAM .5N 51
Knights Enham Dr. GU51: Fleet .9H 27
Knights Enham Rdbt. SP10: A'ver .6N 51
Knights La. RG20: Bal H .1N 7
Knights Lea RG20: Bal H .1M 7
Knights Lodge SO22: Winche .7H 105
Knights Pk. Rd. RG21: B'toke .5A 42
Knights Rd. BH11: Bour .1B 226
GU9: H End .3G 64
Knightstone Ct. PO2: Ports .4G 214
Knightstone Grange SO45: Hythe .7M 193
Knight St. RG21: B'toke .7A 42
Knights Way GU34: Alt .5D 80
Knights Yd. SP11: Hur T .4D 34
Knightwood Av. PO9: Hav .4G 202
SO43: Lyn .2B 148 (2N 189)
Knightwood Cl. BH23: Chri .6F 230
GU14: Farn .1N 49
SO40: Ashu .8H 171
SO43: Lyn .2B 148 (2N 189)
Knightwood Ct. SO19: South .8C 174
Knightwood Cres. SO53: Cha F .6M 131
Knightwood Glade SO53: Cha F .5L 131
Knightwood Leisure Cen. .7L 131
Knightwood M. SO53: Cha F .6M 131
Knightwood Rd. SO45: Hythe .7N 193
SO53: Cha F .4L 131
Knightwood Vw. SO53: Cha F .7A 132
Knockhundred La. GU26: Lip .7K 103
Knockwood La. SO20: N Wal .9N 67
Knole Ct. BH1: Bour .1A 246
Knole Gdns. BH1: Bour .1A 246
Knole Rd. BH1: Bour .9A 228
Knoll Cl. GU51: Fleet .1M 47
Knoll Ct. GU51: Fleet .9M 27
Knoll Gdns. BH24: St I .4C 186
RG20: Enbo R .1B 8
Knoll Mnr. BH2: Bour .9K 227
Knoll Rd. GU15: Camb .7M 19
GU51: Fleet .1M 47
Knoll Wlk. GU15: Camb .7M 19
Knollys Ho. PO1: Ports .1F 240
Knollys Rd. GU11: Alders .8H 49
RG26: Pam H .4M 11
Knook, The GU47: Coll .6F 18
Knottgrass Rd. SO31: Loc H .7B 196
Knowland Dr. SO41: M Sea .7K 235
Knowle, The GU35: Head .1D 102
Knowle Av. PO17: K Vil .2N 197
Knowle Cres. RG20: Kings .2B 6 (6K 9)
Knowle Hill SO50: E'leigh .5F 132
Knowle La. SO50: Hor H .4A 162
Knowle Rd. PO17: Fare .2B 198
RG24: B'toke .3L 41
SO42: Broc .6B 148 (8N 189)
Knowles Av. RG45: Cr'tne .1B 18
Knowles Cl. BH23: Chri .7A 230
GU35: Bor .5J 101
SO16: Nur .6C 158
Knowles Ct. PO3: Ports .8H 215
Knowles Mdw. GU33: Hi Br .4G 141
Knowle Vw. RG28: Whit .7H 55
KNOWLE VILLAGE .2A 198
Knowle Village Bus. Pk. PO17: K Vil .1N 197
Knowlings, The RG28: Whit .6H 55
KNOWLTON .9F 148
Knowlton Gdns. BH9: Bour .2M 227
Knowsley Cres. PO6: Cosh .1H 215
Knowsley Rd. PO6: Cosh .1G 215
Knox Cl. GU52: Ch Cr .4K 47
Knox Rd. PO2: Ports .7D 214
PO9: Hav .8D 202
Knox Ter. *GU34: Alt .4G 80*
(off Orchard La.)
Knyght Cl. SO51: Rom .6N 129
Knyveton Ho. *BH1: Bour .1M 245*
(off Knyveton Rd.)
Knyveton Rd. BH1: Bour .1M 245
Kohat Cl. SP9: Tidw .7B 30 (6F 30)
Kohat Ct. GU11: Alders .9H 49
Kohat Rd. SP9: Tidw .9C 30 (7G 30)
Kohima Cl. GU11: Alders .8K 49
Kootenay Av. SO18: South .3J 175
Kooyong Cl. SO51: E Wel .1B 156
Kornwestheim Way SO50: E'leigh .9C 132
Krooner Rd. GU15: Camb .1K 29

Kynegils Rd.—Lauriston Dr.

Kynegils Rd. SO22: Winche 4H 105
Kynon Cl. PO12: Gos 8L 213
Kyoto Wlk. PO9: Hav 6G 203
Kytes La. SO32: Durl 6E 162

L

Laburnum Av. PO6: Dray 1K 215
Laburnum Cl. GU11: Alders 1J 65
SO52: N Bad 7F 130
Laburnum Ct. SO19: South 7B 174
Laburnum Cres. SO45: Hythe 1M 207
Laburnum Dr. SO23: Kin W 7M 91
SO41: Ever 6M 233
Laburnum Gdns. GU52: Ch Cr 6N 47
Laburnum Gro. PO2: Ports 7F 214
PO11: H Isl 3H 243
SO50: E'leigh 9E 132
Laburnum Ho. BH10: Bour 2K 227
SO30: Hed E 4A 176
Laburnum Pas. GU11: Alders 9J 49
Laburnum Path PO6: Dray 9K 201
Laburnum Rd. GU9: Weyb 3G 64
GU11: Alders 1J 65
PO7: W'lle 3L 201
PO16: Fare 1D 212
SO16: S'ing 7A 160
SO30: Hed E 4A 176
Laburnums, The GU17: Blackw 8D 18
Laburnum Way RG23: B'toke 5M 41
Lacey Rd. PO4: S'sea 1J 241
Lackford Av. SO40: Tott 4L 171
Lackford Way SO40: Tott 4M 171
Lackland Ct. GU51: Fleet 9K 27
(off King John St.)
Lacon Cl. SO18: South 2C 174
Ladies Wlk. SP10: A'ver 3B 70
Ladin Ho. BH8: Bour 8A 228
(off Richmond Pk. Rd.)
Ladram Rd. PO12: Gos 3G 239
LADWELL 9N 125
Ladwell Cl. RG14: New 1C 8
Lady Betty's Dr. PO15: White 3H 197
Ladybridge Rd. PO7: Purb 5K 201
Ladycroft SO24: New A 2C 108
Ladycross Rd. SO45: Hythe 7M 193
Lady Diana Ct. SP11: Ludg 1D 30
Ladygate Dr. GU26: Gray 4J 103
Lady Godley Cl. SP9: Tidw 9C 30
Lady Jane Wlk. SP11: Ludg 1D 30
Lady Pl. Ct. GU34: Alt 5F 80
Ladysmith Cl. BH23: Chri 7A 230
Ladysmith Pl. GU35: Bor 2H 101
Ladyway SP4: Idm 9C 66
Ladywell BH13: Poole 3F 244
Ladywell La. SO24: New A 8F 94
Ladywood SO50: E'leigh 6D 132
Ladywood Av. GU14: Cov 8E 28
Ladywood Ho. PO5: S'sea 3D 240
Laffans Rd. GU11: Alders 5E 48
(not continuous)
RG29: Odi 2F 62
LA Fitness
Fareham 8E 198
(off Pulheim Pde.)
Southampton 9H 159
La Frenaye Pl. SO21: Sth W 2J 91
Lagado Cl. BH14: Poole 5A 244
Lagoon Cl. BH14: Poole 5A 244
Lahore Cl. SP9: Tidw 7C 30 (6G 30)
Lahore Rd. SP9: Tidw 9C 30 (7G 30)
Laidlaw Cl. BH12: Poole 6F 226
Laidlaw Gdns. SO53: Cha F 3N 131
Lainston Cl. SO22: Winche 4G 105
Lake Cnr. BH25: New M 2B 232
(off Fernhill La.)
Lake Ct. RG26: Tadl 5K 11
SO21: Hurs 1L 131
Lake Dr. GU35: Bor 4K 101
SO22: Oli B 2F 126
Lake End Way RG45: Cr'tne 1C 18
Lake Farm Cl. SO30: Hed E 2N 175
Lake Gro. Rd. BH25: New M 2A 232
Lake Ho. SO15: South 4H 173
Lakeland Dr. GU16: Frim 3N 29
Lakeland Gdns. SO40: March 9D 172
Lakelands RG26: Bau 4D 10
Lakelands Dr. SO15: South 4H 173
Lake La. GU10: Dock 2A 84
Laker Ho. SO15: South 3L 173
Lake Rd. BH11: Bour 1F 226
(not continuous)
PO1: Ports 1D 240
SO19: South 8B 174
SO32: Curd 2J 177
SO53: Cha F 4C 132
Laker Sq. SP10: A'ver 8B 52
Lakes, The SO32: Swanm 7C 164
Lakeside BH24: Hight 2M 187
PO13: Lee S 3B 238
PO17: F'ley 4A 198
Lakeside, The GU17: Blackw 9F 18
Lakeside Av. PO3: Ports 9J 215
SO16: Rown 6D 158
Lakeside Bus. Pk. GU47: Sandh 6C 18
Lakeside Cl. GU12: Ash V 7N 49
SP10: Charl 8K 51
Lakeside Country Pk. 3D 160
Lakeside Ct. GU51: Fleet 9N 27
PO4: S'sea 5G 240
Lakeside Dr. RG27: Brams 9A 16
Lakeside Gdns. GU14: Cov 5F 28
PO9: Hav 7G 202
Lakeside Holiday Village PO11: H Isl 5K 243
Lakeside Nth. Harbour PO6: Cosh 1E 214
Lakeside Pines BH25: New M 2C 232
Lakeside Rd. BH13: Poole 4E 244
GU11: Alders 6N 49
GU12: Ash V 6N 49
GU14: Farn 4J 49
Lakesmere Rd. PO8: Horn 4C 182
Lake Vw. RG27: H Win 5C 26
Lakeview Dr. BH24: Hight 2N 187
Lake Vw. Mnr. BH25: New M 3B 232
Lakewood Cl. SO53: Cha F 4B 132
Lakewood Rd. BH23: Highc 5G 231
SO40: Ashu 7J 171
SO53: Cha F 5B 132
Lamb Cl. SP10: A'ver 2B 70
Lambdens Wlk. RG26: Tadl 5H 11
Lambdown App. SP11: Per D 5A 30
Lambdown Ter. SP11: Per D 5A 30 (7H 31)
Lamberhurst Cl. SO19: South 1E 194
Lambert Cl. PO7: W'lle 4M 201
Lambert Cres. GU17: Blackw 9E 18
Lamborne Cl. GU47: Sandh 4C 18
Lamborough La. SO24: Hin A 9F 108
Lambourn Cl. PO14: Fare 9N 197
Lambourne Cl. SO21: Spar 3A 104
SO45: Dib P 8L 193
SP11: Thru 1N 67
Lambourne Dr. SO31: Loc H 6D 196
Lambourne Ho. SO30: Hed E 4M 175
Lambourne Rd. SO18: Wes E 9F 160
Lambourne Way GU10: Tong 3N 65
SP11: Thru 1N 67
Lambourn Sq. SO53: Cha F 6N 131
Lamb Roundabout, The
SP10: A'ver 2A 70
Lambs Cl. RG25: Over 2E 56
Lambs Lease GU33: Liss 2G 140
Lambs Row RG24: Lych 4G 42
Lamb Wlk. PO9: Hav 3C 202
Lamerton Cl. GU35: Bor 3J 101
Lamerton Rd. GU35: Bor 3J 101
Lammas Cl. PO31: Cowes 5N 237
Lammas Rd. SO45: Hythe 7M 193
Lampard La. GU10: Chur 6F 84
Lampards Cl. RG27: Roth 6F 24
Lampeter Av. PO6: Dray 9J 201
Lampool Ho. RG25: Over 2E 56
(off Station Rd.)
Lamports, The GU34: Alt 4G 81
Lamports Ct. GU9: Farnh 9E 64
(off Firgrove Hill)
Lampton Ct. BH9: Bour 5K 227
Lampton Gdns. BH9: Bour 5K 227
Lanark Cl. GU16: Frim 2N 29
Lancashire Cotts. SP11: Hath 1J 51
Lancaster Av. GU9: Farnh 9E 64
Lancaster Cl. BH23: Chri 7E 230
PO13: Lee S 3D 238
PO16: Portc 8K 199
SO31: Burs 9L 175
SP10: A'ver 9M 51
Lancaster Ct. SO30: Wes E 9G 160
Lancaster Dr. GU15: Camb 7M 19
Lancaster Rd. RG21: B'toke 5B 42
SO16: South 8E 158
Lancaster Way GU14: Farn 5L 29
PO7: W'lle 3N 201
Lancer Cl. BH23: Chri 7J 229
Lancer Ct. GU11: Alders 9G 48
Landale Cl. SP11: Enh A 3A 52
LANDFORD 1J 155
Landford Gdns. BH8: Bour 4A 228
Landford Way BH8: Bour 4A 228
LANDFORDWOOD 7J 121
Landguard Rd. PO4: S'sea 4H 241
SO15: South 4J 173
Landon Ct. PO12: Gos 5J 239
Landon Rd. PO13: Gos 8F 212
LANDPORT 1E 240
Landport Gate 6K 5
Landport St. PO1: Ports 1E 240
(Durban Homes)
PO1: Ports 6M 5 (3C 240)
(Lansdowne St.)
PO5: S'sea 6M 5 (3C 240)
Landport Ter. PO1: Ports 6M 5 (3C 240)
Landport Vw. PO1: Ports 2N 5 (1D 240)
Landseer Cl. GU47: Coll 7G 18
RG21: B'toke 8E 42
Landseer Ct. RG26: Bau 4E 10
SP10: A'ver 9M 51
Landseer Rd. BH4: Bour 2G 244
SO19: South 7G 174
Lands End La. GU35: Lind 2K 101
Lands End Rd. SO31: Burs 2M 195
Lane, The BH8: Bour 9N 227
PO4: S'sea 5G 240
PO12: Gos 6J 239
RG26: Tadl 5J 11
SO40: Cad 6N 155
SO43: Lyn 1B 148
SO45: Fawl 5F 208
LANE END
RG29 5G 62
SO21 3G 134
SO24 6K 111
Lane End RG26: B'ley 2G 23
Lane End Dr. PO10: Ems 9M 203
Lanehays Rd. SO45: Hythe 6L 193
Lanes, The BH25: New M 1B 232
Lanesbridge Cl. SO40: Woodl 5F 170
Lanes End PO14: Stub 6M 211
RG24: Chin 1H 43
Langbar Cl. SO19: South 4C 174
Langbrook Cl. PO9: Langs 9F 202
Langdale Av. PO6: Cosh 1J 215
Langdale Cl. GU14: Cov 8G 28
SO16: South 2E 172
Langdale Ct. GU12: Ash V 6N 49
(off Lakeside Cl.)
Langdon Ct. BH14: Poole 1B 244
Langdon Rd. BH14: Poole 1A 244
LANGDOWN 6M 193
Langdown Ct. SO45: Hythe 6M 193
Langdown Firs SO45: Hythe 6M 193
Langdown Lawn SO45: Hythe 7M 193
Langdown Lawn Cl. SO45: Hythe 7M 193
Langdown Rd. SO45: Hythe 6M 193
Langford Ct. PO16: Fare 8D 198
(off Queens Rd.)
Langford La. SP5: Down, Redl 1M 119 (5D 120)
Langford Rd. PO1: Ports 9G 214
Langham Cl. SO52: N Bad 8E 130
Langham Ct. RG27: Sher L 7J 23
Langham Rd. GU34: Alt 5E 80
Langhorn Rd. SO16: S'ing 7A 160
LANGLEY
GU33 7L 115
SO45 9C 208
Langley Chase BH24: Ashl H 3D 186
Langley Cl. GU52: Ch Cr 7L 47
Langley Dr. GU11: Alders 2J 65
GU15: Camb 7N 19
Langley Gdn. SP6: F'dge 8K 151
Langley Gro. RG27: Sher L 7H 23
Langley La. GU33: Liss, Rake 8L 115
Langley Lodge Gdns.
SO45: Blac 9D 208
Langley Rd. BH14: Poole 1C 244
BH23: Chri 5G 230
PO2: Ports 8F 214
SO15: South 4F 172
Langley Wlk. GU14: Farn 3K 49
LANGRISH 9C 138
Langrish Cl. PO9: Hav 3G 203
Langrish Rd. SO16: South 7G 159
Langside Av. BH12: Poole 6E 226
Langstaff Way SO18: South 2E 174
LANGSTONE 1F 216
Langstone Av. PO9: Langs 1F 216
Langstone Bri. PO9: Langs 3G 216
PO11: H Isl 3G 216
Langstone Ct. PO6: Dray 9K 201
Langstone Harbour (Nature Reserve) 6A 216
Langstone High St. PO9: Langs 2F 216
Langstone Ho. PO9: Hav 6G 202
PO16: Fare 1C 212
Langstone Marina Hgts. PO4: S'sea 4L 241
Langstone Rd. PO3: Ports 1H 241
PO9: Langs 1F 216
Langstone Sailing Club 2F 216
Langstone Technology Pk. PO9: Langs 9E 202
Langstone Wlk. PO13: Gos 6D 212
PO14: Fare 9N 197
Langstone Way PO4: S'sea 2J 241
Langton Cl. BH25: B Sea 6C 232
PO13: Lee S 1C 238
SO22: Winche 5J 105
Langton Dene BH4: Bour 2G 244
(off Portarlington Rd.)
Langton Dr. GU35: Head 9C 84
Langton Farm Gdns. PO1: Ports 9F 214
Langton Rd. BH7: Bour 9C 228
SO32: Bis W 3L 163
Langtons Ct. SO24: New A 1G 108
Langtry Ct. SO31: Burs 8L 175
Langtry Pl. PO31: Cowes 5P 237
Lanham La. SO22: Winche 7B 104
Lankhills Rd. SO23: Winche 4K 105
Lansdowne Av. PO7: Wid 6J 201
PO16: Portc 2M 213
SO23: Winche 9K 105
SP10: A'ver 3L 69
Lansdowne Cl. SO51: Rom 4L 129
Lansdowne Ct. BH1: Bour 1N 245
(Bourne Pines)
BH1: Bour 9L 227
(off Lansdowne Rd.)
SO23: Winche 9K 105
SO51: Rom 4L 129
Lansdowne Cres. BH1: Bour 2L 245
Lansdowne Gdns. BH1: Bour 1L 245
SO51: Rom 4L 129
LANSDOWNE HILL 7C 4 (7L 173)
Lansdowne Hill SO14: South 7C 4 (7L 173)
Lansdowne Ho. PO12: Gos 1J 239
Lansdowne M. BH1: Bour 1L 245
Lansdowne Rd. BH1: Bour 9L 227
GU11: Alders 1J 65
GU34: Alt 3G 80
SO15: South 3F 172
Lansdowne St. PO5: S'sea 6M 5 (3C 240)
Lansdown Roundabout, The
BH1: Bour 2L 245
Lansley Rd. RG21: B'toke 3C 42
Lantana Cl. PO7: W'lle 3N 201
Lantern Ct. SO23: Winche 8J 105
Lanyard Dr. PO13: Gos 1F 238
Lapin La. RG22: B'toke 5K 59
Lapthorn Cl. PO13: Gos 4D 212
Lapwing Cl. PO8: Horn 3B 182
PO12: Gos 9K 213
RG22: B'toke 3H 59
Lapwing Dr. SO40: Tott 2J 171
Lapwing Gro. PO16: Portc 9H 199
Lapwing Ri. RG28: Whit 5F 54
Lapwing Rd. PO4: S'sea 2K 241
Lapwing Way GU34: Four M 5H 97
Lara Cl. BH8: Bour 3A 228
Larch Av. SO45: Hard 3A 208
Larch Cl. BH24: St I 4D 186
GU15: Camb 4N 19
GU30: Lip 3D 116
PO13: Lee S 2C 238
SO23: Kin W 6M 91
SO30: Wes E 8H 161
SO41: Hor 3G 232
Larch Ct. PO1: Ports 1E 240
Larchdale Cl. SO31: Wars 9A 196
Larch Dr. RG20: Kings 2B 6
SP10: A'ver 2J 69
Larches Gdns. PO15: Fare 8M 197
Larches Way GU17: Blackw 8D 18
Larchfield Rd. GU52: Fleet 4M 47
Larchfield Way PO8: Horn 5C 182
Larch Rd. GU35: Head D 1D 102
SO16: South 8F 158
Larch Row SP6: Gods 9N 151
Larch Way GU14: Cov 9E 28
SO31: Burs 1K 195
Larchwood RG24: Chin 9G 22
Larchwood Av. PO9: Bed 5B 202
Larchwood Bus. Cen. PO9: Bed 5A 202
Larchwood Ct. SO15: South 5J 173
Larchwood Rd. SO40: Tott 4J 171
Larcombe Rd. GU32: Pet 2K 145
Larg Dr. SO22: Winche 2G 105
Lark Cl. RG22: B'toke 2H 59
SP10: A'ver 8A 52
Larkfield RG24: Chin 1G 42
Larkfield Cl. GU9: Farnh 7B 64
Larkfield Rd. GU9: Farnh 8B 64
Lark Hill Ri. SO22: Winche 1H 127
Larkhill Rd. PO3: Ports 4G 215
Lark Ri. GU30: Lip 1C 116
Lark Ri. Ho. GU51: Fleet 2H 47
Lark Rd. BH23: Mude 8C 230
SO50: E'leigh 2B 160
Larks Barrow Hill RG28: Whit 8G 37
Larksfield Av. BH9: Bour 3N 227
Larkshill Cl. BH25: New M 2C 232
Larkspur Chase SO19: South 5J 175
Larkspur Cl. GU11: Alders 3J 65
SO31: Loc H 7B 196
SO32: Swanm 6C 164
Larkspur Dr. SO40: March 1D 192
SO53: Cha F 6L 131
Larkspur Gdns. RG21: B'toke 8A 42
SO30: Hed E 4N 175
SO45: Holb 4N 207
Larkswood Cl. GU47: Sandh 4C 18
Larkwhistle Farm Rd. SO21: Mich S 4K 77
Larkwhistle Wlk. PO9: Hav 2C 202
Larmer Cl. GU51: Fleet 4J 47
Larwood Sq. SP10: A'ver 8B 52
(off Cricketers Way)
La Sagesse Convent 5K 129
Lascelles Ct. BH7: Bour 8E 228
Lascelles Rd. BH7: Bour 8E 228
Laser Cl. SO31: Wars 8B 196
Laser Quest
Bournemouth 6N 247 (2L 245)
LASHAM 4M 79
Lasham Grn. PO9: Hav 4H 203
(off Sharps Rd.)
Lasham Rd. GU51: Fleet 8H 27
Lasham Wlk. PO14: Fare 9N 197
Lashly Mdw. PO7: H'don 8D 166
Latch Farm Av. BH23: Chri 6K 229
LATCHMERE GREEN 8B 12
LATCHMOOR 2M 223
Latchmoor Ct. SO42: Broc 7D 148
Latchmoor Drove SP5: H'twth, L'ford 9H 121
Latchmore Dr. SO45: Dib 5H 193
Latchmore Forest Gro. PO8: Cowp 7A 182
Latchmore Gdns. PO8: Cowp 7M 181
Latelie Cl. SO31: Net A 4G 194
Latham Av. GU16: Frim 2N 29
Latham Cl. SO50: Fair O 1M 161
Latham Ct. SO15: South 3G 172
Latham Rd. SO50: Fair O 1M 161
SO51: Rom 4M 129
Latimer Ct. BH9: Bour 6K 227
BH13: Poole 3F 244
PO3: Ports 4J 215
Latimer Gate SO14: South 8E 4
Latimer Ho. GU51: Fleet 9K 27
Latimer M. BH9: Bour 6K 227
Latimer Rd. BH9: Bour 6K 227
Latimers Cl. BH23: Highc 5H 231
Latimer St. SO14: South 8E 4 (7M 173)
SO51: Rom 5L 129
Latimer Wlk. SO51: Rom 5L 129
Lauder Cl. GU16: Frim 2N 29
Lauderdale GU14: Cov 1F 48
Launcelot Cl. SP10: A'ver 7N 51
Launcelyn Cl. SO52: N Bad 9E 130
Launceston Cl. PO12: Gos 9L 213
Launceston Dr. SO50: E'leigh 7D 132
Laundry La. GU47: Coll 7G 18
RG27: Heck 9H 15
SO41: M Sea 8L 235
Laundry Rd. SO16: South 8F 158
Laundry Yd. RG28: Whit 5G 54
Laura Cl. SO21: Comp 8G 127
Laurel Bank RG20: Burgh 4D 8
Laurel Cl. BH23: Chri 5F 230
BH24: St L 4B 186
GU14: Cov 9E 28
GU15: Camb 9M 19
PO12: Gos 9L 213
RG23: Oak 1D 58
RG29: N War 8J 45
SO19: South 7B 174
SO31: Loc H 5E 196
SO41: Hor 2F 232
SO45: Hythe 6L 193
Laurel Ct. PO7: W'lle 1M 201
Laurel Gdns. GU11: Alders 3J 65
SO31: Loc H 5E 196
Laurel La. BH24: St L 5B 186
Laurel Rd. PO8: Horn 6C 182
SO31: Loc H 5E 196
Laurels, The GU9: Weyb 3H 65
GU51: Fleet 2M 47
RG21: B'toke 5D 42
SO32: Botl 1C 176
SO42: Broc 8C 148
SP10: A'ver 9L 51
Laurence Ct. SO50: Fair O 1N 161
SP11: Ludg 1D 30
Laurence Grn. PO10: Ems 5M 203
Laurence M. SO51: Rom 4M 129
Lauren M. PO11: H Isl 5E 242
(off Sea Front)
Lauren Way SO40: Calm 1H 171
Laurie Wlk. SO45: Fawl 7D 208
Lauriston Ct. RG21: B'toke 7D 42
Lauriston Dr. SO53: Cha F 3N 131

Lindley Gdns.—Longfield Dr.

Lindley Gdns. SO24: New A 2F 108
Lindoe Cl. SO15: South 3L 173
Lindon Ct. PO4: S'sea 3G 241
Lind Rd. PO12: Gos 6L 239
Lindsay Cl. RG28: Whit 4H 55
Lindsay Ct. BH13: Poole 1E 244
Lindsay Gdns. BH13: Poole 1E 244
Lindsay Mnr. BH13: Poole 1E 244
Lindsay Pk. BH13: Poole 1E 244
Lindsay Rd. BH13: Poole 1D 244
SO19: South 4J 175
Lindsey Ho. *PO5: S'sea* 5E 240
(off Richmond Rd.)
Lindum Cl. GU11: Alders 1J 65
Lindum Dene GU11: Alders 1J 65
Lindurn Ct. BH12: Poole 1E 244
Lindway SO31: P Ga 3D 196
Liners Ind. Est. SO15: South 4H 173
Lines, The RG20: Kings 1B 6 (5K 9)
Lineside BH23: Burt 6M 229
Lines Rd. GU11: Alders 4M 49
LINFORD 4B 188
Linford Cl. BH25: New M 2B 232
Linford Ct. PO9: Hav 2D 202
SO50: Fair O 1N 161
Linford Cres. SO16: South 8J 159
Linford Rd. BH24: Hang, Poul 8M 185
Ling Cres. GU35: Head D 1D 102
Lingdale SO16: Chilw 4L 159
Lingdale Cl. SP10: A'ver 1J 69
Lingdale Pl. SO17: South 2M 173
Lingdale Rd. BH6: Bour 8G 228
Lingen Cl. SP10: A'ver 7M 51
Lingfield Cl. GU34: Alt 6F 80
RG24: Old Bas 6K 43
Lingfield Ct. PO1: Ports 7L 5 (4C 240)
Lingfield Gdns. SO18: South 9D 160
Lingfield Grange BH13: Poole 2F 244
Lingmala Gro. GU52: Ch Cr 6N 47
Ling Rd. BH12: Poole 5A 226
Lingwood Av. BH23: Mude 8A 230
Lingwood Cl. SO16: Bass 4L 159
Lingwood Wlk. SO16: Bass 4L 159
Linhorns La. BH25: New M 9B 222
Link, The GU46: Yat 6M 17
PO7: W'lle 9A 182
SP10: A'ver 1J 69
LINKENHOLT 6G 7
Linkenholt Way PO9: Hav 4C 202
Link Gallery, The *7H 105*
(off Romsey Rd.)
Linklater Path PO1: Ports 9E 214
Linklater Rd. PO1: Ports 9E 214
Link Rd. BH24: Poul 8M 185
GU34: Alt 2G 81
PO17: S'wick 7C 200
RG20: Kings 2C 6
SO16: South 8E 158
Links, The GU35: W'hil 6G 100
PO13: Gos 7E 212
Links Cl. PO9: R Cas 9H 183
Links Dr. BH23: Chri 5G 228
LINKSIDE 9K 85
Linkside Av. BH8: Bour 6B 228
Linkside E. GU26: Hind 9L 85
Linkside Nth. GU26: Hind 9K 85
Linkside Sth. GU26: Hind 1L 103
Linkside W. GU26: Hind 9K 85
Links La. PO9: R Cas 8H 183
PO11: H Isl 4C 242
Links Rd. BH14: Poole 3B 244
SO22: Winche 5H 105
Links Vw. Av. BH14: Poole 3C 244
Links Vw. Way SO16: Bass 5L 159
Links Way GU14: Cov 9E 28
Link Way PO14: Stub 7M 211
RG23: Oak 1D 58
Linkway GU15: Camb 9L 19
GU52: Fleet 5L 47
RG45: Cr'tne 1B 18
Linkway Pde. GU52: Fleet 5L 47
Linnet Cl. BH24: Hight 2M 187
GU31: Pet 2B 146
PO8: Cowp 6M 181
RG22: B'toke 9J 41
Linnet Ct. BH25: New M 4A 232
PO12: Gos 1H 239
Linnets, The PO16: Portc 9H 199
SO40: Tott 2J 171
Linnet Sq. SO50: E'leigh 2B 160
Linnets Rd. SO24: New A 2E 108
Linnets Way GU34: Alt 3F 80
Linnies La. SO41: Sway 8H 223
Linsford Bus. Pk. GU16: Mytc 9N 29
Linstead Rd. GU14: Cov 4G 28
Linsted La. GU35: Head 9N 83
Linton Cl. RG26: Tadl 6J 11
Linton Dr. SP10: A'ver 9M 51
LINWOOD 1B 188
Linwood Cl. SO45: Hythe 7M 193
Linwood Rd. BH9: Bour 7M 227
Lion & Lamb Way GU9: Farnh 8D 64
Lion & Lamb Yd. GU9: Farnh 8D 64
Lion Brewery, The PO2: Ports 8E 214
Lion Cl. RG25: Over 3D 56
Lion Ct. RG24: B'toke 4G 42
Lionheart Cl. BH11: Bour 1B 226
Lionheart Way SO31: Burs 9K 175
Lion Ho. PO1: Ports 3L 5
Lion Rd. GU14: Farn 1K 49
PO1: Ports 1H 5 (9A 214)
Lions Fld. GU35: Oakh 3C 100
Lions Ga. SP6: F'dge 1J 153
Lions Hall SO23: Winche 9L 237 (7K 105)
Lions Hill Way BH24: Ashl H 4A 186
Lions La. BH24: Ashl H 3A 186
Lion St. PO1: Ports 3L 5 (2C 240)
Lions Wood BH24: St L 4B 186
Lion Ter. PO1: Ports 4L 5 (2C 240)
(not continuous)
Lion Way GU52: Ch Cr 6N 47
LIPHOOK 4E 116
Liphook By-Pass GU30: B'sht, Lip 2N 115
Liphook Golf Course 6C 116
Liphook Ho. PO9: Hav 4H 203
Liphook Rd. GU27: Hasl 9N 103
GU27: Hasl, Linc, Lip 3H 117
GU30: Lip 3H 117
GU30: Pass 4A 102
GU35: Head 4A 102
GU35: Lind 2L 101
GU35: W'hil 7H 101
Liphook Station (Rail) 4E 116
Lipizzaner Flds. PO15: White 1E 196
Lippen La. GU32: W Meo 5P 135
SO32: Warn 5P 135
Lipscombe Cl. RG25: Herr 2M 79
Lipscombe Ri. GU34: Alt 3F 80
Lisa Ct. RG21: B'toke 7B 42
Lisbon Rd. SO15: South 4J 173
Liskeard Dr. GU14: Farn 6J 29
Lisle Cl. SO22: Oli B 2E 126
SO41: Lymi 3D 234
LISLE COURT 3J 235
Lisle Ct. SO22: Winche 8J 105
Lisle Ct. Rd. SO41: Lymi 2H 235
Lisle Way PO10: Ems 6L 203
Lismoyne Cl. GU51: Fleet 1L 47
LISS 1E 140
Liss Dr. GU51: Fleet 9H 27
Lissenden BH13: Poole 2E 244
LISS FOREST 8F 114
Liss Rd. PO4: S'sea 3G 241
Liss Station (Rail) 1E 140
Lister Rd. PO6: Cosh 9G 200
RG22: B'toke 9A 42
LITCHFIELD 3G 37
Litchfield Cl. SP10: Charl 7K 51
Litchfield Cres. SO18: South 1D 174
Litchfield Dr. GU51: Fleet 9H 27
Litchfield Ho. RG26: Tadl 5H 11
Litchfield Rd. SO18: South 1D 174
SO22: Winche 2H 105
Litchford Rd. BH25: A'ley 2D 232
Lith Av. PO8: Horn 2C 182
Lith Cres. PO8: Horn 1C 182
Lith La. PO8: Cath 2A 182
PO8: Horn 1B 182
Litten, The RG20: Kings 2B 6
Lit. Abshot Rd. PO14: Abs 9E 196
Lit. Aldershot La. RG26: Bau 4B 10
Little Angels Playworld 6B 18
Little Anglesey PO12: Gos 5K 239
Lit. Anglesey Rd. PO12: Gos 5J 239
Little Ann *SP4: Win E* 3A 86
(off Main Rd.)
Lit. Ann Rd. SP11: Abb A 5G 68
Lit. Arthur St. PO2: Ports 9F 214
Lit. Ashton La. SO32: Bis W 9G 134
Lit. Austins Rd. GU9: Farnh 9F 64
Lit. Bagmore La. RG25: Herr 2K 79
Lit. Barn Pl. GU33: Liss 1G 140
Lit. Barrs Dr. BH25: New M 2C 232
Little Basing RG24: Old Bas 4G 43
Little Binfields RG24: Old Bas 2H 43
LITTLE BULLINGTON 4C 76
Lit. Bull La. SO32: Wal C 9N 163
Little Burn SO41: Sway 5J 223
Little Cl. PO13: Gos 4E 212
Lit. Coburg St. PO1: Ports 2E 240
Little Copse GU46: Yat 6N 17
GU52: Fleet 4L 47
SP10: A'ver 3L 69
Lit. Copse Chase RG24: Chin 1F 42
Little Cnr. PO7: Den 7G 181
Little Ct. BH13: Poole 5D 244
BH14: Poole 6A 244
Little Cft. GU46: Yat 8N 17
Littlecroft Av. BH9: Bour 3M 227
Lit. Dean Ct. SO20: S Bri 2G 88
Lit. Dean La. RG25: Up G 4B 62
Lit. Dene Copse SO41: Penn 4B 234
LITTLEDOWN
BH7 6D 228
SP11 7E 6
Littledown Av. BH7: Bour 7B 228
Littledown Cen. 6D 228
Littledown Ct. BH1: Bour 5N 247 (1L 245)
Littledown Dr. BH7: Bour 7B 228
Little Drove SP6: Woodg 2A 154
Lit. Drove Rd. SO20: Chil 5F 74
Little Fallow RG24: Lych 3G 43
Littlefield Cres. SO53: Cha F 6K 131
Littlefield Rd. GU34: Alt 4G 80
Lit. Forest Mans. BH1: Bour 7N 247 (2L 245)
Lit. Forest Rd. BH4: Bour 9H 227
Little Fosters BH13: S'bks 7C 244
Lit. Fox Dr. SO31: P Ga 4E 196
Little Gays PO14: Stub 6K 211
Lit. George St. PO1: Ports 9F 214
Little Green PO12: Gos 5J 239
Littlegreen Av. PO9: Hav 5G 203
Lit. Green Orchard PO12: Gos 4J 239
Little Hackets PO9: Hav 4E 202
Lit. Hambrook St. PO5: S'sea 7M 5 (4C 240)
Little Hartleys RG27: Hoo 2K 45
Lit. Hayes La. SO21: Itc A 9J 93
Little Hoddington RG25: Up G 3B 62
Lit. Hoddington Cl. RG25: Up G 3B 62
LITTLE HOLBURY 3N 207
Lit. Holbury Pk. Homes SO45: Holb 3N 207
Lit. Hyden La. PO8: Clan 3B 168
Lit. Kimble Wlk. SO30: Hed E 4N 175
Lit. Knowle Hill RG19: Ashf H 5L 9
RG20: Kings 1D 6 (5L 9)
Lit. Lance's Hill SO19: South 3D 174
Little La. PO12: Gos 5J 239
LITTLE LONDON
RG26 1N 21
SO20 1A 86 (4A 88)
SP11 2C 52
Lit. London Rd. RG7: Sil 6A 12
Little Mead PO7: Den 7H 181
Little Meads SO51: Rom 5K 129
Littlemill La. SP6: Dame 3P 149
Lit. Minster St. SO23: Winche 8M 237 (7L 105)
Little Moor GU47: Sandh 4E 18
Littlemoor Av. BH11: Bour 2B 226
Lit. Oak Rd. SO16: Bass 7L 159
LITTLE PARK 4G 68
Littlepark Av. PO9: Bed 6B 202
Lit. Park Cl. SO30: Hed E 4M 175
Lit. Park Farm Rd. PO15: Seg 4F 196
Littlepark Ho. PO9: Bed 6B 202
LITTLE POSBROOK 3J 211
Lit. Quob La. SO30: Wes E 9J 161
Little Reynolds SO40: Tott 5K 171
LITTLE SANDHURST 4C 18
LITTLE SHODDESDEN 7M 31
Lit. Shore La. SO32: Bis W 4N 163
LITTLE SOMBORNE 5J 89
Lit. Southsea St. PO5: S'sea 7M 5 (4C 240)
LITTLETON 1F 104
Littleton Gro. PO9: Hav 5F 202
Littleton La. SO21: Spar 2E 104
SO22: Lit 9E 90
Littleton Rd. SO22: Lit 2F 104
Little Vigo GU46: Yat 9L 17
Lit. Wellington St. GU11: Alders 9J 49
Little Wood SO51: W Wel 2C 120 (1N 155)
Lit. Woodfalls Dr. SP5: Woodf 9C 120
Littlewood Gdns. SO30: Wes E 1H 175
SO31: Loc H 6B 196
Little Woodham A 1642 Living History Village 2E 238
Lit. Woodham La. PO13: Gos 2E 238
Littleworth Rd. GU10: Seal 9N 65
Litton Gdns. RG23: Oak 1D 58
Litzo, The BH5: Bour 2B 246
Liverpool Ct. PO13: Gos 2F 238
Liverpool Rd. PO1: Ports 2F 240
PO14: Fare 2B 212
Liverpool St. SO14: South 1D 4 (3M 173)
Livery Rd. SP5: Mid W, W Win 5G 86
Livesay Gdns. PO3: Ports 1G 241
Livia Cl. SP10: A'ver 6A 52
Livingstone Rd. BH5: Bour 1E 246
BH12: Poole 8A 226
BH23: Chri 7N 229
PO5: S'sea 4E 240
SO14: South 2M 173
SP10: A'ver 9D 52
LivingWell Fitness Club
Portsmouth 2L 215
Llangar Gro. RG45: Cr'tne 1C 18
Lloyd Av. SO40: March 9D 172
Loader Cl. BH9: Bour 6L 227
SO23: Kin W 8N 91
Loane Rd. SO19: South 7D 174
Lobelia Ct. PO7: W'lle 3A 202
Lobelia Rd. SO16: S'ing 7A 160
Locarno Rd. PO3: Ports 6H 215
Loch Rd. BH14: Poole 9C 226
Lock App. PO6: P Sol 1B 214
Locke Cl. SP11: Grat 5K 67
LOCKERLEY 4A 122 (2N 121)
Lockerley Cl. SO41: Lymi 4E 234
Lockerley Cres. SO16: South 1E 172
LOCKERLEY GREEN 2N 121
Lockerley Rd. PO9: Hav 6G 202
SO51: Dun 5B 122
SP5: E Tyt 9N 87
Locke Rd. GU30: Lip 2F 116
SO30: Hed E 2N 175
Locke Ter. PO12: Gos 2L 239
Lockhams Rd. SO32: Curd 2H 177
Lock Rd. GU11: Alders 6M 49
Locksbridge La. RG26: B'ley 2E 22
Locks Drove SP11: Ibt, Wild 3L 33
LOCKS HEATH 6D 196
Locks Heath Cen. SO31: Loc H 6D 196
Locksheath Cl. PO9: Hav 3D 202
Locks Heath Pk. Rd. SO31: Loc H 8E 196
Lock's La. SO21: Spar 3A 104
Locksley Ct. SO15: South 3L 173
Locksley Rd. SO50: E'leigh 2C 160
Locksmead RG21: B'toke 6E 42
Lock Sq. SP10: A'ver 8B 52
Locks Rd. SO31: Loc H 7D 196
Locks Sailing Club 2L 241
Lockswasy Rd. PO4: S'sea 3J 241
Lockswood Keep SO31: Loc H 5D 196
Lockswood Rd.
SO31: Loc H, Sar G, Wars 8B 196
Lock Vw. PO6: P Sol 1B 214
Lockwood Cl. GU14: Cov 4G 29
Loddon Bus. Cen. RG24: B'toke 4F 42
Loddon Centre, The RG24: B'toke 3F 42
Loddon Ct. RG21: B'toke 9C 42
Loddon Dr. RG21: B'toke 6D 42
Loddon Ho. RG21: B'toke 5D 42
Loddon Mall RG21: B'toke 6C 42
Loddon Rd. GU14: Cov 6F 28
Loddon Vale Indoor Bowling Club, The 6M 41
Lode Hill SP5: Down 1L 119 (7B 120)
Lode Hill Caravan Site
SP5: Down 7C 120
Lodge, The PO7: W'lle 3A 202
SO15: South 3L 173
Lodge Av. PO6: Cosh 9H 201
Lodge Cl. BH14: Poole 1C 244
GU11: Alders 2L 65
SP10: A'ver 1L 69
Lodge Ct. BH14: Poole 1C 244
Lodge Dr. SO45: Dib P 8L 193
SP11: Weyh 8D 50
Lodge Drove SP5: Woodf 9C 120
Lodge Gdns. PO12: Gos 4J 239
RG20: Pen 3B 8
Lodge Gro. GU46: Yat 7B 18
Lodge Hill PO17: Newt 4K 179
Lodge La. SO42: Beau 1C 236
SP11: Chu F 9A 32
Lodge Rd. BH23: Chri 6H 229
PO9: Bed 8B 202
SO14: South 3M 173
SO31: Loc H 6E 196
SO41: Penn 3B 234
Lodge Va. SO51: E Wel 1B 156
Lodsworth GU14: Cov 9F 28
Lodsworth Cl. PO8: Clan 7D 168
Lodsworth Ho. PO1: Ports 1E 240
Loewy Cres. BH12: Poole 4B 226
Lofting Cl. SO50: B'stke 1J 161
Logan Cl. SO16: South 6E 158
Loggon Rd. RG21: B'toke 9B 42
Lomax Cl. SO30: Hed E 1N 175
Lombard Av. BH6: Bour 9G 229
Lombard Ct. PO1: Ports 7K 5
Lombard St. PO1: Ports 7J 5 (4B 240)
Lombardy Cl. PO13: Gos 6G 212
Lombardy Ri. PO7: W'lle 4N 201
Lomond Cl. PO2: Ports 8E 214
RG23: Oak 9C 40
Londesborough Pl.
SO41: Lymi 4D 234
Londesborough Rd. PO4: S'sea 4F 240
Londlandes GU52: Ch Cr 7K 47
London Av. PO2: Ports 6E 214
London La. BH23: Avon 5J 219
SP11: Facc 7K 7
London Mall PO2: Ports 6F 214
LONDON MINSTEAD 8M 155
London Rd. GU15: Camb 8H 19
GU17: Blackw, Min 2A 28
GU30: B'sht, Lip 2E 116
GU31: Hi Br, Pet 8A 140
GU33: Hi Br, Liss, Rake 4G 141
GU34: Holy 3H 81
PO2: Ports 3F 214
PO6: Cosh 9G 201
PO7: Purb, W'lle, Wid 3K 201
PO7: Wid 7J 201
PO8: Clan, Horn 1D 182
(not continuous)
PO8: Cowp 8A 182
RG21: B'toke 7D 42
RG24: Old Bas 7F 42
RG25: Over 2E 56
RG27: Elve 3F 26
RG27: H Win 5C 26
RG27: H Win, Hoo, Nat S 7F 42
RG27: Nat S 7F 42
RG28: Free, L'stoke, Whit 5H 55
RG29: Odi 8L 45
(not continuous)
SO15: South 2C 4 (4L 173)
SO20: S Bri 2G 88
SO21: M'dvr 9K 77
SO23: Kin W, Winche 2M 105
SP5: Firs 4D 86
SP10: A'ver 9C 52
SP11: A'ver, And D 1D 70
London St. RG21: B'toke 7C 42
RG28: Whit 5G 55
SP10: A'ver 2A 70
London Tavern Caravan Park, The
BH24: Poul 8M 185
Lone Barn La. SO32: Corh 7K 135
Lone Valley PO7: Wid 6K 201
Longacre Cl. GU33: Liss 1F 140
Long Acre Ct. PO1: Ports 9F 214
Longacre Ri. RG24: Chin 1F 42
Longacres PO14: Titch C 5F 196
Long Barn Rd. SO21: Spar 5N 89
SP11: E Ant 6B 52
Long Barrow Cl. SO21: Sth W 3J 91
Longbarrow Cl. BH8: Bour 5C 228
Long Beech Dr. GU14: Cov 9E 28
SO40: Tott 4K 171
Long Bottom SP11: Bidd 4N 31
Longbourn Pl. RG24: B'toke 3N 41
Longbridge GU9: Farnh 8E 64
Longbridge Cl. RG27: Sher L 3M 23
SO40: Calm 9K 157
Longbridge Ct. SO40: Calm 9K 157
Longbridge Ho. PO5: S'sea 5M 5
Longbridge Ind. Pk. SO14: South 7A 174
Longbridge Rd. RG26: B'ley 1G 22
Long Cl. SO41: Penn 3A 234
SP5: Down 1J 119 (7A 120)
Longclose Rd. SO30: Hed E 3A 176
Long Cl. West SP5: Down 1J 119 (7A 120)
LONG COMMON 9C 162
Long Copse SO45: Holb 5B 208
Long Copse Chase RG24: Chin 1F 42
Long Copse Ct. PO10: Ems 5M 203
Long Copse La. PO10: Ems, Westb 5M 203
Longcroft GU10: Ben'ly 7K 63
PO9: Hav 8E 202
Longcroft Cl. RG21: B'toke 7B 42
Longcroft Rd. RG20: Kings 1A 6 (5K 9)
Long Cross Hill GU35: Head 2A 102
Long Cross La. RG22: B'toke 4J 59
Long Curtain Rd. PO5: S'sea 9K 5 (5B 240)
Longdean Cl. PO6: Cosh 8B 200
Longdon Dr. PO13: Lee S 9B 212
LONG DOWN 2N 191
Long Down GU31: Pet 9A 140
Longdown GU52: Fleet 5L 47
Longdown Activity Farm 8K 171
Longdown Lodge GU47: Sandh 5D 18
Longdown Rd. GU47: Sandh 4C 18
Long Dr. PO13: Gos 7E 212
SO30: Wes E 9J 161
Long Drove SP5: E Gri 9F 86
Longfield RG23: Oak 8D 40
Longfield Av. PO14: Fare 1N 211
Longfield Caravan Site
BH23: Hurn 3E 218
Longfield Cl. GU14: Farn 4J 29
PO4: S'sea 2K 241
RG25: Nth W 9B 58
Longfield Dr. BH11: Bour 1E 226

Lynch Rd.—Manor Rd.

Lynch Rd. GU9: Farnh .8F **64**
Lyn Ct. RG21: B'toke .6E **42**
Lyndale Cl. SO41: M Sea .7L **235**
Lyndale Dr. GU51: Fleet .2B **48**
Lyndale Rd. SO31: P Ga .5E **196**
Lynden Cl. PO14: Fare .9L **197**
Lynden Ct. PO11: H Isl .3E **242**
Lynden Ga. SO19: South .7E **174**
Lyndford Ter. GU52: Fleet .4L **47**
LYNDHURST .2C **148** & 2N **189**
Lyndhurst Av. GU11: Alders .4L **65**
GU17: Blackw .7E **18**
Lyndhurst Cl. PO11: H Isl .5G **242**
SO22: Winche .2H **105**
Lyndhurst Dr. RG22: B'toke .4L **59**
Lyndhurst Ho. PO9: Hav .3E **202**
Lyndhurst Rd. BH23: Bock, Bran, Wat .2B **230**
BH23: Chri .6C **230**
BH24: Bur .6E **188**
GU51: Fleet .8H **27**
PO2: Ports .6G **214**
PO12: Gos .3J **239**
SO40: Ashu .1F **190**
SO42: Beau .7E **206**
SO42: Broc .9D **148**
SP5: L'ford .8J **121**
(not continuous)
Lyndock Cl. SO19: South .8C **174**
Lyndock Pl. SO19: South .8C **174**
Lyndon Gate BH2: Bour .8G **247**
Lyndons, The GU30: Pass .7N **101**
Lyndsey Cl. GU14: Cov .8D **28**
Lyndum Cl. GU32: Pet .9M **139**
Lyndum Pl. GU35: Lind .2L **101**
Lyne Pl. PO8: Horn .4B **182**
Lynes Ct. BH24: Ring .1J **187**
Lyne's La. BH24: Ring .1J **187**
Lynford Av. SO22: Winche .4J **105**
Lynford Way SO22: Winche .4J **105**
Lynn Cl. SO18: Wes E .8F **160**
Lynn Cres. PO14: Titch C .8G **196**
Lynn Rd. PO2: Ports .8G **214**
Lynn Way GU14: Cov .5H **29**
SO23: Kin W .9N **91**
Lynric Cl. BH25: B Sea .7B **232**
Lynton Ct. SO40: Tott .4L **171**
Lynton Cres. BH23: Chri .3G **229**
Lynton Gdns. PO16: Fare .6B **198**
Lynton Ga. PO5: S'sea .9N **5** (5D **240**)
Lynton Gro. PO3: Ports .8H **215**
Lynton Mdw. SO20: Chil .4F **74**
Lynton Rd. GU32: Pet .9L **139**
GU35: Bor .4J **101**
SO30: Hed E .3N **175**
Lynwood Av. PO8: Cowp .7L **181**
Lynwood Cl. GU35: Lind .2M **101**
Lynwood Ct. SO22: Winche .4K **105**
SO41: Lymi .3D **234**
Lynwood Dr. SP10: A'ver .1L **69**
Lynwood Gdns. RG27: Hoo .2G **45**
Lynx Cl. SO50: B'stke .1K **161**
Lynx Ct. GU14: Farn .1L **49**
Lynx Ho. PO6: Cosh .2F **214**
Lyon Av. BH25: New M .3C **232**
Lyon Rd. BH12: Poole .4C **226**
Lyons Pl. SO30: Hed E .5M **175**
Lyon St. SO14: South .1E **4** (4M **173**)
Lyon Way GU16: Frim .3L **29**
Lyon Way Ind. Est. GU16: Frim .3L **29**
Lyric Pl. SO41: Lymi .2E **234**
Lysander Cl. BH23: Chri .7E **230**
Lysander Ct. PO1: Ports .5J **5** (3B **240**)
Lysander Way PO7: W'lle .1A **202**
Lyson's Rd. GU11: Alders .1J **65**
Lyss Ct. GU33: Liss .1E **140**
Lysses Ct. PO16: Fare .8E **198**
Lysses Path PO16: Fare .8E **198**
Lyster Rd. SP6: F'dge .9K **151**
Lystra Rd. BH9: Bour .3L **227**
Lyteltane Rd. SO41: Lymi .4D **234**
Lytham Cl. GU35: W'hil .5G **100**
Lytham Rd. SO18: South .1E **174**
Lythe La. GU32: Stro .7G **139**
Lyton Path RG26: Bau .8E **10**
Lyttel Combe RG27: Hoo .2K **45**
Lytton Rd. BH1: Bour .9N **227**
RG21: B'toke .6D **42**
SO45: Hythe .7N **193**
Lyvers La. SP5: E Gri .9F **86**

M

M3 Trade Pk. SO50: E'leigh .8C **132**
Mabbs La. RG27: H Win .8B **26**
Mabelmyll Cft. RG27: Hoo .2K **45**
Mabey Av. BH10: Bour .4H **227**
Mabey Cl. PO12: Gos .5L **239**
Mablethorpe Rd. PO6: Cosh .8F **200**
Macadam Way SP10: A'ver .9H **51**
Macandrew Rd. BH13: Poole .6D **244**
Macarthur Cres. SO18: South .2E **174**
Macaulay Av. PO6: Cosh .8A **200**
Macallum Rd. SP11: Enh A .2A **52**
McCartney Wlk. RG22: B'toke .3L **59**
Macdonald Rd. GU9: Up H .3D **64**
McDonalds Almshouses *GU9: Farnh .9C 64*
(off West St.)
McFauld Way RG28: Whit .6H **55**
McGovern M. SO31: Wars .9A **196**
McIntyre Rd. BH23: Bour A .7C **218**
McKay Cl. GU11: Alders .8L **49**
McKernan Ct. GU47: Sandh .5B **18**
McKinley Rd. BH4: Bour .3G **244**
Macklin Ho. SO22: Winche .8J **237**
Maclaren Rd. BH9: Bour .3K **227**
Maclean Rd. BH11: Bour .3D **226**
Macnaghten Rd. SO18: South .3B **174**
Macnaghten Woods GU15: Camb .7N **19**
McNaughton Cl. GU14: Cov .9E **28**
Macpennys Woodland Garden .6E **220**
Macrae Rd. GU46: Yat .7M **17**
McWilliam Cl. BH12: Poole .6G **226**
McWilliam Rd. BH9: Bour .4L **227**
Madden Cl. PO12: Gos .4H **239**
Maddison St. SO14: South .6C **4** (6L **173**)
Maddocks Hill SO24: Rop .2C **110**
Maddoxford La. SO32: Botl .9C **162**
Maddoxford Way SO32: Botl .1C **176**
Madeira Cl. RG24: B'toke .2E **42**
Madeira Ct. BH1: Bour .5N **247** (1L **245**)
Madeira Rd. BH1: Bour .6N **247** (1L **245**)
BH14: Poole .9B **226**
PO2: Ports .5F **214**
Madeira Wlk. PO11: H Isl .4F **242**
SO41: Lymi .3F **234**
Madeley Rd. GU52: Ch Cr .5N **47**
Madeline Rd. GU31: Pet .9M **139**
Madison Av. BH1: Bour .8A **228**
Madison Cl. PO13: Gos .8G **212**
Madison Ct. PO16: Fare .8E **198**
Madocks Way PO8: Cowp .6M **181**
Madox Brown End GU47: Coll .6G **18**
Madrid Rd. SP10: A'ver .9B **52**
Madrisa Ct. SO41: Lymi .2E **234**
Mafeking Rd. PO4: S'sea .4G **241**
Maffey Ct. SO30: Botl .3D **176**
Magazine La. SO40: March .8E **172**
Magazine Rd. GU14: Farn .3F **48**
Magdala Rd. PO6: Cosh .1G **215**
PO11: H Isl .4E **242**
Magdalen Ct. PO2: Ports .5F **214**
Magdalene Rd. GU47: Owl .3H **19**
Magdalene Way PO14: Titch C .7F **196**
Magdalen Hill SO23: Winche .7M **105**
Magdalen La. BH23: Chri .8K **229**
Magdalen M. SO23: Winche .8P **237**
Magdalen Rd. PO2: Ports .5E **214**
Magdalen Row GU32: Pet .1L **145**
Magellan Cl. SP10: A'ver .9D **52**
Magellan Ho. SO14: South .8F **4**
Magennis Cl. PO13: Gos .9F **212**
Magenta Ct. PO13: Gos .1E **238**
Magister Dr. PO13: Lee S .2C **238**
Magistrates' Court
Aldershot .9H **49**
Bournemouth .1L **245**
Fareham .8D **198**
Portsmouth .5N **5** (3D **240**)
Southampton .1D **4** (4M **173**)
Magna Rd. BH11: Bour .1C **226**
Magnolia Cl. BH6: Bour .9K **229**
GU47: Owl .4F **18**
PO14: Fare .9A **198**
SO45: Dib .5H **193**
SP10: A'ver .2L **69**
Magnolia Ct. BH4: Bour .2H **245**
BH25: New M .3C **232**
RG24: B'toke .2B **42**
Magnolia Gro. SO50: Fair O .1B **162**
Magnolia Ho. BH10: Bour .2K **227**
Magnolia Rd. SO19: South .5D **174**
Magnolia Way GU52: Fleet .4M **47**
PO8: Cowp .6C **182**
Magnus Dr. RG22: B'toke .3K **59**
Magpie Cl. BH8: Bour .3N **227**
GU10: Ews .2N 63
(off Badger Way)
GU35: Bor .5K **101**
PO16: Portc .9G **199**
RG22: B'toke .2H **59**
Magpie Dr. SO40: Tott .3J **171**
Magpie Gdns. SO19: South .6G **174**
Magpie Gro. BH25: New M .4A **232**
Magpie La. PO13: Lee S .9B **212**
SO50: E'leigh .1C **160**
Magpie Rd. PO8: Ids .5J **183**
Magpie Wlk. PO8: Cowp .6L **181**
PO8: Horn .6G **183**
Mahler Cl. RG22: B'toke .2A **60**
Maida Rd. GU11: Alders .7K **49**
Maiden La. SO41: Lymi .5E **234**
Maidenthorn La. RG25: Nth W .9B **58**
Maidford Gro. PO3: Ports .4K **215**
Maidment Cl. BH11: Bour .2C **226**
Maidstone Cres. PO6: Cosh .8F **200**
Mailing Way RG24: B'toke .3N **41**
Main Dr. PO17: S'wick .3B **200**
SO42: Beau .1G **236**
SO45: Exb .1G **236**
Mainline Bus. Cen. GU33: Liss .1E **140**
Main Rd. GU10: B Oak .10M **63**
GU35: K'ly .7G **82**
PO1: Ports .2H **5** (1A **240**)
PO10: S'brne .9N **203**
PO13: Gos .4F **212**
RG26: Tadl .7J **11**
SO21: Col C .3L **133**
SO21: Ott .2F **132**
SO21: Owls .5C **134**
SO22: Lit .9E **90**
SO40: March .9E **172**
SO40: Tott .6L **171**
SO41: E End .4A **236**
SO41: Portm, Wal .9G **224**
SO42: Beau .4A **236**
SO45: Dib .2F **192**
SO45: Hard .2A **208**
SO50: Fis P .4M **133**
SP4: Ames .6A **66**
SP4: Win D, Win E, Win G .4A **86**
Mainsail Dr. PO16: Fare .9D **198**
Mainstone SO51: Rom .7K **129**
Mainstream Ct. SO50: B'stke .9H **133**
Main St. RG19: Green .1G **9**
Maisemore Gdns. PO10: Ems .1K **217**
Maitland Ct. SO41: Lymi .3D **234**
Maitland Rd. GU14: Farn .3K **49**
Maitlands, The BH4: Bour .8G **247** (3H **245**)
Maitlands Cl. GU10: Tong .4N **65**
Maitland St. PO1: Ports .9E **214**
Maize Cl. SP11: E Ant .6B **52**
Maizemore Wlk. PO13: Lee S .1B **238**
Majestic Rd. RG22: B'toke .4J **59**
SO16: Nur .8A **158**
Majorca Av. SP10: A'ver .9B **52**
Majorca Mans.
BH2: Bour .6J **247** (2J **245**)
Makins Ct. SO24: New A .1E **108**
Malcolm Cl. SO31: Loc H .6E **196**
SO53: Cha F .3C **132**
Malcolm Ho. PO2: Ports .4G **214**
Malcolm Rd. SO53: Cha F .3C **132**
Malcomb Cl. BH6: Bour .2K **247**
Malcroft M. SO40: March .9F **172**
Malden Ho. PO12: Gos .9L **213**
Maldive Rd. RG24: B'toke .2E **42**
Maldon Cl. SO50: B'stke .9H **133**
Maldon Rd. PO6: Cosh .9E **200**
SO19: South .5C **174**
Malham Gdns. RG22: B'toke .5K **59**
Malibres Rd. SO53: Cha F .4D **132**
Malin Cl. PO14: Stub .5L **211**
SO16: South .7D **158**
Malins Rd. PO2: Ports .9E **214**
Mall, The BH24: Bur .7E **188**
PO2: Ports .7E **214**
SO53: Cha F .5C **132**
SP9: Tidw .9A **30** (8F **30**)
SP10: A'ver .2N 69
(off Borden Gates)
Mallard Cl. BH8: Bour .5N **227**
BH23: Mude .8C **230**
GU27: Hasl .9N **103**
RG22: B'toke .3H **59**
SO24: New A .9F **94**
SO32: Bis W .3K **163**
SO41: Hor .3H **233**
SO51: Rom .4M **129**
SP10: A'ver .8A **52**
Mallard Ct. *GU11: Alders .3J 65*
(off Boxhalls La.)
Mallard Gdns. PO13: Gos .6D **212**
SO30: Hed E .9N **161**
Mallard Pl. GU14: Cov .4J **29**
Mallard Rd. BH8: Bour .5A **228**
PO4: S'sea .2J **241**
PO9: R Cas .9H **183**
Mallard Rd. Retail Pk. BH8: Bour .5A **228**
Mallards GU34: Alt .3F **80**
Mallards, The PO9: Langs .1F **216**
PO16: Fare .6C **198**
Mallards Rd. SO31: Burs .2K **195**
Mallard Way GU46: Yat .7L **17**
Mallett Cl. SO30: Hed E .9B **162**
Mallory Cl. BH23: Chri .6B **230**
Mallory Cres. PO16: Fare .6C **198**
Mallory Rd. RG24: B'toke .2D **42**
Mallow Cl. BH23: Chri .6E **230**
GU35: Lind .2M **101**
PO6: Cosh .9G **201**
PO7: W'lle .3N **201**
SO31: Loc H .7C **196**
Mallow Rd. SO30: Hed E .4L **175**
Mallows, The BH25: A'ley .2E **232**
Malls Shopping Centre, The RG21: B'toke .6C **42**
Malmesbury Cl. BH23: Chri .9K **229**
SO50: Fair O .1N **161**
Malmesbury Ct. BH8: Bour .8N **227**
SO31: Net A .4E **194**
Malmesbury Flds. RG22: B'toke .2M **59**
Malmesbury Gdns. SO22: Winche .4H **105**
Malmesbury Ho. *SP9: Tidw .8E 30*
(off Kennet Rd.)
Malmesbury Lawn PO9: Hav .3C **202**
Malmesbury Mews *BH8: Bour .9N 227*
(off Malmesbury Pk. Pl.)
Malmesbury Pk. Pl. BH8: Bour .9N **227**
Malmesbury Pk. Rd. BH8: Bour .8L **227**
Malmesbury Pl. SO15: South .3J **173**
Malmesbury Rd. BH24: St L .5B **186**
SO15: South .3J **173**
SO51: Rom .4L **129**
Malmsbury Rd. GU35: W'hil .5J **101**
Maloney M. PO11: H Isl .6K **243**
Malory Cl. SO19: South .4H **175**
Malpass Rd. SO21: Wor D .5G **90**
Malshanger La. RG23: Oak .7A **40**
Malta Cl. RG24: B'toke .2C **42**
Malta Rd. PO2: Ports .8F **214**
Maltby's GU34: Selb .7L **99**
Malthouse, The SO51: Rom .4L **129**
Malthouse Apartments, The
PO12: Gos .1M **239**
Malthouse Cl. GU52: Ch Cr .6K **47**
SO21: E'ton .1C **106**
SO51: Rom .4L **129**
Malthouse Ct. GU30: Lip .2E **116**
Malthouse Gdns. PO13: Gos .7E **212**
SO40: March .9E **172**
Malthouse La. PO16: Fare .8D **198**
RG26: Tadl .7K **11**
SO24: Bigh .6L **95**
SP11: Chu S, Co Du .2N **31**
SP11: Sman .2B **52**
Malthouse Mdws. GU30: Lip .2E **116**
Malthouse M. GU34: Holy .2J **81**
Malthouse Rd. PO2: Ports .8E **214**
Malthouse Wlk. *SP11: Ludg .1C 30*
(off Tidsworth Rd.)
Maltings, The GU30: Lip .2F **116**
GU31: Pet .1M **145**
GU35: W'hil .6H **101**
PO7: H'don .9D **166**
PO16: Fare .7F **198**
RG26: B'ley .2G **22**
Maltings Cl. GU34: Alt .6F **80**
Malt La. SO32: Bis W .4M **163**
Malus Cl. PO14: Fare .1B **212**
Malvern Av. PO14: Fare .1A **212**
Malvern Cl. BH9: Bour .3L **227**
RG22: B'toke .8J **41**
SO32: Bis W .4N **163**
Malvern Ct. *BH9: Bour .4L 227*
(off Malvern Rd.)
BH23: Chri .6B 230
(off Dorset Rd.)
Malvern Dr. SO45: Dib P .6J **193**
Malvern Gdns. SO30: Hed E .9A **162**
Malvern M. PO10: Ems .8M **203**
Malvern Rd. BH9: Bour .3L **227**
GU14: Cov .5F **28**
GU17: Min .3B **28**
GU33: Hi Br .3G **141**
PO5: S'sea .6E **240**
PO12: Gos .2H **239**
SO16: South .9H **159**
Malvern Way *SP4: Port .9B 66*
(off Southbourne Way)
Malwood Av. SO16: South .8J **159**
Malwood Cl. PO9: Hav .3G **203**
Malwood Gdns. SO40: Tott .2J **171**
Malwood Rd. SO45: Hythe .5L **193**
Malwood Rd. W. SO45: Hythe .5L **193**
Manaton Way SO30: Hed E .1M **175**
Manawey Bus. Units
GU12: Alders .1N **65**
Manchester Rd. PO1: Ports .2F **240**
SO31: Net A .4E **194**
SO41: Sway .4H **223**
Mancroft Av. PO14: Stub .6M **211**
Mandalay *GU9: Up H .3C 64*
(off Lawday Pl. La.)
Mandale Cl. BH11: Bour .2E **226**
Mandale Rd. BH11: Bour .3D **226**
Mandarin Way PO13: Gos .1E **238**
Mandela Way SO15: South .3A **4** (5K **173**)
Manderley SO41: M Sea .9L **235**
Mandora Rd. GU11: Alders .7K **49**
Manica Cl. GU35: Bor .4J **101**
Mankhorn La. SP11: Bidd .5N **31**
Manley James Cl. RG29: Odi .8L **45**
Manley Rd. SO31: Burs .9K **175**
Mann Cl. RG28: Whit .6H **55**
Manners, The SO31: Net A .3F **194**
Manners La. PO4: S'sea .3F **240**
Manners Rd. PO4: S'sea .3F **240**
Manning Av. BH23: Chri .5E **230**
Manningford Cl. SO23: Winche .3L **105**
Mannings Heath Rd.
BH12: Poole .5A **226**
Mannington Hall *BH4: Bour .3G 245*
(off Portarlington Rd.)
Mannington Pl. BH2: Bour .7J **247**
Manns Cl. SO18: Wes E .9G **160**
Mannyngham Way SO51: Tims .6K **123**
Manor, The *BH1: Bour .2N 245*
(off Derby Rd.)
Manor Av. BH12: Poole .6A **226**
Mnr. Barns La. RG40: F'std .2J **17**
Manor Bri. Ct. SP9: Tidw .7D **30** (6G **31**)
Manor Cl. GU10: Tong .3N **65**
GU27: Hasl .9N **103**
GU34: Alt .2G **81**
PO9: Hav .8F **202**
PO17: Wick .8C **178**
RG22: B'toke .4J **59**
SO23: Winche .6M **105**
SO31: Old N .9K **175**
SO40: Tott .4L **171**
SO41: M Sea .8L **233**
SP6: F'dge .1J **153**
SP9: Shi B .2B **66** (1G **66**)
SP11: Abb A .6G **68**
Manor Copse SP10: K Enh .5A **52**
Manor Cotts. RG28: Free .4M **55**
Manor Ct. BH24: Ring .9J **185**
GU52: Ch Cr .7M **47**
PO9: Hav .8E **202**
PO15: Seg .5G **196**
Manor Cres. GU27: Hasl .9N **103**
PO6: Dray .1J **215**
SO31: Burs .9K **175**
Manor Farm .6C **176**
Manor Farm SP5: Bish .2E **118**
Mnr. Farm Barns GU34: E Wor .8M **81**
Mnr. Farm Cl. BH25: New M .5A **232**
SO50: B'stke .1J **161**
Manor Farm Country Pk. .7A **176**
Mnr. Farm Grn. SO21: Twyf .8K **127**
Mnr. Farm Gro. SO50: B'stke .1J **161**
Mnr. Farm La. SO51: Mich .4K **123**
SP5: Br Ch .3A **118**
Mnr. Farm M. GU10: Dock .4B **84**
Mnr. Farm Rd. SO18: South .1B **174**
SP6: F'dge .9F **150**
Manor Farmyard BH8: Bour .3E **228**
Manor Flds. GU30: Lip .2F **116**
Manor Gdns. BH24: Ring .9J **185**
BH25: New M .3C **232**
Manor Ho. RG24: Lych .3G **42**
Manor House, The
GU15: Camb .7M **19**
Manor Ho. Av. SO15: South .4D **172**
Manor Ho. Flats GU10: Tong .4N **65**
Manorhurst *BH4: Bour .1G 244*
(off Snowdon Rd.)
Manor La. RG24: Old Bas .5J **43**
SO51: Tims .7K **123**
Manor Lea GU27: Hasl .9N **103**
Mnr. Lodge Rd. PO9: R Cas .8G **182**
Manor M. PO6: Dray .9K **201**
MANOR PARK .9M **155**
Manor Pk. Av. PO3: Ports .8H **215**
Manor Pk. Cotts. *GU34: Alt .5G 80*
(off Kingsmead)
Manor Pk. Dr. GU46: Yat .8N **17**
Manor Park Est. GU12: Alders .1L **65**
Manor Pk. Ind. Est. SO40: Tott .3A **172**
Manor Quay SO18: South .3B **174**
Manor Ri. SP11: An V .5L **69**
Manor Ri. Flats SP11: An V .5L **69**
Manor Rd. BH1: Bour .2M **245**
BH23: Chri .8K **229**

Manor Rd.—Matthew Rd.

Manor Rd. BH24: Ring .1K **187**
BH25: A'ley, New M .3B **232**
GU9: Farnh .6G **64**
GU11: Alders .2H **65**
GU14: Farn .8M **29**
GU34: Alt .2G **80**
PO1: Ports .9F **214**
PO11: H Isl .3E **242**
RG24: Sher J .9N **21**
SO16: Chilw .3J **159**
SO21: Twyf .8K **127**
SO32: Durl .3G **163**
SO41: M Sea .8L **233**
SO45: Dib .4F **192**
SO45: Holb .4A **208**
SO50: B'stke .1J **161**
SP5: E Tyt .8N **87**
SP10: A'ver .9M **51**
Manor Rd. Nth. SO19: South .6C **174**
Manor Rd. Sth. SO19: South .7C **174**
Manor Ter. SO31: Old N .9J **175**
Manor Vw. SP5: Land .8K **121**
Manor Vs. PO17: Wick .7C **178**
Manor Wlk. GU12: Alders .1K **65**
Manor Way PO11: H Isl .5G **242**
PO13: Lee S .1A **238**
SO50: E'leigh .8C **132**
Manor Wharf SO18: South .3A **174**
Mansbridge Cotts. SO18: S'ing .7D **160**
Mansbridge Rd. SO18: S'ing .7C **160**
SO50: E'leigh .2E **160**
Manse La. RG26: Tadl .7K **11**
Mansel Cl. BH12: Poole .7G **227**
Mansel Ct. SO16: South .9D **158**
Mansell Cl. SO45: Dib P .8K **193**
Mansell Ct. RG28: Whit .4G **55**
Mansel Rd. E. SO16: South .1D **172**
Mansel Rd. W. SO16: South .9C **158**
Mansergh Wlk. SO40: Tott .2H **171**
Mansfield Av. BH14: Poole .1A **244**
Mansfield Cl. BH14: Poole .1A **244**
Mansfield Ct. *BH4: Bour .3G 245*
(off Portarlington Rd.)
Mansfield La. SO32: Shed .6L **177**
Mansfield Pk. GU34: Meds .4J **97**
Mansfield Rd. BH9: Bour .5J **227**
BH14: Poole .1A **244**
BH24: Ring .1J **187**
(not continuous)
PO13: Gos .8E **212**
RG22: B'toke .9N **41**
Mansion Ct. PO4: S'sea .6F **240**
Mansion Dr. RG27: Brams, Haze .2M **25**
Mansion Rd. PO4: S'sea .6F **240**
SO15: South .4H **173**
Manston Ct. SO16: South .7E **158**
Mansvid Av. PO6: Cosh .1J **215**
Mantle Cl. PO13: Gos .9F **212**
Mantle Sq. PO2: Ports .6C **214**
Mant's La. SO23: Winche .9P **237** (7M **105**)
Manydown Pk. RG23: W Law .6E **40**
Maple Av. GU14: Cov .7F **28**
Maple Cl. BH23: Highc .7H **231**
BH25: B Sea .7C **232**
GU17: Blackw .8E **18**
GU34: Alt .3F **80**
GU47: Sandh .4B **18**
PO10: Ems .7M **203**
PO13: Lee S .2C **238**
PO15: Fare .8M **197**
SO24: New A .2E **108**
SO31: Burs .1K **195**
SO51: Rom .6B **130**
Maple Ct. PO11: H Isl .3D **242**
RG22: Wort .7K **41**
Maple Cres. PO8: Clan .5C **168**
RG21: B'toke .4C **42**
SP11: Ludg .1F **30**
Maple Dr. PO7: Den .7H **181**
SO23: Kin W .7M **91**
SP5: Firs .4E **86**
Mapledurham La. GU32: W'ton .5J **145**
MAPLEDURWELL .7M **43**
Maple Gdns. GU46: Yat .8N **17**
SO40: Tott .4J **171**
Maple Gro. RG26: Tadl .5H **11**
Maple Ho. PO9: Hav .7G **202**
Maplehurst Chase RG22: B'toke .4K **59**
Maple Leaf Cl. GU14: Cov .9H **29**
Maple Leaf Dr. GU35: Bor .3J **101**
Maple Ri. PO15: White .1G **196**
Maple Rd. BH9: Bour .6K **227**
PO5: S'sea .5E **240**
SO18: South .3C **174**
SO45: Hythe .9N **193**
Maplers Dr. GU51: Fleet .9K **27**
Maples, The SO53: Cha F .4A **132**
Maple Sq. SO50: E'leigh .2C **160**
Mapleton Rd. SO30: Hed E .4A **176**
Mapletons, The RG29: Odi .8M **45**
Mapletree Av. PO8: Horn .5C **182**
Maple Wlk. GU12: Alders .2M **65**
GU31: Pet .3M **145**
SP10: A'ver .3K **69**
Maple Way GU35: Head D .1D **102**
Maple Wood PO9: Bed .8B **202**
Maplewood RG24: Chin .9F **22**
Maplewood Cl. SO40: Tott .4J **171**
Maplin Rd. SO16: South .9C **158**
Marabout Cl. BH23: Chri .7N **229**
Maralyn Av. PO7: W'lle .3M **201**
Marathon Pl. SO50: B'stke .1M **161**
Marbrean Cl. SP6: F'dge .9F **150**
Marchant Rd. SP10: A'ver .2L **69**
Marchant's Hill (Activity Cen.) .9M **85**
March Cl. SP10: A'ver .9A **52**
Marchesi Ct. PO14: Stub .4M **211**
MARCHWOOD .9E **172**
Marchwood BH1: Bour .2N **245**
Marchwood By-Pass SO40: March, Tott .4M **171**
SO45: Dib .7A **172**
Marchwood Ct. *PO12: Gos .4F 238*
(off Tower Cl.)
Marchwood Ho. RG27: Winchf .9G **27**
Marchwood Ind. Pk. SO40: March .7F **172**
Marchwood Rd. BH10: Bour .3G **227**
PO9: Hav .3E **202**
SO15: South .4G **173**
SO40: Elin .6A **172**
Marchwood Ter. *SO40: March .8E 172*
(off Main Rd.)
Marchwood Village Cen. SO40: March .9E **172**
Marchwood Yacht Club .7F **172**
Marcus Cl. SO50: B'stke .1M **161**
Mardale Rd. SO16: South .2C **172**
Mardale Wlk. SO16: South .2C **172**
Marden Paddock SO42: Broc .7C **148** (8N **189**)
Marden Way GU31: Pet .1N **145**
Mardon Cl. SO18: S'ing .6C **160**
Mare La. SO21: More, Owls .3B **134**
Mareth Cl. GU11: Alders .9K **49**
Margam Av. SO19: South .5D **174**
Margaret Cl. PO7: W'lle .9L **181**
Margaret Rd. RG22: B'toke .7M **41**
Margaret Rule Hall PO1: Ports .4N **5**
Margarita Rd. PO15: Fare .7A **198**
Margate Rd. PO5: S'sea .3E **240**
Margery's Ct. PO1: Ports .4K **5** (2B **240**)
Margha Rd. SP9: Tidw .8C **30** (7G **30**)
Marguerite Cl. RG26: B'ley .1G **22**
Mariann Ct. BH6: Bour .1G **246**
Marianne Cl. SO15: South .4E **172**
Marianne Rd. BH12: Poole .6G **226**
Marie Av. SP5: Down .2H **119** (7N **119**)
Marie Cl. BH12: Poole .7B **226**
Marie Ct. PO7: W'lle .1M **201**
Marie Rd. SO19: South .7G **175**
Marigold Cl. PO15: Fare .7A **198**
RG22: B'toke .2J **59**
Marina, The BH5: Bour .2B **246**
Marina Bldgs. *PO12: Gos .3K 239*
(off Stoke Rd.)
Marina Cl. PO10: Ems .1N **217**
Marina Ct. BH5: Bour .2B **246**
Marina Dr. SO31: Hamb .7L **195**
Marina Gro. PO3: Ports .9J **215**
PO16: Portc .1L **213**
Marina Keep PO6: P Sol .2B **214**
Marina Towers BH5: Bour .2B **246**
Marina Vw. BH23: Chri .9J **229**
Marine Cotts. PO12: Gos .2K **239**
Marine Ct. BH25: B Sea .7M **231**
PO4: S'sea .5H **241**
SO45: Hythe .5L **193**
Marine Ct. Mans. *PO13: Lee S .1A 238*
(off Marine Pde. W.)
Marine Dr. BH25: B Sea .7N **231**
Marine Dr. E. BH25: B Sea .8A **232**
Marine Dr. W. BH25: B Sea .7M **231**
Marine Pde. SO14: South .6N **173**
Marine Pde. E. PO13: Lee S .2A **238**
Marine Pde. W. PO13: Lee S .9N **211** & 1A **238**
Marine Point BH25: B Sea .7A **232**
Marine Prospect BH25: B Sea .7A **232**
Marine Rd. BH6: Bour .2G **247**
Mariners Cl. RG26: Tadl .7K **11**
SO31: Hamb .5L **195**
Mariners Ct. BH23: Mude .8C **230**
SO41: Lymi .4F **234**
Mariners Dr. GU14: Farn .6L **29**
Mariners M. SO45: Hythe .5M **193**
Mariners Reach BH25: B Sea .7B **232**
Mariners Wlk. PO4: S'sea .2J **241**
Mariners Way PO12: Gos .4M **239**
SO31: Wars .8N **195**
Marine Ter. SP11: Hur T .4D **34**
Marine Wlk. PO11: H Isl .4J **243**
Marion Rd. PO4: S'sea .6F **240**
Maritime Av. SO40: March .7F **172**
Maritime Chambers SO14: South .9F **4**
Maritime Wlk. SO14: South .9F **4** (8N **173**)
Maritime Way SO14: South .9E **4** (8M **173**)
Marjoram Cl. GU14: Cov .8D **28**
Marjoram Cres. PO8: Cowp .7B **182**
Marjoram Way PO15: White .2G **197**
Markall Cl. SO24: Cher .9F **108**
Markan Rd. SP4: Idm .9C **66**
Mark Anthony Ct. PO11: H Isl .4E **242**
Mark Cl. PO3: Ports .4G **215**
SO15: South .3G **172**
Mark Ct. PO7: W'lle .1M **201**
Marken Cl. SO31: Loc H .6C **196**
Market Bldgs. SO16: S'ing .7B **160**
Market Chambers *RG21: B'toke .7C 42*
(off Church St.)
Market Hill PO31: Cowes .5P **237**
Market La. SO23: Winche .8M **237** (7L **105**)
Market Pde. PO9: Hav .8F **202**
Market Pl. BH24: Ring .1J **187**
RG21: B'toke .7C **42**
RG28: Whit .5G **54**
SO14: South .7D **4** (7M **173**)
SO51: Rom .5L **129**
SP6: F'dge .1J **153**
Market Quay PO16: Fare .8D **198**
Market Sq. GU34: Alt .5F **80**
Market St. GU34: Alt .5F **80**
SO23: Winche .8M **237** (7L **105**)
SO50: E'leigh .2F **160**
(not continuous)
Market Way PO1: Ports .2N **5** (1D **240**)
Markham Ct. GU15: Camb .7M **19**
Markham Rd. BH9: Bour .6L **227**
Mark La. RG21: B'toke .7C **42**
SP10: A'ver .8H **51**
SP11: Pen C .9G **51**
Mark's La. BH25: Bash .9B **222**
Markson Rd. SO21: Sth W .3G **90**
Marks Rd. BH9: Bour .3K **227**
PO14: Stub .6A **212**
Marks Tey Rd. PO14: Stub .3M **211**
Mark Way SO51: Lock .1M **121**
Markway Cl. PO10: Ems .8K **203**
Marlands Lawn PO9: Hav .3C **202**
Marlands Shop. Cen.
SO14: South .4C **4** (6L **173**)
Marlborough Cl. GU51: Fleet .3B **48**
PO7: W'lle .4L **201**
Marlborough Ct. *BH4: Bour .2G 245*
(off Marlborough Rd.)
BH12: Poole .1F 244
(off Princess Rd.)
SO45: Dib P .7K **193**
SO53: Cha F .8M **131**
Marlborough Gdns. RG23: Oak .9D **40**
SO30: Hed E .8N **161**
Marlborough Gro. PO16: Portc .1L **213**
Marlborough Ho. PO1: Ports .3J **5**
SO15: South .2L **173**
Marlborough Mans. *BH7: Bour .8E 228*
(off Christchurch Rd.)
MARLBOROUGH PARK .4N **49**
Marlborough Pk. PO9: Hav .6H **203**
Marlborough Pines *BH4: Bour .2G 245*
(off Marlborough Rd.)
Marlborough Pl. SO41: Lymi .1D **234**
Marlborough Ri. GU15: Camb .7N **19**
Marlborough Rd. BH4: Bour .7G **247** (2G **244**)
BH14: Poole .1A **244**
PO12: Gos .1H **239**
SN8: Co Du .1H **31**
SO15: South .2G **173**
SO53: Cha F .3C **132**
SP4: Bul C .3B **66**
Marlborough Row PO1: Ports .1J **5** (1B **240**)
Marlborough St. SP10: A'ver .1N **69**
Marlborough Trad. M. RG24: Chin .1E **42**
Marlborough Vw. GU14: Cov .7E **28**
Marldell Cl. PO9: Hav .4G **203**
Marles Cl. PO13: Gos .8F **212**
Marley Av. BH25: New M .2N **231**
GU27: Hasl .3N **117**
Marley Cl. BH25: New M .3A **232**
MARLEY COMMON .3N **117**
Marley La. GU27: Hasl, K'ly G .1N **117**
Marley Mt. SO41: Sway .6F **222**
Marlhill Cl. SO18: South .9D **160**
Marlin Cl. PO13: Gos .1F **238**
Marline Rd. BH12: Poole .8B **226**
Marl La. SP6: F'dge, Sand .8F **150**
Marlow Cl. PO15: Fare .5A **198**
Marlow Dr. BH23: Chri .3G **229**
Marlowe Cl. RG24: B'toke .3D **42**
Marlowe Ct. PO7: W'lle .9L **181**
SO19: South .9D **174**
Marlow Rd. SO32: Bis W .3K **163**
Marlpit Dr. BH23: Walk .4J **231**
Marlpit La. BH25: Bash .7B **222**
Marl's La. RG24: B'toke, Sher J .7C **22**
Marls Rd. SO30: Botl .3B **176**
Marmion Av. PO5: S'sea .5E **240**
Marmion Grn. BH23: Chri .7B **230**
Marmion Rd. PO5: S'sea .5D **240**
Marne Ho. PO14: Fare .9A **198**
Marne Rd. SO18: South .3E **174**
SP4: Bul C .3B **66**
Marnhull Ri. SO22: Winche .7G **105**
Marpet Cl. BH11: Bour .1D **226**
Marples Way PO9: Hav .8D **202**
Marquis Way BH11: Bour .1A **226**
Marram Cl. SO41: Lymi .9E **224**
Marrelswood Gdns. PO7: Purb .5K **201**
Marrowbrook Cl. GU14: Cov .9J **29**
Marrowbrook La. GU14: Cov .1H **49**
Marrow Meade GU51: Fleet .9K **27**
Marryat Ct. BH23: Highc .7K **231**
BH25: New M .3A **232**
Marryat Rd. BH25: New M .3A **232**
Marsden Ct. RG28: L'stoke .4N **55**
Marsden Rd. PO6: Cosh .9C **200**
Marsh, The SO45: Hythe .4M **193**
SP6: Brea .3L **151**
Marshal Cl. GU34: Alt .6E **80**
Marshall Cl. GU14: Cov .5H **29**
Marshall Ct. SO15: South .3L **173**
Marshall Dr. SO30: Wes E .1K **175**
Marshall Gdns. RG21: B'toke .4C **42**
Marshall Rd. GU47: Coll .6F **18**
PO11: H Isl .5J **243**
Marshall Sq. SO15: South .3L **173**
SP10: A'ver .8B 52
(off Cricketers Way)
Marsh Cl. GU35: Bor .4L **101**
PO6: Dray .2K **215**
Marsh Ct. *BH6: Bour .2G 246*
(off Clifton Rd.)
Marshcourt RG24: Lych .3G **43**
Marsh Ct. Rd. SO20: S Bri .3F **88**
Marshfield Cl. SO40: March .9C **172**
Marshfield Ho. PO6: Dray .1L **215**
Marsh Gdns. SO30: Hed E .9N **161**
Marsh Ho. SO14: South .7E **4** (7M **173**)
Marshlands Cl. BH23: Chri .8N **229**
Marshlands Rd. PO6: Farl .1L **215**
Marshlands Spur PO6: Farl .1M **215**
Marsh La. BH23: Chri .8N **229**
(Purewell)
BH23: Chri .4J **229**
(St Catherine's Hill La.)
GU10: Ben'ly .7L **63**
PO14: Stub .6K **211**
RG27: Eve .6J **17**
SO14: South .7F **4** (6M **173**)
SO41: Lymi .9D **224**
SO45: Fawl .4F **208**
SP6: Brea .3K **151**
Marsh Pde. *SO45: Hythe .5M 193*
(off The Marsh)
Marshwood Av. PO7: W'lle .2A **202**
Marston Cl. BH25: New M .1C **232**
Marston Dr. GU14: Farn .5K **29**
Marston Ga. SO23: Winche .6M **237** (6L **105**)
Marston Gro. BH23: Chri .5G **230**
Marston La. PO3: Ports .4J **215**
Marston Rd. BH25: New M .1C **232**
GU9: Farnh .8B **64**
SO19: South .5H **175**
Marston Wlk. RG24: B'toke .2B **42**
Marsum Cl. SP10: A'ver .6M **51**
Martello Cl. PO12: Gos .4F **238**
Martello Ho. BH13: Poole .6D **244**
Martello Pk. BH13: Poole .6D **244**
Martello Rd. BH13: Poole .4C **244**
Martello Rd. Sth. BH13: Poole .5D **244**
Martello Towers BH13: Poole .6D **244**
Martells, The BH25: B Sea .7C **232**
Martells Ct. PO1: Ports .6K **5** (3B **240**)
Martha Ct. BH12: Poole .7C **226**
MARTIN .9C **118**
Martin Av. PO7: Den .6H **181**
PO14: Stub .6N **211**
Martin Cl. PO13: Lee S .9B **212**
RG21: B'toke .4D **42**
SO32: Swanm .7D **164**
Martindale Ter. *SO16: South .2D 172*
(off Severn Rd.)
Martin Down National Nature Reserve .9B **118**
MARTIN DROVE END .7B **118**
Martin Drove End SP6: Mart .8B **118**
Martinet Dr. PO13: Lee S .2C **238**
Martingale Ct. GU11: Alders .9G **49**
Martin Rd. PO3: Ports .8H **215**
PO9: Hav .5G **202**
PO14: Stub .6N **211**
Martins, The SO50: Fair O .2A **162**
Martins Cl. GU17: Blackw .9F **18**
GU34: Alt .3G **80**
Martins Flds. SO21: Comp .5G **127**
Martin's Hill Cl. BH23: Burt .5M **229**
Martins Hill La. BH23: Burt .5M **229**
Martins La. SO20: Chil, S Bri .4G **75**
SO40: Woodl .5C **170**
Martin Snape Ho. PO12: Gos .3M **239**
Martins Pk. GU14: Cov .5F **28**
Martins Ri. SP5: W'psh .5H **121**
Martin's Rd. SO42: Broc .6D **148**
Martin St. SO32: Bis W .4L **163**
Martins Wood RG24: Chin .9G **22**
Martin Way GU16: Frim .3N **29**
SP10: A'ver .8A **52**
Martlesham Rd. SP4: Ames .6A **66**
Martlet Cl. PO13: Lee S .2C **238**
Martley Gdns. SO30: Hed E .9N **161**
MARTYR WORTHY .9E **92**
Marvic Ct. PO9: Hav .3E **202**
Marvin Cl. SO30: Botl .3B **176**
Marvin Way SO18: South .4G **175**
SO30: Botl .3B **176**
Marwell Activity Cen. .8B **134**
Marwell Cl. BH7: Bour .7D **228**
Marwell Dr. SO21: Owls .7B **134**
Marwell Rd. GU51: Fleet .8H **27**
Marwell Wildlife .7B **134**
Maryat Way PO15: White .9F **176**
Marybridge Cl. SO40: Tott .4L **171**
Mary Coombs Ct. PO11: H Isl .4G **242**
Mary Drake Cl. SO45: Holb .5A **208**
Maryfield SO14: South .6F **4** (6N **173**)
Mary Key Cl. SO19: South .1E **194**
Maryland Cl. SO18: South .8D **160**
Maryland Ct. SO41: M Sea .8H **235**
Maryland Gdns. SO41: M Sea .8H **235**
Mary La. GU34: New V .7N **97**
RG25: Nth W .8A **58**
Mary Mitchell Cl. *BH24: Ring .1J 187*
(off Lyne's La.)
Mary Mitchell Ct. *BH23: Chri .8J 229*
(off King's Av.)
Mary Rose Cl. PO15: Fare .6A **198**
Mary Rose Ct. RG21: B'toke .7A **42**
Mary Rose M. GU34: Alt .3G **81**
Mary Rose Mus. .2H **5** (1A **240**)
Mary Rose Street, The
PO1: Ports .4N **5** (2D **240**)
Marzan Rd. PO3: Ports .6J **215**
Masefield Av. PO6: Cosh .8A **200**
Masefield Cl. SO50: E'leigh .9D **132**
Masefield Cres. PO8: Cowp .7N **181**
Masefield Gdns. RG45: Cr'tne .2D **18**
Masefield Grn. SO19: South .4H **175**
Maskell Way GU14: Cov .9E **28**
Maslen M. RG22: B'toke .6K **59**
Mason Cl. GU46: Yat .8A **18**
Mason Ct. RG20: Wol H .2A **8**
Mason Pl. GU47: Sandh .5B **18**
Mason Rd. GU14: Cov .6G **29**
Mason's Wlk. PO7: Den .5F **180**
Masons Yd. SO23: Winche .8L **237**
Mason Way GU11: Alders .3K **65**
Masseys La. SO42: Beau .9B **206**
Masten Cres. PO13: Gos .8E **212**
Masters Ct.
BH2: Bour .6G **247** (2H **245**)
Masterson Cl. BH23: Chri .7N **229**
Matapan Rd. PO2: Ports .4E **214**
MATCHAMS .9E **186**
Matchams Cl. BH24: Match .9E **186**
Matchams Karting .1D **218**
Matchams La. BH23: Hurn .8E **218**
BH24: Match .8E **218**
Matchams Leisure Pk. .1E **218**
Matchams Leisure Pk. Golf Driving Range .9E **186**
Matheson Rd. SO16: South .5E **158**
Mathew Ter. GU11: Alders .9L **49**
Mathias Wlk. RG22: B'toke .4M **59**
Matilda Dr. RG22: B'toke .3K **59**
Matilda Pl. SO23: Winche .6M **237** (6L **105**)
Matinee Ho. GU11: Alders .9J **49**
Matley Gdns. SO40: Tott .3H **171**
Matrix Ho. RG21: B'toke .6D **42**
Matrix Pk. PO15: Titch .6H **197**
Matthew Ct. BH6: Bour .1G **246**
Matthew Rd. GU11: Alders .2G **64**

Matthews Cl.—Merrieleas Dr.

Matthews Cl. GU14: Farn 3M 49
PO9: Bed 6C 202
Matthews La. SO42: Beau 1B 236
Matthews Pl. PO7: W'lle 3M 201
Matthews Rd. GU15: Camb 5L 19
Matthews Way GU51: Fleet 1L 47
RG23: Oak 1E 58
MATTINGLEY 4K 25
Mattingley Dr. GU51: Fleet 8H 27
Mattock Way RG24: Chin 9F 22
Maturin Cl. SO41: Lymi 3E 234
Maude Av. PO14: Titch C 8G 196
Maudit Ho. *GU51: Fleet* 9K 27
(off Rykmansford Rd.)
Maundeville Cres. BH23: Chri 6G 229
Maundeville Rd. BH23: Chri 6H 229
Maunsell Way SO30: Hed E 8M 161
Maureen Cl. BH12: Poole 7A 226
Maurepas Way PO7: W'lle 1L 201
Mauretania Ho. SO14: South 4A 174
Mauretania Rd. SO16: Nur 7A 158
Maurice Rd. BH8: Bour 6A 228
PO4: S'sea 3K 241
Mauritius Cl. RG24: B'toke 2E 42
Maury's La. SO51: W Wel 1A 120 (9M 121)
Mavins Rd. GU9: Farnh 9F 64
Mavis Cres. PO9: Hav 7F 202
Mavis Rd. BH9: Bour 5M 227
Maw Cl. RG22: B'toke 2A 60
Maxine Cl. GU47: Sandh 4D 18
Maxstoke Cl. PO5: S'sea 2E 240
Maxwell Ct. BH11: Bour 1D 226
Maxwell Rd. BH9: Bour 6L 227
BH13: Poole 6D 244
PO4: S'sea 4H 241
SO19: South 7E 174
May Av. SO41: Lymi 1D 234
Maybray King Way SO18: South 3D 174
Maybrick Cl. GU47: Sandh 4B 18
Maybrook RG24: Chin 8G 22
Maybury Cl. GU16: Frim 4M 29
MAYBUSH 9D 158
Maybush Ct. SO16: South 1F 172
May Bush La. SO32: Sob H 2K 179
Maybush Rd. SO16: South 9D 158
May Cl. GU35: Head 3A 102
GU47: Owl 5F 18
RG24: Old Bas 5K 43
SO45: Holb 5B 208
May Copse SO45: Holb 5B 208
May Ct. BH9: Bour 6J 227
May Cres. GU12: Ash 1N 65
SO45: Holb 5B 208
Maycroft Ct. SO15: South 2L 173
Maydman Sq. PO3: Ports 1H 241
Mayfair BH4: Bour 3G 244
Mayfair Camping Site SO30: Wes E 7A 162
Mayfair Ct. *GU51: Fleet* 9J 27
(off Turners Way)
SO30: Botl 3D 176
Mayfair Gdns. BH11: Bour 2E 226
SO15: South 3L 173
Mayfair Ho. *RG21: B'toke* 6C 42
(off Festival Pl.)
Mayfield Av. BH14: Poole 2C 244
SO40: Tott 2L 171
Mayfield Av. Ind. Pk. SP11: Weyh 8A 50
Mayfield Cl. GU9: Bad L 4K 65
PO14: Stub 5N 211
SP9: Shi B 2A 66 (1F 66)
Mayfield Ct. RG27: Eve 5G 17
Mayfield Ridge RG22: B'toke 5K 59
Mayfield Rd. BH9: Bour 4K 227
GU14: Cov, Farn 5H 29
GU15: Camb 3K 29
PO2: Ports 6F 214
PO12: Gos 4L 239
SO17: South 8N 159
SP6: F'dge 9F 150
Mayfield Ter. *PO13: Lee S* 2B 238
(off Russell Rd.)
Mayflower Cl. PO14: Stub 7M 211
RG24: Chin 1F 42
SO41: Lymi 3G 234
SO53: Cha F 7N 131
Mayflower Ct. SO16: South 2G 172
Mayflower Cruise Terminal 6H 173
Mayflower Dr. GU46: Yat 6K 17
PO4: S'sea 2K 241
Mayflower Memorial 8C 4
Mayflower Rd. GU35: W'hil 6H 101
SO15: South 2G 173
Mayflowers, The SO16: Bass 7M 159
Mayflower Theatre 3B 4 (5L 173)
Mayfly Cl. SP6: F'dge 9J 151
Mayford Rd. BH12: Poole 8F 226
May Gdns. BH11: Bour 3C 226
BH23: Walk 4K 231
Mayhall Rd. PO3: Ports 7H 215
Mayhill La. SO32: Drox, Swanm 5E 164
Maylands Av. PO4: S'sea 2H 241
Maylands Rd. PO9: Bed 7B 202
May La. SO41: Pil 6G 224
Mayles Cl. PO17: Wick 7C 178
Mayles Cnr. PO17: K Vil 1N 197
Mayles La. PO15: K Vil 3N 197
PO17: K Vil, Wick 9A 178
Mayles Rd. PO4: S'sea 2J 241
Maylings Farm Rd. PO16: Fare 6B 198
Maynard Cl. PO13: Gos 4E 212
Maynard Pl. PO8: Horn 3B 182
Maynard Rd. SO40: Tott 3M 171
Maynard's Wood RG24: Chin 1F 42
Mayo Cl. PO1: Ports 9E 214
May Pl. RG21: B'toke 7C 42
Maypole Vs. SO50: E'leigh 4F 132
Mayridge PO14: Titch C 6F 196
May Rd. SO15: South 3H 173
Mays Firs SP6: Hale 1D 154
Mays La. PO14: Stub 5M 211
May St. RG21: B'toke 6A 42
May Tree Cl. SO22: Winche 1G 126
Maytree Cl. SO31: Loc H 6D 196
SO50: Fair O 1A 162
Maytree Gdns. PO8: Cowp 7M 181
May Tree Rd. SP10: A'ver 9K 51
Maytree Rd. PO8: Cowp 7M 181
PO16: Fare 8C 198
SO18: South 4E 174
SO53: Cha F 2A 132
Mayvale Cl. SO40: March 9E 172
Mazion *BH12: Poole* 6A 226
(off Ringwood Rd.)
Meacher Cl. SO40: Tott 2L 171
Mead, The GU14: Farn 9K 29
GU30: Lip 1D 116
GU32: Pet 2K 145
GU33: Liss 1E 140
PO13: Gos 5D 212
RG24: Old Bas 5J 43
SO45: Hythe 6K 193
Meadbrook Gdns. SO53: Cha F 6A 132
Mead Cl. SO51: Rom 5A 130
SP10: A'ver 2M 69
Mead Ct. *SO53: Cha F* 6A 132
(off Meadbrook Gdns.)
Mead Cres. SO18: S'ing 8B 160
Meadcroft Cl. SO31: Wars 9A 196
MEAD END
PO7 7H 181
SO41 6G 223
Meadend Cl. PO9: Hav 4H 203
Mead End Rd. PO7: Den 7H 181
SO41: Sway 6G 222
Meade Rd. SP11: Ludg 1E 30 (5L 31)
Mead Gdns. RG27: H Win 5A 26
Meadham La. RG25: Over 9J 9
RG26: Hann 9K 9
Mead Hatchgate RG27: Hoo 1G 44
Mead Hedges SP10: A'ver 3L 69
(not continuous)
Mead La. GU9: Farnh 8D 64
GU31: Buri 8L 145
Meadow, The BH25: New M 6L 231
PO7: Den 6G 180
Meadow Av. SO31: Loc H 5D 196
SP6: F'dge 9H 151
Meadow Bank GU9: Farnh 8D 64
SO21: Spar 5N 89
Meadowbank Rd. PO15: Fare 8N 197
Meadow Cl. BH23: Bran 7C 220
BH23: Sop 8L 219
BH24: Bur 8D 188
BH24: Ring 8L 185
GU17: Haw 9F 18
GU30: Lip 2E 116
PO11: H Isl 5F 216
SO24: New A 1F 108
SO30: Wes E 9J 161
SO32: Wal C 7N 163
SO40: Tott 5M 171
SO51: W Wel 1C 120 (9N 121)
SO52: N Bad 9F 130
SP6: F'dge 9H 151
Meadow Ct. BH9: Bour 3L 227
GU14: Cov 8H 29
GU51: Fleet 2L 47
PO10: Ems 9M 203
SP5: W'psh 5J 121
SP6: F'dge 9J 151
Meadow Ct. Cl. BH9: Bour 3L 227
Meadow Crest Wood
SO42: Broc 6A 148 (8M 189)
Meadowcroft Cl. SO21: Ott 1G 132
Meadow Dr. SP11: G Cla 9N 69
Meadow Edge PO7: Wid 7J 201
Meadow End GU30: Lip 1E 116
Meadow Gdns. SO32: Wal C 7A 164
Meadow Gate Av. GU14: Farn 1H 49
Meadow Gro. SO53: Cha F 8A 132
Meadowhead Rd. SO16: Bass 8L 159
Meadow Ho. GU17: Haw 9G 19
Meadowland BH23: Chri 8A 230
RG24: Chin 9F 22
SO23: Kin W 8M 91
Meadow Lands GU32: Pet 2L 145
Meadowlands BH24: Ring 4K 187
PO9: R Cas 7J 183
PO9: Warb 8G 203
SO41: Lymi 2B 234
Meadow La. BH23: Burt 4M 229
RG27: H Win 6B 26
SO31: Hamb 7L 195
SO50: E'leigh 1E 160
Meadowmead Av. SO15: South 3F 172
Meadow Mobile Home Park, The
RG27: Sher L 3L 23
Meadow Pl. PO9: Hav 3E 202
Meadowridge RG22: B'toke 4L 59
Meadow Rise PO8: Cowp 7B 182
RG25: Nth W 9B 58
SO22: Lit 2F 104
Meadow Rd. BH24: Ring 9L 185
BH25: New M 2C 232
GU14: Farn 5K 29
RG21: B'toke 9B 42
SO41: Penn 4C 234
SP4: Bul 3A 66
Meadows, The BH25: New M 5A 232
GU10: Chur 7H 85
GU47: Coll 8G 19
PO7: W'lle 1K 201
PO16: Fare 6E 198
RG27: Sher L 3L 23
SO18: S'ing 7C 160
SO31: Sar G 4D 196
SO43: Lyn 3B 148 (3N 189)
SO51: Rom 3M 129
Meadows Bus. Park, The GU17: Blackw 8G 18
Meadowside RG25: Up G 3B 62
Meadowside Cl. SO18: S'ing 7C 160
Meadowside Ct. RG24: B'toke 3M 41
Meadowside Leisure Cen. 1G 197
Meadow St. PO5: S'sea 7M 5 (4C 240)
Meadowsweet PO7: W'lle 9B 182
Meadowsweet Way PO6: Cosh 8E 200
SO50: Hor H 4N 161
Meadow Vw. GU35: Bor 4K 101
GU52: Ch Cr 6K 47
RG28: Whit 5F 54
SO21: M'dvr 7J 77
SO24: Rop 1D 110
SP5: Bish 2D 118
Meadowview Cl. SP11: Per D 5B 30
Meadow Vw. Rd. BH11: Bour 2C 226
Meadow Wlk. GU33: Liss 1E 140
GU51: Fleet 4J 47
PO1: Ports 2N 5 (1D 240)
PO13: Gos 3D 212
Meadow Way BH24: Ring 9L 185
BH25: B Sea 7B 232
GU12: Alders 8N 49
GU17: Blackw 8E 18
GU30: Lip 1E 116
SO22: Winche 1G 126
SO45: Fawl 5E 208
SP10: A'ver 1K 69
Mead Pk. Sq. SO20: Mid Wa 4B 72
Mead Rd. SO23: Winche 1J 127
SO41: Penn 4B 234
SO53: Cha F 6A 132
SP10: A'ver 2M 69
Meads, The SO51: Rom 5K 129
SO53: Cha F 7M 131
Mead Vw. SP11: G Cla 8N 69
Mead Way PO16: Fare 6D 198
Meadway GU16: Frim 2N 29
PO7: W'lle 9A 182
Meadway, The BH23: Chri 4F 230
Mears Rd. SO50: Fair O 2A 162
Measures Ga. SO21: Stoke C 7F 76
Meath Cl. PO11: H Isl 6J 243
Mede Cl. RG25: Over 3E 56
Medieval Merchant's House 8C 4
Medina Chambers
SO14: South 9C 4 (8L 173)
Medina Cl. SO53: Cha F 7C 132
Medina Ct. PO13: Lee S 9N 211
SP10: A'ver 8B 52
(off Itchen Ct.)
Medina Gdns. RG23: Oak 1D 58
Medina Ho. PO16: Fare 1C 212
Medina Rd. PO6: Cosh 9E 200
SO15: South 1G 173
Medina Way BH23: Fri C 8E 230
Medlar Cl. BH23: Burt 5N 229
SO30: Hed E 4A 176
Medlar Dr. GU17: Haw 1H 29
Medley Pl. SO15: South 3F 172
Medlicott Way SO32: Swanm 7D 164
Medonte Cl. GU51: Fleet 3N 47
MEDSTEAD 1G 96 (9K 79)
Medstead and Four Marks Station
Watercress Line (Mid-Hants Railway)
4J 97
Medstead Dr. GU51: Fleet 8J 27
Medstead Rd. GU34: Bee 8N 79
PO9: Hav 6F 202
Medwall Grn. SO19: South 5H 175
Medway Av. RG23: Oak 9D 40
Medway Ct. RG21: B'toke 6E 42
SP10: A'ver 8B 52
Medway Dr. GU14: Cov 6G 28
SO53: Cha F 4M 131
Meerut Rd. SO42: Broc 6C 148 (8N 189)
SP9: Tidw 8C 30 (7G 30)
Meeting Ho. La. BH24: Ring 1J 187
Megana Way SO51: Brai 8B 124
Megan Ct. PO6: Cosh 1G 215
Megan Rd. SO30: Wes E 9H 161
Meggeson Av. SO18: South 9D 160
Megson Dr. PO13: Lee S 9C 212
Meitner Cl. RG26: B'ley 9G 12
Melbourne Ct. *BH5: Bour* 9E 228
(off Seabourne Rd.)
Melbourne Gdns. SO30: Hed E 4N 175
SP4: Bul C 3C 66
Melbourne Ho. PO1: Ports 1D 240
Melbourne Pl. PO5: S'sea 5M 5 (3C 240)
Melbourne Rd. BH8: Bour 8N 227
BH23: Chri 5H 229
SO30: Hed E 4N 175
Melbourne St. SO14: South 6G 4 (6N 173)
Melbury Av. BH12: Poole 7B 226
Melbury Cl. SO41: Lymi 3D 234
Melbury Ct. SO17: South 1M 173
Melchet Cl. SO51: Sher E 6L 121
MELCHET PARK 6L 121
Melchet Rd. SO18: South 2G 174
Melchet Vw. SO51: Sher E 6L 121
Melcombe Ho. PO31: Cowes 5N 237
Melford Ct. BH1: Bour 6N 247 (2L 245)
Melford Gdns. RG22: Wort 9J 41
Melgate Cl. BH9: Bour 5K 227
Melick Cl. SO40: March 8E 172
Melick Way PO7: W'lle 8K 181
Meliot Ri. SP10: A'ver 6N 51
Melksham Cl. GU47: Owl 4F 18
Mellersh Cl. GU52: Ch Cr 7K 47
MELLISHES BOTTOM 8G 179
Mellor Cl. PO6: Cosh 9E 200
Melrose Av. GU14: Cov 7E 28
Melrose Cl. GU14: Cov 7E 28
GU35: Bor 5J 101
PO4: S'sea 3J 241
Melrose Ct. BH25: A'ley 3D 232
SO23: Winche 8K 105
SO40: Calm 1J 171
Melrose Gdns. PO12: Gos 9H 213
Melrose Rd. SO15: South 9J 159
Melrose Wlk. RG24: B'toke 3A 42
Melton Ct. BH13: Poole 1E 244
Melville Cl. SO16: South 6H 159
Melville Gdns. BH9: Bour 6K 227
SO31: Sar G 3C 196
Melville Rd. BH9: Bour 6J 227
PO4: S'sea 5L 241
PO12: Gos 9J 213
Melville Ter. *GU9: Farnh* 8D 64
(off Fox Yd.)
Melvin Jones Ho. PO14: Stub 4M 211
Memorial Bungs. RG28: L'stoke 5M 55
Memorial Rd. RG27: Hoo 3G 44
Memorial Sq. PO1: Ports 4N 5 (2D 240)
Mendip Cl. BH25: New M 4D 232
RG22: B'toke 8J 41
Mendip Ct. *BH23: Chri* 6B 230
(off Dorset Rd.)
Mendip Gdns. SO45: Dib P 7J 193
Mendip Rd. GU14: Cov 5G 28
SO16: South 2E 172
Mendips Rd. PO14: Fare 9A 198
Mendips Wlk. PO14: Fare 9N 197
MENGHAM 4G 242
Mengham Av. PO11: H Isl 5G 243
Mengham Ct. PO11: H Isl 4H 243
Mengham La. PO11: H Isl 4G 243
Mengham Rd. PO11: H Isl 4G 242
Mengham Rythe Sailing Club 4K 243
Menin Ho. PO15: Fare 7M 197
Menin Way GU9: Farnh 9F 64
Menslands La. PO7: H'don 2A 180
Menzies Cl. SO16: South 6E 158
MEON 4G 211
Meon Cl. GU14: Cov 6F 28
GU32: Pet 9L 139
PO8: Clan 7D 168
PO13: Gos 6D 212
RG26: Tadl 4G 11
SO51: Rom 5B 130
Meon Ct. SO18: South 2H 175
Meon Cres. SO53: Cha F 6B 132
Meon Gdns. SO32: Swanm 6D 164
Meon Ho. PO16: Fare 1C 212
Meon Rd. BH7: Bour 8E 228
PO4: S'sea 3H 241
PO14: Titch 4G 211
RG23: Oak 1D 58
SO51: Rom 5B 130
Meonside Ct. PO17: Wick 7C 178
MEONSTOKE 8N 135
Meon Valley Golf Course 2N 177
Meon Wlk. RG21: B'toke 6D 42
Meonwara Cres. GU32: W Meo 8E 136
Mercer Cl. RG22: B'toke 7L 41
Mercer Way SO51: Rom 4N 129
Merchants Pl.
SO23: Winche 7N 237 (6L 105)
Merchants Row *PO1: Ports* 7J 5
(off White Hart Rd.)
Merchants Wlk. SO14: South 8C 4 (7L 173)
Merchistoun Rd. PO8: Horn 3B 182
Mercia Av. SP10: Charl 7K 51
Mercury Cl. GU35: Bor 4K 101
SO16: South 7E 158
Mercury Gdns. SO31: Hamb 5L 195
Mercury Marshes Local Nature Reserve 5L 195
Mercury Pl. PO7: Purb 7M 201
Merdon Av. SO53: Cha F 4A 132
Merdon Cl. SO53: Cha F 4B 132
Mere Cft. PO15: Seg 6G 197
Meredith Cl. BH23: Chri 7A 230
Meredith Gdns. SO40: Tott 4K 171
Meredith Lodge PO7: W'lle 2N 201
Meredith Rd. PO2: Ports 5F 214
Meredith Towers SO19: South 6J 175
Meredun Cl. SO21: Hurs 6N 125
Merepond La. GU34: Priv 2L 137
Merganser Cl. PO12: Gos 9K 213
Meriden Cl. BH13: Poole 6D 244
Meriden Ct. *SO23: Winche* 4L 105
(off Northlands Dr.)
Meriden Rd. PO5: S'sea 5M 5 (3C 240)
Meridian Cen. PO9: Hav 8F 202
Meridian Office Pk. RG27: Hoo 3H 45
Meridians, The BH23: Chri 8J 229
Meridians Cross SO14: South 9F 4 (8N 173)
Meridian Way SP4: Ames 5A 66
Meriton Ct. *BH1: Bour* 9L 227
(off Lansdowne Rd.)
Merivale GU51: Fleet 3J 47
Merlewood Cl. BH2: Bour 1K 245
Merley Dr. BH23: Highc 6J 231
Merlin Cl. BH24: Hight 2M 187
PO8: Cowp 6M 181
SO32: Bis W 3L 163
Merlin Ct. GU16: Frim 3M 29
GU34: Four M 5J 97
Merlin Dr. PO3: Ports 4H 215
Merlin Gdns. PO16: Portc 8K 199
SO30: Hed E 3M 175
Merlin Lodge SO19: South 7B 174
Merlin Mead RG22: B'toke 4H 59
Merlin Mews *SO32: Bis W* 4M 163
(off Houchin St.)
Merlin Quay SO19: South 6A 174
Merlin Rd. GU14: Farn 1K 49
GU34: Four M 5J 97
RG20: Bis G 1G 9
(off Harrier Rd.)
Merlins Cl. GU9: Farnh 9E 64
Merlin Way BH23: Mude 9C 230
GU14: Cov 9F 28
SO53: Cha F 5L 131
Mermaid PO1: Ports 3K 5
Mermaid Ct. BH5: Bour 2B 246
Mermaid Rd. PO14: Fare 3B 212
Mermaid Way SO14: South 9F 4 (8N 173)
Merriatt Cl. RG21: B'toke 9C 42
Merrick Way SO53: Cha F 4M 131
Merridale Rd. SO19: South 6C 174
Merrie Gdns. SP6: Woodg 2A 154
Merrieleas Cl. SO53: Cha F 5A 132
Merrieleas Dr. SO53: Cha F 5A 132

Merriemeade Cl.—Minnitt Rd.

Merriemeade Cl. SO45: Dib P . . . 8K **193**
Merriemeade Pde. SO45: Dib P . . . 8K **193**
Merrileas Gdns. RG22: B'toke . . . 2J **59**
MERRITOWN . . . 8B **218**
Merritown La. BH23: Hurn . . . 8A **218**
Merritt Ct. SO53: Cha F . . . 9B **132**
Merrivale Av. BH6: Bour . . . 9H **229**
Merrivale Cl. SO45: Hythe . . . 6K **193**
Merrivale Rd. PO2: Ports . . . 5F **214**
Merron Cl. GU46: Yat . . . 8M **17**
Merrow Av. BH12: Poole . . . 7F **226**
Merrow Chase *BH13: Poole* . . . *6D 244*
(off Haven Rd.)
Merrow Cl. PO16: Portc . . . 9J **199**
Merrydown La. RG24: Chin . . . 1H **43**
Merryfield PO14: Titch C . . . 5F **196**
RG24: Chin . . . 9F **22**
Merryfield Av. PO9: Hav . . . 4D **202**
Merryfield Cl. BH23: Bran . . . 7C **220**
Merryfield La. BH10: Bour . . . 2G **226**
Merryfield Rd. GU31: Pet . . . 9A **140**
SO24: Monk . . . 4H **111**
Merry Gdns. SO52: N Bad . . . 7F **130**
MERRY OAK . . . 5D **174**
Merryoak Grn. SO19: South . . . 5D **174**
Merryoak Rd. SO19: South . . . 6D **174**
Merrytree Cl. SO51: W Wel . . . 1B **120**
Merryweather Est. BH24: Poul . . . 9M **185**
Merryweather Way RG24: B'toke . . . 1C **42**
Mersea Gdns. SO19: South . . . 6E **174**
Mersey Ct. SP10: A'ver . . . 8B **52**
Mersham Gdns. SO18: South . . . 3E **174**
Merstone Rd. PO13: Gos . . . 6E **212**
Merthyr Av. PO6: Dray . . . 8J **201**
Merton Av. PO16: Portc . . . 2M **213**
Merton Cl. GU47: Owl . . . 3H **19**
SP6: F'dge . . . 8J **151**
Merton Ct. BH23: Highc . . . 7J **231**
PO5: S'sea . . . 4E **240**
Merton Cres. PO16: Portc . . . 2L **213**
Merton Gro. BH24: Ring . . . 9J **185**
Merton Rd. PO5: S'sea . . . 4D **240**
RG21: B'toke . . . 5A **42**
SO17: South . . . 8N **159**
Meryl Rd. PO4: S'sea . . . 3K **241**
Meryon Rd. SO24: New A . . . 2E **108**
Mescott Mdws. SO30: Hed E . . . 9M **161**
Mesh Pond SP5: Down . . . 1H **119** (7N **119**)
Mesh Rd. SO51: Mich . . . 3H **123**
Messner St. RG24: B'toke . . . 2D **42**
Metcalfe Av. PO14: Stub . . . 5N **211**
Meteor Rd. PO10: T Isl . . . 5N **217**
Methuen Cl. BH8: Bour . . . 9N **227**
Methuen Rd. BH8: Bour . . . 9M **227**
GU33: Longc . . . 3H **115**
PO4: S'sea . . . 4H **241**
Methuen St. SO14: South . . . 1D **4** (3M **173**)
Metuchen Way SO30: Hed E . . . 6N **175**
Meudon Av. GU14: Farn . . . 9K **29**
Mews, The BH2: Bour . . . 7H **247** (2H **245**)
GU31: Pet . . . 9M **139**
PO1: Ports . . . 1F 240
(off Clive Rd.)
PO5: S'sea . . . 5E 240
(off Collingwood Rd.)
PO9: Hav . . . 5E **202**
(Riders La.)
PO9: Hav . . . 8F **202**
(The Pallant)
PO12: Gos . . . 3N **239**
RG26: B'ley . . . 2J **23**
SO16: Rown . . . 5E **158**
SO45: Blac . . . 9D **208**
SO53: Cha F . . . 9A **132**
SP10: A'ver . . . 3A **70**
Mews Ct. SO21: Ott . . . 1F **132**
Mewsey Ct. PO9: Hav . . . 2D **202**
Mews La. SO22: Winche . . . 8J **237** (7K **105**)
Meybury Cl. BH23: Bran . . . 8C **220**
Mey Cl. PO7: W'lle . . . 2A **202**
Meynell Cl. SO50: E'leigh . . . 9D **132**
Meyrick Cl. BH23: Bran . . . 8C **220**
Meyrick Ct. BH2: Bour . . . 9K **227**
Meyrick Dr. RG14: New . . . 1C **8**
Meyrick Gate *BH2: Bour . . . 1K 245*
(off Wimborne Rd.)
Meyrick Ho. PO2: Ports . . . 7D **214**
Meyrick Pk. Cres. BH3: Bour . . . 8K **227**
Meyrick Park Golf Course . . . 5K **247** (1J **245**)
Meyrick Pk. Mans. BH2: Bour . . . 5L **247** (1K **245**)
Meyrick Rd. BH1: Bour . . . 2M **245**
PO2: Ports . . . 7D **214**
PO9: Hav . . . 8D **202**
Micawber Ho. PO1: Ports . . . 9E **214**
Michael Crook Cl. PO9: Bed . . . 6C **202**
Michael Ho. SP11: Enh A . . . 2A **52**
Michaelmas Cl. GU46: Yat . . . 9N **17**
Michaelmas Drove SP11: Weyh . . . 9B **50**
Michaelmas Pl. SO32: Swanm . . . 5D **164**
Michaels Way SO45: Hythe . . . 5L **193**
SO50: Fair O . . . 1A **162**
MICHELDEVER . . . 7J **77**
Micheldever Cl. RG28: Whit . . . 7H **55**
Micheldever Dr. GU51: Fleet . . . 9H **27**
Micheldever Gdns. RG28: Whit . . . 7H **55**
Micheldever Rd. RG28: Whit . . . 6G **55**
SP10: A'ver . . . 2A **70**
SP11: A'ver . . . 2A **70**
MICHELDEVER STATION . . . 4J **77**
Micheldever Station (Rail) . . . 4J **77**
Michelgrove Rd. BH5: Bour . . . 2B **246**
MICHELMERSH . . . 4J **123**
Michelmersh Cl. SO16: Rown . . . 6D **158**
Michelmersh Grn. BH8: Bour . . . 4A **228**
Michigan Way SO40: Tott . . . 2H **171**
Mickleham Cl. BH12: Poole . . . 6F **226**
Mickle Hill GU47: Sandh . . . 4C **18**
MIDANBURY . . . 1D **174**
Midanbury B'way. SO18: South . . . 1D **174**
Midanbury Ct. SO18: South . . . 2C **174**
Midanbury Cres. SO18: South . . . 1D **174**
Midanbury La. SO18: South . . . 3C **174**
Midanbury Wlk. SO18: South . . . 2D **174**
Midas Cl. PO7: Purb . . . 5N **201**
MIDDLE BOCKHAMPTON . . . 9A **220**
Middlebridge St. SO51: Rom . . . 6L **129**
Middlebrook SO32: Bis W . . . 3M **163**
Middle Brook St.
SO23: Winche . . . 8N **237** (7L **105**)
(not continuous)
Middle Church La. GU9: Farnh . . . 8D **64**
Middle Cl. RG26: Pam H . . . 4L **11**
Middle Comn. Rd. SO41: Penn . . . 3A **234**
Middle Ct. *PO1: Ports . . . 9F 214*
(off Inverness Rd.)
Middlecroft La. PO12: Gos . . . 1H **239**
Middle Gordon Rd. GU15: Camb . . . 8L **19**
Middle Hill GU11: Alders . . . 8J **49**
Middle La. BH24: Ring . . . 1K **187**
SP6: Mart . . . 8B **118**
Middle Mead PO14: Fare . . . 9L **197**
RG27: Hoo . . . 2G **44**
Middle Mdw. GU33: Liss . . . 1F **140**
Middlemoor Rd. GU16: Frim . . . 3N **29**
Middle Old Pk. GU9: Farnh . . . 6B **64**
Middle Pk. Way PO9: Hav . . . 5D **202**
Middle Rd. BH10: Bour . . . 1G **226**
SO19: South . . . 7D **174**
SO22: Winche . . . 6J **237** (6J **105**)
SO31: P Ga . . . 4E **196**
SO41: Lymi . . . 3D **234**
SO41: Sway . . . 5J **223**
SO41: Tip . . . 7E **222**
SO52: N Bad . . . 7F **130**
Middlesex Rd. PO4: S'sea . . . 4J **241**
Middle St. PO5: S'sea . . . 5N **5** (3D **240**)
SO14: South . . . 3M **173**
MIDDLETON . . . 4M **71**
Middleton SP5: Mid W . . . 5G **87**
Middleton Cl. PO14: Fare . . . 1A **212**
SO18: South . . . 9E **160**
Middleton Gdns. BH7: Bour . . . 8C **228**
GU14: Cov . . . 6G **28**
RG21: B'toke . . . 4C **42**
Middleton M. BH25: New M . . . 5A **232**
SO31: P Ga . . . 4E **196**
Middleton Ri. PO8: Clan . . . 7D **168**
Middleton Rd. BH9: Bour . . . 4J **227**
BH24: Ring . . . 9K **185**
GU15: Camb . . . 7N **19**
SP5: Mid W . . . 4G **87**
Middleton Wlk. PO14: Fare . . . 1A **212**
MIDDLE WALLOP . . . 9N **67**
Middleway, The SP11: And D, Longp . . . 9G **52**
MIDDLE WINTERSLOW . . . 5G **87**
Midfield Cl. PO14: Fare . . . 1B **212**
Midgham Rd. SP6: F'dge . . . 3F **152**
Midhurst Ct. SO53: Cha F . . . 7A **132**
Midhurst Ho. PO1: Ports . . . 1E **240**
Midhurst Rd. GU30: Lip . . . 3E **116**
GU31: Pet . . . 8C **140**
Midland Rd. BH9: Bour . . . 5K **227**
Midlands Est. SO30: Wes E . . . 9G **161**
Midlane Cl. RG21: B'toke . . . 9B **42**
Midlington Hill SO32: Drox . . . 4H **165**
Midlington Rd. SO32: Drox . . . 4K **165**
Mid Summer Pl. SP4: Ames . . . 4A **66**
Midway SO45: Hythe . . . 6L **193**
Midway Rd. PO2: Ports . . . 3F **214**
Midways PO14: Stub . . . 7M **211**
Midwood Av. BH8: Bour . . . 5C **228**
Mike Hawthorn Dr. GU9: Farnh . . . 7E **64**
Milbeck Cl. PO8: Cowp . . . 7A **182**
Milborne Cres. BH12: Poole . . . 7C **226**
Milburn Cl. BH4: Bour . . . 1G **244**
Milburn Rd. BH4: Bour . . . 1F **244**
Milbury Cres. SO18: South . . . 4E **174**
Mildenhall BH4: Bour . . . 3H **245**
Mildmay Ct. RG29: Odi . . . 8L **45**
SO23: Winche . . . 8P **237**
Mildmay St. SO22: Winche . . . 9H **105**
Mildmay Ter. RG27: H Win . . . 6C **26**
Milebush Rd. PO4: S'sea . . . 2K **241**
Mile End La. SO32: Meon . . . 7A **142**
Mile End Rd. PO1: Ports . . . 9D **214**
PO2: Ports . . . 8D **214**
(not continuous)
Miles Ct. PO11: H Isl . . . 6K **243**
Milesdown Pl. SO23: Winche . . . 7M **105**
Miles La. SP5: W'psh . . . 3J **121**
Miles Pl. SO31: Wars . . . 8D **196**
Milestone Point *PO9: Hav . . . 8F 202*
(off West St.)
Milestones, Hampshire's Living History Mus. . . . 6N **41**
Milford Cl. PO9: Bed . . . 6D **202**
Milford Ct. PO4: S'sea . . . 3J **241**
PO12: Gos . . . 4F **238**
SO41: M Sea . . . 8L **235**
Milford Cres. SO41: M Sea . . . 7L **235**
Milford Dr. BH11: Bour . . . 1D **226**
Milford Gdns. SO53: Cha F . . . 6C **132**
Milford Ho. SO23: Winche . . . 9K **105**
MILFORD ON SEA . . . 8L **235**
Milford Pl. SO41: M Sea . . . 8L **235**
Milford Rd. BH25: New M . . . 5C **232**
PO1: Ports . . . 2E **240**
SO41: Ever, Lymi, Penn . . . 6M **233**
Milford Trad. Est. SO41: M Sea . . . 8L **235**
Military Rd. PO1: Ports . . . 1M **5** (1C **240**)
PO3: Ports . . . 3G **214**
PO6: Dray . . . 8K **201**
PO12: Gos . . . 7K **239**
(Fort Rd., not continuous)
PO12: Gos . . . 6J **213**
(Heritage Way)
PO12: Gos . . . 3G **238**
(Privett Rd.)
PO13: Lee S . . . 4E **238**
PO16: Fare . . . 7F **198**
Milkingpen La. RG24: Old Bas . . . 5J **43**
Milk La. PO7: W'lle . . . 3K **201**
Milkwood Ct. SO40: Tott . . . 3J **171**
Milky Down BH24: Hight, Poul . . . 1N **187**
Milky Way GU31: Buri, Old D . . . 8M **145**
Millais Gdns. . . . 4H **85**
Millais Rd. SO19: South . . . 7C **174**
Millam Ct. PO11: H Isl . . . 3E **242**
Milland La. GU30: Mill . . . 7C **116**
Milland Rd. SO23: Winche . . . 8M **105**
Millard Cl. RG21: B'toke . . . 4A **42**
MILLBANK . . . 5A **174**
Millbank Ho. SO14: South . . . 4A **174**
Millbank St. SO14: South . . . 5A **174**
Millbank Wharf SO14: South . . . 5A **174**
Millbridge Gdns. SO19: South . . . 6F **174**
Millbridge Rd. GU46: Yat . . . 5L **17**
MILLBROOK . . . 3F **172**
Millbrook Cl. GU33: Liss . . . 1F **140**
RG27: Sher L . . . 7H **23**
SO53: Cha F . . . 7N **131**
Millbrook Dr. PO9: Hav . . . 3G **203**
Millbrook Flyover SO15: South . . . 3D **172**
Millbrook Ho. SO30: Hed E . . . 2B **176**
Millbrook Point Rd. SO15: South . . . 5E **172**
(not continuous)
Millbrook Rd. SO15: South . . . 3D **172**
Millbrook Rd. E. SO15: South . . . 4H **173**
Millbrook Rd. W. SO15: South . . . 4G **172**
Millbrook Station (Rail) . . . 4G **173**
Millbrook Towers SO16: South . . . 9D **158**
Millbrook Trad. Est. SO15: South . . . 4E **172**
Millburns, The SO51: Tims . . . 6K **123**
Mill Chase Leisure Cen. . . . 4L **101**
Mill Chase Rd. GU35: Bor . . . 3L **101**
Mill Cl. GU27: Hasl . . . 9N **103**
PO7: Den . . . 6J **181**
PO11: H Isl . . . 6F **216**
RG27: Sher L . . . 3M **23**
SO16: Nur . . . 6C **158**
SP11: Wher . . . 2E **74**
Mill Cnr. GU51: Fleet . . . 7A **28**
Mill Ct. GU34: Up Froy . . . 10G **63**
SP6: F'dge . . . 1H **153**
Millcourt SO50: Fair O . . . 1A **162**
Mill Drove SN8: Co Ki . . . 1G **30**
Mill End PO10: S'brne . . . 9N **203**
SP6: Dame . . . 7A **150**
Millennium Centre, The GU9: Farnh . . . 9C **64**
Millennium Cl. PO7: W'lle . . . 4M **201**
Millennium Ct. PO7: W'lle . . . 4M **201**
RG21: B'toke . . . 6A **42**
Miller Cl. BH25: A'ley . . . 2D **232**
Miller Ct. BH12: Poole . . . 6A **226**
BH23: Chri . . . 8J **229**
Miller Dr. PO16: Fare . . . 6B **198**
Miller Gdns. BH6: Bour . . . 9E **228**
Miller Rd. BH23: Chri . . . 7N **229**
Millers La. SO20: Mid Wa . . . 3A **72**
SO22: Pitt . . . 2C **126**
Miller's Pond Gdns. SO19: South . . . 7D **174**
Millers Quay Ho. *PO16: Fare . . . 9D 198*
(off Lwr. Quay Rd.)
Millers Rd. RG26: Tadl . . . 5H **11**
Millers Vw. SO31: Burs . . . 8L **175**
Millers Way SO45: Dib P . . . 7L **193**
Millers Yd. SO21: Sut S . . . 7D **76**
Mill Est. Yd. SO16: Nur . . . 6B **158**
Mill Field Local Nature Reserve . . . 4H **43**
Millgate Ct. GU9: Farnh . . . 7F **64**
Mill Ga. Ho. *PO1: Ports . . . 4K 5*
(off St George's Sq.)
MILL GREEN . . . 2K **9**
Millgreen La. RG19: Head . . . 2K **9**
Millhams Rd. BH10: Bour . . . 1G **226**
Millhams St. BH23: Chri . . . 8L **229**
Millhams St. Nth. BH23: Chri . . . 8L **229**
Mill Hill SO24: New A . . . 9F **94**
SO30: Botl . . . 4D **176**
Mill Hill Av. SP9: Tidw . . . 6C **30**
Mill Ho. Bus. Cen. SO19: South . . . 6B **174**
Mill Ho. Cen. SO40: Tott . . . 3N **171**
Mill Ho. Gdns. PO7: Den . . . 6H **181**
Milliken Cl. SO45: Fawl . . . 6D **208**
Millins Cl. GU47: Owl . . . 4G **18**
MILL LANE . . . 1K **63**
Mill La. BH21: Cran, Edmo . . . 7K **149**
BH23: Highc . . . 6K **231**
BH23: Hurn . . . 9E **218**
BH24: Bur . . . 6F **188**
GU10: Fren . . . 1D **84**
GU30: Pass . . . 6N **101**
GU31: S Hart . . . 9G **147**
GU32: Pet . . . 7A **140**
GU32: Ste . . . 6L **139**
GU33: Emp, Hawk . . . 6M **113**
GU34: Alt . . . 4H **81**
GU35: Head, Lind . . . 3M **101**
GU46: Sandh, Yat . . . 5N **17**
GU47: Sandh . . . 5N **17**
PO1: Ports . . . 9D **214**
PO7: Purb . . . 7F **200**
PO9: Bed . . . 8C **202**
PO9: Langs . . . 1E **216**
PO10: S'brne, Westb . . . 8N **203**
PO12: Gos . . . 1K **239**
PO15: Titch . . . 6K **197**
PO17: Wick . . . 5C **178**
RG7: Rise . . . 5H **15**
RG7: Stra S . . . 7J **13**
RG20: Ecc . . . 5G **9**
RG27: H Wes . . . 4B **24**
RG27: Rise . . . 5H **15**
RG27: Sher L . . . 8K **13**
RG29: N War . . . 6H **45**
SO16: Nur . . . 7L **157**
SO21: Abb W . . . 9A **92**
SO24: Bis S . . . 1J **109**
SO32: Botl . . . 8G **162**
SO32: Drox . . . 2K **165**
(not continuous)
SO41: E End . . . 1N **235**
SO41: Lymi . . . 2F **234**
Mill La. SO41: Penn, Sway . . . 8L **223**
SO42: Broc . . . 7D **148**
SO43: Mins . . . 9N **155**
SO51: Rom . . . 5K **129**
SO51: Sher E, W Wel . . . 7N **121**
SP5: Bish . . . 3D **118**
SP5: E Win, Mid W . . . 4H **87**
SP11: Longp . . . 2A **76**
Mill La. Ind. Est. GU34: Alt . . . 4H **81**
Mill Mdw. SO41: M Sea . . . 7J **235**
Millmere GU46: Yat . . . 6N **17**
Mill Path SP9: Tidw . . . 6B **30** (6F **30**)
Mill Pond, The SO45: Holb . . . 2N **207**
Mill Pond Rd. PO12: Gos . . . 1K **239**
Mill Quay PO10: S'brne . . . 1N **217**
Mill Race Vw. SP5: Down . . . 1K **119** (7A **120**)
Mill Ri. SO51: Dun . . . 4D **122**
Mill Rd. BH23: Chri . . . 6K **229**
GU33: Liss . . . 1E **140**
PO7: Den . . . 6H **181**
PO7: W'lle . . . 3L **201**
PO12: Gos . . . 1J **239**
PO16: Fare . . . 9C **198**
RG7: Rise . . . 2J **15**
RG24: B'toke . . . 3L **41**
SO15: South . . . 3E **172**
SO40: Tott . . . 3N **171**
Mill Rd. Nth. BH8: Bour . . . 3A **228**
Mill Rd. Sth. BH8: Bour . . . 4A **228**
Mill Rd. Ter. GU33: Liss . . . 1E **140**
Mill Rythe Holiday Village PO11: H Isl . . . 1J **243**
Mill Rythe La. PO11: H Isl . . . 9G **217**
Mills, The BH12: Poole . . . 8C **226**
Millside *SO32: Corh . . . 8N 135*
(off Warnford Rd.)
Mills Rd. PO2: Ports . . . 7E **214**
Mill Stream GU9: Weyb . . . 4G **65**
Millstream, The GU27: Hasl . . . 1N **117**
Millstream Cl. SP10: A'ver . . . 3M **69**
Millstream Ct. BH24: Ring . . . 1J **187**
Millstream Ri. SO51: Rom . . . 5K **129**
Millstream Trad. Est. BH24: Ring . . . 3K **187**
Mill St. PO14: Titch . . . 9K **197**
SO50: E'leigh . . . 8F **132**
Mill Vw. RG29: Grey . . . 9F **44**
Millvina Cl. SO40: Woodl . . . 6F **170**
Mill Way SO40: Tott . . . 5L **171**
Millway SO32: Durl . . . 6E **162**
Millway Cl. SP10: A'ver . . . 2L **69**
Millway Rd. SP10: A'ver . . . 2L **69**
Millyford Cl. BH25: New M . . . 6M **231**
Milne Cl. SO45: Dib P . . . 7H **193**
Milner Ct. SO15: South . . . 2H **173**
Milne Rd. SP4: Bul C . . . 3B **66**
Milner Pl. SO22: Winche . . . 8J **105**
Milner Rd. BH4: Bour . . . 3G **245**
Milnthorpe La. SO22: Winche . . . 9H **237** (7J **105**)
Milsons, The SO20: S Bri . . . 3F **88**
MILTON . . . 3H **241**
Milton Av. SP10: A'ver . . . 9K **51**
Milton Bus. Cen. BH25: New M . . . 4N **231**
Milton Cl. BH14: Poole . . . 2B **244**
RG24: B'toke . . . 3D **42**
Milton Ct. PO4: S'sea . . . 2H **241**
Milton Gate *BH25: New M . . . 5A 232*
(off Old Milton Rd.)
Milton Gro. BH25: New M . . . 4C **232**
SO31: Loc H . . . 7E **196**
Milton La. PO4: S'sea . . . 2G **240**
Milton Locks PO4: S'sea . . . 3L **241**
Milton Mead BH25: New M . . . 4A **232**
Milton Pde. PO8: Cowp . . . 8M **181**
Milton Pk. Av. PO4: S'sea . . . 3J **241**
Milton Rd. BH8: Bour . . . 9L **227**
BH14: Poole . . . 2B **244**
PO3: Ports . . . 1H **241**
PO4: S'sea . . . 2H **241**
PO7: W'lle . . . 9L **181**
PO8: Cowp . . . 8M **181**
SO15: South . . . 1A **4** (4K **173**)
SO50: E'leigh . . . 7F **132**
SP4: Ames . . . 6A **66**
Milverton Cl. BH23: Highc . . . 5G **231**
SO40: Elin . . . 5N **171**
Milverton Ct. SO18: South . . . 3F **174**
Milverton Ho. PO5: S'sea . . . 3D **240**
Milverton Rd. SO22: Winche . . . 6H **237** (6H **105**)
SO40: Elin . . . 4N **171**
Milvil Ct. PO13: Lee S . . . 1A **238**
Milvil Rd. PO13: Lee S . . . 1A **238**
Mimosa Cl. GU35: Lind . . . 2M **101**
PO15: Seg . . . 6H **197**
Mimosa Ct. SP10: A'ver . . . 3L **69**
Mimosa Dr. SO50: Fair O . . . 1B **162**
Minchens La. RG26: B'ley . . . 1F **22**
Mincingfield La. SO32: Durl . . . 7G **162**
Minden Cl. RG24: Chin . . . 1F **42**
SP10: A'ver . . . 7M **51**
Minden Ho. PO14: Fare . . . 9B **198**
SO51: Rom . . . 5N 129
(off Chambers Av.)
Minden Pl. GU34: Four M . . . 5J **97**
Mindens, The *SP9: Shi B . . . 2B 66*
(off Salisbury Rd.)
Minden Way SO22: Winche . . . 9G **104**
Minehurst Rd. GU16: Mytc . . . 8N **29**
Minerva Cl. PO7: Purb . . . 7M **201**
Minerva Cres. PO1: Ports . . . 6J **5** (3B **240**)
Minerva Dr. PO12: Gos . . . 9L **213**
Ministry Rd. RG19: Green . . . 1H **9**
MINLEY . . . 3N **27**
Minley Cl. GU14: Cov . . . 8G **28**
Minley Ct. PO9: Hav . . . 4H **203**
Minley Gro. GU51: Fleet . . . 9N **27**
Minley La. GU17: Min . . . 2N **27**
Minley Link Rd. GU14: Cov . . . 8D **28**
Minley Rd. GU14: Cov . . . 6E **28**
GU17: Min . . . 5M **27**
(not continuous)
GU51: Fleet . . . 6M **27**
Minnitt Rd. PO12: Gos . . . 3N **239**

A-Z Hampshire 301

Minores Rd.—Mountbatten Gdns.

Minores Rd. SP9: Tidw ... 8E **30** (7G **31**)
Minshull Ct. SP10: A'ver ... 1M **69**
MINSTEAD ... 9M **155**
Minstead Av. SO18: South ... 2G **175**
Minstead Cl. RG26: Tadl ... 7H **11**
SO22: Winche ... 2H **105**
Minstead Ct. *SO17: South ... 2M 173*
(off Westwood Rd.)
Minstead Dr. GU46: Yat ... 8M **17**
Minstead Rd. BH10: Bour ... 3G **226**
PO4: S'sea ... 4J **241**
Minstead Studys Cen. ... 8L **155**
Minster Cl. GU14: Farn ... 2M **49**
PO15: Fare ... 7M **197**
Minster Ct. *BH12: Poole ... 1E 244*
(off Princess Rd.)
GU15: Camb ... 9H **19**
(Tuscam Way)
GU15: Camb ... 6M **19**
(York Rd.)
SO15: South ... 4H **173**
Minster Gallery ... *8M 237*
(off Gt. Minster St.)
Minster La. SO23: Winche ... 8M **237** (7L **105**)
MINT, THE ... 8G **115**
Minter Ct. RG26: Tadl ... 4F **10**
Mintern Cl. SO50: B'stke ... 7H **133**
Minterne Grange BH14: Poole ... 6A **244**
Minterne Rd. BH9: Bour ... 4L **227**
BH14: Poole ... 6A **244**
BH23: Chri ... 8A **230**
Minters Ct. *SO23: Winche ... 7L 237*
(off Cross St.)
Minter's Lepe PO7: Purb ... 6M **201**
Minton M. BH2: Bour ... 9K **227**
Mint Rd. GU33: Liss ... 9F **114**
Mint Yd. SO23: Winche ... 8M **237**
Mintys Hill SP6: R'bne ... 2C **150**
Mirabella Cl. SO19: South ... 8B **174**
Mirage BH13: S'bks ... 8B **244**
Mirror Cl. SO31: Wars ... 8C **196**
MISLINGFORD ... 1F **178**
Mislingford Rd. SO32: Swanm ... 7E **164**
Misselbrook La. SO52: N Bad ... 8J **131**
Missenden Acres SO30: Hed E ... 2N **175**
Mission La. PO8: Cowp ... 7A **182**
Mistletoe Gdns. SO31: Sar G ... 4B **196**
Mistletoe Rd. GU46: Yat ... 9N **17**
Mistral SO14: South ... 7N **173**
Mitchell Av. RG27: H Win ... 7B **26**
Mitchell Cl. BH25: B Sea ... 7B **232**
PO15: Seg ... 4G **196**
RG26: Pam H ... 3L **11**
SO19: South ... 7B 174
(off Hazel Rd.)
SP10: A'ver ... 9H **51**
Mitchell Dr. SO50: Fair O ... 9N **133**
Mitchell Gdns. RG22: B'toke ... 3L **59**
Mitchell Point SO31: Hamb ... 7J **195**
Mitchell Rd. PO9: Bed ... 6B **202**
SO50: E'leigh ... 1F **160**
Mitchells Cl. SO51: Rom ... 5M **129**
SP5: Woodf ... 2M **119**
Mitchell Way PO3: Ports ... 5J **215**
SO18: S'ton A ... 5D **160**
Mitford Rd. SO24: New A ... 1D **108**
Mitre Copse SO50: B'stke ... 1K **161**
Mitre Ct. BH23: Chri ... 7K **229**
Mizen Way PO13: Gos ... 1F **238**
Mizzen Ho. PO6: P Sol ... 1B **214**
Moat Cl. RG26: B'ley ... 9G **12**
SO45: Holb ... 5N **207**
Moat Ct. BH4: Bour ... 9F **226**
PO12: Gos ... 4F **238**
Moat Dr. PO12: Gos ... 4F **238**
Moat Hill SO18: South ... 8D **160**
Moat La. BH25: B Sea ... 5A **232**
Moat Wlk. PO12: Gos ... 4F **238**
Mobile Home Pk. PO8: Horn ... 8D **168**
MOCKBEGGAR ... 2M **185**
Mockbeggar La. BH24: Ibsl, Mock ... 2J **185**
Model Farm La. SP5: P'tn ... 6E **86**
Moffat Rd. BH23: Chri ... 7N **229**
Moffats Cl. GU47: Sandh ... 5C **18**
Moggs Mead GU31: Pet ... 1N **145**
Mole Cl. GU14: Cov ... 6F **28**
Molefields SO41: M Sea ... 7L **235**
Mole Hill PO7: W'lle ... 4N **201**
Molesworth Rd. PO12: Gos ... 3L **239**
(not continuous)
Mollison Ri. PO15: White ... 3G **197**
Molyneaux Rd. BH25: A'ley ... 3E **232**
Momford Rd. SO22: Oli B ... 2F **126**
Monachus La. RG27: H Win ... 5C **26**
Monarch Cl. PO7: W'lle ... 2A **202**
RG22: B'toke ... 4J **59**
SO31: Loc H ... 7D **196**
Monarch Ct. *BH4: Bour ... 2G 245*
(off Marlborough Rd.)
Monarch Way SO22: Winche ... 8G **104**
SO30: Wes E ... 9K **161**
Monastery Rd. SO18: South ... 3C **174**
Monckton Rd. PO3: Ports ... 6H **215**
PO12: Gos ... 6K **239**
Mon Cres. SO18: South ... 3G **174**
Moneyer Rd. SP10: A'ver ... 7M **51**
Moneyfield Av. PO3: Ports ... 8H **215**
Moneyfield La. PO3: Ports ... 8H **215**
Moneyfield Path PO3: Ports ... 7J **215**
Mongers Piece RG24: Chin ... 8H **23**
Monier Williams Rd. SO21: Bar S ... 6N **71**
Moniton Est. RG22: Wort ... 7K **41**
Monkey La. GU34: C'more ... 7E **112**
Monkey Puzzle Rdbt. GU14: Cov ... 9G **29**
Monks Brook Cl. SO50: E'leigh ... 2C **160**
Monks Brook Ind. Pk. SO53: Cha F ... 7N **131**
Monks Cl. GU14: Farn ... 8L **29**
(not continuous)
SP9: Tidw ... 7C **30** (6G **30**)
Monks Ct. SO41: Lymi ... 4F **234**
Monkshanger GU9: Farnh ... 8G **65**
MONK SHERBORNE ... 6K **21**
Monk Sherborne Ho. RG26: M She ... 7K **21**
Monk Sherborne Rd. RG24: Sher J ... 6K **21**
RG26: Cha A, Rams ... 5F **20**
RG26: M She ... 6K **21**
Monks Hill PO10: Westb ... 3N **203**
PO13: Lee S ... 8M **211**
Monkshood Cl. BH23: Chri ... 5D **230**
Monks Orchard GU32: Pet ... 8M **139**
Monks Path GU14: Farn ... 7M **29**
SO18: S'ing ... 8C **160**
Monks Pl. SO40: Tott ... 4K **171**
Monks Ri. GU51: Fleet ... 2J **47**
Monks Rd. SO23: Winche ... 5L **105**
SO31: Net A ... 3F **194**
Monks Wlk. GU9: Farnh ... 9H **65**
PO12: Gos ... 7J **213**
SO45: Dib P ... 9K **193**
Monks Way BH11: Bour ... 1A **226**
PO14: Stub ... 7L **211**
SO18: S'ing ... 7C **160**
SO50: E'leigh ... 2C **160**
Monks Well GU10: Farnh ... 9K **65**
Monkswell Grn. BH23: Chri ... 8N **229**
Monks Wood GU32: Pet ... 8M **139**
Monks Wood Cl. SO16: Bass ... 5N **159**
Monkswood Cres. RG26: Tadl ... 6H **11**
MONKTON ... 6E **148**
Monkton Ct. BH4: Bour ... 1G **245**
Monkton Cres. BH12: Poole ... 6C **226**
Monkton Drove BH21: Wim G ... 6E **148**
Monkton Hgts. *BH5: Bour ... 1A 246*
(off Boscombe Spa Rd.)
Monkton La. GU9: Farnh, Hale ... 5G **64**
SO40: Tott ... 4K **171**
Monkton Pk. GU9: Farnh ... 6H **65**
MONKWOOD ... 4J **111**
Monkwood Cl. PO9: Hav ... 4D **202**
Monkworthy Cl. BH24: Ashl H ... 3C **186**
Monkworthy Dr. BH24: Ashl H ... 3C **186**
Monmouth Cl. BH24: Ring ... 2K **187**
SO53: Cha F ... 6N **131**
Monmouth Ct. BH24: Ring ... 1J **187**
Monmouth Gdns. SO40: Tott ... 5K **171**
Monmouth Rd. PO2: Ports ... 6E **214**
Monmouth Sq. SO22: Winche ... 8F **104**
Monnow Gdns. SO18: Wes E ... 1F **174**
Monroe Cl. PO12: Gos ... 4G **238**
Mons, The SO23: Winche ... 7K **237**
Mons Av. SP4: Bul C ... 3B **66**
Mons Barracks GU11: Alders ... 6L **49**
Mons Cl. GU11: Alders ... 4N **49**
Mons Ct. SO23: Winche ... 7K **237** (6K **105**)
Monson Ho. PO1: Ports ... 1F **240**
Montacute Cl. GU14: Farn ... 8M **29**
Montacute Ho. PO7: W'lle ... 1M **201**
Montagu Cl. PO12: Gos ... 8L **213**
Montague Av. SO19: South ... 7H **175**
Montague Cl. GU15: Camb ... 8K **19**
SO19: South ... 7H **175**
Montague Ct. SO45: Dib P ... 9K **193**
Montague Gdns. GU31: Pet ... 1B **146**
Montague Pl. RG21: B'toke ... 8C **42**
Montague Rd. BH5: Bour ... 1E **246**
PO2: Ports ... 7F **214**
SO50: B'stke ... 9H **133**
Montague Wallis Ct. PO1: Ports ... 4K **5** (2B **240**)
Montagu Pk. BH23: Highc ... 7J **231**
Montagu Rd. BH23: Highc ... 7K **231**
Montana Ct. PO7: W'lle ... 3N **201**
Monteagle La. GU46: Yat ... 8L **17**
(not continuous)
Montecchio Way GU34: Holy ... 2J **81**
Montefiore Dr. SO31: Sar G ... 4C **196**
Monteray Dr. SO41: Hor ... 2G **233**
Monterey Dr. PO9: Hav ... 5G **203**
SO31: Loc H ... 7D **196**
Montfort Ct. SO51: Rom ... 5B **130**
Montfort College SO51: Rom ... 5B **130**
Montfort Hgts. SO51: Rom ... 5B **130**
Montfort Rd. SO51: Rom ... 6B **130**
Montgomerie Rd. PO5: S'sea ... 3E **240**
Montgomery Av. BH11: Bour ... 3F **226**
SO40: Tott ... 2K **171**
Montgomery Cl. GU47: Sandh ... 5D **18**
SO22: Winche ... 9G **105**
Montgomery Ho. *SP9: Tidw ... 6C 30*
(off Sidbury Circular Rd.)
Montgomery Path GU14: Cov ... 9H **29**
Montgomery Rd. GU14: Cov ... 9H **29**
PO9: Hav ... 8G **202**
PO13: Gos ... 4E **212**
SO18: South ... 3E **174**
SP11: Enh A ... 3A **52**
Montgomery Wlk. PO7: W'lle ... 4L **201**
Montgomery Way SO53: Cha F ... 9N **131**
Montpelier Cl. SO31: P Ga ... 6F **196**
Montreal Ct. GU11: Alders ... 1H **65**
Montreal Wlk. GU30: Lip ... 3E **116**
Montrose Av. PO16: Portc ... 8N **199**
Montrose Cl. GU16: Frim ... 2N **29**
GU35: W'hil ... 6K **101**
GU51: Fleet ... 3N **47**
SO30: Botl ... 4B **176**
Montrose Dr. BH10: Bour ... 4F **226**
Montserrat Pl. RG24: B'toke ... 1D **42**
Montserrat Rd. PO13: Lee S ... 1A **238**
RG24: B'toke ... 1D **42**
Monument Chase GU35: W'hil ... 6K **101**
Monument Ct. SO14: South ... 9D **4**
Monument La. PO17: Boar, Fare ... 4K **199**
SO41: Wal ... 1G **234**
MONXTON ... 4C **68**
Monxton Grn. PO9: Hav ... 3H **203**
Monxton La. SP11: A'ver, Weyh ... 8C **50**
Monxton Pl. RG27: Sher L ... 7H **23**
Monxton Rd. SP10: A'ver ... 1H **69**
SP11: A'ver ... 2F **68**
SP11: Grat ... 4M **67**
Monxton Rd. Rdbt. SP11: A'ver ... 1H **69**
Moody Rd. PO14: Stub ... 7L **211**
Moody's Hill SP5: W Dean ... 1J **121**
Moon Cl. SO40: March ... 9D **172**
Moonhills La. SO42: Beau ... 6G **206**
Moonrakers Way BH23: Chri ... 5G **230**
Moonscross Av. SO40: Tott ... 6M **171**
Moor Cl. GU35: W'hil ... 4G **100**
GU47: Owl ... 4G **19**
Moorcot Cl. PO6: Cosh ... 8E **200**
Moor Ct. La. SO21: Spar ... 6N **89**
Moorcroft Av. BH23: Burt ... 3M **229**
Moorcroft Cl. SO21: Sut S ... 7D **76**
MOORDOWN ... 4K **227**
Moordown Cl. BH9: Bour ... 3L **227**
Moore Av. BH11: Bour ... 2E **226**
Moore Cl. BH25: New M ... 5A **232**
GU52: Ch Cr ... 6M **47**
SP10: A'ver ... 9N **51**
Moore Cres. SO31: Net A ... 2G **194**
Moore Gdns. PO12: Gos ... 3H **239**
Moore Rd. GU52: Ch Cr ... 6M **47**
Moorfield Gro. BH9: Bour ... 4K **227**
Moorfields Rd. BH13: Poole ... 5D **244**
Moorfoot Gdns. RG22: B'toke ... 8K **41**
MOORGREEN ... 9K **161**
Moorgreen Park SO30: Wes E ... 9K **161**
Moorgreen Rd. PO9: Hav ... 4G **203**
SO30: Wes E ... 9J **161**
Moorhams Av. RG22: B'toke ... 4J **59**
Moorhead Ct. SO14: South ... 8A **174**
Moorhill Gdns. SO18: South ... 3J **175**
Moorhill Rd. BH24: Bur ... 8D **188**
SO30: Wes E ... 2H **175**
Moorings, The BH3: Bour ... 6H **227**
BH23: Chri ... 9J **229**
GU26: Hind ... 4N **103**
PO16: Fare ... 1D **212**
RG21: B'toke ... 6E **42**
Moorings Way PO4: S'sea ... 2J **241**
Moorland Av. BH25: B Sea ... 6A **232**
Moorland Cl. SO31: Loc H ... 5D **196**
SO45: Dib P ... 6J **193**
Moorland Ga. BH24: Ring ... 3K **187**
Moorland Rd. BH1: Bour ... 1A **246**
PO1: Ports ... 1F **240**
Moorlands Cl. GU26: Hind ... 3N **103**
GU51: Fleet ... 3N **47**
SO42: Broc ... 7A **148** (8M **189**)
Moorlands Cres. SO18: South ... 2F **174**
Moorlands Pl. GU15: Camb ... 8J **19**
Moorlands Rd. GU15: Camb ... 9J **19**
SO32: Swanm ... 4C **164**
Moor La. SP5: W'psh ... 7F **120**
Moorlea BH8: Bour ... 9M **227**
Moor Pk. PO7: W'lle ... 9B **182**
Moor Pk. La. GU9: Farnh ... 7G **65**
GU10: Farnh ... 8J **65**
Moor Pk. Way GU9: Farnh ... 8H **65**
Moor Rd. GU14: Farn ... 4J **29**
GU16: Frim ... 4N **29**
GU27: Hasl ... 1L **117**
GU33: Longc ... 5G **115**
Moors, The GU10: Tong ... 3N **65**
Moors Cl. BH23: Hurn ... 8E **218**
SO21: Col C ... 3K **133**
Moorside SO23: Winche ... 7P **237**
Moorside Cl. BH11: Bour ... 3F **226**
GU14: Cov ... 3J **29**
Moorside Gdns. BH11: Bour ... 3F **226**
Moorside Rd. BH11: Bour ... 3E **226**
SO23: Winche ... 5N **105**
Moors Nature Reserve, The ... 5A **164**
Moors Valley Country Park and Forest ... 9B **184**
Moors Valley Country Park Vis. Cen. ... 9A **184**
Moors Valley Golf Course ... 8A **184**
Moors Valley Railway
Kingsmere Station ... 8A **184**
MOORTOWN ... 3K **187**
Moortown Av. PO6: Dray ... 8K **201**
Moortown La. BH24: Crow, Ring ... 4K **187**
Moorvale Rd. BH9: Bour ... 4L **227**
Moor Vw. RG24: Old Bas ... 4J **43**
Moot Cl. SP5: Down ... 3L **119** (8B **120**)
SP10: A'ver ... 6A **52**
Moot Gdns. SP5: Down ... 3K **119** (8A **120**)
Moot La. SP5: Down ... 3K **119** (8A **120**)
SP6: Hale, Woodg ... 1A **154**
Mopley SO45: Blac ... 9D **208**
Mopley Cl. SO45: Blac ... 9D **208**
Moral Rd. GU17: Min ... 3B **28**
Morant Arms *SO42: Broc ... 7D 148*
(off Brookley Rd.)
Morant Ct. BH25: New M ... 3C **232**
Morant Rd. BH24: Poul ... 8L **185**
Moraunt Cl. PO12: Gos ... 8L **213**
Moraunt Dr. PO16: Portc ... 1K **213**
Moray Av. GU47: Coll ... 5F **18**
Mordaunt Dr. RG45: Cr'tne ... 2D **18**
Mordaunt Rd. SO14: South ... 3M **173**
Morden Rd. BH9: Bour ... 5J **227**
Morecombe Ct. PO5: S'sea ... 3E **240**
Moreland Cl. GU34: Alt ... 6G **80**
Moreland Rd. PO12: Gos ... 2K **239**
Morelands Ct. PO7: Purb ... 5N **201**
Morelands Rd. PO7: Purb ... 5M **201**
Moresby Ct. PO16: Fare ... 8D **198**
MORESTEAD ... 3C **134**
Morestead Rd.
SO21: Chilc, More, Winche ... 9M **105**
(not continuous)
Moreton Cl. GU10: Chur ... 7G **85**
GU52: Ch Cr ... 7L **47**
Moreton Rd. BH9: Bour ... 2M **227**
Morgan Ct. BH2: Bour ... 5K **247**
GU14: Cov ... 8E 28
(off Whetstone Rd.)
Morgan Le Fay Dr. SO53: Cha F ... 5L **131**
Morgan Rd. PO4: S'sea ... 3K **241**
SO30: Hed E ... 5N **175**
Morgan's Dr. PO14: Stub ... 3M **211**
Morgan's La. SP4: Win D ... 3A **86**
SP5: Pent ... 1G **148**
Morgans Ri. Rd. SP5: M Val ... 1M **119** (7C **120**)
MORGAN'S VALE ... 1M **119** (7C **120**)
Morgans Va. Rd. SP5: M Val ... 2M **119** (8C **120**)
Morgaston Rd. RG26: B'ley, M She ... 6M **21**
Morland Rd. GU11: Alders ... 3K **65**
SO15: South ... 1H **173**
Morland's Rd. GU11: Alders ... 6M **49**
Morley Cl. BH5: Bour ... 9D **228**
BH23: Burt ... 3M **229**
GU46: Yat ... 8L **17**
SO19: South ... 4D **174**
Morley Cres. PO8: Cowp ... 7A **182**
Morley Dr. SO32: Bis W ... 3M **163**
Morley Gdns. SO53: Cha F ... 4A **132**
Morley Rd. BH5: Bour ... 9D **228**
GU9: Farnh ... 9E **64**
PO4: S'sea ... 5H **241**
RG21: B'toke ... 1B **60**
Morleys La. SO51: Ampf ... 9H **125**
Morn Hill Caravan Site SO21: Winche ... 6F **106**
Morningside Av. PO16: Portc ... 8N **199**
Mornington Cl. RG26: Bau ... 4D **10**
SP10: A'ver ... 4N **69**
Mornington Dr. SO22: Winche ... 4G **104**
Mornington Rd. GU35: W'hil ... 4F **100**
PO31: Cowes ... 5N 237
(off Cliff Rd.)
Mornish Rd. BH13: Poole ... 3D **244**
Morpeth Av. SO40: Tott ... 2M **171**
Morrell Cl. SO32: Wal C ... 8A **164**
Morris Cl. PO13: Gos ... 3D **212**
SO45: Dib ... 5J **193**
Morrison Av. BH12: Poole ... 7D **226**
Morris Ri. RG24: Chin ... 1F **42**
Morris Rd. GU14: Farn ... 3M **49**
SO15: South ... 3A **4** (5K **173**)
Morris St. RG27: Hoo ... 3E **44**
Morse Cl. GU35: W'hil ... 6H **101**
Morse Ct. SO31: Net A ... 3E **194**
Morse Rd. RG22: B'toke ... 7N **41**
Morshead Cres. PO16: Fare ... 6B **198**
Mortimer Cl. BH23: Mude ... 8C **230**
RG27: H Win ... 8A **26**
SO23: Kin W ... 9M **91**
SO31: Net A ... 3F **194**
SO40: Tott ... 1K **171**
Mortimer Gdns. RG26: Tadl ... 6J **11**
Mortimer La. RG7: Stra S ... 4J **13**
RG21: B'toke ... 6B **42**
Mortimer Lawn PO9: Hav ... 2D **202**
Mortimer Rd. BH8: Bour ... 5M **227**
PO6: Cosh ... 8D **200**
SO19: South ... 6C **174**
SO30: Botl ... 3D **176**
Mortimers Dr. SO50: Fair O ... 1A **162**
Mortimers Ind. Units SO51: Ower ... 5E **156**
Mortimers La. SO32: Lwr U ... 9C **134**
SO50: Fair O ... 1N **161**
Mortimer Station (Rail) ... 1K **13**
Mortimer Way SO52: N Bad ... 9E **130**
MORTIMER WEST END ... 1C **12**
Mortimore Rd. PO12: Gos ... 1H **239**
Morton Ho. GU30: Lip ... 1F **116**
Morval Cl. GU14: Cov ... 8G **28**
Mosaic Cl. SO19: South ... 6K **175**
Mosbach Pl. SO41: Lymi ... 2E **234**
Moscrop Ct. RG21: B'toke ... 7B **42**
Mosedale Wlk. SO16: South ... 2D **172**
Moselle Cl. GU14: Cov ... 7F **28**
Moselle Ct. SO15: South ... 5H **173**
Moser Gro. SO41: Sway ... 4H **223**
Mosquito Way GU14: Farn ... 1H **49**
(not continuous)
Moss Cl. GU33: Liss ... 1F **140**
Moss Dr. SO40: March ... 8E **172**
Mosse Ct. PO17: Wick ... 7C **178**
Mossleigh Av. SO16: Rown ... 6E **158**
Mossley Av. BH12: Poole ... 5D **226**
Moss Rd. SO23: Winche ... 6M **105**
Motcombe Rd. BH13: Poole ... 3E **244**
Moths Grace RG24: B'toke ... 3M **41**
MOTTISFONT ... 3F **122**
Mottisfont Abbey & Gardens ... 2F **122**
Mottisfont Cl. SO15: South ... 4F **172**
Mottisfont Lodge SO51: Rom ... 5M **129**
Mottisfont Rd. SO50: E'leigh ... 8E **132**
Moulin Av. PO5: S'sea ... 5F **240**
Moulsham Copse La. GU46: Yat ... 6L **17**
Moulsham Grn. GU46: Yat ... 6L **17**
Moulsham La. GU46: Yat ... 6L **17**
Moulshay La. RG27: Sher L ... 7K **23**
Mound Cl. PO12: Gos ... 4J **239**
Moundsmere Cl. RG25: Pres C ... 5F **78**
MOUNT, THE ... 3A **8**
Mount, The BH24: Poul ... 9M **185**
GU35: Head ... 1C **102**
GU51: Fleet ... 1M **47**
PO13: Gos ... 7G **212**
SO16: Bass ... 7L **159**
SO16: South ... 1F **172**
Mountain Ash Cl. SO18: South ... 3G **175**
Mount Av. BH25: New M ... 5B **232**
Mountbatten Av. SO51: Rom ... 5M **129**
Mountbatten Bldg. SO17: South ... 7M **159**
Mountbatten Bus. Cen. SO15: South ... 5J **173**
Mountbatten Bus. Pk. *PO6: Farl ... 1L 215*
(off Jackson Cl.)
Mountbatten Centre, The ... 5E **214**
Mountbatten Cl. BH23: Mude ... 9C **230**
PO13: Gos ... 4E **212**
Mountbatten Ct. BH25: New M ... 3A **232**
GU11: Alders ... 9J 49
(off Victoria Rd.)
SO22: Winche ... 3J **105**
SP10: A'ver ... 9C **52**
Mountbatten Dr. PO7: W'lle ... 3K **201**
SO31: Sar G ... 4C **196**
Mountbatten Gallery
Portsmouth ... 4N **5** (2D **240**)
Romsey ... 3M **157**
Mountbatten Gdns. BH8: Bour ... 4C **228**

Mountbatten Ho.—Newlands Rd.

Mountbatten Ho. PO1: Ports 2J 5 (1B 240)
RG21: B'toke 5E 42
SO15: South 2C 4
Mountbatten Lodge *GU9: Farnh* *8D 64*
(off The Hart)
Mountbatten M. GU15: Camb 6L 19
Mountbatten Pl. SO23: Kin W 7N 91
Mountbatten Retail Pk.
SO15: South 4A 4 (6K 173)
Mountbatten Ri. GU47: Sandh 4B 18
Mountbatten Rd. BH4: Bour 4F 244
BH13: Poole 4F 244
SO40: Tott 3K 171
SO50: E'leigh 7E 132
Mountbatten Sq. PO4: S'sea 5J 241
Mountbatten Way PO1: Ports 1M 5 (9C 214)
SO15: South 5H 173
Mt. Carmel Rd. SP11: Pale 6J 67
Mountclere *BH4: Bour* *4G 244*
(off Alumhurst Rd.)
Mount Cl. BH25: New M 5B 232
RG20: High 4A 8
SO22: Winche 3J 105
Mount Dr. PO15: Fare 9L 197
SO53: Cha F 8C 132
Mounters La. GU34: Alt 7D 80
Mountfield SO45: Hythe 5K 193
Mt. Grace Dr. BH14: Poole 6A 244
Mt. Heatherbank BH1: Bour 6L 247
Mt. Hermon Rd. SP11: Pale 6K 67
Mount Ho. Cl. SO45: Hythe 4M 193
Mountjoy Ct. PO1: Ports 7J 5 (4B 240)
Mount La. SO51: Lock 3N 121
MOUNT PLEASANT
GU34 ....6F 80
SO41 ....7N 223
Mt. Pleasant BH24: Ring 1K 187
GU9: Farnh 9C 64
GU47: Sandh 4C 18
RG26: Tadl 5G 11
RG27: H Win 6C 26
RG28: Free 4M 55
SO23: Kin W 9M 91
SO51: Rom 6L 129
SP11: Amp 3B 68
Mt. Pleasant Camping Pk. BH23: Hurn 6F 218
Mt. Pleasant Dr. BH8: Bour 5C 228
BH23: Bran 6E 220
RG26: Tadl 5G 11
Mt. Pleasant Ind. Est. SO14: South 3N 173
Mt. Pleasant La. SO41: Lymi 7N 223
Mt. Pleasant Rd. GU12: Alders 9L 49
GU34: Alt 5F 80
GU35: Lind 2L 101
PO12: Gos 5K 239
SO14: South 1F 4 (3N 173)
Mount Rd. BH11: Bour 2F 226
RG20: High 3A 8
Mountsom's La. GU34: Up Farr 3F 98
Mounts Way GU51: Fleet 9H 27
Mount Temple SO51: Rom 5N 129
Mount Vw. GU11: Alders 1J 65
SO50: E'leigh 8F 132
Mountview Av. PO16: Portc 8N 199
Mount Vw. Cl. SO22: Oli B 1F 126
Mount Vw. Rd. SO22: Oli B 1F 126
Mount Zion BH1: Bour 2L 245
Mourne Cl. RG22: B'toke 7K 41
Mousehole La. SO18: South 2D 174
SO45: Hythe 6M 193
Mousehole Rd. PO6: Cosh 8A 200
Mowatt Rd. GU26: Gray 5M 103
Mowbray Rd. SO19: South 6F 174
Moxhams SP6: F'dge 1J 153
MOYLES COURT 3M 185
Mozart Cl. RG22: B'toke 2N 59
Muccleshell Cl. PO9: Hav 5G 202
Mucklands La. GU34: Bent 7K 79
Muddyford Rd. SP5: Redl 1M 119 (7C 120)
MUDEFORD 9C 230
Mudeford BH23: Mude 9B 230
Mudeford Grn. Cl. BH23: Mude 9B 230
Mudeford La. BH23: Chri, Mude 8A 230
(not continuous)
Mudeford Quay BH23: Mude 9C 230
Mudeford Sailing Club 9A 230
Mude Gdns. BH23: Mude 9C 230
Mude Valley Nature Reserve 8C 230
Mud La. RG27: Eve 4C 16
Muir Ho. SO45: Dib P 8K 193
Mulberries, The GU9: Farnh 6H 65
Mulberry Av. PO6: Cosh 9H 201
PO14: Stub 7M 211
Mulberry Cl. GU47: Owl 5F 18
PO12: Gos 3K 239
RG45: Cr'tne 1E 18
SO45: Blac 8C 208
Mulberry Cnr. SO53: Cha F 8M 131
Mulberry Ct. GU34: Four M 4K 97
SO30: Wes E 9J 161
Mulberry Gdns. SP6: F'dge 2H 153
Mulberry Gro. SO41: Ever 6L 233
Mulberry La. PO6: Cosh 1H 215
SO31: Sar G 4B 196
Mulberry Lodge PO10: Ems 7M 203
Mulberry Mead RG28: Whit 5G 55
Mulberry M. BH6: Bour 9G 228
Mulberry Path PO6: Cosh 1H 215
Mulberry Rd. SO40: March 9E 172
Mulberry Wlk. SO15: South 2H 173
Mulberry Way GU14: Cov 7F 28
RG24: Chin 9G 22
Mulfords Hill RG26: Tadl 4H 11
Mull Cl. RG23: Oak 9C 40
Mullen Cl. SO19: South 6C 174
Mullenscote Pk. Homes SP11: Weyh 9A 50
MULLENSPOND 1N 67
Mullins Cl. BH12: Poole 6G 226
RG21: B'toke 3C 42
Mullion Cl. PO6: P Sol 1C 214
Multisports Swimming 3D 160
Mulvany Ct. *PO5: S'sea* *2E 240*
(off Cumberland Rd.)
Mumby Rd. PO12: Gos 2M 239
Mundays Row PO8: Horn 1C 182
Munnings Cl. RG21: B'toke 8E 42
Munnings Ct. SP10: A'ver 9M 51
Munnings Dr. GU47: Coll 7F 18
Munro Cres. SO15: South 3E 172
Munro Way GU11: Alders 3M 49
Munster Rd. BH14: Poole 2B 244
PO2: Ports 6E 214
Murefield Rd. PO1: Ports 2E 240
Muria Est. SO14: South 5A 174
Muriel Rd. PO7: W'lle 1M 201
Murley Rd. BH9: Bour 6L 227
Murray Cl. PO15: Fare 7A 198
SO19: South 4J 175
SP10: A'ver 4M 69
Murray Rd. GU14: Cov 9H 29
PO8: Horn 4B 182
Murray's La. PO1: Ports 1H 5 (1A 240)
Murrays Rd. GU11: Alders 5M 49
MURRELL GREEN 9L 25
Murrell Green Bus. Pk. RG27: Hoo 1L 45
Murrell Grn. Rd. RG27: H Win 7L 25
Murrells La. GU15: Camb 1K 29
Murrills Est. PO16: Portc 9N 199
Mursell Way SO31: Hou 3J 195
MUSCLIFF 2M 227
Muscliffe Ct. PO9: Hav 4H 203
Muscliffe La. BH9: Bour 2L 227
Muscliffe Rd. BH9: Bour 5K 227
Muscott Cl. SP9: Shi B 2A 66 (1F 66)
Museum of Archaeology 9D 4 (8M 173)
Museum of Army Flying 5A 72
Museum of Electricity 7L 229
Museum of the Iron Age 1A 70
Museum Rd. PO1: Ports 6L 5 (3C 240)
Musgrave Cl. RG22: B'toke 2M 59
Musgrove Gdns. GU34: Alt 4E 80
Musket Copse RG24: Old Bas 5H 43
Mussett Cl. SO40: Tott 3L 171
Muss La. SO20: Ki S 8B 86 (6G 88)
Mustang Av. PO15: White 2E 196
Mustard Way SP11: E Ant 6B 52
Myers Cl. SO32: Swanm 6D 164
Mylen Bus. Cen. SP10: A'ver 1L 69
Mylen Rd. SP10: A'ver 1L 69
Myllers Lond RG27: Hoo 2K 45
My Lord's La. PO11: H Isl 4H 243
Myrtle Av. PO16: Portc 1M 213
SO40: Tott 4K 171
Myrtle Cl. PO13: Gos 5E 212
SO41: Hor 2G 233
Myrtle Dr. GU17: Blackw 8F 18
Myrtle Gro. PO3: Ports 9J 215
Myrtle Rd. BH8: Bour 8N 227
SO16: South 7G 158
MYTCHETT 9N 29
Myvern Cl. SO45: Holb 5B 208

N

Naafi Rdbt. GU11: Alders 9K 49
Nada Rd. BH23: Chri 5F 230
Nadder Rd. SP9: Tidw 8D 30 (7G 31)
Nahalsen Cl. SP4: Port 9B 66
Nailsworth Rd. PO6: Cosh 8C 200
Naini Tal Rd. SP9: Tidw 8C 30 (7G 30)
Nairn Cl. GU16: Frim 2N 29
Nairn Ct. BH3: Bour 7J 227
Nairn Rd. BH3: Bour 8J 227
BH13: Poole 6C 244
Naish Ct. PO9: Hav 2C 202
Naish Dr. PO12: Gos 7J 213
Naish M. BH25: B Sea 7B 232
Naish Rd. BH25: B Sea 7M 231
Namu Rd. BH9: Bour 5J 227
Nancy Rd. PO1: Ports 2F 240
Nantanbury SP5: Down 2K 119
Napier Cl. GU11: Alders 4N 49
PO13: Gos 2F 238
RG45: Cr'tne 1E 18
Napier Cres. PO15: Fare 8M 197
Napier Rd. PO5: S'sea 5E 240
PO8: Horn 4C 182
RG45: Cr'tne 1E 18
SO19: South 5J 175
Napier Wlk. SP10: A'ver 9C 52
Napoleon Av. GU14: Farn 6K 29
Napoleon Dr. RG23: B'toke 4L 41
Narborough Ho. PO12: Gos 9M 213
Narrow La. BH24: Poul 9N 185
SO51: Rom 5L 129
Narvik Rd. PO2: Ports 4E 214
Naseby Cl. PO6: Cosh 8B 200
Naseby Rd. BH9: Bour 5L 227
Nash Cl. GU14: Cov 8H 29
RG21: B'toke 4D 42
SO45: Dib P 8J 193
Nashe Cl. PO15: Fare 6N 197
Nashe Ho. PO15: Fare 6M 197
NASHES GREEN 1M 79
Nashe Way PO15: Fare 6M 197
Nash Mdws. RG29: S War 4D 62
Nash Rd. SO45: Dib P 8J 193
Nasmith Cl. PO12: Gos 3G 238
Natasha Gdns. BH12: Poole 7A 226
Nately Rd. RG27: Up N 8D 44
RG29: Grey 8D 44
NATELY SCURES 4C 44
Nat Gonella Sq. *PO12: Gos* *3M 239*
(off Walpole Rd.)
National Motor Museum, The 6D 206
Nations Hill SO23: Kin W 8M 91
Navarac Ct. BH14: Poole 2A 244
Navigators Way SO30: Hed E 1N 175
Navy Rd. PO1: Ports 1J 5 (1B 240)
Nea Cl. BH23: Chri 6F 230
NEACROFT 9D 220
Neacroft Cl. BH25: New M 6M 231
Nea Dr. BH24: Har 3D 184
Nea Meadow Nature Reserve 6G 230
Nea Rd. BH23: Chri 6G 230
NEATHAM 2L 81
Neath Rd. RG21: B'toke 6E 42
Neath Way SO53: Cha F 7M 131
Needles Ct. SO41: M Sea 8J 235
Needles Ho. PO16: Fare 1C 212
Needlespar Ct. SO31: Wars 7C 196
Needles Point BH1: Bour 2N 245
SO41: M Sea 8K 235
Needles Vw. BH6: Bour 2H 247
Neelands Gro. PO6: Cosh 9N 199
Neilson Cl. SO53: Cha F 5A 132
Nelson Av. PO2: Ports 6E 214
PO16: Portc 1K 213
Nelson Centre, The PO3: Ports 6J 215
Nelson Cl. BH25: New M 3A 232
GU9: H End 2F 64
GU12: Alders 1L 65
PO10: S'brne 9N 203
SO20: S Bri 3F 88
SO45: Holb 5A 208
SO51: Rom 4M 129
Nelson Ct. BH23: Chri 8J 229
PO14: Fare 2B 212
SO45: Hythe 8N 193
Nelson Cres. PO8: Horn 3C 182
Nelson Dr. BH23: Mude 8B 230
GU31: Pet 8N 139
PO4: S'sea 2K 241
(not continuous)
Nelson Gate SO15: South 3A 4 (5K 173)
Nelson Hill SO15: South 5K 173
Nelson Ho. *PO12: Gos* *3N 239*
(off South St.)
Nelson Ind. Pk. SO30: Hed E 1M 175
Nelson La. PO17: Fare 6L 199
Nelson Monument 6K 199
Nelson Pl. SO41: Lymi 3F 234
Nelson Rd. BH4: Bour 1E 244
BH12: Poole 1E 244
GU9: H End 2F 64
PO1: Ports 9E 214
PO5: S'sea 4D 240
PO12: Gos 3K 239
SO15: South 4H 173
SO23: Winche 7N 105
SO50: B'stke 8H 133
Nelsons Gdns. SO30: Hed E 8N 161
Nelson St. GU11: Alders 9J 49
SO14: South 7G 4 (8N 173)
Nelson Wlk. SP10: A'ver 9C 52
Nelson Way GU15: Camb 9H 19
Nene Ct. SP10: A'ver 8B 52
Nepaul Rd. SP9: Tidw 7C 30 (6G 30)
Nepean Cl. PO12: Gos 6K 239
Neptune Ct. PO1: Ports 6J 5 (3B 240)
PO13: Gos 6F 212
SO16: South 7E 158
Neptune Ho. SO14: South 9F 4
Neptune Rd. GU35: Bor 5K 101
PO14: Fare 3B 212
PO15: Fare 7M 197
Neptune Way SO14: South 9F 4 (8N 173)
Nerissa Cl. PO7: W'lle 1A 202
Nerquis Cl. SO51: Rom 4A 130
Nesbitt Cl. PO13: Gos 5D 212
Nessus St. PO2: Ports 8E 214
Nest Bus. Pk. PO9: Hav 5H 203
Nestor Cl. SP10: A'ver 9M 51
Netherfield Cl. GU34: Alt 4E 80
PO9: Warb 8G 203
Netherfield Pl. RG24: B'toke 3N 41
Netherhall Gdns. BH4: Bour 2G 245
Netherhill La. SO32: Botl 1E 176
Netherhouse Ct. GU51: Ch Cr 5J 47
Netherhouse Moor GU51: Ch Cr 4J 47
Nether St. GU34: Alt 4F 80
NETHERTON 7H 7
Netherton Rd. PO12: Gos 9H 213
SP11: Facc, Hur T, Net 7H 7
Nether Vell-Mead GU52: Ch Cr 7K 47
NETHER WALLOP 1A 88
NETLEY ABBEY 4F 194
Netley Abbey (remains of) 3E 194
Netley Castle SO31: Net A 3E 194
Netley Cliff SO31: Net A 4F 194
Netley Cliff Sailing Club 4F 194
Netley Cl. SO53: Cha F 9N 131
Netley Ct. PO12: Gos 8L 213
Netley Firs Cl. SO19: South 6K 175
Netley Firs Rd. SO30: Hed E 5L 175
NETLEY HILL 5K 175
Netley Hill Est. SO19: South 6K 175
Netley Lodge Cl. SO31: Net A 4G 194
NETLEY MARSH 4G 170
Netley Marsh Workshops SO40: Net M 3G 170
Netley Pl. PO5: S'sea 9N 5
Netley Rd. PO5: S'sea 9N 5 (5D 240)
PO14: Titch C 8F 196
Netley Sailing Club 6G 195
Netley Station (Rail) 3G 195
Netley St. GU14: Farn 3K 49
Netley Ter. PO5: S'sea 9N 5 (5D 240)
Nettlebeds La. SO24: Bigh, Old A 4J 95
Nettlecombe Av. PO4: S'sea 6F 240
Nettlestone SO31: Net A 2G 194
Nettlestone Rd. PO4: S'sea 5H 241
Netton Cl. SP5: Bish 3C 118
Netton St. SP5: Bish 3C 118
Neuvic Way RG28: Whit 6H 55
Nevada Cl. GU14: Cov 9F 28
Neva Rd. SO18: South 2D 174
Neville Av. PO16: Portc 2M 213
Neville Cl. RG21: B'toke 9C 42
SP10: A'ver 3A 70
Neville Ct. PO12: Gos 2K 239
RG24: B'toke 4F 42
Neville Dr. SO51: Rom 3M 129
Neville Duke Rd. GU14: Cov 4H 29
Neville Gdns. PO10: Ems 6L 203
Neville Rd. PO3: Ports 9H 215
Nevil Shute Rd. PO3: Ports 5H 215
New Abbey Ho. SP11: Weyh 8B 50
Newall Rd. SP11: A'ver 2G 68
NEW ALRESFORD 9F 94
Newark Rd. GU17: Min 3A 28
New Barn Cl. GU51: Fleet 4J 47
New Barn Cotts. SO21: Craw 4C 90
New Barn Farm La. PO8: Blen 8D 168
New Barn La. GU31: Buri 1J 169
GU34: Alt 6F 80
SO21: Craw 4B 90
SP11: Wher 9E 70
Newbarn Rd. PO9: Bed 6B 202
Newbolt Cl. PO8: Cowp 7M 181
Newbolt Rd. PO6: Cosh 8N 199
NEWBRIDGE 4N 155
Newbridge SO31: Net A 3G 195
New Bridge La. RG21: B'toke 6E 42
Newbridge Rd. SO40: Cad 4N 155
Newbridge Way SO41: Penn 5C 234
NEW BRIGHTON 6M 203
New Brighton Rd. PO10: Ems 8M 203
Newbroke Rd. PO13: Gos 8F 212
New Bldgs. SP11: Chu C 4D 32
Newburgh St. SO23: Winche 6K 237 (6K 105)
Newbury By-Pass
RG20: Burgh, Newt, Wa W 1B 8
Newbury Cl. SO50: B'stke 1M 161
Newbury Dr. BH10: Bour 5H 227
Newbury La. SP11: Charl, Pen M 7G 50
Newbury Pl. SO31: Wars 7C 196
Newbury Rd. RG19: Head 1H 9
RG20: Kings 2A 6 (6K 9)
(Canon's Ct.)
RG20: Kings 1A 6 (1H 9)
(Union La.)
RG28: Whit 5G 55
SO15: South 1H 173
SP10: A'ver, K Enh 5A 52
SP11: Enh A 1N 51
Newbury Rd. Junc. RG24: B'toke 4M 41
Newbury St. RG28: Whit 5G 55
SP10: A'ver 1A 70
NEW CHERITON 1K 135
Newchurch Rd. RG26: Tadl 4G 10
Newcliffe Gdns. SO30: Hed E 5M 175
New Cliff Ho. SO19: South 9C 174
Newcomb Cl. SP10: A'ver 4M 69
Newcombe Rd. BH6: Bour 8H 229
SO15: South 1A 4 (4K 173)
Newcomen Ct. PO2: Ports 6D 214
Newcomen Rd. PO2: Ports 6D 214
Newcome Pl. GU12: Alders 3M 65
Newcome Rd. GU9: Weyb 4G 64
PO1: Ports 1F 240
New Copse GU34: Meds 8K 79
New Cotts. GU10: Farnh 5J 63
SO16: South 9B 158
New Ct. BH24: Ring 1H 187
PO15: Seg 4G 196
Newcroft Gdns. BH23: Chri 6K 229
New Cut PO11: H Isl 5F 216
New Dawn Cl. GU14: Cov 9F 28
New Down La. PO7: Purb 7H 201
New Drove SP11: Ludg 2C 30 (5K 31)
Newenham Rd. SO41: Lymi 4E 234
New Farm Ind. Est. SO24: New A 2D 108
New Farm Rd. SO21: E Str 7L 77
SO24: New A 1D 108
Newfield Av. GU14: Cov 6G 28
Newfield Rd. GU33: Liss 8F 114
New Forest Cider 8D 188
New Forest Dr.
SO42: Broc 6A 148 (8M 189)
New Forest Ent. Cen. SO40: Tott 5L 171
New Forest Golf Course 1D 148
New Forest Mus. 2C 148
New Forest National Pk. 1K 219
New Forest Reptile Cen. 3K 189
New Forest Safari 7E 188
New Forest Wildlife Pk. 1L 191
NEWFOUND 7E 40
Newgate La. PO14: Fare 5C 212
Newgate La. Ind. Est. PO14: Fare 2D 212
(not continuous)
Newgate M. BH2: Bour 6J 247
New Greenham Arts 1H 9
NEW GREENHAM PARK 1G 9
New Greenham Pk. Leisure Cen. 1H 9
NEWGROUNDS 5A 154
New Haig Rd. SP4: Bul C 3B 66
New Hampshire Blvd.
PO1: Ports 5J 5 (3B 240)
New Ho. La. SP11: Apple 3A 50
New Inn Cotts. *SO42: Beau* *1B 236*
(off New Inn La.)
New Inn Ct. SO31: Sar G 3B 196
New Inn Flds. GU35: Slea 7K 83
New Inn La. SO40: Bart 4B 170
SO42: Beau 1B 236
New Inn Rd. SO40: Bart 4B 170
Newitt Pl. SO16: Bass 5L 159
Newlands GU52: Fleet 5M 47
PO15: Fare 8M 197
Newlands Av. PO12: Gos 3J 239
SO15: South 3H 173
Newlands Cl. GU46: Yat 8N 17
SO45: Blac 7C 208
SO53: Cha F 7K 131
Newlands Copse SO45: Blac 7D 208
Newlands La. PO7: Den, Purb 8G 180
Newlands Mnr. SO41: Ever 7L 233
Newlands Rd. BH7: Bour 8D 228
BH23: Chri 7B 230
BH25: New M 5C 232
GU15: Camb 3K 29
PO7: Purb 4L 201
SO45: Fawl 6C 208

A-Z Hampshire 303

New La.—Northington

New La. BH25: Bash .9A 222
GU31: S Hart .9G 147
GU34: Holy .9E 62
PO9: Hav .7G 202
SO20: Ki S .6G 89
SO41: M Sea .8M 235
Newlease Rd. PO7: W'lle .4N 201
Newlyn Wlk. SO51: Rom .3N 129
Newlyn Way BH12: Poole .7C 226
PO6: P Sol .1B 214
Newman Bassett Ho.
RG23: B'toke .5L 41
Newman Ct. RG22: B'toke .2M 59
Newman La. GU34: Alt .4H 81
Newman La. Ind. Est. GU34: Alt .3H 81
Newmans Copse Rd. SO40: Tott .6N 171
Newmans Ct. GU9: Up H .3C 64
Newmans Hill PO17: Mis .2D 178
Newman St. SO16: South .2G 172
Newmans Way SP4: Bul .3A 66
Newmarket Cl. SO50: Hor H .4A 162
New Market Sq. RG21: B'toke .6C 42
Newmer Ct. PO9: Hav .3C 202
New Mill Cotts. GU27: Hasl .9M 103
New Mill La. RG27: Eve .3B 16
New Mill Rd. RG27: Eve .3B 16
RG40: F'std .3B 16
NEW MILTON .4B 232
New Milton Health & Leisure Cen. .4A 232
New Milton Indoor Bowls Club .3B 232
New Milton Station (Rail) .3B 232
Newmorton Rd. BH9: Bour .2L 227
Newney Cl. PO2: Ports .4G 214
NEWNHAM .2C 44
Newnham Ct. PO9: Hav .4H 203
Newnham La. RG24: Old Bas .3J 43
RG27: Newn .3J 43
Newnham Pk. RG27: Hoo .3F 44
Newnham Rd. RG27: Hoo, Newn .3D 44
New North Dr. RG27: Sher L .5M 23
New Paddock Cl. GU34: Holy .1J 81
New Pde. BH10: Bour .3J 227
PO16: Portc .9M 199
New Pk. Rd. BH6: Bour .1F 246
Newport Cl. SO53: Cha F .8M 131
Newport La. SO51: Brai .7A 124
Newport Rd. GU12: Alders .1L 65
PO12: Gos .2H 239
New Priory Gdns. PO16: Portc .9L 199
New Rd. BH10: Bour .1J 227
BH12: Poole .8B 226
BH24: Mock .1L 185
BH24: Ring .4K 187
GU17: Haw .9G 18
GU27: Hasl .1N 117
GU35: W'hil .6H 101
GU47: Sandh .5C 18
GU52: Ch Cr .5N 47
PO2: Ports .9F 214
PO8: Clan .7C 168
PO8: Love .4M 181
PO9: Bed, Hav .7D 202
PO16: Fare .8C 198
RG21: B'toke .6C 42
RG26: B'ley .4B 22
RG26: Lit L, Pam G .9K 11
RG26: Tadl .6F 10
RG27: Eve .6J 17
RG27: H Win .6B 26
RG27: Hoo .3G 44
RG29: N War .7J 45
SO14: South .4D 4 (5M 173)
SO20: Mid Wa .9M 67
SO21: Col C .3K 133
SO21: Mich S .4J 77
SO22: Lit .9F 90
SO31: Net A .3E 194
SO31: Swanw .1C 196
SO31: Wars .9A 196
SO32: Bis W .1N 163
SO32: Meon .9N 135
SO32: Swanm .8B 164
SO40: Ashu .7H 171
SO41: Key .8N 235
SO45: Blac .7C 208
SO45: Hard .9A 194
(not continuous)
SO45: Hythe .5M 193
SO50: B'stke .1M 161
SO51: Rom .4N 129
SO51: Tims .6K 123
SP5: L'ford .1K 155
SP6: R'bne .2B 150
New Rd. Cotts. *GU34: Selb .7L 99*
(off Selborne Rd.)
New Rd. East PO2: Ports .8G 215
New Royal Theatre .4M 5 (2D 240)
News Centre, The PO3: Ports .3G 214
Newstead Rd. BH6: Bour .1G 247
New St. BH24: Ring .2K 187
RG7: Stra S .5M 13
RG21: B'toke .7C 42
SO20: S Bri .2F 88
(off High St.)
SO41: Lymi .2E 234
SP10: A'ver .8A 52
New St. Cl. SP10: A'ver .1A 70
New St. M. SO41: Lymi .2E 234
New Ter. SO16: Bass .6M 159
NEWTON .6G 121
Newton Bungs. *SP5: W'psh .5H 121*
(off The Street)
Newton Cl. PO14: Stub .4M 211
SP5: W'psh .5H 121
NEWTON COMMON .7N 97
Newton La. GU34: New V .7D 98
SO51: Rom .5L 129
SP5: W'psh .6G 121
Newton Morrell BH14: Poole .2B 244
Newton Pk. SP10: A'ver .9H 51
Newton Pl. PO13: Lee S .9A 212
Newton Rd. BH13: Poole .5C 244
BH25: B Sea .6C 232
GU14: Farn .6M 29
SO18: South .1C 174
SO21: Twyf .6L 127
NEWTON STACEY .2K 75
Newton Toney SP4: New T .6E 66
Newton Toney Rd. SP4: All, New T .7D 66
NEWTON TONY .6E 66
NEWTON VALENCE .8G 99
Newton Way GU10: Tong .3N 65
NEWTOWN
BH12 .7A 226
GU30 .3E 116
GU34 .5E 80
PO11 .3E 242
PO12 .3L 239
PO17 .4L 179
RG20 .1E 8
SO14 .1F 4 (4N 173)
SO19 .9F 174
SO31 .9A 196
SO32 .3K 163
SO43 .9L 155
SO51 .9B 122
Newtown PO16: Portc .9M 199
RG26: Tadl .4G 11
SP5: Br Ch .3A 118
Newtown Cl. SP10: A'ver .2L 69
NEWTOWN COMMON .1E 8
Newtown Ct. SO31: Wars .8N 195
Newtown La. BH24: Mock .9M 153
PO11: H Isl .3E 242
Newtown Nature Reserve .9G 236
Newtown Rd. GU30: Lip .3E 116
GU47: Sandh .5D 18
RG20: Newt .1E 8
SO19: South .8E 174
SO31: Wars .1N 209
SO50: E'leigh .8E 132
SO51: Awb, Sher E .2A 128
Newtown Vs. SP11: Ludg .1F 30 (5L 31)
New Valley Rd. SO41: M Sea .8J 235
New Villas RG20: Bal H .1M 7
New Ward Rd. SP4: Bul C .3B 66
New Wokingham Rd. RG45: Cr'tne .1C 18
Nichola Ct. BH12: Poole .7A 226
Nicholas Cl. BH23: Walk .4K 231
Nicholas Ct. PO11: H Isl .4E 242
PO13: Lee S .2A 238
Nicholas Cres. PO15: Fare .7B 198
Nicholas Gdns. BH10: Bour .4G 226
Nicholas Rd. SO45: Blac .9C 208
Nicholl Pl. PO13: Gos .6E 212
Nichol Rd. SO53: Cha F .3B 132
Nicholson Gdns. *PO1: Ports .2E 240*
(off Boarhunt Cl.)
Nicholson Pl. SO24: New A .1D 108
Nicholson Wlk. SO16: Rown .5C 158
Nicholson Way PO9: Hav .6E 202
Nichols Rd. SO14: South .3F 4 (5N 173)
NICHOLS TOWN .3E 4 (5M 173)
Nickel Cl. SO23: Winche .6M 105
Nickel St. PO5: S'sea .7M 5 (4C 240)
Nickleby Gdns. SO40: Tott .3H 171
Nickleby Ho. PO1: Ports .9E 214
Nickleby Rd. PO8: Clan .5B 168
Nickson Cl. SO53: Cha F .4N 131
Nicolson Cl. SP4: Ames .5A 66
Nicotiana Ct. *GU52: Ch Cr .7K 47*
(off Rye Cft.)
Nightingale Av. SO50: E'leigh .2A 160
Nightingale Cl. GU14: Cov .6E 28
PO9: R Cas .9G 183
PO12: Gos .1H 239
SO22: Winche .8F 104
SO31: Burs .1K 195
SO51: Rom .5N 129
SO51: W Wel .1A 120 (9M 121)
Nightingale Ct. PO6: Cosh .9J 201
SO15: South .4H 173
Nightingale Cres. SO32: Shi H .2B 178
Nightingale Dr. SO40: Tott .2J 171
Nightingale Gdns. GU47: Sandh .5D 18
RG24: B'toke .3L 41
RG27: Hoo .2G 45
Nightingale Gro. SO15: South .3H 173
Nightingale Ho. SO31: Net A .5G 195
SO51: Rom .4N 129
Nightingale M. SO31: Loc H .6E 196
SO31: Net A .5G 195
Nightingale Pk. PO9: Warb .8H 203
Nightingale Ri. RG25: Over .3E 56
Nightingale Rd. GU32: Pet .2K 145
GU35: Bor .5K 101
PO5: S'sea .9M 5 (5C 240)
PO6: Cosh .8G 200
SO15: South .3H 173
Nightingale Wlk. SO31: Net A .5G 194
Nightjar Cl. GU10: Ews .2N 63
PO8: Horn .3A 182
Nile Rd. SO17: South .9M 159
Nile St. PO10: Ems .9M 203
Nimrod Dr. PO13: Gos .9F 212
(not continuous)
Nine Acres GU32: Ste .4A 140
Nine Elms La. PO17: Fare .5F 198
Ninian Cl. SO50: Fair O .2N 161
Ninian Pk. Rd. PO3: Ports .6H 215
Ninian Path PO3: Ports .6H 215
Niton Cl. PO13: Gos .6E 212
Noads Cl. SO45: Dib P .7L 193
Noads Way SO45: Dib P .8K 193
Noar Hill GU34: Selb .2K 113
Noar Hill Nature Reserve .2L 113
Nobbs La. PO1: Ports .6K 5 (3B 240)
Nobes Av. PO13: Gos .5E 212
Nobes Cl. PO13: Gos .6F 212
Noble Cl. BH11: Bour .5D 226
Noble Rd. PO14: Titch C .9G 196
SO30: Hed E .4A 176
NOBS CROOK .5L 133
Nobs Crook RG27: Hoo .2J 45
SO21: Col C .4L 133
Noctule Ct. PO17: K Vil .1N 197
Noel Cl. SO42: Broc .7D 148
Noel Rd. BH10: Bour .5F 226
Nomad Cl. SO18: South .1F 174
NO MAN'S LAND .6C 106
NOMANSLAND .2J 155
Nook, The GU47: Sandh .5C 18
PO13: Gos .7G 212
SO50: E'leigh .7F 132
Nook Caravan Park, The
SO31: Loc H .5E 196
Norbury Cl. SO53: Cha F .5N 131
Norbury Gdns. SO31: Hamb .7J 195
Norcliffe Cl. BH11: Bour .3F 226
Norcliffe Rd. SO17: South .2M 173
Norcroft Ct. SO16: South .9H 159
Norden Cl. RG21: B'toke .5C 42
Norden Ho. RG21: B'toke .5D 42
Norden Way PO9: Hav .4C 202
Nordik Gdns. SO30: Hed E .5N 175
Nore Cres. PO10: Ems .8K 203
Nore Farm Av. PO10: Ems .8K 203
Noreuil Rd. GU32: Pet .1K 145
Norfolk Av. BH23: Chri .4J 229
Norfolk Ct. SO53: Cha F .9A 132
Norfolk Cres. PO11: H Isl .5D 242
Norfolk Ho. PO9: Hav .8G 202
Norfolk M. PO11: H Isl .4E 242
Norfolk Rd. PO12: Gos .9H 213
SO15: South .2J 173
Norfolk St. PO5: S'sea .7N 5 (4D 240)
Norgett Way PO16: Portc .2K 213
Norham Av. SO16: South .9H 159
Norham Cl. SO16: South .9H 159
Norland Rd. PO4: S'sea .4F 240
Norlands Dr. SO21: Ott .9G 126
Norley Cl. PO9: Hav .4E 202
NORLEYWOOD .7M 225
Norleywood BH23: Highc .6H 231
Norleywood Rd. SO41: E End, Norl .6K 225
Norman Av. BH12: Poole .8D 226
Norman Cl. GU35: Bor .4K 101
PO16: Portc .2M 213
Norman Ct. GU9: Farnh .9E 64
PO4: S'sea .5F 240
Norman Ct. La. SP11: Up C .4M 69
NORMANDY .5F 234
Normandy Cl. SO16: Rown .5D 158
SO41: Sway .5H 223
Normandy Ct. PO17: Wick .6D 178
SO31: Wars .8N 195
Normandy Dr. BH23: Chri .7N 229
Normandy Gdns. PO12: Gos .3H 239
Normandy Ho. *SO51: Rom .5N 129*
(off Chambers Av.)
Normandy La. SO41: Lymi .4F 234
Normandy Rd. PO2: Ports .4E 214
Normandy St. GU34: Alt .4F 80
Normandy Way SO40: March .7E 172
SP6: F'dge .9H 151
Norman Gdns. BH12: Poole .8E 226
SO30: Hed E .5L 175
Norman Ho. SO14: South .4A 174
Normanhurst Av. BH8: Bour .5A 228
Norman Rd. PO4: S'sea .4F 240
PO11: H Isl .5H 243
PO12: Gos .2J 239
SO15: South .5J 173
SO23: Winche .8K 105
SO45: Blac .8D 208
Normans Flats SO23: Winche .8K 105
Normans Way BH25: A'ley .3D 232
Normanton Cl. BH23: Chri .5J 229
Normanton Rd. RG21: B'toke .4C 42
Norman Way PO9: Bed .7C 202
Normay Ri. RG14: New .1C 8
Norn Hill RG21: B'toke .5D 42
Norn Hill Cl. RG21: B'toke .5D 42
Norrie Ct. RG24: B'toke .3L 41
Norris Cl. BH24: Ashl H .4B 186
GU35: W'hil .6G 100
SO51: Rom .2B 130
Norris Gdns. BH25: New M .5B 232
PO9: Warb .9G 203
SO21: Sth W .3H 91
Norrish Ct. *PO1: Ports .9F 214*
(off Inverness Rd.)
Norris Hill SO18: South .1C 174
Norris Hill Rd. GU51: Fleet .3A 48
GU52: Fleet .3A 48
Norrish Rd. BH12: Poole .9A 226
Norset Rd. PO15: Fare .7M 197
North Acre SP11: Longp .2A 76
NORTHAM .4A 174
Northam Bri. SO14: South .4A 174
SO18: South .4A 174
Northam Bus. Cen. SO14: South .4A 174
Northam M. PO1: Ports .2E 240
Northampton La. SO45: Blac .8C 208
Northam Rd. SO14: South .4E 4 (5N 173)
(not continuous)
Northam St. PO1: Ports .1E 240
Northanger Cl. GU34: Alt .4E 80
Northarbour Rd. PO6: Cosh .1E 214
Northarbour Spur PO6: Cosh .9E 200
North Av. GU9: H End .3F 64
PO2: Ports .3F 214
NORTH BADDESLEY .8G 130
Nth. Battery Rd. PO2: Ports .6C 214
North Bay PO10: T Isl .5N 217
NORTH BOARHUNT .9J 179
NORTH BOCKHAMPTON .8B 220
NORTHBOURNE .1H 227
Northbourne Av. BH10: Bour .1H 227
Northbourne Cl. SO45: Dib P .8M 193
Northbourne Gdns. BH10: Bour .1J 227
Northbourne Pl. BH10: Bour .1H 227
Northbourne Rdbt. BH10: Bour .1J 227
NORTHBROOK
SO21 .7J 77
SO32 .3N 163
Northbrook Av. SO23: Winche .7M 105
Northbrook Bower SO32: Bis W .3N 163
Northbrook Cl. PO1: Ports .9E 214
SO23: Winche .7N 105
Northbrook Ct. SO23: Winche .7N 105
Northbrook Cres. RG24: B'toke .3L 41
Northbrook Ho. SO32: Bis W .3N 163
Northbrook Ind. Est. SO16: South .9H 159
Northbrook Rd. GU11: Alders .2K 65
SO14: South .3F 4 (5N 173)
NORTH CAMP .4M 49
North Camp Station (Rail) .3N 49
Nth. Camp Sta. Rdbt. GU14: Farn .3N 49
NORTH CHARFORD
SP6, South Charford .9N 119
SP6, Woodfalls .9C 120
Nth. Charford Drove SP6: Brea .8L 119
Northcliffe Ho. SO16: Nur .5A 158
North Cl. GU12: Alders .1N 65
GU14: Farn .4J 29
PO9: Hav .9G 202
PO12: Gos .3H 239
SO41: Lymi .2E 234
SO51: Rom .3B 130
NORTH COMMON .9A 122
North Comn. La. SO41: Lymi .8N 223
SP5: L'ford .8H 121
Northcote Rd. BH1: Bour .1M 245
GU14: Cov .6H 29
PO4: S'sea .4F 240
SO17: South .9A 160
Northcott Cl. PO12: Gos .4H 239
Northcott Gdns. GU14: Cov .7F 28
Nth. Ct. PO1: Ports .9F 214
SO15: South .2G 172
North Cres. PO11: H Isl .4H 243
Northcroft Ct. *RG29: S War .4D 62*
(off Alton Rd.)
Northcroft Rd. PO12: Gos .1H 239
Nth. Cross St. PO12: Gos .3M 239
Northdene Rd. SO53: Cha F .7A 132
North Dr. BH25: Oss .8M 221
PO17: S'wick .3A 200
SO22: Lit .1F 104
North East Cl. SO19: South .5G 174
North East Rd. SO19: South .6E 174
North E. Sector BH23: Bour A .6B 218
NORTH END
PO2 .7E 214
RG20 .2L 7
SO24 .7E 108
SP6 .3P 149
North End BH23: Avon .3J 219
SO20: Brou .1A 86 (4A 88)
SP4: All .7D 66
North End Av. PO2: Ports .6E 214
North End Cl. SO53: Cha F .8A 132
North End Gro. PO2: Ports .6E 214
North End La. BH24: Har .6G 152
SP6: F'dge .6G 152
Northend La. SO32: Drox .1J 165
Northern Access Rd. SO45: Fawl .6G 209
(not continuous)
Northern Anchorage SO19: South .7B 174
Northern Av. SP10: A'ver .9N 51
Northern Pde. PO2: Ports .5E 214
Northern Retail Pk. SP10: A'ver .9N 51
Northern Rd. PO6: Cosh .2G 214
SO45: Fawl .6J 209
Northerwood Av.
SO43: Lyn .2A 148 (2N 189)
Northerwood Cl. SO52: N Bad .8E 130
Northesk Ho. PO1: Ports .1E 240
Northey Rd. BH6: Bour .8H 229
NORTH FAREHAM .5D 198
Nth. Farm Cl. GU14: Cov .4H 29
Nth. Farm Rd. GU14: Cov .4H 29
NORTH FARNBOROUGH .8K 29
North Fld. RG25: Over .1D 56
Northfield Av. PO14: Fare .1B 212
Northfield Caravan Pk.
PO16: Portc .7K 199
Northfield Cl. GU12: Alders .1M 65
GU52: Ch Cr .5A 48
PO8: Horn .9C 168
SO32: Bis W .2K 163
Northfield La. GU34: Bin .8C 80
Northfield Pk. PO16: Portc .8K 199
Northfield Rd. BH24: Poul, Ring .8K 185
GU52: Ch Cr .5N 47
RG27: Sher L .3L 23
SO18: South .8D 160
SO41: M Sea .8M 235
Northfields SO21: Twyf .6L 127
Northfields Farm La.
PO17: Wick .5D 178
North Front SO14: South .4D 4 (5M 173)
(not continuous)
North Fryerne GU46: Yat .5N 17
Northgate Av. PO2: Ports .8G 215
Northgate La. RG25: Elli .9C 60
Nth. Ga. Rd. GU14: Farn .1L 49
Northgate Way RG22: B'toke .4J 59
NORTH GORLEY .6M 153
North Greenlands SO41: Penn .4C 234
North Gro. Ho. PO5: S'sea .4E 240
North Hants Golf Course .8M 27
NORTH HARBOUR .2C 214
Nth. Harbour Bus. Pk. PO6: Cosh .1D 214
North Haven Yacht Club .9A 244
NORTH HAYLING .5J 217
North Head SO41: M Sea .9H 233
North Hill PO16: Fare .6D 198
PO17: S'wick .7C 200
North Hill Cl. SO22: Winche .4K 105
North Hill Ct. SO22: Winche .4K 105
NORTH HOUGHTON .4E 88
NORTHINGTON .9A 78

Northington Rd.—Oakwood Ct.

Northington Rd. SO21: Itc A 8J 93
SO24: Nort 6L 93
NORTH KINGSTON 6M 187
NORTHLANDS 7J 121
Northlands Cl. SO40: Tott 2K 171
Northlands Dr. SO23: Winche 4L 105
Northlands Gdns. SO15: South 3K 173
Northlands Rd. SO15: South 3K 173
SO40: Tott 2L 171
SO50: E'leigh 9E 132
SO51: Rom 6B 130
North La. GU12: Alders 8M 49
GU31: Buri 7K 145
GU31: S Hart 8G 146
PO8: Chal 6J 169
PO8: Clan 5B 168
SO42: Beau 9E 192
SP5: Nom 2J 155
SP5: W Tyt 6L 87
Northleigh Cnr. SO18: S'ing 6C 160
Nth. Lodge Rd. BH14: Poole 1C 244
North Mall GU51: Fleet 2L 47
Northmead GU14: Farn 8K 29
North Mdw. *PO12: Gos* 1M 239
(off Weevil La.)
Northmere Dr. BH12: Poole 7D 226
Northmere Rd. BH12: Poole 8C 226
Nth. Millers Dale SO53: Cha F 3M 131
Northmore Cl. SO31: Loc H 4E 196
Northmore Rd. SO31: Loc H 4E 196
NORTHNEY 4J 217
Northney La. PO11: H Isl 4J 217
Northney Rd. PO11: H Isl 3G 216
NORTH OAKLEY 2H 39
Northolt Gdns. SO16: South 6F 158
Northover Ct. BH3: Bour 7H 227
Northover La. SO41: Tip 8F 222
Northover Rd. PO3: Ports 8J 215
SO41: Penn 2A 234
North Pde. GU35: Bor 1H 101
North Pk. Bus. Cen.
PO17: K Vil 1N 197
NORTH POULNER 7M 185
Nth. Poulner Rd. BH24: Poul 8L 185
NORTH RIPLEY 3N 219
North Rd. BH7: Bour 9B 228
GU11: Alders 4M 49
GU32: Pet 9M 139
PO8: Horn 9C 168
PO17: S'wick 7B 200
SO17: South 1A 174
SO23: Kin W 6M 91
SO40: March 8F 172
SO42: Broc 7D 148
SO45: Dib P 7J 193
SP4: Ames 6A 66
North Rd. Caravan Site SP4: Ames 6A 66
North Rd. E. PO17: S'wick 3B 200
North Rd. W. PO17: S'wick 3B 200
North Row RG26: B'ley 9G 12
Northshore BH13: S'bks 9A 244
Nth. Shore Rd. PO11: H Isl 3D 242
Northside La. SO24: Bis S, Gund 8M 95
North Solent Nature Reserve 9F 208 & 8H 209
North Sq. PO17: K Vil 2A 198
NORTH STONEHAM 4B 160
NORTH STREET
SO24 8E 96
SP6 1L 151
North St. GU31: Rog 9L 141
PO1: Ports 1E 240
(Cornwallis Cres.)
PO1: Ports 3K 5 (2B 240)
(Sarah Robinson Ho.)
PO9: Bed 7D 202
PO9: Hav 8F 202
PO10: Ems 8M 203
PO10: Westb 5N 203
PO12: Gos 3M 239
(not continuous)
RG20: Kings 2B 6 (6K 9)
SO24: Bis S 1K 109
SO41: Penn 4C 234
North St. Arc. PO9: Hav 8F 202
Nth. Stroud La. GU32: R'dean, Stro 3D 144
NORTH SYDMONTON 2H 9
NORTH TIDWORTH 7C 30 (6G 30)
NORTH TOWN 8N 49
Northtown Trad. Est. GU12: Alders 1N 65
Nth. Trestle Rd. SO45: Fawl 2F 208
Northumberland Ct. BH24: Ring 1J 187
Northumberland Rd. GU35: W'hil 6J 101
PO5: S'sea 3F 240
SO14: South 3G 4 (5N 173)
(not continuous)
North Vw. SO22: Winche 6J 237 (6J 105)
North Vw. Rd. RG26: Tadl 6K 11
NORTH WALLINGTON 7F 198
North Wallington PO16: Fare 7E 198
North Walls
SO23: Winche 6M 237 (6L 105)
NORTH WALTHAM 9A 58
Nth. Waltham Rd. RG23: Oak 3B 58
NORTH WARNBOROUGH 7J 45
North Way PO9: Hav 8E 202
SP10: A'ver 8C 52
Northway PO13: Gos 4E 212
PO15: Titch 6H 197
SP4: Port 9D 66
Northways PO14: Stub 6N 211
NORTH WEIRS 7A 148 (8M 189)
North Weirs SO42: Broc 6A 148 (8M 189)
North West Ind. Area
BH23: Bour A 6A 218
Northwick RG27: Eve 6J 17
Northwood Cl. SO16: Bass 5M 159
North Wood Ho. *BH4: Bour* 2G 244
(off Poole Rd.)
Northwood La. PO11: H Isl 7G 216
Northwood Pk. 1C 104
Northwood Rd. PO2: Ports 4F 214
Northwood Sq. PO16: Fare 7D 198
Nortoft Rd. BH8: Bour 8M 227
NORTON 5E 76
Norton Cl. BH23: Chri 7N 229
PO7: W'lle 2L 201
PO17: S'wick 3A 200
SO19: South 7C 174
Norton Dr. PO16: Fare 6C 198
Norton Gdns. BH9: Bour 5J 227
Norton Ho. RG22: B'toke 8L 41
Norton Ride RG24: Lych 4G 43
Norton Rd. BH9: Bour 6J 227
PO17: S'wick 3A 200
RG7: Rise 2G 14
Norton Welch Cl. SO52: N Bad 8G 130
Norway Cl. BH9: Bour 5K 227
Norway Rd. PO3: Ports 4G 215
Norwich Av. BH2: Bour 6H 247 (2H 245)
GU15: Camb 1N 29
Norwich Av. West
BH2: Bour 6G 247 (2H 245)
Norwich Cl. RG22: B'toke 3K 59
SO31: Sar G 5B 196
Norwich Ct. BH2: Bour 7J 247
Norwich Mans. BH2: Bour 6H 247 (2H 245)
Norwich Pl. PO13: Lee S 9A 212
Norwich Rd. BH2: Bour 7J 247 (2J 245)
PO6: Cosh 8E 200
SO18: South 9D 160
Norwood Pl. BH5: Bour 9E 228
Nottingham Pl. PO13: Lee S 9A 212
Nouale La. BH24: Poul 1N 187
Novello Cl. RG22: B'toke 3M 59
Novello Gdns. PO7: W'lle 3M 201
Noyce Dr. SO50: Fair O 2A 162
Noyce Gdns. BH8: Bour 4E 228
Nubia Cl. PO31: Cowes 5N 237
Nuffield Dr. GU47: Owl 4H 19
Nuffield Health Club
Farnham 4G 65
Portsmouth 5E 214
(off Alex Way)
Nuffield Theatre
Southampton 8M 159
Nugent Rd. BH6: Bour 1J 247
Nunns Pk. SP5: W'psh 5H 121
Nuns Rd. SO23: Winche 5L 105
Nuns Wlk. SO23: Kin W 1N 105
SO23: Winche 5L 105
Nunton Drove SP5: Nun, Ods 5J 119
Nursery Cl. GU51: Fleet 3B 48
PO10: Ems 6M 203
PO13: Gos 5D 212
RG24: Chin 9H 23
RG27: Hoo 1G 44
Nursery Fld. GU33: Liss 2D 140
Nursery Gdns. PO8: Horn 5A 182
SO19: South 4F 174
SO22: Winche 7H 237 (6H 105)
SO51: Rom 5N 129
SO53: Cha F 9A 132
Nursery Gro. SO30: Hed E 5N 175
Nursery Ho. SO53: Cha F 6A 132
Nursery La. PO14: Stub 6M 211
Nursery Rd. BH9: Bour 3L 227
BH24: Ring 2K 187
GU34: Alt 3G 80
PO9: Bed 7C 202
SO18: South 1B 174
SO24: New A 1F 108
Nursery Ter. RG29: N War 7J 45
Nurse's Path SO21: Twyf 7L 127
NURSLING 6C 158
Nursling Cres. PO9: Hav 4G 203
Nursling Grn. BH8: Bour 4A 228
Nursling Ind. Est.
SO16: Nur 7A 158
Nursling St. SO16: Nur 6B 158
NURSTED 5B 146
Nutash PO14: Titch C 5F 196
NUTBANE 2F 50
Nutbane Cl. SP10: A'ver 2K 69
Nutbane La. SP11: C'vle 3F 50
Nutbean La. RG7: Swal 1K 15
Nutbeem Rd. SO50: E'leigh 1E 160
Nutbourne GU9: Weyb 3G 65
Nutbourne Ho. PO6: Farl 1L 215
Nutbourne Rd. PO6: Farl 1L 215
PO11: H Isl 5L 243
NUTBURN 7G 130
Nutburn Rd. SO52: N Bad 7G 130
Nutchers Drove SO20: Ki S 8B 86 (6G 88)
NUTCOMBE 5N 103
Nutcombe La. GU26: Hind 7N 103
Nutfield Ct. GU15: Camb 6M 19
SO16: South 8D 158
Nutfield Pl. PO1: Ports 1E 240
Nutfield Rd. SO16: Rown 5C 158
Nuthatch Cl. *GU10: Ews* 2N 63
(off Sparrow Hawk Cl.)
PO9: R Cas 9H 183
RG22: B'toke 4H 59
NUTLEY 2E 78
Nutley Cl. BH11: Bour 2D 226
GU35: Bor 5J 101
GU46: Yat 8N 17
Nutley Dr. GU51: Fleet 9J 27
Nutley La. RG25: Dumm 9H 59
Nutley Rd. PO9: Hav 4D 202
Nutley Way BH11: Bour 3D 226
Nutmeg Ct. GU14: Cov 7E 28
Nutsey Av. SO40: Tott 9K 157
Nutsey Cl. SO40: Tott 8L 157
Nutsey La. SO40: Tott 9L 157
Nutshalling Av. SO16: Rown 6C 158
Nutshalling Cl. SO40: Calm 9J 157
Nutshell La. GU9: Up H 4E 64
Nutwick Rd. PO9: Hav 6H 203
Nutwood Way SO40: Tott 9L 157
NYEWOOD 4K 147
Nyewood Av. PO16: Portc 8M 199
Nyewood Industries GU31: Nye 4K 147
Nyria Way PO12: Gos 3M 239

O

Oakapple Gdns. PO6: Farl 9M 201
Oak Av. BH23: Chri 6G 229
GU47: Owl 4F 18
Oak Bank SP10: A'ver 3N 69
Oakbank Rd. SO19: South 7B 174
SO50: B'stke 8G 133
Oak Cl. PO8: Cowp 8M 181
RG20: Kings 2C 6 (6L 9)
RG21: B'toke 6E 42
RG23: Oak 1D 58
RG25: Over 3D 56
RG26: Bau 5D 10
SO15: South 2B 172
SO32: Uph 8E 134
SO43: Lyn 3B 148
SO45: Dib P 8K 193
SP5: Far 8F 86
SP9: Tidw 7E 30
Oak Coppice Cl. SO50: B'stke 1L 161
Oak Coppice Rd.
PO15: White 1G 196
Oak Cotts. GU27: Hasl 9N 103
(not continuous)
Oak Ct. GU9: Farnh 9D 64
GU14: Farn 2N 49
PO15: Fare 7M 197
Oakcroft La. PO14: Stub 3M 211
Oakdene GU34: Alt 3E 80
PO13: Gos 7F 212
SO17: South 9N 159
SO40: Tott 3J 171
Oakdene Ct. SO50: Fair O 1N 161
Oakdene Rd. PO4: S'sea 3K 241
Oakdown Rd. PO14: Stub 5N 211
Oak Dr. GU31: Pet 3L 145
SO50: Fair O 1N 161
Oakenbrow SO41: Sway 5H 223
SO45: Dib P 7J 193
Oaken Copse GU52: Ch Cr 7N 47
Oaken Copse Cres. GU14: Farn 5K 29
Oakes, The PO14: Stub 4L 211
Oak Farm Cl. GU17: Blackw 8E 18
Oakfield SO41: Lymi 3E 234
Oakfield Ct. PO9: Hav 4H 203
Oakfield Gdns. SO16: South 1G 173
Oakfield Pl. GU14: Cov 8E 28
Oakfield Rd. GU17: Haw 9G 19
RG26: Pam H 4L 11
SO40: Bart 3B 170
SO40: Tott 3M 171
Oakfields GU15: Camb 8K 19
RG24: Lych 3G 43
SO50: E'leigh 5E 132
Oakfields Cl. RG20: Ecc 5G 9
Oakford Ct. BH8: Bour 3A 228
Oak Gdns. BH11: Bour 5F 226
SO41: Ever 6L 233
Oakgreen Pde. GU34: Four M 4K 97
Oak Grn. Way SO18: South 2E 174
OAK GROVE 7G 19
Oak Gro. Cres. GU15: Camb 7H 19
Oakgrove Gdns. SO50: B'stke 1J 161
Oakgrove Rd. SO50: B'stke 1J 161
OAKHANGER 3C 100
Oak Hanger Cl. RG27: Hoo 2H 45
Oakhanger Rd. GU35: Bor 3F 100
Oak Hill SO24: New A 2F 108
Oakhill SO31: Burs 9M 175
Oakhill Cl. SO31: Burs 9M 175
SO53: Cha F 7C 132
Oakhill Ct. SO53: Cha F 7C 132
Oak Hill Rd. RG25: Pres C 4F 78
Oakhill Rd. GU35: Head D 2D 102
Oakhill Ter. SO31: Burs 9M 175
Oak Ho. SO41: Lymi 9D 224
Oakhurst BH13: Poole 2F 244
BH23: Chri 7B 230
(off Newlands Rd.)
GU26: Gray 4M 103
Oakhurst Cl. SO31: Net A 3G 195
Oakhurst Dr. PO7: W'lle 1A 202
Oakhurst Gdns. PO7: Wid 7J 201
Oakhurst Rd. SO17: South 8M 159
Oakhurst Way SO31: Net A 3G 195
Oakland Av. GU9: Weyb 3G 64
Oakland Dr. SO40: March 9E 172
Oakland Rd. RG28: Whit 5G 54
Oaklands GU46: Yat 7N 17
PO7: W'lle 3A 202
RG27: H Win 7B 26
SO21: Sth W 3H 91
SO41: Lymi 4F 234
Oaklands, The SO53: Cha F 9A 132
Oaklands Av. SO40: Tott 3M 171
Oaklands Cl. SO22: Winche 8F 104
SP6: F'dge 9H 151
Oaklands Gdns. PO14: Titch C 8F 196
Oaklands Gro. PO8: Cowp 7L 181
Oaklands Ho. PO6: Cosh 7A 200
Oaklands Mead SO40: Tott 2M 171
Oaklands Pk. RG27: Hoo 4E 44
Oaklands Rd. GU32: Pet 9L 139
PO9: Hav 8G 202
Oaklands Swimming Pool 6E 158
Oaklands Way PO14: Titch C 8F 196
RG23: B'toke 5L 41
SO16: Bass 7L 159
SO45: Dib P 7H 193
Oakland Ter. RG27: H Win 6C 26
Oak La. BH24: Ring 9L 185
Oaklea Cl. PO7: Wid 7J 201
Oaklea Dr. RG27: Eve 3B 16
Oak Leaf Cl. SO40: March 1D 192
Oakleafe Pl. SO53: Cha F 6A 132
Oaklea Gdns. RG26: B'ley 2J 23
Oakleigh Cres. SO40: Tott 4L 171
Oakleigh Dr. SP5: L'ford 1J 155
Oakleigh Gdns. SO51: Rom 5N 129
Oakleigh Way BH23: Highc 7H 231
OAKLEY 9C 40
Oakley Cl. SO45: Holb 4A 208
Oakley Ct. SO16: South 2G 172
Oakley Dr. GU51: Fleet 3M 47
Oakley Gdns. PO7: Wid 6K 201
Oakley Hgts. BH2: Bour 5K 247 (1J 245)
Oakley Ho. PO5: S'sea 7N 5 (4D 240)
SO15: South 3L 173
Oakley John Wlk. SO19: South 4D 174
Oakley La. RG23: Oak 1C 58
SO51: Houg, Mott 1F 122
Oakley Pl. *RG27: H Win* 6C 26
(off High St.)
Oakley Rd. GU15: Camb 9K 19
GU35: Bor 2J 101
PO9: Hav 4D 202
RG25: Nth W 6A 58
RG26: Hann 9L 9
SO16: South 1E 172
SO51: Mott 2E 122
Oak Lodge GU35: Bor 5J 101
PO2: Ports 6D 214
Oakmead RG26: B'ley 9F 12
Oakmead Gdns. BH11: Bour 2C 226
Oakmeadow Cl. PO10: Ems 6N 203
Oakmead Sports Cen. 2D 226
Oakmont Dr. PO8: Cowp 8N 181
Oakmore Pk. SO50: Hor H 5B 162
Oakmount Av. SO17: South 1L 173
SO40: Tott 2M 171
SO53: Cha F 8B 132
Oakmount Mans. SO17: South 1L 173
Oakmount Rd. SO53: Cha F 5C 132
Oak Pk. Dr. PO9: Hav 6G 202
Oak Pk. Golf Course 3M 63
Oak Pk. Ind. Est. PO6: Cosh 9E 200
OAKRIDGE 4C 42
Oakridge RG20: Enbo R 1B 8
Oakridge Ho. RG21: B'toke 4D 42
Oakridge Rd. RG21: B'toke 4A 42
SO15: South 2C 172
Oakridge Towers RG21: B'toke 4D 42
Oak Rd. BH8: Bour 8N 227
BH25: A'ley 3D 232
GU14: Farn 9L 29
PO8: Clan 6C 168
PO15: Fare 7N 197
SO19: South 8B 174
SO31: Burs 1K 195
SO32: Bis W 3N 163
SO45: Dib P 8J 193
SP6: Ald 5C 152
Oaks, The GU14: Cov 9F 28
GU33: G'ham 4E 114
GU34: Meds 9L 79
GU46: Yat 8N 17
GU51: Fleet 2J 47
PO8: Cowp 8A 182
RG26: Tadl 5G 11
SO19: South 5D 174
SO31: Burs 1K 195
SP10: A'ver 1L 69
(off Lynwood Dr.)
Oaks Coppice PO8: Horn 4A 182
Oaks Dr. BH24: St L 5A 186
OAKSHOTT 9K 113
Oakshott Dr. PO9: Hav 4G 203
Oak St. PO12: Gos 3L 239
Oakthorn Cl. PO13: Gos 1E 238
Oak Tree Cl. GU12: Alders 2N 65
GU35: Head 3B 102
RG26: Tadl 4H 11
SO20: Chil 5F 74
SO21: Col C 4K 133
Oaktree Ct. SO16: Bass 8K 159
SO41: M Sea 8J 235
Oak Tree Dr. GU33: Liss 1F 140
PO10: Ems 5L 203
Oaktree Dr. RG27: Hoo 1H 45
Oaktree Gdns. SO30: Hed E 4M 175
Oak Tree La. GU27: Hasl 9M 103
Oak Tree Pde. *BH23: Bran* 7D 220
(off Ringwood Rd.)
Oaktree Pde. BH23: Bran 6D 220
Oaktree Pk. SO30: Wes E 7H 161
Oak Tree Rd. GU35: W'hil 6H 101
SO18: South 1B 174
Oaktrees GU9: Up H 4D 64
Oak Tree Vw. GU9: H End 4G 64
Oak Tree Way SO50: E'leigh 7E 132
Oaktree Way GU47: Sandh 4C 18
Oakum Ho. PO3: Ports 1H 241
Oak Vale SO30: Wes E 8F 160
Oakville Mans. SO15: South 3B 4
Oak Wlk. SO50: Fair O 1N 161
Oak Way GU12: Alders 2M 65
Oakway GU10: Ben'ly 7K 63
Oakway Dr. GU16: Frim 3N 29
Oakwood BH3: Bour 7J 227
GU52: Ch Cr 7M 47
RG24: Chin 9G 22
(Alderwood)
RG24: Chin 9F 22
(Maplewood)
Oakwood Av. BH25: New M 2C 232
PO9: Bed 6B 202
SO21: Ott 1G 133
Oakwood Centre, The PO9: Hav 5H 203
Oakwood Cl. BH9: Bour 4M 227
BH24: Ashl H 3C 186
SO21: Ott 9G 127
SO31: Wars 9A 196
SO51: Rom 3A 130
SO53: Cha F 3B 132
Oakwood Ct. RG27: H Win 6B 26
SO30: Wes E 8J 161
SO53: Cha F 3B 132

Oakwood Dr.—Orchard Ter.

Oakwood Dr. GU34: Alt .5D 80
SO16: South .6H 159
Oakwood Ho. GU14: Cov .4H 29
(off Nth. Farm Cl.)
Oakwood Pl. RG45: Cr'tne .1C 18
Oakwood Rd. BH9: Bour .4L 227
BH23: Highc .5G 231
PO2: Ports .4F 214
PO11: H Isl .4F 242
SO53: Cha F .4B 132
Oakwood Way SO31: Hamb .6L 195
Oakwoood Ct. BH25: New M .3C 232
Oasis, The BH13: Poole .1E 244
Oast Ho. Cres. GU9: Hale .4E 64
Oasthouse Dr. GU51: Fleet .8A 28
Oast Ho. La. GU9: Hale .5F 64
Oast La. GU11: Alders .3K 65
Oasts, The RG29: L Sut .4E 62
Oates Rd. BH9: Bour .5J 227
Oatfield Gdns. SO40: Calm .1J 171
Oatlands SO51: Rom .4M 129
Oatlands Cl. SO32: Botl .1C 176
Oatlands Rd. SO32: Botl .1C 176
Oatley Wlk. SO45: Fawl .6D 208
Oat Rd. SP11: E Ant .6B 52
Oatsheaf Pde. GU51: Fleet .3L 47
Oban Cl. RG23: Oak .9C 40
Oban Rd. BH3: Bour .7J 227
O'Bee Gdns. RG26: Bau .4E 10
Obelisk Rd. SO19: South .8B 174
Obelisk Way GU15: Camb .7L 19
Oberfield Rd. SO42: Broc .6A 148 (8M 189)
Oberon Cl. PO7: W'lle .1A 202
Ober Rd. SO42: Broc .6B 148 (8N 189)
Oberursel Way GU11: Alders .9H 49
Occupation La. PO14: Titch .9H 197
Oceana Blvd. SO14: South .8D 4
Oceana Cres. RG22: B'toke .6H 59
Oceanarium .9M 247 (3K 245)
Ocean Breeze BH4: Bour .4G 245
Ocean Cl. PO15: Fare .7N 197
Ocean Ct. PO11: H Isl .5E 242
Ocean Hgts. BH5: Bour .2C 246
Oceanic Way SO40: March .7G 172
Ocean Pk. PO3: Ports .6J 215
Ocean Quay SO14: South .5A 174
Ocean Rd. PO14: Fare .3B 212
SO14: South .9M 173
Ocean Terminal .9E 4 (8M 173)
OCEAN VILLAGE .9F 4 (8N 173)
Ocean Village Innovation Cen. SO14: South .9F 4
(off Ocean Way)
Ocean Way SO14: South .9F 4 (8N 173)
Ochil Cl. RG22: B'toke .8K 41
Ockendon Cl. PO5: S'sea .6N 5 (3D 240)
Ockham Hall GU35: K'ly .7G 83
Ocknell Gro. SO45: Dib .6H 193
O'Connell Rd. SO50: E'leigh .1C 160
O'Connor Rd. GU11: Alders .4N 49
Octavia Gdns. SO53: Cha F .5D 132
Octavia Hill SO22: Winche .8H 105
Octavian Cl. RG22: B'toke .3K 59
Octavia Rd. SO18: S'ing .7C 160
Octavius Ct. PO7: W'lle .9B 182
Odd La. RG7: Sil .4F 12
Odell Cl. PO16: Fare .6B 198
Odeon ABC Cinema
Bournemouth .7M 247 (2K 245)
Odeon Cinema
Andover .2N 69
Basingstoke .6M 41
Bournemouth .7M 247 (2K 245)
Port Solent .2C 214
Southampton .6A 4 (6K 173)
Odette Gdns. RG26: Tadl .4J 11
ODIHAM .8K 45
Odiham Castle (Remains of) .7G 45
Odiham Cl. SO16: South .7E 158
SO53: Cha F .9N 131
Odiham Rd. GU10: Up H .3B 64
RG7: Rise .2G 14
RG27: Rise .3G 15
RG27: Winchf .8A 26
RG29: Odi .5M 45
Odway La. GU31: Buri .8L 145
Officers Quarters, The PO12: Gos .2M 239
Officers Row RG26: B'ley .2J 23
OGDENS .7A 154
Oglander Rd. SO23: Winche .4L 105
Ogle Rd. SO14: South .5C 4 (6L 173)
O'Gorman Av. GU14: Farn .1K 49
O'Jays Ind. Pk. PO3: Ports .6H 215
Okeford Ho. BH9: Bour .7K 227
Okement Cl. SO18: Wes E .9F 160
Okingham Cl. GU47: Owl .3F 18
Olaf Cl. SP10: A'ver .6A 52
Olave Cl. PO13: Lee S .1A 238
Old Acre Rd. GU34: Alt .6E 80
OLD ALRESFORD .6F 94
Old Aylesfield Bldgs. GU34: Alt .8B 62
Old Barn Cl. BH23: Chri .4G 229
BH24: Ring .1M 187
RG25: Nth W .9A 58
Oldbarn Cl. SO40: Calm .9J 157
Old Barn Cres. PO7: H'don .9D 166
Old Barn Farm Caravan Pk. GU30: Lip .1G 117
Old Barn Gdns. PO8: Love .4N 181
Old Barn La. BH23: Chri .4G 229
GU10: Chur .6K 85
Old Barn Rd. BH23: Chri .4G 229
OLD BASING .4J 43
Old Basing Mall RG21: B'toke .6C 42
Old Beggarwood La. RG22: B'toke .5J 59
Oldberg Gdns. RG22: B'toke .2A 60
Old Bitumen Rd. SO45: Fawl .4F 208
Old Blandford Rd. SP5: Com B .3G 118
Old Boat Yard, The BH23: Chri .6H 229
Old Brickfield Rd. GU11: Alders .3K 65
Old Brick Kiln Trad. Estate, The
RG26: Rams .5G 20
Old Brickyard, The GU31: Nye .4J 147
Old Brickyard Rd. SP6: Sand .9E 150
Old Bridge Cl. SO31: Burs .9M 175
Old Bridge Ho. Rd. SO31: Burs .9M 175
Old Bridge Rd. BH6: Bour .6G 228
GU10: Run .6K 65
PO4: S'sea .5F 240
OLD BURGHCLERE .7D 8
Oldbury Ct. SO16: South .9C 158
Oldbury Ho. PO5: S'sea .6N 5
Oldbury Way PO14: Fare .9M 197
Old Canal PO4: S'sea .3J 241
Old Canal, The PO4: S'sea .3J 241
Old Canal Pl. RG21: B'toke .6E 42
Old Chapel La. RG26: Cha A .4H 21
Old Christchurch La.
BH1: Bour .6M 247 (2K 245)
Old Christchurch Rd.
BH1: Bour .7L 247 (2K 245)
(not continuous)
SO41: Ever .5L 233
Old Coach Rd. SP4: Bul .3A 66
SP9: Shi B .1C 66 (1G 67)
Old Coach Road, The SP11: Abb A .7G 68
Old College Wlk. PO6: Cosh .2H 215
Old Commercial Rd. PO1: Ports .9D 214
Old Common SO31: Loc H .5D 196
Old Common Gdns. SO31: Loc H .5D 196
Old Common Rd. RG21: B'toke .7E 42
Old Common Way SP11: Ludg .1D 30 (5K 31)
Old Compton La. GU9: Farnh .8G 65
Old Convent, The GU10: Dock .5N 83
Old Copse Rd. PO9: Hav .7G 202
Oldcorne Hollow GU46: Yat .8K 17
Old Cottage Cl. SO51: W Wel .1B 120 (9N 121)
Old Courthouse, The BH14: Poole .9A 226
Old Cove Rd. GU51: Fleet .9N 27
Old Cracknore Cl. SO40: March .8E 172
Old Cricket M. SO15: South .2L 173
Old Cross Rd. SO40: Cad .6N 155
(off Southampton Rd.)
Old Dairy Cl. GU51: Fleet .2M 47
Old Dean Rd. GU15: Camb .6M 19
OLD DITCHAM .7B 146
Old Down SO21: More .3C 134
Old Down Cl. RG22: B'toke .2J 59
Old Down La. SO21: More .3C 134
Old Down M. SP10: A'ver .9M 51
Old Down Rd. SP10: A'ver .9M 51
Olde Farm Dr. GU17: Blackw .7D 18
Oldenburg PO15: White .1E 196
Oldenburg Cl. SP10: A'ver .7M 51
Old English Dr. SP10: A'ver .6M 51
Old Farm Cl. BH24: Poul .7M 185
Old Farm Copse SO51: W Wel .1C 120 (9N 121)
Old Farm Dr. RG22: B'toke .8J 41
SO18: South .3D 160
Old Farmhouse Cl. SP9: Shi B .2B 66 (1G 66)
Old Farmhouse M. SO41: Lymi .1E 234
(off Lwr. Buckland Rd.)
Old Farm La. PO14: Stub .7M 211
Old Farm Wlk. SO41: Lymi .3D 234
Old Farm Way PO6: Farl .1M 215
Old Farnham La. GU9: Farnh .9E 64
GU10: Farnh .5M 63
Oldfield Cl. GU35: Bor .5J 101
Oldfield Vw. RG27: H Win .7B 26
Old Flour Mill, The PO10: Ems .9N 203
Old Forge, The RG26: Bau .4E 10
SO32: Shed .3N 177
Old Forge Cl. BH24: Poul .8M 185
SP6: Ald .4B 152
Old Forge End GU47: Sandh .6D 18
Old Forge Gdn. SO20: Brou .1A 86
Old Forge Rd. GU52: Ch Cr .8K 47
Old Fromans Farm SO20: Ki S .8A 86 (6F 88)
Old Garden Cl. SO31: Loc H .7F 196
Old Gardens SO22: Winche .4K 105
Oldgate Gdns. PO2: Ports .4G 214
Old Gosport Rd. PO16: Fare .9D 198
Old Green La. GU15: Camb .6L 19
Old Heath Way GU9: Up H .3E 64
Old Hill, The SP11: Wher .1E 74
Old Hillside Rd. SO22: Winche .4G 104
Old Iron Foundry SO20: Ki S .8A 86
Old Ively Rd. GU14: Farn .3C 48
(not continuous)
Old Ivy La. SO18: Wes E .9F 160
Old Kempshott La. RG22: Wort .9J 41
Old Kennels Cl. SO22: Oli B .2E 126
Old Kennels La. SO22: Oli B .2E 126
Old Kiln Cl. GU10: Chur .6H 85
Old Kiln La. GU10: Chur .5H 85
Old La. GU10: Dock .4N 83
GU11: Alders .3J 65
GU12: Alders .8N 49
PO8: Cath .9B 168
RG19: Ashf H .2N 9
Old Lane, The GU10: Chur .8H 85
Old Litten La. GU32: Frox, Ste .2J 139
Old London Rd. PO2: Ports .4G 214
SO20: S Bri .2G 88
Old Lyndhurst Rd. SO40: Cad .6N 155
Old Magazine Cl. SO40: March .8E 172
Old Malthouse La. SP4: Firs, Ford .4A 86
Old Maltings, The SO41: Lymi .2D 234
Old Manor Farm PO9: Bed .8B 202
Old Manor Way PO6: Cosh .1J 215
Old Micheldever Rd. SP11: A'ver .4F 70
Old Mill Ho. BH24: Ring .2J 187
Old Mill La. GU31: Pet .8A 140
PO7: H'don .8L 167
PO8: Love .3J 181
Old Mill Way SO16: South .1F 172
OLD MILTON .5A 232
Old Milton Grn. BH25: New M .5A 232
Old Milton Grn. Pde. BH25: New M .5A 232
Old Milton Rd. BH25: New M .5A 232
Old Monteagle La. GU46: Yat .7L 17
Old Mulberry Cl. BH10: Bour .5E 226
OLD NETLEY .9J 175
Old Oak Cl. SP11: E Ant .6B 52
Old Odiham Rd. GU34: Alt .8B 62
Old Orchard, The RG29: S War .4C 62
Old Orchards SO41: Lymi .4F 234
Old Palace Farm SO20: Ki S .9B 86 (7G 88)
Old Park Cl. GU9: Up H .4C 64
Old Park La. GU9: Farnh .5C 64
GU10: Up H .3B 64
(not continuous)
SO20: Mid Wa .4B 72
Old Park Rd. SO24: Bis S .2N 109
Old Parsonage Ct. SO21: Ott .1G 132
Old Pharmacy Ct. RG45: Cr'tne .1D 18
Old Pond Cl. GU15: Camb .3L 29
OLD PORTSMOUTH .7J 5 (4B 240)
Old Potbridge Rd. RG27: Winchf .2N 45
Old Priory Cl. SO31: Hamb .7L 195
Old Priory Rd. BH6: Bour .1J 247
Old Pump Ho. Cl. GU51: Fleet .1N 47
Old Railway, The PO12: Gos .2L 239
Old Reading Rd. RG21: B'toke .5D 42
Old Rectory, The RG29: S War .4D 62
(off Alton Rd.)
Old Rectory Cl. GU34: E Wor .7N 81
PO10: Westb .6N 203
Old Rectory Ct. SO40: Elin .5A 172
Old Rectory Gdns. GU14: Farn .8M 29
SO21: Abb W .9A 92
Old Rectory La. SO21: Twyf .6L 127
Old Rectory Rd. PO6: Farl .9M 201
Old Redbridge Rd. SO15: South .2B 172
Old Reservoir Rd. PO6: Farl .1L 215
Old River PO7: Den .7G 181
Old Rd. PO12: Gos .4L 239
SO14: South .9F 4 (8N 173)
SO51: Rom .3N 129
Old Road, The PO6: Cosh .2G 214
Old Romsey Rd. SO40: Cad .6N 155
Old St John's M. BH9: Bour .3K 227
Old Salisbury La. SO51: Rom, Shoo .2C 128
(not continuous)
Old Salisbury Rd. SO51: Ower .4E 156
SP11: Abb A .6H 69
Old School, The RG28: Whit .5G 54
(off Fairclose)
SO32: Bis W .4L 163
Old School Cl. GU51: Fleet .2M 47
RG27: H Win .6C 26
SO19: South .6E 174
SO31: Net A .2G 195
SO45: Hard .2N 207
Old School Ct. PO16: Fare .7E 198
Old School Dr. PO11: H Isl .5H 243
Old School Gdns. SO30: Wes E .9J 161
Old School La. GU46: Yat .7M 17
Old School Pl. SO20: Brou .1A 86
(off Chapel La.)
Old School Rd. GU33: Liss .1E 140
RG27: Hoo .3E 44
Old School Ter. GU51: Fleet .2M 47
(off Old School Cl.)
Old Shaftesbury Drove SP2: Nethe .1G 119
SP5: Com B .1G 118
Old Shamblehurst La. SO30: Hed E .9N 161
OLD SHIRLEY .1F 172
Old Sidings GU34: Lwr Farr .5C 98
Old Spring La. SO32: Swanm .6D 164
Old Stable M. SO22: Lit .9E 90
Old Stable Yard, The RG21: B'toke .7C 42
Old Stacks Gdns. BH24: Ring .2M 187
Old Star Pl. PO1: Ports .3J 5 (2B 240)
Old Station App.
SO23: Winche .8P 237 (7M 105)
Old Station Rd. SO21: Itc A .9H 93
Old Station Way GU35: Bor .2F 100
Old Stockbridge Rd.
SO20: Grat, Mid Wa, Ov Wa .5K 67
SO20: Ov Wa .5K 67
Old Stocks Oak GU33: Liss .9D 114
Old Stoke Rd. SO21: Stoke C .2L 91
Old St. PO14: Stub .7K 211
(not continuous)
Old Swanwick La. SO31: Lwr Swan .1A 196
Old Tannery, The SP5: Down .1L 119
(off High St.)
Old Ter. SO16: Bass .6M 159
Old Thornford Rd. RG19: C Cmn .1J 9
Old Thorns Golf Course .3N 115
Old Timbers PO11: H Isl .4F 242
Old Town M. GU9: Farnh .8C 64
Old Turnpike PO16: Fare .6D 198
Old Van Diemans Rd. PO7: Purb .4K 201
Old Vicarage Cl. BH10: Bour .1J 227
Old Vicarage La. SO20: Ki S .8B 86 (6G 88)
SO41: Sway .6K 223
Old Vineries, The SP6: F'dge .1G 152
Old Vyne La. RG26: Bau .3F 20
Old Ward Rd. SP4: Bul C .3A 66
Old Well Close, The SO19: South .7G 174
Old Welmore GU46: Yat .8M 17
Old Winchester Hill Fort .6D 142
Old Winchester Hill La. GU32: W Meo .1A 142
Old Winchester Hill Nature Reserve .5D 142
Old Winton Rd. SP10: A'ver .2A 70
Oldwood Chase GU14: Cov .9D 28
Old Worting Rd. RG22: B'toke, Wort .7L 41
Old Wymering La. PO6: Cosh .9F 200
Oleander Cl. SO31: Loc H .4D 196
Oleander Dr. SO40: Tott .2H 171
Olinda St. PO1: Ports .1F 240
Olive Cres. PO16: Portc .2M 213
Olive Gro. SP11: Pale .6K 67
Olive Leaf Ct. PO11: H Isl .2H 243
Oliver Ct. PO12: Gos .3L 239
Olive Rd. SO16: South .7F 158
Oliver Ri. GU34: Alt .4F 80
Oliver Rd. PO4: S'sea .4H 241
SO18: S'ing .8B 160
SO41: Penn .3C 234
OLIVER'S BATTERY .1F 126
Oliver's Battery Cres. SO22: Oli B .1F 126
Oliver's Battery Gdns. SO22: Oli B .2F 126
Oliver's Battery Rd. Nth. SO22: Winche .9F 104
Oliver's Battery Rd. Sth. SO22: Oli B .2F 126
Olivers Cl. RG26: B'ley .2H 23
SO40: Tott .3H 171
Olivers Ct. PO2: Ports .8F 214
Oliver's La. RG26: B'ley .9H 13
Oliver's Wlk. RG24: Lych .4G 43
Olivia Cl. PO7: W'lle .9A 182
Olympic Way SO50: Fair O .9L 133
Omdurman Rd. SO17: South .9M 159
Omega Enterprise Pk. SO53: Cha F .6A 132
Omega Ho. PO5: S'sea .2E 240
Omega Pk. GU34: Alt .5H 81
Omega St. PO5: S'sea .2E 240
Omni Bus. Cen. GU34: Alt .5H 81
Onibury Cl. SO18: South .1E 174
Onibury Rd. SO18: South .1E 174
Onslow Cl. RG24: B'toke .2F 42
Onslow Rd. PO5: S'sea .6E 240
SO14: South .1E 4 (4M 173)
Ontario Way GU30: Lip .3E 116
Openfields GU35: Head .2A 102
Ophir Gdns. BH8: Bour .9M 227
Ophir Rd. BH8: Bour .9M 227
PO2: Ports .6E 214
Optrex Bus. Pk. RG27: Roth .8D 24
Oracle Dr. PO7: Purb .6M 201
Orange Gro. PO13: Gos .7F 212
SP11: Pale .6K 67
Orange La. SO20: Ov Wa .8M 67
Orange Row PO10: Ems .9M 203
Oratory Gdns. BH13: Poole .5D 244
Orchard, The BH23: Bran .7E 220
PO6: Cosh .1G 215
PO7: Den .6G 180
RG25: Over .3D 56
RG26: Tadl .5K 11
RG27: Hoo .1G 45
SO16: Bass .6N 159
SO16: Chilw .2K 159
SO32: Bis W .4N 163
SO41: M Sea .8K 235
SO45: Dib P .6J 193
SO50: E'leigh .1E 160
SP9: Shi B .2A 66
Orchard Av. SO50: B'stke .2K 161
Orchard Bus. Pk. RG20: Kings .4J 9
Orchard Caravan Park, The
SO40: Woodl .5D 170
Orchard Cl. BH10: Bour .4H 227
BH21: Edmo .8K 149
BH23: Chri .8K 229
BH24: Ring .9K 185
GU9: Bad L .4K 65
GU17: Haw .3H 29
GU29: Els .8N 147
GU31: E Har .8K 147
PO8: Horn .4C 182
PO11: H Isl .5F 242
PO12: Gos .7J 213
SO21: Col C .3K 133
SO21: Sth W .3G 90
SO24: New A .2F 108
SO32: Botl .9C 162
SO40: Tott .5M 171
SO45: Fawl .5F 208
SO52: N Bad .7E 130
SP6: F'dge .9J 151
Orchard Ct. BH25: New M .3C 232
GU10: Cron .3L 63
GU15: Camb .2K 29
(off Orchard Way)
SO30: Botl .3B 176
Orchard Dean SO24: New A .9F 94
Orchard Dr. GU35: Lind .3M 101
Orchard End SP4: Bul .3A 66
Orchard Flds. GU51: Fleet .2L 47
Orchard Gdns. BH10: Bour .4G 226
GU12: Alders .2L 65
SP6: F'dge .1J 153
Orchard Ga. GU47: Sandh .5D 18
PO6: Dray .9J 201
Orchard Gro. BH25: New M .5B 232
PO8: Cowp .7N 181
PO16: Portc .1J 213
Orchard Ho. GU10: Tong .3N 65
GU34: Alt .5G 80
(off Orchard La.)
SO14: South .7D 4 (7M 173)
Orchard La. GU34: Alt .4G 80
PO10: S'brne .9N 203
SO14: South .7E 4 (7M 173)
SO51: Rom .5L 129
Orchard Lea RG27: Sher L .4L 23
Orchardlea SO32: Swanm .8D 164
Orchard Leigh BH25: New M .4C 232
Orchard Mead BH24: Ring .9K 185
Orchard M. BH10: Bour .4G 226
BH23: Chri .8K 229
Orchard Mt. BH24: Ring .9K 185
(off Southampton Rd.)
Orchard Pl. RG28: Whit .5G 54
(off Church St.)
SO14: South .8D 4 (7M 173)
Orchard Rd. GU9: Bad L .4J 65
GU14: Farn .8J 29
PO4: S'sea .3F 240
PO9: Hav .9F 202
PO11: H Isl .5G 243
RG22: B'toke .7L 41
SO21: Sth W .3G 90
SO31: Loc H .7C 196
SO50: Fair O .1N 161
SP5: M Val .1M 119 (7C 120)
SP10: A'ver .9L 51
Orchards, The BH24: Ring .2M 187
Orchard St. BH2: Bour .7K 247 (2J 245)
Orchards Way SO17: South .9M 159
SO30: Wes E .1H 175
Orchard Ter. GU34: Alt .4G 80
(off Orchard La.)

Orchard Wlk. BH2: Bour 7K **247** (2J **245**)
BH10: Bour 4G **226**
RG27: Brams 9A **16**
SO22: Winche 4H **105**
SO23: Winche 6M **237**
Orchard Way GU12: Alders 2L **65**
GU15: Camb 2K **29**
GU31: Pet 3M **145**
SO45: Dib P 7K **193**
Orcheston Rd. BH8: Bour 8M **227**
Orchid Cl. PO17: K Vil 2N **197**
Orchid Ct. *SP10: A'ver* *3K **69***
(off Floral Way)
Orchid Dr. SP11: Ludg 2D **30** (5K **31**)
Orchid Way BH23: Chri 7M **229**
Ordnance Bus. Pk. PO13: Gos 5F **212**
Ordnance Ct. PO3: Ports 3H **215**
Ordnance La. SP11: Weyh 8B **50**
Ordnance Rd. GU11: Alders 9K **49**
PO12: Gos 3M **239**
SO15: South 1D **4** (4M **173**)
SP9: Tidw 8D **30** (7G **31**)
Ordnance Rdbt. GU11: Alders 9K **49**
Ordnance Row PO1: Ports 4J **5** (2B **240**)
Ordnance Survey Head Office 7B **158**
Ordnance Way SO40: March 7F **172**
Oregon Cl. SO19: South 6E **174**
Orford Cl. BH23: Chri 2G **229**
Orford Ct. PO6: Cosh 1G **215**
Orford Rd. SP4: Ames 6A **66**
Oriana Way SO16: Nur 7A **158**
Oriel Bus. Pk. GU34: Alt 4H **81**
Oriel Dr. PO14: Titch C 8F **196**
Oriel Hill GU15: Camb 9M **19**
Oriel Rd. PO2: Ports 6E **214**
Oriental Ter. SO14: South 8D **4** (7M **173**)
Orient Dr. SO22: Winche 3G **104**
Orion Av. PO12: Gos 9L **213**
Orion Cl. PO14: Stub 6N **211**
SO16: South 7E **158**
Orion Ind. Cen. SO18: S'ing 6D **160**
Orion's Point SO14: South 2D **4** (4M **173**)
Orkney Cl. RG24: B'toke 2E **42**
SO16: South 7D **158**
Orkney Rd. PO6: Cosh 8G **201**
Orme Ct. PO16: Fare 8C **198**
Ormesby Dr. SO53: Cha F 3N **131**
Ormond Cl. SO50: Fair O 9M **133**
Ormonde Rd. BH13: Poole 3E **244**
Ormsby Rd. PO5: S'sea 4D **240**
Ornamental Farm 3G **202**
Orpen Rd. SO19: South 7G **175**
Orpine Cl. PO15: Titch 6J **197**
Orsmond Cl. PO7: W'lle 3N **201**
Orwell Cl. GU14: Cov 6G **29**
PO12: Gos 9L **213**
SO16: South 1D **172**
Orwell Cres. PO14: Titch C 7F **196**
Orwell Rd. GU31: Pet 2L **145**
Osborn Ct. PO3: Ports 4J **215**
Osborn Cres. PO13: Gos 4D **212**
Osborne Cl. GU34: Alt 5D **80**
PO7: W'lle 2A **202**
RG21: B'toke 4B **42**
SO31: Net A 4H **195**
Osborne Ct. GU14: Farn 3L **49**
GU51: Fleet 3L **47**
SO41: M Sea 8J **235**
Osborne Dr. GU52: Fleet 4N **47**
SO53: Cha F 7C **132**
Osborne Gdns. SO17: South 1A **174**
SO50: Fair O 1B **162**
Osborne Ho. SO14: South 8F **4**
Osborne M. SO50: E'leigh 5G **132**
Osborne Rd. BH9: Bour 6J **227**
BH14: Poole 2A **244**
BH25: New M 3B **232**
GU14: Farn 2L **49**
GU32: Pet 9M **139**
PO5: S'sea 9N **5** (5D **240**)
PO12: Gos 2M **239**
PO13: Lee S 1A **238**
SO31: Wars 9N **195**
SO40: Tott 3N **171**
SP10: A'ver 2M **69**
Osborne Rd. Nth. SO17: South 1A **174**
Osborne Rd. Sth. SO17: South 2N **173**
Osborne Vw. Rd. PO14: Stub 7K **211**
Osborn Ind. Est. RG27: Hoo 3H **45**
Osborn Mall PO16: Fare 8E **198**
Osborn Rd. GU9: Farnh 6F **64**
PO16: Fare 8D **198**
Osborn Rd. Sth. PO16: Fare 8D **198**
Osborn Sq. PO16: Fare 8E **198**
Osborn Way RG27: Hoo 3H **45**
Osbourne Ho. BH25: New M 3B **232**
SO51: W Wel 1B **120**
Osbourne Lodge BH2: Bour 6H **247** (2H **245**)
Osier Cl. PO2: Ports 6D **214**
Osier Rd. GU32: Pet 2K **145**
Oslands La. SO31: Lwr Swan 2A **196**
Osler Cl. RG26: B'ley 1G **23**
Oslo Towers SO19: South 1C **194**
Osnaburgh Hill GU15: Camb 8K **19**
Osprey Cl. BH23: Mude 9C **230**
PO6: Farl 1N **215**
RG20: Bis G 2G **9**
SO16: South 6G **158**
SO40: March 9D **172**
Osprey Ct. PO4: S'sea 2J **241**
PO16: Portc 9H **199**
Osprey Dr. PO11: H Isl 4H **243**
Osprey Gdns. GU11: Alders 3J **65**
PO13: Lee S 1B **238**
Osprey Quay PO10: S'brne 1N **217**
Osprey Rd. RG22: B'toke 1H **59**
OSSEMSLEY 6N **221**
Ossemsley Sth. Dr. BH25: Oss 7N **221**
Osterley Cl. SO30: Botl 4B **176**
Osterley Rd. SO19: South 5C **174**
Ostlers, The SO41: Hor 3H **233**

Oswald Cl. BH9: Bour 4J **227**
Oswald Rd. BH9: Bour 4J **227**
SO19: South 8B **174**
Othello Dr. PO7: W'lle 1A **202**
Ottawa Dr. GU30: Lip 3E **116**
OTTERBOURNE 2F **132**
Otterbourne BH2: Bour 5H **247** (1H **245**)
Otterbourne Cres. PO9: Hav 4D **202**
RG26: Tadl 7H **11**
Otterbourne Golf Course 8D **126**
Otterbourne Hill SO21: Ott 3E **132**
Otterbourne Ho. SO21: Ott 1F **132**
Otterbourne Ho. Gdns. SO21: Ott 2F **132**
Otterbourne Park Wood & Nature Reserve 3F **132**
Otterbourne Rd. SO21: Comp, Ott, Shaw 9G **127**
SO21: Comp, Winche 5H **127**
Otterbourne Wlk. RG27: Sher L 7J **23**
Otter Cl. GU12: Alders 8M **49**
PO13: Gos 2F **238**
SO50: B'stke 1L **161**
Otters Wlk. BH25: New M 9C **222**
OTTERWOOD 8K **207**
Ouse Cl. SO53: Cha F 4M **131**
Ouse Ct. *SP10: A'ver* *8B **52***
(off Nene Ct.)
Outer Circ. SO16: South 7F **158**
Outlands La. SO30: Curd 4G **176**
Outram Rd. PO5: S'sea 4E **240**
OUTWICK 3J **151**
Oval, The GU33: Liss 1E **140**
SP10: A'ver 7B **52**
Oval Gdns. PO12: Gos 3H **239**
Oval Rd. SO51: Lock 4A **122**
Oven Camp Site, The PO11: H Isl 2F **242**
Overbrook SO45: Hythe 7L **193**
Overbrook Way SO52: N Bad 7D **130**
Overbury Rd. BH14: Poole 2A **244**
Overcliffe Mans. BH1: Bour 2M **245**
Overcliff Ri. SO16: Bass 7K **159**
Overdale Pl. GU35: W'hil 6J **101**
Overdale Ri. GU16: Frim 1N **29**
Overdale Wlk. GU35: W'hil 6J **101**
Overdell Ct. SO15: South 1A **4** (3K **173**)
Over Links Dr. BH14: Poole 3B **244**
Overlord Cl. GU15: Camb 5L **19**
Overstrand Cres. SO41: M Sea 9K **235**
OVERTON 2E **56**
Overton Cl. GU11: Alders 4L **65**
Overton Ct. GU10: Tong 4N **65**
Overton Cres. PO9: Hav 4D **202**
Overton Hill RG25: Over 2E **56**
Overton Ho. RG25: Over 2E **56**
Overton Rd. SO21: Mich S 4J **77**
Overton Station (Rail) 9E **38**
OVER WALLOP 8M **67**
Oviat Cl. SO40: Tott 3H **171**
OVINGTON 2N **107**
Ovington Av. BH7: Bour 7F **228**
Ovington Ct. SO18: South 2H **175**
Ovington Dr. GU51: Fleet 9J **27**
Ovington Gdns. BH7: Bour 7F **228**
Ovington Rd. SO50: E'leigh 2E **160**
Owen Cl. PO13: Gos 9E **212**
Owen Ho. *PO3: Ports* *1G **241***
(off Whitcombe Gdns.)
Owen Rd. SO50: E'leigh 1D **160**
Owens Rd. SO22: Winche 5K **105**
Owen St. PO4: S'sea 5H **241**
Owen Way RG24: B'toke 3M **41**
OWER
SO45 8J **209**
SO51 5F **156**
Ower Farm La. SO32: Uph 7G **134**
Ower La. SO45: Cals 8J **209**
OWER SERVICE AREA 4F **156**
OWLSMOOR 4G **18**
Owlsmoor Rd. GU47: Coll, Owl 5F **18**
Owls Rd. BH5: Bour 2A **246**
Owl Wlk. SO21: Owls 7B **134**
OWSLEBURY 5C **134**
Owslebury Bottom SO21: Owls 4C **134**
Owslebury Gro. PO9: Hav 4F **202**
Oxburgh Cl. SO50: E'leigh 7D **132**
Ox Drove RG20: Ashm 6N **7**
RG20: Burgh 3D **8**
SO21: Craw 2L **89**
SO20: Craw 2L **89**
SO21: More 2C **134**
SO21: Sth W 3K **91**
SP5: Br Ch, Com B 6A **118**
SP11: And D, Pic P 9E **52**
SP11: Kimp 9K **31**
Ox Drove, The RG25: Pres C 7F **78**
SO24: Ch Can, Up Wield 8D **78**
Ox Drove Ri. SP11: Pic P 7G **53**
Ox Drove Way SO24: Up Wield 9G **79**
Oxenbourne Down (Local Nature Reserve) 1E **168**
Oxenbourne La. GU32: E Meon 5A **144**
Oxenden Ct. GU10: Tong 2N **65**
Oxenden Rd. GU10: Tong 2N **65**
Oxendown SO32: Meon 9N **135**
Oxenham Mdws. SO20: Mid Wa 4A **72**
OXENWOOD 5A **6**
Oxenwood Grn. PO9: Hav 3D **202**
Oxey Cl. BH25: New M 5B **232**
Oxford Av. BH6: Bour 9E **228**
SO14: South 3E **4** (4M **173**)
Oxford Cl. PO16: Fare 7B **198**
Oxford La. BH11: Bour 1F **226**
SO32: Drox 3G **165**
Oxford M. SO14: South 8E **4** (7M **173**)
Oxford Rd. BH8: Bour 1M **245**
GU14: Farn 2L **49**
GU47: Owl 3G **19**
PO5: S'sea 4F **240**
PO12: Gos 2H **239**
SO14: South 3M **173**
SO21: Sut S 7D **76**
Oxford St. SO14: South 8E **4** (7M **173**)

Oxford Ter. SO41: Sway 5K **223**
Oxford Way RG24: B'toke 2B **42**
Oxlease Cl. SO51: Rom 3N **129**
Oxlease La. RG25: Herr 9F **60**
Oxleys Cl. PO14: Fare 9L **197**
Oxted Ct. PO4: S'sea 2J **241**
Oysell Gdns. PO16: Fare 8H **199**
Oyster Cl. RG22: B'toke 3K **59**
Oyster Est. PO6: Farl 1L **215**
Oyster M. BH13: Poole 3E **244**
PO1: Ports 7J **5** (4B **240**)
Oyster Quay PO6: P Sol 1C **214**
SO31: Hamb 7L **195**
Oyster St. PO1: Ports 7J **5** (4B **240**)
Oyster Vw. PO13: Lee S 9N **211**
Ozier Rd. SO18: South 9E **160**

P

Paccombe SP5: Redl 1M **119** (7C **120**)
Pacific Cl. SO14: South 8N **173**
Packenham Rd. RG21: B'toke 8A **42**
Pack La. RG22: B'toke 9J **41**
RG23: Oak, Wort 8D **40**
Packridge La. SO51: Toot 2D **158**
Padbury Cl. PO2: Ports 4G **215**
Paddington Cl. BH11: Bour 2B **226**
Paddington Gro. BH11: Bour 3B **226**
Paddington Ho. *RG21: B'toke* *6C **42***
(off Festival Pl.)
Paddington Rd. PO2: Ports 7G **214**
Paddock, The BH25: New M 7L **231**
GU26: Gray 3J **103**
GU35: Head 2A **102**
PO12: Gos 4J **239**
PO14: Stub 4M **211**
RG20: Kings 2A **6** (6K **9**)
RG27: H Win 5C **26**
SO21: Itc A 9J **93**
SO23: Kin W 9N **91**
SO40: Calm 9J **157**
SO41: Sway 5J **223**
SO42: Broc 7C **148**
SO50: E'leigh 6F **132**
SP6: Frog 7A **154**
Paddock Cl. BH24: St I 4C **186**
SO21: Sth W 3J **91**
SP4: Win D 3A **86**
Paddock Ct. RG27: H Win 7B **26**
Paddock End PO7: Den 7G **181**
Paddock Fld. SO20: Chil 3G **74**
Paddock Flds. RG24: Old Bas 4J **43**
SO20: Mid Wa 4B **72**
Paddock Gdns. SO41: Lymi 1D **234**
Paddock Rd. RG22: B'toke 8M **41**
Paddocks, The BH10: Bour 2H **227**
SO45: Fawl 5F **208**
Paddock Vw. SO22: Lit 1E **104**
Paddock Wlk. PO6: Cosh 9B **200**
RG22: B'toke 8M **41**
Paddock Way GU30: Lip 1D **116**
GU32: Pet 2K **145**
SO24: New A 2E **108**
Padfield Cl. BH6: Bour 8H **229**
Padget Rd. BH24: Poul 8M **185**
Padnell Av. PO8: Cowp 7A **182**
Padnell Pl. PO8: Cowp 8B **182**
Padnell Rd. PO8: Cowp 7A **182**
Padstow Pl. SP6: F'dge 2H **153**
Padwell Rd. SO14: South 3M **173**
Padwick Av. PO6: Cosh 9H **201**
Padwick Cl. RG21: B'toke 7B **42**
Padwick Ct. PO11: H Isl 4E **242**
Paffard Cl. PO13: Gos 9E **212**
Page Cl. SO45: Holb 6B **208**
Pages Bungs. RG21: B'toke 6D **42**
Pages La. SO42: Beau 1B **236**
Paget Cl. SP9: Tidw 6B **30** (6F **30**)
Paget Ho. SO16: Nur 5A **158**
Paget Rd. BH11: Bour 2E **226**
PO12: Gos 5J **239**
Paget St. SO14: South 7G **4** (7N **173**)
Pagham Cl. PO10: S'brne 9N **203**
Pagham Gdns. PO11: H Isl 5M **243**
Paice La. GU34: Meds 3E **96**
Paices Hill RG7: A'mas 2F **10**
Paignton Av. PO3: Ports 8H **215**
Paignton Rd. SO16: South 1E **172**
Paimpol Pl. SO51: Rom 6L **129**
Pain's Rd. PO5: S'sea 3E **240**
Painswick Cl. PO6: Cosh 9D **200**
SO31: Sar G 3C **196**
Painter Cl. PO3: Ports 5J **215**
Painters Fld. SO23: Winche 1J **127**
Painters Mdw. SP11: Pic P 7F **52**
Painters Pightle RG27: Hoo 2F **44**
Paisley Rd. BH6: Bour 9F **228**
Pakenham Dr. GU11: Alders 8J **49**
Palace Cinema, The 4F **80**
Palace Cl. SO20: Ki S 9A **86** (7F **88**)
Palace Ga. RG29: Odi 8K **45**
Palace Ga. Farm RG29: Odi 8K **45**
Palace House 7E **206**
Palace La. SO42: Beau 7E **206**
Palace M. SO32: Bis W 4M **163**
Pale La. GU52: Elve 8G **27**
RG27: Winchf 3E **46**
Palermo Ct. BH2: Bour 7H **247** (2H **245**)
PALESTINE 6K **67**
Palestine Rd. SP11: Pale 6J **67**
Palfrey Rd. BH10: Bour 2H **227**
Paling Bus. Pk. SO30: Hed E 6M **175**
Palk Rd. PO9: Bed 7D **202**
Pallant, The PO9: Hav 8F **202**
Pallant Gdns. PO16: Fare 7F **198**
Pallet Cl. SO21: Col C 4K **133**
Pallot Cl. SO31: Burs 9K **175**
Palma Apartments BH25: New M 7L **231**
Palm Ct. PO5: S'sea 5D **240**
Palmer Dr. SP10: A'ver 1C **70**

Palmer Pl. BH25: New M 2B **232**
Palmers Cl. SO50: Fair O 1A **162**
Palmer's Rd. PO10: Ems 8M **203**
Palmers Rd. Ind. Est. PO10: Ems 8M **203**
Palmerston Av. BH23: Chri 8N **229**
PO16: Fare 8D **198**
Palmerston Bus. Pk. PO14: Fare 1C **212**
Palmerston Cl. GU14: Cov 9F **28**
Palmerston Ct. *PO5: S'sea* *5D **240***
(off Clarence Pde.)
SO23: Winche 9K **105**
Palmerston Dr. PO14: Fare 1C **212**
Palmerston Hgts. BH1: Bour 9B **228**
Palmerston Ho. SO14: South 7D **4**
SO51: Rom *5N **129***
(off Fryers Cl.)
Palmerston Indoor Bowls Club 1C **212**
Palmerston Mans. *PO5: S'sea* *5D **240***
(off Palmerston Rd.)
Palmerston M. BH1: Bour 9B **228**
Palmerston Pl. SP10: A'ver 1C **70**
Palmerston Rd. BH1: Bour 9B **228**
BH14: Poole 1B **244**
PO5: S'sea 5D **240**
PO11: H Isl 3G **242**
SO14: South 4D **4** (5M **173**)
Palmerston St. SO51: Rom 5L **129**
Palmerston Way PO12: Gos 5G **239**
Palmers Yd. RG20: Ecc 4H **9**
Palm Hall Cl. SO23: Winche 7N **105**
Palm Rd. SO16: South 8F **158**
Palmyra Rd. PO12: Gos 9J **213**
Palomino Dr. PO15: White 2E **196**
Pamber Dr. GU51: Fleet 9J **27**
PAMBER END 3L **21**
Pamber Forest (Nature Reserve) 7M **11**
PAMBER GREEN 9L **11**
PAMBER HEATH 4L **11**
Pamber Heath Rd. RG26: Pam H 5K **11**
Pamber Rd. RG7: Sil 4N **11**
RG26: Cha A 4H **21**
Pamela Av. PO6: Cosh 8A **200**
Pamplyn Cl. SO41: Lymi 2C **234**
Pangbourne Av. PO6: Cosh 1J **215**
Pangbourne Cl. SO19: South 6E **174**
Pankridge St. GU10: Cron 3L **63**
Pannall Rd. PO12: Gos 9J **213**
Panorama BH14: Poole 2B **244**
Panorama Rd. BH13: S'bks 9A **244**
Pan St. PO1: Ports 1N **5** (1D **240**)
Pansy Rd. SO16: Bass 7M **159**
Pantheon Rd. SO53: Cha F 5D **132**
Pantile Dr. RG27: Hoo 2J **45**
Pantiles, The SP6: F'dge 1G **153**
Pantings La. RG20: High 4A **8**
Panton Cl. PO10: Ems 6L **203**
Panwell Rd. SO18: South 3E **174**
Papermakers RG25: Over 3E **56**
Paper Mill La. GU34: Alt 4G **80**
Parade, The BH6: Bour 2H **247**
BH25: A'ley 3E **232**
GU16: Frim 4M **29**
GU46: Yat 7A **18**
PO1: Ports 2J **5** (1B **240**)
PO13: Gos 5D **212**
PO14: Stub 5M **211**
PO31: Cowes 5P **237**
RG21: B'toke 5D **42**
RG26: Tadl 4H **11**
Parade Ct. PO2: Ports 3F **214**
Paradise La. PO10: Westb 5N **203**
PO16: Fare 8G **198**
(not continuous)
SO32: Bis W, Wal C 5A **164**
SO40: Woodl 4D **170**
Paradise St. PO1: Ports 2N **5** (1D **240**)
Parcel Dr. RG24: B'toke 4N **41**
Parchment, The PO9: Hav 8F **202**
Parchment St. SO23: Winche 8M **237** (7L **105**)
(not continuous)
Pardoe Cl. SO30: Hed E 5N **175**
PARDOWN 3D **58**
Pardown RG23: Oak 3D **58**
Parfitts Cl. GU9: Farnh 8C **64**
Parham Cl. BH25: New M 3N **231**
Parham Dr. SO50: E'leigh 8D **132**
Parham Ho. GU30: Lip 1F **116**
Parham Rd. BH10: Bour 4G **226**
PO12: Gos 1L **239**
Parish Cl. GU9: Up H 4C **64**
Parish Ct. SO41: Lymi 2E **234**
Parish Rd. GU14: Farn 3L **49**
Park, The BH25: New M 7L **231**
SO32: Drox 2J **165**
Park & Ride
East Winchester (Barfield) 8M **105**
East Winchester (St Catherine's) 9M **105**
Leisure Park 6M **41**
Portsmouth 1D **214**
South Winchester 4J **127**
Park App. PO17: K Vil 2A **198**
Park Av. GU15: Camb 9L **19**
PO7: Purb, Wid 7K **201**
RG24: Old Bas 6J **43**
SO23: Winche 6N **237** (6L **105**)
SO41: Lymi 2D **234**
Parkbury BH13: Poole 2E **244**
Park Cl. BH23: Burt 3M **229**
BH25: A'ley 1D **232**
BH25: B Sea 7A **232**
GU10: Hol P 9M **63**
GU35: K'ly 7H **83**
PO12: Gos 1H **239**
RG23: Oak 9C **40**
SO23: Winche 4L **105**
SO40: March 9C **172**
SO41: M Sea 8L **235**
SO42: Broc 6D **148**
SO45: Hythe 5N **193**
Park Cl. Rd. GU34: Alt 3G **80**
Park Corner Rd. RG27: H Win 5C **26**

Park Cottage Dr.—Penarth Av.

Park Cottage Dr. PO15: Seg 6J **197**
Park Cotts. SP5: Redl 1M **119** (7C **120**)
Park Ct. BH13: Poole 2F **244**
GU9: Farnh 7F **64**
PO5: S'sea 7N **5** (4D **240**)
SO15: South 4H **173**
SO23: Winche 4L **105**
SO41: M Sea 8J **235**
SO51: Rom 7B **130**
Park Crematorium, The GU12: Alders 4M **65**
Park Cres. PO10: Ems 8K **203**
Park Drove SO20: Ov Wa 7N **67**
Parker Cl. PO12: Gos 7J **213**
Parker Gdns. PO7: Wid 7K **201**
Parker Rd. BH9: Bour 7K **227**
Parkers Cl. BH24: Poul 8M **185**
SP5: Down 1J **119** (6A **120**)
Parkers Trade Pk. GU32: Pet 1K **145**
Park Farm Av. PO15: Fare 5M **197**
Park Farm Cl. PO15: Fare 6N **197**
Park Farm Ind. Est. GU16: Camb 3L **29**
Park Farm Rd. PO7: Purb 5L **201**
Parkfield Ho. PO6: Cosh 7A **200**
RG45: Cr'tne 1E 18
(off Cambridge Rd.)
Parkfields GU46: Yat 8N **17**
Park Gdns. BH23: Chri 7A **230**
RG21: B'toke 8D **42**
PARK GATE 4E **196**
Park Gate BH25: New M 4B **232**
Park Gate Bus. Cen. SO31: P Ga 3E **196**
Parkgate Mnr. BH2: Bour 6J **247**
Park Gate M. BH2: Bour 7J **247**
Park Glen SO31: P Ga 5F **196**
Park Gro. PO6: Cosh 1G **215**
Park Hill GU52: Ch Cr 6L **47**
RG24: Old Bas 5H **43**
Parkhill SO21: W Str 5L **77**
Parkhill Cl. GU17: Blackw 9F **18**
SO45: Holb 5A **208**
Parkhill Rd. GU17: Blackw 9F **18**
Park Ho. PO5: S'sea 9N **5** (5D **240**)
SO23: Winche 6N **237**
Park Ho. Farm Way PO9: Hav 5B **202**
Parkhouse M. SP4: Chol 3G **66**
Parkhouse Rd. SP9: Shi B 2A **66** (1F **66**)
Parkhurst Flds. GU10: Chur 7H **85**
Parkland Cl. BH31: Ver 5A **184**
Parkland Dr. BH25: B Sea 6A **232**
Parkland Gro. GU9: Weyb 2H **65**
Parkland Pl. BH25: New M 4B **232**
SO17: South 2M 173
(off Westwood Rd.)
Parklands *BH4: Bour 9G 226*
(off Branksome Hill Rd.)
BH4: Bour 2G **244**
(Grosvenor Rd.)
PO7: Den 7G **180**
SO18: South 1C **174**
SO31: Sar G 5D **196**
SO40: Tott 2N **171**
Parklands Av. PO8: Cowp 5A **182**
PO8: Horn 5A **182**
Parklands Bus. Pk. PO7: Den 7G **180**
Parklands Cl. PO12: Gos 1K **239**
SO53: Cha F 5A **132**
Parkland Way SP4: Port 9B **66**
Park La. BH10: Bour 2K **227**
BH21: Wim G 7G **148**
GU10: Chur 7D **84**
GU15: Camb 8L **19**
GU34: Lwr Froy 8H **63**
PO6: Cosh 9H **201**
PO7: W'lle 9B **182**
PO8: Cowp 8A **182**
PO9: Bed 7C **202**
PO9: Hav 1C **202**
PO14: Stub 5M **211**
PO16: Fare 6D **198**
RG7: Mort, Stra S 4F **12**
RG19: Head 2L **9**
RG24: Old Bas 6J **43**
RG40: F'std 2C **16**
SO15: South 3B **4** (5L **173**)
SO21: Abb W 9A **92**
SO21: Ott 3F **132**
SO21: Twyf 8L **127**
SO24: Rop 5B **110**
SO32: Drox 2K **165**
SO32: Swanm 3D **164**
SO40: March 8B **172**
SO41: M Sea 8J **235**
SO42: Beau 4D **236**
SO45: Holb 4N **207**
SO50: E'leigh 3F **132**
SP5: Mid W 8G **87**
SP6: Ald 4C **152**
SP11: Quar 3L **67**
Park Lodge *BH8: Bour 7M 227*
(off Richmond Pk. Rd.)
Park Mans. BH8: Bour 7N **227**
PO6: Cosh 1H **215**
Park M. SO31: P Ga 4E **196**
Park Mt. SO24: New A 9F **94**
Park Pde. PO9: Hav 5E **202**
Park Pl. GU17: Haw 1H **29**
GU52: Ch Cr 6L **47**
Park Prewett Rd. RG24: B'toke 3L **41**
Park Rd. BH8: Bour 1L **245**
BH25: A'ley 1D **232**
BH25: New M 5A **232**
GU9: Farnh 6F **64**
GU11: Alders 2K **65**
GU14: Farn 2N **49**
GU15: Camb 1K **29**
GU31: S Hart 9F **146**
GU32: Pet 1M **145**
GU47: Sandh 6E **18**
PO1: Ports 5K **5** (3B **240**)
PO7: Den 5G **180**
PO7: Purb 5K **201**
Park Rd. PO11: H Isl 3C **242**
PO12: Gos 5K **239**
SO15: South 4H **173**
SO22: Winche 4K **105**
SO23: Winche 4K **105**
SO32: Bis W 3K **163**
SO41: Lymi 2D **234**
SO41: M Sea 8L **235**
SO53: Cha F 4A **132**
SP6: F'dge 9J **151**
SP9: Tidw 8D **30** (7G **31**)
Park Rd. Nth. PO9: Hav 7E **202**
Park Rd. Rdbt.
GU14: Farn 3N **49**
Park Rd. Sth. PO9: Hav 8F **202**
Park Row GU9: Farnh 7D **64**
Park Royal PO2: Ports 5F **214**
Parkside BH23: Chri 5F **230**
BH24: Ring 2K **187**
GU9: Up H 4E **64**
PO9: Bed 7C **202**
SO40: Tott 5M **171**
Parkside Av. SO16: South 2C **172**
Parkside Cl. PO7: Purb 5K **201**
Parkside Gdns. BH10: Bour 4J **227**
SO22: Winche 4G **105**
Parkside La. SO24: Rop 4B **110**
Parkside Rd. BH14: Poole 1A **244**
RG21: B'toke 8D **42**
Parkside Wlk.
BH25: New M 4B 232
(off Park Vw.)
PARKSTONE 1A **244**
Parkstone Av. BH14: Poole 1A **244**
PO4: S'sea 6F **240**
Parkstone Dr. GU15: Camb 9L **19**
Parkstone Golf Course 3B **244**
Parkstone La. PO4: S'sea 5F **240**
Parkstone Rd. SO24: Rop 4D **110**
Park St. GU15: Camb 7L **19**
GU35: Bor 4J **101**
PO5: S'sea 6M **5** (3C **240**)
PO12: Gos 2K **239**
SO16: South 2G **173**
Park Terraces PO12: Gos 3L **239**
Park Vw. BH7: Bour 8B **228**
BH25: New M 4B **232**
PO9: R Cas 1H **203**
RG7: Bee H 1B **14**
RG28: Whit 6F **54**
SO14: South 4E **4**
SO21: Shaw 7J **127**
SO30: Botl 3D **176**
SO30: Hed E 3M **175**
SO50: E'leigh 9E 132
(off Newtown Rd.)
Parkview BH2: Bour 5K **247**
Parkview Cl. SP10: A'ver 8L **51**
Park Vw. Ct. BH8: Bour 7N **227**
Park Vw. Ho. *GU11: Alders 9J 49*
(off High St.)
PO16: Fare 5D **198**
Park Vs. GU17: Haw 2H **29**
SP6: Dame 6A **150**
Parkville Rd. SO16: S'ing 7B **160**
Park Vista GU32: E Meon 3L **143**
Park Wlk. PO15: Fare 6N **197**
SO14: South 4D **4** (5M **173**)
Parkwater Rd. SP5: W'psh 5N **121**
Park Way PO9: Hav 8E **202**
SO50: Fair O 1B **162**
Parkway GU15: Camb 1L **29**
PO15: White 2H **197**
PO16: Fare 6D **198**
RG45: Cr'tne 1C **18**
Parkway, The PO13: Gos 6D **212**
SO16: Bass 6M **159**
Parkway Ct. SO53: Cha F 5B **132**
Parkway Dr. BH8: Bour 6B **228**
Parkway Gdns. SO53: Cha F 5A **132**
Parkway Retail Pk. BH8: Bour 1M **245**
Parkwood Cen. PO7: W'lle 1M **201**
Parkwood Cl. RG24: Chin 8G **23**
SO30: Hed E 3A **176**
Parkwood La. *BH5: Bour 9E 228*
(off Seabourne Rd.)
Parkwood Rd. BH5: Bour 9D **228**
Parley Golf Course 8A **218**
Parley Grn. La. BH23: E Par 8A **218**
Parley Rd. BH9: Bour 4L **227**
Parliament Pl. SO22: Oli B 1G **126**
Parmiter Ho. *SO23: Winche 6M 105*
(off Wales St.)
Parnell Ct. SP10: A'ver 9J **51**
Parnell La. SO51: Brai, Mich 3L **123**
Parnell Rd. SO50: E'leigh 1D **160**
Parnholt La. SO51: Brai 3C **124**
Parr Rd. PO6: Cosh 9E **200**
Parry Cl. PO6: Cosh 9N **199**
Parry Ct. PO12: Gos 2L **239**
Parry Rd. SO19: South 6H **175**
Parsonage Barn La. BH24: Ring 9K **185**
Parsonage Cl. GU32: Pet 8A **140**
GU34: Up Farr 4E **98**
SP6: F'dge 1J **153**
Parsonage Est. GU31: Rog 9L **141**
Parsonage Hill SP5: Far 8E **86**
Parsonage La. SO32: Durl 5E **162**
Parsonage Pk. Dr. SP6: F'dge 9H **151**
Parsonage Rd. BH1: Bour 7N **247** (2L **245**)
SO14: South 4N **173**
Parsonage Way GU16: Frim 3N **29**
Parsons Cl. GU11: Alders 9L **49**
GU52: Ch Cr 6L **47**
PO3: Ports 4G **215**
Parsons Fld. GU47: Sandh 5D **18**
Parsons La. GU26: Hind 1L **103**
Part La. RG7: Rise 1J **15**
Partnership Bus. Park, The
PO4: S'sea 2G **241**
Partridge Av. GU46: Yat 7L **17**
Partridge Cl. BH23: Mude 9C **230**
GU10: Ews 2N 63
(off Badger Way)
GU16: Frim 3N **29**
PO16: Portc 9G **199**
RG22: B'toke 3H **59**
SO21: Bar S 5A **76**
Partridge Down SO22: Oli B 2F **126**
Partridge Dr. BH14: Poole 4A **244**
Partridge Gdns. PO8: Cowp 6L **181**
Partridge Grn. BH25: New M 9C **222**
GU34: Alt 3F **80**
Partridge Hill SP5: L'ford 9L **121**
Partridge Rd. SO42: Broc 8C **148** (9N **189**)
SO45: Dib P 8L **193**
Partridge Wlk. BH14: Poole 4A **244**
Partry Cl. SO53: Cha F 4M **131**
Passage La. SO31: Wars 8M **195**
PASSFIELD 6A **102**
Passfield Av. SO50: E'leigh 1C **160**
Passfield Cl. SO50: E'leigh 1C **160**
Passfield Ent. Cen. GU30: Pass 7N **101**
Passfield Mill Bus. Pk. GU30: Pass 6N **101**
Passfield Rd. GU30: Pass 7A **102**
Passfield Wlk. PO9: Hav 4H **203**
Passford Hill SO41: Bold 8D **224**
Passingham Wlk. PO8: Cowp 6A **182**
Pasteur Rd. PO6: Cosh 9F **200**
Pastures, The PO7: Den 6F **180**
PO14: Titch C 5F **196**
SO23: Kin W 6M **91**
SO24: Cher 8E **108**
SO50: E'leigh 1E 160
(off Cranbury Rd.)
Pasture Wlk. SP11: E Ant 6B **52**
Pat Bear Cl. SO15: South 2B **172**
Patchins, The BH14: Poole 5A **244**
Patchway Dr. PO14: Fare 9M **197**
Paternoster Ho. SO23: Winche 8N **237**
Paternoster Row SO23: Winche 8N **237** (7L **105**)
Paterson Cl. RG22: B'toke 3L **59**
Paterson Rd. GU33: Longc 4H **115**
Pathfinders, The GU14: Cov 9E **28**
Patricia Cl. SO30: Wes E 9H **161**
Patricia Dr. SO30: Hed E 3A **176**
Patrick Howard Dobson Ct. PO8: Cowp 6N **181**
Patrick's Cl. GU33: Liss 1F **140**
Patrick's Copse Rd. GU33: Liss 1F **140**
Patten Av. GU46: Yat 8M **17**
Patterdale Ho. PO6: Cosh 8C **200**
Pattersons La. PO8: Blen 4E **182**
Pattinson Cres. SP11: A'ver 2G **69**
Paul Cl. GU11: Alders 2G **65**
Paulet Cl. GU51: Fleet 9K **27**
SO18: South 1E **174**
Paulet Lacave Av. SO16: Nur 5C **158**
Paulet Pl. RG24: Old Bas 5J **43**
SO22: Winche 9J **105**
Pauletts La. SO40: Calm 9H **157**
Paul's Fld. RG27: Eve 5G **17**
PAULSGROVE 9C **200**
Paulsgrove Ent. Cen. PO6: Cosh 9C **200**
Paulsgrove Ind. Cen. PO6: Cosh 9C **200**
Paulsgrove Rd. PO2: Ports 8G **214**
Pauls La. SO41: Sway 7L **223**
Paulson Cl. SO53: Cha F 4A **132**
Paultons Golf Centre & Golf Course 4C **156**
Paultons Park 5C **156**
Paultons Park Watermill 5E **156**
Pauncefoot Hill SO51: Rom 1H **157**
Pauncefote Rd. BH5: Bour 9D **228**
Pauntley Rd. BH23: Chri 8A **230**
Pavan Gdns. BH10: Bour 3G **226**
Pavilion Cl. SO50: Fair O 3N **161**
Pavilion Ct. SO15: South 3K **173**
Pavilion Gdns. SO45: Blac 7C **208**
Pavilion La. GU11: Alders 8G **48**
Pavilion on the Park 1B **160**
Pavilion Rd. GU11: Alders 1G **64**
SO30: Botl, Hed E 2A **176**
Pavilions End, The GU15: Camb 1M **29**
Pavilion Theatre
Bournemouth 8M **247** (3K **245**)
Pavilion Way PO12: Gos 2M **239**
Paviours GU9: Farnh 7D **64**
Pawmers Mead GU52: Ch Cr 8K **47**
Pax Hill GU10: Ben'ly 7J **63**
Paxton Cl. RG22: B'toke 3K **59**
SO30: Hed E 5A **176**
Paxton Ct. SO31: Loc H 7D **196**
Paxton Rd. PO14: Fare 8B **198**
Paynes Cl. RG19: Head 3K **9**
SO20: Brou 1A **86**
Paynes Hay Rd. SO51: Brai 5A **124**
Paynes La. SO20: Brou 1A **86** (4A **88**)
SO50: Fair O 9N **133**
Paynes Mdw. RG24: Lych 3H **43**
Paynes Pl. SO30: Hed E 9N **161**
Payne's Rd. SO15: South 4H **173**
(not continuous)
Peabody Rd. GU14: Farn 2M **49**
Peace Cl. BH23: Bran 7C **220**
Peach Gro. SP11: Pale 6K **67**
Peach Rd. SO16: South 7F **158**
Peach Tree Cl. GU14: Farn 5J **29**
Peacock Cl. PO16: Portc 9G **199**
Peacock La. PO1: Ports 7K **5** (4B **240**)
Peacock Pl. SO23: Winche 6N **105**
Peacock Trad. Est. SO50: E'leigh 8C **132**
Peak, The PO9: R Cas 7J **183**
Peak Cl. SO16: South 2E **172**
Peak Dr. PO14: Fare 9N **197**
Peake Cl. RG24: Lych 4G **43**
PEAKED HILL 8L **49**
Peake New Rd. SO32: Warn 6P **135**
Peakfield GU10: Fren 1E **84**
PO7: Den 6F **180**
Peak La. PO14: Fare 1N **211**
SO32: Bis W, Uph 8F **134**
Peak Rd. PO8: Clan 6A **168**
Pealsham Gdns. SP6: F'dge 9H **151**
Pearce Ct. PO12: Gos 2L **239**
Pearcesmith Ct. BH25: B Sea 7N **231**
Pearces Pl. RG20: Kings 2B **6**
Pear Cl. BH12: Poole 1F **244**
Pearl Gdns. BH10: Bour 2G **227**
Pearl Rd. BH10: Bour 2G **227**
Pearman Ct. SO41: Penn 4C **234**
Pearman Dr. SO41: Lymi 4F **234**
SP10: A'ver 1C **70**
Pearson Av. BH14: Poole 9A **226**
Pearson Gdns. BH10: Bour 1H **227**
Pearson Ho. PO12: Gos 9M **213**
Pear Tree Av. GU51: Fleet 1L **47**
Peartree Av. SO19: South 6C **174**
Pear Tree Cl. BH23: Bran 7D **220**
GU35: Lind 3L **101**
SO32: Botl 9C **162**
SO51: W Wel 1A **120**
SP6: Ald 4C **152**
Peartree Cl. PO14: Stub 5N **211**
SO19: South 6B **174**
Peartree Ct. SO41: Lymi 4E **234**
Pear Tree Dr. SP5: L'ford 2J **155**
Peartree Gdns. SO19: South 4E **174**
PEARTREE GREEN 6C **174**
Pear Tree Rd. GU35: Lind 3L **101**
Peartree Rd. SO19: South 6B **174**
SO45: Dib P 7K **193**
Pear Tree Way RG21: B'toke 4D **42**
Pease Cft. GU31: S Hart 9G **146**
Peatmoor Cl. GU51: Fleet 1K **47**
Pebble Cl. PO11: H Isl 5H **243**
Pebble Ct. PO11: H Isl 6K **243**
SO40: March 8E **172**
Pebbles BH6: Bour 2J **247**
Pebmarsh Rd. PO6: Cosh 9E **200**
Pecche Pl. RG24: Old Bas 1H **43**
Peckham Av. BH25: New M 4B **232**
Peckham Cl. PO14: Titch C 7F **196**
Pedam Cl. PO4: S'sea 4H **241**
Peddlars Gro. GU46: Yat 7A **18**
Peddlars Wlk. BH24: Ring 1J **187**
Peel Cl. BH12: Poole 9A **226**
GU35: W'hil 6H **101**
SO51: Rom 3B **130**
PEEL COMMON 6C **212**
Peel Ct. BH23: Chri 8J **229**
GU14: Farn 3L **49**
RG27: H Win 6B **26**
Peel Gdns. RG20: Kings 1A **6** (5K **9**)
Peel Pl. PO5: S'sea 6N **5** (3D **240**)
Peel Rd. PO12: Gos 2L **239**
Peel St. SO14: South 5A **174**
Peewit Hill SO31: Burs 7L **175**
Peewit Hill Cl. SO31: Burs 7L **175**
Pegasus Av. GU12: Alders 8N **49**
SO41: Hor 4H **233**
Pegasus Cl. GU27: Hasl 1M **117**
PO13: Gos 2F **238**
SO16: South 7E **158**
SO31: Hamb 7K **195**
Pegasus Ct. BH1: Bour 9L **227**
BH25: New M 3B **232**
GU12: Alders 1N **65**
GU51: Fleet 1L **47**
RG28: Whit 4G **54**
Pegasus Rd. GU14: Cov 5H **29**
Peggotty Ho. PO1: Ports 9E **214**
Peggotty Pl. GU47: Owl 3G **18**
Peggs Way RG24: B'toke 3M **41**
Pegham Ind. Pk. PO15: F'ley 3M **197**
Peked Mede RG27: Hoo 2K **45**
Pekelond RG27: Hoo 2K **45**
Pelham BH13: Poole 1E **244**
Pelham Cl. BH23: Chri 8N **229**
GU35: W'hil 6J **101**
RG24: Old Bas 6J **43**
Pelham Rd. PO5: S'sea 8N **5** (4D **240**)
PO12: Gos 2K **239**
Pelham Rd. Pas. PO5: S'sea 7N **5** (4D **240**)
Pelham Ter. PO10: Ems 9N **203**
Pelican Cl. PO15: Fare 7N **197**
Pelican Ct. SO21: Hurs 6N **125**
SP10: A'ver 9A **52**
Pelican Mead BH24: Hight 2M **187**
Pelican Rd. PO14: Fare 3B **212**
RG26: Pam H 3L **11**
Pellows, The RG20: Kings 2C **6** (6L **9**)
Pelton Rd. RG21: B'toke 5A **42**
Pemberley Pl. *RG24: B'toke 3N 41*
(off Priestley Rd.)
Pembers Cl. SO50: Fair O 1A **162**
Pemberton Rd. SO43: Lyn 2C **148**
Pembrey Cl. SO16: South 6E **158**
Pembridge Ho. SP6: F'dge 1K **153**
Pembridge Rd. SP6: F'dge 8K **151**
Pembroke B'way. GU15: Camb 8L **19**
Pembroke Chambers PO1: Ports 7K **5**
Pembroke Cl. PO1: Ports 7K **5** (4B **240**)
SO40: Tott 2N **171**
SO50: E'leigh 7D **132**
SO51: Rom 5M **129**
Pembroke Ct. BH23: Highc 7J **231**
PO13: Gos 7E **212**
SO17: South 1M **173**
SP10: A'ver 1A **70**
Pembroke Cres. PO14: Stub 6K **211**
Pembroke Pde. GU46: Yat 6A **18**
Pembroke Pl. BH4: Bour 3F **244**
Pembroke Rd. BH4: Bour 3F **244**
BH12: Poole 7B **226**
PO1: Ports 7K **5** (4B **240**)
(not continuous)
RG23: B'toke 6K **41**
SO19: South 6F **174**
Pembury Pl. GU12: Alders 1L **65**
Pembury Rd. PO9: Warb 9G **203**
PO14: Stub 4N **211**
Pemerton Rd. RG21: B'toke 4D **42**
SO22: Winche 3H **105**
Penarth Av. PO6: Dray 9J **201**

Penarth Cl.—Pintail Cl.

Penarth Cl. SO19: South 4G 174
Penbere Cl. RG26: Pam H 3L 11
Pen Cl. SP10: A'ver 2B 70
Pen Craig BH13: Poole 2F 244
Pendarvis Ct. GU26: Gray 4L 103
Pendennis BH1: Bour 1N 245
Pendennis Cl. RG23: B'toke 5K 41
Pendennis Ct. RG23: B'toke 5K 41
Pendennis Rd. PO6: Cosh 8A 200
Pendle Cl. SO16: South 2E 172
Pendle Grn. SO51: Lock 2N 121
Pendleton Gdns. SO45: Blac 7C 208
Pendula Way SO50: B'stke 7J 133
Penelope Ct. BH23: Highc 7K 231
Penelope Gdns. SO31: Burs 9K 175
Penfold Cft. GU9: Farnh 6H 65
Penfold Way PO9: Hav 3C 202
Penford Paddock SO32: Bis W 4N 163
Pengelly Av. BH10: Bour 1J 227
Pengilly Rd. GU9: Farnh 8D 64
Penhale Gdns. PO14: Titch C 8E 196
Penhale Rd. PO1: Ports 2F 240
Penhale Way SO40: Tott 5L 171
Penhurst Rd. PO9: Bed 7B 202
Peninsula Hgts. BH13: Poole 6C 244
Peninsula Rd. SO22: Winche 9J 237 (7J 105)
Peninsular Pl. RG45: Cr'tne 1E 18
Peninsula Sq. SO23: Winche 8K 237 (7K 105)
Penistone Cl. SO19: South 8E 174
Penjar Av. PO7: Purb 5K 201
Penk Ridge PO9: Bed 9N 201
Pennant Hills PO9: Bed 7B 202
Pennant Pk. PO16: Fare 6E 198
Pennant Way BH23: Chri 7B 230
Pennard Way SO53: Cha F 8M 131
Penn Cl. BH25: B Sea 5N 231
Pennefather's Rd. GU11: Alders 8H 49
Pennerly Ct. PO9: Hav 2D 202
Penner Rd. PO9: Hav 1E 216
Penn Hill Av. BH14: Poole 2B 244
Penn Hill Ct. BH14: Poole 2C 244
Pennine Cl. RG22: B'toke 8K 41
Pennine Ct. *BH23: Chri* *6B 230*
(off Hunt Rd.)
Pennine Gdns. SO45: Dib P 7J 193
Pennine Ho. SO16: South 3E 172
Pennine Rd. SO16: South 3D 172
Pennine Wlk. PO14: Fare 1A 212
Pennine Way GU14: Cov 5F 28
PO13: Lee S 3C 238
RG22: B'toke 8K 41
SO53: Cha F 8B 132
Pennings Rd. SP9: Tidw 6C 30 (6G 30)
PENNINGTON 3C 234
Pennington Cl. SO21: Col C 4K 133
SO41: Penn 4C 234
Pennington Cross SO41: Lymi 4D 234
Pennington Oval SO41: Penn 4B 234
Pennington Way PO15: Fare 6N 197
Penns Pl. GU31: Pet 9C 140
Penns Rd. GU32: Pet 9L 139
Penns Wood GU14: Farn 2M 49
Penn Way PO12: Gos 4G 239
Penny Black La. RG24: B'toke 3N 41
Penny Ct. BH24: Poul 9M 185
PO12: Gos *2L 239*
(off Ferrol Rd.)
Pennycress SO31: Loc H 7B 196
Penny Hedge BH25: B Sea 6C 232
Penny Hill SN8: Co Du 2H 31
Penny Hill Caravan Pk. GU17: Min 2M 27
Penny La. BH1: Bour 1B 246
SO20: S Bri 3G 88
Penny Pl. PO7: Purb 6M 201
Pennyroyal GU51: Fleet 2H 47
Pennys Cl. SP6: F'dge 8J 151
Pennys Cres. SP6: F'dge 8J 151
Penny's Hatch RG20: Kings 2C 6
Pennys La. BH21: Cran 6J 149
SP5: Far 8F 86
SP6: F'dge 9J 151
Penny's Mead *BH21: Cran* *6J 149*
(off Penny's La.)
Penny St. PO1: Ports 8J 5 (4B 240)
Penny Way BH23: Fri C 8E 230
Pennywell Gdns. BH25: A'ley 2E 232
Penrhyn BH1: Bour 1A 246
Penrhyn Av. PO6: Dray 9J 201
Penrhyn Cl. GU12: Alders 1K 65
SO50: E'leigh 7D 132
Penrith Rd. BH5: Bour 1D 246
RG21: B'toke 7B 42
Penrose Cl. PO2: Ports 6E 214
Penrose Way GU34: Four M 5H 97
Penryn Dr. GU35: Head D 2E 102
Pensdell Farm Cotts. RG25: Clid 1C 60
Penshurst Way SO50: E'leigh 6E 132
Pentagon, The SO45: Fawl 6E 208
Pentere Rd. PO8: Horn 4A 182
Pentice, The SO23: Winche 8M 237
Pentire Av. SO15: South 1J 173
Pentire Way SO15: South 9J 159
Pentland Cl. RG22: B'toke 8K 41
SO45: Dib P 7J 193
Pentland Pl. GU14: Cov 5G 28
Pentland Ri. PO16: Portc 8M 199
Pentney Cl. RG25: Over 3D 56
PENTON CORNER 9G 50
Penton Ct. PO9: Hav 3H 203
PENTON GRAFTON 7F 50
PENTON HARROWAY 8G 50
Penton La. SP11: C'vle, Pen G 2E 50
PENTON MEWSEY 6G 50
Penton Pl. SO23: Winche 8M 105
Penton Rd. SO21: Twyf 6L 127
Pentons Cl. GU34: Holy 1K 81
Pentons Hill SP6: Frog 4N 153
Penton Way RG24: B'toke, Sher J 1C 42
PENTRIDGE 2G 148
Pentridge Way SO40: Tott 5K 171
Penwith Dr. GU27: Hasl 2M 117
PENWOOD 3B 8
Penwood Grn. PO9: Hav 4H 203
Penwood Hgts. RG20: Pen 3B 8
Penwood Rd. RG20: Wa W 1C 8
Peper Harow PO8: Horn 4B 182
Peppard Cl. SO18: South 3E 174
Pepper Cl. PO11: H Isl 2G 243
Peppercorn SO41: Sway 5K 223
Peppercorn Cl. BH23: Chri 6A 230
Peppercorn Way SO30: Hed E 8M 161
Pepys Av. SO19: South 5H 175
Pepys Cl. PO4: S'sea 4G 240
PO12: Gos 6K 239
Percival Cl. PO13: Lee S 2C 238
Percivale Rd. SO53: Cha F 8L 131
Percival Pl. RG24: Old Bas 6J 43
Percival Rd. PO2: Ports 8G 215
Percy Chandler St. PO1: Ports 1E 240
Percy Cl. SO45: Hythe 4L 193
Percy Rd. BH5: Bour 1B 246
PO4: S'sea 3F 240
PO12: Gos 3L 239
SO16: South 2F 172
Peregrine Cl. SO40: Tott 4J 171
Peregrine Rd. BH23: Mude 8C 230
RG20: Bis G 1G 9
Peregrines, The PO16: Portc 9H 199
Perham Cres. SP11: Ludg 1E 30
PERHAM DOWN 4B 30 (6J 31)
Perins Cl. SO24: New A 2D 108
Periwinkle Cl. GU35: Lind 2M 101
Perkins Ho. PO1: Ports 3L 5
Pern Dr. SO30: Botl 3D 176
Peronne Cl. PO3: Ports 3G 214
Peronne Rd. PO3: Ports 3G 214
Perowne St. GU11: Alders 9H 49
Perran Rd. SO16: South 1C 172
Perring Av. GU14: Cov 4G 29
Perring Rd. GU14: Farn 2J 49
Perrin Lock Ct. *BH23: Chri* *8J 229*
(off King's Av.)
Perry Dr. GU51: Fleet 2J 47
Perryfield Gdns. BH7: Bour 6E 228
Perryhill Dr. GU47: Sandh 4B 18
Perry Way GU9: Up H 3D 64
GU35: Head 3B 102
Perrywood Cl. SO45: Holb 5A 208
Perrywood Gdns. SO40: Tott 2H 171
Perseus Pl. PO7: Purb 6M 201
Perseus Ter. PO1: Ports 6J 5 (3B 240)
Pershore Cl. SO31: Loc H 7D 196
Pershore Rd. RG24: B'toke 2C 42
(not continuous)
Persian Dr. PO15: White 2E 196
Persley Rd. BH10: Bour 2H 227
Perth Cl. BH23: Chri 5H 229
Perth Ho. PO1: Ports 2E 240
Perth Rd. PO4: S'sea 3J 241
PO13: Gos 5F 212
SP11: Per D 4B 30 (6J 31)
Pervin Rd. PO6: Cosh 9G 201
Peshawar Cl. SP9: Tidw 7B 30 (6F 30)
Pesthouse La. RG28: Whit 4G 54
Peststead La. SO32: Sob 7L 165
Peter Ashley Activity Cen. 8L 201
Peter Ashley La. PO6: Dray 8L 201
Peterborough Rd. PO6: Cosh 8F 200
SO14: South 3M 173
Peterhouse Cl. GU47: Owl 3H 19
Peters Cl. SO31: Loc H 6B 196
Peterscroft Av. SO40: Ashu 9G 171
PETERSFIELD 1M 145
Petersfield RG23: Oak 2D 58
Petersfield Bus. Pk. GU32: Pet 1K 145
Petersfield Cl. RG24: Chin 8J 23
Petersfield Golf Course 5B 140
Petersfield Grn. SP9: Tidw 8C 30 (7G 30)
Petersfield Ho. *PO1: Ports* *1E 240*
(off St Faith's Rd.)
Petersfield La. PO8: Clan 5C 168
Petersfield Mus. 1M 145
Petersfield (Old) Golf Course 3N 145
Petersfield Pl. BH7: Bour 7E 228
Petersfield Rd. BH7: Bour 8D 228
GU31: Buri 7K 145
GU33: G'ham, Longc 5D 114
GU35: W'hil 2F 114
PO9: Hav 7E 202
SO21: Winche 7A 106
SO23: Winche 7M 105
SO24: Cher, Hin A 1J 135
SO24: Monk, Rop 2A 110
Petersfield Station (Rail) 9L 139
Petersfield Swimming Pool 1N 145
Petersfield Town FC 9N 139
Petersham Cl. PO7: W'lle 9L 181
Petersham Ho. *PO5: S'sea* *6E 240*
(off Clarendon Rd.)
Peterson's Tower 9K 223
Peters Rd. SO31: Loc H 6B 196
Petit Rd. BH9: Bour 3L 227
Petrel Cft. RG22: B'toke 2H 59
Petrel Wlk. PO13: Gos 6D 212
Petrie Rd. PO13: Lee S 1B 238
Petticoat La. SP5: Redl 1N 119
Pettinger Gdns. SO17: South 2B 174
Petty Cl. SO51: Rom 5N 129
Pettycot Cres. PO13: Gos 5D 212
Petty's Brook Rd. RG24: Chin 8H 23
Petunia Cl. RG22: B'toke 2J 59
Petworth Cl. RG22: B'toke 4K 59
Petworth Gdns. SO16: South 6G 159
SO50: E'leigh 7E 132
Petworth Rd. PO3: Ports 1J 241
Pevensey Cl. SO16: South 1C 172
Peveral Wlk. RG22: B'toke 7M 41
Peveral Way RG22: B'toke 8M 41
Peverel Ct. GU30: Lip 1D 116
Peverells Rd. SO53: Cha F 5C 132
Peverells Wood Av. SO53: Cha F 5C 132
Peverells Wood Cl. SO53: Cha F 5D 132
Peveril Cl. BH24: Ashl H 2C 186
Peveril Rd. SO19: South 6C 174
Pewsey Cl. RG23: Wort 8J 41
Pewsey Pl. SO15: South 9J 159
Pexalls Cl. RG27: Hoo 2K 45
Pheaben's Fld. RG26: B'ley 1F 22
Pheasant Cl. GU34: Four M 6G 97
RG22: B'toke 2H 59
SO21: Bar S 5B 76
Pheasant Copse GU51: Fleet 1J 47
Pheasantry Dr. RG27: Brams 9A 16
Pheasants Mead SO20: Mid Wa 3A 72
Pheby Rd. RG22: B'toke 9M 41
Phi Ho. SO16: Chilw 2H 159
Philip Rd. PO7: W'lle 4N 201
Phillimore Rd. SO16: S'ing 7B 160
Phillips Cl. GU10: Tong 2N 65
GU35: Head 2B 102
SO16: Rown 5D 158
Phillips Cres. GU35: Head 2B 102
Philpott Dr. SO40: March 9E 172
Phoenix, The 1J 101
Phoenix BH14: Poole 1A 244
Phoenix Bldgs. PO3: Ports 6H 215
Phoenix Cl. SO31: Burs 9L 175
Phoenix Ct. GU11: Alders 1J 65
RG20: Kings 2B 6
RG27: H Win 8A 26
Phoenix Film Theatre, The 8M 159
PHOENIX GREEN 8A 26
Phoenix Grn. RG27: H Win 8A 26
Phoenix Ho. SO30: Hed E 2B 176
Phoenix Ind. Pk. SO50: E'leigh 1G 160
Phoenix Pk. Ter. RG21: B'toke 5C 42
Phoenix Sq. PO2: Ports 4F 214
Phoenix Ter. RG27: H Win 8A 26
Phoenix Way PO13: Gos 7E 212
Phyldon Cl. BH12: Poole 9A 226
Phyldon Rd. BH12: Poole 8A 226
Physic Garden, The 1M 145
Piazza, The *BH1: Bour* *1B 246*
(off Palmerston Rd.)
Pickaxe La. RG29: S War 6C 62
Picket Cl. SP6: F'dge 9J 151
PICKET HILL 5B 188
PICKET PIECE 8F 52
PICKET POST 4C 188
Picketts Hill GU35: Head, Slea 7K 83
Picket Twenty SP11: A'ver 1D 70
(not continuous)
Picket Twenty Way SP11: A'ver 2E 70
Pickford Ho. *GU11: Alders* *9K 49*
(off Pickford St.)
Pickford Rd. BH9: Bour 5J 227
Pickford St. GU11: Alders 9K 49
Pickwick Cl. SO40: Tott 3H 171
Pickwick Ho. PO1: Ports 9E 214
Picton Ho. PO5: S'sea 5N 5 (3D 240)
PO7: W'lle 9K 181
Picton Rd. SP10: A'ver 4M 69
Pidham La.
GU32: E Meon, R'dean 3B 144
Pier App. BH2: Bour 8M 247 (3K 245)
Pier Head Rd. PO2: Ports 8B 214
Pierrefonde's Av. GU14: Farn 7J 29
Pier Rd. PO5: S'sea 9L 5 (5C 240)
Pier St. PO13: Lee S 1A 238
Pier Theatre, The 9M 247 (3K 245)
Pigeonhouse Fld. *SO21: Sut S* *7D 76*
(off Stockbridge Rd.)
Pigeon Ho. La. PO7: Purb 3E 200
Pigeonhouse La. RG25: Far W 8N 59
Pigeonhouse Yd. *SO21: Sut S* *7D 76*
(off Stockbridge Rd.)
Pigeons Cl. RG26: B'ley 2H 23
Piggott Pl. GU31: Pet 8A 140
Pig Shoot La. BH23: Hurn 2C 228
Pike Cl. GU11: Alders 9L 49
PIKESHILL 1A 148 (2N 189)
Pikes Hill SO43: Lyn 1A 148 (2N 189)
Pikes Hill Av. SO43: Lyn 1A 148 (2N 189)
Pilbrow Ct. PO12: Gos 3H 239
Pilchards Av. SO50: Fair O 9M 133
PILCOT 5G 46
Pilcot Rd. GU51: Cr V 5G 46
RG27: Cr V, Dogm 5G 46
Pilgrim Pk. (Caravan Pk.)
BH24: Poul 9M 185
Pilgrim Pl. SO18: S'ing 7C 160
SO41: Lymi 3E 234
Pilgrims Cl. BH25: A'ley 2D 232
SO53: Cha F 7L 131
Pilgrims Gate SO22: Winche 5J 105
SO32: Bis W 3L 163
Pilgrims Ho. SO22: Winche 5J 105
Pilgrims Way GU35: Head 2A 102
PO14: Stub 7L 211
SP10: A'ver 8B 52
Pillar Box Gdns. RG24: B'toke 3N 41
PILLEY 6F 224
PILLEY BAILEY 5G 225
Pilley Bailey SO41: Pil 5G 225
Pilley Hill SO41: Pil 6E 224
Pilley St. SO41: Pil 6F 224
Pill Hill SP5: W'psh 5H 121
Pilning Cl. PO14: Fare 9M 197
Pilot Hight Rd. BH11: Bour 2E 226
Pilots Vw. *SP4: Ames* *5A 66*
(off Porton Rd.)
Pimpernel Cl. SO31: Loc H 7B 196
Pimpernel Way *PO7: W'lle* *9K 181*
(off Melick Way)
RG24: Lych 4G 42
Pine Av. BH6: Bour 1F 246
BH12: Poole 7D 226
GU15: Camb 9M 19
Pine Bank GU26: Hind 3N 103
Pinebeach Ct. BH13: Poole 5E 244
Pinecliffe Av. BH6: Bour 1F 246
Pinecliffe Rd. BH25: New M 7L 231
Pinecliff Rd. BH13: Poole 5E 244
Pine Cl. BH25: B Sea 6N 231
GU15: Camb 6G 19
SO21: Sth W 3J 91
SO22: Oli B 2F 126
SO40: Ashu 7J 171
SO45: Dib P 7L 193
SO52: N Bad 7E 130
SP5: L'ford 1J 155
Pine Ct. GU11: Alders 9J 49
GU34: Four M 6J 97
PO10: Ems 5M 203
Pine Ct. Bus. Cen. BH1: Bour 2L 245
Pine Cres. BH23: Highc 7G 230
SO53: Cha F 3A 132
Pine Dr. BH13: Poole 2D 244
BH24: St I 4C 186
GU17: Haw 1G 29
PO8: Clan 6C 168
SO18: South 3H 175
Pine Dr. E. BH13: Poole 3E 244
SO18: South 3J 175
Pinefield Rd. SO18: South 9D 160
Pinefields Cl. RG45: Cr'tne 1D 18
Pine Grange BH1: Bour 2L 245
Pine Gro. GU52: Ch Cr 6N 47
PO9: Hav 8G 203
Pinegrove Rd. SO19: South 7D 174
Pinehill Ri. GU47: Sandh 5E 18
Pinehill Rd. GU35: Bor 5J 101
RG45: Cr'tne 1D 18
Pineholt Cl. BH24: St I 3D 186
Pine Ho. BH25: New M 3B 232
Pinehurst RG26: Tadl 6H 11
SO17: South 1M 173
SO41: M Sea 8J 235
Pinehurst Av. BH23: Mude 9B 230
GU14: Farn 1K 49
Pinehurst Cl. PO7: W'lle 8C 182
Pinehurst Cotts. GU14: Farn 1K 49
Pinehurst Pas. GU14: Farn 1K 49
Pinehurst Rd. GU14: Farn 1J 49
SO16: Bass 4L 159
Pinehurst Rdbt. GU14: Farn 9K 29
Pinelands BH1: Bour 1N 245
Pinelands Ct. BH8: Bour 7N 227
SO16: South 7H 159
Pinelands Mobile Home Pk. RG7: A'mas 1L 11
Pinelands Rd. SO16: Chilw 3L 159
Pine Lea SO32: Bis W 2K 163
Pine Mnr. Rd. BH24: Ashl H 3A 186
Pinemount Rd. GU15: Camb 9M 19
Pine Pk. Mans. BH13: Poole 1E 244
Pine Rd. BH9: Bour 5K 227
GU34: Four M 4K 97
SO32: Bis W 3N 163
SO51: Rom 6B 130
SO53: Cha F 3N 131
SP6: Ald 5C 152
Pines, The BH1: Bour 5N 247 (1L 245)
(Benjamin Ct.)
BH1: Bour 1M 245
(Knyveton Rd.)
BH13: Poole 3E 244
PO16: Fare 8J 199
SO16: South 8G 159
SP10: A'ver 1M 69
Pineside BH9: Bour 6L 227
Pines Rd. GU30: Lip 2A 116
GU51: Fleet 1L 47
Pinetops Cl. SO41: Penn 3B 234
Pine Tree Cl. PO31: Cowes 5N 237
Pine Tree Gdns. PO8: Cowp 8A 182
Pine Tree Glen BH4: Bour 2G 244
Pine Trees Cl. PO14: Fare 9N 197
Pine Tree Wlk. PO8: Horn 8D 168
Pine Va. Cres. BH10: Bour 3J 227
Pine Vw. GU35: Head D 1E 102
Pine Vw. Cl. GU9: Bad L 5J 65
SP5: Woodf 9C 120
Pineview Cl. SO31: Burs 9L 175
Pine Vw. Gdns. BH10: Bour 2K 227
Pine Wlk. GU33: Liss 8F 114
SO16: Chilw 4K 159
SO31: Sar G 4D 196
SP10: A'ver 3K 69
Pine Way SO16: Bass 4L 159
Pinewood PO13: Gos 7G 212
RG24: Chin 9E 22
SO16: Bass 5L 159
Pinewood Av. BH10: Bour 1H 227
PO9: Bed 6B 202
Pinewood Cl. BH10: Bour 1H 227
BH23: Walk 4J 231
GU47: Sandh 5B 18
PO14: Stub 4N 211
RG26: Bau 4D 10
SO51: Rom 3B 130
Pinewood Ct. GU51: Fleet 1M 47
Pinewood Cres. GU14: Cov 7E 28
SO45: Hythe 7N 193
Pinewood Dr. RG20: Newt 2E 8
SO45: Hythe 7N 193
Pinewood Hill GU51: Fleet 1M 47
Pinewood Lodge *PO16: Fare* *7D 198*
(off Southampton Rd.)
Pinewood Pk. GU14: Cov 5E 28
SO19: South 5K 175
Pinewood Rd. BH13: Poole 4F 244
BH23: Highc 5H 231
BH24: St I 4C 186
SO41: Hor 3F 232
Pinkerton Rd. RG22: B'toke 9L 41
Pinkney La. SO43: Lyn 4M 189
Pink Rd. PO2: Ports 8F 214
Pinks Hill PO16: Fare 7F 198
Pinks La. RG26: Bau 4E 10
Pinnacle, The BH1: Bour 7N 247
Pinnell Cl. RG22: B'toke 4J 59
Pinset Camp Site SO22: Winche 6E 104
Pinsley Dr. PO17: S'wick 3A 200
Pintail Cl. RG22: B'toke 3H 59

Pinto Cl.—Pounds Ga.

Pinto Cl. PO15: White 2F 196
Pipers Ash BH24: Poul 9M 185
Pipers Cl. SO40: Tott 4K 171
Pipers Cft. GU52: Ch Cr 7M 47
Pipers Dr. BH23: Chri 7C 230
Pipers Mead PO8: Clan 6A 168
Pipers Patch GU14: Farn 8K 29
Pipers Wood Ind. Pk.
PO7: W'lle 1K 201
Piping Cl. SO21: Col C 4K 133
Piping Grn. SO21: Col C 4K 133
Piping Rd. SO21: Col C 4K 133
Pipistrelle Wlk. PO17: K Vil 1A 198
Pipit Cl. PO8: Horn 4A 182
PO12: Gos 9K 213
Pippin Cl. BH23: Chri 4H 229
SO41: Lymi 4E 234
Pippin Gro. SP11: Apple 4B 50
Pippin Sq. RG27: H Win 8B 26
Pipson La. GU46: Yat 8N 17
Pipsons Cl. GU46: Yat 7N 17
Pirbright Rd. GU14: Farn 9L 29
Pirelli St. SO14: South 5B 4 (6L 173)
Pirelli Way SO50: E'leigh 1E 160
Pirrie Cl. SO15: South 1J 173
Pitcairn Cl. RG24: B'toke 1D 42
Pitcairn M. PO4: S'sea 5J 241
Pitchponds Rd. SO31: Wars 9N 195
Pitcot La. SO21: Owls 5C 134
Pitcroft La. GU31: Buri 7M 145
PO2: Ports 8E 214
(not continuous)
Pitcroft Rd. PO2: Ports 7E 214
Pitfield La. RG7: Mort 1H 13
Pitfold Av. GU27: Hasl 9M 103
Pitfold Cl. GU27: Hasl 9N 103
Pither Rd. RG29: Odi 2E 62
Pithouse La. RG19: Ashf H 4N 9
Pitman Cl. RG22: B'toke 9K 41
Pitmore Cl. SO50: E'leigh 4F 132
Pitmore La. SO41: Penn, Sway 5K 223
Pitmore Rd. SO50: E'leigh 4F 132
Pitreavie Rd. PO6: Cosh 2G 215
PITT 9F 104
Pittard Rd. RG21: B'toke 8A 42
Pitter Cl. SO22: Lit 1F 104
Pitt Hall Cotts. RG26: Rams 7B 20
Pitt Hill La. PO7: H'don 9F 166
Pitthouse La. BH23: Hurn 6G 218
Pitt La. GU10: Fren 2C 84
Pittmore Rd. BH23: Burt 4M 229
PITTON 6E 86
Pitton Rd. SP5: Far 8E 86
Pitt Rd. SO15: South 4H 173
Pitts Deep La. SO41: E End 5B 236
Pitts La. SP5: Bish 3D 118
SP10: A'ver 3N 69
Pitts Pl. BH25: A'ley 4E 232
Pitts Rd. GU11: Alders 7K 49
Pitt Way GU14: Cov 7H 29
Pit Wlk. SP4: New T 5F 66
Pitymoor La. PO17: S'wick 5C 200
Place Ct. GU11: Alders 3L 65
Place Cres. PO7: W'lle 4N 201
Place Flats SP11: Weyh 8D 50
Place Ho. Cl. PO15: Fare 8M 197
Place La. SO21: Comp 5J 127
Place Watermill 9L 229
PLAITFORD 9L 121
PLAITFORD GREEN 7M 121
Plaitford Gro. PO9: Hav 5B 202
Plaitford Wlk. SO16: South 1E 172
Planet Ice
Basingstoke 6L 41
Gosport 7G 213
Plantagenet Cres. BH11: Bour 1B 226
Plantation SO41: Ever 6M 233
Plantation, The RG27: Sher L 4L 23
SO32: Curd 1H 177
SP5: Mid W 5G 86
Plantation Ct. SO41: Lymi 2D 234
Plantation Dr. BH23: Walk 4J 231
SO40: March 9D 172
PLANTATION HILL 7M 9
Plantation Rd. BH23: Hurn 4E 218
BH24: Match 4E 218
GU33: Hi Br 4G 141
RG26: Tadl 3F 10
SO51: W Wel 2M 155
SP9: Tidw 9D 30 (7G 31)
SP10: A'ver 2L 69
Plantation Row GU15: Camb 8K 19
Plantation Way GU35: W'hil 6F 100
Plant Cl. SO51: E Wel 1B 156
Plant Pk. Rd. BH24: Match 5F 186
Plassey Cres. BH10: Bour 1G 226
Plassey Rd. SP9: Tidw 7C 30 (6G 30)
(not continuous)
PLASTOW GREEN 3L 9
Platform Rd. SO14: South 9D 4 (8M 173)
Platoff Rd. SO41: Lymi 6E 234
Player Ct. SP6: F'dge 9J 151
Players Cres. SO40: Tott 5L 171
Playfair Rd. PO5: S'sea 3E 240
Playfields Dr. BH12: Poole 8C 226
Plaza Pde. SO51: Rom 5M 129
Plaza Theatre, The 5M 129
Pleasance Way BH25: New M 3A 232
Pleasant Hill RG26: Tadl 5H 11
Pleasant Rd. PO4: S'sea 3J 241
PLEASANT VIEW 7F 174
Plemont Cl. BH12: Poole 5C 226
Pless Rd. SO41: M Sea 9H 233
Plestor, The GU34: Selb 7L 99
Plough Gdns.
SO20: Brou 2A 86 (5A 88)
Plough La. RG27: Brams, Haze 1L 25
SO32: Sob H 9L 165
Plough Rd. GU46: Yat 6A 18
Plough Way SO22: Winche 1H 127
SP11: E Ant 7B 52
Plover Cl. PO14: Stub 6L 211
RG22: B'toke 1J 59
SO16: South 6G 158
SP10: A'ver 8A 52
Plover Dr. SO41: M Sea 8M 235
Ploverfield SO31: Burs 1M 195
Plover La. RG27: Eve 4B 16
Plover Reach PO4: S'sea 2J 241
Plover Rd. SO40: Tott 3J 171
Plovers Down SO22: Oli B 2F 126
Plovers Rd. PO8: Horn 3A 182
Plovers Way GU34: Alt 2G 80
PLPH Rd. SO45: Fawl 3E 208
Plumer Rd. GU33: Longc 3H 115
Plum Fell La. GU34: Selb 8L 99
Plumley Wlk. PO9: Hav 2D 202
Plumpton Gdns. PO3: Ports 5J 215
Plumpton Gro. PO7: W'lle 9B 182
Plumpton Way GU34: Alt 6F 80
Pluto Rd. SO50: E'leigh 9D 132
Plymouth Dr. PO14: Stub 6K 211
Plymouth St. PO5: S'sea 3D 240
Poachers Fld. RG29: S War 4D 62
Pococks La. GU33: Hawk 7M 113
Poets Way SO22: Winche 6H 105
Poinsettia Cl. PO15: Seg 6H 197
Point, The
Eastleigh 9E 132
Point, The BH5: Bour 2B 246
Pointout Cl. SO16: Bass 8K 159
Pointout Rd. SO16: Bass 8K 159
POKESDOWN 9D 228
Pokesdown Station (Rail) 9D 228
Poland La. RG29: Odi 5L 45
Polden Cl. GU14: Cov 5G 28
POLECAT 6N 103
POLECAT CORNER 1J 61
Polesden Cl. SO53: Cha F 4N 131
Poles La. SO21: Hurs, Ott 7N 125
SO41: Lymi 5E 234
POLHAMPTON 9G 39
Police Sta. La. SO32: Drox 2K 165
Polkerris Way GU52: Ch Cr 7N 47
Pollard Cotts. RG20: Bal H 1M 7
POLLARDS MOOR 1A 170
Pollards Moor Rd. SO40: Copy 1A 170
Pollocks Path GU26: Hind 5M 103
Polmear Cl. GU52: Ch Cr 7N 47
POLYGON 2A 4 (4K 173)
Polygon, The SO15: South 3A 4 (5K 173)
Polygon Ct. SO15: South 3A 4 (5K 173)
Polymond Ho. SO14: South 8C 4
Pomeroy Cres. SO30: Hed E 9M 161
Pompey Centre, The PO4: S'sea 2G 240
Pond Cl. BH25: New M 3B 232
RG25: Over 4D 56
SO40: March 8E 172
Pond Cotts. RG25: Clid 3B 60
Pond Cft. GU46: Yat 7A 18
Pondhead Cl. SO45: Holb 5A 208
Pond La. GU10: Chur 4E 84
PO8: Clan 5B 168
SP11: Grat 5L 67
Pond Piece PO7: Den 7G 180
Pond Rd. GU14: Farn 1K 49
GU35: Head D 3C 102
RG26: B'ley 2H 23
SO31: Sar G 3C 196
Pondside Flats SO42: Beau 7E 206
Pondside La. SO32: Bis W 3L 163
(not continuous)
PONDTAIL 3A 48
Pondtail Cl. GU51: Fleet 3A 48
Pondtail Gdns. GU51: Fleet 3A 48
Pondtail Rd. GU51: Fleet 3A 48
Pond Vw. Cl. GU51: Fleet 1N 47
Ponsonby Ho. PO5: S'sea 5N 5 (3D 240)
Ponsonby Rd. BH14: Poole 1B 244
Pook La. PO9: Warb 1G 217
(not continuous)
PO17: Fare 5D 198
Pookles La. GU34: E Wor 6N 81
POOKSGREEN 8B 172
Pooksgreen SO40: March 8B 172
Poole Commerce Cen. BH12: Poole 9D 226
Poole Hill BH2: Bour 7J 247 (2J 245)
Poole La. BH11: Bour 2D 226
Poole La. Rdbt. BH11: Bour 2C 226
Poole Rd. BH2: Bour 7G 247 (2H 245)
BH4: Bour 7G 247 (1F 244)
BH12: Poole 1D 244
SO19: South 6C 174
Pool Rd. GU11: Alders 3L 65
RG27: H Win 5B 26
Poors Farm Rd. RG24: Old Bas 3M 43
Popes Ct. SO40: Tott 3M 171
Pope's Hill RG20: Kings 2A 6 (6K 9)
Popes La. SO32: Lwr U 8D 134
SO40: Tott 3M 171
POPHAM 3N 77
Popham Ct. PO9: Hav 3C 202
Popham La. RG25: Nth W 9A 58
Poplar Cl. BH23: Bran 7E 220
BH23: Highc 6K 231
GU14: Cov 7E 28
RG26: Bau 5D 10
RG27: Sher L 3L 23
Poplar Cres. BH24: Ring 1L 187
Poplar Dr. PO14: Fare 9A 198
SO40: March 9C 172
Poplar Gro. PO11: H Isl 3G 243
Poplar La. BH23: Bran 6E 220
Poplar Rd. BH25: A'ley 2E 232
SO19: South 4D 174
Poplars, The SO32: Wal C 8A 164
Poplar Wlk. GU9: H End 3F 64
GU31: Pet 3L 145
PO3: Ports 1H 241
Poplar Way BH24: Ring 1L 187
SO30: Hed E 4A 176
SO52: N Bad 7E 130
POPLEY 2D 42
Popley Ponds Local Nature Reserve 1C 42
Popley Way RG24: B'toke 3A 42
Poppy Cl. BH23: Chri 6D 230
SO31: Loc H 7C 196
SP10: A'ver 2J 69
Poppy Ct. BH6: Bour 1G 246
Poppy Fld. RG24: Lych 3H 43
Poppyfields SO53: Cha F 6M 131
Poppy Gdns. PO15: Fare 6M 197
Poppyhills Rd. GU15: Camb 5N 19
Poppy Rd. SO16: S'ing 6A 160
Porchester Cl. SP10: Charl 7K 51
Porchester Rd. SO19: South 7C 174
Porchester Sq. *RG21: B'toke* *6C 42*
(off Festival Pl.)
Porlock Rd. SO16: South 1B 172
Portacre Ri. RG21: B'toke 8A 42
Portadene BH4: Bour 8G 247 (3H 245)
Portal Cl. SP11: A'ver 2H 69
Portal Rd. PO13: Gos 5E 212
SO19: South 6F 174
SO23: Winche 8M 105
SO40: Tott 3K 171
SO50: B'stke 9H 133
Portarlington Cl. BH4: Bour 3H 245
Portarlington Ct. *BH4: Bour* *2G 245*
(off Portarlington Rd.)
Portarlington Rd. BH4: Bour 7G 247 (2G 244)
PORTCHESTER 9M 199
Portchester Castle 2A 214
Portchester Ct. BH8: Bour 9M 227
Portchester Crematorium PO16: Portc 8K 199
Portchester Hgts. PO16: Portc 8M 199
Portchester La. PO17: Fare, S'wick 6M 199
Portchester Pl. BH8: Bour 9M 227
Portchester Ri. SO50: E'leigh 5E 132
Portchester Rd. BH8: Bour 8L 227
PO2: Ports 8F 214
PO16: Portc 8H 199
Portchester Sailing Club 2A 214
Portchester Station (Rail) 9M 199
Portcullis Ho. SO14: South 9E 4 (8M 173)
Portelet Cl. BH12: Poole 5B 226
Portelet Ho. SO16: South 8C 158
Portelet Pl. SO30: Hed E 5N 175
Porteous Cres. SO53: Cha F 6D 132
Porter Cl. *RG29: Odi* *2E 62*
(off Wooldridge Cres.)
Porter Rd. RG22: B'toke 1A 60
Portersbridge M. SO51: Rom 5L 129
Portersbridge St. SO51: Rom 5L 129
Porters Cl. RG25: Dumm 9F 58
SP10: A'ver 9K 51
Porter's La. SO14: South 8C 4 (7L 173)
Portesbery Hill Dr. GU15: Camb 7N 19
Portesbery Rd. GU15: Camb 7M 19
Portesham Gdns. BH9: Bour 2M 227
Portfield Cl. BH23: Chri 6K 229
Portfield Ind. Est. PO3: Ports 5H 215
Portfield Rd. BH23: Chri 7J 229
PO3: Ports 5H 215
SP5: Bish 1E 118
Port Hamble SO31: Hamb 6L 195
PORTHSEA ISLAND 2G 241
Portiswood Cl. RG26: Pam H 5K 11
Portland Bldgs. PO12: Gos 3L 239
Portland Cl. GU32: Pet 8A 140
Portland Dr. GU52: Ch Cr 7L 47
PO12: Gos 4F 238
Portland Gro. SP10: A'ver 1N 69
Portland Ho. PO12: Gos 3M 239
Portland Pl. BH2: Bour 1K 245
Portland Rd. BH9: Bour 5L 227
PO5: S'sea 9N 5 (5D 240)
PO7: W'lle 2M 201
Portland Sq. GU33: Liss 1E 140
Portland St. PO1: Ports 4L 5 (2C 240)
PO16: Fare 8D 198
SO14: South 5C 4 (6L 173)
Portland Ter. PO5: S'sea 9N 5 (5D 240)
SO14: South 4C 4 (6L 173)
Portland Way PO17: K Vil 2A 198
Port La. SO21: Hurs 6N 125
Portman Cres. BH5: Bour 1E 246
Portman M. BH7: Bour 9C 228
Portman Rd. BH7: Bour 9C 228
Portman Ter. BH5: Bour 1E 246
PORTMORE 8G 225
Portobello Gro. PO16: Portc 8M 199
PORTON . . . . . 9C 66 & 1C 86
Porton Rd. SP4: Ames 4A 66
Port Royal St. PO5: S'sea 2E 240
Port Royal St. Ind. Est. PO5: S'sea 2E 240
Portsbridge Rdbt. PO6: Cosh 2F 214
Portsdown Av. PO6: Dray 9K 201
Portsdown Hill Rd.
PO6: Cosh, Dray, Farl 7E 200
PO9: Bed 8J 201
PO17: Fare 6K 199
Portsdown Rd. PO6: Cosh 8N 199
PO16: Portc 8N 199
PORTSEA 3J 5 (2B 240)
Portside Cl. SO40: March 7F 172
PORTSMOUTH 4N 5 (2D 240)
Portsmouth (Park & Ride) 1D 214
Portsmouth Cathedral 7J 5 (4B 240)
Portsmouth Cl. GU34: Alt 7D 80
Portsmouth Cres. RG22: B'toke 9M 41
Portsmouth Ent. Cen. PO3: Ports 5J 215
Portsmouth FC 2G 241
Portsmouth Ferry Terminal
PO2: Ports 8D 214
Portsmouth Golf Course 7M 201
Portsmouth Gymnastics Cen. 5E 214
Portsmouth Harbour Cruising Club 5C 214
Portsmouth Harbour Station (Rail)
. . . . . 4H 5 (2A 240)
Portsmouth Harbour Yacht Club 1B 214
Portsmouth History Cen. *4N 5*
(off Guildhall Sq.)
Portsmouth Indoor Tennis Cen. 5L 5 (3C 240)
Portsmouth Rd. GU15: Camb 3M 29
GU16: Frim 3M 29
GU26: B'sht, Lip 9F 102
GU26: Hind 6L 103
GU30: B'sht, Lip 9F 102
GU30: Lip, Mill 5D 116
GU33: Rake 9M 115
PO6: Cosh 2G 214
PO8: Horn 5B 182
PO13: Lee S 3B 238
SO19: South 7B 174
SO31: Burs 9L 175
SO50: Fis P 6M 133
Portsmouth Sailing Club 6H 5 (3A 240)
Portsmouth & Southsea Station (Rail)
. . . . . 3N 5 (2D 240)
Portsmouth Visitor Info. Cen. 3H 5 (2A 240)
Portsmouth Wlk. RG22: B'toke 9M 41
Portsmouth Way RG22: B'toke 9M 41
PORT SOLENT 1B 214
Portsview Av. PO16: Portc 8M 199
Portsview Gdns. PO16: Portc 8M 199
PORTSWOOD 1N 173
Portswood Av. SO17: South 2N 173
Portswood Cen. SO17: South 1N 173
Portswood Dr. BH10: Bour 2L 227
PORTSWOOD PARK 2N 173
Portswood Pk. SO17: South 2N 173
Portswood Rd. PO2: Ports 3F 214
PO9: Hav 3D 202
SO17: South 2N 173
Port Vw. Caravan Pk. BH23: Hurn 5E 218
Portview Rd. SO18: South 9D 160
Port Way PO6: P Sol 9B 200
Portway RG7: Rise 3G 14
RG26: Bau 4D 10
Portway Cl. SO18: South 3F 174
SP10: A'ver 1K 69
Portway Ind. Est. SP10: A'ver 9J 51
(Caxton Cl., not continuous)
SP10: A'ver 9H 51
(Telford Gate)
Portway Pl. RG23: B'toke 6K 41
Portway Rdbt. SP10: A'ver 8J 51
Posbrooke Rd. PO4: S'sea 3H 241
Posbrook La. PO14: Titch 3H 211
Post Corner RG24: B'toke 3N 41
Postern Cl. PO16: Portc 9M 199
Postern Ct. SO14: South 7C 4 (7L 173)
Post Horn La. RG27: Roth 7E 24
Post Office La. BH24: St I 3D 186
RG25: Dumm 9F 58
Post Office Rd. BH1: Bour 7L 247 (2K 245)
PO7: Purb 4K 201
RG17: Ink 1H 7
Potash Ct. PO9: Hav 8E 202
POTBRIDGE 3N 45
Potbridge Rd. RG29: Odi 4M 45
Potkiln Ho. GU51: Fleet 8L 27
Pot La. RG24: Old Bas 4N 43
Potley Hill Rd. GU46: Yat 7B 18
Potteries, The GU14: Cov 6F 28
PO16: Fare 6D 198
Potters Av. PO16: Fare 5C 198
Potters Fld. GU33: Liss 1F 140
Potters Ga. GU9: Farnh 8C 64
Potters Heron Cl. SO51: Ampf 1K 131
Potters Heron La. SO51: Ampf 1K 131
Potters Ind. Pk. GU52: Ch Cr 6A 48
Potters La. RG27: Stra T 1N 23
Potters Wlk. *RG21: B'toke* *6C 42*
(off Festival Pl.)
Pottery Way BH14: Poole 3A 244
Pottery Cl. PO7: Den 7G 180
Pottery Drove SO20: Ov Wa 8K 67
Pottery Junc. BH12: Poole 9C 226
Pottery La. RG17: Ink 1G 7
Potwell Ct. PO7: W'lle 4M 201
Potwell La. PO7: Purb 5F 200
POULNER 8M 185
Poulner Cl. SO19: South 9E 174
Poulner Ct. PO9: Hav 3C 202
Poulner Pk. BH24: Poul 8M 185
Poultons Cl. RG25: Over 3D 56
Poultons Rd. RG25: Over 3D 56
Pound, The SO20: Brou 2A 86
Pound Cl. BH24: Ring 9K 185
GU35: Head 2B 102
PO13: Gos 8F 212
RG26: B'ley 1F 22
SO20: Ov Wa 8M 67
SO24: Up Wield 8H 79
Pound Cotts. SO32: Meon 8N 135
Pound Ga. GU34: Alt 3G 80
Pound Ga. Dr. PO14: Titch C 8F 196
POUND GREEN 1D 20
Pound Hill SO24: New A 9E 94
Pound Ho. PO1: Ports 3L 5
Pound La. *BH23: Chri* *8L 229*
(off High St.)
BH24: Bur 8D 188
RG20: Burgh 4D 8
SO32: Meon 8N 135
SO40: Copy 9C 156
SO40: Tott 7L 171
SO51: Ampf 1G 131
SO51: Plai 8M 121
SO51: Sher E 6N 121
SP6: Dame 3N 149
Pound Lea PO11: H Isl 2G 243
Pound Mdw. RG27: Sher L 4M 23
RG28: Whit 5H 55
Pound Rd. GU12: Alders 1L 65
PO17: S'wick 7C 200
RG25: Over 3E 56
SO20: Ov Wa 8M 67
SO23: Kin W 7N 91
SO31: Old N 9J 175
SO41: Penn 3B 234
Pounds Ga. PO1: Ports 3K 5

Pounds Ter.—Queens Ct.

Pounds Ter. PO1: Ports 2K **5** (1B **240**)
POUND STREET 3C **8**
Pound St. SO18: South 3E **174**
Pound Tree Rd. SO14: South 5D **4** (6M **173**)
Poveys Mead RG20: Kings 3C **6** (6L **9**)
Powell Cres. SO40: Tott 5M **171**
Powell Rd. BH14: Poole 2A **244**
Powerleague
Basingstoke 1M **59**
Power Rd. PO1: Ports 1F **240**
Powerscourt BH2: Bour 8G **247**
Powerscourt Rd. BH25: B Sea 7M **231**
PO2: Ports 8F **214**
Powis Cl. BH25: New M 3C **232**
Powlett Rd. SO41: Lymi 3E **234**
Powlingbroke RG27: Hoo 2K **45**
Powntley Copse GU34: Alt 7B **62**
RG29: S War 7B **62**
Poyner Cl. PO16: Fare 7D **198**
Poynings Cres. RG21: B'toke 9D **42**
Poynings Pl. PO1: Ports 7K **5** (4C **240**)
Poynters Cl. SP10: A'ver 8M **51**
Poyntz Rd. RG25: Over 2D **56**
Precinct, The PO7: W'lle 2M **201**
PO11: H Isl 4G **243**
SO30: Hed E .4N **175**
SO45: Holb 4A **208**
Precosa Rd. SO30: Botl 5B **176**
Prelate Way PO14: Titch C 7F **196**
Premier Bus. Pk. PO14: Fare 2D **212**
Premier Centre, The SO51: Rom 6C **130**
Premier Gym 1N **173**
Premier Pde. SO18: South 8D **160**
Premier Way SO51: Rom 7C **130**
Prentice Cl. GU14: Farn 4K **29**
Prescelly Cl. RG22: B'toke 7K **41**
Preshaw Cl. SO16: South 7H **159**
Preshaw Est. SO32: Uph 5J **135**
Presidents Ct. *PO12: Gos* *8L 213*
(off Vanguard Rd.)
PRESTON CANDOVER 5E **78**
Preston La. BH23: Burt 4N **229**
Preston Rd. PO2: Ports 8G **214**
Preston Way BH23: Chri 6F **230**
Prestwood Cl. BH25: B Sea 5A **232**
Prestwood Rd. SO30: Hed E 4N **175**
Pretoria Cl. GU33: Longc 4J **115**
Pretoria Rd. PO4: S'sea 4G **241**
SO30: Hed E .5M **175**
SP11: Fabe 2F **30** (5L **31**)
Preymead Ind. Est. GU9: Bad L 3K **65**
Pricketts Hill PO17: Wick 3B **178**
SO32: Shed 3B **178**
Prideaux-Brune Av. PO13: Gos 4E **212**
Priest Cft. SO45: Blac 6C **208**
Priest Cft. Dr. SO45: Blac 6C **208**
Priest Down RG22: B'toke 5K **59**
Priestfields PO14: Titch C 7F **196**
Priestlands SO51: Rom 4L **129**
Priestlands Cl. SO40: Net M 4G **170**
Priestlands La. SO41: Lymi 3C **234**
Priestlands Pl. SO41: Lymi 3D **234**
Priestlands Rd. SO41: Penn 3C **234**
Priest La. BH23: Sop 8L **219**
Priestley Cl. SO40: Tott 3K **171**
Priestley Rd. BH10: Bour 5F **226**
RG24: B'toke .3N **41**
Priestwood Cl. SO18: South 3H **175**
Primate Rd. PO14: Titch C 6G **196**
Primrose Cl. PO13: Gos 3E **212**
SO30: Hed E .5N **175**
SO53: Cha F 8L **131**
Primrose Ct. BH1: Bour 9A **228**
PO7: W'lle 3A **202**
SP10: A'ver *3K 69*
(off Floral Way)
Primrose Dr. RG27: H Win 5C **26**
Primrose Gdns. GU14: Cov 9G **28**
RG22: B'toke .5K **59**
Primrose La. GU33: Rake 9J **115**
SP5: Woodf 8C **120**
Primrose Rd. SO16: Bass 7M **159**
SP11: Ludg 1D **30**
Primrose Wlk. GU46: Yat 7L **17**
GU51: Fleet 1L **47**
Primrose Way BH23: Chri 5D **230**
GU47: Sandh .4D **18**
SO31: Loc H .7C **196**
SO51: Rom 4B **130**
Primula Rd. GU35: Bor 4K **101**
Prince Albert Gdns. *SP10: A'ver* *2N 69*
(off The Elms)
Prince Albert Rd. PO4: S'sea 4H **241**
Prince Alfred St. PO12: Gos 4K **239**
Prince Charles Cl. SP11: Ludg 1D **30** (4K **31**)
Prince Charles Cres. GU14: Farn 4K **29**
Prince Cl. SP10: A'ver 8C **52**
Prince Dr. GU47: Sandh 4C **18**
Prince George St. PO1: Ports 3K **5** (2B **240**)
PO9: Hav 8F **202**
Prince of Wales Av. SO15: South 3F **172**
Prince of Wales Cl. PO7: W'lle 2A **202**
Prince of Wales Ct. *GU11: Alders* *9H 49*
(off Queen Elizabeth Dr.)
Prince of Wales Ho. *SP11: Ludg* *1D 30*
(off Andover Rd.)
Prince of Wales Rd. BH4: Bour 1F **244**
PO12: Gos 3L **239**
Prince of Wales Wlk. GU15: Camb 7L **19**
Prince of Wales Way
SO20: Mid Wa 3A **72**
Prince Regent Ct. PO5: S'sea 6N **5**
Prince Regent Pl. GU14: Farn 2L **49**
Prince Rd. PO14: Fare 2B **212**
SO16: Rown .5D **158**
Prince's Av. GU11: Alders 6K **49**
Prince's Bldgs. SO23: Winche 7N **237**
Princes Cl. GU35: W'hil 6H **101**
SO32: Bis W .3L **163**
SP5: Redl 1N **119** (7D **120**)
Princes Cotts. GU32: E Meon 4L **143**
Princes Ct. BH5: Bour 1B **246**
BH12: Poole 1E **244**
PO1: Ports 9E **214**
SO14: South 4A **174**
Princes Cres. RG22: B'toke 8N **41**
SO43: Lyn 2D **148**
Princes Dr. PO7: W'lle 9A **182**
Prince's Esplanade PO31: Cowes 5M **237**
(not continuous)
Princes Hall 9J **49**
Princes Hill SP5: Redl 1N **119** (7D **120**)
Princes Ho. *PO5: S'sea* *7M 5*
(off King's Ter.)
SO14: South *4A 174*
(off Graham St.)
PRINCE'S MARSH 3D **140**
Princes Mead (Shopping Cen.)
GU14: Farn 8K **29**
Princes Pl. BH25: A'ley 2D **232**
PO1: Ports 9D **214**
SO22: Winche 9J **105**
Princes Rd. GU32: Pet 9K **139**
SO15: South 4J **173**
SO51: Rom 4L **129**
Princess Av. BH23: Chri 8L **229**
Princess Cl. SO30: Wes E 9J **161**
Princess Ct. SO23: Winche 6M **237** (6L **105**)
Princess Dr. GU34: Alt 5D **80**
Princess Gdns. PO8: Horn 3B **182**
Princess Ga. BH12: Poole 1E **244**
Princess Louise Sq. GU34: Alt 7D **80**
Princess Mary Gdns.
SP11: Ludg 1D **30** (5K **31**)
Princess M. BH12: Poole 1E **244**
Princess Rd. BH4: Bour 1F **244**
BH12: Poole 1E **244**
SO40: Ashu 8H **171**
Princess Royal Cl. SO41: Lymi 2D **234**
Prince's St. PO1: Ports 9E **214**
SO14: South 4A **174**
Princess Way GU15: Camb 7L **19**
Princes Way GU11: Alders 9J **49**
Prince William Ct. SO50: B'stke 1K **161**
Prinstead Cl. SO23: Winche 8M **105**
Prinsted Cres. PO6: Farl 1L **215**
Prinsted Wlk. PO14: Fare 9N **197**
Printers Row SO23: Winche 7L **237**
Printing Ho. Ct. *GU11: Alders* *9K 49*
(off Sebastopol Rd.)
Prior Cl. BH7: Bour 9C **228**
Priors Barton SO23: Winche 9K **105**
Priors Cl. BH23: Fri C 7E **230**
GU14: Farn 4J **29**
RG20: Kings 2B **6**
Priors Ct. GU12: Ash 1N **65**
PRIORS DEAN 6H **113**
Priorsdean Av. PO3: Ports 1H **241**
Priorsdean Cres. PO9: Hav 5D **202**
Priors Dean Rd.
sO22: Winche .2H **105**
Priors Hill La. SO31: Old N 1J **195**
Priors Keep GU52: Fleet 3N **47**
Prior's La. GU17: Blackw 8C **18**
Priors Rd. RG26: Tadl 3G **10**
Priors Row RG29: N War 7J **45**
Priors Way SO22: Oli B 2F **126**
Priors Way, The
SO24: Monk 5J **111**
Priors Wood RG45: Cr'tne 1N **17**
Priory, The SO32: Bis W 4L **163**
Priory Av. SO17: South 1B **174**
Priory Cl. GU51: Fleet 3J **47**
SO17: South 1B **174**
SO32: Bis W 3L **163**
Priory Ct. BH6: Bour 9F **228**
GU15: Camb .8H **19**
PO4: S'sea 3F **240**
PO6: Cosh 9N **199**
SO32: Bis W .3L **163**
Priory Cres. PO4: S'sea 3H **241**
Priory Gdns. PO7: W'lle 9M **181**
PO16: Portc 1L **213**
RG24: Old Bas 4J **43**
SO23: Winche .7M **237**
Priory Gate 9M **237**
Priory Ho. SO14: South 4E **4** (5M **173**)
Priory Ind. Pk. BH23: Chri 7D **230**
Priory La. GU10: Fren, Tilf 1K **85**
GU34: Selb 6A **100**
RG27: H Win .8A **26**
RG28: Free 2L **55**
Priory M. BH23: Chri 8L **229**
Priory Quay BH23: Chri 9M **229**
Priory Rd. BH2: Bour 8K **247** (3J **245**)
PO4: S'sea 5H **241**
PO12: Gos 8K **213**
PO15: Fare 7N **197**
PO17: S'wick .3B **200**
SO17: South .1A **174**
SO31: Net A .3F **194**
SO50: E'leigh .2D **160**
Priory School Sports Hall 3F **240**
Priory St. GU14: Farn 8M **29**
Priory Tennis Sports Cen. 3F **240**
Priory Vw. *PO5: S'sea* *3F 240*
(off Victoria Rd. Nth.)
Priory Vw. Pl. BH9: Bour 3L **227**
Priory Vw. Rd. BH9: Bour 3L **227**
BH23: Burt 3M **229**
Prisma Pk. RG24: B'toke 3F **42**
Prite La. SO24: Cher 6E **108**
Private Rd. SO41: Lymi 1E **234**
Privet La. SP11: Fyf, Rede 7N **31**
Privet Rd. BH9: Bour 6J **227**
GU35: Lind 2M **101**
PRIVETT
GU34 . . . . .3L **137**
PO12 . . . . .3G **239**
Privett Cl. RG24: Lych 3H **43**
Privett Ho. PO1: Ports 2K **5** (1B **240**)
Privett Pl. PO12: Gos 3G **239**
Privett Rd. GU32: Frox 3D **138**
PO7: Wid 6L **201**
PO12: Gos 3G **238**
PO13: Lee S 4E **238**
PO15: Fare 7M **197**
Privett Way GU32: Pet 2L **145**
Prochurch Rd. PO8: Cowp 6B **182**
Proctor Cl. SO19: South 5H **175**
Proctor Dr. PO13: Lee S 3C **238**
SO52: N Bad .9E **130**
Proctor La. PO1: Ports 2G **240**
Promenade BH13: Poole, S'bks 9B **244**
(not continuous)
BH23: Fri C 9D **230**
PO1: Ports 8J **5** (4B **240**)
PO5: S'sea 9K **5** (5B **240**)
PO12: Gos 6H **239**
PO13: Lee S 9N **211**
Promenade, The PO2: Ports 7E **214**
PO10: Ems 1M **217**
SO45: Hythe .4M **193**
Promenade Ct. PO13: Lee S 1A **238**
Prospect Av. GU14: Farn 6K **29**
Prospect Commercial Pk. SO24: New A 2E **108**
Prospect Hill GU35: Head 8A **84**
Prospect Ho. SO19: South 5D **174**
Prospect La. PO9: Hav, R Cas 4H **203**
Prospect Pl. SO45: Hythe 4M **193**
SO53: Cha F 6A **132**
Prospect Rd. GU14: Cov, Farn 8J **29**
PO1: Ports 9D **214**
SO24: New A .2D **108**
Prospect Vs. RG22: B'toke 9A **42**
Protea Gdns. PO14: Titch 8K **197**
Provene Cl. SO32: Wal C 7A **164**
Provene Gdns. SO32: Wal C 7N **163**
Providence Ct. PO1: Ports 9E **214**
Providence Hill SO31: Burs 8L **175**
Providence Pk. SO16: Bass 6L **159**
Provost St. SP6: F'dge 1J **153**
Prowse Cl. PO13: Lee S 9A **212**
Pruetts La. GU31: Liss, Pet 4E **140**
GU33: Hi Br, Liss 4E **140**
Prunella Pl. PO7: W'lle 9K **181**
Prunus Cl. SO16: South 6H **159**
Przewalski Wlk. SO21: Owls 7B **134**
PUCKNALL 6E **124**
Puckridge Hill Rd. GU11: Alders 5G **48**
Pudbrooke Gdns. SO30: Hed E 2M **175**
Pudbrook Ho. SO30: Botl 4C **176**
Pudding La. SO23: Winche 1M **105**
Puddle Slosh La. SP6: F'dge 9G **150**
Puffin Cl. RG22: B'toke 4H **59**
SO16: South 6G **159**
Puffin Cres. PO14: Stub 4L **211**
Puffin Gdns. PO13: Gos 5D **212**
Puffin Wlk. PO8: Cowp 6L **181**
Pug's Hole SP5: W Tyt 8L **87**
Pulens Cres. GU31: Pet 9B **140**
Pulens La. GU31: Pet 8A **140**
Pulheim Pde. PO16: Fare 8E **198**
Pullman Way BH24: Ring 2K **187**
Pumphouse Way RG24: B'toke 3M **41**
Pump La. PO8: Horn 5A **182**
PO13: Gos 7E **212**
Pundle Grn. SO40: Bart 4B **170**
Punsholt La. SO24: W Tis 7F **110**
SO24: W Tis, W Tis 2F **136**
Purbeck Ct. BH5: Bour 2E **246**
BH23: Chri *6B 230*
(off Dorset Rd.)
Purbeck Dr. PO14: Fare 9N **197**
Purbeck Ho. BH8: Bour 1M **245**
Purbeck La. BH21: Cran 8L **149**
Purbeck Rd. BH2: Bour 7J **247** (2J **245**)
BH25: B Sea .7M **231**
Purbeck Wlk. PO14: Fare 9N **197**
PURBROOK 5K **201**
Purbrook Chase Pct. PO7: Purb 6M **201**
Purbrook Cl. SO16: South 7H **159**
Purbrook Gdns. PO7: Purb 4K **201**
Purbrook Heath Rd. PO7: Purb 4G **200**
Purbrook Rd. PO1: Ports 2F **240**
RG26: Tadl 5G **11**
Purbrook Way PO7: Purb 5N **201**
PO9: Hav 5B **202**
Purcell Cl. PO7: W'lle 4M **201**
RG22: B'toke .1A **60**
Purcell Rd. SO19: South 7H **175**
Purchase Rd. BH12: Poole 7F **226**
Pure Gym 4E **174**
PUREWELL 8N **229**
Purewell BH23: Chri 8N **229**
Purewell Cl. BH23: Chri 8A **230**
Purewell Ct. BH23: Chri 7A **230**
Purewell Cross BH23: Chri 8A **230**
Purewell Cross Rd. BH23: Chri 7M **229**
Purewell Gate BH23: Chri 8M **229**
Purewell Mews BH23: Chri 8M **229**
Purkess Cl. SO53: Cha F 5B **132**
Purkiss Cl. SO40: Woodl 5C **170**
Purley Way GU16: Frim 4N **29**
SO51: Plai 9L **121**
Purlieu Dr. SO45: Dib P 7J **193**
Purlieu La. SP6: Gods 4A **154**
Purmerend Cl. GU14: Cov 7E **28**
Purrocks, The GU32: Pet 8M **139**
Purser's La. SO24: Bram 2E **136**
Purslane Gdns. PO15: Titch 6H **197**
Purvis Cl. SP4: Ames 5A **66**
Purvis Gdns. SO19: South 8F **174**
Pussex La. BH23: Hurn 7D **218**
Putmans La. GU31: S Hart 6E **146**
Puttenham Rd. RG24: Chin 9H **23**
Puttocks Cl. GU27: Hasl 1M **117**
Pycroft Cl. PO11: H Isl 5J **217**
SO19: South 5E **174**
Pye La. BH21: Cran 6M **149**
PYESTOCK 2C **48**
Pyestock Cres. GU14: Cov 8E **28**
Pye St. PO1: Ports 2N **5** (1D **240**)
Pyland's La. SO31: Burs 7M **175**
Pyle Cl. PO8: Cowp 6A **182**
PYLEHILL 8N **133**
Pyle La. PO8: Horn 5E **182**
Pylewell Rd. SO45: Hythe 4M **193**
Pyotts Copse RG24: Old Bas 2H **43**
Pyotts Ct. RG24: Old Bas 2H **43**
PYOTT'S HILL 2H **43**
Pyott's Hill RG24: Old Bas 1H **43**
Pyramid Cen. PO3: Ports 5J **215**
Pyramid Pk. PO9: Hav 1E **216**
Pyramids Leisure Centre, The 6E **240**
Pyrford Cl. PO7: W'lle 8M **181**
PO12: Gos 4G **239**
Pyrford Gdns. SO41: Lymi 4E **234**
Pyrford M. SO41: Lymi 4E **234**
Pytchley Cl. PO14: Stub 6K **211**

Q

QEII Cruise Terminal 1N **193**
QM Sports Cen. 8C **42**
Quadrangle, The GU16: Frim 4L **29**
SO50: E'leigh 8E **132**
SO51: Rom 6C **130**
Quadrant SP6: F'dge 2J **153**
Quail Way PO8: Horn 4A **182**
Quaker Ct. BH24: Ring 2J **187**
Quandra Point PO3: Ports 5J **215**
Quantock Cl. RG22: B'toke 8K **41**
Quantock Ct. *BH23: Chri* *6B 230*
(off Hunt Rd.)
Quantock Rd. SO16: South 2D **172**
Quantocks, The SO45: Dib P 7J **193**
Quarely Rd. PO9: Hav 3C **202**
QUARLEY 3L **67**
Quarr Ho. SO41: Sway 4J **223**
Quarry Chase BH4: Bour 2G **245**
Quarry La. GU46: Yat 8A **18**
Quarry Rd. SO23: Winche 7M **105**
Quarterdeck, The BH5: Bour 2C **246**
PO12: Gos 2N **239**
Quarterdeck Av. PO2: Ports 7C **214**
Quarters Rd. GU14: Farn 1K **49**
Quartremaine Rd. PO3: Ports 5J **215**
Quartremaine Rd. Ind. Est. PO3: Ports 6J **215**
Quavey Rd. SP5: Redl 2N **119** (8D **120**)
Quay, The BH23: Chri 9M **229**
SO31: Hamb .7L **195**
Quay 2000 SO17: South 2A **174**
Quay Ct. BH23: Chri 6J **229**
Quay Haven SO31: Lwr Swan 2A **196**
Quay Hill SO41: Lymi 2F **234**
Quay Ho. *PO1: Ports* *7H 5*
(off Seagers Ct.)
Quay La. PO12: Gos 7K **213**
(Priory Rd.)
PO12: Gos 3N **239**
(Warrior Ct.)
SO31: Lwr Swan 2A **196**
Quayle Dr. BH11: Bour 1D **226**
Quay Point PO6: Cosh 9D **200**
Quay Rd. BH23: Chri 8L **229**
SO41: Lymi 2F **234**
Quays, The
(The Eddie Read Swimming & Diving Complex)
. . . . .7B **4** (7L **173**)
Quayside SO30: Botl 4D **176**
Quayside Commerce Cen. *PO16: Fare* *9D 198*
(off Old Gosport Rd.)
Quayside Rd. SO18: South 3A **174**
SO45: Fawl 7K **209**
Quayside Wlk. SO40: March 7E **172**
Quay St. PO16: Fare 9E **198**
(not continuous)
SO41: Lymi 2F **234**
Quay West PO12: Gos 7K **213**
QUEBEC 5E **146**
Quebec Cl. GU30: Lip 3E **116**
Quebec Gdns. GU17: Haw 9F **18**
SO31: Burs 9K **175**
Queen Anne PO1: Ports 3J **5**
Queen Anne's Dr. PO9: Bed 7C **202**
Queen Anne's Ga. GU9: H End 3F **64**
Queen Anne's Wlk. *RG21: B'toke* *6C 42*
(off Festival Pl.)
Queen Elizabeth II Jubilee Activities Cen.
. . . . .7A **176**
Queen Elizabeth Av. SO41: Lymi 2D **234**
Queen Elizabeth Country Pk. 8H **145**
Queen Elizabeth Country Pk. Cen. 2F **168**
Queen Elizabeth Ct. SO17: South 8A **160**
Queen Elizabeth Dr. GU11: Alders 9H **49**
Queen Elizabeth Rd. GU15: Camb 4M **19**
Queen Elizabeth The Queen Mother Hall
PO4: S'sea 2L **241**
Queen Katherine Rd. SO41: Lymi 3F **234**
Queen Mnr. Rd. SP5: Lave 6A **86**
Queen Mary Av. BH9: Bour 4K **227**
GU15: Camb .8J **19**
RG21: B'toke .5C **42**
Queen Mary Cl. GU51: Fleet 9L **27**
Queen Mary Rd. PO16: Portc 1M **213**
Queen Rd. PO14: Fare 2B **212**
Queens Av. BH23: Chri 9L **229**
GU11: Alders .8J **49**
SP10: A'ver 1N **69**
Queens Bldgs. SO14: South 6E **4** (6M **173**)
Queensbury Mans. BH1: Bour 7N **247** (2L **245**)
Queensbury Pl. GU17: Haw 1E **28**
Queens Cl. PO13: Lee S 1A **238**
SO45: Hythe .6N **193**
SO51: Rom 5N **129**
SP11: Ludg 1D **30**
Queens Cotts. SP11: S M Bo 9K **35**
Queens Ct. BH4: Bour 5G **247**
BH8: Bour 6M **227**
BH25: A'ley 3E **232**
GU9: Up H 3D **64**
GU14: Farn 3L **49**

Redlands La.—Robertson Way

Redlands La. GU10: Cron, Ews 2L 63
PO10: Ems 5M 203
(not continuous)
PO14: Fare 8B 198
PO16: Fare 8B 198
Red La. GU35: Head D 9D 84
RG7: A'mas, Pad C 1K 11
RG25: Pres C 3J 79
SO32: Lwr U, Uph 6C 134
SP5: Mid W 4H 87
SP5: W Tyt 8K 87
Red Leaves SO32: Wal C 9A 164
Red Lion La. GU9: Farnh 9D 64
RG21: B'toke 7C 42
RG25: Over 2D 56
Red Lion M. RG29: Odi 8L 45
Red Lion St. *SO32: Bis W 4M 163*
(off Brook St.)
Red Lodge SO53: Cha F 9N 131
Red Lodge Community Pool 7K 159
REDLYNCH 1N 119 (7C 120)
Redlynch Cl. PO9: Hav 5H 203
Redmill Dr. PO13: Lee S 9B 212
Redmoor Cl. SO19: South 4D 174
Rednal Ho. PO5: S'sea 2E 240
Red Oaks GU10: Rowl 8N 63
Red Oaks Dr. SO31: P Ga 4E 196
Redon Way SP10: A'ver 9M 51
Redoubt Ct. PO14: Fare 2B 212
Red Post La. SP11: A'ver, Weyh 9D 50
RED RICE 8H 69
Red Rice Rd. SP11: Red R, Up C 8H 69
Redrise Cl. SO45: Holb 5N 207
Redshank Rd. PO8: Horn 3A 182
Red Shoot Camping Pk. BH24: Lin 1B 188
Redvers Buller Rd. GU11: Alders 4L 49
Redvers Cl. SO41: Lymi 3E 234
Redvers Rd. BH23: Chri 7A 230
Redward Rd. SO16: Rown 6E 158
Redwing Ct. PO4: S'sea 2K 241
Redwing Gdns. SO40: Tott 2J 171
Redwing Rd. PO8: Clan 7C 168
RG22: B'toke 3H 59
Redwood RG24: Chin 9F 22
Redwood Cl. BH24: Ring 1L 187
SO30: Wes E 9G 161
SO41: Lymi 1C 234
SO45: Dib P 6H 193
Redwood Ct. PO7: W'lle 1M 201
Redwood Dr. PO16: Portc 9K 199
Redwood Gdns. SO40: Tott 4J 171
Redwood Gro. PO9: Hav 5G 202
Redwood La. GU34: Meds 9L 79
Redwood Lodge PO16: Fare 7D 198
Redwoods Way GU52: Ch Cr 6N 47
Redwood Way SO16: Bass 5M 159
Reed Cl. GU11: Alders 6M 49
Reed Dr. SO40: March 8E 172
Reeder Cl. SP6: F'dge 1H 153
Reedling Dr. PO4: S'sea 2K 241
Reedmace Cl. PO7: W'lle 3A 202
Reeds La. GU33: Liss 8J 115
Reeds Mdw. GU32: Lang 9D 138
Reed's Pl. PO12: Gos 2J 239
Reeds Rd. PO12: Gos 9K 213
Reef, The BH5: Bour 2B 246
Reefside *BH5: Bour 1B 246*
(off Florence Rd.)
Rees Hall PO5: S'sea 8M 5
Rees Rd. SO21: Wor D 5G 90
Reeves Cl. SO51: W Wel 1B 120 (9N 121)
Reeves Rd. GU12: Alders 1L 65
Reeves Way SO31: Burs 9K 175
Regal Cl. PO6: Cosh 9G 201
Regal Hgts. RG29: Odi 8K 45
Regal Wlk. SO50: E'leigh 9F 132
Regency Ct. BH1: Bour 1N 245
PO1: Ports 6J 5 (3B 240)
Regency Cres. BH23: Chri 6J 229
Regency Gdns. PO7: W'lle 3L 201
Regency Ho. BH1: Bour 5N 247
Regency Pl. BH24: Ring 9K 185
PO15: Fare 8A 198
Regent Centre, The 8L 229
Regent Cl. GU51: Fleet 3M 47
SO21: Ott 9G 127
Regent Ct. PO1: Ports 9E 214
RG21: B'toke 5D 42
SO17: South 1M 173
SO23: Winche 4L 105
(off Northlands Dr.)
Regent Dr. BH7: Bour 6C 228
Regent Ho. SO30: Hed E 8N 161
Regent Pl. PO5: S'sea 8M 5 (4C 240)
Regent Rd. SO53: Cha F 6B 132
Regents Ct. BH13: Poole 2E 244
PO9: Langs 9F 202
PO17: K Vil 2A 198
SO16: South 2G 172
SP10: A'ver 9D 52
Regents Ga. SO31: Sar G 4B 196
Regents Gro. SO15: South 1G 173
Regents M. GU32: Pet 9K 139
Regent's Pk. Gdns. SO15: South 3G 172
Regent's Pk. Rd. SO15: South 4F 172
Regents Pl. GU47: Sandh 5E 18
PO12: Gos 1M 239
Regents Trade Pk. PO13: Gos 3E 212
Regent St. GU51: Fleet 3M 47
SO14: South 5C 4 (6L 173)
Regent Way BH23: Chri 8L 229
Regiment Cl. GU14: Cov 9E 28
Reginald Mitchell Ct. SO50: E'leigh 8D 132
Reginald Noble Ct. BH4: Bour 1F 244
Reginald Rd. PO4: S'sea 4H 241
Reid St. BH23: Chri 7K 229
Reigate Ho. PO1: Ports 1E 240
Reith Way SP10: A'ver 9H 51
Relay Rd. PO7: W'lle 1L 201
Reldas, The *PO1: Ports 7J 5*
(off Oyster St.)
Reliant Cl. SO53: Cha F 7N 131
Rembrandt Cl. RG21: B'toke 8E 42
Remembrance Gdns. RG24: Chin 1F 42
Renda Rd. SO45: Holb 4A 208
Rennie Ga. SP10: A'ver 9J 51
Renny Rd. PO1: Ports 2F 240
Renoir Cl. RG21: B'toke 8E 42
Renouf Cl. SO41: Penn 3C 234
Renown Cl. SO53: Cha F 7N 131
Renown Gdns. PO8: Cowp 5N 181
Renown Ho. *PO12: Gos 3L 239*
(off The Anchorage)
Renown Way RG24: Chin 8G 22
Repton Cl. PO12: Gos 3G 238
Repton Gdns. SO30: Hed E 9A 162
(not continuous)
Reservoir La. GU32: Pet 8M 139
SO30: Hed E 4L 175
Resolution Ho. *PO12: Gos 3L 239*
(off The Anchorage)
Rest A While Pk. BH24: St L 5B 186
Rest-a-Wyle Av. PO11: H Isl 2G 243
Restharrow BH1: Bour 1L 245
Restormel Cl. RG23: B'toke 5K 41
Retreat, The BH23: Chri 8N 229
GU51: Ch Cr 5K 47
PO5: S'sea 4D 240
SO40: Tott 5N 171
SO50: E'leigh 8F 132
Retreat Holiday Caravan Park, The
PO11: H Isl 5L 243
Reuben's Cres. RG26: Tadl 6H 11
Revelstoke Av. GU14: Farn 6K 29
Revenge Cl. PO4: S'sea 1K 241
Revenge Ho. PO12: Gos 3L 239
Rewlands Dr. SO22: Winche 3G 105
Rex Ind. Est. SO53: Cha F 7B 132
Reynards Cl. RG26: Tadl 5H 11
Reynolds Cl. RG21: B'toke 7F 42
Reynolds Ct. SO51: Rom 6N 129
SP10: A'ver 8M 51
Reynolds Dale SO40: Tott 5K 171
Reynolds Grn. GU47: Coll 7F 18
Reynolds Ho. *RG22: B'toke 9L 41*
(off Pinkerton Rd.)
Reynolds Rd. GU14: Farn 3D 48
PO12: Gos 5L 239
SO15: South 2H 173
SO50: Fair O 2A 162
Reynolds St. GU51: Fleet 8K 27
Reyntiens Vw. RG29: Odi 9L 45
Rhine Banks GU14: Cov 7F 28
Rhinefield Cl. PO9: Hav 5C 202
SO42: Broc 6B 148 (8N 189)
SO50: B'stke 1K 161
Rhinefield Rd. BH25: Woot 5N 221
SO42: Broc 6K 189
Rhiners Cl. SO41: Sway 5J 223
Rhodes Sq. SP10: A'ver 7B 52
Rhyll Gdns. GU11: Alders 1H 65
Rhyme Hall M. SO45: Fawl 5F 208
Rhys Ct. PO4: S'sea 3H 241
Ribble Cl. SO53: Cha F 7B 132
Ribble Ct. SO16: South 1D 172
SP10: A'ver 8B 52
(off Itchen Ct.)
Ribble Gdns. PO16: Portc 9J 199
Ribble Pl. GU14: Cov 6G 28
Ribble Way RG21: B'toke 6E 42
Ribbonwood Hgts. BH14: Poole 1A 244
Ricardo Cres. BH23: Mude 8C 230
Ricardo Way SO41: Bold 8D 224
Richard Cl. GU51: Fleet 4K 47
Richard Ct. PO3: Ports 1H 241
Richard Gro. PO12: Gos 7J 213
Richard Moss Ho. SO23: Winche 6M 237
Richard Newitt Courts SO16: Bass 6M 159
Richards Cl. BH10: Bour 4H 227
SO31: Loc H 6D 196
SO45: Fawl 6D 208
Richards Ct. SO15: South 1G 173
SO30: Wes E 9G 160
Richards Fld. RG24: Old Bas 1H 43
Richardson Cl. RG26: B'ley 2G 22
Richardson Dr. PO15: Fare 7N 197
Richard Taunton Pl. SO17: South 9M 159
Richborough Dr. SP10: Charl 7J 51
Riches M. PO16: Fare 8C 198
Richlans Rd. SO30: Hed E 4N 175
Richmond PO1: Ports 2J 5
Richmond Cl. GU14: Cov 9F 28
GU35: W'hil 5J 101
GU52: Fleet 5L 47
PO11: H Isl 3D 242
SO40: Calm 1H 171
SO53: Cha F 3A 132
Richmond Ct. BH8: Bour 7N 227
BH25: New M 3B 232
GU51: Fleet 3L 47
SO41: M Sea 8J 235
Richmond Cres. SP9: Tidw 8E 30 (7H 31)
Richmond Dene *BH2: Bour 1K 245*
(off Wimborne Rd.)
Richmond Dr. PO11: H Isl 3D 242
Richmond Gdns. BH1: Bour 6M 247 (2K 245)
PO7: Purb 4K 201
(off Crofton Cl.)
SO17: South 1N 173
Richmond Gdns. Shopping Cen.
BH1: Bour 6M 247 (2K 245)
Richmond Hgts. BH1: Bour 5M 247
Richmond Hill BH2: Bour 7L 247 (2K 245)
Richmond Hill Dr. BH2: Bour 6L 247 (2K 245)
Richmond Hill Ga. BH2: Bour 6L 247
Richmond Ho. BH2: Bour 6L 247 (2K 245)
GU47: Coll 6G 19
SO22: Winche 6K 237 (6K 105)
Richmond La. SO51: Rom 3N 129
Richmond Pk. SO21: Ott 9H 127
Richmond Pk. Av. BH8: Bour 7M 227
Richmond Pk. Cl. BH8: Bour 8A 228
Richmond Pk. Cres. BH8: Bour 7N 227
Richmond Pk. Lodge *BH8: Bour 8N 227*
(off Richmond Pk. Rd.)
Richmond Pk. Rd. BH8: Bour 7M 227
Richmond Pl. PO1: Ports 4L 5 (2C 240)
PO5: S'sea 5D 240
Richmond Ri. PO16: Portc 8L 199
Richmond Rd. BH14: Poole 9A 226
GU47: Coll 5G 19
PO5: S'sea 5E 240
PO12: Gos 3J 239
PO13: Lee S 9N 211
RG21: B'toke 5B 42
SO15: South 4H 173
Richmond St. SO14: South 7E 4 (7M 173)
Richmond Ter. PO5: S'sea 9N 5
Richmond Wood Rd. BH8: Bour 7M 227
Richville Rd. SO16: South 2F 172
Rickett La. RG27: H Wes 4D 24
Ridding Cl. SO15: South 1G 173
Riddings La. RG19: Head 2M 9
Riders La. PO9: Hav 5E 202
(not continuous)
Rideway Cl. GU15: Camb 9K 19
RIDGE 2J 157
Ridge, The SP5: Redl, Woodf 3M 119 (9C 120)
SP6: Gods 4B 154
Ridge Cl. PO8: Clan 7C 168
RG22: B'toke 5L 59
RIDGE COMMON 7J 139
Ridge Comn. La. GU32: Ste, Stro 9H 139
Ridgefield Gdns. BH23: Chri 6F 230
Ridge La. RG27: Newn, Roth 2D 44
SO30: Botl 7G 176
SO51: Rom 2H 157
Ridgemoor Cl. GU26: Hind 2N 103
Ridgemount Av. SO16: Bass 2N 159
Ridgemount La. SO16: Bass 6L 159
Ridges, The RG40: Cr'tne, F'std 1K 17
Ridges Vw. SP11: Lit L 2C 52
Ridge Top La. GU32: Frox, Ste, Stro 7D 138
Ridgeway SO22: Winche 9G 104
Ridgeway, The GU34: Alt 6F 80
PO16: Fare 8G 198
Ridgeway Cl. PO6: Cosh 8A 200
SO50: Fair O 9N 133
SO53: Cha F 7C 132
Ridgeway La. SO41: Lymi 4D 234
Ridgeway Office Pk. GU32: Pet 2K 145
Ridgeway Pde. GU52: Ch Cr 6M 47
Ridgeway Wlk. SO53: Cha F 7C 132
Ridgewood Cl. SO45: Dib 5H 193
Ridgway PO9: Hav 8D 202
Ridings, The GU33: Liss 1G 140
PO2: Ports 4G 214
SO32: Wal C 7A 164
SO50: B'stke 1L 161
Ridley Cl. GU52: Fleet 4L 47
SO45: Holb 4A 208
Ridley Rd. BH9: Bour 6K 227
Ridleys Piece RG29: S War 4D 62
Ridout Cl. BH10: Bour 5F 226
Rifle Way GU14: Cov 9E 28
Rigby Rd. SO17: South 2N 173
Riggs Gdns. BH11: Bour 4D 226
Riley La. RG24: Old Bas 4J 43
Riley Rd. SO21: Wor D 5J 91
Rimbault Cl. GU11: Alders 4M 49
Rimbury Way BH23: Chri 6K 229
Rimes La. RG26: Bau 7F 10
Rimington Gdns. SO51: Rom 2A 130
Rimington Rd. PO8: Cowp 7M 181
Rindle Cl. GU14: Cov 8E 28
Ring, The SO16: Chilw 4K 159
Ringbury SO41: Lymi 9D 224
Ringlet Way SO23: Winche 6N 105
Ringsgreen La. GU32: Frox 3G 139
Ringshall Gdns. RG26: B'ley 1F 22
Ringway Centre, The
RG21: B'toke 4A 42
Ringway East RG21: B'toke 4E 42
Ringway Ho. RG24: B'toke 4E 42
Ringway Nth. RG21: B'toke 4L 41
RG24: B'toke 4L 41
Ringway Sth. RG21: B'toke 9B 42
Ringway West RG21: B'toke 4N 41
RINGWOOD 1J 187
Ringwood Brewery 2J 187
Ringwood Dr. SO52: N Bad 7D 130
Ringwood Health & Leisure Cen. 1K 187
Ringwood Ho. PO9: Hav 4F 202
Ringwood La. BH21: Wim G 7G 148
Ringwood Raceway 1E 218
Ringwood Rd. BH11: Bour 3B 226
BH12: Poole 6A 226
BH23: Avon, Sop 7K 219
BH23: Bran, Hin, Walk 6C 220
(not continuous)
BH24: Bur 6C 188
BH24: St I, St L 7A 186
(not continuous)
BH31: Ver 4A 184
GU14: Farn 5L 29
GU17: Blackw 7E 18
PO4: S'sea 4J 241
SO40: Bart, Net M, Tott 4D 170
SO43: St Cr 8K 155
SP6: Ald 5C 152
SP6: Bick, F'dge 2K 153
SP6: N Gor 6M 153
SP6: N Gor, S Gor 9K 153
Ringwood Rd. Retail Pk.
BH11: Bour 3C 226
Ringwood Town & Country Experience 8J 185
Ringwood Trad. Est. BH24: Ring 2K 187
RIPLEY 5M 219
Ripley Gro. PO3: Ports 8H 215
Ripley Ter. RG27: Sher L 7J 23
Ripon Ct. PO13: Gos 2F 238
SO50: Hor H 4A 162
Ripon Gdns. PO7: W'lle 9B 182
Ripon Rd. BH9: Bour 6L 227
GU17: Min 3B 28
Ripplesmore Cl. GU47: Sandh 5D 18
Ripplewood SO40: March 9F 172
Ripstone Gdns. SO17: South 8N 159
Rise, The PO7: Wid 7L 201
RG40: F'std 3D 16
RG45: Cr'tne 1B 18
SO42: Broc 7C 148 (8N 189)
RISELEY 2G 14
Riseley Bus. Pk. RG7: Rise 2G 15
Risinghurst M. RG24: B'toke 2B 42
Ritchie Cl. PO11: H Isl 4G 242
Ritchie Ct. SO19: South 6F 174
Ritchie Rd. BH11: Bour 2F 226
Rival Moor Rd. GU31: Pet 1B 146
Rivendale *SO15: South 4H 173*
(off Payne's Rd.)
River Cl. GU34: Four M 5J 97
River Ct. BH23: Bour A 7D 218
SO41: Lymi 2F 234
Riverdale Av. PO7: W'lle 2A 202
Riverdale Cl. SP6: F'dge 9J 151
Riverdale La. BH23: Chri 8K 229
Riverdene Pl. SO18: South 2B 174
Riverdown Rd. GU32: W Meo 3C 136
River Gdns. SO41: M Sea 8L 235
River Glade BH23: Chri 3G 228
River Grn. SO31: Hamb 7L 195
Riverhead SO24: Bis S 2L 109
Riverhead Cl. PO4: S'sea 2J 241
River Hill GU34: Bins 1F 82
River La. PO15: F'ley 3M 197
Riverlea Rd. BH23: Chri 8K 229
Rivermead SP4: Idm 9C 66
Rivermead Cl. SO51: Rom 5K 129
Rivermead Ct. PO10: Ems 6N 203
Rivermead Gdns. BH23: Chri 4H 229
Rivermead Ho. SO51: Rom 5K 129
Rivermead Rd. GU15: Camb 2K 29
Rivermede GU35: Bor 3K 101
River M. SO50: B'stke 9H 133
SP6: F'dge 1J 153
River Pk. Leisure Cen. 6N 237 (5L 105)
River Rd. GU46: Yat 5L 17
SP6: Gods 9N 151
Rivers Cl. GU14: Farn 2N 49
Riversdale Cl. SO19: South 1C 194
Riversdale Gdns. PO9: Hav 7F 202
Riversdale Rd. BH6: Bour 1K 247
Riverside BH10: Bour 2K 227
BH24: Ring 2J 187
GU34: Alt 5H 81
SO50: B'stke 9H 133
SP11: G Cla 7N 69
Riverside Av. BH7: Bour 4E 228
PO16: Fare 6F 198
Riverside Bus. Pk. GU9: Farnh 7F 64
SO41: Lymi 2F 234
Riverside Caravan Pk. SO31: Hamb 4L 195
Riverside Cl. GU14: Cov 7H 29
GU33: Liss 1E 140
RG24: Old Bas 3J 43
RG25: Over 2E 56
SO40: Bart 4C 170
Riverside Ct. GU9: Farnh 7E 64
SO18: South 2B 174
(Harcourt Rd.)
SO18: South 3A 174
(Manor Wharf)
Riverside Gdns. SO51: Rom 6K 129
Riverside Grn. SO20: Ki S 6G 88
Riverside Ho. SO23: Winche 7P 237
Riverside Indoor Bowling Club 5L 105
Riverside Ind. Pk. GU9: Farnh 7F 64
Riverside La. BH6: Bour 9J 229
Riverside M. PO17: Wick 7C 178
Riverside Pk. BH23: Chri 9K 229
GU9: Farnh 7F 64
Riverside Pk. (Watchmoor Pk.)
GU15: Camb 1J 29
Riverside Pl. SP6: F'dge 1J 153
Riverside Rd. BH6: Bour 9J 229
Riverside Ter. PO10: Ems 9N 203
Riverside Wlk. GU31: Pet 1N 145
(not continuous)
Riverside Way GU15: Camb 1J 29
Riverslea Mews BH23: Chri 8N 229
Rivers Reach SO41: Lymi 3F 234
River's St. PO5: S'sea 3E 240
River Vw. GU34: Alt 4G 80
Riverview SO40: Tott 5M 171
River Vw. Cl. SO20: Chil 4E 74
River Vw. Ho. SO19: South 7B 174
River Vw. Rd. SO18: South 9B 160
Riverview Ter. SO31: Lwr Swan 1A 196
River Wlk. SO18: South 8C 160
River Way BH23: Chri 5G 228
PO9: Hav 6G 202
SP10: A'ver 8A 52
Riverwey Ind. Pk. GU34: Alt 4H 81
Riviera BH1: Bour 2M 245
Riviera Ct. BH2: Bour 6H 247 (2H 245)
BH13: Poole 6D 244
RJ Mitchell Centre, The
SO19: South 6B 174
R L Stevenson Av. BH4: Bour 2F 244
Roads Hill PO8: Cath 1N 181
Road Vw. PO2: Ports 8D 214
Robard Ho. SO31: Burs 9K 175
Robere Ho. SO19: South 7C 174
Robert Cecil Av. SO18: S'ing 7C 160
Robert Mack Ct. PO1: Ports 4K 5 (2C 240)
Robert Mays Rd. RG29: Odi 9J 45
Roberts Cl. PO17: Wick 6C 178
SO23: Kin W 6M 91
SO41: Ever 5M 233
Robertshaw Ho. SO43: Lyn 1B 148
Robertson Cl. GU34: Alt 7D 80
Robertson Rd. SO24: New A 2E 108
Robertson Way GU12: Ash 1N 65

Roberts Rd.—Rowanside Cl.

Roberts Rd. BH7: Bour 8D 228
GU12: Alders 1L 65
GU15: Camb 7J 19
GU33: Longc 4H 115
PO12: Gos 1H 239
SO15: South 5J 173
SO21: Bar S 5A 76
SO40: Tott 5M 171
SO45: Hythe 5L 193
SP11: Ludg 2C 30 (5K 31)
Robert Whitworth Dr. SO51: Rom 3M 129
Robin Cl. GU34: Alt 2G 80
RG22: B'toke 2J 59
Robin Cres. BH25: Bash 1M 231
Robin Gdns. BH23: Chri 6K 229
PO8: Cowp 6L 181
SO40: Tott 2J 171
Robin Gro. BH25: New M 4A 232
Robin Hood Cl. GU14: Farn 5J 29
Robinia Cl. PO7: W'lle 2A 202
Robinia Grn. SO16: South 6H 159
Robin La. GU47: Sandh 5D 18
Robin Pl. SO31: Net A 3F 194
Robin's Bow GU15: Camb 9K 19
Robins Cl. PO14: Stub 5M 211
Robins Ct. *SO24: New A 1F 108*
(off Station App.)
Robins Gro. Cres. GU46: Yat 7L 17
Robin's Mdw. PO14: Titch C 8F 196
Robinson Ct. PO13: Lee S 2A 238
PO16: Portc 8L 199
Robinson Rd. PO14: Stub 7L 211
Robinson Way GU35: Bor 5K 101
PO3: Ports 6K 215
Robin Sq. SO50: E'leigh 1A 160
Robins Way BH23: Mude 9D 230
Robin Way SP10: A'ver 8A 52
Robsall Cl. BH12: Poole 7C 226
Rocheford Cl. SP5: Mid W 4H 87
Rochester Cl. RG22: B'toke 2K 59
Rochester Ct. PO13: Gos 2F 238
Rochester Gro. GU51: Fleet 3L 47
Rochester Rd. BH11: Bour 2F 226
PO4: S'sea 4G 241
Rochester St. SO14: South 5A 174
Rochford Rd. PO6: Cosh 9E 200
RG21: B'toke 6B 42
Rockall Cl. SO16: South 6D 158
ROCKBOURNE 2C 150
Rockbourne Cl. PO9: Hav 5C 202
Rockbourne Gdns. BH25: New M 6M 231
Rockbourne La. SP6: Dame, R'bne 3P 149
Rockbourne Rd. RG27: Sher L 7H 23
SO22: Winche 2H 105
SP5: Com B 7F 118
SP6: Com B, R'bne 7F 118
SP6: R'bne, Sand 3C 150
Rockbourne Roman Villa (remains of) 4C 150
Rockdale Dr. GU26: Gray 4M 103
Rockdale Ho. GU26: Gray 4M 103
Rockery, The GU14: Cov 9F 28
Rockery Cl. SO45: Dib 5H 193
Rockfield Way GU47: Coll 5F 18
ROCKFORD 5M 185
Rockford Cl. BH6: Bour 2J 247
Rockford Ho. SO50: Fair O 3M 161
Rock Gdns. GU11: Alders 1H 65
Rock Ho. La. GU10: Farnh 7H 65
Rockingham Way PO16: Portc 9K 199
Rockleigh Dr. SO40: Tott 6K 171
Rockleigh Rd. SO16: South 8J 159
Rockmoor La. SP11: Litt 6E 6
Rockram Cl. SO40: Bart 3B 170
Rockram Gdns. SO45: Dib 6H 193
Rockrose Ct. SP11: Ludg 2D 30
Rockrose Way PO6: Cosh 7B 200
Rockstone Ct. SO14: South 1E 4 (4M 173)
Rockstone La. SO14: South 1D 4 (4M 173)
Rockstone Pl. SO15: South 1C 4 (4L 173)
Rockville Dr. PO7: W'lle 2M 201
Rockwood Ct. PO10: Ems 8M 203
Rodbourne Cl. SO41: Ever 6L 233
Rodfield La. SO21: Chilc 1F 134
SO24: Ovin 9M 107 (1F 134)
Roding Cl. RG21: B'toke 6E 42
Rodlease La. SO41: Bold 4E 224
Rodmel Ct. GU14: Farn 2N 49
Rodney Cl. BH12: Poole 6E 226
PO13: Gos 9E 212
Rodney Ct. SO19: South 6G 175
SP10: A'ver 9C 52
Rodney Dr. BH23: Mude 8B 230
Rodney Ho. PO12: Gos 3M 239
Rodney Rd. PO4: S'sea 2G 241
Rodney Way PO8: Horn 4B 182
Rodwell Cl. BH10: Bour 1G 227
Roebuck Av. PO15: F'ley 3N 197
Roebuck Cl. BH25: New M 3C 232
PO6: Cosh 1G 214
Roebuck Dr. PO12: Gos 9L 213
Roedeer Copse GU27: Hasl 9N 103
Roe Downs Rd. GU34: Meds 1G 97
Roentgen Rd. RG24: B'toke 4F 42
Roeshot Cres. BH23: Chri 5G 230
Roeshot Hill BH23: Chri 5E 230
Roewood Cl. SO45: Holb 5A 208
Roewood Rd. SO45: Holb 5A 208
ROGATE 9L 141
Rogate Gdns. PO16: Portc 8L 199
Rogate Ho. PO1: Ports 1E 240
Rogate Rd. GU33: Hi Br 4G 141
Roger Penny Way SO43: B'haw, Broo 3G 154
SP5: Redl 5A 154
SP6: Gods 5A 154
Rogers Cl. PO12: Gos 1K 239
SO50: B'stke 8J 133
Rogers Ct. GU34: Alt 5F 80
Rogers Ho. PO13: Lee S 2B 238
Rogers Mead PO11: H Isl 5F 216
Rogers Rd. SO50: B'stke 8J 133
Roi-Mar Home Pk. BH8: Bour 2A 228
Roke La. RG29: Odi 1G 62
SO32: Bis W 1K 163
Roker Way SO50: Fair O 2M 161
Rokes Pl. GU46: Yat 7K 17
Roko Health & Fitness
Portsmouth 5H 215
Roland Cl. PO8: Horn 4B 182
Roll Ct. SO16: Bass 6M 159
Rollesbrook Gdns. SO15: South 2A 4 (4K 173)
Rollestone Rd. SO45: Holb 5N 207
Rolling Mill Mews SO50: E'leigh 1D 160
Rolls Dr. BH6: Bour 1L 247
Roman Cl. SO53: Cha F 5C 132
Roman Dr. SO16: Chilw 4K 159
Roman Gdns. SO45: Dib P 8J 193
Roman Grn. PO7: Den 6F 180
Roman Gro. PO16: Portc 2M 213
Roman Ho. RG23: B'toke 6K 41
Roman Mdw. SP5: Down 2K 119 (7A 120)
Roman Quay SP6: F'dge 1J 153
Roman Ride RG45: Cr'tne 1N 17
Roman Rd. RG23: B'toke, Wort 7J 41
SO16: Bass, Chilw 3L 159
SO20: S Bri 2E 88
SO21: Twyf 7L 127
SO45: Dib P 6H 193
SO45: Hard 2N 207
Roman Row SO32: Bis W 3N 163
Romans Bus. Pk. GU9: Farnh 7F 64
Romans Fld. RG7: Sil 4A 12
Romans Ga. RG26: Pam H 4M 11
Roman's Rd. SO23: Winche 9L 237 (8K 105)
Roman Way GU9: Farnh 6G 64
PO9: Bed 7C 202
RG23: Wort 7J 41
SO21: Bar S 5B 76
SO45: Dib P 8J 193
SP10: A'ver 6A 52
Romany, The GU14: Farn 2C 48
Romany Folklore Mus. 8L 99
Romayne Cl. GU14: Cov 7J 29
Romero Hall SO15: South 3L 173
Romford Rd. SO31: Wars 9A 196
Romill Cl. SO18: Wes E 8F 160
Romley Ct. GU9: Farnh 9F 64
Romney Cl. BH10: Bour 3J 227
Romney Ct. *BH4: Bour 2G 245*
(off Portarlington Rd.)
Romney Rd. BH10: Bour 2J 227
SP11: E Ant 6B 52
ROMSEY 5L 129
Romsey Av. PO3: Ports 1J 241
PO16: Portc 9J 199
Romsey By-Pass SO51: Rom 6K 129
Romsey Cl. GU11: Alders 4L 65
GU17: Blackw 7E 18
RG24: B'toke 2B 42
SO50: E'leigh 9E 132
Romsey Ct. SO15: South 4J 173
Romsey Golf Course 4B 158
Romsey Ind. Est. SO51: Rom 4L 129
Romsey Rd. PO8: Horn 9C 168
SO16: Nur, South 4B 158
SO20: Brou 2A 86 (5A 88)
SO20: Ki S 9A 86 (8E 88)
SO20: N Wal 9M 67
SO22: Pitt, Winche 8H 237 (1C 126)
SO23: Winche 8H 237 (7H 105)
SO40: Cad, Copy 6N 155
SO43: Lyn 1B 148 (2N 189)
SO50: E'leigh 9E 132
SO51: Awb, Lock 4A 122
SO51: E Wel, W Wel 1B 120 (9N 121)
SO51: Ower 5F 156
SP4: Ames 6A 66
SP5: W'psh 5H 121
SP11: Cott, Full, G Cla, Wher 8B 70
Romsey Sports Cen. 6M 129
Romsey Station (Rail) 4M 129
Romyns Ct. PO14: Fare 8B 198
Ronald Bowker Ct.
SO22: Winche 6H 237 (6J 105)
Ronald Pugh Ct. SO18: S'ing 7C 160
Rondle Wood GU30: Mill 6N 141
Rookcliff SO41: M Sea 8J 235
Rookcliff Way SO41: M Sea 8J 235
Rooke Ho. PO1: Ports 3K 5
Rookery, The PO10: S'brne 8N 203
RG20: High 4A 8
RG28: Whit 5G 55
SP5: Com B 2G 119
SP5: W Dean 1J 121
Rookery Av. PO15: White 2E 196
(not continuous)
Rookery Grange SO31: Swanw 2E 196
Rookery La. SO20: Brou 2B 86 (5B 88)
SP6: Brea 2J 151
Rookesbury Pk. Caravan Club Site
PO17: Wick 5F 178
Rookes Cl. PO8: Horn 4B 182
Rookes La. SO41: Lymi 4D 234
Rookes M. GU31: Pet 9N 139
Rook Farm Way PO11: H Isl 3F 242
Rook Hill Rd. BH23: Fri C 8D 230
Rook La. SO21: M'dvr 7J 77
Rookley SO31: Net A 2G 195
Rooksbridge SO45: Dib 6H 193
Rooksbury Cft. PO9: Hav 4G 202
Rooksbury Mill Ct. SP10: A'ver 3L 69
Rooksbury Rd. SP10: A'ver 3L 69
Rooksdown Av. RG24: B'toke 3L 41
Rooksdown La. RG24: B'toke 3K 41
(not continuous)
Rooks Down Rd. SO22: Winche 9H 105
Rooksfield RG20: Bis G 2G 9
Rooksway Gro. PO16: Portc 9H 199
Rookswood GU34: Alt 3F 80
Rookswood Cl. RG27: Hoo 2H 45
Rookwood SO41: M Sea 8J 235
Rookwood Av. GU47: Owl 3G 18
Rookwood Cl. SO50: E'leigh 6F 132
Rookwood Gdns. SP6: F'dge 1G 152
Rookwood La. GU34: Meds 4D 96
SO24: Rop 5D 96
Rookwood Vw. PO7: Den 5G 180
Rope Hill SO41: Bold 6C 224
Rope Quays PO12: Gos 2M 239
Rope Wlk. SO31: Hamb 7L 195
Rope Walk, The PO16: Fare 9D 198
Ropewalk Ho. SO23: Winche 6M 237
Rope Yarn La. SP11: Stoke 6J 35
ROPLEY 2E 110
Ropley Cl. RG26: Tadl 6G 11
SO19: South 1E 194
ROPLEY DEAN 1B 110
Ropley Rd. BH7: Bour 7F 228
GU34: E Tis 1N 111
PO9: Hav 4H 203
ROPLEY SOKE 7F 96
Ropley Station
Watercress Line (Mid-Hants Railway) 1A 110
Rosary Gdns. GU46: Yat 7N 17
Roscrea Cl. BH6: Bour 1L 247
Roscrea Dr. BH6: Bour 1L 247
Rosebank Cl. RG26: Tadl 5H 11
SO16: Rown 6D 158
Rosebank Lodge SO16: Rown 6D 158
Rosebay Cl. SO50: Hor H 5N 161
Rosebay Ct. PO7: W'lle 4N 201
Rosebay Gdns. RG27: Hoo 1J 45
Roseberry Cl. RG22: B'toke 5K 59
Rosebery Av. PO6: Cosh 1H 215
SO45: Hythe 7M 193
Rosebery Cl. BH31: Ver 4A 184
Rosebery Cres. SO50: E'leigh 6F 132
Rosebery Rd. BH5: Bour 9D 228
SO24: New A 1E 108
Rose Bowl County Golf Course, The 2K 175
Rosebrook Ct. SO18: South 3C 174
Rosebud Av. BH9: Bour 4L 227
Rose Cl. RG22: B'toke 2K 59
SO30: Hed E 2N 175
SO45: Hythe 7M 193
Rosecott PO8: Horn 4D 182
Rose Cotts. GU52: Ch Cr 8L 47
Rose Ct. PO12: Gos 1J 239
Rosecrae Cl. BH25: New M 2A 232
Rosedale GU12: Alders 9L 49
Rosedale Av. SO51: Rom 5N 129
Rosedale Cl. BH23: Chri 8A 230
PO14: Titch 9J 197
Rosedene Gdns. GU51: Fleet 1L 47
Rosedene La. GU47: Coll 7F 18
Rosedene Lodge BH12: Poole 9F 226
Rose Estate, The RG27: Hoo 3H 45
Rosefield Ct. RG27: H Win 5C 26
Rose Gdns. BH9: Bour 4K 227
GU14: Cov 9G 28
Rose Hill PO8: Cowp 4A 182
Rosehill Cl. BH23: Bran 6D 220
Rosehill Dr. BH23: Bran 6C 220
Rosehip Cl. SO50: Fair O 2L 161
Rosehip Way RG24: Lych 4G 42
Rose Hodson Ct. RG20: Kings 1A 6 (5K 9)
Rose Hodson Pl. RG23: B'toke 4L 41
Roselands *BH1: Bour 9J 227*
(off Lansdowne Rd.)
PO8: Horn 5A 182
SO30: Wes E 2H 175
Roselands Cl. SO50: Fair O 9M 133
Roselands Gdns. SO17: South 9M 159
Rose La. SP11: Fyf 9N 31
Roseleigh Dr. SO40: Tott 4L 171
Rosemary Cl. GU14: Cov 7F 28
SO23: Winche 7P 237 (6M 105)
Rosemary Ct. BH23: Highc 7K 231
SO40: Tott 3H 171
(off Alkman La.)
Rosemary Dr. RG26: Tadl 7H 11
Rosemary Gdns. BH12: Poole 7A 226
GU17: Blackw 8E 18
PO15: White 1G 197
SO30: Hed E 5N 175
Rosemary Hall Cl. GU12: Ash 1N 65
Rosemary La. GU10: Rowl 8N 63
GU17: Blackw 8D 18
PO1: Ports 4J 5 (2B 240)
Rosemary Pl. SO45: Blac 9D 208
Rosemary Price Ct. SO30: Hed E 2N 175
Rosemary Rd. BH12: Poole 7A 226
Rosemary Wlk. PO13: Lee S 1B 238
Rosemary Way PO8: Horn 6B 182
Rosemoor Gro. SO53: Cha F 3N 131
Rosemount Ct. SO30: Wes E 9G 160
Rosemount Rd. BH4: Bour 3F 244
Rosendale Rd. SO53: Cha F 8B 132
Rose Rd. SO14: South 2M 173
SO40: Elin 4N 171
Rosery, The PO12: Gos 6K 239
Rosetta Rd. PO4: S'sea 3J 241
Rose Wlk. GU51: Fleet 1L 47
Rosewall Rd. SO16: South 8E 158
Rosewarne Ct. SO23: Winche 5L 105
Rosewood PO13: Gos 7G 212
RG24: Chin 9F 22
Rosewood Gdns. BH25: New M 2A 232
PO8: Clan 6C 168
SO40: March 9F 172
Rosewood Rd. GU35: Lind 2M 101
Rosida Gdns. SO15: South 2A 4 (4K 173)
Rosina Cl. PO7: W'lle 1B 202
Roslin Gdns. BH3: Bour 7H 227
Roslin Hall BH1: Bour 2N 245
Roslin Rd. BH3: Bour 7J 227
Roslin Rd. Sth. BH3: Bour 7H 227
(not continuous)
Roslyn Ho. PO5: S'sea 7N 5 (4D 240)
Rosoman Ct. SO19: South 6D 174
Rosoman Rd. SO19: South 6D 174
Rossan Av. SO31: Wars 9A 196
Ross Cl. RG21: B'toke 9B 42
Rossetti Cl. RG24: B'toke 3D 42
Ross Gdns. BH11: Bour 1A 226
SO16: South 9F 158
Ross Glades BH23: Chri 8J 227
Rossington Av. SO18: South 3D 174
Rossington Way SO18: South 3D 174
Rossini Cl. RG22: B'toke 2N 59
Rossiters La. SO40: Woodl 5D 170
Rossiters Quay BH23: Chri 8M 229
Rossley Cl. BH23: Chri 4G 230
Rosslyn Cl. SO52: N Bad 8F 130
Ross Mews SO31: Net A 4E 194
ROSSMORE 7D 226
Rossmore Gdns. GU11: Alders 1G 65
Rossmore Pde. BH12: Poole 6A 226
Rossmore Rd. BH12: Poole 6A 226
Ross Rd. BH24: Poul 7M 185
Ross Way PO13: Lee S 9B 212
Roston Cl. SO18: Wes E 8E 160
Rostrevor La. PO4: S'sea 6F 240
Rostron Cl. SO18: Wes E 9G 160
Rosyth Rd. SO18: South 3D 174
Rotary Ho. SO15: South 1J 173
Rothay Ct. RG21: B'toke 6E 42
Rothbury Cl. SO19: South 6E 174
SO40: Tott 1K 171
Rothbury Pk. BH25: New M 4C 232
Rotherbank Farm La. GU33: Liss 8F 114
Rotherbrook Ct. GU32: Pet 2K 145
Rother Cl. GU31: Pet 9B 140
GU47: Sandh 5E 18
SO18: Wes E 1F 174
Rothercombe La. GU32: Stro 9G 138
Rother Dale SO19: South 7J 175
Rotherfield Pk. 1B 112
Rotherfield Pk. Est. GU34: E Tis 1A 112
Rotherfield Rd. BH5: Bour 2E 246
BH23: Highc 5J 231
Rother Ho. GU33: Liss 2E 140
Rother Rd. GU14: Cov 6G 29
ROTHERWICK 7E 24
Rotherwick Cl. PO9: Hav 4H 203
Rotherwick Ct. GU14: Farn 3L 49
Rotherwick Ho. GU51: Fleet 8J 27
Rotherwick La. RG27: H Wes, Roth 4B 24
Rotherwick Rd. RG26: Tadl 6H 11
Rothesay Dr. BH23: Highc 7G 230
Rothesay Rd. BH4: Bour 8G 227
PO12: Gos 9J 213
Rothsbury Dr. SO53: Cha F 6N 131
Rothschild Cl. SO19: South 9C 174
Rothville Pl. SO53: Cha F 2N 131
Rothwell Cl. PO6: Cosh 8B 200
Rothwell Ho. RG45: Cr'tne 1E 18
ROTTEN GREEN 7J 27
Rotten Grn. La. RG27: Elve 7K 27
Rotten Hill RG25: Over 4N 55
RG28: L'stoke 4N 55
Rotterdam Dr. BH23: Chri 7N 229
Rotterdam Towers SO19: South 1D 194
Rotunda Est. GU11: Alders 9K 49
ROUGHDOWN 7A 208
Roughdown La. SO45: Blac, Holb 7A 208
Roumelia La. BH5: Bour 1B 246
Roundabouts, The GU33: Liss 9F 114
Roundaway La. SP11: Tang 9E 32
Round Cl. GU46: Yat 8B 18
Round Copse SO45: Dib 6H 193
Roundhaye Gdns. BH11: Bour 1D 226
Roundhaye Rd. BH11: Bour 1D 226
ROUND HILL 8G 49
Round Hill SP6: F'dge 1J 153
Roundhill Cl. SO18: South 1E 174
Roundhouse Ct. PO11: H Isl 5H 243
SO41: Lymi 3D 234
(off Queen St.)
Roundhouse Dr. SO40: Tott 4H 171
Roundhouse Mdw. PO10: S'brne 1N 217
Roundhuts Ri. SO23: Winche 6N 105
Roundmead Rd. RG21: B'toke 7B 42
Round Tower, The 7H 5 (4A 240)
Roundtown RG25: Tun 2J 61
Roundway PO7: W'lle 1N 201
Roundway Ct. SP10: A'ver 1L 69
Roundways BH11: Bour 3C 226
Rounton Rd. GU52: Ch Cr 5M 47
Routs Way SO16: Rown 4D 158
Row, The *RG27: H Win 6C 26*
(off High St.)
SP5: Redl 1M 119 (7D 120)
Rowallan Av. PO13: Gos 8E 212
Rowan Av. PO8: Cowp 8B 182
Rowan Cl. BH23: Chri 6F 230
BH24: St L 4A 186
GU15: Camb 5N 19
GU51: Fleet 2A 48
PO13: Lee S 2B 238
PO15: White 1G 196
RG26: Tadl 5J 11
SO16: South 8F 158
SO21: Sth W 3J 91
SO31: Burs 1K 195
SO32: Swanm 7D 164
SO40: Tott 4K 171
SO41: Sway 6J 223
SO51: Rom 6B 130
Rowan Ct. PO4: S'sea 3G 241
SO16: South 9H 159
SO19: South 7D 174
SO53: Cha F 6C 132
Rowan Dale GU52: Ch Cr 6L 47
Rowan Dr. BH23: Chri 6F 230
Rowan Gdns. SO30: Hed E 4A 176
Rowan Ind. Pk. GU34: Alt 4H 81
Rowan Rd. GU35: Lind 3K 101
PO9: Hav 6H 203
RG26: Tadl 6J 11
Rowans, The GU26: Hind 5M 103
SO40: March 9E 172
Rowans Cl. GU14: Cov 3G 29
Rowanside Cl. GU35: Head D 3E 102

Rowans Pk.—St Davids Cl.

Rowans Pk. SO41: Lymi ... 3D 234
Rowan Tree Cl. GU33: Liss ... 1F 140
Rowan Way PO14: Fare ... 9L 197
ROW ASH ... 2K 177
Rowbarrow Droke SO42: Beau ... 3L 205
Rowborough Rd. SO18: South ... 2D 174
Rowbury Rd. PO9: Hav ... 3D 202
Rowdell Cotts. SO24: Rop ... 1D 110
Rowden Cl. SO51: W Wel ... 2B 120 (1N 155)
Roweashe Way SO31: Loc H ... 6C 196
Rowe Gdns. BH12: Poole ... 7D 226
Rowena Ct. *PO5: S'sea* ... 4E 240
(off Outram Rd.)
Rowena Rd. BH6: Bour ... 9J 229
Rowes All. PO1: Ports ... 6H 5
Rowes La. SO41: E End ... 4A 236
Rowhay La. SO32: Lwr U, Uph ... 8D 134
Rowhill Av. GU11: Alders ... 1H 65
Rowhill Cl. GU14: Cov ... 8E 28
Rowhill Copse Local Nature Reserve ... 2G 64
Rowhill Cres. GU11: Alders ... 2H 65
Rowhill Dr. SO45: Dib ... 6H 193
Rowhills GU9: H End ... 2F 64
Rowhills Cl. GU9: Weyb ... 3H 65
Rowin Cl. PO11: H Isl ... 5K 243
Rowland Rd. PO6: Cosh ... 8N 199
PO15: Fare ... 7B 198
Rowlands Av. PO7: W'lle ... 9M 181
ROWLANDS CASTLE ... 8J 183
Rowlands Castle Golf Course ... 8H 183
Rowlands Castle Rd. PO8: Horn, Ids ... 4D 182
Rowlands Castle Station (Rail) ... 8J 183
Rowlands Cl. RG7: Mor W ... 1B 12
SO53: Cha F ... 8M 131
Rowlands Sq. GU32: Pet ... 2L 145
Rowlands Wlk. SO18: South ... 9E 160
ROWLEDGE ... 8N 63
Rowley Cl. SO30: Botl ... 2C 176
Rowley Ct. SO30: Botl ... 2C 176
Rowley Dr. SO30: Botl ... 2C 176
Rowlings Rd. SO22: Winche ... 3H 105
ROWNER ... 7E 212
Rowner Cl. PO13: Gos ... 7E 212
Rowner Cres. RG27: Sher L ... 7H 23
Rowner La. PO13: Gos ... 6E 212
Rowner Rd. PO13: Gos ... 6C 212
(not continuous)
Rowner Swimming Cen. ... 1E 238
Rowner Wlk. PO13: Gos ... 8E 212
(not continuous)
Rownest Wood La. SO21: W'cott ... 4N 77
ROWNHAMS ... 4D 158
Rownhams Cl. SO16: Rown ... 5D 158
Rownhams Ct. SO16: South ... 8E 158
Rownhams Ho. SO16: Rown ... 5D 158
Rownhams La. SO16: Rown ... 2E 158
SO16: South ... 6E 158
(not continuous)
SO52: N Bad ... 7E 130
Rownhams Pk. SO16: Rown ... 3D 158
Rownhams Rd. BH8: Bour ... 3N 227
PO9: Hav ... 4D 202
SO16: South ... 9E 158
SO52: N Bad ... 9F 130
Rownhams Rd. Nth. SO16: South ... 5E 158
ROWNHAMS SERVICE AREA ... 3E 158
Rownhams Way SO16: Rown ... 5D 158
Rowse Cl. SO51: Rom ... 3M 129
Row Wood La. PO13: Gos ... 7D 212
Roxan M. SO17: South ... 9A 160
Roxbee Cox Rd. GU14: Farn ... 1B 48
Roxborough *BH4: Bour* ... 2G 245
(off Portarlington Rd.)
Roxburghe Cl. GU35: W'hil ... 5J 101
Roxburgh Ho. SO31: Loc H ... 6D 196
Royal Air Force Yacht Club ... 7L 195
Royal Albert Wlk. PO4: S'sea ... 5F 240
Royal Apartments PO11: H Isl ... 5E 242
Royal Arc. BH1: Bour ... 1B 246
Royal Clarence Yd. PO12: Gos ... 1M 239
Royal Cl. BH23: Chri ... 6J 229
RG22: B'toke ... 5J 59
Royal Ct. SO17: South ... 9N 159
Royal Crescent, The SP9: Tidw ... 7D 30 (6G 31)
Royal Cres. Rd. SO14: South ... 8F 4 (7N 173)
Royal Dr. GU35: Bor ... 1K 101
Royale Cl. GU11: Alders ... 2L 65
Royal Gdns. PO9: R Cas ... 9G 183
SO15: South ... 3E 172
Royal Garrison Church ... 8K 5 (4B 240)
Royal Ga. PO4: S'sea ... 5J 241
Royal Green Jackets Museum, The
... 7K 237 (6K 105)
Royal Hampshire Regiment Mus.
... 8L 237 (7K 105)
Royal Huts Av. GU26: Hind ... 3N 103
Royal London Pk. SO30: Hed E ... 2M 175
Royal Lymington Yacht Club ... 3G 235
Royal Marines Mus. ... 5J 241
Royal Military Academy Sandhurst ... 6J 19
Royal Military Police Mus. ... 3B 200
Royal Motor Yacht Club ... 9A 244
Royal Naval Cotts. PO17: S'wick ... 3A 200
Royal Naval Mus. ... 2H 5 (1A 240)
Royal Navy Submarine Mus. ... 4N 239
Royal Oak Cl. GU46: Yat ... 7A 18
Royal Oak Ct. PO14: Fare ... 9B 198
Royal Oak Pas. SO23: Winche ... 7M 237
Royal Oak Rd. BH10: Bour ... 1G 226
Royal Pde. GU26: Hind ... 3N 103
Royal Southampton Yacht Club
Channel Way ... 8A 174
Gins La. ... 3F 236
Royal Southern Yacht Club ... 7L 195
Royal Sovereign Av. PO14: Fare ... 3C 212
Royal Victoria Country Pk. ... 5H 195
Royal Victoria Country Pk. Heritage Cen.
... 5G 195
Royal Victoria Country Pk. Visitors Cen.
... 5G 195
Royal Victoria M. BH4: Bour ... 2H 245
Royal Way PO7: W'lle ... 2A 202
Royal Winchester Golf Course ... 7F 104
Royal Winchester M. SO22: Winche ... 6G 105
Royce Cl. SP10: A'ver ... 9H 51
Roydon La. SO41: Bold ... 3D 224
Roydon Cl. SO22: Winche ... 9J 105
Roy's Cl. SP11: Ludg ... 1D 30
Roy's Copse SO45: Dib ... 5H 193
Roysdean Mnr. *BH1: Bour* ... 1N 245
(off Derby Rd.)
Roy's La. SO32: Sob H ... 9L 165
Royston Av. SO50: E'leigh ... 7E 132
Royston Centre, The GU12: Ash V ... 3N 49
Royston Cl. SO17: South ... 9N 159
Royston Ct. SO40: Tott ... 1L 171
Royston Pl. BH25: B Sea ... 6C 232
Rozel Ct. SO16: South ... 8D 158
Rozeldene GU26: Hind ... 4N 103
Rozelle Cl. SO22: Lit ... 1E 104
Rozelle Rd. BH14: Poole ... 1A 244
Rozel Mnr. BH13: Poole ... 3F 244
Rubens Cl. BH25: New M ... 3C 232
RG21: B'toke ... 9E 42
Ruby Cl. SO40: Tott ... 1H 171
Ruby Rd. SO19: South ... 4E 174
Rudd Hall Ri. GU15: Camb ... 1M 29
Rudd La. SO51: Brai, Tims ... 5K 123
Rudd Way SO14: South ... 7F 4 (7N 173)
Rudgwick Cl. PO16: Portc ... 9K 199
Rudmore Ct. PO2: Ports ... 7D 214
Rudmore Rd. PO2: Ports ... 8D 214
Rudmore Rdbt. PO2: Ports ... 8E 214
Rudmore Sq. PO2: Ports ... 8D 214
Rudolph Ct. PO7: Purb ... 4K 201
Ruffield Cl. SO22: Winche ... 4G 105
Rufford Cl. GU52: Fleet ... 5M 47
SO50: E'leigh ... 6E 132
Rufford Gdns. BH6: Bour ... 9H 229
Rufus Cl. SO16: Rown ... 5C 158
SO53: Cha F ... 4C 132
Rufus Ct. SO43: Lyn ... 2C 148
Rufus Gdns. SO40: Tott ... 3J 171
Rufus Stone ... 7K 155
Rugby Cl. GU47: Owl ... 4G 18
Rugby Rd. PO5: S'sea ... 3F 240
Rumbridge Gdns. SO40: Tott ... 3N 171
Rumbridge St. SO40: Tott ... 4M 171
Rune Dr. SP10: A'ver ... 6M 51
RUNFOLD ... 6L 65
Runfold Rdbt. GU10: Bad L ... 4M 65
Runfold St George GU10: Bad L ... 5K 65
Runnymede PO15: Fare ... 5N 197
SO30: Wes E ... 1H 175
Runnymede Av. BH11: Bour ... 1C 226 & 1B 226
Runnymede Ct. GU14: Farn ... 5J 29
SO30: Wes E ... 1H 175
Runton Rd. BH12: Poole ... 9D 226
Runway, The BH23: Chri ... 7D 230
Runwick La. GU10: Farnh ... 6M 63
Rushden Way GU9: H End ... 3F 64
Rushes, The RG21: B'toke ... 6E 42
SO40: March ... 8E 172
Rushes Farm GU32: Pet ... 9L 139
Rushes Rd. GU32: Pet ... 9L 139
Rushfield Rd. GU33: Liss ... 2E 140
Rushford Warren BH23: Mude ... 9B 230
Rushington Av. SO40: Tott ... 4M 171
Rushington Bus. Pk. SO40: Tott ... 5L 171
Rushington Ct. SO40: Tott ... 5L 171
Rushington La. SO40: Tott ... 5L 171
RUSHMERE ... 9F 166
Rushmere La. PO7: Den, H'don ... 3F 180
Rushmere Rd. BH6: Bour ... 7F 228
Rushmere Wlk. PO9: Hav ... 3D 202
RUSHMOOR ... 2L 85
Rushmoor Arena (Army Show Ground) ... 7G 48
Rushmoor Cl. GU52: Fleet ... 4M 47
Rushmoor Ct. GU14: Farn ... 3L 49
Rushmoor Gym ... 3L 65
Rushmoor La. GU34: Bent ... 6H 79
SO24: Bent, Lwr W ... 6H 79
Rushmoor Rd. GU11: Alders ... 6F 48
Rushmoor Stadium ... 4J 29
Rushpole Ct. SO45: Dib ... 6H 193
Rushton Cres. BH3: Bour ... 8K 227
Ruskin Av. BH9: Bour ... 3M 227
Ruskin Cl. RG21: B'toke ... 8F 42
Ruskin Ct. RG45: Cr'tne ... 1B 18
Ruskin Rd. PO4: S'sea ... 3H 241
SO50: E'leigh ... 8E 132
Ruskin Way PO8: Cowp ... 6N 181
Rusland Cl. SO53: Cha F ... 5N 131
Russell Churcher Ct. PO12: Gos ... 9H 213
Russell Cl. PO13: Lee S ... 1B 238
Russell-Cotes Art Gallery & Museum
... 8N 247 (3L 245)
Russell Cotes Rd. BH1: Bour ... 8N 247 (3L 245)
Russell Ct. BH25: New M ... 3B 232
GU11: Alders ... 9J 49
(off Frederick St.)
GU17: Blackw ... 8F 18
SO40: March ... 8E 172
Russell Dr. BH23: Chri ... 8N 229
SO51: Dun ... 4D 122
Russell Equestrian Cen. ... 7G 160
Russell Gdns. BH24: St I ... 3E 186
Russell Mt. BH4: Bour ... 1G 245
Russell Pl. PO16: Fare ... 8C 198
SO17: South ... 1N 173
SO40: Tott ... 2K 171
Russell Rd. PO9: Hav ... 6F 202
PO13: Lee S ... 2B 238
RG21: B'toke ... 8C 42
SO23: Winche ... 4L 105
Russell St. PO12: Gos ... 1J 239
SO14: South ... 7E 4 (7M 173)
Russell Way GU31: Pet ... 2N 145
Russel Rd. BH10: Bour ... 1H 227
Russet Cl. GU10: Tong ... 3N 65
SO24: New A ... 2E 108
SO32: Swanm ... 7D 164
Russet Gdns. GU15: Camb ... 1M 29
Russet Glade GU11: Alders ... 2F 64
Russet Ho. SO30: Hed E ... 4M 175
Russett Cl. RG7: Rise ... 2G 14
SO41: Lymi ... 4F 234
Russett Rd. GU34: Alt ... 5G 80
Russetts Dr. GU51: Fleet ... 3M 47
Rustan Cl. SO30: Hed E ... 4N 175
SO50: Fair O ... 1A 162
Rustic Glen GU52: Ch Cr ... 6L 47
Rustington Ho. *PO1: Ports* ... 2D 240
(off Up. Arundel St.)
Ruth Cl. GU14: Cov ... 7E 28
Rutherford Cl. RG20: High ... 4A 8
Rutherford Ho. PO12: Gos ... 9M 213
Rutherford Rd. RG24: B'toke ... 3E 42
Rutland Cl. GU11: Alders ... 8J 49
Rutland Ct. SO18: South ... 3E 174
Rutland Gdns. SO31: Burs ... 9L 175
Rutland Mnr. BH13: Poole ... 1E 244
Rutland Rd. BH9: Bour ... 6M 227
BH23: Chri ... 5J 229
Rutland Ter. GU11: Alders ... 8J 49
Rutland Way SO18: South ... 1E 174
Rutledge Dr. SO22: Lit ... 1F 104
Ruxley Cl. SO45: Holb ... 4A 208
Ryan Gdns. BH11: Bour ... 1F 226
Ryan Mt. GU47: Sandh ... 5C 18
Rycroft Mdw. RG22: B'toke ... 6J 59
Rydal Cl. BH23: Chri ... 2G 229
GU14: Cov ... 9F 28
GU35: Bor ... 2J 101
PO6: Cosh ... 8C 200
RG22: B'toke ... 9J 41
Rydal Dr. GU52: Ch Cr ... 6K 47
Rydal Ho. *BH4: Bour* ... 3G 245
(off Portarlington Rd.)
PO6: Cosh ... 8C 200
Rydal Rd. PO12: Gos ... 8J 213
Ryde Ct. GU12: Alders ... 1L 65
Ryde Gdns. GU46: Yat ... 7L 17
Ryde Pl. PO13: Lee S ... 3C 238
Ryde Ter. SO14: South ... 7N 173
Ryebeck Rd. GU52: Ch Cr ... 6M 47
Rye Cl. GU14: Cov ... 6G 29
GU51: Fleet ... 7A 28
SO53: Cha F ... 6L 131
RYE COMMON ... 1J 63
Rye Comn. La. GU10: Cron ... 1K 63
Rye Cft. GU52: Ch Cr ... 7K 47
Ryecroft PO9: Warb ... 8H 203
PO14: Titch C ... 7F 196
Ryecroft Av. BH11: Bour ... 1C 226
Ryecroft Gdns. GU17: Blackw ... 9G 18
Ryedale SO40: Ashu ... 7J 171
Ryedown La. SO51: E Wel ... 8C 128
Ryefield Cl. GU31: Pet ... 1B 146
Ryeland Cl. GU51: Fleet ... 7A 28
Ryeland Way SP11: E Ant ... 6C 52
Ryelaw Rd. GU52: Ch Cr ... 6M 47
Rye Paddock La. SO45: Fawl ... 4F 208
Rye Way SP11: E Ant ... 6B 52
Rykmansford Rd. GU51: Fleet ... 6K 27
Rylandes Ct. SO16: South ... 8E 158
Ryle Rd. GU9: Farnh ... 9D 64
Ryon Cl. SP10: A'ver ... 6N 51
Ryves Av. GU46: Yat ... 8K 17

S

Sabre Ct. GU11: Alders ... 9G 49
Sabre Rd. PO10: T Isl ... 5N 217
Sackville St. PO5: S'sea ... 6N 5 (3D 240)
(not continuous)
Saco Ct. *GU14: Farn* ... 2L 49
(off Reading Rd.)
Saddleback Rd. GU15: Camb ... 5N 19
Saddleback Way GU51: Fleet ... 8N 27
Saddler Cnr. GU47: Sandh ... 6D 18
Saddlers Cl. SO21: Sut S ... 7D 76
SO50: E'leigh ... 6E 132
SP6: F'dge ... 1J 153
Saddlers M. SP11: Fyf ... 9N 31
Saddlers Scarp GU26: Gray ... 3J 103
Saddlewood GU15: Camb ... 9L 19
Sadlers La. SO45: Dib P ... 8M 193
Sadlers Rd. RG17: Ink ... 1E 6
Sadlers Wlk. PO10: S'brne ... 9N 203
Saffron Cl. RG24: Chin ... 8H 23
Saffron Ct. *BH11: Bour* ... 3B 226
(off Saffron Way)
GU14: Cov ... 8E 28
SO31: Loc H ... 7B 196
Saffron Dr. BH23: Chri ... 6D 230
Saffron Way BH11: Bour ... 3B 226
PO15: White ... 1G 196
Sage Cl. PO7: W'lle ... 3A 202
Sages La. GU34: Priv ... 8K 111
Sailor's La. SO32: Corh ... 8J 135
Sainfoin La. RG23: Oak ... 2D 58
Sainsbury Cl. SP10: A'ver ... 3M 69
Sainsbury Lodge *PO1: Ports* ... 2F 240
(off Lucknow St.)
St Agathas Rd. SO31: Hamb ... 5L 195
St Agathas Way PO1: Ports ... 2N 5 (1D 240)
St Albans Av. BH8: Bour ... 7M 227
St Albans Cres. BH8: Bour ... 6M 227
St Albans Rd. BH8: Bour ... 7M 227
PO4: S'sea ... 4G 241
PO9: Hav ... 5G 202
SO14: South ... 3F 4 (5N 173)
St Albans Rdbt. GU14: Farn ... 3L 49
St Aldhelms BH14: Poole ... 1D 244
St Aldhelm's Cl. BH13: Poole ... 2D 244
St Aldhelm's Pl. BH13: Poole ... 1D 244
St Aldhelm's Rd. BH13: Poole ... 1D 244
St Alphege Gdns. SP10: A'ver ... 8M 51
St Andrew Cl. PO8: Horn ... 9C 168
St Andrews BH23: Chri ... 8J 229
St Andrews Bldgs. SO31: Hamb ... 7K 195
St Andrews Cl. SO51: Tims ... 7K 123
SO52: N Bad ... 7D 130
St Andrews Ct. PO1: Ports ... 5M 5 (3C 240)
St Andrews Grn. *SO32: Meon* ... 8N 135
(off Allens La.)
St Andrews Pk. SO50: Hor H ... 5N 161
St Andrews Rd. GU35: W'hil ... 5G 100
PO5: S'sea ... 4E 240
PO6: Farl ... 9N 201
PO11: H Isl ... 5H 243
PO12: Gos ... 3K 239
RG22: B'toke ... 8M 41
(not continuous)
SO14: South ... 3D 4 (5M 173)
SP9: Tidw ... 8C 30 (7G 30)
St Andrew's Way GU16: Frim ... 5N 29
St Anne's Av. BH6: Bour ... 9H 229
St Annes Cl. SO22: Winche ... 9G 105
SP11: G Cla ... 8M 69
St Annes Gdns. SO19: South ... 8C 174
SO41: Lymi ... 3D 234
St Anne's Gro. PO14: Fare ... 1B 212
St Anne's Ho. *SO51: Rom* ... 6L 129
(off Banning St.)
St Annes La. SO32: Shed ... 3N 177
St Annes M. SO14: South ... 2M 173
St Anne's Rd. SO19: South ... 8C 174
St Ann's Cl. SP10: A'ver ... 2M 69
St Ann's Ct. BH1: Bour ... 9B 228
St Ann's Cres. PO12: Gos ... 1J 239
St Ann's Rd. PO4: S'sea ... 4G 241
PO8: Horn ... 3C 182
St Anthony's Rd. BH2: Bour ... 9K 227
St Antony's BH4: Bour ... 8G 247 (3H 245)
St Aubin's Av. SO19: South ... 5E 174
St Aubins Cl. GU34: Four M ... 5J 97
St Aubin's Pk. PO11: H Isl ... 4D 242
St Aubyns La. BH24: Hang ... 4A 188
St Augustine Gdns. SO17: South ... 1B 174
St Augustine Rd. PO4: S'sea ... 5G 240
St Augustine's Cl. GU12: Alders ... 1M 65
St Augustin's Rd. BH2: Bour ... 9K 227
St Austell Cl. SO50: B'stke ... 9J 133
St Austins GU26: Gray ... 4M 103
St Barbara's Cl. RG26: B'ley ... 2J 23
St Barbara Way PO2: Ports ... 4G 215
St Barbe Cl. SO51: Rom ... 6N 129
St Barbe Mus. ... 2E 234
St Bartholomew's Gdns. PO5: S'sea ... 4E 240
St Bede's Ct. SO23: Winche ... 5L 105
St Benedicts Cl. GU11: Alders ... 1J 65
St Bernard Ho. SO14: South ... 7E 4
St Birinus Gdns. SP10: A'ver ... 7M 51
St Birinus Rd. SP5: Woodf ... 2M 119 (8C 120)
St Birstan Gdns. SP10: A'ver ... 8M 51
St Blaize Rd. SO51: Rom ... 4A 130
St Boniface Ct. SO52: N Bad ... 9F 130
St Boniface Gdns. BH10: Bour ... 3H 227
St Bonnet Dr. SO32: Bis W ... 3M 163
St Brelade Pl. SO16: South ... 8C 158
St Brelades BH14: Poole ... 4A 244
St Brelades Av. BH12: Poole ... 4B 226
St Catherines Ct. BH1: Bour ... 2N 245
PO11: H Isl ... 4C 242
ST CATHERINE'S HILL ... 3H 229
St Catherine's Hill ... 1L 127
St Catherine's Hill La. BH23: Chri ... 4J 229
St Catherine's Hill Nature Reserve
Christchurch ... 3H 229
Winchester ... 1L 127
St Catherine's Pde. BH23: Chri ... 5J 229
St Catherine's Path BH6: Bour ... 2H 247
St Catherine's Rd. BH6: Bour ... 1J 247
PO11: H Isl ... 4C 242
SO18: South ... 1B 174
SO23: Winche ... 8M 105
SO50: E'leigh ... 7E 132
St Catherine's Ter. BH6: Bour ... 2H 247
St Catherine St. PO5: S'sea ... 6E 240
St Catherines Vw. SO23: Winche ... 9M 105
SO30: Hed E ... 4L 175
St Catherines Way BH23: Chri ... 3G 229
PO16: Fare ... 8G 199
SO21: Winche ... 9N 105
St Catherines Wood GU15: Camb ... 9L 19
St Chad's Av. PO2: Ports ... 6F 214
St Christopher Av. PO16: Fare ... 6D 198
St Christophers Cl. GU12: Alders ... 9M 49
RG22: B'toke ... 8L 41
SO52: N Bad ... 8E 130
St Christophers Gdns.
PO13: Gos ... 6E 212
St Christopher's Pl. GU14: Cov ... 9H 29
St Christophers Rd. GU14: Cov ... 9J 29
PO9: Bed ... 5C 202
St Clair Rd. BH13: Poole ... 7C 244
St Clares Av. PO9: Hav ... 2D 202
St Clares Ct. PO9: Hav ... 3D 202
St Clements Cl. SO51: Rom ... 4L 129
St Clements Ct. BH1: Bour ... 9A 228
GU14: Farn ... 5K 29
St Clements Gdns. BH1: Bour ... 9A 228
St Clements Rd. BH1: Bour ... 9A 228
St Clement St.
SO23: Winche ... 8L 237 (7K 105)
St Clements Yd. SO23: Winche ... 8M 237
St Colman's Av. PO6: Cosh ... 9H 201
St Contest Way SO40: March ... 1E 192
ST CROSS ... 9K 105
St Cross Ct. SO23: Winche ... 9K 105
St Cross Hospital SO23: Winche ... 1K 127
St Cross Mede SO23: Winche ... 1J 127
St Cross Rd. GU9: Farnh ... 7E 64
GU10: Cron ... 3L 63
SO23: Winche ... 9L 237 (2J 127)
St Cuthbert's Cl. SO31: Loc H ... 5E 196
St Cuthbert's La. SO31: Loc H ... 5E 196
St Davids Cl. GU9: Weyb ... 4H 29
GU14: Cov ... 4H 29
RG29: Odi ... 9J 45
SO40: Calm ... 1J 171

A-Z Hampshire 315

Salisbury Rd. BH1: Bour 1B 246
BH14: Poole 9A 226
BH23: Burt, Sop, Wink 9L 219
BH24: Blas, Ell, Ibsl, Ring 9J 185
GU14: Farn 8L 29
GU17: Blackw 8E 18
PO4: S'sea 5G 240
PO6: Cosh 1H 215
SO17: South 8M 159
SO20: Brou 2A 86 (3N 87)
SO24: New A 1E 108
SO40: Calm, Tott 7G 156
SO51: Ower 6F 156
(Romsey Rd.)
SO51: Ower 2B 156
(Whinwhistle Hill)
SO51: Rom, Shoo 3D 128
SO51: W Wel 1A 120 (6G 121)
SP4: Bul 3A 66
SP5: Com B 2G 119
SP5: Down 1J 119 (5A 120)
SP5: L'ford, W'psh, Down 6G 121
SP6: Brea, B'gte, F'dge 1K 153
SP9: Shi B 1B 66 (3G 66)
SP9: Tidw 3G 66
SP10: A'ver 3K 69
SP11: Abb A, An V 3B 72
SP11: Pale 6K 67
Salisbury Rd. Arc. SO40: Tott 3M 171
Salisbury St. BH21: Cran 6J 149
SO15: South 2C 4 (4L 173)
SP6: F'dge 1J 153
Salisbury Ter. PO13: Lee S 2B 238
Salmon Dr. SO50: B'stke 1K 161
Salmond Rd. SP11: A'ver 1H 69
Salmons Rd. RG29: Odi 9J 45
Salona Cl. SO53: Cha F 5D 132
Saltaire Apartments BH6: Bour 2J 247
Salterns Av. PO4: S'sea 2J 241
Salterns Cl. PO11: H Isl 4J 243
Salterns Ct. BH14: Poole 5A 244
Salterns Est. PO16: Fare 1D 212
Salterns La. PO11: H Isl 4H 243
PO16: Fare 1D 212
SO31: Burs 3L 195
SO45: Fawl 4F 208
Salterns Nature Reserve, The 6F 234
Saltern's Rd. PO13: Lee S 8L 211
PO14: Stub 8L 211
Salterns Way BH14: Poole 5A 244
Salter Rd. BH13: S'bks 9A 244
Salters Acres SO22: Winche 3G 104
SALTERS HEATH 4M 21
Salters Heath Rd. RG26: M She 6K 21
Salters La. SO22: Winche 4F 104
Saltgrass La. SO41: Key 9N 235
Salthouse Apartments, The
PO12: Gos 1M 239
(off Salt Meat La.)
Saltings, The PO6: Farl 1M 215
PO9: Langs 2F 216
Salt La. SO32: Uph 6G 134
Saltmarsh La. PO11: H Isl 2E 242
Saltmarsh Pk. SO41: Lymi 1F 234
Saltmarsh Rd. SO14: South 8G 4 (7N 173)
Saltmead SO17: South 9A 160
Salt Meat La. PO12: Gos 1M 239
Saltram Rd. GU14: Farn 1N 49
Salvia Cl. PO7: W'lle 3A 202
Salwey Rd. SO30: Botl 5A 176
Samantha Cl. BH10: Bour 3J 227
Samber Cl. SO41: Lymi 2C 234
Sam Ford Pl. SO50: E'leigh 1E 160
Sammy Miller Motorcycle Mus. 1N 231
Sampan Cl. SO31: Wars 8B 196
Samphire Cl. SO41: Lymi 1D 234
Sampson Rd. PO1: Ports 2H 5 (1A 240)
PO14: Fare 2B 212
Sampson's Almshouses GU9: Farnh 9B 64
Samson Cl. PO13: Gos 9F 212
Samuel Rd. PO1: Ports 1G 240
Sam Whites Hill SP11: Up C 5L 69
San Carlos App. GU11: Alders 9L 49
Sancreed Rd. BH12: Poole 7C 226
Sanctuary Cl. SO19: South 4F 174
Sandalwood Cl. PO8: Clan 6C 168
SANDBANKS 9A 244
Sandbanks Dr. RG22: B'toke 3K 59
Sandbanks Rd. BH14: Poole 5A 244
Sandbourne Ct. BH4: Bour 3G 244
Sandbourne Rd. BH4: Bour 4G 244
Sand Cl. SO51: W Wel 1B 120
Sandcroft Cl. PO12: Gos 4G 238
Sandecotes Rd. BH14: Poole 1A 244
Sandell Ct. SO16: Bass 6N 159
Sandel Pl. *SP4: Ames* 5A 66
(off Butterfield Rd.)
Sanderling BH5: Bour 2A 246
Sanderling Ct. BH1: Bour 9K 227
BH5: Bour 2A 246
Sanderling Lodge PO12: Gos 2M 239
Sanderling Rd. PO4: S'sea 2K 241
Sanderlings BH24: Hight 2M 187
Sanderlings, The PO11: H Isl 5G 243
Sanderson Centre, The PO12: Gos 2K 239
SANDFORD 8N 187
Sandford Av. PO12: Gos 3F 238
Sandford Cl. BH9: Bour 3N 227
RG20: Kings 2C 6
Sandford Ct. BH6: Bour 1G 247
GU11: Alders 1H 65
Sandford Rd. GU9: Up H 3D 64
GU11: Alders 1H 65
RG26: Tadl 5G 10
Sandford Springs Golf Course 2D 6 (6M 9)
Sandham Memorial Chapel 4D 8
Sandhaven Ct. BH13: S'bks 9A 244
Sandheath Rd. GU26: Hind 9L 85
Sand Hill GU14: Farn 5K 29
Sand Hill Ct. GU14: Farn 5K 29
Sandhill La. PO13: Lee S 9C 212
Sandhills *BH5: Bour* 1D 246
(off Parkwood Rd.)
Sandhills Caravan Pk. BH23: Mude 9D 230
SANDHURST 6D 18
Sandhurst Ct. PO5: S'sea 4E 240
Sandhurst La. GU17: Blackw 7D 18
Sandhurst Rd. GU46: Yat 6B 18
RG45: Cr'tne 2D 18
SO15: South 2A 4 (4K 173)
Sandhurst Sports Cen. 5G 18
Sandhurst Station (Rail) 6C 18
San Diego Rd. PO12: Gos 1K 239
Sandilands Way SO45: Hythe 8M 193
Sandisplatt PO14: Fare 9M 197
Sandle Copse SP6: F'dge 9E 150
Sandleford Rd. PO9: Hav 2D 202
SANDLEHEATH 9D 150
Sandleheath Ind. Est. SP6: Sand 9E 150
Sandleheath Rd. SP6: Ald 1C 152
Sandle Mnr. Dr. SP6: F'dge 9F 150
Sandlewood Cl. SO40: Calm 2J 171
Sand Martin Cl. RG26: Cha A 4H 21
SO50: E'leigh 2B 160
Sandmartin Cl. BH25: B Sea 7A 232
Sandon Lodge BH8: Bour 7N 227
Sandown Cl. GU17: Blackw 8F 18
GU34: Alt 6G 80
PO12: Gos 4F 238
Sandown Ct. *BH1: Bour* 2N 245
(off Christchurch Rd.)
Sandown Cres. GU11: Alders 3K 65
Sandown Dr. GU16: Frim 2M 29
Sandown Hgts. PO14: Fare 9M 197
Sandown Rd. BH23: Chri 8A 230
PO6: Cosh 1F 214
SO15: South 1G 172
Sandpiper Cl. PO8: Horn 3A 182
SO40: March 9D 172
Sandpiper Rd. SO16: South 6F 158
Sandpipers PO6: Farl 1M 215
Sandpiper Way RG22: B'toke 3H 59
Sandpit Hill RG20: New 1C 8
Sandpit La. RG7: Swal 1L 15
SO41: E End 5B 236
Sandport Gro. PO16: Portc 1K 213
Sandringham Cl. BH9: Bour 2M 227
GU34: Alt 5D 80
SO53: Cha F 8L 131
Sandringham Ct. BH2: Bour 8L 247
BH8: Bour 8N 227
RG22: B'toke 8M 41
SO15: South 4F 172
(off Regent's Pk. Rd.)
Sandringham Gdns. BH9: Bour 2M 227
Sandringham Ho. SP10: A'ver 7N 51
Sandringham La. PO1: Ports 2F 240
Sandringham Rd. BH14: Poole 2A 244
GU32: Pet 9M 139
PO1: Ports 2F 240
PO14: Fare 9L 197
SO18: South 1C 174
SANDS, THE 9N 65
Sands, The GU35: W'hil 5F 100
Sandsbury La. GU32: Stro 8J 139
Sands Cl. GU10: Seal 8M 65
Sands Drove RG17: Ink 1F 6
Sands Rd. GU10: Run 7L 65
Sandy Balls Holiday Cen. SP6: Gods 9N 151
Sandy Beach Est. PO11: H Isl 6M 243
Sandy Brow PO7: Purb 5L 201
Sandy Cl. GU31: Pet 1B 146
Sandycroft SO31: Wars 8A 196
SANDY CROSS 6N 65
SANDY DOWN 3C 224
Sandy Down SO41: Bold 3B 224
Sandyfield Cres. PO8: Cowp 7M 181
Sandy Hill Rd. GU9: Up H 3C 64
Sandykeld BH1: Bour 2A 246
Sandy La. BH6: Bour 9E 228
BH23: Chri 4H 229
BH24: St I 4C 186
GU10: Rush 2J 85
GU14: Cov 6E 28
GU15: Camb 7N 19
GU27: Lip 8L 103
GU32: Ste 5A 140
GU33: Rake 2K 141
GU35: K'ly 7G 83
GU47: Sandh 4B 18
GU52: Ch Cr 7M 47
PO14: Titch 9J 197
RG26: Pam H 6K 11
RG27: H Win 7C 26
SO32: Shed, Wal C 2M 177
SO43: Lyn 3B 148 (3N 189)
SO50: Fair O 1M 161
SO51: Brai, Rom 1N 129
SO52: N Bad 7G 131
(not continuous)
SP5: Redl 1N 119 (7D 120)
Sandy Mead Rd. BH8: Bour 5C 228
Sandy Plot BH23: Burt 5M 229
Sandy Point PO11: H Isl 5N 243
Sandy Point Nature Reserve 6M 243
Sandy Point Rd. PO11: H Isl 6L 243
(not continuous)
Sandys Cl. RG22: B'toke 8N 41
Sandys Rd. RG22: B'toke 7N 41
Sandys Rd. Rdbt. RG22: B'toke 7N 41
Sandy Way BH10: Bour 3J 227
Sankey La. GU51: Fleet 8B 28
San Remo Towers BH5: Bour 2B 246
Sanross Cl. PO14: Stub 7K 211
Santina Cl. GU9: H End 2F 64
Saor M. SP10: A'ver 1M 69
Sapley La. RG25: Over 3D 56
Saplings, The SO45: Holb 3N 207
Sapphire Cl. PO12: Gos 9K 213
Sapphire Ct. SO14: South 9G 4 (8N 173)
Sapphire Ridge PO7: W'lle 2A 202
Saracen Cl. SO41: Penn 5C 234
Saracens Rd. SO53: Cha F 5D 132
Sarah Cl. BH7: Bour 6E 228
Sarah Robinson Ho. PO1: Ports 3K 5 (2B 240)
Sarah Sands Cl. BH23: Chri 6N 229
Sarah Way GU14: Farn 8K 29
Sarisbury Cl. RG26: Tadl 5G 11
Sarisbury Ga. SO31: P Ga 4E 196
SARISBURY GREEN 3B 196
Sark Rd. BH12: Poole 6B 226
Sark Way RG24: B'toke 2E 42
Sarnia Ct. SO16: South 7D 158
SARSON 3B 68
Sarson Cl. SP11: Amp 3B 68
Sarson La. SP11: Amp, Weyh 9B 50
Sartoris Cl. SO31: Wars 8A 196
Sarum Cl. SO20: Mid Wa 9M 67
SO22: Winche 7G 105
SP9: Shi B 2A 66 (1F 66)
Sarum Ct. BH14: Poole 1A 244
SO22: Winche 7H 105
Sarum Hill RG21: B'toke 7B 42
Sarum Ho. SO40: Tott 1K 171
SP10: A'ver 2N 69
Sarum Rd. RG26: Tadl 4G 10
SO22: Winche 7B 104
SO53: Cha F 6C 132
Sarum Vw. SO22: Winche 7F 104
Sarum Wlk. SO41: Lymi 9D 224
Satchell La. SO31: Hamb, Hou 3J 195
Saturn Cl. SO16: South 7E 158
Saulfland Dr. BH23: Chri 6F 230
Saulfland Ho. BH23: Chri 6F 230
Saulfland Pl. BH23: Chri 6F 230
Saunders Cl. PO13: Lee S 9C 212
Saunders Gdn. RG26: Tadl 5H 11
Saunders Ho. PO6: Cosh 8N 199
Saunders La. SO51: Awb 8E 122
Saunders Mdw. SN8: Co Du 1H 31
Saunders M. PO4: S'sea 5J 241
Saunton Gdns. GU14: Farn 6J 29
Savernake Cl. PO13: Gos 6F 212
SO51: Rom 3A 130
Savile Cres. GU35: Bor 4J 101
Saville Cl. PO12: Gos 4H 239
SO50: B'stke 7H 133
Saville Gdns. PO16: Fare 6C 198
Savoy Cl. SP10: A'ver 2A 70
Savoy Ct. PO4: S'sea 6F 240
Savoy Gro. GU17: Haw 1F 28
Sawmills, The SO32: Durl 6E 162
Sawyers Cl. SO22: Winche 5F 104
Sawyer's Hill PO7: Den 2H 181
Saxe Ct. PO17: K Vil 2A 198
Saxholm Cl. SO16: Bass 5L 159
Saxholm Dale SO16: Bass 5L 159
Saxholm Way SO16: Bass 5L 159
Saxley Ct. PO9: Hav 3C 202
Saxonbury Rd. BH6: Bour 8H 229
Saxon Centre, The BH23: Chri 7L 229
Saxon Cl. PO8: Cath 8C 168
PO16: Portc 8K 199
SO31: Wars 8B 196
Saxon Ct. SO50: Hor H 4N 161
SP9: Tidw 7D 30
SP10: A'ver 7N 51
Saxon Cft. GU9: Farnh 9E 64
Saxonford Rd. BH23: Fri C 7E 230
Saxon Gdns. SO30: Hed E 5L 175
Saxon Ho. SO14: South 4A 174
Saxonhurst SP5: Down 2L 119 (7B 120)
Saxonhurst Cl. BH10: Bour 1J 227
Saxonhurst Gdns. BH10: Bour 2J 227
Saxonhurst Rd. BH10: Bour 2H 227
Saxon King Gdns. BH6: Bour 1L 247
Saxon Leas SP5: Mid W 5H 87
Saxon Mdw. SP5: Down 2K 119 (7B 120)
Saxon Pl. SO41: Lymi 9D 224
Saxon Ri. SN8: Co Du 1H 31
Saxon Rd. SO15: South 5J 173
SO20: Mid Wa 4A 72
SO23: Winche 5L 105
SO45: Blac 7D 208
Saxon Sq. Shop. Cen. BH23: Chri 8L 229
Saxon Wlk. SO53: Cha F 7C 132
Saxon Way RG24: Lych 4G 42
SO51: Rom 5A 130
SP6: Ald 5D 152
SP10: A'ver 7M 51
Saxony Cres. SO21: Spar 6N 89
Saxony Way GU46: Yat 9M 17
Sayers Cl. GU16: Frim G 5N 29
Sayers Rd. SO50: B'stke 1H 161
Scafell Av. PO14: Fare 9N 197
Scallows La. SO51: W Wel 8N 121
Scamblers Mead SP11: Pen G 7F 50
Scantabout Av. SO53: Cha F 5C 132
Scarff Ct. PO11: H Isl 5H 243
Scarlatti Rd. RG22: B'toke 2A 60
Scarlet Oaks GU15: Camb 1N 29
Scarlett's Rd. GU11: Alders 8J 49
Sceptre Ct. SP10: A'ver 9D 52
Scholars Cl. SP11: Ludg 1D 30
Scholars Retreat SO41: M Sea 9G 233
Scholars Wlk. GU14: Farn 6J 29
PO6: Dray 1K 215
School Cl. RG22: Wort 7J 41
SO41: Penn 3C 234
SO53: Cha F 7N 131
SP11: Ver D 8E 6
School Flds. GU35: K'ly 7G 82
School Hill GU47: Sandh 4C 18
RG45: Cr'tne 1F 18
SO32: Sob 5L 165
School La. BH11: Bour 1F 226
BH23: Thorn 3G 220
BH24: Ring 1K 187
BH24: St I 3D 186
GU10: Ben'ly 7K 63
GU10: Ews 2N 63
GU32: Pet 7A 140
GU33: Liss 1E 140
School La. GU46: Yat 7L 17
PO2: Ports 9E 214
PO7: Den 5D 180
PO10: Ems 9M 203
PO10: Westb 4N 203
RG7: Rise 2J 15
RG7: Sil 4A 12
SO20: Brou 1A 86 (4A 88)
SO20: N Wal 9N 67
SO21: Itc A 8J 93
SO23: Winche 1L 105
SO24: Bis S 1K 109
SO24: Rop 2D 110
SO31: Hamb 8L 195
SO41: Lymi 2E 234
SO41: Lymi, Pil 6F 224
SO41: Lymo, M Sea 8M 233
SO43: Mins 8L 155
SO53: Cha F 8M 131
SP6: Gods 5A 154
SP11: S M Bo 9L 35
School Pl. SO19: South 6C 174
School Rd. BH23: Thorn 3F 220
GU10: Rowl 8N 63
GU26: Gray 4K 103
GU27: Hasl 1N 117
GU35: Bor 3J 101
PO12: Gos 7H 213
PO17: Wick 7C 178
RG7: Rise 1J 15
SO21: Twyf 7K 127
SO31: Burs 9L 175
SO40: Elin 4N 171
SO45: Fawl 5E 208
SO45: Hythe 5M 193
SO51: Rom 3B 130
SO51: W Wel 2C 120 (1N 155)
SP5: Lover 9D 120
SP5: Nom 2J 155
Schooners Cl. PO13: Lee S 1B 238
Schooner Way PO4: S'sea 1K 241
SO31: Wars 8B 196
Schroeder Cl. RG21: B'toke 9B 42
Schubert Rd. RG22: B'toke 2N 59
Scimitars, The PO14: Stub 5L 211
Scotland Cl. SO50: Fair O 1B 162
Scotland Hill GU47: Sandh 4C 18
Scotney Ct. PO9: Hav 3H 203
Scotney Rd. RG21: B'toke 4C 42
Scots Ct. RG27: Hoo 1J 45
Scott Cl. BH12: Poole 5D 226
PO14: Stub 4M 211
SO20: Ki S 9B 86 (7G 88)
SP10: A'ver 9D 52
Scotter Rd. BH7: Bour 8E 228
SO50: B'stke 9H 133
Scotter Sq. SO50: B'stke 9H 133
Scott Ho. PO2: Ports 6D 214
RG21: B'toke 5D 42
Scott-Paine Dr. SO45: Hythe 5N 193
Scott Rd. BH12: Poole 5D 226
PO1: Ports 2H 5 (1A 240)
PO3: Ports 3G 215
SO19: South 9D 174
SO50: E'leigh 1D 160
Scotts Cl. SO21: Col C 4L 133
SP5: Down 1J 119 (7A 120)
Scotts Cnr. *RG21: B'toke* 1A 60
(off The Harrow Way)
Scott's Ct. GU14: Farn 5K 29
Scott's Grn. BH23: Chri 6B 230
Scottshills La. BH23: Chri 7N 229
(not continuous)
Scouts La. SP5: W Tyt 6K 87
SCRAG HILL 6E 130
Scratchface La. PO7: Purb 5N 201
(not continuous)
PO9: Bed 7A 202
RG25: Herr 2K 79
Scrubbs La. SO24: Bis S 5H 109
Scullards La. SO14: South 5C 4 (6L 173)
Sculpture Park, The 5K 85
Scures Hill RG27: Nat S 4C 44
Scures Rd. RG27: Hoo 2F 44
Scythe Cl. SP11: E Ant 6B 52
Seabird Way PO16: Fare 1D 212
Seabourne Pl. BH5: Bour 9E 228
Seabourne Rd. BH5: Bour 9D 228
Sea Breeze *BH6: Bour* 2J 247
(off St Catherine's Rd.)
Sea Breeze Gdns. PO4: S'sea 4K 241
Seabreeze Way SO41: Down 8H 233
SeaCity Mus. 4C 4 (5L 173)
Seacliff Ct. BH6: Bour 1G 246
Seacole Gdns. SO16: South 9H 159
Seacombe Grn. SO16: South 1C 172
Seacombe Rd. BH13: S'bks 9A 244
Seacote BH6: Bour 2J 247
Seacourt Tennis Club 5F 242
Sea Crest Rd. PO13: Lee S 2B 238
Seacroft Av. BH25: B Sea 6N 231
Seafarers Wlk. PO11: H Isl 6M 243
SEAFIELD 4L 239
Seafield Cl. BH25: B Sea 7A 232
Seafield Dr. BH6: Bour 9H 229
Seafield Pk. Rd. PO14: Stub 7L 211
Seafield Rd. BH6: Bour 1G 247
BH23: Fri C 8E 230
BH25: B Sea 6N 231
PO3: Ports 7H 215
PO16: Portc 1K 213
SO16: South 9C 158
Seafields PO10: Ems 9L 203
Seafield Ter. PO12: Gos 4L 239
Seafire Rd. PO13: Lee S 2C 238
Seaford Cl. SO31: Burs 9K 175
Sea Front PO11: H Isl 4C 242
Sea Front Est. PO11: H Isl 5H 243
Seagarth Cl. SO16: South 8J 159
Seagarth La. SO16: South 8J 159
Seagers Ct. PO1: Ports 7H 5 (4A 240)

Seagrim Rd.—Sherwood Av.

Seagrim Rd. BH8: Bour 3N 227
Sea Gro. Av. PO11: H Isl 5G 242
Seagrove Rd. PO2: Ports 7E 214
Seagull Cl. PO4: S'sea 1K 241
RG22: B'toke 2H 59
Seagull La. PO10: Ems 8M 203
(not continuous)
Seagull Rd. BH8: Bour 5N 227
Seagulls, The PO13: Lee S 3C 238
Seahorse Wlk. PO12: Gos 2M 239
Sea Kings PO14: Stub 5L 211
Sea La. PO14: Stub 8M 211
Sealark Rd. PO12: Gos 9K 213
Seale La. GU10: Seal 6M 65
Seal Rd. RG21: B'toke 6C 42
SEAMAN'S CORNER 8L 155
Seaman's La. SO43: Mins 8L 155
Seamead PO14: Stub 8M 211
Sea Mill Gdns. PO1: Ports 4K 5 (2B 240)
Seamoor La. BH4: Bour 2F 244
Seamoor Rd. BH4: Bour 2F 244
Sea Pines SO41: M Sea 8J 235
Searing Way RG26: Tadl 4G 11
Searle Dr. PO12: Gos 9M 213
Searle Rd. GU9: Farnh 9E 64
Searles Cl. SO24: New A 1F 108
Searl's La. RG27: Hoo, Roth 8H 25
Sea Rd. BH5: Bour 2B 246
BH6: Bour 2J 247
BH25: B Sea 6N 231
SO19: South 7B 174
SO41: M Sea 8L 235
Seascape BH6: Bour 2F 246
(off Southbourne Overcliff Dr.)
Seaside Wlk. BH5: Bour 1C 246
Seathrift Cl. PO13: Lee S 1A 238
Seathwaite Ho. PO6: Cosh 8C 200
Seaton Av. PO3: Ports 8H 215
Seaton Cl. BH23: Highc 6K 231
PO14: Stub 6M 211
SO18: Wes E 1G 174
SO41: Lymi 1E 234
Seaton Gdns. BH9: Bour 6L 227
Seaton Rd. BH23: Highc 6K 231
GU15: Camb 8K 19
SEA VIEW 5G 243
Sea Vw. BH5: Bour 2B 246
(off Boscombe Spa Rd.)
Seaview Av. PO16: Portc 8N 199
Seaview Ct. PO12: Gos 4F 238
PO13: Lee S 2B 238
Sea Vw. Est. SO31: Net A 4F 194
Sea Vw. Rd. BH23: Walk 5L 231
BH25: New M 7L 231
PO6: Dray 8K 201
PO11: H Isl 4J 243
Sea Vixen Ind. Est. BH23: Chri 7C 230
Seaward Av. BH6: Bour 1E 246
BH25: B Sea 7N 231
Seaward Gdns. SO19: South 6C 174
Seaward Path BH13: Poole 5E 244
Seaward Rd. SO19: South 6C 174
Seaward Twr. PO12: Gos 3N 239
Seaway BH25: New M 6C 232
Seaway Av. BH23: Fri C 7E 230
Seaway Cres. PO4: S'sea 3L 241
Seaway Gro. PO16: Portc 2L 213
Seaweed Cl. SO19: South 1C 194
Seawinds SO41: M Sea 9H 233
Sebastian Gro. PO7: W'lle 1A 202
Sebastopol Rd. GU11: Alders 9K 49
Second Av. PO6: Cosh 9F 200
PO6: Farl 1L 215
PO9: Hav 7H 203
RG7: A'mas 3J 11
SO15: South 2C 172
Second Marine Av. BH25: B Sea 8B 232
Second St. SO45: Hard 9C 194
Sedbergh Ho. SO16: South 1C 172
Sedbergh Rd. SO16: South 1C 172
Seddon Cl. BH25: B Sea 6C 232
Sedgefield Cl. PO6: Cosh 9A 200
SO40: Tott 2J 171
Sedgeley Gro. PO12: Gos 8J 213
Sedgemead SO31: Net A 4F 194
Sedgemead Ct. SO31: Net A 4F 194
Sedgemoor GU14: Farn 5K 29
Sedgewick Cl. PO13: Gos 8E 212
Sedgewick Ct. SO50: B'stke 9H 133
Sedgewick Rd. SO19: South 5G 174
Sedgley Cl. PO5: S'sea 3E 240
Sedgley Rd. BH9: Bour 6J 227
Sedgwick Rd. SO50: B'stke 9H 133
Seebys Oak GU47: Coll 7F 18
Seeviours Ct. RG28: Whit 5G 54
Segars La. SO21: Twyf 8K 127
SEGENSWORTH 5G 197
Segensworth East Ind. Est. PO15: Seg 4G 197
(not continuous)
Segensworth Nth. Ind. Est. PO15: Seg 4H 197
Segensworth Rd. PO15: Seg, Titch 5G 196
(not continuous)
Segensworth West Ind. Est. PO15: Seg 4F 196
Selangor Av. PO10: Ems 8J 203
Selborne Av. GU11: Alders 3K 65
PO9: Hav 4D 202
SO18: South 2G 174
Selborne Cl. GU17: Blackw 7E 18
GU32: Pet 8M 139
RG27: Hoo 2H 45
Selborne Ct. SO16: Bass 6M 159
SO51: Rom 3B 130
Selborne Gdns. PO12: Gos 3J 239
Selborne Pl. SO22: Winche 9H 105
Selborne Pottery 7L 99
Selborne Rd. GU33: G'ham 5C 114
GU34: Alt, Selb 7E 80
SO40: Tott 2K 171
Selborne Wlk. RG26: Tadl 5H 11
SO18: South 2G 174
Selborne Way GU35: W'hil 5F 100
SELBOURNE 7L 99
Selbourne Dr. SO50: E'leigh 8E 132
Selbourne Rd. PO9: Hav 8E 202
Selbourne Ter. PO1: Ports 2F 240
Selbourne Vs. PO1: Ports 2F 240
Selby Wlk. RG24: B'toke 2C 42
Seldon Cl. SO22: Oli B 1F 126
Selfridge Av. BH6: Bour 2L 247
Selfridge Cl. BH6: Bour 2L 247
Selhurst Ho. PO1: Ports 1E 240
Selhurst Way SO50: Fair O 2N 161
Sellwood Rd. SO31: Net A 3G 194
Sellwood Way BH25: New M 6M 231
Selma Ct. PO5: S'sea 5E 240
Selman Cl. SO45: Hythe 5N 193
Selsdon Av. SO51: Rom 4A 130
Selsey Av. PO4: S'sea 5H 241
PO12: Gos 8J 213
Selsey Cl. PO11: H Isl 5M 243
SO16: South 8D 158
SELSMORE 4J 243
Selsmore Av. PO11: H Isl 5J 243
Selsmore Rd. PO11: H Isl 4G 243
Selworth La. SO32: Sob 8K 165
Selwyn Dr. GU46: Yat 7L 17
Selwyn Gdns. SO50: E'leigh 7E 132
Sembal Ho. SO15: South 2A 4 (4K 173)
Sengana Cl. SO30: Botl 4B 176
Senlac Rd. SO51: Rom 5A 130
Sennen Pl. PO6: P Sol 1B 214
Sentinel Cl. PO7: W'lle 9B 182
Sepen Meade GU52: Ch Cr 7K 47
Seps 4 Rd. SO45: Fawl 4G 209
September Cl. SO30: Wes E 1H 175
Serendipity Sam's Play & Party Cen. 3L 129
Serenity BH6: Bour 2J 247
(off St Catherine's Rd.)
Serle Cl. SO40: Tott 3H 171
Serle Gdns. SO40: Tott 4K 171
Sermon Rd. SO22: Winche 5F 104
Serotine Cl. PO17: K Vil 2A 198
Serpentine Rd. PO5: S'sea 5D 240
(Clarence Pde.)
PO5: S'sea 9N 5 (5D 240)
(Elphinstone Rd.)
PO7: Wid 6K 201
PO16: Fare 6D 198
Service Rd. PO6: Cosh 9E 200
SETLEY 2A 224
Setley Gdns. BH8: Bour 3B 228
Setley Ridge Vineyard 1A 224
Seton Dr. RG27: Hoo 3F 44
Sett, The GU16: Frim G 6N 29
GU46: Yat 8L 17
Setters Cl. SO21: Col C 4K 133
Set Thorns Rd. SO41: Sway 5K 223
Settle Cl. SO16: South 2G 172
Settlers Cl. PO1: Ports 1E 240
Sevenoaks Dr. BH7: Bour 7D 228
Sevenoaks Rd. PO6: Cosh 9F 200
Seven Thornes La. GU26: Lip 7L 103
Seventh St. RG19: Green 1G 9
(off Warehouse Rd.)
Seventon Rd. RG25: Nth W 9A 58
Severals, The RG24: Sher J 9N 21
Severn Cl. GU47: Sandh 5E 18
PO6: Cosh 8C 200
(not continuous)
PO16: Portc 9J 199
Severn Ct. SP10: A'ver 8B 52
(off Itchen Ct.)
Severn Gdns. RG23: Oak 1D 58
Severn Rd. GU14: Cov 6G 28
SO16: South 2D 172
Severn Way RG21: B'toke 6E 42
SO30: Wes E 9H 161
Seville Cres. SP10: A'ver 9B 52
(not continuous)
Seward Ct. BH23: Highc 6J 231
Seward Grn. SO45: Hythe 6N 193
Seward Ri. SO51: Rom 4B 130
Seward Rd. SO45: Hythe 6N 193
Seymour Cl. PO2: Ports 9E 214
SO16: South 8H 159
SO40: Calm 1J 171
SO53: Cha F 7C 132
Seymour Ct. GU51: Fleet 1M 47
RG29: Odi 8L 45
(off Seymour Pl.)
RG45: Cr'tne 1A 18
Seymour Gdns. BH24: Poul 8L 185
Seymour Ho. SO16: South 8J 159
Seymour La. SO52: N Bad 8E 130
Seymour Pl. RG29: Odi 8L 45
Seymour Rd. BH24: Poul 8L 185
GU35: Head D 3E 102
PO13: Lee S 3B 238
RG22: B'toke 9L 41
SO16: South 8H 159
Shackleton Ho. PO2: Ports 6F 214
Shackleton Rd. PO13: Gos 8F 212
Shackleton Sq. BH23: Bran 6D 220
SP10: A'ver 7B 52
(off Cricketers Way)
Shadwell Ct. PO2: Ports 6D 214
Shadwell Rd. PO2: Ports 6E 214
Shady Nook GU9: Up H 4D 64
Shaftesbury Av. PO7: Purb, W'lle 5L 201
SO17: South 1N 173
SO53: Cha F 8A 132
Shaftesbury Ct. BH3: Bour 8K 227
(off Wimborne Rd.)
GU14: Farn 3L 49
GU35: Bor 5J 101
(off Forest Rd.)
Shaftesbury Mt. GU17: Haw 1E 28
Shaftesbury Rd. BH8: Bour 8N 227
PO5: S'sea 9N 5 (5D 240)
PO12: Gos 3L 239
(not continuous)
Shaftesbury St. SP6: F'dge 1H 153
Shaggs Mdw. SO43: Lyn 2B 148 (2N 189)
Shakespeare Av. SO17: South 2N 173
SP10: A'ver 9K 51
Shakespeare Bus. Cen. SO50: E'leigh 8F 132
Shakespeare Dr. SO40: Tott 9K 157
Shakespeare Gdns. GU14: Cov 7F 28
PO8: Cowp 7M 181
Shakespeare Mews PO14: Titch 9K 197
(off East St.)
Shakespeare Rd. BH6: Bour 7G 229
PO1: Ports 1F 240
RG24: B'toke 3D 42
SO50: E'leigh 7D 132
Shakespeare Ter. PO1: Ports 7K 5
Shalbourne Ri. GU15: Camb 8M 19
Shalbourne Rd. PO12: Gos 9J 213
Shalcombe SO31: Net A 2G 194
SHALDEN 9A 62
Shalden Cl. SO16: South 7H 159
SHALDEN GREEN 8B 62
Shalden Grn. Rd. GU34: Shal 9A 62
Shalden La. GU34: Shal 5N 79
Shalden Rd. GU12: Alders 2M 65
Shaldon Rd. PO9: Hav 3H 203
Shaldon Way GU51: Fleet 3J 47
Shales Rd. SO18: South 3F 174
Shallows, The SP6: Brea 4M 151
Shallows La. SO41: Bold, Pil 7D 224
Shamblehurst La. SO30: Hed E 9N 161
Shamblehurst La. Nth. SO32: Hed E 9A 162
Shamblehurst La. Sth. SO30: Hed E 2N 175
Shamrock Cl. GU16: Frim 4M 29
PO12: Gos 3M 239
Shamrock Ent. Cen. PO12: Gos 7H 213
Shamrock Quay SO14: South 5B 174
Shamrock Rd. SO19: South 7B 174
Shamrock Vs. SO17: South 1A 174
Shamrock Way SO45: Hythe 3M 193
Shanklin Cl. GU12: Alders 1L 65
Shanklin Cres. SO15: South 1K 173
Shanklin Pl. PO14: Fare 9M 197
Shanklin Rd. PO4: S'sea 3F 240
SO15: South 9J 159
Shannon Cl. PO15: Fare 7N 197
Shannon Ct. PO12: Gos 8L 213
(off Hayling Cl.)
SP10: A'ver 8B 52
Shannon Ct. Rd. GU26: Hind 6L 103
Shannon Ho. SO14: South 5A 174
(off Kent St.)
Shannon Rd. PO14: Fare 3C 212
PO14: Stub 4L 211
Shannon Way SO53: Cha F 6M 131
Shapland Av. BH11: Bour 1C 226
Shapley Heath RG27: Winchf 1A 46
SHAPPEN BOTTOM 8E 188
Shappen Hill La. BH24: Bur 8D 188
Shapton Cl. SO45: Holb 4N 207
Sharlands Rd. PO14: Fare 2C 212
Sharon Ct. PO12: Gos 2L 239
Sharon Rd. SO30: Wes E 9G 160
(not continuous)
Sharpley Cl. SP6: F'dge 8H 151
Sharpness Cl. PO14: Fare 9M 197
Sharp Rd. BH12: Poole 7E 226
Sharps Cl. PO3: Ports 5J 215
Sharps Rd. PO9: Hav 4H 203
Sharvells Rd. SO41: M Sea 7J 235
Shavards La. SO32: Meon 8N 135
Shaves La. BH25: New M 1B 232
Shaw Cl. SO18: Wes E 9E 160
SO40: Tott 3K 171
SP10: A'ver 1J 69
Shawcross Ind. Pk. PO3: Ports 3H 215
Shawfield Rd. PO9: Hav 8G 203
SHAWFORD 7J 127
Shawford Cl. SO16: Bass 7K 159
SO40: Tott 3H 171
Shawford Down Nature Reserve 6H 127
Shawford Gdns. BH8: Bour 4A 228
Shawford Gro. PO9: Hav 4C 202
Shawford Rd. BH8: Bour 3A 228
SO21: Shaw, Twyf 7J 127
Shawford Station (Rail) 7J 127
Shaw La. RG26: Bau 7E 10
Shaw Pk. RG45: Cr'tne 2D 18
Shaw Pightle RG27: Hoo 2F 44
Shaw Rd. BH24: Poul 7M 185
Shayer Rd. SO15: South 1H 173
Sheardley La. SO32: Drox 3A 166
Shearer Cl. PO9: Hav 3C 202
Shearer Rd. PO1: Ports 9F 214
Shear Hill GU31: Pet 8A 140
Shears Brook Cl. BH23: Bran 6D 220
Shears Ct. RG22: B'toke 2J 59
Shears Rd. SO50: B'stke 9J 133
SP11: E Ant 6B 52
Shearwater Av. PO16: Portc 8G 199
Shearwater Cl. PO13: Gos 6D 212
Shearwater Dr. PO6: Farl 1N 215
Sheddon Pl. SO21: Spar 4B 104
SHEDFIELD 3N 177
Sheeling Cl. GU12: Alders 8M 49
Sheep Drove SO20: N Wal 2M 87
Sheep Fair SP10: A'ver 1B 70
Sheep Fair Cl. SP10: A'ver 1B 70
Sheephouse GU9: Farnh 9E 64
Sheepmoor Dr. GU51: Fleet 9L 27
Sheep Pond La. SO32: Drox 9L 135
Sheep St. GU32: Pet 1M 145
Sheepwash Ct. RG24: B'toke 4M 41
Sheepwash La. PO7: Den 9F 180
RG20: Newt 2D 8
RG26: Rams 6F 20
Sheepwash Rd. PO8: Cowp, Horn 7C 182
PO8: Horn 4D 182
Sheerwater Ct. PO11: H Isl 6K 243
SHEET 7A 140
Sheffield Cl. GU14: Cov 8H 29
SO50: B'stke 7H 133
Sheffield Ct. PO13: Gos 1E 238
Sheffield Rd. PO1: Ports 2F 240
Shelbourne Cl. BH8: Bour 8N 227
Shelbourne Rd. BH8: Bour 8M 227
Sheldon's La. RG27: Hoo 2F 44
Sheldons Rd. RG27: Hoo 2G 44
Sheldrake Gdns. SO16: South 6G 159
SO41: Hor 3J 233
Sheldrake Rd. BH23: Mude 9C 230
Shelford Rd. PO4: S'sea 2J 241
Shell Ct. SO40: March 8E 172
Shellcroft SO31: Wars 9A 196
Shelley Av. PO6: Cosh 8N 199
Shelley Cl. BH1: Bour 9B 228
BH23: Chri 7E 230
BH24: Ashl H 3A 186
GU51: Fleet 3M 47
RG24: B'toke 3D 42
SO21: Itc A 9H 93
SO22: Winche 6H 105
Shelley Ct. GU15: Camb 8L 19
SO15: South 3A 4 (5K 173)
Shelley Gdns. BH1: Bour 9B 228
PO8: Cowp 7M 181
Shelley Hamlets BH23: Chri 7F 230
Shelley Hill BH23: Chri 7F 230
Shelley Ho. BH25: New M 4B 232
Shelley La. SO51: Ower 1D 156
Shelley Mnr. BH5: Bour 1C 246
(off Beechwood Av.)
Shelley Ri. GU14: Farn 6H 29
Shelley Rd. BH1: Bour 9B 228
BH12: Poole 9B 226
SO19: South 4H 175
SO40: Tott 9K 157
SO50: E'leigh 2D 160
Shelley Rd. E. BH7: Bour 9B 228
Shelleys La. GU34: E Wor 7M 81
Shelley Wlk. GU46: Yat 8L 17
Shelley Way SO41: M Sea 7K 235
Shell La. GU34: C'more 3B 112
Shelton Rd. BH6: Bour 8F 228
Shenley Cl. PO15: Fare 7M 197
Shenstone Ct. BH25: New M 5B 232
Shepards Cl. PO14: Fare 9M 197
Shepheard's Way PO12: Gos 5L 239
Shepherd & Flock Rdbt. GU9: Farnh 7G 65
Shepherd Cl. BH23: Highc 5H 231
Shepherds Cl. SO22: Oli B 1F 126
SO40: Bart 4B 170
(not continuous)
Shepherds Down SO24: New A 2E 108
Shepherds Farm La. SO32: Bis W, Corh 8L 135
Shepherds Fld. SO21: Mar W 8E 92
Shepherds Hey Rd. SO40: Calm 1H 171
Shepherds Hill BH24: Har 3E 184
Shepherds La. BH24: Har 3D 184
SO21: Comp, Hurs 7D 126
Shepherds Purse Cl. SO31: Loc H 7B 196
Shepherds Ri. SP11: Ver D 8E 6
Shepherds Rd. SO23: Winche 6N 105
SO40: Bart 4B 170
Shepherds Row SP10: A'ver 2B 70
Shepherds Spring Cotts. SP10: A'ver 8N 51
Shepherds Spring La. SP10: A'ver 1N 69
Shepherds Wlk. GU14: Cov 5G 28
RG23: Oak 9D 40
Shepherds Way BH7: Bour 7D 228
GU30: Lip 4E 116
RG45: Cr'tne 1A 18
SO16: Nur 6B 158
SO41: Ever 5L 233
Shepherd Way PO9: Hav 3C 202
Sheppard Cl. PO8: Horn 4A 182
RG28: Whit 6G 55
Sheppard Rd. RG21: B'toke 9B 42
Sheppard Sq. SP10: A'ver 8B 52
(off Cricketers Way)
Sheraton Av. RG22: B'toke 3K 59
Sheraton Cl. GU17: Haw 9G 18
Sherborne Ct. SO50: E'leigh 6D 132
Sherborne Rd. GU14: Farn 2M 49
RG21: B'toke 4B 42
RG24: Sher J 9N 21
SO17: South 9N 159
SHERBORNE ST JOHN 9N 21
Sherborne Way SO30: Hed E 4N 175
Sherbrooke Cl. PO13: Lee S 1C 238
SO23: Kin W 7N 91
Sherecroft Gdns. SO30: Botl 3E 176
Sherfield SP4: Win D 3A 86
Sherfield Av. PO9: Hav 4G 202
Sherfield Cl. BH8: Bour 4A 228
SHERFIELD ENGLISH 6N 121
Sherfield English La. SO51: Plai 8L 121
SP5: L'ford 9L 121
SHERFIELD GREEN 3L 23
Sherfield Ho. SO15: South 1A 4
SHERFIELD ON LODDON 4M 23
Sherfield Rd. RG26: B'ley 1G 22
RG27: Sher L 2H 23
Sheridan Cl. GU11: Alders 2J 65
SO19: South 5H 175
SO22: Winche 9G 104
Sheridan Cres. RG26: Bau 4E 10
Sheridan Gdns. PO15: White 1F 196
SO40: Tott 3K 171
Sheridan Rd. GU16: Frim 4M 29
Sheringham Rd. BH12: Poole 9D 226
PO6: Cosh 8E 200
Sherington Cl. GU14: Farn 6K 29
Sherland Pl. PO14: Fare 1A 212
(off Longfield Av.)
Sherley Grn. SO31: Burs 9L 175
Sherlock Homes SO41: Lymi 3D 234
Sherlock Lea RG27: Eve 6H 17
Sherrard Way GU16: Mytc 9N 29
Sherringham Cl. SO45: Fawl 5F 208
Sherrington Way RG22: B'toke 9A 42
Sherwin Cres. GU14: Farn 4K 29
Sherwin Wlk. PO12: Gos 4J 239
Sherwood Av. SO30: Hed E 6N 175

Solent Ho.—Sparky's Pl.

Solent Ho. PO9: Hav .6G 202
PO16: Fare .1C 212
Solent Ind. Cen. SO15: South .4H 173
Solent Ind. Est. SO30: Hed E .1M 175
Solent Lodge BH25: New M .5A 232
Solent Mead SO41: Lymi .3E 234
Solent Mdws. SO31: Hamb .8L 195
Solent Meads Golf Course .1L 247
Solent Pines BH1: Bour .2N 245
SO41: M Sea .8H 235
Solent Retail Pk. PO9: Hav .8E 202
Solent Rd. BH6: Bour .2K 247
BH23: Walk .4K 231
BH25: New M .7M 231
PO6: Dray .9K 201
PO9: Hav .8D 202
PO14: Stub .7K 211
SO15: South .7A 4 (6K 173)
SO45: Dib P .9K 193
Solent Sky Aviation Mus. .8G 4 (7N 173)
Solent Vw. BH6: Bour .2K 247
PO13: Lee S .9N 211
PO16: Portc .8K 199
SO41: Lymi .3H 235
SO45: Cals .8K 209
Solent Vw. Ct. SO41: Penn .4C 234
Solent Village PO15: White .3H 197
Solent Way PO12: Gos .4G 239
PO15: White .3F 196
SO41: M Sea .8M 235
Solly Cl. BH12: Poole .7C 226
Solomons La. SO32: Shi H, Wal C .9A 164
Solstice Pk. SP4: Ames .5A 66
Solstice Pk. Av. SP4: Ames .5A 66
Solutions Sports Cen. .4D 4 (5M 173)
Solway Ho. SO14: South .4A 174
(off Kent St.)
Somborne Ct. SO17: South .1M 173
(off Westwood Rd.)
Somborne Dr. PO9: Hav .4F 202
Somborne Ho. SO19: South .9D 174
Somborne Pk. Rd. SO20: Lit Som, S Bri .3H 89
SOMERFORD .6B 230
Somerford Av. BH23: Chri .6D 230
Somerford Bus. Pk. BH23: Chri .7C 230
Somerford Cl. SO19: South .4E 174
Somerford Rd. BH23: Chri .8A 230
Somerford Rdbt. BH23: Chri .6C 230
Somerford Way BH23: Chri .7A 230
SOMERLEY PARK .4F 184
Somerley Pk. Golf Course .4E 184
Somerley Rd. BH9: Bour .7L 227
Somerley Vw. BH24: Ring .9K 185
Somers Cl. SO22: Winche .9H 105
Somerset Av. GU35: Bor .4J 101
SO18: South .3G 174
Somerset Ct. GU14: Farn .2L 49
PO12: Gos .8K 213
SO15: South .4H 173
Somerset Cres. SO53: Cha F .9B 132
Somerset Ho. PO7: W'lle .9K 181
Somerset Rd. BH7: Bour .9C 228
BH23: Chri .7H 229
GU14: Farn .2L 49
PO5: S'sea .6E 240
SO17: South .9A 160
Somerset Ter. SO15: South .4H 173
Somers Rd. PO5: S'sea .3D 240
(not continuous)
Somers Rd. Nth. PO1: Ports .2E 240
Somerston Flats PO9: Hav .8G 202
SOMERS TOWN .3D 240
Somers Way SO50: E'leigh .3D 160
Somerton Av. SO18: South .3F 174
Somerton Cl. BH25: A'ley .3E 232
Somervell Cl. PO12: Gos .5J 239
Somervell Dr. PO16: Fare .6B 198
Somerville Ct. BH25: New M .3A 232
SP10: A'ver .9C 52
Somerville Cres. GU46: Yat .7A 18
Somerville Pl. PO2: Ports .6D 214
Somerville Rd. BH2: Bour .7H 247 (2H 245)
BH24: Poul .9M 185
SO23: Kin W .6N 91
Somme Rd. SP11: Per D .2A 30 (5J 31)
Sommers Ct. SO19: South .7B 174
Sonata Ho. PO6: P Sol .1B 214
Sonnet Way PO7: W'lle .1B 202
Sonning Cl. RG22: B'toke .3H 59
Sonninge Cl. GU47: Coll .5F 18
Sonning Way BH8: Bour .4M 227
Soper Gro. RG21: B'toke .5C 42
Soper's Bottom SP11: Rag A .3C 50
Sopers La. BH23: Chri .8K 229
(not continuous)
Sopers Row RG24: Old Bas .5H 43
SOPLEY .9L 219
Sopley Cl. BH25: New M .6M 231
Sopley Common (Nature Reserve) .7F 218
Sopley Ct. PO9: Hav .3H 203
Sopley Farm Bldgs. BH23: Sop .9L 219
Sopwith Cl. BH23: Mude .8D 230
SO20: Ki S .9B 86 (7G 88)
Sopwith Pk. SP10: A'ver .9H 51
Sopwith Rd. SO50: E'leigh .9D 132
Sopwith Way SO31: Swanw .1B 196
Sorrel Cl. GU14: Cov .7E 28
PO7: W'lle .3A 202
SO31: Loc H .7C 196
SO51: Rom .3B 130
Sorrel Dr. PO15: White .2G 197
Sorrell Ct. BH23: Chri .6D 230
Sorrell's Cl. RG24: Chin .9G 23
Sorrell Way BH23: Chri .6D 230
Sorting La. RG24: B'toke .3M 41
Sotherington La. GU33: Blackm .9M 99
GU34: Selb .9M 99
South Acre GU31: S Hart .9G 147
SOUTHAMPTON .4C 4 (5L 173)
Southampton Airport Parkway Station (Rail)
.5D 160
Southampton City Art Gallery .3C 4 (5L 173)
Southampton Cl. GU17: Blackw .7E 18
Southampton Crematorium SO16: Bass .5N 159
Southampton FC .4G 4 (5N 173)
Southampton Golf Course .5K 159
Southampton Hill PO14: Titch .8J 197
Southampton Ho. PO9: Hav .4G 202
SOUTHAMPTON INTERNATIONAL AIRPORT
.5E 160
Southampton Outdoor Sports Cen. .7J 159
Southampton Rd. BH24: Poul, Ring .1J 187
PO6: Cosh .9N 199
PO14: Titch .5F 196
PO15: Seg .4E 196
PO16: Fare .7D 198
SO31: P Ga, Titch C .4E 196
(not continuous)
SO40: Bart, Cad .6N 155
(not continuous)
SO41: Bold, Lymi .6C 224
SO42: Broc .2A 224
SO43: Lyn .2C 148
SO45: Dib, Hythe .5K 193
SO50: E'leigh .3E 160
SO51: Rom .5M 129
SP5: Alder, Whad, W'psh .3D 120
SP6: Blis, F'dge, Gods .1K 153
Southampton Row PO1: Ports .3K 5 (2B 240)
Southampton Snowsports Cen. .6K 159
Southampton Solent University
East Park Terace Campus .4D 4 (5M 173)
Sir James Matthews Building
.3C 4 (5L 173)
Warsash Maritime Cen. .1M 209
Southampton Station (Rail) .4A 4 (5K 173)
Southampton St. GU14: Farn .3K 49
SO15: South .1C 4 (4L 173)
Southampton Water Activities Cen. .7A 174
Sth. Atlantic Dr. GU11: Alders .8L 49
South Av. BH25: New M .4C 232
GU9: H End .4F 64
PO2: Ports .4F 214
SO45: Fawl .5C 208
SOUTH BADDESLEY .9L 225
Sth. Baddesley Rd. SO41: Lymi .2G 235
South Bay PO10: T Isl .5N 217
SOUTH BOCKHAMPTON .2A 230
SOUTHBOURNE .2H 247
Southbourne Av. PO6: Dray .9J 201
SO45: Holb .4A 208
Southbourne Cliff Dr. BH6: Bour .2J 247
Southbourne Cl. SP4: Port .9B 66
(off Southbourne Way)
Southbourne Coast Rd. BH6: Bour .2H 247
Southbourne Gro. BH6: Bour .1F 246
Southbourne La. Central BH6: Bour .1F 246
(off Chestnut Av.)
Southbourne La. E. BH6: Bour .1F 246
(off Grand Av.)
Southbourne La. W. BH6: Bour .1E 246
(off Fishermans Av.)
Southbourne Overcliff Dr. BH6: Bour .2F 246
Southbourne Prom. BH6: Bour .2F 246
Southbourne Rd. BH6: Bour .8E 228
SO41: Lymi .3C 234
Southbourne Sands BH6: Bour .2G 246
Southbourne Way SP4: Port .9B 66
Southbrook Cl. PO9: Langs .9F 202
Southbrook Cotts. SO21: M'dvr .7J 77
Southbrook M. SO32: Bis W .3M 163
Southbrook Pl. SO21: M'dvr .7J 77
(off Rook La.)
Southbrook Rd. PO9: Langs .9F 202
SO15: South .4A 4 (5K 173)
Southby Dr. GU51: Fleet .2N 47
SOUTH CAMP .7L 49
SOUTH CHARFORD .9N 119
Sth. Charford Drove SP6: Brea .8K 119
Southcliff PO13: Lee S .9A 212
Southcliff Ct. BH6: Bour .2J 247
Southcliffe Rd. BH23: Fri C .8D 230
BH25: New M .7M 231
South Cliff Rd. BH2: Bour .9L 247 (3K 245)
Southcliff Rd. SO14: South .1D 4 (3M 173)
South Cl. PO9: Hav .9G 202
PO12: Gos .5H 239
SO24: New A .1D 108
SO51: Rom .3B 130
Southcote Ho. BH1: Bour .1N 245
(off Vale Rd.)
Southcote Rd. BH1: Bour .1M 245
South Ct. SO15: South .2G 172
SO31: Hamb .7J 195
SO41: M Sea .8K 235
Southcroft Rd. PO12: Gos .2H 239
Sth. Cross St. PO12: Gos .3M 239
Southdale Ct. SO53: Cha F .6A 132
Southdene Rd. SO53: Cha F .7A 132
SOUTH DOWN .8H 127
Southdown Ct. BH23: Chri .6B 230
(off Dorset Rd.)
Sth. Down La. SO21: E Str .7L 77
Southdown Pl. SO21: Comp .7G 127
Southdown Rd. PO6: Cosh .9H 201
PO8: Cath, Horn .9C 168
(not continuous)
RG26: Tadl .4G 11
SO21: Shaw .7H 127
Southdowns SO24: Old A .6F 94
Southdown Vw. PO7: W'lle .8K 181
South Dr. BH25: Bash, Oss .9M 221
RG27: Sher L .6L 23
SO22: Lit .2E 104
SO51: Rom .1H 129
SP9: Tidw .8G 30
South E. Cres. SO19: South .6E 174
South E. Rd. SO19: South .6E 174
South E. Sector BH23: Bour A .7D 218
SOUTH END .4P 149
SOUTHEND .2M 179
South End Cl. SO21: Hurs .7N 125
Southend La. SO32: Sob H .2M 179
South End Rd. SP10: A'ver .3A 70
Southend Rd. RG21: B'toke .6B 42
Southern Gdns. SO40: Tott .3L 171
Southernhay PO7: Den .6G 180
Southernhay Ct. SO41: M Sea .8K 235
Southern Haye RG27: H Win .7B 26
Southern La. BH25: New M .6A 232
Southern Oaks BH25: New M .5A 232
Southern Rd. BH6: Bour .1F 246
GU15: Camb .8L 19
GU35: Bor .2H 101
RG21: B'toke .7C 42
SO15: South .4A 4 (6K 173)
SO30: Wes E .2H 175
SO41: Lymi .3D 234
SO45: Fawl .7K 209
Southern Way GU9: Farnh .9E 64
GU14: Cov .9F 28
Southey Rd. BH23: Chri .6B 230
SOUTH FARNBOROUGH .2M 49
Southfield BH24: Ring .2K 187
Southfield La. BH24: Bur .8F 188
Southfield M. BH24: Ring .2K 187
Southfields Cl. SO32: Bis W .3M 163
Southfield Wlk. PO9: Hav .2C 202
South Front SO14: South .5E 4 (6M 173)
SO51: Rom .5M 129
Southgate M. SO23: Winche .9L 237 (7K 105)
Southgate St. SO23: Winche .8L 237 (7K 105)
Southgate Vs. SO23: Winche .9L 237
SOUTH GORLEY .8M 153
South Gro. GU51: Fleet .8A 28
SO41: Lymi .3F 234
SOUTH HAM .8N 41
Sth. Ham Ho. RG22: B'toke .8L 41
Sth. Hampshire Ind. Pk. SO40: Tott .9K 157
South Ham Rd. RG22: B'toke .7N 41
SOUTH HARTING .9G 146
SOUTH HAY .4D 82
SOUTH HAYLING .5E 242
SOUTH HILL .8C 132
South Hill RG25: Up G .3B 62
SO16: Bass .7M 159
SO32: Drox .3J 165
SP6: Ald .4D 152
South Hurst GU35: W'hil .6J 101
Southill Av. BH12: Poole .8A 226
Southill Gdns. BH9: Bour .5L 227
Southill Rd. BH9: Bour .5L 227
BH12: Poole .8A 226
SOUTHINGTON .2C 56
Southington Cl. RG25: Over .3C 56
Southington La. RG25: Over .2C 56
Sth. Kinson Dr. BH11: Bour .2E 226
Southlands PO6: Cosh .9H 201
RG24: Chin .9F 22
SO41: Penn .4C 234
Southlands Av. BH6: Bour .1J 247
South La. GU31: Buri .8K 145
PO8: Blen, Chal .1G 183
PO8: Clan .6B 168
SP5: Down .2J 119 (7A 120)
SP5: Nom .2J 155
Southlawns Wlk. BH25: B Sea .5A 232
Southlea RG25: Clid .2B 60
Southlea Av. BH6: Bour .9J 229
Southleigh Farm PO9: Hav .6K 203
Southleigh Gro. PO11: H Isl .3F 242
Southleigh Rd. PO9: Hav, Warb .8H 203
PO10: Ems .6L 203
South Lodge PO15: Fare .8L 197
South Mall GU51: Fleet .2L 47
South Mdw. RG45: Cr'tne .2F 18
Southmead Rd. GU11: Alders .2K 65
PO15: Fare .8N 197
Sth. Millers Dale SO53: Cha F .5N 131
Sth. Mill Rd. SO15: South .3E 172
Southmoor La. PO9: Hav .9D 202
South Normandy PO1: Ports .6K 5 (3B 240)
South Pde. PO4: S'sea .6E 240
PO5: S'sea .6E 240
SO40: Tott .3M 171
South Pk. Ct. PO9: Hav .8F 202
South Pk. Rd. BH12: Poole .6E 226
South Pl. PO13: Lee S .3C 238
South Point SO31: Hamb .7J 195
South Ridge RG29: Odi .9L 45
South Rd. BH1: Bour .9B 228
GU30: Lip .5E 116
GU47: Owl .1G 18
PO1: Ports .9F 214
PO6: Dray .1L 215
PO8: Horn .1C 182
(not continuous)
PO11: H Isl .4F 242
PO17: S'wick .3B 200
(East Rd.)
PO17: S'wick .7B 200
(Hilltop Rd.)
RG20: Kings .2C 6 (6L 9)
RG45: Cr'tne .1G 18
SO17: South .2A 174
SO20: Brou .5B 88
SO21: Owls .7B 134
SO24: New A .1D 108
SOUTHROPE .2M 79
Southrope Grn. RG25: Herr .2M 79
SOUTHSEA .9N 5 (5D 240)
Southsea Caravan Activity Pk.
PO4: S'sea .5L 241
Southsea Castle & Mus. .6D 240
Southsea Esplanade PO4: S'sea .6G 240
Southsea Model Village .6G 240
Southsea Ter. PO5: S'sea .8M 5 (4C 240)
Southsea Works Ind. Est. PO4: S'sea .2H 241
Southside Cotts. SO20: Longs .2F 88
Southside Rd. SP11: Longp .4N 71
South Spur PO17: S'wick .7C 200
South Sq. PO17: K Vil .2A 198
Sth. Stoneham Ho. SO18: S'ing .8B 160
South St. GU9: Farnh .8E 64
GU14: Farn .2N 49
PO5: S'sea .7M 5 (4D 240)
PO9: Hav .9F 202
PO10: Ems .9M 203
PO12: Gos .4K 239
PO14: Titch .9J 197
SO24: Rop .2D 110
SO41: Penn .4C 234
SO45: Hythe .6M 193
SO50: E'leigh .3E 160
SP5: Br Ch .3A 118
SP10: A'ver .3N 69
SOUTH SWAY .9L 223
Sth. Sway La. SO41: Sway .7K 223
South Ter. PO1: Ports .3J 5 (2B 240)
SOUTH TIDWORTH .9D 30 (7G 31)
SOUTH TOWN .2G 97
Sth. Town Rd. GU34: Meds .1G 96
Sth. Trestle Rd. SO45: Fawl .3G 209
SOUTH VIEW .4C 42
South Vw. BH2: Bour .9K 227
PO8: Cowp .6A 182
SO22: Winche .7J 237 (6J 105)
Southview SO32: Drox .2K 165
South Vw. Cl. SO21: Sut S .7D 76
South Vw. Cotts. RG27: Hoo .2G 44
South Vw. Gdns. SP10: A'ver .2A 70
Southview M. RG21: B'toke .4D 42
Southview Pk. Homes SO22: Oli B .2G 126
South Vw. Pl. BH2: Bour .8J 247 (3J 245)
Southview Ri. GU34: Alt .3E 80
South Vw. Rd. BH23: Chri .8K 229
SO15: South .2J 173
SO22: Oli B .2F 126
Southview Rd. GU35: Head D .2D 102
South Vw. Ter. SP11: S M Bo .2N 53
Southville Rd. BH5: Bour .9E 228
South Wlk. GU12: Alders .9M 49
Southwark Cl. GU46: Yat .7M 17
SP9: Tidw .8E 30
SOUTH WARNBOROUGH .4D 62
Southwater PO13: Lee S .9N 211
South Way SP10: A'ver .8C 52
Southway GU15: Camb .9K 19
PO13: Gos .5E 212
PO15: Titch .6H 197
SP4: Port .9D 66
Southways PO14: Stub .6N 211
SOUTH WEIRS .8A 148 (9M 189)
South Weirs SO42: Broc .8A 148 (9M 189)
Southwell Pk. Rd. GU15: Camb .8K 19
Sth. Western Cres. BH14: Poole .3A 244
Sth. Western Ho. SO14: South .8F 4 (7N 173)
SOUTHWICK .3A 200
Southwick Av. PO16: Portc .8N 199
Southwick By-Pass PO17: S'wick .3M 199
Southwick Cl. SO22: Winche .2H 105
Southwick Ct. PO14: Fare .2C 212
Southwick Hill Rd. PO6: Cosh .7E 200
Southwick Ho. PO1: Ports .1E 240
(off Crasswell St.)
PO3: Ports .1H 241
(off Cotton Rd.)
Southwick Park Golf Course .4B 200
Southwick Pl. BH6: Bour .7F 228
Southwick Rd. BH6: Bour .8F 228
PO6: Cosh .4A 200
PO7: Den .6F 180
PO17: N Boa, Wick .7D 178
PO17: S'wick .4A 200
South Winchester (Park & Ride) .4J 127
South Winchester Golf Course .1E 126
Southwinds SO21: Stoke C .7F 76
SOUTH WONSTON .3H 91
SOUTHWOOD .9F 28
Southwood Av. BH6: Bour .1F 246
BH23: Walk .5J 231
Southwood Bus. Cen. GU14: Cov .8F 28
Southwood Cl. BH23: Walk .5J 231
Southwood Cres. GU14: Cov .8F 28
Southwood Gdns. SO31: Loc H .6C 196
Southwood Golf Course .1G 49
Southwood La. GU14: Cov .9F 28
GU51: Fleet .9B 28
Southwood Rd. GU14: Cov .9F 28
GU17: Min .3A 28
GU34: Shal .9A 62
PO2: Ports .4F 214
PO11: H Isl .5J 243
Sovereign Av. PO12: Gos .9L 213
Sovereign Cen. BH1: Bour .9B 228
Sovereign Cl. BH7: Bour .6C 228
PO4: S'sea .2L 241
SO40: Tott .2J 171
Sovereign Ct. GU51: Fleet .2L 47
(off Victorian Rd.)
SO17: South .1L 173
SO50: E'leigh .1E 160
Sovereign Cres. PO14: Titch C .8D 196
Sovereign Dr. PO4: S'sea .2K 241
SO30: Hed E .4A 176
Sovereign Ga. PO1: Ports .1D 240
(off Staunton St.)
Sovereign La. PO7: Purb .6M 201
Sovereign Sq. BH1: Bour .1B 246
(off Christchurch Rd.)
Sovereign Way SO50: E'leigh .6D 132
Sowcroft La. RG29: S War .7D 62
Sowden Cl. SO30: Hed E .3M 175
Sowley La. SO41: E End .1N 235
Spain, The GU32: Pet .1L 145
Spain La. GU34: Las .3J 79
Spalding Rd. SO19: South .5J 175
Spaniard's La. SO51: A'field, Lee .9M 129
SPANISH GREEN .2A 24
Sparc Ho. GU17: Min .5E 28
Sparkford Cl. BH7: Bour .6B 228
SO22: Winche .9J 237 (8J 105)
Sparkford Rd. SO22: Winche .9J 237 (8J 105)
Sparky's Pl. BH1: Bour .9A 228

320 A-Z Hampshire

Spa Rd.—Statham Sq.

Spa Rd. SO14: South 6C 4 (6L 173)
Sparrow Cl. PO8: Cowp 6N 181
Sparrow Ct. PO13: Lee S 9B 212
Sparrowgrove SO21: Ott 9G 127
Sparrowhawk Cl. GU10: Ews 2N 63
PO3: Ports 4H 215
Sparrow Sq. SO50: E'leigh 1B 160
SPARSHOLT 3B 104 (6N 89)
Sparsholt Cl. PO9: Hav 4C 202
Sparsholt La. SO21: Hurs 3N 125
SO21: Spar 7A 104
SO22: Winche 8A 104
Sparsholt Rd. SO19: South 1D 194
Spartan Cl. PO10: T Isl 5N 217
PO14: Stub 3N 211
Spartina Dr. SO41: Lymi 9E 224
Sparvells RG27: Eve 5H 17
Sparvell Way GU15: Camb 7L 19
Spats La. GU35: Head D 8B 84
Spear Rd. SO14: South 2M 173
SPEARYWELL 1D 122
Speckled Wood Rd. RG24: B'toke 2C 42
Specks La. PO4: S'sea 2H 241
Speedfields Pk. PO14: Fare 3D 212
Speedwell Cl. SO31: Loc H 7C 196
SO53: Cha F 7N 131
Speedwell Dr. BH23: Chri 6D 230
Speggs Wlk. SO30: Hed E 4N 175
Spellers Way BH23: Chri 8A 230
Speltham Hill PO7: H'don 9E 166
Spencer Cl. GU12: Alders 1K 65
GU16: Frim G 6N 29
GU34: Four M 4J 97
GU52: Ch Cr 6A 48
PO11: H Isl 4G 242
RG26: Pam H 4L 11
Spencer Ct. BH25: New M 4B 232
PO5: S'sea 5E 240
PO14: Stub 6A 212
Spencer Dr. PO13: Lee S 2B 238
Spencer Gdns. PO8: Cowp 6M 181
SO52: N Bad 7F 130
Spencer Rd. BH1: Bour 1N 245
BH13: Poole 5C 244
BH25: New M 3B 232
PO4: S'sea 5G 241
PO10: Ems 5L 203
SO19: South 4H 175
SO50: E'leigh 1C 160
Spenlow Cl. PO2: Ports 9E 214
Spenser Cl. GU34: Alt 3G 81
SO31: Wars 9A 196
Spenser Ct. GU35: W'hil 6J 101
Sperrin Cl. RG22: B'toke 8K 41
Spetisbury Cl. BH9: Bour 3M 227
Spey Ct. SP10: A'ver 8B 52
Spice Quay PO1: Ports 7H 5 (4B 240)
Spicer Ct. BH2: Bour 7J 247 (2J 245)
Spicer Ho. PO1: Ports 2L 5
Spicer La. BH11: Bour 1C 226
Spicers GU34: Alt 5G 80
Spicers Ct. SO22: Winche 6K 237 (6K 105)
Spicers Hill SO40: Tott 5L 171
Spicer St. PO1: Ports 1D 240
Spicers Way SO40: Tott 4L 171
Spicewood PO15: Fare 7A 198
Spiers Cl. RG26: Tadl 5K 11
Spiers La. SO24: Ch Can 7D 78
SO24: Old A 3G 94
Spinacre BH25: B Sea 6C 232
Spindle Cl. PO9: Hav 6J 203
Spindle Warren PO9: Hav 6J 203
Spindlewood RG24: Chin 8G 22
Spindlewood Cl. BH25: B Sea 5B 232
SO16: Bass 5M 159
Spindlewood Way SO40: March 1E 192
Spinnaker Cl. PO11: H Isl 3E 242
PO13: Gos 9F 212
Spinnaker Ct. PO1: Ports 7H 5
SO31: Net A 3F 194
Spinnaker Dr. PO2: Ports 4E 214
Spinnaker Grange PO11: H Isl 4J 217
Spinnaker Ho. PO6: P Sol 1B 214
Spinnaker M. SO31: Wars 8A 196
Spinnakers, The PO13: Lee S 2A 238
(off Beach Rd.)
Spinnaker Sailing Club 5L 185
Spinnaker Tower 5H 5 (3A 240)
Spinnaker Vw. PO9: Bed 8A 202
Spinner Dr. PO9: Hav 3C 202
Spinners Garden 7E 224
Spinney, The BH12: Poole 8E 226
BH24: Ashl H 2C 186
GU26: Gray 3J 103
GU27: Hasl 1M 117
GU46: Yat 6M 17
GU51: Fleet 3J 47
PO7: Den 7G 180
PO8: Horn 4A 182
PO13: Gos 7F 212
PO16: Fare 8H 199
RG24: B'toke 3M 41
(Peggs Way)
RG24: B'toke 4N 41
(Priestley Rd.)
RG27: Hoo 1G 45
SO16: Bass 5L 159
SO21: Comp 6G 127
SO24: Bram 9L 109
SO40: Calm 1J 171
SO50: B'stke 1L 161
SO50: E'leigh 1E 160
(off Desborough Rd.)
Spinney Caravan Park, The SO24: New A 9E 94
Spinney Cl. BH24: St L 4A 186
PO8: Cowp 7M 181
Spinney Ct. RG24: B'toke 3M 41
Spinney Dale SO45: Hythe 7N 193
Spinney Gdns. SO45: Hythe 7N 193
Spinney M. RG24: B'toke 3M 41
Spinney Rd. SP11: Ludg 1C 30
Spinney Wlk. SO18: South 8D 160
Spinney Way BH25: New M 9B 222
Spire Cl. PO14: Titch C 6F 196
RG24: B'toke 1C 42
Spirit Health Club
Eastleigh 9C 132
Farnborough 3K 49
Southampton 7B 4 (7L 173)
Spitalfields Rd. GU34: Alt 4F 80
SPITALHATCH 4H 81
Spital Hatch GU34: Alt 4H 81
Spitfire Ct. SO19: South 7A 174
Spitfire End SO23: Winche 6A 106
Spitfire La. SO20: S Bri 2C 88
Spitfire Link SO21: Winche 7A 106
Spitfire Loop SO18: S'ton A 4D 160
Spitfire Quay SO19: South 6A 174
Spitfire Way SO31: Hamb 7K 195
Spithead Av. PO12: Gos 6L 239
Spithead Hgts. PO4: S'sea 4M 241
Spithead Ho. PO16: Fare 1C 212
Spittlefields BH24: Ring 1L 187
Spokane Cl. GU11: Alders 2H 65
Spoonwood Ct. RG24: B'toke 3M 41
Sports Centre, The 6C 42
Sportsman Pl. SO30: Wes E 1J 175
Spouts La. SO51: W Wel 8M 121
Spradbury La. RG19: Head 3K 9
SPRAT'S DOWN 8H 209
Sprats Hatch La. RG27: Dogm, Winchf 5C 46
SPRATT'S DOWN 6A 54
Spray Leaze SP11: Ludg 1F 30
Spray Rd. RG17: Ink 1E 6
SN8: Ham 1E 6
Spreadbury Dr. GU51: Fleet 9L 27
Sprents La. RG25: Over 3E 56
Spring, The PO7: Den 7G 181
Spring Arts & Heritage Centre, The 8G 202
Springbank Rd. BH7: Bour 6C 228
SPRINGBOURNE 8N 227
Springbourne Ct. BH1: Bour 9A 228
Spring Cl. RG24: Sher J 8N 21
SO19: South 6D 174
SO50: Fair O 1N 161
Spring Ct. PO13: Lee S 2B 238
SO15: South 5K 173
Spring Cres. SO17: South 2N 173
Springcroft PO13: Gos 3D 212
Springcross Av. GU17: Haw 1F 28
Springdale Ct. SO40: Tott 3M 171
Springfarm Rd. GU27: Hasl 1N 117
Springfield RG23: Oak 9E 40
SO31: Sar G 6A 196
Springfield Av. BH6: Bour 1K 247
BH23: Chri 4G 229
RG27: H Win 5B 26
SO45: Holb 4B 208
Springfield Cl. PO9: Bed 7B 202
PO17: Wick 6C 178
SO41: Lymi 3G 234
SP10: A'ver 1C 70
Springfield Ct. SO19: South 8D 174
Springfield Cres. SP5: Woodf 3M 119 (8C 120)
Springfield Dr. SO40: Tott 4L 171
Springfield Gdns. BH25: A'ley 4E 232
Springfield Gro. SO45: Holb 4B 208
Springfield La. GU51: Fleet 2K 47
Springfield Rd. RG26: Pam H 4L 11
Springfields SP11: Ludg 1C 30
Springfields Cl. SO21: Col C 3K 133
Springfield Ter. GU33: Liss 1E 140
(off Mill Rd.)
Springfield Way PO14: Stub 7M 211
Spring Firs SO19: South 7D 174
Springford Cl. SO16: South 7G 159
Springford Cres. SO16: South 8G 159
Springford Gdns. SO16: South 7G 159
Springford Rd. SO16: South 8G 159
Spring Gdn. La. PO12: Gos 2L 239
Spring Gdns. BH12: Poole 9B 226
GU14: Farn 5J 29
PO1: Ports 4M 5 (2D 240)
PO10: Ems 9M 203
RG20: Wa W 1B 8
SO24: New A 2E 108
SO30: Hed E 4A 176
SO52: N Bad 7E 130
Spring Gro. SO31: Burs 9L 175
Spring Hill La. SP11: S M Bo 9L 35
Springhill Rd. SO53: Cha F 6A 132
Spring Hills SO19: South 5G 175
Springholm Cl. GU9: Bad L 4K 65
Spring Ho. Cl. SO21: Col C 3L 133
Springlakes Ind. Est. GU12: Alders 8N 49
Spring La. BH25: A'ley 4E 232
GU9: Up H 3C 64
RG7: Rise 2E 14
RG7: Swal 1F 14
RG20: Burgh 4D 8
SO21: Col C 3K 133
SO32: Swanm 7D 164
SO50: B'stke 8H 133
Spring La. W. GU9: Up H 4C 64
Spring Leaze SP11: Stoke 7H 35
Springles La. PO15: Titch 4K 197
Springmead SO41: Lymi 3F 234
Springmead Ct. GU27: Hasl 1M 117
(off Copse Rd.)
GU47: Owl 4G 19
Spring Mdw. SN8: Co Du 2H 31
Spring M. SP10: A'ver 9A 52
(off Shepherds Spring La.)
Springpark Ho. RG21: B'toke 5D 42
Spring Pl. SO51: Rom 5L 129
Spring Rd. BH1: Bour 9N 227
SO19: South 4D 174
SO31: Sar G 3C 196
SO41: Lymi 3F 234
SO45: Hythe 5M 193
Springs, The RG7: Stra S 5J 13
Spring St. PO1: Ports 3N 5 (2D 240)
SPRINGVALE 7N 91
Spring Vale PO8: Cowp 6B 182
SO32: Swanm 6C 164
Springvale Av. BH7: Bour 6C 228
SO23: Kin W 8M 91
Springvale Rd. SO23: Kin W, Winche 1L 105
Spring Wlk. BH1: Bour 9A 228
PO1: Ports 2N 5 (1D 240)
Springwater Cl. BH11: Bour 3E 226
Springwater Dr. BH23: Chri 8N 229
Springwater Rd. BH11: Bour 3E 226
Spring Way SO24: New A 2E 108
Springwell PO9: Hav 8F 202
Springwell La. RG27: H Win 3C 26
Springwood Av. PO7: W'lle 3N 201
Spring Woods GU47: Sandh 4E 18
GU52: Fleet 4L 47
Spruce Av. GU35: W'hil 4F 100
PO7: W'lle 2A 202
Spruce Cl. SO21: Sth W 2J 91
SO31: Wars 9A 196
SP10: A'ver 2J 69
Spruce Dr. SO19: South 5J 175
SO40: Tott 2H 171
Spruce Wlk. PO13: Lee S 1B 238
Spruce Way GU51: Fleet 2B 48
Spur, The PO12: Gos 5H 239
PO17: Wick 6C 178
Spurgeon Rd. BH7: Bour 8E 228
Spur Hill Av. BH14: Poole 2B 244
Spurlings Ind. Est. PO17: Fare 6G 198
Spurlings Rd. PO17: Fare 5F 198
Spur Rd. BH14: Poole 2B 244
PO6: Cosh 9G 200
PO7: W'lle 2M 201
(not continuous)
Spurs Ct. GU11: Alders 9G 49
Spybush La. SO24: Old A 9C 78
Square, The BH1: Bour 7L 247 (2K 245)
BH21: Cran 6J 149
GU10: Rowl 8N 63
GU14: Farn 1K 49
GU26: Gray 4M 103
GU30: Lip 2D 116
GU31: S Hart 8G 146
GU32: Pet 1M 145
PO10: Westb 6N 203
PO12: Gos 8L 213
PO14: Titch 9J 197
PO17: Wick 7C 178
RG19: Green 1H 9
RG20: Bis G 1H 9
RG21: B'toke 5D 42
RG24: B'toke 3M 41
SO20: N Wal 1A 88
SO23: Winche 8M 237 (7L 105)
SO31: Hamb 7L 195
SO41: Penn 3C 234
SO45: Fawl 5F 208
SO50: Fair O 1N 161
SO51: Awb 9B 122
SP11: Hur T 4D 34
Squarefield Gdns. RG27: Hoo 1J 45
Square Tower, The 7H 5 (4A 240)
Squarey Cl. SP5: Down 3K 119 (8A 120)
Squires Wlk. SO19: South 9C 174
Squirrel Cl. GU47: Sandh 5D 18
SO31: P Ga 4F 196
SO50: B'stke 1K 161
Squirrel Ct. GU12: Alders 8N 49
Squirrel Dr. RG23: B'toke 7H 59
SO19: South 7E 174
Squirrel La. GU14: Cov 7J 29
Squirrels, The BH13: Poole 2E 244
Squirrels Ct. BH23: Chri 4G 228
Squirrels Wlk. SO45: Dib P 7L 193
Stable Cl. PO14: Titch C 7G 196
RG27: Hoo 2F 44
SP11: Ludg 2C 30 (5K 31)
Stable La. GU31: Pet 1M 145
(off Bowen La.)
Stable Rd. GU35: Bor 1H 101
Stables, The BH1: Bour 1B 246
BH23: Chri 7J 229
SO31: Loc H 7D 196
Stables Rd. SP9: Tidw 8G 30
Stable Vw. GU46: Yat 6N 17
Stacey Cl. BH12: Poole 7A 226
Stacey Ct. PO9: Hav 2D 202
Stacey Gdns. BH8: Bour 4C 228
Staff College Rd. GU15: Camb 7J 19
Stafford Ho. GU11: Alders 9K 49
(off Station Rd.)
Stafford Rd. BH1: Bour 2L 245
GU32: Pet 8M 139
PO5: S'sea 4E 240
SO15: South 3J 173
Staff Rd. GU12: Alders 9L 49
SO51: Mich 5H 123
Stagbrake Cl. SO45: Holb 5N 207
Stag Bus. Pk. BH24: Ring 3K 187
Stag Cl. BH25: New M 2N 231
SO50: B'stke 1K 161
Stag Dr. SO30: Hed E 2A 176
Stag Gates SO45: Blac 7C 208
Stag Hill RG22: B'toke 9M 41
Stag Oak La. RG24: Chin 8F 22
Stagshorn Rd. PO8: Horn 3C 182
Stags La. SO21: More 4C 134
Stag Way PO15: F'ley 4N 197
Stainer Cl. SO19: South 7N 175
Stainers La. SO21: Sth W 3G 91
Stairs Hill GU33: Emp 2N 113
Staith Cl. SO19: South 5G 174
Stake La. GU14: Cov 8J 29
STAKES 4M 201
Stakes Hill Rd. PO7: Purb, W'lle 2M 201
Stakes La. SO32: Bis W, Durl, Uph 1H 163
SO32: Bis W, Uph 7N 135
Stakes Rd. PO7: Purb 4K 201
Stalham Rd. BH12: Poole 8D 226
Stallard Cl. PO10: Ems 8L 203
Stallards La. BH24: Ring 1J 187
Stalybridge Cl. SO31: P Ga 3D 196
Stamford Av. GU16: Frim 3N 29
PO11: H Isl 4E 242
Stamford Rd. BH6: Bour 9F 228
Stamford St. PO1: Ports 1F 240
Stamford Way SO50: Fair O 2N 161
Stampsey Ct. PO2: Ports 6E 214
STAMSHAW 6E 214
Stamshaw & Tipner Leisure Cen. 6D 214
Stamshaw Prom. PO2: Ports 4E 214
Stamshaw Rd. PO2: Ports 6E 214
STANBRIDGE EARLS 1H 129
Stanbridge La. SO51: Awb, Rom 9F 122
Stanbridge Rd. PO9: Hav 6H 203
Stanbury Cl. SP11: Thru 1N 67
Stanbury Rd. SP11: Fyf, Thru 9M 31
Stancomb Broad La. GU34: Meds 4A 96
(not continuous)
Stancombe La. GU34: Shal 9A 62
Stancomb La. GU34: Meds 3E 96
Standard Way PO16: Fare 6E 198
Standen Rd. SO16: Nur 6B 158
Standfast La. GU33: Hawk 5N 113
STANDFORD 6M 101
Standford Hill GU35: Stan 6M 101
Standford La. GU30: Pass 6M 101
GU35: Head, Stan 3M 101
GU35: Stan 6M 101
Standford St. SO14: South 6G 4 (6N 173)
Standing Hill SP5: W Tyt 8K 87
STANDON 3N 125
Stanfield RG26: Tadl 4H 11
Stanfield Cl. BH12: Poole 7B 226
Stanfield Rd. BH9: Bour 6J 227
BH12: Poole 7B 226
Stanford Cl. PO6: Cosh 9E 200
Stanford Ct. PO9: Hav 4H 203
SO19: South 7H 175
STANFORD END 2D 14
Stanford Gdns. SO41: Lymi 4D 234
Stanford Hill SO41: Lymi 3D 234
Stanford Ri. SO41: Sway 5J 223
Stanford Rd. RG22: B'toke 2L 59
SO41: Lymi 3D 234
Stanham Cl. SO21: Wor D 5H 91
Stanhope Dr. PO31: Cowes 5N 237
(off Queen's Rd.)
Stanhope Ga. GU15: Camb 8J 19
PO5: S'sea 9N 5 (5D 240)
Stanhope Rd. GU15: Camb 9H 19
PO1: Ports 3N 5 (2D 240)
Stanier Way SO30: Hed E 8N 161
Staniforth Ct. BH23: Chri 8N 229
Stanley Av. PO3: Ports 8J 215
Stanley Cl. PO12: Gos 7J 213
PO15: Fare 8A 198
RG26: Bau 4E 10
SP5: Bish 3C 118
Stanley Dr. GU14: Cov 9E 28
Stanley Holiday Cen. BH25: New M 9D 222
Stanley La. PO5: S'sea 5D 240
Stanley Rd. BH1: Bour 9N 227
BH23: Highc 6J 231
PO2: Ports 7D 214
PO10: Ems 9N 203
SO17: South 1A 174
SO40: Tott 1K 171
SO41: Lymi 4F 234
SO45: Holb 4B 208
Stanley St. PO5: S'sea 5D 240
STANMORE 9H 105
Stanmore La. SO22: Winche 8G 104
Stannington Cl. BH25: New M 4C 232
Stannington Cres. SO40: Tott 2M 171
Stannington Way SO40: Tott 2M 171
STANPIT 8A 230
Stanpit BH23: Chri 8A 230
Stanpit Marsh Nature Reserve 9N 229
Stanstead Rd. SO50: E'leigh 8D 132
STANSTED 1N 203
Stansted Cl. PO9: R Cas 8J 183
Stansted Cres. PO9: Hav 3H 203
Stansted Rd. PO5: S'sea 3E 240
STANSWOOD 1L 237
Stanswood Grange RG27: Sher L 7H 23
Stanswood Rd. PO9: Hav 3D 202
SO45: Cals, Fawl 2K 237
Stanton Dr. GU51: Fleet 3K 47
Stanton Rd. BH10: Bour 4G 227
GU32: Pet 9L 139
SO15: South 3E 172
Stanton Rd. Ind. Est.
SO15: South 3F 172
Staple Ash La. GU32: Frox 6C 138
Staple Cl. PO7: W'lle 9L 181
Staplecross La. BH23: Burt 6N 229
Stapleford Cl. SO51: Rom 3A 130
Stapleford La. SO32: Durl 6C 162
Staple Gdns.
SO23: Winche 7L 237 (6K 105)
Staplehurst Cl. SO19: South 9F 174
Staplers Reach PO13: Gos 6D 212
Stapleton Rd. PO3: Ports 8H 215
Staplewood La. SO40: March 2A 192
(not continuous)
Stapley La. SO24: Rop 3E 110
Stares Cl. PO13: Gos 9E 212
Star Hill GU10: Chur 6F 84
RG27: H Win 4E 26
Star Hill Caravan Site
RG27: H Win 2F 26
Star Hill Dr. GU10: Chur 5F 84
Starina Gdns. PO7: W'lle 1B 202
Star La. BH24: Ring 1J 187
RG20: High 4A 8
Starling Cl. RG22: B'toke 2H 59
Starling Sq. SO50: E'leigh 1B 160
Star Post Rd. GU15: Camb 5N 19
Statham Sq. SP10: A'ver 7B 52

Station App.—Stroud Common

Station App. BH25: New M 3B 232
GU14: Farn 7K 29
GU16: Frim 4M 29
GU17: Blackw 9G 19
GU34: Four M, Meds 4H 97
(not continuous)
GU51: Fleet 9N 27
PO1: Ports 4J 5 (2B 240)
PO10: Ems 8M 203
PO16: Fare 8C 198
RG21: B'toke 5C 42
SO21: Itc A 8H 93
SO24: New A 1F 108
SO42: Broc 7D 148
SO51: Rom 4M 129
SP10: A'ver 1L 69
SP11: Grat 5K 67
SP11: Ludg 1D 30 (5K 31)
Station Cl. PO17: Wick 6C 178
SO21: Itc A 8H 93
Station Cotts. SO42: Beau 8K 191
Station Downside RG27: Winchf 2C 46
Station Hill GU9: Farnh 8E 64
RG21: B'toke 5C 42
RG25: Over 9E 38
RG27: Winchf 1B 46
SO21: Itc A 9H 93
SO23: Winche 6L 237 (6K 105)
SO24: Rop 1A 110
SO30: Curd 3F 176
SO31: Burs 2M 195
SO32: Curd 3F 176
Station La. SO53: Cha F 6A 132
Station Mall RG21: B'toke 6C 42
Station M. SO51: Rom 4M 129
Station Rd. BH14: Poole 1A 244
BH23: Chri 7K 229
BH23: Hin 3G 231
BH24: Bur 8F 188
BH25: New M 3B 232
GU10: Ben'ly 8K 63
GU11: Alders 9K 49
GU14: Farn 8K 29
GU16: Frim 3L 29
GU30: Lip 4D 116
GU31: Pet 9M 139
GU32: Pet 9L 139
GU32: W Meo 9D 136
GU33: Liss 9D 114
GU34: Alt 4G 80
GU34: Bent 6L 79
GU35: Bor 2H 101
PO3: Ports 8H 215
PO6: Dray 2K 215
PO11: H Isl 3D 242
PO12: Gos 9H 213
PO16: Portc 9M 199
PO17: Wick 6C 178
RG7: Mort 1K 13
RG20: E Woo, Wol H 2A 8
RG23: Oak 1B 58
RG25: Clid 3B 60
RG25: Over 2E 56
RG27: Hoo 2G 45
RG27: Winchf 2C 46
RG28: Whit 4G 55
SO15: South 2B 172
SO16: Nur 6N 157
SO19: South 8D 174
SO20: Chil 5E 74
SO20: Ov Wa 8L 67
SO23: Winche 6K 237 (6K 105)
SO24: New A 9F 94
SO31: Burs 1M 195
SO31: Net A 1A 194
SO31: P Ga 4D 196
SO32: Bis W 4M 163
SO32: Drox, Sob 5L 165
SO41: Sway 5J 223
SO51: Rom 5L 129
SP4: New T 6E 66
SP6: Ald 4C 152
SP6: F'dge 9F 150
SP9: Tidw 9D 30 (7G 31)
SP11: Grat 5K 67
Station Rd. Nth. SO40: Tott 3A 172
Station Rd. Sth. SO40: Tott 3A 172
Station St. PO1: Ports 3N 5 (2D 240)
SO41: Lymi 2F 234
Station Ter. SO21: Shaw 7J 127
Station Theatre 3D 242
Station Yd. SP6: Ald 4B 152
Staunton BH2: Bour 8M 247
Staunton Av. PO11: H Isl 4D 242
Staunton Country Pk. 1F 202
Staunton Country Pk. Vis. Cen. 3F 202
Staunton Hgts. PO9: Hav 4E 202
Staunton Rd. PO9: Hav 7E 202
Staunton St. PO1: Ports 1D 240
Stavedown Rd. SO21: Sth W 3G 90
Stead Cl. PO11: H Isl 4H 243
Steamer Point Local Nature Reserve 7G 230
Steamer Point Vis. Cen. 8F 230
Stedman Rd. BH5: Bour 9E 228
Steele Cl. SO53: Cha F 8B 132
Steele's Rd. GU11: Alders 7K 49
Steels Drove SP6: Woodg 2A 154
(off High St.)
Steels La. SP6: Dame 4P 149
Steel St. PO5: S'sea 7M 5 (4C 240)
STEEP 6L 139
Steep Cl. PO16: Portc 8L 199
SO18: South 2G 175
Steeple Dr. GU34: Alt 4F 80
Steeple Way PO14: Titch C 6G 196
STEEP MARSH 4N 139
Steepways GU26: Hind 1K 103
Steerforth Cl. PO2: Ports 8E 214
Steerforth Copse GU47: Owl 3G 19
Steinbeck Cl. PO15: White 1F 196
Stella Ct. BH23: Highc 7K 231
Stem La. BH25: Bash, New M 3N 231
Stem La. Ind. Est. BH25: New M 3N 231
Stem La. Trad. Est. BH25: New M 3N 231
Stenbury Dr. RG25: Pres C 5E 78
Stenbury Way SO31: Net A 2G 195
Stephen Cl. PO8: Cowp 8B 182
Stephen Ct. SO45: Holb 5B 208
Stephendale Rd. GU9: Farnh 6F 64
Stephen Langton Dr. BH11: Bour 1B 226
Stephen Lodge PO5: S'sea 8N 5 (4D 240)
Stephen Martin Gdns. SP6: F'dge 9H 151
Stephen Rd. PO15: Fare 8B 198
Stephens Ct. SO51: Rom 6L 129
Stephenson Cl. PO12: Gos 5J 239
SP10: A'ver 9J 51
Stephenson Rd. PO15: Titch 7H 197
RG21: B'toke 5N 41
SO40: Tott 8K 157
Stephenson Way SO30: Hed E 8M 161
Stephens Rd. RG26: Tadl 5J 11
Stephen's Wlk. BH24: Ring 1J 187
(off Lyne's La.)
Stephyns Dr. GU51: Fleet 8L 27
Steplake La. SO51: Sher E 6M 121
Step Ter. SO22: Winche 7J 237 (6J 105)
Sterling Gdns. GU47: Coll 5G 19
Sterling Pk. SP10: A'ver 9J 51
Steuart Rd. SO18: South 3B 174
Stevens Drove SO20: Houg 4C 88
Stevens Grn. SP11: S M Bo 1M 53
Stevens Hill GU46: Yat 8A 18
Stevenson Cres. BH14: Poole 2B 244
Stevenson Lodge BH4: Bour 2G 244
Stevenson Rd. BH6: Bour 2K 247
SO21: Bar S 4A 76
STEVENTON 6L 57
Steventon Rd. SO18: South 3G 175
Stewart Borrow Ho.
PO8: Cowp 7L 181
Stewart Cl. BH8: Bour 9N 227
Stewart Ho. SO53: Cha F 3A 132
Stewart Mews BH8: Bour 9N 227
(off Stewart Cl.)
Stewart Pl. PO1: Ports 9F 214
Stewart Rd. BH8: Bour 8L 227
RG24: B'toke 2F 42
Stewarts Grn. PO7: H'don 8D 166
Stibbs Way BH23: Bran 6D 220
Stiles Dr. SP10: A'ver 1C 70
Stillions Cl. GU34: Alt 5G 80
Stillmeadows SO31: Loc H 7D 196
Stillmore Rd. BH11: Bour 3B 226
Stillwater Pk. BH24: Poul 7M 185
Stilwell Cl. GU46: Yat 7A 18
Stinchar Dr. SO53: Cha F 7M 131
Stinsford Cl. BH9: Bour 2M 227
Stirling Av. PO7: W'lle 2N 201
Stirling Cl. BH25: New M 3C 232
GU14: Cov 9J 29
GU16: Frim 2N 29
SO40: Tott 2N 171
Stirling Ct. BH1: Bour 2A 246
(off Manor Rd.)
BH4: Bour 3G 245
(off Portarlington Rd.)
BH8: Bour 7M 227
BH25: New M 3C 232
PO15: Fare 6A 198
Stirling Cres. SO30: Hed E 1N 175
SO40: Tott 2N 171
Stirling Rd. BH3: Bour 7J 227
Stirling St. PO2: Ports 8E 214
Stirling Wlk. SO51: Rom 5L 129
Stirling Way BH23: Mude 8D 230
STOCKBRIDGE 2F 88
Stockbridge Bridge Nature Reserve 3H 89
Stockbridge Cl. PO9: Hav 4H 203
RG24: Chin 8J 23
Stockbridge Dr. GU11: Alders 4L 65
Stockbridge Rd. GU51: Fleet 8J 27
RG25: Nth W 1N 77
SO20: Ki S 8B 86 (6G 88)
SO21: Craw, Spar 4M 89
SO21: Sut S 7D 76
SO22: Lit, Winche 6J 237 (2E 104)
SO23: Winche 6L 237 (2E 104)
SO51: Tims 6J 123
SP5: Lo Cnr 2J 87
SP11: Red R 5G 73
Stockbridge Rd. E. SO21: Sut S 5F 76
Stockbridge Way GU46: Yat 9N 17
Stocker Cl. RG21: B'toke 9B 42
Stocker Pl. PO13: Gos 7F 212
Stockers Av. SO22: Winche 4H 105
STOCKHEATH 5F 202
Stockheath La. PO9: Hav 7E 202
Stockheath Rd. PO9: Hav 5E 202
Stockheath Way PO9: Hav 6F 202
Stockholm Dr. SO30: Hed E 5N 175
Stocklands SO40: Calm 9J 157
Stock La. SP5: L'ford 7J 121
Stockley Cl. SO45: Holb 5A 208
Stockport Rd. SP4: Ames 7A 66
Stocks La. GU34: Priv 4H 137
SO32: Meon 8N 135
Stockton Av. GU51: Fleet 9L 27
Stockton Cl. PO6: Cosh 8D 200
SO30: Hed E 3A 176
Stockton Pk. GU51: Fleet 1L 47
Stockwell Pl. SO21: Spar 3B 104
Stockwood Ct. BH2: Bour 9K 227
(off St Winifred's Rd.)
Stockwood Way GU9: Weyb 3H 65
Stoddart Av. SO19: South 4D 174
Stodham La. GU31: Liss, Pet 4D 140
GU33: Hi Br, Liss 4D 140
GU33: Liss 3D 140
STOKE
PO11 7G 216
SP11 7H 35
STOKE CHARITY 7F 76
Stoke Charity Rd. SO21: Kin W 2L 91
SO23: Kin W 2L 91
STOKE COMMON 7J 133
Stoke Comn. Rd. SO50: B'stke 7J 133
STOKE FARTHING 3B 118
Stoke Gdns. PO12: Gos 3L 239
Stoke Ga. SP11: Stoke 7H 35
Stoke Hgts. SO50: Fair O 9M 133
Stoke Hill SP11: Stoke 8G 34
Stoke Hills GU9: Farnh 7E 64
Stoke Ho. RG26: Tadl 4H 11
Stoke La. SP11: Stoke 5F 34
Stoken La. RG27: H Win 5M 25
STOKE PARK 1K 161
Stoke Pk. Dr. SO50: B'stke 8H 133
Stoke Pk. Rd. SO50: B'stke 8H 133
Stoke Prior BH4: Bour 2G 245
(off Poole Rd.)
Stoke Rd. PO12: Gos 3K 239
SO16: South 1F 172
SO23: Winche 3L 105
SP11: Hur T, Stoke 5E 34
SP11: Sman, Stoke 3D 52
Stokesay Cl. SO45: Hythe 9M 193
Stokes Bay Mobile Home Pk.
PO12: Gos 5F 238
(not continuous)
Stokes Bay Rd. PO12: Gos 5F 238
Stokes Bay Sailing Club 6H 239
Stokes Ct. SO15: South 1A 4
SO32: Swanm 6D 164
Stokes La. RG24: Sher J 9K 21
RG26: Bau 4C 10
RG26: M She 9K 21
Stokesway PO12: Gos 3L 239
Stoke Wood Cl. SO50: Fair O 1M 161
Stokewood Leisure Cen. 7L 227
Stokewood Rd. BH3: Bour 8K 227
STONE 2K 237
Stonechat Cl. GU31: Pet 2B 146
Stonechat Ct. BH23: Chri 7B 230
Stonechat Dr. SO40: Tott 2H 171
Stonechat Rd. PO8: Horn 4A 182
Stone Cl. SP5: Mid W 5H 87
SP10: A'ver 3L 69
Stonecrop Cl. SO31: Loc H 7C 196
Stonecross Ho. PO2: Ports 8E 214
Stonedene Cl. GU35: Head D 3D 102
Stonefield Pk. SO20: Chil 8J 75
Stone Gdns. BH8: Bour 4D 228
Stoneham Cemetery Rd. SO18: S'ing 7D 160
Stoneham Cl. GU32: Pet 9K 139
SO16: S'ing 6B 160
Stoneham Ct. SO16: Bass 6N 159
Stoneham Gdns. SO31: Burs 9K 175
Stoneham Golf Course 5N 159
Stoneham La. SO16: S'ing 6B 160
SO50: E'leigh 2C 160
Stoneham Pk. GU32: Pet 9K 139
Stoneham Way SO16: S'ing 7B 160
Stonehill Pk. GU35: Head D 3D 102
Stonehill Rd. GU35: Head D 3E 102
STONEHILLS 5G 208
Stonehills RG25: Stev 5L 57
SO45: Fawl 5G 209
Stonehouse Ri. GU16: Frim 3N 29
Stonehouse Rd. GU30: Lip 2F 116
Stone La. PO12: Gos 3K 239
(not continuous)
Stonelea Gro. RG29: N War 5J 45
Stoneleigh BH13: Poole 5D 244
Stoneleigh Av. SO41: Hor 2G 232
Stoneleigh Cl. PO16: Portc 9K 199
Stonemasons Ct. SO23: Winche 7M 237
STONER HILL 5H 139
Stoner Hill Rd. GU32: Frox 3H 139
Stoners Cl. PO13: Gos 5D 212
Stone Sq. PO9: Hav 5F 202
Stone St. GU12: Alders 2M 65
PO5: S'sea 7M 5 (4C 240)
Stone Ter. SO21: Ott 3E 132
Stoney Bottom GU26: Gray 4L 103
Stoney Cl. GU46: Yat 9N 17
Stoney Ct. SO22: Winche 4J 105
Stoney Croft Rise SO53: Cha F 1A 160
STONEY CROSS 8J 155
Stoney Cross SP11: Ludg 1D 30
Stoney Drove SP11: Ver S 7F 6
Stoneyfields GU9: Farnh 9G 64
Stoney La. GU34: Meds 3J 97
SO22: Winche 4H 105
Stoney M. SO22: Winche 4J 105
STONY BATTER 8M 87
STONYFORD 7F 156
STONY HEATH 3D 20
Stony La. BH23: Burt, Chri 3L 229
BH23: Chri 7M 229
GU32: Frox 4E 138
PO1: Ports 2H 5 (1A 240)
SP6: Dame 4N 149
Stony La. Sth. BH23: Chri 8M 229
STONYMARSH 4G 123
Stonymoor Cl. SO45: Holb 5A 208
Stookes Way GU46: Yat 9L 17
Stopples La. SO41: Hor 2G 232
Storrington Rd. PO8: Clan 6D 168
Stourbank Rd. BH23: Chri 8K 229
Stourcliffe Av. BH6: Bour 1F 246
Stour Cl. GU31: Pet 2L 145
SO18: Wes E 8F 160
SO51: W Wel 1A 120 (9M 121)
Stour Ct. BH12: Poole 1E 244
(off Princess Rd.)
Stourcroft Dr. BH23: Chri 4G 229
Stourfield Rd. BH5: Bour 1E 246
Stour Gdns. BH10: Bour 2J 227
Stourhead Cl. GU14: Farn 8M 29
SP10: A'ver 2L 69
Stour Rd. BH8: Bour 8N 227
BH23: Chri 9J 229
RG23: Oak 1D 58
Stourton BH4: Bour 2G 245
(off Marlborough Rd.)
Stourvale Av. BH23: Chri 6G 229
Stourvale Gdns. SO53: Cha F 7B 132
Stourvale M. BH6: Bour 8F 228
Stourvale Pl. BH5: Bour 9E 228
Stourvale Rd. BH5: Bour 9E 228
BH6: Bour 9E 228
Stour Valley Nature Reserve 1K 227
Stourview Ct. BH6: Bour 9F 228
Stour Wlk. BH8: Bour 2A 228
Stour Way BH23: Chri 4G 228
Stourwood Av. BH6: Bour 2F 246
Stourwood Lodge BH6: Bour 1F 246
Stourwood Rd. BH6: Bour 1G 246
Stouts La. BH23: Bran 6D 220
Stovold's Way GU11: Alders 2H 65
Stow Cres. PO15: Fare 7N 197
Stowe Cl. SO30: Hed E 1A 176
Stowe Rd. PO4: S'sea 3K 241
Stradbrook PO13: Gos 7D 212
Stragwyne Cl. SO52: N Bad 7E 130
Straight Mile SO51: Ampf 3C 130
STRAITS, THE 5G 82
Strand SO14: South 6D 4 (6M 173)
Strand, The PO4: S'sea 6E 240
PO11: H Isl 6J 243
Stranding St. SO50: E'leigh 9D 132
Strategic Pk. SO30: Hed E 3K 175
Stratfield Av. RG26: Tadl 6H 11
Stratfield Ct. RG26: Tadl 5J 11
Stratfield Dr. SO53: Cha F 3N 131
Stratfield Gdns. PO9: Hav 2D 202
STRATFIELD MORTIMER 1J 13
Stratfield Pk. PO7: W'lle 1K 201
Stratfield Pl. BH25: New M 3N 231
Stratfield Rd. RG21: B'toke 4B 42
STRATFIELD SAYE 5M 13
Stratfield Saye House 5B 14
STRATFIELD SAYE PARK 5B 14
Stratfield Saye Rd. RG7: Stra S 8H 13
STRATFIELD TURGIS 9B 14
Stratford Ct. GU9: Farnh 9E 64
SO16: Bass 6M 159
SO23: Winche 4L 105
(off Northlands Dr.)
Stratford Ho. PO5: S'sea 6N 5 (3D 240)
Stratford Pl. SO41: Lymi 1D 234
SO50: E'leigh 8F 132
Stratford Rd. PO7: W'lle 1A 202
STRATFORD TONY 2F 118
Stratford Tony Rd. SP5: Com B 2G 118
Strathfield Rd. SP10: A'ver 4M 69
Strathmore Ct. GU15: Camb 7M 19
Strathmore Rd. BH9: Bour 2L 227
PO12: Gos 3L 239
Stratton Cl. PO6: Cosh 9D 200
SO21: E Str 7M 77
Stratton La. SO21: E Str 7M 77
SO24: Nort 7M 77
Stratton Rd. BH9: Bour 2N 227
RG21: B'toke 9A 42
SO15: South 1H 173
SO23: Winche 7M 105
Stratton Wlk. GU14: Farn 5J 29
Strauss Rd. RG22: B'toke 2L 59
Stravinsky Rd. RG22: B'toke 2A 60
Strawberry Flds. RG26: B'ley 9G 13
SO30: Hed E 4L 175
SO42: Beau 1B 236
Strawberry Grn. PO2: Ports 7F 214
Strawberry Hill SO31: Loc H 6C 196
Strawberry Mead SO50: Fair O 2L 161
Stream Cotts. GU16: Frim 3M 29
(off Frimley Gro. Gdns.)
Stream Ho. Dr. GU34: Selb 7L 99
Streamleaze PO14: Titch C 7F 196
Streamside GU51: Fleet 3M 47
Street, The GU10: Dock 2A 84
GU10: Fren 1E 84
GU10: Tong 5N 65
GU31: S Hart 9G 146
GU34: Bins 1D 82
GU34: Lwr Farr, Up Farr 4D 98
GU51: Cr V 6H 47
RG24: Old Bas 5H 43
RG26: B'ley 2E 22
RG27: Eve 4D 16
RG27: Roth 7E 24
RG29: Grey 9F 44
RG29: L Sut 4E 62
RG29: N War 8H 45
SP5: Far 8F 86
SP5: W Win 5F 86
SP5: W'psh 5H 121
STREET END
RG27 6F 24
SO32 9G 134
Street End RG27: Elve 8G 27
SO52: N Bad 7G 130
Street Mdw. RG29: S War 4D 62
(off Lees Hill)
Streets La. BH24: Crow 4M 187
Streetway Cl. SP11: Pale 5K 67
Streetway Rd. SP11: Grat, Pale 6K 67
Strete Mt. BH23: Chri 7A 230
Stride Av. PO3: Ports 1H 241
Strides La. BH24: Ring 1J 187
Strides Way SO40: Tott 3H 171
String La. RG7: Sil 6M 11
RG26: Pam H 6M 11
Strode Gdns. BH24: St I 3E 186
Strode Rd. PO2: Ports 6D 214
Strokins Rd. RG20: Kings 1B 6 (5K 9)
Strongs Cl. SO51: Rom 4A 130
Stronsay Cl. GU26: Hind 2N 103
STROUD 9H 139
Stroud Cl. PO6: Cosh 8B 200
RG24: Chin 1F 42
RG26: Pam H 4L 11
STROUD COMMON 1G 145

Strouden—Tadley Bottom

STROUDEN 5B 228
Strouden Av. BH8: Bour 5M 227
Strouden Ct. PO9: Hav 2D 202
Strouden Ct. Pct. PO9: Hav 2D 202
Stroud End GU32: Stro 9H 139
Strouden Rd. BH9: Bour 5L 227
Stroud Gdns. BH23: Chri 8A 230
Stroud Grn. La. PO14: Stub, Fare 3N 211
RG27: Roth 8C 24
Stroud La. BH23: Chri 8A 230
GU17: Blackw 9C 18
GU51: Cr V 6H 47
Stroudley Av. PO6: Dray 2K 215
Stroudley Rd. RG24: B'toke 3F 42
Stroudley Way SO30: Hed E 9A 162
Stroud Pk. Av. BH23: Chri 8A 230
Stroudwood Rd. PO9: Hav 6F 202
SO32: Lwr U 9C 134
Struan Cl. BH24: Ashl H 2C 186
Struan Ct. BH24: Ashl H 2D 186
Struan Dr. BH24: Ashl H 2D 186
Struan Gdns. BH24: Ashl H 2C 186
Stuart Bridgewater Ho.
SO18: South 3E 174
Stuart Cl. GU14: Cov 7J 29
PO14: Stub 6M 211
Stuart Ct. PO6: Cosh 9G 201
SP10: A'ver 7N 51
Stuart Cres. SO22: Winche 8J 105
Stuart Ho. *SO22: Winche 7G 105*
(off Highcroft Rd.)
Stuart Rd. BH23: Highc 6K 231
Stubbings Mdw. (Caravan Pk.)
BH24: Ring 1H 187
STUBBINGTON 5N 211
Stubbington Av. GU35: W'hil 6H 101
PO2: Ports 7F 214
Stubbington Grn. PO14: Stub 5M 211
Stubbington La. PO13: Lee S 8M 211
PO14: Stub 5N 211
Stubbington Way SO50: Fair O 1A 162
Stubb La. SO21: Owls 3F 134
Stubbs Ct. SP10: A'ver 8M 51
Stubbs Drove SO30: Hed E 3A 176
Stubbs Folly GU47: Coll 6F 18
Stubbs Moor Rd. GU14: Cov 7H 29
Stubbs Rd. RG21: B'toke 9D 42
SO19: South 8G 174
STUCKTON 3L 153
Stuckton Rd. SP6: F'dge, Stuc 1K 153
Stud Farm SP11: S M Bo 9L 35
Studland Cl. SO16: South 1C 172
Studland Dene *BH4: Bour 4G 245*
(off Studland Rd.)
Studland Dr. SO41: M Sea 7J 235
Studland Ind. Est. RG20: Bal H 1N 7
Studland Rd. BH4: Bour 4G 244
PO13: Lee S 1A 238
SO16: South 2C 172
Studley Av. SO45: Holb 4A 208
Studley Cl. BH23: Highc 6L 231
Studley Ct. BH25: New M 6M 231
Stukeley Rd. RG21: B'toke 7A 42
Sturdee Cl. GU16: Frim 3N 29
Sturmey Dr. GU51: Fleet 8L 27
Sturminster Ho. SO16: South 1F 172
Sturminster Rd. BH9: Bour 2M 227
Sturt La. BH8: Bour 3E 228
Sturt Rd. GU9: Up H 3D 64
GU27: Hasl 9N 103
Styles, The SP5: Bish 3D 118
Sudbury Rd. PO6: Cosh 9E 200
Suetts La. SO32: Bis W 5B 164
Suffolk Av. BH23: Chri 5J 229
SO15: South 3J 173
Suffolk Cl. SO53: Cha F 1A 160
Suffolk Cotts. PO12: Gos 4K 239
Suffolk Dr. PO15: White 2E 196
SO53: Cha F 9A 132
Suffolk Grn. SO53: Cha F 1A 160
Suffolk Rd. BH2: Bour 6G 247 (2H 245)
(not continuous)
PO4: S'sea 4H 241
SP10: A'ver 2M 69
Suffolk Rd. Sth. BH2: Bour 5G 247 (1H 245)
Sugar La. SP11: Longp 4N 71
Sullivan Cl. GU14: Farn 8K 29
PO6: Cosh 9N 199
Sullivan Rd. GU15: Camb 8J 19
RG22: B'toke 2N 59
SO19: South 6H 175
Sullivan Way PO7: W'lle 4M 201
Sultan Rd. PO1: Ports 9D 214
PO2: Ports 9D 214
PO10: Ems 8M 203
Sulzers Rdbt. GU14: Farn 9K 29
Sumar Cl. PO14: Stub 3N 211
Summer Down La. RG23: Oak 4N 39
RG26: Hann 4N 39
Summerfield Cl. BH23: Burt 4M 229
Summerfield Gdns. SO16: S'ing 6B 160
Summerfields BH7: Bour 7C 228
RG24: Chin 8H 23
SO31: Loc H 8E 196
Summerhill BH13: S'bks 9A 244
Summerhill Rd. PO8: Cowp 7N 181
Summerhouse Ct. GU26: Gray 4M 103
Summerlands Rd. SO50: Fair O 1N 161
Summerlands Wlk. PO9: Hav 4H 203
Summer La. SO42: Beau 7K 207
SO45: Exb 1G 236
Summerleigh Wlk. PO14: Stub 3N 211
Summerlug SP4: Win E 3A 86
Summers Av. BH11: Bour 1F 226
Summersfield Ter. GU33: Liss 2E 140
Summer's La. BH23: Burt 5N 229
Summers St. SO14: South 4A 174
Summertrees Ct. BH25: A'ley 2E 232
Summit Av. GU14: Cov 8D 28
Summit Way SO18: South 1D 174
Sumner Ct. GU9: Farnh 7E 64
Sumner Rd. GU9: Farnh 7E 64
GU31: Buri 7K 145
Sunbeam Way PO12: Gos 4K 239
Sunbury Cl. BH11: Bour 1E 226
GU35: Bor 4K 101
Sunbury Ct. BH2: Bour 6K 247
BH4: Bour 2G 245
(off Marlborough Rd.)
PO15: Fare 5A 198
Sun Ct. *PO5: S'sea 3E 240*
(off Sedgley Cl.)
Suncourt Vs. PO12: Gos 8H 213
Sunderland Dr. BH23: Chri 7D 230
Sunderland Pl. GU14: Farn 1K 49
Sunderton La. PO8: Clan 6B 168
Sundew Cl. BH23: Chri 5E 230
BH25: A'ley 2E 232
Sundowner SO14: South 7N 173
Sundridge Cl. PO6: Cosh 9F 200
Sunflower Cl. RG22: B'toke 3K 59
Sunflower Way SP11: E Ant 6B 52
Sun Hill *PO31: Cowes 5P 237*
(off Market Hill)
Sun Hill Cres. SO24: New A 2F 108
Sun La. RG7: Rise 2F 14
SO24: New A 2F 108
Sunlight Gdns. PO15: Fare 7A 198
Sunningdale *BH4: Bour 2G 244*
(off Portarlington Rd.)
BH23: Chri 8J 229
SO45: Hythe 6L 193
Sunningdale Cl. PO13: Gos 7E 212
SO50: B'stke 1K 161
Sunningdale Cres. BH10: Bour 2G 226
Sunningdale Gdns.
SO18: South 3F 174
Sunningdale Mobile Home Pk.
SO21: Col C 3K 133
Sunningdale Rd. PO3: Ports 1H 241
PO16: Portc 1M 213
Sunnybank SP11: A'ver 3E 68
Sunnybank Rd. GU14: Cov 6F 28
Sunnydale Farm Camping & Caravan Site
SO31: Old N 1G 195
Sunnydown Rd. SO22: Oli B 2E 126
Sunnyfield Ri. SO31: Burs 9L 175
Sunnyfield Rd. BH25: B Sea 6B 232
Sunnyheath PO9: Hav 5E 202
Sunnyhill SN8: Co Du 2G 31
Sunny Hill Ct. BH12: Poole 9B 226
Sunny Hill Rd. GU11: Alders 9F 48
Sunnyhill Rd. BH6: Bour 9E 228
BH12: Poole 9B 226
Sunnylands Av. BH6: Bour 1J 247
Sunnyleigh M. BH8: Bour 9N 227
Sunny Mead RG23: Oak 2D 58
Sunnymead Dr. PO7: W'lle 8K 181
Sunnymoor Rd. BH11: Bour 5E 226
Sunnyside GU51: Fleet 1K 47
SO31: Loc H 6F 196
Sunnyside Cl. SP10: Charl 8K 51
Sunnyside Pk. (Caravan Site) BH24: St I 3F 186
Sunnyside Rd. BH12: Poole 7B 226
GU35: Head D 3E 102
Sunnyside Wlk. PO9: Hav 2D 202
Sunnyview Cl. GU12: Alders 1L 65
Sunny Wlk. PO1: Ports 3H 5 (2A 240)
Sunny Way SO40: Tott 3M 171
Sunray Est. GU47: Sandh 5C 18
Sunridge Cl. BH12: Poole 8E 226
Sunridge Shades BH14: Poole 2A 244
Sun Rise Way SP4: Ames 5A 66
Sunset Av. SO40: Tott 2L 171
Sunset Lodge BH13: Poole 3E 244
Sunset Rd. SO40: Tott 2L 171
Sunshine Av. PO11: H Isl 5H 243
Sunshine Caravan Pk. GU35: W'hil 4E 100
Sun St. PO1: Ports 4K 5 (2B 240)
SUNTON 1H 31
Suntrap Gdns. PO11: H Isl 5H 243
Sunvale Av. GU27: Hasl 9M 103
Sunvale Cl. GU27: Hasl 9M 103
SO19: South 7F 174
Sun Valley Ind. Pk. SO23: Winche 5N 105
Sunwood Dr. RG27: Sher L 7H 23
Sunwood Rd. PO9: Hav 4D 202
Surbiton Rd. SO50: E'leigh 7F 132
Surrey Av. GU15: Camb 9J 19
Surrey Cl. BH23: Chri 4J 229
SO40: Tott 5K 171
Surrey Ct. BH4: Bour 1G 245
SO15: South 4H 173
SO53: Cha F 9B 132
Surrey Gdns. BH4: Bour 1G 245
Surrey Glade *BH4: Bour 1G 244*
(off Surrey Rd.)
Surrey Heath Mus. 7M 19
Surrey Ho. BH2: Bour 5H 247 (1H 245)
Surrey Lodge BH4: Bour 5G 247 (1H 245)
Surrey Point SO16: Bass 8K 159
Surrey Rd. BH2: Bour 5G 247 (1H 245)
BH4: Bour 5G 247 (1G 245)
BH12: Poole 9E 226
SO19: South 8B 174
SO53: Cha F 9A 132
Surrey Rd. Sth. BH4: Bour 1G 245
Surrey St. PO1: Ports 3N 5 (2D 240)
Sussex Cl. BH9: Bour 2M 227
Sussex Ct. PO5: S'sea 8N 5 (4D 240)
PO12: Gos 8L 213
Sussex Gdns. GU31: Pet 2M 145
GU51: Fleet 8N 27
SUSSEX PLACE 5C 4 (6M 173)
Sussex Pl. PO1: Ports 1D 240
PO5: S'sea 8N 5 (4D 240)
Sussex Rd. GU31: Pet 2M 145
PO5: S'sea 8N 5 (4D 240)
SO14: South 5D 4 (6M 173)
SO53: Cha F 9B 132
Sussex St. SO23: Winche 7L 237 (6K 105)
Sussex Ter. PO5: S'sea 8N 5 (4D 240)
Sutcliffe Sq. *SP10: A'ver 7B 52*
(off Cricketers Way)
Sutherland Cl. GU35: W'hil 6J 101
SO51: Rom 3A 130
Sutherland Ct. *SP10: A'ver 9N 51*
(off Artists Way)
Sutherland Rd. PO4: S'sea 4F 240
SO16: South 6E 158
Sutherlands Ct. SO53: Cha F 6A 132
Sutherlands Way SO53: Cha F 5N 131
SUTTON 9J 149
Sutton Cl. PO3: Ports 4J 215
PO8: Cowp 7L 181
Sutton Ct. PO14: Fare 8B 198
Suttones Pl. SO15: South 1C 4 (3L 173)
Sutton Fld. GU35: W'hil 6H 101
Sutton Gdns. SO23: Winche 7M 237 (6L 105)
Sutton Manor M. *SO21: Sut S 7D 76*
(off Stockbridge Rd.)
Sutton Pk. Rd. SO21: Sut S 7D 76
Sutton Pl. SO42: Broc 7D 148
Sutton Rd. BH9: Bour 5M 227
PO8: Cowp 7L 181
RG21: B'toke 4C 42
SO40: Tott 1L 171
SUTTON SCOTNEY 7D 76
SUTTON SCOTNEY SERVICE AREA 7D 76
Suttonwood La. SO24: Bigh 7N 95
Suvla La. *SP4: Bul C 3B 66*
(off Old Ward Rd.)
Swains Cl. RG26: Tadl 5H 11
Swains Rd. RG26: Tadl 5H 11
Swaits Mdw. RG19: Head 2J 9
Swaledale Gdns. GU51: Fleet 8N 27
Swale Dr. SO53: Cha F 5M 131
Swale Rd. GU14: Cov 6G 28
Swallow Cl. GU34: Alt 2G 80
GU46: Yat 7L 17
PO9: Hav 6H 203
RG22: B'toke 2H 59
SO40: Tott 4J 171
SP9: Tidw 8D 30 (7G 31)
Swallow Ct. PO8: Clan 5B 168
PO13: Lee S 9B 212
Swallow Dr. SO41: M Sea 8L 235
Swallowfields SP10: A'ver 7A 52
Swallow Sq. SO50: E'leigh 1B 160
Swallow Wood PO16: Fare 5D 198
SWAMPTON 9L 35
Swanage Cl. SO19: South 6C 174
Swanage Rd. PO13: Lee S 1A 238
Swan Centre, The SO50: E'leigh 1F 160
Swan Cl. PO10: Ems 9N 203
SO31: Lwr Swan 2A 196
Swancote PO16: Portc 9H 199
Swan Ct. *GU17: Haw 9G 19*
(off Toad La.)
GU32: Pet 1M 145
PO13: Gos 4D 212
RG27: H Win 6C 26
SP10: A'ver 1A 70
Swan La. GU47: Sandh 6D 18
SO23: Winche 6L 237 (6K 105)
Swanley Cl. SO50: E'leigh 7E 132
Swan Mead BH24: Hight 2M 187
Swan M. RG29: N War 7J 45
SWANMORE 6D 164
Swanmore Av. SO19: South 7F 174
Swanmore Bus. Pk. SO32: Swanm 6B 164
Swanmore Cl. BH7: Bour 7E 228
SO22: Winche 3G 105
Swanmore College Sports Complex 7B 164
Swanmore Golf Cen. 9E 164
Swanmore Golf Course 9E 164
Swanmore Pk. SO32: Swanm 3E 164
Swanmore Rd. BH7: Bour 8E 228
PO9: Hav 2D 202
SO32: Bis W, Swanm 4B 164
SO32: Drox 4H 165
Swan Quay PO16: Fare 9F 198
SO18: South 2B 174
Swansbury Dr. BH8: Bour 4E 228
Swan St. *BH21: Cran 6J 149*
(off High St.)
GU32: Pet 1L 145
RG20: Kings 3A 6 (6K 9)
Swans Wlk. PO11: H Isl 4J 243
Swanton Cl. PO14: Stub 5N 211
Swanton Gdns. SO53: Cha F 5N 131
Swan Way GU51: Ch Cr 4J 47
SWANWICK 2E 196
Swanwick Bus. Cen. SO31: Lwr Swan 2A 196
SWANWICK HILL 3F 196
Swanwick La. SO31: Lwr Swan, Swanw 1N 195
Swanwick Nature Reserve 9C 176
Swanwick Shore Rd. SO31: Lwr Swan 2A 196
Swanwick Station (Rail) 3E 196
Swanwick Wlk. RG26: Tadl 5H 11
SWARRATON 9A 78
Swarraton Rd. PO9: Hav 6G 202
Swattons Cl. SP4: Bul 3A 66
SWAY 6J 223
Sway Ct. PO9: Hav 4H 203
SO41: Sway 7K 223
Sway Gdns. BH8: Bour 4A 228
Sway Pk. Ind. Est. SO41: Sway 6J 223
Sway Rd. BH25: Bash, New M 9B 222
SO41: Lymi, Penn 1M 233
SO41: Tip 9B 222
SO42: Broc 1N 223 & 9C 148
Sway Station (Rail) 6J 223
SWAYTHLING 7B 160
Swaythling Rd. PO9: Hav 3D 202
SO18: Wes E 8F 160
SO30: Wes E 8F 160
Swaythling Station (Rail) 7B 160
Swedish Houses RG26: Tadl 6J 11
Sweep, The BH24: Ring 1J 187
Sweetbriar Gdns. PO7: W'lle 4N 201
Sweethills Cres. PO15: White 1E 196
Swelling Hill SO24: Rop 9G 96
Sweyns Lease SO42: Beau 1B 236
Swift Cl. PO8: Horn 3A 182
PO13: Lee S 9B 212
SO22: Winche 9H 105
SO50: E'leigh 1B 160
SP10: A'ver 8A 52
Swift Ct. GU51: Fleet 2M 47
Swift Gdns. SO19: South 9B 174
Swift Hollow SO19: South 9B 174
Swift Rd. GU9: Up H 3E 64
PO10: T Isl 5N 217
SO19: South 9B 174
(not continuous)
Swift's Cl. GU10: Farnh 9K 65
Swinburn Gdns. PO8: Cowp 6N 181
Swincombe Ri. SO18: Wes E 1F 174
Swindon Ho. *SP9: Tidw 7D 30*
(off Wylye Rd.)
Swing Swang La. RG24: B'toke 4F 42
(not continuous)
Swiss Rd. PO7: W'lle 2M 201
Switch Ho. Rd. SO45: Fawl 6J 209
Swithuns Ct. SO16: Nur 5A 158
Swivelton La. PO17: Boar 5J 199
Sword Cl. PO8: Clan 6B 168
PO12: Gos 5G 239
Swordfish Cl. PO13: Lee S 8M 211
Swordfish Dr. BH23: Chri 7D 230
Sword Sands Path PO3: Ports 9K 215
Sword Sands Rd. PO3: Ports 9K 215
Sycamore Av. SO53: Cha F 3A 132
Sycamore Cl. BH23: Chri 6G 229
GU16: Frim 3N 29
GU47: Sandh 5D 18
PO8: Clan 6D 168
PO8: Cowp 7M 181
PO13: Gos 7G 212
PO14: Titch C 8F 196
SO31: Burs 1K 195
SO41: M Sea 7J 235
SO51: Rom 6B 130
SO52: N Bad 7E 130
SP9: Tidw 8E 30
Sycamore Cotts. *GU15: Camb 1K 29*
(off Blenheim Pl.)
Sycamore Ct. BH24: Poul 7M 185
SO16: South 9G 158
SP6: F'dge 1J 153
Sycamore Cres. GU51: Ch Cr 5K 47
Sycamore Dr. GU16: Frim 2N 29
PO11: H Isl 3E 242
SO23: Kin W 7M 91
SO45: Holb 3N 207
Sycamore Grange GU51: Fleet 2L 47
Sycamore Pk. GU34: Alt 4H 81
Sycamore Rd. GU14: Farn 1L 49
(not continuous)
GU35: Lind 3L 101
SO16: South 9F 158
SO32: Bis W 4A 164
SO41: Hor 2G 233
SO45: Hythe 6L 193
Sycamores, The BH4: Bour 5G 247
GU14: Farn 9M 29
GU17: Blackw 8D 18
SO45: Hythe 5M 193
Sycamore Wlk. GU31: Pet 3L 145
SO30: Botl 3D 176
SP10: A'ver 3K 69
Sycamore Way RG23: B'toke 4M 41
Sydenham Ct. PO1: Ports 2E 240
Sydenham Ter. PO1: Ports 2E 240
Sydmanton Rd. SO51: Rom 6N 129
SYDMONTON 7F 8
Sydmonton Ct. PO9: Hav 3H 203
Sydney Av. SO31: Hamb 6J 195
Sydney Ho. PO1: Ports 1D 240
Sydney Loader Pl. GU17: Blackw 7C 18
Sydney Rd. BH23: Chri 5H 229
GU35: Bor 4J 101
PO12: Gos 3K 239
SO15: South 1G 172
SO50: B'stke 8H 133
Syers Cl. GU33: Liss 1E 140
Syers Rd. GU33: Liss 1E 140
Sylmor Gdns. BH9: Bour 4L 227
Sylvan Av. SO19: South 4G 174
Sylvan Cl. BH24: St L 4A 186
SO41: Hor 4J 233
Sylvan Ct. GU14: Farn 2M 49
Sylvan Dr. SO52: N Bad 8E 130
Sylvaner Ct. RG21: B'toke 5C 42
Sylvan La. SO31: Hamb 8L 195
Sylvan Ridge GU47: Sandh 4C 18
Sylvan Rd. BH12: Poole 8A 226
Sylvans, The SO45: Dib P 6J 193
Sylvan Vw. PO7: W'lle 3N 201
Sylvan Way GU52: Ch Cr 6L 47
Sylvan Wood BH23: Highc 7G 230
Sylvia Cl. RG21: B'toke 8B 42
Sylvia Cres. SO40: Tott 1L 171
Symes Rd. SO51: Rom 5A 130
Symonds Cl. SO53: Cha F 8B 132
Symonds St. SO23: Winche 9M 237 (7L 105)
Sympson Rd. RG26: Tadl 5K 11
Syon Pl. GU14: Farn 8M 29
Sywell Cres. PO3: Ports 5J 215

T

Tadburn Cl. SO51: Rom 5N 129
SO53: Cha F 7B 132
Tadburn Grn. SO51: Rom 6L 129
Tadburn Meadows Local Nature Reserve 4A 130
Tadburn Rd. SO51: Rom 5N 129
Tadfield Cres. SO51: Rom 5N 129
Tadfield Rd. SO51: Rom 5N 129
TADLEY 5J 11
TADLEY BOTTOM 5K 11

Thornleigh Rd.—Treloar Rd.

Thornleigh Rd. SO19: South ... 8C 174
Thornley Rd. BH10: Bour ... 2H 227
THORNS BEACH ... 5D 236
Thorns La. SO41: E End ... 4C 236
SO42: Beau ... 5D 236
Thornton Av. SO31: Wars ... 8N 195
Thornton Cl. PO7: Wid ... 7J 201
RG26: B'ley ... 2J 23
SO24: New A ... 1E 108
Thornton End GU34: Holy ... 2J 81
Thornton M. RG45: Cr'tne ... 1E 18
Thornton Rd. PO12: Gos ... 8K 213
Thornybush Gdns. GU34: Meds ... 3K 97
Thornycroft Av. SO19: South ... 8B 174
Thornycroft La. RG22: B'toke ... 6M 41
Thornycroft Rdbt. RG21: B'toke ... 6N 41
Thorold Ct. SO18: South ... 1C 174
Thorold Rd. GU9: Farnh ... 7E 64
SO18: South ... 2C 174
SO53: Cha F ... 3C 132
Thorpe Gdns. GU34: Alt ... 4D 80
Thorrowgood Ho. PO2: Ports ... 8E 214
Threadgill Way SP9: Shi B ... 2A 66 (1F 66)
Three Acre Cl. BH25: B Sea ... 6N 231
Three Acre Dr. BH25: B Sea ... 6A 232
Three Acres PO7: Den ... 7H 181
THREE ASHES ... 6C 12
Three Castles Path RG25: Elli ... 1J 79
Three Colts La. SP5: Bish ... 2E 118
Threefield La. SO14: South ... 7E 4 (7M 173)
Three Horse Shoes La. SO24: Bram ... 3F 136
Three Oaks SO19: South ... 5J 175
Three Stiles Rd. GU9: Farnh ... 7B 64
Three Tun Cl. PO1: Ports ... 4K 5 (2B 240)
Three Ways Cl. PO14: Stub ... 3N 211
Thresher Cl. PO7: W'lle ... 9C 182
Threshers Cnr. GU51: Fleet ... 8A 28
Throgmorton Rd. GU46: Yat ... 8K 17
THROOP ... 2A 228
Throop Cl. BH8: Bour ... 4D 228
Throop Rd. BH8: Bour ... 1A 228
Throopside Av. BH9: Bour ... 2A 228
Thrush Cl. RG22: B'toke ... 1H 59
Thrush Rd. BH12: Poole ... 5A 226
Thrush Wlk. PO8: Cowp ... 7M 181
THRUXTON ... 1N 67
Thruxton Aerodrome ... 1L 67
Thruxton Airfield Rd. SP11: Thru ... 2L 67
Thruxton Ct. SO19: South ... 5C 174
Thruxton Motor Racing Circuit ... 1L 67
Thruxton Rd. PO9: Hav ... 4C 202
Thuiller Rd. SO21: Bar S ... 6N 71
Thumwood RG24: Chin ... 9G 23
Thundery Hill GU10: Seal ... 6N 65
Thurbern Rd. PO2: Ports ... 6F 214
Thurlow Cl. *SP4: Ames* ... *5A 66*
(off Raleigh Cres.)
Thurmell Cl. SO30: Hed E ... 6N 175
Thurmell Wlk. SO30: Hed E ... 6N 175
Thurmond Cres. SO22: Winche ... 8G 105
Thurmond Rd. SO22: Winche ... 8G 104
Thursby Rd. BH23: Highc ... 5H 231
Thursley Rd. GU10: Chur ... 5L 85
Thurston Cl. SO53: Cha F ... 5B 132
Thurston Ho. GU51: Fleet ... 2K 47
Thurston Pl. RG21: B'toke ... 1A 60
Thurstons GU34: Bins ... 1D 82
Thwaite Rd. BH12: Poole ... 9F 226
Thyme Av. PO15: White ... 1G 196
Thyme Cl. RG24: Chin ... 7G 23
Thyme Ct. GU14: Cov ... 7E 28
Tibb's Mdw. *SP11: Co Du* ... *2N 31*
(off Butts Hill)
Tiberius Cl. RG23: B'toke ... 4L 41
Tiberius Rd. SP10: A'ver ... 7A 52
TICHBORNE ... 5C 108
Tichborne Cl. GU17: Blackw ... 8F 18
Tichborne Down SO24: New A ... 2E 108
Tichborne Gro. PO9: Hav ... 4D 202
Tichborne Pl. GU12: Alders ... 2M 65
Tichborne Rd. SO18: South ... 2H 175
SO50: E'leigh ... 3D 160
Tichborne Way PO13: Gos ... 6F 212
Ticklecorner La. RG7: Mort ... 3H 13
Tickleford Dr. SO19: South ... 1E 194
Tickner Cl. SO30: Botl ... 5B 176
Ticonderoga Gdns. SO19: South ... 9C 174
Tidcombe Grn. PO9: Hav ... 2C 202
Tidemill Cl. BH23: Chri ... 6K 229
Tides Reach SO18: South ... 2B 174
Tides Way SO40: March ... 8E 172
Tideway Gdns. PO4: S'sea ... 3K 241
TIDPIT ... 9D 118
TIDWORTH ... 8D 30 (7H 31)
TIDWORTH CAMP ... 8A 30 (7F 30)
Tidworth Garrison Golf Course ... 8F 30
Tidworth Leisure Cen. ... 8D 30 (7G 31)
Tidworth Rd. PO9: Hav ... 5F 202
SN8: Co Du ... 2G 31
SP4: All, Bosc, Idm, Port ... 9B 66
SP4: Bul C ... 2D 66
SP11: Ludg ... 2A 30 (5J 31)
Tiffany Cl. SO41: Hor ... 2G 233
Tiffield Cl. PO3: Ports ... 4K 215
Tiger Moth Cl. PO13: Lee S ... 1C 238
Tiger Rd. PO1: Ports ... 9A 214
Tigwells Fld. RG29: S War ... 4D 62
Tilbrook Rd. SO15: South ... 2F 172
Tilburg Rd. BH23: Chri ... 7N 229
Tilbury's Cl. GU35: Bor ... 4J 101
Tildbury Cotts. SO21: Up B ... 4C 76
Tilden Rd. SO21: Comp ... 8H 127
Tile Barn Cl. GU14: Farn ... 7J 29
Tilebarn La.
SO42: Broc ... 1N 223 & 1A 224
Tile Barn Row RG20: Wol H ... 3A 8
Tilebourne Cl. SO51: Tims ... 6L 123
Tilford Rd. GU9: Farnh ... 9F 64
GU10: Chur, Rush ... 5L 85
GU26: Hind ... 6L 85
PO8: Love ... 4N 181
Till Cl. SP11: E Ant ... 6B 52
Tiller Gdns. BH11: Bour ... 1E 226
Tiller Rd. PO7: W'lle ... 9K 181
Tillingbourn PO14: Titch C ... 6F 196
Tillingbourne Ct. *BH12: Poole* ... *1E 244*
(off Princess Rd.)
Tillington Gdns. PO8: Clan ... 7D 168
TILLY DOWN ... 3B 50
TILMORE GARDENS ... 8M 139
Tilmore Gdns. GU32: Pet ... 8M 139
Tilmore Rd. GU32: Pet ... 9M 139
Tilney Cl. GU34: Alt ... 4E 80
Timber Cl. *GU9: Farnh* ... *8D 64*
(off The Hart)
Timbercroft Cl. GU34: Four M ... 6H 97
Timberlake Ct. RG21: B'toke ... 6C 42
Timberlake Rd. RG21: B'toke ... 6D 42
(Goat La.)
RG21: B'toke ... 6B 42
(Victory Rdbt.)
Timberlane PO7: Purb ... 5L 201
Timberley Cl. SO45: Holb ... 4A 208
Timberley Ho. *PO1: Ports* ... *2E 240*
(off Railway Vw.)
Timberley La. SP5: Redl ... 8E 120
Timberley Pl. RG45: Cr'tne ... 1A 18
Timbermill Ct. SP6: F'dge ... 2J 153
Timbers, The PO15: Fare ... 8M 197
Timor Cl. PO15: White ... 1E 196
RG24: B'toke ... 2D 42
Timothy Cl. BH10: Bour ... 1H 227
Timothy's Fld. SP11: Abb A ... 6F 68
Timothy Wlk. PO7: W'lle ... 8K 181
Timpson Rd. PO1: Ports ... 1F 240
TIMSBURY ... 7K 123
Timsbury Cres. PO9: Bed ... 6E 202
Timsbury Dr. SO16: South ... 1E 172
Timson Cl. SO40: Tott ... 4J 171
Tincleton Gdns. BH9: Bour ... 2M 227
Tindal Cl. GU46: Yat ... 7N 17
Tindale Rd. SO16: South ... 9D 158
Tinker All. SO18: S'ton A ... 4E 160
TINKERS CROSS ... 7H 151
Tinker's La. GU34: Bent ... 7L 79
Tinley Gdns. RG29: Odi ... 8L 45
Tinneys Cl. SP5: Woodf ... 9C 120
Tins, The SO41: Lymi ... 2D 234
Tintagel Cl. RG23: B'toke ... 5L 41
SO16: South ... 5H 159
SP10: A'ver ... 7N 51
Tintagel Dr. GU16: Frim ... 3N 29
Tintagel Way PO6: P Sol ... 1C 214
Tintern Cl. PO6: Cosh ... 8B 200
RG24: B'toke ... 3A 42
Tintern Gro. SO15: South ... 5K 173
Tintern Rd. PO12: Gos ... 3J 239
Tin Yd. La. BH23: Bock ... 1N 229
TIPNER ... 5C 214
Tipner Grn. PO2: Ports ... 5D 214
Tipner La. PO2: Ports ... 5C 214
Tipner Rd. PO2: Ports ... 6D 214
Tipper La. GU31: S Hart ... 9G 146
Tippett Gdns. RG22: B'toke ... 3A 60
TIPTOE ... 7E 222
Tiptoe Grn. *PO9: Hav* ... *3H 203*
(off Burghclere Rd.)
Tiptoe Rd. BH25: Woot ... 6B 222
Tipton Ho. PO5: S'sea ... 3D 240
Tiptree Cl. SO50: E'leigh ... 7E 132
Tisted Ct. PO9: Hav ... 4H 203
Titanic Engineers Memorial ... 3C 4 (5M 173)
Titchborne Ho. SO30: Hed E ... 3N 175
TITCHFIELD ... 9K 197
Titchfield Abbey ... 7K 197
Titchfield By-Pass PO14: Titch ... 8J 197
Titchfield Cl. RG26: Tadl ... 6J 11
TITCHFIELD COMMON ... 8F 196
Titchfield Cres. RG27: Sher L ... 7J 23
Titchfield Grange PO15: Seg ... 6H 197
Titchfield Haven Nature Reserve ... 6J 211
Titchfield Haven Nature Reserve Vis. Cen.
... 7J 211
Titchfield Hill PO14: Titch ... 9K 197
(not continuous)
Titchfield La. PO15: F'ley, Wick ... 9M 177
PO17: Wick ... 9M 177
TITCHFIELD PARK ... 6H 197
Titchfield Pk. Rd. PO15: Seg ... 6G 197
Titchfield Rd. PO14: Stub, Titch ... 9K 197
Tithe, The PO7: Den ... 6G 180
Tithe Barn SO41: Lymi ... 1E 234
Tithelands La. SO24: Bram ... 1A 136
Tithe Mead SO51: Rom ... 3M 129
Tithe Mdw. RG22: B'toke ... 5L 59
Tithewood Cl. SO53: Cha F ... 2N 131
Tithing Rd. GU51: Fleet ... 8L 27
Tittymouse La. SP11: Weyh ... 8C 50
Titus Gdns. PO7: W'lle ... 1A 202
Tiverton Ct. *BH4: Bour* ... *2G 244*
(off Marlborough Rd.)
PO16: Fare ... 7D 198
Tiverton Rd. RG23: B'toke ... 6K 41
Tivoli Cl. SO53: Cha F ... 5D 132
Tivoli Ct. PO2: Ports ... 8G 215
Toad La. GU17: Haw ... 9G 19
Tobago Cl. RG24: B'toke ... 2C 42
Tobruk Cl. SP11: Enh A ... 3A 52
Tobys Gdn. GU31: Pet ... 1M 145
Toby St. PO1: Ports ... 2N 5 (1D 240)
Tockington Ct. GU46: Yat ... 7N 17
Todber Cl. BH11: Bour ... 3B 226
Todhurst Ho. PO1: Ports ... 2E 240
Todmore GU33: G'ham ... 3E 114
Toft Mans. BH1: Bour ... 2N 245
Tokar St. PO4: S'sea ... 5H 241
Tokio Rd. PO3: Ports ... 7H 215
Toledo Gro. SP10: A'ver ... 9B 52
Tolefrey Gdns. SO53: Cha F ... 6L 131
Tollard Cl. BH12: Poole ... 6C 226
Tollard Ct. BH2: Bour ... 9K 247
Tollbar Way SO30: Hed E ... 1L 175
Tollgate SO53: Cha F ... 1A 160
Tollgate, The PO16: Fare ... 7D 198
Tollgate Cl. RG23: Oak ... 8D 40
Tollgate Estates SO51: Rom ... 1H 129
Tollgate Rd. SO31: Lwr Swan ... 1A 196
SP10: A'ver ... 9K 51
Tollway RG24: Chin ... 8H 23
Tolpuddle Gdns. BH9: Bour ... 2M 227
Tolpuddle Way GU46: Yat ... 8B 18
Tomkyns Cl. SO53: Cha F ... 6L 131
Tomlins Av. GU16: Frim ... 2N 29
Tomlins Cl. RG26: Tadl ... 6H 11
Tommy Grn. Wlk.
SO50: E'leigh ... 9D 132
Toms La. BH24: Lin ... 1B 188
Tonbridge St. PO5: S'sea ... 5D 240
Tonge Rd. BH11: Bour ... 1F 226
TONGHAM ... 4N 65
Tongham Mdws. GU10: Tong ... 3N 65
Tongham Rd. GU10: Bad L ... 5M 65
GU10: Run ... 6L 65
(not continuous)
GU12: Alders ... 2M 65
Tonnant Cl. PO14: Stub ... 6N 211
Toogoods Way SO16: Nur ... 6C 158
Toomer Cl. SO45: Fawl ... 6D 208
TOOTHILL ... 2D 158
Toothill Rd. SO51: Toot ... 2B 158
Topaz Dr. SP10: A'ver ... 1K 69
Topaz Gro. PO7: W'lle ... 1B 202
Top Green SO51: Lock ... 2N 121
Topiary, The GU14: Cov ... 9G 28
RG24: Lych ... 3H 43
Topiary Gdns. SO31: Loc H ... 5E 196
Topiary Pl. GU9: Up H ... 3E 64
Top La. BH24: Ring ... 1K 187
Torbay Rd. BH14: Poole ... 2A 244
Torberry Dr. GU31: Pet ... 2A 146
Torch Cl. SO50: B'stke ... 1M 161
Tor Cl. PO7: Purb ... 6N 201
PO16: Fare ... 8G 198
Torcross Cl. SO19: South ... 8C 174
Torfrida Ct. PO4: S'sea ... 4K 241
Tormead SO45: Hythe ... 6L 193
Tornay Gro. SO52: N Bad ... 8E 130
Toronto Ct. SO16: South ... 2E 172
Toronto Pl. PO12: Gos ... 2K 239
Toronto Rd. PO2: Ports ... 9F 214
Torquay Av. PO12: Gos ... 8J 213
SO15: South ... 2J 173
Torque Cl. SO19: South ... 6J 175
Torre Cl. SO50: E'leigh ... 6E 132
Torridge Gdns. SO18: Wes E ... 8F 160
Torrington Cl. GU35: Lind ... 2M 101
SO19: South ... 6E 174
Torrington Rd. PO2: Ports ... 5F 214
Tor Rd. GU9: Farnh ... 8B 64
Tortuga Wlk. RG24: B'toke ... 2E 42
Tortworth Cl. PO14: Fare ... 9N 197
Tor Way GU31: Pet ... 1M 145
Torwood Gdns. SO50: B'stke ... 1K 161
Tosson Cl. SO16: South ... 2D 172
Totally Tennis ... 7D 42
TOTE HILL ... 8A 122
TOTFORD ... 8B 78
TOT HILL ... 3D 8
TOT HILL SERVICE AREA ... 3C 8
Totland Cl. GU14: Farn ... 6J 29
SO16: South ... 2D 172
Totland Ct. SO41: M Sea ... 8J 235
Totland Rd. PO6: Cosh ... 1F 214
PO13: Gos ... 6E 212
Totnes Cl. SO50: E'leigh ... 7D 132
Totsome Cotts. PO17: K Vil ... 2A 198
Tottehale Cl. SO52: N Bad ... 9E 130
Tottenham Cl. RG26: B'ley ... 9G 13
Tottenham Rd. PO1: Ports ... 1F 240
Tottenham Wlk. GU47: Owl ... 4F 18
Totters La. RG27: H Win, Odi ... 9M 25
RG29: Odi ... 9M 25
TOTTON ... 3N 171
Totton & Eling Bowls Cen. ... 3H 171
Totton & Eling Heritage Cen. ... 4A 172
Totton & Eling Tennis Cen. ... 3H 171
Totton By-Pass SO40: Tott ... 4M 171
Totton Health & Leisure Cen. ... 6C 170
Totton Station (Rail) ... 3N 171
Totton Wlk. PO9: Hav ... 3D 202
Totton Western By-Pass
SO40: Calm, Tott ... 1G 171
SO51: Ower ... 6G 156
Tourist Info. Cen.
Aldershot ... 9J 49
Andover ... 1A 70
Bournemouth ... 7M 247 (2K 245)
Christchurch ... 8L 229
Cowes ... 5P 237
Fareham ... 8D 198
Fordingbridge ... 1J 153
Gosport ... 3N 239
Lymington ... 2E 234
Lyndhurst ... 2C 148
Petersfield ... 1M 145
Ringwood ... 1J 187
Romsey ... 5L 129
South Hayling ... 5E 242
Southampton ... 3C 4 (5L 173)
Winchester ... 8N 237 (7L 105)
Tournai Cl. GU11: Alders ... 4N 49
Tournerbury Golf Course ... 2H 243
Tournerbury La. PO11: H Isl ... 3G 243
Tourney Rd. BH11: Bour ... 1C 226
Tovey Ct. SP10: A'ver ... 9C 52
Tovey Pl. SO23: Kin W ... 8N 91
Towans, The BH13: S'bks ... 9A 244
Tower Arts Cen. ... 7F 104
Tower Cl. GU26: Hind ... 3N 103
GU30: Lip ... 2D 116
PO12: Gos ... 4F 238
(not continuous)
SP10: Charl ... 7K 51
Tower Ct. BH1: Bour ... 1K 245
BH2: Bour ... 9J 247 (3J 245)
SO23: Winche ... 6L 237 (6K 105)
SO31: Wars ... 8N 195
Tower Gdns. SO16: Bass ... 7L 159
Towergate Ind. Pk. SP10: A'ver ... 2K 69
Tower Hill GU14: Cov ... 9J 29
Tower Hill Ct. RG20: Kings ... 2A 6
Tower Ho. SO19: South ... 8C 174
Tower La. SO50: E'leigh ... 1G 160
Tower Lane Ind. Est. SO50: E'leigh ... 2G 160
Tower Pl. SO30: Wes E ... 1H 175
Tower Rd. BH1: Bour ... 9B 228
BH13: Poole ... 3F 244
GU26: Hind ... 3N 103
GU30: Lip ... 2D 116
PO4: S'sea ... 4G 241
SO23: Winche ... 6L 237 (6K 105)
Tower Rd. W. BH13: Poole ... 4E 244
Towers, The SO31: Net A ... 4E 194
Towers Dr. RG45: Cr'tne ... 1D 18
Towers Gdn. PO9: Langs ... 2F 216
Tower Skyline Plaza, The *RG21: B'toke* ... *6C 42*
(off Alencon Link)
Tower St. GU34: Alt ... 6E 80
PO1: Ports ... 7H 5 (4A 240)
PO10: Ems ... 9M 203
SO23: Winche ... 7L 237 (6K 105)
TOWN CENTRE ... 6C 42
Town Centre East Junc. RG24: Old Bas ... 6F 42
Town Cl. SO24: Rop ... 1E 110
Towngate M. BH24: Ring ... 2K 187
Town Hall Ct. RG28: Whit ... 5G 54
Town Hall Rd. PO9: Hav ... 8F 202
Townhill Farm District Cen. SO18: Wes E ... 9F 160
TOWNHILL PARK ... 9F 160
Townhill Way SO18: Wes E ... 8F 160
Town La. GU32: Pet ... 8A 140
Town Mill RG25: Over ... 2E 56
Town Mill La. RG28: Whit ... 5H 55
Town Quay PO1: Ports ... 6H 5 (3B 240)
SO14: South ... 8C 4 (7L 173)
TOWNS END ... 2B 20
TOWNSEND ... 4D 228
Townsend SP5: P'tn ... 6E 86
Townsend Cl. BH11: Bour ... 1F 226
RG21: B'toke ... 7A 42
Townsend La. SP6: Mart ... 9A 118
Townside Pl. GU15: Camb ... 7M 19
Town Sq. GU15: Camb ... 7L 19
Town Sta. Rdbt. SP10: A'ver ... 2N 69
Townsville Rd. BH9: Bour ... 4M 227
Town Wall ... 7C 4
Towpath Mead PO4: S'sea ... 3K 241
Toynbee Cl. SO50: E'leigh ... 9E 132
Toynbee Rd. SO50: E'leigh ... 9E 132
Tozer Cl. BH11: Bour ... 4D 226
Trade St. RG20: Wol H ... 3N 7
Trafalgar Cl. SO53: Cha F ... 7N 131
Trafalgar Ct. BH23: Mude ... 9B 230
GU9: Farnh ... 9D 64
PO5: S'sea ... *5E 240*
(off Richmond Rd.)
PO14: Fare ... 1B 212
Trafalgar Hall PO5: S'sea ... 5N 5
Trafalgar Pl. PO1: Ports ... 1F 240
SO41: Lymi ... 2F 234
Trafalgar Ri. PO8: Clan ... 6B 168
Trafalgar Rd. BH9: Bour ... 7K 227
SO15: South ... 4H 173
Trafalgar Sail
Portsmouth ... 3H 5 (1A 240)
Trafalgar Sq. PO12: Gos ... 2K 239
SP4: Win G ... *3B 86*
(off Trenchard Av.)
Trafalgar St. SO23: Winche ... 8L 237 (7K 105)
Trafalgar Vs. *GU14: Cov* ... *8E 28*
(off Brownsover Rd.)
Trafalgar Way GU15: Camb ... 9H 19
SO20: S Bri ... 3F 88
SO45: Hythe ... 8N 193
Trafford Rd. GU16: Frim ... 4M 29
SO50: Fair O ... 2M 161
Trajan Wlk. SP10: A'ver ... 7A 52
Trampers La. PO17: Newt, N Boa ... 9J 179
Tranby Rd. SO19: South ... 6C 174
Tranmere Cl. SO41: Lymi ... 4F 234
Tranmere Rd. PO4: S'sea ... 3J 241
Traveller's End SO22: Winche ... 5H 105
Travis La. GU47: Sandh ... 6E 18
Treadgold Mus. ... 3K 5 (2B 240)
Treadwheel Rd. PO8: Ids ... 4G 183
Treagore Rd. SO40: Calm ... 1J 171
Treamar Cl. SO16: South ... 2E 172
Treasury Ct. SO23: Winche ... 7L 237
Treble Cl. SO22: Oli B ... 1F 126
Trebor Av. GU9: Farnh ... 9F 64
Tredegar Rd. PO4: S'sea ... 4G 241
Tredenham Cl. GU14: Farn ... 3L 49
Treebys Cl. BH23: Burt ... 5N 229
Treeside BH23: Chri ... 4E 230
Treeside Av. SO40: Tott ... 3N 171
Treeside Dr. GU9: Weyb ... 3G 64
Treeside Rd. SO15: South ... 2H 173
Treeside Way PO7: W'lle ... 9M 181
Treetops *BH4: Bour* ... *1G 244*
(off Surrey Rd.)
Trefoil Cl. PO7: W'lle ... 2N 201
RG27: H Win ... 5B 26
Trefoil Way BH23: Chri ... 6E 230
Tregantle M. PO12: Gos ... 3J 239
Tregaron Av. PO6: Cosh ... 9J 201
Tregenna Ho. GU30: Lip ... 2D 116
Tregolls Dr. GU14: Farn ... 9L 29
Tregonwell Cl. BH2: Bour ... 7K 247
Tregonwell Ct. BH2: Bour ... 7J 247
Tregonwell Rd.
BH2: Bour ... 7K 247 (2J 245)
Trelawney Ct. BH8: Bour ... 9L 227
Trellis Dr. RG24: Lych ... 3H 43
Treloar Rd. PO11: H Isl ... 6M 243

Treloen Ct.—Up. St Michael's Gro.

Treloen Ct. BH8: Bour .9L 227
(off Wellington Rd.)
Treloyhan Cl. SO53: Cha F .8B 132
Tremona Ct. SO16: South .9G 158
Tremona Rd. SO16: South .8G 159
Trenchard Av. SP4: Win G .3B 86
Trenchard Pk. GU35: Bor .3J 101
Trenchard Rd. SP11: A'ver .1H 69
Trenchmead Gdns.
RG24: B'toke .3L 41
Trenley Cl. SO45: Holb .5A 208
Trent Cl. GU14: Cov .6G 29
SO18: South .1D 174
Trent Ct. SP10: A'ver .8B 52
Trentham Av. BH7: Bour .6E 228
Trentham Cl. BH7: Bour .6E 228
Trent Ho. SO14: South .5A 174
Trent Rd. SO18: South .1D 174
Trent Wlk. PO16: Portc .9J 199
Trent Way PO13: Lee S .2B 238
RG21: B'toke .6E 42
SO30: Wes E .9H 161
Tresham Cres. GU46: Yat .7K 17
Tresillian Cl. BH23: Walk .4K 231
Tresillian Gdns. SO18: Wes E .9F 160
Tresillian Way BH23: Walk .4K 231
Trevis Rd. PO4: S'sea .3K 241
Trevone BH25: New M .3C 232
(off Herbert Rd.)
Trevone Cl. SO40: Tott .5L 171
Trevor Rd. PO4: S'sea .4F 240
Trevose Cl. PO13: Gos .7E 212
SO53: Cha F .8B 132
Trevose Cres. SO53: Cha F .7B 132
Trevose Way PO14: Titch C .8E 196
Triangle, The BH2: Bour .7J 247 (2J 245)
BH25: New M .6L 231
PO11: H Isl .5L 243
SO18: South .1B 174
SP5: W'psh .5H 121
(off The Green)
Triangle Gdns. SO16: Nur .8C 158
Triangle La. PO14: Titch .4H 211
Tribe Rd. PO12: Gos .2J 239
Trident Bus. Pk. SO45: Hythe .5N 193
Trilakes Animal Pk. .6B 18
Trimaran Rd. SO31: Wars .8B 196
Trimmers GU9: Farnh .9C 64
Trimmers Cl. GU9: Up H .3D 64
Trimmer's Ct. PO1: Ports .6H 5 (4B 240)
Trimmers Fld. GU9: Farnh .9G 64
Trimmers Wood GU26: Hind .1M 103
Trimms Drove SP6: Woodg .2A 154
(off High St.)
Trims Ct. RG25: Over .2D 56
Tringham Ho. BH7: Bour .6E 228
Trinidad Cl. RG24: B'toke .2C 42
Trinidad Cres. BH12: Poole .6A 226
Trinidad Ho. BH12: Poole .6A 226
PO6: Cosh .7N 199
Trinity BH1: Bour .6N 247
GU47: Owl .3G 19
Trinity Chu. La. PO31: Cowes .5P 237
Trinity Cl. PO12: Gos .3M 239
Trinity Ct. SO15: South .4H 173
SO21: Col C .4M 133
SO40: March .8E 172
SO40: Tott .9L 157
SO53: Cha F .6B 132
Trinity Flds. GU9: Up H .3C 64
Trinity Gdns. PO16: Fare .8C 198
SO23: Winche .7N 237 (6L 105)
Trinity Gate BH2: Bour .5M 247
Trinity Grn. PO12: Gos .3N 239
Trinity Hill GU9: Up H .3C 64
GU34: Meds .9K 79
Trinity Ind. Est. SO15: South .3E 172
Trinity Ri. SP11: Pen M .6F 50
Trinity Rd. BH1: Bour .5N 247 (1L 245)
GU34: Meds .8K 79
SO14: South .3E 4 (5M 173)
Trinity St. PO16: Fare .7D 198
Trinity Vw. Rd. SP9: Tidw .8C 30
Tripps End Caravan Site SO30: Hed E .3A 176
Tristan Cl. SO45: Cals .9J 209
Tristram Cl. SO53: Cha F .8L 131
Triton Centre, The SO51: Rom .7C 130
Triumph Cl. PO15: Fare .7N 197
Triumph Rd. PO14: Fare .3B 212
Troak Cl. BH23: Chri .6A 230
Trojan Way PO7: Purb .6N 201
Troon Cres. PO6: Dray .8K 201
Trooper Bottom GU32: Frox .2H 139
Trosnant Rd. PO9: Hav .7E 202
Trotsford Mdw. GU17: Blackw .9E 18
TROTTON MARSH .6N 141
TROTTS .7A 172
Trotts La. SO40: March .6B 172
Trotwood Cl. GU47: Owl .3G 19
Troublefield Nature Reserve .7D 218
Trout La. SO20: N Wal .1A 88
Trout Rd. GU27: Hasl .9N 103
Trowbridge Cl. SO16: Rown .6D 158
Trowbridge Ct. SO23: Winche .7M 237
Trowe's La. RG7: Bee H .1B 14
RG7: Swal .1H 15
Trueman Sq. SP10: A'ver .7B 52
(off Cricketers Way)
Truman Rd. BH11: Bour .1F 226
Truncheaunts La. GU34: E Wor .8H 81
Trunk Rd. GU14: Cov .8E 28
Truro Ct. PO13: Gos .1E 238
Truro Pl. RG22: B'toke .2K 59
Truro Ri. SO50: B'stke .9J 133
Truro Rd. PO6: Cosh .8A 200
Truscott Av. BH9: Bour .7L 227
Trussell Cl. SO22: Winche .3H 105
Trussell Cres. SO22: Winche .3H 105
Trust Cl. RG27: Hoo .2F 44
Tryplets GU52: Ch Cr .8K 47
Trystworthy BH2: Bour .5J 247
Tubb's La. RG20: High .4A 8
RG26: Cha A .4J 21
Tucks Cl. BH23: Bran .6C 220
TUCKTON .9J 229
Tuckton Cl. BH6: Bour .1G 247
Tuckton Gdns. BH6: Bour .9H 229
Tuckton Rd. BH6: Bour .1G 247
Tudor Av. PO10: Ems .5L 203
Tudor Cl. GU26: Gray .5M 103
PO11: H Isl .5F 242
PO13: Gos .8F 212
PO16: Portc .8K 199
RG26: B'ley .2D 22
SO40: Calm .2J 171
SP6: Ald .5D 152
Tudor Ct. BH1: Bour .9L 227
GU30: Lip .1E 116
PO5: S'sea .6E 240
PO6: Cosh .9G 201
PO14: Fare .1C 212
RG26: Tadl .5H 11
SP10: A'ver .7N 51
Tudor Cres. PO6: Cosh .2G 214
Tudor Dr. GU46: Yat .9N 17
Tudor Gdns. SO30: Hed E .5L 175
Tudor Hall GU15: Camb .7N 19
Tudor House & Garden .7C 4 (7L 173)
Tudor Sailing Club .6L 215
Tudor Way GU52: Ch Cr .7M 47
SO23: Kin W .7M 91
Tudor Wood Cl. SO16: Bass .7L 159
Tuffin Cl. SO16: Nur .6B 158
TUFTON .8F 54
Tukes Av. PO13: Gos .4D 212
Tulip Cl. RG22: B'toke .3J 59
Tulip Gdns. PO9: Bed .7C 202
SO31: Loc H .6C 196
Tulip Rd. SO16: Bass .7A 160
Tulls La. GU35: Stan .5N 101
Tumulus Cl. SO19: South .6J 175
Tunball La. SN8: Fos .7B 6
Tunbridge Cres. GU30: Lip .1D 116
Tunbridge La. GU30: B'sht .6C 102
GU30: B'sht, Lip .9D 102
Tunnel La. RG29: N War .7H 45
Tunstall Cl. SO19: South .6J 175
Tunstall Rd. PO6: Cosh .8E 200
SO19: South .6J 175
TUNWORTH .4L 61
Tunworth Cl. GU51: Fleet .8K 27
Tunworth Ct. PO9: Hav .4H 203
RG26: Tadl .5J 11
(off Tunworth M.)
Tunworth M. RG26: Tadl .5J 11
Tunworth Rd. RG25: Mapl, Tun .7M 43
Tupman Ho. PO1: Ports .9E 214
Turbary Cl. BH12: Poole .6B 226
Turbary Common Nature Reserve .4D 226
Turbary Gdns. RG26: Tadl .4H 11
Turbary Pk. Av. BH11: Bour .3D 226
Turbary Retail Pk. BH11: Bour .3C 226
Turbary Rd. BH12: Poole .7B 226
GU51: Fleet .8L 27
TURGIS GREEN .1B 24
Turgis Rd. GU51: Fleet .8K 27
Turin Ct. SP10: A'ver .6A 52
(not continuous)
TURKEY ISLAND .3B 178
Turk's La. RG7: Mort .1E 12
Turk St. GU34: Alt .5F 80
(not continuous)
TURMER .1G 185
Turnberry Cl. BH23: Chri .8J 229
Turnberry Dr. RG22: B'toke .5J 59
Turner Av. PO13: Gos .7F 212
Turner Cl. RG21: B'toke .7F 42
Turner Ct. SP10: A'ver .9M 51
Turner Pl. GU47: Coll .7F 18
Turner Rd. PO1: Ports .9E 214
Turners Av. GU51: Fleet .8J 27
Turners Farm Cres. SO41: Hor .4H 233
Turner's Grn. La. RG27: Elve .8H 27
(not continuous)
Turner Sims Concert Hall .8M 159
Turners Oak Ct. SO15: South .1H 173
Turners Way GU51: Fleet .9J 27
Turnhill Ct. SP11: Enh A .3A 52
Turnpike Down SO23: Winche .6N 105
Turnpike Rd. SP11: A'ver .2E 70
Turnpike Way RG23: Oak .9C 40
SO30: Hed E .2M 175
Turnstone End GU46: Yat .7L 17
Turnstone Gdns. SO16: South .6G 158
Turtin Dr. GU51: Fleet .8L 27
Turtle Cl. PO14: Stub .4L 211
Turvy King Ct. PO7: Den .6G 181
Tuscam Way GU15: Camb .9H 19
Tuscan Wlk. SO53: Cha F .6C 132
Tuscany Way GU46: Yat .9M 17
PO7: W'lle .1B 202
Tussocks, The SO40: March .8E 172
Tutland Rd. SO52: N Bad .8E 130
Tutor Cl. SO31: Hamb .6K 195
Tutts La. SO51: W Wel .1B 120 (9N 121)
Tweedale Rd. BH9: Bour .3N 227
Tweed Cl. GU14: Cov .6G 29
SO53: Cha F .5M 131
Tweed Ct. PO9: Hav .5E 202
Tweed La. SO41: Bold .6D 224
Tweedsmuir Cl. GU14: Cov .9F 28
RG22: B'toke .7K 41
Twelve Acre Cres. GU14: Cov .7F 28
Twelve Trees Ho. RG45: Cr'tne .1E 18
(off Cambridge Rd.)
Tweseldown Race Course .6A 48
Tweseldown Rd. GU52: Ch Cr .7N 47
Twiggs End Cl. SO31: Loc H .5C 196
Twiggs La. SO40: March .3C 192
Twiggs La. End SO40: March .4B 192
Twinley La. RG28: Col H, Free .7L 37
Twisell Thorne GU52: Ch Cr .7K 47
Twiss Sq. SO23: Winche .3L 105
Twittens Way PO9: Hav .8F 202
Two Acres Caravan Pk.
PO11: H Isl .5L 243
Two Gate La. RG25: Over .3E 56
Two Gate Mdw. RG25: Over .2E 56
Two Riversmeet Golf Course .8M 229
Two Riversmeet Leisure Cen. .8M 229
Two Ways Ct. GU35: W'hil .6H 101
TWYFORD .7L 127
Twyford Av. PO2: Ports .5E 214
(not continuous)
SO15: South .1H 173
Twyford Cl. BH8: Bour .4A 228
GU51: Fleet .8K 27
Twyford Ct. SO23: Winche .4L 105
Twyford Dr. PO13: Lee S .9B 212
Twyford Ho. SO15: South .3L 173
Twyford Rd. SO50: E'leigh .9F 132
Twyford Waterworks .7N 127
Twynes Mdw. RG27: Hoo .2K 45
Twynham Av. BH23: Chri .7K 229
Twynham Cl. SP5: Down .3K 119 (8A 120)
Twynham Ct. BH6: Bour .1J 247
(off Twynham Rd.)
Twynham Rd. BH6: Bour .2H 247
(not continuous)
Twynhams Hill SO32: Shi H .2C 178
TYE .7J 217
Tyfield RG24: Sher J .9N 21
Tyhurst Pl. SP10: A'ver .3N 69
Tyler Ho. PO9: Hav .4E 202
Tylers Cl. SO41: Lymi .1D 234
Tyleshades, The SO51: Rom .6N 129
Tylney La. RG27: Newn, Roth .2D 44
Tylney Pk. Golf Course .8D 24
Tylston Mdw. GU30: Lip .1D 116
Tyndale Cl. BH9: Bour .2N 227
Tyne Cl. GU14: Cov .6G 28
SO53: Cha F .7M 131
Tyne Ct. SP10: A'ver .8B 52
Tynedale Cl. PO12: Gos .8H 213
Tynefield Caravan Site
PO15: Titch .5J 197
Tyneham Av. BH12: Poole .6A 226
Tyne Way SO30: Wes E .9J 161
Tynwald Ct. BH23: Chri .8J 229
Tyrells Ct. SP10: A'ver .1B 70
Tyrells La. BH24: Bur .6D 188
Tyrrel Lawn PO9: Hav .2D 202
Tyrrell Gdns. BH8: Bour .4D 228
Tyrrells Ct. BH23: Bran .6D 220
Tyrrel Rd. SO53: Cha F .5A 132
Tyseley Rd. PO5: S'sea .2D 240
Tythe Cl. SP11: E Ant .6B 52
Tytherley Grn. BH8: Bour .4A 228
PO9: Hav .3H 203
Tytherley Rd. SO18: South .2G 174
SP5: Mid W .5J 87

U

Ubsdell Cl. BH25: New M .3B 232
Ullswater SO50: E'leigh .2E 160
Ullswater Av. GU14: Cov .9G 28
SO18: Wes E .1F 174
Ullswater Cl. GU9: Up H .4C 64
GU35: Bor .2J 101
Ullswater Gro. SO24: New A .2F 108
Ullswater Ho. PO6: Cosh .8C 200
Ullswater Rd. SO16: South .1D 172
Ulric Ho. GU51: Fleet .7L 27
Undercliff Dr. BH1: Bour .9M 247 (3L 245)
BH5: Bour .3L 245
Undercliff Gdns. SO16: Bass .7K 159
Undercliff Rd. BH5: Bour .2B 246
Underdown Av. PO7: Wid .7L 201
Undershore SO41: Lymi .8F 224
Undershore Rd. SO41: Wal .1F 234
Underwood Av. GU12: Ash .1N 65
Underwood Cl. SO16: Bass .7K 159
Underwood Rd. SO16: Bass .7K 159
SO50: B'stke .8H 133
Unicorn PO1: Ports .3K 5
Unicorn Ga. PO1: Ports .1M 5 (1C 240)
Unicorn Rd. PO1: Ports .1M 5 (1C 240)
PO13: Lee S .9N 211
Union Cl. GU47: Owl .3G 18
Union La. RG19: Head .5K 9
RG20: Kings .1A 6 (5K 9)
SO32: Drox .1J 165
Union Pl. PO1: Ports .1E 240
SO15: South .4J 173
SO41: Lymi .2E 234
Union Ri. GU33: Longc .4J 115
Union Rd. GU9: Farnh .8E 64
PO9: Hav .8E 202
SO14: South .4A 174
Union St. GU11: Alders .9J 49
GU14: Farn .8J 29
PO1: Ports .3K 5 (2B 240)
PO16: Fare .8E 198
SO23: Winche .7P 237 (6M 105)
SP10: A'ver .1A 70
(off East St.)
Union Ter. GU11: Alders .9J 49
Unity Ct. SO50: E'leigh .1F 160
Universal Marina SO31: Sar G .3N 195
University Cres. SO17: South .8N 159
University of Bournemouth
Christchurch Rd. .2M 245
University of Portsmouth
ARDSU .9F 200
Eldon Bldg. .5N 5 (3D 240)
Frewen Library .6L 5 (3C 240)
Langstone Campus .2L 241
Marine Sciences .3M 241
Mercantile House .5M 5 (3C 240)
Omega Cen. .2E 240
St George's Building .6L 5 (3B 240)
University of Portsmouth
St Michael's Rd. .5M 5 (3C 240)
University House .5M 5 (3C 240)
University Quarter .3L 5 (2C 240)
Wiltshire Building .5M 5 (3C 240)
University of Southampton
Avenue Campus .9M 159
Highfield Campus .8M 159
Maritime Centre of Excellence .7L 159
National Oceanography Cen. .9N 173
Winchester School of Art .6N 237 (6M 105)
University of Southampton Sports Ground
.4D 160
University of Winchester
Chute House Campus .6C 42
King Alfred Campus .9H 237 (7J 105)
West Downs Campus .6H 105
University Parkway SO16: Chilw .2H 159
University Rd. SO17: South .7N 159
University Rdbt. BH10: Bour .6G 227
Unwin Cl. SO19: South .9B 174
Upavon Cl. RG23: Wort .8J 41
Up Fallow RG24: Lych .4H 43
UP GREEN .7J 17
Up Green RG27: Eve .7J 17
UPHAM .8E 134
Upham St. SO32: Lwr U, Uph .9D 134
Uphill Rd. SO22: Lit .1F 104
Upland La. GU33: Hawk .7M 113
Upland Rd. GU15: Camb .6M 19
UPLANDS .6C 198
Uplands Av. BH25: B Sea .6B 232
Uplands Cl. GU47: Sandh .5D 18
Uplands Cres. PO16: Fare .6D 198
Uplands Gdns. BH8: Bour .4N 227
Uplands La. GU34: Four M .6H 97
Uplands Rd. BH8: Bour .5M 227
GU9: Farnh .9G 65
PO6: Dray .8K 201
PO7: Den, Wor E .4C 180
PO9: R Cas .8J 183
SO22: Winche .3J 105
Uplands Way SO17: South .9M 159
Upmill Cl. SO30: Wes E .8F 160
UP NATELY .6C 44
Upnor Cl. SP11: Per D .4B 30 (6J 31)
Up. Adhurst Ind. Pk. GU31: Pet .6D 140
Up. Anstey La. GU34: Alt .10C 62
Up. Arundel St. PO1: Ports .2D 240
Up. Banister St. SO15: South .1C 4 (4L 173)
Up. Barn Copse SO50: Fair O .9M 133
Up. Bere Wood PO7: W'lle .3N 201
Up. Broadmoor Rd. RG45: Cr'tne .1E 18 & 1F 18
Up. Brook Dr. SO31: Loc H .7B 196
Up. Brook St. SO23: Winche .8M 237 (7L 105)
(not continuous)
Up. Brownhill Rd. SO16: South .8E 158
Up. Bugle St. SO14: South .7C 4 (7L 173)
UPPER BULLINGTON .5C 76
UPPER BURGATE .6K 151
UPPER CANTERTON .7L 155
Up. Charles St. GU15: Camb .7L 19
Up. Chestnut Dr. RG21: B'toke .8A 42
Up. Church La. GU9: Farnh .8D 64
Up. Church Rd. SO32: Shed .3A 178
UPPER CHUTE .2N 31
UPPER CLATFORD .5L 69
Up. College Ride GU15: Camb .5N 19
Up. Common Rd. SO41: Penn .2N 233
Up. Cornaway La. PO16: Portc .7K 199
(not continuous)
Up. Crabbick La. PO7: Den .5D 180
Up. Crescent Rd. SO52: N Bad .7E 130
Up. Deacon Rd. SO19: South .4F 174
Upper Drove SP10: A'ver .1J 69
Up. Elms Rd. GU11: Alders .1J 65
Up. Farm Rd. RG23: Oak .2D 58
UPPER FARRINGDON .4E 98
Up. Farringdon Rd. GU34: Lwr Farr .4D 98
UPPER FROYLE .8G 63
Up. Froyle Dr. GU51: Fleet .9J 27
Up. Gordon Rd. BH23: Highc .5J 231
GU15: Camb .8M 19
UPPER GREEN
GU35 .7G 83
RG17 .1H 7
Up. Grove Rd. GU34: Alt .6F 80
UPPER HALE .4E 64
Up. Hale Rd. GU9: Hale, Up H .3C 64
Up. Hammer La. GU26: Hasl .7L 103
Upper Heyshott GU31: Pet .1N 145
Up. High St. SO23: Winche .6K 237 (6K 105)
Up. Hinton Rd. BH1: Bour .7M 247 (2K 245)
Up. House Ct. PO17: Wick .6B 178
UPPER KINGSTON .5M 187
Up. Lamborough La. SO24: Cher .8G 108
Up. Lanham La. SO24: Old A .9F 78
Upper Mkt. St. SO50: E'leigh .9F 132
Upper Mead SO20: Mid Wa .4B 72
Up. Mead Cl. SO50: Fair O .1A 162
Up. Moors Rd. SO50: B'dge .4K 133
Upper Mt. GU33: Liss .2D 140
Up. Mount St. GU51: Fleet .9J 27
Up. Mullins La. SO45: Hythe .6K 193
Up. Neatham Mill La.
GU34: Holy .2J 81
Up. New Rd. SO30: Wes E .1H 175
Up. Northam Cl. SO30: Hed E .4L 175
Up. Northam Dr. SO30: Hed E .4J 175
Up. Northam Rd. SO30: Hed E .3L 175
Up. Norwich Rd. BH2: Bour .7J 247 (2J 245)
Up. Old Pk. La. GU9: Farnh .5B 64
Upper Old St. PO14: Stub .4L 211
Up. Park Rd. GU15: Camb .8M 19
UPPER PARKSTONE .9A 226
UPPER PENNINGTON .3A 234
Upper Piece PO7: Den .7H 181
UPPER RATLEY .9E 122
Upper Rd. BH12: Poole .7A 226
Up. St Helens Rd. SO30: Hed E .6M 175
Up. St Michael's Gro. PO14: Fare .9B 198

Up. St Michael's Rd.—Viscount Dr.

Up. St Michael's Rd. GU11: Alders 2K 65
Up. School Dr. GU27: Hasl 1N 117
Up. Shaftesbury Av. SO17: South 9N 159
Up. Sherborne Rd. RG21: B'toke 4B 42
UPPER SHIRLEY 9J 159
Up. Shirley Av. SO15: South 1H 173
UPPER SLACKSTEAD 4G 124
Up. Soldridge Rd. GU34: Meds 5E 96
Up. South Vw. GU9: Farnh 7E 64
Upper Spinney SO31: Wars 9N 195
UPPER STREET 2J 151
Upper St. GU51: Fleet 2L 47
Up. Stroud Cl. RG24: Chin 1F 42
UPPER SWANMORE 3E 164
Up. Terrace Rd. BH2: Bour 7K 247 (2J 245)
UPPER TIMSBURY 5K 123
Up. Toothill Rd. SO16: Rown 2D 158
Up. Union St. GU11: Alders 9J 49
Up. Union Ter. GU11: Alders 9J 49
Up. Verran Rd. GU15: Camb 1M 29
Upper Wardley GU30: Mill 9E 116
Upper Wardown GU31: Pet 9A 140
Up. Weston La. SO19: South 8E 174
Up. Weybourne La. GU9: H End, Weyb 2F 64
Upper Wharf PO16: Fare 9E 198
UPPER WIELD 8G 79
Up. Wield Dr. GU51: Fleet 8K 27
UPPER WOOTON 1E 40
UPPER WYKE 1H 53
Uppleby Rd. BH12: Poole 9A 226
(not continuous)
Upron Fld. Cl. RG22: B'toke 3K 59
UP SOMBORNE 5K 89
Up Street RG25: Dumm 9D 58
RG25: Nth W 9A 58
UPTON
SO16 5B 158
SP11 9G 6
Upton Cl. GU14: Farn 9M 29
PO9: Hav 2D 202
Upton Cres. RG21: B'toke 4B 42
SO16: Nur 4C 158
UPTON GREY 3A 62
Upton Grey Cl. SO22: Winche 3H 105
Upton Grey Dr. GU51: Fleet 9K 27
Upton Grey Rd. RG25: Up G 3A 62
RG29: Grey 9E 44 (3A 62)
Upton Ho. SO16: South 1E 172
Upton La. SO16: Nur 6N 157
Upton Rd. SP11: Hur T, Ibt, Upt 9G 6
Urchfont Ho. SP9: Tidw 8E 30
(off Bourne Rd.)
Usborne Cl. PO13: Lee S 9B 212
Utrecht Ct. BH23: Chri 7N 229
Uxbridge Cl. SO31: Sar G 3C 196

V

Vadne Gdns. PO12: Gos 1K 239
Vaggs La. SO41: Hor 8E 222
Valcourt BH4: Bour 1H 245
(off Branksome Wood Rd.)
Valdean Home Pk. SO24: New A 9F 94
Vale, The PO5: S'sea 5D 240
PO8: Horn 1C 182
RG23: Oak 1D 58
SO31: Loc H 7E 196
SO45: Hythe 6L 193
Vale Cl. BH14: Poole 1C 244
Vale Ct. BH1: Bour 1N 245
(off Vale Rd.)
Vale Dr. SO18: South 1D 174
Vale Gro. PO12: Gos 9J 213
Vale Hgts. BH14: Poole 9C 226
Vale Lodge BH1: Bour 9A 228
Valencia Cl. BH23: Chri 2G 229
Valencia Way SP10: A'ver 9A 52
Valentine Av. SO19: South 7G 175
Valentine Cl. PO15: Fare 6M 197
Valentine Ct. PO7: W'lle 1A 202
SO19: South 7G 175
Valerian Av. PO15: Titch 6J 197
Valerian Cl. SO50: Hor H 5N 161
Valerian Rd. SO30: Hed E 4N 175
Vale Rd. BH1: Bour 1N 245
BH14: Poole 1C 244
GU15: Camb 9J 19
SO23: Winche 8N 105
SP5: Woodf 2M 119 (8C 120)
Valetta Pk. PO10: Ems 9L 203
Valette Rd. BH9: Bour 2L 227
Valeview Mobile Homes SO41: Sway 8G 222
Vale Way SO23: Kin W 6M 91
Valewood La. GU26: Gray 3L 103
Valiant Gdns. PO2: Ports 4E 214
Valiant Way BH23: Chri 7D 230
Valley, The SO22: Winche 8G 105
Valley Cl. BH23: Chri 3H 229
PO7: Wid 6K 201
SO21: Col C 4K 133
SO45: Blac 7D 208
SP5: Woodf 2M 119 (8C 120)
Valley Court, The SO22: Winche 8H 105
Valleydene SO45: Dib P 7L 193
Valley La. BH23: Thorn 3G 220
Valley Mead SP11: An V 4J 69
Valley Pk. Dr. PO8: Clan 7D 168
Valley Ri. SO31: Sar G 5B 196
SP11: Up C 5L 69
Valley Rd. BH8: Bour 4B 228
SO22: Lit 1F 104
SO40: Tott 5M 171
SO53: Cha F 5A 132
Valley Side GU30: Lip 1D 116
Valley Vw. BH12: Poole 7F 226
GU47: Sandh 6C 18
Valley Wlk. SO32: Uph 6G 134
Valley Way RG26: Pam H 4L 11
Valmeade Cl. RG27: Hoo 2H 45
Valroy Cl. GU15: Camb 7M 19
Valsheba Dr. PO14: Stub 7L 211
Vanburgh Gdns. RG22: B'toke 3K 59
Vanburgh Ho. SO30: Hed E 2A 176
Vanburgh Way SO53: Cha F 3N 131
Van Dyck Cl. RG21: B'toke 8F 42
Vanguard Ct. PO4: S'sea 4L 241
Vanguard Rd. BH8: Bour 5B 228
PO12: Gos 8L 213
SO18: South 2E 174
Vanners La. RG20: Croc H 1N 7
Vannes Pde. PO16: Fare 8D 198
(off Harper Way)
Vanstone Rd. PO13: Gos 8F 212
Vantage Way BH12: Poole 4A 226
Vardy Cl. SO19: South 7H 175
Varna Rd. GU35: Bor 4K 101
SO15: South 5H 173
Varndell Rd. RG27: Hoo 2F 44
Varney Cl. GU14: Cov 7G 29
Varos Cl. PO12: Gos 1J 239
Vaudrey Cl. SO15: South 1H 173
Vaughan Cl. SO19: South 5J 175
Vaughan Rd. SO45: Dib 5H 193
Vaughans GU34: Alt 5G 80
Vauxhall Way GU32: Pet 1L 145
Veals La. SO40: March 2F 192
Vear's La. SO21: Col C 4L 133
Vecta Cl. BH23: Fri C 8E 230
Vectis Cl. GU34: Four M 5H 97
Vectis Ct. SO16: Bass 7L 159
Vectis Rd. BH25: B Sea 7M 231
PO12: Gos 4G 239
Vectis Way PO6: Cosh 1G 214
Velder Av. PO4: S'sea 2H 241
Vellan Ct. SO16: South 1C 172
Velmead Cl. GU52: Fleet 4N 47
Velmead Rd. GU52: Fleet 4M 47
Velmore Rd. SO53: Cha F 8N 131
Velsheda Ct. SO45: Hythe 3M 193
Velvet Lawn Rd. BH25: New M 2A 232
Venerable Rd. PO14: Fare 3C 212
Vengeance Rd. PO13: Lee S 9A 212
Venice Cl. PO7: W'lle 1A 202
Venice Ct. SP10: A'ver 7A 52
(not continuous)
Venison Ter. SO20: Brou 1A 86
Venning Av. BH11: Bour 1C 226
Ventnor Ct. SO16: Bass 6A 160
Ventnor Rd. PO4: S'sea 3F 240
PO13: Gos 5D 212
Ventnor Ter. GU12: Alders 1L 65
Ventnor Way PO16: Fare 8G 198
Ventry Cl. BH13: Poole 1D 244
Venture Ct. PO3: Ports 3H 215
Venture Ind. Pk. PO3: Ports 3H 215
PO13: Gos 5F 212
Venture Rd. SO16: Chilw 2J 159
Venture Rdbt. RG21: B'toke 8D 42
Venture Sidings PO4: S'sea 2G 240
Verandah Cotts. RG27: H Win 6C 26
(off High St.)
Verbena Cres. PO8: Cowp 6B 182
Verbena Way SO30: Hed E 4A 176
Verden Way SP10: A'ver 7M 51
Verdi Cl. RG22: B'toke 2M 59
Verdon Av. SO31: Hamb 6J 195
Verger Cl. PO14: Titch C 6F 196
Verge Wlk. GU11: Alders 3J 65
Verica Gdns. RG26: Pam H 3L 11
Verity Sq. SP10: A'ver 7B 52
Vermont Cl. SO16: Bass 7L 159
Vernalls Cl. BH10: Bour 1H 227
Vernalls Ct. BH25: A'ley 1D 232
Vernalls Gdns. BH10: Bour 1H 227
Verne, The GU52: Ch Cr 6M 47
Verne Cl. PO15: White 9E 176
Verner Cl. GU35: Head 3A 102
Verney Cl. BH11: Bour 3F 226
SP4: Ames 5A 66
(off Butterfield Dr.)
Verney Rd. BH11: Bour 3E 226
VERNHAM BANK 8D 6
VERNHAM DEAN 8D 6
Vernham Rd. SO22: Winche 4H 105
VERNHAM ROW 7D 6
Vernhams M. RG24: B'toke 3M 41
VERNHAM STREET 7F 6
Verno La. BH23: Chri 5E 230
Vernon Av. PO4: S'sea 2H 241
(not continuous)
Vernon Cl. PO12: Gos 2J 239
SO32: Bis W 1N 163
SP4: Ames 5A 66
Vernon Ct. GU9: Farnh 8C 64
PO2: Ports 6F 214
Vernon Hill SO32: Bis W 1M 163
Vernon M. PO4: S'sea 2H 241
Vernon Rd. PO3: Ports 6H 215
PO12: Gos 2J 239
Vernon Theatre 3B 148
Vernon Wlk. SO15: South 2C 4
Verona Av. BH6: Bour 9G 228
Verona Rd. SO53: Cha F 5C 132
Veronica Cl. RG22: B'toke 3J 59
Veronica Dr. GU51: Cr V 6J 47
Verran Rd. GU15: Camb 1M 29
Verulam Pl. BH1: Bour 6M 247 (2K 245)
Verulam Rd. SO14: South 3N 173
Verwood Cres. BH6: Bour 1K 247
Verwood Rd. BH24: A'ley 9E 184
PO9: Hav 3H 203
Veryan PO14: Fare 8A 198
Vesey Cl. GU14: Farn 7J 29
Vespasian Ct. SO18: South 3A 174
Vespasian Gdns. RG24: B'toke 3L 41
Vespasian Quay SO18: South 2A 174
Vespasian Rd. SO18: South 3B 174
SP10: A'ver 7A 52
Vespasian Way SO53: Cha F 6C 132
Vesta Way SO53: Cha F 5C 132
Vestry Cl. SP10: A'ver 1M 69
Vetch Cl. BH23: Chri 6D 230
Vetch Fld. RG27: Hoo 2J 45
Viables Craft Cen. 1B 60
Viables Ind. Est. RG22: B'toke 1B 60
Viables La. RG22: B'toke 1C 60
Viables Rdbt. RG22: B'toke 1A 60
Vian Cl. PO13: Gos 4E 212
Vian Ct. BH25: New M 3A 232
Vian Pl. SO23: Kin W 7N 91
Vian Rd. PO7: W'lle 3L 201
Vicarage Dr. SO30: Hed E 5M 175
Vicarage Farm Bus. Pk. SO50: Fair O 7N 133
Vicarage Gdns. GU26: Gray 4L 103
GU52: Ch Cr 7L 47
SO41: Hor 3H 233
(not continuous)
Vicarage Gro. RG27: Hou G 2H 25
Vicarage Hill GU34: Alt 5F 80
RG27: H Win 7C 26
Vicarage La. GU9: Farnh 8D 64
GU9: Up H 3E 64
GU27: Hasl 9N 103
GU46: Yat 6M 17
PO7: H'don 8E 166
PO14: Stub 5M 211
RG27: Hou G 3F 24
SO24: Rop 2C 110
SO32: Curd 3F 176
SO32: Swanm 6D 164
SO40: Copy 1B 170
SO41: Hor 3H 233
Vicarage Pk. SP5: M Val 2M 119 (8C 120)
Vicarage Rd. BH9: Bour 4J 227
GU17: Haw 9G 19
GU34: Alt 6E 80
GU46: Yat 6L 17
SO40: March 9E 172
SP5: Lover 8E 120
Vicarage Ter. PO12: Gos 8H 213
Vicarage Way BH23: Burt 4N 229
Vice La. SO43: B'haw 3L 155
Viceroy Rd. SO19: South 7E 174
Vickers Bus. Cen. RG24: B'toke 3N 41
Vickers Cl. BH8: Bour 4E 228
Vickery Way BH23: Chri 6N 229
Victena Rd. SO50: Fair O 1N 161
Victor Ct. SO18: South 4H 175
Victoria Av. BH9: Bour 5J 227
GU15: Camb 8J 19
PO1: Ports 8L 5 (4C 240)
PO7: Wid 6J 201
PO11: H Isl 4F 242
Victoria Bldgs. SO32: Bis W 3L 163
Victoria Cl. SO31: Loc H 8D 196
Victoria Ct. BH6: Bour 1F 246
GU51: Fleet 2L 47
PO11: H Isl 4E 242
SO32: Durl 4F 162
SP10: A'ver 2M 69
Victoria Cres. BH12: Poole 8B 226
Victoria Dr. GU17: Blackw 9E 18
Victoria Gdns. BH24: Ring 2K 187
GU14: Cov 8F 28
GU51: Fleet 2L 47
SP6: F'dge 1G 153
Victoria Gate SO23: Winche 5K 105
Victoria Glade SO31: Net A 4G 195
Victoria Gro. PO5: S'sea 4E 240
Victoria Hill Rd. GU51: Fleet 2K 47
Victoria Ho. SO23: Winche 6L 237
Victoria Lodge SO17: South 1N 173
Victoria M. PO17: K Vil 2A 198
SO31: Net A 4F 194
Victoria Pk. Pl. BH9: Bour 5K 227
(off Victoria Pk. Rd.)
Victoria Pk. Rd. BH9: Bour 5J 227
Victoria Pl. BH1: Bour 9N 227
GU30: Lip 6G 116
PO12: Gos 3K 239
RG22: B'toke 7K 41
SO41: Lymi 4E 234
SO51: Rom 5L 129
(off Love La.)
SP11: Hur T 4D 34
Victoria Rd. BH1: Bour 9N 227
BH12: Poole 9A 226
BH23: Chri 9A 230
GU9: Farnh 8E 64
GU11: Alders 9J 49
GU14: Farn 8J 29
GU34: Alt 4F 80
GU47: Owl 4G 18
GU51: Fleet 2K 47
PO1: Ports 1H 5 (1A 240)
PO7: W'lle 2M 201
PO10: Ems 8L 203
PO11: H Isl 6F 216
SO19: South 9B 174
SO23: Winche 5K 105
SO31: Net A 3E 194
SO32: Bis W 3L 163
SO41: M Sea 8H 235
SO50: E'leigh 7F 132
SP6: F'dge 1G 152
Victoria Rd. E. GU34: Alt 4G 80
Victoria Rd. Nth. PO5: S'sea 4E 240
Victoria Rd. Sth. PO5: S'sea 5E 240
Victoria Sq. PO13: Lee S 1A 238
Victoria St. PO1: Ports 9D 214
PO12: Gos 2L 239
RG21: B'toke 7C 42
SO14: South 5A 174
Victoria Ter. GU26: Gray 4L 103
(off Crossways Rd.)
PO6: Cosh 1G 215
PO10: Ems 8N 203
Victoria Wlk. SO30: Wes E 9J 161
Victoria Way GU30: Lip 2D 116
Victor Rd. PO3: Ports 9G 215
Victor St. SO15: South 1G 173
Victory Av. PO8: Horn 4A 182
Victory Bus. Cen. PO1: Ports 2F 240
(off Somers Rd. Nth.)
Victory Cl. SO53: Cha F 7N 131
Victory Ct. BH5: Bour 2B 246
BH8: Bour 9N 227
(off Lowther Rd.)
PO7: W'lle 1M 201
PO13: Gos 7F 212
Victory Cres. SO15: South 3G 173
Victory Gate 3H 5 (2A 240)
Victory Grn. PO2: Ports 6D 214
Victory Ho. PO6: P Sol 1B 214
Victory Indoor Bowls Club 5E 214
Victory Retail Pk. PO1: Ports 9D 214
Victory Rd. PO1: Ports 4J 5 (2B 240)
PO14: Stub 6N 211
SO15: South 4G 173
Victory Rdbt. RG21: B'toke 6B 42
Victory Sq. SO15: South 3G 173
Victory Trad. Est. PO3: Ports 6H 215
Victory Way SO16: Rown 4D 158
Viewpoint BH4: Bour 4F 244
RG21: B'toke 5E 42
Vigo La. GU46: Yat 8M 17
Vigo Rd. SP10: A'ver 1A 70
Vigo Rd. Rdbt. SP10: A'ver 1A 70
Viking Cl. BH6: Bour 1K 247
PO14: Stub 5L 211
SO16: South 7D 158
SO45: Blac 8D 208
Vikings, The SO51: Rom 5B 130
Viking Way BH6: Bour 1K 247
BH23: Mude 9C 230
PO8: Horn 8C 168
SP10: A'ver 6A 52
Villa Gdns. PO7: W'lle 1M 201
Village, The RG28: Litc 3G 37
RG40: F'std 2H 17
SP5: W Tyt 8L 87
Village Cl. PO14: Stub 6M 211
Village Ga. PO14: Titch 8J 197
Village Hotel & Leisure Club
Farnborough 1K 49
Village M. SO40: March 9E 172
Village Rd. PO12: Gos 5H 239
Village St. GU32: Pet 7A 140
GU34: Bent 6L 79
SO20: Chil 4F 74
SP11: G Cla 7N 69
Village Way GU46: Yat 6N 17
Ville De Paris Rd. PO14: Fare 3C 212
Villeneuve St. SO50: E'leigh 9C 132
Villette Cl. BH23: Chri 5K 229
Villiers Ct. PO5: S'sea 5D 240
(off Palmerston Rd.)
SO23: Winche 8L 237
Villiers Rd. PO5: S'sea 5D 240
(not continuous)
SO15: South 3H 173
SO45: Dib P 9L 193
Vimoutiers Ct. SP6: F'dge 1H 153
Vimy Ho. PO14: Fare 9A 198
Vince Cl. BH11: Bour 1F 226
Vincent Av. SO16: South 9H 159
Vincent Cl. BH25: New M 4B 232
Vincent Ct. BH9: Bour 7K 227
GU51: Fleet 2M 47
Vincent Dr. SP10: A'ver 2A 70
Vincent Gro. PO16: Portc 1L 213
Vincent Rd. BH25: New M 3A 232
SO15: South 2H 173
Vincent's Gro. SO15: South 2G 173
Vincent St. SO15: South 2H 173
Vincent's Wlk. SO14: South 6D 4 (6M 173)
Vindomis Cl. GU34: Holy 1K 81
Vine Bank SO18: South 2G 174
Vine Cl. BH7: Bour 7D 228
GU11: Alders 5J 49
SO31: Sar G 6A 196
Vine Coppice PO7: W'lle 5M 201
Vine Farm Cl. BH12: Poole 6G 226
Vine Farm Rd. BH12: Poole 6F 226
Vine Gdns. SO32: Bis W 3L 163
Vinegar Hill SO41: M Sea 7K 235
Vine Rd. SO16: South 8F 158
Vinery, The BH25: New M 3C 232
Vinery Cl. RG28: Whit 5G 55
Vinery Gdns. SO16: South 9H 159
Vinery Rd. SO16: South 9H 159
Vineside PO13: Gos 7G 212
Vine St. GU11: Alders 1J 65
Vine Tree Cl. RG26: Tadl 6K 11
Vineyard Cl. SO19: South 7B 174
Vineyards, The SO52: N Bad 8F 130
Viney Av. SO51: Rom 4A 130
Viney Rd. SO41: Lymi 5E 234
Vinnells La. GU32: W Meo 6E 136
Vinneys Cl. BH23: Burt 4M 229
SO42: Broc 7D 148
Vinns La. RG25: Over 3C 56
Vinson Rd. GU33: Liss 1F 140
Violet Av. PO14: Stub 6L 211
Violet Cl. RG22: B'toke 3J 59
SO53: Cha F 6M 131
Violet Ct. PO7: W'lle 8K 181
SP11: Ludg 1C 30
Violet La. BH25: New M 2B 232
RG26: Bau 6C 10
Violet Rd. SO16: Bass 7M 159
Virgin Active
Farnborough 9E 28
Virginia Cl. BH12: Poole 7A 226
BH31: Ver 4A 184
SP4: Ames 5A 66
Virginia Gdns. GU14: Farn 1L 49
Virginia Pk. Rd. PO12: Gos 1H 239
Viscount Cl. BH11: Bour 1A 226
Viscount Ct. BH5: Bour 1B 246
BH11: Bour 1B 226
SP10: A'ver 9D 52
Viscount Dr. BH23: Mude 7D 230

Viscount Gdns.—Watermain Rd.

Viscount Gdns. SO50: E'leigh 3D 160
Viscount Wlk. BH11: Bour 1A 226
Vista, The BH4: Bour 4G 244
Vita Rd. PO2: Ports 5F 214
Vitellius Gdns. RG24: B'toke 3L 41
Vitre Gdns. SO41: Lymi 4E 234
Vivaldi Cl. RG22: B'toke 3N 59
Vivash Rd. PO1: Ports 2F 240
Vivian Cl. GU52: Ch Cr 5N 47
Vivian Rd. RG21: B'toke 4D 42
Vixen Cl. PO14: Stub 6L 211
SO40: Ashu 6J 171
Vixen Dr. GU12: Alders 8N 49
Vixen Wlk. BH25: New M 9C 222
Vockins Cl. SP9: Tidw 6C 30
Vokes Cl. SO19: South 5F 174
Vosper Rd. SO19: South 8B 174
Voyager Pk. PO3: Ports 6H 215
VT House SO30: Hed E 2A 176
Vue Cinema
Basingstoke 6C 42
Camberley 7L 19
Eastleigh 1F 160
Portsmouth 5J 5
Vulcan, The PO1: Ports 5J 5 (3B 240)
Vulcan Cl. GU47: Sandh 6C 18
SO15: South 3E 172
Vulcan Ct. GU47: Sandh 6C 18
Vulcan Ho. *GU14: Farn* *1L 49*
(off Wallis Sq.)
Vulcan Rd. SO15: South 3E 172
Vulcan Way BH23: Chri 7D 230
GU47: Sandh 6C 18
Vyne, The 6C 22
Vyne Cl. GU34: Alt 4F 80
Vyne Mdw. RG24: Sher J 8A 22
Vyne Rd. RG21: B'toke 5C 42
RG24: Sher J 8A 22
RG26: B'ley 4D 22
Vyse La. SO14: South 8C 4 (7L 173)

W

Wade Cl. GU14: Cov 4H 29
Wade Ct. Rd. PO9: Hav 9G 202
Wade Hill Drove SO40: Calm 7G 156
Wade La. PO9: Hav 1G 216
Wade Rd. RG24: B'toke 4F 42
Wadham GU47: Owl 4H 19
Wadham Rd. PO2: Ports 6E 214
Wadhurst Gdns. SO19: South 1E 194
Wadhurst Rd. SO30: Hed E 4N 175
Wadleys Drove BH21: Cran 6K 149
Wadmore Cl. SO45: Hythe 5N 193
WADWICK 4N 35
Wadwick Bottom SP11: Binl, S M Bo, Wad 8L 35
Waggoners Way GU26: Gray 4J 103
Waggoners Wells La. GU26: Gray 4J 103
Wagner Cl. RG22: B'toke 2N 59
Wagon La. RG27: Hoo 1H 45
Wagon Yd. GU9: Farnh 8D 64
Wagtail Cl. SO50: E'leigh 1B 160
Wagtail Dr. BH25: New M 4A 232
Wagtail Rd. PO8: Horn 3A 182
Wagtail Way PO16: Portc 9H 199
Wainscott Rd. PO4: S'sea 5H 241
Wainsford Cl. SO41: Penn 3B 234
Wainsford Rd. SO41: Ever, Penn 4M 233
Wainwright Cl. PO6: Dray 2K 215
Wainwright Gdns. SO30: Hed E 8N 161
Wait End Rd. PO7: W'lle 3M 201
Waitland Cl. PO7: W'lle 3L 201
Wakefield Av. BH10: Bour 1J 227
PO16: Fare 6B 198
Wakefield Ct. PO7: Purb 6N 201
SO18: South 1E 174
Wakefield Pl. *PO12: Gos* *5J 239*
(off Stephenson Cl.)
Wakefield Rd. SO18: South 1E 174
Wakeford Cl. RG26: Pam H 4L 11
Wakeford Ct. RG26: Pam H 3L 11
SO51: Rom 5M 129
Wakeford Pl. SO31: Wars 8D 196
Wakefords Cl. GU11: Alders 5M 49
Wakefords Copse GU52: Ch Cr 8N 47
Wakefords Pk. GU52: Ch Cr 8N 47
(not continuous)
Wakefords Way PO9: Hav 3G 203
Wake Lawn PO4: S'sea 4K 241
Wakely Gdns. BH11: Bour 1E 226
Wakely Rd. BH11: Bour 1E 226
Walberant Bldgs. PO3: Ports 4G 214
Walberton Av. PO6: Cosh 9H 201
Walberton Ct. PO6: Cosh 9H 201
Walburton Way PO8: Clan 7D 168
Walcott Av. BH23: Chri 5J 229
Waldegrave Cl. SO19: South 9B 174
Walden Gdns. PO8: Horn 3B 182
Walden Rd. PO2: Ports 6D 214
Waldon Gdns. SO18: Wes E 9F 160
Waldorf Hgts. GU17: Haw 1F 28
Waleron Rd. GU51: Fleet 8L 27
Wales St. SO23: Winche 7P 237 (6M 105)
Walford Rd. PO6: Cosh 8D 200
WALHAMPTON 1F 234
Walhampton Golf Course 2H 235
Walhampton Hill SO41: Wal 1F 234
Walhampton Obelisk 2G 234
Walk, The RG27: Sher L 5M 23
SO22: Winche 7K 237 (6K 105)
Walker Gdns. SO30: Hed E 1N 175
Walker Pl. PO13: Gos 7F 212
SO31: Hamb 7K 195
Walker Ri. SO20: N Wal 9N 67
Walker Rd. PO2: Ports 6D 214
Walkers Cl. SO50: Fair O 1A 162
Walker's La. Nth. SO45: Blac 7C 208
Walker's La. Sth. SO45: Blac 9D 208
Walker's Ridge GU15: Camb 9N 19
WALKFORD 4K 231
Walkford La. BH25: New M 4M 231
Walkford Rd. BH23: Walk 5K 231
Walkford Way BH23: Walk 5K 231
Walkwood Av. BH7: Bour 6E 228
Wallace La. SO42: Beau 1B 236
Wallace Rd. PO2: Ports 8G 214
SO19: South 9D 174
Wallace Way GU11: Alders 8H 49
Walldown Rd. GU35: W'hil 7J 101
Walled Gardens, The RG29: S War 4D 62
Walled Mdw. SP10: A'ver 1A 70
WALLINGTON 7F 198
Wallington Ct. PO14: Fare 1B 212
PO16: Fare 6F 198
Wallington Dr. SO53: Cha F 4N 131
Wallington Hill PO16: Fare 7E 198
Wallington Orchard PO16: Fare 6F 198
Wallington Rd. PO2: Ports 7G 215
Wallington Shore Rd. PO16: Fare 8F 198
(Cams Hill)
PO16: Fare 7E 198
(North Wallington)
Wallington Way PO16: Fare 7E 198
Wallin's Copse RG24: Chin 1G 42
Walliscott Rd. BH11: Bour 5E 226
Wallis Ct. RG23: B'toke 5M 41
Wallisdean Av. PO3: Ports 9J 215
PO14: Fare 9B 198
WALLISDOWN 5D 226
Wallisdown Hgts. BH11: Bour 5D 226
Wallisdown Rd. BH10: Bour 5F 226
BH11: Bour 4B 226
BH12: Poole 4B 226
Wallisdown Rdbt. BH12: Poole 5E 226
Wallis Dr. RG26: B'ley 2J 23
Wallis Gdns. PO7: W'lle 9M 181
Wallis Rd. BH10: Bour 5F 226
PO7: W'lle 9M 181
RG21: B'toke 8C 42
Wallis Sq. GU14: Farn 1L 49
Wall La. RG7: Sil 3B 12
Wallop Dr. RG22: B'toke 4J 59
Wallop Drove SO20: N Wal 2M 87
Wallop Rd. SO20: Ov Wa 6K 67
SP11: Grat, Ov Wa 6K 67
Wallrock Wlk. PO10: Ems 5M 203
Walls Caravan Pk. RG27: Hoo 1J 45
Walls Ct. GU16: Frim 4N 29
Wallside Cotts. GU30: Lip 1E 116
Walmer Cl. SO50: E'leigh 5E 132
Walmer Rd. PO1: Ports 2F 240
Walnut Av. SO18: S'ing 6C 160
Walnut Cl. BH25: New M 3A 232
GU11: Alders 2J 65
GU34: Alt 3F 80
GU46: Yat 9N 17
SO16: South 1E 172
SO53: Cha F 2A 132
Walnut Dr. PO14: Stub 6L 211
Walnut Gro. SO16: South 2E 172
SO22: Winche 5H 105
Walnuts, The GU52: Ch Cr 6K 47
Walnut Tree Cl. PO11: H Isl 4F 242
SO21: Sth W 3H 91
Walnut Tree Ground SP11: Fyf 9N 31
Walnut Tree Rd. SP10: A'ver 2M 69
Walnut Way RG21: B'toke 4D 42
SO16: Nur 6C 158
Walpole Gdns. RG27: H Win 5C 26
Walpole La. SO31: Lwr Swan 1B 196
Walpole Rd. BH1: Bour 9A 228
PO12: Gos 3M 239
SO22: Winche 9G 104
Walpole Ter. PO12: Gos 4K 239
Walpole Wlk. BH1: Bour 9A 228
Walsall Rd. PO3: Ports 1H 241
Walsford Rd. BH4: Bour 9G 227
Walsh Rd. RG26: B'ley 2G 23
Walsingham Cl. PO6: Cosh 8E 200
Walsingham Dene BH7: Bour 6C 228
Walsingham Gdns. SO18: South 8D 160
Waltham Bus. Pk. SO32: Swanm 7C 164
WALTHAM CHASE 8A 164
Waltham Cl. BH7: Bour 8E 228
GU47: Owl 4F 18
PO16: Portc 7L 199
SO32: Drox 1J 165
Waltham Ct. RG25: Over 2E 56
Waltham Cres. SO16: South 7G 159
Waltham La. RG25: Nth W, Over, Stev 4F 56
Waltham Rd. BH7: Bour 7E 228
RG25: Over 2E 56
Waltham St. PO5: S'sea 5M 5 (3C 240)
Walton Cl. GU51: Fleet 3L 47
PO7: W'lle 4M 201
PO12: Gos 3J 239
RG22: B'toke 1N 59
Walton Ct. PO1: Ports 6K 5
PO15: Fare 5N 197
Walton Pl. SO22: Winche 9H 105
Walton Rd. BH10: Bour 4G 227
PO6: Farl 2J 215
PO12: Gos 3J 239
SO19: South 6H 175
Walton Rd. Ind. Est. PO6: Farl 2K 215
Waltons Av. SO45: Holb 4A 208
Walworth Ent. Cen. SP10: A'ver 9C 52
Walworth Ind. Est. SP10: A'ver 8D 52
Walworth Rd. SP10: A'ver 8C 52
SP11: Pic P 8C 52
Walworth Rdbt. SP10: A'ver 9C 52
Wandesford Pl. PO12: Gos 7J 213
Wangfield La. SO32: Curd 1E 176
Wansbeck Cl. SO53: Cha F 7N 131
Wansdyke, The RG17: Ink 1F 6
Wanstead Cl. BH24: Poul 8L 185
Wantage Rd. GU47: Coll 5F 18
Warbler Cl. PO8: Horn 3A 182
SO16: South 5G 159
Warbleton Rd. RG24: Chin 9H 23
WARBLINGTON 8H 203
Warblington Av. PO9: Warb 8H 203
Warblington Cl. RG26: Tadl 6J 11
SO53: Cha F 9M 131
Warblington Ct. PO1: Ports 6K 5 (3B 240)
Warblington Pl. PO3: Ports 1H 241
Warblington Rd. PO10: Ems 1L 217
Warblington Station (Rail) 7H 203
Warblington St. PO1: Ports 6K 5 (3B 240)
WARBORNE 7F 224
Warborne La. SO41: Pil, Portm 6G 224
Warbrook Ct. PO9: Hav 4H 203
Warbrook La. RG27: Eve 5D 16
Warburton Cl. SO19: South 6J 175
Warburton Rd. SO19: South 5J 175
Ward Av. PO31: Cowes 5P 237
Ward Cl. SP10: A'ver 8N 51
Ward Ct. PO11: H Isl 4E 242
Ward Cres. PO10: Ems 6N 203
Warden Cl. SO30: Wes E 1H 175
Wardens Cl. PO11: H Isl 2F 242
Warders Ct. PO12: Gos 2K 239
Ward Ho. PO1: Ports 2K 5 (1C 240)
Wardle Rd. SO50: Highb 5H 133
WARDLEY 9E 116
Wardley Grn. GU30: Mill 9F 116
Wardley La. GU30: Mill 9E 116
Ward Rd. PO4: S'sea 5H 241
Wardroom Rd. PO2: Ports 7C 214
Wareham Ct. BH7: Bour 8E 228
Warehouse, The BH2: Bour 7K 247
Warehouse Rd. RG19: Green 1G 9
Warfield Av. PO7: W'lle 2M 201
Warfield Cres. PO7: W'lle 2M 201
Wargrove Dr. GU47: Coll 5F 18
Warley La. SO21: More 4C 134
Warlock Cl. SO19: South 7H 175
Warminster Ho. *SP9: Tidw* *7D 30*
(off Wylye Rd.)
Warmwell Cl. BH9: Bour 3M 227
Warnborough Ct. PO9: Hav 3H 203
Warner Cl. RG24: B'toke 1C 42
SO30: Hed E 9N 161
Warner Ct. GU47: Coll 6G 18
SO23: Winche *4L 105*
(off Northlands Dr.)
SP10: A'ver 1M 69
Warner M. SO30: Botl 3D 176
Warnes La. BH24: Bur 8D 188
WARNFORD 5P 135
Warnford Cl. PO12: Gos 3H 239
Warnford Ct. SO15: South 3L 173
Warnford Cres. PO9: Hav 4D 202
Warnford Gro. RG27: Sher L 7H 23
Warnford Rd. BH6: Bour 7E 228
BH7: Bour 7E 228
SO32: Corh 8N 135
Warren, The GU9: H End 2G 64
GU11: Alders 1H 65
GU30: Pass 7A 102
RG26: Tadl 5G 11
SO45: Holb 3N 207
SP11: Per D 5B 30
Warren Av. BH23: Mude 9B 230
PO4: S'sea 2H 241
SO16: South 9F 158
SO53: Cha F 7C 132
Warren Cl. BH24: A'ley 3G 187
GU9: Farnh 7G 64
GU35: W'hil 5F 100
GU47: Sandh 5C 18
GU52: Fleet 4N 47
PO11: H Isl 3C 242
RG27: H Win 7C 26
SO16: South 9F 158
SO53: Cha F 7C 132
WARREN CORNER
GU10 ....2N 63
GU32 ....1H 139
Warren Cnr. GU10: Ews 2N 63
SO21: Mich S 4J 77
Warren Ct. BH2: Bour 9K 227
Warren Cres. SO16: South 9F 158
Warren Dr. BH24: A'ley 3G 186
SP11: Abb A 6F 68
Warren Edge Cl. BH6: Bour 2J 247
Warren Edge Ct. *BH6: Bour* *2J 247*
(off Warren Edge Rd.)
Warren Edge Rd. BH6: Bour 2J 247
Warren Gdns. SO51: Rom 3A 130
Warren La. BH24: A'ley 3G 187
GU32: Frox, Pr De 1H 139
(not continuous)
SO21: Owls 1D 134
SO42: Beau 4E 236
WARREN PARK 3C 202
Warren Pk. SO41: Down 8H 233
Warren Pl. SO40: Calm 9J 157
Warren Ri. GU16: Frim 2N 29
Warren Rd. BH4: Bour 3F 244
BH14: Poole 1B 244
GU33: Liss 7F 114
GU33: Longc 4J 115
SO23: Winche 6N 105
Warren Side GU31: S Hart 9G 146
Warrens La. SP5: Ch St 5A 120
Warren Way RG22: B'toke 8L 41
Warrington M. GU11: Alders 2G 64
Warrior Bus. Centre, The PO6: Farl 1M 215
Warrior Cl. SO53: Cha F 8N 131
Warrior Ct. PO12: Gos 3N 239
Warrior Pk. Ind. Est. SO53: Cha F 8N 131
Warrys Cl. SO45: Hythe 9M 193
WARSASH 8A 196
Warsash Cl. PO9: Hav 3E 202
Warsash Ct. SO31: Wars 8N 195
Warsash Gro. PO13: Gos 6D 212
Warsash Rd. PO14: Titch, Titch C 9G 197
SO31: Loc H, Wars 8N 195
Warspite Cl. PO2: Ports 4E 214
Warton Cl. *SO42: Beau* *1B 236*
(off Chapel La.)
Warton Rd. RG21: B'toke 5D 42
Warwick Av. BH25: New M 3C 232
(not continuous)
Warwick Cl. GU11: Alders 2L 65
PO13: Lee S 3C 238
RG28: Whit 5G 54
SO23: Winche 4K 105
SO53: Cha F 8M 131
Warwick Ct. BH8: Bour 7M 227
PO10: Ems *9M 203*
(off High St.)
SO23: Winche *4L 105*
(off Northlands Dr.)
Warwick Cres. PO5: S'sea 3D 240
Warwick Ho. *SO14: South* *4A 174*
(off Kent St.)
Warwick Pl. BH7: Bour 9D 228
SO51: W Wel 1B 120
Warwick Rd. BH7: Bour 9D 228
BH14: Poole 2A 244
GU14: Farn 3F 48
RG23: B'toke 5L 41
SO15: South 9J 159
SO40: Tott 2M 171
Warwicks La. BH21: Sut 9K 149
Warwick Way PO17: Wick 6C 178
Wasdale Cl. GU47: Owl 3F 18
PO8: Horn 9C 168
Wash Brook RG27: Hoo 1G 45
Washbrook Rd. PO6: Cosh 9E 200
WASH COMMON 1C 8
Washford Cl. GU35: Bor 3L 101
Washford La. GU35: Bor, Lind 2L 101
(not continuous)
Washington Av. BH1: Bour 8A 228
Washington Rd. PO2: Ports 8E 214
PO10: Ems 8M 203
Washington Ter. PO10: Ems 8M 203
WASH WATER 1C 8
Wash Water RG20: Wa W 1A 8
WASING 1D 10
Watchetts Dr. GU15: Camb 2L 29
Watchetts Lake Cl. GU15: Camb 1M 29
Watchetts Rd. GU15: Camb 9K 19
Watch La. RG28: Free 4M 55
Watchmoor Point GU15: Camb 9J 19
Watchmoor Rd. GU15: Camb 1J 29
Watchmoor Trade Cen. GU15: Camb 9J 19
Watcombe Rd. BH6: Bour 1G 246
Waterbeech Dr. SO30: Hed E 2N 175
Waterberry Dr. PO7: W'lle 9K 181
Waterbrook Est. GU34: Alt 4J 81
Waterbrook Rd. GU34: Alt 4H 81
Water Cl. SO23: Winche 9N 237 (7L 105)
Watercress Ct. *GU34: Alt* *4G 81*
(off Dickers La.)
Watercress Line (Mid-Hants Railway)
Alresford Station 1F 108
Medstead and Four Marks Station 4J 97
Ropley Station 1A 110
Watercress Mdw. SO24: New A 2D 108
Watercress Way GU34: Meds 3K 97
WATERDITCH 1D 230
Waterditch Rd. BH23: Wat 1D 230
WATER END 4A 44
Water End La. RG24: Old Bas 4N 43
Water End Pk. (Caravan Site)
RG24: Old Bas 4A 44
Waterford Cl. SO41: Lymi 3F 234
Waterford Gdns. BH23: Highc 7J 231
Waterford La. SO41: Lymi 3F 234
Waterford Pl. BH23: Highc 7J 231
Waterford Rd. BH23: Highc 6K 231
BH25: A'ley 3D 232
Waterfront Bus. Pk. GU51: Fleet 9N 27
Water Gdns. BH8: Bour 9L 227
Watergate PO12: Gos 3N 239
Watergate La. SP4: Bul 3A 66
Waterhouse Cl. SO21: Twyf 6L 127
Waterhouse La. SO15: South 3G 172
Waterhouse Mead GU47: Coll 6F 18
Waterhouse Way SO15: South 3G 172
Wateridge Rd. RG21: B'toke 3D 42
Water La. BH6: Bour 7G 228
GU9: Farnh 6G 65
GU14: Farn 5J 29
GU34: Alt, E Wor, W Wor 6H 81
SO15: South 3B 4 (5L 173)
SO21: Abb W 1A 106
SO21: Owls 6B 134
SO23: Winche 8P 237 (7M 105)
SO24: Bis S 2L 109
SO24: Itc S 1N 107
SO40: Tott 2K 171
SO45: Dib P 7K 193
SO50: Hens 6B 134
Waterlily Cl. RG21: B'toke 6E 42
Waterlock Gdns. PO4: S'sea 3L 241
Waterloo Av. RG23: B'toke 4L 41
Waterloo Cl. PO8: Cowp 7L 181
Waterloo Ct. RG28: Whit 5G 55
SP10: A'ver 2N 69
Waterloo Ind. Est. SO30: Hed E 1M 175
WATERLOO PARK 8K 49
Waterloo Pl. RG45: Cr'tne 1D 18
Waterloo Rd. BH9: Bour 7K 227
GU12: Alders 1L 65
PO9: Hav 7F 202
PO12: Gos 6L 239
RG45: Cr'tne 1C 18
SO15: South 4H 173
SO41: Lymi 2F 234
Waterloo St. PO5: S'sea 5N 5 (3D 240)
Waterloo Ter.
SO15: South 2C 4 (4L 173)
SP11: An V 5K 69
WATERLOOVILLE 2M 201
Waterlooville Golf Course 8B 182
Waterlooville Leisure Cen. 9K 181
Waterloo Way BH24: Ring 2K 187
Watermain Rd. BH24: Match 3C 218

West Cl.—Wheelers Hill

West Cl. BH6: Bour 1K 247
GU9: H End 3F 64
SO41: Penn 4B 234
WEST COMMON 1J 237
West Comn. SO45: Blac 9B 208
Westcot Rd. SO45: Holb 5N 207
West Ct. PO1: Ports 9F 214
PO4: S'sea 4H 241
SO15: South 2G 172
Westcroft Pde. BH25: New M 4B 232
Westcroft Rd. PO12: Gos 2H 239
WEST DEAN 1J 121
Westdeane Ct. RG21: B'toke 7A 42
W. Dean Rd. SP5: W Tyt 5J 87
Westdown Rd. BH11: Bour 1E 226
West Downs Cl. PO16: Fare 5C 198
West Downs Student Village
SO22: Winche 6H 105
West Dr. SO50: B'stke 8H 133
WEST END
GU34 3C 96
PO14 1A 212
SO30 1H 175
West End Rd. RG24: Sher J 8M 21
West End Cen. 9H 49
(off Queen's Rd.)
West End Cl. SO22: Winche 7J 237 (6J 105)
WEST END GREEN 5J 13
West End Gro. GU9: Farnh 8C 64
West End La. GU10: Fren 9N 63
GU34: Meds 2C 96
West End Local History Mus. 1H 175
West End Rd. SO18: South, Wes E 3E 174
SO19: South 6K 175
SO30: Wes E 1H 175
SO31: Burs 6K 175
West End Ter. SO22: Winche 7J 237 (6J 105)
Westerham BH13: Poole 2E 244
Westerham Cl. PO6: Cosh 9F 200
Westerham Rd. BH4: Bour 2F 244
Westering SO51: Rom 3B 130
Westerleigh BH4: Bour 3G 245
(off West Cliff Rd.)
Westerley Cl. SO31: Wars 8B 196
Western Av. BH10: Bour 1H 227
BH13: Poole 2C 244
BH25: B Sea 6M 231
PO10: Ems 9K 203
SO15: South 5E 172
SP10: A'ver 1N 69
Western Cl. BH10: Bour 1H 227
Western Ct. PO16: Fare 8C 198
Western Cross RG29: Odi 9K 45
Western District Cut SO15: South 3J 173
Western Esplanade
SO14: South 4A 4 (5K 173)
(Central Sta. Bri.)
SO14: South 8C 4 (7L 173)
(Town Quay)
SO15: South 6A 4 (6K 173)
Westerngate BH13: Poole 2F 244
Western La. RG29: Odi 8K 45
Western Pde. PO5: S'sea 8M 5 (4C 240)
PO10: Ems 1L 217
Western Rd. BH13: Poole 3E 244
GU11: Alders 1G 65
GU33: Liss 1E 140
GU35: Bor 1H 101
PO6: Cosh 9D 200
(not continuous)
PO9: Hav 7E 202
PO16: Fare 8D 198
SO22: Winche 6J 237 (6J 105)
SO30: Wes E 1H 175
SO41: Lymi 2D 234
SO45: Fawl 6J 209
SO53: Cha F 3C 132
SP10: A'ver 2N 69
Western Ter. PO2: Ports 6D 214
Western Way PO12: Gos 4G 238
PO16: Fare 8C 198
RG22: B'toke 9M 41
Westers La. RG29: S War 6C 62
W. Farm Cl. SN8: Co Du 1H 31
WESTFIELD 4F 242
Westfield BH2: Bour 5H 247
Westfield Av. PO11: H Isl 4F 242
PO14: Fare 9B 198
West Fld. Cl. RG26: Tadl 5K 11
Westfield Cl. SO31: Hamb 7J 195
SO50: Hor H 4A 162
Westfield Comn. SO31: Hamb 7H 195
Westfield Cnr. SO18: S'ing 6C 160
Westfield Ct. GU51: Fleet 2M 47
SP10: A'ver 2A 70
Westfield Cres. SO53: Cha F 8A 132
Westfield Dr. SO32: Swanm 9F 164
Westfield Drove SO24: B'wth 3H 135
Westfield Gdns. BH23: Chri 5D 230
SO41: Ever 5M 233
Westfield Ind. Est. PO8: Horn 3D 182
PO12: Gos 3J 239
Westfield La. GU10: Wrec 7N 63
Westfield Oaks PO11: H Isl 4F 242
West Fld. Rd. SO23: Kin W 6N 91
Westfield Rd. BH6: Bour 1H 247
GU15: Camb 2K 29
PO4: S'sea 4H 241
PO12: Gos 2H 239
RG21: B'toke 8D 42
SO15: South 3F 172
SO22: Lit 1F 104
SO40: Tott 2M 171
SO41: Lymi 4F 234
SO53: Cha F 9A 132
Westfields RG20: W Wo 1J 7
West Fryerne GU46: Yat 5N 17
Westgate BH4: Bour 9G 226
(off Branksome Wood Rd.)
Westgate GU11: Alders 9H 49
PO14: Stub 7M 211
Westgate Cl. RG23: B'toke 5K 41
Westgate Hall 8C 4
Westgate M. SO30: Wes E 1J 175
Westgate Mus. 7L 237
Westgate Pk. BH4: Bour 2F 244
Westgate St. SO14: South 8C 4 (7L 173)
Westglade GU14: Cov 8F 28
WEST GREEN 7M 25
West Grn. GU46: Yat 6L 17
West Green House Gdns. 7L 25
West Green Rd. RG27: H Win 5M 25
WEST GRIMSTEAD 2D 120
Westgrove SP6: F'dge 1H 153
WEST HAM 6M 41
West Ham Cl. RG22: B'toke 7L 41
West Ham Ct. RG22: B'toke 7L 41
West Ham Est. RG22: B'toke 7N 41
West Ham La. RG21: B'toke 6N 41
RG22: Wort 7K 41
West Ham Rdbt. RG22: B'toke 6M 41
West Hants Club 7J 227
WEST HARTING 6F 146
West Haye Rd. PO11: H Isl 6K 243
West Hayes SO22: Winche 7H 105
SO41: Lymi 3F 234
West Hayling Nature Reserve 4E 216
WEST HEATH
GU14 7H 29
GU34 3F 20
W. Heath La. RG26: Bau, Rams 4F 20
W. Heath Rd. GU14: Cov 8H 29
WEST HILL
BH2 7J 247 (2J 245)
SO22 8J 237 (7J 105)
West Hill Ct. SO15: South 3A 4 (5K 173)
West Hill Dr. SO22: Winche 7H 237 (6J 105)
SO45: Hythe 4L 193
West Hill Gdns. GU51: Fleet 1J 47
WEST HILL PARK 9J 197
West Hill Pk. SO22: Winche 6H 105
West Hill Pl. BH2: Bour 7J 247 (2J 245)
(not continuous)
West Hill Rd. BH2: Bour 7H 247 (2H 245)
West Hill Rd. Nth. SO21: Sth W 2J 91
West Hill Rd. Sth. SO21: Sth W 3J 91
West Hoe La. SO32: Bis W 3B 164
W. Horton Cl. SO50: B'stke 1K 161
W. Horton La. SO50: B'stke 2K 161
WEST HOWE 2C 226
W. Howe Cl. BH11: Bour 2E 226
W. Howe Ind. Est. BH11: Bour 3C 226
West Hundreds, The GU51: Fleet 9J 27
WEST HURN 9C 218
Westland Cl. SP4: Ames 5A 66
(off Raleigh Cres.)
Westland Ct. GU14: Cov 8F 28
Westland Dr. PO7: Purb 5M 201
PO13: Lee S 2C 238
Westland Gdns. PO12: Gos 4J 239
Westlands BH23: Bran 7C 220
Westlands Dr. BH13: Poole 5D 244
Westlands Gro. PO16: Portc 1L 213
Westlands Ho. RG21: B'toke 7B 42
West La. BH23: Bran 7B 220
PO11: H Isl 3E 242
RG29: N War 6H 45
SO41: Ever 5M 233
SO52: N Bad 7D 130
WEST LEIGH 4G 203
West Leigh Pk. 5G 203
WESTLEY 2A 104 (6N 89)
Westley Cl. SO22: Winche 5H 105
Westley Ct. Rd. SO21: Spar 6N 89
Westley Gro. PO14: Fare 9B 198
Westley La. SO21: Spar 6N 89
WEST LISS 9D 114
West Lodge PO13: Lee S 9N 211
Westlyn Rd. RG26: Pam H 4L 11
Westman Rd. SO22: Winche 4H 105
West Mansion BH4: Bour 2G 244
Westmarch Bus. Cen. SP10: A'ver 8A 52
Westmarch Ct. SO17: South 9A 160
W. Marlands Rd. SO14: South 4C 4 (5L 173)
Westmead GU9: Farnh 8D 64
(off The Hart)
GU14: Farn 9K 29
Westmead Cl. PO11: H Isl 4D 242
WEST MEON 8D 136
WEST MEON WOODLANDS 3D 136
West M. PO17: K Vil 2A 198
W. Mills Rd. SP6: F'dge 1H 153
Westminster Cl. GU51: Fleet 1M 47
RG22: B'toke 3K 59
Westminster Ct. BH25: B Sea 7A 232
Westminster Gdns. PO14: Titch C 6F 196
Westminster Ga. SO22: Winche 9F 104
Westminster Ho. RG21: B'toke 6C 42
(off Festival Pl.)
Westminster Pl. PO1: Ports 9E 214
Westminster Rd. BH13: Poole 4F 244
SO41: M Sea 9H 233 & 7H 235
Westminster Rd. E. BH13: Poole 4F 244
Westmoreland Ct. SO41: Hor 3G 233
Westmorland Way SO53: Cha F 6C 132
WESTON
GU32 4H 145
SO19 9D 174
Weston Av. PO4: S'sea 3J 241
Weston Cl. RG25: Up G 3A 62
SO19: South 9D 174
WESTON COLLEY 7G 77
WESTON COMMON 6G 175
WESTON CORBETT 7N 61
Weston Ct. PO1: Ports 2E 240
(off Canal Wlk.)
SO19: South 1D 194
SP11: Enh A 2A 52
Weston Cres. SO18: South 3G 174
Weston Down La. SO21: We Co 7H 77
Weston Dr. BH1: Bour 2M 245
Weston Gro. Rd. SO19: South 8B 174
Weston Ho. GU32: Pet 1L 145
Weston La. GU32: W'ton 4H 145
SO16: Nur 7N 157
SO19: South 1C 194
SO21: M'dvr, We Co 7H 77
SP5: Mid W 5G 86
Weston Pde. SO19: South 1C 194
WESTON PATRICK 5A 62
Weston Rd. GU31: Pet 1N 145
RG25: Up G 4A 62
SO50: E'leigh 9E 132
Weston Sailing Club 2D 194
W. Overcliff Dr. BH4: Bour 9G 247 (3G 244)
Westover La. BH24: A'ley 2G 187
Westover Retail Pk.
BH9: Bour 2L 227
Westover Rd. BH1: Bour 7M 247 (2K 245)
GU51: Fleet 2N 47
PO3: Ports 8J 215
SO16: South 2B 172
SO41: M Sea 8K 235
West Pk. SP11: Apple 4B 50
West Pk. Dr. SP6: Dame 6A 150
West Pk. La. SP6: Dame 3P 149
West Pk. Lodge SO17: South 1M 173
(off Westwood Rd.)
West Pk. Rd. SO15: South 4B 4 (5L 173)
West Point PO13: Lee S 1A 238
W. Point Bus. Pk. SP10: A'ver 9H 51
West Portway SP10: A'ver 8H 51
West Quay Retail Pk.
SO15: South 5A 4 (6K 173)
West Quay Rd. SO15: South 5A 4 (6K 173)
(Southern Rd.)
SO15: South 7K 173
(West Quay Rd. Ind. Est.)
West Quay Rd. Ind. Est.
SO15: South 7A 4 (7K 173)
West Quay Shop. Cen.
SO15: South 5C 4 (6L 173)
Westray Cl. RG21: B'toke 4E 42
West Ridge GU10: Seal 5N 65
Westridge RG20: High 4A 8
Westridge Ct. SO17: South 1N 173
Westridge Rd. SO17: South 1N 173
West Rd. BH5: Bour 9D 228
BH23: Bran 6C 220
GU14: Farn 4K 29
GU15: Camb 8M 19
PO10: Ems 9K 203
PO17: S'wick 3B 200
SO19: South 8C 174
SO21: Bar S 5A 76
SO30: Hed E 4K 175
SO41: M Sea 9H 233
SO45: Dib P 8J 193
SO45: Hard 8B 194
Westrow Gdns. SO15: South 3K 173
Westrow Rd. SO15: South 3K 173
Westside SP4: All 7D 66
Westside Cl. RG22: B'toke 8M 41
Westside Vw. PO7: W'lle 9K 181
WEST SOUTHBOURNE 1F 246
West Sta. Ter. BH2: Bour 6G 247
(off Queens Rd.)
WEST STRATTON 6K 77
W. Stratton La. SO21: W Str 6K 77
West St. BH24: Ring 1H 187
GU9: Farnh 9B 64
GU31: Rog 9K 141
PO1: Ports 7H 5 (4A 240)
PO7: H'don 9D 166
PO9: Bed, Hav 7D 202
PO10: Ems 9M 203
PO14: Titch 9J 197
PO16: Fare 8C 198
(not continuous)
PO16: Portc 9K 199
(not continuous)
PO17: S'wick 3N 199
RG20: Burgh 4D 8
RG26: Tadl 5J 11
RG29: N War, Odi 8H 45
SO14: South 7C 4 (7L 173)
SO24: New A 9F 94
SO32: Sob 6K 165
SO45: Hythe 4L 193
SP6: F'dge 1H 153
SP10: A'ver 1N 69
(not continuous)
West St. Cl. RG26: Tadl 5J 11
WEST TISTED 7F 110
W. Tisted Cl. GU51: Fleet 9K 27
WEST TOWN 4E 242
WEST TYTHERLEY 8L 87
West Undercliff Prom.
BH2: Bour 9J 247 (4G 244)
BH4: Bour 4G 244
West Vw. BH21: Wim G 7G 148
GU35: W'hil 6G 100
SP10: A'ver 2N 69
West Vw. Dr. SO20: Chil 5F 74
West Vw. Rd. BH23: Chri 8A 230
GU35: Head D 3E 102
Westview Rd. SO22: Spar 4E 104
Westward Ho. RG27: Eve 5G 16
Westward Rd. SO30: Hed E 2N 175
West Way BH9: Bour 4M 227
SO41: Penn 4C 234
SP10: A'ver 9C 52
Westway PO15: Titch 6H 197
West Way Cl. BH9: Bour 5M 227
Westways PO9: Bed 9N 201
PO14: Stub 6N 211
Westways Cl. SO16: Nur 6C 158
WEST WELLOW 1B 120 (9N 121)
West Wick SP5: Down 1H 119
WEST WINTERSLOW 5F 86
Westwood Bus. Pk. SO40: Tott 8K 157
Westwood Cl. PO10: Ems 7N 203
Westwood Ct. SO17: South 1M 173
SO30: Wes E 1J 175
SO40: Tott 9L 157
Westwood Gdns. SO53: Cha F 4C 132
WEST WOODHAY 1K 7
Westwood Ho. GU30: Lip 1E 116
(off Tudor Ct.)
Westwood Mans. SO17: South 1M 173
WESTWOOD PARK 1M 173
Westwood Rd. PO2: Ports 4F 214
SO17: South 2L 173
SO31: Net A 2F 194
SO43: Lyn 1B 148 (1N 189)
Westwoods Pk. BH25: Bash 1M 231
Westwood Vw. SO24: Kilm 2L 135
Westwood Woodland Pk. 1E 194
WEST WORLDHAM 9L 81
Wetherby Ct. SO40: Tott 2J 171
Wetherby Gdns. GU14: Farn 3L 49
SO40: Tott 2J 171
SP10: Charl 8L 51
Wetherdown GU31: Pet 1N 145
Wey Bank GU10: Ben'ly 8L 63
Weybank Cl. GU9: Farnh 8E 64
WEYBOURNE 4G 65
Weybourne Rd.
GU9: Farnh, Weyb 5G 64
GU11: Alders 5G 65
Weybridge Cl. SO31: Sar G 3C 196
Weybridge Mead GU46: Yat 6A 18
Weybrook Ct. RG24: Sher J 8M 21
Weybrook Pk. Golf Course 2L 41
Wey Cl. GU15: Camb 8K 19
Weydon Farm La. GU9: Farnh 9D 64
Weydon Hill Cl. GU9: Farnh 9D 64
Weydon Hill Rd. GU9: Farnh 9D 64
Weydon La. GU9: Farnh 9D 64
Weydon Mill La. GU9: Farnh 9E 64
Weyford Cl. GU35: Lind 2L 101
WEYHILL 8D 50
WEYHILL BOTTOM 7D 50
Weyhill Cl. PO9: Hav 4D 202
PO16: Portc 8L 199
RG26: Tadl 6H 11
Weyhill Gdns. SP11: Weyh 9D 50
Weyhill Rd. SP10: A'ver 1J 69
SP11: A'ver, Pen C, Weyh 8D 50
WEYHILL SERVICE AREA 9F 50
Weylands Cl. GU30: Lip 1E 116
Wey Lodge Cl. GU30: Lip 2F 116
Weymouth Av. PO12: Gos 8H 213
Weymouth Rd. BH14: Poole 9A 226
PO2: Ports 7E 214
Weyside GU9: Farnh 8E 64
Weyside Pk. GU34: Alt 3H 81
Weysprings Cl. RG21: B'toke 6E 42
Weywood Cl. GU9: Weyb 3H 65
Weywood La. GU9: Weyb 3G 65
Whaddon Chase PO14: Stub 6L 211
Whaddon Ct. PO9: Hav 3C 202
Whaddon La. SO21: Owls 5C 134
Whale Island Way PO2: Ports 7D 214
Whalesmead Cl. SO50: B'stke 2K 161
Whalesmead Rd. SO50: B'stke 1K 161
Whaley Rd. PO2: Ports 7C 214
Wharf, The RG29: Odi 7M 45
Wharf Cl. BH12: Poole 8C 226
Wharfdale Rd. BH4: Bour 5G 247 (1G 245)
(not continuous)
BH12: Poole 8B 226
WHARF HILL 9N 237 (8L 105)
Wharf Hill SO23: Winche 9P 237 (8M 105)
Wharf Mill SO23: Winche 9P 237
Wharf Rd. PO2: Ports 8D 214
SO19: South 7B 174
Wharncliffe Gdns. BH23: Highc 7J 231
Wharncliffe Ho. SO19: South 7B 174
Wharncliffe Rd. BH5: Bour 1A 246
BH23: Highc 7H 231
SO19: South 7B 174
Whartons Cl. SO40: Ashu 7J 171
Whartons La. SO40: Ashu 6J 171
Whately Rd. SO41: M Sea 9G 233
What Vere La. GU34: Holy 10E 62
Wheat Cl. SO53: Cha F 6L 131
Wheatcroft Dr. SO18: South 1F 174
Wheatcroft Rd. PO13: Lee S 1B 238
Wheatear Dr. GU31: Pet 1B 146
Wheatears Dr. SO51: W Wel 1B 120
Wheatham Rd. GU33: Liss 2N 139
WHEAT HOLD 4N 9
Wheatland Cl. SO22: Winche 9H 105
Wheatlands PO14: Titch C 5F 196
Wheatlands Av. PO11: H Isl 6L 243
Wheatlands Cres. PO11: H Isl 6L 243
WHEATLEY 3G 82
Wheatley Grn. PO9: Hav 3C 202
Wheatley La. GU34: Bins 1F 82
GU35: K'ly 1F 82
Wheatley Rd. GU11: Alders 8H 49
Wheatleys Cl. RG25: Stev 6K 57
Wheaton Grange BH4: Bour 5G 247 (1H 245)
Wheaton Rd. BH7: Bour 9D 228
Wheatplot Pk. Homes
BH10: Bour 1K 227
WHEATSHEAF COMMON 6C 116
Wheatsheaf Ct. GU35: Head 1B 102
SO30: Hed E 4M 175
Wheatsheaf Dr. PO8: Cowp 7L 181
WHEATSHEAF ENCLOSURE 6D 116
Wheatstone Rd. PO4: S'sea 4F 240
Wheeler Cl. PO12: Gos 1K 239
RG28: Whit 6H 55
Wheelers Hill RG27: Hoo 2J 45

Wheeler's La. BH11: Bour 1A 226
(not continuous)
Wheelers Mdw. SO31: Old N 9J 175
Wheelers Wlk. SO45: Blac 8D 208
Wheelers Yd. SO21: Sut S 7D 76
(off Oxford Rd.)
Wheeler Way RG24: B'toke 1B 42
Wheelhouse Pk. Caravan Pk.
SO52: N Bad 3M 131
Wheelwright M. SP5: Down 2H 119
Wheelwrights RG20: High 3A 8
Wheelwrights La. GU26: Gray 3J 103
Wheely Down Rd. SO32: Warn 5M 135
Whernside Cl. SO16: South 2E 172
WHERWELL 2E 74
Wherwell Ct. PO9: Hav 4H 203
Wherwell Dr. GU51: Fleet 9J 27
Whetstone Rd. GU14: Cov 8E 28
Whichers Cl. PO9: R Cas 1H 203
Whichers Ga. Rd. PO9: R Cas 1H 203
Whimbrel Cl. PO4: S'sea 2L 241
Whimbrel Ct. BH23: Mude 8C 230
Whinchat Cl. PO15: Fare 5M 197
RG27: H Win 5B 26
SO16: South 5G 158
Whinfield Rd. SO45: Dib P 8K 193
Whin Holt GU52: Fleet 5M 47
Whins Cl. GU15: Camb 9K 19
Whins Dr. GU15: Camb 9K 19
Whinwhistle Rd. SO51: E Wel 2B 156
Whippingham Cl. PO6: Cosh 9E 200
Whipps Hill SP6: R'bne 4D 150
Whistler Cl. RG21: B'toke 8E 42
SO19: South 7G 174
Whistler Gro. GU47: Coll 7F 18
Whistler Rd. SO19: South 7G 174
Whistlers La. RG7: Sil 4A 12
Whiston Ho. PO12: Gos 9L 213
Whitaker Cres. SO41: Penn 3C 234
Whitaker Way GU26: Gray 4K 103
Whitby Cl. BH23: Chri 2G 229
GU14: Farn 2N 49
Whitby Ct. SO41: M Sea 8H 235
Whitby Rd. SO41: M Sea 8H 235
WHITCHURCH 5G 54
Whitchurch Cl. GU11: Alders 4M 65
Whitchurch Ct. SO19: South 7D 174
Whitchurch Rd. GU51: Fleet 9K 27
Whitchurch Silk Mill 6G 54
Whitchurch Station (Rail) 4G 55
Whitcombe Cl. SO40: Tott 3L 171
Whitcombe Gdns. PO3: Ports 1G 241
Whiteacres Cl. PO12: Gos 2K 239
White Acres Rd. GU16: Mytc 8N 29
White Av. GU33: Longc 4H 115
White Barn Cres. SO41: Hor 3H 233
Whitebeam Cl. PO8: Horn 5C 182
PO14: Fare 9A 198
RG22: Wort 7J 41
SO21: Col C 4L 133
Whitebeam Gdns. GU14: Cov 9E 28
White Beam Ri. PO8: Clan 6C 168
Whitebeam Rd. SO30: Hed E 4A 176
Whitebeam Way SO52: N Bad 7F 130
Whitebines GU9: Farnh 8F 64
White City RG20: Wol H 2A 8
Whitecliffe Av. PO3: Ports 9H 215
Whitecliffe Ct. PO12: Gos 3F 238
White Cloud Pk. PO4: S'sea 4G 241
White Cloud Pl. PO4: S'sea 4G 241
White Cott. Cl. GU9: Hale 4F 64
Whitecroft SO45: Hythe 7M 193
Whitecroft La. SO43: Lyn 1B 148
Whitecross Gdns. PO2: Ports 5G 214
Whitedell La. PO17: Fare 5F 198
White Dirt La. PO8: Cath 9B 168
Whiteditch Rd. SN8: Co Du 3G 31
Whitedown GU34: Alt 6E 80
Whitedown La. GU34: Alt 6D 80
Whitedown Rd. RG26: Tadl 5F 10
White Farm Cl. BH10: Bour 6H 227
White Farm La. SN8: B'mre 4D 6
Whitefield Lodge BH25: New M 3B 232
Whitefield Rd. BH25: New M 3B 232
SO45: Holb 5A 208
White Gates SO32: Durl 6E 162
Whitehall BH23: Chri 9L 229
Whitehall La. SO20: Lit Som 5J 89
White Harmony Acres Ind. Est.
SO30: Wes E 6J 161
White Hart BH23: Chri 7K 229
(off Barrack Rd.)
White Hart All. PO1: Ports 7J 5 (4B 240)
Whitehart Flds. BH24: Poul 9M 185
White Hart Ind. Est. GU17: Blackw 9G 18
White Hart La. PO16: Portc 1K 213
RG21: B'toke 7D 42
RG26: Cha A 4G 21
SO40: Cad 6N 155
(off Romsey Rd.)
White Hart M. GU30: Lip 4D 116
(off Portsmouth Rd.)
White Hart Rd. PO1: Ports 7J 5 (4B 240)
PO12: Gos 3K 239
SO50: Fair O 2N 161
Whitehaven PO8: Horn 4D 182
PO16: Portc 1K 213
Whitehaven Home Pk. SO45: Blac 8C 208
Whitehayes Cl. BH23: Burt 4N 229
Whitehayes Rd. BH23: Burt 4M 229
Whitehead Cl. RG24: Lych 4G 43
White Heather Ct. SO45: Hythe 3M 193
White Hill RG20: Burgh, W'way 6C 8
RG20: Ecc 5G 9
RG20: Kings 8J 9
RG25: Over 8J 59
RG29: Wel 5G 62
SP11: Hath 8K 33
Whitehill SP5: P'tn 6E 86
Whitehill Cl. GU15: Camb 6M 19
SO18: South 2G 175
WHITEHILLL 5J 101
Whitehill La. SO24: Bis S, New A 2G 108
Whitehill Pk. GU35: W'hil 7K 101
Whitehill Rd. GU35: Stan 6L 101
Whitehorn Dr. SP5: L'ford 1J 155
White Horse La. PO7: Den 3H 181
RG40: F'std 1G 16
White Horses BH25: B Sea 7N 231
Whitehouse SO41: M Sea 9K 235
White Ho. Cl. RG22: B'toke 9M 41
Whitehouse Cl. GU14: Farn 6K 29
White Ho. Gdns. GU32: Pet 8L 139
GU46: Yat 6M 17
Whitehouse Gdns. SO15: South 4F 172
White Ho. Wlk. GU9: H End 3F 64
White Knights BH25: B Sea 7A 232
White Ladies Cl. PO9: Hav 8G 202
Whitelands BH23: Thorn 3F 220
White La. RG25: Up G 1A 62
RG25: W Cor 7M 61
RG26: Hann, N Oak 6J 39
SO21: Twyf 5L 127
Whitelaw Rd. SO15: South 3G 173
Whiteleaf La. PO7: H'don 4C 166
Whitelegg Way BH10: Bour 1J 227
WHITELEY 1F 196
Whiteley Farm Rdbt. PO15: White 9H 177
Whiteley La. PO15: Titch 6J 197
PO15: White 1H 197
SO31: Burr 8E 176
Whiteley Village Shop. Cen.
PO15: White 1H 197
Whiteley Way PO15: White 9H 177
White Lion Courtyard BH24: Ring 1J 187
(off Millstream Ct.)
White Lion Wlk. PO12: Gos 2M 239
White Lion Way GU46: Yat 6N 17
White Lodge Gdns. PO16: Fare 5A 198
Whitemoor La. SO40: Wins 7E 156
SO51: Ower 7D 156
Whitemoor Rd. SO42: Broc 6A 148 (8M 189)
WHITENAP 6B 130
Whitenap Cl. SO51: Rom 6A 130
Whitenap La. SO51: Rom 6A 130
White Oak Wlk. PO9: Hav 4H 203
White Oak Way SP11: An V 5J 69
WHITEPARISH 5H 121
White Rd. GU15: Camb 7H 19
SO50: B'stke 8H 133
Whites Cl. RG27: Hoo 2F 44
Whites Ct. PO2: Ports 7E 214
Whites Hill SO21: Owls 5B 134
Whiteshoot SO20: Brou 2A 86 (4A 88)
Whiteshoot Hill SP5: Redl, Woodf 9C 120
Whiteshoot Rd. SO20: N Wal 4M 87
Whiteshute La. SO22: Winche 2H 127
SO23: Winche 9J 105
Whites La. SO45: Fawl 5F 208
Whites Pl. PO12: Gos 2K 239
Whites Rd. GU14: Farn 2N 49
SO19: South 5E 174
White Star Pl. SO14: South 7F 4 (7N 173)
Whitestone Cl. SO16: South 2E 172
Whitestones RG22: B'toke 4L 59
White Swan Ct. SO21: Sut S 7D 76
(off Oxford Rd.)
White Swan Rd. PO1: Ports 4M 5 (2C 240)
Whites Way SO30: Hed E 9M 161
Whitethorn Rd. PO11: H Isl 4H 243
Whitethorns GU9: H End 2F 64
(off Lwr. Weybourne La.)
White Tree Cl. SO50: Fair O 3A 162
Whitewater BH5: Bour 2B 246
Whitewater Ri. RG27: Hoo 1J 45
SO45: Dib P 7L 193
Whitewater Rd. GU51: Fleet 8L 27
RG29: N War 7J 45
White Way SP5: P'tn 6D 86
White Way, The SO32: Ext 6L 135
White Wings Ho. PO7: Den 7G 181
Whitewood RG24: Chin 9G 22
Whitfield Pk. BH24: Ashl H 3E 186
Whitgift Cl. RG22: B'toke 5K 59
Whithedwood Av. SO15: South 2J 173
Whitlet Cl. GU9: Farnh 9D 64
Whitley Ct. GU11: Alders 9J 49
(off Grosvenor Rd.)
Whitley Rd. GU46: Yat 9N 17
Whitley Row PO4: S'sea 2K 241
Whitley Way BH25: New M 1C 232
Whitlock Ri. SP5: Bish 2D 118
Whitmarsh La. RG24: Chin 9J 23
RG27: Sher L 9K 23
Whitmoor Va. Rd. GU26: Gray, Hind 9H 85
Whitmore Cl. GU47: Owl 5F 18
Whitmore Grn. GU9: H End 4G 64
Whitmore Va. GU26: Gray 9G 84
Whitmore Vale Rd. GU26: Gray 3J 103
WHITNAL 8M 37
Whitney Rd. RG24: B'toke 4F 42
WHITSBURY 9J 119
Whitsbury Cl. BH8: Bour 4A 228
Whitsbury Rd. PO9: Hav 4G 203
SP6: F'dge 6G 151
Whitstable Rd. PO6: Cosh 9F 200
Whittingham Ct. BH5: Bour 9E 228
Whittington Cl. SO45: Hythe 7L 193
Whittington Ct. PO10: Ems 9M 203
Whittle Av. PO15: Seg 4F 196
Whittle Cl. GU47: Sandh 4C 18
Whittle Cres. GU14: Cov 5H 29
Whittle Rd. SP10: A'ver 9H 51
WHITWAY 5C 8
Whitwell SO31: Net A 2G 195
Whitwell Rd. PO4: S'sea 6F 240
Whitworth Cl. PO12: Gos 3K 239
Whitworth Ct. SO18: South 2B 174
Whitworth Cres. SO18: South 2B 174
Whitworth Rd. PO2: Ports 8G 215
PO12: Gos 3J 239
SO18: South 2B 174
Whyke Ct. PO9: Hav 7E 202
Whynot La. SP10: A'ver 1L 69
Whyte Av. GU12: Alders 2M 65
Whyte Cl. SO45: Holb 5N 207
Whyteways SO50: E'leigh 8E 132
WICK
BH6 1K 247
SP5 1J 119 (7N 119)
Wick 1 Ind. Est. BH25: New M 4N 231
Wick 2 Ind. Est. BH25: New M 4N 231
Wick Cl. BH25: New M 4N 231
Wick Dr. BH25: New M 4N 231
Wicket, The SO45: Hythe 7L 193
Wicket Rd. BH10: Bour 1G 226
Wick Farm BH6: Bour 9L 229
Wickfield Av. BH23: Chri 8L 229
Wickfield Cl. BH23: Chri 8L 229
Wick Grn. BH6: Bour 9L 229
WICKHAM 6C 178
Wickham Cl. GU34: Alt 6D 80
GU52: Ch Cr 5K 47
RG26: Tadl 5H 11
Wickham Ct. GU52: Ch Cr 5K 47
PO12: Gos 4F 238
SO40: Tott 3L 171
Wickham Cft. PO17: Wick 7C 178
Wickham Ho. SO17: South 1M 173
Wickham Park Golf Course 6A 178
Wickham Pl. GU52: Ch Cr 5K 47
Wickham Rd. BH7: Bour 9D 228
GU15: Camb 5N 19
GU52: Ch Cr 5K 47
PO16: Fare 5D 198
PO17: Fare 1D 198
SO32: Curd 3F 176
SO32: Drox 8J 165
Wickham St. PO1: Ports 3J 5 (2B 240)
Wickham Vineyard 2L 177
Wickham Way RG27: Sher L 7J 23
Wick Hill La. RG40: F'std 1J 17
Wick La. BH6: Bour 9K 229
BH23: Chri 9L 229
SP5: Down 1H 119 (7L 119)
Wicklea Rd. BH6: Bour 1L 247
Wicklow Cl. RG22: B'toke 8K 41
Wicklow Dr. SO53: Cha F 7M 131
Wickmeads Rd. BH6: Bour 1K 247
Wickor Cl. PO10: Ems 7N 203
Wickor Way PO10: Ems 6N 203
Wick Point Mews BH23: Chri 9L 229
Wicor Mill La. PO16: Portc 1K 213
Wicor Path PO16: Portc 2M 213
(Bayly Av.)
PO16: Portc 1J 213
(Heritage Gdns.)
Widbury Rd. SO41: Penn 4C 234
Widden Cl. SO41: Sway 5J 223
Widdicombe Av. BH14: Poole 3C 244
Widecombe Dr. SO45: Hythe 5K 193
Wide La. SO18: S'ing, S'ton A 6C 160
SO50: E'leigh 4D 160
Wide La. Cl. SO42: Broc 7C 148
Wide Lane Sports Complex 4D 160
Widgeon Cl. PO12: Gos 9K 213
SO16: South 5G 159
Widgeon Ct. PO16: Portc 9H 199
Widgeons GU34: Alt 3F 80
Widget Cl. BH11: Bour 4F 226
Widlers La. SO32: Uph 8E 134
WIDLEY 7K 201
Widley Ct. PO14: Fare 2C 212
Widley Ct. Dr. PO6: Cosh 1H 215
Widley Gdns. PO7: Wid 6L 201
Widley Rd. PO2: Ports 6D 214
PO6: Cosh 9H 201
Widley Wlk. PO7: Purb 7G 201
Widmore Rd. RG22: B'toke 9L 41
Wield Cl. PO9: Hav 5C 202
Wield Industries SO24: Lwr W 7H 79
Wield Rd. GU34: Meds 7H 79
RG25: Pres C 5E 78
Wigan Cres. PO9: Bed 7B 202
Wights Wlk. RG22: B'toke 3K 59
Wight Vw. PO13: Lee S 9N 211
Wightway M. SO31: Wars 8N 195
WIGLEY 5F 156
Wigmoreash Drove SN8: B'mre, Ham 3F 6
Wigmore Ho. PO1: Ports 1E 240
Wigmore Rd. RG26: Tadl 4F 10
Wilberforce Cl. SO22: Winche 8G 105
Wilberforce Rd. PO5: S'sea 8N 5 (4D 240)
PO12: Gos 6L 239
Wilby La. PO3: Ports 4K 215
Wilcon Ct. SO50: Hor H 4A 162
Wilcot Cl. SP4: Ames 6A 66
Wild Arum Way SO53: Cha F 7L 131
Wildburn Cl. SO40: Calm 9J 157
Wild Cherry Way SO53: Cha F 6M 131
Wilde Cl. SO40: Tott 3K 171
WILDERN 2N 175
Wildern Cl. SO31: Loc H 6C 196
Wildern Ct. SO30: Hed E 2M 175
Wilderness Hgts. SO18: Wes E 1G 175
Wilderness Rd. GU16: Frim 2N 29
Wildern La. SO30: Hed E 2N 175
Wildern Leisure Cen. 3N 175
Wilders Cl. GU16: Frim 1N 29
Wilderton Rd. BH13: Poole 2D 244
Wilderton Rd. W. BH13: Poole 1E 244
Wildfell Cl. BH23: Chri 5K 229
Wild Flowers Dr. PO15: Titch 6H 197
Wildground La. SO45: Hythe 8M 193
Wild Grounds Nature Reserve 9D 212
WILDHERN 9L 33
Wild Herons RG27: Hoo 2J 45
WILDMOOR 7N 23
Wildmoor La. RG27: Sher L 4M 23
Wildmoor Wlk. PO9: Hav 4H 203
Wildown Gdns. BH6: Bour 2J 247
Wildown Rd. BH6: Bour 2K 247
Wild Ridings PO14: Fare 9L 197
Wild Rose Cres. SO31: Loc H 7B 196
Wildwood Dr. RG26: Bau 4D 10
Wildwood Gdns. GU46: Yat 9M 17
Wilfred Rd. BH5: Bour 1C 246
Wilkins Cl. PO8: Clan 5B 168
Wilkins Gdns. BH8: Bour 8N 227
Wilkinson Dr. BH8: Bour 4D 228
Wilkinson Way GU9: Weyb 5H 65
Wilkins Rd. SO30: Hed E 1N 175
Wilks Cl. SO16: Nur 6B 158
Willbury Rd. GU9: Farnh 6G 64
Willems Av. GU11: Alders 9H 49
Willems Rdbt. GU11: Alders 9H 49
Willersley Cl. PO6: Cosh 8D 200
WILLESLEY WARREN 5B 38
Will Hall Cl. GU34: Alt 6D 80
Will Hall Farm GU34: Alt 5D 80
William Booth Ho. PO1: Ports 2L 5 (2C 240)
William Cl. BH23: Walk 4J 231
PO14: Stub 7N 211
William Ct. BH23: Highc 7K 231
GU14: Farn 2L 49
(off Cambridge Rd. W.)
PO3: Ports 1H 241
William Farthing Cl. GU11: Alders 9J 49
William George Ct. PO13: Lee S 2A 238
William Hitchcock Ho. GU14: Farn 5K 29
William Ho. SO16: South 6F 158
SP11: Enh A 2A 52
William Macleod Way SO16: South 1F 172
William Panter Ct. SO50: E'leigh 1E 160
William Price Gdns. PO16: Fare 7D 198
William Rd. BH7: Bour 7C 228
SO41: Lymi 1E 234
William's Bus. Pk. BH25: New M 4N 231
Williams Cl. PO13: Gos 9F 212
SO45: Holb 5B 208
Williams Ct. BH4: Bour 2G 245
Williams Ind. Pk. BH25: New M 4N 231
Williamson Cl. SP11: Ludg 1C 30
Williams Rd. PO3: Ports 5J 215
William St. SO14: South 5A 174
Williams Way GU51: Fleet 2A 48
William Tite Ct. PO12: Gos 1H 239
William Way GU34: Alt 3G 80
Willian Pl. GU26: Hind 1N 103
Willington Cl. GU15: Camb 7K 19
Willis Av. SO52: N Bad 8G 130
Willis La. GU34: Four M 7L 97
Willis Museum, The 7C 42
Willis Rd. PO1: Ports 3N 5 (2D 240)
PO12: Gos 3L 239
(not continuous)
SO16: S'ing 6B 160
Willis Ter. GU32: Pet 1L 145
Willis Waye SO23: Kin W 9M 91
Willment Marine & Business Pk.
SO19: South 6B 174
Willments Ind. Est. SO19: South 7A 174
Willoughby Cl. GU34: Alt 4E 80
Willoughby Way RG23: B'toke 5M 41
Willow Av. SP6: F'dge 9H 151
Willowbourne GU51: Fleet 2H 47
Willow Cl. BH4: Bour 9F 226
BH24: St L 4A 186
GU16: Mytc 8N 29
GU30: Lip 3F 116
GU35: Bor 4K 101
PO9: Hav 8G 202
SO30: Hed E 4A 176
SO30: Wes E 9J 161
Willow Cnr. RG26: Bau 4E 10
Willow Ct. BH7: Bour 7F 228
GU16: Frim 3M 29
GU34: Alt 5E 80
PO14: Fare 8A 198
SO16: South 8F 158
Willow Cres. GU14: Farn 5K 29
Willowdale Cl. GU32: Stro 9G 138
Willowdene Cl. BH25: A'ley 3D 232
PO9: Bed 5B 202
Willow Dr. BH23: Chri 9K 229
BH24: Ring 3K 187
GU31: Pet 3M 145
SO40: March 1E 192
Willowford GU46: Yat 7N 17
Willow Gdns. GU30: Lip 3F 116
SO52: N Bad 7E 130
Willow Grn. SO21: Col C 4L 133
Willow Gro. SO50: Fair O 1A 162
SP10: A'ver 2M 69
Willow Herb Cl. SO31: Loc H 7B 196
Willow La. BH23: Bran 4F 220
GU17: Haw 9F 18
Willow Mead BH8: Bour 2A 228
SO30: Hed E 2M 175
Willowmead Cl. RG14: New 1C 8
Willow Pl. PO12: Gos 2K 239
Willow Rd. GU33: Liss 1E 140
RG26: Tadl 5H 11
SO32: Bis W 4A 164
Willows, The BH25: B Sea 6C 232
GU10: Run 6L 65
PO2: Ports 6D 214
PO7: Den 6F 180
RG23: Oak 2C 58
RG29: N War 7J 45
SO30: Wes E 9J 161
SO53: Cha F 9A 132
SP10: A'ver 3M 69
Willows Cl. SO32: Swanm 7D 164
Willows End GU47: Sandh 5D 18
Willowside PO8: Cowp 5N 181

Wolverton Common—Wyck La.

WOLVERTON COMMON .9A 10
Wolverton Gdns. GU32: W Meo .8D 136
Wolverton La. RG26: Wolve .6N 9
Wolverton Rd. BH7: Bour .9C 228
PO9: Hav .4E 202
RG26: Axm, Bau, Wolve, Wolv C .6N 9
SO14: South .3F 4 (5N 173)
Wolverton Towns End RG26: Bau, Wolve .2A 20
Wolvesey Castle .9N 237 (7L 105)
Wolvesey Palace .9N 237 (7L 105)
Wolvesey Pl. SO53: Cha F .8M 131
Wolvesey Ter. SO23: Winche .9P 237 (8M 105)
Wonderholme Pde. BH10: Bour .4F 226
WONSTON .7E 76
Wonston Cl. SO21: Sut S .7D 76
Wonston Ct. PO9: Hav .3H 203
Wonston La. SO21: Wons .1G 90 (9D 76)
Wonston Rd. SO16: South .7G 159
SO21: Sut S .7D 76
Woodbarn, The GU9: Farnh .9E 64
(off Alfred Rd.)
Woodberry La. PO9: R Cas .8J 183
PO10: R Cas, Westb .1L 203
Woodbind Wlk. SO31: Loc H .7C 196
Woodbine Cl. GU47: Sandh .6E 18
Woodbine La. RG20: Burgh .2D 8
Woodbourne GU9: Weyb .3G 65
Woodbourne Cl. GU33: Liss .1F 140
GU46: Yat .7N 17
PO15: Fare .8N 197
Woodbridge Dr. GU15: Camb .6M 19
Woodbridge La. GU32: E Meon .3A 144
Woodbridge Rd. GU17: Blackw .8D 18
Woodbury BH1: Bour .8N 247 (3L 245)
SO42: Broc .7A 148 (8M 189)
Woodbury Av. BH8: Bour .4B 228
GU32: Pet .8L 139
PO9: Langs .9F 202
Woodbury Cl. BH23: Chri .3H 229
Woodbury Ct. RG7: Fa H .1A 16
Woodbury Gro. PO8: Cowp .5N 181
Woodbury Rd. RG22: B'toke .3K 59
Wood Cl. RG22: B'toke .4K 59
SO19: South .7G 175
Woodcock Bottom & Whitmore Vale .2K 103
Woodcock La. SO41: Hor .3H 233
Woodcocks Cres. BH7: Bour .6D 228
WOODCOT .4D 212
Woodcot Caravan Pk.
PO11: H Isl .5K 243
Woodcot Cres. PO9: Hav .3G 203
Woodcote Grn. GU51: Fleet .3J 47
Woodcote La. PO14: Fare .5C 212
SO32: Uph .7E 134
Woodcote Rd. SO17: South .8A 160
Woodcot Gdns. GU14: Cov .8F 28
WOODCOTT .1B 36
Woodcott Ter. GU12: Alders .2M 65
Woodcroft RG23: Oak .2D 58
Woodcroft Gdns. PO8: Cowp .5N 181
Woodcroft La. PO8: Cowp .5N 181
Woodcroft M. GU32: Pet .9L 139
Woodcutters Dr. PO8: Cowp .6M 181
WOODEND .2H 179
Wood End GU14: Farn .9M 29
RG24: Chin .1F 42
RG45: Cr'tne .1B 18
Woodend Rd. BH9: Bour .6J 227
BH24: Crow .6A 188
Wood End Way SO53: Cha F .6M 131
Wooden Ho. La. SO41: Pil .5H 225
Wooderson Cl. SO50: Fair O .9M 133
WOODFALLS .3M 119 (8C 120)
Woodfern SP6: Gods .9N 151
Woodfield GU35: K'ly .7G 83
Woodfield Av. PO6: Farl .8M 201
Wood Fld. Cl. GU34: E Wor .7N 81
Woodfield Cl. RG20: Enbo R .1B 8
Woodfield Cotts. GU32: Frox .2H 139
Woodfield Dr. SO22: Winche .8F 104
Woodfield Gdns. BH23: Chri .5F 230
Woodfield Ho. PO2: Ports .5F 214
Woodfield Pk. Rd. PO10: S'brne .8N 203
Woodfield Rd. BH11: Bour .1E 226
Woodford Cl. BH24: Ring .1M 187
Woodford Ct. BH7: Bour .9C 228
Woodford Rd. BH1: Bour .1N 245
Woodgarston Dr. RG22: B'toke .4J 59
Woodgarston La. RG26: Up Woott .3E 40
Woodgaston La. PO11: H Isl .7J 217
Woodgate GU51: Fleet .9A 28
Woodglade Cl. SO40: March .9E 172
WOODGREEN .2A 154
Woodgreen Av. PO9: Bed .7D 202
Woodgreen Dr. BH11: Bour .2B 226
Woodgreen Rd. SO22: Winche .2H 105
SP6: Brea, Woodg .4M 151
Woodgreen Wlk. SO40: Calm .1H 171
Woodhall Way PO15: Fare .6A 198
Woodhayes Av. BH23: Chri .4G 230
Woodhay Wlk. PO9: Hav .3H 203
Wood Hill La. RG29: L Sut, Odi .4E 62
WOODHOUSE .3C 52
Wood Ho. BH13: Poole .2E 244
Woodhouse La. PO8: Ids .4G 183
PO8: Ids, R Cas .6H 183
PO9: R Cas .6H 183
RG19: Ashf H .2M 9
SO30: Botl .3A 176
WOODINGTON .6C 128
Woodington Cl. PO9: Hav .3G 203
Woodington Nature Reserve .8B 128
Woodington Rd. SO51: E Wel .6C 128
Woodland, The SO53: Cha F .3M 131
Woodland Av. BH5: Bour .1D 246
Woodland Cl. PO13: Gos .1E 238
SO18: South .3H 175
SO51: E Wel .1B 156
Woodland Ct. RG23: B'toke .5H 59
Woodland Cres. GU14: Farn .6L 29
Woodland Dr. RG26: B'ley .2J 23
SP5: Mid W .4G 87
Woodland Drove SO21: Col C .1L 133
Woodland Gdns. SO45: Blac .8C 208
Woodland Grange BH1: Bour .5N 247 (1L 245)
Woodland M. SO30: Wes E .1H 175
Woodland Pl. SO15: South .3K 173
Woodland Ri. GU52: Ch Cr .6K 47
WOODLANDS
SO24 .1D 108
SO40 .6E 170
Woodlands BH3: Bour .8K 227
BH6: Bour .1F 246
BH13: Poole .1E 244
GU46: Yat .1N 27
GU51: Fleet .1L 47
PO16: Fare .7F 198
RG20: Pen .3B 8
RG24: Chin .8H 23
RG25: Over .2D 56
Woodlands, The GU35: W'hil .7J 101
SO23: Kin W .9N 91
Woodlands Av. GU9: Weyb .3H 65
PO10: Ems .6L 203
Woodlands Bus. Village
RG21: B'toke .5E 42
Woodlands Caravan Pk. SO41: Hor .3G 233
Woodlands Cl. BH23: Bran .7C 220
GU17: Haw .3G 28
SO31: Sar G .3C 196
SO45: Dib P .8K 193
SO53: Cha F .2B 132
Woodlands Ct. GU34: Alt .6D 80
GU47: Owl .4H 19
SO23: Winche .5L 105
SO45: Dib P .8K 193
Woodlands Dr. SO31: Net A .3H 195
SO40: Woodl .6D 170
Woodlands Drove SO40: Ashu .7F 170
Woodlands Gdns. SO51: Rom .3A 130
Woodlands Gro. PO7: Purb .4L 201
Woodlands La. GU33: Liss .3G 140
PO11: H Isl .2E 242
Woodlands Rd. BH25: B Sea .7N 231
GU14: Cov .6F 28
GU15: Camb .8K 19
RG26: Bau .4D 10
SO40: Ashu, Woodl, Net M .6E 170
SO42: Broc .9C 148 (9N 189)
Woodland St. PO1: Ports .1F 240
Woodlands Wlk. GU17: Haw .3G 28
PO4: S'sea .2K 241
Woodlands Way BH24: St I .4C 186
PO9: Hav .5F 202
SO15: South .2L 173
SO31: Burs .1K 195
SO52: N Bad .8E 130
SP10: A'ver .1B 70
Woodland Vale SO19: South .6F 174
Woodland Vw. PO8: Love .4N 181
SO31: Burs .1K 195
SO41: Down .8H 233
Woodland Wlk. BH5: Bour .1D 246
(not continuous)
GU12: Alders .8M 49
Woodland Way BH23: Highc .6F 230
BH25: New M .9C 222
SO41: M Sea .8J 235
Wood La. GU14: Cov .9J 29
GU34: Selb .7K 99
GU51: Fleet .2A 48
PO17: S'wick .3B 200
RG27: Up N .6C 44
SO24: Bram .9L 109
SO41: M Sea .8J 235
SO42: Beau .6B 206
Woodlane Cl. SO24: Bram .9M 109
Woodlark Gdns. GU31: Pet .1B 146
Woodlark Glade GU15: Camb .6M 19
Wood Lawn Cl. BH25: B Sea .6A 232
Woodlea Cl. SO22: Winche .4J 105
Woodlea Gdns. SO30: Wes E .1J 175
Woodlea Pk. GU34: Meds .4J 97
Woodlea Way SO51: Ampf .2L 131
Woodleigh GU51: Fleet .3M 47
Woodleigh Cl. PO9: Hav .6J 203
(not continuous)
Woodleigh Ct. BH2: Bour .5J 247
WOODLEY .2B 130
Woodley Cl. SO51: Rom .2B 130
Woodley Cl. Flats SO51: Rom .2B 130
Woodley Gdns. SO41: Lymi .1D 234
Woodley Grange SO51: Rom .3B 130
Woodley La. SO51: Rom .4N 129
Woodley Rd. PO12: Gos .3L 239
SO19: South .7B 174
Woodleys RG20: Ecc .5G 9
Woodley Way SO51: Rom .2B 130
Woodling Cres. SP6: Gods .9N 151
Wood Lodge SO40: Calm .1H 171
Woodman Cl. SO21: Spar .4B 104
Woodmancote Rd. PO4: S'sea .3H 241
WOODMANCOTT .4A 78
Woodman Ct. GU51: Fleet .3L 47
Woodmanfield RG25: Up G .3B 62
Woodman La. SO21: Spar .3B 104
Woodmere Cft. RG22: B'toke .3H 59
Woodmill La. SO18: S'ing .8B 160
Woodmill Outdoor Activities Cen. .8B 160
Woodmoor RG40: F'std .3J 17
Woodmoor Cl. SO40: March .9F 172
Wood Pk. SP11: Ludg .1E 30 (5L 31)
Woodpath PO5: S'sea .4D 240
Woodpath Ho. PO5: S'sea .4D 240
Woodpecker Cl. GU10: Ews .2N 63
GU35: Bor .5J 101
PO9: Warb .8H 203
RG22: B'toke .2H 59
Woodpecker Copse
SO31: Loc H .6E 196
Woodpecker Dr. SO40: March .9D 172
Woodpeckers SO23: Winche .4L 105
Woodpeckers Dr. SO22: Winche .4G 104
Woodpecker Way PO3: Ports .4H 215
SO50: E'leigh .1B 160
Woodrisings, The BH2: Bour .5H 247 (1H 245)
Wood Rd. GU9: Up H .3E 64
GU15: Camb .3K 29
GU26: Hind .1M 103
SO40: Ashu .8H 171
Woodroffe Dr. RG22: B'toke .1L 59
Woodroffe Wlk. PO10: Ems .5M 203
Wood Row BH8: Bour .2B 228
Woodrow PO7: Den .6F 180
Woodruff Cl. BH23: Chri .6E 230
Woodrush Cres. SO31: Loc H .7B 196
Woods, The BH9: Bour .6H 227
(off Talbot Rd.)
Woodsedge PO7: W'lle .3A 202
WOODSIDE
SO41 .4E 234
SO43 .9L 155
Woodside GU14: Farn .5K 29
GU15: Camb .6H 19
GU17: Haw .2E 28
PO5: S'sea .4D 240
PO13: Gos .3D 212
SO16: Chilw .1K 159
SP11: Ver D .8D 6
Woodside Av. SO41: Lymi .5E 234
SO50: E'leigh .9C 132
Woodside Cl. GU35: Bor .4J 101
SO40: March .9D 172
SO41: Lymi .4E 234
Woodside Ct. GU14: Cov .7F 28
(off Guillemont Flds.)
SO17: South .2N 173
Woodside Cres. GU35: Bor .4J 101
SO16: Chilw .1J 159
Woodside Gdns. GU51: Fleet .2A 48
RG24: Chin .8H 23
SO40: Ashu .7J 171
Woodside La. BH25: A'ley .1D 232
GU34: Lwr Farr .3A 98
SO41: Lymi .4E 234
Woodside Pk. GU35: Bor .4J 101
Woodside Rd. BH5: Bour .1E 246
BH14: Poole .2A 244
GU9: Weyb .3G 65
GU14: Farn .4H 49
SO17: South .2N 173
SO50: E'leigh .8C 132
SO52: N Bad .8E 130
Woodside Way SO30: Hed E .5L 175
Woods La. RG25: Clid .3N 59
RG29: Grey .7F 44
Woodstock Av. PO8: Horn .5A 182
Woodstock Cl. PO14: Fare .8A 198
SO30: Hed E .5A 176
Woodstock Ct. RG21: B'toke .6B 42
SO22: Winche .3J 105
Woodstock Dr. SO17: South .1M 173
Woodstock La. BH24: Ring .1K 187
Woodstock Mead RG22: B'toke .4K 59
Woodstock Rd. BH23: Burt .4N 229
PO9: Bed .7C 202
PO12: Gos .4L 239
Woodstocks GU14: Farn .6L 29
Woods Vw. Rd. BH9: Bour .6H 227
Woodthorpe Gdns. SO31: Sar G .3C 196
Woodvale PO15: Fare .7N 197
Woodvale Gdns. BH25: A'ley .2D 232
Woodvale Rd. GU14: Farn .3K 49
Woodview Cl. SO16: Bass .5M 159
Woodview Pk. Caravan Pk.
SO30: Curd .3F 176
Woodville Cl. GU17: Blackw .8D 18
RG24: Chin .9G 22
Woodville Dr. PO1: Ports .7L 5 (4C 240)
Woodville La. RG24: Chin .1G 42
Woodville Ri. RG24: Chin .1G 42
Woodville Rd. PO9: Bed .7B 202
SO45: Fawl .5F 208
Wood Wlk. RG26: Rams .7B 20
Woodward Cl. PO12: Gos .3H 239
Woodway GU15: Camb .8K 19
WOODYATES .1F 148
Woofferton Rd. PO6: Cosh .8B 200
Wooland Ct. GU52: Ch Cr .7K 47
Wooldridge Cres. RG29: Odi .2E 62
Woolfield La. GU32: Frox .2B 138
Woolford Cl. SO22: Winche .8G 105
Woolford Way RG23: B'toke .5M 41
Wool Gro. SP10: A'ver .2B 70
Woolley Ho. SO14: South .4E 4
Woolley Sq. SP10: A'ver .7B 52
Woolmead, The GU9: Farnh .7E 64
Woolmead Rd. GU9: Farnh .7E 64
Woolmead Wlk. GU9: Farnh .7E 64
(off Woolmead Rd.)
Woolmer Ct. PO9: Hav .4H 203
WOOLMER HILL .8L 103
Woolmer Hill Rd. GU27: Hasl .7L 103
Woolmer La. BH24: Blas .7K 185
GU30: B'sht .6C 102
Woolmer Pond (Nature Reserve) .1G 114
Woolmer Rd. GU33: Longc .2F 114
Woolmer St. PO10: Ems .5L 203
Woolmer Trad. Est. GU35: Bor .4H 101
Woolmer Vw. GU26: Gray .4M 103
Woolmer Way GU35: Bor .5N 101
Woolner Av. GU32: Pet .9M 139
PO6: Cosh .9H 201
Woolsbridge Rd.
BH24: Ashl H, St L .2C 186
WOOLSTON .9B 174
Woolston Ct. PO12: Gos .4G 238
Woolston Pl. RG27: Sher L .7H 23
Woolston Rd. PO9: Hav .3C 202
SO31: Net A .1F 194
Woolston Station (Rail) .7B 174
WOOLTON HILL .2A 8
Woolton Lodge Gdns.
RG20: Wol H .2A 8
Woolverton SO22: Winche .5H 105
Woolwich Cl. SO31: Burs .8K 175
Wooteys Way GU34: Alt .3F 80
WOOTTON .5B 222
Wootton SO31: Net A .2G 195
Wootton Cl. RG23: W Law .4H 41
Wootton Farm Rd. BH25: Woot .5N 221
Wootton Gdns.
BH1: Bour .6N 247 (2L 245)
Wootton Hgts. BH1: Bour .2L 245
(off Wootton Mt.)
Wootton La. RG23: W Law .7F 40
RG26: Up Woott .2E 40
Wootton Mt. BH1: Bour .6N 247 (2L 245)
Wootton Rd. PO13: Lee S .3C 238
SO41: Tip .7D 222
Wootton Rough BH25: Woot .7C 222
WOOTTON ST LAWRENCE .4G 41
Wootton St. PO6: Cosh .1G 214
Worbarrow Gdns. BH12: Poole .6A 226
Worcester Av. RG22: B'toke .3K 59
Worcester Cl. GU14: Farn .5K 29
PO5: S'sea .3E 240
Worcester Ct. GU51: Fleet .9L 27
(off King John St.)
PO13: Gos .1E 238
Worcester Pl. SO19: South .8F 174
SO41: Lymi .4F 234
Wordsworth Av. BH8: Bour .5B 228
GU46: Yat .8L 17
PO6: Cosh .8N 199
Wordsworth Cl. RG24: B'toke .3D 42
SO22: Winche .6H 105
SO32: Bis W .3A 164
Wordsworth Pl. PO15: White .9F 176
Wordsworth Rd. SO15: South .1H 173
Workhouse La. GU32: E Meon .3L 143
Workman's La. SO31: Wars .2B 210
Works, The BH2: Bour .7J 247
(off Up. Norwich Rd.)
Workshop Rd. PO17: S'wick .7B 200
Worldham Golf Course .6J 81
Worldham Hill GU34: E Wor .7M 81
Worldham Rd. PO9: Hav .3H 203
WORLDS END .5B 180
Worrell Dr. BH12: Poole .6A 226
Worrell Sq. SP10: A'ver .7B 52
(off Cricketers Way)
Worsam Ct. RG22: B'toke .7K 41
Worsley Rd. GU16: Frim .4N 29
PO5: S'sea .8N 5 (4D 240)
Worsley St. PO4: S'sea .5H 241
Worthing Av. PO12: Gos .8H 213
Worthing Rd. PO5: S'sea .5E 240
Worthy Ct. PO9: Hav .4H 203
WORTHY DOWN .5G 91
Worthy La. SO23: Winche .5K 105
Worthy Rd. BH25: New M .3B 232
SO23: Winche .5L 105
WORTING .7J 41
Worting Rd. RG21: B'toke .7M 41
RG22: B'toke, Wort .7L 41
RG23: Newf, Wort .8E 40
Worting Rd. Rdbt.
RG22: B'toke .7L 41
Wortley Rd. BH23: Highc .7J 231
Wote St. RG21: B'toke .7C 42
Wouldham Cl.
SP11: Per D .4B 30 (6J 31)
Wraysbury Pk. Dr. PO10: Ems .5M 203
Wrecclesham Hill GU10: Wrec .7N 63
Wrekin, The GU14: Farn .2N 49
Wrekin Cl. RG22: B'toke .8K 41
Wren Centre, The PO10: Ems .6N 203
Wren Cl. BH23: Mude .9D 230
BH24: Hight .2M 187
BH25: New M .4A 232
GU34: Alt .3G 80
GU46: Yat .7L 17
RG22: B'toke .2H 59
SO22: Winche .9H 105
Wren Cres. BH12: Poole .9E 226
Wren Gdns. SP6: Ald .4E 152
Wren Rd. SO50: E'leigh .2C 160
Wren Way GU14: Farn .5H 29
Wrenway PO16: Portc .9H 199
Wrexham Gro. PO8: Cath .8B 168
Wright Cl. PO15: White .3J 197
Wrights Cl. SO21: Sth W .3H 91
Wright's Hill SO19: South .8E 174
Wright's La. RG17: Comb .3G 6
SN8: Ham .3G 6
Wrights Wlk. SO31: Burs .9K 175
Wrights Way SO21: Sth W .3H 91
Wright Way SO45: Fawl .7J 209
Writers Cl. GU26: Hind .1L 103
Wroxham Rd. BH12: Poole .9D 226
Wryneck Cl. SO16: South .5F 158
Wulwyn Ct. RG45: Cr'tne .1B 18
Wyatt Ct. GU47: Coll .6F 18
PO12: Gos .1M 239
Wyborn Cl. PO11: H Isl .5G 243
Wych La. PO13: Gos .4D 212
Wychwood Cl. BH2: Bour .1J 245
Wychwood Dr. BH2: Bour .9K 227
SO45: Blac .9C 208
Wychwood Grange BH2: Bour .9K 227
Wychwood Gro. SO53: Cha F .4C 132
Wychwood Pl. SO22: Winche .4K 105
WYCK .4A 82
Wyck La. GU34: Bins, E Wor, Wyck .3N 81
(not continuous)

HOSPITALS, HOSPICES and selected HEALTHCARE FACILITIES covered by this atlas.

N.B. Where it is not possible to name these facilities on the map,
the reference given is for the road in which they are situated.

49 ALMHURST ROAD 3F 224
    49 Almhurst Road
    BOURNEMOUTH
    BH4 7LJ
    Tel: 01202 706143

ALDERNEY HOSPITAL 5A 226
    Ringwood Road
    POOLE
    BH12 4NB
    Tel: 01202 735537

ALTON COMMUNITY HOSPITAL 7D 80
    Chawton Park Road
    ALTON
    GU34 1RJ
    Tel: 01420 82811

ANDOVER WAR MEMORIAL
    COMMUNITY HOSPITAL 9L 51
    Charlton Road
    ANDOVER
    SP10 3LB
    Tel: 01264 358811

BASINGSTOKE & NORTH HAMPSHIRE HOSPITAL 3N 41
    Aldermaston Road
    BASINGSTOKE
    RG24 9NA
    Tel: 01256 473202

BROADMOOR HOSPITAL .1G 18
    Kentigern Drive
    CROWTHORNE
    RG45 7EG
    Tel: 01344 773111

CHASE COMMUNITY HOSPITAL 5J 101
    Conde Way
    BORDON
    GU35 0YZ
    Tel: 01420 488801

CHRISTCHURCH HOSPITAL 6J 229
    Fairmile Road
    CHRISTCHURCH
    BH23 2JX
    Tel: 01202 486361

CLARE PARK SPIRE HOSPITAL 4M 63
    Crondall Lane
    FARNHAM
    GU10 5XX
    Tel: 01252 850216

COUNTESS MOUNTBATTEN HOUSE 9J 161
    Botley Road
    SOUTHAMPTON
    SO30 3JB
    Tel: 02380 477414

COUNTESS OF BRECKNOCK HOUSE (HOSPICE) 9L 51
    Andover War Memorial Hospital
    Charlton Road
    ANDOVER
    SP10 3LB
    Tel: 01264 835288

EMSWORTH VICTORIA HOSPITAL 9M 203
    North Street
    EMSWORTH
    PO10 7DD
    Tel: 01243 376041

FAREHAM COMMUNITY HOSPITAL 4D 196
    Brook Lane
    Sarisbury Green
    SOUTHAMPTON
    SO31 7DQ
    Tel: 01489 587 400

FARNHAM HOSPITAL & CENTRE FOR HEALTH 7F 64
    Hale Road
    FARNHAM
    GU9 9QL
    Tel: 01483 782000

FLEET COMMUNITY HOSPITAL 1K 47
    Church Road
    FLEET
    GU51 4LZ
    Tel: 01483 782700

FORDINGBRIDGE HOSPITAL 1J 153
    Bartons Road
    FORDINGBRIDGE
    SP6 1JD
    Tel: 01425 652255

FRIMLEY PARK HOSPITAL .2M 29
    Portsmouth Road
    Frimley
    CAMBERLEY
    GU16 7UJ
    Tel: 01276 604604

GOSPORT WAR MEMORIAL HOSPITAL 3J 239
    Bury Road
    GOSPORT
    PO12 3PW
    Tel: 02392 524611

HAMPSHIRE BMI CLINIC 5F 42
    Basing Road
    Old Basing
    BASINGSTOKE
    RG24 7AL
    Tel: 01256 357111

HOLY CROSS HOSPITAL 8N 103
    Hindhead Road
    HASLEMERE
    GU27 1NQ
    Tel: 01428 643311

HYTHE HOSPITAL 7M 193
    Beaulieu Road
    SOUTHAMPTON
    SO45 4ZB
    Tel: 02380 846046

JACKSPLACE HOSPICE 7C 76
    Stockbridge Road
    Sutton Scotney
    WINCHESTER
    SO21 3JE
    Tel: 01962 760060

KING'S PARK HOSPITAL 9C 228
    Gloucester Road
    BOURNEMOUTH
    BH7 6JF
    Tel: 01202 303757

LEIGH HOUSE 6B 106
    Alresford Road
    WINCHESTER
    SO21 1HD
    Tel: 01962 825800

LEWIS MANNING HOSPICE .6A 244
    1 Crichel Mount Road
    POOLE
    BH14 8LT
    Tel: 01202 708470

LYMINGTON NEW FOREST HOSPITAL 9E 224
    Wellworthy Road
    LYMINGTON
    SO41 8QD
    Tel: 01590 663000

MILFORD ON SEA WAR MEMORIAL HOSPITAL 8L 235
    Sea Road
    Milford-on-Sea
    LYMINGTON
    SO41 0PG
    Tel: 01590 648100

MOORGREEN HOSPITAL 9K 161
    Botley Road
    SOUTHAMPTON
    SO30 3JB
    Tel: 02380 475200

NHS WALK-IN CENTRE (BITTERNE) 3E 174
    Bitterne Health Centre
    Commercial Street
    SOUTHAMPTON
    SO18 6BT
    Tel: 02380 426356

NHS WALK-IN CENTRE (BOSCOMBE) 9B 228
    Boscombe & Springbourne Health Centre
    11 Shelley Road
    BOURNEMOUTH
    BH1 4JQ
    Tel: 01202 727969

NHS WALK-IN CENTRE (GUILDHALL WALK, PORTSMOUTH)
. . . . .5N 5
    27 Guildhall Walk
    PORTSMOUTH
    PO1 2DD
    Tel: 02392 751006

NHS WALK-IN CENTRE (SOUTHAMPTON - CENTRAL)
. . . . .1F 4
    Brinton's Terrace
    Fanshawe Wing
    Royal South Hants Hospital
    SOUTHAMPTON
    SO14 0YG
    Tel: 02380 716539

NHS WALK-IN CENTRE (ST. MARY'S, PORTSMOUTH) . . .2H 241
    Milton Road
    PORTSMOUTH
    PO3 6DW
    Tel: 0845 076 5551

NAOMI HOUSE HOSPICE 7C 76
    Stockbridge Road
    Sutton Scotney
    WINCHESTER
    SO21 3JE
    Tel: 01962 760060

NUFFIELD HEALTH BOURNEMOUTH 9L 227
    67 Lansdowne Road
    BOURNEMOUTH
    BH1 1RW
    Tel: 01202 291866

OAKHAVEN HOSPICE 5D 234
    Lower Pennington Lane
    LYMINGTON
    SO41 8ZZ
    Tel: 01590 613025

PARKLANDS HOSPITAL 2M 41
    Aldermaston Rd.
    BASINGSTOKE
    RG24 9RH
    Tel: 01256 817718

PETERSFIELD HOSPITAL 1L 145
    Swan Street
    PETERSFIELD
    GU32 3LB
    Tel: 01730 263221

PHYLLIS TUCKWELL HOSPICE 9G 64
    Waverley Lane
    FARNHAM
    GU9 8BL
    Tel: 01252 729400

PORTSMOUTH SPIRE HOSPITAL 4K 203
    Bartons Road
    HAVANT
    PO9 5NP
    Tel: 02392 456000

PRINCESS ANNE HOSPITAL .8G 158
    Coxford Road
    SOUTHAMPTON
    SO16 6YD
    Tel: 02380 777222

Hospitals, Hospices and selected Healthcare Facilities

PRIORY HOSPITAL SOUTHAMPTON, THE 2F **192**
    Hythe Road
    Marchwood
    SOUTHAMPTON
    SO40 4WU
    Tel: 02380 840044

QUEEN ALEXANDRA HOSPITAL 8G **200**
    Southwick Hill Road
    Cosham
    PORTSMOUTH
    PO6 3LY
    Tel: 02392 286000

RAVENSWOOD HOUSE 1A **198**
    Knowle
    FAREHAM
    PO17 5NA
    Tel: 01329 836000

ROMSEY HOSPITAL 4N **129**
    Winchester Hill
    ROMSEY
    SO51 7ZA
    Tel: 01794 834700

ROWANS HOSPICE 5J **201**
    Purbrook Heath Road
    Purbrook
    WATERLOOVILLE
    PO7 5RU
    Tel: 02392 250001

ROYAL BOURNEMOUTH HOSPITAL 5E **228**
    Castle Lane East
    BOURNEMOUTH
    BH7 7DW
    Tel: 01202 303626

ROYAL HAMPSHIRE COUNTY HOSPITAL 8H **237** (7J **105**)
    Romsey Road
    WINCHESTER
    SO22 5DG
    Tel: 01962 863535

ROYAL SOUTH HANTS HOSPITAL 1E **4** (4M **173**)
    Brinton's Terrace
    SOUTHAMPTON
    SO14 0YG
    Tel: 023 8063 4288

ST ANN'S HOSPITAL 7C **244**
    69 Haven Road
    POOLE
    BH13 7LN
    Tel: 01202 492128

ST JAMES HOSPITAL 2K **241**
    Locksway Road
    PORTSMOUTH
    PO4 8LD
    Tel: 02392 822444

ST MARY'S HOSPITAL 1G **241**
    Milton Road
    PORTSMOUTH
    PO3 6AD
    Tel: 02392 866505

ST MARY'S NHS TREATMENT CENTRE 2H **241**
    Milton Road
    PORTSMOUTH
    PO3 6DW
    Tel: 03332 001823

ST MICHAEL'S HOSPICE 2N **41**
    Basil de Ferranti House
    Aldermaston Road
    BASINGSTOKE
    RG24 9NB
    Tel: 01256 844744

ST WALERIC 4L **105**
    Park Road
    WINCHESTER
    SO23 7BE
    Tel: 01962 841941

SARUM ROAD BMI HOSPITAL 7G **105**
    Sarum Road
    WINCHESTER
    SO22 5HA
    Tel: 01962 844555

SOUTHAMPTON GENERAL HOSPITAL 9G **159**
    Tremona Road
    SOUTHAMPTON.
    SO16 6YD
    Tel: 02380 777222

SOUTHAMPTON SPIRE HOSPITAL 9H **159**
    Chalybeate Close
    SOUTHAMPTON
    SO16 6UY
    Tel: 02380 775544

SOUTHAMPTON TREATMENT CENTRE 1E **4** (4M **173**)
    Level C
    Royal South Hants Hospital
    Brinton's Terrace
    SOUTHAMPTON
    SO14 0YG
    Tel: 0845 194 9750

TATCHBURY MOUNT HOSPITAL 9G **157**
    Tatchbury Mount
    Calmore
    SOUTHAMPTON
    SO40 2RZ
    Tel: 02380 874000

WESSEX NUFFIELD HEALTH HOSPITAL 3E **132**
    Winchester Road
    Chandler's Ford
    EASTLEIGH
    SO53 2DW
    Tel: 02380 266377

WESTERN COMMUNITY HOSPITAL 1E **172**
    Walnut Grove
    SOUTHAMPTON
    SO16 4XE
    Tel: 02380 475401

WOODHAVEN 9G **157**
    Tatchbury Mount
    Calmore
    SOUTHAMPTON
    SO40 2RZ

The representation on the maps of a road, track or footpath is no evidence of the existence of a right of way.

The Grid on this map is the National Grid taken from Ordnance Survey® mapping with the permission of the Controller of Her Majesty's Stationery Office.

SAFETY CAMERA INFORMATION

PocketGPSWorld.com's CamerAlert is a self-contained speed and red light camera warning system for SatNavs and Android or Apple iOS smartphones/tablets. Visit www.cameralert.co.uk to download.

Safety camera locations are publicised by the Safer Roads Partnership which operates them in order to encourage drivers to comply with speed limits at these sites. It is the driver's absolute responsibility to be aware of and to adhere to speed limits at all times.

By showing this safety camera information it is the intention of Geographers' A-Z Map Company Ltd., to encourage safe driving and greater awareness of speed limits and vehicle speed. Data accurate at time of printing.

Printed and bound in the United Kingdom by Polestar Wheatons Ltd., Exeter.